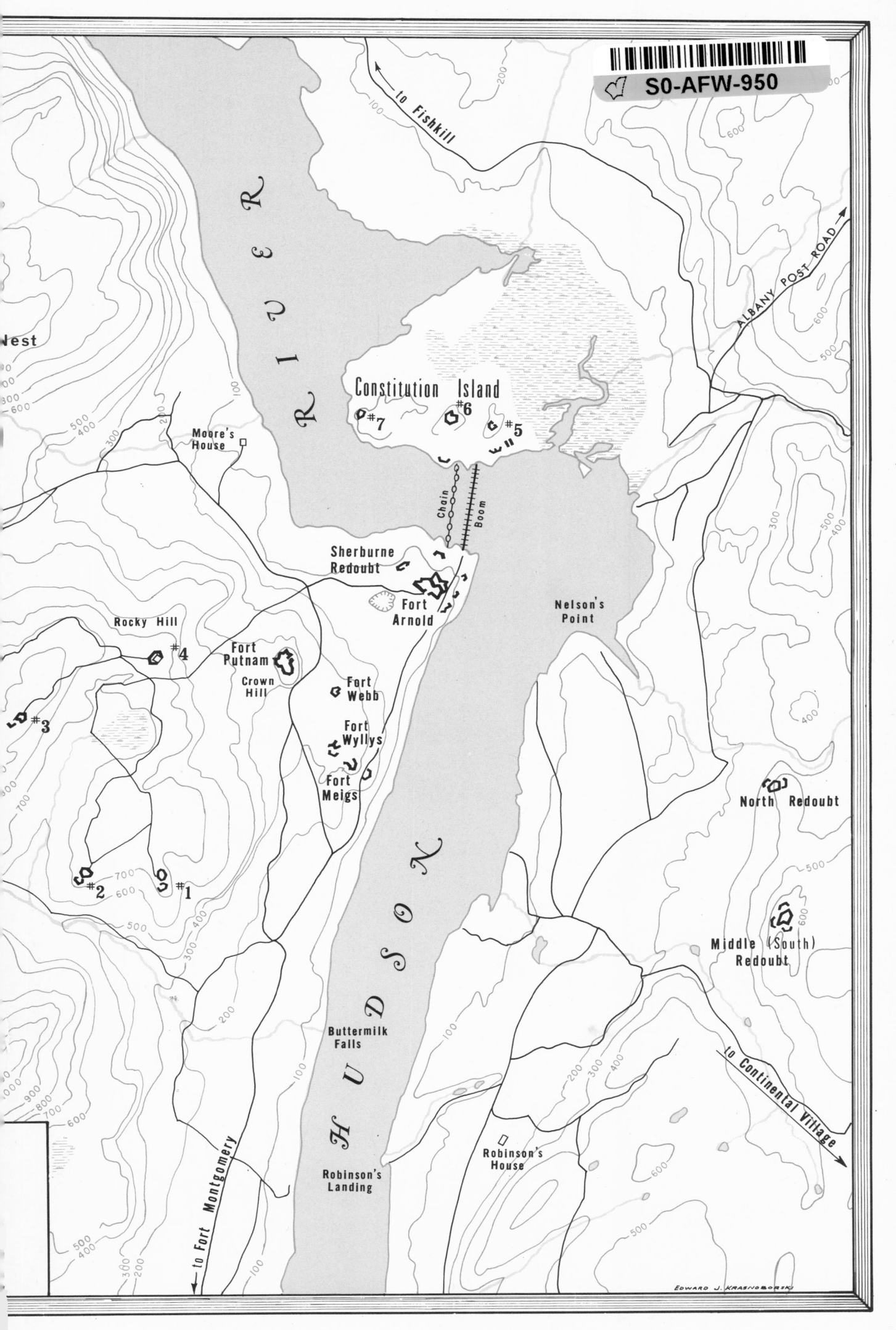

RIVER

to Fishkill

West

Albany Post Road

Constitution Island

#7

#6

#5

Moore's House

Chain

Boom

Sherburne Redoubt

Fort Arnold

Nelson's Point

Rocky Hill

Fort Putnam

#4

Crown Hill

Fort Webb

Fort Wyllys

North Redoubt

Fort Meigs

#3

Middle (South) Redoubt

#2

#1

HUDSON

Buttermilk Falls

Robinson's House

to Continental Village

to Fort Montgomery

Robinson's Landing

Edward J. Krasnoborski

THE RIVER AND THE ROCK

An Original Title in

The West Point Military Library

EDITED BY

Colonel Thomas E. Griess, U.S.M.A.

AND

Jay Luvaas, Allegheny College

CONTRIBUTIONS IN MILITARY HISTORY, NO. 1

The History of Fortress West Point, 1775-1783

THE RIVER AND THE ROCK

by DAVE RICHARD PALMER

Lieutenant Colonel, United States Army / Department of Military Art and Engineering, United States Military Academy

Greenwood Publishing Corporation
New York

Copyright © 1969 by Dave Richard Palmer

Library of Congress Catalog Card Number: 77–79061
SBN: 8371–1497–7

Greenwood Publishing Corporation
211 East 43rd Street, New York, N.Y. 10017

Printed in the United States of America

Dedicated to the memory of those fallen
comrades of the West Point Class of 1956
who found "a soldier's resting place
beneath a soldier's blow" in Vietnam.

CONTENTS

General George Clinton in a fort above the Hudson River. Courtesy of the West Point Library.

ILLUSTRATIONS

PREFACE

O_{NE} launches a project like this for a variety of reasons. First, no definitive history of Fortress West Point has ever before been done. Moreover, there exist in print nearly as many errors and misconceptions about it as facts. Then too, the story itself is most compelling. But perhaps the foremost reason is the realization that the history of West Point in the American Revolutionary War is actually a history in miniature of the entire war. West Point on the Hudson River was a hub from which the spokes of war radiated and returned; it was a lodestone for personalities and events, a pivot point of tactics and strategy, a center of controversy and construction, a witness to both base treason and lofty patriotism.

Many of the factors that fettered the Patriots throughout the War of Independence are nowhere better illustrated than in the painfully frustrating but eventually successful exertions to protect Henry Hudson's River. Inexperienced leadership, lack of military know-how, a shortage of funds and equipment, a dearth of professional engineers, and near-ruinous political interference are only some of the difficulties faced by those responsible for the prosecution of the defenses. Not surprisingly, many of the reasons for ultimate American victory are neatly evidenced in the story of the ultimately successful defense of the Hudson: the steadfastness of George Washington; British blunders; assistance from foreign powers; the difficulty of campaigning in eighteenth-century America; and a smile from Lady Luck. The complications faced in the Hudson Highlands were not peculiar to that one region but were common throughout America during the war. A nation unprepared for war, with leaders untrained to command, could not have expected to avoid mistakes, defeats, frustrations, confusion. That all adversities were weathered and that most were turned to profit are the reasons the colonists won the war. The long travail and eventual success at West Point mirrored the larger struggle and the greater victory of the Thirteen Colonies. And that is justification enough for telling the tale.

No one can complete a work of this sort without the able and unselfish assistance of others, and I am sincerely grateful to all those who helped, individuals and institutions alike. In the latter category, I want especially to recognize the courtesy and professionalism of the staffs of the New-York Historical Society Library, the Library of Congress, the West Point Museum, the West Point Library, the New York Public Library, the National Archives, the Duke University Library, and the Constitution Island Association, headed by Mrs. Genevieve H. Lewis.

At the top of a list of individuals would have to come Colonel Thomas E. Griess, Professor of the History of the Military Art at the United States Military Academy. Colonel Griess first suggested the subject, then extended many valuable leads during the research, and later encouraged and prodded me in the writing. The book would not have been written but for his influence. Colonel Charles H. Schilling provided enthusiastic support and that all-important element, time. A trio of scholars at Duke University—Professors Theodore Ropp, John R. Alden, and Harold T. Parker—might recognize the impact of their teachings in the work. Several persons read and commented on various portions of the manuscript: Gerald C. Stowe, Edward W. Hermann, Donald F. Clark, John H. Mead, Lieutenant Colonel John W. Woodmansee, Lieutenant Colonel Merle G. Sheffield, Mrs. W. T. Glover, and Mrs. Barbara J. Ackerson. Their discerning remarks enriched and refined the manuscript. Messrs. Stowe, Hermann, Clark, Mead, and Sheffield also provided invaluable research assistance. Mr. Constantine Sidamon-Eristoff paused in his "pursuit of potholes" long enough to open his splendid library to me. Mr. Edward J. Krasnoborski worked diligently to prepare accurate maps and charts which add both authenticity and art to the book. Mrs. Thelma M. Baker typed the manuscript—not once but twice—and spent long hours checking and correcting my spelling and punctuation. Mrs. Sally L. French, Mrs. Mary E. Grace, Mrs. Grace C. Monahan, and Mr. Roger J. Hassler pitched in enthusiastically to help meet some of the preparation deadlines, while Mrs. Dorothy H. Waterfield and Mr. Emanuel M. Pirotta provided administrative assistance. The final product is a markedly better one because of the guidance of Mr. H. C. Cohen of Greenwood Publishing Corporation, and for the genuine advice tendered by Professor Jay Luvaas of Allegheny College.

Most significantly, I must acknowledge and praise the forbearance and assistance of Lu Palmer, my wife. Her aid in proofreading the manuscript and in acting as a sounding board vies in value with her provision of an environment conducive to writing. And there was always Allison, who helped in her own inimitable way.

The combined efforts of these persons and others contributed to the making of a better book. If any errors remain they are wholly mine.

West Point, N.Y.   —D. R. P.
January, 1969

ICE AND INDIANS;
PIRATES AND
PATRIOTS

AFTER bearing gifts of gold, myrrh, and frankincense to the Christ Child in Bethlehem, the three Magi, awed by their encounter with the Infant, made their way from the City of David to the far points of the compass. One, called Anasis, came by some mysterious route—probably supernatural—to the wild jumble of mountains which would someday be known as the Hudson Highlands. There, on the summit of High Tor, he erected an altar for worship according to his special rite. The Indians, angered that this strange visitor was ignoring their own all-powerful sun god, plotted to slip up the flank of High Tor and destroy both the intruder and his "pagan" altar. They would have done it, too, but for a miracle. Just at the last moment, as the paint-streaked savages closed in on their prey, the sky darkened and thunder rolled and the very earth split asunder, swallowing the hostile warriors. Water eventually filled the vast, heaven-created chasm, forming a magnificent river.

Thus, in a legend recorded in 1933 by Hudson River historian Paul Wilstach, is explained the birth of the "River of Legends."

It is easy to understand why the early explorers, traders, and settlers had to seek in myth an explanation of the Hudson River's incongruous path through the Hudson Highlands. That waterway, rising some three hundred miles from the sea, in a storybook Adirondack lake endowed with a storybook name, Lake Tear of the Clouds, behaves as rivers should through most of its course. It pours rapidly but correctly down from the mountains, gaining strength and speed and size, until it reaches Albany. There, fed by the Mohawk River from the west and finding itself only six feet above sea level, the previously turbulent stream calms down, deepens, and broadens.

1

Beauty lost as the waters grow sedate is more than regained as they become stately. From Albany to the Hudson Highlands—a unique strip of mountains running roughly east-west approximately fifty miles above New York City—one cannot fault the river's logic. But when the current reaches that great granite barrier, reason seems to fail. Water is supposed to take the path of least resistance, and that path would be to bypass the Highlands to the west and to flow into the Atlantic through a sister stream in New Jersey.

Rather than seek a route around the mountains, the Hudson slices bravely through them in a narrow, twisting, picturesque gorge. Stone cliffs drop directly into the water in many places, while precipices attainable only to a skilled climber overlook the river's tortuous fifteen-mile passageway through the rugged heights. In *A Book of the Hudson*, Washington Irving wrote of the "awful defiles" created when the "gigantic Titans had erst waged their impious war with heaven, piling up cliffs on cliffs, and hurling vast masses of rocks in wild confusion." One amazed American officer, on first viewing the area during the Revolutionary War, confided to his journal that only a poet or a painter could adequately describe the "huge mountains, rocky cliffs, and venerable forests in one confused mass." Other travelers were similarly impressed with the majesty and strength of the terrain along the Hudson's corridor through the Highlands. But, romantic and wondrous as were the "precipitate mountains to the water's edge," they were also a strong natural obstacle to military or commercial movement. For that reason, the Hudson-created canyon through the Highlands was destined to become a focal point of the War of Independence.

Actually, the true birth of the Hudson Gorge, if not so sudden or so clear, is eminently more fascinating than the legendary beginning. In point of time, it is not within the scope of mortal imagination to comprehend just how old are the gray, crystalline rocks of the Highlands. Nor is it within reach of our most modern scientific methods to measure their age even to the nearest 10 million years. Enough, perhaps, to say that few geological formations in the world are older.

To begin with, there was a vast sea called, after man developed his passion for naming all things, the Grenville Ocean. For unrecorded ages, out of that ocean settled an ever-increasing layer of ooze which became a thousand feet and more thick. Slowly but constantly the colorless sediment solidified to complete the first step in forming the Hudson Highlands. Then, some 700 million years ago, the calm of the Grenville Ocean was abruptly broken; for the next 100 million years or so cataclysmic eruptions from the deep bowels of the earth struck time and again with a terrible pressure and a searing, rock-melting heat. The sedimentary stone was changed into its present forms of schist, gneiss, and granite. And nothing in 600 million years since has been able to alter the basic structure of those rocks. While melting and squeezing the previously level ocean bed, those internal igneous explosions lifted and twisted it. A jagged, tortured patch of mountains resulted—forerunners of the Hudson Highlands.

As if the 100 million years of unchecked fury had left her utterly spent, Nature subsided and let her gentler methods take over; wind and water waged their steady war of erosion against the granite heights. Oceans came and receded. New layers of rock formed on the old. Loose splinters of the mountains, undercut and worn by powerful winds, tumbled from the peaks. Prehistoric rains washed and smoothed the rugged slopes. Waves smashed and plucked. But above it all, endless ocean or featureless erosion plain, the highest spires of the craggy gray mountains stood uncovered—arrogant islands in the vastness.

Recovered by a slumber lasting a quarter of a billion years, Nature roused herself and lashed out once more from the center of the earth. In an unrestrained spasm of energy, she uplifted at a stroke (by her clock) the Taconic Mountains, a belt of sharp ridges running from southwest to northeast and stretching through the present northeastern portion of the United States. The sturdy peaks, which had for so long withstood the elements found themselves, tumbled and pitched on edge, a part of this newer and grander range.

Once more oceans came and went as the plastic surface of the earth slowly fluctuated. Once more waves and wind and rain worked at reducing the stubborn rocks. And once more, when the oceans attained their greatest depth, the ancestors of the Highlands remained just above the surface. Then that second long stillness was broken. In a mighty and sudden effort the Acadian Mountains were thrust up, signaling the start of a restless and quavering period that would endure for the next 80 million years. The murky seas that bubbled around the Highlands during those eons were laden with animal life, including long, sharklike creatures. Ultimately a paroxysm of violence raised the Appalachian Mountains and at long last ended the uneasy era. After 80 million years of disruption the Taconic Mountain Range was shattered. Only portions remained; among them were the Berkshires, the Green Mountains, and the thrice-struck Hudson Highlands.

A general land elevation accompanying the Appalachian upheaval raised the Hudson Highlands above sea level for the last time. But the forces of erosion never rest. Through succeeding millions of quiet years the elements gathered and deposited sediment around the array of disordered, jagged peaks. Eventually the summits of the Highlands hills looked out, as mere bumps, over a vast, monotonous, unrelieved peneplain. Slowly, ever so slowly, the surface of the earth began to rise. As slowly, a sluggish stream began to collect rain water draining from the south slopes of the Highlands. It meandered to the ocean through a marshy, deltalike land. That dirty, shallow, lazy stream would develop into the majestic Hudson River.

Eons passed. Years are too small a scale to measure the changes taking place; decades—even centuries—little better. Animals walked, then flew. Eventually, dinosaurs waddled in the sticky mire of the Hudson delta. Imperceptibly, the surface of the earth inland from the ocean continued to rise. The wandering, slow-moving river settled into a fixed bed and began to flow ever more rapidly. Gradually, inch by inch—perhaps inch by century —it ate its way backward into the tousled ridges at its headwaters. Grudgingly the crystalline rocks conceded this new invasion. Finally, only the massive ridge of Storm King–Breakneck separated the northernmost rivulet of the Hudson from its brother waterway in the north. Then, after having withstood the best Nature had to offer for half a billion years, the Grenville granite succumbed to the nibbling headwaters of the Hudson River. The water worked through and annexed the northern streams.

Strengthened by the addition of new watercourses, and sped along by the still-rising land, the Hudson immediately set about consolidating its conquest of the mighty mountains. At first fitfully, then more steadily, the current dug deeper and deeper into its own bedrock. Downward progress was retarded only once, when the burrowing river reached the solid, close-grained mass which today we know as West Point. After scouring flat the top of that unbroken bulk—and incidentally making a parade ground for future generations of cadets—the waters searched out a path around the point. Taking advantage of an irregular weakness, they cut a zig-zag course between West Point and Constitution Island. With that defiant obstacle bypassed, the torrent, unabated, cut lower yet until—about a million years ago—a chasm had been carved more than 700 feet below the level of the present river bed. It must have been a breathtaking view had there been anyone around to appreciate it.

Next came the ice. Preceded by an arctic chill killing plants and animals in its path, a great glacier slid down from the north. Beginning somewhere in the region of a bay that would one day also bear the name of Henry Hudson, the mass of ice began to radiate southward, following, like water, paths of least resistance. One tongue, finding the Hudson Valley, sped ahead of the main sheet. It entered and filled the deep, beautiful gorge through the Highlands. That channel, though, was too constricted, causing ice to pile up until it eventually spilled over the tops of the Highlands themselves. At its greatest height, the surface of the ice was about one mile above the peaks.

Carrying boulders, sand, and dirt, and bearing down with an immeasurable weight, the glacier acted as an enormous, natural sheet of sandpaper. Northern slopes and summits of the Highlands show effects even today of the sanding. They are generally smooth and evenly rounded, whereas the southern flanks, plucked of loose boulders by the glacier, are irregular and precipitate. Giving under the immense burden of ice, the land itself sank. Fortunately, the glacier began to thaw and to retreat toward its arctic home before the Highlands were pushed beneath the surface of the sea.

Though receding, the glacier was not yet ready to quit punishing the Highlands. It would have, indirectly, a final fling. As the cold white sheet withdrew, huge ice chunks, broken free from the forward edge, lodged to melt in valleys or were carried by rivers out to sea. Several larger than normal blocks converged on the narrow gap between Storm King and Breakneck after the main body of ice had retreated north of those two ridges. Reinforced with glacial debris, the ice caused a solid jam in the defile. As water from the melting glacier rose behind it, the ice and boulder barricade grew higher and thicker. The frigid lake increased in size as the glacier continued slowly to melt its way northward. Pressure on the dam intensified until—probably after a midsummer thunder shower—it burst with a sharp, resounding crack, letting loose a foaming, crushing cascade of

View looking up the Hudson River from a hill above West Point. Drawn by
Archibald Robertson about 1796. Courtesy of the West Point Museum. **5**

ice and water which rushed headlong in a 300-foot crest through the Highlands. It was a fitting finale to the ice age.

After that first, angry surge of the flood had vented itself, the river remained a rampaging torrent for hundreds, maybe thousands, of years. Until the glacier finally freed the St. Lawrence, the Hudson was the sole exit for the entire northern watershed, including the Great Lakes. During that era the water level was over a hundred feet above West Point's plain. About ten thousand years ago the St. Lawrence took its share of the burden and the Hudson fell to near its present level. The land, pushed down by the glacier, remained only slightly higher than the waves of the Atlantic. Therefore, when the volume of fresh water flowing through the Hudson's channel was so drastically reduced, salt water entered, and the once raging river became a tidal estuary while its once remarkable granite gorge was filled up with several hundred feet of silt. The river was then very much as we know it today.

About that time man first gazed upon the river. A single, lithe scout peered over it from the west bank. He was Asian. His remote ancestors had crossed the Bering Strait, on a land bridge, and had worked their way south and east. He still retained oriental features, especially high cheek bones and straight, black hair, but he had grown tall and supple during the long migration. Through narrowed eyes he watched impassively as the current flowed past; then, as the water stopped and the tide pushed it back upstream, his eyes opened and he became excited! A legend carried by the first Asians and handed down from generation to generation proclaimed that they were fated to wander until they found a wondrous water flowing in two directions. Promptly titling the newly discovered river "The-Water-Which-Runs-Two-Ways," Indians took up residence in the Hudson Valley.

Those first Indians, Algonquins all, staked out claims along both banks of the broad river and, proving that they were every bit as civilized as other human beings, soon began to war among themselves. Mohicans on the east bank became tribal enemies of Mincees on the west shore, while Tappans watched the sun rise over the island of their chosen foes, the Manhattans. But one should not jump to the conclusion that these Algonquins were warlike; they were not. Indeed, life along the Hudson was so pleasant that those first dusky inhabitants had little real inclination to fight one another. Furthermore, the Hudson, serving as a wide no-man's-land, separated would-be warriors and provided a ready-made excuse to avoid massive tribal assaults. It was no obstacle, however, to excursions for captives. That was generally the form of warfare waged along the Hudson— seizure of an enemy brave or two for sacrificial purposes, reprisals, counter-reprisals, and so on.

A prisoner's fate was rarely a pleasant one. Sometimes he was kept as a slave; less often, he was adopted into the new tribe; but usually death at the torture stake awaited him. When a captive was to be killed, everyone in the village gathered for the spectacle. In his youth, each warrior, preparing for the day when he might be captured, had learned a death song. In defiance of his captors and tormentors, he would chant it as long as possible, going along with the grisly game. His captors would try to prolong the suffering by administering tortures so as to induce the most excruciating pain while not quite causing unconsciousness. Older children were allowed to begin the ceremony by burning patterns on the chest of the unfortunate Indian. Squaws next stripped his flesh in long, careful bands. A brave, usually the one who had made the capture, scalped his victim and placed glowing coals, one by one, on the exposed skull. The eyes of the poor wretch were gouged out, but not until after he was forced to watch himself be emasculated. And through it all, the mournful death chant continued. Properly done, and with full cooperation from a sturdy prisoner, such entertainment could last two or three days.

Through centuries, the tribes lived contentedly along the silver river. Fish and game were plentiful. Squaws scratched good plots for corn. Tobacco was grown and copper was worked. Raids by and against nearby tribes were diversions rather than dangers. This idyllic life was disturbed only by the threat of the fierce Mohawks. From time to time, out of the west, those ferocious members of the Iroquois nation would strike the villages along the Hudson, slaughtering and exacting tribute. However, content with having once more cowed the gentler Algonquins, they always returned to their western lands. All things considered, life was good as the unnumbered years rolled by.

Of course it could not last. The white man came—first merely looking, then trading trinkets for furs, then moving in, and in the end evicting the red man.

History is silent on the identity of the first European to see "The-Water-Which-Runs-Two-Ways." He may even have been a Viking. John Cabot, an Italian explorer working for England and sailing only five years after Columbus had crossed the blue ocean, could have discovered the river, but his records are less than accurate. An Italian employed by France, Giovanni da Verrazano, came across the mouth of the river in 1524, but did not explore it. He named it "Grand River." The following year, Estevan Gomez, a Portuguese citizen sailing for Spain, journeyed to the wide waterway and may have gone part way up it. "San Antonio," he dubbed the waters. Unknown traders, probably French and Dutch, followed the scent of fur as far as the site of Albany. Their fate and, for that matter, their fortune have never been ascertained. The river remained a mystery until an English sea dog, hired by the Dutch, set out to seek a short cut to Cathay.

Out from Amsterdam, on Saturday, 25 March 1609, sailed the Dutch yacht, the *Halve Maen* or *Half Moon*. Henry Hudson, the experienced captain of the 80-ton vessel, steered for the North Star while keeping a wary eye on his crew—a malcontented and mixed lot of English and Dutch. Soon blocked by floes of ice and threats of mutiny from penetrating the Arctic Circle, Hudson changed course, touched at Cape Cod, and then turned south. On 21 August, off the coast of Virginia not far from the struggling, two-year-old settlement of Jamestown, the ship's cat began running from one side of the deck to the other, mewing strangely. Crew members could see nothing. After carefully pondering that omen, Hudson decided to reverse course and proceed northward. Poking the nose of his shallow-draft ship into Chesapeake Bay and the Delaware River, the captain correctly surmised that neither could be the long-sought short route to China. He continued along the coast until, on a foggy September morning, an eerie fire, seeming to float above the horizon, lured the curious explorer landward. The source of that mysterious flame has never been discovered, but when the sun scattered the morning haze, Sandy Hook showed up dead ahead. Sailing into "a great stream out of the bay," Hudson anchored within sight of high hills and verdant forests. That night Robert Juet, one of the English officers, wrote in his log book, "This is a very good land to fall with, and a pleasant land to see."

More than a week was passed in exploring the bay and trading with Indians. Hudson, politely returning a visit made by the native chieftains to the *Half Moon*, went ashore in full ceremonial procession. He was serenaded by savages who gathered around and "sung in their fashion." Unhappily, the harmonious setting did not prevail. Later, with or without provocation, warriors in canoes attacked five sailors in the ship's longboat. Rain had extinguished the fire for their matchlocks, leaving the five at the mercy of Indian arrows. Nightfall and some hearty rowing saved them, but not before one of their number was killed and two others painfully wounded. To guard against future incidents, Hudson took two braves hostage, outfitted them with red coats, and confined them in the ship. Things became tense in New York Bay; it was time to continue the voyage.

Autumn's first bright leaves were appearing when the little ship, hampered by a northerly wind, began the journey upstream after midday on 12 September. Next day the wind remained contrary, but the *Half Moon* rode several miles with the tides. Far from being discouraged, the crew was growing eager—such tidal action in so large a body of water could indicate that they were in a strait connecting the Atlantic with the Pacific. And that alluring ocean might—just might—lie beyond those haze-enveloped mountains looming on the northern horizon. The 14th dawned bright and clear and brought a spanking, southeast wind. Billowing sails rushed the excited explorers all the way from upper Manhattan Island to a site near modern Peekskill before the afternoon was half over. Wanting to use all the friendly wind, Hudson determined to attempt the treacherous-looking passage through the forbidding mountains that day. With "high land on both sides," the *Half Moon* threaded the strange route, successfully negotiated the S-turn between West Point and Constitution Island, and, to the jubilant cries of her crew, steered northward toward open water as dusk began to settle. Anchoring at dark under the bulking eminence of Storm King, Henry Hudson very likely felt closer to success than he ever had—or would. In the last moments of daylight he had plainly seen that the waterway widened suggestively beyond the mountains now towering over him. Moreover, the tides were obviously still active, and the fish-filled water was salty. He probably slept little.

Teasingly, a thick river fog enshrouded them at dawn. With triumph possibly within reach, and a southerly wind wasting, the impatient explorers chafed as they rode at anchor. Intrigued with thoughts of what the day might bring, the sailors guarding the two hostages grew lax. In a trice, the redskins had squirmed through a porthole and were swimming ashore. No chase was given, for at that moment the mist began clearing and the crew turned out to get under way. Safely on shore, and seeing the *Half Moon* departing, the Indians shouted "in scorne" and made vulgar gestures (the journal of the voyage leaves it to our imagination to picture what the savages might have thought was vulgar). Maybe it is appropriate that the Indians chose that moment to escape and to mock the white men, for, as the day wore on, it must have become more and more obvious to Hudson that he was on a river, not a passageway to the Pacific. In consolation, natives living near that night's anchorage turned out to be "very loving people."

After reaching the vicinity of the confluence of the Hudson and Mohawk Rivers, the English navigator, disappointed but resigned, turned his Dutch ship southward. No longer hurried by vain hopes of reaching the Pacific, he conducted a more leisurely return trip. Days were spent walking along the shore, bantering with Indians, and investigating possible sites for settlements. Amazed by the profusion of trees, counting great quantities of chestnuts, noting the abundant slate and stone for houses, and finding the soil to be suitable for farming, Robert Juet wrote that the area north of the Highlands would be "a very pleasant place to build a towne on." The chief of the "loving people," quite likely eager to get another dram of the white man's intoxicating water, intercepted the *Half Moon* and pleaded with Hudson to come ashore for a visit. The captain, tired now of river exploration and impatient to cross the Atlantic before the onset of winter storms, declined the invitation. Not even two maidens, "of the age of sixteene or seventeene yeares," were inducement enough; the high poop of the *Half Moon* disappeared downstream, leaving the "loving people" and their maidens behind. We are not told what the crew thought.

Catching a good wind, the *Half Moon* made the stretch through the Highlands on the first day of October, but the breeze died suddenly, leaving her becalmed off Stony Point. There Hudson had his last adventure on the river which would bear his name. When Indians from the mountains came to trade, one crept into a cabin and grabbed a pillow, two shirts, and two bandoleers. Seen escaping, he was shot and killed. The explosion frightened the other Indians. They all leapt from the ship and swam away. All, that is, but one; he swam near the longboat and attempted to overturn it. Grabbing a cutlass, the ship's cook cut off the redskin's hand at the wrist. Splashing helplessly with the bloody stub, he sank. Incensed, his fellow braves lined the banks to fire arrows at the offending white men. They even paddled to within arrow range in canoes. Arrows, though, were no match for gunpowder; the Indians had the worst of the exchange and the Europeans, gathering a fresh breeze, sailed away unharmed.

Henry Hudson left New York Harbor on 4 October, landing in England six weeks later. He had not located a route to the Far East, but by exploring the stream he had christened "River of the Mountains," he had become one of the world's most famous failures.

Hudson's story spread quickly and far in the Old World. Dutch fortune seekers came to the "River of the Mountains" the very next year, and the next. Soon permanent trading posts were established. Settlers were not far behind. In 1620 the Pilgrims requested permission to start their new life on the shores of the Hudson. Turned down, they opted for Massachusetts. Three years later, thirty French-speaking Protestant families came to the New World. Fort Orange was raised on the long hill where Albany now stands, Esopus (Kingston) was planted, and clearings were made on the islands at the mouth of the river Henry Hudson had explored. In 1625 forty-five settlers joined these first families. A year more and Peter Minuit arrived holding a commission to govern New Netherlands and a sack of beads to buy Manhattan. Officially, the river was renamed "Mauritius" in honor of the great soldier-statesman, Prince Maurice of Orange. Practical pioneers, though, called it "North River" to differentiate between it and the Delaware, the "South River."

Although a new flare-up in the chronic war between Mohawks and Mohicans hindered progress above the Highlands, settlements south of those mountains flourished. By 1628, Manhattan proudly claimed 270 people and several windmills; not thirty years later there were in the town on the tip of the island over a hundred quaint houses and about a thousand quarrelsome persons. Trade prospered, ships were built, new settlements sprang up, and the feudal Patroon system was instituted. The first great manors of the Hudson were founded.

But, inevitably, the Indian war could not be limited to the Indians. Despite the fact that Dutch and Mohican relations had been generally good, many settlers saw in the Indian war an opportunity to weaken the local tribes. As hundreds of refugee Mohicans streamed down the Hudson to escape marauding Mohawks, William Kieft, a particularly inept governor, thought he saw his chance. At midnight, 25 February 1643, militia massacred about 120 sleeping men, women, and children. Understandably, the Mohicans never again trusted or adored the Dutch. Intermittent warfare between whites and reds would plague the Hudson Valley for many decades to come.

Peg-legged, pompous Peter Stuyvesant replaced the brutal Kieft in 1647. The new governor was able, aggressive, and quickly unpopular. He wasted no time before putting his personal stamp on the colony. Manhattan became New Amsterdam. Selling liquor to Indians was forbidden; worse, a tax was slapped on alcoholic beverages consumed by the heavy-drinking burghers themselves. Schools were opened, bucket brigades were organized, fences repaired and painted. Conciliatory gestures were made to calm the Indians. Improved relations were arranged with other colonies. Tactless and overbearing, Stuyvesant nonetheless governed the opinionated inhabitants of New Netherlands with a comprehensive, firm, long-needed efficiency. When a severe earthquake struck the length of the Hudson Valley in 1663, local wags claimed that it was "old silver leg" trying to straighten the river's channel through the Highlands.

Stuyvesant's rule—and Holland's—ended fifty-five years, almost to the day, after Hudson claimed the "sweet smelling" territory for the Netherlands. Colonel Richard Nicolls, an Englishman working for England, sailed into the harbor at the head of an expedition of 450 men and four ships. New Amsterdam became New York without a drop of blood being spilled.

English rule and English settlers altered the flavor of the New World province. New Netherlands, like New Amsterdam, became New York; Fort Orange was renamed Albany; Esopus was called Kingston; and the noble river finally received the name of its explorer. Not surprisingly, the two cultures clashed. Even such a seemingly reconcilable matter as how properly to celebrate Christmas produced bitter sparks. It was with unrestrained joy, then, that the burghers welcomed a Dutch force which reconquered the province in 1673. Briefly, Netherlands sovereignty was restored, but the ecstatic Dutch inhabitants had scant opportunity to profit from their release. Six months later, at a European treaty table, New York was turned back to Britain. The infuriated American Dutchmen had nothing to do but chew through the stems of their long clay pipes and make the best of it. Although they became English subjects, their peculiar habits and peculiar stubbornness left an impact on the Hudson Valley that would not be worn away.

With that colonizing genius possessed in such great measure by the English, Royal officials bent their efforts toward making New York a peaceful and profitable province. As events would prove, it would be easier to fashion fortunes than to establish tranquility in the New World. But they tried. Most Indian chiefs, finding these new white men more to their liking, agreed to cooperate. Mohawks and Mohicans, at English insistence, called off their lengthy war. For the first time in decades, human blood did not redden the Hudson's surface. Counties were laid out; courts were instituted; and—that ultimate sign of civilization—post offices were established. By the last decade of the seventeenth century, New York was not only prospering, it was booming.

Underneath, however, all was not well. Unrest, feeding on economic agitation and anti-Catholic sentiment, sprang into full rebellion. In June 1689, Jacob Leisler, wine merchant and militia captain, seized the city. The following March he sent an expedition of 160 men up the Hudson to capture Albany. With the fall of that northern town, the "Democrats," as Leisler's followers styled themselves, controlled all of New York. At Leisler's call, representatives of five colonies met at New York City in May 1690. Even though the purpose of the gathering was limited to consideration of a combined assault against the French and Indians in Canada, a significant precedent of united colonial action was set by that first colonial congress. The resulting expedition was something less than spectacular; it succeeded merely in reaching Lake Champlain before dwindling provisions and shrinking perseverance forced it back. As a matter of fact, all of Leisler's luck was running out. Early in 1691 he was captured, tried, and executed by a force sent out from England. Nevertheless, his two-year rule of a New York "Republic" had conjured up dual specters of colonial independence and combined colonial military action. He had lived eighty-five years too soon.

After the Leisler affair, New Yorkers turned their attention to money matters only to discover that their town was an expanding center for a burgeoning, lucrative, new business—piracy. With the blessings and protection of then Governor Benjamin Fletcher, the lower Hudson became a booming haven for buccaneers. Numerous dark coves and tree-shrouded streams along the river assured immunity, while the governor's benevolence and letters of marque assured success. What was worse, the pirates did not limit their activities to high-seas robbery. An entry in Albany's records for 1696 complained that "pirates in great numbers infest the Hudson at its mouth and waylay vessels on their way to Albany, speeding out from covers and from behind islands and again returning to the rocky shores, or ascending the mountains along the river to conceal their plunder." Tainted gold poured into New York, making the fortunes of many an otherwise proper and respected businessman. As the scandalous affair reached such proportions that the Hudson was bidding well to achieve the notoriety enjoyed by the Barbary Coast, the Ministry in England took steps to squelch it. Richard Coote, Earl of Bellomont, arriving with a mandate to break up the piracy ring, succeeded Fletcher. A well-armed vessel was fitted out and turned over to one of New York's more distinguished gentlemen, Mr. William Kidd. He was charged with bringing the "pirates, free booters, and sea rovers to justice." Kidd's approach to the problem of clearing the seas was rather unusual—he efficiently began picking off the fattest merchantmen himself, leaving little for the other pirates to steal. Thus was launched the career of Captain Kidd, king of sea robbers.

Before his capture and subsequent swinging, Kidd returned to the Hudson with a treasure variously estimated at about a million dollars in mid-twentieth-century purchasing power. Its disposition has never been completely explained. It could have been buried anywhere along the Hudson from a location south of Albany to the sands of Gardiner's Island. Kidd Point (or, more prosaically, Jones' Point) opposite Peerskill is the leading contender for the treasure cache in the Highlands. Generations of young men—and some not so young—have dug for that hidden fortune. It may be that the next generation will uncover it.

A decade after Kidd's bones glistened on a gibbet, war and hard times in Germany finally brought the resilient peoples of the Rhine Valley to despair. They decided to migrate to America. But to what location? After checking all available sources, the Germans were struck and convinced by similarities between descriptions of the Hudson Valley and their own Rhineland. And so the Palatine Germans, the "tarmakers," came to the august river. They chose to build their homes just north of the Highlands on a site that, precisely one century earlier, explorers from the *Half Moon* had selected as "a very pleasant place to build a towne on." They called it Newburgh. Following quickly on the heels of those first Germans came thousands of their countrymen. They were joined, too, by French Huguenots seeking freedom from religious persecution. Unnumbered Englishmen crowded in. Blacks, some free, most slaves, became abundant. A few Indians also were held in slavery. Dutchmen continued to join their New World relatives, apparently having decided that English rule could be tolerated after all. Many of all nationalities came as indentured servants. All in all, New York in the first two-thirds of the eighteenth century was a magnet of great power for Europe's disaffected. They came seeking freedom, planning a new life, searching fortune, and praying for peace. Whatever they achieved of the first three, they did not find peace in the Hudson Valley.

Of wars, the colonies had more than enough, even for the most reckless adventurers. Indians, increasingly reluctant to see their hunting grounds devoured, and waxing ever fonder of the white man's firewater, could be depended upon to go on the warpath from time to time. A sudden loss of hair was a disease endemic in the New World; the scalping knife joined great and small poxes, bloody fluxes, and childbirth as major hazards to good health. But the red men could have been tolerated, perhaps even tamed, if the white men could have kept the peace among themselves. They could not.

Leaving European lands did not mean leaving European wars. Conflicts between Old World enemies inevitably involved New World colonies. As France and England resumed their ancient feud, America was added to the long list of battlegrounds. When the "Glorious Revolution" of 1688 drove James II from the throne and replaced him with William and Mary, Americans were caught up in the ebb and flow of a struggle that would endure most of a century.

Colonists, far from the source of antagonism and often confused over the origins of the fighting, supported their monarch—but they insisted on naming the conflicts as they saw them. The War of the League of Augsburg became King William's War; Queen Anne's War was the American version of the War of the Spanish Succession; the War of the Austrian Succession had its counterpart on this side of the Atlantic in King George's War. This bewildering procession of wars, interspersed with Indian outbreaks on the frontiers and clashes with the Spaniards in Florida, settled almost nothing in America. France controlled Canada in 1688, at the outbreak of the fighting, and retained it sixty years later when the treaty of Aix-la-Chapelle temporarily ended the bloodshed. Actually, battles in the colonies were not especially bloody; blundering officials often failed to bring opposing forces together, and militiamen, imbued with the importance of living to fight another day, too seldom remained in the proximity of the foe on those occasions when he was encountered. But important patterns were set, it should be carefully noted. The Hudson River–Lake Champlain route became the highroad of war; men from all the colonies sailed bravely northward to invade Canada, while Bourbon soldiers started south on the same path to strike the colonies. That neither side was ever quite successful did not detract from the importance each attached to the route itself. Colonial cooperation was the second pattern to evolve. Though the various colonies could never have been accused of having been overly friendly toward one another, the danger of a common enemy did draw them closer. Moreover, the seeming inability—or indifference—of the mother country to provide protection gave all Americans an awareness of the benefits of mutual defense.

The stage was set for the final colonial clash, the French and Indian War. This one, called the Seven Years' War in Europe, would finally remove French authority from North America. Ironically, unlike previous conflicts, it would start in America and spread to Europe. And, perhaps poetically, it was triggered by a rash, twenty-two-year-old Virginia militia officer who led an expedition against French forces supposedly encroaching on the frontiers of his colony. The young officer was Colonel George Washington.

Eight colonies had sent representatives to a congress in Albany to discuss steps for a combined defense. Unfortunately, the delegates had been unable to agree on a plan of unity proposed by Benjamin Franklin, and indeed were discussing it when war began. Nonetheless, one more step toward colonial unity had been taken. And once again that step had been taken on the banks of the Hudson.

Bumbling among leaders and bickering amidst units was a feature of the French and Indian War—as it had been of all previous wars in Pioneer America. But this time there was a difference; more forces and better generals were sent out from England and a sincere effort was mounted to oust the French. Predictably, the Hudson was again chosen as the axis of a major invasion of Canada. French forces halted one column at Fort Ticonderoga in 1758, but a year later General Jeffery Amherst captured the Lake Champlain fort and, in another year, marched into Montreal. By 1763 the French had admitted defeat and, at long last, were driven from America. The King's loyal subjects in the colonies richly deserved their much desired peace. Peace hopes were illusory, though, even then.

In spite of wars, people along the Hudson's shores had increasingly prospered and procreated, had cleared large farms and begun numerous industries, had started businesses and built towns. The entire valley of the Hudson bustled with activity, with the striking exception of the Hudson Highlands. Few men were eager to scratch for a living in that rocky soil when good land was available farther north. Population and civilization advanced rapidly above and below the grim mountains, leaving the ghostly peaks to nod in nearly complete primordial loneliness. That is not to say that they were totally neglected. Some men, wealthy and in search of summer homes, chose the Highlands specifically for their splendid isolation. Beverley Robinson, past friend and future foe of George Washington, was one. Another was Stephen Moore, whose ostentatious home on the flats beneath West Point was widely known as "Moore's Folly." A few men, too poor to move on, erected wretched, solitary huts and attempted to squeeze survival from the stony fields. Young Timothy Dwight, later to become President of Yale College, paid a visit to the area and was shocked by his encounter with the inhabitants. "No human being," he wrote, "can be imagined as more ignorant or uncultivated or to exhibit more strongly the marks of poverty and barbarism." These indigent farmers were never very numerous and, as a rule, they did not remain long. In short, while the colony of New York flourished, the Hudson Highlands remained wild and inhospitable.

Roads were poor. In a time when highways were hardly more than muddy lanes cleared through virgin forests, when a law had to be passed requiring road builders to remove every stump over one foot high, when a journey on even the best of roads was exhausting and undependable, it is not surprising that most commerce and travel was by river. Two roads connected New York to Albany, one on each bank of the Hudson. They were not good ones even by the standards of the time. Consequently, river traffic was heavy and the number of ships on the Hudson grew as New York's population increased. One particular vessel, the Hudson River sloop, was specifically developed to cope with the tricky winds and variable tides encountered in the twisting passage through the Highlands. Trade burgeoned in warm months, but came to a virtual standstill when the river froze. Sensible men did not venture to pass the Highlands in the dead of winter; even the mail was carried by Indian runners hired for the cold season. In a very real sense, the Hudson had become the spinal column of the colony.

The impact of the Highlands was there for any discerning man to see. From dictating the path of war to influencing sloop design to inspiring the choice of settlements to hiring mail carriers, the imposing presence of the gray, rocky heights was a considerable factor of life in New York. And, as would soon become obvious, there were discerning men upon whom that significant fact was not lost.

Events moved at an alarming pace after the French left America. The threat of military exploitation by the French was replaced with the threat of economic exploitation by the English. At least that is how Americans understood the matter. Stamp Act, Sugar Act, Boston Massacre, and tea parties; redcoat, Regulator, Minuteman, and Tories—all merged confusingly in a heady, emotion-filled, fateful decade. Hotheads shouted for war; calmer men counseled patience. Those officials in England who could have prevented the Revolution seemed unaware of the seriousness of the explosive situation in the colonies. To handle his infuriated, independent-minded American subjects, George III needed expert, mature guidance from his cabinet. Unfortunately, serving him then was probably the most inefficient cabinet, and certainly some of the most ineffectual ministers, in British history.

In late April 1775 the first wild tales of Lexington and Concord reached the banks of the Hudson. That river, already steeped in history and soaked in blood, was poised on the edge of its greatest adventure. The lofty, granite summits of the Highlands had survived the wear of half a billion years to reach that moment. Where the Hudson and the Highlands cross would become a key location—maybe *the* key location—during the War of Independence. In fact, it would be called the "Key to the Continent."

PART ONE

THE FROWN OF ADVERSITY

1

DECISION IN MAY

IT WAS a long way from Fort Ticonderoga to Philadelphia. A week's trip would have been considered good time for a hard-riding messenger. Moreover, the sprawling, cosmopolitan capital of Pennsylvania had nothing in common with the compact, French-constructed fortress standing sentinel over a short but strategic portage between Lake Champlain and Lake George in the forested wilderness of upper New York. And yet, events at each site on one fateful day in May were to have a far-reaching impact on both shape and outcome of the American Revolution.

As dawn's first vague glimmer of light rolled over red tiles on the fort's south barracks, Ethan Allen, Benedict Arnold, and a hastily assembled crew of "Green Mountain Boys" crouched beneath Ticonderoga's dilapidated stone walls. A sudden rush, a startled sentry, a hoarse shout for surrender, and the fortress fell to American arms. The rudely awakened British commander—unaware of the bloody clash which had taken place three weeks earlier at the Massachusetts villages of Lexington and Concord —demanded to know under whose orders such an affront had been conducted. Allen thundered that he was acting in the name of "the Great Jehovah and the Continental Congress." It is not likely that he had a commission from the former, and certain that he had none from the latter, for the Continental Congress convened that very same day, 10 May 1775, in faraway Philadelphia.

Commotion paced the cobblestone streets in the City of Brotherly Love. Fresh details and accounts of the "shot heard round the world" constantly flowed in from New England. With each new version Americans saw their victory over the redcoats grow in magnitude. Open warfare, a threat for so many years, now loomed as a most distinct possibility. Gaudily attired militia units, finding a purpose other than social for their being, drilled in newborn earnestness. Young ladies discovered overnight the powerful attraction, and prestige, of a beau in uniform. Drummer boys drummed. Couriers managed to assume an air of sinister urgency as they clattered into town. Matrons wagged. Printers could not match the demand for news. Merchants fretted over the fate of Boston-bound cargoes. Excited citizens gathered in the taverns and talked knowingly of war and peace and Parliament and representation. And a number of very serious men, chosen to represent their states in the Second Continental Congress, weighed carefully the changed situation. They had not been elected to control a rebellion against the Crown, but the events of 19 April could not be ignored. As the hour of opening approached, a strange, light-hearted feeling of expectancy—tinged with dread—permeated Philadelphia. Quite clearly, Congress would have to face the terrible question of whether there should be war or reconciliation with the Mother Country.

Eleven states were represented on that first day. Georgia and Rhode Island had no envoys. Assembling in the ground-floor room of the east wing of the Pennsylvania State House, the delegates elected Peyton Randolph of Virginia President. Then, after agreeing to open their sessions with prayer, they adjourned until 10 o'clock next morning. It had been a long ride, many members had just arrived, and they would need to feel one another out in private before beginning business in public.

Thursday, 11 May, was hot and sultry. A dank coolness in the large, attractive chamber was a welcome respite from oppressive waves of heat reflecting from the street. Welcome, that is, until it was decided that all deliberations would be in secret. Behind locked doors, with windows opened no more than a good crack at the top, congressmen soon began to swelter. John Hancock of Massachusetts presented a stack of depositions purporting to prove that redcoats had really fired the first shots at Lexington and Concord. That consumed most of the day. When the reading was over, Congress ordered that Hancock's documents be published in newspapers. They met again on Friday, but adjourned almost immediately. More delegates were expected, especially from pivotal New York, and sparring for position was not yet completed. Discussions continued over cups in cooler taverns and private drawing rooms. Two camps were emerging even then: a war party headed vigorously by the Massachusetts delegation, and a more cautious group seeking conciliation, composed generally of central and southern state representatives. John Adams, a plump-appearing but tough-minded Boston lawyer, paced the hard-line faction, while John Dickinson, a thoroughgoing Pennsylvania Patriot, gravitated to the position of spokesman for conservative members.

On Saturday, a saddlesore agent from one county in Georgia arrived. Rhode Island's representative reported two days later, raising to thirteen the number of colonies participating. Over the weekend, several additional emissaries from New York joined their compatriots. Among them were George Clinton, Robert R. Livingston, Philip Schuyler, and Henry Wisner —all fated to fulfill crucial roles in the forthcoming war in the Hudson

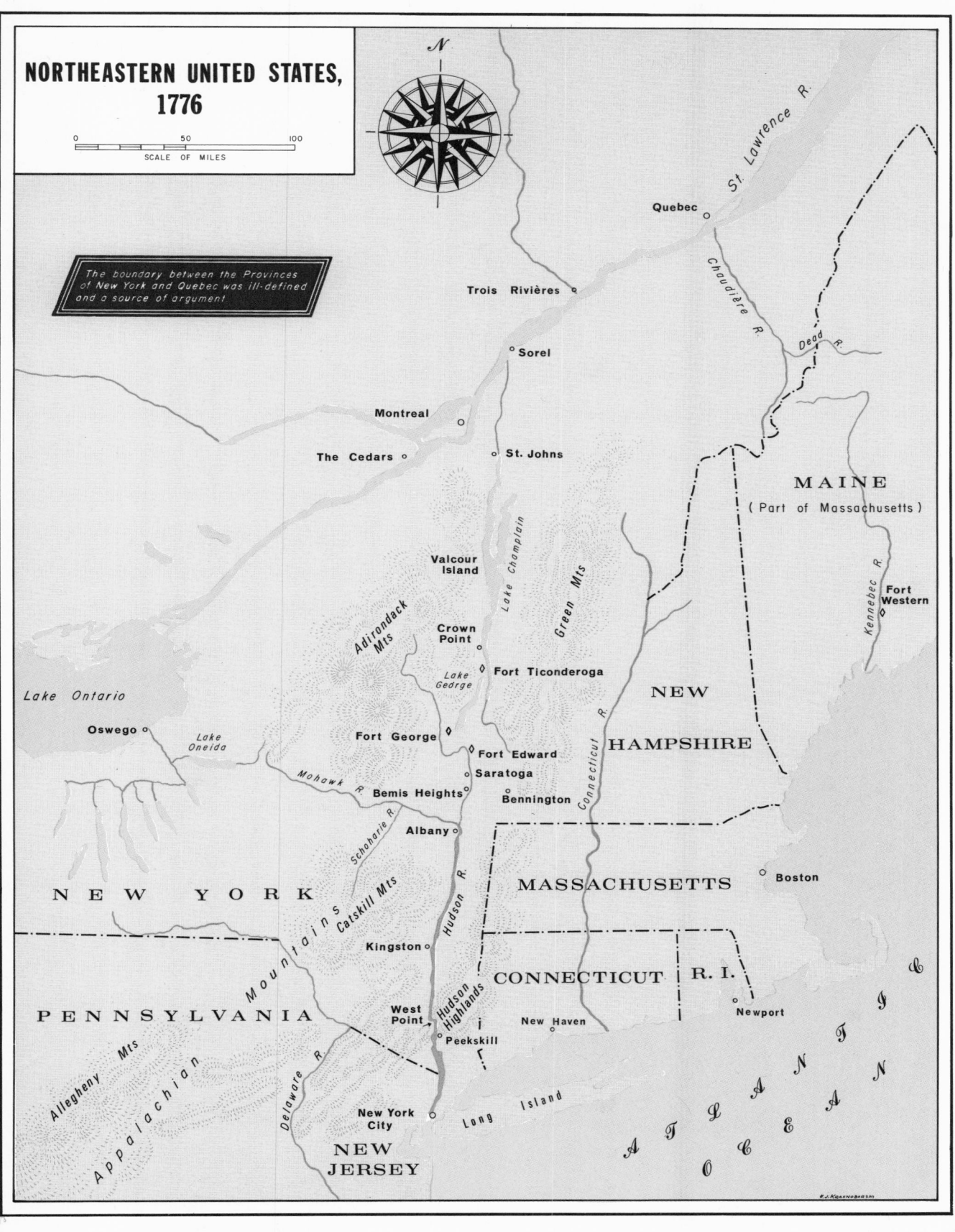

NORTHEASTERN UNITED STATES, 1776

0   50   100
SCALE OF MILES

N

The boundary between the Provinces of New York and Quebec was ill-defined and a source of argument.

Quebec

St. Lawrence R.

Chaudière R.

Dead R.

Trois Rivières

Sorel

Montreal

The Cedars

St. Johns

MAINE
(Part of Massachusetts)

Lake Champlain

Valcour
Island

Green Mts

Kennebec R.

Fort
Western

Crown
Point

*Adirondack
Mts*

*Lake
George*

Fort Ticonderoga

NEW

Lake Ontario

Oswego

*Lake
Oneida*

Fort George

Connecticut R.

HAMPSHIRE

Mohawk R.

Fort Edward

Saratoga

Bemis Heights

Bennington

Schoharie R.

Albany

Boston

NEW   YORK

Catskill Mts

MASSACHUSETTS

Appalachian   Mountains

Kingston

CONNECTICUT

R. I.

PENNSYLVANIA

West
Point

*Hudson
Highlands*

New Haven

Newport

Allegheny Mts

Appalachian

Delaware R.

Peekskill

Hudson R.

New York
City

Long Island

NEW
JERSEY

A T L A N T I C

O C E A N

F. J. Krasnoborski

Valley. When Congress convened at nine o'clock Monday morning, its members were prepared at last to get down to work.

Thoughtful Patriots in New York had correctly surmised that any spreading of the conflict, then conveniently confined to Boston, would involve their own seaport at the Hudson's mouth. With that fear in mind, they sent a message by their last increment of delegates requesting advice from the Continental Congress. Congress' answer was equivocal. New York should act passively, even let soldiers be quartered in city barracks, so long as the troops did nothing to threaten city security or colonial communications. However, all warlike stores should be removed to safe areas and, Congress added, it would be proper to "repel force by force." That answer was an obvious compromise and satisfied neither faction. To appease the activists, Congress further resolved "that a committee be appointed to consider what posts are necessary to be occupied in the Colony of New York, and by what number of troops it will be necessary they should be guarded."[1]

Selection of committee members was a rather simple task. New York's entire delegation was appointed, while Thomas Lynch, a respected South Carolinian, and Samuel Adams, a Massachusetts firebrand, provided geographical balance. As for chairman, a military man was deemed appropriate. One member of Congress stood out alone as an obvious choice, a man qualified by reputation and experience to assume responsibility for military matters. And lest someone overlook his rank, George Washington, Colonel of Virginia Militia, had been wearing his uniform since reaching Philadelphia. For two days Congress continued in its unhurried manner to develop a line of action. New England delegates, sweating in woolen clothes, began to grumble at the lack of progress. After all, New England blood had already been spilled; time for talking was past. But other colonies, less involved, were not to be rushed into joining Boston's "argument" with General Gage. On 17 May Congress even paused to attend graduation exercises at the College of Philadelphia, later the University of Pennsylvania. The *Pennsylvania Packet* of 29 May 1775 reported admiringly that Congress was "the most illustrious assembly [the college] ever beheld." It was indeed a most illustrious body. Eminent within it was Benjamin Franklin, America's (and, many would have added, Europe's) foremost scientist, inventor, writer, and statesman, to cite but a few of his remarkable qualifications. George Washington's mere presence endowed Congress with a certain calm dignity, while John Adams, John Hancock, John Dickinson, Samuel Chase, Richard Henry Lee, Edward Rutledge, and many others made truth of the *Packet*'s high-flown description.

Illustrious Congress might be, precipitate never. After the graduation exercises, it met at noon and cautiously voted to curtail exports to other British possessions in the Americas. That could hardly have been construed as a hostile act; economic sanctions had been used before.[2]

Then, after adjournment, electrifying news of attack and victory at Ticonderoga reached Philadelphia. An entirely new problem confronted Congress. No longer was it simply a question of farmers defending their personal property and individual rights against military depredations;

Americans had taken the offensive and had conquered a great, bastioned fortress defended by the King's regulars. No matter that it had been lightly garrisoned with invalids and half-pay soldiers. It was remembered only that 15,000 British had once been bloodily repulsed there and that it was a strategic point fought over in all previous wars. Ticonderoga was a big name. Pride was the first reaction of most delegates; then, on more sober reflection, consternation. Reconciliation, which had been the drift of Congress, now suddenly seemed removed from reach. Open war was nearer. Washington kept his committee working late that night, studying New York and Hudson River maps at the Conestoga Wagon Inn on Market Street.[3]

Next day, feeling it should somehow do something about the *fait accompli* handed it by Arnold and Allen, Congress resolved that cannon and other stores should be removed to Lake George. Once there, Congress prudently instructed, all booty should be carefully inventoried so that it could be returned to British officials after "restoration of the former harmony between Great Britain and these colonies so ardently wished for by the latter."

It happened just then that a Major Skene of the British army came ashore at the Market Street Wharf. He announced that he was the newly appointed governor of Ticonderoga and Crown Point as well as "Surveyor of the Woods." Tauntingly informed that he should show his commission to Ethan Allen, the major was laughed out of town.

Washington's committee worked by candlelight a second straight night. Among the New Yorkers on the committee were several who had seen at first hand, in the last war, the Hudson's strategic importance. They told of New York's vulnerability to an invasion from Canada and described the river's worth as a barrier to east-west travel. Any effort, they assured Washington, on the part of other colonies to aid New England was doomed to failure should English sail dominate the watercourse. Furthermore, if the river were lost, Americans north of the Hudson Highlands would be left to the frightful mercy of Indians. Military logic was obvious in their arguments. Washington, Lynch, and Adams agreed: the Hudson must be held.

It was no secret that Washington favored a decisive course. Usually a taciturn, unpoetic man, not given at all to penning or speaking inspirational words, he wrote that month to a friend:

> Unhappy . . . it is to reflect that a brother's sword has been sheathed
> in a brother's breast, and that the once happy and peaceful plains of
> America are either to be drenched with blood or inhabited by slaves.
> Sad alternative! But can a virtuous man hesitate in his choice?[4]

One month to the day after Paul Revere's ride, Washington delivered his committee's report. Congress dissolved itself into a committee of the whole to consider it. No decision was reached that day. Nor the next nor the next. After a Sabbath rest, debate was resumed with equal lack of results. Randolph was obliged to leave for Virginia and John Hancock was elected President to replace him, but still the gentlemen in the State House reached no decision. The cleavage within Congress was not as deep as it might have seemed, however. On the end to be achieved, a consensus had been reached. Redress of grievances against a "wicked Parliament" was the goal, not separation from the Crown. As a matter of fact, at inns where delegates gathered to slake their thirst, toasts were drunk to the health of George III. The snag came in searching for means to reach that end. Was appeasement or force the proper path? Washington's report had recommended vigorous steps to be taken to defend New York. Those measures looked ominously warlike to some of the representatives.

Finally, on 25 May, Congress reached agreement. On that day it made its first outright decision to wage war in the name of thirteen colonies against Great Britain. The decision came in the form of six resolutions: first, the colony of New York was to take and fortify a post at Kingsbridge on the northern end of Manhattan Island; second, posts should "be also taken in the Highlands on each side of Hudson's River and batteries erected in such manner as will most effectually prevent any vessels passing" up the river; the remaining four dealt with administrative problems of pay, training, numbers, equipment, and length of service. A day later a seventh was added: New York was advised to "persevere the more vigorously" in preparing her defenses for it was "very uncertain whether the earnest endeavours" toward reconciliation would be successful. John Hancock, forwarding Congress' desires to New York, asked the Provincial Convention of that state to keep the subject as much a secret as possible.[5]

Significant though it is, one should not try to interpret Congress' decision to act to defend the Hudson before all other places as evidence of clairvoyance. New Yorkers, understandably vitally concerned themselves, had made it the first tangible issue of discussion, and Arnold and Allen had highlighted the strategic importance of the waterway by their dramatic, bloodless coup at Ticonderoga. Nevertheless, the very critical importance the river would assume in a wider conflict was recognized by the men in the State House. Defense of the Hudson was not only the first action of war debated and decided upon by the Continental Congress, it was also the first responsibility assigned to George Washington by the lawmakers. It would remain of abiding interest to both the Virginian and the Congress.

Washington had spent the last five evenings during the debate alone in his lodgings in the home of Edward Fitz Randolph. Then, exuberantly celebrating his victory in traditional soldierly fashion, the colonel caroused two weekday nights running in City Tavern.[6]

A 32-gun frigate, *Cerberus*, anchored in Boston Harbor the same day Congress voted to defend the Hudson. Aboard the ship (named, by the way, for the mythical, three-headed dog which guards the gate to Hell) were three members of that Parliament which had so angered Americans. Aside from their Parliamentary affiliations, John Burgoyne, Henry Clinton, and William Howe were also major generals in His Majesty's service. Those three, like the Virginia colonel in Philadelphia, found reason to hoist a happy glass that night. A long voyage was ended and the future, for soldiers, looked bright. In the war fast closing in, each would have an opportunity to cross swords with forces led by George Washington in battles swirling around the Hudson River. Each, in turn, would come to regret it; only Washington would endure.

2

CONSTRUCTION BY COMMITTEE

W*ITH THE* illegal but functioning Continental Congress as an example, New York radicals established their own legislative body. Called at first a Congress, later Convention, it opened on 23 May 1775 in the Exchange Building in New York City. The delegates' position was precarious. Loyalists were strong in the city and the southern counties of the state, technically no formal revolt had begun, and even the most ardent of Whigs could not agree on ultimate aims. Nonetheless, they met, hammered out rules of procedure, and assumed the mantle of legislative authority for the State of New York. Aware—and worried, perhaps—that he and his compatriots were treading around treason, Alexander McDougall moved that "all the Ministers in this City who can pray in English" should be requested to take turns opening each day's session. The motion passed swiftly. Their status thus clarified in Heaven if not in London, the representatives turned to more worldly matters.

Ticonderoga was the first item of discussion. Fearing an irruption from Canada, the Continental Congress had requested that New Yorkers remove the cannon and stores from the great fortress and secure them near the southern tip of Lake George. New York's Convention, after appointing a committee to superintend that transfer of equipment, turned its attention largely to matters of always short money and always touchy relations with neighboring provinces. Then on 29 May two documents arrived to spur the representatives to action. The first was the list of seven resolutions passed by the Continental Congress four days earlier, exhorting New York to block the Hudson. Lending urgency to those directives was the second document, a letter from Colonel Benedict Arnold, dated at Crown Point, 23 May 1775, earnestly requesting reinforcements and warning of an imminent invasion by a force of regulars and Indians aimed at the recapture of Ticonderoga. To help Arnold, the Provincial Convention forwarded his plea for assistance to Philadelphia and ordered that pork, flour, and twenty barrels of rum be sent to sustain the light garrisons on Lake Champlain. It would take more than food and liquor to erect forts along the Hudson River, though. The men in the Exchange Building decided to think about it overnight.[1]

Next day, exhibiting the mercantile rather than military make-up of its members, the Provincial Convention argued long over a committee report on the efficacy of paper currency. After a break in late afternoon, the delegates reassembled for an evening session to consider defending the Hudson. It was relatively easy to agree on raising a fortification at Kingsbridge on Manhattan Island, for every member knew that location, and a committee was promptly appointed to select the precise site.

Defenses in the Hudson Highlands were quite another matter. Not all the delegates were familiar with the area, and not a few were concerned that the cost of such a project might prove exorbitant. Late that night, after lengthy but inconclusive discussions, the weary legislators decided to send two of their number as an exploratory committee to gather information. Colonel James Clinton and Mr. Christopher Tappen, lifelong residents of the area just beyond the Highlands, were to take such assistants as they might need and "go to the Highlands and view the banks of the Hudson River there, and report to this Congress the most proper place for erecting one or more fortifications; and likewise an estimate of the expense that will attend erecting the same."[2]

The Convention displayed wisdom in its choice. Tappen, a stolid Dutchman, was a trustee of Kingston and a clerk of the corporation as well. He understood finances. Clinton, of English ancestry, taller and bolder than Tappen, enjoyed a good reputation as a soldier, having served as a captain in the expedition against Fort Frontenac in 1758 and, two years later, in Lord Jeffery Amherst's campaign down the St. Lawrence to capture Montreal. He was also an experienced surveyor, an occupation requiring a good feel for terrain. Both men knew the country intimately. Clinton had been born and raised at Little Britain just west of Newburgh, within sight of the Hudson Highlands, while Tappen was a native of Kingston farther up the river. Finally, to assure cooperation, the two were brothers-in-law; James Clinton's younger brother, George, had eloped with pretty Cornelia Tappen some five years earlier. He was also the George Clinton who was then sitting in the Continental Congress and who had helped George Washington prepare the study calling for fortifications along the Hudson.

No one was in a hurry. As the two men walked from the Exchange Building into the balmy May night, they agreed to arrange details for the voyage on the morrow. The day just ending had been a very long and vexing one. Next morning they contracted for a boat, secured the assistance of two militia captains, Samuel Bayard and Erasmus Williams, and set Friday, 2 June, as the sailing date. By that scheduling they would be able to spend Sunday with their families above the Highlands. Arrangements made, the two delegates attended Convention sessions on both Wednesday and Thurs-

General James Clinton. Courtesy of Washington's Headquarters Museum.

day. Early Friday they boarded their hired sloop, stood out into the Hudson, and headed upriver.

It is quite likely that the exploratory committee had already made up its mind without benefit of exploration. The tortured path of the river through the rocky defiles of the Highlands was well known to both. Moreover, the Hudson had long been a waterway of war; men had considered closing it before. As soldier, surveyor, and local inhabitant, Clinton was almost surely aware of past estimates that the best choke point along the entire river was where the water was channeled through a sharp S-turn between Martalear's Rock—a stony island connected to the east shore by a swamp—and a higher point thrusting out from the west.

On the trip north they noted prospective sites for fortifications, marking them carefully on a map for future inspection. Stony Point and Verplanck's Point, where the river narrows above Haverstraw Bay and the Highlands begin, were listed as potential positions for early-warning outposts. The men aboard the little sailing vessel must have scrutinized with care Anthony's Nose, a mountain rising almost straight out of the water on the eastern side of the river and towering above nearby hills. It was a widely known landmark because of the great protruding rock halfway up the cliffs which gave the looming mountain an uncannily lifelike human profile—and its name. But Clinton, the soldier, would quickly have seen that despite its very commanding appearance, Anthony's Nose was too steep and too high to have any military significance. However, directly across from the mountain, where Popolopen Creek emptied into the Hudson, were two promising positions which appeared to provide a good sweep of the river. Clinton was not enthusiastic, though, because he was looking for a place where works could be erected on both sides of the river. Had he known that two years later he would be fighting for his very life in a fort on the hill above Popolopen Creek—a fort, moreover, named after him—his interest might have quickened.

Continuing upstream the sloop passed Sugarloaf Mountain, rising in a long, graceful curve on the right, and Buttermilk Falls, spilling foam on the left. There was a glimpse through trees of Beverley Robinson's splendid country home nestled under Sugarloaf. The wild, strong beauty of this stretch had been sampled many times before by Clinton and Tappen, but now, imagining themselves on an English warship trying to beat upriver under hostile fire from the shores, the brothers-in-law were for the first time aware of what a terrible gauntlet Nature had devised.

Looking ahead and slightly to the left they saw the high plain—called even then "the West Point"—rising above them. Partly hidden behind it was Martalear's Rock, soon to be named Constitution Island. Tacking sharply to port as he rounded the point, the vessel's captain fought wind and current and tide to avoid being thrown too near the shore and onto the boulders lurking in shallow water there. Clinton happily observed that the ship was completely at the mercy of imaginary cannon on the bank. It might have been at that moment that he conceived the idea of stretching some sort of obstacle across the water to further impede vessels attempting to pass.

Suddenly coming into view just beyond the West Point, on the same side of the river, was the fancy—"ostentatious" some described it—country home built by a prominent and wealthy merchant from New York City, John Moore. Situated on a lovely spot of flat land nearly at water level, the red structure with its shutters and steeply sloping roof seemed strangely out of place—a touch of too much civilization in this almost primeval wilderness. Local folk called it "Moore's Folly." Crow's Nest Mountain rose abruptly behind, adding both beauty and contrast. Stephen Moore had inherited the house and most of the land on the western shore which so interested Clinton and Tappen.

As the boat emerged from the gap between Storm King and Breakneck, the Hudson Highlands behind, Clinton may have made note of one last possibility for a defensive position. Standing out from the eastern shore was Pollepel Island. Although the river was wide at this point, it was shallow from the island all the way to Plum Point on the western side, a factor to be considered because the river runs deep, very deep, in its chasm through the Highlands.

After a pleasant weekend with their families, the two representatives turned the sloop southward for the return trip. Accompanied by their assistants, they went ashore first at Moore's landing.

On the large, level area behind West Point was a good growth of evergreen trees, interspersed with corn fields and cow pastures, and laced with sparkling, sweet springs. Stone for building was plentiful. Lime, the men knew, could be procured from Newburgh and other settlements to the north. The command of the river was superb from atop the promontory overlooking the zig-zag course around the Point. Clinton would have been quietly pleased could he have known that a bastioned fort, bearing his name, would one day rise where he stood; he would have been chagrined to foresee all that would transpire before that day.

Crossing the Hudson to Martalear's Rock, Clinton and Tappen were delighted to discover that the island was also well suited for fortification. Two small fields, where the ground was level and workable, and an unoccupied house near the marshes on the southeast corner of the island were proof that it was habitable. Fresh water was not so abundant as on the West Point, but a natural site for a powder magazine was found. That did it. They agreed that forts and artillery batteries should be placed on both West Point and Martalear's Rock. Obstructions should also be built to block the water between the two places. Closer inspection of other locations to the south did not alter those initial conclusions.

Docking in New York about midday on Thursday, 8 June, the two delegates were able to resume their seats in an afternoon session beginning at four o'clock. After putting their report into very careful prose and preparing an accompanying map, they submitted their findings to the Provincial Convention on Saturday. It read in part:

> Your Committee . . . report it as their opinion that a post, capable of containing three hundred men, erected on the east bank of Hudson's River, marked A, and another on the west side of said river, to contain two hundred men, marked B, in the annexed map, will answer the

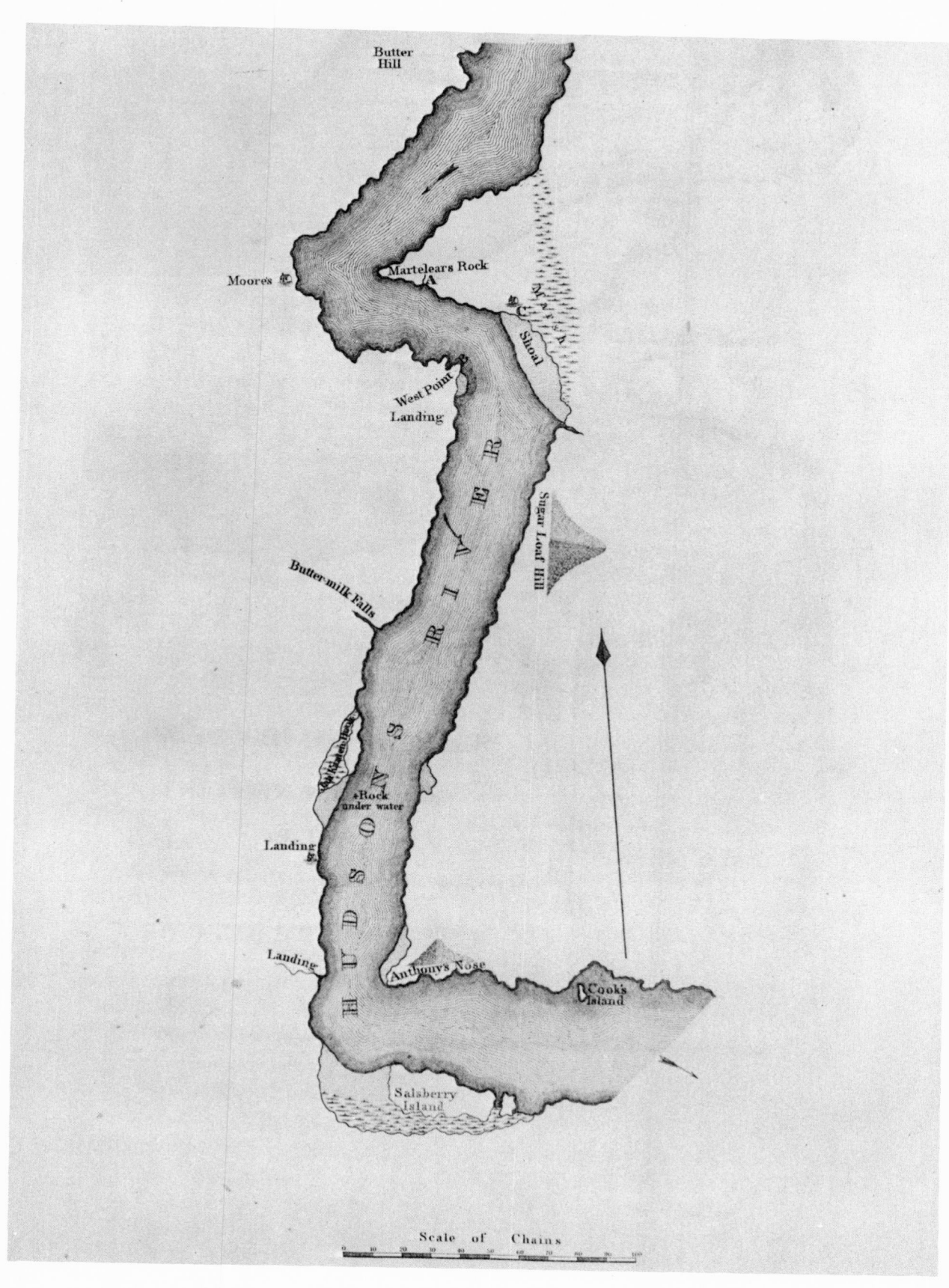

Butter
Hill

Moore's

Martelears Rock

Shoal

West Point
Landing

RIVER

Sugar Loaf Hill

Butter-milk Falls

HUDSON

Rock
under water

Landing

Landing

Anthony's Nose

Cook's
Island

Salsberry
Island

Scale of Chains

*Map of the Highlands drawn to accompany the report of James Clinton
and Christopher Tappen. From American Archives.*

purpose proposed and directed by the Continental Congress, as it is not only the narrowest part of the said river, but best situated, on account of the high hills contiguous to it, as well on the west as east side of the river which cover those parts; so that without a strong easterly wind, or the tide, no vessel can pass it; and the tide on said part of the river is generally so reverse, that a vessel is usually thrown on one side of the river or the other, by means whereof such vessel lay fair and exposed to the places Your Committee have fixed on.[3]

Having delivered themselves of that breathtaking sentence, Clinton and Tappen went on to write of drinking water, construction materials, boats, signals, and the like. Then, somewhat hesitantly, they included the observation that "by means of four or five booms chained together on one side of the river, ready to be drawn across, the passage can be closed up, to prevent any vessel passing or repassing." Booms, in the parlance of the day, were linked, raftlike affairs made of heavy logs or old boats. When connected and stretched across a river they served the same purpose against ships as felled timber, or abatis, did against horses on land. The concept of obstructing a river in that manner was not new. A key inlet at Constantinople had been closed by a chain centuries earlier, and a "Great Chain" had been a factor in the renowned siege of Malta. More recently, the French at Quebec had integrated a boom into their defenses of that river citadel. Clinton, having fought in Canada, had probably heard of Quebec's boom, though it is doubtful that he ever saw it.

Charged also with determining an approximate cost, the two were unsure of the ultimate expense: "Your Committee are unable to make a true estimate of the expense that will attend the erecting the said fortifications. . . ." Their guess was that it would require no less than £1,500. That struck a raw nerve; money was scarce.

The Convention decided to postpone decision while forwarding the results of the survey to the New York delegation in Philadelphia. Perhaps the New Yorkers hoped that Congress might pay for the project, since that body had first raised the subject. If that was their reasoning, the timing was exceedingly poor. On the very day the Convention ordered the report forwarded, Congress was groping painfully for "ways and means of raising money." Then, on following days, Congress busied itself raising and organizing an army. On 15 June it selected George Washington to be Commander-in-Chief of a Continental Army. Not until after Washington made his acceptance speech a day later did Congress take a moment to consider New York's problems. The men in Philadelphia had no ready solution. The best that could be done was to tell New York to ask Connecticut for aid and soldiers.[4]

It may be that each believed the other would assume responsibility for building the Highlands forts. For whatever reason, neither Convention nor Congress took any action on the matter that month—or the next.

Events elsewhere might have helped shove thoughts of the Hudson into the background. The Battle of Bunker Hill was fought on 17 June, a lesson in itself of the value of fortifications. Just over a week later New York City found itself in the awkward situation of hosting on the same day the passage of General Washington on his way to Boston and the arrival of a new Royal Governor, William Tryon. Luckily, Washington passed in the morning and Tryon came in the afternoon; both received honors. Washington, in fact, was welcomed with a formal statement wishing him success in gaining "an accommodation with our Mother Country." The incident typified a certain ambivalence which permeated the thinking of most American leaders that summer—they were preparing for war while halfway expecting peace. War was a fact by then, but a hard one to accept. In any event the Convention adjourned on 8 July. Congress did likewise on the first day of August. Summer passed softly in the Hudson Highlands.

By the middle of August defenses along the Hudson appeared to be a forgotten matter. Offensive actions held the center of attention. Two New York generals, Philip Schuyler and Richard Montgomery, were preparing to invade Canada over the Lake Champlain route while Washington was readying a second force, to be commanded by Benedict Arnold, to strike at Quebec through the Maine woods. There remained about three months suitable for construction work in the Highlands before the onset of winter.

A letter from General Washington abruptly ended the Convention's equanimity. Received and read on 17 August, it relayed intelligence of a suspected British raid on New York City. It turned out to be a false alarm, but served nonetheless to restore a sense of urgency among the delegates. Next day "two prime sailing boats with proper persons" were ordered to reconnoiter ocean waters east of New York in an attempt to get early warning of an invasion. Some member of the Convention also remembered the Hudson Highlands. The delegates rather quickly resolved "that the fortifications formerly ordered by the Continental Congress, and reported by a Committee of this Congress, as proper to be built on the banks of Hudson's River, in the Highlands, be immediately erected." Nothing had been done for over two months—now, in the face of danger, the defenses were to be raised "immediately."[5]

A Commission of five members was appointed to "manage the erecting and finishing" of the works. By failing at the outset to hand authority—and concomitant responsibility—to a single accountable individual, the Convention set the stage for debacle. The Commission was a committee in every sense but name; because not all Commissioners were Convention delegates, the title "committee" could not properly be used. But a committee it was, with all the managerial shortcomings of committees in every age. Committees are safe—they seldom commit vast blunders. By the same token, they rarely do anything brilliant. It has been said that committees do nothing best and are best at doing nothing. Be that as it may, the War of Independence was a struggle conducted in the main by committee action; one should not expect the approach to defending the Hudson to have been any different. Similarly, one should not be surprised to learn that the Commission had mixed success in its endeavors.

Difficulties arose almost immediately in the form of personnel turbulence. Within days two Commissioners resigned. Samuel Bayard, who had accompanied Clinton and Tappen in June, and William Bedlow were selected as replacements. With the additions of John Hanson a week later and

Thomas Grenell in early September, the Commission numbered seven. John Berrien, the only one of the original members actually to perform any duties, was designated purchasing agent in New York City. It was good that Bayard was included, for none of the other members of the exploratory group were available for consultation. They were scattered on various missions. Clinton, fated to play a future role in the Highlands, had vacated his seat in the Convention to recruit and organize a regiment with which he would march into Canada alongside Montgomery.

After reading the report filed by Clinton and Tappen and hearing Bayard describe the sites, the Commission set as its first order of business procuring supplies and equipment and, most important, obtaining cannon. Funds to purchase guns and gear were not to be had, but the items themselves were available in the City Battery. On 22 August, by a 16-to-8 vote, the Convention authorized Commission members to remove whatever was "necessary for completely fortifying and equipping" the Highlands forts. The Commissioners started eagerly to work, only to be pulled up short within three days when the Convention, having second thoughts, ordered them to stop. Next day the unsure legislators reversed themselves once again and permitted the nettled Commissioners to continue. August's last days and the first week in September were devoted to readying all the equipment, assembling transportation, arranging (in vain) for a detachment of soldiers for protection, and hiring an engineer.[6]

Engineers were few in the Thirteen Colonies in 1775, and those with military knowledge were downright rare. General Washington himself was hard pressed to locate a capable engineer officer for the Continental Army. He did find one in Rufus Putnam—who would leave his mark and name in stone at the future West Point—but the Commissioners were less lucky. There was a candidate available, they discovered, a man trained as an engineer in England. He had gained at least some experience with fortifications, having worked for Benedict Arnold repairing Fort Ticonderoga after its capture. Moreover, he desired engineering duty and was, in fact, at that time in Philadelphia seeking a colonel's commission as an engineer in the Continental Army. Perhaps he overvalued his own worth, for he was not accepted on those terms. However, when nothing opened in Philadelphia, Bernard Romans accepted the offer tendered by the Commissioners and set out for New York.

Bernard Romans was a Dutchman turned English and a botanist turned engineer. Born in Holland, trained to engineering in England, the fifty-five-year-old adventurer had recently immigrated to America, where he had pursued various enterprises. A talented artist and map-maker, he had sketched Indians and prepared maps in the generally uncharted regions of Florida. Just a few months earlier, he had plotted the location of ten Spanish treasure ships, sunk off the Florida coast by a hurricane in 1715.[*] His last employment had been as a botanist. The outbreak of war found him in New England arranging for the publication of a book he had written on

---

[*] Map and wealth sat for nearly two centuries until a treasure hunter in the 1960's found the chart in the Library of Congress and brought up the sunken riches.

the natural history of Florida. A strong Dutch temperament quickly became evident when he joined the expedition to Ticonderoga. Irascible, and intolerant of anyone who chanced to disagree with him, Romans made few friends. When he testily dropped out of the march to continue alone, one Edward Mott tartly recorded his departure: "Mr. Romans left us and joined no more; we were all glad, as he had been a trouble to us, all the time he was with us."

New York's Provincial Convention adjourned on 2 September, leaving its affairs in the hands of a Committee of Safety. When Romans arrived from Philadelphia, sometime in the second week of the month, the Committee of Safety briefed the engineer and the Commissioners on construction schedules and financial arrangements. Finally, with fall in the air, Romans and three of the Commissioners, Bayard, Bedlow, and Hanson, set sail for the Highlands.

Scratching around for construction workers and guards, the Committee of Safety remembered the three-month-old instructions from Philadelphia telling New York to ask Connecticut for troops. What ensued is illustrative of events in those early days of the Revolution and is a good example of why things often went wrong. On 13 September the Committee of Safety asked the general commanding the Connecticut soldiers at Harlem to send a company of troops to the Commissioners in the Highlands. Three days later the general informed the Committee that he could take orders only from General Washington or Congress. The New Yorkers quickly sent him a copy of Congress' letter, but the Connecticut general, calling attention to the date, refused to move without more current orders. Exasperated, the Committee of Safety forwarded all the correspondence to Congress, asking them for a ruling on the dispute. Meantime, the Commissioners and Romans remained in the Highlands unprotected by military forces. Militia from New Windsor agreed to help in case of an emergency, but they admitted that with no powder they could do little. At long last there arrived in November two understrength companies, commanded by Captains John Grenell and Benjamin Ledyard.[7]

When Romans and the Commissioners first arrived in the Highlands, the days passed gainfully enough. Moving into the abandoned farmhouse (owned by a Mr. Bunn) on Martalear's Rock, they soon reached agreement on general types of and locations for the planned structures. As the Commissioners began a search for local workers and materials, Romans, attended by a black slave, drew up blueprints for the works. At that point in the war Americans were fighting for their rights, as Englishmen, under the British Constitution. An "iniquitous" Parliament, not George III, was their enemy. The Declaration of Independence was almost a year in the future. Discussing this one evening around the fireplace of the small house they had taken over, the Commissioners decided to christen the fortress they were to build, Fort Constitution. The name stuck; to this day the island remains Constitution Island—a constant reminder that Americans once swore allegiance to English monarchs and the British Constitution.

It soon became evident, to Romans at least, that the concept recommended by Clinton and Tappen, approved by the Provincial Convention, and agreed upon by the Commissioners was all wrong. The confident botanist, not bothering to consult with his employers, designed defenses more to his own liking. Booms or other water obstructions were ignored completely. Firepower alone, in his scheme of things, would stop all vessels. On West Point he envisioned no more than a blockhouse containing four light cannon and a small battery of three guns, the latter six-pounders. Constitution Island would become the main fortress, the paramount position. There was nothing small in his plans for fortifications on the island. Those works were to be edifices wholly worthy of their magnificent setting in the imposing Highlands. Four blockhouses, a like number of batteries, and a bastioned fort were to be the fighting positions. In all, 61 cannon and 20 swivel guns were now to be integrated into eleven different works. The main fort, quickly dubbed the "Grand Bastion," was to be protected by an outer stone wall 30 feet thick, 18 feet high, and nearly 500 feet long. Behind the defenses, barracks, storerooms, a guardroom, and an ammunition magazine would complete the complex. Naïvely, the engineer estimated 150 men could complete the construction in four months at a cost of about £6,000.[8]

Romans completed his drawings on 14 September. Evidently sensing that he would be unable to obtain approval from the Commissioners, he slipped away to New York City. Once there he completed the estimate of expenses and submitted the entire packet for Convention approval on the afternoon of 18 September. The Committee of Safety must have assumed that the Commissioners were aware of and concurred in the engineer's ideas, for on the 19th they accepted without question the revised plan and forwarded the sketches and cost estimates to Philadelphia. After all, John Berrien, the Commission's purchasing agent, had appeared with the Dutchman and had seemed to be in complete accord. Romans, headstrong but happy, departed for a six-day visit to New Haven, perhaps hoping the inevitable anger at his action would have cooled by the time he returned.[9]

In the engineer's absence, time did not stand still in the Highlands. Beverley Robinson, a boyhood friend of George Washington, had married into a wealthy New York family. Of the lands he had acquired by matrimony, a large portion were in the Highlands along the west side of the river. Thinking him the owner of Constitution Island, the Committee of Safety sent notice that a fort was being erected there and offered to buy the land. Robinson, who happened to be staying at the time in his rambling country home near the island, rode down to the site where laborers were already clearing trees and gathering stone. Seeing that the works would not affect his meadowland on the eastern section of the island, he informed the Committee of Safety that a widow, a Mrs. Ogilvie, was owner of the western half. "Was it mine," he stated, "the public should be extremely welcome to it." His generosity was ironic because Beverley Robinson would become the leading Tory warrior in the area and would, almost precisely two years thence, have occasion to tread in conqueror's boots on the ruins and ashes of Fort Constitution. Mrs. Ogilvie, having less prestige than Mr. Robinson, was not approached with an offer of purchase. Nor was Mr. Bunn then asked for the use of his house.[10]

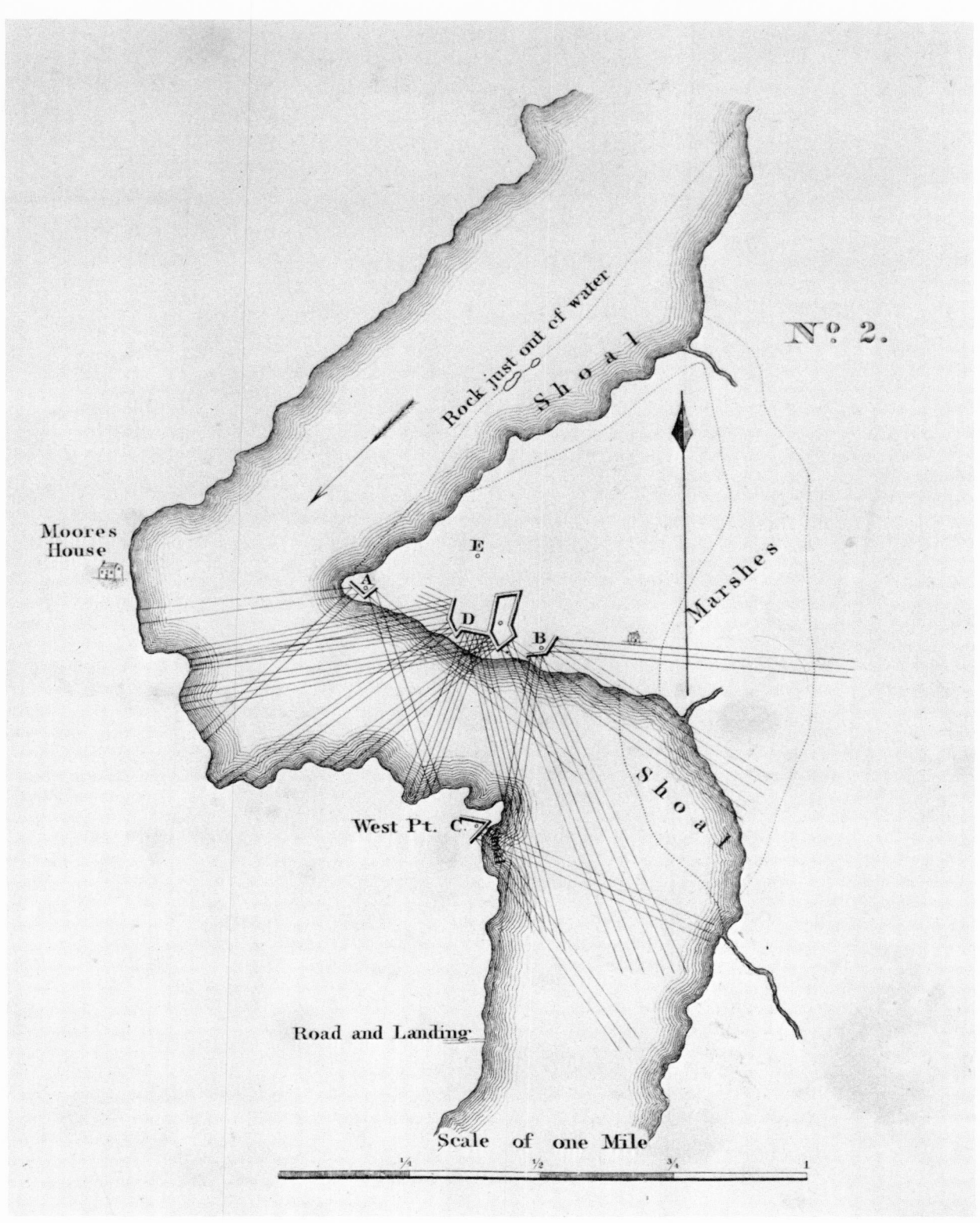

No. 2.

Rock just out of water

Shoal

Marshes

Moores House

E

A

D

B

Shoal

West Pt. C.

Road and Landing

Scale of one Mile

¼   ½   ¾   1

Bernard Romans' concept of the defenses to be erected on Constitution Island. From American Archives.

All the activity in the Highlands was beginning to attract unwanted attention. Royal Governor William Tryon, accompanied by a military escort, sailed up the river to investigate personally. Off Haverstraw, on Saturday, 23 September, he happened across a vessel hired by the Commissioners. In the Governor's presence the captain was carefully interrogated. What kind of fortification was it? What was the ground like? How many guns? Who guarded it? Anxiously, the Commissioners repeated their long-standing request for security forces and hastened construction of the first blockhouse and battery. They also tried to hire workers who could and would come armed.[11]

It is not clear how Bernard Romans thought he would get away with having gone contrary to the Commissioners' wishes. Perhaps, having obtained higher acceptance of his scheme, he simply did not care what the Commissioners thought. At any rate, they were not long in learning of his duplicity. After the Committee of Safety sent the revised plans on to Philadelphia, Berrien informed the Commissioners upriver of what had transpired. His letter reached the three men on Constitution Island on Sunday evening, 24 September. The resulting uproar shattered such Sabbath calm as had descended on the little island. The astounded New Yorkers could hardly believe what they read. They had been duped. Infuriated at the Dutchman's actions and attitude, the three dashed off a sharp, angry letter to New York City.

"We should have esteemed ourselves happy," they began sarcastically, "had we been consulted on this subject before it had been sent forward." Mr. Romans' plan was insufficient, a "temporary expedient" only which might "prove the ruin of the Province." Furthermore, who was in charge? "Inform us," demanded the incensed men, "whether we are under Mr. Romans' direction, or whether he is obliged to consult with us upon the measures to be pursued." Bayard, Bedlow, and Hanson all signed the tart message.[12]

The letter reached its destination Thursday afternoon, barely beating an anxious Romans, who appeared Friday morning. Seizing the initiative, he proposed to contract for the entire project at a price of £5,000. Stipulations were that he be granted absolute management—the Commissioners serving merely to keep him supplied—and that a sum of about £200 be advanced "to be applied to such incidental matters as are immediately wanted, and do not occur directly to the memory." Surprised by the sudden offer, the Committee of Safety voted to wait a day before considering the proposal. So it was that on the final day of September, the determined Dutchman and the harried representatives had a long and rather unpleasant discussion. When his proposal to contract the job was rejected, he countered with a request to be formally appointed as an engineer. The Committee had no power to bestow on him the title of engineer but would pay him for his engineering services. At a rate of "twenty Shillings sterling," he demanded. Twelve was the regular rate, they reminded him; and anyway, he should not "expect more than the pay of a Colonel in the Continental Army." Romans gave in, asking only for an advance in pay. The legislators allowed him £20.

That done, they turned to the touchy problem of assuaging the feelings of Bayard, Bedlow, and Hanson. Reminding those gentlemen that the Provincial Convention had retained the services of Romans by request of the Commissioners themselves, the Committee added, "Mr. Romans is now to proceed to you, and give you his best advice and assistance, as an engineer." Rather wistfully, the members implored that "the works may be carried on with all your joint wisdom, advice, and assistance." With a Dutch botanist and a civilian Commission at odds over the construction of a military post, it is easy to imagine the vigor with which the task was subsequently approached.[13]

Reluctantly, Romans journeyed back to Constitution Island during the first week of October to be met as reluctantly by the still-bridling Commissioners.

Elsewhere in America the next week was an active one. New York's Provincial Convention assembled once more for business, undertaking right away a review of all events which had occurred in its recess. Continental Congressmen in the Pennsylvania State House debated the efficacy of Romans' plans. In Cambridge, Washington was struggling to organize and train the mass of men that still somehow held the British bottled in Boston. Benedict Arnold and a brave band of 1,100 troops were far up the Kennebec River on their hazardous march to Quebec. Richard Montgomery was attempting to capture strategic St. Johns at the northern end of Lake Champlain to open his path to the St. Lawrence. Ethan Allen, co-conqueror of Fort Ticonderoga, was already on his way to England in chains after being captured during an abortive attack on Montreal. But on Constitution Island, Romans and the Commissioners merely glowered at one another.

That same week in Boston, General Gage was busy turning over the command to General William Howe. Howe, victor of the bloody Battle of Bunker Hill, had endured the interminable days since by conducting a siege of his own, a campaign to seduce the flashing blond wife of Joshua Loring. A shrewd strategic move—appointing Loring to the lucrative position of commissary of prisoners—assured Howe that no objections would be heard from that quarter. Obstacles cleared, the general called forth all the wiles and stratagems he had learned in a long career—and won. The second of the three illustrious shipmates on the good ship *Cerberus,* Henry Clinton, was applying himself in like manner with less success. Living in style in John Hancock's splendid Boston home, Clinton hired Mrs. Mary O'Callaghan Baddeley to manage the large household. By his own admission he admired her for more than mere housekeeping talents, but the striking young Irish woman primly held him at bay. John Burgoyne, better at breaching bedroom barricades than Howe and Clinton combined, was perhaps just a little bored with Boston ladies. He was making plans to return to England.

Back on Constitution Island, work slowly resumed on the fortifications according to Romans' specifications. The Provincial Convention, surprisingly, was not unhappy with the progress made on the forts. Feeling that "every step to complete them" had been taken, the New Yorkers informed Congress that all was well. Cannon and material for construction had been transported to the island and several guns were already in place by early October—enough, the Convention thought, "to prevent any enemy from passing through the Highlands."[14]

Chagrined by their unhappy experience over the design of the fortifications and suddenly bold behind their newly emplaced cannon, the Commissioners determined immediately to prevent "any enemy from passing." Because it was difficult to select "enemy" vessels from among the hundreds of commercial ships plying their trade along the Hudson, the Commissioners were faced with a problem. Their solution was direct and simple: *all* vessels passing must "lower the peak of their mainsail, as a token of their being friendly." In other words, if they are not for us they must be against us.

Whether from Tory sentiments or an injured sense of Yankee pride, many of the skippers objected. A trial case was inevitable—and it was not long in coming. On 15 October river captain Robert North approached the narrow passage with defiance burning in his eyes. Upon being hailed from the island to dip his sail, he refused. A cannon shot would be sent his way if he persisted, Samuel Bayard yelled. "That is just what I want," was the return bellow. His bluff called, Bayard angrily ordered a waiting boat, manned by several armed workers, to overtake the sloop and board it. On reaching the vessel the workers found themselves looking at Robert North's flushed face over a pair of cocked pistols. Unless someone could produce an order from the Provincial Convention, North had no intention of either stopping or dipping his sail. He thundered that he would sooner blow the brains out of "that damned rascal, Captain Bayard." In the face of oaths, threats, and certain "unfriendly expressions," the workers prudently declined to test the fierce-looking river skipper. Mainsail and spirit unbowed, North sailed on.[15]

Straightway the irate Commissioners prepared a message to the President of the Provincial Convention, relating their version of the incident and requesting approbation and authority to continue. North, however, outraced the letter to New York. He stormed into a Convention session, complaining bitterly of such high-handed behavior in the Highlands. The lawmakers immediately instructed the Commissioners to desist, reminding them forcefully that the purpose of the establishment on the island was to provide military security, not to exact respect or deference for the Convention or its officers. Convention members undoubtedly wished the Commissioners could be as efficient at erecting forts as raising trouble. Later they spelled out rules of conduct for the Commissioners to abide by in dealing with river traffic. John Hanson took umbrage at the censure, the final blow to his pride. He quit in a huff, vowing never to return to the fortifications. Jonathan Lawrence was ordered up to replace him, while Bayard and Bedlow, embittered but submissive, remained on the job. It was a job, though, growing daily less and less satisfying.

In the meantime, delegates at Philadelphia had been reviewing the status of New York's Highlands forts. A debate erupted over the question of doing more or less. John Adams, the inveterate note-taker, scribbled down the substance of opposing views as the argument progressed. On one hand a faction believed too much time had been wasted already, that simpler forts could be raised faster, and that other locations might be better suited for the purpose than Constitution Island. An opposing group espoused Romans' thesis that a lesser work "would only be beginning a strong-hold for an enemy." Finally Silas Deane took the floor and admonished both sides, reminding them that Congress had sent an order to New York, that New York had hired an engineer, and that the Provincial Convention of that state seemed satisfied with the spot and the plan. It was their affair. Congress, he continued, must either "rescind the whole" or go on as planned. The Continental lawmakers appointed a three-man committee to consider the arguments and prepare instructions for the Convention in New York.

Among the three selected was Robert R. Livingston, New Yorker and member of George Washington's original committee which had first recommended closing the Hudson. He remembered the urgency with which they had worked back in May, and the long nights spent poring over maps of the great river. He had questions. Why was it taking so long to erect forts recommended nearly half a year ago? Shouldn't New York speed up the work, especially with winter so near? Couldn't it be done "more cheaply and expeditiously" with wood rather than stone? What about warning posts? And shouldn't batteries be erected in other places? The committee returned a rather sharp letter for Congress to consider on 7 October.

John Rutledge, speaking in the slow, soft style of men from South Carolina, agreed with the strong letter, but suggested adding a paragraph requiring New York to obstruct the river "by booms or otherwise." After some argument his suggestion was adopted. The communication, firmly hinting that the Provincial Convention should revitalize its efforts to complete the task, was approved. New Yorkers were also directed "to take the most effectual method to obstruct the navigation of the Hudson River, if, upon examination, they find it practicable."[16]

When those instructions reached New York, they were promptly forwarded to the Highlands with directions to the Commissioners to lose no time in carrying out Congress' wishes. Taking cognizance of the personality clash at the work site, the Provincial Convention specifically directed, "You will take Mr. Romans to your assistance."

As it happened, Romans on that very day applied once more to obtain the rank and pay of a colonel. Thinking the entire Provincial Convention might be more sympathetic than the Committee of Safety, he repeated his previous request. Pursuit of a colonel's rank and privileges and an engineer's title and pay were motivation enough, but avarice, too, played a part in his persistence. All the while he had been working on Patriot defenses, the Dutchman had been drawing wages as a botanist of Florida from the Royal Treasury, at the rate of £50 sterling a year. Fear that tidings of his new job could cause the stipend to be suspended was behind his insistence on obtaining a more secure, permanent position. The Convention agreed only to forward the application to Philadelphia.

It might have been that Romans wanted to do nothing to affect adversely his application. Or it could have been the mellowing effect on all hands of the stunning display of autumn fireworks as turning leaves splashed the overwatching mountains in color. For whatever reason, engineer and Commissioners cooperated and reached rare agreement on a reply to the needling suggestions of the Continental Congress. They reckoned that, without doubt, the works in three weeks would be "of sufficient strength to stand the brunt of as large a ship of rank as can come here, and two or three small fry." As for using timber rather than stone in the construction, the area was "miserable timber country" and stone work was faster by "a degree beyond comparison." Neither did the men in Fort Constitution think much of Congress' idea of placing batteries at Moore's house or on a hill near Peekskill. However, another site had excited their interest: "But at Pooploop's Kill, opposite Anthony's Nose, it is a very important pass: the river narrow, commanded a great way up and down, full of counter currents, and subject to almost constant fall winds; nor is there any anchorage at all, except close under the works to be erected." Addressing the problem of blocking the river itself, they thought that would "be an easy matter."[17]

A most dangerous diversion was thus broached. While shrugging off Congressional recommendations for improvement, Romans and the two Commissioners had opened a door leading to the construction of another fortress some distance from Fort Constitution at a moment when supplies, manpower, and time were not sufficient to complete properly the work already begun. Ill-founded optimism—in New York City as well as in the Highlands—led to the erroneous estimate that the works could be completed by December.

That optimism soon returned bitter dividends. Based on rosy reports emanating from New York, Congress assigned additional men to the Highlands for winter quartering. The Convention was thereby forced to order the construction of barracks to house a total of 1,000 troops. In an age when a soldier was fortunate to have 20 square feet—when bunks were only 4 feet wide and three men shared each one—the new requirement was not an extravagant increase. But the overburdened Commissioners were unable to shoulder *any* increase.

Estimates notwithstanding, the construction was going slowly, due as much to the severe handicaps of building in the Highlands as to personality problems. Part of the trouble, of course, must also be laid to a lack of professional engineering know-how. A competent engineer would have seen, at the very least, that he could not meet the announced schedule. As a construction engineer, Romans displayed some talent in his ideas; as a military engineer, he fell far short in both concept and priorities. Building a fort was rather more difficult than repairing one. The fact that Romans insisted on claiming the rank and prerogatives of a Continental colonel, an unauthorized assumption, aggravated his already strained relations with the Commissioners, who were themselves not the most efficient of managers. But not all the shortcomings can be blamed on the men in charge.

Drunkenness was probably a factor. The hardy and hearty colonists looked upon rum as one of the staples of life. It was, in fact, common practice to compute a ration of beer or spirits as part of a working man's salary. At the time of the American Revolution, alcohol was both anesthetic and energizer. Bullets, bread, blankets, and booze were essential ingredients for keeping an army in the field; laborers no less than soldiers required the latter three. Early that winter, when whiskey's wiles were even more in demand, New York lawmakers resolved to expel all retailers of rum from the construction site. That vote, certainly not precipitated by any temperance views, is strong indication that the workers in the Highlands had been more zealous in their pursuit of drink than of work.

Graft might also have been a factor. Many there were in the War of Independence who found the motives of profit and patriotism to be compatible. More than £4,250 had sifted through the hands of the Commissioners in just three months, and precious little there was to show for it. That amount is only the sum of the recorded monetary advances from the New York Convention; it does not include the worth of the cannon, powder, boats, and sundry equipment furnished in kind. One report relayed to officials alleged that Commissioners were paying twelve shillings for a log 14 feet long by 8 inches in diameter. On a good day, at that rate, an enterprising logger could earn nearly twenty times the amount the Provincial Convention was eventually willing to pay the Commissioners themselves. Watchful Patriots in New Windsor loudly accused Commissioner Jonathan Lawrence and his wife of using Constitution Island as a base for lucrative black-market activities in tea. An inspection, a short time later, of food intended for the workers and soldiers discovered culpable purchases of spoiled pork. Packed in kegs, rotten meat had been intentionally covered by a thin layer of edible ham at either end. Whether there was or was not graft, the members of the Convention questioned only the results of efforts to block the Hudson and consistently approved requests for additional funds. Interestingly, the charges of profiteering were no bar to Jonathan Lawrence's subsequent election as a delegate from Queens to the Provincial Convention.[18]

Awful reality came clear to the men on Constitution Island about the same time winter's advance guard of sharp, chill winds whistled over the rocks. The work, after all, would not be finished before the snows arrived. Romans was quick to blame the Commissioners, and they him. Tempers, never very well suppressed, boiled over. Epithets were hurled; "scoundrel" and "villain" were names rattled around the island. Romans moved into a finished blockhouse and refused to speak to the Commissioners, who by then were four, Thomas Grenell having joined.

An angry, vindictive, voluminous correspondence ensued. Romans from his blockhouse and the Commissioners in the abandoned farmhouse assailed one another with quill and paper. Messengers crossed the few yards separating antagonists bearing written ripostes and counterstrokes. "Epistolary altercation" was Romans' apt phrase describing the childish paper war. All sources of friction were aired and argued, point by point. Romans' idiosyncrasies and extravagances and vanities came to light; the

Commissioners' pettiness and inefficiency and poor judgment were roundly explored. It was even pointed out that Romans' slave was as fractious and disliked as the Dutchman himself. All in all, by their petulant argument, Commissioners and engineer did absolutely no good and much harm. November passed. Progress at the construction site was imperceptible.[19]

Word of dissension and disorder in the Highlands leaked back to Philadelphia. Worried, delegates there decided that a commander should be appointed to coordinate and control the entire operation. A wise, if late, conclusion. Then, of all people, Congress recommended for the post John Hanson, the angry ex-Commissioner who had sworn, "I will never go back to the fort." Embarrassed when the *faux pas* was discovered, Congress voted to postpone one week making another nomination. As a matter of fact, the position would remain vacant until George Washington appointed a commander six months later. On 8 November Congress instructed a three-man committee to go to New York to "take an accurate view of the state of our fortifications upon Hudson's river, and make a report of it as soon as it can conveniently be done."[20]

The committee was composed of three of Congress' more distinguished members. Robert R. Livingston, scion of an influential New York family, well-known and admired at twenty-nine, had been interested in and involved with the Hudson River forts from the beginning. John Langdon, a wealthy New Hampshire merchant and an active politician, was five years Livingston's senior. Robert Treat Paine, dean of the trio at forty-four, was also the most famous. A lawyer, he had catapulted to prominence as a prosecutor in the trial of Captain Preston resulting from the "Boston Massacre." His opponent in that trial had been John Adams, now a fellow Patriot and delegate to Congress from Massachusetts. Paine would later be a signer of the Declaration of Independence, which Livingston would help write. Paine's previous military experience consisted only of a stint as chaplain on an expedition to Crown Point in 1760. Neither Livingston nor Langdon had had any military service at all.

Those gentlemen arrived at New Windsor on 16 November and rowed down to Constitution Island next day. Romans and the Commissioners were just then at the peak of their paper duel, but they paused long enough to escort their Congressional visitors through the partially completed works. The three inspectors were shocked at what they saw, in spite of Romans' nervous assurances that only a little more time was needed. Over 200 soldiers and workers were living there and some 71 cannon were counted, but Romans' blockhouse was the sole completed defense the island had. "We must own," they reported to Congress, "that we found the fort in a less defensible situation than we had reason to expect, owing chiefly to an injudicious disposition of the labour, which has hitherto been bestowed on the barracks, the block-house, and the southwest curtain."

Learning that the principle defense of the fortress would be the "Grand Bastion," the committee was startled to discover that, except for the southwest curtain, it had not even been begun. Checking fields of fire of the guns already in place, they perceived—with scarcely concealed disparagement—that an approaching ship would be masked by West Point until nearly upon the island. Then, looking across the river, the nonmilitary committee saw the fatal military flaw in Fort Constitution:

> The fortress is unfortunately commanded by all the grounds about it, and is much exposed to an attack by land; but the most obvious defect is, that the grounds on the West Point are higher than the fortress, behind which point an enemy may land without the least danger. In order to render the pass impassable, it seems necessary that this place should be occupied. . . . [W]e fear nothing short of it will be sufficient to avail us of the winding of the river.[21]

The astute Congressmen clearly sensed that affairs along the Hudson were in a mess. Aware, too, of their own inadequacy in matters military, they closed their report with a pressing recommendation that qualified persons be dispatched to survey the Highlands for "spots on which batteries may be most cheaply, expeditiously, and advantageously raised." They left, firmly convinced that Romans' grandiose fortifications were impressively impotent and that the Commissioners were not capable of supervising such an important project.

When the disturbing truth reached Philadelphia, Congress, knowing that Washington's Chief of Artillery, Colonel Henry Knox, was in New York, tried to intercept him with a request to check the fortifications. It was too late. Knox had already passed the Highlands on his way to Fort Ticonderoga to get cannon for the siege of Boston. It would prove ironic that while Congress was attempting to overtake him with a request to investigate the Highlands defenses, Knox was sharing an overnight room south of Fort Ticonderoga with a captured British officer, Captain John André. Near the same age and having common interests, the big Boston bookseller and the artistic Britisher spent a very pleasant evening together; one dark day in the future both would have cause to remember the meeting. For its part, Congress apparently took no other action to correct the disquieting situation in New York.

Some of the difficulty in righting the problem was due to inaction of the Provincial Convention itself or, more precisely, to the fact that there was no Convention to act through most of November. On 4 November it had adjourned, neglecting to establish a Committee of Safety to function for it. Not until 6 December did a sufficient number of delegates return to permit the conduct of business. Taking up the subject of the dispute at Constitution Island and the resulting snaillike rate of construction, Convention members voted to approach the issue by designating yet another committee. Francis Nicoll, Joseph Drake, and Thomas Palmer were envoys appointed to "endeavor to accommodate the difference subsisting between the Commissioners and the Engineer."

Within a week the conciliatory committee returned its verdict. An imbroglio did, indeed, exist. Worse, the defenses against shipping were inadequate, the buildings were incomplete, the entire plan was too ambitious, the work was poorly supervised. Engineer and Commissioners had apparently succeeded only in obstructing one another. A reduced plan of construction was recommended for the island site, while a strong argument was entered for rapidly raising a fort on the north flank of Popolopen Creek, several miles south of Fort Constitution. "We are clearly of opinion," they wrote, "that this is by far the most advantageous situation in the Highlands for a fortification." West Point was ignored. Before adjourning for Christmas, the New York Convention ordered Thomas Palmer to carry those recommendations to Philadelphia to be laid before the Continental Congress.[22]

Thus ended the hectic year 1775. Freezing weather and heavy snows settled over the Hudson Valley as Thomas Palmer rode for Philadelphia. Henry Knox was at the same time dragging cannon from Fort Ticonderoga to Boston. Under the walls of Quebec, in a blinding snowstorm on the last day of December, Richard Montgomery was killed and Benedict Arnold wounded in a desperate, vain effort to storm the city. On Constitution Island, Romans was sparked to action when word reached him of Palmer's mission to the Continental Congress. The New Year was getting off to an unsettled start.

Romans, irate but ever-faithful to the appropriateness of his own plans, rushed to New York City to defend his ideas. Arguing robustly and with conviction, he partially convinced the Committee of Safety that he had been right after all. Hesitant to make a decision, though, the Committee passed responsibility to the Continental Congress by directing Romans to hurry to Philadelphia, there to plead his case.

The results were predictable. Palmer reached the seat of government first. After hearing his testimony, Congress resolved, on 5 January, that "no farther fortifications be erected at Marter's Rock, on Hudson's river, and that a point of land at Poplopen's Kill, on the said river, be without delay effectually fortified." The Committee of Safety, upon receiving those instructions, obediently halted work on Constitution Island, but, aware of Romans' persuasiveness, delayed issuing further orders to the puzzled Commissioners in the Highlands. Through January nothing happened.

In mid-February, yielding at last to Romans' persistency, the Continental lawmakers reversed their earlier orders by balloting to improve the defenses of Constitution Island. They decreed that another battery of 18 cannon be erected there and that a redoubt, mounting 30 guns, be built on the river bank opposite West Point. West Point, itself, was once more scorned.[23]

Unhappily for the beleaguered botanist, his victory had been a Pyrrhic one. He was replaced as engineer in the Highlands. After garnering a captaincy in the Independent Pennsylvania Artillery Company, he returned to New York briefly two months later in a belated attempt to draw pay for the period of his absence. A letter in his favor from the Continental Congress seems to have been of no avail; New Yorkers, wearied with the worrisome Dutchman, were hardly inclined to reimburse him for not working. Romans departed, leaving few friends and a rather general feeling that "he had been a trouble to us, all the time he was with us."

3

THE SCENE OF WAR SHIFTS

L*ONDON* had not been ready for full-scale fighting. When King and Cabinet instructed General Gage to use force, they had in mind dispersing a mutinous mob of riffraff, not warring with thirteen united colonies. If any minister devoted much deep thought to the unrest in America there is little evidence of the fact. The truth is that America was merely a minor irritation to the Monarch in 1774 and 1775. George III had much more urgent problems at home and in Europe; recalcitrant colonials were among the least of his worries. Of course, neither he nor his close advisors had ever been to America. They did not sense how short was the fuse or how large was the powder keg.

Gage did. He had lived in America almost continuously since 1754. His wife was American. Ordered to Massachusetts to enforce the Boston Port Bill, he had quickly let it be known that more troops would be required. Lord Dartmouth, Secretary of State for American Colonies, could not believe the pessimistic analysis from his commander across the Atlantic. Feeling that an injection of vigor might improve the situation, London dispatched in lieu of soldiers three major generals on the *Cerberus*. Before that trio arrived, however, the bloody events of 19 April and the coup at Ticonderoga served notice that General Gage, on the scene, had better judged the temper of Americans than had men in cozy offices in faraway Whitehall. If doubt remained, the spectacle of snarling Yankees flocking by thousands to besiege Boston should have erased it. And the costly clash at Bunker Hill convinced even the most chuckleheaded minister that a rap on the colonial knuckles would not suffice. The rebellious colonies, it was clear, would have to be subdued by major military operations.

Boston itself was a cul-de-sac. For miles around, rail fences, stone walls, and short hills provided the rebels natural positions from which to pick to pieces any force foolish enough to venture into the country. The death march back from Concord had already demonstrated that. Too, it would be costly in the extreme just to leave Boston; the Americans, commanded by Gage's old friend and former comrade-in-arms, George Washington, had dug impressive entrenchments across the narrow neck connecting Boston proper to the mainland. Then, even if redcoats did break out of the town and manage to survive in the countryside, there was no objective to take to achieve victory. Americans could simply fall back until the British got as far from their fleet and supplies as they dared. Militarily, roads from Boston led nowhere.

As soon as it became evident in Boston and London that some overall strategy was needed, officials scurried to open maps and memories of the wild continent beyond the sea. Where was the strategic center of the colonies, a place to go which would cause the rebellion to fold? None was apparent. Occupation of no city, or cities, would assure victory. Boston was a case in point. Furthermore, to go inland out of reach of the Royal navy would be to invite disaster. America was vast, England's army small. And there was no obstacle against which to trap and smash the rebel army.

Awed by the well-nigh insurmountable problems of conducting a land campaign in eighteenth-century America, several officials seriously recommended war by blockade only. The navy could close every major colonial port and smite the mutinous Americans economically. Dependent on trade for nearly every manufactured item, the colonies would, in the opinion of backers of this theory, soon sue for peace. The plan never got far. For one thing, war with Americans was not popular in England; victory had to be achieved swiftly. For another, England herself was deep in debt; loss of trade with the colonies would hurt merchants at home as well as colonists abroad. And besides, it just wasn't the seemly way to go about things.

The decision was made to subdue the rebels by invasion. Mercenaries were hired from several principalities in Germany to bolster the strength of the army, while plans were formulated to crush Washington in a grand campaign in 1776.

Washington and his committee in Congress had surmised in May 1775 that British strategy would center on the Hudson River. And events would prove them to be entirely correct. Having decided to invade America, King George and his ministers developed a scheme of conquest which relied on controlling that waterway. Only by use of a large river could army and navy elements remain in touch in the interior; only the Hudson led to a decisive objective. As soon as arrangements could be completed in 1776, land and naval forces would take the line of the Hudson, thereby isolating New England, the "heart of the rebellion," from the other colonies. Once sliced off, New England could be put down. This original "line of the Hudson" hypothesis would continue, throughout the war, to intrigue officials responsible for restoring British order in America.

Undoubtedly, the germ of British views of the Hudson had been fermenting long before the Revolutionary War began. The Colonial Wars had amply demonstrated the Hudson's military significance. It was an obvious path from the Atlantic to the frontier and on to Canada; ministers who had never seen North America had access to official reports submitted as late as 1773, spelling out the strategic importance of the Hudson as a link between New York and Canada. Just four days before the fateful shot at Lexington, Lord Dartmouth wrote Gage of the need for a large ground and sea force, based at New York City, prepared to operate on the Hudson to defeat "any attempt to send succour to the New England people from the middle colonies. . . ." Hence, even before the English were fully aware of the seriousness of American resistance, they had considered a general scheme to occupy a line extending from Canada along the Hudson to New York City, then hooking eastward along the coast to Boston.[1]

General Henry Clinton, who as a boy had lived on the banks of the Hudson, prepared a detailed study in the autumn of 1775. Vast results, he thought, would accrue to the Crown if the Hudson were taken immediately. An offensive northward from New York City, joined by a southward expedition from Canada, could be decisive. Noting that the Eastern states received bread from the Middle states, while the Middle states depended on the Eastern for meat, Clinton predicted that both areas would "experience the greatest distresses" should Britain hold the Hudson. Inability of the colonists to assemble or feed their troops would be a valuable benefit to derive from control of the waterway, and, of course, "a ready intercourse . . . with Canada by way of the lakes" would be an "obviously important" advantage.[2]

Howe, too, was convinced of the river's worth. When he replaced Gage, one of the first papers to cross his desk was a request to send assistance to General Guy Carleton, who was then being hard pressed in Canada by the invasion of Montgomery and Arnold. Howe declined. Securing the line of the Hudson, he felt, would prove in the long run more decisive.[3]

Reinforcements were scheduled to arrive in the spring or early summer of 1776, at which time Howe anticipated launching his offensive. In the interim something had to be done to carry the war to the rebels—it was really rather embarrassing that his Majesty's crack troops were held helpless in Boston by such a rabble as Washington could muster. Winter weather and the unpromising geography of the Boston position precluded operations in New England, but Howe saw an opportunity to conduct a campaign against Charleston. That city could be captured during the winter—thus "freeing" Loyalists in South Carolina—and the regiments could return in time for the summer's fighting. Henry Clinton was designated to command the expedition. As the New Year began, Clinton busied himself fitting out a convoy and preparing troops and equipment for the voyage.

Nothing of that nature could be kept secret very long in Boston; word of the impending departure of a body of soldiers and several transports soon reached Washington in nearby Cambridge. At the same time a letter came from Major General Charles Lee warning of the extremely vulnerable condition of New York. Lee, then a respected soldier held in esteem second only to Washington himself, wrote emphatically, "New York must be secured, but it will never, I am afraid, be secured by direct order of the Congress, for obvious reasons. . . . You must step in to their relief." Perturbed by recent reports of rising Tory strength on Long Island and alerted by the obvious British intent to send some of the Boston garrison southward, Washington concluded that New York was the English objective. He did step in. Carefully notifying Governor Jonathan Trumbull of Connecticut and informing the Continental Congress (John Adams, then visiting the army, was invited "to take Pott Luck" and discuss the matter), the Commander-in-Chief took the extraordinary step of ordering a general of the Continental Army to assume command of affairs in a state not yet occupied by the enemy. Charles Lee was directed, on 8 January 1776, to hurry to New York, there "to put the City and the Fortifications up the River in the best posture of defense."[4]

"It is a matter of the utmost importance to prevent the enemy from taking possession of the City of New York and the North River, as they will thereby command the country and the communication with Canada." With Washington's sober words ringing in his ears, Lee struck out for New York. The Commander-in-Chief had also ordered Lee to insure that the Highlands fortifications were "guarded against surprizes from a body of men which might be transported by water near the place and then march'd in upon the back of them." It is particularly prophetic that the General should have included that clause in his very first set of instructions pertinent to the forts up the Hudson.[5]

Bad weather forced Lee to halt at New Haven. There he learned of the repulse of Arnold and Montgomery at Quebec, news making his mission all the more urgent since it meant that New York might ultimately be open to an invasion from the north. To balance that bleak information was the encouraging notification that Governor Trumbull, in response to Washington's plea, had called up two Connecticut regiments to accompany Lee. As he prepared to resume his trip, a disturbing message arrived from the New York Committee of Safety. Lee was not wanted in New York. Citizens there, including several firm Patriots, were horrified at the prospect of his arrival at the head of troops. British men-of-war rode at anchor in the bay and Tories were thick in the town. Brusque actions on the part of the Continental general could goad the British into bombarding the city. Many inhabitants had already fled with their wives and children. Valuables were being removed. Servants buried silver and china. The Committee feared that continued evacuation of families in the bitterly cold weather might "occasion hundreds to perish for want of shelter." For the first time, war and rebellion assumed a real, stark, present meaning to the people of New York City. It had been somehow different and faraway before; Boston and Canada were places to talk about. Now it was uncomfortably near, and the realization was far from pleasant.[6]

Lee's reply, penned in Stamford, was colorful and altogether typical of the man. He would come to New York, regardless, but the population should not worry about a shelling from the ships. "I declare solemnly, that if they make a pretext of my presence to fire on the town, the first house set in flames by their guns shall be the funeral pile of some of their best friends." Nature took a hand, though, and presented New Yorkers a reprieve: chronic gout and flaming rheumatism halted Lee at Stamford. In great pain, feverish, unable to walk, he neither slept nor ate for a week.

Meanwhile, General Clinton had loaded his expeditionary force and dropped out of Boston Harbor on 20 January. As Charles Lee struggled against snow and sickness to reach New York, Henry Clinton fought high seas and icy decks en route to the same destination. Probably Clinton had the worse time of it: seasickness kept him exposed and shivering at the rail much of the voyage.

Fifty miles north of New York City, at Fort Constitution, conditions were worsening. Frigid winds, coming straight out of the north, buffeted the island. Not without reason had early Dutch settlers called the gap between Breakneck Ridge and Storm King Mountain, "wind-gate." Ice floes had started forming in December and by January the river was frozen solid. Boats gave way to sleds and snowshoes. Workers and soldiers huddled together for warmth in the partially completed barracks, spending most of their energy gathering and chopping firewood, a chore that should have been completed weeks earlier. Construction work, in any event, was not feasible. The ground was frozen too hard for digging, and mortar could not be mixed in such cold weather.

Spirits dropped with the temperature. Disillusioned by the confusion and negligible progress of the autumn months and seeing little likelihood of completing the task that winter, workers slipped away by twos and threes. The two companies of Minutemen, chaffing at their unpleasant conditions, felt they should receive extra pay for the fatigue duty required of them. Morale was not enhanced when the Provincial Convention refused to grant it. Laborers and soldiers alike might have put to good use some of the rum that the Convention had banned from the Highlands. The few structures which had been finished were poorly put together and required repairs almost from the moment they were placed in use. The roof of the powder magazine leaked so badly that fires had to be kept burning constantly in order to keep the powder dry. Tending bonfires among the powder kegs was not a duty likely to improve the attitude of the frost-nipped, sullen men on Constitution Island.

Command problems continued to plague the efforts to raise forts. Congress had not yet appointed a commander, although the Convention had submitted several recommendations. The Minutemen, feeling it beneath their dignity to take orders from the Commissioners, participated when it pleased them. Romans was gone, a fact seeming to raise the general level of cooperation but one that left a void in engineering expertise. Late in 1775 the Commissioners had asked the Provincial Convention for wages. That body, freer with men than money, granted a salary but only after cutting the number of Commissioners from seven to three. That helped. Berrien continued in the city, while Bedlow and Grenell remained on Constitution Island. But still a commander was needed. Frustrated at the failure of the Continental Congress to act, the Committee of Safety on 16

January named Isaac Nicoll, Colonel of the Orange County Minutemen, to command at the fortifications until "the arrival of a proper Continental Officer."[7]

As the first month of 1776 ended, Fort Constitution was no farther along than it had been in December, and nothing at all had been done on the site above Popolopen Creek.

Aching and wan, General Lee completed most of his trip to New York in a litter, riding only when dignity demanded and pain permitted. To his amazement, New York Patriots warmly greeted him as he entered the city on Sunday afternoon, 4 February. The reason for their turnabout soon became apparent. At anchor in the harbor was Henry Clinton's fleet from Boston. Clinton's arrival just hours before Lee's had thoroughly frightened the populace of New York City. They fully expected an invasion then and there. It was promptly granted that Lee should take possession of the town as well as the dominant heights on Long Island. New York troops were put under his command along with a regiment from New Jersey. Counting the two Connecticut regiments, Lee deployed some 2,500 men to repulse any British effort to come ashore.

But Clinton had no intention of landing his troops. He had come to New York to rest from the rigors of a winter voyage and to take on fresh provisions before proceeding southward. He had not seen Manhattan since 1749, so in a way it was a homecoming. Young Henry had been thirteen years old when he first came to New York. His reception then had been markedly different from this one, for his father at that time had been the newly appointed Royal Governor of the Province. As a lad he had enjoyed the city and the nearby countryside, not to mention the privileges accruing to the son of the governor. Entering military service at an age and rank befitting his position, the young blood became a lieutenant at fifteen, a captain at sixteen. During his six-year sojourn in America, he got to be well acquainted with two distant cousins, James and George Clinton. George, in fact, was hired as a clerk by Governor Clinton. Henry left, at nineteen, to seek his fortune elsewhere. Now, over a quarter of a century later, he had returned, a paunchy, middle-aged man, not permitted to touch land where once his father ruled.

Not that it was necessary to go ashore. The present governor, William Tryon, had deemed it wise to quit New York several months earlier. Ever since, his "executive mansion" had been in the bay aboard the English sloop of war, *Duchess of Gordon*. Clinton therefore had no trouble paying his respects. For eight days he and his convoy remained in the harbor, keeping Patriot nerves and Tory hopes on edge. Knowing that New York was slated to be the scene of operations in the coming summer, Clinton, an able if not a brilliant soldier, devoted his time to gaining intelligence of rebel defenses. New York City itself, he quickly saw, was a death trap for its defenders. The Royal navy could land troops in any of several places north of American positions on Manhattan Island, thereby sundering the Patriots' one slender link to safety at Kingsbridge. Tryon, who had carefully watched the stumbling efforts to raise defenses in the Highlands, briefed Clinton on the status of the construction on Constitution Island. Pleased to learn that the critical works were so far in arrears, the general made a mental note to seize them early in the coming campaign while they were yet unfinished. He correctly judged the Hudson's noble route through the Highlands to be the key to attaining and maintaining the line of the Hudson. Defended or not, Manhattan would be relatively simple to capture; defended properly, the Hudson Highlands promised to be quite a serious obstacle. Those hills should be taken first, he reasoned, for Manhattan could be captured anytime. On 12 February, to the audible relief of Convention members, Clinton left for his ultimate destination, Charleston.[8]

In the flurry of excitement at the Hudson's mouth, the miserable men and stalled work at Fort Constitution were more or less forgotten. But the day after it was known for sure that Clinton had departed, Commissioner Berrien passed along word from the Convention that "no time ought to be lost in contracting for and getting the timber and other necessaries to the place for erecting the new fortress." Bedlow was flabbergasted. "I know not how to act," he immediately fired back; "having no directions what kind of fortress is intended, I cannot tell what timber and necessaries will be wanted." It was imperative that an engineer be found to lay out the new fortress. Romans had been absent, haggling in Philadelphia, since the first of the year. A search was initiated for a replacement, without results. Men with engineering talents were few to begin with, while demands for them had multiplied prodigiously as the war deepened. There at dead center the matter rested until final word came from Philadelphia on 22 February. Continental delegates, having reviewed all the information and questioned both Thomas Palmer and Bernard Romans, prescribed that certain defenses at Constitution Island were to be completed and that construction on the new fort at Popolopen Creek should be expedited. January and most of February had been a period spent in perplexity; no one, least of all the Commissioners responsible for the project, knew exactly what was desired. Now at last the decision had been made. The Convention named Thomas Palmer to be a Commissioner, instructed him to "apply to General Lee for an engineer," and told him to start work on the new fort forthwith.[9]

Palmer found Lee sympathetic to his request for an engineer. Lee sent Captain William Smith, chief engineer at the time in the city, to assist the Commissioners. Smith made a hurried journey, leaving New York City on 27 February and returning on 29 February. During a busy two days he prescribed an outline for a new work east of Fort Constitution, marked a position for another on the east bank a mile south of the island, and staked out the trace of a fortification to be raised on the cliff just north of the mouth of Popolopen Creek. That latter bastion, it had already been determined, would be named for "the brave General Montgomery." After Romans, the courteous and capable Smith was a most refreshing and impressive individual. The Commissioners wanted to retain him. Lee, leaving New York for other duties, agreed that Smith should stay. However, his future duties were in the city; construction of the Highlands forts continued without benefit of engineer guidance.[10]

On the last day of that long February, after Smith had begun the cold trek down the Post Road to New York, William Bedlow, Jonathan

Lawrence, and Thomas Palmer gathered round the fireplace in the new commissary building, which served also as headquarters on the island. Gilbert Livingston, a representative to the Provincial Convention from Dutchess County, was with them. He had accompanied Palmer and Smith to the Highlands and had been prevailed upon to remain behind. Palmer, an energetic and zealous proponent of erecting forts along the river as well and as soon as possible, quickly had the other three equally enthused. They wrote the Provincial Convention that very day sending assurances that "nothing shall be wanting on our part" to prosecute the plans laid out by Smith. Inasmuch as several miles separated the sites of Fort Constitution and fort-to-be Montgomery, they decided to split up, with Bedlow and Lawrence supervising affairs at Constitution Island, while Palmer and Livingston were to work at Popolopen Creek. The Convention rapidly approved that arrangement and formally added Livingston to the Commission.

Colonel Isaac Nicoll, commander of state soldiers in the Highlands forts, slightly damped Palmer's optimism by reminding the four men of realities. His command was "greatly in want" of food and fuel. It had been two months since the troops had tasted fresh food. There were not enough pots and dishes to send any to Popolopen Creek. No shelter was available near the proposed work site. Not all the Minutemen were armed. And besides, he counted on no more than 150 men, hardly the number that would be needed—and many of those were already dour at doing labor without drawing laborers' wages. In the same vein, Bedlow mentioned that unpaid debts were numerous and wages were in arrears. To do more than meet obligations, £500 would be needed.

Undeterred, Palmer pushed on. On 14 March, taking carpenters and masons, he and Livingston went ashore on the north bank of Popolopen Creek to start. Those first workers found sleeping quarters in a sloop anchored in the stream while they built a storehouse and laid the foundation for a barracks to house 160 men. In the meantime Palmer had requested Continental soldiers to garrison the new fort and help erect it. Shortly, the men arrived. Until the barracks could be finished, the incoming troops were squeezed into already crowded boats tied up below the fort. The menu, consisting only of salt pork and hard bread, added distaste to discomfort. Within a week the soldiers grew restless, worked half-heartedly, and started a clamor for better treatment. Startled by the unruly, mutinous attitude of the men, the uneasy Commissioners pleaded with the Convention for rum. "If a supply of that could immediately be sent up," they declared, "it would have a very good effect."[11]

Relenting somewhat from its previous stand prohibiting liquor, the Convention provided for a measure of spirits as well as better food, but at the same time begged the Commissioners to be frugal, "as an extra allowance to fatigue-men is not by order of Continental Congress, and may therefore be a Colony charge." Colonel Nicoll took matters into his own hands when a boatload of peas passed by Constitution Island on 2 April. Stopping the vessel, he let his hungry soldiers confiscate one hundred bushels. Nicoll gave the merchant a receipt and directed him to apply for payment to the Provincial Convention. With his men happily boiling peas, he wrote to the Convention informing that body of his action and explaining once more his plight: no vegetables, sick men, desertions, mutiny. "Necessity has no law," was his excuse.

Thus, fitfully, the tempo of construction picked up as March ended and spring returned to the Hudson Highlands. Gradually food and supplies arrived, alleviating much of the discomfort and raising morale. The Commissioners, having learned from past mistakes, could approach the task with a good degree of confidence and experience. Bedlow had been living in the Highlands and concentrating on fortifications from the very first, while both Palmer and Lawrence had been involved one way or another with blocking the river for the past several months. Even the vexing and undefined command problem was reduced to manageable proportions. Palmer, eager and aggressive, had irritated Nicoll by issuing unauthorized orders to some of the soldiers. Nicoll objected and both men appealed to the Convention. Attempting to placate both parties, the Convention pleased neither, but it did prescribe a workable arrangement. A single, overall commander would have been a better solution, and, of course, a capable engineer was sorely missed. But, all things considered, it looked as if something might be accomplished at long last.

While William Smith had been rapidly laying out forts on heights over the Hudson, another engineer, Lieutenant Colonel Rufus Putnam, was engaged in planning positions to be erected on heights overlooking Boston. Henry Knox, after an epic winter journey, had presented Washington a "noble train of artillery" from Fort Ticonderoga. The Commander-in-Chief planned to emplace the cannon on Dorchester Heights, making Boston untenable. Putnam designed ingenious, prefabricated fortifications; the forts were built overnight, presenting the British with a *fait accompli* when they awoke on 5 March. General Howe judiciously evacuated the town, taking with his army a thousand other persons including the alluring Mrs. Loring and Henry Clinton's chaste housekeeper, Mrs. Baddeley.

At that moment America belonged to Americans. Not a single redcoat remained in the United States. Quebec and Halifax were held by Great Britain, and so was a portion of Florida, but the Thirteen Colonies had militarily won their independence. Washington, knowing the real trial was yet to come, had little time and less inclination to rejoice. His prime mission was to defend America's shores; Howe's to invade and conquer a hostile nation. The British had already concluded to strike at both ends of the Hudson. Analyzing his country's geography, Washington deduced Howe's aims. As soon as it was certain that Howe had no further intentions in Boston, the Commander-in-Chief turned his army and attention to the Hudson River. Accompanied by Mrs. Washington, he arrived in New York on 14 April and at once undertook preparations to defend the province.

As the Continental Army marched and sailed to New York, a prestigious Congressional committee passed through the city on its way to try to persuade the Canadians to become the fourteenth state. Benjamin Franklin, then in his seventy-first year, headed the group. Charles Carroll of Carrollton, considered by many to be the richest man in America, and Samuel

Chase, a Maryland firebrand, were the other two members. All three would return from the futile attempt in time to sign the Declaration of Independence. Carroll's brother, John, a Roman Catholic priest, went along as an unofficial member.

Renting the packet *Rhode-Island* in New York City, the committee sailed up the Hudson on 2 April. Wind and tide were uncooperative; three days were consumed in reaching the Highlands. They tacked right past the worksite above Popolopen Creek, probably unaware that a fort was being built there. It was late in the day on 5 April when the packet approached Constitution Island. Chase and Carroll, "from curiosity," went ashore to inspect the defenses. Franklin had had his fill of forts in the French and Indian War. He remained aboard. Colonel Nicoll was absent, but Bedlow escorted the Congressmen over the island, explaining the concept of various works, answering questions, and enumerating several of the stumbling blocks that had been encountered. The visitors were aghast at what they saw. Thirty cannon were in place, but not "a gunner or an artilleryman in the fort." For food, "nothing but pork, beef, and flour; no vegetables." From Bedlow they heard that "the Minute-men work about six hours in the day, and that with great reluctance." Worst of all, "The fortifications directed by Congress on the 15th of February, and laid out by Mr. Smith, remain wholly neglected." Alarmed, Franklin sent a dispatch that same night, by express, informing Congress of the unsatisfactory condition of the fortifications.[12]

Washington was not long in New York before he was apprised of the true status of the defenses in the Highlands. Colonel Nicoll, for one, wrote him of personnel and equipment shortages. Though Congress took no action on receipt of the report from its committee, word of it probably reached the dismayed Commander-in-Chief. He urged Nicoll to apply the "most diligent attention to the works" and to complete them "with all possible expedition." Realizing that nearly a year had passed since he had first recommended that posts be erected on the river, the General asked the New York Committee of Safety to give him a copy of all resolutions of the Continental Congress relative to the fortifications. Upon reading the combined directives, Washington saw clearly just how poorly administered had been the entire program. He then decided to assume the responsibility himself for the long-pursued objective of closing the Hudson.

His first step was to designate a commander, Colonel Cornelius D. Wynkoop, whom he ordered to take post with his regiment in the Highlands. But on learning that four companies of Colonel James Clinton's 3rd New York Regiment were already stationed at Forts Montgomery and Constitution, the Commander-in-Chief countermanded his instructions to Wynkoop and directed Clinton's deputy, Lieutenant Colonel Henry Beekman Livingston, to assume the command. "You will repair thither and if no superior officer is there, you must take the command, and look to the works now carrying on there, which you must exert yourself in seeing finished as soon as possible." The Provincial Convention acknowledged Washington's authority over the Highlands defenses and, on 8 May, resolved that Colonel Nicoll should be relieved of his responsibilities in favor of Livingston.

A view from West Point of the defenses on Constitution Island. Made by an unknown artist in the spring of 1776. Courtesy of the Cornell University Library.

Evidently, however, no one thought to notify Nicoll. His orders were to command until relieved by "a proper Continental Officer." Livingston's letter from Washington told him to take over "if no superior officer is there." After comparing those two directives, Nicoll refused to be replaced by a lieutenant colonel. Livingston was taken aback. Biting his tongue, he accepted the situation for the time being and devoted his energies to inspecting the forts.[13]

What he saw was distressing. The garrisons were, in his words, "in a most deplorable situation." In a starkly critical report he cited a dire need for medical facilities, boats, fresh food, and the ever-important rum. He protested strongly against the prior disregard for the welfare of the workers and the too-obvious neglect of the defenses. And on top of that, the jolted officer recorded, not a single step had been taken toward obstructing the surface of the waterway itself.[14]

Washington thereupon sent a group of such military experts as he could assemble to look into the matter. Brigadier General Lord Stirling (William Alexander) headed the mission, while Colonels Rufus Putnam and Henry Knox, chiefs respectively of Continental engineers and artillery, both heroes of Dorchester Heights, were detailed to assist him. At the last moment, Captain Winthrop Sargent replaced the busy Knox as artillery advisor. Explaining that he was deeply troubled by conditions in the Highlands, Washington told Stirling to inspect the fortifications and to recommend "such alterations as shall be judg'd necessary for putting them into a fit and proper posture of defense."[15]

Stirling was thorough. In the long, warm days of late May he set out, determined to examine minutely every detail and aspect of the Highlands forts. Although honored as an earl by his fellow Patriots, William Alexander had never proved his claim to the title of the earldom of Stirling. Perhaps "his lordship" was accepted because, in his own right, he was a prominent citizen of New Jersey, a brave and able soldier, and an appealing person. In spite of his fifty years and a more than normal fondness for hard drink, he was one of the more respected Continental generals.

Stirling, Putnam, and Sargent came first to Stony Point and Verplanck's Point. There, at the beginning of the Highlands, they thought a small work should be placed. Arriving next at Fort Montgomery, Stirling watched Continental soldiers and work gangs of impressed "notorious Tories" laboring under the direction of Commissioners Thomas Palmer and Gilbert Livingston. Colonel Rufus Putnam was contemptuous of the engineering ability displayed. He informed Stirling, aside, that one good engineer could "do the whole business as well." Stirling and the artillery officer, Sargent, walked the perimeter of the fort. From the Hudson and along Popolopen Creek, rock-faced cliffs rose sharply to the site some 125 feet above the river. On the third side, too, nature had provided a deep, steep gully. Only to the rear, the west, was there a good, level approach. Defensive barricades would be required on that side to counter an attack from the hills behind the fort. Then the practiced eye of the artilleryman picked up a fact apparently unperceived by the others: across Popolopen Creek was a higher knob that dominated the defenses. Guns there would render

Fort Montgomery untenable. Stirling crossed the creek to check. Finding Sargent's assessment to be true, he paced the rocky eminence and saw that it was large enough to be crowned by a strong fort. In fact, it appeared to him to be the most proper place on the river to "be made the grand post."

Continuing north, the three army officers landed at Constitution Island. In minutes they concluded that the works there were foolishly extravagant and utterly indefensible, being dominated by higher ground all about. "Upon the whole, Mr. Romans has displayed his genius at a very great expense, and to very little public advantage." Rowing across the river and clambering to the top of the West Point, Stirling realized that a fort was needed on the large plain there. He wrote:

> . . . every work on the island is commanded by the hill on the West-Point, on the opposite side of the river, within five hundred yards, where there is a level piece of land near fifty acres in extent. A redoubt on this West-Point is absolutely necessary, not only for the preservation of Fort Constitution, but for its own importance on many accounts.[16]

Returning to New York City on 1 June, Stirling drafted a long, careful account of his findings. For the busy Commander-in-Chief he prepared a resume of the report. Inexplicably, the condensed version carried no mention of West Point. Washington concurred in the recommendations contained in the resume and ordered them implemented. Thus, once again, the key location of West Point was slighted. Colonel Livingston, aware of Stirling's strong feelings regarding West Point, felt an oversight had been made when he received Washington's instructions and found no mention of that location. He wrote to the General on 14 June, informing him that "the work of most consequence is excluded, as it commands at point blank all the fortifications erected on this Island." On that very day, however, Colonel James Clinton was ordered to the Highlands to command those posts of "infinite importance," and Livingston was shifted to Long Island to lead the balance of Clinton's regiment. Lost somewhere in that switch was the knowledge of the consequence of West Point. It almost seemed that fate had decreed West Point should remain unfortified.[17]

Because the Continental Army had assumed the responsibility of the Highlands fortifications, New York discharged the Commissioners on 13 June 1776, and Isaac Nicoll was finally prevailed upon to surrender his command to James Clinton. Almost exactly a year after Clinton and Tappen had recommended sites for forts, Clinton returned to the lovely gorge in the mountains to superintend their construction. He must have wondered how so very little could have been accomplished in a whole year's time.

4

RETREAT AND
PANIC

JULY 1776 was a month of momentous portent for the future of both America and the Highlands defenses. Congress declared America independent on 2 July. On that same day General William Howe disembarked the first of an army of 34,000 men on Staten Island to initiate his campaign to conquer the new nation.

When English and Hessian troops were safely on land, British warships began probing Patriot defenses of the lower Hudson. On Friday the 12th, the *Phoenix,* with forty guns, and the *Rose,* with twenty, and three tenders, caught a strong flood tide and a sharp south wind to run the gauntlet of guns Henry Knox had lined up on Manhattan Island. As the five ships came by in stately column under full sail, American artillery blazed away. Washington, watching the "incessant fire," was thoroughly surprised when the vessels passed practically unscathed. The flotilla continued to Tappan Zee where the river was too wide for rebel cannon on either bank to be effective. There they anchored, neatly cutting all river traffic to the city. To Washington, it was impressive "proof of the incompetency of batteries to stop a ship's passage with a brisk wind and strong tide where there are no obstructions in the Water to impede their motion."[1]

It is a frailty of human nature that danger is fully comprehended only when present or passed. The Patriots were, after all, no more than human; an entire year had been consumed in endlessly discussing obstructions for the Hudson, but none of the words had been converted to deeds. Not until enemy sail filled the river was the need so apparent as to demand immediate response. Provincial Convention delegates were startled into postevent vigilance. They quickly resolved that:

> . . . a Secret Committee be appointed to devise and carry into execution such measures as to them shall appear most effectual for obstructing the channel of Hudson's River, or annoying the enemy's ships in their navigation up the said River; and that this Convention pledge themselves for defraying the charges incident thereto.[2]

Such open generosity regarding money was totally out of character for the economically strapped Convention and is indicative of the degree of concern felt over the project. More evidence lies in the calibre of men chosen for the committee: John Jay and Robert R. Livingston, both just returned from representing New York in the Continental Congress, joined Robert Yates, Christopher Tappen, Gilbert Livingston, and William Paulding, all esteemed members of the Provincial Convention. John Berrien, with a year's experience as purchasing agent for the defunct Highlands Fortifications Commission, took that same position for the Secret Committee. Finally, the Convention provided £5,000 for expenses and authorized its Secret Committee "to impress boats, vessels, teams, wagons, horses, and drivers when they shall find it necessary for the publick service, as well as to call out the militia, if occasion should require." Obviously, they meant business.[3]

Members of the committee went immediately to Washington's headquarters to ask him to name a Continental general as commander of the militia units being called up. The General, by then painfully aware of difficulties inherent in mixing Continental officers and state troops, persuaded the group to appoint one of their own officers. George Clinton, recently returned from a Congressional seat in Philadelphia and already in the Highlands, was their choice. Washington concurred. In the haste of making the appointment no one thought about a commission, but paper work could always be straightened out later.

Jay, Yates, and the two Livingstons left right away by horse for Fort Montgomery, where they were met by scenes of frenzied activity. On hand to welcome them were the Clinton brothers, James and George.

James Clinton had no sooner reached the Highlands back in June than he rapidly injected energy and a sense of urgency into soldiers and workers at the forts. The Commissioners were relieved of all responsibility, but the new Continental commanding officer retained two as engineers, although Bedlow seems to have been the only one actively engaged from then on. Under Clinton's constant prodding, Fort Montgomery began to take shape. The barracks, 80 feet by 20, two stories high, neared completion; an arch was put over the magazine so powder could be stored safely behind its eight-foot-thick walls; salt was piled in a basement under one end of the barracks; carpenters built gun platforms; soldiers cleared ground to the west; Clinton planned a wall to cover the vulnerable back side of the site. In the midst of that welter of work came notification of the Declaration of Independence. That cheered the grimy, isolated men. Then arrived word of the presence in Tappan Zee of British warships. That stunned them.

Colonel Clinton was at Constitution Island when the news broke that

Saturday morning. His first actions were to sound the alarm, initiate the construction of fire rafts previously suggested by George Washington, and to relay the information to his younger brother, Brigadier General George Clinton. George Clinton left New Windsor without delay, called out three regiments on his own initiative, and joined James on the island. He left orders for one militia regiment to assemble at the island, another to report to Fort Montgomery, and a third to stand by near Newburgh. Others were alerted. On 14 July James and George rowed to Fort Montgomery, beginning a fraternal partnership that would endure for more than a year: Colonel James, a Continental officer, commanded the two forts while General George commanded all New York militia in the Highlands. James' great respect for his capable "kid" brother fostered close cooperation between the Continental and the Minuteman.

While jittery soldiers unlimbered cannon and opened powder kegs and otherwise prepared for battle, George Clinton sat down in a corner of the not quite completed barracks at Fort Montgomery to review steps he had already taken. Owners of watercraft had been warned to stand ready to transport troops. Some boats, "the oldest and worst sloops," were being assembled at Constitution Island where they were to be filled with combustibles, fastened together, and stretched across the river to provide a flaming barrier at that point. An assistant was checking into the feasibility of mounting nine-pounders in the bows of galleys. About 700 militia had already come into Fort Montgomery. Sloops were tying up in Popolopen Creek to serve as floating billets. George Clinton, in his first crisis, had had a busy and fruitful weekend.[4]

The Convention on 16 July mobilized the militia for five and a half months, legalizing George Clinton's reflex action. When Washington and the Convention delegates had agreed upon General Clinton to be commander in the Highlands, he, knowing that circumstances did not permit waiting to be asked, had already been running the show there for three days.

Thus, when the first four members of the Secret Committee arrived, the Hudson Hills were a veritable beehive, bustling with excited men. The Clinton brothers and Commissioner-turned-engineer William Bedlow joined the visitors in considering what steps could be taken to obstruct the river. James Clinton had never forgotten his original proposal to stretch a boom across the waters. His idea was discussed and approved with no argument. Then one of the seven suggested a chain—a great iron barrier, floated on logs, reaching across the river to defy wooden sailing ships. They knew links had already been made and shipped north to help close the River Sorel. That notion, too, was accepted. Large, porcupinelike rafts—formed from logs lashed together, their protruding ends sharpened and shod in iron—could be anchored at various spots in front of the chain and boom to slow and harry hostile ships. Sketches were drawn and also agreed upon. Wheels were needed for cannon carriages, at least 200 of them. It finally grew late and the seven imaginative Patriots stopped for the night.

Next day they wrote for the iron links believed to be at Albany and figured that 150 white pine logs would be required to float them. Twenty heavy cannon were needed for frigates which would patrol behind the combined obstacles of chain, boom, and timber frames. Not wasting a moment, the Secret Committee split up to accomplish all the tasks it had assigned itself. Jay set out for the Salisbury Iron Works to get cannon, Yates and Robert Livingston headed for Albany, Gilbert Livingston and Tappen journeyed to Poughkeepsie. The latter four were in search of iron links and blacksmiths, ships and sailors, combustibles and gunners.[5]

Continental frigates were being built in Poughkeepsie under the supervision of three Patriots familiar with ironworking, Jacobus Van Zandt, Samuel Tudor, and Augustine Lawrence. The Secret Committee promptly diverted them to the mission of chain-making. Deputized to fabricate the chain, they were also instructed to put it across the river near Fort Montgomery if practicable. Fort Constitution was listed as an alternate location. While Secret Committee members were scouring the country for ready-made links and ordering bar iron, Jacobus Van Zandt inspected the two proposed sites for the chain. It seemed to him that the barrier should go across between Fort Constitution and West Point and he so informed George Clinton:

> The situation of the forts and cross running of the tides with the bafiling [sic] winds generally here, and with the assistance of what cannon already mounted, we can defend the chain much better here than at Fort Montgomerie; and what will add grate strength to us, by placing number of men on the hills at West Point with musquetery, we can annoy the ships in such manner that no man will be able to stand her decks, provided, the ships should incline more to West Point than the fort side.[6]

Clinton, his hands full controlling units pouring into the Highlands, deferred decision until an opportunity arose to discuss the matter with someone in the Secret Committee.

It was New York's first major mobilization and it was not proceeding smoothly. Barracks were not yet erected to house all the troops and medical facilities were virtually nonexistent. Adding to the turmoil, every town along the river felt itself endangered and clamored for protection. Furthermore, crops were reaching a critical stage and farmers objected to being called away. One Mathew McKenney, when summoned by his lieutenant, said he would do his fighting at home and, to punctuate his words, took off a lieutenant's hat with a swipe of his sword. Several complete companies refused to budge. On the other hand, there were unforeseen problems with those who did answer the call. Lack of training and discipline in the militia organization did not make General Clinton's job easier. The soldiers, overwrought and nervous, fired muskets at every suspicious shadow, a practice as hard on short nerves as it was on scarce reserves of powder. Clinton, proclaiming that "the patriotism of such is much to be suspected," promised "the severest punishment the law will admit of" for offenders. Perhaps linked to their trigger-happy exuberance was the fact that each man had thoughtfully included in his bedroll a bottle of "strong liquor." Nor was field sanitation understood or practiced. Garrison orders had to detail men daily "to remove all filth and nastiness from about the barracks and garrisons." From private to general it was a time of learning.

Where the ideas of one Clinton brother stop and those of the other begin is impossible to discern. They worked in tandem. Who did what is not important anyway; things got done. Before the month was out a breastwork was taking shape on the point of land south of Fort Montgomery. High, hollow signal spires, made of stacked logs and filled with dried brush and kindling, were ready to burn a bright warning of enemy advance. Guard stations and outposts were established, and Fort Montgomery itself was strengthened. Fire rafts had been constructed in Poughkeepsie and would soon be floated down to play a role in choking the river. Afraid that British warships might run past the defenses under cover of darkness, the brothers lined the opposite river bank beneath Anthony's Nose with piles of brush, intending to light them on approach of English sail. These fires would show passing vessels in full silhouette while Patriot guns in the fort would remain nearly invisible. All told, July was a month of great accomplishment in the Hudson Highlands.

Another event occurred in July which was to have a lasting impact on the fortifications. Washington designated an engineer for the Hudson defenses. On 21 July he ordered Lieutenant Thomas Machin to proceed without delay to "Fort Montgomery or Constitution in the High Lands on Hudson's River." The Commander-in-Chief told Machin that he would be the engineer for all present or future defenses of the river and enjoined him to give the duty personal and devoted attention. To the Secret Committee General Washington described Machin as "an ingenious, faithful hand."[7]

The lieutenant was no novice. At thirty-two, he was an experienced and capable engineer and a combat-tested soldier. Schooled in mathematics from childhood, he had entered artillery training during the Seven Years' War. As a brave thirteen-year-old he participated in the fighting in Europe, distinguishing himself in the important Battle of Minden. Back in England after the war, he continued his engineering education and worked on some rather complex civil engineering projects. In 1772 he traveled to America to examine a reported copper lode in New Jersey. The New World appealed to him; he stayed, settling in Boston. Apparently he was a radical from the start, for he soon joined the Boston activists. Reports have him dressed in Indian garb lustily tossing tea chests into the harbor at that famous party. He was definitely at Bunker Hill, fighting bravely and well and suffering an arm wound.

As a Continental officer, he rose rapidly in esteem if not in rank and was handed steadily increasing responsibilities. When Howe evacuated Boston, Machin experimented with various means "for obstructing the Channel of Boston." Until June 1776 he was engaged in engineering work around that city. That labor done, he carefully packed up his instruments and journeyed to New York where Washington sorely wanted capable engineers. Machin, one of the truly unsung heroes of the Revolution, reached Fort Montgomery in late July.[8]

Elsewhere that fateful month, other forces and other people were stirring, moving, setting the stage for a major battle. Far to the north the overextended and undermanned American invasion of Canada had finally been beaten back. General John Burgoyne arrived from England with thousands of fresh troops, including some forty-three hundred German mercenaries, forcing the remnants of the Patriot units to retreat. By July they had withdrawn to Crown Point and General Guy Carleton was poised at the north end of Lake Champlain. Nothing remained between him and Albany but the Lakes, Fort Ticonderoga, and some determined men. A wilderness arms race occupied most of July as both sides paused to construct a fleet. Far to the south, General Henry Clinton's attempt to seize Charleston had been repulsed by the end of June. General Charles Lee, who had faced Clinton across New York Harbor months earlier, had the satisfaction of watching the British fail in their final effort. Through most of July British forces sat outside Charleston, but Clinton eventually put them on transports and returned to New York, landing at Staten Island on the 31st.

Separating the two strong British armies—one on Staten Island, the other near Lake Champlain—stood only Washington in an untenable position in New York City, unfinished forts and obstacles in the Highlands, and the unbuilt fleet near Fort Ticonderoga. The British probably never had a better chance to squelch the rebellion than in the very month independence was proclaimed.

But in British minds there was still a thought that invasion might be avoided. William Howe and his brother, Lord Richard Howe, admiral commanding the Royal fleet in American waters, had come to New York not only as instruments of his Majesty's military might; they were also deputized to seek peaceful solutions and to grant pardons. While Admiral Howe's armed ships were roaming up the Hudson, General Howe sent a flag to Manhattan with a message for "George Washington, Esquire." Coolly, the Continental officer who met the flag, acting on Washington's instructions, refused the message on the basis that he knew of no such person in the American army. Several days later, another English emissary came with a message to *General* Washington and was admitted. However, on learning that the Howe brothers could offer hardly more than forgiveness, Washington ended the interview with the terse observation that "those who had committed no fault wanted no pardon."

Still General Howe delayed attacking the Americans. Summer's long days dragged on. British and Hessian troops encamped on Staten Island grew restless. Enforced idleness and plenty of fresh meat made them "riotous as satyrs." One officer wrote to a relative in England:

> The fair nymphs of this isle are in wonderful tribulation. . . . A girl cannot step into the bushes to pluck a rose without running the most imminent risk of being ravished, and they are so little accustomed to these vigorous methods that they don't bear them with the proper resignation, and of consequence we have most entertaining courts-martial every day. . . .[9]

It soon was obvious to the British General that waiting longer would merely waste valuable time. His troops would never be more ready; and with each day lost, rebel defenses grew stronger.

Wednesday night, 21 August 1776, was one of those times designed for believers of omens. Darkness came early; thunder boomed and shook the earth; lightning seared trees and shattered houses; rain cascaded in blowing sheets from heavy, circling clouds. For three hours men cringed beneath Nature's fantastic display of wild fury. Washington called it "a most violent gust." Some said it was a tornado. Still others an augury. Thursday's dawn came bright and clear, illuminating the long-expected and much-dreaded English invasion force streaming ashore on Long Island.

Americans, meanwhile, had not remained passive in August. Defensive measures—forts, chains, booms, batteries—were of prime importance, of course, and received most emphasis, but it just was not in the nature of the Patriots to remain solely on the defensive. They had to lash out, someway, at the enemy. British troops on Staten Island were out of reach, Washington had realized, but not British shipping on the Hudson.

At 1:15 P.M. on 3 August, four row-galleys came even with *Phoenix* and *Rose* with obvious intent to fight. While hundreds watched from shore the little Patriot vessels—*Lady Washington, Spitfire, Shark,* and *Whiting*— opened a lively fire at close range on their much larger and surprised opponents. For a full half hour smoke rolled over the broad bay as broadsides were exchanged. Shot after shot thudded home, sending splinters flying and opening holes in both English and American hulls. The smaller vessels, less able to stand such slugging, eventually pulled out of range, and Lieutenant Colonel Benjamin Tupper ordered a withdrawal to Dobb's Ferry. Astonished to count only two dead and fourteen wounded, his courage soared and he reported to Washington that they were ready "to give them another drubbing." Repairs had to be made first, however, and before the galleys got another chance, fire boats were sent after the British interlopers on the Hudson.

On the dark night of 16 August, two ships, loaded with pine knots, wood shavings, pitch, and tar, and primed with "spirits of turpentine and salt petre," steered ominously for the two anchored Britishers. They had been especially constructed by one Ephraim Anderson who had vowed to be a "burning and shining light" in behalf of his country. As the silent attackers neared the unsuspecting warships, American crewmen slipped softly into trailing longboats and rowed to shore. *Phoenix* and *Rose* floated gently at anchor, completely unaware of the approaching holocaust. One volunteer remained at the helm of each fire ship in order to hit the target squarely, fasten grappling hooks, and ignite his floating tinderbox. In the dark, however, a smaller English craft was mistaken for *Rose*. It was struck and destroyed, but its sacrifice saved the others. The second fire ship found *Phoenix* and grappled with her, but English tars, alerted by the flaming tender, managed to cast off the burning American boat, narrowly averting catastrophe. That was warning enough. "Sadly frightened," the four surviving ships dropped downriver, running safely through a hail of fire from Fort Washington on the east shore high up on Manhattan Island.[10]

Close on the heels of the daylight attempt by armed galleys and the night assault by fire ships came history's first recorded underwater attack on an enemy ship. A very recent graduate of Yale College, David Bushnell, had invented both a crude submarine and a timing device to explode a powder charge beneath the surface. The ingenious craft, named *American Turtle*, operated and powered by a one-man crew, had a top speed of three knots, could submerge or surface by alternate flooding or pumping, and was so designed that the operator could attach a keg of powder to the bottom of a ship while remaining inside the sub. It was decided to test the invention in action against a ship of the line in New York Harbor. Picking a dark night and slack tide for the experiment, Bushnell chose no other target than *Asia*, a 64-gun man-of-war—and Admiral Howe's flagship. With a volunteer operator, Sergeant Ezra Lee, at the controls, the bobbing craft was towed by whaleboat almost the length of the bay to within range of *Asia*. Sergeant Lee, after much exertion, brought *American Turtle* alongside the hulking ship, submerged and tried to attach the powder keg. An unforeseen difficulty balked him: designed to bite into wood, the fastening screw would not penetrate copper sheathing on the hull. With the timing device armed, Lee decided it would be imprudent to tarry long; he jettisoned the keg and eased away to safety. A little later, a violent explosion kicked a spout of mud and water high into the air, rocking ships and startling crewmen, but doing no damage. Bushnell tried twice more but with even less success. Frustrated, he gave up his submariner career and entered the army as an engineer.

In a major effort to block the Hudson between Manhattan Island and New Jersey, sloops were sunk, other underwater obstacles were built and installed, and two large forts, Washington and Lee, were constructed overlooking the barrier. Those defenses were located where the modern George Washington Bridge spans the river. Obstacles there, however, had slight chance to succeed because the river is too wide and straight. On a flood tide and with a proper wind, British ships could pass with negligible risk, a bitter fact Washington learned not long after all the labor had been expended. Expecting the ships to snag on his obstructions, he watched in "surprize and mortification" as a strong flotilla "ran through without the least difficulty."[11]

Unable to combat the greatly superior English fleet and equally helpless to hinder its movement in the lower Hudson, Patriots had but one hope, one place to close the river: the Hudson Highlands. By the end of summer it was painfully obvious to everyone that defenses in that granite defile constituted the linchpin of American hopes to retain control of the waterway.

Washington fought and lost the Battle of Long Island. He withdrew to Manhattan and the Provincial Convention retired to Fishkill to place the Highlands between them and the British. With concern for personal safety thereby added to public interest in the defenses, the legislators, on the way to Fishkill, dropped off a committee to inspect the state of the forts. If any member of the Convention had been unaware of the fact that conditions were less pleasant in the Highlands than in New York City, his very first experience served as an eye-opener. Meeting in the Episcopal Church of Fishkill on 5 September, the legislators recorded that the church was "very foul with the dung of doves and fowls, without any benches, seats, or other conveniences whatever, which renders it unfit for the use of this Convention." Resettling in the village's Dutch Church, which was presumably cleaner and more convenient, they heard the report of its committee. It was not a heartening account.[12]

Provisions in camp were low, only 764 men could be counted present for duty, and tools were much needed at the work site. A thousand men more should be on hand. And, in the committee's opinion, "to render Fort Constitution tenable, the West-Point, which commands it, ought to be fortified."

It was not that August had been wasted. Much progress had been made; Convention members simply tended to see the requirement for adequate defenses a little more clearly in the light of clearer danger. George Clinton had been called away to help in the fighting raging at the river's mouth, but James, promoted to Brigadier General that month, had remained at the forts, exhorting everyone there to greater effort. Machin, the new engineer, had fitted in smoothly from the start. His drive and practical knowledge were already proving invaluable. His first mission had been to lay out and erect a battery on the knob just south of Fort Montgomery. Next, James Clinton sent him across the Hudson to plan and raise a fort under Anthony's Nose to guard the entrance to Peekskill Creek. The former, the position which would become Fort Montgomery's twin, was christened "Clinton," a name to honor both generals concerned with building it. "Independence" was the name of the redoubt growing up under the shadow of Anthony's Nose, although it was called "Red-Hook" for a time. August in the Hudson Highlands had been abnormally rainy and cold, slowing the work, but at month's end, cannon frowned at the Hudson River from both forts flanking Popolopen Creek, ramparts were taking shape, powder was ensconced in bombproof dungeons, and several new barracks were nearing completion.

Nor had the Secret Committee been standing still. Sloops were being armed. Fire rafts had been constructed. Some four thousand fire arrows were on order. Chain links were floating down from Albany. Ready-made items were dredged up around the state. Robert Livingston, Lord of the Manor, agreed to make more iron bars. Forges up and down the Hudson flamed day and night as blacksmiths shaped and welded heavy links, hooks, and anchors. Typical of the various contracts let was one to Abel Noble and Peter Townsend at the Stirling Ironworks. They were engaged to produce 16 tons of large anchors, 18 tons of bar iron, and 5 tons of steel. To do that, Noble and Townsend kept eleven fires going and hired 152 workers. Loggers cut and trimmed huge trees, making 160 logs, each 50 feet long. Ships were stripped of rope cables. By the last of August all was in motion, but it would take time before the manifold projects could be completed and the finished material consolidated. And not all the hastily conceived and constructed enterprises turned out as planned. James Clinton found the much-ballyhooed fire rafts awkward and unworkable, more bother than benefit. What became of the 4,000 fire arrows is unknown, but apparently no Patriot archer ever sent one zinging toward an enemy sail.[13]

Convention members urged haste in fabricating the chain, ordered large quantities of tools, and called up still more militia. Unfortunately, they unaccountably disregarded their own committee's recommendation to fortify West Point.

Looking nervously both to the south, where Washington and Howe were sparring, and to the north, where General Carleton threatened invasion, James Clinton, the Convention, and the Secret Committee all carried on, into the fall, their sometimes separate, sometimes common endeavors to make the Highlands impregnable and the Hudson impassable. Roads were improved, barricades were strengthened, men were trained to use cannon, and the chain neared completion.

In September the Battle of Harlem Heights was fought. Soon after, accidentally or otherwise, much of New York City was burned. Early in October Howe threatened to cut off Patriot forces by landing behind them, obliging Washington to abandon Manhattan Island and retreat towards the Highlands. As he fell back, apprehension rose in the Highlands forts. Just a few weeks earlier, before the Battle of Long Island, a young English officer had carefully sized up Washington's rag-tag army and had written his opinion to a relative: "I imagine that we shall very soon come to action, and I do not doubt but the consequence will be fatal to the rebels. An army composed as theirs is cannot bear the frown of adversity."[14]

Maddeningly, the weather turned dry after August's surfeit of rain. So little water remained in ponds and streams by early October that trip hammers at the forges could be operated only part time. Just when the chain was most urgently needed, the work was slowest. Anxiously awaiting the chain's completion, but helpless to hurry it, several members of the Secret Committee once more surveyed the Highlands for the best possible location to install it. On 9 October they met and, after long discussion, decided that the chain would function best if stretched from Constitution Island to West Point. Since West Point had not been fortified, they resolved "that a fortification be erected at West Point in order to defend the chain."

That resolution struck James Clinton and Thomas Machin like a thunderbolt! Didn't the Secret Committee know the British were expected daily? And didn't the gentlemen know building a fort took time? Hastily, General Clinton called a conference on Constitution Island two days later. He and Machin carefully pointed out the weaknesses there. West Point could not be fortified overnight and Fort Constitution alone could not protect the chain. Convinced, the Committee voted, on the spot:

> That Mr. Machin immediately prepare a place on each side of the River at Fort Montgomery to fasten the ends of the intended chain to. That he place two or three guns in a small work to be erected for that purpose on the flat place just under the north end of the grand battery, where the fire rafts now lay—also a small work, if time permit, near the water edge on the south side of Pooplopin's Kill.[15]

Again, almost predictably now, West Point was skipped in favor of another location. Undoubtedly, Clinton and Machin were correct in believing it was too late to change the entire scheme of defense, but men had been recommending West Point from the beginning, to no avail. James Clinton, himself, had been the first.

In the final days of October, Howe beat Washington again at the Battle of White Plains, shoving the shattered Continentals to a new line north of Croton River. Washington's back was against the Highlands. At the same time, word came from Ticonderoga of Carleton's defeat of the American fleet under Benedict Arnold at Valcour Island. Everything then pointed to a decisive battle for possession of the Hudson's gorge through the Highlands.

Troubled, and wanting to do something to help, the Committee of Safety impulsively seized on a suggestion of George Clinton's that cannon placed at water level would be most effective against ships. They immediately instructed Colonel Charles DeWitt to install batteries along the river near the high-tide mark. DeWitt agreed to do it, but, with unusual candor, admitted to an "ignorance of the business." Henry Wisner, a member of the Secret Committee, was detailed to assist with the new project. No one was sure where the men or cannon or material would come from, but at least the Committee of Safety could not be accused of doing nothing. Wisner and DeWitt recommended almost a dozen additional sites in a whirlwind tour of the Highlands. It is hard to see how their errand, no matter how well intentioned, could have done other than detract from the greater effort.[16]

Although work on the chain had been "shamefully delayed," the threat of invasion had served to hustle the blacksmiths and the last links were floated down to Fort Montgomery in the first few days of November. With an energy entirely typical of him, Machin turned to the problem of stretching the giant iron chain 1,800 feet across a river strongly affected by tides. A Captain Hazlewood, who had witnessed a smaller but similar operation in the Delaware River, offered some advice, but, basically, it was Machin's puzzle to solve. He selected the terminus points, installed sturdy anchors on land and in the river bottom, and began assembling the chain in short lengths as it arrived. Clevises had been placed at every tenth link to facilitate the construction, while swivels were occasionally inserted to preclude buckling. Machin's technique was to assemble the entire chain, fastening it on logs near the shore under Fort Montgomery. One end was fixed to its braces there and the other snaked up along the river bank. Waiting until near the end of the ebb tide, he pulled the chain across by use of perhaps a score of boats, all rowing hard, helped by the slight tide. Then, in slack tide, the opposite end was fixed. Cautiously, the boatmen backed off to see what would happen when the tide reversed itself. In a few hours they had an answer. As water rushed upriver, pushing the great logs and bubbling around the links, it magnified the tension already pulling the links taut. The iron creaked and groaned as each link and swivel and clevis was subjected to the two-way tug. Then, with a sharp crack, the chain parted, spilling logs and dimming hopes.

Chagrined, the engineer sent his boatmen after the two free-floating ends. When the cumbersome combination of log and iron was secured once again alongside the shore, Machin inspected the break. A swivel, sent down from Ticonderoga, had been the guilty member. Quickly, Machin had it rewelded while he checked every other piece of iron. They looked all right. Next day, when tide conditions were once more proper, the flock of rowboats repeated the process of positioning the chain, this time leaving both ends fixed while swinging the two halves like gate doors to a junction at mid-stream. A second time they backed off and watched. Again, the chain snapped, this time at a clevis. Machin ordered the chain drawn into Popolopen Creek, while the dejected Secret Committee members wrote to Fishkill reporting the failure.[17]

During the time Machin was struggling with the chain, Washington was making up his mind to cross the Hudson and retreat through New Jersey. Howe had shown no disposition to attack again, and Carleton had not followed up his advantage on the northern lakes. The Commander-in-Chief apparently believed the Hudson Highlands could be defended with less than the entire American army, while New Jersey and Pennsylvania now needed a higher degree of protection. But before he left he wanted to be personally satisfied of the capacity of the forts to resist. For the first time, General George Washington visited the defenses he had recommended some eighteen months earlier.

Just before midday, 10 November 1776, Washington left for Peekskill. Behind him, elements of the Continental Army were already crossing at Stony Point. Accompanying him was Brigadier General William Heath, a fat, bald, somewhat pompous Yankee from Massachusetts. Heath was to be the commander of all troops, forts, and installations in the Highlands. On the 11th and part of the 12th, Washington and Heath rode through the hills, inspected forts, talked with officers there, and discussed methods of defense. The General counted 29 cannon overlooking the planned site of the chain, all mounted on garrison carriages and pointed at the river. Nearly 750 men were in the forts near Anthony's Nose, while about 400 men and 30 guns were on Constitution Island. After that tour, Washington was more convinced than ever that the craggy hills could be and should be defended. Seeing the great amount of effort which had been directed at preventing the passage of ships, he astutely grasped the tactical error of concentrating on the river alone. Those works, however efficient, would be helpless should enemy troops slip around to their rear. He insisted that Heath become familiar with "the roads and ways leading through the hills." Before leaving, he instructed his engineer, Colonel Rufus Putnam, to remain for a period of time to assist Heath. Final instructions to the new commander spoke Washington's concern: "You will not only keep in view the importance of securing these passes but the necessity of doing it without delay."[18]

Two thousand Continental troops were to be quartered near Fishkill for the winter. Washington asked the Provincial Convention to provide shelter for them. Happy to have the added protection of such a force, the Provincial Convention readily agreed to undertake the task. But, on beginning, it discovered a severe shortage of lumber and laborers. To counter the first problem they decided to build huts with mud walls. The solution to the second deficit may be America's earliest instance of the utilization of "conscientious objectors" in noncombat activities. Claiming that certain militia units in Albany County, "either through want of zeal in, or disaffection to, the cause of American freedom," had not answered the call to arms, the

Convention ruled it to be "highly just and equitable . . . that such as, through enmity or cowardice, will not step forth as soldiers should contribute an equivalent in labour." Shirking soldiers could build mud houses.[19]

Throughout most of the autumn, New York's Provincial Convention entrusted its work to a Committee of Safety. The reverses in New York City and Canada had progressively shaken the collective sense of security of the Committee members. Then they learned that the chain would not hold, that Washington had departed for New Jersey, and that, on 16 November, Fort Washington had fallen—along with Fort Lee the last defense beneath the Highlands. Fort Lee succumbed four days later. In that moment of crisis, when cool heads and calm hands should have prevailed, the men in Fishkill were panic-stricken. The "frown of adversity" was indeed hard to bear. They commanded the Secret Committee "to report *some* form of a plan" for perfecting the obstructions "with all convenient speed." Then they directed soundings be taken to find a shallow place in the river, presumably for the installation of sunken defenses. Henry Wisner was sent out to complete his job of scattering cannon along the shores "for the annoyance of the enemy's ships, should any attempt to pass." Unmindful of Washington's selection of Heath as the Highlands commander, the Committee of Safety asked General Philip Schuyler to "take on himself the superintendence and direction of such works as he may think necessary . . . for the security of Hudson's River." Fortunately, Schuyler wisely declined. They requested a plan from Benedict Arnold as he passed through on his return from Canada, and even John Jay's absurd proposal of an immense project to fill in the river near Fort Montgomery by pushing Anthony's Nose into it was no longer laughed at.[20]

In a dither to do something—anything—the Committee of Safety leaped on another of George Clinton's suggestions, this one mentioning the desirability of obstructing the river near Pollepel Island. That location had nothing to commend it except water shallow enough to permit the employment of *chevaux-de-frise* and caissons.* The river at Pollepel Island was not only straight, it was too broad to allow adequate cover of the obstacles by cannon fire. Hostile ships would be able to pick their way around the obstructions. That lesson had been learned earlier at Fort Washington—and forgotten so soon. Nevertheless, the Committee of Safety, with General Heath's backing, placed full emphasis on the new plan.

Thomas Machin began drawing the necessary blueprints, while George Clinton marched 500 men to Fort Constitution to accomplish the labor. Boats were confiscated, the countryside was searched for tools, stone was gathered, ironworkers started turning out braces and bolts and pointed tips. On the first dawn of December, a chilly Sunday morning, George Clinton had his men on the island, poised to begin.

Five days later, despite the flurry of activity, not a single caisson had been built because, in George Clinton's words, "The weather has been so

---

* Caissons were sunken wooden boxes, weighted by stone. The *chevaux-de-frise* were tree trunks, wedged in the stone, with one end clad in iron and reaching to the water's surface.

extream bad, which with the want of felling axes, has like to prevented our doing much at the business we were sent upon." As time dragged on, a few huge boxes were made and sunk in a line extending from Pollepel Island to Plum Point. Gradually, though, cold weather, lack of supplies, and fading enthusiasm brought the project to a halt. News filtered down of Carleton's withdrawal; word came up that Howe had crossed the Hudson and was following Washington through New Jersey. The Highlands defenses were not to be tested that year. Everyone relaxed.

Granted a breathing spell, New Yorkers took inventory. Genuine amazement was evinced at the "several fruitless attempts" to shut the door on the Highlands. Small, unfinished positions were sprinkled along the banks of the Hudson from one end to the other of that stream's course through the mountains. The various posts were neither mutually supporting nor self-sufficient. The soldiers were barefoot, hungry, restless. They had not been paid since August. Deserters left in groups. And even the steadfast were proclaiming firm intentions of returning to the hearth when their terms of service expired on 31 December.[21]

All in all, the situation was worse than bleak. Christmas Day in the forts along the Hudson was a cold, cheerless holiday. The New Year held scant hope.

PART TWO

THE YEAR OF THE HANGMAN

5

FIVE LANGUID MONTHS

SUPERSTITIOUS folk started it. And the word spread on the wind. Continental delegates grinned tightly and cracked nervous little jokes when they heard the allusion. Traditionally, the figure seven had been symbolic of a hangman's gibbet; considering that, the coming year boded the very darkest of evils for it ominously contained a triple mark of death. Only once in a thousand years is a twelvemonth represented by three hanging trees, three macabre sevens. The eerie combination forecast good times for hangmen, bad ones for rebels. Late in 1776, with British arms meeting success after success, Washington's army melting away, redcoats and Hessians devouring New Jersey, and fear gnawing in Philadelphia, one need not have drawn on supernatural logic to have believed that 1777 could, indeed, become the Year of the Hangman.

Continental Congressmen might not have been superstitious, but they were cautious. When it became evident that General Howe had shifted the thrust of his campaign from New York to New Jersey, threatening Pennsylvania, the delegates fled southward to the relative security of Baltimore. Meeting there in gloomy session before Christmas, they learned of General Charles Lee's capture and that some three thousand ragged scarecrows were all that remained under Continental colors along the Delaware River. In that emergency, probably the moment most fraught with disaster in the entire war, only one man stood between the British and the abyss, General George Washington. On him Congress conferred extraordinary powers, giving the Virginia general what amounted to a blank check in the forlorn hope that he might perform a military miracle.

He did. In his magnificent ten-day Christmas Campaign, Washington reversed the entire tide of the war. After a long, exasperating series of setbacks, all suffered in defensive battles, the Commander-in-Chief resolved to attack, to lash out, to seize the initiative.

In this effort he was helped by William Howe. English columns should have pursued the beaten Americans across New Jersey and Pennsylvania "into the very laps of the Continental Congress." But Howe was not that cut of soldier; it was not in his indolent mind to push the sword to the hilt if the blade were weighted with ice. Sir William—he had been knighted in reward for his New York exploits—*followed* Washington across New Jersey, put his troops into winter quarters, and settled down in New York City to savor memories of his victories with "feasting, gaming and banqueting" and to enjoy his open dalliance with beautiful "Betsy" Loring. He also sent General Henry Clinton with 6,000 men to seize Newport, Rhode Island, that December—a debatable decision which further dissipated British strength. Washington, a weaker but wiser general after his autumn battles, had an army still in the field, thanks to Howe's inexplicable lethargy. Moreover, in large measure due to the exploits of Benedict Arnold on faraway Lake Champlain, the Hudson remained a Patriot river. By failing either to destroy the rebel army or to isolate New England by breaking through the Hudson Highlands, the British left a spark of resistance—a spark Washington was quick to fan.

No good explanation has ever been made for Howe's failure to take the crucial Highlands passes after Washington crossed the Hudson and marched away into New Jersey in November 1776. They were his for the taking. Carleton's return to Canada was probably a factor. The fast-approaching winter would have been another; perhaps the English commander did not dare risk a campaign in the mountains at a time when a sudden freeze might catch his fleet high up the waterway. Too, he may have been unaware of the inadequacy of defenses along the river. Then again, it could have been that British military moves were somewhat shaped by a lingering if vain hope that the peace feelers so ardently pressed by the Howe brothers would yet bear fruit. Or, the supine surrender to the impulse to secure adequate bases for the winter—for which reason General Clinton had been dispatched to Newport—may have so weakened Sir William that he felt unequal to the task of cracking the Highlands barrier. One reason, as valid as any, could be simply that the British believed Washington was so whipped that he soon must fold; and it was evident that once the Continental Army was destroyed, the fortresses along the Hudson could be grabbed at leisure. Moreover, as a soldier—and Howe was a better general than his record in America might indicate—he would naturally have tended to inform himself about the enemy army, thus instinctively turning away from the river when Washington left it. What is sure is that, for whatever reason, Howe's decision to ignore the Highlands gave Washington the one glimmer of opportunity he needed.

Late on Christmas Day, Patriots crossed an ice-choked Delaware River. Assembling north of Trenton, they marched through blowing rain and sleet and snow to annihilate a Hessian garrison in that town at dawn. Jarred out of complacency, Howe hurriedly sent a strong column under Cornwallis to smash the impudent rebels. Washington gathered his men south of Trenton, shrewdly side-stepped the British lunge, and dashed over frozen roads deeper into New Jersey to Princeton, where he fought and won a second battle. Having gained two much-wanted tactical victories, the Commander-in-Chief capped his campaign with a brilliant strategic stroke. Marching his weary but happy troops into the hills of northern New Jersey, Washington set up a winter cantonment near Morristown where he occupied a perfect flanking position. His location, behind high ridges and dense forests, was virtually unassailable, while British outposts in the low ground to the south would be vulnerable at any time to raids from the Patriot redoubt. Worse, from the British viewpoint, any attempt to march from New York to Philadelphia would be impossible with the Continental Army a threat on the flank. Bowing to the inevitable, Sir William withdrew from most of New Jersey. The entire course of the war had been altered. Defeat had been averted. As a sign of Heavenly approbation—at least so construed by Washington's superstitious soldiery—a solar eclipse occurred on 9 January 1777. Perhaps, just perhaps, it would not be a year for hangmen after all.

Washington's position at Morristown was of great significance to the men in the Hudson Highlands and even more so to the people of New England. With New York City in enemy hands, all military and civilian traffic between New England and the remainder of the states crossed the Hudson at ferry sites near those ancient, rugged mountains. Roads from the crossing points ran along level valleys behind protecting ridges reaching almost to Philadelphia. So long as the Highlands forts held fast and the Continental Army covered the few passes near Morristown, America's one slim lifeline connecting central and eastern colonies was secure.

Even as the hard-fighting handful of Americans under George Washington braved and overcame the combined odds of malevolent weather and superior numbers, other Americans in the Hudson Highlands surrendered to languor and despondency. After the supercharged excitement of the preceding weeks such a letdown was probably no more than normal, but it dismayed those officers whose eyes had been rather rudely opened to the fact that the vaunted Highlands defenses were so very far from completion. A heavy snowfall on 26 December 1776, along with plunging temperatures, forced workers and soldiers alike into such shelter as they could find. All movement was temporarily stalled by deep drifts. Sleet, slanting and hard, followed. For most of the men their ordeal would end on 31 December, the expiration date of their current tours of duty. So, half from celebration, half from necessity, they turned to drink to render the remaining days passable if not pleasant. Discipline all but disappeared on Constitution Island and at Fort Montgomery; James Clinton gnashed his teeth helplessly in the face of insubordination and railed at the militia, "drunk and made so by the officers."

His brother felt more compassion for the hapless soldiers. Watching many of them drift away in search of food, he refused to make them stay. "Indeed they must desert or starve; and however well disposed, they will not submit to the latter," he explained. "It would be cruel as well as unjust to force them back to starve, nor shall I have strength left to do it." General

Heath managed to retain for six weeks the services of several Continentals at a bounty of $10 a man, but money was no inducement to New York militiamen. Most left.[1]

A trickle of replacements from other states trudged into the forts, but, as a rule, they were untrained and unprepared to face the rigors of winter duty. Heath complained bitterly to Washington that his own state of Massachusetts had sent him men "almost naked, and so infected with the itch as to be unfit for service." New York's Committee of Safety, sitting in Fishkill on 1 January 1777, authorized George Clinton to raise "one thousand men by drafts or in other such ways as to him appear most equitable and expeditious." Convention members were "convinced that a thousand men under the command of a brave and vigilant officer would effectually keep the enemy at bay and bring back to their just allegiance to this State such of the inhabitants who from the arts or threats of the enemy have been seduced from it." Nearly every officer was sent to his home county to recruit. The term for draftees was set to run through March, proof that Americans had not, in spite of the most obvious evidence, learned that short-term soldiers were at best an inefficient, short-term answer to the serious problem of providing men for war. As things stood, however, that was a purely academic matter for Clinton. He needed men immediately. Furthermore, it was unlikely that he could lay hands on a thousand men not already serving or excused by virtue of recent duty.

Thomas Machin, the energetic engineer, hit upon a partial solution: scores of tories were being rounded up in the area; forced labor was better than no labor. Thirty prisoners, the "least dangerous" of the Hudson Valley's "disaffected inhabitants," were put to work by him at New Windsor on the fabrication of river obstructions. In the face of all efforts, though, Fort Constitution's garrison dwindled to 156 that January while Fort Montgomery's was fewer by 6.[2]

For the most part, the steadfast souls manning the forts seem to have done little more than survive. Which feat, considering their wretched living conditions, may have been all one could have expected of them. General Heath, who had been so specifically and forcefully ordered by Washington to complete the defenses, devoted to the fortifications not a single word in his memoirs of the period. If that is not conclusive evidence that the commander of the Highlands was not impressed by the need for constructing or improving forts, perhaps his choice of February to take a long vacation to Massachusetts lends credence to such a charge. When the commanding general is disinterested, the men cannot be expected to be otherwise.

James Clinton's time was split between Continental duties in Morristown and Command of the Highlands forts, while brother George found himself saddled with recruiting responsibilities, construction supervision, and the conduct of minor operations against British outposts above Manhattan. Apparently, only one individual continued to devote full attention to furthering the Hudson River obstructions—Lieutenant Machin. When others had been disheartened at the failure of the chain, Machin alone did not despair. Convinced that it would hold with just a few minor modifications, he had already begun to alter it before George Clinton sent him to New Windsor to build *chevaux-de-frise* for the Pollepel Island–Plum Point obstacle line. Now, in January's lull, he turned once more to the former project.[3]

As the engineer saw the problem, it was a matter of improving the method of attaching the chain, not of changing the construction of the chain itself. Each link was made from bar iron 1½ inches square, more than enough, Machin reasoned, to withstand the strain involved. It seemed that the weak points were the clevis or swivel parts, but, barring faulty iron, most of those were deemed strong enough to hold up. Smaller or weaker ones were replaced. The real villain was the tide. Because it had an average variance from high to low water of about five feet, the chain had to be flexible enough to adjust to it. But, being flexible, it had floated with the tide, curving inward and turning the sharpened logs partially cross-ways in the water. Extra pressure thus built up had been sufficient to snap weaker members. Machin's solution was to fix the chain more rigidly across the river by means of numerous lines and anchors. Tidal action, then, could produce less horizontal drift. There would have to be some sway, he figured, to compensate for the vertical rise, but by the use of more and longer cables he sought to reduce movement enough to drop stresses below the critical point. On paper it looked good, but there was no way to test the theory until spring came. Gambling that his concept would work, Machin made such changes as were required in the chain and ordered extra anchors and cables.

Meanwhile, he proceeded with the project dreamed up in the panic of late 1776, establishing a line of underwater obstructions across the wide but shallow stretch of water by Pollepel Island. Using his impressed Loyalist laborers, the hard-driving officer soon produced several huge timber-frame caissons which, filled with rock, were to serve as solid foundations for great, iron-tipped log fingers reaching up to rip holes in wooden-hulled ships. Each caisson was about thirty feet square at bottom and braced "as if it was intended for a house of six stories." Machin contacted Robert Erskine, manager of Ringwood Furnace and future map-maker for the Continental Army, who agreed to manufacture metal parts. By February those iron items were arriving and many of the logs were readied. A thaw on 20 January gave Machin a chance to sound the river bottom between Pollepel Island and Plum Point to determine how many of these obstacles he would need and how tall each one would have to be to break water. His calculations indicated that 98 *chevaux-de-frise* would be required, varying in height from 12 to 47 feet.[4]

No records remain to relate the working conditions or hours of Tories who fell into Machin's vigorous hands, but it is safe to assume they worked as long and as hard as he himself always did. Otherwise he could not have made such progress. Ironically, during this period when Tories toiled so, Patriot laborers worked hardly at all and accomplished nothing of note. George Clinton angrily wrote, "I think the artificers neither go out early enough in the morning, or continue late enough in the evening at work. . . . From nine in the morning until three in the afternoon is not by any means a day's work." He felt obliged to issue instructions telling the workers that "not only the safety of this State, but of the whole continent" depended on diligent and faithful work.[5]

Machin left his post only once during January when he made a brief journey to Morristown on the 29th to confer with Washington about promotion and pay. Responsibilities and performances notwithstanding, he was still a lieutenant. It seemed to him that he deserved a higher rank, especially when other officers were rising so rapidly. Washington concurred. As for pay, he had received none since May 1776. After eight payless months he was feeling a severe financial pinch. The Commander-in-Chief wrote a personal letter to Artillery Chief Henry Knox—Machin was technically an artillery officer—recommending the engineer as "a person of merit" who should be considered for promotion. It is presumed that his salary losses were made good, in part at least, but promotion was not attained. For the first time, but by no means the last, recognition which he so richly deserved passed him by.[6]

Except that a leaf on the calendar had turned, February in the Highlands was hardly discernible from January. Machin pursued his projects, token improvements were made on the forts, men shivered. George Clinton continued to divide his interests between recruiting duties in the state and supervising works of construction and obstruction along the Hudson. General Washington gave some thought to sending James Clinton northward to Ticonderoga once again, but changed his mind, deciding the New Yorker's influence with local militiamen made him more valuable at Fort Montgomery. Only one noteworthy event occurred during the month: Heath went home on the 12th and was replaced by Brigadier General Alexander McDougall.

McDougall, Scottish by birth and ancestry, radical American by environment and inclination, had been an avid and active rebel for several years prior to the war. He had risen to fame when Royal authorities jailed him in 1770 on suspicion of having authored an inflammatory pamphlet. His case became so celebrated that the year he spent in prison was more social event than confinement. After that, wherever appeared that high, square forehead, accented by a receding hairline and puffy eyes, one could expect to hear hot words or hotter action from the self-styled "Son of Liberty." Despite a slight speech impediment, he was a leader in New York's Provincial Convention until he accepted an army commission in 1776. As befitted so distinguished a rabble-rouser, he climbed rapidly in the service, attaining the rank of brigadier general six weeks after entering. The broad-faced Scot had participated in the fighting around New York in the latter half of 1776, but had been confined most of the winter to a sickbed.

In designating McDougall military commander of the Hudson Highlands area, Washington was probably guided by political subtleties as well as military considerations. With George Clinton commanding New York militia units and responsible for obstructing the Hudson, James Clinton in charge of the forts and their garrisons, and the New York Provincial Convention prone to interfere at any time in any phase of the activities, it was helpful that Washington's man there was a New York politician.

General Alexander McDougall. Courtesy of the West Point Library.

If February was a slow month in the Highlands of New York, it was an exceedingly busy one in governmental chambers in London. There, finishing touches were being put to a plan of campaign designed to quench once and for all, in the coming summer, the irritating rebellion of the American Colonies. The plan evolving sprang from two letters Sir William Howe wrote late in 1776 and took its special twist from "thoughts" espoused in person by General John Burgoyne. At the vortex of the planning was Lord Dartmouth's replacement as Secretary of State for American Colonies, Lord George Germain. An ex-general, court-martialed for misconduct at the Battle of Minden and officially judged unfit to serve "in any military capacity whatever," Germain had quite ironically reached the political seat which made him, in effect, director of all military affairs in America. Burgoyne's imagination and ambition combined with Germain's incompetence and prejudice to hatch Great Britain's grand strategy for 1777.

The concept was good; very possibly it was the only one which could have gained victory in America for George III. Basically, the idea was the same as it had been in 1776: first, occupy and hold the line of the Hudson River, isolating New England; then invade and crush that Yankee seedbed of rebellion before turning on other colonies in their turn. Fault lay in the plan devised to accomplish the larger concept. Three columns were all scheduled to strike simultaneously at Albany. Howe was to lead troops up the Hudson from New York City, Burgoyne would head an expedition southward from Montreal, and the third was expected to attack down the Mohawk River Valley from the west. Until they reached Albany there would be no overall Commander—and could be no cooperation between forces separated by hundreds of miles of frontier forest. There was no guarantee of assistance should any one of the three columns need help. It was a plan pregnant with disaster. Even so, bad plans boldly executed more often than not prove better than good plans poorly executed. If his Majesty's generals in America could make it work, there was every reason to expect that his more traitorous subjects would indeed be swinging on a gallows by year's end.

Burgoyne, hopes brimming, sailed from England on 3 April 1777. Bound for Canada with plans and several thousand reinforcements, he fully expected to stamp out rebellion and make himself famous that year. The campaign of 1777 had begun.

Although the enemy's precise plans were unknown, Americans did suspect strongly that the British would make a major effort that year along the Hudson Valley. If that happened the forts and obstructions in the Highlands would play an important, perhaps decisive, role in the campaign. But no one had as yet decided how best to defend those vital hills and defiles. Four main forts—Constitution, Montgomery, Independence, and Clinton—stood in varying stages of completion, while numerous battery sites were to be found, some with cannon, most without. Machin had faith that his revamped chain would hold; few agreed with him. George Clinton remained convinced that the *chevaux-de-frise* at Pollepel Island would do the job. "We have this business in great forwardness," he informed Washington in late February, "and I have not the least doubt but we shall complete it in season nor but that it will be effectual." He went on to say heavy artillery would be needed, and to suggest that the guns could safely be taken from other forts. His intent was to install cannon on Pollepel Island and in a fort planned for Plum Point, a fort Machin was to erect as soon as warmer weather permitted. All in all, the crucial defenses remained practically helpless. Such combat strength as had been amassed in the Highlands was frittered out piecemeal; at no single spot was attention or power focused.[7]

Clinton's February optimism turned to March pessimism. His recruiting endeavors had netted only four hundred men of the thousand needed, and those were slated to be discharged at month's end. As a result there was an insufficient number of troops to perform the most essential guard duties, none to assist civilian laborers on the forts. Moreover, morale amongst those workers and soldiers was at rock bottom. Either pay or living conditions must be bettered, they demanded. Clamoring for improvements, 108 mutinied on 1 March, "quit the work . . . and took up clubs and threatened others if they did not." Their revolt was short-lived only because most of the men remained loyal if disgruntled and refused to sanction mass desertion. Turning from personnel problems to construction projects, Clinton saw an equally dismal picture. The chain was ready, but anchors and cables enough still had not been gathered. *Chevaux-de-frise* to complete the underwater barrier at Pollepel Island had been constructed and were being sunk, but cannon to cover them had yet to be found. The Provincial Convention grew concerned once more and, predictably, dispatched a committee to ascertain "the forwardness of the obstructions in Hudson's River." Clinton, on being informed of the Convention's wishes "that so necessary an affair should meet with no delay," grumpily guessed another month's time would be necessary and took the opportunity to remind the lawmakers that General Washington, not New York, was responsible for the defenses.[8]

To be fair, though, it must be acknowledged that the Convention left the men in the Highlands pretty much alone that spring. They had their own problems. Meeting in Kingston's Court House where they were striving to piece together a constitution for the State of New York, delegates were troubled by the terrible conditions existing in the overcrowded prison beneath them. Indignantly, they recorded that "from the past want of care of the prisoners now confined in the jail immediately underneath the Convention chamber, the same is supposed to have become unwholesome, and a very nauseous and disagreeable effluvia arises, which may endanger the health of the members of this Convention." Corrective action was loudly demanded—and taken. An ingenius solution emerged: "*Resolved,* that for the preservation of their health, the members of this Convention be at liberty at their pleasure to smoke in the Convention Chamber while the house is sitting and proceeding on business." That resolution passed by the narrow margin of three votes, indicating that several stalwart members would have preferred the smell of prison "effluvia" straight rather than diluted by clouds of tobacco smoke. The prisoners, no doubt, felt very sorry to be causing the legislators so much discomfort. But the problem was overcome and the Constitution was written.[9]

In March, Machin made final arrangements to try again to install the chain. Logs to replace those previously lost were dragged and floated to Fort Montgomery early in the month; the meticulous engineer carefully recorded a cost of £8.20.0 in his account book for 7 and 8 March to cover expenses of "Taking the great Chain Logs down to Fort Montgomery with 40 men, 4 days." The logs were assembled in groups, the chain was secured to them, and all was in readiness, except cables, which were still missing. Machin waited impatiently, anxious to test his theory.[10]

For the past several months, Peekskill, a river town boasting over fifty houses, had been a Patriot collection point, a military magazine of considerable worth. An army community, Continental Village, had sprung up a few miles to the north. Much of Washington's horde of powder and equipment and weapons was stored there. Howe, still smarting from professional embarrassment over the inglorious end of his 1776 campaign, determined during the winter to destroy the rebel cache at Peekskill as soon as danger of the river's freezing passed. Quietly, in carefully shrouded secrecy, he loaded troops aboard transports late on Friday night, 21 March 1777. In darkness the convoy started upriver, reaching a safe anchorage near Teller's Point late the next afternoon. Before Sunday's sun was much more than up, the vessels got underway once again, sailed to Peekskill, and began disgorging troops there at noon.

General McDougall was not entirely surprised, for the fleet had been observed on the 22nd and its presence reported. Nonetheless, when he watched enemy troops streaming ashore—estimated at about a thousand strong, but really only half that number—he was unprepared to make a stand. He must have regretted boldly writing just the day before, "You may rest assured particular attention will be paid to the security of those [Highlands] fortresses. Nothing in my power will be wanting." Such stores as could quickly be carted away were removed, the rest burned. Patriots fell back on the Albany Post Road and halted in the pass leading into the Highlands. No pursuit was attempted by the Royal raiders, but they jeered lustily and scornfully at the precipitate American flight. One English secretary briefly described the action in his diary: "The Rebels are runoff in a panic about Peek's Kill having burnt their barracks, magazines for the most part, etc., before they went."

Word of the attack reached Fort Constitution four hours after the redcoats had landed. Quickly the warning beacon was set afire, sending flame and smoke high into the air. George Clinton saw the signal at his home in New Windsor and immediately called out three regiments. Two marched for Fort Montgomery and the third to Constitution Island. By the time those arrangements had been made, night had fallen. Clinton traveled through the darkness, taking no time to sleep, arriving at Fort Montgomery at three o'clock Monday morning. By that afternoon, though, Patriot commanders, with evident relief, had recognized that a raid was all the British had in mind. Marauding British soldiers were recalled and reloaded into transports, which promptly dropped downstream.[11]

At headquarters in Morristown, Washington was highly displeased with the lack of will displayed by Americans defending Peekskill and quite perturbed that the garrison had been so weakly manned. In a bitter letter to the President of Congress, he decried all militia and recruiting officers:

> All that was possible for me to do towards collecting a force at Peekskill, I had attempted before. I had in peremptory terms called upon the officers of Rhode Island and Connecticut to forward on their recruits . . . to that place; I had directed such of the New York Regiments as had not been ordered to Ticonderoga to repair thither, I had requested eight of the Massachusetts Regiments to that post, and lest these should not arrive in time, I urged Govr. Trumbull in a letter of the 6th instt. to send 2000 of his militia to the same place.
>
> But, sorry I am to observe, the militia have got tired, and . . . the most unheard of desertions, or most scandalous peculations, have prevailed among the officers who have been employed in recruiting.[12]

His wrath was not abated when days passed with no word from commanders in the Highlands. "Not being able to account for Genl. McDougall's . . . and Genl. Clinton's . . . silence upon this occasion," he sent an express rider toward Peekskill seeking information. He was far from impressed with the timid performance of Alexander McDougall. The Commander-in-Chief was not by himself; many of McDougall's own officers were critical of his performance, some openly so. If the Hudson was to be a center of fighting, a fighting commander was needed. Mentally running over his list of generals of proven ability under fire, Washington came quickly to the name of Benedict Arnold.[13]

New York, meanwhile, authorized George Clinton full power to call up militia from the counties of Dutchess, Ulster, Orange, and Westchester. At once conferring with the various colonels involved, Clinton decided to mobilize a third of the available manpower. That was easier said than done, however. Throughout April the threat of another sudden raid was constantly in the minds of everyone in the lower Hudson Valley. Yet militia could be brought to service only by the "greatest exertions." Dutchess County, for example, was directed to provide 800 men to garrison forts Montgomery and Constitution; three weeks later not a man had shown up. "It is distressing indeed," complained the disgusted militia general, "that men at this critical period should be so backward in their duty and gives me the utmost pain to be obliged to say that the fault must be with the officers." He had put his finger right at the heart of the problem. America had so far failed to produce qualified leaders in the quantity needed; nowhere was the failure more evident than in the militia where men seldom respected their officers, commonly felt superior to them, often despised them, and infrequently obeyed them. In an incident typical of the times, a Corporal John Lovett flew into a rage upon seeing his wife, a camp follower, talking one day to a lieutenant. Calling her a whore, Lovett "punched his wife with his gun" and bellowed that "he had rather a camp colored man should speak to his wife than an officer!"[14]

A violent civil war erupted that spring in the lower counties of New York. Men of Tory sympathies had always been numerous, although they had been generally quiescent while the Patriots held power. Then, coming close behind Washington's defeats in New York in 1776, the successful raid on Peekskill encouraged many of them. Singly, and sometimes in bands, they shouldered weapons and marched off to join Howe in New York City. Fights flared with Patriots bent on preventing the exodus. To make matters worse, gangs of bandits purporting to support one or the other cause sprang up in the no man's land between the city and the Highlands. Attitudes quickly hardened and jails filled as patrols snared more and more "disaffected people." George Clinton advocated death without mercy for all traitors. The Convention agreed, passing a resolution on 5 May directing that "traitorous inhabitants of this state as shall be found in arms against the authority of the same [are] to be destroyed or otherwise effectually secured." Earlier, they had issued a broadside establishing death as the penalty for enemy spies, recruiters, suppliers, or informers. One Simon Mabee soon thereafter fell into McDougall's hands and was convicted by a court-martial for recruiting Loyalists. McDougall informed the Convention that Mabee "had great appearance of guilt in his countenance, which is a faithful index to the heart." But, cautious about hanging a man without more specific guidance, he asked for elaboration, saying, "Where blood is concerned, the law cannot be too plain." The Convention staunchly confirmed its ruling. Mabee was hanged on 21 April, and from then on hangmen were kept busy.[15]

After the fright of the Peekskill raid had subsided somewhat, Machin concluded that it would not do to wait longer for all the cables to arrive. Men and boats had been in readiness for over a week to fix the chain in place. The engineer accepted whatever risk was involved and ordered the chain installed. Once again the clumsy iron and wood obstacle was snaked across the river and fastened. Anchors were sunk and lines attached. This time when the tide came in the huge chain rose and curved slightly and pulled taut—and held! The Hudson was closed.

It soon became the talk of the Valley, a local curiosity. A chain across the river! Even some of the blacksmiths whose skill had gone into forging and welding the iron shook their heads in disbelief. Militiamen, reporting for duty at Fort Montgomery, wanted first of all to catch a glimpse of the "floating chain." For some, looking from the ramparts of the fort was not sufficient; they were eager to examine the ironwork closer, although security measures prohibited any except designated caretakers getting near it. No matter about regulations—curiosity was more compelling. Many clambered down the steep rocks for a look. Two, a Sergeant Kendrick and a Corporal Wendle, went so far as to talk a sentry out of a boat in order to view Machin's marvel up close. Caught and court-martialed, they were each fined one dollar.

Through most of April the situation remained hectic. British bluffs and feints caused alarm after alarm at the forts. The men "slept on their arms" several nights. Washington told the Clinton brothers to arrange their schedules so that one of them would be in Fort Montgomery at all times. McDougall fully expected another movement up the river, in the form of harassment if not a full-blown attack. George Clinton fretted and called up

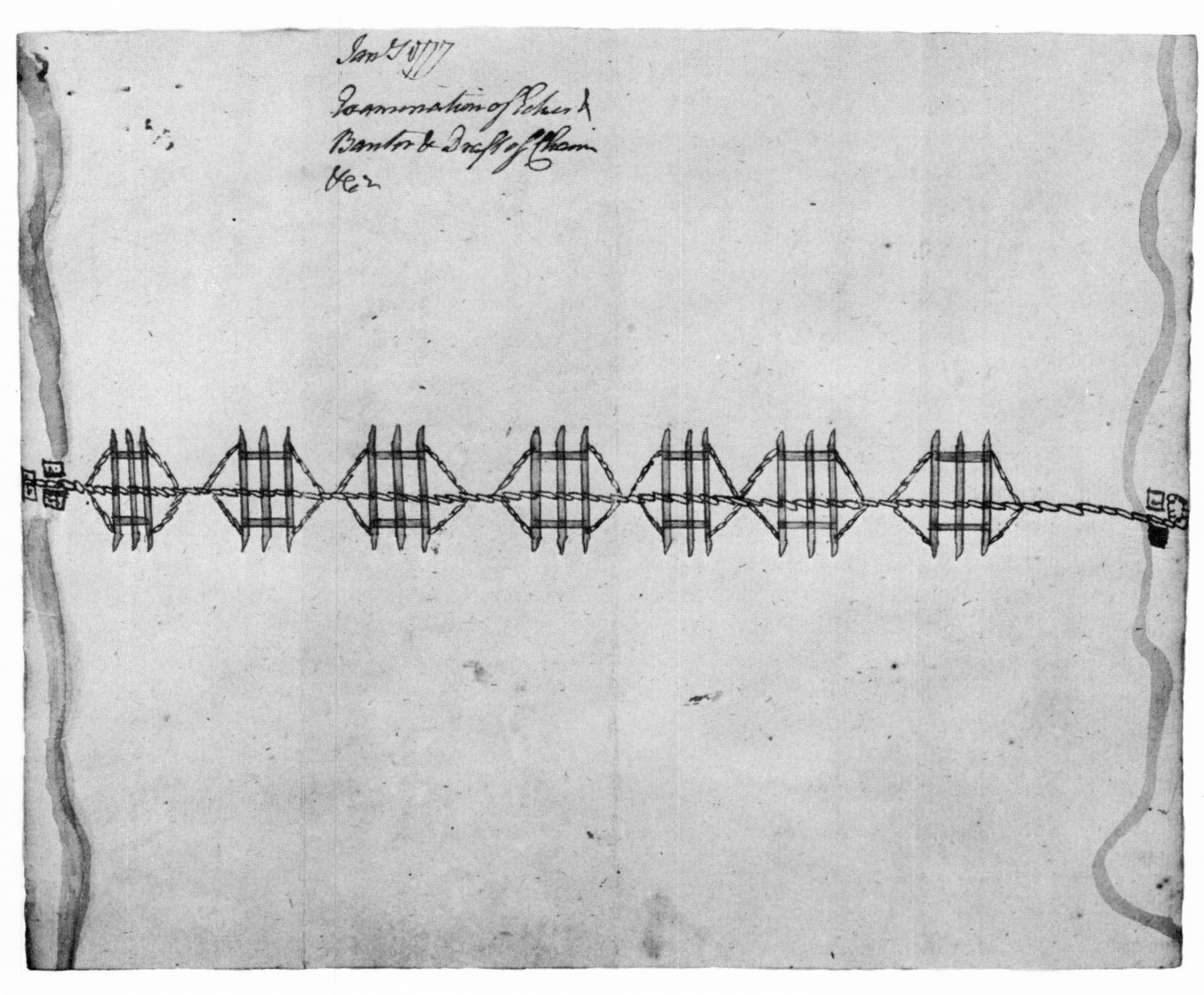

A contemporary sketch of the chain of Fort Montgomery. Probably done by Thomas Machin. Courtesy of the Bear Mountain Park Museum.

more militia. But the attack came elsewhere. Governor William Tryon led a force of 2,000 to Danbury, Connecticut, destroying another rebel supply cache. Conspicuous in rallying the Connecticut militia and organizing a pursuit of the retiring British was Brigadier General Benedict Arnold. The contrast to the Peekskill raid a month earlier was obvious: Arnold had instinctively struck back at the British, inflicting moderate casualties on the raiders; McDougall had withdrawn, not accounting for so much as a single enemy loss. Washington marked the difference.

Actually, as soon as he learned of the Danbury raid, McDougall boldly left James Clinton in charge of the Hudson River forts while he charged off to Connecticut in an attempt to strike the marauders. However, as he drew nearer the enemy his resolve wavered. Calling a council of war —a common enough event in those days, but even so the resort of an unsure commander—he asked his subordinates whether they should continue. The vote was to return to Continental Village because of "the exposed state of Peeks Kill and the great improbability of coming up with [the enemy]." It is likely that the redcoats had too much a headstart to be caught by McDougall's column anyway, but his decision to return without trying could only be compared unfavorably with Arnold's exploits.[16]

Repeated scares began to have the effect of dulling Patriot reactions, causing a false sense of security—maybe even euphoria—gradually to blanket the hills. Then, too, things were actually looking a little better. Militiamen still did not respond wholeheartedly when called to duty, true, but their numbers in the Highlands forts at any one time had increased. And the chain was there, already boasting a month's layer of rust. And all the *chevaux-de-frise* were emplaced. What was more, the forts were at last taking on the appearance of forts. In a letter to Washington, George Clinton reassuringly reported that the defenses were "in great forwardness, and in a few days will become formidable."[17] Washington was not moved. He had learned that false optimism was a disease endemic in the Highlands. If the men on the spot were not seriously worried, the Commander-in-Chief was. He believed the water obstructions to be adequate, but the absence of defenses against an overland attack from the west disturbed him increasingly, nagged at him. He asked George Clinton to station as many men in the western passes as could conceivably be spared from the garrisons. Then, sensing the burgeoning complacency, he quite pointedly ordered McDougall to prepare defenses against a surprise attack on Fort Montgomery.[18]

At that point, Washington also decided to give the Highlands command to a more dynamic soldier. His first choice was Benedict Arnold. That warrior, however, was en route to Philadelphia to contend with Congress over rank. He would not be available.

While the General was browsing over the list of available commanders, the Continental Congress needled him to make greater exertions toward establishing stronger defenses in the Highlands. Washington, piqued by the constant Congressional meddling, tartly replied that all had been done which could be done. "War in theory," he lectured the men in Philadelphia, "and the modes of defense are obvious and easy, but in practice they are more difficult." But more could be accomplished, and the

General from Virginia did not rest. To inject more engineering skill into the construction, he once again detached Colonel Rufus Putnam for temporary duty to help McDougall in the Highlands. Reiterating the importance of defending against an attack from the land side, the Commander-in-Chief specifically told McDougall to "view the passes thro' the mountains on each side of the river, examine the approaches to the forts, the heights that are near to them," and immediately begin such additional works as may be necessary.[19]

Still not satisfied that everything was being done, on 12 May he deputized one of his most trusted lieutenants, Major General Nathanael Greene, to inspect and correct defenses in the Highlands. More precisely, Greene was to insure that the defenses were prepared to resist an attack from either land or water and, even more particularly, to preclude a *coup de main* from the west.

Greene took along Brigadier Generals Henry Knox and Anthony Wayne. Joined by George Clinton and Alexander McDougall (James Clinton had been sent to an outpost near Sydnam's Bridge), they inspected carefully the forts, passes, and water obstructions. In the subsequent report, signed by all five, that all-star group devoted itself almost exclusively to a discussion of water obstructions, neatly side-stepping the vexing question —and Washington's clear instructions—of planning measures to repulse a land attack. After recommending the addition of a boom to go in front of the chain, noting the need for two more cables to reinforce Machin's handiwork, and advocating an increase in the number of warships stationed above the chain, the five generals jointly wrote, "We are very confident, if the obstructions in the river can be rendered effectual, the enemy will not attempt to operate by land, the passes through the Highlands are so exceedingly difficult."[20]

Washington, once he was certain that Arnold was unavailable to command in the Highlands, settled on an old war-horse, Major General Israel Putnam. He made that selection on 12 May. At the same time, along the St. Lawrence, John Burgoyne was assembling his forces for the march south.

6

AN UNCERTAIN SUMMER

WHEN surgeon James Thacher saw Major General Putnam for the first time, he confided to his diary that the "corpulent and clumsy" new commander had "little of the refinements of the well-educated gentleman, but much of the character of the veteran soldier." Referred to rather more scornfully than not as "Old Put," Israel Putnam was one of the most colorful and best known of Continental generals—and one of the least able. Then in his sixtieth year, he was obese, slow of foot, and no more nimble of mind. When he opened his mouth a small chin disappeared in folds of fat. He was an old soldier, literally and figuratively. His early life had been one adventure after another, earning him "Indian fighter" fame as well as renown in the role of battling militia leader in the French and Indian Wars. Among the first to join the Patriot cause, he became a general by virtue of his experience and reputation and led troops boldly if not wisely at Bunker Hill and in the battles in New York in 1776. Astride an appropriately large horse, brandishing British pistols captured from Major Pitcairn on the first day of the war, swearing and sweating profusely, galloping energetically about, Putnam quickly became a battlefield fixture known to all fighting Patriots.

In good-bellied dignity, Putnam rode to Peekskill late in May to assume command. It is clear that Washington would have preferred Benedict Arnold, but why Putnam was second choice is quite unclear. The Commander-in-Chief was plainly aware of Putnam's personality, for he pointedly cautioned McDougall to remember "the old gentleman's temper." Describing the new commander as "active, disinterested, and open to conviction," Washington urged McDougall to provide him all the advice and assistance in his power. Even so, it is likely that General Washington was unaware of the extent of Putnam's infirmities. After all, he had been faithful; no one questioned his physical courage; and his part in the New York fighting had been handled no more ineptly than had George Washington's. The General wanted a fighting officer commanding in the Highlands —and "Old Put" was a fighter.

Before Putnam left for Peekskill, Washington called him to headquarters and personally explained his new responsibilities. He was "to use every possible means in his power for expediting and effecting the works and obstructions" recommended by Nathanael Greene's committee. Particularly, he was to devote "immediate attention to fixing the boom." At the same time, the Commander-in-Chief wrote Congress requesting that body to purchase and forward huge rope cables, "four hundred and fifty fathoms long and of the largest size that can be had," to be stretched diagonally across the river below the chain and boom to add depth to the system of obstacles. Putnam could not have failed to grasp Washington's concern over completing the Hudson's defenses.[1]

Boats, too, were needed. Almost since his arrival in the Highlands, McDougall had been pressing for completion of armed galleys to back up the chain. He had asked Washington for men to crew them but had been turned down. The Provincial Convention, engrossed in writing a constitution and punishing Loyalists, had ignored him. Two galleys, *Lady Washington* and *Shark*, remained of the four gallant little ships which had challenged British warships in Tappan Zee in 1776. On his own initiative, McDougall had repaired and readied them, but still no one would listen to his pleas for men. In May he informed the Continental Navy Board of War, "Besides, the enemy I fear will be able to pass the chain, laid across the river at Fort Montgomery, in the night unless some armed vessels are anchored to the northward of the chain to prevent it." In addition to the unmanned galleys, two Continental frigates had long been building at Poughkeepsie. *Montgomery* and *Congress*, the latter a namesake of the flagship from which Benedict Arnold had so audaciously delayed Carleton's advance on Lake Champlain in 1776, were already programmed to be integrated into the river defenses.

New York's Convention had assumed responsibility for all the vessels during the winter of 1776–1777, but a misunderstanding with the Continental Congress delayed their fitting in the spring. Men and money, perennial problems for the Patriots, were the cause of disagreement. By summertime the frigates and galleys were neither ready nor manned. New York insisted it was a Continental responsibility, while Congress felt the state should meet those expenses. Only imminent danger broke the impasse; in fear of momentary invasion, New York accepted the charges and Washington released Continental soldiers with experience as "watermen" to crew the ships. George Clinton, caught between Convention and Congress, striving to complete the defenses, and anxious to avoid Washington's displeasure, wrote earnestly to the captain of frigate *Montgomery* to exert himself to the utmost to hurry his ship "to the chain at this place." As more inducement to rush, he included, "His Excellency General Washington expects the frigates and galleys are already [here] which renders us more anxious for their speedy arrival."[2]

The outlook in London was far brighter than that in Philadelphia. "In my opinion the Americans will treat before winter," wrote George III on 4 June, anticipating that his scheme would end the rebellion in 1777. A few days later Burgoyne gave the word and his "splendid regatta" sailed from St. Johns. By month's end he had over ten thousand men and scores of cannon ready to fling at Fort Ticonderoga. Howe began the campaign at the Hudson's mouth just as Burgoyne started south toward its headwaters. Moving in strength into New Jersey, hoping to draw Washington into a fight, Sir William made as if to dash for Philadelphia. Not liking the odds, Washington declined the offer to do battle, but he was convinced Philadelphia was Howe's goal and took action accordingly.

Late on 12 June he called a council of war composed of general officers. Their joint advice was to mass more men on Howe's flank to constrain him from continuing overland to Pennsylvania. Deeming a force of "one thousand effective Continental troops," reinforced with militia and "convalescents," as adequate to defend the Highlands forts so long as the bulk of Howe's army remained in New Jersey, Washington ordered Putnam to forward most of the units under his command. They were sent, but the enemy failed to follow Washington's script. Not a week later he told Putnam, "The Enemy's design and movements are truly mysterious." By the 20th Howe had withdrawn his forward elements, leading the American commander to wonder if the original purpose had not been "to induce us to draw off our troops from Peekskill." In haste, he ordered the Highlands troops back and cautioned Putnam to be particularly alert. Two more days and Washington decided, "with tolerable certainty, that the enemy are about to quit the Jerseys and make some expedition by water." The Hudson Highlands "may probably be the object." Then, as suddenly as he had withdrawn, Howe reversed direction, flailing back into New Jersey. Washington was puzzled. He admitted to Congress, "In respect to the enemy's designs or intended movements, they are not to be determined." When Howe, on the final day of June, entirely and unexpectedly evacuated New Jersey, removing all troops to Staten Island, the Americans were left more in the dark than ever.[3]

Next day, at sunset, information from the northern theatre reached headquarters and Washington learned of Burgoyne's preparations to invest Ticonderoga. In a flash the puzzle seemed to fall together: Howe *was* planning a move up the Hudson in conjunction with the large invasion from Canada! Late into the night Washington and his top generals discussed the matter. Orders were issued for two brigades to march at first light to reinforce the Highlands defenses. An express rider rushed to warn Putnam: "No time is to be lost, much may be at stake and I am persuaded if General Howe is going up the river he will make a rapid and vigorous push to gain the Highlands passes." To George Clinton, Washington wrote in the most urgent terms, asking him "to call forth a respectable force of the militia" to defend in the mountains until the Continental Army could arrive. If Burgoyne's attempt was the real thing, Washington felt, Howe's mission must be to strike up the Hudson. On the other hand, should Burgoyne merely be feinting, it would not do to move everything to the Highlands. In a quandary, describing his situation as "truly delicate and embarrasing," the General nervously waited for more conclusive information from northwards.[4]

That information was on its way. Burgoyne, by placing cannon on an overlooking hill, had convinced American defenders that the fortress was untenable. Chagrined, they marched away. Among them was an engineer from Poland who would not forget Burgoyne's bitter lesson.

George Clinton had been most of June in Fort Montgomery, while James Clinton was posted at Sydnam's Bridge on security-detachment duty. When Washington's letter reached the former, he wasted no time in calling forth nine militia regiments and hastening the arming of vessels designed to protect the chain. *Congress* was still in Poughkeepsie, *Montgomery* had no guns as yet, qualified crewmen had not been located for the galleys, and *Shark* was still without a captain. Putnam hastily directed that several cannon from the forts be installed on the ships, named a Lieutenant Shaw to command *Shark,* and screened once more all available soldiers in search of qualified seamen, especially gunners. Meanwhile, the mobilization was proceeding more smoothly than had the one a year before, but that isn't to say Clinton and Putnam did not have their hands full. They did.[5]

At the height of the furor, simultaneous notifications reached George Clinton of his election as first Governor of New York State and of the fall of Fort Ticonderoga. Accepting the governorship, he informed the Convention that military affairs would require his "steady attendance" at Fort Montgomery until a calmer moment. And, in truth, his presence was much needed. The militia, although having responded quickly enough to the alarm, were already mumbling. Their corn was "suffering" and harvest was "coming on." When several men climbed nearby mountain peaks and observed not a single British ship on the river, they grew puzzled, even cynical, over the reason for their mobilization. The terrible news from Ticonderoga only temporarily stilled and sobered them.

The boom was unfinished, although carpenters and blacksmiths labored almost continually on it. Machin was having unforeseen difficulty getting enough iron. Clinton, realizing he could not hope to install the boom before the expected English onslaught, directed the removal of all cables from *Montgomery.* Sailors spliced them into one heavy line. Stretched across the river and tied to fixtures planted for the boom, it served as an added obstacle. Clinton, proudly notifying Washington of that improvisation, said *Congress'* ropes would likewise be used, and informed him that "the redoubts and other works at this post are in as good condition as could be expected."[6]

Fort Ticonderoga's fall sent an ominous shudder reverberating through Washington's headquarters and into the halls of Congress. The great fortress had been in Patriot hands since the earliest days of the war; it had become a symbol of American strength. And now it was gone. The loss alone was bad enough, but when it was learned that Major General Arthur St. Clair had abandoned the bastion without a fight, had in fact slipped away in the night, Americans were mortified. Washington, filled with "chagrin and surprise," found the shocking news beyond "the compass of my reasoning." In Philadelphia, John Adams fumed, "I begin to wish there was not a fort upon the Continent."[7]

Washington ordered Arnold northward—fighting generals were much in demand—while setting his own army in motion toward the Hudson. Reaching the Clove, a "rugged gorge" west of the forts, he paused to see what his opponent would do. Staff officers scurried up and down the river, impressing sloops enough to transport 4,000 men and assembling the flotilla at Robinson's Landing south of Fort Constitution. For over a week the army remained on tenterhooks, inclining first in one direction and then another. Headquarters was a run-down log cabin with a single bed. Washington slept fitfully on the bed while his staff and aides sprawled on the floor around him, but the seriousness of the situation removed concern over such physical inconveniences. Reconnaissance reports and messages from spies painted an altogether confusing picture of enemy intent. No sooner did information arrive of the fleet "standing up towards the North River" than it would be contradicted by word that Howe was sailing up Long Island Sound to New England. Then, before the harried Commander-in-Chief could ponder that intelligence, another messenger would clatter in with news of the British sailing south into the Atlantic. Howe's purpose was to confuse the Americans and he succeeded admirably. John Adams, equally uncharitable to British as well as American generals, commenting on Howe's moves, declared deprecatingly, "I am much in doubt whether he knows his own intentions." Washington continued to camp in the Clove, ready to pounce in any direction, carefully reading each new report, hoping to catch the clue that would tell him how to act.[8]

Nor were the Patriots the only ones puzzled by Howe's maneuvers. He kept his own counsel, not even informing key subordinates. A Hessian officer penned, "We cannot guess what General Howe's intentions may be." But he could not keep secret from everyone his plans. One who learned them was General Henry Clinton upon his return in July from England, where he had become "Sir Henry." Howe confided to the new knight that he intended to go to Philadelphia. Clinton was astonished. Having recently been in London he knew what the grand strategy was and could not understand Howe's unexplained deviation. The Hudson was supposed to be the center of operations, he reminded his superior, but Howe was adamant. On 23 July, Sir William and the fleet and Mrs. Loring dropped down to Sandy Hook and were off.

Clinton remained in New York with a depleted defensive garrison. The entire operation was a major blunder, he was sure. Carefully concealing his words in the body of a cover message, Clinton remonstrated to Burgoyne:

> Sir W. Howe is gone to the Cheasapeake bay with the greatest part of
> the army. I hear he is landed but am not certain. I am left to command
> here with too small a force to make any effectual diversion in your favor.
> I shall try something at any rate. It may be of use to you. I own to you
> I think Sir W.'s move just at this time the worst he could make.[9]

Just before Howe sailed, Washington deduced the British intent to be an attempt at Philadelphia. When spies came in with details of vast quantities of supplies placed aboard the vessels and of horse stalls built on decks, he reasoned that such preparations would not be made for a short strike up the Hudson. Therefore, when the fleet set sail, the Continental Army left the Clove and hastened across northern New Jersey to the Delaware. Nonetheless, Washington had a nagging worry that it was all a ruse. He kept a cautious eye on the Hudson, for "General Howe's in a manner abandoning General Burgoyne is so unaccountable." Reaching the Delaware, the General halted his tired troops. On the last day of July a rider brought evidence of the British fleet's being at the Delaware's mouth. Without hesitation Washington put his men across the river and continued to Philadelphia, only to hear a day later that the English had pulled away from the river and had disappeared once more at sea. His first reaction was that Howe had fooled him, had drawn him away from the Highlands, and was even then racing back to the Hudson. But the men were fatigued, and his hunch might be wrong; he ordered the army to bivouac, while fast horsemen galloped back to the Highlands with the frightening news. For weeks Washington had been chasing a will-o'-the-wisp; he was thoroughly exasperated.

By following the adventures—or misadventures—of a single company during that hectic period, one can get a feel of how bewildering it all was to those in the ranks. Captain Robert Kirkwood's Company of the Delaware Regiment was encamped on Lincoln Mountain 18 miles from Morristown on 4 July. After a celebration commemorating the first full year of independence, the men packed up for a march.

By 10 July Kirkwood's command had reached a new camp "at Clove between 2 mountains." For several days they sat in the wild valley, observing with farmers' interest that it only had "about 20 acres of tillable land." While there, Captain Kirkwood discovered a health hazard in his midst: one of the camp followers was guilty of "giving the men the venerial disorder." She was dunked in a nearby stream until nearly unconscious and then "drum'd out of our encampment." On the 14th the company covered 18 miles up the valley toward New Windsor. On reaching Newburgh, the men "duck'd" another woman, this one for "stealing and insolence." Those were hardy women who chose to follow Washington's army and they took their share of the lumps. After crossing the Hudson, a wondrous waterway to most of the Delaware troops, Kirkwood's company hiked to Fishkill where an orchard became temporary home. After four days of green fruit they were on the road again, this time climbing over steep mountains east of the river to Peekskill. Legs aching, they were not overly appreciative of the stark beauty of the hills. With only a blanket for a bed, the footsore troops were most interested each day in finding a "suitable" camp site, by which was meant dry and rock-free. On 23 July they were "on the road leading to North Castle where we encamped on a verry stony hill."

Paraded to see two men hanged on the 25th, the soldiers were disappointed when the culprits were "granted 3 days longer to live." Next day the company tramped to Verplanck's Point and made preparations to recross the Hudson. At that point all women were obliged to quit the column and cross with the baggage, a normal procedure but one they did not like, for the baggage often took days to catch up. What the troops cared for religion as it was dished out by army chaplains is unknown, but an insight into their feelings may have been recorded in Kirkwood's Orderly Book the day his company passed over the Hudson to Stony Point: "The Reverend Mr. Leonard thought to have deprived himself of his life by cutting his throat with a rasor but unfortunately missed his aim."

Dropping down to Passaic in New Jersey, the company was "afforded two great curiosities." Equal in the minds of the men were the beauty of the cataract which "fell about 100 foot . . . to the surface of the river" and a cradle-bound monstrosity, an adult man with a gigantic head, normal body, and withered limbs who laughed lasciviously at the unit's women, who apparently had not been detained long with the baggage. After marching from the falls they lynched one Richard Ennis for trying to persuade them to "desert to the enemy." Along Kirkwood's trail was strewn a host of angry farmers and townsmen. Loose food, such as chickens and garden vegetables, was considered by the Delaware troops to be public property—and fence rails made excellent cooking fires it was discovered. Washington himself rebuked them. Nor was field sanitation all that could have been desired; at least once during the march Kirkwood threatened, "Any soldier who shall be caught doing his occasions anywhere but in the holes dug for that purpose will be severely punished."

On 4 August, one month after commencing its march, the company completed its great circle around the Hudson Highlands. That night it halted in Hannover almost within sight of its starting point. Kirkwood's orderly clerk noted plaintively that they were "encamped in a stony orchard." In the heat of summer the unit had trudged well over two hundred miles with nothing more to show for its peregrinations than worn-out shoes and blistered, bare feet.[10]

When Howe headed south, everyone in the Highlands experienced a great relaxation of tension. Most of the militia, called up for only a month anyway, left for home and field at the end of July. George Clinton relinquished military duties and assumed his new gubernatorial responsibilities; James Clinton came to Fort Montgomery as his brother's replacement. Israel Putnam saw the lull as a golden opportunity to improve the slack discipline of his soldiers and to impress on local inhabitants the dire consequences of spying or otherwise aiding the enemy.

He had in his clutches two culprits, a soldier, Amos Rose, convicted of the heinous crime of "firing a gun loaded with a ball at Lieutenant Elisha Brewster," and Edmund Palmer, a "noted Tory and robber." Rose was to be "shot to death on Friday," 1 August. On that same day Palmer was to be executed "by hanging him up by the neck till he is dead, dead, dead." Apparently, simple death was not enough; it would be meted out in triplicate.[11]

A double execution; an undisciplined soldier shot, a disloyal civilian hanged. Putnam happily contemplated the tranquilizing impact of the display upon all skulkers in and out of uniform. He envisioned a grand show with all units on parade to observe the event. Those unanticipated and perplexing British movements, however, granted Rose and Palmer a stay of execution. On 28 July Washington ordered Putnam to march two brigades into New Jersey. "Old Put" sent the troops and postponed the execution until there should be more men to observe.

Three days later, Washington learned of the disappearance of Howe's fleet from the Delaware, feared he had been tricked into leaving the Hudson unprotected, and quickly ordered the brigades to retrace their route to Peekskill. Connecticut and New York militia were called out and Putnam was exhorted to make "every possible exertion" to prepare for the enemy.[12]

Governor George Clinton, at his capital in Kingston, received on 5 August Washington's worried message warning of Howe's probable plan to take the Hudson. Clinton had been away from Fort Montgomery less than two weeks, the militia had been home not a week, and the new State Legislature had been sitting only since the first of the month. Nevertheless, the Governor acted unhesitatingly. Three militia regiments, "completely armed and accoutered," were dispatched to Peekskill, four were put in motion for Fort Montgomery, one to Sydnam's Bridge "at the mouth of the Clove." He established an express system linking the Patriot army facing Burgoyne with Washington's force in Pennsylvania by way of slanting valleys west of the Hudson. Then, on the same day, he prorogued the brand new State Legislature, ending his proclamation announcing that action with an emotional, "God save the people," and made arrangements to assume personal command in Fort Montgomery. "I never knew militia to come out with greater alacrity," he reported to Washington four days later from the fort. The same might have been said for the Governor.[13]

Pacing the familiar ramparts that he and brother James had done so much to build, George Clinton felt himself in the eye of a cyclone. Up the Mohawk, frontier settlements were being overrun one after another by an invading force of redcoats and redskins; tales of atrocities and pleas for help filtered back. Above Albany Burgoyne was camped on the banks of the Hudson River looking at the very same water flowing serenely past Fort Montgomery. And Howe was somewhere at sea, probably returning to dash up the river to join Burgoyne. What was worse, Washington was too far away to provide immediate assistance. As he stood there, looking at the chain below him and Fort Clinton across the creek and cannon all around, the Governor must have felt that stark loneliness experienced by men who shoulder heavy responsibility in times of trial.

But not "Old Put." Thoughts of a fight bothered him not in the least. As a matter of fact, he viewed the turn of events as rather fortunate for it gave him a greater audience at Peekskill for his pet project—the dual execution—than he could have hoped for otherwise. He published orders setting 8 August as the death-date. Fifers and drummers were to lead the way and all brigades, colors flying, would march ceremoniously to Gallows Hill to witness the end of Amos Rose and Edmund Palmer.

On the 7th, the British ship, *Mercury,* approached Verplanck's Point south of Peekskill and sent a longboat ashore under a flag of truce. A young officer carried a letter from Sir Henry Clinton to General Putnam. Sir Henry wrote that Edmund Palmer was a lieutenant in his Majesty's service; he questioned Putnam's authority to administer the death penalty; and he closed by threatening reprisal should Palmer be executed. It was a desperate effort to save Palmer's life, but Sir Henry had failed to consider "the old gentleman's temper."

When the American general read Clinton's message, he immediately flew into a violent rage and harangued all those not quick enough to remove themselves. Imagine! The British general sticking his nose into American business! Trembling with righteousness, indignation, and downright anger, he scribbled these abrupt words:

> Edmund Palmer, an officer in the enemy's service, was taken as a spy
> lurking within our lines; he has been tried as a spy, condemned as a
> spy, and shall be executed as a spy, and the flag is ordered to depart
> immediately.

Swiftly folding the paper, Putnam thrust it at a waiting messenger. But before the courier could reach his horse, a shout from the red-faced general stopped him short. "Old Put" had reached the limit of his somewhat limited patience.

A sharp order to an aide; a rattle of guard horses; a hastily procured provisions wagon; and Edmund Palmer was swinging alone and almost unobserved on Gallows Hill. Wearing the satisfied grin of a long-suffering man suddenly released from his tormentor, Putnam scrawled on the bottom of his message, "P.S.—He has been accordingly executed."[14]

Speculation and tension increased day by day as Howe's whereabouts and destination remained a mystery. Coast watchers peered intently to sea for a glimpse of sail that would reveal the lost fleet. Rumors, rampant as usual in such circumstances, had English ships everywhere from Boston to Charleston. Still "in the most perfect ignorance," the Commander-in-Chief started his men moving once again toward the Hudson, this time "by slow and easy marches." On the night of the 10th, when the army had been on the road three days, word overtook Washington that Howe had been sighted 16 leagues south of the Capes of Delaware. The Americans camped in place. Ten days passed interminably, with no word. Washington sent Daniel Morgan to help halt Burgoyne; and waited. On 21 August, believing Howe could not intend to enter the Chesapeake, Washington informed Congress that Charleston must be his destination. Next day he learned that his foe had at last turned up—in the Chesapeake! The Continental Army, after its long summer of seemingly aimless marching and countermarching on hot, grimy roads, reacted with enthusiasm to orders sending it south of Philadelphia to fight.[15]

By that time events had occurred to the northward which changed the whole picture there, too. Burgoyne had been handed a severe setback in the Battle of Bennington on 16 August, while Arnold, by a ruse involving a half-wit, had turned back the hostile column on the Mohawk River. Militia, energized by the very real threat of invasion and inflamed by skillful propaganda, were flocking to the army opposing Burgoyne. That officer, who had come on campaign with a large baggage train carrying everything needed for his personal comfort in the wilderness, including a mistress, was suddenly not so sanguine. Howe, near Philadelphia, was in no position to provide any support, while the garrison in New York City was barely large enough to defend that port. In the Highlands forts it looked as if the critical moments had passed. Many militiamen were released to bring in the harvest. George Clinton himself traveled to Albany to inspect the situation there. The State Legislature prepared to meet again in September.

As for the fortifications, they seem to have been almost entirely neglected during the uncertain summer. A constantly fluctuating troop population was one factor militating against improvements. Machin devoted his attention much of the time to getting timber and iron for the boom, and bricks for works overlooking the *chevaux-de-frise* at Pollepel Island. And it had been discovered that some gaps existed in the *chevaux-de-frise*, necessitating the construction of more caissons—a project proceeding very slowly. It was during this period that he erected "Machin's Battery" on Plum Point. He testified months later that "nothing material was done" to the forts above Popolopen Creek after George Clinton left to become governor. In September even Machin was assigned additional duties as recruiter and artilleryman and was placed in command of a detachment at New Windsor, evidence that no concern was felt over the status of fortifications. And, in spite of Washington's specifically telling Putnam in May to give "immediate attention to fixing the boom," it was not across the river by the end of September. In that month sixteen artificers were "employed at building the capstan, docks, anchors and boom for obstructing the Navigation of Hudson's River at Fort Montgomery." Machin and sixty men brought "down the booms to Fort Montgomery" early in October. Reflecting the rosy attitude prevalent in the Highlands, Governor Clinton informed his legislature on 10 September that all was well, the forts being "in so respectable a state of defense as to promise us security against any attack in that quarter."[16]

But that simply was not so. The forts were not complete. The western wall of Fort Montgomery was hardly more than a trace on the ground—and that was the direction of danger! A small redoubt had been raised behind Fort Clinton, but it alone was inadequate. Captain Gershom Mott, on Constitution Island, complained in September, "We are in want of seasoned timber . . . for carriages for several large cannon." The situation was the same in Fort Montgomery, he added. Perhaps men who had looked at and worked with and lived in the forts every day for months simply could no longer realize that the defenses were incomplete.[17]

Qualified sailors for the several armed vessels had not been found in numbers enough. Israel Putnam, in his direct manner, hit upon a solution: crew them with convicts. What the captains thought about that can easily be imagined. Over their protestations, though, Putnam filled the galleys and frigates by courts-martial. Almost any offense, from desertion to thievery to "behaving in a disorderly manner," carried a penalty that summer in the Highlands of being "sent on board the Continental guard ship of war there to be kept to hard service during the war."[18]

Sir Henry Clinton sat dejectedly in New York City during August and most of September, unable to do more than protect his base there, fuming, searching for an opportunity to launch an assault up the river. His informers told him that virtually all rebel manpower was committed either against Burgoyne high up the river or against Howe in distant Pennsylvania; never again, he reasoned, would the Highlands be so lightly defended. In a letter to Burgoyne, on 11 September, he wrote, "If you think 2,000 men can assist you effectively, I will make a push at Montgomery in about ten days." "I expect reinforcement every day," he added. But, until reinforcements arrived, he was helpless.[19]

That is not to say Sir Henry was entirely unhappy—Mrs. Baddeley had joined him once again. However, apparently finding that running his household, which included thirty servants, was itself a full-time job, she continued to resist his impassioned advances.

Washington, after losing the Battle of Brandywine on 11 September, needed more men. Gambling on Henry Clinton's inability to leave New York City, the Commander-in-Chief ordered Putnam to send all but about a thousand Continentals from the Highlands to the scene of active combat near Philadelphia. On hearing that, Governor Clinton ordered to arms eleven regiments of New York militia, all there were in the southern part of the state. It had been a long, long summer for the militiamen. Some had forgotten how many times they had grabbed musket and bedroll and made a forced march to one or the other of the mean little forts on the river. And the British had never so much as fired one shot at them. "Wolf!" had been cried too often. Those showing up grumbled loudly from the start. Israel Putnam, in sympathy with them, sent several hundred home, to the scarcely concealed disgust of Governor Clinton.[20]

A fleet from England anchored in New York Harbor late on Wednesday, the 24th, carrying 1,700 British and Hessian replacements. Henry Clinton had his men. By the weekend, Putnam received an inflated report of the arrival of "sixty sail of transport . . . with three thousand British and German troops." Spies also carried to Peekskill news of preparations for an attack: bakers working overtime turning out bread, ammunition being loaded on ships, patrols pulling in. Counting up his strength, "Old Put" saw plainly his precarious situation. He sat down and wrote a letter directly to the President of the Continental Congress:

> The post is of as much importance as any upon the Continent, and I will exert myself to the utmost for its defence, weakened as it is—but permit me to tell you, sir, that I will not be answerable for its safety with the strength left me against the force I am sensible the enemy can, and believe will, speedily send against it.[21]

7

THE BATTLE OF FORT MONTGOMERY

A DAMNED starved defensive!" exploded Sir Henry, describing his unenviable situation in New York after Howe had departed. "Mortified" to be left in the city without enough strength to act "either to serve my country or advance my own fame," the paunchy little general rankled with resentment. Coordinated American probes at three points on his perimeter, in August, served to confirm the Englishman's belief in his "total incapacity to do anything" to help General Burgoyne. But when Washington ceased churning around in New Jersey and shifted south to intercept Howe, the danger of a Patriot attack against New York diminished. Feeling more secure, Henry Clinton began to expand the boundaries of his imagination. On 11 September he sent a messenger slipping northward to inform Burgoyne that "a push at [Fort] Montgomery" might be possible. That same evening, he threw 2,000 men on a raid across the Hudson into New Jersey. All they gained, materially, were some horses, a few hundred head of cattle and sheep, and "twenty milch cows, which afforded a seasonable refreshment," but it created another scare in the Highlands with the inevitable ringing of the militia tocsin.[1]

Sir Henry's letter holding out a possibility of help reached General Burgoyne on the morning of 21 September—with what were to prove to be fatal results for the British. Burgoyne and Patriot forces under Horatio Gates had clashed inconclusively two days earlier at Freeman's Farm (called variously the Battle of Freeman's Farm or the First Battle of Saratoga) and the English general was on the point of renewing his attack when Clinton's message arrived. Pondering his alternatives, "Gentleman Johnny" decided to wait where he was until aid came from his comrade below. Chances of his reaching Albany right then were good; by waiting, however, he gave the Americans time to accumulate a force too strong to be pushed aside. At once Burgoyne replied, telling Sir Henry in classic understatement that an attempt to break through the Highlands would be most useful. "Do it, my dear friend, directly." To the messenger, for Clinton's ears only, Burgoyne confided the chilling information that salt provisions would last at most a month more and that the line of communications—and retreat—to the lakes could not be held.[2]

Waiting for reinforcements from England and information from Burgoyne, Sir Henry began to study in detail various methods of cracking the Highlands. It was not a new problem to him for he had first considered it while visiting Governor Tryon in New York Harbor over a year and a half before. Tryon was now a major general serving under Sir Henry and eager for an operation up the river. He, too, had contemplated destroying the rebel works almost from the very beginning. Learning that Israel Putnam had concentrated most of his meager force east of the river, Clinton focused his own attention on the western side. In planning a way to get at the forts he discovered a windfall right in the British camp in the person of Beverley Robinson.

Robinson, a Virginian, came from one of that state's more distinguished families. He was a close friend from youth of another son of the Old Dominion, George Washington. Moving to New York, he had married into the wealthy Philipse family and had since prospered, increasing his wife's generous dowry.* Robinson at first refused to take sides in the struggle between the colonies and the mother country, preferring to live aloof from the argument in his spacious country home in the Highlands opposite West Point. But events swept him up. In February 1777 John Jay informed him, on behalf of a committee selected for "detecting and defeating conspiracies in the State of New York," that he must choose to be either Patriot or Tory. The Patriots would be "exceeding happy to have you with us," he was told. But Robinson could not bring himself to break with his Monarch. Leaving his family in the Highlands, he took refuge in New York City. His choice made, the new Loyalist became a most avid one. In May he raised a regiment, dubbed the Loyal Americans and composed of men, like himself, forced to quit their homes and lands by Patriot pressure. He selected his men as carefully as possible, and specified that no person could be an officer "whose character will not bear the strictest examination." One of his first missions, and a continuing one, had been to gather intelligence of the rebel situation in the Highlands, a job made easier when "Old Put" agreed to permit Mrs. Robinson to send sealed letters to her husband under the protection of flags.[3]

Intimately familiar with all the paths and roads through the mountain maze of his beloved Highlands, Robinson traced on a map a route leading from Stony Point through a cut called Timp Pass to the rear of Fort Clinton and, by forking off at the small settlement of Doodletown and

---

* When young George Washington visited New York in 1756, he escorted Eliza Philipse, the statuesque sister-in-law of his old friend and host, Beverley Robinson. But she was apparently not interested in the shy, stiff Southern farmer who showed no promise of advancing far in the world.

going completely around Bear Mountain, to the back of Fort Montgomery as well. Robinson knew that neither fort was completed on its back side and —a key consideration—the road he indicated was not obstructed by so much as a single rebel outpost. It just might be possible to march unobserved all the way to the forts and take them by surprise. Henry Clinton realized total surprise could never be gained, for American spies would probably detect his preparations, while observers would surely see his fleet moving toward the Highlands. Deception was the answer, he mused. If the Americans could be led to believe he was aiming for Peekskill on the eastern shore—a repeat of the March raid—perhaps the forts would be left relatively vulnerable to a swift descent from the rear. It was at least worth a try; the alternative, a frontal attack from the river up sheer cliffs into the very face of the defenses, was not attractive.[4]

When reinforcements reached him on the 24th, Sir Henry was ready. Preparations were begun while he fretfully awaited some intelligence from the north to clear away the fog of war presently enshrouding that theatre and provide him a reason to attack. It came on 29 September in the form of Burgoyne's message posted on the 21st. Troops began loading. As part of a cover plan, all officers except a select and necessary handful believed Clinton's preparations to be aimed at a strike somewhere up Long Island Sound. One problem arose. Commodore William Hotham, the naval commander, had never been convinced of either the utility or the feasibility of taking the Highlands forts. Now, at the last minute, he balked, throwing plans into temporary turmoil. Clinton cajoled and harangued so compellingly, however, that Hotham reluctantly gave in. The men were packed aboard; the expedition was ready. Three divisions, each numbering about a thousand troops, stood poised to spring. As soon as tides were right, Henry Clinton would pay cousins James and George a visit.

As dusk fell on 3 October one division in transports set sail for Tarrytown while another stepped out overland for the same destination. At dawn next day the two forces converged there, giving the appearance of being on another minor and limited foraging raid. The third division, followed by empty transports to pick up the division which had marched, eased unobtrusively up the river later in the day. Dusty soldiers squeezed back into the uncomfortable boats. "That night the wind being still favorable," the amphibious force sailed swiftly northward hoping darkness and speed would conceal its approach to the Highlands. Before noon on the 5th, Clinton's advance was swarming ashore "near an old causeway on a sandy beach" at Verplanck's Point. As he watched his men splash through shallow water to dry land, a messenger from Burgoyne arrived. That general finally admitted he was in deep trouble. He urgently needed a "diversion." Clinton was exceedingly worried, but could see nothing to do at the moment but continue.[5]

Reports of recent troop arrivals from Europe and persistent indications of an impending military operation alarmed New York's watchful governor. Convinced—rightly so this time—that an attempt was afoot to breach the Highlands, George Clinton ordered his colonels to assemble one half of each regiment and to march to the Highlands forts. The remaining halves were to be ready "on a moment's warning." That was done on the same day General Putnam was writing Congress disclaiming any responsibility for defeat. To be closer to the scene, Governor Clinton left the capital at Kingston for New Windsor. On the 4th, James Clinton forwarded from Fort Montgomery the uneasy information of an enemy incursion to Tarrytown. He was unsure what was happening, for no alarm guns had been fired, picket boats had not reported in, and General Putnam had sent no word. Moreover, he complained nervously to his brother, "there is very few of the militia yet come down."[6]

While Henry Clinton's convoy glided silently north over dark waters, Governor Clinton was up most of the night discharging state and military business. At nine that evening he was at his desk writing of militia and signal guns and the enemy, while making plans to go on the morrow to Fort Montgomery. By three o'clock next morning he had concluded from reading reports filtering in through the night that the English had in mind nothing more than a raid. Henry Clinton's shrewd move to Tarrytown had worked, confusing the Patriots and gaining him several precious hours.[7]

Sunday morning, 5 October 1777, began quietly enough. George Clinton, in a boat approaching Fort Constitution, had time to appreciate the wild display of autumn color crowning the great peaks along the river. When his slowly moving sloop was perhaps a mile above the island, he heard a distant, faint boom. And then another and another. Finally the signal gun at Fort Constitution barked out its message: this time it had happened, the British had come! Redundantly, beacons seconded the message of the signal guns, sending smoke billowing into the October sky from half a dozen hilltops. The anxious general felt helpless. Tides and breezes, which were so favorable to Sir Henry, practically stalled southbound river traffic. Horses were not to be had. Worried and impatient, he set out to trudge the remaining six miles on foot. Upon entering Fort Montgomery in midafternoon, he looked around and "found the garrison weaker than when I left it." And militiamen were responding slowly to the alarm. The Goshen and Cornwall Regiments combined had turned out fewer than a hundred men. Colonel John Lamb had around a hundred Continental artillerymen and Colonel Lewis Dubois commanded three hundred Continentals. Clinton could count on another hundred or so militia by next day, raising his total strength to perhaps six hundred.[8]

Hotham deprecatingly described the resistance offered by the startled Patriot detachment at Verplanck's Point as an "appearance only of opposition." At that he was kind. Men manning the small breastworks there stampeded on sight of the armada bearing down on them, abandoning a 12-pound cannon without even so much as firing a parting shot. Sir James Wallace, commanding the flotilla of row-galleys, continued past the landing site, debouching into Peekskill Bay in order to block any reinforcement from there to the forts. He need not have bothered. "Old Put" had been completely hoodwinked by Sir Henry's feint; he was convinced Peekskill was the objective and was taking steps to have men transferred *from* the forts! Wallace stood to near Fort Independence, "fired upon it and took a boat," and awaited the unfolding of the remainder of the plan. On whose orders it is not clear, but Fort Independence was evacuated.[9]

Confusion and uncertainty reigned inside Patriot lines that night. George Clinton, as a precaution, sent Major Samuel Logan, "an alert officer who was well acquainted with the ground," with a strong reconnaissance party of about a hundred men south through Timp Pass to watch British movements in the river near Stony Point. Not long after Logan's group filed off into darkness, word came from Israel Putnam that the British had taken Fort Independence. He directed Clinton to send sixty men under a captain across the river to secure "the pass between Fort Independence and Anthony's Nose." The Governor obediently complied, dispatching them in the middle of the night. A couple of hours after midnight, several armed ships and transports, making noise and showing lights, sailed up from Verplanck's Point to Fort Independence acting for all the world as if they intended to land troops. Hoping Patriot attention would be drawn north of Peekskill, Henry Clinton was holding loaded transports in the river ready to debark troops at Stony Point at dawn. Before first light, General Putnam rode up to Fort Independence to see for himself what had happened. It was deserted. The elderly officer, puzzled, was at a loss to know just what the British were about, but he remained stubbornly sure Peekskill was the ultimate objective of all the strange nocturnal maneuvering. When dawn came the river valley was locked in a heavy fog made to order for Sir Henry. As Israel Putnam turned his weary mount back toward Peekskill, a local inhabitant rushed up with a tale of seeing British boats crossing to Stony Point. Putnam squinted into the impenetrable fog but could see barely beyond his horse's head. He decided the man must be a Tory, for no one could have seen what he claimed to have glimpsed. He ignored the intelligence.[10]

But other eyes had seen ghostly sail looming in the dense fog. Lieutenant Samuel English and a small detachment of soldiers, damp and cold from early morning mist, huddled on a small rise just north of Stony Point. Their mission was scouting out enemy movements in that area. When Major Logan had reached Timp Pass sometime before midnight, he decided to remain in the defile with the bulk of his reconnaissance party while sending forth smaller groups which could cover the countryside undetected. Besides, he sensed the onset of sickness and doubted his own ability to continue. Lieutenant English threaded his way along pitch-black paths to his position, posted guards close around, and then ordered his men to rest until dawn would make it possible for them to observe enemy activities. Fog rolled in from the river, filled the valleys, and swirled about the silent cluster of Patriots. In the half-light between end of night and start of sunrise, one of the men thought he saw movement on the river. Instantly alert, everyone stared hard into the haze, but only unbroken grayness rewarded their searching eyes. Minutes passed. Tenseness eased. As they were concluding that a mirage of fog and shadow and morning light had been to blame for the false alarm, an eddy of wind parted the fog for a moment to reveal a river all but jammed with hostile ships approaching the beach and ferry landing near Stony Point. Waiting just long enough to be sure troops were actually wading ashore, Lieutenant English and his scouts scurried back to Timp Pass.

When the lieutenant breathlessly choked out his report to Major Logan, an excited discussion ensued. Some officers argued that the proper course of action would be to remain where they were "to give opposition to the enemy as there was but one pass over the mountain and that very narrow and difficult." The path leading up from the valley to Logan's position was steep, rocky, and narrow. And the invaders would have to come that way. A hundred brave men could block the pass. But Logan was "very ill at the time," shaking with fever and suffering from "bloody flux." His orders had been to learn what the English were up to, but to avoid a fight. He had accomplished that. Ending the discussion, he proclaimed his intention of returning to Fort Clinton. A sergeant noted for endurance was directed to run the three miles back to the forts to report Logan's intelligence to Governor Clinton. After the sergeant was off, Logan retraced his steps of the preceding night through Doodletown in the valley and up the southeast lip of Bear Mountain to Fort Clinton.[11]

When Logan's runner reached George Clinton, that officer sat down and penned Putnam an urgent request for assistance. Before he could send it, a courier arrived with a letter from Putnam promising reinforcements if "the enemy . . . mean to attack Fort Montgomery by land." At the bottom of his own message the Governor noted receipt of General Putnam's dispatch and said he could not reply better than with news of Lieutenant English's observations. It was then about eight o'clock. To deliver the important letter, Governor Clinton chose Silvester Waterbury, a civilian commissary agent. That was a mistake. Waterbury was either disloyal or hopelessly inefficient, perhaps both—a fact which might have been suspected earlier from the manner in which he had performed his commissary duties. He defected to the British afterwards. Colonel Samuel B. Webb, commanding a regiment east of the river in the vicinity of Peekskill, termed him "an infamous scoundrel." And Colonel John Lamb, commander of artillery in the forts, definitely suspected him of treachery. Hindsight might indicate he was in cahoots with Major Daniel Hammill, an enemy agent then serving as James Clinton's brigade major. At any rate, Waterbury disappeared across the river and wasted eight hours in unexplained wanderings before delivering the message—eight fatal hours.[12]

The Governor also sent word for the frigate *Congress* to slip its lines at Robinson's Landing and move up to Constitution Island to bolster defenses there. Then, fully expecting aid soon to be forthcoming from forces east of the river, he arranged for boats to stand by to carry them over. When the *Congress'* skipper remonstrated that he had "no more than four men on board fit for duty," George Clinton authorized him to impound some of the "supernumerary" ferryboat operators.

About nine o'clock that morning Major Logan and his men reached the forts, bushed from their night-long reconnaissance. Logan could add nothing to his previous report. Fog had prevented his men from obtaining even a close estimate of British strength and his unfortunate decision to retire had deprived the Americans of any information other than knowledge that some British had landed at Stony Point. Obviously disappointed, and needing information, the Governor sent Lieutenant Paton Jackson with twenty men "to discover the enemy's movements." Jackson, impressed by the urgency of his mission, formed his men hastily and set out at a brisk trot for Timp Pass. Some thirty minutes later, as his column swung unsuspectingly into Doodletown, muskets suddenly blazed from behind walls and bushes, dropping three Americans and scattering the rest. That ambush spilled the day's first blood. Less than two miles away, George Clinton heard the fusillade and knew without waiting for Jackson's survivors to return that Sir Henry's men were already north of Timp Pass.

His reaction was immediate and proper. He soon dispatched 100 men—50 militia under his brother-in-law, Lieutenant Colonel James McClaughry, and an equal number of Continentals commanded by Lieutenant Colonel Jacobus Bruyn—toward Doodletown with the dual mission of assisting Lieutenant Jackson and delaying the enemy's advance. Operating on a hunch, he turned to Thomas Machin—who just happened to be in the forts to superintend the installation of the boom, one of the few jobs he would never complete—and ordered him to select "the most suitable position to obstruct the enemy" on the road running from the rear of Fort Montgomery to the Forest of Dean. Machin hurried out about the same time Bruyn and McClaughry were pounding away from Fort Clinton, heading in quickstep for Doodletown.[13]

Knowing that the battle for the forts would be the decisive phase of his entire campaign, Henry Clinton threw ashore that dawn the bulk and cream of his force. Left holding the base at Verplanck's Point was a weak element consisting mainly of Loyalists. First out of the boats and over the well-packed beach was an advance guard under the direction of Lieutenant Colonel Mungo Campbell. His initial objective was to secure Timp Pass on Dunderberg Mountain, the one bottleneck where the whole attempt could be thwarted. To insure swiftness, Sir Henry ordered all cannon left behind. Comprising Campbell's command were 500 regulars, dispatched from the 52nd and 57th Regiments, and 400 Loyalists. Captain Andraes Emerick's chasseurs, the New York Volunteers of Major Alexander Grant, and Colonel Beverley Robinson's Loyal Americans were Campbell's "provincials." Robinson, although a colonel, was second in command to Campbell because colonial ranks were rated inferior by one grade to those in the English establishment. As the advance guard set out with long strides, a picked body of men dropped their heavy packs and dashed ahead in hopes of reaching Timp Pass before Americans could react to close it. Leading the way was a member of Robinson's regiment identified as Brom Springster, a man raised in that very area. As Springster and the light detachment following him were straining up the south slope of Dunderberg Mountain, Major Logan's 100 scouts were marching away down the mountain's northern flank.

Hardly daring to believe their luck, the redcoats climbed into the cut, hastily organized a defense, and waited for the remainder of the advance guard to come puffing up. The pass showed obvious signs of having been recently occupied by a fairly large body of men, a fact perplexing to the professional soldiers. Why would the Americans not, at the very least, have dropped a delaying force here? Did a trap lurk ahead? Campbell deployed his men along the flanks of the pass to rest until the main body could catch up. In the interim he sent an armed reconnaissance force down into the valley toward Doodletown to investigate the way. Quietly entering Doodletown, that scouting party heard Lieutenant Jackson's column hurrying headlong in their direction. Fearfully, the British dove for cover off the road, narrowly escaping detection. Then, seeing that the little Patriot band contained about an equal number of men, they regained enough composure to fire a ragged volley as Jackson jogged into range. Utterly surprised, those Americans who were not hit bolted. As the smoke slowly cleared, English soldiers found themselves alone except for three crumpled forms on the road. Back at Fort Montgomery, George Clinton's ears perked up as echoes from the firing reached him, and so did Henry Clinton's as he struggled up the last few feet of steep road to Timp Pass.

To call the rocky, rutted, tortuous trail leading up to Timp Pass a road is to praise it unjustly. A report prepared at the time described it as "almost impenetrable." Writing not a generation later, an English historian who had participated in the war had this to say:

> As the path would not admit above three men to march abreast, and by
> its windings would have exposed the troops during their passage to be
> destroyed at the pleasure of any force stationed at the top of the hill, the
> most trifling guard would have been sufficient to have rendered the
> attempt of the British abortive.[14]

Even today, standing in the imposing, fortresslike saddle of Timp Pass, one wonders how Henry Clinton could possibly have passed had the Americans heeded any of George Washington's oft-repeated admonitions to "secure your flanks and rear . . . by stopping up all roads by which you are accessible in any part." But they had not. And, what is worse, Logan, with much more than a "trifling guard," had failed to grasp the significance of the position even when some of his officers pointed it out to him.

As the British column advanced from Stony Point, Loyalists paused long enough to burn homes and barns of Patriots along the way, exacting a fiery retribution for earlier harsh treatment meted out by erstwhile friends and neighbors. Across the river, Israel Putnam observed the swath of flaming buildings, a finger pointing to the forts, and thought it not unusual.[15]

Bruyn and McClaughry had no idea what they would encounter in Doodletown Valley. After that sudden burst of firing, an eerie quiet had descended on the hills. All they heard as they lurched ahead was their own heavy breathing mingled with the steady clatter of bouncing canteens and cartouches, of booted feet drumming irregular music on the stony path. Rounding the flank of Bear Mountain and starting to drop down into the valley, they met several of Jackson's men. The story reported was unclear: all the shaken survivors could be sure of was that an enemy force of unknown size hovered around Doodletown. The Americans continued, but cautiously now, moving by stages, gingerly probing ahead before advanc-

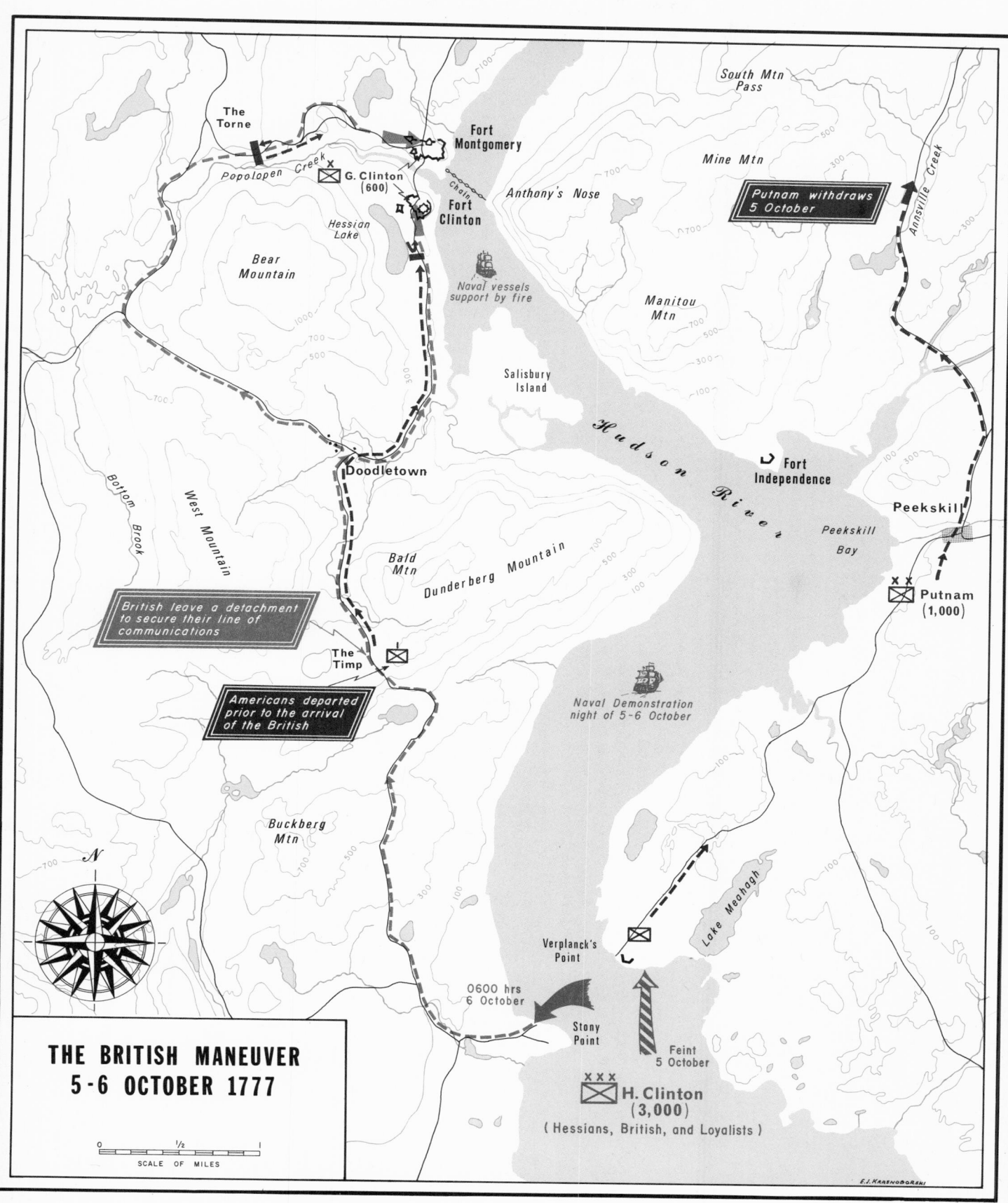

The Torne

Fort Montgomery

South Mtn Pass

Popolopen Creek

⊠ G. Clinton (600)

Chain

Anthony's Nose

Mine Mtn

Putnam withdraws 5 October

Ansville Creek

Fort Clinton

Hessian Lake

Bear Mountain

Naval vessels support by fire

Manitou Mtn

Salisbury Island

Hudson River

Fort Independence

Peekskill

Peekskill Bay

Bottom Brook

West Mountain

Doodletown

Bald Mtn

Dunderberg Mountain

⊠⊠ Putnam (1,000)

British leave a detachment to secure their line of communications

The Timp

⊠

Naval Demonstration night of 5-6 October

Americans departed prior to the arrival of the British

Lake Meahagh

Buckberg Mtn

N

Verplanck's Point

⊠

0600 hrs 6 October

Stony Point

Feint 5 October

⊠⊠⊠ H. Clinton (3,000)
(Hessians, British, and Loyalists)

THE BRITISH MANEUVER
5-6 OCTOBER 1777

0   1/2   1
SCALE OF MILES

E.J. KRASNOBORSKI

Infantry unit   ⊠

Infantry company ⊠

Infantry brigade   ⊠

ing. Minutes passed. The sun, long since having burned away the fog, crawled toward its zenith.

Upon reaching Timp Pass, Henry Clinton ordered Campbell to march west of Bear Mountain to intersect the Forest of Dean Road and from there to assault Fort Montgomery from the rear. Major General John Vaughan, commanding the main body, was to rest his men until Campbell could complete his long circuit and then rush Fort Clinton simultaneously with the attack on Montgomery. Major General William Tryon commanded the reserve and followed Vaughan. Tryon dropped off a battalion to secure Timp Pass, insuring a route of retreat should one be necessary. Clinton himself decided to accompany Vaughan's force. Serving as voluntary aide-de-camp to Sir Henry was a Polish nobleman, Count Grabouski. He had arrived in America, seeking adventure, with the convoy bringing reinforcements not two weeks before.

Campbell missed a clash with Bruyn and McClaughry by no more than minutes. As American point men entered Doodletown, they encountered stragglers from the enemy column which had just left the town. Some harmless shots were exchanged. Campbell pushed on, ignoring the action behind him. Vaughan roused his troops and moved toward the ruckus, while the Americans withdrew slightly to a creek which looked like a good delaying position. A runner hurried off to warn George Clinton of the hostile force aiming for the Forest of Dean Road.[16]

Shortly after noon, edgy defenders in Fort Montgomery saw a flash of color through the woods and heard sounds of approaching horses and men. Fingers tightened on musket triggers. Jitters dissolved into mirth just a moment later, however, when out of the woods burst such an apparition as few of the ragged men had ever beheld. Riding toward the fortress on a handsome horse bedecked with silver-studded bridle and saddle was Lieutenant Colonel William S. Livingston, a young blood of the aristocratic and influential Livingston clan. Dressed in fine clothes, draped in a colorful and flowing cape, proudly carrying a shining sword and sporting a brace of matched pistols, accompanied by body servants, he was properly attended and accoutered for battle—in his own eyes. Awed, sentries pulled aside a portion of the breastwork to let the reinforcement in. Livingston had been in the neighborhood "by accident" and wanted to join in the fight. George Clinton welcomed him.[17]

About the time young Livingston was making his grand entrance, Bruyn's message arrived. Governor Clinton had no more doubts as to enemy intentions: they planned to attack his two forts from the rear. As always in time of stress, he was decisive. He told James Clinton to assume command of Fort Clinton, taking Fort Montgomery as his personal responsibility. Machin he directed to take a force, including the fort's only fieldpiece, to defend the defile selected earlier in the morning. That done, the Governor took stock of his own situation in the strongholds. Fort Clinton was smaller, but nearer to completion; Fort Montgomery was virtually defenseless on the back side except for three small redoubts along the trace of the wall. According to Machin, "part of the walls of the fort were not more than half raised." In all, fewer than six hundred men defended the two forts. Militia were yet trickling in, but many were unarmed. For once, though, powder was not lacking. The full magazine in Fort Montgomery contained, in the eyes of the normally impoverished Patriots, a veritable widow's cruse. George Clinton decided on his defense. He would take some men from Fort Clinton to enable him to man all three of the small redoubts as strong points, his brother would hold Fort Clinton and protect the connecting bridge across Popolopen Creek. In the meantime, detachments were to delay the British forward of the forts for as long as possible. He reckoned he could hold out until sundown, more than sufficient time for reinforcements to arrive.

On that thought, George Clinton looked across the river. He could see empty boats still waiting for reinforcements at Robinson's Landing. What was taking so long? In a hurried scrawl he wrote Putnam again, informing that officer of the situation and pleading with him to hurry to his assistance. The message was sent at 1:30 P.M. by Livingston's servant. Again, as would soon be evident, Governor Clinton trusted a crucial message to an untrustworthy messenger.

Machin, meanwhile, had rounded up nearly a hundred men, including Captain Ephraim Fenno and a crew of artillerymen to work the small, brass fieldpiece. After searching unsuccessfully for axes needed to fell trees, he set out. (Although a Major Newkirk was in command of most of the men, Machin, then a captain-lieutenant, a rank lower than captain, seems to have controlled the entire group—another indication of the trust he engendered as well as an added reason to wonder at his failure to receive deserved promotions.) A little over a mile from Fort Montgomery, Popolopen Creek flows through a narrow, boulder-strewn cleft where Bear Mountain all but nudges sharp-sided Torne Hill. At the tightest point, where only the rushing stream and the rough trail gave any order to the tangled, wild pass, Machin had wisely chosen to make his stand. Constricted, perpetually in shadow, densely cluttered with vines, it is appropriately named Hell Hole. The distance was not far, but the column moved slowly, keeping pace with the perspiring, profane crew manhandling the cannon. Before they had gone far, George Clinton borrowed Livingston's fine horse and rode out to check progress, no doubt growing tired of the interminable waiting, and wishing personally to lay eyes on the enemy. It was good that he did as things turned out. Campbell's guides reached Hell Hole first; for the second time that day Americans were ambushed.

Machin later recalled, "Before I could reconnoitre the ground after posting my men, I found myself nearly surrounded." Captain Fenno whirled the brass gun around and managed to get off eight or nine charges of grapeshot at point-blank range. That kicked the British back and gave the Patriots a moment. The fighting grew confused. Several men were killed outright, many fell wounded into the thick undergrowth. "During all the while," Machin reported, "there was a warm musquetry fire." By instinct, British soldiers crawled around the cannon's field of fire, suddenly swarming down around and behind the Americans. Machin, with what men he could muster, broke out and led a retreat back to the fort. Fenno and several of his gunners were captured after spiking the fieldpiece. British bayonets pursued the disorganized Americans and might have exacted a terrible toll in blood had not Governor Clinton reacted so quickly to the ambush. Sensing in a moment the situation when the firing started, he turned his horse and spurred for the fort. There he hastily organized a covering party. Lieutenant Oliver Lawrence trundled a twelve-pounder on garrison carriage to a small height on the route of retreat "to rake a side way" which the enemy would pass. As Machin's men streamed back, the big gun belched grape at Campbell's charging advance guard, stopping them cold. The cannon was eventually lost, but most of the troops returned.[18]

James Clinton heard the musket firing erupt far up Popolopen Creek, and shortly after the huskier roar of the fieldpiece. Then, as if in answer, a rattle of musketry sounded from the direction of Doodletown. Vaughan had begun his push toward Fort Clinton. He quickly forced Bruyn back from the shallow creek, but the Americans fell away in a fairly disciplined manner. Bruyn and McClaughry had already decided to make their next stand at a stone wall near the south end of Mile Pond (later named Hessian Lake). According to plan they marched there, dropping off an individual now and then to harass the British van. In the excitement no one thought to record the hour, but Machin returned to Fort Montgomery and the British hit the stone wall about the same time, say three o'clock. Campbell paused for his column to close up and then deployed in assault formation. Meanwhile, Vaughan maneuvered Bruyn away from the stone fence. James Clinton stood ready to rush out with a force to help, but, under cover of cannon fire from Fort Clinton, Bruyn and McClaughry fell back "in middling good order." James Clinton sent Bruyn right on through his position, across the bridge and into Fort Montgomery. McClaughry was ordered to take command of the small redoubt some hundred yards southwest of Fort Clinton. In that isolated post McClaughry had eighty men bolstered by three six-pounders. Connecting McClaughry's position with Fort Clinton were a couple of field guns and a small detachment of men behind hastily erected breastworks. While those arrangements were being made, Vaughan's men approached to within cannon range. James Clinton gave the order to fire, and the battle was joined.[19]

Help from Putnam was George Clinton's only hope. But "Old Put" was away from headquarters taking a look at the nearly deserted English lines on Verplanck's Point, trying to fathom the meaning of his opponent's all-day inactivity. Moreover, George Clinton's eight o'clock message was still in Waterbury's pocket and his one-thirty letter was with Livingston's servant who seemed to have no idea he was supposed to hurry. And time was fast running out.

For nearly two hours both Vaughan and Campbell probed the forts and pressed ever closer. Henry Clinton had brought no cannon, so his men were at a disadvantage initially. Musket fire from beyond a hundred yards was wholly ineffective, but cannon shot from the forts raked the British 200 to 300 yards away. It was a galling, unequal exchange, forcing the attackers to move by crawling or sprinting from rock to rock. Vaughan's men worked carefully to within 50 yards of Fort Clinton by "taking advantage of the ground . . . in a loose, irregular manner." However, casualties were few in that painfully slow approach largely because "the American artillery [was] being served with more attention to quickness in firing than accuracy in pointing." Much the same thing was occurring outside Fort Montgomery where Campbell eased his troops to within 80 yards of that fortress. He also attempted to slip some men around the north side to infiltrate over an undefended wall. Captain John Hodge happened to look up from the deck of the *Montgomery* at that moment and saw the creeping troops. Glad to be able to do something, he shifted a twelve-pounder to that side of his vessel "to play upon" them. With round shot from the Patriot ship howling overhead, the enveloping redcoats beat a rapid retreat.[20]

Shortly before five o'clock the Royal navy joined the fray. Sir James Wallace, "crowding all sail" and bending every oar, was able to bring some of his cannon to bear on Fort Clinton. Two galleys even managed to lob several shot into the fort, although it was more nuisance than danger to the garrison. Both forts returned fire from fixed batteries overwatching the river, but with no serious effect. Other warships approached the chain and opened a lively fire on Captain Hodge's four defending craft. Hodge had his flotilla arrayed across the river behind the chain. The *Shark*, mounting four nine-pounders, and the *Camden*, bristling with ten cannon, were stationed near the east end of the chain while frigate *Montgomery*, armed with eight twelve-pounders, lay near the western shore "with her broadside to the enemy." Under the *Montgomery's* stern rode the third row galley, *Lady Washington*. Her main armament was a bow-mounted thirty-two-pounder, the only one in the little armada. Outgunned, Hodge held his fire at first, letting the *Lady Washington* respond at long range with thirty-two-pound shells. Undeterred by the single gun, the Britishers edged closer and their gunners began to find the range. Several solid balls smacked into the *Montgomery's* wooden hull. At that, Hodge signaled all ships to fire and Patriot gun crews blazed away "as fast as they could." The slugfest endured until the sun fell with neither side doing much damage, probably because the river's gorge soon filled with pungent, blinding clouds of smoke.[21]

On bluffs above the brawling sailors, soldiers were raising fog banks of their own when men in Fort Montgomery saw a white flag thrust up in the midst of Campbell's lines. As it waved back and forth to attract attention, firing slackened and stopped. Curious defenders peeped over gun barrels to see what was afoot. A very young drummer—at that close range it was easy to see fright in his eyes—stepped into the open and "beat a parley." Moments later a lieutenant colonel strode out between the lines accompanied only by a soldier holding aloft the flag. Mungo Campbell wanted to talk, George Clinton could clearly see, but he obviously was not speaking or acting for the overall British commander for, even as he stood out there waiting, his countrymen opposing Fort Clinton and manning the fleet kept up a dense and deliberate fire. Campbell, in spite of his gruelling, day-long hike, was impeccably dressed. He wore colorful regimentals and eye-catching insignia of rank with that easy insolence marking him as a person of high social status. Somewhere in Fort Montgomery crouched a rifleman whose finger itched at the temptation to drill that peacock of an officer. Brigadier General George Clinton, by the polite rules of procedure governing the brutal business of war, could not himself answer a flag of a lieutenant colonel. But Lieutenant Colonel Livingston could—and, besides, he was as fancily dressed as the Britisher. Clinton sent Livingston "to meet him without the works and know his business." And just to be sure it was handled properly, the Governor ordered his factotum, Thomas Machin, to go along.

After amenities, Campbell asked for the surrender of the fort "to prevent the effusion of blood" which he assured the American would be the result of an assault. Not stated, but implicit in the gesture, was another eighteenth-century rule of war: when defenders of a besieged fortress failed to respond to a valid request to surrender, the besieger could then put the entire garrison to the sword with a perfectly clear conscience. Livingston, as much an aristocrat in his own right as Campbell, haughtily and out of hand rejected the offer. Americans most certainly would not yield. On the other hand, should the British care to "surrender themselves prisoners of war, they might depend upon being well treated." Campbell's reply was not recorded for posterity. "Very well then," Livingston rejoined, "you may renew the attack as soon as I shall return within the fort." The two men nodded pleasantly, turned their backs on one another, and walked casually to their own lines. The time was about half past five.[22]

Campbell could have entertained no serious thought that the Americans would so easily buckle. He may merely have extended the offer as a formality, though no such courtesy was shown by Vaughan to Fort Clinton's garrison. The cease-fire might have been used as an opportunity to move his men into final assault positions. Or, that little act with the flag may have been a prearranged signal to Vaughan that Campbell was ready to attack the fort. Henry Clinton later wrote about Campbell's "signal" to Vaughan which permitted both columns to coordinate assaults. Be that as it may, Campbell's men were all set to charge when the conference ended. As soon as he returned, a wall of nearly eight hundred men rose and advanced on Fort Montgomery. One of the first shots to ring out from the fort was from the weapon of the farmer who had been so tempted earlier to take a pot shot at the fancy British officer. He must have kept Campbell in his sights while waiting for the truce to end. He got his shot, a good one, killing the enemy commander instantly.

The leaderless assault washed nearly to the redoubts before it fell back in confusion under a withering fire. Ground between the lines was littered with human forms, some rolling in agony, others grotesquely motionless. Beverley Robinson assumed command and quickly reorganized his units for another attempt.

Meanwhile James Clinton found himself too busy to watch the drama across Popolopen Creek. It was obvious that an attack was imminent, and he was running short of powder. That had been no real worry because he knew that the magazine in Fort Montgomery was crammed with powder kegs. He sent a detachment to get a resupply, but they returned minutes after leaving with news that British infiltrators had control of the bridge between the twin forts. Worried, the general ran to the barricades and warned all the men to conserve powder, to fire only when a good target appeared. An aide braved fire to dash across open ground to the separate redoubt with a similar warning for McClaughry. James Clinton had hardly been aware of the pause in firing around Fort Montgomery, but when Campbell's attack was launched the sudden fusillade jerked his head that way. For a moment only, however, for Vaughan's men were up with fixed bayonets, rushing his position.

Across the river, men were at long last stirring. Waterbury, having delayed every minute he thought he safely could, delivered George Clinton's letter at four o'clock—eight hours after it had been sent. Livingston's easy-going servant would not stroll in with his for another several minutes. Putnam was away when the message came, but Colonel Samuel Wyllys, acting on his own, sent all the Continentals he could scrape together pounding up the road to Robinson's Landing under the command of Colonel Return Jonathan Meigs. When "Old Put" returned he approved the action and ordered a militia regiment to follow. While they marched, sounds of battle echoed over the river, seeming to increase in intensity as the minutes passed. Officers, watching the sun fall, were anxious. Lieutenant Colonel Eleazor Oswald, of Lamb's Regiment, wrote to his colonel: "Heaven preserve you all, my dear Colonel! I feel for you, and lament that I can't assist you. . . . A large reinforcement is on their march to your assistance."[23]

"Trusting by order to the bayonet only," thirsting for a good crack at the rebels whose cannon had been almost insufferable—if ineffective—all afternoon, a heavy column crashed into Fort Clinton's south wall. Another swept around McClaughry's redoubt. Point men clawed and chopped to make a breach or get a handhold, others "actually pushed one another up into the embrasures." Casualties piled up. Among those to fall was Count Grabouski, whose search for excitement had been all too quickly rewarded and would have to be continued in another world. The struggle grew fierce, hand to hand. At that infighting, better-trained regulars wielding red-dripping bayonets were superior. The Americans either surrendered or poured out over the opposite wall in a desperate attempt to escape. The highly charged redcoats raised a victory roar heard across the creek in Fort Montgomery—and feared by the Patriots for what it was.[24]

McClaughry had fared better in his redoubt, having shattered the column attacking him. James Clinton, his own command no longer fighting, ran instinctively for the protection of the resisting redoubt. But that was not the right choice. In open ground, as the shadows of twilight lengthened, he discovered himself caught in a crossfire, being shot at by friend and foe alike. Having no other recourse, he sprinted for the bridge in the slim hope of breaking through to join his brother in Fort Montgomery. Racing boldly over the corpse-littered field, he realized that several enemy soldiers were firing as he passed and expected any second to be hit, but somehow he safely cleared the gauntlet. Running recklessly down the steep road, propelled dangerously by gravity, he was unprepared either to stop or defend himself when a dark figure loomed out of deep shadows near the bridge

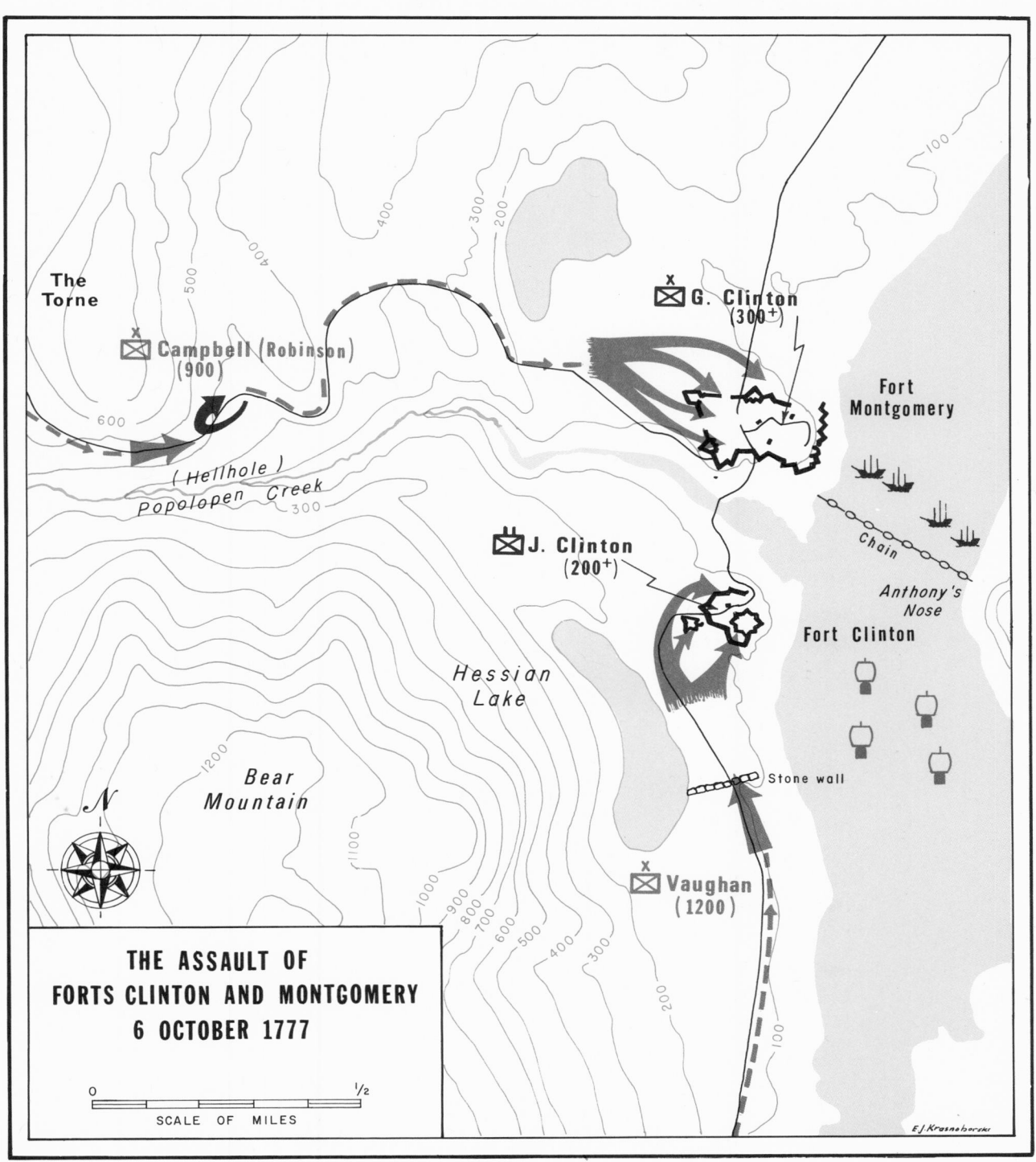

The
Torne

⊠ Campbell (Robinson)
(900)

(Hellhole)
Popolopen Creek

⊠ G. Clinton
(300⁺)

Fort
Montgomery

Chain

Anthony's
Nose

⊠ J. Clinton
(200⁺)

Fort Clinton

Hessian
Lake

Bear
Mountain

N

Stone wall

⊠ Vaughan
(1200)

**THE ASSAULT OF
FORTS CLINTON AND MONTGOMERY
6 OCTOBER 1777**

0   ½
SCALE OF MILES

E.J.Krasnoborski

Infantry regiment ⊠   ⛵ Ship at anchor
Infantry battalion ⊠   ⛴ Ship under sail

and lunged at him with a bayonet. The long knife sank sickeningly into thigh, but Clinton's momentum tore him free and carried him on to the bridge. Stemming the bleeding with both hands, he began the climb up to Fort Montgomery. Behind him McClaughry finally surrendered when Vaughan turned men from Fort Clinton and stormed the redoubt from behind.[25]

Fort Montgomery relied almost solely upon the three small strong points in its weak west wall to hold off the enemy onslaught. Commanding them were Colonel Lewis Dubois, Lieutenant Colonel William Livingston, and Major Samuel Logan, still sick but insisting on being in the fight. After repulsing one attack, they encouraged and commended their men, and prepared for the next. Morale was high until that lusty cheer resounded out of the dense smoke and firing at Fort Clinton. That dread cry clearly signaled the defeat of comrades there. Dubois and others urged Governor Clinton, "in consideration of the important place he filled in the state," to leave while he could. But, even as they discussed the matter, the enemy came on again, bayonets glinting in quick-fading light. The Americans answered by firing platoon volleys, "but soon ran into a promiscuous fire." Major Grant's Volunteers, Americans fighting for the Monarch to whom they had remained loyal, were in the fore of the attack. Eighteen of them fell in that valiant charge, including Grant. But the others pressed forward. Machin watched in fascination as Robinson "formed a solid column from the center by files, under cover of a rock at about 100 paces from the fort, and in that form [ran] up the parapet." Robinson's column smashed over the wall between the center and north redoubt, spilling screeching soldiers into the fortress. The fight was over and so was the day. In darkness broken by flames licking around several buildings, "each man made the best escape he could."[26]

James Clinton limped up into the fortress just in time to find his brother and to encounter swarming enemy troops. The British absolutely must not get their hands on New York's Governor, he shouted, forcefully assuming the attitude of older brother which he had not adopted at any other time in the war. With what men he could grab, the general hastily organized a covering position to give the Governor time to escape. George Clinton half-crawled, half-tumbled down the steep slope to the river where he was fortunate enough to be picked up by a boat. Satisfied that he had held as long as necessary, James Clinton hobbled to the ravine north of the fort and slipped away.[27]

From start to finish, it had taken Sir Henry's men half an hour to storm and carry the two forts. The labor of thirty months had been undone in thirty minutes.

But ignominy and defeat had not fully run their courses. Seeing the forts fall, Captain Hodge ordered his fleet to help survivors and then sail upriver to Constitution Island. Tide and wind were not on the Patriot side, though, and inexperienced crews were no match for the elements. *Lady Washington* got away clean, but *Montgomery, Shark,* and *Camden* floundered helplessly and finally ran aground. The *Camden,* her ten guns intact, was abandoned. Captain Hodge decided to burn *Montgomery* rather than let it fall to the enemy; the *Shark's* skipper followed suit. As the Loyalist historian, Charles Stedman, described the scene:

> The flames suddenly broke forth; and, as every sail was set, the vessels soon became magnificent pyramids of fire. The reflection on the steep face of the opposite mountain [Anthony's Nose], and the long train of ruddy light that shone upon the water for a prodigious distance, had a wonderful effect; whilst the ear was awfully filled with the continued echoes from the rocky shores, as the flames gradually reached the cannon. The whole was sublimely terminated by the explosions, which again left all to darkness.[28]

8

A FORTNIGHT OF DEFEAT

GEORGE CLINTON wasted no time watching the blazing and exploding ships. He quickly shoved to Putnam's headquarters in Peekskill, struggling the whole way in the dark over a narrow road choked with Meig's milling men, reinforcements suddenly finding themselves with no place to reinforce. He conferred with "Old Put" on what to do next. The older man, somewhat abashed by the day's events and weary from nearly thirty-six straight hours in the saddle, all but relinquished leadership to General Clinton. The Governor surmised, while Putnam and Parsons nodded agreement, that Henry Clinton's intention "was to relieve Burgoyne's army by effecting a junction with him." With the forts carried, it was fully to be expected the British would "pass the *chevaux-de-frise* and so proceed by water up the river." The three men rapidly concluded to abandon the posts at Sydnam's Bridge and Peekskill, to fall back to stronger defensive positions above the Highlands; since nothing remained to prevent British passage of the chain, enemy vessels could sail to Robinson's Landing, effectively cutting off any force lingering in Peekskill. Putnam was to withdraw to a mountain pass on the eastern side just three miles south of Fishkill, while the Governor, his "broken but brave forces" bolstered by Colonel Samuel B. Webb's regiment, would cross the river to organize a defense around Machin's Battery and the *chevaux-de-frise*. Through the balance of that second sleepless night, officers made necessary arrangements and issued marching orders. About dawn the army decamped —in such haste that no one supervised the destruction of supplies and equipment left behind.[1]

Few slept in the smoking forts above Popolopen either. There were wounded to care for and dead to cover, captives to guard and sentries to post. Among the 265 Patriot prisoners was Lieutenant Colonel William Livingston, a most pained officer as he watched his sword, pistols, and silver-saddled horse confiscated as spoils of war. Caught too, was Major Hammill. Of all those failing to escape, he was least concerned, for he was, or quickly came to be, in the pay of Sir Henry Clinton and could foresee a rapid release. Lieutenant Jackson, after surviving that opening ambush in Doodletown, was made prisoner in the day's final fight; Samuel Logan, whose bad decision at Timp Pass may have caused it all, was also taken. The Governor's aide, Major Stephen Lush, failed to get away. James McClaughry surrendered, but not before sustaining seven separate wounds to bear witness to his resistance. According to a story probably apocryphal but quite possibly true, Henry Clinton recognized McClaughry as a relative of George Clinton's and inquired, "Where is my good friend George?" The Irishman sharply retorted, "Safe, thank God, beyond the reach of your friendship."

Came dawn on the 7th, a fair day, and curious soldiers and officers went down to inspect the chain and the still unfinished boom. For months they had heard tales of the Patriots' wondrous floating chain. Reality was every bit as imposing as reports. The Englishmen were impressed. "The construction of both," wrote Commodore William Hotham in high praise of his enemy, "gives strong proofs of labour, industry and skill." One row-galley, *Dependence*, testing the barrier, "looked for passage over the chain but found none." Hotham told his ship captains to salvage as much of the iron as possible. The rest was to be destroyed. How much of the expensive metal sailed back to New York City as ballast and what part was dropped into the Hudson has never been revealed.[2]

An unusual problem faced Clinton and his men on the morning of 7 October. After consolidating their position and providing for the wounded, officers detailed work parties for the grisly but necessary aftermath of every battle: burial of the dead.* Attempting to dig graves in and around the forts, soldiers quickly discovered how shallow was the soil and how hard the bedrock. Corpses from Fort Montgomery were then dragged unceremoniously to a small pond nearby, weighted with stone, and dropped into the water. Friend and foe alike were accorded, in death, equal treatment. Some evidence was later unearthed indicating cremation, probably used as a sanitary method of disposing of limbs severed either in battle or by surgeons afterward (amputation being the preferred method of wound treatment in the eighteenth century). At Fort Clinton the problem was the same. And, though no firm documentation supports the conclusion, it is logical to assume the same solution was used. Mile Pond, just behind the fort, was ideally located for such a purpose. Its name soon thereafter became "Hessian Lake," evoking memories of slain German mercenaries

---

* The number to fall in that fight has never been established with even reasonable accuracy. Both sides minimized their own losses while inflating reports of casualties inflicted on the enemy. A good guess, striking a balance between extremes, is that something over a hundred and fifty bodies in all had to be buried a day after the assault. At an investigation six months later, Americans could only surmise that around seventy Patriots had fallen.

resting in a murky grave on its bottom. Senior officers and the ill-fated Count Grabouski were interred in more normal if unmarked graves.[3]

Under a flag of truce, an officer in a small boat went up to Constitution Island later in the day to ask the garrison of that fort to surrender. As the boat approached, an apprehensive sentry fired on the flag, causing rowers frantically to reverse direction and return angrily to Fort Montgomery. Fuming at such an "insolent reception, unknown in any war," Sir Henry ordered the island seized. An hour before noon on 8 October, metal-workers cut the chain. Longboats hauled it ashore. Then three galleys, the *Spitfire, Crane,* and *Dependence,* escorted upriver twenty-two flatboats crowded with soldiers. Hardly a breath of wind blew. Oars laboriously splashed the amphibious force along. As the sun dipped behind Crow's Nest Mountain, throwing slanting rays on the island's natural and man-made battlements, British boats nosed ashore. Red- and blue-clad troops, bayonets gleaming silver, dashed up to the works to find—no one. Fort Constitution was deserted. That lone and dishonorable shot fired on the flag of truce had been the only round expended in protection of the island—a ludicrous defense of a ludicrous fort.[4]

When Forts Montgomery and Clinton had come under attack on the 6th, Fort Constitution's commander, Major Lewis Dubois (not to be confused with the colonel of the same name in Fort Montgomery), took stock of his situation and found it hopeless. Not counting artillerymen under Captain Gershom Mott, Dubois had about a hundred "new levies and militia" and some thirty or more rear-echelon supply types with which to man the island's defenses. Worse, he saw with sudden and shocking clarity what some men had observed and recorded long before: huddled as it was beneath the dominant cliff of West Point, the island was a death trap. A water-borne force could advance under cover of West Point until almost upon the island, then rapidly row across to attack. Or, the English could set cannon on West Point and simply blast Fort Constitution into submission. Dubois despaired. He apparently went to pieces, forfeiting all semblance of direction and discipline.

While the battles downriver raged, boats came to the island to evacuate cannon and supplies. By some unexplained mixup they departed empty. *Congress* slipped her moorings at Robinson's Landing and took station near the island. There, crewed inexpertly by soldiers and convicts, she promptly mired hopelessly in the mud. After his escape from Fort Montgomery, Colonel Lamb stopped long enough to order everything removed. Machin, a bloody bandage concealing a chest wound, also made his way that night to Fort Constitution where he found the officers in a state of consternation and the men "in a mobbish condition." News of defeat below, made vivid by sight of beaten and wounded survivors reeling past in wide-eyed fright, had spread a paralyzing mantle of fear over the garrison. When the *Lady Washington* reported that all other vessels were destroyed, panic flared. Machin pleaded with Mott to remove all the cannon at least, but the leaders had lost control. Early on the 7th, the *Congress'* captain set her afire, punctuating the despair of the defenders. Men began leaving the island by every means available. Shortly afterward those Englishmen in a rowboat had approached waving a white flag stuck on an oar. Indicating how far discipline had slipped, soldiers standing on the landing bravely "repulsed" the boat. Then in a rush the last members of the garrison set fire to barracks and departed. No one stopped to destroy stores or to spike cannon. Six boxes of musket cartridges and some blacksmiths' tools were all they saved. When Henry Clinton's men waded ashore over a day later they found the fort had been "evacuated in the greatest confusion."[5]

Fort Constitution his without a fight, Sir Henry was buoyantly surprised at the ease of his victory. "*Nous y Voici,*" he exulted in an encouraging note to Burgoyne, "and nothing now between us but Gates. I sincerely hope this little success of ours may facilitate your operations." He could not have known that just a day after the masterly capture of Forts Montgomery and Clinton, Burgoyne's fate had been sealed. Desperate, and wholly unaware of Henry Clinton's efforts in his behalf, Burgoyne had launched an attack on the 7th. That assault was stopped and, by virtue of Benedict Arnold's timely arrival on the field, beaten back. "Gentleman Johnny's" game was up. He could no longer do anything more than hang on for a few days. His only hope—and it was a most slender one—was that Henry Clinton might somehow reach and rescue him. But Clinton was operating in the dark; he had no idea just how critical was Burgoyne's situation. London's original strategic plan, allowing columns to operate out of touch with one another and beyond supporting distance, was finally bearing its bitter fruit.[6]

A day after Constitution Island fell, Clinton sent ex-Governor Tryon ashore at Fort Independence with a mixed command of Hessian and English units "to destroy the rebel settlement, Continental Village." Not believing the Americans would docilely vacate the entire area, a strong force marched from Verplanck's Point to aid Tryon. Converging on the deserted Patriot supply depot and bivouac site, the soldiers were taken by surprise to discover wagons laden with equipment of all sorts, full and undamaged storehouses, and enough newly constructed barracks to house 1,500 troops. Even though a drenching, driving rain made burning difficult, everything —wagons and all—was put to the torch. For the second time that year American stores and facilities at Peekskill went up in smoke.[7]

While Tryon was marching to Continental Village, Commodore Hotham ordered Sir James Wallace, in command of a "flying squadron" of row-galleys, to make an attempt at passing Machin's *chevaux-de-frise* at Pollepel Island. Sir Henry and the Commodore both thought Wallace might do "essential service" if he could break through as "there can be nothing [above] to give him any interruption." The attempt failed, though, due largely to "extreme badness of the weather."

After securing Constitution Island, soldiers crossed the river, landing on the flat where stood Stephen Moore's fancy red house. Stephen himself, the only active Patriot in the large Moore family, had not lived in the house since 1775, but it had become a refuge for his relatives, Tories all. His brother Thomas, a former resident of Peekskill, had moved in with his numerous children about the time Romans and the Commissioners were at loggerheads, and had lodged there ever since. Charles, a bachelor, stayed from time to time. One nephew, John, though employed as a British official in New York City, had sent his wife and child to the house. Others drifted in and out. Patriot commanders, workers, and soldiers apparently tolerated their displaced, "disaffected" countrymen, for no incident of reprisal ever occurred. Ironically, the horde of Moores residing in the big house escaped "the dangers and excitements incident to a state of war" until their friends, the redcoats, arrived.

Finding no rebels on West Point, Henry Clinton's men turned to a duty more pleasant than fighting: foraging. Before the angrily protesting members of the household could convince an officer of their allegiance to the Crown, the garden was stripped, chickens were thrust headless into canvas bags, and a cow grazing in the orchard was slaughtered. The hungry men, contented with such a windfall, were not in the least interested in harming the inhabitants. Furthermore, being well disciplined, they knew better than to enter the house itself. Not so the sailors. When an escort vessel tied up at the landing, seamen, seeing that soldiers had taken everything of value outside the home, raced right up to the large front veranda. Bishop Richard Channing Moore, a boy at the time, later recalled the scene:

> . . . they immediately entered the house and, with ruthless violence, tore up the carpets, stripped the beds, stole the teaspoons from the table where the family were seated at their evening meal, and without restraint carried on the work of indiscriminate pillage. One of the band of depredators, more savage than the rest, with fiendish cruelty and dastardly cowardice, presented a fixed bayonet at Mrs. Moore's breast, threatening the life of an unprotected mother surrounded by an interested group of weeping and helpless children![8]

Bad news reached Sir Henry from north and south simultaneously, either late on Thursday, at the height of the rainstorm, or early on 10 October. From above Albany came word of Burgoyne's worsening plight, though not of the lost battle at Bemis Heights; and in New York City, Generals Robertson and Leslie both were taken ill, leaving a Hessian officer in charge. That would not do. With "nobody but drunken General Schmidt to trust the foreposts to," Clinton himself returned to New York City on that day. Before leaving, he wrote Burgoyne, informing him that "there is not a rebel cannon left in the Highlands." Burgoyne, understandably enough, was concerned more with cannon and troops at Saratoga, where there were all too many. Clinton also left orders for Fort Montgomery to be razed while Fort Clinton—renamed Fort Vaughan—was to be strengthened. Because Fort Clinton was on higher ground than Fort Montgomery, the garrison could not be endangered should the rebels reoccupy the latter. Moreover, that consolidation reduced the force required to defend the position.[9]

Meanwhile, Americans in the Highlands were in a high state of agitation. Putnam, convinced in his own mind that British units planned "to make forced marches toward Albany," urged George Clinton to consider moving that way, too. The Governor, though, was more interested in contesting every step of the British advance. From New Windsor he proclaimed he would "defend the *chevaux-de-frise* in the best manner I can and as long." But he did not place his faith entirely upon those water obstructions:

> As soon as ever I find the shipping likely to pass the *chevaux-de-frise* I will by forced march endeavor to gain Kingston and cover that town. I shall have one brass twenty-four pounder and six smaller brass pieces which will make a formidable train. I am persuaded if the militia will join me—which I have reason to hope—I can save the country, a few scattered houses excepted, along the river from destruction and defeat the enemy's design in assisting their northern army.[10]

George Clinton was encouraged when James hobbled in with nothing more than a painful flesh wound which did "not appear to be any ways dangerous." By the 8th, over two hundred survivors of the battle had made their way to New Windsor, including many previously thought to have been captured. On 9 October, with rain beating in sheets on the windows of Widow Falls' Inn, a cousin's wayside tavern where George Clinton had established temporary headquarters, he prepared for George Washington a long and detailed account of the loss of the forts. He ended by acknowledging that "public censure" was likely, and asking that "it may fall on me alone; for . . . the officers and men under me of the different corps behaved with the greatest spirit and bravery." It was a letter which would reach a most sympathetic individual, for the Commander-in-Chief himself, on 4 October, had been repulsed at Germantown. Sir William Howe was in Philadelphia.[11]

By Friday the 10th the Governor's hopes of defending settlements along the west shore had melted, even though Wallace's vessels had drawn back without breaking the *chevaux-de-frise*. Reinforcements expected from New England had not arrived, and probably would not. Militiamen, "anxious about the immediate safety of their respective families," either did not join or insisted on returning home each evening. George Clinton reluctantly informed the Council of Safety at Kingston that his only chance of stopping the enemy would be to deceive them as to his actual strength, explaining, "I thus may deter them from doing what if they should attempt I could not prevent." Ominously, he suggested that small works should be thrown up to cover landings and paths leading to Kingston. He also recommended, "Every man that can fire a gun should be immediately imbodied and employed at those works."[12]

Even though the situation appeared utterly bleak when viewed from the American side, it was anything but promising from the British vantage point. Henry Clinton was groping in the dark, almost entirely unapprised of Burgoyne's activities. Communicating between the two British headquarters was one of the most pressing of problems. Both English generals relied upon daring couriers to smuggle letters through Patriot lines in civilian clothing. That took time, as the penalty for capture was a spy's death. Nor was it a sure method. To increase the odds of successful transmission, the two commanders sent several copies of every missive, each carried by a different volunteer over a different route.

One of these, entrusted with Clinton's exuberant notification of victory in the Highlands, was Daniel (or David) Taylor, a lieutenant who had already safely made a trek from Burgoyne southward. With Clinton's message folded tightly in an egg-shaped silver capsule about the size of a musket ball, Taylor set out under cover of darkness on the night of 8 October, sticking to side roads west of the river. It was his mishap—a fatal one—to choose the road leading past Mrs. Falls' Inn. Fatigued after negotiating the rough Highlands passes, and looking for a safe place to rest, he was happily surprised to run into soldiers wearing familiar red and blue British uniforms. Making himself known to an officer in the detachment, Taylor fully expected to be taken in. In that wish he was not disappointed; he had stumbled into George Clinton's guard. They wasted no time taking him right in to the Governor.

In a quick motion the courier popped the silver ball into his mouth and swallowed it, but not without being observed. George Clinton, anxious for information of the enemy, administered a severe dose of emetic tartar, "calculated to operate either way." Surgeon James Thacher later wrote, "This produced the happiest effect as respects the prescriber; but it proved fatal to the patient." Taylor, however, grabbed the ball as soon as it came up and swallowed it a second time. The Governor, a gruff man even when calm, thundered that Taylor should be "hung up instantly and cut open to search it." Taylor apparently believed him and stopped resisting. Clinton later reported with evident satisfaction, "This brought it forth."

In his confession, Taylor related that among the things he was to tell Burgoyne was that Royal forces held the passes through the Highlands of Hudson's River—styled by Sir Henry, "the Key of America." Actually, a confession was superfluous. When Americans unscrewed the two halves of the silver ball and Henry Clinton's message fluttered out, that was all the proof they needed to convict Taylor as a spy. He was a dead man when he vomited up the evidence. James Thacher summed up the matter with, "Out of thine own mouth thou shalt be condemned." On the 14th Taylor was convicted and sentenced to death by a court-martial sitting in New Windsor. Governor Clinton ordered the execution to take place on 17 October in full view of all available American troops. Other events intervened, however, and Taylor was hanged on an apple tree on 18 October, observed by only a scattering of curious people, not far from what General Vaughan had left standing of the town of Kingston.[13]

In the meantime, Wallace, balked earlier by weather and tide from breaking through the *chevaux-de-frise,* had gathered a small force for another try on Saturday, 11 October. Four armed ships—the small brig *Diligent* and three row-galleys, the *Spitfire, Crane,* and *Dependence*—approached the line of obstacles, carefully made a breach through the frowning, rust-red teeth, and gingerly slipped through one by one. The entire operation was performed under the eyes of hundreds of New Yorkers on shore and to the scarcely stifled, enraged thoughts and words of New York's Governor. The range from Machin's Battery on Plum Point to the English vessels was too great for effective fire to be delivered by the several four-pounders positioned there, but a single brass twenty-four-pounder was fully expected to make the English "very uneasy in the river." That gun, however, had a broken axletree which could not be repaired in time, Not that it mattered much, as there were no round shot available for it in any case. In that moment of trial, Patriot preparations to defend the expensive *chevaux-de-frise* betrayed the rank amateurishness of their military establishment. George Clinton had no time to ponder the complete failure of his personal and favorite project; Wallace's "musquito fleet" was already disappearing upriver. The countryside had to be warned.[14]

Hard-riding and bone-weary horsemen were sent once more to alert riverside towns, this time to announce that hostile ships were above the final barrier. Kingston, where everyone "sixteen years and upwards capable of bearing arms" had been called out, was warned to be especially vigilant. At Pleasant Valley, some eight miles east of Poughkeepsie, Doctor Peter Tappen had his hands full with a group of women and wounded soldiers. Among them were his own wife, expected "every minute [to] be taken in labor," and his sister, the wife of Governor Clinton. Thomas Machin, one of the wounded, had a bad chest injury, but was bearing up "bravely." An express rider reached the woebegone group with advice "to move further back" from the river. Other mounted messengers galloped on foam-flecked horses into every settlement near the Hudson sounding that electrifying warning shouted in another state two and a half years earlier by Paul Revere and William Dawes: "The redcoats are coming!"[15]

Prisoners were taken from their stinking, overcrowded, floating jails at Kingston and sent into Connecticut for security, glad no doubt for the excitement and a breath of clean air. State records were likewise removed. Up and down the river Patriots hid or buried valuables and, where possible, moved families inland. Old men took down ancient rifles and boys practiced with muskets. Tories gloated.

But the alert was premature. Although the river marauders burnt storehouses at Poughkeepsie and set fire to several boats along the way, they were only reconnoitering. The attack itself would follow. On the same day that Wallace was cruising north of Newburgh, Henry Clinton was sending a regiment of Hessian grenadiers, two battalions of Anspachers, and his own 45th Regiment up from New York City to Verplanck's Point. Working feverishly, aware that Burgoyne's fate quite probably hinged on him, he loaded six months' provisions for 5,000 men in boats able to sail to Albany. An attempt, at least, to save the northern army must be made. Those preparations completed, here turned to Fort Clinton (Vaughan) and ordered General Vaughan to embark nearly 2,000 men aboard thirty transports and "feel his way to General Burgoyne." Everything for the expedition was in readiness when Wallace returned on the 14th to report no Patriot resistance whatsoever above the *chevaux-de-frise*—if one discounted desultory and ineffective cannon fire from Machin's Battery. Early Wednesday morning, 15 October, aided by fog, the convoy passed through the obstacles. Some boats snagged temporarily but rocked and wriggled loose without damage. The fleet assembled beyond the barrier and started north. Some observant Patriots remarked that General Vaughan's flagship bore a most inappropriate name—*Friendship*.[16]

Burning everything that floated as they advanced, the British still managed to get almost to Kingston by nightfall. From Esopus Landing, down Rondout Creek from Kingston, Patriot cannon blasted away at the British, dealing no hurt but attracting unwanted attention. George Clinton had dashed ahead for the Capital, leaving his soldiers straining northward in a forced march. Early on the 16th Vaughan attacked American positions at the mouth of Rondout Creek. A lone galley, gallantly firing a single thirty-two-pounder, blocked the creek. On shore, Colonel Levi Pawling commanded a small militia detachment composed in good part of teenagers. They crouched behind hastily erected earth and log breastworks. In Pawling's position were the batteries that had drawn English ire. Swiftly, Vaughan landed and attacked, taking the positions and the guns. *Lady Washington*, the galley, beat a retreat and was later scuttled by her crew high up the creek. Vaughan continued to Kingston, a town he condemned as "a nursery for almost every villain in the country." Scattered resistance was brushed aside. Musket fire from some of the houses, Vaughan reported, "induced me to reduce the place to ashes, which I accordingly did, not leaving a house." Moreover, he added, "a considerable quantity of stores" and several boats went up in flames as well. Just one house, belonging to a Tory, was left standing. British casualties were negligible, and most of those were incurred in an accident during the destruction of the town. Three Negroes, a man and two women, were carried away, but not to freedom. George Clinton, arriving with no troops, was only "an idle spectator" to the defeat and the huge bonfire. His army, after a march of forty miles in twenty-four hours, came panting up from the south only an hour or two after the red-uniformed raiders were safely aboard ships in the very broad and very British Hudson.[17]

All Vaughan's efforts had been in vain. The very next day Burgoyne surrendered his entire army. For all intents and purposes, the campaign of 1777 was over. Vaughan, of course, did not know that, but he and Wallace strongly suspected that the northern army had "retreated if not worse." Wallace was hampered by the deep draft of some of his ships, preventing his attempting a dash all the way to Albany unless he could be sure of meeting Burgoyne. For one more week, while anxiously awaiting some information from the northern army, the King's ships roamed the river from New York City nearly to Albany, laying waste or pillaging whatever they could reach, creating a great swath of devastation and bitterness. George Clinton's own home near the Highlands was one of those looted. The logbook of row-galley *Dependence* is replete with accounts of arson and bombardment.

While his subordinates were burning homes and building hate along the Hudson's shores, Henry Clinton attempted to contact Israel Putnam to entice him into switching sides—for a price. Just why he thought "Old Put" would be susceptible is not clear. Perhaps rumors had reached him of the American's dissatisfaction with either the course of the war or of his part in it. There is no evidence that Putnam ever considered treason, either before or after the contact, but something had aroused the suspicions of at least one American officer, Colonel John Lamb. Lamb did not admire "Old Put" and detested his son and aide-de-camp, Major Daniel Putnam. "I am credibly informed," Lamb was later to say, "that on the day of the attack, Major Putnam, aide-de-camp to the general, was at Mr. Robinson's, looking out of the garrett windows and amusing himself in company with the Miss Robinson with the agreeable scene at Fort Montgomery and Clinton." Lamb went on to say, "Some time after the loss of the forts General Putnam sent his son, the major, with a flag in order to have an interview with Colonel Beverley Robinson, what possible business they transacted I believe remains a profound secret."[18]

Putnam's family had been living in Beverley Robinson's large house opposite West Point, sharing it with Robinson's own family. Mrs. Putnam, then on her death bed (she died on 14 October), had remained behind after the American withdrawal from the Highlands. At Clinton's instigation, Robinson visited the dying woman. In secret he informed her that if her husband had "the least inclination" to help end the rebellion it could be done honorably. He entreated her to relay the word to Putnam. Illness and imminent death probably precluded her ever doing so. Robinson, on pretext of checking his property and visiting with his own family, remained around the house and sent a letter under a flag of truce to Putnam. The general's son replied politely, prompting Robinson to write another. But by then other events had caught up with Henry Clinton's adventure in the Highlands and the project to sway "Old Put" was dropped.[19]

Clinton's first attempt to buy the loyalty of a commander of the Highlands had failed. It would not be his last such effort.

On the very day of Burgoyne's surrender, a letter from Howe found Henry Clinton in the Highlands. Howe was in Philadelphia but he had just been rather roughly handled by Washington at Germantown. He wanted 4,000 reinforcements sent immediately, "unless you may be on the eve of accomplishing some very material and effectual stroke." In that event, and provided it could be accomplished in a few days, Clinton was authorized to prolong his campaign. Clinton still wanted to help Burgoyne, but he was entirely at a loss what to do or even what was needed. Worse, he barely had adequate strength to hold the key defile in the Highlands, defend New York City, and support Vaughan's expedition upriver. Sending any reinforcements at all to Howe would oblige him to give up the Hudson. He knew Howe was wrong. And yet the orders had been explicit. Hoping against hope for good tidings from Burgoyne, Sir Henry waited two more days. Then he despondently returned to his headquarters in the city. Finally, on the 22nd, out of time and out of heart, he ordered Vaughan and Wallace to fall down the river. Soon thereafter, he issued instructions for demolition of all Highlands fortifications except Fort Clinton (Vaughan).[20]

Repassing the Highlands was a more harrowing experience than going up had been. The Patriots realized that Wallace and Vaughan would have to take flight as soon as Burgoyne surrendered. Ammunition and fieldpieces and men flowed down from Gates' army to give the intruders grief. Hotham, anticipating trouble, had stationed several ships so as to secure the narrow passages through the Highlands; the *Mercury* stood off Pollepel Island, the *Cerberus* at Stony Point, the *Tartar* near Fort Montgomery, and the *Preston* next to Peekskill. But above the mountain gorge, the English convoy was on its own. While passing Poughkeepsie on 23 October, Vaughan heard a shout from his lookouts and observed the rebels "posting themselves advantageously behind the heights" of the town. Row-galleys moved in close to shore and fired at the Patriots until all transports had eased safely downstream. As the flotilla neared the trace of *chevaux-de-frise*, five cannon opened up from Plum Point. Three row-galleys shifted over and exchanged fire with the shore batteries for an hour while the transports squirmed through the obstacle. Next, as the retiring vessels drew near Constitution Island, fire from the base of Crow's Nest Mountain raked them yet again in a parting gesture of defiance.[21]

What Mott's men had left undone on Constitution Island, the British completed. With pry bar and gunpowder, soldiers leveled Romans' huge stone walls and gutted his battery sites. Fire completed the destruction. Fort Independence shared the same fate. Montgomery had already been destroyed. On the 25th, Henry Clinton learned for sure of Burgoyne's capture. Bitterly, he ordered Fort Clinton (Vaughan) destroyed. When that last bastion was razed, sweating soldiers filed down the steep path to waiting transports and were off. Then a protecting rear guard withdrew and the Highlands of the Hudson were once more American territory. On the afternoon of 28 October the *Spitfire* and *Crane*, the last vessels out of the Highlands, reached New York. Writing an inglorious footnote to a frustrating fortnight, the *Crane*, having lost both anchors, ran past the landing and grounded on Governor's Island. That seemed to Sir Henry to symbolize the expedition which had begun so brilliantly to end so dismally.[22]

The grandiose castle of a campaign erected by Burgoyne and Germain had crumbled to ruin, sending shudders into every court in Europe. Those famed Hudson River fortifications, built at the cost of so much Patriot time and treasure, had not withstood assault; but England, on the other hand, had been too weak to hold them. Howe had taken Philadelphia —or as some wit would later remark, Philadelphia had taken Howe—but Washington's splendid if unsuccessful battle at Germantown had mightily impressed Europeans with the stubbornness and resilience of American revolutionaries. Finally, the loss of Burgoyne's entire army was a body blow to British prestige that no amount of propaganda could cover. Even as smoke drifted skyward from sites of freshly burned forts on the Hudson's banks, fast packets were speeding across the Atlantic with the amazing news.

It had not been the Year of the Hangman; it was the year of salvation. France, for months a covert ally of America, was emboldened to side overtly with the rebels. Spain later declared war on George III; eventually the Dutch, too, became an active enemy of the British. England was no longer faced with suppressing a colonial uprising, but with waging a world-wide war of major proportions.

A measure of the deep-seated disappointment Sir Henry experienced at the turn of events is to be seen in the subsequent behavior of Mary Baddeley. Having previously turned back all his clumsily pressed, amorous advances, the sympathetic lady was overcome by the general's overwhelming despair when he returned from the Highlands. She became his mistress.

PART THREE

BUILDING WEST POINT

9

FIVE LOST MONTHS

WHEN Sir Henry departed he left in his wake razed forts, smashed and sunken ships, and a host of charred chimney stacks protruding nakedly from embers where once stood homes. With him as booty went 77 cannon, great quantities of iron, 6 tons of powder, several thousand cannon balls, and many more items of equipment, all from the supplies that had been so painfully and slowly accumulated by the Patriots at such sacrifice.[1]

It was good. Although they were unable to realize it and he did not know it, Henry Clinton had done his American enemies a favor. Despite the severe property losses, his coming had been a boon. Weapons taken when Burgoyne's army capitulated more than offset losses in the Highlands, gunpowder could and would be replaced, many boats could be refloated and river shipwrights were already busy laying new keels. Forge operators, the experience of one chain behind them, knew how to fabricate another better than the last. And, of course, rocks and logs and dirt could always be reshaped into the form of forts. So, none of the damage was permanent, and, in the long view, Sir Henry's visit served to pave the way for even stronger defenses. In that respect, his complete destruction of all existing fortifications redounded to Patriot advantage. Obliged to begin anew, engineers and officers would not approach their rebuilding task with vision obscured by blinders of already existing works. For the first time since James Clinton and Christopher Tappen had explored the area in 1775, men unbiased by considerations of labor and material already expended could search for locations and means to close the river. Henry Clinton's legacy was to give the Americans a chance to take a fresh, clean, new look.

Ideally, Patriots should have recognized previous errors and inconsistencies, should have benefited by their costly experiences, and would have discovered straightway where and how to erect better defenses. Ideally, too, they would have pitched into the job jestfully, vigorously. But efficiency was never a hallmark of our revolutionary ancestors; and nowhere was that fact better evidenced than in the Hudson Highlands. American fortification efforts in the five months following Henry Clinton's withdrawal were half farce, half futile, wholly frustrating.

It all began, appropriately enough, on 6 October. While British soldiers were battering their way through improperly designed defenses and a befuddled Israel Putnam was striving to discern just what it was they were doing, the Continental Congress sought to strengthen those very fortifications. Sitting in York, Pennsylvania, after fleeing Philadelphia before Sir William Howe's unchecked advance, Congressmen were startled to receive General Putnam's letter disclaiming responsibility should the Highlands fall. They dispatched an ambiguous letter to General Horatio Gates, then facing Burgoyne above Albany, directing him "to give such assistance for strengthening the defences of Hudson's River as the circumstances of his own department may admit, of which he is to judge." Next, Congress told General Washington "to send one of the four engineers to do duty at Fort Montgomery and the defences on Hudson's River." About the time those messages were being prepared, exultant English troops were raising victory whoops in Forts Clinton and Montgomery. Washington dutifully complied, dictating a letter to Lieutenant Colonel Lewis de la Radière, "I desire you will immediately proceed to Fort Montgomery and there take upon you the direction of such works as shall be deemed necessary by the commanding officer of that department." When Tench Tilghman, one of several aides serving the Commander-in-Chief, laid that letter before Washington for signature, British boats were underway to attack an impotent, empty Fort Constitution.[2]

To Putnam Washington penned, "Congress having recommended it to me to send an engineer to Fort Montgomery, I have instantly dispatched Lt. Colo. Radière upon that service." In what must go down as one of the tersest introductions on record, the General added, "He is the second in command of four gentlemen sent out by Doctr. Franklin and Mr. Deane."

One of Benjamin Franklin's priority missions as Minister to France had been "to secure skilled engineers, not exceeding four," who would be willing to serve in the Continental Army. The French Court complied, surreptitiously of course, with the request. Louis Le Bègue de Presle Duportail was chosen. He in turn selected three men to accompany him: Jean Baptiste de Gouvion, Jean Baptiste Joseph de Laumoy, and Lewis de la Radière. Duportail was a major in the French army, Laumoy and Radière captains, and Gouvion a lieutenant. Franklin agreed that they would be received in the Continental Army one step higher than their French rank, whereupon officials in France advanced all four one grade as they departed. Their reception in Philadelphia in July 1777 was less than warm. Congress and Washington had already been inundated by a horde of foreign fortune hunters and fame seekers whose willingness to serve the rebel cause in return for high pay and even higher rank was the cause of no little embarrassment. Many of them, like the four engineers, came with guarantees of commissions from American emissaries in Europe. All too great a percentage possessed second-rate military abilities, spoke little or no English, and demanded preferential treatment. As much as the new nation needed engineers, Duportail and his companions were looked upon at first as just another group of adventurers.

Nor did they act any differently. Congress, on 8 July, ordained Duportail colonel, Radière lieutenant colonel, and Gouvion major; Laumoy was ill and had not yet reached Philadelphia. Without so much as waiting for the ink to dry on his commission, Duportail pressed Congress to promote him to brigadier general and to raise the others one more grade as well. Congress refused, but it did prescribe that Duportail was to "take rank and command of all engineers heretofore appointed." Congress then directed the new engineers to join Washington. When they did, he promptly sent them back to Philadelphia. A French officer with higher rank but (presumably) lesser talent was already serving with the General, and Duportail was unable to conceal his "jealousy." During August and September, the unhappy Frenchmen worked at odd jobs connected with fortifying Philadelphia, and contemplated returning to France. They remained indignant at Congress' supposed slight, but pursued their quest for quick promotion. When Radière received instructions to repair to the Highlands, he was lobbying for rank. The officer who had been a captain in France only months before, who was now a Continental lieutenant colonel for doing nothing more than crossing the Atlantic, threatened to embark for France in January if he were not elevated to full colonel.[3]

In November Congress asked Washington's advice concerning Duportail and his companions. Should the engineers be promoted or permitted to return to Europe as they threatened? The General cautiously admitted that the four had previously had small opportunity to display their skills and he assumed they would do "essential service" if given a "proper occasion." He evaded the question of promotion, but indicated how scarce were men with engineering talents, and how very valuable. If they did resign, Washington concluded, "I would take the liberty to mention that I have been well informed that the engineer in the Northern Army (Cosieski, I think his name is)[*] is a gentleman of science and merit." Congress decided to retain them.[4]

Exactly when Radière arrived in the Highlands is uncertain. Washington's orders read, "immediately proceed to Fort Montgomery," but the French engineer appears not to have begun his journey quite that promptly. He reported for duty when—or soon after—Henry Clinton destroyed the forts and sailed away. His first mission was to assist in a reconnaissance to determine where the Highlands could best be defended.

[*] The individual referred to is Thaddeus Kosciuszko. Washington never could quite grasp the spelling of the Pole's name even though he tried every feasible way. Some other samples: "Koshiosko," "Kosuisko," "Kosciouski," "Kosciousko," "Kosciusko," "Cosciusko," "Koscuisco," "Koscuiszko." Once, in apparent surrender, he used two different variations in a single letter.

No sooner had Washington learned of Henry Clinton's disengagement than he advised Israel Putnam to request New York and Connecticut militiamen "to assist the Continental troops that remain with you in putting Forts Clinton and Montgomery in repair." Putnam was more interested in conducting forays against the British base in New York than in stacking stones in the Highlands, but, accompanied by James and George Clinton, Radière, and several others, he took a quick look at the ruins. The group studied the terrain and, over Radière's objections, concluded that West Point should be fortified. Putnam explained their joint decision in a letter to Washington dated 7 November 1777:

> Governor Clinton and myself have been down to view the forts, and are both of opinion that a boom, thrown across at Fort Constitution, and a battery on each side of the river, would answer a much better purpose than at Fort Montgomery; as the garrison would be reinforced by militia with more expedition, and the ground much more definable.
>
> All these circumstances considered, we have concluded to obstruct the navigation at the former place, and shall go about it immediately.[5]

Radière had no competing solution, but he protested the choice, wanting "to take more time to examine the ground." Putnam permitted him to conduct a more detailed investigation, and promptly turned his own thoughts to more interesting and active projects.

In Putnam's priority of things, starting construction "immediately" meant "later"—after he had repaid Henry Clinton by raiding Kingsbridge. Such troops as he could grasp he maneuvered through Westchester County toward New York City. As for Washington's suggestion to put militia units to work on the fortifications, it was not in the least practical. Winter was coming and those oft-summoned soldiers were unwilling to stay past the emergency; so far as the minutemen were concerned, the minute was over. James Clinton disconsolately complained, "I find it a very difficult task to keep the militia from strolling home; . . . we are daily sending after them."

In the meantime, Washington asked for troops from the northern theatre to reinforce him near Philadelphia, but received no cooperation from his compatriots. Horatio Gates, in Albany, ignored orders in a conspiratorial effort to wrest power from the Commander-in-Chief; Israel Putnam, in Peekskill, ignored directives in the bull-headed belief that his contemplated attack on New York was more important. When the replacements were slow in arriving, Washington sent an aide, Lieutenant Colonel Alexander Hamilton, speeding northward to hurry them on. On his way to Albany, the brilliant young officer carefully informed "Old Put" of the General's wishes. After a frustrating stay in upper New York, where he was only partially successful in obtaining the needed troops, he returned to New Windsor on 9 November. There, to his utter astonishment, he found Putnam persisting in his "farcical parade against New York." Moreover, those units which Putnam had condescended to forward had not yet marched. They were in disarray—unpaid, unhappy, undisciplined. Control was crumbling. A minor mutiny had erupted; to quell it a captain had felt obliged to run one of his men through, and was shot in return by the soldier's buddy. Moreover, the sickness rate was high. The "itch" was rampant, spreading through the ranks, immobilizing entire units. "Old Put," obsessed with attacking New York City, was oblivious to it all. "Governor Clinton has been the only man who has done anything toward removing them [sending reinforcements southward]; but for want of General Putnam's cooperation has not been able to effect it," the aide stingingly reported. Hamilton was not charged directly with checking the status of work on fortifications, but he inspected nonetheless. Although Putnam's obtuse doings no longer surprised him, he was depressed to learn that nothing was being done. Bitterly, he informed Washington:

> I fear, unless you interpose, the works here will go on so feebly for want of men that they will not be completed in time; whereas it appears to me of the utmost importance it should be pushed with the utmost vigor. Governor Clinton will do everything in his power. I wish General Putnam was recalled from the command of this post, and Governor Clinton would accept it. The blunders and caprices of the former are endless.[6]

As he was writing those acid words, Hamilton was stricken by "fever and violent rheumatic pains." He remained in bed in George Clinton's house until the symptoms departed, but when he attempted to resume his journey the disease returned full force. Reaching the barnlike home of Dennis Kennedy in Peekskill, the aide collapsed, hovering near death for over a month. That ended his mission to New York, but his alarming letter had reached Washington, informing that officer of the incredibly disordered state of affairs along the Hudson.

Despite a campaign in Pennsylvania that cried for all his attention, the Commander-in-Chief found time to approve the plan to erect defenses at West Point. However, he took no step to relieve Putnam, for Congress had already taken matters into its own hands. On 5 November the legislators passed a series of resolutions bearing directly and in detail on military operations, taking in the process a degrading swipe at the General. Congress ordered Horatio Gates to assume command of the Highlands, directed Washington to recall Israel Putnam, and specified that Gates was to have full power "to order such a number of galleys, gunboats, fire-rafts, chains, caissons, and *chevaux-de-frise* to be provided, and such fortifications to be erected, for obstructing and keeping possession of the North River, as he shall judge necessary." Congressmen further instructed Gates "to take effectual care that the fortifications which shall be erected on the North River be not too extensive, and that each be completed with a well, magazines, barracks, bomb-casements, etc., sufficient for a determined defence." General Washington may not have appreciated Congress' interference, but, as always, he bowed to civil authority. Reading the explicit Congressional directive sent to Gates, the Commander-in-Chief assumed that the hiatus in the Highlands would promptly be corrected. He therefore left Putnam in command until Gates should arrive.[7]

An undercurrent in Congress aimed at toppling George Washington was picking up steam and heading toward the climax that would be remembered as the "Conway Cabal." Horatio Gates was a central figure in the conspiracy, backed as he was in Congress by several New England delegates and glowing under munificent praise as the victor of Saratoga. After news of that battle reached Congress, John Adams, who had been nurturing an expanding jealousy of Washington's fame, identified his own position in an unguarded letter to his wife, Abigail:

> Congress will appoint a Thanksgiving; and one cause of it ought to be that the glory of turning the tide of arms is not immediately due to the Commander-in-Chief nor to southern troops. If it had been, idolatry and adulation would have been unbounded; so excessive as to endanger our liberties, for what I know. Now, we can allow a certain citizen to be wise, virtuous, and good, without thinking him a deity or a saviour.[8]

In the weeks following, Congress busied itself with establishing a new Board of War intended to take over a large share of the war's direction, thus further reducing Washington's influence.

Horatio Gates, a smallish man with ability to match, was unfortunately possessed of great ambition. Erecting forts in the Hudson Highlands did not appeal to him in the least. He remained in Albany angling for a better role. George Clinton began work on his own hook to complete more *chevaux-de-frise* for the Pollepel Island-Plum Point line, but nothing else was accomplished. Congress had quite clearly placed the responsibility in Gates' unwilling hands—and he as clearly planned to do nothing. His reward for such obedience was selection as President of the revamped Board of War. As November faded into December, the forts along the silver river were much as Henry Clinton had left them, except that snow was beginning to blanket the charred rubble.[9]

Informed of the total inactivity of Gates and Putnam throughout November, Washington exploded. Writing directly to Gates, he breathed fire in words polite but pointed. Gates was rebuked for not reporting what he was doing toward "repairing the old works or building new," and for not even indicating "when you might be expected down into that part of the country." The infuriated Virginian urged Gates to go to the Highlands "as speedily as possible." Then in a final burst of sarcasm he concluded, "You must be so well convinced of the importance of the North River that nothing more need be said to induce you to set about the security of it with the greatest vigour." In a letter to Putnam he was equally forceful but more direct. Starting by stating that the importance of the Hudson and the necessity of defending it were subjects so obvious "that it is unnecessary to enlarge upon them," the Commander-in-Chief went on to enlarge in some detail:

> These facts at once appear, when it is considered that it runs thro' a whole state; that it is the only passage by which the enemy . . . can ever hope to cooperate with an army . . . from Canada; that the possession of it is indispensably essential to preserve our communication between the Eastern, Middle and Southern States; and further, that upon its security . . . depend our chief supplies of flour for the subsistence of such forces as we may have . . . in the Eastern or Northern Departments or [along the Mohawk Valley].

Bitingly Washington declared, "These facts are familiar to all, they are familiar to you." To hammer his ideas through the "old gentleman's" mental fog, the General repeatedly and imperatively stated his instructions.

> Seize the present opportunity and employ your whole force and all the means in your power for erecting and completing . . . such works and obstructions as may be necessary to defend and secure the river. . . . I shall expect that you will exert every nerve and employ your whole force in future, while and whenever it is practicable, in constructing and forwarding the proper works and means of defence.

Even Putnam should have understood without the slightest doubt what the Commander-in-Chief was saying.[10]

When those epistolary upbraidings were well on their way, an extract from the proceedings of Congress reached headquarters informing Washington of Gates' selection as President of the Board of War. Whatever he may have thought about that business, he was quite pleased to have Gates removed from command of the Highlands fortifications. Without losing a day, he wrote to the one individual in New York whom he most trusted to do the work, Governor George Clinton. Defense of the Hudson is vital, he began, and "there cannot remain a doubt" that the enemy, as soon as winter is over, "will attempt to gain possession of it to prosecute their favorite plans of ruin and devastation." Would the Governor turn his attention "to this infinitely important object" and assist in raising defenses? "Nothing would be more pleasing to me, and I am convinced more advancive of the interest of the States, than for you to take the chief direction and superintendance of this business."[11]

While that higher-level maneuvering transpired, Radière was investigating all the sites between Pollepel Island and Popolopen Creek. He walked through the debris of thirty-months' labor, scrutinizing hills and slopes and river banks that already had been scanned so many times by so many others. Finally he drew up his own concept of where the river should be defended; not, he was convinced, in the place Putnam and the Clinton brothers had agreed upon earlier. In mid-December he sent a sketch straight to Congress—an action he admitted "does not belong directly to the engineer"—and took that opportunity to plead once more for the rank of colonel. It was a request as unnecessary as it was unbecoming, for Congress had at last succumbed to the blandishments of Duportail; it had raised each French engineer one rank. Radière was a colonel. The position he had craved was his; the question was, could he produce?[12]

Bad weather, worse roads, and an unaccountable wait at Israel Putnam's headquarters delayed Washington's letter to Clinton by more than two weeks. All the while that it lingered unread in someone's saddlebags nothing happened toward rebuilding forts. George Clinton, thinking Horatio Gates was still responsible for the defenses, deemed it improper to interfere, but at the same time he knew something should be done, and soon. He anxiously pleaded with Gates to "put things in a proper train." Couldn't he come to the Highlands "only for a few days," at least to get the work started? General Putnam was posturing around New York, "for what purpose he best knows," and could not be depended upon if Gates did not personally take an interest. The Governor might as well have saved his ink; Gates was eyeing larger game. Anyhow, before Gates could have responded to Clinton's entreaty, Washington's letter came asking the Governor to undertake the effort.[13]

Writing thoughtfully at his desk in Poughkeepsie, George Clinton prepared a lengthy reply in which he thoroughly discussed all aspects of the problem and promised faithfully to devote "every leisure hour" to the defenses; but he declined the command on grounds that gubernatorial duties would preclude his giving full attention to the task. On new fortifications, he had explicit advice:

> I am clearly of opinion that a strong fortress ought to be erected on the opposite side of the creek from where Fort Montgomery stood or at the West Point opposite Fort Constitution. The latter I prefer as the most defensible ground and because the navigation of the river there is more difficult and uncertain and the river something narrower than it is at the former place. A new chain should be procured (if possible) and . . . stretched across the river.[14]

One wonders if it crossed his mind that he was suggesting the same thing—in much the same words—that his brother had recommended nearly three years earlier?

Christmas passed. Gates did not show, nor did Putnam. Snow fell. Washington and his already suffering Continentals were building huts in Valley Forge. Putnam had asked for a furlough to look after private affairs subsequent to the death of his wife; Washington agreed so long as General Samuel Parsons remained on duty "carrying on the works upon the river." But as for those works, "hardly anything is yet done at them and little I think is to be expected," was George Clinton's comment in a letter to a friend. "The good man's views," he wrote, referring to Israel Putnam, "are not calculated for things of this sort." The New Year came.[15]

In the first days of 1778, Radière requested Putnam to call a council of war charged with "fixing a plan of defense for Hudson's River." He prepared a grandiloquent memorial designed to convince the council of the logic in "fortifying the hill upon which Fort Clinton was in preference to any other place." His conclusion stated blandly that there were many and strong arguments for erecting a bastion on the eminence where once squatted Fort Clinton, few and weak reasons for building a fort on West Point. Apparently the engineer had spent the better part of December marshaling his arguments, for he produced to bolster his stand three additional studies, all voluminous and detailed, relating to techniques of constructing forts and methods of blocking the river. Steeped in European concepts of attacking massive forts by formal approaches in methodical and ritualistic sieges, Radière saw the problem basically as one of building a fortress that could best withstand a classical siege. There was insufficient space between Fort Clinton and Bear Mountain for such stylized approaches to be conducted, nor would the rocky surface itself permit the digging of parallels and trenches. Behind West Point, on the other hand, stretched a large plain of gravelly soil admirably suited for siege works. Therefore, it was simply out of the question to raise a bastion anywhere but on the ruins of Fort Clinton.

The Frenchman's template for sieges, taken straight out of a book, made that conclusion inevitable.[16]

"Old Put" felt himself on shaky ground. Paperwork was not his strength. Radière stood alone against all the Americans, but that stack of memorials, prepared by a "man of science," and purportedly taken from the teachings of Vauban, the immortal French military engineer, was foreboding. Stopping in Fishkill on his way to set up headquarters in Moore's House on West Point, Putnam worriedly queried George Clinton. The Governor's curt reply was, "I have already given my opinion in favor of West Point and I have hitherto heard no sufficient reasons to change my sentiments." Furthermore, Clinton was singularly unimpressed by Radière. He thought the Frenchman smart in terms of "scientific" training but "deficient in point of practical knowledge," which, in the Governor's mind, made the engineer "unfit . . . for the present task."[17]

That stand only deepened Putnam's concern. He next requested advice from the New York Legislature. On 8 January that body appointed a committee "to confer with him relative to the necessary works to be constructed for the defences of the passes in the Highlands." Nine men were chosen. At once they met with Israel Putnam and James Clinton to hear the reasoning of Radière. Nothing was decided. Noting unnecessarily that "a disagreement in sentiment" existed between the generals and the engineer, the committee recommended that commissioners be appointed "to view the several passes on Hudson River . . . and advise in fixing the places where such fortifications should be erected." That suggestion was readily adopted and five commissioners named. Four of them departed on an inspection tour almost immediately. To William Bedlow, a commissioner himself back in 1775–1776 and now a paymaster for New York State, history must have seemed to be repeating itself: commissioners in the Highlands; committees from the state government; a stubborn engineer; disagreement; no sign of progress.

After carefully examining both of the proposed sites and listening to Radière expound his case, the commissioners voted unanimously for West Point. Fort Clinton, they felt, could not be rebuilt before spring whereas a fortified post at West Point could be raised in winter. Importantly, a chain would be more effective there than at the southern location. Militia could better support West Point, although a citadel on that promontory would indeed be more vulnerable to a siege across the light soil on the large plain behind it. Finally, batteries at water level could also be located to protect both ends of the chain if it stretched from West Point to Constitution Island. That report was delivered in on 14 January 1778, but the decision had been taken two days earlier.[18]

Commissioners, the engineer, and generals had all assembled late on the 12th. Learning that he would be backed by the Yorkers, Putnam designated West Point as the site to be defended.

Radière exploded in Gallic fury. The ignorant Americans did not comprehend the finer points of siege warfare! He was disgusted. All his fine memorials, careful sketches, blueprints—wasted. To Duportail, General Washington, Congress—in fact to anyone who might help reverse the decision—he dashed off hurried letters making it plain what a mistake was being made. Such lack of tact did not endear the Frenchman to his American commanders nor increase his popularity with contemporaries. For once displaying some wit, Israel Putnam called him "an excellent paper engineer," and stated, "I am confident if Congress would have found business for him with them, our works would have been as well constructed and much more forward than they now are." Muttering unhappily in French, "It is better to fortify a place less good than to do nothing at all," and other phrases which were never translated, Radière went to West Point and began marking outlines for a future fortress. It was the middle of January.[19]

Ice was thick on the Hudson. Teams hauling loaded sleighs safely traversed it, both man and beast glad to swap narrow, steep, twisting trails through the hills for the broad, level ice-way. Officers assembled a regiment of the brigade of Brigadier General Samuel Holden Parsons when word arrived that the French engineer had completed his initial survey. Major Samuel Richards marched the regiment over the river and up the sharp cliff to the plain. The day was 20 January 1778. Snow was two feet deep. Major Richards remembered it this way:

> Coming on to the small plain surrounded by high mountains, we found it covered with a growth of yellow pines ten or fifteen feet high; no house or improvement on it, the snow waist high. We fell to lopping down the tops of scrub pines and treading down the snow, spread our blankets, and lodged in that condition the first and second nights. Had we not been hardened by two years of previous service, we should have thought it difficult to endure this.[20]

American soldiers had come to West Point. There would never be a day from that moment to this when the encircling granite hills would cease to echo the tread of marching feet, the camaraderie of camp, the boom of reveille gun.

Some rough lumber that had escaped burning lay scattered around the old fort sites. It was gathered and brought to West Point, but by far the bulk of the building material had first to be cut. Each day details with axes trudged off to "draw logs from the edge of the mountains and procure the luxury of log huts." Other men picked rushes from the swamp behind Constitution Island to thatch roofs. Soon log cabins, crude but snug, nestled "just below the summit of the upper bank that they might be partially sheltered from the northwest wind."

By the time that first garrison had housed itself, January was all but gone. George Washington, with troubles aplenty in Valley Forge, grew increasingly concerned over the snail's pace of progress in the Highlands. His patience stretching visibly thin, he had queried Putnam on 15 January, "I shall be glad to know whether anything is now doing or whether anything of consequence has yet been done towards repairing the works and replacing and completing the obstructions in the North River." Ten days later he received Putnam's epistle informing him of the decision to defend at West Point. The Commander-in-Chief may not have remembered the exact date, but he must have recalled that "Old Put" had promised to "go about immediately" doing precisely the same thing at the same place some

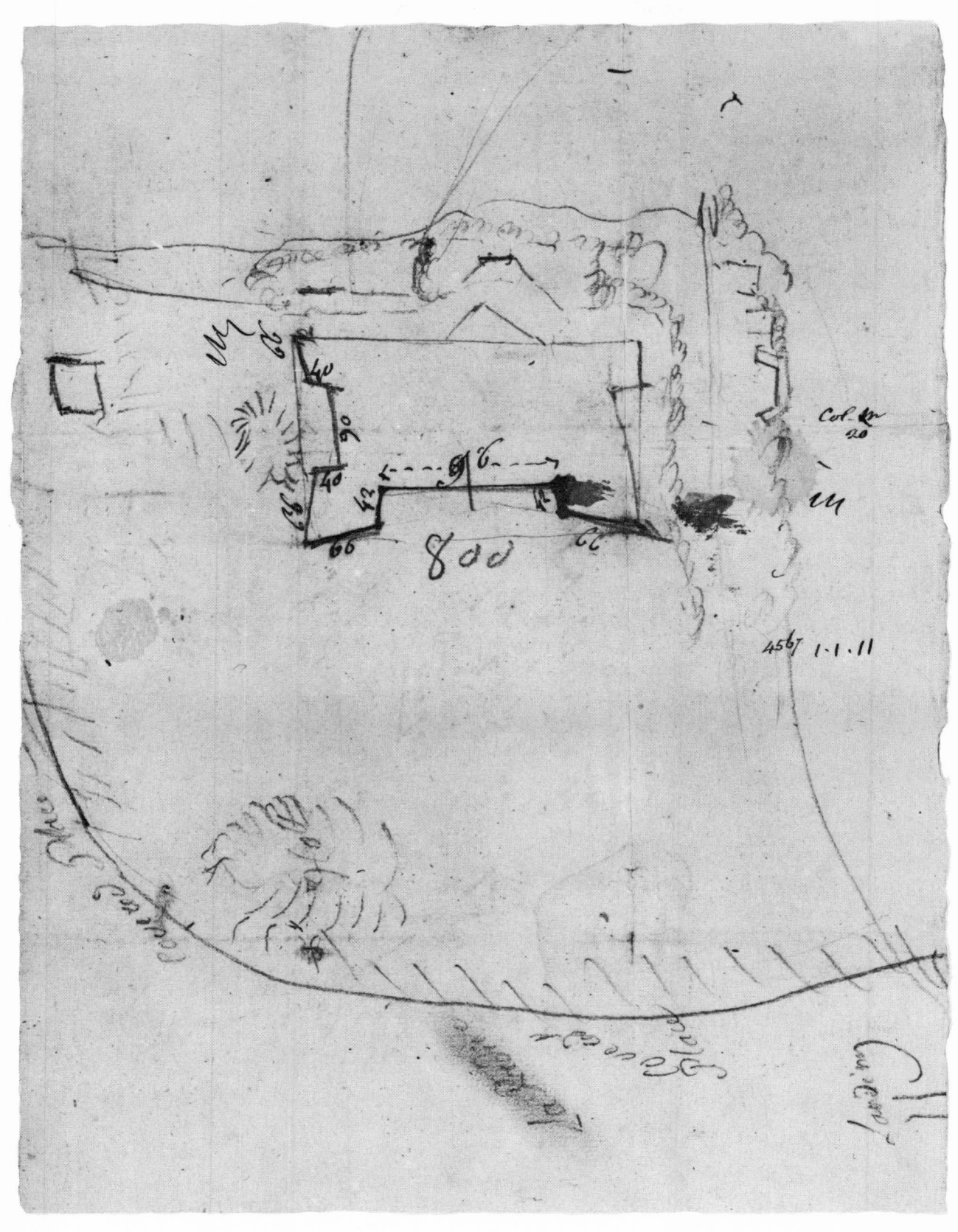

Earliest known sketch of Fort Arnold (Clinton) at West Point. Sketched in February or March 1778. The name nearly rubbed out at the bottom, center, is "La Radière." Courtesy of the New-York Historical Society Library.

141

ten weeks earlier! Obviously upset with Putnam's procrastination, and not without justification, Washington was "very apprehensive that the season will entirely pass away before anything material will be done for the defence of Hudson's River." Time was running by; if the river were not closed by spring, British forces could have it for the asking. "I most earnestly desire," he asserted, "that the strictest attention may be paid to every matter which may contribute to finishing and putting [the works] in a respectable state before the spring." On the same date he wrote directly to Radière urging him to accept and support the decision to fortify West Point. "If we remain much longer disputing about the proper place, we shall lose the winter," he explained.[21]

Hoping to mollify the General, Putnam described in glowing terms all the advances recently made. Water batteries and a large fort to protect them had been "laid out." A road leading from the high plain to a river landing had been made "with great difficulty." "Barracks and huts for about three hundred men are completed, and barracks for about the same number are covered." Men continued to work on *chevaux-de-frise* to strengthen the Pollepel Island barrier. A chain and the necessary anchors "are contracted for." Parts of the Fort Montgomery boom, "sufficient for this place," were available. Radière's great fort was to have walls 14 feet high, 21 feet thick, and 600 feet in interior length. Almost as an afterthought, in the letter's last sentence, Putnam mentioned that he was departing for Connecticut the next day, leaving General Parsons in command. Boiled down to essentials, Putnam's message stated that he was handing Parsons a West Point innocent of any defenses whatsoever and devoid of structures other than some quarters for the troops. Worse, he did not consider it necessary to furnish Parsons with "any account of what is prepared or where the various works are carrying on; what workmen are employed; what materials are now ready or tools to work with." On taking over, General Parsons reported "everything in confusion . . . perfect chaos."[22]

"Old Put's" departure was not lamented by New Yorkers. Governor Clinton and his legislators had been quite anxious to get on with a program of construction in the Highlands; Putnam's lethargy and hesitancy had aggravated them. For their part they had provided money, workers, and advice, and had even settled an argument between the general and his own engineer. In return, nothing much had happened so far as they could see. Parsons discovered a distinct lack of cooperation from local inhabitants and blamed it on "their tempers [being] soured with the general who commands the department." Robert R. Livingston summed up New York sentiment in a private letter to General Washington dated 14 January: "I respect his bravery and former services, and sincerely lament that his patriotism will not suffer him to take that repose to which his advanced age and past services justly entitle him." Replying after Putnam was gone, Washington admitted that "the prejudices of all ranks in [New York] against him are so great that he must at all events be prevented from returning."[23]

Command arrangements remained unsettled through the winter, thanks largely to Congress' irritating habit of taking the initiative from Washington in making military appointments, often without so much as conferring with him first. On 18 February, after George Clinton had already rejected Washington's request that he take charge of construction in the Highlands, Congressmen voted "that Governor Clinton be authorized and requested to superintend the business of obstructing, fortifying, and securing the passes of Hudson's River." That left General Parsons on very unsure footing, even though Clinton once more declined the request. Asking Washington to clarify the situation, Parsons cited Congress' resolves of 5 November 1777 and 18 February 1778, as well as Washington's several letters to Putnam to show that, technically, *no one* had command in the Highlands. "I most ardently wish to aid Governor Clinton or any gentleman appointed to superintend the work," he wrote, exasperation evident in his tone; "at present no one has the direction, I suppose it to be because no man chooses to be responsible for the post; I have kept the troops at work because I found them here when I took command."[24]

Nor was a command vacuum Parsons' only problem. Weather was bad in late February and early March. No work at all was accomplished during 7 of those days. Snow piled up and the ground froze deeper. Food and clothing were in short supply. At Valley Forge Washington reported "a famine in camp." His men were "naked and starving." He asked George Clinton to marshal New York's resources to provide "any assistance, however trifling." Governor William Livingston of New Jersey, taking such requests to heart, suggested a novel source of clothing. Noting that "the rural ladies in [Bergen County] pride themselves in an incredible number of petticoats," he recommended that those undergarments be requisitioned for Continental service. "I have only to observe," he justified his rather unchivalrous thought, "that the generality of the women in that county, having for above a century *worn the breeches,* it is highly reasonable that the men should now . . . make booty of petticoats." At first blush, the mental picture of hardened Continental soldiers marching guard in female underwear is ludicrous, but clothing of any sort would have been gladly accepted by men freezing for the lack of it. Their suffering was indeed extreme. General Washington proclaimed—hinting darkly, perhaps—that he could not "enough admire the incomparable patience and fidelity of the soldiery, that they have not been ere this excited by their sufferings to a general mutiny and dispersion." Conditions in the Highlands, miserable enough, were good by comparison with Valley Forge; it may be, then, that "patience and fidelity" were present in shorter measure, because a mutiny of sorts erupted at West Point. The artificers (skilled workers) refused to labor under adverse conditions except on their own terms. Parsons brooked no such nonsense. Taking into consideration that they had been "a refractory set of men for a long time and seem to have agreed that they will not work 'till their own terms and particular inclinations are complied with," he rounded them up at bayonet point and court-martialed the lot. In future they performed better, but meanwhile irreplaceable time had been lost.[25]

Incidentally, it was during this period that the Moores of West Point left the land their father had settled, never to return. In actuality, if not legally, West Point became government property. General Parsons believed that so long as Tories continued to live there, the enemy would obtain information on the new fortress. Furthermore, as houses were scarce, the Red House would serve the Patriot cause well as a headquarters for the commander and his staff. Charles Moore, upon being told to vacate, asked for permission to move into Beverley Robinson's home as the Robinson family had recently left the Highlands for New York. That request was denied; Robinson's home, too, had been converted to public use, which, at that time, meant army use. Late that winter the Moores joined thousands of other refugees uprooted by the war. Soldiers' boots echoed in the corridors and rooms of "Moore's Folly."

Besides command confusion and inclement weather and reluctant workers, trouble with the engineer bubbled over in March. All along a rupture had lurked just below the surface. From the first Radière had made but slight effort to conceal his disdain for Americans and their miserable military talents while missing no opportunity to preen his own virtues. On top of that open sense of superiority add his habit of dashing off complaining letters to Congress and Commander-in-Chief, and the regard he engendered among those men responsible for conducting construction in the Highlands begins to come into focus. His contentious stand for Fort Clinton as opposed to West Point, in the face of unanimous disagreement and continuing long after the decision had been made, earned him no friends. Then, lending impetus to the resentment sprouting up against him, he had created a minor furor early in January by transgressing the always touchy subject of command relationships. His commission as engineer did not authorize him to command troops. Nonetheless, discovering himself temporarily the senior officer at New Windsor, he had assumed the role of commander and forthwith thrown another officer, an American, into jail. An immediate howl of protest arose. Israel Putnam shortly put him in his place, but feelings had been bruised all around. Thus it was that when the French engineer and the American officers at West Point approached the task of erecting defenses there was an atmosphere of mutual animosity. But all of those squabbles were background; the final breach came from disagreement over the design of the fortress at West Point.[26]

Radière envisioned a massive masonry work done in dimension and design suitable to European standards. In his mind's eye he saw a great crag of a fortress perched far out on the point, looming high above the river and constructed to withstand a siege of two or three weeks' duration. The ring of hills looking down from the west on the projected stronghold he recognized as potentially dangerous positions from which an enemy could command his bastion, but his solution was to enlarge and strengthen the western walls of the fort. When he first traced outlines in the snow, no one thought to question him. But as plans were drawn up, the impracticality of his scheme became apparent. Even General Putnam thought it might be "too large to be completed by the time expected." Putnam, as a matter of fact, sent a letter which was considered in Congress, complaining of the engineer's entire behavior and performance. On 4 March Congress delegated responsibility for the Highlands fortifications to the Board of War. The Board was "to give such directions to Colonel Radière" as were dictated by the good of the service. Next day, Horatio Gates, in his capacity as

President of the Board of War, informed the commander in the Highlands that his Board well understood "the inefficacy of the endeavors of Colonel la Radière and two other French engineers [Duportail and Gouvion] to raise the works they had injudiciously planned elsewhere." Then Gates concisely summed up the dilemma Americans faced in dealing with their French friends:

> . . . and the Board are thoroughly convinced that, if the actual construction of the works on the North River be left to Colonel la Radière, they will not be completed till the next campaign is ended, altho' 5000 men should be at his direction. At all events therefore, the Board desire you to employ that engineer as far as you shall find him really useful and no farther. We would wish to avoid offense to any foreigners who have interested themselves in our cause; we would treat them with all possible respect: But we must not sacrifice or hazard our safety from a point of delicacy.[27]

In other words, humor him as much as possible, gain all feasible benefit from his knowledge, but don't let his wild ideas carry you too far afield.

Parsons and others discussed the matter with the Frenchman in logic clean and simple: not much time remained before the ice would break up permitting British ships to sail upriver; to build the ponderous citadel proposed would take months when only days or at most weeks were available. Furthermore, funds for such a vast project were nonexistent. Colonel Radière retired to his quarters in Moore's house, ordered his clerk, a recent deserter from the British, to spread out once more his drawings. He studied them, broodingly contemplating a less ambitious plan. But his heart was not in it; the Americans had forced West Point upon him and now they were trying to tell him how to build the fort as well. Crossing the ice to Parsons' headquarters in Beverley Robinson's home, the stubborn Frenchman adamantly requested permission to leave in order to place his arguments before higher authority. Although warmer weather in early March led General Parsons to believe ground could be broken in a few days, he authorized Radière's departure. To Washington he explained:

> Colonel Radière finding it impossible to complete the fort and other defenses intended at this post in such manner as to effectually withstand attempts of the enemy to pass up the river early in the spring, and not choosing to hazard his reputation on works erected on a different scale, calculated for a short duration only, has desired leave to wait on your excellency and Congress, which I have granted him.[28]

It had been anything but an enjoyable winter for Parsons. Nothing had seemed to go right, he had few resources to accomplish so grave a responsibility, and resistance sprang from all sides. The deep gray gloom of that time of year at that place—something noted even today at modern West Point—did nothing to add cheer to a cheerless situation. In response to an inquiry from a friend, he wrote:

> You ask me where I can be found? This is a puzzling question; the camp is at a place on Hudson's River called West Point, opposite where Fort Constitution once stood. The situation is past description, surrounded with almost inaccessible mountains, and craggy rocks which overtop the

highest hills, at present covered with piles of snow. . . . The surrounding prospect affords [a] great variety of hills, mountains, rocks, which seem to shut up every avenue to us . . . ; to a contemplative mind which delights in a lonely retreat from the world . . . 'tis as beautiful as Sharon, but affords to a man who loves the society of the world a prospect nearly allied to the shades of death; here I am to be found at present in what situation of mind you will easily imagine.[29]

Serving to compound that doleful outlook, another missive from Washington reached West Point as Radière rode away. General Parsons knew without opening it that the Commander-in-Chief would urge his "strictest attention to a work of so much consequence."

Much of March was gone. Ice still clogged the river, but not a single man-made obstacle had been added. Moreover, artillery had yet to be sited over the waterway. It had been intended all along to arm West Point with British cannon captured at Fort Ticonderoga in 1777. Heavier guns especially were desired. Men had labored to prepare them for movement south on the frozen river, but like so many other things that went wrong that winter, they were not shipped. Much against Washington's advice, Congress had planned a winter invasion of Canada. It proved to be entirely abortive, never progressing above Albany, but the diversion delayed movement of the cannon. By late March, long after the ice had broken up, men in the Highlands had no idea where the cannon were. Not that it made much difference; there was no place to mount guns had they been present. A site for a fort had been selected, but the first spade of earth remained to be turned. On paper a magnificent fortress existed, but it was beyond, far beyond, the Patriots' limited time and pinched means. And the engineer, obstinately convinced that everyone else was in error, had quit just when work was ready to start. Henry Clinton's destructive visit was now five months in the past—five lost months.[30]

10

THE GREAT CHAIN

NOT EVERYTHING went wrong during

those ill-spent five months. It seems always to have been assumed that regardless of which location was fortified, another chain would be drawn across the river. The commissioners appointed by New York's Legislature to advise Putnam had listed among their reasons for recommending West Point:

> Three hundred feet less of chain will be requisite at this place than at Fort Clinton. It will be laid across in a place where vessels going up the river most usually lose their headway. Water batteries may be built on both sides of the river for protecting the chain and annoying the ships coming up the river, which will be completely commanded from the walls of the fort.[1]

And two months before that, Israel Putnam and the Clinton brothers had seen the benefits of closing the river at West Point by means of "a boom, thrown across at Fort Constitution." In December, George Clinton had recommended that "a new chain should be procured if possible." No evidence exists to indicate anyone ever thought the river could be blocked without a chain. The only questions were where and how to fabricate one. Since the eventual location of the fortress was of no concern to ironworkers, forges could be fired and the task begun right away.

Early in January Colonel Hugh Hughes, a deputy quartermaster for the Continental Army, was working closely with New York State authorities to coordinate construction of floating batteries, gun boats, and a chain. By midmonth George Clinton was searching for "a number of anchors and cables to fix the rafts for buoying the New Chain intended to be drawn across the river." A joint committee of the Senate and Assembly of New York's Legislature turned its full attention to the river defenses, grandly expostulating that "every possible exertion ought to be made to finish the water obstructions." For the making of a chain, the lawmakers decreed, "all the ironworks in the country which have proper metal and conveniences for the purpose should be immediately employed at making different parts of it."[2]

In conferences the design of the chain was discussed and debated. Everything about the Fort Montgomery chain had been satisfactory, the experts concluded, except its size and strength. Colonel Hughes, armed with advice from Machin and George Clinton, decided to make the new parts from heavier metal. Whereas the old links had been about an inch and a half through, bar iron for the new ones would be drawn two and a quarter inches square, more than doubling the cross-sectional area and hence the tensile strength. Clevises and swivels would also be correspondingly larger. The design settled, Hughes and Machin set out for Chester, New York, to "agree for the new chain" with Peter Townsend, manager of the Sterling Ironworks.[3]

Hughes hit a snag immediately. Townsend had not yet been paid for the last chain and, as a hard-headed businessman, he could not let patriotism interfere with good business procedures; if Hughes wanted another chain, he must first fork over funds outstanding on the last one. Unhappily, money was at the head of a long list of things the quartermaster was unable to procure. The Continental Army's war chest was bare. Dejectedly, Hughes hurried to Poughkeepsie to plead with Governor Clinton. With £5,000, he explained, there should be "little or no difficulty in getting all the iron that is necessary." Without it, however, "the business of a chain for the security of the river must be retarded." It had only been two days since the Legislature had recommended in such strong language that "every possible exertion" should be made. George Clinton put them to the test. Warning that "the least delay in the prosecution of this important business may be attended with the most fatal consequences," he earnestly recommended the granting of the amount requested. Passing resolutions required no funds; implementing them did. Not surprisingly, New York was unable to provide Hughes all he needed. The State's "situation in the money way" was hardly better than the Continental Army's. Indeed, specie was so scarce and paper depreciating so rapidly that the members of the legislature soon began to take a portion of their own pay in wheat and flour. "Faced with insuperable difficulties for want of cash," Hughes nevertheless persevered. Incurring debts in both New York and Connecticut, the hard-working officer somehow scraped together enough money—£4,027—to allow Townsend to reconcile his divergent motives of profit and patriotism. Later, in February, the Continental Congress voted $50,000 to George Clinton "towards defraying the charge" of securing the "passes of the North or Hudson's River."[4]

On 2 February 1777, while a snowstorm raged outside Townsend's

The surviving links of the Great Chain, displayed on the plain of West Point. U.S. Army photograph.

house, Colonel Hughes and the ironmonger sat down around a roaring log fire to hammer out details of a contract for the chain:

ARTICLES OF AGREEMENT between Noble, Townsend & Company, Proprietors of the Sterling Iron Works, . . . and Hugh Hughes, D. Q. M. G. to the army of the United States. . . .

That the said Noble, Townsend & Company . . . engage to have made and ready to be delivered . . . on or before the first day of April, . . . or as much sooner as circumstances will admit, an Iron Chain . . . in length five hundred yards,—each link about two feet long, to be made of the best Sterling Iron, two inches and one quarter square, . . . with a swivel to every hundred feet, and a clevis to every thousand weight in the same manner of the former chain.

Also, Townsend agreed to produce "at least twelve tons of anchors . . . as soon as the completion of the chain will permit." Hughes consented to pay at the rate of £440 per ton in Continental money. Figuring the total weight of links, clevises, swivels, and anchors at about 65 tons, the price for iron alone amounted to nearly £30,000—not cheap by any consideration and exceedingly costly when the purchaser is destitute.[5]

Hughes and George Clinton agreed to exempt sixty workers from military duty for nine months, "providing such persons shall be steadily employed in the business of iron-making and working at the said works." No explanation was made for granting nine months' exemption for two months' work. Probably it was inducement to get men to labor for lower wages, evidence again of the scarcity of money. Peter Townsend's son, writing many years after the event, recalled that his father left that same night for the Sterling Ironworks and fired the furnaces. Whether or not he began quite so quickly, he certainly lost little time. In very short order, forges were blazing around the clock in a race to complete the chain by April.

From the start, Thomas Machin, the "ingenious, faithful hand" Washington had long ago ordered to the Highlands, was charged with the responsibility for assembling and fixing the chain. Before Israel Putnam left his Highlands post, he addressed a series of questions to Governor Clinton, one of which was, "Who would you recommend to have direction of making and sinking the *chevaux-de-frise?*" Naming Machin, the Governor explained that no one else knew how many "are yet wanted and where to be sunk so as to perfect the obstructions." Clinton went on to advise, "The preparations for drawing the chain and boom across the river ought in my opinion also to be under his direction as he fixed the last chain, which was well done, and of course understands that business." Quite some time before that was written, however, Machin was already on the job. New Year's Day found him "exploring Hudson's River" for a site to place a chain, while his account of expenses on 20 January shows that immediately after he and Hughes first met with Townsend he was "getting timber for the chain." Knowing what had to be done, he had tarried for neither money nor contract. The chain was his project, a fact understood and accepted by everyone. In a move obviously intended to clarify the position of Machin vis-à-vis Radière, and as obviously telling Radière to keep out of Machin's hair, the Board of War "particularly" ratified the "appointment of Captain Machin to superintend the making of the chain."[6]

Townsend kept his smiths hard at work through February and into March, apparently suffering no major breakdowns or shortages. On 25 February General Parsons braved choking drifts "to visit the ironworks and find the situation of the chain." All must have been in reasonable order and progressing satisfactorily for the general made no complaints.

In the first week of March, Machin traveled to New Paltz, "getting the logs to use for the chain." It was planned to drag the huge logs to New Windsor where they would be shaped and sharpened, then dried and treated with tar and oakum. There also, sections of the chain would be stapled to them. Although West Point was nearer the Sterling Ironworks than was New Windsor, geography dictated the longer route. A level valley floor connected Townsend's forges with New Windsor whereas steep and snowbound ridges intersected a direct line from the ironworks to West Point. As Machin was obtaining tree trunks 40 to 50 feet in length, and cutting them into 16-foot sections, Townsend began shipping the first links by sleigh. Colonel Hughes stepped in, however, and temporarily halted movement of the iron, fearing that taking the chain to the Hudson before "the works are in some measure defensible" would risk unnecessarily its loss in a raid. Furthermore, he had learned that teamsters were demanding and getting £50 per ton "for the transportation of iron to the river, which is a most astonishing price." A pause in deliveries would give him a chance to seek out cheaper teams. Also, river ice could be expected soon to break up, permitting boats to assume much of the burden of moving supplies, which would in turn free local teams and hopefully drive the exorbitant price down. A harried quartermaster in that bargain-basement war had to cut every possible corner when it came to fiscal affairs.[7]

Machin and Hughes were also combing the countryside for "cordage" and "white-rope." Hemp, like nearly everything else, was in short supply. It was needed to make lines to steady the chain. Agents ranged into Connecticut as well as up and down the river, acting under the broad guidance that rope of "all sizes would be wanted." Gradually, piece by piece, it was accumulated. Splicers worked for weeks converting the miscellaneous bits into sturdy, dependable rope cables.[8]

A letter from George Washington came into Alexander McDougall's hands on 21 March. It directed McDougall, now a major general, to proceed to the Highlands where he was to assume command "of the different posts in that department." In battles around Philadelphia, McDougall had convinced Washington that he was a real fighter after all. His first order of business would be to conduct an investigation into the loss of Forts Montgomery and Clinton; that done, he was to turn his attention "to the completion of the works or at least to putting them in such a state that they may be able to resist a sudden attack of the enemy." McDougall did not like his assignment to the Highlands, but he accepted the duty without complaint. He arrived in Fishkill on the 25th and immediately opened a "Court of Enquiry." When that business was over, he journeyed to West Point and concerned himself with the erection of defenses there. Chaining a river was nothing new to him—he had commanded in the Highlands a year earlier when the Fort Montgomery chain had been successfully installed.[9]

It had been intended originally to stretch the chain from a spot on the West Point shore about four hundred yards upriver from jutting Gee's Point, the easternmost portion of the promontory. There the river was narrowest, approximating the five hundred yards cited in the contract for the chain. By April a capstan had been built on that spot (just east of modern-day North Dock) and preparations were well along on anchor points and fixtures for guys from shore. Someone, perhaps McDougall himself, raised the question of the need for a battery or redoubt to protect that end of the chain. None had been planned. All battery sites were several hundred feet farther downriver under the frowning fort going up on the top of West Point. It was a good question; there was a requirement for a position of some kind to overwatch the chain's vulnerable juncture with the shore. But it was already April. The British could strike up the river before even a small work could be completed. Engineer advice was needed. Colonel Radière was back at West Point by then and the Polish Engineer, Colonel Thaddeus Kosciuszko, was also on hand—but the man everyone most naturally turned to was Captain-lieutenant Thomas Machin. (Between trips relating to the chain, that active officer had also found time to go "in pursuit of deserters.") Machin came to West Point at McDougall's request on 10 April. He was joined by Governor Clinton, General James Clinton, General Parsons, and General McDougall. They carefully examined the irregular shoreline where Flirtation Walk now wends and "determined to fix the chain under the cover of the fire of the fort, for the present, as it would be some time before the work could be finished to cover a battery where the capstan is now fixed." Machin assured them that the chain could be attached in the small cove directly below the large fort and in front of a battery (later called Chain Battery) already in place. Although considered then as a temporary expedient, the location selected by Machin was used throughout the war.[10]

Machin returned right away to New Windsor where he resumed putting everything together. Colonel Hughes had permitted Townsend to ship the remainder of the chain toward the end of March. It was stacked up near the mouth of Murderer's Creek in sections of ten links and a clevis. Swivels and anchors lay nearby in a separate pile. Forty straining men took four days to drag and roll and float the massive, treated logs into position. Once at the site the logs were combined by fours into rafts and held together by 12-foot timbers. Then followed the back-breaking task of connecting sections of chain and tugging them onto the rafts. That done, the whole affair was floated down to West Point and beached in front of Moore's house on 16 April.[11]

Some unforeseen difficulty arose. For one thing, the river's width at the new location was greater by a hundred yards than at the original site; perhaps enough extra links and clevises had not been turned out. Whatever the need, Machin had to make a special trip to the Sterling Ironworks to superintend the construction of new parts. When he returned in late April, all pieces of the chain were ready. On the last day of the month, repeating the operation he had performed three times before at Fort Montgomery, the engineer coordinated the efforts of a fleet of boats and a bevy of men on shore, tugging on lines or straining on capstan arms, to ease the chain across the river. It was made fast on both Constitution Island and West Point, anchor lines were snugged taut, and the boats backed away. The new chain, the Great Chain, was a reality. George Clinton dispatched a congratulatory note to Thomas Machin, relating his pleasure "to learn that the chain is across the river, and that you had the good fortune to accomplish it so expeditiously and so much to your satisfaction."[12]

11

AN ENGINEER FROM POLAND

WHILE Thomas Machin was struggling successfully to chain the Hudson, General Parsons began to see a flicker of hope that he might make some headway toward erecting a fortress to complement the iron barrier. His optimism started when Radière quit.

The French engineer was not gone a week before Parsons was prepared to commence work on the fort and water batteries. "We shall begin to break ground in two days," he informed George Clinton, "when we shall be able to employ five hundred men more than we now have to great advantage; in ten days or a fortnight, we can employ five hundred more." That is, by the first of April he intended to have things in full swing. Parsons specifically requested that Colonel Rufus Putnam's regiment be one of those detailed to perform labor at West Point, saying, "He will be very useful, being much acquainted with the duty of an engineer." Wanting only units that could be trusted to do a maximum of building with a minimum of bickering, he begged the Governor to reject the assignment of the "Congress' Own," a group described as a "regiment of infernals." Meanwhile, Parsons needed an engineer to get things going pending arrival of Rufus Putnam or some assigned engineer. With no hesitation, he turned to the ubiquitous Thomas Machin, writing on 11 March, "As Colonel la Radière has left us, I wish you, if you can be absent from New Windsor for a day, to come to this post tomorrow or the day after, to advise about the proper method of fortifying this place."[1]

Machin got that letter the next day. Hurriedly completing several items of business—including matters relating to the management of George Clinton's farm, another task he had undertaken—he rushed off to West Point. There, under his supervision, the first spade of earth was turned, the fort begun. He could not remain, but before returning to his duties on chain, *chevaux-de-frise*, and country estate, he organized the workers and gave Parsons a suggested schedule of construction. Towering bluffs rising steeply out of the river provide a degree of protection from that direction, he reasoned; therefore, it is most important to raise first of all the sides of the fort facing the large, level plain. Begin there. Those two walls and a bastion at their juncture should have first priority. One battery near water level should be built at the same time in order better to hinder the passage of ships should the British attempt a raid before the chain is installed. Parsons agreed wholeheartedly with the advice. Proudly he informed Washington that by early April he expected "to have two sides and one bastion of the fort in some state of defense." Better yet, even before March was gone, there was "a prospect of having five or six cannon mounted in one of our batteries."[2]

Far away, other events were transpiring that eventually corrected the previously turbulent and unsatisfactory command arrangements in the Highlands. Unable any longer to brook the confusion stemming from Congress' insistence on naming commanders from time to time, Washington himself chose Alexander McDougall. "As I consider it essential to the nature of the command," he explained, "that one officer should have the general control and direction of all the posts in the Highlands and their dependencies, and be answerable for them, you are to consider yourself possessed of this general control and direction and to act accordingly." (Two centuries later, cadets at West Point studying the History of the Military Art would know that Washington was applying the principle of war, Unity of Command.) After promising to return McDougall to the main army if he could "get things in a proper train by the opening of the campaign," the Commander-in-Chief sent a message to Congress. In it he requested Congress' cooperation in recognizing the total responsibility and authority of a single commander at that important place. A week later Congress acquiesced. One officer, who responded to Washington, was thenceforward to exercise control over all factors relating to the defense of the Hudson Highlands. That was a major step forward, albeit nearly three years late.[3]

Another propitious event, though not of Washington's making, occurred that March. From the earliest days of the war, defenses along the Hudson River had suffered from the nationwide shortage of engineers. Bernard Romans had proved as impractical as he was intractable; Radière sprang from an identical mold; Machin had turned in yeoman work which for some mysterious reason was neither acknowledged nor rewarded. Others, such as William Smith and Rufus Putnam, put in appearances now and then. Each new engineer added his own improvements and imperfections. No need was more real or apparent or pressing than the requirement for a capable and permanent engineer. When Radière rode pouting into Valley Forge, the matter came to a head. General Horatio Gates had been well served in the Saratoga campaign by a young Polish officer who was agreeable, tactful, apparently devoted to Gates (an important consideration at that particular time), and, by all judgments, a most able engineer.

156   *Colonel Thaddeus Kosciuszko. Courtesy of the West Point Museum.*

By virtue of his power as President of the Board of War, Gates ordered Thaddeus Kosciuszko to report to West Point. He was "to be employed as shall be thought proper in his capacity of an engineer."[4]

Kosciuszko received the order and promptly set out for the Highlands. In that blustery March of 1778 the Pole was just thirty-two years old and had been in America since shortly after the Declaration of Independence. His European childhood and background had been rather typical for a son of a minor nobleman. Following graduation in 1771 from the Royal School in Warsaw, he had been commissioned a captain in the Polish army and had then attended a school of artillery and military engineering in France. He had returned briefly to Poland, but seeing scant opportunity for advancement—and spurred away by an unfortunate love affair—he journeyed once more to Paris. The young idealist soon became enthused with the philosophical concepts of freedom and liberty and saw the American Revolution as an embodiment of his beliefs. Early in 1776 he borrowed passage money for the United States. His first employer was the State of Pennsylvania. For them he labored on forts and obstructions to close the Delaware River south of Philadelphia, gaining practical experience that would be invaluable in his later work on the Hudson. His performance on the Delaware defenses so influenced Congress that, on 18 October 1776, it appointed him "an engineer in the service of the United States, with the pay of sixty dollars a month, and the rank of colonel."

Transferred to Ticonderoga, he very favorably impressed Americans there. Despite his rather limited military experience, he immediately recognized that Fort Ticonderoga would be untenable should the English choose to haul cannon to the top of nearby Mount Defiance. His advice to fortify that strategic peak was not followed. Although many historians believe that defending the hill would have overextended the relatively small Patriot garrison, Americans on the spot soon had dramatic if traumatic cause to recall the Pole's recommendation. When John Burgoyne came south in 1777 he dragged cannon to the top of an undefended Mount Defiance, just as Kosciuszko had foreseen. General Arthur St. Clair, commanding the fortress, had no choice but retreat. In subsequent fighting around Saratoga, Kosciuszko expertly prepared field fortifications along Bemis Heights, winning great acclaim for his part in those vital victories leading up to Burgoyne's surrender. Horatio Gates, in particular, had been highly impressed; whatever his own abilities, Gates had been a regular officer in the British army for some years and was better equipped than most American generals to recognize talent in the half-art, half-science skills requisite in an eighteenth-century military engineer.

The slender, ski-nosed foreigner went first to Poughkeepsie where he met George Clinton on 26 March. He continued to West Point, bearing Clinton's written approbation: "I believe you will find him an ingenious young man and disposed to do everything he can in the most agreeable manner." Parsons, who knew of Kosciuszko by reputation, was delighted to greet him as West Point's new engineer. Dining together the first evening, the two men quickly formed a good degree of mutual regard and respect. Both were pleased with the assignment. Delight became dismay the very next day, however, when who should stroll into headquarters but Colonel Radière![5]

Radière was walking proof of the mischief that could occur when different agencies assigned men to the Highlands. Washington had not been informed of Kosciuszko's orders. After listening to Radière's story, the General had assumed that a personality conflict between Israel Putnam and the Frenchman had been to blame for the latter's departure from his post in the Highlands. That problem would seem to have been resolved when McDougall replaced "Old Put." Thereupon, Washington sent Radière back with instructions to resume his mission in the Highlands. To McDougall he wrote, "This will be delivered to you by Colonel de la Radière . . . who was employed to superintend the fortifications on the North River, but, from some misunderstanding between him and the late commanding officer, . . . he determined to renounce the work and return to camp." Then the Virginian added, hopefully perhaps, "I can safely recommend him to you as a man who understands his profession, and make no doubt of his giving you satisfaction both in projecting and executing the works required for the defence of the river."[6]

The Commander-in-Chief may have had no doubts, but Parsons was full of them. He wanted no part of Radière. It was too late that day to turn away the unwanted engineer, but Parsons told him he must travel on to Fishkill on the morrow where General McDougall was holding an investigation into the loss of the Highlands the past October. McDougall would have to decide. That night Parsons put his very strong opinion on paper in a letter to the Scot:

> Colonel Kosciuszko, sent to this place, is particularly agreeable to the gentlemen of this State and all others concerned at this post: you will, sir, readily find by a little enquiry that altho' Colonel la Radière appears to be a man of some learning and ingenuity, an attachment to his opinion in his profession and some other matters have rendered him not so suitable as some other persons to have the principle direction at this post. . . . As we are very desirous of having Colonel Kosciuszko continue here and both cannot live upon the Point, I wish your honor to adopt such measures as will answer the wishes of the people and garrison; and best serve the public good. Colonel la Radière will be with you tomorrow."[7]

The Frenchman and the Pole probably spent a most uncomfortable evening avoiding one another.

Even though the 29th was a Sunday, Radière went to Fishkill. McDougall received him graciously and attempted to salve his bruised feelings. Gigantic, jovial Henry Knox was also a dinner guest, so it is nearly certain that a large meal was devoured amidst booming laughter and hearty tales. McDougall, probably with an assist from Knox, prevailed upon Radière to remain in the area, to provide what help he could whenever it might be needed. He promised in the meantime to ask General Washington for a decision. Because Kosciuszko's commission as colonel preceded Radière's by nearly a year, McDougall was bound to treat the Pole as chief engineer pending Washington's judgment.[8]

Anger was Washington's first reaction to the foul-up. Curtly he wrote, "The presence of Colonel de la Radière rendering the services of Mr. Kosciouski as engineer at Fishkill unnecessary, you are to give him orders to join this army without loss of time." Then one of his aides must have informed the General that higher authority had sent Kosciuszko to West Point. Abashed, and a mite calmer, he added, "P. S. However desirous I am that Mr. Kosciousko should repair to this army, if he is especially employed by order of Congress or the Board of War, I would not wish to contravene their commands." McDougall was thus left just where he had started—with two engineers and no decision as to which to keep. On 13 April he tried again. "Mr. Kosciousko is esteemed by those who have attended the work at West Point to have had more practice than Colonel de la Radière, and his manner of treating the people more acceptable than that of the latter; which induced General Parsons and Governor Clinton to desire the former may be continued at West Point." Pointedly he told Washington that, although Kosciuszko outranked Radière, the emotional Frenchman "disputes rank with the former, which obliges me to keep them apart." Washington replied on 23 April, "As Colonel la Radière and Colonel Kosiusko will never agree, I think it will be best to order la Radière to return, especially as you say Kosiusko is better adapted to the genius and temper of the people." Radière remained only long enough to see Machin fix his chain across the river. Early in May he departed. Kosciuszko, after having performed in the role for over a month, was now in fact chief engineer at West Point. It was a post he would hold for well over two more years. West Point finally had a steady and efficient engineer.[9]

During the dispute, Parsons had kept the garrison hard at work on the defenses. As snow melted and ice loosened its grip on the river, soldiers by the hundreds streamed into the Highlands to build with their hands a mighty fortress. George Clinton mobilized portions of several militia regiments, directing them "immediately to march to West Point." Lafayette, at that time commanding in Albany, dispatched additional Continental regiments to West Point, including Colonel Rufus Putnam's. Putnam's men, three hundred in number, made the voyage jammed into four sloops half-filled with lumber. Other vessels, entirely loaded with wooden beams, escorted them. There was no doubt that the Massachusetts men were expected to do construction work as they trudged up the steep road from the landing to West Point's plain on 31 March. Lafayette left his northern post, returning through the Highlands to the main army at Valley Forge,* but his replacement, Thomas Conway (whose name would be remembered in history mainly for its alliterative effect when combined with "cabal"), continued his predecessor's policy of cooperating with the commander in the Highlands by shifting troops that way. Drenching April rainstorms struck in the first week of the new month, but the soldiers continued to

---

* Traveling in elegance with seven horses and four "domestics," Lafayette elicited a caustic notation in McDougall's diary. The Scot was apparently pained at being obliged to feed so many mouths.

labor, drying out around blazing fires at night and warding off effects of the chilly, wet weather with increased doses of rum.[10]

There was plenty to do and, for once, enough material to do it with. During February and March, although nothing much was being accomplished on the fort itself, Colonel Hughes and Governor Clinton had energetically searched for construction materials, while General Parsons had kept his soldiers busy felling trees and dragging them "out of ye mountains." By the end of February alone he could report over "1000 sticks of timber are cutt . . . and about 1000 or 1500 fascines" were ready. It would seem that the officer who said the "work was incessant" was not exaggerating. The same officer recalled that as soon as the snow melted "we set ourselves to collect the rough stone, which we found on the surface of the ground, to use in erecting the fortification." With plentiful building material on hand, supervised professionally by Kosciuszko, and driven by Parsons, the men performed admirably. By 8 April, Governor Clinton could record, "The works . . . are now carried on with a degree of spirit that promises their speedy completion."[11]

The year's first real scare came at the beginning of April, providing nerve-wracking but free incentive to the builders in the mountains. On 2 April McDougall uncovered a number of men claiming to be deserters from the English but actually hired "to spy out our situation." His own spies slipped in with the alarming word that the British had "two bomb ketches . . . to bomb you out." At once, seriously concerned over the vulnerability of the fortress at West Point, he directed Parsons to exert every effort "to enclose such parts of the works as are accessible to the enemy." Don't waste time trying "to complete the heights of the parapets to the plane," he wrote, "but apply your whole strength to enclose the works." Parsons posted lookouts on Anthony's Nose and turned every other hand to throwing up at least a semblance of breastworks all around the site. A day later he reported that task completed. McDougall remained worried. He told George Clinton, "I have little doubt of the enemy's intention to pay us a visit; because it will advance their views and no season [is] more proper than before our works and obstructions are finished." But for all the excitement, it turned out to be merely one more false alarm.[12]

McDougall, accompanied by Radière, went to West Point for the first time on 8 April. Next day, George and James Clinton joined them. After a thorough investigation of the works, they were satisfied with everything except the proposed location of the chain. When Machin came on the 10th and agreed that the barrier could as well be fastened underneath the fortress, that change was readily adopted.

After noon, Machin and the Governor left to attend to other business, while McDougall, James Clinton, Parsons, and Radière climbed "Rock and Crown Hills in the rear of our works." In accordance with his policy of keeping Radière and Kosciuszko separated, McDougall did not invite the Pole along. McDougall asked for opinions regarding construction of redoubts or forts on those hills. Radière was already on record as believing it was unnecessary or undesirable. As none of the others claimed any expertise in the engineering profession, the result of the conference was not surprising. McDougall that evening wrote in his diary, "They all agreed it was inexpedient to make any works on those hills, and the direction of cannon from there would be very uncertain." When the four scrambled back down, Kosciuszko heard the results of their expedition. Standing on the site of the great bastion rising on West Point's plain, he looked up at the hills just over a half a mile away. They loomed commandingly above him. Thoughts of Mount Defiance and Fort Ticonderoga must have tumbled through his head. Always tactful, he probably unobtrusively drew Parsons aside after dinner and talked to him. His logic was persuasive. For that matter, neither James Clinton nor Parsons was hard to convince: memory of the loss of Forts Clinton and Montgomery was too fresh. Those forts had fallen to attack from the rear. Before McDougall returned to Fishkill, he had changed his mind. He became quite satisfied that "the heights near it are such that the fort is not tenable if the enemy possess them. For this reason we are obliged to make some work on them." Radière had lost again. His love for the Pole did not increase.[13]

With Kosciuszko it was no sooner decided than done. He quickly drew up plans to defend the two hills sitting directly southwest of the main bastion on the plain and separated from each other by a gully through whose marshy bottom ran a spring-fed stream. (Dammed up, the stream is now Lusk Reservoir.) Colonel Rufus Putnam marched his regiment, the 5th Massachusetts, up the steep flank of Crown Hill to begin construction of a strong fort there. The top of the sharp hill was small and round, roughly two hundred feet in diameter. Kosciuszko's design called for the fort to cover the entire area, its walls to be an extension upward of the hill's nearly vertical cliffs. Crown Hill was itself virtually unapproachable except from the direction of the plain; it was without doubt the strongest natural position at West Point. Rufus Putnam described the site as "a high hill, or rather rock, which commands the plain and point. The rock on the side next the point is not difficult to ascend, but on the other side . . . the rock is 50 feet perpendicular."[14]

Across the stream, some thousand feet distant, ran the crest of a longer and lower ridge. There the engineer determined to establish three redoubts, one behind the other. Lacking Crown Hill's sharp sides, the rather level ridge would require defense in depth. Guns from the fort that Rufus Putnam was to build would be able to support the lower forts. Parsons sent three regiments of his own Connecticut Brigade to erect those positions. Each of the regiments took responsibility for one site. In order, running from the plain southwestward, were the units of Colonel Samuel B. Webb, Colonel Samuel Wyllys, and Colonel Return Jonathan Meigs. Wyllys and Meigs were on hand, but Webb was then a prisoner of the British. Colonel Henry Sherburne's regiment remained behind on the plain to build a redoubt overlooking the spot where it was expected the chain would one day be permanently fixed. At a later date, McDougall would name each of the new works for the colonel whose regiment erected it. James Clinton took charge of building the great fort on the plain, supervising New York militiamen and some Continentals. Like the other works, that bastion was not named right away, but most people assumed it would be called Fort

Clinton when the day of christening arrived. They were premature by two and a half years.

McDougall wrote out his concept of the defensive plan on 11 April 1778. It was a plan which stood up throughout the war with only minor modifications.

> The hill which Colonel Putnam is fortifying is the most commanding and important of any that we can now attend to. . . . The easternmost face of this work must be so constructed as to command the plain on which Colonel Putnam's regiment is now encamped [level land in the general vicinity of the present football stadium] and annoy the enemy if he should force the works now erecting by Colonel Meigs' and Colonel Wyllys' regiments, as well as to command [Webb's Redoubt]. . . .
>
> The next principal ground to be occupied for the safety of the post is the rising ground . . . near the northwest corner of the Long Barracks. . . . This redoubt [Sherburne's] is so important that it must be finished without delay. The chain to be fixed on the west side in or near the Gap of the Snook, commanded by the fire from the east curtain of [Sherburne's Redoubt]. The water batteries now erected on the point to be completed as soon as possible and two cannon placed in each. . . . The security of the fort depends so much on the heights in the rear . . . that the commanding officer at West Point should take his quarters on the hill Colonel Putnam is now fortifying. . . . [In event of attack, each regiment will take post in the work it is now constructing.] Should the enemy force the regiments of Colonels Wyllys, Meigs, and Webb from their works, it will be most advancive to the defense . . . that those corps retire to defend to the last extremity the avenues leading to Colonel Putnam's redoubt. . . .[15]

In later months redoubts would be built even farther out to cover the approaches to Fort Putnam, and Constitution Island would once again be fortified. But for the moment, Kosciuszko had laid out a most ambitious amount of work—more, as it turned out, than could be accomplished that summer—which would remain the backbone of the system of fortifications at West Point.

With each passing day the weather grew warmer, and fear of an English attack climbed with the temperature. Men toiled zealously. The hills grew more barren as trees were cut promiscuously, walls of the works climbed higher, and the number of cannon staring out over the river increased. By mid-April the main fort, still without a formal name, was "so enclosed as to resist a sudden assault of the enemy." A friend of Kosciuszko's informed General Gates that the engineer had "made many alterations, which are universally approved of. . . . if the enemy let us alone two weeks longer, we shall have reason to rejoice at their moving this way." The enemy did let them alone. Work continued apace. Everyone could see progress, and exult in it. To be sure, there were hitches and headaches. Militiamen quit, or were drawn away for other purposes, bringing forth James Clinton's exasperated complaint at one point, "Our fort is now almost at a stand since the departure of the militia." Draft horses and oxen were extremely scarce commodities, necessitating their forceful impressment into duty. But, all in all, April 1778 passed into history as one of the most productive periods the Hudson Hills would ever witness. On the last day of the month Thomas Machin put his chain across. It was a fitting achievement to cap a fine start.[16]

May began with a bang. In the final days of April, word of the treaty with France had arrived in the Highlands. Everyone rejoiced. The war was as good as won! They had beaten George III! Independence for the United States was assured! If their optimism was ill-founded, their joy was genuine. Officers raised uncounted glasses of Madeira in happy and repeated toasts to King Louis and George Washington and France and each of the thirteen states and anything else that crossed their minds. The men took respite from work to swill grog. Spirits had never been higher along the Hudson. In Fishkill, on 2 May, revelers "provided an ox which is to be roasted whole." Shortly afterward, the glorious alliance with France was "celebrated at the Point." The hard-working and happy warriors feasted on burnt cow and raw rum. One officer in particular "was uncommonly gay," entertaining his enthusiastically applauding compatriots far into the night, pouring forth a "great shower of puns . . . in his nocturnal cogitations." McDougall, who always displayed "much of the Scotch character," was, when plied with wine, "affable and facetious." On such occasions he often humorously described his "national peculiarities and family origin," an act which never failed to convulse his audience in laughter. On finishing, he would draw himself erect and add, in a voice tinged with mirth, marred by a speech impediment, and dripping with a Scottish burr, "Now, gentlemon, you have got the history of Sawney McDougall, the milk-mon's son." With the Scot and other officers taking turns providing spontaneous entertainment, the boisterous celebration continued, we might surmise, nearly till dawn. It was a moment to be remembered. A wild, deliciously delirious time.[17]

It was too good to last. Reality returned. After all, Englishmen still held New York and Philadelphia and all of Canada. French soldiers, if they arrived, could hardly be expected for months. If a reminder were needed, it came in the form of a letter from General Washington. "I very much fear," wrote he to McDougall, "that we . . . shall relapse into a state of supineness and perfect security." Given "the desperate state of British affairs," the enemy might think it "worth a desperate attempt to extricate themselves." The Commander-in-Chief then warned McDougall that "near two hundred sail of light transports" had left Philadelphia, constituting a potential threat to the Hudson forts.[18]

Fear of attack made everyone start taking second looks at the defenses. For a time some even began to fear the fortress was improperly designed and executed. From Fishkill, on 11 May, McDougall, a natural worrier, sent a jittery message to George Clinton: "I am far from being pleased with Mr. Korsuaso's [Kosciuzsko's] constructing the batteries, and carrying on the works, and I fear they will not answer the expectation of the country. I wish therefore to have an hour's conversation with you on this subject as soon as you can spare one." Four days later, Lieutenant Colonel William S. Livingston informed the Governor rather anxiously, "The works here want much alteration, and demand your inspection, otherwise we shall again be kidnapped." (Following his capture at Fort Montgomery, Livingston had escaped from a British prison and was then serving horseless at West Point.) The problem, whatever it may have been, was presumably corrected, for it was never again mentioned.[19]

After receiving a letter from Washington setting forth the situation of the army to include an account of conditions in the Highlands, Congress resolved on 15 April to send Horatio Gates to command in the northern theatre. Mindful of Washington's strictures on unity of command—although leaving the appointment to the General would have been more in accord with his thinking—Congress carefully defined Gates' command as encompassing any and all troops in the entire theatre. He was granted almost total power in the area, being cautioned only to take care "that the fortifications be not too expansive." Congress remembered Romans and Radière and their vast plans and all the squabbling. Washington had already promised McDougall that he would be relieved for duty in the field, but there is no evidence that he asked for Gates. As a matter of fact, selecting Gates was not an especially wise move on the part of Congress; New Yorkers were generally against him as a result of his controversy with Schuyler a year before. When Governor Clinton heard the news, he bluntly declared, "We were well pleased with General McDougall and the exchange, therefore, is not considered a favor."[20]

Prior to Gates' arrival, the forts were formally christened. All were dubbed with the name of the person whose troops had performed the labor of construction—except the main stronghold on the plain. It was not named for James Clinton. That incident makes an interesting though unproven story. McDougall, a New Yorker, had no love for Gates. As a dedicated Patriot he could do nothing to injure or weaken Gates' command of West Point, but no such restriction precluded his needling the squat little Virginian. The fact that Gates had been more or less discredited in his abortive attempt to unseat Washington made him a more appealing target to an old rabble-rouser like McDougall. The Scotsman was mulling that over when inspiration rode into Fishkill in the person of crippled Benedict Arnold. Arnold, on his way to Valley Forge, rested two days with McDougall. His left leg, so grievously wounded the past October, had not yet healed. It was no secret that Arnold and Gates were bitter enemies. Why not name the main fortress at West Point for Arnold, forcing Gates to face his enemy's name every day he remained in the Highlands? Without even stretching one's imagination, it is easy to picture McDougall chuckling over his splendid joke as Arnold resumed his journey.

Whether or not that reconstruction of the birth of a name for Fort Arnold is correct, the following facts are known: James Clinton was initially charged with the responsibility of building that fort; all other forts or redoubts raised at that time were named after the officers in charge of them; the fort was referred to as Fort Clinton before May 1778; Arnold stayed with McDougall from 11 to 13 May; by 15 May, letters from West Point called the bastion "Fort Arnold." For most of the summer a disagreement lingered, some using the name "Arnold," others "Clinton." It is safe to say Arnold's presence inspired the christening of the fort after him; it is a good guess that Gates' known dislike for Arnold did not greatly disincline McDougall to choose that name.[21]

The last time Congress ordered Horatio Gates to the Highlands he had been riding high on a swell of popularity and could afford to ignore instructions. Since then he had lost considerable prestige in the clash with Washington. No longer was he a big enough man to do as he pleased. Even so, more than a month passed before he reached Fishkill. McDougall, waiting impatiently to relinquish command, chaffed at the delay. "General Gates is not yet arrived, nor do I learn when tis likely he will," he exclaimed angrily on 11 May. More dolefully he ventured, "I think I am not well treated by him and Congress." He was not lonely, though. Benedict Arnold had hardly departed before Parsons came up for an overnight visit. Then Nathanael Greene reined in. Greene, a Quaker with nonpacifist notions, was justly considered Washington's most brilliant general. His advice probably carried more weight than that of anyone else in the councils of war.* Greene remained two nights, departing on the 16th. Finally, at 11 o'clock on the morning of 18 May, Gates and his large entourage made their appearance. Next day McDougall escorted the new commander to West Point. There he carefully pointed out the concept of defenses, not neglecting loudly to mention newly dubbed Fort Arnold. Kosciuszko, beaming at the reunion with his old commander, led the way. The briefings were completed late on the 20th. McDougall happily scrawled in his diary, "Resigned the command this evening to General Gates." A measure of his boundless pleasure to be leaving the Highlands can be found in several entries *not* recorded in the diary. From 21 through 25 May it is blank. Then, on the 26th, the diary ends with a single note which speaks eloquently of his activities that week: "4½ gallons rum."[22]

Gates seems not to have made any alterations in the scheme of construction. He had faith in Kosciuszko, and he was apparently satisfied with steps already undertaken. Progress was indeed being made. By the end of May gunboats were in the river, Machin was well along on a boom to supplement the chain, more cannon were reaching the Highlands day by day, and the fortifications at West Point were showing the results of constant labor applied under the expert guidance of the Polish engineer.

Patriots decided that spring to convert Beverley Robinson's country home into a hospital. When Surgeon James Thacher moved his medical equipment into the large house on 11 June, he remarked: "Robinson's house, with the out-buildings, is found very convenient for a hospital; the farm and gardens are very extensive, affording excellent pasturing for horses and cows, and containing three or four large orchards abounding in

---

* Although Greene has been rightly accorded the honor of being, behind Washington, the best strategist of the war—some historians place him first—his advice on Hudson River forts was uniformly bad. It was largely at his urging that Washington attempted to defend Forts Washington and Lee in 1776 (lost causes both) and it will be remembered that his recommendation concerning defenses in the Highlands in 1777 was to concentrate on the river obstructions since the hills behind were too rough for an attacker to penetrate.

fruit of various descriptions." Thacher did not so much appreciate the environment, however. He accused Robinson of being "guided altogether by a taste for romantic singularity and novelty" in selecting the location. "It is surrounded on two sides by hideous mountains and dreary forests, not a house in view, and but one within a mile."[23]

As curious an observer as he was an inveterate recorder, Thacher waited only a day before scaling Sugarloaf Hill, a peak shooting steeply up behind the hospital. After an arduous climb, he "contemplated with amazement the sublime scene" stretched out before his view.

> Looking down as from a cloud, we beheld the Hudson, resembling a vast canal cut through mountains of stupendous magnitude; a few boats playing on its surface were scarcely visible. But to the pen of the poet, and the pencil of the painter, be consigned the task of describing the wonders of nature there exhibited in the form of huge mountains, rocky cliffs, and venerable forests, in one confused mass. From this summit, too, we have a most interesting view of the fortress and garrison of West Point. Fort Putnam, on its most elevated part, the several redoubts beneath, and the barracks on the plain below, with numerous armed soldiers in active motion, all defended by the most formidable machinery of war, combine to form a picturesque scenery of peculiar interest, which can be heightened only when from the cannon's mouth issue fire and smoke, and the earth trembles with its roar and thunder.[24]

The newly arrived man of medicine might have preferred a more civilized spot, but he was nonetheless mightily impressed with the majesty of the Hudson Highlands and the strength of West Point.

June arrived hot. Old-timers who had spent a long lifetime in the Hudson Valley could not recall a more blistering June. Temperatures soared several days above the 100-degree mark. Humidity was high. Men were struck down by the heat. Across New Jersey and into Pennsylvania the same smothering heat wave clasped broiling arms over the land. The muggy conditions were so unbearable at West Point that men could not stir at midday without fear of heatstroke. Working hours were set from five to 10:00 A.M. and from 3:00 P.M. to sundown. Even with a five-hour siesta break, the days were ten sweaty hours long. Men tired and sagged. The construction rate lagged. Morale sank. Rum was issued each day just after dawn and again at sunset, but thirsty soldiers found extra supplies of their own. A drunken riot erupted in the evening of 29 June, prompting Brigadier General John Glover, then commanding the garrison at West Point, to clamp down on the men and forbid outsiders from "selling spiritous liquors, cider, etc., to the soldiers in this garrison." Brawling stopped, but probably due as much to sultriness as soberness.[25]

In Philadelphia, where British and Hessian troops had enjoyed a very pleasant winter in contrast to the horrendous conditions of Valley Forge, Sir Henry Clinton was the new commander. Sir William Howe had been recalled to England after the fiasco of 1777. Faced by war against Frenchmen as well as Americans, Sir Henry had to give up either New York or Philadelphia. His strength was insufficient to hold both and still permit the conduct of operations. It was a rather easy decision: New York was much the more important. By 18 June his army was lurching overland across New

Jersey toward the Hudson, slowed considerably by burned bridges, a burning sun, and a burdensome baggage train.

Washington, his army newly trained and eager for a fight, set out in pursuit. At Monmouth Court House, on 28 June, he hit Clinton's long column. In a vicious battle, with heat causing more casualties than bullets, the Continentals mauled a rear guard but were unable to prevent the escape of the main body. Henry Clinton got to New York City and George Washington moved to a position below the Highlands along the Hudson. That was precisely the respective positions of the two armies late in 1776. Washington, hoping a French fleet would arrive to enable him to attack the Englishmen, wrote elatedly, "It is not a little pleasing, nor less wonderful to contemplate, that after two years of maneuvering and undergoing the strangest vicissitudes that perhaps ever attended any one contest since creation, both armies are brought back to the very point they set out from."[26]

The movement of both major armies back to the Hudson quite naturally altered arrangements at West Point. With the entire Continental Army serving as a buffer between New York and the Highlands, security was no longer a major worry. Workers could toil without looking over their shoulders. On the other hand, in anticipation of making an assault on New York City, Washington withdrew most of the Continentals. Gates marched "the main body of the army" from West Point to Peekskill in late June, leaving Brigadier General John Glover commanding. Glover complained loudly, wanting to serve in the field with his brigade. To complicate matters, he became very ill. Gates asked George Clinton to assume command, but the Governor had his hands full with Indian raids on the frontier. On 29 June, Washington reminded Gates of his responsibility to prepare and defend the posts in the Highlands. Gates contented himself with telling an unwell General Glover "to give your whole attention to the completing of, first the out works at West Point, and then the body of the place." Through most of June and July, understandably enough, progress slackened. Heat, anticipation of a fight in New York, absence of an effective commander, and a shortage of manpower saw to that.[27]

Meanwhile, Thomas Machin was assembling the final parts and pieces for a boom to reinforce his chain. Huge sharpened logs were floated to West Point. Iron clamps and connections came by the cartload from Sterling Furnace. General Glover provided soldiers experienced in iron-working to help assemble the obstacle in late June. Sometime shortly afterward, the boom was completed and drawn across the river.* Resembling a great rope ladder, it could have served as a plank bridge across the Hudson if boards had been laid from log to log, but it was not so used. Quite likely guards and repairmen and visiting dignitaries did walk on it, but records throughout the war show that communications between Constitution Island and West Point were by boat. Security measures, alone, would

---

* Two logs and attached iron parts of the boom were recovered from the river bottom in the middle of the last century and can be viewed in Washington's Headquarters Museum, Newburgh, New York.

have been enough to keep sutlers, ordinary soldiers, and the general public away from both boom and chain. The sole purpose of the boom was to function as a buffer for the chain, to slow or snag a ramming vessel before it reached the final barrier. It was not a bridge.[28]

George Washington first visited the new works at West Point on 16 July 1778. As he rode up to Fort Arnold a tattered honor guard snapped to attention and artillerymen boomed out a ragged thirteen-gun salute, "the number of the United States." The Commander-in-Chief had little time for pleasantries—a French fleet under Admiral D'Estaing was standing off New York Harbor and a major battle seemed to be in the offing. Before the battle he wanted to see for himself how stout were his defenses in the Highlands, to get firsthand an idea of "the number of men sufficient for their security." Kosciuszko guided the distinguished visitor around the works, describing the role of each in the overall pattern of defense and pointing out strengths and weaknesses of each one. All the forts were constructed of dirt and wood, there not having been time for masonry work. Lining the shore around the Point were Chain, Lanthorn, Green, and South Batteries, containing a total of eleven cannon. Near where the chain was held fast to Constitution Island stood another battery containing six guns. On the plain itself, Fort Arnold with nine cannon and Sherburne's Redoubt with five constituted the defenses. High to the southwest loomed Fort Putnam, mounting six artillery pieces and overwatching redoubts Meigs, Webb, and Wyllys and their total of four guns. Fifteen or more pieces not yet mounted raised West Point's grand total to nearly sixty. Most of those had been captured at Fort Ticonderoga in 1777. The preoccupied leader was apparently satisfied with what he saw for he changed nothing and later commended Kosciuszko. Duportail, Chief of Engineers, was not with the General, however, so Washington deferred judgment at that time. The need for a commander was most evident and he did take action to improve that void, which Gates himself should have seen to long before. Upon returning to headquarters he issued orders solving Glover's pique at being separated from his Brigade. That general was to march his unit "to Fort Clinton on West Point" to join *him*. Glover gloomily complied, putting his men in motion. But before they could arrive, Washington changed his mind and directed Colonel William Malcolm "immediately to repair to Fort Arnold at West Point and take upon you the command of that post." Even the Commander-in-Chief was not sure of the fort's name, thanks to McDougall's last-minute joke on Gates.[29]

Less than a week after inspecting West Point, Washington's hopes of retaking New York were dashed. D'Estaing refused to risk his fleet on the sandy shoal outside New York Harbor. He sailed for Newport instead. Deeply disappointed, Washington sent troops to reinforce General John Sullivan in Rhode Island and encamped with the rest of his army below the Highlands. From that moment began Washington's personal control of affairs and fortifications at West Point. Theretofore, he had always relied upon subordinates to direct the vital defenses; thenceforward, he himself kept a finger in virtually every phase of activities in the fortress.

When French sail disappeared into the Atlantic, the Virginian turned with renewed interest to the Hudson. In that receptive mood, then, he was shocked at the explosion of Colonel Malcolm soon after he had assumed command of West Point. Lieutenant Colonel Aaron Burr had marched Malcolm's regiment to West Point, arriving there on 23 July. Malcolm, whose wife came to West Point with him, had followed his men by a couple of days. He rapidly made the rounds of the various positions, immediately met socially with all his officers, and quickly decided that West Point was in abominable shape, a shambles. "I was sent to this command," he remonstrated, "which I found in just as bad order as ever your imagination can conceive. If the enemy do come, I shall fight them in the field, which is my only chance. The works are not worth a farthing."[30]

12

THE GIBRALTAR OF AMERICA

S *UCH IS* the formidable state and strength of this post that it has received the appellation of the American Gibraltar, and when properly guarded may bid defiance to an army of twenty thousand men." With those words, James Thacher described West Point after it was completed.[1]

But in the fourth August of the war, West Point was a long way from finished; what work had been done up to then had been performed in great haste in order to have some sort of works up should the British attack. By far the greater labor lay ahead, a fact Colonel Malcolm had readily grasped. At first he had been overwhelmed by the magnitude of the task, but he soon grew grudgingly reconciled to it as evidenced in a letter written to Parsons on 3 August:

> Here I am holding committee among spades and shovels. Why was I banished? However, I begin to be reconciled. . . . We are driving on downwards; the more we do the more we find we have to do. Why did you not begin to move the mountain, rather than add to its magnitude.[2]

Accepting the job of building West Point did not mean he had to like it. "Send me news and newspapers," he pleaded, "anything to keep us alive; this is actually t'other end of the world."

As a matter of fact, Colonel Malcolm could not have avoided becoming energetically interested in completing the defenses had he tried. George Washington saw to that. The General, in a very real sense, took West Point under his wing. Shocked and disappointed that so little had been accomplished by so many over such a long period of time, and undoubtedly unnerved at how very close the British had come in 1777 to taking the

Hudson away from him, he apparently decided to assume personal control of the location he considered to be the key to the continent. Commanders there would from then on correspond directly with him; the most minute problem affecting the garrison or the fortress was never too trivial to be brought before the Commander-in-Chief. As busy as he was, he took time to oversee almost everything related to the defenses. For example, in the one month of August 1778 he concerned himself with such diverse and detailed items as the content of workers' rations, pay of artificers, condition of arms, internal personnel management, shoemaking, expenses of the commander, confinement of prisoners, discipline, crews for gunboats, design of the forts, experiments with a fire "machine," strength of the garrison, Kosciuszko's work, the number of cannon available, and even Malcolm's policy of granting furloughs. In all, during this period, he wrote or dictated more than two letters a week touching some way on the forts along the Hudson. Later he would live at West Point. Never would he relinquish control or interest— the chain, for instance, could only be drawn up in winter and replaced in spring at his order. Once, when it appeared that the laborers were lagging, it was none other than General Washington who commanded his supply agent to "send a tolerable good supply of rum as soon as possible to the stores at West Point [or] the works which are so important will be retarded." "Father of West Point" is an appellation which would not be inaccurately applied to the Father of our Country.[3]

With that high-level encouragement, Malcolm got busy. Artificers whom he believed were "idling away their time" were soon very "properly employed." Kosciuszko began a bombproof magazine inside Fort Arnold for the storage of powder; that important commodity had previously been stacked in sheds above ground and in ships moored in the river below. Military units were combed to locate masons to quarry stone for facing and strengthening the works. Malcolm even offered to pay the stoneworkers extra to speed that labor along. Appearances were not overlooked; the new colonel specified that "men for guard are to be brought to the parade clean shaved and powdered." Discipline grew tighter; punishment was regularly dealt out, but even there construction priorities were kept uppermost in mind. A court-martial found one John Purnold guilty of desertion. His punishment was sixty lashes on the bare back and hard labor "by being chained to a wheel barrow" for as long as his regimental commander cared to keep him at it. The same court found a John Gowdy guilty of drunkenness and sentenced him to "attend Purnold, to fill his barrow." The deserter and the drunk were allowed, even in punishment, to help by hauling dirt and rocks for West Point's defenses.[4]

George Clinton came to Malcolm's aid on the matter of manpower. New York's jails were overflowing. Would the colonel care to have some Tories to do forced labor on the forts? He most certainly would, so long as they were of "sound wind and limb." The Governor's ideas of using "these gentry correspond with my opinion to a hair." He assured Clinton that they would be carefully guarded because, he noted eagerly, "they are fine fellows to work." Revolutionary governments cannot be expected to be overly solicitous of the rights or feelings of professed or potential enemies.

Tories were put to work, although some not yet in jail were given a choice between toiling a month or providing an able-bodied replacement. Tories in the Hudson Valley were, after all, accustomed to such treatment. They had done much to help raise the old fortifications, they were to do the same for West Point. In addition to local men, several British and Hessian soldiers—deserters as well as prisoners—were employed in the Highlands. Seventeen labored in Fort Arnold alone.[5]

Sometime that August, Kosciuszko stood in the center of Fort Putnam observing carpenters and masons at work and happened to glance up at Rocky Hill, not half a mile away to the west and a good two hundred feet higher. Artillery located there would have everything inside Fort Putnam at its mercy. In spite of the heat, he made his way to the summit of that knob. Sitting thoughtfully on the edge of a sheer rock cliff, he watched the workers beneath him in Fort Putnam and clearly observed those farther down on the plain. Once again, painful memories of Mount Defiance and Fort Ticonderoga flooded his consciousness. That convinced him. Rocky Hill must be fortified. Quickly his practiced eye took in the terrain. Steep slopes protected the hill on three sides. On the fourth the ground was easier with a slight hollow to cover an attacking force until it burst out right in the defenders' faces. An elevated cannon platform would cover that dip, however. With a preliminary sketch in his pocket, he clambered back down to his desk to draw up a blueprint.

It was at this time, during the fortress' very beginning, that General Washington started a tradition at West Point which has survived two centuries and exists still: academic and practical research and study. West Point became a center for experimentation and remained one throughout the Revolutionary War. On 11 August Washington ordered Malcolm to provide "such a number of hands as may be necessary" to assist Captain John Stevens. Stevens was the inventor of a screw propeller and was right then trying to design and build "a machine in the river, at West Point, for the purpose of setting fire to any of the enemy's shipping that might attempt a passage up it." Just what became of that particular invention is unknown, but while Stevens was toying with it, the Commander-in-Chief authorized another research project. Hearing that James Jay, John Jay's brother, was "desirous of making some experiments in gunnery," he ordered Colonel John Lamb to assist in the study. It wasn't much, but it was a beginning that would blossom.[6]

After Malcolm had been in command a month, Washington sent General Duportail, his Chief of Engineers, to check his progress. From headquarters in White Plains, the Commander-in-Chief ordered the French engineer to "proceed as speedily as convenient to the Highlands and examine the several fortifications carrying on there for the defence of the North River." He asked for a "full report" but cautioned Duportail to be practical: "consider the labor and expence which have been already incurred, the advanced season of the year, and the resources of the country. . . ." Perhaps Washington suspected Duportail might use this inspection as an excuse to attempt a vindication of Radiére's expansive plans. Other duties delayed Duportail's departure until 7 September. When he appeared that

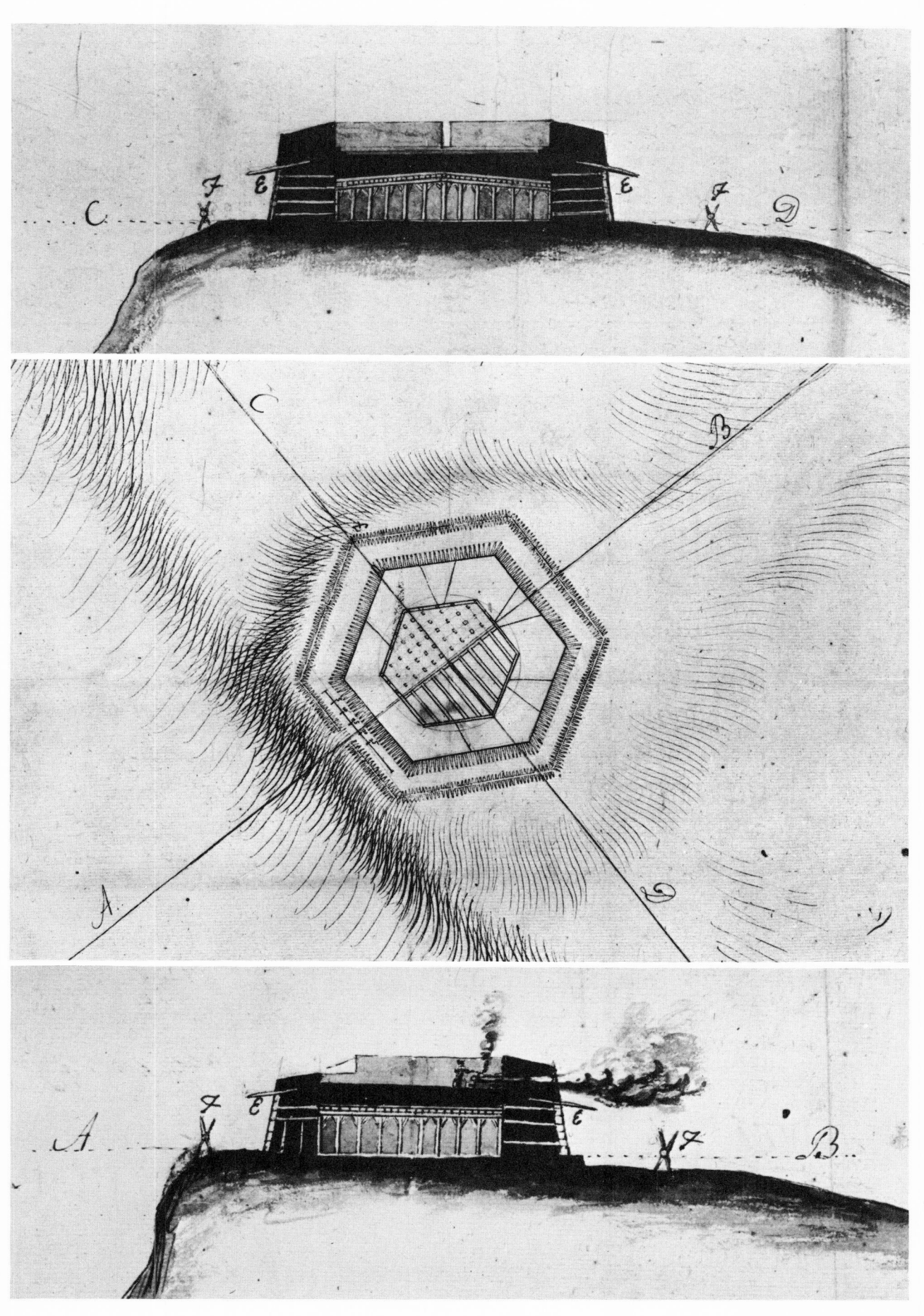

Kosciuszko's plan for the construction of Redoubt 4. Courtesy of the New-York Historical Society Library.

day on the Point, he carried a message of explanation from General Washington, who was evidently quite aware of the heartburn his French engineers suffered over Kosciuszko. "It is my wish," the letter read, "that Colonel Koshiosko may communicate everything to this gentleman. . . ."[7]

The Pole had no desire whatsoever to discuss anything with the Frenchman who was wearing the general's star he believed he himself should have had. Conveniently, he was away from West Point when Duportail visited, although he might have wished later that he had remained at his post. Three days before, he had gone to White Plains with the avowed and actual purpose of testifying at the hearings being conducted on General St. Clair's 1777 evacuation of Fort Ticonderoga. While there he found himself serving as General Gates' second in a duel with James Wilkinson. In pursuit of honor, those two attempted three times to shoot each other with pistols, but managed to do no damage at all. The duel should have been over, but Kosciuszko became embroiled in an argument with his opposite number, John Carter. They swapped heated words, almost going to the duelling field themselves. In the end, though, they were content to carry on a verbal exchange in print. The normally mild-mannered Polish engineer was still angry when he returned to West Point. There, on reading Duportail's report, he really approached his bursting point.

Duportail was a good engineer. He had gained and merited Washington's respect and confidence. His most blameworthy habit was his constant maneuvering for rank and position for himself and his French cohorts —and one should be careful before classing ambition and consideration of subordinates as traits to be avoided. When he came to West Point he approached his mission with commendable if not quite complete professional detachment. He balanced what had been done with what he felt needed to be accomplished, and prescribed something in the middle that he believed was feasible yet effective. His report was proper. Indeed, his observations and recommendations constituted definite improvements to the scheme of fortifications. But he could not avoid taking several pokes at the Pole. He mentioned Kosciuszko's name four times, each instance disparagingly. Borrowing a book from Washington, he managed to spell it three different ways in the four tries—and never correctly. The professional competence of his report is marred by the thread of pettiness running through it.[8]

Not only West Point's forts, but the chain, Constitution Island, and the barrier at New Windsor were on his inspection agenda. The ineffective *chevaux-de-frise* at Pollepel Island, conceived in a moment of panic in 1776, drew the engineer's scorn. He thought the obstacles themselves appeared very weak. They were. Henry Clinton had already proved that. Moreover, the river appeared "very wide in this part for a defense of *chevaux-de-frise.*" It was. "I can with difficulty persuade myself that a ship would be much embarrassed by them," was his caustic comment. He recommended that until West Point should be completed, the Pollepel Island defenses should be forgotten. It was a good recommendation.

"As to the chain itself," he thought it a key portion of the defenses, but recommended that it be suspended "three feet below the surface of the water." Floating on the surface, it seemed exposed "to be laid hold of by machines prepared for the purpose on board the vessels which may approach." Even more dangerous, he thought, "would be the breaking it by cannon shot—when a vast number comes to be fired on both sides in a contest between enemy ships and the batteries." He suggested it could "be very easily executed—by having another chain made fast at each end to the great one, and carried above the floats." That recommendation was prudently ignored.

Perceiving it to be "equally necessary to secure the chain on the left-hand shore of the river," Duportail noted that a single, open battery was the only work on Constitution Island. Three small redoubts and another battery would make the Patriots "completely masters of the island." One redoubt, to contain about sixty men, should be built on the site of the old blockhouse "to afford an immediate defense to the chain and its extremity." Another should be erected "on an eminence in the rear of the newly constructed battery," while the third should be placed on a hill "which commands all the other rising ground in the island." Those two positions "ought to be made for 150 men or 200 at most." The additional battery he envisioned going up on the remains of one previously standing near the water level. It would be "perfectly well placed for battering the enemy's ships." His ideas concerning the island were excellent. It is ironic that, as men had so long concentrated on Constitution Island to the exclusion of the western point of land, focus on West Point should in turn have caused the island to be ignored. In actuality, to close the river properly both were needed—either alone had a blind spot; together they were mutually reinforcing. It is to Duportail's credit that he recognized that fact. With minor alterations, the island was fortified as he suggested; three redoubts and two batteries.

The Frenchman's judgment on the West Point works was somewhat more mixed. "Fort Arnold [designed and laid out by Radiére] appears to me to be pretty well situated and traced—but if the intention of Colonel Kosciusko is to leave the sides next the river at the present height (as appears to be the case) I cannot approve it." Nor did he like the Pole's work on the new bombproof. Sherburne Redoubt was "extremely well placed for battering the vessels which should approach the chain," but the parapet needed to be raised and the embrasures covered. Instead of the redoubt and batteries "in front of the Redoubt Willis, . . . and which require for their defense four or five hundred men," Duportail preferred one small, enclosed strongpoint. "But for the present," he granted, "matters may be left as they are." Fort Wyllys itself he didn't like at all. It was in the wrong place, did not cover all avenues of approach, was too large. Worse, Fort Putnam could not cover all of it with fire. "It will be best perhaps to rebuild this fort altogether," he strongly urged. At any event, the wall facing Fort Putnam should not be raised to protect the interior, "which I am told Colonel Kosciousko purposes, because it must be prodigiously elevated to answer that purpose." Rather, Duportail would construct a traverse and "reject a third of the work on the south as altogether useless."

Fort Putnam he recognized as "the key of all the others." Claiming it could be made almost impregnable, Duportail said, "This fort has nothing to fear but a bombardment or escalade." To make it impervious to bombardment, a bombproof "sufficient for three fourths of the garrison, magazines, hospital, etc." should be constructed. "I am told," he added, "Colonel Koshucsko purposes at this time to begin one; but which will not suit more than 70 or 80 men." Rocky Hill loomed above Fort Putnam, the engineer noted. When told that Kosciuszko had already drawn up plans for a redoubt there, he hastily wrote, "There is indeed a height which commands [Fort Putnam], but it would be very difficult for an enemy, even when master of it to bring heavy cannon there. Besides it would be too far to make a breach." Obviously the spectre of Mount Defiance did not lurk in his memory as it did in Kosciuszko's. The Rocky Hill project was temporarily killed.

All in all, it was a fine paper he sent to Washington. Most of his ideas were good, many were adopted. But the immediate result was harmful because he had been unable to curb his dislike of the Polish engineer whom Americans deemed superior to a fellow Frenchman.

Radière himself still rankled over those blows to his ego. From White Plains, where he was working as an engineer with the main army, yet close enough to the Highlands to be reminded constantly of his previous embarrassment, he got wind of a rumor that the Pole would be advanced to brigadier general. Immediately he petitioned Congress, claiming priority and imploring consideration ahead of his competitor. Taking sides just before coming to West Point, Duportail had approached Washington with a plea that Radière be ruled senior to Kosciuszko. The Commander-in-Chief deferred the matter to Congress, but let that body know his opinion that only Duportail should outrank the Pole. The upshot was that neither officer gained a promotion. At times the General must have wondered if foreign advisors were truly worth all the worry. One thing was sure—steps should be taken to assure that America would never again be forced to rely on outsiders for professional military advice. Washington was convinced that a school, a military academy, would have to be established so the United States could train its own engineers.[9]

Everything came to a head when Kosciuszko returned to West Point and read Duportail's report. Convinced, with some justification, that Duportail thought him the "worst of engineers," he tried to get away from the source of antagonism. His old friend, Horatio Gates, was being transferred to New England. Kosciuszko asked to be taken along. Gates promptly wrote Washington, requesting that the engineer be assigned to him because the works at West Point were so far advanced. The Commander-in-Chief knew better than Gates how very much remained to be done. And from his previous experience he knew how important it was to retain continuity in engineering advice while in the midst of construction. He turned Gates down, saying,

> Colonel Kosciusko has had the chief direction and superintendence of the works at West Point, and it is my desire that he should remain to carry them on. New plans and alterations at this time would be attended with many inconveniences, and protract the defences of the river. These . . .

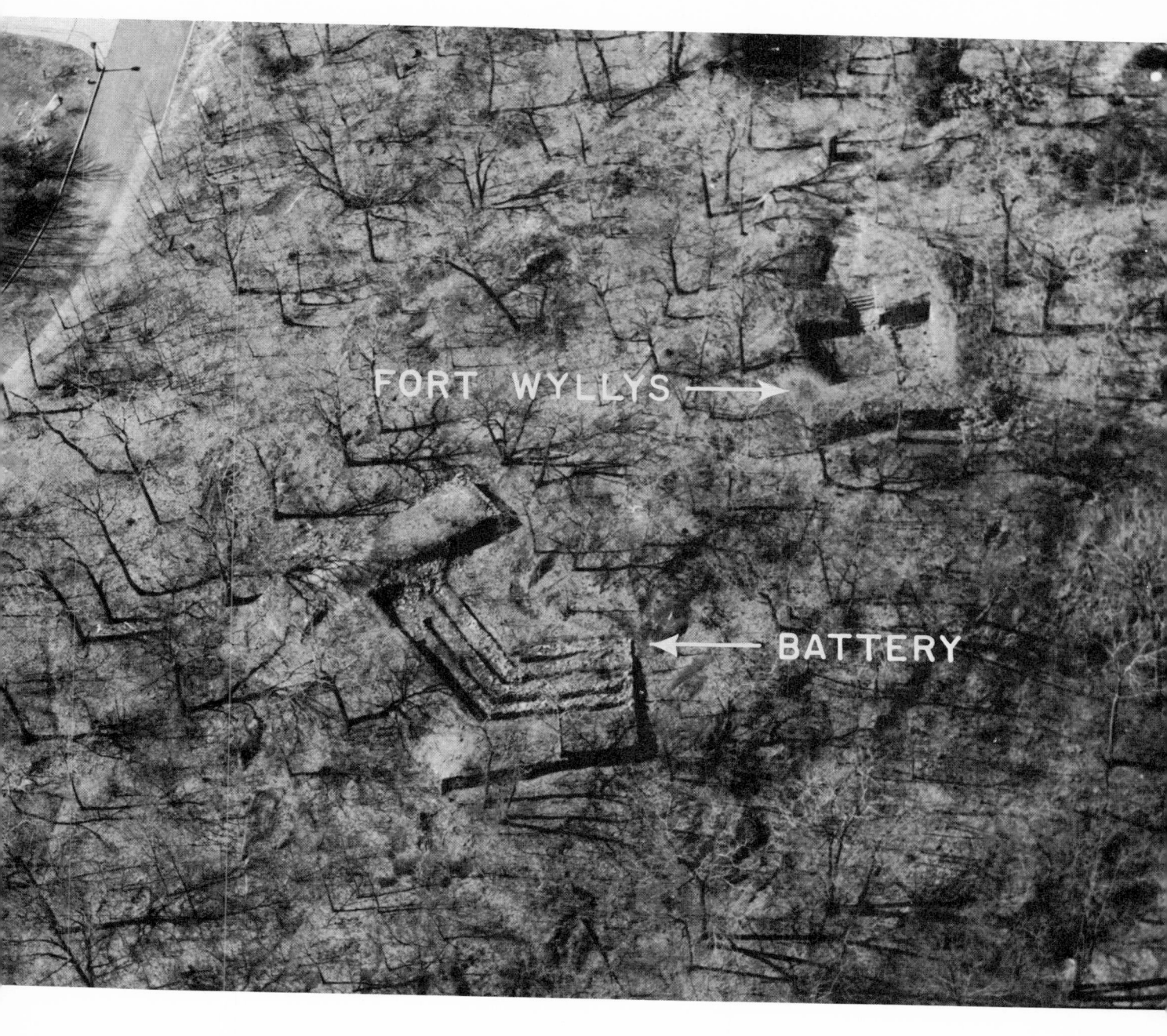

FORT WYLLYS →

← BATTERY

Aerial view showing the ruins of Redoubt Wyllys, 1966. U.S. Army photograph.   177

might take place in case of his absence under the management of another engineer.[10]

Kosciuszko was crushed. "My happiness is lost," he wrote Gates. To another friend he lamented, "I am the most enhappy man in the world, because all my Yankees the best friends is gone to Whit Plains or to eastern and left me with the Skoches or Irishes impolites as the saviges." He placed the blame where it belonged, saying, "I should go to the eastern with General Gates but General Washington was obstacle of going me ther and I am verry sorry of it." The Pole could only seek solitary solace in a lovely rock garden which he had constructed on the side of a cliff beneath Fort Arnold. He must have retired to his retreat often in those days.[11]

His foreign engineers hostile toward one another and unhappy with him, Washington took action to mollify them and yet keep the work at West Point on track. Less than a week after receiving Duportail's report, he and his French Chief of Engineers rode together to West Point. Washington carefully and painstakingly examined every fort, each battery, every building. He looked at the chain and viewed Rocky Hill. He peered over cannon to observe their field of fire. Personally, he investigated each proposed site for new works. Then, in a masterpiece of tact, he praised with pen both Duportail and Kosciuszko. His letter, written in Fort Arnold on 19 September, was addressed to Duportail. He put his thoughts on paper because both engineers had some difficulty understanding English and also because it would provide each of them with a record of his words. In phrases as carefully chosen as any he ever wrote, Washington told Duportail that he highly approved of his suggestions for improvements. Then, after slipping in a mere mention of the fact that Congress itself had sent Kosciuszko to West Point, he ruled that the great progress already made "would render any alteration in the general plan a work of too much time." Next, the General blandly told Duportail, "The favorable testimony which you have given of Colonel Kosciousko's abilities prevents uneasiness on this head." Duportail, of course, had paid no such compliment, not intentionally at least. But he could hardly refute it. Then, as sop for the Frenchman, Washington reminded him that, as the senior engineer in the Continental Army, he could always supervise the Pole's work. Moreover, he directed that the defenses on Constitution Island should be laid out as Duportail had recommended. The letter worked, apparently, for as Washington rode away that afternoon the Polish engineer was pleased and so was the Frenchman. Each believed he had won the argument. By such performances did Washington hold his fragile army together.[12]

Leaves on the rocky hillsides were turning again. The campaign of 1778, such as it was, was over. The French fleet, which had raised so much premature jubilation, had seemingly been of no assistance. In fact, licking his wounds in Boston, Admiral D'Estaing was being assailed in most bitter terms by many Americans. Washington's great dream of evicting Sir Henry Clinton from New York was a casualty along with many other shattered hopes. Seeing no possibility for further action that year, the General decided to get his army early into winter quarters. He selected a great arc along the Hudson Highlands stretching from Danbury, Connecticut, to

Middlebrook, New Jersey. Fredericksburg, above the Highlands, was to be his own headquarters. West Point was the keystone in that disposition. Marching orders were issued after mid-September.

Among the instructions to the army was an order to Israel Putnam to "proceed to West Point to reinforce the garrisons in the Highlands and aid in the completion of the works with all possible expedition." Whether someone complained at the prospect of "Old Put's" return or whether Washington himself had second thoughts is not known. But he soon changed his mind. Upon visiting West Point with Duportail, he became convinced that Putnam was not suited to the command there. "On consideration," he informed Putnam from West Point, "it appears to me best that you should encamp with the division under your command on the east side of the river." Colonel Malcolm would remain in command for the time being, while the Commander-in-Chief, at Fredericksburg, would virtually command everything in the Highlands himself.

Memories of 1777 were revived on the last day of September; and notification was served of George Washington's newly assumed control. The General had earlier posted men to "keep a careful and constant look out on the North River, and . . . give the earliest notice possible to the commander at West Point" of any suspicious movement of British transports. When reports poured in at month's end of preparations being made in New York City that indicated an imminent strike up the river, Washington had no intention of celebrating the anniversary of the fall of Forts Clinton and Montgomery with a repeat performance. He ordered General Putnam to close Timp Pass. "You will therefore detach a field officer with about one hundred men to guard the pass leading from Haverstraw to Fort Montgomery." The alarm proved false, but with Washington looking over Putnam's shoulder the Highlands defenses were not about to be taken by surprise.[13]

As the troops were finding or building barracks and Washington was settling down in his new headquarters, Thomas Machin paid him a visit. Machin was still a captain-lieutenant and had not been paid regularly since 1776. His work in the Highlands had been satisfactory, he thought, but he had been superseded first by Radière, then by Kosciuszko. He wanted his back pay and requested permission to return to regular military duty as his engineering talents were not being used. To support his claim, he showed Washington a certificate prepared in his behalf by Governor Clinton. The Governor listed all his many activities during more than two years in the Highlands, the most recent of which had been refloating the *Lady Washington* by designing huge leather bellows to pump her out. "In justice to Captain Machin," Clinton summarized, "I am bound to add that while he was under my command he discovered great diligence and industry in forwarding the different works committed to his care and that in the execution of them he experienced an uncommon share of personal labor and fatigue being often necessarily exposed to work in the water in very cold weather." Later he strengthened his statement, saying that Machin "frequently endangered his health by working in the water when it was floating with ice." Washington agreed with the engineer and arranged for a just price to be set on his services. Not long after, Machin joined James Clinton in the Indian fighting then flaring along New York's western frontier. His remarkable service as an engineer in the Hudson Highlands was terminated. So far as the defenses along the river were concerned, he faded away into the pages of history as inconspicuously as he had emerged. Someday some historian will attempt a biography of that amazingly unsung man, and he may then receive the recognition that is his due.[14]

As the fall months passed, Colonel Malcolm came to enjoy his post more and more. Unperturbed by threats of attack, protected as they were by the entire Continental Army, he and Kosciuszko directed all their energy to improving the fortifications. Satisfaction with progress achieved was evident in correspondence from various persons. Malcolm, himself, best expressed the prevalent mood in a light letter to George Clinton concerning impressed Tory laborers:

> Last night I received a fine reinforcement of Tories from Peekskill and this morning they are at work. From the information of Lieutenant Connelly who brought them in, I expect a world of solicitations in their favor, and I imagine they will apply to your Excellency. I expect the more so, because I am tormented with the Orange County Justices whenever any miscreants are brought in from the mountains.
>
> Now, as I only want to get a whiles worth out of them, and as it is the very least atonement they can make for their crimes, I request that your Excellency will evade the interest that I know will be made for them, by boobies as bad as they. I have never kept any of those fellows above three months and then give them a discharge and certificate that they are white washed. . . . amuse your stupid justices that they may not torment me with their foolish demands and we shall make you a good fort bye and bye.[15]

Apparently, local magistrates did not wholly approve of Malcolm's method of cleansing Tories, and neither did those involved enjoy being "white washed" by labor on the forts.

Life at West Point soon settled into a routine not unlike that found on army posts the world over. Construction was no longer performed at panic pace, but according to a well-conceived plan. All concerned could take more pride in their work, and as a result had more to be proud of.

The men lived in huts laid out in two long rows on the plain, or in Long Barracks, a two-story structure between Fort Arnold and Sherburne Redoubt. As winter approached they saw wisdom in patching cracks, especially in the northern walls. Lumber was extremely scarce, of course, but soldiers have always been able to improvise. Orderly books provide a clue that a certain amount of midnight requisitioning was going on. Once Malcolm resorted to offering a ten-dollar reward to anyone "who will discover the villain that hath stolen the aprons from the cannon in the redoubts." Recruiting never slackened in George Washington's army, but it always accelerated near the end of the year when many enlistments normally expired. Proselyting became prevalent at West Point. A favorite gambit was for officers from one unit slyly to escort men from another to the sutler's tent, get them drunk, and sign them up then and there. Malcolm soon put a stop to that. Other similarly vexing little problems required his constant attention. Laundry women, for example, charged too much, forcing the commandant to establish a price ceiling on their service. And day-to-day living, especially in an era that did not appreciate sanitation, demanded a persistent awareness on the part of the post commander. At one point he proclaimed, "The necessary [is] to be covered every evening . . . and every man in garrison are ordered to make use of them only—if any dirty fellow is detected [violating] this so necessary a regulation, he shall be ignominiously punished." All in all, Malcolm had a big task, great responsibility, and he liked it.[16]

Not that all was tedium and routine. At least one unit held a ball in November. Officers sent wagons out, "collected the girls in the neighborhood, and had a kickup in the evening." It must have been a social success for we are told the same group held "a second dance on the following Friday." For once, men in the Highlands were not gripped in a sombre mood. And quite obviously they did not share the outlook of the Continental Congress, which had just one month earlier resolved to dismiss anyone holding office who shall "act, promote, encourage, or attend" any play or theatrical entertainment.[17]

A break in the routine occurred in late November when Burgoyne's hapless troops, captured over a year earlier, were ferried across the Hudson just above West Point. Those prisoners, the so-called Convention Army, were being moved westward deeper into the interior of the country. Washington entertained several German officers as they passed. American soldiers looked with some curiosity and not a little sympathy at the pathetic survivors of a campaign that seemed to have been won so long ago. Washington, ever cautious now with the security of West Point, ordered Malcolm to put the garrison on full alert while the large body of prisoners were "near and passing the river."

Shortly after that interlude, Washington directed McDougall once more to take command of the Highlands. The Scot was to establish his own headquarters at Peekskill and place a brigade at West Point. "I need not observe to you," the General clearly observed to him, "that West Point is to be considered the first and principle object of your attention." McDougall promptly although reluctantly obeyed, ordering Brigadier General John Paterson to march to West Point. Malcolm was incensed. He fired off a letter to General Washington protesting his relief. Washington patiently explained that the move was in no way intended as a slap at him, but that more troops were needed to insure the defense of the post, therefore requiring a general to supervise them. McDougall cautiously told Paterson to take a few days to familiarize himself with the post until Malcolm's anger should vent itself. Malcolm was not at all happy. He wrote several angry letters to George Clinton, hoping the Governor would help. He couldn't, and Paterson duly took the role of commandant. George Washington, if he bothered to recount all the personality problems that had erupted at the peculiar bend in the river, might have wondered if it was just human nature or if the location itself somehow bred dissension.[18]

Kosciuszko gained an assistant in the change. Lieutenant Colonel Jean Baptiste Gouvion, the most junior of the four French engineers, came to the Highlands with McDougall. At McDougall's request, Washington specifically detailed the Frenchman to work there under supervision of the Pole. The arrangement seems to have worked out quite successfully; Gouvion was a much more personable chap than either Radière or Duportail and he apparently was content to work for Kosciuszko. McDougall quite preferred Gouvion to Radière, describing the former as "a modest and worthy young gentleman."[19]

As cold weather closed in, the engineer put finishing touches to that season's work. During the winter, he knew from experience, it was largely a waste of time to attempt exterior construction. Much, however, could be accomplished inside the forts and storage facilities and barracks. During the fall, in accord with Duportail's recommendations, Constitution Island had become once more a scene of construction activity. A small redoubt with a bombproof had been begun atop the westernmost knob of the island and two more were being built closer to the chain. On the West Point side, workmen had been busy, too. Fort Putnam now boasted a larger bombproof and a cistern to catch and store rain water. Fort Webb was well on the way to completion. Before the snows came, it had a stone wall all around and contained a bombproof magazine. Iron and brass guns were mounted throughout—in the four water batteries perched just above high-tide mark near the western end of the chain, across the river on Constitution Island, in Fort Arnold and Sherburne Redoubt on the plain, and in each of the four forts on higher ground to the west of Fort Arnold. By Christmas of 1778, the interlocking system of fortifications that constituted fortress West Point was mostly in being if not completed. On the west side of the river, only those redoubts which would later be called "1," "2," and "3" had not yet been planned. A fort for Rocky Hill (later called "4") had been designed but construction had not been initiated.[20]

McDougall was not at all pleased with his assignment. He knew too well the problems and the boredom and the pitfalls of command in the Highlands. Greeting his very arrival, however, came a flurry of high excitement. On his first day at West Point, 4 December 1778, while he was preparing "to inspect the state of this post and to give the necessary orders for the winter," the British suddenly moved in strength up the river. The next few days were hectic as troop columns converged on the river, gunners puzzled over how to fire from unfinished batteries, militiamen streamed in to help hold the river forts, and McDougall strove to coordinate the diverse groups of men while at the same time attempting to discern what his enemy had in mind. That trip, though, the redcoats were content to land at Stony Point and burn the structures there. They quickly embarked again and withdrew down the river. Inspired by that scare, McDougall viewed his job with renewed interest and considerable concern.[21]

Nearly a year had gone by since he had watched the works first take shape. During those intervening months great amounts of labor and money had been poured into the defenses at West Point. And yet they stood incomplete. Should the British launch a determined effort to seize the fortress, McDougall reasoned anxiously, he would be powerless to repel them. Mulling that over, he foresaw his reputation washing away. Americans had been led to believe even then that West Point was another Gibraltar. It was not, the Scot knew, but what would be the fate of any general unable to defend the Gibraltar of America? He candidly set forth his fears in a letter to Washington:

> It is a capricious, censorious and perilous hour for general officers—I am determined not to be made the scapegoat of any ignorant, wicked, or inattentive servant of the country, appointed by the cabals or intrigues of any set of men—I have directed Lieutenant Colonel Gouvion to repair to West Point with me to make an accurate report of the present state of the works. . . . This done I shall report to Congress and your Excellency; and order the engineer on the ground to keep a journal of my orders directing the works, the strength and materials he shall have, and the progress of the work from day to day; and if the supreme council of the country will not enable me to execute their orders, they must take the consequences with their constituents. . . .[22]

Spoken like a true politician, which he was, or had been until he became a soldier. Although his major motivation seemed to be self-serving, designed primarily to protect his reputation, McDougall's efforts to cover himself could hardly have any but a positive impact on the fortifications. Lethargy and indifference would have been ruinous; enthusiasm and interest from whatever source were welcome.

A week later, having discovered what a great amount of labor remained to be done to perfect the defenses at West Point, McDougall ordered the young French engineer to proceed "on the first fair day" to West Point to conduct an extremely detailed inspection. (Carefully, he made multiple copies of his instructions to prove, if need be, that he had really tried to improve the fortress). Gouvion was to assume mentally the role of an English general with 7,000 men and an adequate supporting flotilla. With that force, he was asked, "What would be your plan of operation to reduce the works or to remove or pass the chain?" McDougall instructed him to reconnoitre the land for miles around, to decide what strength would be necessary to close the passes, and to examine the hills west of West Point. Specifically, he was to determine "whether there are any hills to the westward of our westernmost work on which it will be necessary to erect additional works." He was to look into the type construction and the quality of materials used, and to consider the works with respect to "their independent and relative quality to each other for defense." To speed the rate of construction on Constitution Island, would it not be "most expedient to secure the chain and boom" there by building blockhouses? That type of position, McDougall thought, could stand up to cannon fire "with the addition of sand bags to strengthen the faces . . . fronting the river." The general wanted to know if Fort Arnold could absorb a battering by two eighteen-pounders for two hours. And there was much more. Had Gouvion executed and reported on everything in his instructions, we would have on record the most complete and authenic description in existence of Revolutionary War West Point. Apparently, however, he did not make the inspection. No report has survived and only three days later McDougall sent the engineer on a mission to Haverstraw and King's Ferry where he remained throughout the winter. Nonetheless,

McDougall's instructions indicate the areas of his concern as well as his unwillingness to accept the status quo.[23]

Two lesser but more immediate problems quickly surfaced, diverting McDougall's attention momentarily from the grander subject of the concept of defense. The first was the simple to see but hard to solve question of how to billet the garrison during the winter. A survey showed that West Point possessed barracks space for 54 officers and 1,516 men. And that figure was reached by squeezing men into every cubic foot available. In Moore's house, for example, the quartermaster intended to crowd 64 soldiers into four rooms, each of which measured maybe 12 by 15 feet. For the overflow, there was no solution but to tent. Unlucky soldiers marched off to a canvas camp, muttering bitterly as they foresaw another miserable winter. Fortunately, with the exception of a severe cold snap just before Christmas, that winter was unusually mild. Tents were bearable. Too, masons and carpenters were able to work most days, thereby opening additional huts and barracks all along. The December cold wave itself was the cause of the second problem.[24]

The chain and boom were caught by ice in the river. They were nearly lost. Never before had anyone been obliged to take a chain *out* of the river. A year before, the British had saved the Patriots that particular puzzle by removing the chain themselves in October. It had been generally acknowledged, however, that the chain could not remain across the river when it froze. Shifting ice would destroy it. Washington, in fact, had told Malcolm early in November to "put all things in readiness to take up the chain and boom" as soon as advanced weather eliminated any serious risk of an enemy attack. Perhaps with the change of command Malcolm assumed it was Paterson's responsibility, but the new commandant apparently neither knew nor thought anything about it. On his visit sometime in mid-December, McDougall noticed the chain and promptly issued orders for its immediate removal. He gave Kosciuszko very minute instructions on the method to be used.[25]

General Paterson then planned to remove the two water obstacles on 21 December as soon as two extra sloops arrived from New Windsor. The boats failed to reach West Point that day, but a sudden drop in temperature did, causing ice to form along the edges of the river and between the chain links. Worried officers gathered near Chain Battery to discuss the problem. In a matter of hours the river would be a solid sheet and the chain would probably be lost. One of the colonels suggested swinging it to the West Point side for the time being. It seemed the only course. Rapidly, boats were in the freezing water, hundreds of troops lined the bank to help haul in rope cables. The huge chain was cut free from its blocks on Constitution Island and released from anchor lines. Carefully and slowly men eased the eastern end of the chain upriver in an arc, bringing it to the rocky bank at West Point where it was fixed. What was done with the boom is unclear, but it was placed in a different area where it was out of danger when the river did freeze.[26]

Alarm gripped McDougall when he heard what had happened. He did what he could, dispatching an officer experienced in handling boats under adverse conditions and firing off urgent letters to impress Paterson with the importance of putting the chain in "a state of safety." He himself made a flying trip to West Point, but, observing that Kosciuszko and Paterson were doing everything possible, he returned to fret in Peekskill. If he knew anything about the causes of ulcers, he probably thought darkly about West Point.

As the river grew its coat of ice, the anxious officers watched the combined elements of tide and temperature snap the chain in two or three places. Fortunately, the weather continued cold and the ice soon became solid, preventing the loss of any of the segments. The boom remained intact in its haven. On Christmas day it was obvious that for the moment both were safe, but everyone agreed it would be best "to pay our attention to getting up the chain."[27]

McDougall, relieved, replied that so long as the iron monster remained safe, he did not "wish to risk the men's limbs by working on it in this severe weather." By the 28th the ice was solid enough to support pedestrian traffic to New Windsor. While awaiting a thaw, Kosciuszko designed a "machine to hoist the chain" aboard boats as soon as it should be freed from the ice. Realizing it would be impossible to tow the entire obstacle through a river chocked with ice floes, he planned to pick up the chain a few links at a time. "The chain is safe," he assured General McDougall, "and can be very easy taken up when the cold abates. The boom lies where it was and will be taken up." The thaw came on the 29th. By 30 or 31 December, the Pole was extricating about seventy-five links a day. With some understatement, General Paterson described it as "a heavy piece of work." By the second day of 1779, some four hundred links and a proportionate number of logs were piled up in front of Moore's house.[28]

Removing the chain cost the life of one man. Apprehensive that "the river would break up the chain" during darkness, Paterson kept sailors on guard at night in boats tied to the great barrier. The evening of 3 January witnessed a brawl between two drunken crewmen during which one of them was knocked sprawling into the frigid, black river. He drowned.

When at last the chain and boom were deposited on dry land, McDougall cast a heartfelt sigh of relief. That unhappy episode had consumed one life, much worry, a lot of hard and cold work, and valuable time which could have been better spent working on the defenses. It had been a terrible fright, one not soon forgotten. Almost a year later, in early November 1779, McDougall still remembered vividly. He then nudged Washington, "It will soon be time to draw in the chain; lest we run the hazard of losing it which was near the case last year, from the lateness of the season, besides employing the garrison on the ice during the severe weather to get it out."[29]

The first couple of months in 1779 were rather uneventful. The weather was not even much of a topic of conversation for it remained surprisingly mild. Life was boring almost beyond endurance at West Point. Lieutenant Colonel Aaron Burr, Executive officer of Malcolm's regiment, found it far too quiet for his restless soul. He departed in January. "West Point is as barren of news as the mountains that surround it," wailed Kosciuszko. Another officer, Ebenezer Huntington had already gone on record with a similarly disparaging view of West Point: ". . . this post doth not afford any news and let me add, it cannot give a pleasant prospect nor afford anything agreeable to sustain life. . . ." McDougall, who had been hard pressed to find shelter for all his men, brooded. Depressed by the shortage of material, he lamented, "My condition is not much better than the Israelites in Egypt who were ordered to make brick without straw." "I am determined it is the last winter I shall be imprisoned in the Highlands to be a drudge for others," he vowed. Dreary though the existence might have been, McDougall worked hard to strengthen the defenses as much as he could and to safeguard the health and morale of his men. Some of his efforts provided a degree of humor. After one inspection tour of a smoky, smelly barracks housing several men, he was so overcome by the stench that he had posters tacked up in every building encouraging the men to change clothes regularly. There were more than enough women in camp to keep their uniforms washed, he asserted. Then he proclaimed pointedly, "A man is seldom aware of the noxious matter that comes through his own skin, but if he takes up a shirt that has been worn a few days by another person, he is frequently offended." Just in the event of a winter attack, the general ordered Paterson to fill empty flour barrels with dirt and use them to line the open east side of Fort Arnold. And so the long weeks passed, routinely, quietly, and all too slowly for most of the officers and men.[30]

After the chain had been deposited on land, Kosciuszko inspected the float logs which had been in the river since the previous spring. Over half were ruined from their long immersion. Late in February, details were sent into the nearby country to cut white pine replacements. As the logs were dragged back, they were coated with pitch and the chain was painstakingly reassembled. When April neared, McDougall began to grow nervous. He prodded, but Paterson stoically informed the nervous Scot that "it takes some time to pitch the logs." In the doldrums of that soft winter, life and labor settled into an easy cadence, not to be rushed until brighter weather regenerated the land and the people—not to mention the enemy threat.

In March 1778, Timothy Dwight had climbed up Sugarloaf Mountain for a look at West Point. He had not enjoyed the vista. The "deep brown" color of the mountains gave an aspect "of universal death." Everything was "majestic, solemn, wild and melancholy" and he observed "not a single cheerful object within the horizon." Had he climbed the hill again in March 1779, the scene striking his eyes would have changed considerably. Forts and barracks in tiers from river level to mountain top covered West Point and Constitution Island. Thousands of men would have been living under his gaze. And nearly every tree at or near West Point was missing, having gone into one of the scores of buildings or having warmed those thousands of men. If not yet a Gibraltar in strength, West Point was taking on something of the bare and formidable appearance of that famous Rock.

13

STEUBEN AND STONY POINT

HISTORY has a way of turning up coincidences. Steuben, who would strengthen the spine of the Continental Army, and West Point, which would strengthen the spine of the continent itself, both joined the Patriot cause at the same time. On his way from Boston to Pennsylvania to present himself to Congress, Baron Friedrich Wilhelm Augustus von Steuben crossed the frozen Hudson River at Fishkill on a bitterly cold day in late January 1778. Soldiers from General Parsons' brigade were then busy making huts on the plain at West Point.

Ragged and shivering Continentals stopped to stare at the spectacle presented by the passage of Steuben's party. The Baron and three aides, all dressed in brand new uniforms of buff and blue, were mounted on spirited horses. Trailing behind came a caravan of sleighs carrying supplies and a dozen servants. To complete the picture, the Prussian's huge Italian greyhound, Azor, loped along beside the column. And if all that weren't sufficiently strange to make Yankee heads turn, the knowledge that they were glimpsing a general who had actually fought with Frederick the Great was more than enough.

It is not recorded what Steuben thought as he passed West Point. He surely would have taken a closer look could he have foreseen that he would spend so many months there in the next five years. But his trained eye must have noted the great natural defensive strength of the Hudson Highlands. And he may have had even then a sound enough grasp of American geography to have perceived the strategic importance of the Hudson River. He was later to write that the British could have only one objective which would determine the fate of America—West Point. "Let us . . . hold West

Point," he stated unequivocally, "and the end of our campaign will be glorious."

Steuben's title of nobility might have been false, his rank questionable, but his abilities were true. Benjamin Franklin, the wise old ambassador who selected him, had judged the German well. Reporting to Congress in York, Pennsylvania, Steuben ran into much the same coolness that the French engineers had encountered. Then near fifty years of age, and fully cognizant of the imperfections of human nature, he saw right off how things stood. Hiding his disappointment at not being greeted with open arms, he boldly made the lawmakers a sporting deal. He volunteered to serve with neither rank nor salary. If the rebellion should fail or if his contributions should be deemed in any manner unsatisfactory, he would claim no compensation beyond expenses. On the other hand, if the Patriots were to win and if Congress should feel he had been an asset, then he would expect ample reward. Flabbergasted to meet a foreigner who did not argue for pay or position, Congress agreed to the gamble and sent him off to join Washington at Valley Forge.[1]

In that appallingly miserable encampment the Baron found an army as innocent of organization as it was ignorant of training. But he found in the tall, stern man at its head a commanding general who was well aware of his army's deficiencies and wanted desperately to correct them. Washington made Steuben acting Inspector General and charged him with converting the horde of tatterdemalions into an effective army. That Steuben did so, and how he did it, are stories known to every schoolboy. He quickly gained an appreciation for the fiercely independent Patriots. Telling an American soldier to do something, he learned, was insufficient. "I am obliged to say, 'This is the reason why you ought to do that,' and then he does it." When Washington rode away from Valley Forge in 1778 to tackle Henry Clinton at Monmouth, a disciplined and trained army marched smartly behind him. By then Steuben had already been accepted as a major general in the Continental Army. His gamble had paid off, and so had Congress'.

Training the men at Valley Forge was but a start. Washington wanted his entire army brought under a single system. Steuben spent his days inspecting and drilling and his nights writing. From memory he scrawled in French those parts of the Prussian regulations that seemed pertinent to the American Army. Aides translated his phrases into English. By April 1779 he had published a book, *Regulations for the Order and Discipline of the Troops of the United States*. It was adopted as official doctrine for the entire Continental Army and received the widest dissemination possible. Soldiers referred to it as "Steuben's *Blue Book*."

Events of late spring and early summer in 1779 were to subject both Steuben and his *Blue Book* to a crucial examination. Those events pivoted on West Point and the Hudson Highlands.

March had turned to April with no appreciable change in the somnolent pace of garrison life at West Point. Kosciuszko had won his struggle to obtain and prepare enough new logs to float the chain, but he was temporarily stymied for want of "two large coils of cable and one sloop, without which we cannot proceed." As the pleasant April days passed, McDougall's

Baron von Steuben. Courtesy of the West Point Museum.

189

growing fear of being caught unprepared by a British raid translated itself into a gradually increasing emphasis on construction work. He recalled most vividly the unhappy episode at Peekskill two years earlier. The hungry garrison saw its duty hours stretched out as the days lengthened. By the end of the month, with an assist from warmer weather and the arrival of necessary equipment, such diligence had accomplished much. Even the pessimistic Scot recognized the progress. He informed Washington that the various forts and redoubts on West Point itself were so far advanced as to discourage an enemy attempt against them. Steps had also been taken to solve the chronic food shortage. So long as the great river brimmed with fish, it was foolish for men at West Point to go hungry. Seines were furnished those soldiers "who understand fishing" and an officer was detailed to supervise catching and dividing fish.[2]

Not that full bellies necessarily made the troops any happier. They didn't like fish. Seafood in lieu of beef ran contrary to their taste. In fact, at a later date, a group of field-grade officers met and formally protested such action, claiming that it was not in any way agreeable to the army to receive fish as a part of the ration. Nevertheless, they had to admit that a pound of fish on the table beat a pound of beef on a due slip. The army ate Hudson River fish.[3]

The spring surge in construction spent itself by May. For want of materials and equipment the pace of improvement slowed nearly to a halt. Carpenters had no nails, boatmen no oars, blacksmiths were without iron, messengers traveled on foot for lack of horses. The chain was successfully pulled across the river,* and the most important positions were more or less defensible, but the entire fortress complex was nowhere near completion. Kosciuszko knew it, and he also knew that until the inconsistent supply system was improved very little more could be accomplished. Either from ignorance of the situation or a desire to undercut the Polish engineer, or maybe both, Duportail that month complained in a letter to John Jay that Kosciuszko's work was something less than satisfactory. The petty sniping of the French engineers had been going on so long, however, that no one paid him any heed.[4]

In New York City, Sir Henry Clinton had been for months peering intently up the Hudson River at West Point. Now he was nearly ready to jump. Throughout 1778 he had been obliged to remain relatively quiet in America while England girded herself for a struggle in Europe. The changed nature of the war—from suppression of rebellion to waging a world-wide conflict—had forced Clinton to evacuate Philadelphia, to cower passively behind his defenses in New York City when the French fleet appeared, and even to dispatch part of his forces on an expedition to the Caribbean. An attack up the Hudson had been simply beyond his strength. This year, though, expecting reinforcements, Sir Henry intended to launch a campaign. By striking at West Point he planned not only to deal the

---

* Although the evidence is unclear, it appears that the boom was never again used. Perhaps Patriots thought it was unnecessary so long as the chain remained attached under Fort Arnold rather than beneath Sherburne Redoubt.

Patriots a severe blow there, but also to draw Washington into battle "in an angle between the mountains and the river, on terms replete with risk on his part and little or none on mine." Calculating that his reinforcements would arrive by late May, he devised a plan which was shrewd enough to work, although very dependent on precise timing. Part of his army would remain in the city while a strong force sailed to Virginia to ravage that colony, drawing American eyes southward. That expedition would then return swiftly to New York, where it would be joined by most of the city's garrison in a swoop up the river to seize Stony Point and Verplanck's Point. At that very moment, Sir Henry expected, fresh troops from Europe would arrive, giving him strength enough to maintain momentum and take West Point. With Washington looking the other way and unaware that royal strength would be suddenly magnified, surprise and celerity just might carry English colors triumphant onto the plain of West Point. It was a bold plan. It could have worked.[5]

Washington's splendid intelligence net picked up the preparations. On 24 May he warned McDougall: "It would seem as if the enemy really has some expedition in view, possibly against the posts under your command. . . . It appears to me far from improbable that an attempt to surprise the forts may be in contemplation." Half a week later the General received word that for several days "the enemy have been putting on board of transports a great number of shells and other military stores." He sent Parsons' brigade to reinforce McDougall and reminded the Scot of West Point's importance: "The completion of the works at West-point has [been] prudently made a principal part of our system; and I am persuaded every thing has been done by you for this purpose."[6]

Even with that prior warning, Sir Henry's plan—or, rather, the first phase of it—worked to perfection. In his own words:

> The troops being embarked for the enterprise up the North River, . . . those from the Virginia expedition arrived just in time to join them. And the whole proceeded together on the 30th of May, accompanied by the frigates, galleys, and gunboats . . . under the direction of Sir George Collier. . . . The wind being fortunately fair, our progress was quick; and Major General [John] Vaughan was in consequence enabled to land . . . on the 31st about eight miles below Verplanck's [and march] into the rear of Fort Lafayette, a small but complete work of four guns on the east side the river garrisoned by seventy men. In the meantime, three battalions of infantry and a detachment of Jagers . . . were put on shore on the west side within three miles of Stony Point. . . .[7]

At the English approach, the outpost on Stony Point set its blockhouse afire and retreated. Sir Henry laboriously dragged cannon to the top of the abandoned height during that night. At dawn, 1 June, those guns opened a heavy fire on Fort Lafayette. Ships joined in. Blasted from the front and cut off from the rear, the Patriots capitulated. A Captain John André carried the surrender summons to the Americans. It would not be André's last visit to Verplanck's Point.

So far so good. "But where, alas, were the promised succors to enable me to prosecute my plan?" Sir Henry's scheme, entirely dependent on the punctual arrival of a sailing squadron, itself at the mercy of winds and 3,000 miles of ocean current, fell through. "Had they arrived at this time," he later wrote, ". . . I have not the smallest doubt but I might have availed myself with the fullest success of the then very critical circumstances and situation of the enemy."

Whether or not the British could have snatched the river from Patriot hands if the trans-Atlantic reserves had put in a timely appearance is now a wholly academic question. They did not arrive. What is important is that George Washington was thoroughly disturbed by the English advance. He feared Clinton might indeed take advantage of the "divided and separated state" of the Continental Army to deliver a blow before the Americans could react. As late as 3 June he was ignorant of the return of the British force that had been in Virginia—for once his secret service had failed him—but even so he reckoned West Point was probably his foe's objective. Hastily, he began concentrating divisions in the Highlands. By 4 June, as the situation cleared, he became convinced that West Point was in truth seriously endangered. He sent an officer galloping to that post to assure McDougall, "I am determined at the utmost hazard to support the fort and I expect it will hold out to the last extremity." Unwilling to trust so vital a position to militia, feeling certain that part-time soldiers would not obey orders to defend at all costs, Washington prescribed that "no part of the garrison ought to be militia." Some twenty-five hundred men were at West Point, including fifty crewmen of the *Lady Washington,* the armed galley posted behind the great chain. They were eager. General Parsons claimed, "The garrison are in high spirits and are very desirous of receiving the enemy's attack." Meanwhile, as Henry Clinton waited in vain for reinforcements, Washington hustled other thousands of Continentals into the hills near West Point.[8]

Henry Clinton, realizing that his occupation of King's Ferry forced the Americans to resort to an east-west line of communications which detoured long miles through Fishkill, "fully expected Mr. Washington would have risked an action for its recovery." He noisily removed part of his force but kept it poised to pounce if the American commander bit at the bait left at King's Ferry. However, the Briton finally complained, his raid "had no other effect on that general than to cause him to hastily assemble his troops . . . and march with them behind the mountains" to cover West Point. For his part, Washington had no intention of being lured south. He had guessed Clinton's overall plan: "If the enemy expect any considerable reinforcement, it is not improbable they are waiting its arrival, and will then prosecute their operations on the river and against the forts that protect its communications."[9]

Through June the two commanders stared at one another, their armies practically holding hands at the southern edge of the Highlands, neither quite daring to take the first step.

Washington used the time to strengthen West Point. Besides sending men, he went to see for himself what was needed. From his headquarters at Smith's Tavern in Smith's Clove (a notorious Tory hangout), the Commander-in-Chief personally rode to the stronghold on 15 June. He returned four days later to inform McDougall that as he himself would be in command of the Highlands, McDougall should take up residence at West Point where he was to have "the immediate command of the forts."

Ever convinced that men performed better with a good slug of rum under their belts, the General did not neglect to order his commissaries to keep the garrison "amply supplied" with that important liquid. He knew his men. Major Sebastian Bauman of Lamb's artillery, for example, had loudly lamented the absence at West Point of the "common necessaries." He was "without quarters, without any bedding, and sometimes without eating; and if nature had not provided water (which is in great quantity here) would be without drink too." But all of those shortages were endurable. What really galled Bauman was the absence of grog. "As for liquors I have none, my daily drink is water. Which I think is rather hard for a man in years . . . and who never before this has experienced so mean nutriment." Rum was indeed a necessity.[10]

Washington was not the only officer who knew how to get the most from grumbling soldiers. McDougall, too, was a keen manipulator of men. One way to accomplish more, he reasoned, was to start earlier in the mornings. When the troops began to balk at the daily, hot, hard, climb from the plain up to Fort Putnam, the Scot shrewdly used their natural aversion to extra labor to spur them up and on. "By way of encouragement to the soldiers," he proclaimed, "those which first come on the parade will be sent to Fort Arnold and the last to Fort Putnam." In other words, those starting to work earliest would not have to make the steep ascent, while laggards would actually have more to do.[11]

Another step that Washington took to reinforce the post, attaching to the garrison his Chief of Engineers, has led not a few historians to leap to a conclusion which is probably erroneous. On first hearing of the English advance up the Hudson, he dispatched Duportail to the Highlands with an explanation to McDougall that the Frenchman's "knowledge of his profession and military qualifications in general will render him very useful to you if he arrives in time." Duportail would provide advice and assistance, Washington wrote, "but it is also my desire that he may be vested with a command in the garrison according to his rank." On reading that sentence, one is at first likely to conclude that the General doubted Kosciuszko's ability and was insuring against the Pole's arguing with the Frenchman at a moment when full cooperation was necessary. That no love was lost between the two engineers was certainly no secret to Washington. However, the matter of command channels had absolutely nothing to do with his request. As a brigadier general and Chief of Engineers, Duportail already had full control over Colonel Kosciuszko. Washington himself had made that plain to both men. Another reason, less obvious but more likely, was Duportail's penchant for command. All the European advisors continually agitated to be given full charge of troops from time to time. No good officer is ever really content with any job short of command in combat. Washington understood that desire and obliged his European officers whenever he could. Every foreign general, at one point or the other, had such an opportunity. Washington must have reasoned that West Point could use all the engineering expertise he could throw that way—which was true—and he probably saw a chance to let Duportail serve for a short while as a commander. The Virginian did not believe he could trust troops in the field to his engineer, but if West Point were besieged, Duportail was a natural choice to help in the defense. In that age, countersiege operations were as much an engineer's responsibility as were sieges themselves. At any rate, the attachment lasted only a few days. By 9 June the Chief of Engineers was back at headquarters with Washington.[12]

At month's end, the American leader determined to take what has been called the "Revolution's boldest venture." The Patriots had not tasted victory since 1777. So far, the French alliance had produced only disappointment. A revolution has to maintain momentum, Washington sensed; it feeds on action. The lull of 1778 had served merely to lower morale. America needed a victory to talk about. Moreover, the British had remained insolently at Stony Point and Verplanck's Point for a month, in effect thumbing their noses at the Continental Army cowering in the nearby hills.

Few places were less appealing to attack than Stony Point. A narrow, steep-sided rock, it juts starkly into the Hudson River, an arrowhead of a peninsula looming like a medieval castle, 150 feet above the water's surface. Three sides were washed by British-controlled river, the fourth was separated from dry land by a tidal marsh traversed by a single elevated road or causeway. The English had increased the rock's natural strength with breastworks and batteries. A garrison of over six hundred men, supported by armed vessels, defied all would-be attackers. Sir Henry confessed that he "looked on the place as perfectly secure." No one would be foolish enough to try storming the position, while a siege would draw the rebels into the open for a fight they did not want. That is how everyone thought and that is why Washington resolved to take Stony Point. The very audacity of the venture, he mused, would help gain surprise. And a successful attempt could not fail to buoy the army's sinking spirits.

His objective chosen, the Commander-in-Chief mentally scanned his list of generals for a commander. The individual heading the attack must be bold beyond boldness, a leader able to lead men in a seemingly suicidal charge, an officer willing to scorn death, a man maybe a little fanatical yet inspirational. That description fit none other than "Mad" Anthony Wayne.

The troops. They must be trained, hand-picked, disciplined. They cannot be volunteers, for surprise is essential and nothing will more surely alert the enemy than news of a select group of volunteers preparing for some special undertaking. No, the men must know only at the very last minute that they are going to attempt the impossible. They shall be normally selected light infantry, but they will be drilled and drilled until they can with confidence execute a night bayonet charge against a prepared position. Each will be as professional a warrior as any legionnaire ever to campaign under Caesar, as any grenadier ever to march with the Great Frederick. Baron Steuben himself will train them on the West Point plain.

Grabbing paper, George Washington drafted two missives. To Anthony Wayne he wrote an official message telling him to take command of the four battalions of light infantry then encamped on Sandy Beach not far from the ruins of Fort Montgomery. The rest of Wayne's troops would be organized and sent to him as soon as possible. His primary mission would be "to oppose any movement of the enemy against the forts." Then, in a private letter, the Commander-in-Chief informed his subordinate that an attack of the British posts at King's Ferry "is a matter I have much at heart." Wayne was to reconnoitre immediately and recommend a course of action. Washington next talked to Steuben. The Prussian thought the men could be adequately sharpened if General Wayne believed the project feasible. The Baron immediately crossed the river and galloped to Major General William Heath's headquarters to "make some arrangements." That general commanded forces east of the Hudson—forces from which light infantry troops would be drawn. The drillmaster intended to begin training those men right away.[13]

As Steuben organized his training schedule and "Mad" Anthony surreptitiously surveyed methods of attacking Stony Point, the army snuggled down in the protecting mountains and prepared to celebrate the Fourth of July. "This day," The Commander-in-Chief announced, "being the anniversary of our *glorious Independence,* will be commemorated by the firing of thirteen cannon from West Point at one o'clock P.M." After the thirteen guns had boomed out one by one, bouncing muted echoes through the hills, orders were read granting pardon to all prisoners under sentence of death. Only one imperfection marred the day's festivities: Washington —and the soldiers, too, we may be sure—regretted his inability to dole out extra liquor. "I wish we had it in our power to distribute a portion of rum to the soldiers, to exhilarate their spirits upon this occasion, but unfortunately our stock is too scanty to permit." He did not dwell on the celebration overly long, however: that very morning an initial report had arrived from General Wayne. Washington made plans to rendezvous with him for a firsthand look at Stony Point.[14]

On 6 July, accompanied by a small guard, the General rode south. North of Bear Mountain Wayne was waiting. Together the two continued, dropping down into Doodletown, moving single file through Timp Pass, and reaching a rise overlooking Stony Point. Excitedly—Wayne never approached anything in life calmly—the tanner from Pennsylvania pointed out his plan to the Virginia planter. Minute piled on minute as the generals, standing apart from aides and guards, gesticulated and pointed, squinting now and then through Washington's telescope and conversing in quiet tones. When the interview was over, the Commander-in-Chief was convinced it might be done. "The works are formidable" he acknowledged, "but perhaps on fuller examination they may be found accessible." Dropping Wayne off at Sandy Beach, he returned to New Windsor.

The plan shifted into high gear. Light infantry units were brought up to full strength; Wayne resumed efforts "to gain a more accurate knowledge" of the position's flanks and rear; Rufus Putnam, then stationed on Constitution Island, was ordered with a reconnaissance party to "examine the enemy's works on Verplanck's Point." Steuben accelerated his training.[15]

The bogus baron had established a pattern of drilling on the snowy fields of Valley Forge that he had little altered since. Personally putting a unit through its paces, he would storm and shout in a colorful mixture of French, German, and poor English. His matchless profanity was a constant source of mirth to the clumsy men he was struggling to convert into soldiers. Steuben would shout, cajole, demonstrate, gesticulate, grow livid with frustration, swear, and occasionally break into a big smile when some maneuver went well. An often-repeated story relates an instance when even his trilingual profanity was not sufficient for the task. During a particularly exasperating performance by a particularly awkward lot of men, Steuben had quickly expended his small store of English, lapsing then into French and German oaths. After shouting every imprecation he could think of in all three languages, he still had not adequately expressed his manifold disgust. Turning to an American aide, he ordered him to swear at them in English, explaining loudly, "*Viens*, Walker, *mon ami, Sacre!* Goddam de *gaucheries* of dese *badauts! Je ne puis plus.* I can curse dem no more."

That scene is familiar to every historian of the Revolutionary War, but not all have recognized it for what it probably was. The routine, repeated with minor alterations over and over, never failed to convulse the men in laughter. Steuben, a shrewd judge of his American charges, probably realized that the miserable men in Valley Forge sorely needed humor, but he also knew that he had to win their confidence and interest if his ideas and teachings were to take root. Whether or not he purposely staged his little performances may never be known, but the results were everything he could have hoped for. When word was spread that the Prussian general was to drill a unit, curious troops flocked to the parade ground to witness the entertainment—and in the process to soak up more military lore.

West Point's plain witnessed similar scenes that July. Steuben's English was much improved and his repertoire of American oaths was proportionately larger. There is no indication that he ever needed an aide that summer to assist him in the task of cursing at men executing their exercises clumsily. His regulations, the *Blue Book,* were arriving from the printer in Philadelphia. As copies became available, Wayne's light infantry had first priority, one going to every officer in the grade of captain or higher. Most of these men had either been drilled before by the Prussian or had been exposed to officers who had. For that reason they shaped up quickly. Heavy rains ate into the short time available—lightning killed one soldier and injured several others on Constitution Island—but Steuben kept the troops on the soggy fields between downpours. He emphasized bayonet practice. Men thrust and parried for hours. Arms and shoulders grew weary; muskets seemed to double and treble in weight. Yet, at a grating shout from the German, the long knives snapped up in unison, aiming thirstily at the jugular of an imaginary foeman. If a soldier failed to respond, whirled too slowly, or missed a command, closely watching officers pounced on him. He did not often fail twice. By the 12th Steuben was smiling more often than swearing. The men were ready. Next day, Washington dispatched to Wayne the contingents of light troops commanded by Colonel Return Jonathan Meigs, Major William Hull, and Major Hardy Murfree. Steuben sent forth from West Point men trained and dedicated and disciplined: in short, professional soldiers. They marched south late on the 14th without tents or other encumbering equipment, but heavily laden with pride and confidence and knowledge. In the forthcoming battle they would put the Baron's teachings to the ultimate test.[16]

Stony Point alone would be assailed. Attempting to coordinate a simultaneous attack against Verplanck's Point might prove too difficult. Besides, secrecy could best be maintained by adhering to a simpler plan. Washington concluded to strike Fort Lafayette after and if Wayne's assault succeeded.

By the time he received his final batch of troops, Wayne was intimately familiar with Stony Point and its defenses. Major Henry ("Light-Horse Harry") Lee had been gathering information for the past month; dashing Captain Allen McClane had entered the fort in disguise to make a close-up reconnaissance; a deserter divulged the important information that a sandy beach on the south side was lightly defended; and Wayne himself had carefully checked all approaches to the position.

Lieutenant Colonel Henry Johnson held the rock with his own 17th Regiment reinforced by a grenadier company, fifteen guns, and a group from the Loyal Americans Regiment. The total was over six hundred men. Two lines of abatis formed the foremost defenses, partially completed trenches ran between several battery sites farther back, and a redoubt stood squarely on the highest point of the peninsula. Ships patrolled the river to detect and repulse any water-borne attack. All in all, Colonel Johnson commanded a tough garrison in a strong position. He felt quite safe.

Morning, 15 July 1779. Wayne ordered his 1,300 men, together for the first time, to assemble for inspection. The troops were to appear "fresh shaved and well powdered" and to have in their possession equipment and rations. The general wanted to ascertain whether the Light Infantry Corps was ready for battle, the various units were informed. Earlier, Wayne had sent a detachment down the much-traveled route past Doodletown and over Dunderberg. Its mission was to seal off Stony Point. No person should enter or leave the fort and all males in the area were to be placed under guard until further orders.

Noon. The inspection was over. Men stood relaxed in ranks, awaiting the signal to disperse. A command came, but it put the four regiments in motion marching southward. Every man and most of the officers were completely surprised. As the column swung past the ruins of Fort Montgomery and turned west, the troops gradually sensed that "Mad" Anthony intended to put their martial skills to work. They entered Hell Hole between Bear Mountain and the Torne, marched through the dark gorge, and followed Popolopen Creek until it turned sharply northward at a fork. Taking a southwesterly track, Wayne led his tall, tough men past the Doodletown trail and on to Clement's Sawmill in a valley behind West Mountain. There they rested and filled canteens. Resuming the march, the column climbed to the top of a long ridge running almost due south between Black and West Mountains. Then the general shifted direction, striking out over a wild mountain trail toward the Hudson. "Light-Horse

Harry" was now in the lead, faultlessly conducting the long column through a forest maze into an assembly area about a mile and a half west of Stony Point. The hike to that point had been somewhat over ten miles long.[17]

Sunset. Weary troopers, still in the dark concerning their objective, settled down around a farmhouse owned by a David Springsteel. They ate, washing supper down with a gill of rum, and wondered. No farm dogs barked; they had all been killed earlier by Lee's men to lessen chances of discovery. Wayne and several officers moved forward for a last look in the fading light at their routes to the objective. The British appeared to be wholly unsuspecting.

Eleven o'clock. Dating a letter dramatically, "Springsteel's, 11 o'clock P.M. 15th July 1779 and near the hours and scene of carnage," Wayne informed Sharp Delaney, his brother-in-law, "This will not reach your eye until the writer is no more." Expecting to die in the forthcoming battle, the Pennsylvanian damned the "folly and parsimony" of Congress and asked Delaney to care for his wife and two children. Outside, units were assembled to hear for the first time what their mission would be. Officers, squinting under the dimmed light of partially covered lanterns or candles, read copies of Wayne's battle order. What the men heard was a harsh and uncompromising command to storm Stony Point with cold steel. If any soldier was "so lost to every feeling of honor" as to retreat a single foot or skulk in the face of danger, he would immediately be put to death by the nearest officer. Anyone caught with a loaded musket could expect a similar fate. Weapons were to remain shouldered until bayonet range was reached. Upon passing the abatis, everyone would yell over and over, "The fort's our own!" The first five into the enemy works would get a cash prize, starting at $500 for the first man. Pondering the task, the light infantrymen may have doubted their ability to crack the strong little fortress. Maybe, like their commander, they expected to meet death. But they did not flinch. Discipline did not permit it. Each man carefully checked his bayonet and fitted it firmly onto the end of his musket; now they knew why the Prussian general had been so insistent on bayonet drill during training.[18]

Half past eleven. In two columns the Light Infantry Corps filed off. White slips of paper fastened to caps helped the men keep closed up; during the expected melee in the darkened fort, anyone not wearing that distinguishing mark was to be bayoneted. The columns were organized identically. A lieutenant and 20 volunteers were in the van to serve as forlorn hopes—in modern parlance, suicide squads. Their job would be to open a gap in the abatis regardless of cost. Behind each forlorn hope marched an advance party of 150 men. That body would charge through the gap made by the 20 volunteers, widen it, and pave the way for the main body of the column to crash into the heart of the fort. Wayne envisioned a twin penetration at water's edge on each flank of the defenses. A demonstration force comprised of Major Murfree's infantry and Lee's horsemen was to draw enemy attention away from the flanks toward the center by charging down the causeway, shouting and shooting. The main attack was the southern column. On its success depended the outcome of the entire assault. Consequently, Wayne himself accompanied it. It is of some signifi-

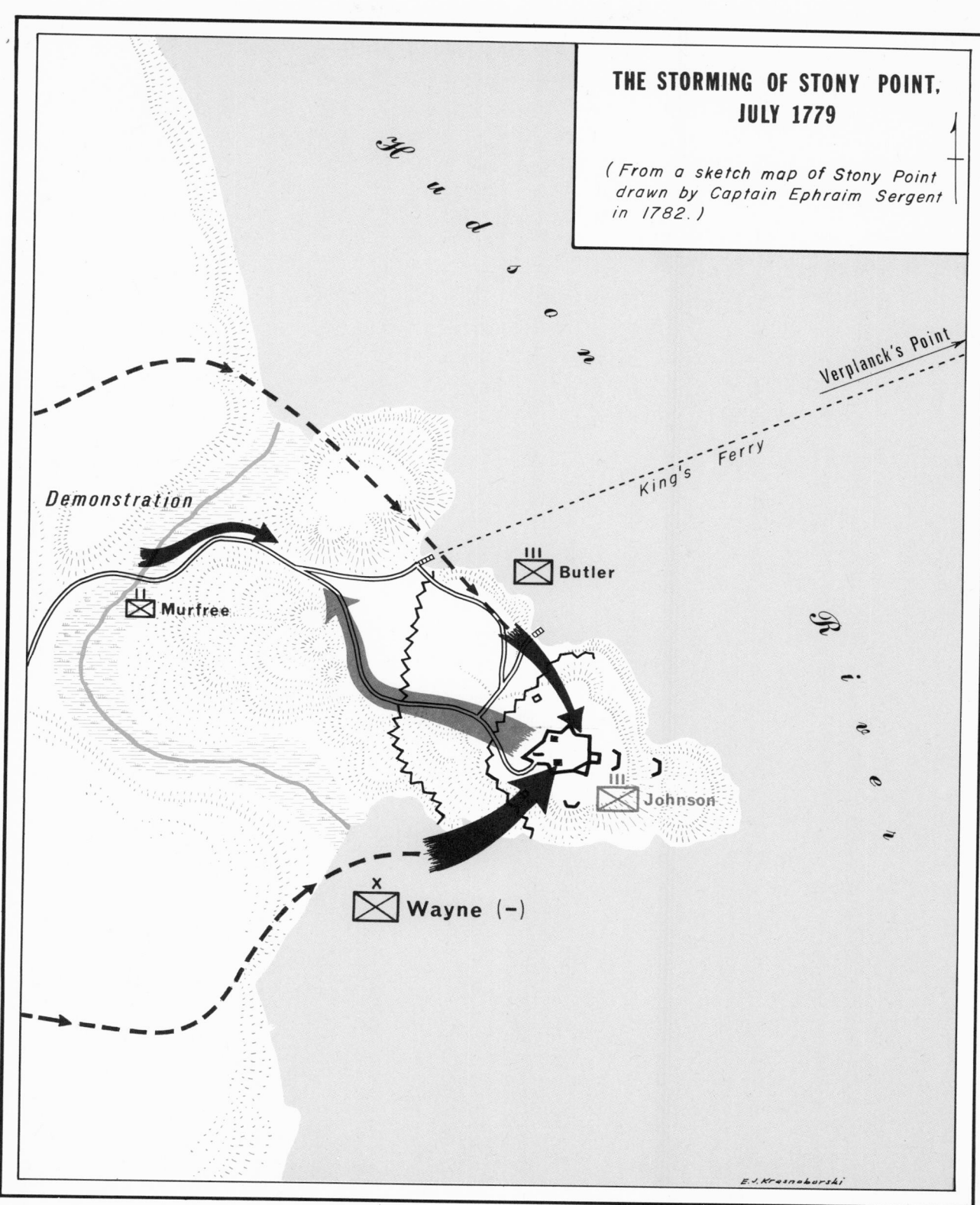

THE STORMING OF STONY POINT,
JULY 1779

(From a sketch map of Stony Point
drawn by Captain Ephraim Sergent
in 1782.)

Hudson

Verplanck's Point

King's Ferry

Demonstration

Butler

Murfree

River

Johnson

X
Wayne (-)

E.J.Krasnoborski

Infantry brigade   ⊠ˣ
Infantry regiment   ⊠ᴵᴵ
Infantry battalion ⊠ᴵᴵᴵ

cance that the troops of Colonel Meigs and Major Hull, only three days away from Steuben's drill field, composed the main body of the main attack.

Midnight. Both columns, moving by separate routes, reached the tidal flats. Without a break in pace, the forlorn hopes waded into the morass of mud and weed and water. The tide was in. Sinking deeper into ooze with each step, shorter soldiers soon felt water lapping at their necks. Still the grim, silent figures pressed on, guiding now on the bold outline of the promontory silhouetted against the sky. As they neared their objective, a sentry on the south shore either heard splashing or saw dim forms in the water. He fired. That shot sounded like a cannon blast as it rent the night silence. The Patriots pushed harder through mud tugging heavily at their feet. Surprise had been lost; speed became essential.

Alerted, nervous guards all along the western lines suddenly saw phantom Americans looming up everywhere. Sighting a few real attackers and many hostile shadows, the outposts blazed away indiscriminately into the night. Wayne and his men surged forward, angry that they had been discovered so soon. As it happened their anger was wasted, for that one alert sentry had actually improved Patriot chances. Colonel Johnson, leaping from bed, knew from the sounds of firing only that an enemy force of unknown size was probing his defenses. Since neither attacking column returned fire, nothing warned him specifically of the danger to his flanks. As he hastily pulled on high boots, a sudden volley of shots poured into the English center. Through the uproar he clearly heard shouting along the road crossing the marsh. Murfree and Lee were doing their jobs well. The English commander, a man of action, sized up the situation and concluded that the rebels were attempting to penetrate his center. As soon as his partly dressed soldiers could assemble, Johnson personally took about three hundred men—six companies—and led them charging down the road to meet the imagined American onslaught. It was a fatal move.

Meanwhile, both attacking columns reached the abatis. "Forlorn hopes" scrambled over and into the defenses, while axmen began chopping a breach in the logs. English outpost detachments fired muskets at point-blank range with murderous effect. Americans dropped. Lieutenant James Gibbons, commanding the northern forlorn hope, lost seventeen of his twenty men. Lieutenant George Knox, Gibbons' counterpart in the south, saw many of his men fall. General Wayne himself was temporarily put out of action by a musket ball that grazed his head. Other men scrambled over the fallen. Officers, in the fore, suffered especially heavy casualties. Disregarding losses and inspired by their leaders, the superbly disciplined troops crowded forward, sweeping into the defenses, all shrieking bansheelike, "the fort's our own!"

And so it was. The two main bodies washed into the center of the position, ruthlessly bayoneting all defenders who refused to surrender immediately. Shocked by the suddenness and savagery of the American attack, Britishers began throwing weapons down and crying for quarter. Colonel Johnson, whose wild counterattack had thrashed out into empty air, found himself cut off from his own fort. About thirty minutes after that first shot it was all over. Stony Point had been taken. Washington's calculated risk had been handsomely rewarded.

Elated by the rapid victory, Wayne reversed the captured English artillery pieces. Aboard the 14-gun British sloop *Vulture* and across the water on Verplanck's Point, aroused Englishmen stared intently into the darkness trying to discern the outcome of the battle. Their curiosity was emphatically settled when solid shot from the rocky eminence began splashing nearby. The *Vulture*, which would a year later figure prominently in a dark drama involving West Point, dropped downriver. A courier went racing away to notify Sir Henry. At 2 A.M., "Mad" Anthony penned a brief but exuberant note to General Washington: "The fort and garrison with Colonel Johnson are ours. Our officers and men behaved like men who are determined to be free."[19]

George Washington had journeyed to Fort Montgomery on the 15th, but he apparently missed seeing Wayne. Knowing the expedition was well on its way, he ordered Brigadier General Peter Muhlenberg to "put your brigade in motion about midnight" and march to Stony Point to assist Wayne if the attack should miscarry. Having done all he could, the Commander-in-Chief returned to New Windsor where he would await results. When Wayne's cryptic message arrived early on the 16th, the normally stoic officer was overjoyed. Immediately, he alerted units to march toward Peekskill in anticipation of bagging Verplanck's Point as well. To Major General Robert Howe he entrusted the command of that operation. Those arrangements made, he threw a long leg over his freshest horse and set out at a fast clip to see for himself the magic that had been performed. Steuben rode happily beside him.[20]

Captain Benjamin Fishbourne, Wayne's aide, had amplified his general's terse announcement of victory, but Washington was still surprised at the magnitude of the win. For the price of a hundred casualties, among them fifteen dead, the Continentals had inflicted greater blood losses on the enemy and had taken nearly five hundred captives. He dismounted within the position, obviously delighted, beaming, congratulating the men. The captured equipment and supplies, including cannon, should be appraised, he ordered, the value in dollars to be distributed among the troops.

Raising his spyglass, the General hungrily observed the hostile garrison on Verplanck's Point. Nathanael Greene was with the Commander-in-Chief, rejoicing, too, in the warm afterglow of the brilliant stroke. The two generals conferred. Was Verplanck's Point worth a try? They decided it was. Quickly, with Greene drafting a part of the message, Washington commanded Robert Howe to "march down your troops and open a battery against their blockhouse" with all haste. "After beating the blockhouse about their ears," Howe was to send in a summons for surrender.[21]

To preserve secrecy, no troops other than Wayne's had been readied. Nor had other generals been notified. Therefore, Washington's earlier orders, those on the 16th, had caught Howe unawares. Many of the Continental generals could have reacted rapidly enough to have accomplished the task despite the short notice, but not Robert Howe. Naming him to command the effort was an error on Washington's part. The North Carolinian was not qualified to perform as a major general, as soon became sadly apparent.

Howe was a playboy, a ladies' man, a bachelor finding it difficult to make the transition from stalking virtue to storming breastworks. By reputation, his was "the worst character you ever heard thro' the whole" of North Carolina. Displaying a rather questionable interest in his habits, a young lady had breathlessly described him as "a sort of woman-eater that devours everything that comes in his way." She also reported, ". . . no woman can withstand him." Howe could shine equally in the company of the philosopher or the libertine, "a favorite of the man of sense and the female world," noted a Boston lawyer. A well-to-do planter and a minor politician when the war erupted, Robert Howe was thrust all too quickly into a position of prominence to which he was all too unsuited. Until April 1779, his service had been in the southern theatre, service as undistinguished as it was acrimonious. Nothing he did seemed to work out right, and he learned not at all from his mistakes. When the outcry in the south grew too loud, he was moved north. His first job was to take Verplanck's Point—a mission he executed with customary lack of efficiency.[22]

Even while Washington and Greene penned letters from Stony Point, setting the stage for Howe to move against the fort at the other terminus of King's Ferry, that general was writing to Washington. He had brought no entrenching tools and somehow did not have his artillery in the same place as his ammunition and was therefore sorry to announce his inability to beat up the British position. The color rose in George Washington's pock-marked cheeks. Sarcastically, he dictated a reply: "I am sorry for the difficulties you seem to be under. I had no doubt but that the cannon and ammunition would proceed together, as one without the other could be of no service." Wounded by Washington's cutting words, Howe wrote a hurried reply that doubtless served merely to reinforce the General's scorn: "Oh: My Dear General what a soul piercing wound has the unexpected inevitable delay of yesterday given to dear sir your very respectful and truly affectionate. R. Howe."[23]

That lost day killed what chances there might have been for capturing Verplanck's Point before Sir Henry could react. Soon, English cavalry and light troops were pounding northward by forced march on the eastern shore, while British vessels beat against an unfavorable north wind, striving to reach the beleagured garrison. On the 18th Washington directed William Heath, who had taken charge of the forces east of the river in Howe's stead, to fall back into the hills north of Peekskill. Verplanck's Point would have been a perfect trap for the Patriots had the British been able to get between them and the mountains.

Nor could Americans remain at Stony Point. Defenses there were ordered razed after all cannon were evacuated to West Point. The prisoners were marched away—except five who had deserted American units to join the forces of the King. They received revolutionary justice: a Saturday court-martial and a Sunday hanging. Washington himself departed on the 18th, his pleasure with the Stony Point victory only slightly dimmed by frustration over Howe's debacle.

Lady Washington, the row-galley which had previously seen so much action on the river, came from West Point to carry away the captured artillery pieces. However, she was operating shorthanded and without proper equipment "to take in the heavy cannon." As a result, she was unable to accomplish the job quickly or efficiently. When the veteran vessel, after an overlong delay in loading the guns, eased away from the peninsula on Sunday, British artillerymen on Verplanck's Point were waiting. Directing massed fire on the slowly moving target, English gunners scored several damaging hits. Her crew grounded the listing galley near Stony Point where she was burned to preclude capture. It was an ignominious end to a gallant ship. All told, for Americans of either persuasion, that was an unhappy Sunday at Stony Point. As deserters swayed limply in the wind, smoke from the burning boat drifted over the gallows, a sombre ending to a sparkling episode.[24] But small disappointments were forgotten in the celebration of Wayne's exploit. America had needed something to brag about—and brag she did. The magnificent little show was a worthy win in its own right, but Patriot propagandists puffed it up as a major victory, a decisive clash, a turning point. And maybe it was, psychologically. Continentals, notoriously inept with the bayonet, had attacked and overwhelmingly defeated a dug-in garrison of his Majesty's best troops. And they had done it at night at bayonet point.

Steuben had one more duty to perform with regard to Stony Point: when Captain Henry Archer, a volunteer aide to Wayne, was selected to carry the official report of the battle to Congress, the Inspector General coached him on the manner in which he should comport himself. Enter the capital city with colors flying and trumpets sounding, make a show to draw people to the street, and grandly proclaim the wondrous victory of American arms. Archer did as he was told, explaining later with some embarrassment that those "were Baron Steuben's instructions and I pursued them literally, though I could not help thinking it had a little of the appearance of a puppet show."[25]

Anthony Wayne received the thanks of Congress, a gold metal, and lasting fame. Both advance guard commanders were granted silver medals. Lieutenants Knox and Gibbons earned brevet promotions. Two officers and three sergeants picked up cash awards for being the first to enter the defenses. "The gallant troops by whom the post was reduced" split some $160,-000. Wayne and his men deserved every last bit of the credit and praise they received. It should be marked, however, that without the training and discipline imparted to the troops by the Inspector General, such an exploit would not have been possible.

The Baron received his reward in the esteem Washington and the gritty Continentals held for him. The men best expressed their respect in a creed that made the rounds of campfires. Written in the jocular yet serious vein adopted by soldiers of every era, it starts with a statement of belief in God, Country, and George Washington, and ends with:

> . . . we believe that Baron Steuben has made us soldiers, and that he is capable of forming the whole world into a solid column . . . we believe in his *Blue Book* . . . and we believe in our bayonets. Amen!

14

WASHINGTON AT
WEST POINT

HAVING pulled off the dazzling coup at Stony Point, General Washington immediately focused all his energies on the West Point defenses. The English, he felt, would now redouble their efforts to capture the Hudson forts in order to erase the stigma of humiliating defeat. The Virginian explained simply, "Sir Harry may wish to retaliate for the loss of that post." While disposing his entire army to protect West Point, the General ordered McDougall to bring the garrison itself to full alert status. "The artillery is also to be distributed," he said, "and every minute arrangement made at once, that everything may be in the most perfect readiness at the shortest notice." Touring the Point on 19 July, he decided to establish his own headquarters there. In that way he could clearly emphasize the fortress' importance and at the same time could better supervise its defense. A battle for West Point might very well prove to be the climactic conflict of the Revolutionary War. The Commander-in-Chief's place was obviously at the central position. Returning to New Windsor to gather papers and belongings, he announced on the 20th, "I propose either this evening or tomorrow to pitch my tent somewhere near West Point."[1]

The great man's lodgings, of course, would not be a humble tent. Working feverishly, servants removed clothing and equipment belonging to the current occupants of Stephen Moore's large, red house and gave the dwelling a thorough cleaning from top to bottom. By Tuesday the 20th the spacious structure was gleaming, ready to receive its most distinguished tenant. That afternoon several of the General's guards loaded the headquarters baggage aboard a sloop and sailed to West Point. After sleeping on deck the first night, they unloaded the gear, arranged Washington's personal furnishings, and pitched their own tents in the orchard. Elizah Fisher, a soldier in the guards, described his new home as "Morses folley a little distant from West Point foart." Washington, after completing necessary correspondence on his last Wednesday in New Windsor, including a long letter to Congress describing the seizure of Stony Point, traveled to West Point late in the day. It was to be his home for the rest of summer and through autumn.[2]

The new resident had no time just then to inspect his latest quarters. More important considerations vied for limited time, namely, preparing West Point to withstand a British thrust. Even before Stony Point, he had ordered to the mountain fastness every soldier in the army who by trade had been a mason. Under Kosciuszko's supervision these men had been occupied in lining the redoubts and batteries with stone. But more labor was called for. Washington's first general orders published from the Moore house established details totaling in all nearly eight hundred men "to be daily employed on the works."[3]

The General also became convinced of the requirement for more depth in the defenses. Standing one day in July on the western parapet of Fort Putnam, he was disturbed by "the long hill in front of" and higher than Fort Putnam. The "long hill" was actually a large ridge shaped like an inverted V with Rocky Hill at the apex and the fingers running away to the south and southwest. "The possession of this hill," he stated, "appears to me essential to the preservation of the whole post and our main effort ought to be directed to keeping the enemy off of it." He ordered Major General Arthur St. Clair, with his entire division, to "consider this hill in all its relations and make yourself completely master of its defense." It was probably pure chance that caused him to select St. Clair for that mission, but it is interesting to recall that St. Clair was the officer who had been forced to evacuate the defenses at Ticonderoga largely because he had failed to heed Kosciuszko's advice to fortify Mt. Defiance. Submitted nearly a year ago, Kosciuszko's recommendation for a redoubt on Rocky Hill had been summarily rejected by Duportail. Now the Commander-in-Chief himself was ordering done what should have been begun months before. General Duportail might have seen a smirk flash across Colonel Kosciuszko's face when Washington made that decision.[4]

Nor did the General limit his attention only to the west side of the river. The high ground across the waterway was totally undefended. Forts on those hills would force an attacker to deploy early, helping keep him at arm's reach from West Point itself. "General Duportail will be pleased to appoint engineers to superintend and direct the new works on the heights east and west of the river and have them forwarded with all possible dispatch," Washington specified. Exactly which officers the Chief of Engineers named is unknown, but both Gouvion and another Frenchman, Béchet de Rochefontaine, were already at West Point and involved in the construction. Most likely they were handed the task. Major General Heath was responsible for the works to be raised east of the river, while McDougall took charge of those erected on the hills above West Point.[5]

By Saturday, 24 July, Washington was satisfied with the locations

The Red House. A detail from a painting, "Washington Valley," by
Mrs. Marilyn Sorenson. From the author's collection.   205

chosen for the new redoubts and approved of the concept of construction; but he was highly exasperated at the confusing practice of referring to various works by vague directional or geographical terms. There were simply too many different sites. He therefore directed, "General Heath will please to give names to the redoubts he is establishing on the heights east of the river, and General McDougall to those on the west side and on [Constitution] Island that the whole may be readily distinguished and known." After pondering the problem three days, McDougall finally settled on numbers. "The Redoubt erecting on the south point of the hill north of Buttermilk Falls" would be known simply as "1." West of that stood "2." The third was "on the heights above Ferrol's," while Rocky Hill held the fourth. From south to north on Constitution Island ran "5" through "7." Heath was more poetic. "Sugar Loaf Redoubt" adorned Sugarloaf Hill. North Redoubt stood "on the heights back of Nelson's" and Middle Redoubt occupied the southern portion of the same hill. All other batteries, redoubts, and forts retained the names McDougall had given them back in 1778.[6]

Thus within a week of Washington's arrival at West Point, the fortress reached the greatest limit of its expansion. Every defensive position had been planned. From then until war's end those several works would be improved and maintained, but no new ones would be erected. Sixteen enclosed positions and ten major battery sites formed three roughly concentric defensive rings around the great chain. Each fort was capable both of defending itself and providing support by fire to its neighbors. No more formidable a position had ever been seen in the New World.

As it had evolved, West Point was a fortress far ahead of its time. The urgings and efforts of engineers trained in the European school to create a single massive work had failed; Yankee ingenuity—abetted admittedly by Continental poverty and a Polish engineer—had devised a system of outlying forts depending upon depth, mutual support, and use of terrain to defeat a besieger. Such a system would not come into vogue in Europe until the nineteenth century, when citadels like Metz and Sedan and Verdun would be constructed. Those vast complexes were on a much larger scale, of course; so, too, however, were the sizes of armies involved. West Point, the Gibraltar of America, was a prototype, a forerunner of things to come.

It is ironic that untutored eighteenth-century Americans worked out a miniature nineteenth-century European fortress because they had to do it in spite of strong protests from their French engineers. But it is not at all surprising that the Frenchmen protested, for they were looking backward to the seventeenth century. When Duportail and his fellow engineers thought of the scattered West Point works they inwardly shuddered. Although they were all avid disciples of Vauban, French military engineers over the decades had lost sight of the essence of the famous engineer's teachings and had come to accept his form as doctrine. Whereas Vauban preached flexibility, his successors applied his designs inflexibly. A fortress should make use of and strengthen the natural terrain, Vauban would have said; his followers believed the fort to be an end in itself. By the late 1700's, most European military engineers practiced a style of construction a hundred years out of date. When one of their number, Montalembert, attempted to update their knowledge and art he was actually ostracized. Not until the second year of the American Revolutionary War was he permitted to publish a modernizing tract. Americans, blissfully ignorant of European methods and woefully short of funds needed to build on a European scale, had followed the dual dictates of necessity and common sense to design a defensive system ideally suited to its unique location and special mission in the Hudson Highlands.

What is more, the quality of design and workmanship in the several sites was in no wise impaired by the novel overall scheme of defense. Erected under the direct, unbroken guidance of Thaddeus Kosciuszko, the many positions shared certain similarities even though no two were identical. The practical Pole shaped each stronghold to conform best to its nearby terrain, using wherever he could nature's sheer walls and rocky obstacles. But the actual construction of each was carried out in accordance with careful criteria established by the engineer. Batteries were built by raising an exterior stone scarp wall that varied in height as necessary to provide a level firing platform on the spot chosen. The stonework was all dry masonry with an inward talus. Capping the scarp wall stood a parapet fabricated of fascines or timber, or perhaps of soil held in place by fascines and logs. Thickness and height differed according to the degree of danger from enemy artillery. Gun platforms were elevated on stone piers or placed upon timber sleepers sunk in the earth. Cannon fired either from embrasures or in barbette. Redoubts were formed in the same manner, except for the scarp wall which was raised enough above the terrain to afford control of the surrounding area. Inner revetment walls on all redoubts were also of dry masonry. Many of the redoubts were bolstered by a detached battery located just outside the walls. Banquettes were provided for the troops, and, in most instances, bombproofs were built. Shielding all the redoubts were various combinations of palisades, pickets, *chevaux-de-frise*, and moats. Abatis encircled batteries and redoubts alike. All in all, the separate works constituting fortress West Point displayed a remarkable level of engineering sophistication. Observers were invariably impressed.[7]

Chastened and spurred by Washington's obvious repudiation of his views on how to fortify West Point, Duportail grudgingly accepted the fact that the defenses would remain as they were and launched himself into a thorough study of the entire defensive complex. Trying to look at the rock-ribbed position the way Sir Henry Clinton must have viewed it, Duportail listed all feasible avenues of approach open to a would-be attacker. Then, one by one, he examined each to determine its likelihood of success and to plot the most proper American reaction. He completed his study on 20 August.[8]

"Since all that has been done at West Point is aimed at blocking the river to prevent the enemy from ascending it with his warships," the French engineer began, "the chain is the principal element and the fortifications are only made to back it up." It appeared to Duportail that a large and heavily loaded ship, fitted out with a "vertical piece of iron" at the prow, might break the chain if it could strike it at full sail. (Nowhere in the report is mention made of the boom; a peculiar omission which would indicate the boom was not in place at that time.) To increase the ability of the chain to withstand such a shock, the engineer recommended "the winding of one end around a cylinder" so that it could give more under the impact. There should be two chains, he thought, one two feet under the surface and the other eight feet deep. And, lastly, crossbars should be fixed to the downstream ends of the great logs to provide a barrier which would help slow a ship before it could strike the chain itself. To preclude a nighttime sneak attack with explosive charges designed to cut the chain, Duportail prescribed patrol boats, alert batteries, preconstructed piles of wood and kindling along both banks to provide quick illumination, and a ready stock of replacement parts should such an attack be successful.

As for overland assaults against the fortress, Duportail could envision four possible alternatives. However, under closer scrutiny, only one seemed to have any real chance of success: an advance along the route which General Washington had instinctively selected as the most dangerous. By seizing the prominent ground where Redoubts 1 through 4 were being built, an enemy could command Forts Putnam, Webb and Wyllys, which would force the evacuation of the latter two. Having accomplished that much, the English could neutralize Fort Putnam by fire from Rocky Hill while moving batteries along the ridge once defended by Webb and Wyllys. From there, they could open fire on Fort Arnold "without even having taken Fort Putnam." However, Duportail noted, Fort Putnam is "always the central point" which must be captured before an attack can succeed against Fort Arnold. That would be most difficult, he reasoned, unless the British could advance their artillery quickly and with little loss to Rocky Hill. And, when the present dispositions were completed, especially after a battery could be raised near Redoubt 1, the redcoats would be all but unable to accomplish that feat. "It seems to me," he concluded, "that we have assured the defense of this mountain as much as it is necessary to do, in view of the number of troops the enemy can sacrifice to the attack of West Point."

No sooner was the Commander-in-Chief satisfied with security arrangements for West Point than he began to have less passive thoughts. Stony Point had been a delicious morsel to whet his appetite for attack and victory. The British had reoccupied the rocky peninsula with a garrison twice as large as the one that had been lost; and Verplanck's Point now had 700 defenders. Could Continentals attack there again? On 26 July Washington called a council of war to address that question. Unanimously his generals voted to defend West Point with every resource, but only one, Samuel Parsons, urged a second assault against Stony Point and Verplanck's Point. The others thought it would not be worth the cost even if it succeeded. Washington went along with the advice. Dropping plans for a second Stony Point, he redoubled efforts to complete the newly approved defenses, assigning men in numbers enough to work in shifts from reveille gun until sunset. But his natural spirit of aggressiveness could not be stilled; he continued to search for means to smite his foe. Hastening completion of the new redoubts at West Point fitted perfectly with that offensive instinct: as soon as the fortress should be "in such a state of defence as will give it security with its own garrison," he expected to put "the rest of the army at liberty to operate with confidence elsewhere."[9]

Casting around for some objective within his pinched means, Washington quickly came up with Paulus (or Powles') Hook. An isolated outpost across the Hudson from Manhattan, it was close enough to British headquarters to create a stir if it were taken. He turned for a leader to his energetic young officer, "Light-Horse Harry" Lee. On 19 August, Lee successfully surprised and overran the post. Next to draw the restless Virginian's gaze was an encampment of Englishmen near Kingsbridge. He told Robert Howe to determine "whether it is practicable to beat up their quarters with a reasonable prospect of success." In his imagination, Washington saw a daring midnight dash on horseback to catch the enemy in bed. A combination of Howe's lethargy, a shortage of horses, and the appearance of the long-awaited British reinforcements caused this operation to abort.[10]

The Patriots need not have feared the arrival of those troops. Henry Clinton had already decided to shift his operations southward away from the exasperating Mr. Washington and those accursed Hudson Highlands. But even if he had not made that decision, renewed action against Washington's army or West Point quickly became impossible. Most of the four thousand or so replacements arrived prostrated by a most virulent fever. They could not campaign. And the worst was yet to come. August had been a damp month and the people of New York City had developed fevers of their own; thus they had but slight resistance to the newly imported malady. When infected sailors and soldiers came ashore, the pestilence rapidly spread, reaching epidemic proportions in just days. The result was calamitous: "so sickly a season never was known in the memory of the oldest person." Some six thousand soldiers were hospitalized, placing any plan of attack completely out of the question. And the sickness lingered. In December a doctor wrote, "The diseases at first most prevalent were intermittent and bilious fevers, which were succeeded by a most invincible flux that still rages in our hospitals." While Washington labored to complete West Point he could launch galling pinpricks at English outposts with relative impunity. Sir Henry was helpless to retaliate.[11]

Seldom had the situation seemed more to favor the Americans. Anticipating momentarily the arrival and cooperation of a large French fleet, Washington was holding over ten thousand trained troops coiled in the hills around West Point. Heartened psychologically by the small but important wins at Stony Point and Paulus Hook, the Continentals were spoiling for a fight. Moreover, news of French victories in the West Indies reinforced the general mood of elation. The enemy, weakened by disease, no longer seemed to constitute a great threat, while West Point assumed more and more an aura of impregnability each day. In Washington's gleeful words, "A flood of good news is pouring in upon us." While awaiting the French, General Washington was a happy and relaxed individual, fully enjoying himself in Stephen Moore's ostentatious house on the river.[12]

Glimpses of the contented, pleasurable days at West Point are to be found in his writings. Humor and gaiety became a part of the environment at headquarters. The General regularly played ball with his aides, catching

Equestrian statue of George Washington. It stands on the plain at West Point. U.S. Army photograph.

and throwing sometimes for hours. He entertained often, serving dinner in the shade of a huge canvas stretched on long poles within a few feet of the river's edge. Displaying a keen wit not often exercised during the years of fighting, he wrote the following letter in mid-August:

> I have asked Mrs. Cochran and Mrs. Livingston to dine with me tomorrow; but ought I not to apprize them of their fare? As I hate deception, even where the imagination only is concerned; I will.
>
> Itisneedlesstopremisethatmytableislargeenoughtoholdthe ladies; of this they had occular proof yesterday. To say how it is usually covered is rather more essential, and this shall be the purport of my letter. Since our arrival at this happy spot, we have had a ham (sometimes a shoulder) of bacon to grace the head of the table; a piece of roast beef adorns the foot; and a small dish of greens or beans (almost imperceptible) decorates the center.
>
> When the cook has a mind to cut a figure (and this I presume he will attempt to do tomorrow) we have two beefstake-pyes or dishes of crabs in addition, one on each side of the center dish, dividing the space, and reducing the distance between dish and dish to about six feet, which, without them, would be near twelve apart. Of late he has had the surprizing luck to discover that apples will make pyes; and it's a question if, amidst the violence of his efforts, we do not get one of apples instead of having both of beef.
>
> If the ladies can put up with such entertainment, and will submit to partake of it on plates once tin but now iron; (not become so by the labor of scouring) I shall be happy to see them.[13]

His use of the phrase "this happy spot" is in direct contrast to the almost unanimous damning of the isolated location by previous residents and visitors.

Dinner with George Washington was an event to be remembered. Beginning at midafternoon, the General, his aides, and invited guests would assemble in the dining marquee where a bevy of servants hovered in attendance. Specially designed tablecloths, embossed with a distinctive decoration, covered the long table. The tall, stately host strode to his chair and the meal began. Visitors never failed to be amazed at the Virginian's capacity for food and the length of time he spent at table. A Frenchman, the Marquis de Chastellux, left this account of such a dinner:

> The repast was in the English fashion, consisting of eight or ten large dishes of butcher's meat, and poultry, with vegetables of several sorts, followed by a second course of pastry, comprised under the two denominations of pies and puddings. After this the cloth was taken off, and apples and a great quantity of nuts were served, which General Washington usually continues eating for two hours, toasting and conversing all the time. These nuts . . . are served half open, and the company are never done picking and eating them. The conversation was calm and agreeable.[14]

When Washington scraped his chair back at half past seven in the evening, the Marquis, stuffed and uncomfortable after the long meal, rose in relief. To his consternation, however, servants entered immediately to shorten the table, and "convert it into a round one." Seeing his surprise, one of the aides explained that it was being prepared for the evening meal. An hour later all were summoned again to eat. The Marquis returned, "protesting against this supper," but Washington, amused, told his guest "he was accustomed to take something in the evening." That second repast consisted of a few light dishes, some fruit, "and above all, a great abundance of nuts, which were as well received in the evening as at dinner." As soon as the food was finished, the cloth was removed and bottles of claret and Madeira were passed around. From then until about eleven o'clock, the men drank and conversed. The talk, "always free and always agreeable," as often as not centered on the opposite sex. Wobbling weakly to bed, the first-time visitor prayed that breakfast might be light.[15]

Washington loved the company of women, especially young and pretty ones. Dancing was one of his favorite sports and flirting seems not to have been far behind. His Excellency could, and often did, dance for two or three hours at a stretch with favorite partners such as Nathanael Greene's vivacious wife, "Kitty," and massive but lively Lucy Knox. The genteel general was completely at ease in the company of ladies. Mrs. Theodoric Bland, married to another Virginia officer, described for a friend a visit to headquarters in 1777. Washington quickly charmed her "by his ability, politeness, and attention." He took her riding in the afternoon, when, as she said, he "throws off the hero and takes on the chatty, agreeable companion." Writing intimately, Mrs. Bland next informed her friend, "He can be downright impudent sometimes—such impudence, Fanny, as you and I like." This is not to say every woman appreciated his attention. Officers at headquarters merrily repeated the tale of his rebuff by Mrs. George Olney. Seeing more the goat than the general, she angrily screeched that "if he did not let go her hand, she would tear out his eyes, or the hair from his head; and that though he was a general, he was but a man." Because Martha was not with him at West Point, he hosted no large dancing parties, but local ladies graced his marquee quite often and he did not let his wife's absence diminish his acting the gallant. When John Jay prepared to depart for Spain that fall, his attractive bride Sarah asked the famous general for a lock of hair. Obligingly, his Excellency clipped off a strand and presented it to her. Feminine laughter—and perhaps an occasional squeal—wafted over the shimmering Hudson that summer and autumn.[16]

Good humor and close attention to the fairer sex were traits marking everyone at headquarters during those sunny weeks. On 24 August, for example, Alexander Hamilton sent this letter to Governor George Clinton:

> The bearer of this is an old woman, and of course the most troublesome animal in the world. She wants to go into New York. It was in vain we told her no inhabitant could be permitted by us to go within the enemy's lines without permission from the civil power. Old and decrepit as she is, she made the tour of the family and tried her blandishments upon each. . . . nothing would satisfy her except a line from General Washington to the Governor. As she showed a disposition to remain with us till she carried her point with true female perseverance—as we are rather straitened in our quarters, and not one of the gentlemen of the family would agree to share his bed with her, and as you must at all events have a visit from her, I at last promised her a letter to you—the direct and sole end of which is to get rid of her.

I dare say your Excellency will think you make a very good bargain for the state by getting rid of her also in the manner she wishes. She seems to be in distress, and to have a claim upon our compassion.[17]

The presence and prestige of America's most renowned Mason brought Freemasonry at West Point to a peak. During his lengthy sojourn in the Highlands, the General attended several lodge meetings, causing overall attendance to jump remarkably. Beverley Robinson's house was the site of most of the weekly gatherings, although a few were held at West Point itself. One of the largest of those conducted on the Point was staged on 24 July, only three days after Washington established his headquarters there. Lodge records indicate some eighty visitors joined regular members to hear a sermon by Reverend Enos Hitchcock, Chaplain of Paterson's brigade. Taking his text from I John 3:11, Hitchcock harangued his audience with the Biblical injunction to "love one another." The assembled Brothers listened politely, but, warriors all, were not overly impressed by the message. Washington, the leader of one great rebellion, was in attendance; Daniel Shays, fated to head a future uprising, was also there. The meetings may not have reformed the revolutionaries, but they provided a source of comradeship and entertainment which helped make the long days and weeks more endurable.[18]

While at West Point, the General attempted to stamp out cursing. It was an "unmeaning and abominable custom," he emphatically proclaimed. He had attempted from time to time to suppress it in his army, never with much success. Riding around West Point, he was shocked to hear with his own ears "that it prevails, *if possible*, more than ever." The name of the Lord was "incessantly imprecated and prophaned in a manner as wanton as it is shocking." Angrily, he told his officers "to check a vice which is as unprofitable as it is wicked and shameful." For a while, unpolished and lusty soldiers were reduced to venting anger and punctuating strongly expressed thoughts with that era's version of "darn," or maybe an occasional risqué "dadgummit." They longed all the more for the good old four-letter expletives with which they had heretofore liberally sprinkled their speech. The troops were unstinting in their adoration for the tall Virginian, but he *did* have some "gosh-darn" strange ideas. History does not record Baron von Steuben's personal reaction to the order, but it can be assumed he obeyed. Nonetheless, it must have been rather traumatic to him to reduce his already limited English vocabulary so drastically.[19]

If the Commander-in-Chief was dismayed by what he heard, he was no more pleased by what he saw. During the sweltering August days, troops swam often in the cool Hudson. Watching them loitering in the river, Washington grew concerned. In an age when men washed infrequently, a prevalent belief held that soaking in water softened a person. The soldiers were "continually in the water and many of them for hours together." In general orders Washington prescribed, "There is to be no bathing between the hours of 8 and 5, and the custom of remaining long in the water is to be discontinued, as it is too relaxing and injurious to health." There was another reason for his concern. Ladies visiting the General, dining in his open marquee near the river, found disconcerting the sight of hundreds of naked soldiers frolicking on and leaping off the rocks of West Point. He stuffily amplified his orders: "It is also expected that the soldiers in this kind of recreation will observe more decency than they usually practice."[20]

Even completely clothed, the troops were hardly more than decent. Major Bauman described the appearance of his own artillerymen as they were viewed by Washington at a muster: "Some without coats, some without hats, some without shoes and stockings, and some without a shirt. In short, they appeared like ragamuffins and not like soldiers. . . ." But the weather was balmy—a drought kept the days dry and nights warm—and men could laugh at their nakedness.[21]

The social event of the fall was the visit of Chevalier de La Luzerne, French Minister to the United States. En route from Boston to Philadelphia, the minister visited Washington at West Point in September. When the Commander-in-Chief met Luzerne and his party at Fishkill, he impressed the Frenchmen as being "naturally and spontaneously polite." Boarding a sloop for West Point, the large group of dignitaries set out with Washington himself at the tiller. A squall blew up, but the General, according to one of the Frenchmen, kept the vessel steering true, eliciting much admiration from his guests. Gun salutes greeted their arrival and an enthusiastic if untalented band gamely struck up tuneful French airs. Dinner in the large tent at river's edge filled the visitors with gastronomical appreciation and wonder. As night closed in, huge bonfires were lighted on Constitution Island, sending sparkling reflections rippling across the river, forming a beautiful backdrop for the ritualistic rounds of toasting.

Next morning at four o'clock, a reveille cannon shook the hills awake. Immediately, drums, fifes, and trumpets opened a raucus early-morning melody beside the Red House. Host and guests rolled out of bed, wondering if all the noise was really necessary.* They dressed, breakfasted, and mounted horses for a tour of the defenses. Washington personally served as guide. Barbe-Marbois, one of Luzerne's secretaries, recorded the inspection:

> The fort on the right [Arnold] is commanded by a hill, and other heights to the number of four command it, rising up as if in stories. They have felt obliged to fortify all these heights to protect the principal fort from being regularly attacked. We visited them in order, in spite of the steepness of the cliffs. Perhaps it is unfortunate that they have had to multiply these forts and complicate the defense in that way, but at the price of this inconvenience the position has been put in a respectable condition.[22]

When all the forts had been viewed, the party descended to the plain to watch brigades, raggedly dressed but smartly drilled, march and maneuver in accordance with Steuben's drill regulations. That demonstration ended in time for Washington and Luzerne to hold a lengthy conference concerning strategy, after which everyone crossed the river to take dinner with General Duportail. The Chief of Engineers had set up a tent similar to

* Cadets at the Military Academy are still awakened in this manner; the bandsmen are affectionately called "Hellcats."

Washington's on the north shore of the Bay of the Assassins, where the village of Cold Spring now stands. Following the French banquet, boats brought the weary group back across an orange and blue river, once more illuminated by leaping fires. On the 17th, Luzerne departed for Philadelphia, carrying strong and fond memories of both Washington and West Point. Seeing his visitor off, the American leader rode part way down the road with him.[23]

Also in September, tidings came of the arrival in American waters of Admiral D'Estaing and a French fleet. Washington was ecstatic. Now he could attack New York. Right away he wrote the admiral, proposing a junction of their forces in a move against the city. Included in his thinking was a plan to have the French "run two or three frigates up the North River" to cut off the retreat of British garrisons at Stony and Verplanck's Points. On the night of the 12th, deserters came in with rumors—unfounded as it turned out—of D'Estaing's presence off Sandy Hook. Huge Henry Knox happily boomed, "If this be true, the probablity is in favor of offensive operations against New York immediately." However, as weeks passed with no further information, the Commander-in-Chief, becoming anxious at time's slipping away, sent Alexander Hamilton and General Duportail southward in hopes of contacting the friendly fleet. It was all in vain. D'Estaing intended to proceed no farther north than Savannah, Georgia.[24]

In conjunction with Americans under Major General Benjamin Lincoln, the French admiral laid siege to the British base at Savannah. The rapid approach of the hurricane season and slow progress in the trenches caused D'Estaing to launch a premature assault of the enemy lines on 9 October. The allies were bloodily repulsed. For the second year in a row, the French fleet departed, leaving in its wake angry Americans volubly blaming their reverses on French failures.

Nearly a month passed before news of that dolorous event reached the Hudson, a month of suspense, but one of high hopes. Watching Sir Henry closely, Washington was inspirited to observe him suddenly withdraw from Stony Point and Verplanck's Point, evacuate Rhode Island, mass his forces in New York, and sink ships to block the channel off Sandy Hook. If the English were so worried, he reasoned, it could only mean D'Estaing was near at hand. Expecting a decisive battle at almost any time, he halted work on the fortifications at West Point and placed the entire army in a posture to march at a moment's notice. Americans reoccupied King's Ferry. On tenterhooks, the Patriots waited. Days passed. Then weeks. By the end of October, Washington was becoming seriously concerned. Time for a campaign was running out. "We are most anxiously waiting for accounts from the southward," he wrote, "having received no official intelligence from thence since the 7th of September which barely announced Count D'Estaing's arrival upon the coast."

Meanwhile, all other news was good. General John Sullivan returned triumphantly from his campaign against the Iroquois. "He had been completely successful, having totally destroyed the country of the Six Nations with a very trifling loss on our side," Washington gloated. Colonel Daniel Brodhead was also victorious in an expedition against the red foe living "upon the heads of the Allegheny River." Washington, an old Indian fighter himself, was "in hopes that these severe blows will effectually intimidate the Indians and secure the future peace of our frontier." And farther west, young George Rogers Clark had won the vast territory of the Ohio by his daring and brilliant operations there. A major victory now in New York would assure the year 1779 a preeminent place in American history.[25]

November's wind blew brown leaves from English cherry trees in the orchard behind the Red House and chased them through the tents of the Commander-in-Chief's guard. Washington's hopes faded. He recalled Hamilton and Duportail, sadly admitting that the attack against New York City could not take place. "It is too late to begin it." Four days later, on the 15th, he learned finally of the defeat at Savannah. The year was done. All that remained was to arrange for winter quarters.

Having encamped so long in the Highlands, the army had consumed almost all local food and forage. It would be necessary to move elsewhere to bivouac. Washington selected Morristown, New Jersey, a site safely back in the hills but conveniently close to West Point. Whatever else happened, that bulwark on the Hudson, built with so much sweat and time and expense, could not be left in the slightest danger. A strong garrison would have to remain and the main army would have to be near enough to support it. On hearing that the field army would quit the Highlands, Nathanael Greene, then serving as Quartermaster General for the Continental Army, vigorously advised Washington to spare no expense to insure holding West Point. "The importance of the North River," the shrewd strategist wrote redundantly but truthfully, "is an object of such importance that the force and supplies necessary for this purpose must be had at all events."[26]

Duportail returned in time to devote a week to the planning of barracks, although his attention was diverted by the sad requirement to arrange the personal affairs of Colonel Radière, who died suddenly at New Windsor on 30 October. Despite his intransigence, Radière had contributed to the building of West Point and to the fight for American independence. His death was lamented.

The Frenchman, those sad duties over, then joined Henry Knox and McDougall in surveying all the works to determine an efficient disposition of artillery for the cold season. By 23 November they gave Colonel Lamb a breakout of guns by number and caliber, ordering him to make the necessary shifts. McDougall, still actually in command of West Point, pressed urgently for men and material to build shelter before freezing weather should arrive. To the Scot, Washington formally gave the mission of resuming construction at West Point. Lumber and carpenters had been diverted from barracks to prepare boats for the invasion that was never launched. The artificers were returned to McDougall and supply agents began looking for more planks. Firewood, too, was sorely needed; fatigue parties hustled back into the hills to chop a supply. In addition to the defenses and barracks, Washington warned McDougall about the chain. It must "remain down as long as possible consistent with its safety," but by no means should it be left on the river as long as last year. In short, McDougall should exert himself "to get matters in general at this post in the best possible train."[27]

General Washington's last two weeks in the Moore house were filled with preparations to shift his army and to move himself. The final portion of his stay might have been clouded with disappointment over the failure of the French navy, but nature compensated by arranging a dry, warm Indian summer. The days were golden, the air clear and crisp.

Washington, always a staunch advocate of firm discipline, left his mark at West Point. Culprits could expect just but harsh treatment from the General. Even as he prepared to depart, he remained a stern superintendent. Late that last month, four soldiers of the 1st North Carolina regiment were found guilty of "assaulting the house of Mr. Uriah McTheil [Mekeel?], firing several shot through it, wounding Thomas Brown and robbing him, likewise plundering the house of several articles of wearing apparel, fowls, butter, cheese, etc." One, named Wiley Borough, confessed and received only a hundred lashes. The other three were sentenced to death. Washington, to magnify the impact of the execution, pardoned two, Peter Burgis and William Mullen, but had them act as executioners for their partner in crime, Reason Rickets. On 20 November, with hundreds of soldiers looking on from the rim of Execution Hollow, Rickets was shot to death by his two weeping buddies. The lesson was not lost on the sober observers.[28]

Just before leaving, the General ordered William Heath to replace McDougall, who was ailing with bladder stones. Heath was chosen after Horatio Gates declined the command. In a very long and quite specific letter, Washington outlined Heath's duties, enjoining him to "neglect nothing conducive to [West Point's] security." Prosecute the works now erecting, he prescribed, "with all the vigor and expedition in your power."[29]

On 30 November, the great chain was removed from the Hudson and stacked where Washington's dining marquee had stood. Mounting his horse under a bright sun, the Virginian paused for a moment, surveyed the rusty links, glanced once at the home he had so enjoyed—"this happy spot"— waved his hat in salute to those remaining, and spurred his mount up the steep road behind "Moore's Folly."

PART
THE BLACK YEAR
FOUR

15

THE TERRIBLE WINTER

SOMEWHERE far to the north, where the Arctic Circle crosses Hudson Bay, a blizzard was born. It roared southward, freezing and killing, sweeping down the Hudson Valley. After noon on Sunday, 2 January 1780, it crashed into and over West Point with a fury unmatched in the memory of any person living. Temperatures plunged so quickly that boats were caught and frozen in midstream. Men who had begun crossing the river by oar completed their passage by foot. Snow too deep and blowing to be measured smothered the Highlands. Unfortunate troops seeking shelter in tents found the canvas structures blown down about their ears and in several instances saw them carried flapping and whirling away across the plain. In either case the men "were quite buried in snow and not dug out" for a day or two. For nearly three days the "storm continued very fierce indeed!" The Hudson froze solid all the way to the ocean and ice grew thick enough to support the heaviest cannon. An entire cavalry troop cantered across from Staten Island to the southern tip of Manhattan. Even in the agony of enduring it, men marveled at the ferocity and unparalleled cold of that terrible blast from the north.[1]

Subzero temperatures, howling winds, and blinding snow paralyzed the post at West Point. Men struggled only to survive. They pooled what wood was available, crowded into a few huts selected to have fires, and huddled close together for warmth. Every stitch of clothing was worn and blankets were draped around shoulders, and still they were miserably cold. But at least they were inside. It was all but impossible to go out of doors in the face of the storm. "No man could endure its violence many minutes without the danger of his life," recorded James Thacher. Late on the third day the blizzard abated somewhat and a few men braved the breath-snatching, brittle cold to break trails to woodbins. In a simple but pathetic entry on 5 January, Doctor Samuel Adams eloquently told his diary of the ordeal he had undergone: "—got wood—oh! the pleasure of a good fire—."

That great storm served notice that it was going to be a hard winter. When it was over, survivors would look back on it as the worst ever.

Even before the blizzard the weather had been bad. When Washington and his entourage rode off for Morristown on the last day of November, the sunny period at West Point ended. McDougall, unhappy at finding himself once more commanding in the Highlands as the cold months approached, and impatient for General Heath to relieve him, had set about the task of finding or building cover for the garrison as early as mid-November. Every man with masonry experience was placed under Kosciuszko's supervision in an effort to complete the barracks already begun as soon as possible. The Scot called all commanders together and had them draw straws. Winners marched their men directly into finished huts and barracks; losers put their units in tents pending completion of new barracks. But it was already too late. A day after Washington's departure the sky turned gray and a light snow filled the air. And the next day enough fell to carpet the plain with nearly half a foot. The barracks were not finished, nor were they likely to be. Lumber was missing and winter was present.[2]

Realizing the battle to be as good as lost, McDougall made the best disposition possible under the circumstances. He ordered troops to move into the forts and redoubts to live in the bombproofs. The quartermaster was told to squeeze "officers and men as close in the rooms as will comport with decency to the former and health to the latter." A hundred men marched into Fort Putnam, crowding into the bombproof there, while their officers moved into the small cabin that normally housed sentries. Another eighty troops were packed into Fort Arnold's bombproof. And so on, until each work with any cover was crammed. Men were still left in tents. The Scotsman, anxious to complete the barracks begun on the plain, had units then in tents cast lots for the partially finished buildings "in order that the officers and men may be vigilant in completing those which are not finished." On the 5 December it snowed again and Heath arrived to replace McDougall.[3]

Conditions steadily worsened. Freezing rain fell from the 10th to the 13th. Blowing with stunning fury, a sudden gale tore fifty boats from their moorings, scattering them up and down the river. A week before Christmas "a most violent cold snow storm" dumped 18 inches on the plain. There had been no bread for ten days. Men remained inside patching cracks to keep out the north wind and muttering darkly. Troops in tents realized that they would probably spend the winter in them. Another cold snap hit on the 20th and temperatures remained low for several days. Food ran out. Christmas, men went hungry. "No bread in the garrison," was Dr. Adams' terse comment. On the 28th another "severe snow storm" heaped drifts higher around the huts. Then sleet pelted down. On the last day of 1779, Heath later recalled, "There was a great body of snow on the ground." Dr. Adams, who indicated his degree of emphasis by adding exclamation marks, recorded the weather on the first day of 1780—the Black Year—as "fair and exceeding cold!!!" The stage was set for the great blizzard. But that awful storm was only the second of many harsh blows at West Point in that dark year. The first, inauspiciously enough, came on New Year's Day.[4]

Early that morning General Heath sat down at his desk in Beverley Robinson's house and began a New Year's message to his suffering troops. "The Major General wishes the year may be productive of success, honor and happiness to the army. . . ." (It would be productive of defeat, dishonor, and unhappiness.) He continued wistfully, ". . . he hopes all of them, after visiting their friends from whom they have been long absent, will re-enlist, return, and join their brothers, at whose side they have fought, bled, and conquered." Finishing the paper with an authorization to issue every man four ounces of rum, he handed it to an aide for distribution in the daily orders. At that moment a runner, out of breath and perspiring despite the bitter cold, reached him with alarming news: there had been a mutiny at West Point!

Abominable weather, leaking tents, foul-smelling bunks shared with three other men, no pay, rags for shoes, poor food or none, prospects of more months like the one just past. It was too much to take. Claiming their enlistments were up, about a hundred men of the Massachusetts Line, mostly from the 4th Brigade, set off that morning in a body for Massachusetts and home. Before they got far, two captains gathered up faithful troops, pursued the deserters, and brought them back. Heath pardoned the most, but punished some with up to a hundred lashes. The general leniency shown, however, was tacit acknowledgment of the miseries the soldiers were enduring. Mass desertion on the first day of the year seemed a dark omen, a portent of worse to come. The seed of mutiny planted that January 1st would sprout and grow and spread and ripen, nurtured like a mushroom in darkness, to burst in infamy a year later.[5]

As soon as men could stir in the wake of the numbing arctic storm, officers had them out clearing supply roads to the sources of food and fuel. Mountain trails were impassable, but sled paths were marked out on river ice. Such provisions as could be located were brought in. Essentially, the men returned to normal winter rationing, sarcastically but truthfully called a "system of starving."

Doctor Adams' first two patients after the wind and cold slackened enough for the sick to seek aid exhibited symptoms resulting from earlier efforts to ward off the chill: they showed up at the hospital with "the venereal disease." Behind them, however, came frostbite cases. Tales abound of barefoot soldiers leaving trails of blood through snowdrifts and along icy roads each winter of the War of Independence. And sadly enough, they are true tales. But not during that terrible winter of 1779–1780; a bare foot froze before it bled, and was lost. Without clothing, men hunkered around fires in their huts. Uniforms and boots and cloaks became more or less communal property. Those men on detail took whatever was available, while others remained naked in barracks. Several had served their enlistment, but had not enough clothes to go home. At Morristown, Anthony Wayne sardonically commented that, as Congress seemed to think hats not a necessary "part of uniform, they mean to leave us uniformly bare-headed —as well as bare-footed—and if they find that we can *bare* it tolerably well in the two extremes, perhaps they may try it in the *center*." At West Point few would have thought that humorous. Living conditions were more miserable and crowded than ever; the wind had solved much of the problem of deciding who would sleep in tents by blowing many of them away. In huts men were packed tighter. Earlier strictures pertaining to decency and health gave way to the more pressing need to put a roof over everyone.[6]

The days and nights were long, dull, and always cold. Men played fitfully at cards, or whittled. Those lucky enough to be literate read, or wrote. They rotated the chore of running out for rations or chopping wood. Mostly they crowded close to the fireplace, and shivered, and waited.

Fire was inevitable. Hastily constructed chimneys were neither designed for nor capable of coping with such constantly roaring fires as the wretched soldiers stoked. On 9 January part of North Redoubt burned, escaping total destruction only because the men valiantly risked their lives to remove powder kegs and to contain the blaze. Men immediately began patching up the damage, but "squalls of snow" and even colder temperatures on the 13th brought a temporary halt to the frigid labor. In the middle of the night on 26 January a large barracks building on the plain, used by the quartermaster, caught fire, flaring so quickly that nothing was saved. The inhabitants themselves sprinted wildly away, escaping without casualties, but many—men and women alike—were left all but nude in the snow. After they were crowded into other already bulging buildings, Heath set up strict measures to prevent a recurrence. Roving guards, including officers, walked constantly at night from building to building; flues were inspected and corrected; in spite of the cold, fires were limited in size. The precautions worked. North Redoubt flamed up once more that winter, the fire burning for two days before being extinguished, but no other fires occurred.[7]

Washington, ever fearful of losing the great fortress on the Hudson, read a possibility of something sinister into the rash of fires. Worriedly he wrote Heath, "From the frequency of fires at West Point and its dependencies, one would think there was something more than accident, and yet, from the enquiry, they do not appear to be the effect of design. It is possible." The Commander-in-Chief then suggested that "there may be fire engines in some of the towns up the river, one of which you might perhaps obtain upon application." No evidence of arson was ever discovered, but orders were published specifying that anyone apprehended committing that crime would "instantly suffer death."[8]

In the camp of Washington's main army at Morristown, conditions were similarly desperate for shelter and maybe more so for food. Joseph Plumb Martin, a soldier in the Connecticut Line, remembered his ordeal there vividly:

> I do solemnly declare that I did not put a single morsel of victuals into my mouth for four days and as many nights, except a little black birch bark which I gnawed off a stick of wood, if that can be called victuals. I saw several of the men roast their old shoes and eat them, and I was afterward

informed by one of the officers' waiters that some of the officers killed and ate a favorite little dog that belonged to one of them. . . . If "suffering" like this did not "try men's souls," I confess that I do not know what could.[9]

Almost as pressing a problem as food and fire was the matter of camp cleanliness. It is not surprising, in view of the penetrating cold, that unclad soldiers were averse to going far from their barracks to relieve themselves. In short order, with hundreds of men and women living closely packed on the plain, the entire encampment began to take on the appearance of a great, flat, open latrine. Heath huffily wrote, "The commandant observes that the men . . . ease themselves about on the snow and ground in an unsoldierlike manner." He had trenches hacked out of the frozen ground and made the men attend lectures on how to use them. To no avail. On a raw night, with an arctic wind whipping across the plain, troops risked punishment rather than run some distance through snow to the exposed latrines. Heath was livid with anger that he should be disobeyed. Moreover, his Yankee sense of orderliness was pained "at the abominable and brutish custom of soldiers easing themselves near the barracks. . . ." "For the sake of decency as well as cleanliness . . . this vile practice will be discontinued," he thundered. Then, bowing to reality, he had vaults sunk right next to each building. That apparently solved the problem.[10]

In the meantime, Washington was concerned over the excellent avenue of approach a solidly icebound river provided the British. They could easily load men and cannon into sleds at New York and be nearly to West Point before the garrison could react. Learning in late January that the enemy had "lately collected a large parcel" of sleighs, the General cautioned Heath to be wary and "to keep men in every work where there is cover, and to direct the officer commanding in them to bar their gates carefully every night and to take every precaution against a surprise. . . ." By now every general officer in the army was aware of Washington's obsession with West Point, and all seemingly accepted in stride such minute meddling in business quite properly their own. Heath complied fully. An emergency supply of food was locked up in Fort Putnam, guards were increased (although not clothing to cover them); officers locked gates each night; reconnaissance patrols ranged far downriver, some surely on ice skates; inspectors checked the entire warning system; strangers were placed under surveillance; sergeants inspected arms. West Point would not be caught short.[11]

In that entire dreadful winter, only one man was satisfied. James Jay was still happily performing his artillery experiments.* On the frozen river he had a perfectly level firing range. Conditions were ideal. He could make exact range measurements from the spot of firing to the point of impact. One day in the early part of February he was allowed fifteen shots, a

---

* James Jay was an individual of noteworthy scientific achievement whose inventions and experiments were of considerable interest to Washington, and of some use. He had provided the Commander-in-Chief with, among other things, a supply of invisible ink "for the purpose of private correspondence"—espionage activities. Washington encouraged and supported his artillery experiments at West Point.

diversion that provided some entertainment to the weather-locked garrison. The men gathered to watch him blaze away with a captured twelve-pounder, sending cannon balls bouncing and skittering along the solid surface of the river in a shower of ice splinters.[12]

As weeks passed with no relaxation of the glacial stranglehold, food diminished in both quantity and variety. Wheat was relatively plentiful but could not be ground into flour until a thaw freed mill wheels. Peas were substituted for bread. Butter, when it could be had, cost ten dollars a pound. Meat was virtually unheard of. Potatoes were a special treat, "an article of great luxury here—worth taking pains to send 15 miles for and paying dear for them, too." Men grew gaunt. Food constantly filled dreams, rarely bellies. There had been a time when they could joke about their system of starving. No more. Laughter lost ground to bitterness. Even the most naïve, most patriotic of soldiers came to realize that they were actually dying slowly of malnutrition in a land of plenty. America was a nation rich in food. In the towns and across the countryside, the population was on the whole well-off—even fat. But in army camps, where huddled soldiers enduring beyond endurance, stalked the specter of starvation. Empty stomachs churned; resentment rose.[13]

Asking George Clinton for help, Heath described the plight of his woebegone charges, and warned of consequences which could be expected unless relief were found:

> The garrison of West Point have during the winter been at a scanty allowance of bread, and often without any at all. This has been the case for these four or five days past. The garrison . . . are obliged to be on almost constant fatigue, dragging materials for their barracks and all their fuel on hand sleds more than a mile. Some of the troops are yet in tents and . . . have been obliged to endure hunger and cold. . . . These they have endured and performed with a patience scarcely to be conceived. But, your Excellency well knows the disposition of soldiers as well as of mankind in general, . . . a crisis may come if a remedy . . . is not afforded.[14]

Though Heath did not say it, soldiers were not alone in their increasing uneasiness. Officers, too, turned sullen. Many resigned. Most considered quitting, although some tug of duty or honor or country kept them in. But doubts lurked.

For all who could manage, of all ranks, the winter was a time for vacation, a chance to go home. A reunion with wife and children before the next campaign; an opportunity to sleep in a clean bed and eat decently; a time to compare conditions in camp with those elsewhere and wonder whether one's countrymen knew or cared what the army was doing; a time to ponder how many more years the family could struggle along without a father. The coming campaign would be the sixth. How many more would there be? And how many would be enough? Disquieting questions, unsettling questions, and there were no answers—only uncertainties.

Many never saw the spring. Weakened by an inadequate diet, almost constantly chilled, living in overcrowded and filthy barracks, the forlorn garrison was more than normally susceptible to those diseases which always hovered over army camps in that era. The small burial ground, nestled against the hills across the plain, expanded noticeably that winter.* Emaciated corpses, stripped of clothes to cover the living, were laid to rest in shallow, frozen graves, attended only by a few friends and a shivering work party disrespectfully eager to fill the hole and retreat indoors to a warm fire. That macabre scene was one not likely to enhance morale.

On 21 February General Heath announced, "Impaired health and close application to business have rendered it indispensably necessary that the general should have a short relaxation and change of air." Major General Robert Howe, the North Carolina playboy, took his place. Howe quickly moved into Beverley Robinson's snug house. According to Dr. Adams' diary, he did not visit the miserable garrison at West Point until the weather turned warmer two weeks later.[15]

The deep freeze began to ease on George Washington's birthday. A warm rain fell, eating into snow and melting ice. On 1 March it was still warm, and foggy. That day the ice broke. Shattering explosions, sounding for all the world like a cross between a cannon blast and a thunderbolt, rent the damp air as the great ice sheet cracked and split. Rising from the river in sharp roars, one after another, booming into the hills, the reports echoed and reechoed around the rocks. That icy cacophony signaled an end to winter—not misery, just winter.

* Maps of the Military Academy drawn in the early nineteenth century clearly show the location of the Revolutionary War cemetery where Washington Hall, the present Cadet Dining Hall, now stands.

16

*DARK DAYS
AND
PRUSSIAN ADVICE*

WHEN THE ice began to break, boatmen rushed to reach vessels that had been locked in the river since the first day of the great storm. Most were saved but not a few were stove in either by compression during freezing or by being crunched between two massive floes after the ice sheet was sundered. For a month more the waterway was clogged with ice chunks, making crossing hazardous and precluding installation of the chain.

Following a false alarm of British advance on 12 March, Howe became worried. The thaw that loosened the ice pack had given way to more snows and frigid weather. If such conditions persisted, spring could easily catch the Patriots with the chain still on shore. Howe ordered Kosciuszko to prepare the chain for immediate emplacement. On inspecting the logs, the Pole was shocked to discover many of them ruined. They had become waterlogged last season and had not been replaced when the chain was withdrawn, for deep snow had covered the great obstacle as soon as it was placed on land. During the bitterly cold winter no one had thought about chain logs—and even if they had, thinking about them was all that could have been done. Watching artificers work on the barrier, Howe reached the conclusion that it was not properly made. He wrote Washington suggesting major changes in design although he realized the season was late. Fortunately, the Commander-in-Chief did not concur. "Your ideas respecting the chain have not escaped me," the General replied. "But although I have thought of its insufficiency and looked towards its improvement, yet I could not conceive much reasonable hope of any considerable alteration. With so much to do in our circumstances, it was impossible to do all." Washington believed extra anchors and cables might help, but the main thing was to place the obstacle across the river and worry about changes later. Working feverishly, Kosciuszko began changing the worst logs and making minor repairs on metal parts. Howe prodded, "Colonel Koskuiszko will exert himself to hasten the chain, and report the moment it is ready." Every officer who had experience in "putting it down" was summoned to help. Finally on 31 March the engineer was ready. Ice was still in the river, and the chain had precious little flotation, but Howe felt it was necessary to stretch it right then. Every man who could possibly be spared gathered to work lines on shore or bend an oar in the river. Even "officers and their waiters" joined in. Unhappily, all efforts were in vain. Additional logs were required. On 5 April, after changing a few more floats, and with no ice remaining, Kosciuszko tried again, this time successfully.[1]

That annual spring chore accomplished, engineer and commander turned their attention to completion of the fortifications. Kosciuszko kept a detail of 80 to 100 men laboring every day at West Point, while Lieutenant Colonel Gouvion supervised perhaps half as many at King's Ferry strengthening Stony Point and Verplanck's Point. To the engineer's dismay, it was soon discovered that a disproportionate amount of labor would be required merely to reach the level of construction attained when work was stopped the preceding autumn. The elements had done significant damage to all works, while snowbound inhabitants had all but destroyed several structures. Wooden parts not properly guarded had been stripped to provide shelter or fire. Checking his calendar, the Pole discovered that he had first come to West Point exactly two years before. The task seemed endless. Strive as he might, nothing ever seemed to be finished. Supplies, as always, were scarce. Men worked lackadaisically, their energy sapped by the efforts of surviving the winter. Maps and plans got lost in the mails, requiring incessant rework. Building West Point was like running on a treadmill. Frustration was a constant companion. The entire garrison shared Kosciuszko's mood of utter discouragement.[2]

To snap the men out of the doldrums and to get on with the job, a firm hand was needed at the helm. Robert Howe was not that hand. Although he styled himself "a disciplinarian by inclination," his record belies his words. Officers found guilty of serious violations of duty received only reprimands; when he ordered soldiers to cease shooting at pigeons flying around the forts they ignored him; he himself complained that reports were neglected, details unfilled, orders blatantly disregarded; subordinates seldom bothered to transmit instructions. When several troopers were caught and convicted of plundering, Howe pardoned them—in spite of a request from their own officers that they be punished. The North Carolinian preferred pleading to punishment, imploring rather than compelling. On 9 April General Howe openly acknowledged that discipline was poor and begged his officers for understanding and assistance. A floundering ship needs an iron grip on the wheel; in periods of depression and deprivation, soldiers need direction and discipline, not supplication.[3]

To his credit Howe did try both the carrot and the stick, but he had neither means for the former nor meanness for the latter. In an attempt to provide some form of diversion, Major Sebastian Bauman of the artillery conducted "an exhibition of fire-works" on the plain and collaborated with James Jay in conducting interesting artillery experiments. Freemasons regularly staged lodge meetings in Moore's house, establishing that "most happy harmony peculiar to our Honorable Society." And at least once a number of officers with thespian talents staged an evening performance of *Cato,* which, we are told, was "pretty well done." But West Point was a grim post with a hungry, cold, restless garrison. Food for stomachs, clothes for backs, pay for pockets—these were what the men wanted. And in the absence of those items, a discipline-inspired sense of dedication could alone make living conditions seem tolerable. Toward achieving that end, Howe also made an effort. In late April his scouts picked up John Lakeman, a deserter to the enemy, and William Burtis, a spy. On the 25th representatives from every company were marched to the edge of Execution Hollow to watch the two strung up. Before the bodies were cut down, General Howe delivered a long harangue against deserting to the enemy. In words which would take on a strangely ironic ring just a few months hence, his voice carried over the West Point plain, "No sentiments of honor or religion can possibly actuate the bosom of that wretch who can perpetrate a crime in which *perfidy, perjury,* or *treason* to the United States of America are [contained]." He trusted that witnessing such a "melancholy event" as the dual hanging would have the "proper effect upon the minds of the soldiers." They may indeed have decided not to spy or desert to the enemy, but they also knew quite well that under Howe no stiff penalty was likely for lesser crimes.[4]

If possible, conditions and morale had worsened by May. Inflation wracked the country. Continental paper currency was virtually worthless; those who would accept it often exchanged it at the ridiculous rate of about four thousand paper dollars to one of silver or gold. To our language was added the expression, "not worth a continental." For all that, however, many soldiers had not been paid even one of those valueless paper dollars for six months. Debt was endemic, verging on epidemic. Desertions outstripped enlistments. "I assure you," Washington told the President of Congress, "every idea you can form of our distresses will fall short of reality." There could be seen "in every line of the army the most serious features of mutiny and sedition." The long-suffering soldiers were "reduced again for want of meat. On several days of late, the troops have been entirely destitute of any, and for a considerable time past they have been at best at half, a quarter, an eighth allowance of this essential article of provision." That was in the main army. He also wrote that the garrison was "in as great distress at West Point to the full." The sacrifices of the men in the Highlands drew Washington's compassion. He wrote Howe, "The distresses of the troops under your command give me great pain and what adds to it is, I have it not in my power to administer to their relief." Dr. James Thacher penned, "Our poor soldiers are reduced to the very verge of famine; their patience is exhausted by complicated sufferings, and their spirits are almost broken."[5]

As if to say that she sympathized in full measure with the bleak days the Patriots were enduring, Nature herself staged a remarkably symbolic protest, a black day. The sun came up red on 19 May. A few showers fell. Slowly a vast black cloud formed from New Jersey to Boston. By nine that morning one "could not see to read large print in a room with the windows open." Fowls went to roost. At noon "a lighted candle in a room with 3 windows open cast shadows on the wall." The Connecticut House of Representatives considered adjourning, some members firmly believing the end of the world was upon them. One practical Yankee scotched such talk with a profound stand: "I am against adjournment. Either the day of judgment is at hand or it is not. If it is I wish to be found in the line of duty." They did adjourn, but only because it was too dark to work. After clearing slightly in the afternoon, skies once more blackened. That night, "was as dark, perhaps, as it ever was at any time anywhere on earth except *Egypt*." Modern city dwellers will recognize the symptoms of a gigantic and severe case of smog. Smoke and debris from vast forest fires had combined with a dank atmospheric inversion to create the phenomenon, but to ordinary folk of that age there was something sinister etched in those Stygian skies. Was it an omen of impending disaster? Did the sword of Damocles hang over the Patriot cause?[6]

Not a week later mutiny struck again. Two Connecticut regiments paraded spontaneously at dusk on 25 May and in mass decided to march home. They were fed up with the war and with their treatment. Short rations, no pay, abysmal conditions, and the long war had brought them to the threshold of outright rebellion. Colonel Return Jonathan Meigs, whose name adorned a redoubt at West Point built by many of these same men, attempted to reason with them. A bayonet sliced through flesh along his ribs, ending the colonel's blandishments. Other officers turned out the Pennsylvania Line to block the New Englanders' route of march. Sobered at seeing their colonel wounded and subdued by the thought of a clash with the Pennsylvanians, the malcontents "returned with grumbling instead of music." Mass mutiny was averted, but not the deep passions from which it sprang. Late into the night small pockets of disgruntled soldiers lingered on the parade field. "We . . . still kept upon the parade in groups, venting our spleen at our country and government, then at our officers, and then at ourselves for our imbecility in staying there and starving in detail for an ungrateful people who did not care what became of us. . . ." Had the officers been able to look just a few months into the future they would have been most reluctant to trust the Pennsylvania Line in such a delicate task as suppressing mutinous countrymen.[7]

From start to finish May had been a most unhappy month. In keeping with that pattern, its last day brought Washington news of the greatest single disaster to overtake American arms in the entire war. Major General Benjamin Lincoln had lost Charleston, South Carolina, thus surrendering nearly five thousand defenders to a jubilant Sir Henry Clinton. Among Lincoln's garrison had been over twenty-six hundred irreplaceable Continentals. That major defeat was a blow to the Patriots. America's knees were buckling under the cumulative blows, her eyes glazing over. Morale, already believed to have been at rock bottom, plunged lower. Black could be blacker. In England, earlier that same month, George III had taken cognizance of the appallingly low state of morale among the rebels. If no great disaster befell Britain, the Monarch opined, the United States would sue for peace that summer. For once, his Majesty was not too far wrong concerning his erstwhile subjects.[8]

The abject depth of despair sweeping Patriot ranks as the year approached its halfway mark has never been more succinctly expressed than in the sharp words of an officer close to Washington, Alexander Hamilton:

> . . . our countrymen have all the folly of the ass and all the passiveness of the sheep in their compositions. They are determined not to be free and they can neither be frightened, discouraged nor persuaded to change their resolution. If we are saved France and Spain must save us. I have the most Pigmy-feeling at the idea, and I almost wish to hide my disgrace in universal ruin.[9]

On the very day that Hamilton spoke of universal ruin, Washington wrote of "the ruin which may be produced by languid measures" from the states and the people. But, indicative of his ability to remain calm in the midst of turmoil, he issued orders, at the same time, "to have ovens erected at West Point" because "there is so great a saving by delivering out bread instead of flour."

Learning that Sir Henry was returning with his fleet and thousands of men to New York, General Washington was alarmed for the safety of West Point. "There is every reason to believe that [General Henry Clinton], encouraged by his success to the southward and by the distresses of the garrison, . . . may resolve upon an immediate attempt upon West Point," he warned Howe. To bolster the garrison, Washington rushed to the Hudson what flour and cattle he could gather. Writing to Governor Jonathan Trumbull of Connecticut, the Commander-in-Chief urged him to have his state militia assist in preparing field fortifications and obstacles for West Point, saying, "This is too serious a danger not to demand instant exertions to obviate it." Ten days later, when the situation was clearer, he informed General Howe, "You do well to consider the post of West Point as the capital object of your attention. . . . This is peculiarly necessary at the present moment, as there are circumstances that authorize a suspicion of something being intended against the post." (There was, indeed, a plot afoot, but the honest and dedicated Virginian could never have imagined the form it was taking.) In order better to insure cooperation from the New York militia, Washington ordered James Clinton to drop everything else and "return with the utmost expedition to West Point." Washington had always considered that losing the Hudson River would probably be a mortal wound to his war effort; now, in this dark year, loss of the waterway could spell sudden death.[10]

George Washington did not know Robert Howe well and was unsure of his abilities. Howe's handling of the garrison had impressed no one and the Commander-in-Chief clearly recalled the bungled effort to take Verplanck's Point nearly a year ago. He began to cast around for a replacement or, at least, a strong lieutenant. Brigadier General James Clinton was a trusted fighter, but it might be some time before he would arrive. Too, in this critical hour, it seemed best to send another major general. Benedict Arnold, Washington knew, wanted the command, and New Yorkers wanted him to have it. They knew and trusted him, and also knew that West Point's preservation was crucial to the defense of New York. In May Philip Schuyler had expressed doubt that Robert Howe could do the job, telling Washington that his state would "wish to see its banner entrusted" to Benedict Arnold. On 12 June Arnold himself raised the subject during a stop at Washington's headquarters. Upon returning from a visit to Connecticut, he informed his chief, he would be pleased to accept the West Point command since his old leg wound would prevent his taking an active role in the field. Washington was worried about West Point right then, however. In a month or so he hoped to attack New York City, leaving no one in the fortress "but invalids because it would be entirely covered by the main army." He felt the energetic Arnold would not be happy in so sedentary a job. The matter was held in abeyance, but Arnold departed thinking he would get the post. For the immediate crisis the Commander-in-Chief selected Alexander McDougall to assist Howe at West Point.[11]

Arnold stopped at West Point on 16 June to visit Howe. Upon his request for a tour of West Point, "which I never saw before," the North Carolinian conducted the famous fighter to all the various posts on the west side of the river. Howe later was to recall that Arnold "spoke so particularly of the Rocky Hill work [Redoubt 4] and with what ease it would be taken as struck me oddly even then, though I had not the least suspicion of him." Arnold continued to Connecticut and Howe resumed preparations for the attack both he and Washington believed was imminent.[12]

Undisciplined troops at the Point plagued efforts to strengthen the various defenses. Fascines, constructed and emplaced with so much effort and expense, were torn down by the men and burned in cooking fires. A mild rebuke was the only punishment dealt out. Even camp followers had grown impudent by June. For example, Sarah Warren was found guilty one day that month of "scandalyzing Captain-Lieutenant Archibald's character." For stepping so out of line, women had been stripped bare to the waist and whipped at other encampments, but under the easygoing environment of West Point, Sarah was cavalierly sentenced "to ask Captain Archibald's pardon before such officers as he shall think necessary." Beginning his fourth month in command, Howe could still naïvely complain that his orders were being disobeyed. Reports from various sources reached Washington, all indicating the need of tighter control in the Highlands. Baron von Steuben, in his role as Inspector General, had been en route to West Point to investigate the problems there when a sudden enemy move into New Jersey had prompted Washington to place him in command of an element of the army at Springfield, New Jersey. On 20 June he requested permission to resume his march to the Highlands. West Point, he strongly believed, was what Sir Henry was after. General Washington immediately approved the request.[13]

Handling Howe could become a touchy matter, Washington realized.

He believed that "to remove him . . . at this period must be too severe a wound to the feelings of any officer to be given but in cases of real necessity." However, the unkempt house at West Point definitely needed a thorough cleaning. Taking Alexander Hamilton aside, General Washington discussed the fine points of protocol with the smart young aide and stressed the necessity of circumventing them in this instance in order to get the job done. Hamilton understood perfectly and managed the situation satisfactorily if unofficially. After Steuben reached the Highlands, the aide wrote him:

> As you are at West Point, the General wishes you to remain there till the present appearances come to some result. He has confidence in your judgment and wishes you to give your advice and assistance to the Commanding officer. As you have no command in the post, you can only do this in a private friendly way; but I dare say, General Howe will be happy to consult you.
>
> You will consider this as a private letter in which I rather convey you the General's wishes than his commands.[14]

In other words, Steuben was to be an advisor—a delicate role affording no glory but many frustrations, entailing responsibility without authority. Not until two centuries later, when descendants of Patriot officers would themselves be cast in the role of advisors to a foreign army, could American officers truly appreciate the finesse required in such a situation.

When the Prussian drillmaster rode into the Highlands stronghold, trailed by his huge greyhound, Azor, he found the troops busy enough. McDougall was there, injecting Scottish fire and vigor into the garrison. James Clinton's brigade was also arriving. Kosciuszko had already replaced many of the soaked logs with new ones, freshly tarred and seasoned, and the chain floated easily once again, although more logs would be needed soon to keep it in that condition. Cannon had been distributed more equally to the various works and ammunition was marked to be sent on a moment's notice to redoubts having no magazines of their own. The Pole himself was personally supervising work on Redoubt Wyllys while Captain Daniel Niven, who had just replaced an ill Villefranche, was putting the finishing touches to Redoubts 1, 2, and 3. Lightning rods—"electrical spires"— adorned the tops of powder magazines, indicating a degree of sophistication the Prussian had not expected. The jail was overflowing, being about as crowded as the barracks, but a new one had been laid out. Spies were having a hard time of it still; Steuben saw two new bodies dangling limply from the gibbets in Execution Hollow. On the surface, West Point appeared to be in good hands. Steuben knew, though, to look beneath the surface.[15]

While his Prussian Inspector General was probing the problems of West Point, Washington never slackened his own efforts to stiffen the garrison. He asked Governor Clinton to help, and the New Yorker readily did so by sending in militia. Howe was instructed to bring his strength up to 2,500 men, all fit for action. The Commander-in-Chief also warned, "Keep yourself compact whatever temptations may be thrown out to induce you to detach." Again, "Put everything in activity . . . and be well upon your guard." When a spy's report indicated Henry Clinton was poised to attack northward, Washington became more specific:

> There is one point I think of essential importance to your arrangements; the distribution of your magazines to the different works that each may have provision and water and stores sufficient to stand a siege. The nature of the post is such that each work depends very much upon itself; nor is the communication from one to another as well secured as might be wished. The advanced works in particular ought to be well provided. I should be glad each of these might have within itself a sufficiency of every thing for a defence of at least sixty days.[16]

One senses in his every word and action Washington's anxiety for the essential post on the Hudson. Disgruntled with the slowness of normal commissary procedures, he detached big Henry Knox to take flour from Trenton to West Point, authorizing him to impress wagons because "the exigency is so pressing."

When Robert R. Livingston suggested that West Point might be more "safely confided to General Arnold, whose courage is undoubted," than to Robert Howe, Washington replied that, "as General McDougall and Baron Steuben (Men of approved bravery) are both with [Howe] and the main army is in supporting distance," Arnold was not needed. As a matter of fact, by the end of June Washington had concluded that West Point was not likely to be attacked. He sent to West Point the Connecticut Line, including those units recently involved in mutiny, and ordered Howe to release the militia. An attack on New York City now seemed to be within his reach if the expected French fleet should show. Howe could safely be left at West Point so long as the capable Steuben remained there peering over his shoulder.[17]

Quietly and so smoothly that few historians have ever noted the transition, the Baron put iron and grit into the garrison at West Point, changing the previously unruly mob of men into sharp, trustworthy soldiers. A careful reading of orderly books of units stationed on the Point at that time reveals the unmistakable stamp of Prussian discipline and thoroughness—factors notably absent before Steuben's arrival. Soldiers on detached duty were recalled; drill periods were held at dawn and again at dusk, and all men attended, even orderlies of senior officers; recruits were given training before they were allowed to perform any duties (a precaution we think normal nowadays, but one seldom taken then); officers were required to conduct drill periods in person; and Major General Steuben oversaw it all. Nothing escaped the sharp eye of the Inspector General. He made men stand erect and walk proudly; he taught them to salute properly; and he insisted that officers learn the names of their soldiers. Drummers and fifers played music at all drills. Elite light infantry units were organized and exercised. The Baron followed up his instructions with a gruelling series of inspections in which he personally checked and queried every man. Reports were turned in on time, sealed and hand-carried. Inventories were made and a uniform system of bookkeeping was instituted. Camp sanitation was improved. "An officer must inspect the tents daily," he said, "to insure there are no bones or other filth in or near them." He even attempted to solve the uniform shortage by declaring that the hunting shirt was an acceptable substitute. When expected shipments of small arms from France failed to materialize, the Prussian took weapons from noncombatants and redistributed them among the fighting men, a logical but hitherto untaken step. Through it all, such friction as may have developed between him and Howe was so carefully suppressed that no hint of any has ever come to light. Howe complied with all advice, apparently pleased to have it.[18]

Orders were published and enforced. On 9 July an orderly clerk, in spelling quaint enough to deserve preservation, recorded the following instructions:

> The plucking green appels or green frute of aney sorts from the orcheds of the inhabitens is absolutely far bidden it is hurtfull to the health of the men very injurious to the property of our fellow cityzens and distructive to the sider which would be otherwise made from the appels and which would be a great advantage in the army in future.[19]

Steuben knew that words alone were not enough; bite had to follow bark. To catch violators, he posted a sergeant, two corporals, and sixteen men to guard the orchard near headquarters. Men stopped "plucking green appels."

The jail was too comfortable, he thought. It was bad enough, but hardly worse than a regular barracks. Confinement, then, was more a vacation from drill and labor than a punishment. Also, control over prisoners had been so slack that hardened types could not be secured in the regular guardhouse. Just what Steuben did is unknown, but a jail sentence at West Point suddenly became something to be avoided. Soldiers actually made their escape from the prison on the Point and surrendered to jailers elsewhere in hopes of having an easier confinement.[20]

Nor did the women at West Point escape his scrutiny. Howe had seen nothing wrong in permitting a flock of prostitutes to live in with the troops; Steuben saw it as a source of trouble. One of his first moves was to ban all unmarried women from the fortress. Neither the soldiers nor the strumpets liked the order. Impudently claiming to be married, the girls stayed. But Steuben was a jump ahead of them. He required all wives to get marriage certificates and specified further that any wife not willing to take in washing, at a prescribed rate, would be ejected. Many of the whores, unwilling to earn a living with their hands, left in search of posts with more complaisant commanders. Others bribed a local justice of the peace into issuing false marriage certificates. When the Baron learned what was happening, he had an answer: the West Point commander would simply refuse to recognize any marriage certificate issued by a New York justice of the peace. To get married, a man would have to return to his home state. The Prussian's crusade apparently worked, for the subject was not raised again.[21]

A startling difference in forms of punishment in July clearly shows an influence other than Howe's, although he technically approved all of them. On the 16th two New Hampshire soldiers were sentenced to run a gauntlet

*Troops drilling in front of Long Barracks. A detail from a watercolor
by W. S. Sturgill. Courtesy of the West Point Army Mess.*

237

of 500 men in open order, all bearing "switches." To be sure the beating was well laid on, the culprits had to advance with a bayonet at their throats to "regulate their steps." Running a similar gauntlet without a bayonet retarding one's pace was punishment for "abusing and clinching" a noncommissioned officer. For bounty jumping, two soldiers were placed on their knees in Execution Hollow and shot to death. Deserters were hanged. Lesser offenses brought whippings and hard labor. Stealing equipment was worth being "picketed fifteen minutes" (an especially harsh torture which often resulted in permanent injury) as well as a hundred lashes. Soldiers are not stupid. The men very rapidly grasped the significance of the punishments. Orders were obeyed with a new-found alacrity and eagerness; the number of violations of regulations markedly declined. "I have as much as circumstances would permit," the Baron told Washington on 28 July, "exerted myself to introduce some discipline into this part of the army which I am sorry to say was almost without."[22]

By modern standards such harsh penalties might seem brutal and cruel, but in that age they were not extraordinary. Steuben carefully informed Washington of his actions and progress. Twice the Commander-in-Chief expressed satisfaction with "the measures you are taking." And Alexander Hamilton wrote, "I dare say all you are doing will be found right. I shall join my *beau pere* to save you from the cord." Exemplary punishment, to include death in extreme cases, was a method Washington might have disliked but which he himself had resorted to at times. By the end of July the soldiers at West Point had been snapped into line. From an untrustworthy rabble they had been converted into crack troops on whom the General could depend. Prussian discipline administered by a professional officer had accomplished a near miracle of transformation.[23]

It was just in time. On 27 July Washington ordered Howe to march the entire garrison, except a New Hampshire brigade and some militia, southward to join the main army for a projected attack on New York City. A French army under the Comte de Rochambeau had landed two weeks earlier at Newport, Rhode Island. With help from Rochambeau and the support of a French fleet, prospects for a decisive battle loomed large. On 30 July General Washington rode to the Highlands and watched some of the troops honed to such a fine edge by the Baron swing off toward Peekskill. He stopped for the night at Howe's headquarters in the Robinson house. There he made last-minute arrangements to throw his army across the Hudson at Stony Point in order to menace Kingsbridge. Next day, in rather high spirits, he set off for Peekskill. For a moment only, some gray broke through the blackness of 1780.[24]

17

THE DARK EAGLE

NATANIS, an Indian chieftain holding sway over the brooding forests at the headwaters of the Kennebec River, joined Colonel Benedict Arnold's brave band in 1775 as it passed through his territory to invade Canada. Following the custom of the time, Natanis gave Arnold an Indian name—Dark Eagle. In a welcoming oration, of which the redskins were fond, Natanis foretold Arnold's fate:

> The Dark Eagle comes to claim the wilderness. The wilderness will
> yield to the Dark Eagle, but the Rock will defy him. The Dark Eagle will
> soar aloft to the sun. Nations will behold him and sound his praises. Yet
> when he soars highest his fall is most certain. When his wings brush the
> sky then the arrow will pierce his heart.[1]

How much of that remarkable prediction was written after Arnold's treason and attributed by legend to Natanis we will never know. But it was a very accurate prophecy. Arnold was an eagle among Revolutionary War generals, a combat leader without peer. He was more than a fighter, he was a winning fighter. Nations did sound his praise. And when he was at the pinnacle of fame, when his eagle wings brushed the sky, the arrow of avarice pierced his heart. He fell with a resounding crash on the Rock Natanis said would defy him—the rock of West Point.

Major General Benedict Arnold had not served actively with the army since October of 1777. For thirty-four months he had been recuperating from a crippling wound received near Saratoga. Now, in the summer heat and dust of the Black Year, the dark-complexioned hero announced himself ready once more to campaign with Washington. When the Commander-in-Chief rode down from Robinson's house on 31 July to supervise the army's crossing of the Hudson, Arnold met him at King's Ferry. The General was extremely pleased to see him. Arnold had always been his most dependable leader in a scrape; and a major battle, perhaps the decisive fight of the war, was anticipated. George Washington dreamed of massing his own forces with Rochambeau's French army to drive Sir Henry Clinton from New York City—a move the Virginian thought would win the war. Arnold had other dreams. He wanted to attain command of West Point in order to sell it to Sir Henry—a move he thought would lose the war, but make him wealthy.

The story of Arnold at West Point simply cannot begin on that muggy day with the two men astride horses on a slight knoll, chatting and watching the grimy Continental Army ferrying over the Hudson. By the summer of 1780 Arnold was renowned as a courageous and a winning warrior—a significant distinction in a war which had seen but few American victories. Unfortunately, his ability on the battlefield was not matched by prowess in other arenas of human conflict. And therein lies the key to his downfall. Both the fame and the greed that brought him to that spot on the Hudson had deep roots in the past; roots which must be explored to comprehend fully the terrible shock and numbing consternation created by his crime.

Born in Norwich, Connecticut, in 1741, he was the fourth Arnold to bear the name Benedict. The first of his ancestors to come to America made the trip from England early in the seventeenth century. Since then the family had prospered in the New World; the original Benedict Arnold had been governor of Rhode Island for many years. Curiously enough, few family names provide more irony than Arnold's—it is derived from an old English word meaning "honor." His early years were not happy ones. A pious mother countered an alcoholic father in a home which became progressively more debt-ridden. When declining family fortunes dictated a premature end to young Benedict's schooling, he was apprenticed to an apothecary. But learning the druggists' trade could not compete with the excitement of the Seven Years' War; recruiters for the 1759 campaign against the French found in the restless youth an easy mark.

Arnold's initial hitch in the army brought him no glory, but it provided a most accurate omen. He deserted. Desertion in those times, however, did not carry quite the stigma it has later gained; he was permitted to join again the following year. He saw no combat, but served the full commitment of that second enlistment.

In 1761 the young Yankee resolved to enter business in New Haven as a merchant in drugs and books. His medicines ranged from "Francis' Female Elixir" to "Greenough's Tincture for the Teeth," his printed works from *Tom Jones* to *Paradise Lost*. Bolstered by such intriguing wares, his establishment flourished until the deepening estrangement between the mother country and the colonies over questions of taxation began to hurt all small businessmen. With his spinster sister Hannah tending the store, Arnold himself sailed a sloop on trading missions to the Caribbean Islands. Those voyages furnished him experience in seamanship that he would later employ in naval clashes on Lake Champlain. They also provided the setting of at least one duel. He satisfied his honor in a fight with pistols against a British sea captain. The old salt's shot went wild while Arnold's ball nicked his antagonist. He sailed, too, up the St. Lawrence to Quebec and Montreal. In the approaching war he would reap unusual profits from the knowledge gained on those mercantile visits to Canada.

As relations between England and America fluctuated, so did Arnold's business; as his trade grew more precarious, so did his temper. Smuggling in those troubled years was viewed by most New Englanders as an upright occupation. Flouting the laws of an "iniquitous" Parliament was considered more clever than criminal. Arnold was no exception. In 1766 a disgruntled crewman, after having been refused certain demanded wages, attempted to inform customs officials that Arnold was a smuggler. The irate merchant hurriedly organized a mob of idle sailors to discourage the would-be informer. The "traitorous" employee was seized, stripped, and whipped. Arnold paid a small fine for such ready discipline, but nothing for smuggling.

He fought another duel, this time with sabers, but with the same happy outcome for the feisty little trader. Then came marriage, some improvement in financial status, participation in radical (later called patriotic) activities, and election to the captaincy of a militia company. He received that last honor just five weeks before smoke at Lexington and Concord signaled the start of the War of Independence.

On Friday, 21 April 1775, a galloping rider brought to New Haven the electrifying news of the stand made by Massachusetts militiamen two days earlier against the detested "lobster-backs." At that moment Arnold was transformed from a quarrelsome New England merchant into a dynamic Patriot leader. Although a town meeting timorously voted against assisting the rebels in the neighboring colony, the headstrong company commander paid his townsmen and elders no heed. Assembling fifty of his men, he proposed marching immediately to join the angry horde outside Boston. His troops clamorously agreed. Gathering on the town green early next morning, the company enthusiastically prepared for departure. Arnold, though short and inclining to stoutness, was nonetheless resplendent in a scarlet coat. His close-set eyes shot fire and enthusiasm past a long, slightly hooked nose. After satisfying himself that his soldiers were adequately armed and equipped, the proud officer called on the town selectmen to provide powder and musket balls. When they refused, Arnold raged that he would have the keys to the magazine in five minutes or he would break down the door and help himself. He got the keys.

On the march to Cambridge Arnold encountered Samuel H. Parsons, another officer whose name was destined to be written in the history of West Point. The two excited soldiers discussed the feasibility of attacking Fort Ticonderoga, the old French bastion on Lake Champlain in New York. As soon as his company had been added to the throng besieging Boston, Arnold described Ticonderoga's exposed and vulnerable situation to the Massachusetts Committee of Safety. That body promptly made Arnold a colonel, authorized him to raise troops in western New England, and instructed him to seize Fort Ticonderoga. Returning to Connecticut, the

242   *General Benedict Arnold. Courtesy of the West Point Library.*

new colonel discovered that the Council of War of his own state had deputized a Vermonter, Ethan Allen, to take the fort. Unable to persuade Connecticut officials to revoke their appointment of Allen, and worried lest he miss the glory which would surely crown the conqueror of Ticonderoga, Arnold hastened northward to intercept Allen and his Green Mountain Boys.

By hard riding he overtook the expedition minutes before the boats were to shove off for the fort. It was after midnight and the attack was planned for dawn. The Connecticut officer, armed with a commission from Massachusetts, confronted the Vermonter, who carried an appointment from Connecticut, and demanded the command of a force poised to assault a British fort in the colony of New York. Allen was puzzled. The Green Mountain Boys soon solved the problem, however; they would serve under no leader but their own Ethan. As time was crucial, a compromise was grudgingly reached. Arnold would accompany Allen, but would issue no orders. Brisk rowing and a forced march allowed the invaders to reach the defenses just as the sky was turning gray. Bursting into the courtyard of the rotting fortress, Allen is reputed to have roared his now famous call for surrender "in the name of the Great Jehovah and the Continental Congress." In view of his celebrated propensity for profanity and his loosely defined religious beliefs, it is quite likely that he employed the Deity's name in a rather more forceful manner. At any rate, the British commander was wholly convinced. Co-victors in a bloodless coup, the towering, green-jacketed Allen and the short, scarlet-coated Arnold walked side by side through the gate.[2]

Instead of the great glory he had sought, Arnold discovered only bitter humiliation. Entering the fort at Allen's side was his sole honor at Ticonderoga. He may have possessed command on paper, but it was Allen who owned the troops and thereby enjoyed the command in reality. Moreover, the mountain men resented the cocky outsider. Embarked on a week-long drunken binge—which had begun the moment the victorious Vermonters broke into the fort's very ample liquor stores—Allen's undisciplined horde found amusement in taking pot shots at the colonel from Connecticut. Arnold dodged well-directed insults and poorly aimed buckshot for four days until a schooner loaded with fifty of his men finally arrived. With that meager force he set sail for St. Johns, the last English position on the lake. There he surprised and captured the garrison, confiscated a sloop and several smaller boats, and burned all remaining vessels before withdrawing to Ticonderoga. As men recruited for Arnold trickled into the fort, and as Allen's drifted home, Arnold became the commander in fact.

Assisted by Bernard Romans, the same engineer who would later plan foolish fortifications on Constitution Island, Arnold attempted to repair the neglected walls of the fort. Meanwhile, looking northward to the even grander prize of Canada, he wrote numerous letters urging an invasion of that vast area before it could be reinforced from England. He was successful in neither endeavor. Before he could either ready the fort or coax his more cautious countrymen into an invasion, a committee of the Massachusetts Congress arrived to investigate his activities and to appoint a commander over him. Arnold was mortified. He indignantly resigned his Massachusetts commission and left Ticonderoga.

Suffering from gout, he decided to stop in Albany to recuperate and write a report to the Continental Congress. While there, he received word of the death of his wife. A bitter and dejected man was Arnold as he headed for New Haven. He had completed the first leg on his trek to treason.

But not even the painful combination of gall, gout, and grief could extinguish the fire of excitement in Arnold's breast. Within weeks he had shoved resentment to the back of his mind and was laboring with Washington over plans to invade Canada by way of the Kennebec River in Maine. Arnold, by then a Continental colonel, was asked to lead the effort. Again glory beckoned; again Arnold was eager. His force, about 1,100 strong, consisted of two battalions of infantry and three companies of riflemen. Captain Daniel Morgan, a veteran soldier from Virginia, was at the head of the riflemen. A young gentleman named Aaron Burr joined as a "casual." By mid-September all preparations had been completed. Washington wished them well and the adventure began.

A niche in history's hall of heroic American exploits was most surely earned by that little army and its intrepid leader. In the face of an approaching Canadian winter it was an act of courage merely to attempt the trip to Quebec; to complete that march was a severe measure of Arnold's leadership. Fettered from the first by leaking boats, floods, and ruined supplies, the column was soon shaken by desertion when the entire rear guard of three companies followed its fainthearted commander back to Cambridge. The others, hungry but determined, remained steadfast. As the ominously reduced force pushed ever deeper into the desolate wilderness, already weakened men were further exhausted by the necessity of making frequent and arduous portages. They were cruelly starved by meager or missing rations, and constantly benumbed by immersion in frigid streams and exposure to chilling rains. By late October the situation was desperate. Arnold commanded gaunt scarecrows, not men. The were making meals of bark and boiled moccasins. Dysentery and drowning had opened gaps in the ranks. The healthy were too few and too weak to carry the ill. Accompanied by a picked group of the strongest, Arnold left his wretched assemblage and forged ahead. Reaching a French settlement on the Chaudière River, he rushed food back to the pitiable survivors in the forest. The disintegrating expedition was saved. On 10 November Arnold and approximately five hundred men restored to fighting trim gazed at the walls of Quebec from the south shore of the St. Lawrence. Disease, death, and desertion had halved his strength, but he had reached Quebec. And the city standing before him was defended by a mere handful of royal troops.

Had Arnold and his bedraggled band captured Quebec the entire course of the Revolutionary War might very possibly have been altered. Canada could well have entered the conflict as the fourteenth state, while Arnold himself would probably have found a place in history far different from the one he now holds. But it was not to be. A winter storm and a shortage of boats delayed the crossing by four days. In impotent fury,

Arnold watched as British reinforcements reached the city. The Americans did cross and invest the town, but by then defenders outnumbered besiegers. If the march from Massachusetts had started just a week earlier it is hard to imagine that Arnold could have failed to seize Quebec.

Brigadier General Richard Montgomery united his own army with Arnold's in December and assumed command of the combined force. Montgomery had led a successful invasion from Lake Champlain to Montreal and then down the St. Lawrence. When the impavid Irishman met Arnold, the Patriots were virtual masters of all Canada save Quebec. Montgomery planned to make the northern province entirely American by storming the King's last stronghold on the first bad night. He couldn't wait, for his army was on the verge of disappearing as enlistments ran out. The right weather arrived in the form of a driving December blizzard. On the last day of 1775, Montgomery was slain and Arnold wounded in a valiant but vain effort to place the Continental colors over the citadel. The loss of Montgomery was sincerely lamented throughout the Continental Army. To commemorate his contributions and his sacrifice to the cause of liberty, the fort which was raised a few months after his death on the north bank of Popolopen Creek was given his name.

In spite of the repulse, Arnold stubbornly refused to admit defeat. From his cot he directed for three more months the investment of a numerically superior English garrison. In recognition of his deeds the Continental Congress promoted the heroic officer to brigadier general, but hardly had notification of the promotion arrived before he was replaced by a senior officer. Sixty-six-year-old Brigadier General David Wooster, a fellow townsman of Arnold's, supplanted him on April Fools' Day. Arnold's pride was again pierced. Claiming trouble with his slowly healing left leg, he requested and received a leave of absence. Arnold rode to Montreal bitter beyond words at being eased out of a command for which he had worked so hard and had sacrificed so much. The second lap of his fateful race to infamy had been run.

The daring invasion which Montgomery and Arnold had carried so near to fruition collapsed almost overnight. Smallpox and short enlistments steadily reduced the American strength, while British numbers were increased by reinforcements from England. When General Guy Carleton sallied out of Quebec in May, the Patriots panicked. Leaving weapons and wounded, they streamed back to Montreal. Meanwhile, at a place west of Montreal called The Cedars, in an action that won no laurels for American arms, some five hundred men were surrendered with hardly a hint of resistance. Mounting a sortie from Montreal, Arnold rescued the men, but the disgrace was only slightly mitigated. Thus menaced from two directions, the demoralized rebels were compelled to retreat to Ticonderoga. At St. Johns, the site of Arnold's successful raid a year earlier, dispirited and defeated remnants of the American army embarked for the voyage down Lake Champlain. If a person were inclined to accuse Fate of enjoying a private joke when Aaron Burr accompanied Benedict Arnold on the march to Quebec, then that person will find his accusation vindicated by the final scene of the American invasion of Canada. The last Continental detachments put St. Johns to the torch and shoved off into the reflecting red waters of Lake Champlain just as columns of redcoats came into view through the dense, green forest. Two lonely horsemen remained on Canadian soil to cover the departure of the rear guard. As the British van slowly picked its way past flaming buildings toward the lake, General Benedict Arnold and Captain James Wilkinson shot their horses and escaped by canoe.

Sulking still, Arnold did not improve his reputation that summer in Fort Ticonderoga. Accolades won on the battlefield faded before accusations made after the guns grew silent. When one of his subordinates was acquitted by a court-martial of a charge of disobedience lodged by Arnold, the hot-headed general offered to meet any member of the court on the "field of honor." Such improper challenges won few friends. Allegations of plundering personal property in Canada were leveled at the irate Connecticut Yankee. Whether true or not, those charges led to mean, petty bickering that further lowered esteem for Arnold. As it was, Ticonderoga held no fond memories for Benedict; and the summer of 1776 was certainly no more pleasant than that of 1775 had been.

Arnold was rescued from his unseemly arguments by the great peril suddenly confronting the Thirteen Colonies. General William Howe and a large army were wresting New York City from Washington, while Carleton, at St. Johns, was constructing a fleet to transport him to Ticonderoga. A juncture of the two generals would accomplish the very thing the Americans so dreaded—severance of the colonies along the line of the Hudson. Washington would try to stop Howe on the lower Hudson, but an aggressive leader with a knowledge of seamanship was needed to turn back the northern prong of the Royal pincers. America needed Benedict Arnold.

As skipper of all American forces on the lake, the irrepressible Arnold was once more an inspiring commander. What matter that there was nothing to command? He would build a fleet, recruit and train crews, and go to meet the enemy. Racing frantically against time, for Carleton had an earlier start, he succeeded.

On 11 October Arnold's outgunned and outmanned flotilla engaged the British near Valcour Island. Hammered by the superior fleet and harassed by Indians firing from shore, Arnold conducted the battle with great verve and tenacity if not with conventional naval tactics. His own vessel, the *Congress*, was at the center of the fight as a constant example to the others. He himself limped about the deck shouting directions here, aiming a cannon there, barking orders above the din of battle, and encouraging the men to match his bravery. Both sides suffered severe loss and damage.* Finally, after mutual exhaustion, the conflict was broken off as a draw. But the Americans were in no shape to engage again. Aided by a dense fog and a dark night, Arnold slipped away to a station eight miles farther south. After making repairs and assessing his casualties, he determined to sail for

---

* One of the sunken American vessels, the *Philadelphia*, was preserved in the mud of the lake. It can be seen today in the Smithsonian Institution in Washington, D.C.

Crown Point and protection. To shield the retreat of his disabled boats, the general-turned-admiral fought again near Split Rock. Attesting to the heat of the struggle is the statistic that twenty-seven of the seventy-three crewmen aboard Arnold's command ship were killed or wounded. His task finished, the enemy delayed, Arnold beached his razed, near-helpless hulks and burned them with flags flying.

Although defeated tactically, the bantam Patriot navy had won a magnificent strategic victory. Carleton had been sorely weakened and decisively delayed. With winter so near, the British general did not dare attempt further operations in that wild country. He prudently withdrew to Canada. Many writers have claimed that Carleton's decision, forced on him by Arnold, prevented the defeat of the Revolution. While that contention can be no more than conjecture, we do know that Carleton's failure set the stage for the utter and complete defeat of Burgoyne a year later at Saratoga.

Basking in well-deserved praise, Arnold went home to New England to enjoy a period of much-needed relaxation. No officer had been more active than he in the first year and a half of the war.

Two events occurred during that winter of rest which were to have a profound impact on the career of the doughty little warrior. The first was a noble gesture on his part which, many months later, would return to haunt him. Always generous with friends, Arnold was quick to come to the aid of Colonel John Lamb when he learned that his old comrade was in need. Lamb, recently exchanged after a long detention following his capture in the hapless attempt to acquire Quebec, had been commissioned to raise a battalion of artillery, but he had neither funds nor credit. Arnold advanced him £1,000. That loan enabled Lamb to recruit his unit. Of all Arnold's investments, this one was probably his worst—but one of America's best. The second incident had a more immediate effect. Without consulting the Commander-in-Chief, Congress promoted five officers to major general, omitting Arnold from the list. All were junior to Arnold in both rank and results. Predictably, he was furious. Washington admitted feeling "uneasiness" at the omission of his most pugnacious general. He wrote to Richard Henry Lee, then in Congress, that the Continental Army did not have "a more active, a more spirited, and sensible officer" than Benedict Arnold. Washington's intervention was to no avail, however. Arnold decided to journey to Philadelphia to plead his case in person. It was at this point that the General tried to give Arnold the command of the Hudson Highlands. But as that unhappy officer was bent on establishing his position before Congress, Israel Putnam was proffered the important post on the Hudson.[3]

Before he could depart for Pennsylvania, Arnold added to his bulging military reputation by participation in yet another battle. In April 1777, Royal Governor William Tryon of New York led 2,000 men on a raid to Danbury, Connecticut, to destroy rebel supplies. From his home in New Haven, Arnold rushed to the scene to help organize efforts to interdict the British column. When General David Wooster—the man who had replaced Arnold at Quebec—fell with a mortal wound, Arnold assumed command of the mixture of Continentals and militia who, like himself, had flocked to the area. In the fierce fighting that ensued, Arnold personally led the hasty Patriot attempts to head off the retreating raiders. Two horses were shot from under him, a musket ball sliced the fabric of his coat, and he narrowly escaped a British bayonet. John Lamb—making the first but not the final payment on Arnold's loan—supported the fearless general with artillery, receiving in the process a painful flesh wound. Tryon and his troops escaped, although not without penalty. Once more Arnold's gallantry was the talk of the taverns. The Continental Congress decided that he did merit promotion to major general after all. For Arnold, though, the sweet always came with the bitter; Congress declined to adjust his date of rank, a step leaving him still junior to the other recently promoted major generals. Not satisfied with promotion alone, Arnold went to Philadelphia.

While in that city, the new major general's cup of humiliation was filled to the brim. Not only did the gentlemen in the government refuse to restore his seniority, they would not accept his accounting for funds which had been issued to defray expenses during the Canadian episode. Acrimonious arguments erupted between Arnold and his supporters, on one side, and his detractors on the other. John Adams, who remained neutral, told his wife, "General Arnold . . . has been basely slandered and libeled." The squabbling dragged on into July. It was Arnold's third consecutive summer spent in controversy. When Congress remained adamant, that officer, cut to the quick and thoroughly disgusted by the treatment he had received, submitted his resignation. Thus was reached the third of four stages in his path to perfidy.[4]

However, Arnold's contributions to his country were not yet ended. A letter arrived from Washington on 11 July—the same day his embittered general had resigned—asking that Congress complete its business with Arnold so that he might be sent to the northern frontier of New York. General John Burgoyne was leading a large force of Englishmen, Germans, Indians, and Canadians from Lake Champlain toward the Hudson. Starting where Carleton had been stopped the preceding autumn, Burgoyne had already seized Ticonderoga and most of the lesser posts on the path to Albany. Meanwhile, a smaller column of redcoats and redskins was driving down the Mohawk Valley from the west. Sir William Howe, coiled in New York City with a great body of troops, was expected momentarily to strike up the Hudson to cap the three-pronged maneuver. Washington needed every man to cope with the threat; and none of the Commander-in-Chief's other generals could match the redoubtable Benedict Arnold.* Forgetting the resignation, Arnold eagerly rode northward to his greatest glory—and to still another galling episode.[5]

Joining the Northern Army as second in command to Major General

---

* A modern parallel might be seen in the attitude of General Dwight D. Eisenhower toward his controversial but successful subordinate, George S. Patton. Refusing to submit to clamors that Patton be fired, Eisenhower retained the battler in whose fighting capacity he had "implicit faith and confidence." Both Patton and Arnold were deeply motivated by such trust and always became keenly charged at the prospect of action. Moreover, it would be difficult to name two more indomitable and aggressive American combat generals than George Patton and Benedict Arnold.

Philip Schuyler, Arnold assisted first in delaying Burgoyne's approach through the thick New York forests. Soon thereafter Schuyler determined to dispatch an expedition up the Mohawk in an attempt to blunt that arm of the British attack. When no brigadier would volunteer for the hazardous task, Arnold stepped forth. His troops consisted of a thousand whole men and one half-wit. Learning that the savages held the half-wit in awe as some sort of supernatural being, the ingenious general duped the hostile Indians into precipitant flight. The English, thus abandoned, soon followed their wild allies. In just ten days, Arnold had erased the threat of any cooperation with Burgoyne from western New York and had temporarily restored peace to that bloody frontier.

More a hero than ever, Arnold returned to the main army above Albany to find a new commander and a changed situation. Major General Horatio Gates had replaced Schuyler, while Burgoyne, though closer to the Hudson, was no longer so confident of victory. "Gentleman Johnny" had lost a detachment at Bennington and was despairing of receiving assistance from the depleted garrison in New York City. More importantly, militia reinforcements had swelled the American ranks to the point that a heavy numerical superiority had been achieved over the diminished invaders. Thaddeus Kosciuszko was on hand to prepare Patriot entrenchments while a survivor of the march to Quebec, Colonel Daniel Morgan, had brought in riflemen to bolster the Continental lines. Arnold was given command of the left wing. On 19 September an indecisive battle was fought at Freeman's Farm. Arnold and Gates argued heatedly over the conduct of the conflict with the result that Arnold was removed from command. The passionate but petty quarrel earned respect for neither officer.

Burgoyne was desperate. His supplies were depleted and the line of retreat had been cut. Hoping against hope for some action from New York City toward the Hudson Highlands, he resolved to gamble everything on one last assault on the dug-in rebels. On 7 October was fought the battle of Bemis Heights. When he initiated that final struggle, Burgoyne did not know of Sir Henry Clinton's successful attack of Forts Montgomery and Clinton the day before. Nor did he know that Fort Constitution was defenseless, thereby leaving the Hudson open to the King's navy.

When the two armies clashed, Gates, who would prove his courage three years later at Camden, was in a safe position two miles to the rear; Arnold, who would prove his loyalty three years later at West Point, was brooding in a tent. As the fighting raged, Arnold simmered. Finally, maddened by frustration and the scent of gunpowder, he leaped on his brown mare, brandished his sword, and galloped pell-mell to the smoke and sound of the guns. The British advance had already been checked. A Patriot counterattack at that stage could turn a mere tactical victory into a strategic success, but Gates' plans had been solely defensive. And from his haven far to the rear, that commander was unable to direct an offense. At that crucial moment Benedict Arnold reached the front. It has been variously suggested that he was drunk, or had taken opium, or was momentarily insane, or that he simply wished to die. Explanations for his astounding actions are beside the point; enough to state the facts as they happened.

Had the award been known then, it is safe to assume that Arnold would have earned the Medal of Honor for his work that day.

Charging to the head of one brigade, Arnold urged an attack against the Hessians opposing them. He had neither command nor authority, but no one dared question the wild-eyed, screeching general. The Patriots responded and the Germans retreated. Burgoyne then attempted to withdraw all his units. He was not to escape so easily, though, from the maniac now leading the Americans. Arnold, intent on driving in for the kill, found two more brigades and threw them against the center of the English position. Then, after miraculously escaping harm while traversing the entire field between the opposing lines, he led a violent and victorious assault on a fortified band of Canadians. Looking around for more troops to lead, he spied Morgan's riflemen. Placing himself in front of the frontiersmen, the magnificent warrior led his last charge in the uniform of the United States. As he crashed into the enemy barricades, a volley brought down his horse and a musket ball smashed the bone in the same leg which had been hit at Quebec. Arnold and the sun fell together. Darkness and the loss of their leader stalled the American surge. Burgoyne was permitted to extricate his battered army, but he had been bled beyond recovery. He surrendered his entire army at Saratoga. British prestige was shattered. France, followed eventually by Spain and the Netherlands, openly sided with the Thirteen Colonies and the American War became a world-wide war.

If the ball which shortened his left leg had entered his heart instead, Benedict Arnold would be remembered today as one of this nation's greatest heroes. As it was, he lived to become one of its greatest villains.

Never before had his star of fame sparkled so brilliantly. The praise-hungry soldier was finally satiated. The throbbing pain in his twice-wounded leg was eased by the gratitude and acclamation of his countrymen. He was lifted high, indeed, before the final fall. Though hampered still by the unhealed wound, he reported to Valley Forge for duty in May 1778. En route he had stopped long enough in the Hudson Highlands to have a fort at West Point named for him. Before fat but faithful Henry Knox, Arnold formally pledged his allegiance to the United States of America. Unable to participate in active campaigning, the crippled hero was selected to be military commander of Philadelphia when the British evacuated that town. Unfortunately, with regard to Arnold, the "City of Brotherly Love" was singularly misnamed.

For all his vaunted successes in military combat, Benedict Arnold was from first to last totally inept in the political arena. His rasping voice, a certain lack of tact, and an overbearing manner did not exactly grease his path. Before long he was embroiled in arguments, large and small, with several prominent Philadelphians. His expansive style of living—and the financial maneuvers necessary to support such rich tastes—seemed indecorous in comparison to the harsh conditions then generally existing in the American army. Charges of malfeasance of duty and allegations of favoritism to Tories were brought against Arnold by the powerful and aroused Council of Pennsylvania. His marriage to a beautiful teenager with Loyalist sentiments did nothing to enhance the thirty-eight-year-old general's image. He was denied a blissful honeymoon when the Continental Congress chose that moment to decline to absolve him of charges leveled by the Pennsylvanians. A court-martial was prescribed to resolve the issue. Washington set 1 May 1779 as the date for the trial.[6]

Military operations intervened, however, and the trial was not held until Christmastime. A dictum among lawyers states that a man who defends himself is defended by a fool; if so, Arnold appointed a fool as defense counsel. Guilty on two of eight charges was the verdict of a month-long proceeding. Arnold was sentenced to receive a reprimand from the Commander-in-Chief, a punishment Washington executed rather mildly the following April.[7]

We need not sympathize with the chastened officer over the tardiness of justice. He had definitely crossed the threshold from loyalty to treason by May of 1779. That is, shortly after he had been scheduled for a court-martial, only weeks following his marriage to pretty Peggy Shippen, and just four years since his first battle. Many must have been the factors which seduced the once resolute Patriot to the side of the Crown: complete disgust with an ungrateful government; a sense of failure in spite of great deeds; a dire need—to match his love—for money; and a delightful young wife who longed for better things. Those would be the most prominent. His melancholy and contentious affairs in Philadelphia had been the fourth and final part of his course to treachery.

A furor would have arisen if Arnold had simply removed himself from the American cause and joined the British, but it would have soon abated. The Revolutionary War could as well have been known as the first American Civil War. Individuals were often victims of divided loyalties in those turbulent times. It was not unusual for families to be split: Benjamin Franklin and his son provide a famous example. Simple desertion by so illustrious a general would have shocked the colonists, and they surely would not have condoned it, but it would have been comprehensible at least. Eventually it would have been accepted. That, though, is not what Benedict Arnold had in mind. When he went, he would take America with him, and make some money in the process. He hoped to enrich himself and to damage America in the deal. There is the substance of his infamy: the Revolution's greatest combat hero was not only preparing to forsake the United States, he was conniving to sell his country for the best price possible.

And that is how West Point enters the narrative. Twice Arnold had saved the Hudson; now he would strive to sell it.

Through a spy, Arnold contacted Captain John André in New York City. André, an old and close friend of Arnold's new bride, was Sir Henry Clinton's aide. The turncoat offered his services to the King on condition that he be amply rewarded, a stipulation to which the British eagerly acceded. From that first contact sprang the methods of secret correspondence to be employed; coded words from Blackstone's *Commentaries*, seemingly innocent letters between André and Peggy, and invisible ink. Arnold was anxious to make a firm commitment for a specific price, but cautious couriers and English doubts frustrated his efforts. Consummating a treason when distrust and distance separated the conspirators was not the simplest of tasks. To indicate his "honesty," Arnold divulged some minor military secrets. Clinton, on his part, suggested that Arnold might take a command in the army and contrive to surrender it, but he would not be more precise concerning British intentions—an understandable precaution. By then it was July of 1779. Three months of the dangerous sparring had gained no results. Arnold, never one to be patient, elected to terminate the preliminaries by setting his price. It was £10,000. With just a hint that the price was right if the object to be surrendered should be important enough, André proposed a personal meeting with the American officer, and, for an opener, he mentioned that the British were interested in "procuring an accurate plan of West Point. . . ."[8]

Until Clinton would definitely pledge to meet his demands, Arnold would not budge. Once again he was a trader. He had good merchandise and he would get a good price for it. He broke off the correspondence for a few months to let the British commander mull over the proposition. His court-martial, more monetary quarrels with Congress, spiraling debts, and thwarted hopes for a naval command prodded him in the spring of 1780 to renew serious efforts to pry money from the Royal treasury. This time, however, he would take a different approach. He would first obtain a command and then bargain. Accordingly, he began scheming to win an assignment to West Point. Through Philip Schuyler, a staunch but innocent friend, he indirectly informed Washington, in May, that he would accept the command in the Highlands. Although two and a half years had passed since he had stopped the British ball at Bemis Heights, he claimed that his condition would not permit active participation in the field. Washington was noncommittal, but Arnold was confident, nevertheless. Writing under the name of Mr. Moore, he informed André, on 15 June, of his expected assumption of command at West Point upon returning from a visit to his home. "Mr. Moore thinks it would be a good stroke," he added, "[if the British were] to get between General Washington and West Point."[9]

The next day, on his way to Connecticut, he stopped at West Point. Major General Robert Howe, the president of the court-martial that had found Arnold guilty, was then commanding. Humoring a request for a close look at the defenses, Howe rode with his guest on a lengthy tour of the forts and redoubts. Arnold pointed to some of the weaknesses he observed as the two clattered along the rocky redoubt trails, but, in the privacy of his room in Fishkill that night, he was more explicit in a letter to his anticipated employer:

> I called on General Howe at West Point, which I never saw before—was greatly disappointed both in the works & garrison. There is only fifteen hundred Soldiers, which will not half man the works, but General Clinton's Brigade of twelve hundred Men are ordered to join the garrison and are on their march from Albany. It is hoped they will arrive before the English can make an attack, which it is thought they have in contemplation. This Place has been greatly neglected General Howe tells me there is not ten days provision for the garrison. . . . It is surprising a Post of so much importance should be so totally neglected. The works appear to me (though well executed) most wretchedly planned to answer

the purpose designed, viz to maintain the Post and stop the passage of the River. The Point is on a low piece of ground comparatively to the chain of Hills which lie back of it. The highest is about half a mile from Fort Putnam, which is strong. On Rocky Hill there is a small redoubt to hold two hundred men and two six pounders pointed on the other works. The wall six foot thick and defenceless on the Back, and I am told the English may land three miles below and have a good road to bring up heavy Cannon to Rocky Hill. This redoubt is wretchedly executed, only seven or ten foot high and might be taken by a handful of men. I am convinced the Boom or chain thrown across the River to stop the Shipping cannot be depended on. A single Ship large and heavy-loaded with a strong wind and tide would break the chain.[10]

As bait to dangle before Sir Henry, this report was beautifully phrased. West Point, "a Post of so much importance," was soon to be reinforced by enough troops to permit an adequate manning of the defenses. Although the works were "well executed," they were "wretchedly planned." The fortress, Arnold shrewdly intimated, could be seized even if at full strength by a general who knew the weaknesses and had assistance from within. Subtly sketched is the alluring prospect of a cheap victory over the supposedly impregnable Highlands fortifications. Benedict Arnold, the merchant, had not lost his marketing talent.

Pennsylvania's disdain for Arnold was more than matched by New York's high regard of him, a respect the traitorous hero did not hesitate to use. Philip Schuyler, an influential Yorker, had already suggested to Washington that his state would be pleased to have Arnold at West Point. Both Arnold and his wife worked on Robert R. Livingston, a man whose name had often been linked with the Hudson forts. In late June, Livingston informed the Commander-in-Chief that General Howe did not have the confidence of New York. He urged Washington to replace him with "General Arnold, whose courage is undoubted, who is the favorite of our militia, and who will agree perfectly with our Governor." With such powerful backing it is not surprising that the cunning general was confident of achieving the position.[11]

But if Arnold was sure of West Point, he was less certain of his British partners. The absence of General Clinton and Major André (recently promoted) on an expedition to South Carolina had complicated the delicate correspondence. Agreement on the worth of treason had not been reached. On 11 July, Arnold baldly repeated his demand for £10,000.

A day later he wrote, "I expect soon to command W. Pt and most seriously wish an interview with some intelligent officer in whom a mutual confidence could be placed." That letter was hardly on its way before he received a note from André stating that Sir Henry wanted West Point. André also suggested that Arnold come near the British lines for a clandestine conference. Apparently sensing that the bargaining balance had swung to him, Arnold replied that he would expect a lump sum payment of £10,000 and a lifetime annuity of £500 even should the enterprise fail. For success, his price went up sharply:

> If I point out a plan of cooperation by which Sir Henry shall possess
> himself of West Point, the Garrison, &c. &c. &c. twenty thousand pounds

Sterling I think will be a cheap purchase for an object of so much importance. At the same time I request a thousand pounds to be paid my Agent—I expect a full and explicit answer—The 20th I set off for West Point.[12]

The response, written on 24 July, but which did not come into Arnold's hands until near the end of August, was all he could have hoped for. If West Point with all its arms, stores, and 3,000 men should be handed over, the "sum even of 20,000 pounds should be paid you." Henry Clinton assured Arnold that he would not be neglected in the event of failure, but the Englishman balked at granting a guaranteed amount.[13]

Working both friend and foe for funds, Arnold obtained an advance of $25,000 from Congress to permit him to take the field. Leaving Peggy and their four-month-old son in Philadelphia, he joined the army at Peekskill. Left behind also was the intricate channel of communications which had been devised to conduct the correspondence with André. It would be weeks before he could reestablish his connections from the new location in the Highlands.

An abrupt shock awaited the jaunty little traitor. Confident that the job at West Point was his, Arnold searched out Washington on the banks of the Hudson to confirm the appointment. Contemplating an attack on New York City, the Commander-in-Chief planned to strip the Highlands of all able-bodied officers and men, depending on the position of the main army above New York City to shield those posts. When Arnold asked what his role would be, he must have been thunderstruck to hear that he was expected to take a field command. Later, in describing the encounter, Washington remembered that Arnold's "countenance changed and he appeared to be quite fallen; and instead of thanking me, or expressing any pleasure at the appointment, never opened his mouth." Arnold rode away too shocked to protest.[14]

The next day's General Orders, stating that Major General Arnold would command the left wing of the army, only sharpened the anguish of the flabbergasted plotter. His meticulously woven plans had been shattered. (Pretty Peggy Arnold heard the news at a dinner party in Philadelphia. A full-fledged accomplice, she knew the stakes in the game her husband was playing. She was convulsed in hysterics, something passed off by other guests as merely the reaction of a young bride and new mother to the fear of her husband's impending entry into combat.) It is not too mysterious, given those circumstances, that the three-year-old wound quite suddenly and painfully worsened. Limping into Washington's presence, Arnold proclaimed himself unfit for the field. He virtually begged for assignment to West Point. Washington had always held Arnold in the highest regard for his great battlefield prowess and unmatchable courage. Now he looked down in amazement at his once-fearless combat leader pleading cowardly for a soft job at the very moment when a major clash with the British seemed imminent. What the General thought we do not know, but he did acquiesce. General Orders on 3 August announced that West Point and its dependencies would be entrusted to Benedict Arnold.[15]

18

RENDEZVOUS WITH THE
VULTURE

RAIN, dreary and heavy, beat upon the battlements of West Point. The depleted garrison sat gloomily around fires waiting for the summer deluge to let up. In that dank setting Major General Arnold arrived ing the Highlands, moving into Beverley Robinson's house. Garrison orders on 5 August proclaimed the password for the day was "Arnold," the countersign, "West Point." The Eagle had come to the Rock.[1]

Arnold's first thoughts were directed toward the sensitive but necessary requirement to open a clandestine channel of communications between West Point and New York City. Until he could do so, messages to and from Sir Henry Clinton would have to travel the time-consuming route via Philadelphia where Peggy acted as a switching point. On his first day in command, he wrote to Robert Howe asking the North Carolinian for the names of spies he had employed. Howe declined to provide such a list, explaining that he was honor-bound never to disclose their names to anyone. He added, though, that Arnold might find Joshua Hett Smith of Haverstraw helpful in locating men for secret service.[2]

Next on Arnold's agenda was lining up assistants and arranging to have Peggy join him. As rain continued to pour down on that first day, the new commander continued to write. Major David Franks was already serving as aide, but another officer was needed. Arnold asked Lieutenant Colonel Richard Varick if he would want the job, throwing out as enticement, "Mrs. Arnold will soon be with me." Peggy's presence would make the lonesome Highlands more appealing to the young man. It would be best, he had calculated, to have his wife close by when time came to join the enemy. With escape in mind, he had chosen to live in the Robinson house rather than in the Moore house on West Point. Not only would it be farther from the scene of action, but it was also better sited for a getaway. The traitor must have chuckled at Robert Howe's solicitous urging that West Point would be a much safer location to establish home and headquarters.[3]

Meanwhile, West Point itself could not be ignored without causing eyebrows to raise. Arnold's reputation as a dynamic leader required him to exert himself to give the appearance of carrying out his responsibilities as commander in the Highlands. Right away he tended to that chore. He asked for returns, ordered that a field-grade officer inspect every sentry after eleven each night, directed repairs on buildings, improved the method of baking bread, increased the number of guards, stiffened control of boats, reformed the handling of sick soldiers. In short, he made it clear that the new general was firmly in control. But he never lost sight of his basic purpose—high treason. Within days he asked Washington for "a map of the country from this place to New York, particularly on the east side of the river, which would be very useful to me." As commander in the Highlands, he might very properly need the map; as a traitor, he quite probably would have to make his escape down the east side of the Hudson.[4]

When Arnold moved into the Robinson house, General Howe warned him that the place was infested with rats, "a damnable lot of marauding animals." So far as Thaddeus Kosciuszko was concerned, Arnold was one rodent too many. The Polish engineer had never lost his loyalty to Horatio Gates, a loyalty requiring a distinct dislike for Arnold ever since those vituperative days in 1777 at Saratoga. After Benjamin Lincoln's resounding defeat at Charleston, Congress had ordered Gates to command in the southern theatre. Gates wanted the Pole to accompany him, and Kosciuszko was very willing to go. He had been at West Point well beyond two years and was more than ready for a change. On 6 August Washington informed Arnold that Kosciuszko would be transferred. His replacement was to be Major Villefranche, recently recovered from an illness and a "gentleman fully acquainted with his business." Kosciuszko left on the 7th, to the mutual satisfaction of both Arnold and himself.[5]

Villefranche immediately and enthusiastically entered into his new responsibility. By 8 August he had surveyed all the works and reported to Arnold "there is a vast deal to do to complete them." His initial inspection finished, the Frenchman shifted energetically to the unending task of correcting deficiencies. Within a week one daily detail of 10 officers, 12 sergeants, and 400 men were laboring to improve Forts Putnam and Wyllys and Redoubt 2. Ten musicians played to enthuse the workers. Another 60 men toiled on positions across the river. When work on the forts had been satisfactorily begun, the engineer took a close look at the chain. "I have been today to visit the chain and it is highly incumbent to have that part which is sunk relifted by putting new pieces of wood under it as soon as possible," he wrote Major Franks on 19 August. He asked Franks to speak to Arnold about it, for the work "should be done immediately without which in a short time it will be so sunk that it cannot be lifted without great trouble and expense of time."[6]

Benedict Arnold was pleased with his new engineer's energy because

A view of West Point in 1780. From a drawing by Pierre L'Enfant.
Courtesy of the West Point Museum.

it put the best possible face on his own actions and gave him extra time to devote to treason. He openly supported and encouraged Villefranche as much as possible, although it obviously was not to his own best interests to let the forts be improved too much. Persistent rumors have Arnold removing a link from the chain, but they are pure poppycock. He did attempt to obtain teams to drag the chain ashore, basing his request on Villefranche's report that the "middle part of the chain" was sinking, but a shortage of horses prevented his doing that in August. Moreover, sometime before the 25th of that month, a woodcutting detail happened on the supply of chain logs stacked at Moore's house and, before anyone could stop them, had chopped the precious floats up for fuel. After that misadventure there was no pressing reason to worry about the iron barrier until new logs could be prepared. Arnold might have had in the back of his mind removing the chain just prior to a British raid, but by the end of August he had not even been able to contact Sir Henry, much less plan the details of weakening or surrendering West Point.[7]

A good case could be constructed, however, to show that Arnold actually weakened the great stronghold by hampering Villefranche's efforts to rework and strengthen the forts. The engineer estimated his manpower requirements to be at least three hundred men on the west side alone if he were satisfactorily "to carry on the works." Arnold himself informed Washington (and the British) in September of the sad state of the defenses:

> Fort Arnold is . . . in a ruinous condition, incomplete, and subject to take fire from shells or carcasses.
> Fort Putnam, stone, wanting repairs, wall on the east side broke down, and rebuilding from the foundation . . . on the west side broke in many places. . . . A commanding piece of ground 500 yards west, between the fort and No. 4—on Rocky Hill.
> Fort Webb, built of fascines and wood, a slight work, very dry and liable to be set on fire. . . .
> Fort Wyllys, built of stone, 5 feet high, [and on top of that] plank filled with earth . . . no bombproofs, the batteries [are outside] the fort.
> Redoubt No. 1—On the south side wood 9 feet thick . . . no cannon in the works . . . no ditch or pickett. Cannon on two batteries. No bombproofs.
> Redoubt No. 2—. . . No boombproofs.
> Redoubt No. 3—a slight wood work 3 feet thick, very dry, no bombproof, a single abatis, the work easily set on fire—no cannon.
> Redoubt No. 4, a wooden work. . . . No bombproof . . . a slight abatis, a commanding piece of ground 500 yards west.[8]

By retarding construction and impeding repairs, thus precluding substantial improvements, he could in effect weaken the fortress simply by keeping it weak. Delay is the deadliest form of denial. Arnold delayed the necessary work.

Of course, some progress had to be permitted, but not too much. Villefranche no sooner rounded up a sizable work force than Arnold reduced it significantly. Two hundred men were packed off to Fishkill on 16 August to chop wood; forty soldiers were detailed a week later to help raise sunken gunboats. Through the month Arnold found reason after reason to detach troops, a dozen here, twenty there, a hundred some place else. Colonel Lamb, who became commandant on 14 August, complained loudly over the practice. "If such drafts as are called for are made from the garrison we shall neither be able to finish the works that are incomplete nor be in a situation to defend those that are finished." He was right, of course —a fact Arnold fully realized. By the first part of September, fewer than fifty laborers were employed in the forts at West Point. Should the British attack soon, they would be opposed by an unready fortress commanded by an officer who had already told them where the vulnerable points were.[9]

Not everyone was pleased with the new commanding general. Major Sebastian Bauman, for one, thought the general practice of continually changing top commanders was harmful and wondered aloud about a major general "who issues public orders for the internal police of this garrison." Bauman was worried for the safety of the post. Arnold's aides, meanwhile, were beginning to have doubts about Arnold himself. His avaricious arrangements with regard to rations as well as his irascible manner were giving them pause for consideration. The general, claiming to have due several thousand back rations, insisted on drawing all he could. He locked the food in a room of his headquarters and sold various portions from time to time. At a period when provisions for the garrison were relatively scarce, Arnold's selfish actions were frowned upon by his aides; but he bluntly told them to mind their own business, what he did with his rations was no concern of theirs. He even had the nerve to apply to Governor Clinton for fresh meat when West Point's supply ran low, claiming it would otherwise be necessary to "break in upon our small stock of salt provisions." When Colonel Lamb also grumbled, Arnold returned some salt to the commissary, but he continued to peddle wine and meat.[10]

The situation at West Point was actually deteriorating despite the ostentatious flurry of activity. When troops trained by Steuben had marched away they were replaced largely by militia. Major Bauman wrote disgustedly that West Point was "under the care of ingovernable and undisciplined militia." The fort appeared for all the world "like a wild Tartar camp." Doctor Adams snorted in his diary, "The militia soldiers [are] very uncleanly—[the] Point smells more disagreeably than ever I before knew it." An idea of the degree of discipline can be gained from incidents such as woodcutters chopping up chain logs, pigs being allowed to run loose, fences burned in cooking fires, and extortion practiced openly by military ferryboat operators and prison guards. Bauman lamented that West Point was far from "that shining fortification all America thinks." In his eyes, it was hardly "an insurmountable barrier against the excursion of its enemy."[11]

But problems of fortifications, chains, rations, discipline, and the like were all entirely secondary to the greedy general living in Robinson's house. His most pressing need by far was to reestablish correspondence with the British in New York City.

Not long after getting settled, Arnold became reacquainted with a man he had first met in Philadelphia in 1778, Joshua Hett Smith. Smith had a reputation as an active Patriot, having served in the militia and as a member of the Provincial Convention in 1776–1777. Recently he had been very energetically assisting Robert Howe in gathering secret intelligence from New York City. However, William Smith, Joshua's brother, had chosen to support the King. William was in 1780 the Royal Chief Justice of New York, a circumstance which aroused mistrust of Joshua in certain Patriot quarters. Those doubts, voiced strongly by his own aides, made no difference to Arnold. Whether or not Smith was loyal (he was, in a wishy-washy way) to the American cause was immaterial, for Arnold dared not confide his dark plans to anyone other than Henry Clinton or an officer close to the English commander. Smith's role was to be that of an unsuspecting go-between, a means to convey secret messages to Sir Henry. Treason requires caution. Arnold moved slowly, first currying Smith's friendship and trust.

He had nothing to send to New York City just then anyway. Until a reply came from the British commander, agreeing to his demands for £20,000 as the charge for handing over West Point, and naming an officer to conduct negotiations, Arnold could only sit tight. Perhaps the Englishman would reject his offer. The suspense of waiting for that letter might explain his irritable nature during the first three weeks in the Highlands. In freakish weather on 24 August, word came. Dr. Adams described the heat of that evening with triple exclamation marks, "Remarkably hot indeed!!!" But earlier in the afternoon thunderstorms had lashed the area and, from dark clouds, "hail as big as musket balls" had pelted the forts. Lightning flashed, showing the way for a drenched messenger galloping from Fishkill with correspondence from Mrs. Arnold. No twentieth-century movie-maker could more appropriately have staged the scene, for nestled in the innocent-looking pouch from Peggy was Sir Henry's answer.[12]

The traitor must have trembled while walking nonchalantly to his study where he could decode the message. Working by candlelight while lightning and thunder created an appropriately ominous panorama in light and sound, silhouetting in flashes West Point's squat forts across the river, Arnold pieced together the words he longed to see. Writing for Sir Henry Clinton (exactly one month ago, the general noted ruefully), André had responded favorably to the American's price in the event of success, but balked at paying £10,000 if the project should fail. West Point, 3,000 men, and all the artillery and stores of the garrison were the prizes Sir Henry wanted, and he would pay well for them. A hint that Arnold would not be left destitute "in case of detection or failure" was held out; that was a gamble the American would have to take. The deal was thereupon settled in Arnold's mind.

All that remained was to meet a British emissary to make arrangements and then to consummate the final act of betrayal. But that was easier in the saying than in the doing; Arnold still had no way to correspond. Even the Philadelphia channel was now closed, for Major Franks had departed just the day before to escort Peggy and her infant to the Hudson.

Arnold's first opportunity did not appear until nearly a week had passed. It came in the form of William Heron, a close friend of Samuel Parsons. Heron told Parsons he wanted to go into the city to collect a debt and asked his friend to arrange it. Parsons sent him to Arnold with the endorsement, "Mr. Heron is a neighbor of mine, for whose integrity and firm attachment to the cause of the country I will hold myself answerable. . . ." Arnold determined to use Heron as his messenger. As it turned out, however, both American generals were wrong in placing their trust in Heron. Arnold's secretive manner in discussing the message and the obviously feigned hand with which it was addressed aroused Heron's suspicion. He carried the letter into New York with him, but did not deliver it. Instead, he gave the strange missive to General Parsons upon returning. Parsons read the note and was fooled by the commercial wording—as Arnold had intended should a stranger read it—into thinking it was merely some sort of a business venture. He laid the document aside where it was forgotten until after the treason. What is strange is not that Heron became mistrustful and failed to deliver the letter, but that he grew suspicious and did *not* deliver it. For Heron was a British spy. With Arnold's message in his pocket, he visited Joshua Smith's brother and divulged what information he knew. Turning the letter over would have been a natural thing for a spy to do. Maybe he simply forgot about it. At any rate, Arnold's first attempt at communication failed.[13]

The second effort was equally unproductive. Having learned that Colonel Elisha Sheldon employed a double spy, Elizah Hunter, Arnold conceived the idea of having André assume the role of being one of his own spies. Through Sheldon, via Hunter, word could be transmitted to André. Under the guise of intelligence gathering, Arnold anticipated arranging a conference at Sheldon's headquarters near the British lines. Hunter was delayed, however, forcing the anxious conspirator to look for yet another messenger. Mrs. Mary McCarthy, a refugee from Quebec, came to him on 3 September, bearing a pass signed by Governor George Clinton authorizing her to journey to New York. Addressing a letter to John Anderson (André's cover name), Arnold asked Mrs. McCarthy to deliver it. Couched again in commercial language, the message told André to contact Arnold through Colonel Sheldon. To Varick, the general explained plausibly enough that he was attempting to contact a spy in New York in hopes of gaining intelligence. Mrs. McCarthy may have been just a little bewildered at such effuse courtesy when a lieutenant, a sergeant, and seven privates conveyed her and her two children all the way to Manhattan in an army boat under the protection of a flag from General Arnold. Not trusting to any single mode of delivery, the enterprising general employed yet another device. Peggy had previously been on the receiving end of finery smuggled out of New York City, and a package was even then waiting for her there. Through Sheldon, and later General Parsons, Arnold arranged to have the package sent out in hopes André could transmit a message by that means. Those were nerve-wracking days for the Highlands commander—a wrong move could ruin him, but it was absolutely essential that he arrange a conference at the earliest opportunity.[14]

George Washington was undergoing as much or more mental anguish, but for entirely different reasons. Striving to save the nation Arnold was conniving to sell, the Commander-in-Chief had much the more difficult road to follow that September. His great scheme, his burning dream, of recapturing New York City went aglimmering for want of French cooperation. Spirits which had been temporarily buoyed by the prospect of battle, plunged into despair. Moreover, ministers in France were beginning to believe their treasury could no longer support the heavy burden of war with England. Americans, they were saying, would have to do more for themselves. Then, on 4 or 5 September, word reached Washington of the Patriot debacle at Camden, South Carolina. Horatio Gates had at last displayed his true military talents by rushing headlong and ineptly into the bloodiest American blunder of the war. At the opening shot his militia had bolted. The Continentals had held fast, but fighting alone and in a poor position, they had been annihilated. Gates himself fled early from the fight. Actually, he did better than run; he set a record for personal retreat. Scathingly, Alexander Hamilton asked if there had ever been "so precipitous a flight? One hundred and eighty miles in three days and a half. It does admirable credit to the activity of a man at his time of life. But it disgraces the general and the soldiers." Consternation, complete, open-mouthed, and unbelieving, was the universal reaction to news of the crushing defeat. The Patriots' will to resist was visibly eroding. Mutiny, the worst winter in memory, starvation, a Congress able only to inhibit rather than help military efforts, rampant inflation, soldiers crying for food and clothing, more mutiny, the heaviest loss of the war, failure of French allies, and now the war's bloodiest setback. America was reeling. One more body blow in that black year and the Thirteen Colonies might give up the struggle. They were near the point of exhaustion, close to total collapse. Just one more blow. . . . In the Hudson Highlands, Benedict Arnold was assiduously preparing to deliver it.[15]

The British were aware of the precarious rebel situation and very calculatingly attempted to take advantage of it. Lord Germain had told Henry Clinton late in 1779, ". . . the gaining over some of the most respectable members of the Congress, or officers of influence and reputation among their troops, would, next to the destruction of Washington's army, be the speediest means of subduing the rebellion and restoring the tranquillity of America." In July 1780 Sir Henry predicted "the rebellion would end in a crash" rather than die of a consumption. He noted with glee "the present very distressed state of the disaffected colonists" and hoped "to increase and accelerate the confusion" which he saw beginning "everywhere to appear in the rebel counsels." He was convinced that the defection of Arnold combined with the loss of West Point would be an irresistible psychological stroke which would finish the rebellion at once. Viewed from the vantage point of two centuries in time, his conclusion appears quite plausible.[16]

On the second day of September Washington got wind of British preparations for an expedition. He quickly relayed the information to Arnold, warning him, ". . . their object will be an attack on the main army or an attempt on the post in the Highlands. I wish you therefore to put the latter in the most defensible state which is possible." Arnold could guess better than his commander what was the English objective, and, in his own way, he had already seen to the defenses of West Point. The letter drew a smirk, nothing more. He was obsessed at the moment with attempts to contact a British agent and the delightful prospect of the arrival of his lovely young wife.

Arnold was a man of vigorous appetites. In Peggy Shippen he had found a partner whose passion matched his own. Their prolonged separation had increased his desire to have her once more by his side, an eagerness he took no pains to conceal. A couple of days before her arrival he wrote to General Robert Howe, himself a man of considerable repute in matters amorous:

> I thank you, my dear sir, for your friendly wishes to me and Mrs. Arnold . . . and for the favorable opinion you are pleased to entertain of the state of our connubial connection. Be assured, Sir, no sensations can have a comparison with those arising from the reciprocity of concern and mutual felicity existing between a lady of sensibility and a fond husband. I myself had enjoyed a tolerable share of the dissipated joys of life, as well as the scenes of sensual gratification incident to a man of nervous constitution; but, when set in competition with those I have since felt and still enjoy, I consider the time of celibacy in some measure misspent."[17]

Peggy was her husband's "greatest treasure," a youthful paramour, a trusted accomplice in treason. His young aides might smile knowingly at his evident eagerness to see her, but at least a part of his impatience sprang from the need to have someone with whom he could discuss the progress of perfidy. And there was at least one other factor contributing to his impatience—jealousy. Peggy was flirtatious, full of life, and apparently saw no reason why marriage and motherhood should change her ways. Hannah Arnold wrote broodingly to her brother of "sighing swains" and mentioned disapprovingly that Robert R. Livingston, the New York Chancellor, was a "dangerous companion for a particular lady in the absence of her husband." The wife of George Meade, Arnold's Philadelphia neighbor, had abruptly reined that gallant in, preventing his "showing Mrs. Arnold those attentions I would wish to have done." Other hints of "frequent private assignations and of numberless *billets doux*" undoubtedly worried the middle-aged and absent husband. On the 5th, he sent a horseman out on the road to Philadelphia to meet her and went himself on the 8th to Joshua Smith's house hoping to have word of her approach. But Peggy did not leave Philadelphia until the 6th. Arnold had to cool his heels waiting for his wife as well as for Henry Clinton's agent. The first week in September had been a tryingly long one for an eager husband and an anxious traitor.[18]

Returning dejectedly to Robinson's house the next day, a Saturday, Arnold was obliged to make small talk with three guests, including the scientist, James Jay. His forced liveliness became real, though, when he thumbed through the correspondence which had arrived in his absence. There, waiting for him, was a message from Anderson. Anderson (André) had received the letter carried by Mrs. McCarthy and had replied right away, sending his response by flag to Colonel Sheldon. André told Sheldon he would come under a flag to Dobb's Ferry at noon on Monday where he "should be happy to see Mr. G———." Arnold's cover name in the delicate correspondence was Gustavus. That much was all right. But the letter continued, "Should I not be allowed to go, the officer who is to command the escort, between whom and myself no distinction need be made, can speak on the affair." André did not want to pass American lines in civilian garb, an act punishable by hanging if he should be caught. The officer "between whom and myself no distinction need be made" was to be, of course, André himself. Sheldon's curiosity was aroused. How could a British officer overtly carry intelligence from a spy? To throw Sheldon off the track, Arnold shrewdly suggested to Anderson (André) that his original message might have been intercepted because Anderson's reply appeared to have been "dictated by the enemy." Carefully he wrote, "I cannot suppose you would be so imprudent as to trust a British officer . . . with our private concerns altho of a commercial nature." Anderson would have to come himself to Sheldon's headquarters from where he would be brought to Gustavus (Arnold), but "by no means hint to [Sheldon] or any other person your intentions in coming out as it may *prevent our speculation.* . . ." Sending that off on Sunday to caution André to watch his tongue and to calm Sheldon, Arnold realized that it would not be received in time to stop André from going to Dobb's Ferry the next day. Accordingly, he himself prepared to meet the flag of truce there.[19]

The American general was not sure on what pretext he could properly meet a British officer, but he resolved to go anyway on the assumption that the British could provide some logical justification for the conference. They could. Colonel Beverley Robinson was more nearly Arnold's rank and owned the house the American general was living in. It would hardly appear irregular for him to be concerned with furnishings and grounds and other affairs having to do with his property—so concerned, in fact, that he would wish to talk over the matter with the present occupant. Arnold could arrange with André the turnover of West Point, but report having had only a property discussion with Robinson. For the second time in the war, Beverley Robinson and his house figured in treasonous calculations.

Sunday night, the 10th, Arnold slept at Smith's house. Next morning, late, he entered his barge and headed downriver toward Dobb's Ferry. André and Robinson waited there on the eastern shore. Never again would conditions be more propitious for talks. But someone had neglected to tell British gunboats prowling the river at that point to expect an American officer. On sighting the lone vessel approaching the meeting site, the gunboats jumped it. Barely escaping with his life, Arnold managed to beach his barge and take refuge in a blockhouse on the western bank. All day he waited there for André to make some sign while the British officer stood across the river vainly watching for a signal from the American. Neither dared take the first step. For that matter, neither was really sure the other was there. At nightfall, when the aggressive gunboats fell down the river, Arnold returned full of disappointment to Robinson's house, Robinson and André to New York.

Angrily, Benedict Arnold decided to put a stop to the impudent activities of the British gunboats. Personal pique of the moment demanded it, but so did the maintenance of his front as a staunch Patriot. English boats "come up almost every day and insult the post" at Dobb's Ferry, he told Lamb. Could the West Point commander spare a couple of cannon to drive them away? Lamb sent two nine-pounders by boat, but the vessel could not reach its destination just then, for "the *Vulture* . . . lies at or near Dobb's Ferry." Those guns were to have no part in the events of succeeding days, but the idea Arnold had planted would sprout fruit exceedingly strange and bitter.[20]

Back at his desk, the frustrated turncoat picked up the pieces of his plot. Sheldon was no longer at the post below, so Arnold informed Major Benjamin Tallmadge of the likelihood of a visit from a spy out of New York. "If Mr. John Anderson . . . should come to your quarters, I have to request that you will give him an escort of two horsemen to bring him on his way to this place, and send an express to me, that I may meet with him." Sheldon's replacement, Lieutenant Colonel John Jameson, was also alerted. On the 13th, Arnold assembled information which would eventually be handed to André. Villefranche's estimate of men needed to defend the forts, not including artillerymen, was 2,430; Major Bauman's return of ordnance showed 89 cannon and 16 mortars on station in the Highlands forts. Figuring the number of gunners needed to work them, Arnold then estimated his overall strength at 3,086—a total very neatly above the 3,000 men Sir Henry had indicated would be worth a full £20,000. He included, too, the orders assigning battle stations to various units, his own appreciation of defects in the defenses, and a statement of Washington's to a recent council of war. Then, turning to other duties, he answered a query from the Commander-in-Chief with bold words which secretly he must have considered humorous, forecasting that American affairs "may be totally changed in a short time by a variety of circumstances. . . ." Putting treason aside momentarily for pleasanter thoughts, he traveled to Smith's house on the 14th to meet Peggy. The reunited couple spent the night as guests of Smith and his wife.[21]

Next day, after talking to Smith, Arnold wrote André proposing a new plan. The Englishman could still approach either Jameson or Tallmadge if he wished to come by land, but a meeting on the Hudson itself could be arranged. "I will send a person in whom you may confide, by water, to meet you at Dobb's Ferry on Wednesday the 20th instant between 11 and 12 o'clock at night, who will conduct you to a place of safety where I will meet you." Joshua Smith would be that person. Thinking Arnold wanted to meet a secret agent, Smith readily agreed to act as go-between. In mercantile phrases, the general commanding in the Highlands described how lucrative the capture of West Point would be—not that the British needed encouragement. "Meet me if possible," he urged. "You may rest assured that if there is no danger in passing your lines, you will be perfectly safe where I propose the meeting. . . ." Arnold was to prove to be a particularly poor prophet.[22]

Arnold took his wife that day to Robinson's house. Both expected the stay to be brief, but neither foresaw in what manner their sojourn would terminate in just ten days.

After Peggy was settled, Arnold perused his correspondence and found a message from General Washington. "I shall be at Peekskill on Sunday evening on my way to Hartford to meet the French admiral and general," Washington wrote. Arnold was to guard the crossing site with fifty men under a captain and "to endeavor to have a night's forage for about forty horses." Call it premonition if you will, but the Commander-in-Chief closed his letter by saying, "You will keep this to yourself, as I want to make my journey a secret." Arnold, of course, would do no such thing. How much might the King pay for the capture of George Washington? The prospect was staggering! Immediately Arnold encoded the information: "General Washington will be at King's Ferry Sunday evening next on his way to Hartford, where he is to meet the French admiral and general, and will lodge at Peekskill." Time was short, but Sir Henry might be able to throw a force up rapidly enough to overwhelm Washington's small guard in the night or perhaps while he was crossing the Hudson. That insidious message and the letter to André were sent on Saturday "by a very honest fellow." As it turned out, Henry Clinton did not have time to react to Arnold's intelligence, but let it be said that the traitor had tried. Arnold pictured himself as an American Monk; for pieces of sterling, though, the role of Judas was not beneath him.[23]

Intrigue thickened over the weekend. While Arnold's "honest fellow" was carrying his letter southward, the 14-gun sloop of war *Vulture* sailed north. Sunday morning the 300-ton vessel, her brown varnished sides separated from the water by a wide black streak, anchored off Teller's Point at the southern part of Haverstraw Bay. On board was Colonel Beverley Robinson. The British planned once more to try to arrange a meeting between Arnold and his ousted landlord. Pretending not to be sure who was living in his house, Robinson addressed two letters, one to Israel Putnam and the other to Benedict Arnold. He asked for a meeting in order to make a request of a confidential nature, ostensibly concerning his property. Casually, he mentioned the name of a person involved in the lengthy negotiations between Arnold and André, James Osborne. That would let Arnold know Robinson's real purpose.[24]

Saturday, Smith and his wife and two nephews came to the Highlands for a visit at Arnold's request. It was natural that the Arnolds should repay the Smith's hospitality, but somewhat unusual that they would do it so soon. The real purpose was to get Smith's family away from home so Arnold and André could meet there in secret. Arnold hosted a large, early dinner Sunday in honor of Peggy's arrival. His two aides, the Smiths, and several officers from West Point, including his old friend John Lamb, were in attendance. During the meal, a courier brought in Robinson's letter. Arnold's heart raced as he read it and saw Osborne's name. Controlling his emotions admirably, he casually folded the note and stuck it in a pocket, explaining blandly that Robinson had requested an interview. Lamb, always suspicious of any overtures from Loyalists and remembering Robinson's attempts to contact Israel Putnam in 1777, adamantly advised Arnold to take no part in "an improper correspondence." General Richard Montgomery had once described Lamb as "bad tempered, troublesome, and turbulent." While Lamb was attacking Quebec with Arnold in 1775, a blast of grapeshot had carried away the left half of his face, leaving him horribly disfigured. Now, when his blood rose, the scars became purple swatches highlighting a deep, dark hollow of an eye-socket hanging limply over a shattered cheekbone. Few people would or could argue face-to-face with the artilleryman. Lamb stormily claimed that the only proper course was to let General Washington decide how to handle the case. There the conversation ended, but Arnold must have been impressed with Lamb's vehemence. To forestall criticism he did ask the General's advice that afternoon. Washington firmly told him to have nothing to do with the Loyalist officer who once had been the Virginian's close friend.

When Washington crossed from Stony Point to Verplanck's Point late that Sunday afternoon, he could see the *Vulture,* sails furled on all three masts, riding serenely at anchor downriver. He would have sad cause just one week later to remember the warship. A story related by Barbe-Marbois long afterward tells of Washington's peering so intently through his spy-glass at the hostile ship that Arnold grew worried and voluntarily brought up the subject of Robinson's presence. The General probably did study the enemy vessel while being ferried over the Hudson, and Arnold did mention Robinson's letter. Whether he was motivated by a guilty conscience, however, is not known. Arnold must have been rather nervous in Washington's presence. He did not remain long with him in Peekskill, thinking perhaps of the possibility of an English raid. He took his leave as soon as he conveniently could and rode back to his own headquarters. It was the last time the two men met. The superb fighter and the magnificent leader had between them virtually carried the War of Independence for its first three years. Now, in the dark year of 1780, Arnold had but one more major scene to play —and in a way it would be his greatest.

Whether it was sixth sense, Arnold's vagueness, some intelligence from his secret service agents, or merely another manifestation of his perpetual concern for West Point's safety, his Excellency felt uneasy after Benedict Arnold's departure. Next morning, the 18th, he revealed his apprehension in a letter to Nathanael Greene, who was commanding the army in Washington's absence. Warning Greene of the recent arrival of enemy reinforcements, he also passed on a report indicating Sir Henry had "ordered the whole flying army to New York and that 70 transports were ready to receive them." Worriedly, he told his lieutenant to move the field army to Tappan to be nearer the Hudson. West Point, he feared, was not strong enough to resist an assault. Believing the garrison to be "so weak that it seems essential to reinforce it," Washington directed Greene to "send a good Continental regiment" to the Highlands. Then, having done all he could to calm the niggling doubt in the back of his mind, the Virginian rode on to his rendezvous with the French.[25]

With Washington out of the way, Arnold promptly ignored his advice and wrote to Robinson. Varick thought the letter too friendly to be sent to an enemy; Arnold agreed to change the wording to make it more impersonal. But when the watchful aide was out, Arnold penned a personal note telling the Loyalist that a man whose "secrecy and honour" could be depended upon would come aboard the *Vulture* on Wednesday, 20 September. Robinson was to keep the ship on station until then to avoid suspicion. And could André be on the *Vulture* that Wednesday night? A letter to Anderson from Gustavus was attached. Washington would return on the following Saturday, Arnold scribbled, warning Robinson that meetings could not be held that weekend. Under a flag, and delivered by an unsuspecting American officer, the messages reached Robinson that same day, a Monday. To reduce river traffic, thereby lessening chances of confusion and discovery, Arnold specified in general orders that "no person whatever" could cross the river without a pass.[26]

Tuesday, Joshua Hett Smith returned from depositing his family out of harm's way in Fishkill. Arnold apparently told him then that he would definitely have to row out to the *Vulture* the night of the 20th. The gabby New Yorker had already concurred in the plan. The general wrote out a pass permitting Smith, John Anderson (André), and two servants "to pass and repass the guards near King's Ferry at all times." Arnold also gave his unwitting accomplice an order for a boat. On Wednesday, the day set, Smith rode to his house, stopping at Verplanck's Point to chat with Lieutenant Colonel James Livingston, but making no strong effort to get a boat. Smith was the hollow reed in Arnold's scheme. A dreamer, a busybody, a man who yearned to be in on big things, he apparently had insufficient force of character to execute actions of such magnitude. He asked a tenant farmer, Samuel Cahoon, to row down the river "a piece" that night. Cahoon did not want to go. Moreover, there was no boat. Smith's irresolute solution was to send Cahoon to Arnold with that negative information. Cahoon, riding all night, reached the Robinson House at first light. Smith got a good night's sleep. André passed the long hours in vain, pacing the deck of the *Vulture*.

André had reached the ominously named sloop on Wednesday, the designated day. When dawn broke Thursday he was quite upset. Twice he had kept an appointment and both times the other party had failed to show. To remain aboard a second day would likely create talk, but André decided to risk it. Feigning sickness as an excuse, he stayed on. The day before, an American outpost had fired on one of the *Vulture's* flags. Seizing that event as pretext, Captain Andrew Sutherland, commanding the ship, sent another flag ashore, ostensibly to protest the improper action. Sutherland's complaining letter, addressed to the enemy commander, Arnold, was written by André and countersigned "John Anderson." Arnold could not fail to know that André was aboard.

Arnold did not need the hint. In a fury after learning at dawn that his plans had miscarried, he hurriedly dressed and traveled to Verplanck's Point in his barge. There he read the message from Sutherland, recognized André's writing, talked in a withdrawn manner to Livingston about "firing upon a party of theirs," and crossed to Stony Point. If the general had not been so preoccupied, Livingston might have told him what he had in mind for the good ship *Vulture*. Arnold himself found the boat Smith should have picked up a day earlier, directed it to be drawn up Haverstraw Creek, and proceeded by horse to Smith's house. There he browbeat Samuel Cahoon and his brother into rowing out to the *Vulture* that night. The Cahoons objected stoutly, especially Samuel who had been up all the night before conveying Smith's despairing message to Arnold, but there was no denying the fiery, feisty little general. Near midnight, they muffled oars in sheepskin and rowed down to the enemy ship. "We were hailed by the vessel," Samuel Cahoon remembered, "and Mr. Smith answered 'Friends,' and said we were from King's Ferry and bound to Dobb's Ferry." The small boat drew alongside the British warship and Smith climbed aboard.

The most dependable account of what transpired in the captain's cabin between Smith, André, Sutherland, and Robinson comes from a letter of Robinson's written on Sunday, the 24th, to Henry Clinton:

> Mr. Smith had a paper from Arnold . . . for the purpose of forwarding some letters to New York on private business. He had a second paper as a pass to bring with him two servants and . . . Mr. John Anderson—he had a third small scrap of paper on which was written nothing more than "Gustavus to John Anderson."
>
> Upon considering all these matters Major André thought it was best for him to go alone as both our names was not mentioned in any one of the papers, and it appeared to him (as indeed it did to me) that Arnold wished to see him; I therefore submitted to being left behind and Major André went off with Smith, between 12 and 1 o'clock Thursday night. Smith told me Arnold would be about one o'clock at a place called the old Trough or Road . . . with a spare horse to carry him to his house; and it is with the greatest concern that I must now acquaint your excellency that we have not heard the least account of him since he left the ship.[27]

He could have added that André went ashore dressed in scarlet regimentals with only a cloak thrown over his shoulders to disguise himself. But it was already too late for worry. As Robinson wrote those words of concern, André was a prisoner in American hands; and the entire, elaborate scheme had failed.

The night was moonless. Fighting an ebb tide in a boat rather too large for two men to handle, the weary Cahoon brothers took longer than had been expected to make shore. When they did reach the rendezvous point, Benedict Arnold was waiting. After a year and a half of secret correspondence the American general and the British major finally talked face to face. Arnold was so famous a figure that the Briton must have felt he knew him. Through Peggy, Arnold would have learned much about the young Englishman. André had sketched her when she was a coquettish young lady in Philadelphia. Author as well as artist, he had more recently satirized Arnold's past as a pharmacist in a derogatory ballad, "The Cow Chase." But, "hid among firs" on the Hudson's bank in that black night, the two conspirators had little time for pleasantries. What they said there has never been discovered. A tentative date for the attack was probably agreed upon; André could have told Arnold that Sir Henry even then had a force poised to launch up the river. A method of attack was most likely a part of the conversation. Arnold would have told André where to strike at the defenses: overrun Redoubt 4, making Fort Putnam untenable, he recommended, and then seize that work which was the key to all others. Arnold would dispose the garrison so as to aid the plan and at a critical moment could either capitulate or throw the command structure into such turmoil that resistance would be negligible. Money was mentioned, Arnold still holding out for £10,000 should the plan fail. At 4:00 A.M., Smith interrupted to warn the two engrossed plotters "of the approaching dawn of day." It was too late for André to return to the *Vulture* that night. Besides, the Cahoons were bushed and balky. Arnold and André rode to Smith's house. Joshua Smith and his tenants went by boat to Haverstraw Creek, arriving there at six o'clock just as the first rays of sun touched the hills.

The two men on horseback reached the house first. Dismounting, they entered to wait for their host. A candle was lighted; they looked at one another for the first time. At that moment the sound of cannon fire bounced across the wide river, shattering the early morning calm. Both men raced for a window. Those retorts signaled the failure of Arnold's plot to sell West Point and sounded André's death knell. Arnold's rendezvous with the *Vulture* had been one day too late.

19

"TREASON OF THE BLACKEST DYE!"

IT HAD been too much for Lieutenant Colonel Livingston to take. Perhaps it was the sheer insolence of the English vessel that so aggravated him. The *Vulture* had come to anchor off Teller's Point on the 17th and had remained there ever since, in effect daring the Americans to do anything about it. Livingston had no guns big enough to inflict serious damage, but he simply could not sit still without making at least a gesture of defiance. He asked Colonel Lamb for ammunition.

That stormy officer sent it, but snorted sarcastically, "Firing at a ship with a four-pounder is, in my opinion, a waste of powder as the damage she will sustain is not equal to the expense." Never would Lamb be more wrong. Livingston shrewdly waited for slack tide and still wind. Just as the ship became visible at first light on the 22nd he "began a heavy cannonade with shot and shell." Becalmed, the *Vulture* was helpless. Sutherland returned the fire with his six-pounders, but the contest was unequal from the start. The British warship was a large, stationary target while the two Patriot guns were small and protected by an earthwork. Beverley Robinson described Livingston's cannonade from the vantage point of the receiving end: "It was near high water, the tide very slack and no wind, so that it was impossible . . . to get the ship out of their reach sooner. Six shot hulled us, one between wind and water, many others struck the sails, rigging, and boats on deck. Two shells hit us, one fell on the quarterdeck, another near the main shrouds. Captain Sutherland is the only person hurt, and he very slightly on the nose by a splinter." *Vulture's* log adds, "—the standing and running rigging shot away in many places, 2 of the iron stantions on the gangways broke by their shot—several of their shells broke over us and many of the pieces dropt on board. . . ." Pressing a handkerchief to his cut nose, Captain Sutherland withstood the fire for thirty minutes, hoping all the while for a breeze. Then, unable either to silence the American guns or continue to absorb such a pounding, he ordered longboats into the water to tow the ship out of range. As the *Vulture* slowly eased away, Patriot gunners redoubled their efforts, grew careless, and let a spark reach open powder. The resulting explosion ended the battle, but the *Vulture* continued downriver to a safe anchorage.[1]

From a second-floor window in Smith's house, André and Arnold had a splendid view of the exchange. A man as excitable as Arnold was must have had a few well-chosen imprecations to hurl in the direction of his too aggressive subordinate. André was probably frightened at the flare-up below; and he could only have been disheartened to see the *Vulture* changing station. Smith joined the two conspirators in time to watch a part of the clash and observe the *Vulture* departing. All three realized that it would be next to impossible for André to return the way he had come. After the blazing exchange of fire, American guardboats would be swarming in the river, their crews unusually suspicious of anyone wanting to visit the English ship. Arnold made arrangements for Smith to escort the Englishman by land to British lines, but he apparently left the final decision on how to go up to André and Smith. After giving André several papers pertaining to the defenses of West Point, the general returned to Robinson's house, angry that his plans had gone awry, but serene enough in the belief that his personal passes and Smith's knowledge of the roads would insure André's safe passage.

It was not to be. André, traveling overland, would be captured. Long ago Arnold had loaned his old friend, John Lamb, money to recruit an artillery unit. The very guns and powder and artillerymen that had driven the *Vulture* from her station were from Lamb's outfit. No more ironic event transpired in the entire War of Independence than that of Benedict Arnold's attempted treachery being foiled by his past patriotism.

Towards evening, with the *Vulture* still far downriver, Smith decided to go by land. André, it seems, was not too pleased with the prospect, but he shucked his officer's jacket and donned a claret-colored coat of Smith's. That act doomed him to hang should he be captured. "At the decline of the sun" they mounted and rode to Stony Point. Crossing to Verplanck's Point, the pair encountered Lieutenant Colonel Livingston who politely extended an invitation "to stay awhile and take supper or a drink of grog." The colonel was feeling self-satisfied over his surprise reveille ceremony for the *Vulture*. Smith, garrulous and jovial, declined, saying they had to press on. André remained silent. About eight miles farther, near Crompond, a detachment of militia stopped them. The local officer was a little doubtful of the two, but apparently only because Arnold's pass properly listed Smith's given name as Joshua, whereas the militiaman knew of him as "Joseph." Whether solicitous or suspicious, the officer told Smith it was too dangerous to continue after dark and advised the two riders to remain there for the night. They did, sharing a bed. Smith slept soundly; André restlessly.

Saturday, 23 September, was a warm and pleasant day. Trees were beginning to assume autumn coats. At West Point only Arnold and his wife knew that a British force stood poised to assault the post, perhaps as early as the 28th. Sir Henry awaited only information of the defenses and confirmation of Arnold's role, both of which Major André was to bring back. Reinforced recently by men and ships under Sir George Rodney, Clinton was ready to snatch whatever opportunity presented itself—in fact, almost 3,000 men were already embarked. In the garrison itself, Colonel Lamb's major immediate worry was loose pigs. He prepared a message for next day's garrison orders on the subject: "Any hogs that are found running about the Point after 12 o'clock tomorrow [Monday] will be killed. . . ." A good two hours before that deadline, Benedict Arnold would have departed West Point in fear of his life.[2]

Smith and André were on the road before daylight. After another seven or eight miles and breakfast, Smith reined in and informed André he would have to cover the final fifteen miles to White Plains alone. The no man's land in that area was crisscrossed by marauding and competing bands of robbers called "cowboys" or "skinners" according to whether they generally favored the Loyalists or the Patriots. Smith, a talker not a doer, found his courage failing him. André struck out alone for White Plains while Smith turned his horse north. Hearing from a boy a report of some rebel horsemen having been seen on the White Plains Road, the English officer spurred his mount down the route to Tarrytown. Shortly before ten o'clock, on the approach to a bridge just above Tarrytown and safety, he rode into an ambush set by three "volunteer militiamen" out looking for loot. André, unarmed, halted at their command.

Expecting to encounter only Loyalists in that area, the young officer apparently tipped his hand immediately by admitting he was British. Upon learning their true leanings he produced Arnold's pass, but it was then too late. Taking his watch and money, the three "Patriots" ordered him to strip, thinking he might have other valuables concealed. A practiced spy, which Major André was not, would never hide bulky papers in a boot, that being the first item of clothing to be searched. When the three skinners found the documents relating to West Point, they realized they were onto something larger than just a few dollars in booty. André attempted to bribe them, but they were afraid he would fail to honor his promise after being released. The greedy trio held a short conference in which they decided to take him to Lieutenant Colonel John Jameson at North Castle. Maybe Jameson would pay a prize. A biographer of Arnold has described that decision thus: "Those three bushwackers were unsavory characters bent on a type of enterprise condemned by both armies. Still, the best that can be said of them is enough: they may have saved the republic that Saturday morning."[3]

Incredibly, Jameson almost fell in with the plot. He had been told to watch for a man named Anderson. Here Anderson was; what was more, he bore Arnold's pass. Jameson, however, had been on the alert for an agent who would come *from* New York; this one was traveling *toward* the city. Moreover, he carried papers which even Jameson recognized as being "of a very dangerous tendency." Pondering the problem, he concluded it to be beyond his ken. Arnold could decide. The colonel prepared a message for

General Arnold explaining the circumstances of Anderson's capture and ordered a lieutenant to escort the prisoner to Robinson's house. André's relief, upon hearing that decision, was all but impossible to conceal. Once in Arnold's care he could surely arrange some means of escape. But it was equally important to get the implicating papers away from eyes more discerning than Jameson's. He earnestly implored the American to send along all documents. Jameson was not entirely the fool. If the prisoner who had so much the appearance of a spy wanted something so badly, Jameson analyzed, maybe it was the wrong thing to do. He sent André empty-handed. When the prisoner and his guard were gone, Colonel Jameson sat down to compose a letter to Washington:

> Inclosed you'll receive a parcel of papers taken from a certain John Anderson who has a pass signed by General Arnold. . . . I have sent the prisoner to General Arnold. He is very desirous of the papers and everything being sent with him, but as I think they are of a very dangerous tendency, I thought it more proper your Excellency should see them.[4]

The colonel sent that missive by a courier, hoping to intercept Washington at Danbury on his return from Hartford.

About then Major Benjamin Tallmadge arrived at North Castle. He had been for years involved in espionage work for Washington. Spies and plots were a part of his life. On hearing the strange story he realized in a flash that Arnold was a traitor. It may be that he, not Jameson, was responsible for the documents being sent to Washington. At any rate, he did vehemently urge Jameson to stop André and recall the message to Arnold. Never noted for being bright, and now hopelessly confused by the whole affair, Jameson equivocated. He ordered the prisoner returned, but insisted upon informing Arnold. A fast rider overtook the column escorting André somewhere in the vicinity of Peekskill. The Britisher was brought back to North Castle. Jameson thereupon ordered Lieutenant Solomon Allen to carry his message on to General Arnold. By then, however, it was late; the lieutenant waited overnight, departing early Sunday morning.

André, meanwhile, learned of Jameson's letter informing Washington of his capture. Fearing the noose, he penned an explanation to the Commander-in-Chief, giving his true identity and claiming to have been "betrayed . . . into the vile condition of an enemy in disguise within your posts." He did not mention Arnold. About that time the fatal documents were returned to North Castle after having missed Washington at Danbury. The General had already passed through on his way to West Point. A captain, carrying both André's letter and the documents, was dispatched to find Washington in the Highlands. If the Commander-in-Chief had learned of the treason before word of its failure reached Arnold, the swarthy traitor would probably have been captured. But the very idea of Benedict Arnold's being a traitor was too far-fetched to be believed even when the evidence was seen in black and white. Not Arnold, renowned and redoubtable, hero of a dozen battlefields, battler without peer, already a legend of the Revolution. There must be some rational explanation, thought everyone except Tallmadge. For that reason, neither of the messengers traveled with any sense of urgency. Both stopped when Sunday night approached. Monday would be early enough, they felt, to complete their missions.

Meantime, Arnold was spending an unpleasant weekend, although he remained entirely unaware of André's fate. Upon his return Friday he had found both aides upset because he had once again seen Smith, whom Varick so distrusted. When Smith himself rode in on Saturday to inform General Arnold that Anderson was safely past the American outposts, the dispute erupted again. At dinner, Varick, Franks, Smith, and Arnold engaged in a heated argument until Peggy, "observing her husband in a passion," pleaded with the men to drop the matter. Arnold and his aides next had words in the office, which doubled as Varick's bedroom, resulting in Franks' angry departure for Newburgh. Later that evening, Arnold calmed down and thought better of his actions. It would not do to stir up trouble at this point. He contritely told Varick that he and Franks were probably correct in thinking Smith a "rascal." Knowing he no longer had any need for Smith, the general vowed "never to go to his house again or to be seen with him but in company."[5]

Sunday was quiet but tense, a warm day with "several smart showers" in the afternoon. Arnold and his young wife were surely becoming increasingly nervous as the climax of betrayal approached. Varick, seriously ill, stayed in bed. Peggy brought tea and comforted him as much as she could. Franks did not return. In Fishkill, George Washington and his party arrived to spend the night at the home of a Dr. McKnight. Coincidentally, Joshua Smith was also at Dr. McKnight's for dinner. Arnold prepared for Washington's visit on the morrow. Aboard the *Vulture*, far downriver, Robinson and Sutherland were extremely worried after both Friday and Saturday nights had passed with no word from André. André himself spent the day in awful suspense. Jameson fretted, still unsure what his course of action toward the unwanted prisoner should have been. At West Point, troops silently hoped the owners would not catch all their loose hogs—fresh pork would be a treat. On the road, two messengers, several miles apart, stopped to get out of the rain, each obviously convinced his missive was not important enough to require riding in bad weather or at night.

Monday morning dawned crisp and clear, a gorgeous autumn day. Washington, as was his custom, rose early and resumed his journey. Henry Knox, the great gunner (the adjective attesting more to bulk than ability, although he was amply endowed with both) rode at one side. Lafayette was on the other. Trailing along behind clattered a bevy of aides. Guards cantered ahead, protectively inspecting possible ambush sites. The Commander-in-Chief had paid a quick visit to the Highlands in July, but had not actually inspected the defenses since leaving Moore's house nearly a year ago. He intended to take a close look at the forts and redoubts on this trip. Reaching the familiar trail leading up to North Redoubt, the General unexpectedly wheeled his horse in that direction. A dismayed chorus sounded from his companions. Mrs. Arnold was probably holding breakfast; wouldn't it be better to eat before beginning the inspection? "I know that all you young men are in love with Mrs. Arnold," the General chided. If they were so eager to see her, he teased, they were excused to ride ahead,

H.M.S. Vulture. *This model, made on an exact scale of one-quarter inch to the foot, is in the West Point Museum. The builder, Mr. Bernhard Schulze, worked from photostats of the original working drawings used to construct the sloop in 1775.*

but he intended to check North and Middle Redoubts before continuing. With good-natured grumbling, the entire party turned up the stony trail behind Washington. Major James McHenry and Captain Samuel Shaw, aides of Lafayette and Knox respectively, were sent ahead to tell the mistress of the house not to wait breakfast. Pleased with the mission, the two young officers broke into a gallop.

When they arrived, about nine o'clock, Peggy was primping upstairs and Arnold was at the table. Would the two aides care to join him? They would. The early ride in the clean, cool air had made them ravenous. As they were eating, Lieutenant Soloman Allen hitched his horse and strode into the house. Arnold, knowing Varick was ill, motioned the lieutenant to give him the packet. Opening Jameson's message, the startled general saw words that were hardly believable. Anderson captured . . . Arnold's pass in his possession . . . information on the West Point defenses . . . Washington notified. . . .

Washington notified! Blood beat in Arnold's ears. His face flushed. Mouthing some excuse, he abruptly pushed back from the table and started upstairs. After a step, he whirled back, pulled Lieutenant Allen aside, and strictly enjoined him not to mention Anderson's capture to anyone. He then bolted up the stairs to his wife's room in remarkably good time for a cripple. Scarcely had he stammered out the thunderous news to an incredulous Peggy before advance riders (probably sent by Alexander Hamilton who had taken a different route and was unaware that his chief had paused to check redoubts on the way) pulled up to announce General Washington's imminent arrival. Franks, back from Newburgh in time to get in on the excitement, rapped on the Arnold's bedroom door with the news. Leaving his distraught wife, Arnold rushed downstairs, shouting as he ran for a horse to be saddled. Throwing a cloak around his shoulders, he hurriedly informed Franks that he was going to West Point to prepare a reception for General Washington and would return in about an hour. Leaping on the hastily saddled animal, the plump little Connecticut Yankee careened over a slight hill and raced dangerously down a steep path to Robinson's Landing. His bargemen, seeing the general approaching at breakneck speed, scurried aboard just before he sprang from his mount and jumped into the boat. "Downriver," he managed to gasp to the surprised boat crew, "and be fast about it!" Catching his breath, he explained lamely that he must hurry in order to get back in time to meet General Washington.[6]

Actually, Washington did not reach the Robinson house for nearly thirty minutes after Arnold's sudden departure. About half-past ten he swung off his horse expecting to be met by the commander of the Highlands fortresses. No one was there except Major Franks, nervously greeting the Commander-in-Chief and explaining none too concisely that Arnold was at West Point, Mrs. Arnold was indisposed, and Varick was ill. Washington attempted to put Franks at ease by ordering breakfast and announcing his intention to meet Arnold at West Point after eating. Downing a quick meal while Franks readied a boat, Washington might have considered Arnold's absence as out of the ordinary, but he had no reason to suspect anything foul. He was in all probability looking forward to visiting the "happy spot" that had been home for so many months during a more pleasant year. Leaving Hamilton behind to handle correspondence, Washington took Knox and Lafayette to assist in the inspection. At eleven o'clock or a little later, they stepped off the boat onto the landing beneath Fort Arnold, surprised to discover no one to meet them other than an open-mouthed sentry. He, in turn, was quite obviously astounded to see General Washington suddenly appear at his post.

Colonel Lamb, flustered and out of breath, his scars glowing crimson, ran down to report to the General. No, he had not seen Arnold all day. Knox and Lafayette exchanged glances. Something was amiss. Much later Washington remembered, "The impropriety of his conduct when he knew I was to be there struck me very forcibly and my mind misgave me; but I had not the least idea of the real cause." Shrugging his large shoulders, Washington surmised Arnold would probably join them during the inspection; he told Lamb to lead the way. The trusting Virginian could have believed any explanation but the truth. At that very moment, Arnold's eight sweating bargemen were rowing him within range of the *Vulture*. Clambering to the white-painted deck of the British ship, he told a startled Beverley Robinson that the entire scheme had been thwarted and André was a prisoner. The time was 11:30 A.M. As reward for their hard work in getting him down the river in what must have been record time, Arnold turned his loyal bargemen over to the English.[7]

For two hours Washington probed and looked and queried. He peered into half-empty magazines, found rust on iron wheels, walked through shoddy barracks, climbed onto crumbling parapets, gazed wonderingly at the sinking chain. Uneasiness about Arnold's unusual behavior gradually gave way to consternation over the run-down condition of the post. In many ways the defenses were weaker than when he had left the preceding November. The excuses he heard from Lamb and Villefranche and Bauman and others were all the same: shortages of supplies, the harsh winter, neglect of the forts in favor of other projects, too few men and too many details, a constantly shifting troop population. After two hours, Washington had seen enough. Thoroughly alarmed, he ordered Lamb and Villefranche to return with him to participate in a discussion with Arnold concerning corrective action which must be taken at once. As the General departed, an honor guard presented arms while Bauman's cannoneers proudly fired a thirteen-gun salute. Preoccupied, Washington and the other officers were whisked across the shimmering river in Lamb's distinctive, green-striped barge, the *Bennington*.[8]

While the Commander-in-Chief had been across the river, Peggy Arnold became hysterical, ranting madly that the men about her intended to kill her baby. The young woman may actually have been out of her senses—there was more than enough justification and she had given indication in the past of emotional instability. On the other hand, she might have been play-acting to evade suspicion of complicity—there is also evidence that she was much too level-headed to become lost in hysteria. Either way, she thoroughly wrenched the emotions of every male in the house and avoided censure as a conspirator with her husband for a century and a half.

The Beverley Robinson house. From The Public Papers of George
Clinton.

About an hour after George Washington and his party had left for West Point, Varick heard a terrifying shriek from the upstairs hallway. Bounding up the steps three at a time he found Peggy, nude but for an unbuttoned dressing gown, racing wildly about the corridor. She was pulling at her loose, flowing hair, screaming wildly. The gossamer negligée floated behind her as she ran, producing a vision "not to be seen," as Varick primly put it, "even by gentlemen of the family, much less by many strangers." Catching sight of the aide, she ran to him and fell on her knees, clutching at his legs and pleading tearfully with him to spare her babe. The shocked young officer was unable to pry her loose. Major Franks and Dr. William Eustis, the headquarters surgeon, reached the scene together at that moment. The three men were able with difficulty to carry the still raving girl to bed. Dr. Eustis managed to calm her somewhat, but told the aides she might die, her condition was so critical.

Varick sat on the side of her bed hoping to keep her soothed. He related their conversation:

> When she seemed a little composed she burst again into pitiable tears and exclaimed to me, alone on her bed with her, that she had not a friend left here. I told her she had Franks and me, and General Arnold would soon be home from West Point with General Washington. She exclaimed: "No, General Arnold will never return; he is gone, he is gone forever; there, there, there, the spirits have carried him up there, they have put hot irons in his head"—pointing that he was gone up to the ceiling. This alarmed me much. I felt apprehensive of something more than ordinary having occasioned her hysterics and utter frenzy.[9]

Sometime later, when she learned Washington had returned, her hysterics (or histrionics) recurred. Screeching unintelligibly something about a blazing iron pressing into her forehead, she cried that "no one but General Washington could take it off." Weeping, apparently in agony, she begged Varick to bring the General to her bedroom. Both aides by this time suspected Arnold had deserted to the enemy, but they were afraid to approach Washington lest their suspicions prove unfounded. Varick decided the Commander-in-Chief should see Mrs. Arnold's frenetic condition; maybe then the General himself would raise the subject of Arnold's absence.

The aide need not have been so punctilious; by then Washington already knew of Arnold's perfidy. His first question on returning to Robinson's house had been of Arnold. Hamilton had heard nothing. Worried, but still never dreaming of treachery, the General, grimy after the inspection, walked to a room set aside for him to prepare for dinner. As the Virginian washed, Colonel Jameson's second messenger arrived. He handed Hamilton the account of Anderson's capture, André's letter divulging his real identity, and the incriminating packet of documents found in the Englishman's boot. Hamilton, at once discerned their meaning. Rushing to the General's room, he knocked urgently, entered, and spread the evidence out on a table. Washington, dressed only in riding boots and breeches, began to read. The aide said not a word. The truth, terrible and incredible, struck George Washington full force. Arnold a traitor!

For a moment Hamilton saw the Commander-in-Chief not as the towering, severe man of monuments, but sagging, shocked; the General's uncovered torso went limp as his soul absorbed the painful reality. The most splendid warrior in the American army had deserted the cause. Emotion worked on the great man's face.

Sharply he pulled himself together. He began to jerk his clothes on while assessing the situation. Arnold may have had accessories. No one not absolutely free of suspicion could be made aware that Washington knew of the treason. That meant, for the time being, only members of his own party could be alerted. Benedict Arnold had fled by barge, the General recalled, and must surely have made good his escape by now. But some unforeseen circumstance could have delayed him along the way. There was a slight chance. He ordered Hamilton and McHenry to ride as swiftly as possible to Verplanck's Point to capture the traitor if he had not already passed that place.

Knox and Lafayette were summoned. "Arnold has betrayed us!" he informed them without preliminary. "Whom can we trust now?" The three considered various courses of action, but finally concluded it would be best to carry on as if nothing were afoot until Hamilton and McHenry should ascertain beyond a doubt that Arnold had gotten away.

There really was no rush. Arnold's precipitate and frantic flight indicated the British had planned no attack until after André's return to New York City. With his schemes disarranged by André's capture, Henry Clinton could hardly launch an immediate expedition up the river for a day or two at the earliest. All of Washington's guard was put on full alert around the Robinson house—probably with orders that no one would be permitted to enter *or* leave—and the three generals calmly went down to dinner. It was then that Varick met the Virginian with a request to visit Mrs. Arnold.

Washington sadly climbed the stairs to Peggy's room. He had known the pert girl since she was fourteen and it hurt him to visit her under these conditions. Varick ushered him in. The scene confronting the General—a notorious pushover for lovely young ladies—was predicated to melt the heart of a man far tougher than Washington. Propped up on pillows, dishevelled dark hair cascading becomingly about her shoulders, covered loosely by the diaphanous dressing gown, clutching her infant to her breast, the pitiable (or shrewd) young woman personified "the sweetness of beauty, all the loveliness of innocence." Washington stood awkwardly at the foot of the bed, but the weeping girl did not recognize his presence. At last Varick said simply, "There is General Washington."[10]

The General moved up beside her. She looked him long in the face and shouted "No!" *That* man was not Washington, she sobbed. Compassion tugging at the corners of his straight mouth, he leaned over and softly assured her that he really was General Washington.

"No!" she wailed, covering her baby with slim, bare arms, "That is the man who was agoing to assist Colonel Varick in killing my child!"

When the anguished officer reached out to touch her she writhed away, wide-eyed, waving her arms, and repeated the story about the spirits carrying her husband away and placing hot irons in his head. As she pointed to the ceiling her flimsy garment fell completely away. Washington reddened, paused helplessly for a moment, then turned on his heel and left the room. At that moment he hated Arnold, hated him as he had never hated anyone in his life. Of Peggy's innocence he had not the slightest doubt; her overwrought condition (or charade) had amply reinforced his natural propensity to dissociate women and war.

Dinner was glum. The food was hardly touched. Knowing or sensing something was wrong, everyone was ill at ease. Washington watched each of the guests, wondering to himself if another traitor sat at the table. Varick and Franks? Perhaps. They would have to be put under arrest as a precaution. Villefranche and Gouvion? It was virtually certain that Arnold would not have confided in so delicate a matter with Frenchmen. Lamb, the sour old campaigner with half a face? After spending much of the day with the guileless colonel, Washington was convinced he was not involved in the plot. Letting his mind roam beyond the Highlands, he was satisfied that Jameson could be trusted because he had sent in the information on André. Lieutenant Colonel James Livingston, whose unexpected firing on the *Vulture* had made the capture of André possible, was at that point an unknown quantity. For the moment, since he commanded at crucial King's Ferry, he would have to be replaced. Nathanael Greene commanded the main army in Washington's absence. He could be depended upon if anyone could. It grew dark outside.

Toward the end of the "melancholy dinner," or maybe shortly after it was over, a note arrived from Alexander Hamilton. He and McHenry had reached Verplanck's Point too late. Arnold, the aide informed Washington, was aboard the *Vulture* and had written to the Commander-in-Chief a letter which was enclosed. Although the young man did not believe it likely, he thought it possible that "Arnold has made such dispositions with the garrison as may tempt the enemy in its present weakness to make the stroke this night, and it seems prudent to be providing against it." Hamilton told his chief he would ask General Greene to alert the main army "without making a bustle" and "to detach a brigade this way" immediately. He would also try to locate Colonel Meigs to tell him to march his 6th Connecticut Regiment toward the Point.[11]

Arnold's letter to his old friend and commander began by claiming he had "ever acted from a principle of love to my country." Then the traitor asked Washington to protect Mrs. Arnold. "She is as good, and as innocent, as an angel, and is incapable of doing wrong." And would it be too much of an imposition "to ask that my clothes and baggage, which are of little consequence, may be sent to me" in the city? After honor, wife, clothes, and signature, the fallen eagle remembered the guiltless people likely to be burnt by his actions. Varick, Franks, and Joshua Smith, he added in a P.S., "are totally ignorant of any transactions of mine that they had reason to believe were injurious to the public."[12]

Washington, realizing Arnold was out of his grasp, began disposing his forces to foil any possible attempt of Sir Henry's to seize West Point by a sudden plunge upriver. With Hamilton not yet returned, he pressed into service Knox's aide, Samuel Shaw. Dictating first to Shaw, then to Robert Harrison, the General got off nine messages between seven and seven-thirty that evening. He ordered Lamb to take command of the posts at Stony Point and Verplanck's Point in place of Livingston. The latter officer was to "come without the least delay" to Robinson's house where guards could keep him out of circulation until his complicity or innocence might be proven. Greene was left in charge of the main army, but Washington directed him to "put the division on the left in motion as soon as possible" toward King's Ferry.* To Colonel Nathaniel Wade of the Massachusetts militia, the Commander-in-Chief wrote:

> General Arnold is gone to the Enemy. . . . from this circumstance and Colonel Lamb's being detached on some business, the command of the garrison [of West Point] for the present devolves on you. I request you will be as vigilant as possible, and as the enemy may have it in contemplation to attempt some enterprise, even tonight, against these posts, I wish you to make, immediately after receipt of this, the best disposition you can of your force, so as to have a proportion of men in each work on the west side of the river. You will see or hear from me further tomorrow.[13]

Washington next ordered Meig's 6th Connecticut to "march without a moment's delay," half to occupy "North and Middle Redoubts on the heights above this place as soon as possible" and the remaining half to go directly to West Point. Militia from Fishkill were summoned and a courier galloped away to recall a large woodcutting detail from Staatsburgh.[14]

Finally, the pacing general got around to André. He directed Jameson to pay "every precaution and attention . . . to prevent Major André from making his escape." Under as large a guard as might be necessary absolutely to preclude his escape or rescue, the Britisher was to be brought to West Point. Furthermore, the General dictated, "he does not appear to stand upon the footing of a common prisoner of war and therefore he is not entitled to the usual indulgences they receive, and is to be most closely and narrowly watched."[15]

As riders disappeared in all directions to spread the alert, the tense cluster of officers was startled by a bright flash of light from the direction of West Point. Rushing to the porch, Washington arrived in time to see an arcing shower of sparks rise high into the air over the fortress. And then another. After the excitement of that wild day, the men standing around the Commander-in-Chief in Beverley Robinson's spacious yard were prepared to believe anything. Then someone, maybe Villefranche, laughed and informed the puzzled onlookers that it was nothing more fearful than Major Sebastian Bauman and his fireworks. And so it was. The men at West Point had remained entirely ignorant of the major events of the day. After all duties were accomplished, everyone not on guard or sick had gathered on

---

* Greene's orders that night, issued at eleven o'clock, stated, "The Pennsylvania division to march immediately. The rest of the army to be put in perfect readiness to move on the shortest notice."

the plain to be treated to one of Bauman's periodic fireworks displays. It was apparently one of his better performances. Dr. Adams returned from the show to note admiringly in his diary how the major "threw a number of rockets."[16]

Relieved, and perhaps chuckling at man's gullibility, Washington returned to his room to await the arrival of replies and individuals. Colonel Wade received Washington's warning shortly before eleven o'clock—a delay probably due to the difficulty of crossing to West Point after all boats were drawn in for security reasons. Immediately, he roused the garrison. Men dressed, grabbed weapons, and raced for designated battle stations. By 2:00 A.M. the forts and redoubts were fully manned and ready. Those positions would become home for the men for several days. On the 26th, Washington told Wade to fill every water cask and distribute provisions to all the works; and more troops piled in to help man the defenses.[17]

The Commander-in-Chief remained at Robinson's house through the 26th and 27th. He personally assumed responsibility for the Highlands, while Greene continued in command of the maneuver army. Gradually the picture of conspiracy cleared and emerged. It became obvious that Arnold had had no accomplices, unless Joshua Smith had been one. With each day danger of a British blow abated. Soon West Point was so reinforced and the Americans so ready that Washington decided he could safely return to the main army. On the 28th he established his headquarters at Tappan. Alexander McDougall, who knew West Point and the Hudson Highlands intimately, and who thoroughly detested service there, was tabbed to replace Washington.

Knowing the Scot's dislike of the place, General Washington assured him his stay would be for a short period only—in fact, just until Major General St. Clair could arrive. McDougall stepped in forcefully. His first instructions to the defenders bespoke a fierce determination to hold West Point at all costs: in event of an attack, he ordered, the garrison would "defend the works to the last extremity." A couple of days later he decided the likelihood of an English assault had passed. After five days of total alert, not to mention five nights of sleeping on their arms, the soldiers at the Point were permitted to relax. Even then, though, a stronger than normal guard was posted and detachments were sent to the site of old Fort Montgomery and to the cove above Buttermilk Falls (now Highland Falls) to provide early warning.[18]

Franks escorted Peggy Arnold, at last in full control of her clothes and senses, back to Philadelphia. A heavy rain drummed on the roof of her carriage as she left the Hudson Highlands on 27 September. Her husband had arrived in rain. Departing in profound despair, she carried with her the heartfelt if misguided sympathies of every gentleman in Washington's entourage. From the cynical perspective of the twentieth century, one is inclined to credit her performance as among the most successful strip teases in history, probably deserving equal billing with Salome's.

The fate of André provided a tear-studded sequel to the sorry story of sedition. When André reached Robinson's house early on the 26th, after riding since midnight under heavy guard and in pouring rain, he was

To the Officer commanding at West Point
and its dependencies —

Sir,

You will immediately make a distribution of the Troops under your command to
~~the several Post~~ that the whole may be in a state of
defence at the shortest notice — You will also have
each work supplied with Ten days provision, wood,
water and stores and keep up constantly that supply — and you will take every other precaution for
the security of the Post. — The Enemy will have
acquired from General Arnold a perfect knowledge of the defences, and will be able to take
their measures with the utmost precision. This
makes it essential our vigilance and care
should be redoubled for its preservation — You
will do every thing in your power to gain information of the Enemy's designs, and give me intelligence as early as possible of any movements
against you —

A party of militia who have been
employed cutting wood and another as guards
to the stores at Fish kill that have been called
in are to return to their destination.

Colonel Gouvion will remain a few
days at this Post to assist in the necessary arrangements —

Given at Head Quarters
Robinsons House
Sept: 27th 1780

G Washington

Washington's instructions for West Point after Arnold's escape.
Courtesy of the West Point Library.   285

promptly hustled over the river to West Point for safeguarding. Washington did not interview him, although he personally interrogated every American who happened to be under the slightest suspicion. Joshua Smith had been captured and was already at the Robinson house when André was brought in. He, too, was sent to West Point. Because of the special nature of the two prisoners—and Washington's special interest in them—they were placed for extra security in a fortification rather than a building. Fort Putnam was the site selected. That was an appropriate choice for it had been André's fond hope to lead the British charge planned to have struck that very fort. Two days the prisoners languished there. On the 28th, the spy and the suspected traitor preceded the Commander-in-Chief by barge to Tappan. Next day, referring to André, Washington ordered a board of general officers "to report a precise state of his case, together with your opinion of the light in which he ought to be considered, and the punishment that ought to be inflicted."[19]

Nathanael Greene was president of the board. Lord Stirling, von Steuben, Lafayette, Robert Howe, and St. Clair were the major generals. Eight brigadiers completed the panel: James Clinton, Glover, Edward Hand, John Stark, Parsons, Knox, Jedidiah Huntington, and John Paterson. Greene, Stirling, and Clinton had been involved with the Highlands fortifications since early in the war. Parsons had been the first commander of West Point; four others had commanded there, and three more would. Twice Steuben had been called upon to assist the garrison. Knox and Lafayette had been with Washington when the treason had been discovered. Knox had shared a bed with André in 1775. It was hardly a disinterested board. But then André's case was clearly open-and-shut. By weight of evidence and force of his own admission, he was condemned. He had entered American lines to obtain intelligence. After getting the information, he attempted to escape in disguise and under a feigned name. He was caught red-handed. And he had confessed. The verdict was inevitable and unanimous: ". . . Major André, Adjutant General to the British army, ought to be considered as a spy from the enemy and . . . ought to suffer death." Washington approved the sentence on 1 October, saying only that the execution would be "in the usual way." Hanging, of course, was the ignoble death set aside for spies.[20]

Henry Clinton loved young André like a son. He attempted in every honorable and feasible way to compel Washington to commute the sentence. The American leader did postpone the execution, letting Clinton know by very clear signs that the Patriots would happily surrender André —in return for Arnold. Sir Henry might have been tempted, but he could not make the swap. Arnold's fate at the hands of his recent comrades can be imagined by observing what the English themselves did to persons convicted of high treason. In matters legal and judicial, it should be remembered, the English-speaking colonists were much attuned to traditions of the Mother Country. Only four months later, in January 1781, a man in London was found guilty of high treason. He was sentenced "to be hanged by the neck, but not till dead; then to be cut down, and his bowels taken out and burnt before his face, his head to be taken off, his body cut into four quarters, and to be at his Majesty's disposal."

André, realizing he would die, blanched at hanging. He begged to be shot—a more suitable death for a gentleman. Washington could not allow it. A spy's lot was to dangle from a rope. If the Americans were to use other means it would be tacit acknowledgment that André was not a spy, and propagandists could claim his death had been murder. Few Americans thirsted to take André's life. Indeed, many felt Washington was wrong. Arnold was the villain, they believed, and André the innocent victim. Dr. James Thacher, who observed the execution, sympathetically described the English officer's last moments:

> . . . the victim, after taking off his hat and stock, bandaged his own eyes with perfect firmness, which melted the hearts and moistened the cheeks, not only of his servant, but of the throng of spectators. The rope being appended to the gallows, he slipped the noose over his head and adjusted it to his neck, without the assistance of the awkward executioner. Colonel Scammell now informed him that he had an opportunity to speak, if he desired it; he raised the handkerchief from his eyes, and said, "I pray you to bear me witness that I meet my fate like a brave man." The wagon being now removed from under him, he was suspended and instantly expired. . . .[21]

With Arnold gone and André dead, Washington took stock of his army's morale and tried to feel the pulse of the nation. The shock of Arnold's dastardly act, the General feared, could cast the country into a whirlpool of despair from which it might not recover. Through the long, black year, morale had edged closer and closer to the point of no return. The United States was tottering, standing weakly on the brink. Washington half expected—and braced for—the worst.*

But the human soul is hard to probe, difficult to understand, impossible to predict. Arnold's treason had precisely the opposite effect on Americans: it revitalized the Revolution.

Consternation, incredulousness, amazement; those were the first emotions to sweep the army and the nation. ". . . An event . . . which will strike you with astonishment . . ."—Washington. ". . . A scene that shocked me more than anything I have met with . . ."—Hamilton. ". . . One of the most extraordinary events in modern history . . ."—Dr. Thacher. "I should as soon have thought West Point had deserted as he . . ."—Private Martin. Close behind that stunning, stilling wave of surprise crested a breaker foaming with anger and condemnation, churning with rage and wrath. "Treason of the Blackest dye!" thundered Nathanael Greene. Arnold was "lost to every sentiment of honor." A veritable hate wave boiled over the land. Arnold was despised, detested, reviled. Carica-

---

* If he could have listened in on conversations that very month in France, Washington would have been even more worried. By late summer 1780, America's European ally had discovered it would have to float huge, unpopular war loans to continue financing the war. Pressures increased for an accommodation. In September, Louis XVI was seriously thinking of peace, a step that would have left the United States high and dry.

tures were drawn and spat upon, or worse. Washington himself literally seethed with hatred for the renegade. Arnold became virtually overnight a nonperson, such was the deep resentment, the universal loathing. After the Continental Congress received George Washington's notification of the desertion, it forthwith began the process of eliminating the now odious memory of an erstwhile hero, resolving "to erase from the register of the names of the officers of the army of the United States the name of Benedict Arnold."[22]

Behind those two instinctive, reflex emotions gathered a surge of thankfulness. Americans were quick to realize what the loss of West Point could have meant. They easily saw a Heavenly hand in the entire affair. "Happily the treason has been timely discovered to prevent the fatal misfortune," Greene told his troops. "The providential train of circumstances which led to it affords the most convincing proof that the liberties of America are the object of divine protection." Congress proclaimed a day of public thanksgiving and prayer to pay homage to "Almighty God" who had bestowed blessings upon the American people, "especially in the late remarkable interposition of His watchful providence . . . at the moment when treason was ripened for execution." Thomas Paine, whose inflammatory words seldom failed to fire and inspire Americans, said the important thing was not Arnold as a person but the very enormity of his anticipated crime and the "providence evident in the discovery." Doctor Adams thoughtfully told his diary, "I think the providential discovery of so deep and dangerous a plot well worthy of our notice, and from which we may draw a happy omen for America." On 27 September, two days after the treason was discovered, General Orders for the main army prescribed the day's parole to be "West Point." Countersigns were "Fortune" and "Favours." "America" was the watchword. The combination of words was no accident; by saving West Point, Fortune had clearly shown she favored America. Congress proclaimed it. Officers announced it. Preachers preached it. Men believed it. Across the land hope was lifted once again. The fatal grip of the dark year was broken.[23]

Ironically, Benedict Arnold had accomplished what no one else had been able to do. By failing to sell West Point, he awakened interest in a dulled populace, aroused emotion in numbed souls, created hope from despair. It was his final and, in a manner of speaking, his greatest service to America.

On the Rock of West Point the Dark Eagle had indeed crashed, but his fall had reversed the strong, bleak tide of the Black Year. From that moment on the situation improved. One could not call the salvation of West Point the decisive event in the War of Independence (although had Arnold's scheme worked, it might have been just that), but it was definitely a turning point, a low point in the pendulum swing of events beyond which the arc constantly rises.

Within a year, the war would be won.

PART FIVE

BACKWATER AND BACKLASH

20

FROM MUTINY TO VICTORY

AS SOON as André's trial was over, Washington instructed Major General Arthur St. Clair to hurry to West Point. St. Clair was not especially eager to take on that responsibility, but he relieved Mc-Dougall on 4 October. A few days later, Nathanael Greene requested the position; he was eager to assume the heavy burden. Washington consented, but he cautioned the Rhode Islander "of the uncertainty of that post's being long removed from my immediate command." In other words, the Commander-in-Chief would continue to regard West Point as his personal baili-wick. Greene accepted the possibility. On 9 October he rode into the for-tress. His first act upon assuming command was to rename Fort Arnold; the great bastion built by James Clinton finally became Fort Clinton.[1]

Greene's stay was brief. Having attempted to manipulate military af-fairs in the southern theatre without consulting the Commander-in-Chief, a chastened Congress discovered the situation there well-nigh beyond recov-ery. A large Patriot army had been captured at Charleston, another wiped out at Camden. Royal troops under Cornwallis held sway in the three southernmost states and seriously endangered Virginia. No American force was even in the field to oppose them. Congress' last effort had been to appoint Horatio Gates, an utter mediocrity, to command in that faraway theatre. He had rapidly rewarded them with the fiasco at Camden. Seeing no way out of the quagmire, the legislators tossed the whole mess to George Washington. He, in turn, had no choice but to send his top general south-ward. Although it meant Nathanael Greene would have to forego the West Point command that he had coveted, he was the logical and the best choice. Dutifully, but with apparent misgivings, he prepared to depart. Until

William Heath should reach the Hudson, McDougall (how he cursed West Point and the fate that repeatedly drew him to those barren rocks!) was to hold the fort. Mrs. McDougall fastened a jaunty cockade on Greene's hat as he departed after having spent only ten days at the Point.

If Arnold's failure to sell the key to the continent was the first step in a stairway to victory, Washington's appointment of the fighting Quaker was the third. The second, unknown at the time to either Washington or Greene, was a remarkable, spontaneous victory at King's Mountain, South Carolina, on 7 October. Wanting a taste of combat, men from the mountain region west of the Blue Ridge assembled and marched east. Reinforced to a strength of nearly one thousand by other Patriot riflemen, the frontiersmen cornered Major Patrick Ferguson and some nine hundred Loyalists on flat-topped King's Mountain and promptly annihilated them. Satisfied with their one foray of the war, the over-mountain men marched proudly home. That entirely unexpected battle temporarily stalled the British surge in the south, giving Nathanael Greene time to reach the Carolinas.

Once there, he set out aggressively to shape system out of chaos. In order better to feed his men during the initial reorganization phase, he divided his small force, remaining himself with one half and sending the other westward under rough, crusty Brigadier General Daniel Morgan. In a classic battle fought not far from King's Mountain at a place known as the Cowpens, Morgan mauled a superior enemy force. After a bleak year of defeat piled upon defeat, it was almost unbelievable that Americans were winning again. Spirits climbed. Indeed, it began to seem that some inexorable force was drawing the Patriots onward to victory.

Not that there were no setbacks. Washington had to weather one of his greatest crises that winter: mass mutiny.

When alarm and excitement over the Arnold affair died down, the Virginian contemplated a raid against New York City. But, at virtually the last moment, he reluctantly concluded that it was impractical. Efforts to stir the French army in Newport likewise came to naught. With sharp winds already evoking memories of the preceding year's terrible cold, the time was at hand to look for winter quarters. Gouvion deftly removed the great chain on 14 November, a signal to all that the period for fighting was at an end. Spreading his army once again in an arc in the hills about West Point, Washington steeled himself to face another agonizing season of starvation —the Continental Army's sixth.

From the start conditions were poor. In spite of Arnold's large wood-cutting details, there was no firewood in camp. Men began burning wooden portions of their defenses, forcing the post commander to place a temporary ban on all fires. Details were sent to fetch logs, but scantily clad troops shivered in the meantime. The shortage of food was even worse. McDougall appealed to Governor Clinton for flour on 2 October, claiming the garrison had but a five-day stock of bread with no prospect of resupply. Clinton was unable to help. "The garrison this night is without an ounce of flour," Nathanael Greene wrote on his second day at the Point. General Heath, replacing Greene on 17 October, spoke of "a great want of flour." James Thacher, attached to a Massachusetts brigade building huts "in the rear of

West Point," stated flatly, "We are threatened with starvation." Displacing his dispensary to New Windsor, Doctor Adams briefly recorded, "Left off from the Point without any regret." Virtually fireless and foodless, it was far from being a happy place.[2]

Clothing was not to be had. Nor medicine. "The brave soldiers, who were but illy clad and destitute of blankets," Heath remembered, "were in a shivering condition." A Frenchman, observing how raggedly clothed most of the soldiers were, colorfully described their situation: ". . . their clothes were truly invalids." Itch was rampant, but lard and sulfur, ingredients for a salve to cure it, were unobtainable. Washington sent officers home on furlough and released men early from their enlistments—being careful to discharge only the least healthy and the most naked—because he could neither feed nor clothe nor care for them. Although his regiments were "never half complete in men," they were always "perfectly so in every species of want." Sarcastically, the Commander-in-Chief suggested it would "be well for the troops if, like chameleons, they could live upon air, or like the bear suck their paws for sustenance during the rigor of the approaching season."[3]

Inflation, of course, had rendered currency all but worthless, but there existed also a severe money shortage. Soldiers could only dimly recall being paid. George Washington, asking and receiving no salary, but whose expenses Congress was supposed to pay, was forced to dip into his own pocket to meet daily obligations. The army has "neither money nor credit adequate to the purchase of a few boards for doors to our log huts," he complained. Away from the army camps, food was plentiful if one had money to purchase it. Islands of want in a bountiful sea, the winter cantonments were rife with discontent. Soldiers, not comprehending why such conditions should exist, began to forage on their own, stealing poultry and killing cattle to satiate hunger. To stop that practice—conduct self-defeating in the long run—Heath restricted everyone at West Point to the post proper after "Retreat" each day, and to their billets after "Tattoo." Officers as well as men turned angry. On New Year's Day, 1781, Dr. Samuel Adams sat down to his diary and poured out his bitterness: he saw himself and his fellow officers as "a set of poor miserable dogs without a single shilling in our pockets—consider this ye money catchers at home and think what you deserve for your sordid avarice and your treatment of your army!"[4]

Fortunately, the weather was mild, exceptionally so when compared with the past winter. New Year's Day was "cloudy but remarkably warm!" January 11 was "much more like April then January," and a week or so later the days were "pleasant as May." Some snow fell in December and January, but the river did not freeze. Perhaps the balmy weather was yet another sign of Heavenly approbation for the Patriot cause?[5]

All things considered, however, the black year was ending about where it had begun. True, recent events on the battlefield had been favorable. And the weather had been kind. But those well-remembered winter companions, hunger and sickness and poverty and nakedness, stalked the camps of the Continentals. It had been that way for each of six winters now. Human beings can endure only so much and remain human, can accept only so long the unacceptable. At some point they must rise in anger and frustration to shake off that which is intolerable.

On the first day of the new year, resentful soldiers in the Pennsylvania line mutinied. Raw rum in empty bellies emboldened them, honest grievances provided an all-too-obvious cause, a few rabble-rousers ignited them. Shouldering muskets and trailing six pieces of artillery, they marched off for Philadelphia to tell Congress what they wanted. When officers attempted to halt them, the mutineers merely brushed them aside, killing two captains and wounding others. Anthony Wayne, whom the men highly respected, followed the column as it proceeded through New Jersey, looking closely for a chance to divert it or to talk some sense into the strangely disciplined mob. The determined troops had no intention of going over to the enemy, nor of deserting; they were rebelling against an inefficient administrative system, not against their country. That much was encouraging. Nonetheless, they were in a full and defiant state of mutiny. Left unchecked, mutiny could have spread cancerlike through the entire army, more effectively destroying the Revolution than anything the British could possibly do.[6]

An aide sent by Wayne bounded off a spent horse in front of Washington's New Windsor headquarters at noon on 3 January. Dashing inside, he found the surprised Commander-in-Chief and blurted out the shocking report "of the unhappy and alarming defection of the Pennsylvania line." Once he comprehended the magnitude of the mutiny, Washington's first, instinctive thought was for the safety of West Point. If the rebellion should spread to New England regiments then encamped in the Highlands, the results could be disastrous. Furtively, he sent out trusted officers to take the pulse of the garrison, meanwhile cautiously summoning "a small escort of horse" to bolster his own guard. He then made tentative plans to rush to the scene of mutiny "if nothing alarming appears here."[7]

But he could not leave. Through the night officers reported, warning him "not to leave this post in the present situation of things, temper of the troops, and distress of the garrison for want of flour, clothing, and, in short, everything." More than three weeks before, an officer at West Point had written with surprising prescience, "That a part of our army, charged with the defense of a post so highly important to America, should be left in such an unprovided and destitute condition is truly a matter of astonishment; and unless a remedy can be found our soldiers will abandon the cause of their country. . . ." That was precisely what worried Washington. He dispatched a rider to Governor Clinton, urgently requesting the New Yorker's help. If the Continentals marched away, New York militia would be needed to hold the fortress. Silently, the anxious Virginian cursed the unseasonably warm weather. Unfrozen, the Hudson beckoned attack of an undefended West Point.[8]

British troops were, in fact, stirring. Henry Clinton had learned of the mutiny before Washington. Hopeful of a windfall, he alerted several units, forming an expedition to move as circumstances and opportunity might direct. Meanwhile, he sent spies into the countryside to bring back a clearer picture. One Ezekiel Yeomans slipped into the city on the 11th with a report of a troop rebellion at West Point. It had been beaten down, Yeomans said, but the spirit of insurrection was strong in the Highlands. The information was wrong, of course, but Sir Henry leaped at the supposed opportunity, directing Chief Justice William Smith to prepare an address to the soldiers in the Highlands fastness. He promised pardon and back pay as a reward for anyone who would desert. Soldiers and ships were immediately put on standby to race up the river in the event American troops left the great fortress untended. A few days later, accurate intelligence arrived from the Highlands and the scheme was dropped. Smith's paper was never delivered to the steadfast men of West Point—but Washington's fears had not been far-fetched.[9]

Serious as the mutiny of the Pennsylvanians was, Washington saw a revolt at West Point as a worse danger. Leaving it up to Anthony Wayne to quell the former, he turned his personal attention to preventing the latter. Teams were ruthlessly impressed to gather flour from a depot at Ringwood, boats were sent upriver in search of provisions, big Henry Knox went galloping off into New England to beg for "an immediate supply of money and clothing." George Clinton joined Washington, swearing "to render your Excellency every assistance in my power." The Governor emphatically seconded the General: West Point's garrison, not the mutineers in New Jersey, was properly the primary concern. Every resource at George Washington's command was directed toward easing shortages at that key post on the Hudson. The records do not say, but it is quite likely that units elsewhere went without as their supplies were diverted to West Point. The effect was immediate and noticeable. Before word of the mutiny reached troops stationed at the Point, one of them wrote: "We have now no longer reason to complain of our accommodations; the huts are warm and comfortable, wood in abundance at our doors, and a tolerable supply of provisions. Our only complaint is want of money."[10]

Days passed. In New Jersey, the mutineers halted at Princeton to bargain with representatives sent out from a frightened Congress. In the Hudson Highlands, New England troops remained quiet. Discipline, Washington felt, was nonetheless taking a terrible beating. The spectacle of soldiers throwing off authority—no matter how just their complaints—and treating with Congress and officers under threat of force was sure to have a deleterious impact on the rest of the army, whose tribulations were every bit as rigorous. The General decided to suppress forcefully the mutinous units. He told Heath to assemble every general and regimental commander for a meeting at West Point.

At exactly 10:00 A.M. on 11 January, Washington climbed out of his barge and walked up the curving path to Moore's house. He bade the officers gathered there to sit down and, getting straight to the point, presented his plan. A thousand men, well shod and carefully fed, would march swiftly from West Point to Princeton to subdue the Pennsylvanians. The Commander-in-Chief realized the danger in asking men basically in sympathy with the mutiny to spill the blood of comrades. Could the soldiers at West Point be depended upon? It was "almost the universal opinion" of those officers present that they could. That settled the matter.

Washington ordered Heath to ready the expedition. West Point's defenses would necessarily be weakened temporarily, but Washington thought the risk acceptable. Those men remaining would simply have to be "uncommonly watchful . . . to the security of the post in the absence of the detachment."[11]

As the General rose to depart, Robert Howe walked up and requested permission to command the detachment. By virtue of seniority, he contended, it was his right. Washington was surprised. Howe had not shown any great inclination for the harsh resolve this mission was likely to require; perhaps he wanted to disprove the impression that he was too easygoing. The Commander-in-Chief thought either Samuel Parsons or John Glover better suited for the dirty job, and hinted as much to the North Carolinian. Howe persisted. Reluctantly, Washington left it up to Heath, agreeing to abide by his choice. Heath, following protocol, selected Howe.

The detachment was picked. Priority on new shoes and solid food went to them. Quartermasters gathered tents and equipment. Cooks prepared and packed four days' provisions. Heath, however, began immediately to doubt "the fidelity and firmness of the soldiers." Pessimistic reports from a camp girl, a trusted sergeant, and one of the commander's waiters caused the concern. Howe and others, though, continued to have faith in the men. Washington could not be sure. If they had to march, he wrote, "God only knows what will be the consequences." As it turned out, the men were not tested then. Congressional emissaries gave in to the mutineers' demands, ending the revolt, but beginning a period of dreadful uncertainty. Appeasement postpones, never cures. Disobedience had paid off. Many ties bind an army, hold it together in the face of adversity, render it unflinching even unto the point of death. Patriotism, comradeship, a just cause, pride, and leadership are some. But the most important, the one remaining when all others fade, is discipline. No matter how patriotic or proud, undisciplined men invariably flee from the mortal danger of the battlefield. In the final analysis, it is discipline that overcomes the natural fear springing from man's instinct for survival. And the discipline of the Continental Army was now in question. If mutiny could work for the Pennsylvanians, why not for others? Where would the next uprising strike? Aware of the "real grievances" existing yet, Washington fully expected "a repetition of similar or even more dangerous disturbances." A conference between the American leader and his French counterpart, Rochambeau, was long overdue, but Washington did not dare leave his army even for a few days. "The moment I do not think my presence at West Point essential," he wrote the Frenchman, "shall be devoted to a visit to your Excellency."[12]

Twenty-two sergeants from the 2nd Massachusetts, then part of the garrison at West Point, petitioned their colonel on 17 January for money, food, and clothing due them. Washington considered their plea for redress to have been "conceived in decent terms and presented with respect," but at that particular time he thought anything looking in any way "like combination ought to be discountenanced." The sergeants never felt his displeasure, however, for the very day he read their mild petition, he was engulfed in January's second major revolt.[13]

Coats were not necessary on Sunday the 21st. A clear, warm sun and a pleasant southerly breeze sent temperatures zooming to unheard-of highs. That evening, crowning the splendid day, beautiful northern lights brightened the horizon with a midwinter display of color. Washington and two aides, Alexander Hamilton and David Humphreys, watched enthralled from the porch of their house in New Windsor. When the bright aurora borealis twinkled out about ten o'clock, the three retired to prepare for bed.[14]

Shortly thereafter, a messenger astride a foam-flecked horse raced up the road toward headquarters. Hearing the urgent clatter in the courtyard, the aides rushed to the entrance hallway. Washington instinctively pulled his boots back on. It was the message all three had been expecting but had hoped would never come—another body of soldiers had defied military authority. Washington rapidly scanned the hurried note: New Jersey troops encamped at Pompton, in their home state, had revolted during the evening of the 20th. Marching towards Trenton, they were making demands "similar to those of the Pennsylvania line." The angry men "are much disguised with liquor," but so far "no blood has been spilt." Colonel Israel Shreve, their grossly fat and equally inept commander, had been entirely unable to "prevail upon them to desist." The Commander-in-Chief did not hesitate a moment. He had previously decided that any mutiny succeeding that of the Pennsylvanians must be immediately and brutally stamped out, "or the army is ruined." His aides, knowing his mind, had paper and quill out by the time he finished reading the message. Rapidly he dictated orders.

Colonel Shreve must "endeavor to collect all those of your regiments who have had virtue enough to resist the pernicious example of their associates" and, if he was able, "to compel the mutineers to unconditional submission." A commissioner from the New Jersey government, known to be near the site of insurrection, was entreated "to employ all your influence to inspire the militia . . . to cooperate with us, by representing the fatal consequences of the present temper of the soldiery not only to military subordination, but to civil liberty." He told Heath, at West Point, of his determination "at all hazards to put a stop to such proceedings, which must otherwise prove the inevitable dissolution of the army." He ordered Heath to prepare immediately a force of "five or six hundred of the most robust and best clothed men." That body would "march from West Point to compel the mutineers to submission." The Commander-in-Chief, himself, would come to the Point early in the morning to convey his personal wishes to the officers and men. The pacing officer continued to bark out tight, terse commands as the hour hand passed eleven. He alerted supply officers. Tents and entrenching tools, horses for artillery, flour and salted beef—all would be needed at once and at any cost. It was just possible, he suddenly thought, that someone might grant concessions to the rebellious soldiers. That could not be permitted for then the problem would have to be faced all over again. To General John Sullivan, Chairman of a Congressional

Committee sent to deal with the Pennsylvania malcontents, he wrote, "I shall as quick as possible, at all events, march a detachment to compel the mutineers to submission, and I beg leave strongly to recommend that no terms may be made with them." Then the General went to bed.[15]

Next morning, at West Point, Washington checked arrangements. Robert Howe was to command the expedition composed of men from Massachusetts, Connecticut, and New Hampshire. Massachusetts troops, under Lieutenant Colonel Ebenezer Sprout, would march from West Point to Ringwood where they were to pick up Major Benjamin Throop's Connecticut men. More Connecticut soldiers and the New Hampshire contingent were to march to King's Ferry, cross, and proceed via Suffern to Ringwood. Artillery would also rendezvous there. Washington's instructions to Howe were to the point, clear, and explicit:

> The object of your detachment is to compel the mutineers to unconditional submission, and I am to desire you will grant no terms while they are with arms in their hands in a state of resistance. The manner of executing this I leave to your discretion according to circumstances. If you succeed in compelling the revolted troops to a surrender you will instantly execute a few of the most active and most incendiary leaders.[16]

There was nothing else he could do. He returned to New Windsor to wait.

Heavy snow fell Monday night. Tuesday, the Massachusetts men set out, making slow progress through the drifts. They found shelter that night by crowding into houses and barns at the Forest of Dean. All day the 24th and again the 25th they plodded through the deep, damp snow. "Having no horse," Thacher wrote, "I experienced inexpressible fatigue, and was obliged several times to sit down on the snow." Ringwood was reached Thursday. Mrs. Erskine, the cartographer's widow, entertained the officers "with an elegant supper and excellent wine." Through the 26th, Howe rested his men, waited for artillery and reinforcements to arrive, and prepared a surprise night attack.

The suspense at New Windsor was unbearable. Washington wrote Howe on the 25th, saying he was "extremely anxious to know the true state of matters" and informing the North Carolinian that he planned to "set out tomorrow towards you; but not with a design of superseding your command." Eight o'clock in the morning of the 26th he left by two-horse sleigh for Ringwood. With Lafayette at his side, the General pushed on throughout the day and evening, reaching Mrs. Erskine's not long before midnight.

Howe had a jolt waiting for his commander. A well-meaning officer had promised pardon if the rebellious soldiers would "return to their duty and conduct themselves in a soldierly manner." To the chagrin of both Washington and Howe, they had returned to their original huts at Pompton; one could hardly punish men who had already been pardoned. However, Howe had learned, after their arrival in Pompton the unruly soldiers had remained surly and had refused to give up their arms. They had not kept their part of the bargain, Howe reasoned, therefore the pardon no longer had force. He planned to attack them anyway. When Washington heard the entire story, he readily concurred. He firmly believed "the existence of the army called for an example." An hour after midnight, Howe's expedition marched toward Pompton, eight miles away.[17]

By dawn, men at the head of the column could see the silent, log huts, half covered with snow. Howe called an hour's halt. Here was the moment of truth. Would American soldiers attack their comrades? Was the tie of discipline stronger than the bond of comradeship? Howe formed his men in a compact line and explained the "heinousness of the crime of mutiny, and the absolute necessity of military subordination." He told the New Englanders what he planned to do. Then he ordered them to load their muskets. James Thacher, watching intently, was relieved when the troops "obeyed with alacrity, and indications were given that they were to be relied on."

Deploying his men and artillery on all sides, Howe summoned the mutineers to surrender. Surrounded and surprised, the New Jersey men meekly gave up. Doctor Thacher recorded their punishment:

General Howe ordered that three of the ringleaders should be selected for condign punishment. These unfortunate culprits were tried on the spot. Colonel Sprout being president of the court-martial, standing on the snow, and they were sentenced to be immediately shot. Twelve of the most guilty mutineers were next selected to be their executioners. This was a most painful task; being themselves guilty, they were greatly distressed with the duty imposed on them, and when ordered to load, some of them shed tears. The wretched victims, overwhelmed by the terrors of death, had neither time nor power to implore the mercy and forgiveness of their God. . . . The first that suffered was a sergeant, and an old offender; he was led a few yards' distance and placed on his knees; six of the executioners, at the signal given by an officer, fired, three aiming at the head and three at the breast, the other six reserving their fire in order to dispatch the victim should the first fire fail; it so happened in this instance; the remaining six then fired, and life was instantly extinguished. The second criminal was, by the first fire, sent into eternity in an instant. The third, being less criminal, by the recommendation of his officers, to his unspeakable joy, received a pardon. This tragical scene produced a dreadful shock and a salutary effect on the minds of the guilty soldiers.[18]

Washington, too, thought the harsh example had "completely subdued" any disposition to mutiny and had brought about "a genuine penitence."

By the time men from West Point's garrison were settled back in their huts, General Washington sensed an overall improvement in his army's attitude and condition. Fear of a general uprising had startled the states to action, while his forceful handling of the affair had improved the status of discipline and morale within the Continental Army itself. "The states seem to be somewhat roused from their late supine condition," he stated hopefully. Moreover, "Congress have called in the most pressing manner for money and supplies; and we hope more vigorous and effectual exertions will be the consequence." The mutinies had represented a step backward, but two forward had been taken in the process. The favorable outcome was made possible by the fidelity of common soldiers. A modern historian, writing of the mutiny, said, "In the hard conflict between sympathy for their comrades and duty to their country the troops from West Point neither complained nor held back."[19]

Calm returned to the Hudson Highlands after that tumultuous month. The monotonous routine of garrison life replaced the high excitement of treason and mutiny. Fortuitously, winter remained mild. Men ate more regularly. Conditions were actually abominable, but, by standards which the Continental Army had come to expect in its winter quarters, the soldiers were relatively well off.

More small victories were racked up and Washington wrang each one for all the propaganda value it was worth. Late in January Lieutenant Colonel William Hull led a raiding detachment from Parson's brigade into Morrisania (now the Bronx), where an enemy force was taken by surprise. Burning barracks and bridges and destroying forage, the Americans left perhaps a score of enemy dead. Withdrawing as swiftly as he had come, Hull carried back fifty-two prisoners and a herd of livestock. His losses were, in Washington's words, "inconsiderable . . . except in the death of Ensign Thompson." From the southern theatre was relayed a story which enlivened many a barracks bull session. By a rapid maneuver, Lieutenant Colonel William Washington cornered over a hundred armed Loyalists in a fortified log barn near Rugeley's Mills, South Carolina. The fort was impervious to musket fire and the Patriots had no artillery. Behind a rise, however, the quick-thinking colonel had his men shape a pine log to look like a cannon. Rolling the "Quaker gun" on carriage wheels to a distant crest where the besieged Tories could see it, Colonel Washington gruffly gave them a choice of surrendering or being blown to bits. Believing him, they capitulated. While such exploits raised Patriot pride, news of Benedict Arnold's marauding expedition into Virginia roused rebel ire. All told, American morale continued to climb measurably as spring approached.

Fortress West Point was never far from George Washington's thoughts. Deciding a better road over the mountains to New Windsor would improve his ability to supply and support the post, he ordered one constructed. Coincidentally, Thomas Machin happened to be in the area and the Commander-in-Chief tapped the experienced Highlands hand to lay out the new route. Experiments, though Washington admitted they were something of a bother, still received his strong backing. Bauman conducted additional artillery trials and a Frenchman, Captain Lewis Garanger, gained permission to demonstrate some special but unspecified gunnery tests to verify his widely broadcast claim to possess some superior technique or knowledge. (Oddly, Lieutenant David Bushnell, inventor of the submarine and floating mines, was at West Point then, but he had apparently lost his urge to experiment. He was content to work as an engineer at improving the fortress.) There was much to be done in the way of refurbishing the forts and redoubts and batteries after the neglect of the preceding year. Obeying a directive from the Commander-in-Chief, Lieutenant Colonel Gouvion had prepared a report on the status of all works on the Point. It was submitted early in November, but Heath had done very little to correct the deficiencies noted; winter, mutiny, and his own disinclination toward engineering work had held him back. Three of the four redoubts above Fort Putnam needed batteries, and none had bombproofs. The engineer also recommended raising another strong point between Redoubts 3 and 4 to protect "the road coming from the furnace." More construction was called for to improve Wyllys, Clinton, and Putnam. So, too, did the defenses on Constitution Island and along the river need additional labor.

By all appearances, the only suggestion Heath acted upon was one requiring no action. "Sherburne redoubt," the engineer wrote, "was built in fascines in beginning the works, and now falls down, but it is of so little consequence that it is not to be repaired." Heath happily left it alone. Aware of the bald New Englander's past record of slovenly supervision of repairs and maintenance, Washington himself pushed the work that spring, prodding the commander and checking progress. As time to refloat the chain approached, the Virginian looked into the engineer's program for preparing new logs. He reminded Heath when it was time to have the gunboat refitted and placed back in the river. If Heath objected to such close supervision, he kept his complaints to himself.[20]

With a desire bordering on mania, Washington ached to capture Benedict Arnold. Reports of the traitor's depredations in Virginia infuriated him; Mount Vernon itself was endangered by the hated rogue. Once again he called upon troops from West Point; on 15 February he ordered Heath to assemble about a thousand light infantry for a march to Virginia. The men should be "robust and in other respects well chosen," and outfitted with good shoes. Continentals from elsewhere, along with local militia, were called upon to fill their places in the defenses. To Lafayette, Washington gave command of the expedition. The young French general was to move his force rapidly southward in an effort to catch the infamous marauder napping. Should Arnold "fall into your hands," Washington told Lafayette, you will execute him "in the most summary way." Lafayette arrived too late to get Arnold, but his presence in Virginia would pay a magnificent if unexpected dividend some months later by helping to pen Cornwallis in Yorktown.[21]

Meanwhile, Washington was thinking in terms of a joint American-French attack against New York City. For nearly a year, thousands of French soldiers had camped at Newport under General Rochambeau. This was the fourth year of alliance between France and the Patriots, but so far the two allies had been unable to coordinate their efforts. Dislike and distrust had been the most noted offspring of the coalition. Furthermore, Washington was by now aware of the growing reluctance in France to continue the expensive war. It looked like 1781 would be the final year of active French participation unless a decisive battle could be fought—and won. With those thoughts running through his head, he rode to Newport in March for a conference with Rochambeau. Returning to New Windsor after an absence of nearly three weeks, he was no nearer his dream of an attack against the British base in New York, but he had had the satisfaction of observing a large French fleet set sail to go to the assistance of Lafayette in Virginia. By month's end, though, he learned that the Frenchmen had brushed into a British squadron off the Chesapeake and had hastily returned to Newport. Sadly, the Commander-in-Chief informed McDougall, "The expedition against Arnold has failed."

Another conference was held between Washington and Rochambeau in Wethersfield, Connecticut, on 22 May. The American argued mightily for a combined assault against the English in New York; the Frenchman was noncommittal, while seeming to prefer a move to the Southland. Rochambeau knew a large French fleet with reinforcements was en route to America, due to arrive in July or August, but he withheld the information from his ally. The meeting was not cordial. Upon parting, the two generals had agreed only to combine their armies at the Hudson above New York City. Washington saw that agreement as a step toward attacking the city, Rochambeau as a leg on the journey south. Washington also thought they had settled upon sending the Newport fleet to Boston when the French army marched to the Hudson. He was furious, therefore, when the Duc de Lauzun, a dashing ex-lover of Marie Antoinette, arrived in New Windsor to report Rochambeau's decision to hold the vessels in Newport. The combined campaign was off to a shaky start.

Henry Clinton got wind of Washington's anticipated operations against his New York enclave and worriedly called on Cornwallis, then in Virginia, to send back some troops and withdraw with the remainder of his force to a post on the coast. Cornwallis obediently headed for Yorktown with Lafayette hanging on his heels. When the French reached the Hudson on 6 July, Clinton was more concerned than ever.

For over a month Rochambeau and Washington reconnoitered the approaches to Manhattan, contemplating possible courses of action. But until the large friendly fleet arrived, any attack was out of the question. They waited. Finally in mid-August a messenger galloped in with a letter from the French admiral. A great amphibious force consisting of over 25 sail of the line and 3,200 land troops, under command of Admiral de Grasse, would arrive on 3 September and would remain until the middle of October. The only problem was that de Grasse was sailing for the Chesapeake!

Dark thoughts coursed Washington's brain. He may have wanted to violate his own injunction against swearing. Once again he had to forsake his dream of retaking New York City, for an opportunity to operate in conjunction with a French fleet could not be ignored. With an alacrity which does credit to his flexibility, he ordered the two armies southward. Rochambeau was most pleased to obey.

In late August the French army crossed the Hudson at King's Ferry, awing the ragtag Americans with their resplendent white uniforms and flawless marching ability. Washington and Rochambeau took tea in Joshua Hett Smith's house on the 21st, a pause evoking memories of the near-loss of West Point. While the long, white columns were being ferried over the river, Rochambeau asked Washington to show him West Point, the famed fortress which had so stirred every visitor. The French commander "was not willing to pass so near West Point as nine miles without seeing it." At eight o'clock on the 23rd, the two allied commanders accompanied by several other officers, rode up to the defenses. Proudly, Washington pointed out the various works and described the theory of depth upon which the fortification was based. Rochambeau was duly impressed. One of his young officers, a cartographer named Alexandre Berthier, prepared a map of the complex for him.* The inspection over, and both armies west of the Hudson, the campaign was resumed. After a feint down the west side of the river to fool Henry Clinton, the two armies disappeared, marching rapidly southward. When they returned in triumph to the Hudson, the war would be all but won.

West Point had not been left untouched by all the preparations and plans and events of the spring and summer. In fact, it had been a much more than normally turbulent period for the post. First the mutinies and then the allied maneuvering had created excitement. Another factor assuring frequent release from boredom was a constant stream of visitors, especially "strangers of rank." West Point had become a show place. Everyone wanted to see the reputedly impregnable fortress. To a man, guests were amazed at "the prodigious labor necessary to transport and pile up steep rocks, huge trunks of trees, and enormous hewn stones" into works both "beautiful and well contrived." In fact, callers came so often that Congress, on Washington's recommendation, voted extra money to the West Point commander to permit him to cope with the heavy burden of entertaining. Spring's warmer weather brought out tourists in greater numbers, multiplying the hours spent in ceremony and show. But in spite of the manifold distractions, all essential functions of the garrison had to continue. The same warm winds which attracted visitors served notice that it was time once more to stretch the great chain across the river.[22]

Stapled to fresh logs, "the great chain was hauled from off the beach near the Red House at West Point and towed down to the blocks" by 280 men on 10 April. Next day, it was "properly fixed with great dexterity, and fortunately without any accident." The chain was a calendar for West Point's garrison. When it went in the water, spring was officially at hand; when it came up, winter followed. Spring had come once more to the Hudson River. And with it arrived a perennial spring problem, the need for replenishing exhausted food reserves. Provisions which had been earmarked for emergencies only, designed to permit the fortress to withstand an English siege, had been devoured to permit the men to withstand the siege of winter. Heath decried the shortage, telling Washington, "The reserves will be gone in a few days if relief does not arrive, and hunger must inevitably disperse the troops." The Virginian, who had been fighting the British with one hand and starvation with the other for six years, "determined to make one great effort more." He sent Heath in May into his native New England to plead with state governments to forward food.[23]

In the first of a series of personnel changes, Washington chose Robert Howe to replace Heath. The North Carolina general had performed well during the mutiny crisis, raising the Virginian's regard for him. Moreover,

---

* Berthier became famous in the Napoleonic Wars as Napoleon's indispensable chief of staff, his alter ego. A copy of his map of West Point can be seen in the USMA Library; the original is in the Princeton University Library.

with the massed French and Continental forces between New York City and the Highlands, little fear was felt for the security of the Point. Indeed, General Washington proposed in June to strip West Point's garrison of all but 440 soldiers, and those to be "the weakliest and worst men." He never actually let the number drop that low, but most of the trained and dependable troops were withdrawn to be replaced by militia or convalescents. Alexander McDougall superseded Howe in June. Washington, bracing for a barrage of protest, beat the Scot to the punch by informing him the Point was not "designed as a permanent command assigned you" and assuring him that he would get a field command at a proper time. To keep McDougall occupied, and the reduced garrison on its toes, Washington specified that the new commander should "visit the redoubts twice or thrice a week at uncertain periods," hold regular roll calls, store "ten days' wood, water, and provisions" in each redoubt, keep two sentries on every parapet, and maintain the works "perfectly clean and sweet." Moreover, boats were being gathered from up and down the river for the proposed attack on New York City. They were to be stored and guarded at West Point. Unable to gripe in his own behalf, McDougall complained loudly about the quality of men comprising the garrison. George Washington admitted they were poor specimens. He understood fully how "the persons employed by the different states to recruit their troops seem to pay more attention to complete the number required than to furnish able-bodied men for the service." But worse was yet to come. McDougall hadn't seen anything yet.[24]

At first, sentries on the road leading to West Point noticed nothing unusual about the slowly moving column of troops as it neared the outpost line. They watched, displaying no more than an interest born of boredom, as it wended its way up the grimy road in the August heat. Perhaps the convoy had more wagons than normal, thus accounting for the heavy dust and slow pace, but otherwise it looked like any other hot, tired body of soldiers. The first extraordinary detail discerned as the column drew closer was a surprising number of cripples. Then, with a start, one observer saw that *all* the newcomers were disabled. Men without arms walked, those missing a leg rode. Some had an eye gone, or a jaw shot away. A handful had been severely burned. As the disfigured men entered the post, people stopped to stare. The strange convoy was composed of an entire regiment of cripples. The Corps of Invalids had arrived to guard West Point.

McDougall's reaction was predictably immediate and angry: he had troubles enough already; these men would eat but could not work; many were unable to defend themselves, let alone the fortress. Washington listened to his wailing politely before replying, "The bringing forward the Corps of Invalids from Philadelphia and Boston was a matter of necessity and not choice; we must therefore submit to some inconveniences and put them to duties of the lightest kind."

The Commander-in-Chief felt sincere compassion for the wretched regiment. Its ranks were composed of old soldiers who had survived the rigors of a battle wound and the even more dangerous subsequent treatment by eighteenth-century surgeons. Those lost arms and eyes and legs had been left on bloody battlegrounds by Patriots fighting under Washing-

Detail from a map made for Rochambeau by Alexandre Berthier in 1781. A legend explains: "A. Profile of the wooden redoubts constructed at West Point. B. Profile of an embrasure in Fort Clinton showing how the fraises can be raised to close the embrasure." Courtesy of Princeton University Library.

305

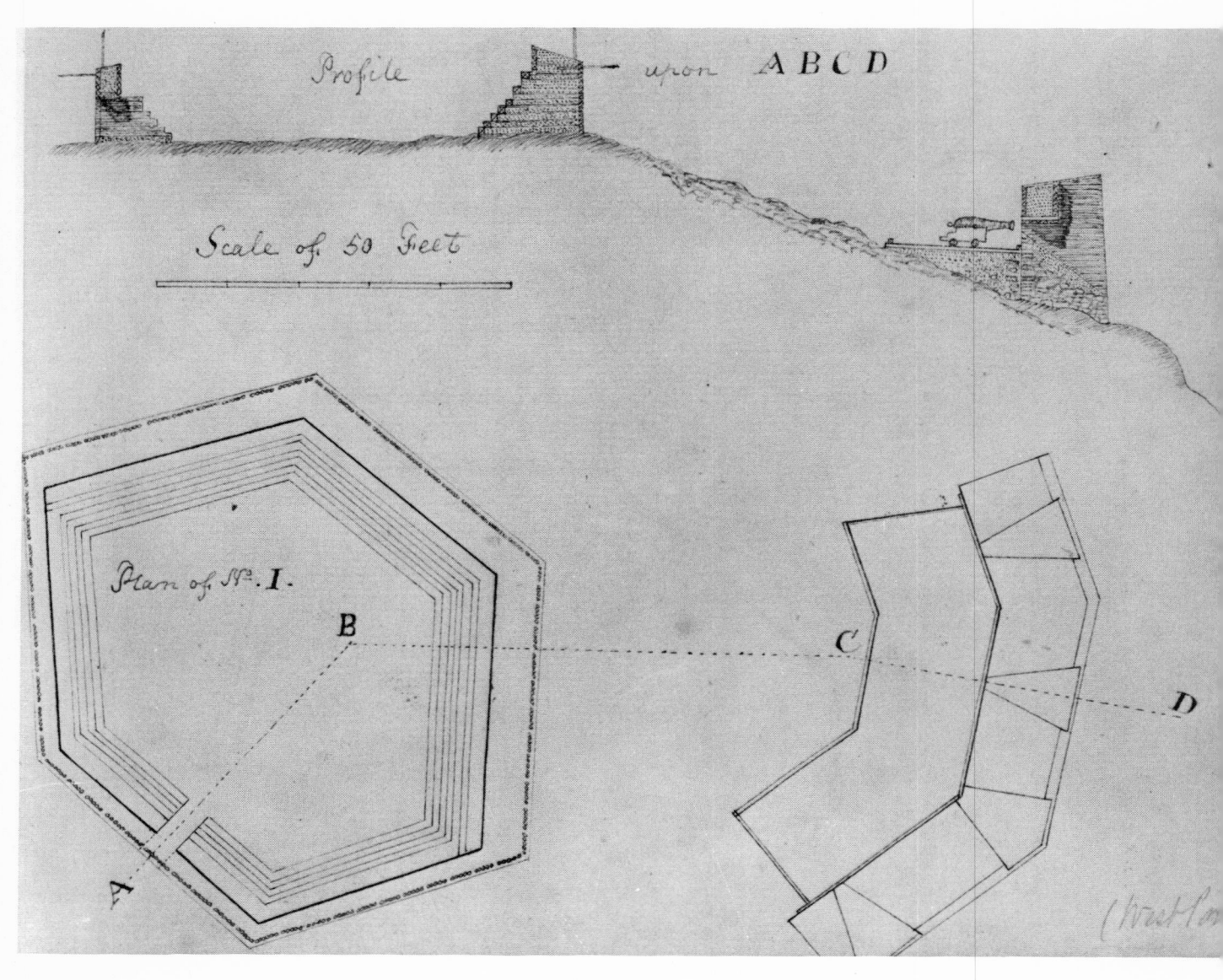

Profile ⟶ upon *A B C D*

Scale of 50 Feet

Plan of Nº. I.

B

C

A

D

Plans of Redoubts 1 and 2. Drawn in 1782 by Captain Ephraim Sergent.

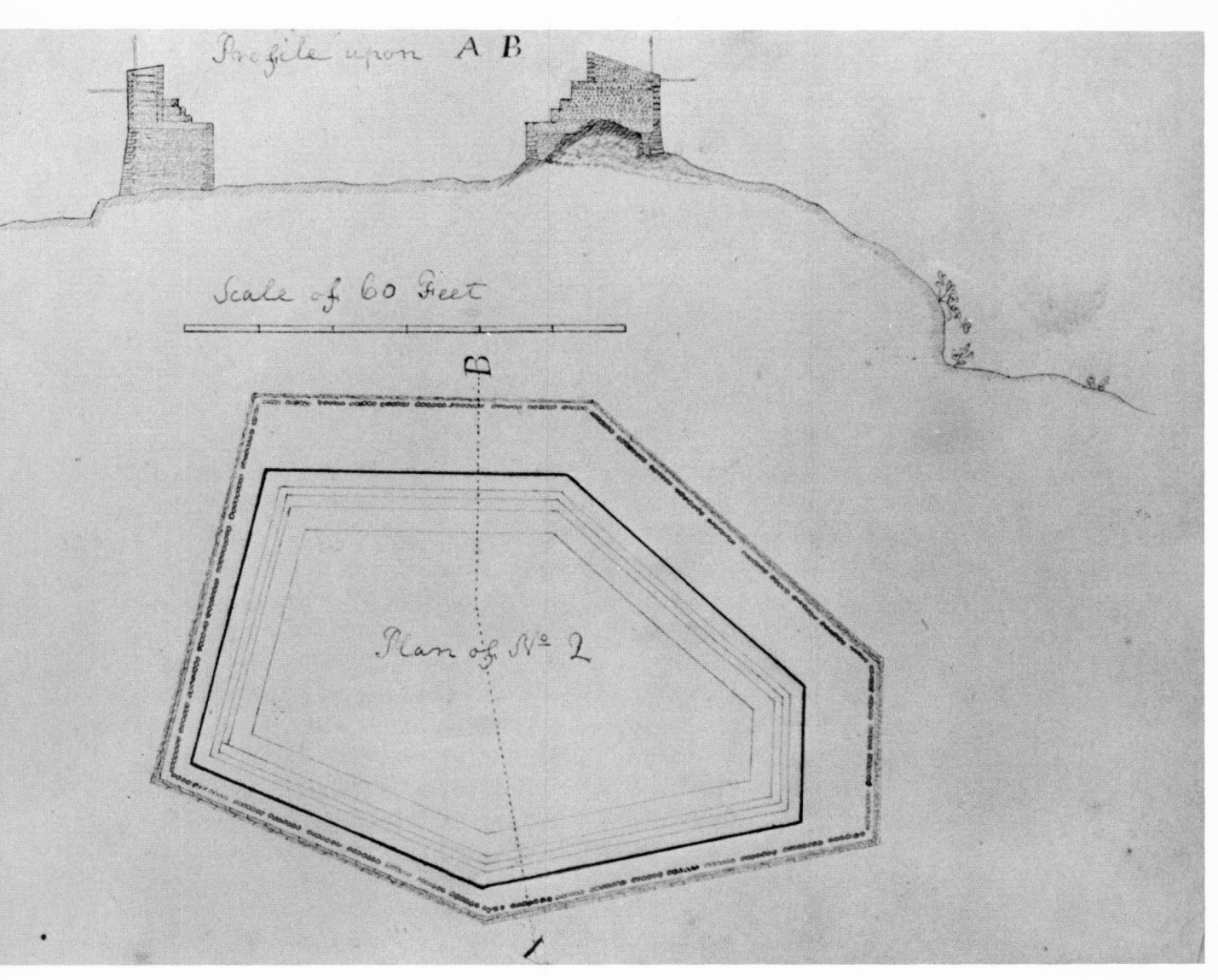

Profile upon A B

Scale of 60 Feet

B

Plan of Nº 2

307

ton's command. To a degree, he held himself responsible for them. Before they embarked on the journey to West Point, the Virginian had written their colonel, Lewis Nicola, directing him to pay the greatest attention "to the convenience and accommodation of this body of veterans, both on their march and in quarters." He also averred, "The pleasant and healthy situation of [West Point] which is remarkable for the salubrity of its air; the accommodations of a stationary post; and the importance of trusting its defence to a body of tried men; all point out very forcibly the propriety of employing your Corps as a part of the garrison." The General might have been solicitous for their health and comfort, but he was also practical enough to think "every man capable of doing garrison duty should be marched to West Point."[25]

McDougall snorted unhappily as he watched the cripples hobble about the post. Just as he was thinking nothing would ever surprise him again, his mouth suddenly fell open—he saw one of the invalids in a skirt. They even had disabled camp followers! A large woman wearing an artillery coat, her left arm shriveled and dangling limply, had strolled into his view. Sharply he asked Colonel Nicola why he permitted a camp woman to wear a uniform. Grinning broadly, the colonel explained that the woman was Margaret Corbin, a half-pay private, a "soldier" by act of Congress. She had been grievously wounded while helping her husband work an artillery piece in Fort Washington back in 1776. Her husband had been killed, but "Molly," her left breast horribly shredded and her arm nearly cut away by grapeshot, had lived. She was a bona fide member of the Corps. Her credentials were unimpeachable, Nicola assured the general. What was more, she could curse and swill grog better than most of the men. The Scotchman walked off, shaking his head.

Although no one foresaw the result, when the Corps of Invalids came to West Point the first step toward the establishment of the United States Military Academy at that rocky stronghold had been taken. Congress had founded the Corps in 1777, basically to provide a home for otherwise destitute veterans. The lawmakers thought a regiment of eight companies could be relied upon to guard towns and garrisons and hospitals, freeing able-bodied men for the field. But the Corps had the additional mission of serving "as a military school for young gentlemen." All subalterns of the invalid regiment were required to attend a school of mathematics. Moreover, every officer was assessed one day's pay per month to purchase "a regimental library of the most approved authors on tactics and the *petite guerre*." The old soldiers were expected to tutor young officer candidates. It somehow seems very proper, now, that the very first American organization designed to produce officers should have been assigned to West Point. It was to be a permanent home.[26]

When events drew him southward, George Washington remembered his promise to Alexander McDougall and offered him a field command. But, after all his protestations, the Scot preferred to remain in the Highlands. (In Virginia he would have been too far from his political base, an important consideration to the New Yorker who was a member of Congress as well as a general.) William Heath came again to command in the Highlands, armed with a clear mission to consider the security of the river citadel "the first object of your attention." Seventeen New England regiments, the Corps of Invalids, a legion of horse, a regiment of artillery, and "all such state troops and militia as are retained in service" comprised Heath's command. In 1777 Washington had gambled by leaving with Israel Putnam a detachment too small to defend the Highlands; he was not going to repeat that error in 1781. While fighting in Virginia, he wanted to have no undue worries over the Hudson's safety.[27]

Excitement departed with the allied army. Having lived in perpetual readiness and expectation most of the summer, officers and men left in the Highlands quickly found themselves submerged in unaccustomed quiet. All eyes were on the southern theatre. For once, the Hudson was in the backwater of war. Americans devoted themselves to gathering provisions and cutting wood, the British to consolidating posts in order to free men to reinforce Lord Cornwallis should he need help. Boredom came when bustle left.

Among those returning to West Point was Doctor Samuel Adams. Probably no one but McDougall disliked the place more than Adams. "Returning to this inhospitable point . . . affords no pleasing sensations," he grouched. Within a week he was weary of the tedium of life in the treeless fortress, writing, "Time rather hangs heavily on one hand." Each day was like the one before and the one after. Sharply at 8:30 every morning, drummers mounted the parapet of Fort Clinton to beat "The Pioneers' March." Men worked until drums rolling "Roast Beef" signaled them to lunch at noon. An hour later the hated drummers sounded again the call to toil. "Retreat" and then "Tattoo" ended labor and the day respectively. Anything to vary that almost inexorable routine was welcome. A group of about forty friendly Indians visited the Point, dancing wildly before dinner on the level ground near Moore's house, appearing "as much like devils as men." But they were just passing through, a moment's diversion. To kill some of the long hours, several individuals took to hiking along the redoubt trails. After checking all the forts for his own curiosity, Adams voted for Fort Wyllys as "the most complete work on the Point." Still the days were long. "Attended my patients," the doctor recorded on 18 October, "—a thing done every day but only mentioned for want of more interesting occurrences." On the fourth anniversary of Burgoyne's surrender, General Paterson "gave an elegant entertainment to all the officers of his brigade." The men, too, celebrated. Crewmen on the sloops managed to have a particularly gay time. Inebriated sailors fought each other in brawls ending when one or more of them fell from the deck to the bottom of the hold. A doctor would then be summoned, but he usually found the unconscious seamen "more drunk than hurt." No one seemed to care—it was a way to let off steam. For two interminable months, the garrison waited, listening intently for the outcome of Washington's struggle with Cornwallis.[28]

Then a rumor of victory flashed from town to town, reaching West Point on 24 October. "A happy event if true," was the conservative reaction. Men hardly dared believe it. Six days later "authentic intelligence arrived." Cornwallis had surrendered his entire army!

The garrison erupted into a violent, joyous orgy, the likes of which has not been seen since at West Point. First, Colonel John Crane threw a party for every officer in his artillery regiment. McDougall led the festivities at Crane's house. With a band of musicians playing exuberantly, the officers shouted and danced with complete abandon. Adams later told his diary, "If our joy on the glorious occasion may be measured by the quantities of liquor and wine we drank, it is beyond dispute that we were exceeding glad." The whooping men celebrated all that night. When Crane's liquor was consumed they returned to their rooms and huts to haul out private stores. At dawn they were still rejoicing, pausing only long enough to applaud the noise of "thirteen heavy cannon discharged at sunrise." After drinking a little coffee with a very hung-over Colonel Crane, the jubilant revelers took some wine and "cold collations" with General McDougall. Then, bringing their own plates and utensils, they all joined General Heath for a joyful lunch at one large table set up on the plain. At one o'clock, Colonel Rufus Putnam lined up two battalions and had them fire a rippling *feu de joie* four times over, after which thirteen huge guns boomed their happy message once again. Heath recalled fondly how in the afternoon "great festivity and social mirth prevailed." Officers were not alone in their uninhibited display of glee; soldiers, too, "had an extra boon on the occasion." In a transport of joy, Heath freed and pardoned every prisoner on the Point,* drawing a ringing "huzza!" from all the officers and unrecorded but surely heartfelt and jubilant cries from prisoners as they joined in the festivities. That evening saw "many droll capers cut," to include a wending, singing procession "in search of General Paterson" who must have finished celebrating earlier than most or else had found more private means of merrymaking. "Nor was numbers of men backward in getting drunk in honor of the day," Doctor Adams recorded when he sobered up.[29]

Gradually, nature and alcohol took its toll and the unrestrained binge petered out. Those three mad days were followed, not surprisingly, by one or two soft ones, but every trooper in the garrison wore a great grin to match his swollen head. The unbelievable had happened: the British were beaten.

---

* His action established a precedent of granting total amnesty on special occasions which is now a cherished tradition—especially among wayward cadets—at the Military Academy.

21

STRATEGY...

BEAMING after their Yorktown victory, singing Continentals marched proudly back to their station on the Hudson River and prepared for winter. Except for two drawn-out years of waiting, the war was over. Great Britain was defeated. Not that the ultimate outcome was so obvious to Americans; many sensed the war had turned a decisive corner, but not even the most optimistic foresaw an immediate end to the conflict. Washington had to assume more battles would be fought, more campaigns conducted, more winters withstood. His instinctive move, therefore, was to return to his old haunt in the rugged hills near the great river.

"English command of the Hudson River would prove fatal" to the Patriot cause. Thus, unequivocally, did George Washington sum up his view of the strategic importance of that waterway in the American Revolutionary War. Quite clearly, the Commander-in-Chief was from first to last convinced he could ill afford to lose the river; and he was joined in that conviction by nearly every other Patriot leader. Because the Americans did win the war, and because the British were never able to establish control over Henry Hudson's River, it has been assumed down through the years that the General was correct in his assessment. Lately, however, the value of the Hudson has become the subject of an emerging controversy. A few historians have begun to wonder if it was so important after all. Some have flatly refuted Washington's appraisal. One has stated categorically that "there was no strategic center, in fact no strategic centers, in America, the capture of which would give Britain victory." Addressing himself specifically to the subject of the Hudson River, an eminent scholar believes "mere severance of the communications between New England and the states to the southwest would have left the Yankees unconquered and defiant" and would not have brought about their collapse. Another's views are strong enough to lead him to speak of the "stupidity" of the British desire to split the colonies at the line of the Hudson.[1]

What is the truth? Would loss of the Hudson to the British have meant the concomitant loss of the War of Independence? Or would such a defeat have been merely another setback for the Patriots, painful, perhaps, but not decisive? In short, was retention of the Hudson River really the master link in Washington's strategy or is that simply another myth from the era of the Revolution? Surprisingly, historians have not bothered methodically and analytically to investigate this question. They have either accepted uncritically the thesis of the Hudson's role as "master" of the Revolutionary War, or, without benefit of thorough research, have labelled that thesis a "myth." So important a subject deserves closer examination.[2]

To appreciate the peculiar importance of the Hudson at the time of the break from England, it must be remembered that North America was then a near primordial land, pricked ever so slightly by civilization. Perhaps the dominant geographical fact of the rebellious British colonies was their vast size in relation to population. Most of the people were to be found near the sea in a large arc sweeping from Boston to Savannah. In this 1,100-mile stretch of territory were dispersed some 2.5 million persons—fewer than live today in the single borough of Brooklyn. Also worthy of note are statistics showing that there were but four towns of more than 10,000 inhabitants in all the thirteen colonies when the war began. Significantly, the Hudson River almost perfectly bisected the population of the colonies; the geographical center of population was somewhere in northern New Jersey.

Roads—what few there were—can only be described as having been exceedingly poor. Not until after the Revolution did turnpikes and plank roads, not to mention bridges, snake out to link the cities and towns. Travelers of the late eighteenth century depended on fords or ferries more or less joined by muddy, rough, narrow roads which were, in essence, no more than lanes cleared through the forests. One early law, in an attempt to improve pioneer roads, required the removal of all stumps over one foot high. Travel was time-consuming, exhausting, undependable, and even dangerous. Peggy Arnold's trip from Philadelphia to West Point—a mere four-hour automobile jaunt today—consumed nearly a week by carriage in 1780. In such a land settlers were forced to rely on rivers for transportation. It is no accident, therefore, that the forward edge of civilization followed streams inland. Roads, too, followed rivers; at first leading from the tiny settlements to the water and later paralleling the river routes.

An appreciation of the paucity of roads and the role of rivers in colonial America provides a clearer understanding of the importance of the Hudson. Navigable by seagoing vessels to Albany, that watercourse had opened the area above the Highlands to settlement. Westward from Albany, the Mohawk River Valley was being cleared and peopled, while northern Connecticut profited by the easy egress to the Atlantic. The significance of the Hudson was not missed by colonial officials. The Surveyor General, reporting on New York in 1773, said the Hudson, after slight improvements, could connect with both Lake Ontario and Lake Champlain. "If this was done," he prophesied, "Hudson's River would lead into one of the most extensive inland navigations in the world." In all preceding colonial wars—and this fact did not pass unnoticed by American generals—the Hudson had figured prominently. A cursory map study will confirm New York's singular position among the colonies. It alone fronted on the Atlantic Ocean, the Great Lakes, the St. Lawrence River, and tributaries leading to the Mississippi River Valley. The Hudson–Lake George–Lake Champlain Portage was the most important path from Canada to New York, while the route from the St. Lawrence to Lake Ontario gave ready access to the entire western reaches of New York. And a portage from Lake Ontario to the Mohawk River led again to the Hudson.[3]

Economically, Americans existed at little more than subsistence level. Though relatively wealthy in agricultural produce, they lacked manufactured items. Colonial factories were constantly improving the quality and quantity of output, but they were unable to match demand. By way of example, the great percentage of all weapons and powder used during the war were imported from Europe. Trade, therefore, was immensely important.

The "granary" of the colonies was bounded generally by the Connecticut River on the northeast and the Potomac River on the south. The Connecticut River Valley exported wheat and corn; the Mohawk and Schoharie Valleys usually had a surplus of grain; Baltimore shipped flour and wheat throughout the war; one of Washington's reasons for remaining in Valley Forge in 1777–1778 was to be near the Pennsylvania supply of flour; and Virginia raised a surfeit of wheat, causing the merchants of Alexandria, in 1781, to ask for state controls. It should be noted, here, that the Hudson River sliced through the eastern portion of the rebel granary, leaving the bulk of the flour producing area to the south and west.

Livestock was, of course, raised throughout the colonies, but that bred in Connecticut was particularly important during the War of Independence. Connecticut's livestock exports before and during the Revolutionary War were considerable. Horses, cattle, pigs, and sheep were raised for export and constituted the bulk of Connecticut's out-of-state trade. In general, then, it is accurate to say Washington relied on lands east of the river for meat, on those west of it for bread.

That, briefly, is the America which was startled by the shots at Lexington and Concord. Its few people, living near the ocean and rivers, subsisted for the most part on what they alone could grow and make. Its poorly charted lands were as poorly served by inadequate roads. And its young factories and mills were incapable of providing sufficient implements of war. This was the meager setting for the American Revolution; and it is the background against which one must ponder the Hudson's value.

First, what was the overall British view of the waterway?

From the very start, English strategists recognized the uniqueness of the Hudson. The historian of the British Army, J. W. Fortescue, clearly described the dilemma facing any English general striving to attack the Continental Army:

> . . . there was no stronghold inland which could command any great tract of country, and therefore no certain line of operations. The enemy had but to retire inland, if pressed, and the invader could not safely follow them, from the impossibility of maintaining his line of communications. *The one exception to the rule was the line of the Hudson. . . .*[4]

The Hudson held out the promise of permitting offensive operations, while fertile lands within reach of its banks could help feed the royal army. Owning the Hudson, the British could have linked hands with their forces in Canada, thus isolating New England. (Their abiding desire to capture and control the river has already been brought out, especially in previous chapters dealing with the campaigns of 1776, 1777, 1779, and 1780.)

Another important—though relatively little-known—reason for British interest in the river was the access it would have afforded to their Indian allies on the frontier. In all probability, the English did not relish exciting the Indians to war any more than did the colonists. The issue was debated conscientiously, but was resolved by 1777. "I have ever been of the opinion," wrote Burgoyne from Canada, "that it is a mistaken idea of humanity in not employing the Indians. I am afraid that it will be proved so, as if they are not for your Majesty's service, they will act as enemies." A later counselor, probably Lord George Germain, added, ". . . the Indians are from interest the faithful allies of Great Britain and the natural enemies of the Americans. . . . A diminution of the number of the Americans and a repulsion of them towards the sea coast is their true interest." Indians were to be used.[5]

British control of the Hudson would have opened for the tribes free access to all of New York, the eastern part of New England, and the newly settled areas in northern Pennsylvania. Also, it would have facilitated British efforts to supply and support Indian depredations elsewhere. The English were well aware of the possibilities. A memorandum in the hands of George III predicted, "The possession of the N. River wou'd open our communication with the Indians, who then might act in concert, and attack such places at such times as we might direct." General William Howe praised the benefits to accrue from the occupation of Albany. The prime gain, he said, would be the opening of "free intercourse with the Indians" without which the British could expect no help from them. George III's plan for 1779 concluded that the results of British occupation of the Hudson would be to strangle the colonies, gain supplies and support, and bring in the Indians. Sir Henry Clinton, defending his judgment during the fateful campaign of Yorktown in 1781, summarized New York's (and the Hudson's) importance to the British: "I cannot agree . . . that the Chesapeake should become the seat of war . . . at the expence of abandoning New York; as I must ever regard this post to be of the utmost consequence whilst it is thought necessary to hold Canada, with which, and the Northern Indians, it is so materially connected." Beyond a doubt the English saw the Hudson as a route to the redskins, and they anticipated employing the waterway in that manner should it fall into their hands.[6]

It cannot be claimed that the English were unanimously agreed on the best method for defeating the colonies. Sir William Howe, after all, chose a Pennsylvania campaign rather than a Hudson expedition in 1777; moreover, he directed the evacuation of the Hudson Highlands after Sir Henry had captured them in October of that year. Also, there were some who agreed with General Edward Harvey, the Acting Commander in Chief of the British Army, who, as early as 1775, wondered whether a British force could ever conquer America. Counsels are seldom united on the mode of waging war. Even so, it is difficult, if not impossible, to find a single, responsible British official who distinctly repudiated the "line of the Hudson" strategy. By far the greater proportion of officers openly agreed with the sentiments expressed by one of Burgoyne's captured officers, who, while being transported down the Hudson, ruefully noted, ". . . had we kept possession of the North River, the war would have been by this time, nearly terminated in favor of Great Britain." And, quite interestingly, Benedict Arnold was hardly fitted for his new, red coat before he appended the weight of his word to the perennial plan to seize the Hudson. There were but two ways to win the war, he stated:

> The first is to collect the whole army and beat Washington, secure the posts which command the Hudson, which could be done in a few days by regular approaches, and cut off the Northern from the Southern Colonies. The supplies of meat for Washington's army are on the east side of the river and the supplies of bread on the west; were the Highlands in our possession, Washington would be obliged to fight or to disband his army for want of provisions.[7]

A modern British historian, Piers Mackesy, looking at the War of Independence from the perspective of two centuries and with benefit of all the recently opened and published documentary sources, corroborates the judgment of his eighteenth-century countrymen. Without hesitation, he writes, "For the enemy, British control of the Hudson would have been disastrous."[8]

So much then for the English. What did the river mean to the Patriots?

On the American side, it is clear Washington and his generals were sincerely convinced that loss of the Hudson would: (1) provide the British an easy route of communications through the continent; (2) open up a large fertile region to the enemy; (3) imperil the neighboring states; (4) permit free intercourse between the English and the Loyalists; (5) isolate New England, thus splitting America's population and resources; and (6) expose the Indians to royal control. Not surprisingly, this list reads like a British set of reasons for taking the Hudson. The first four items are self-evident and need no amplification. A brief resume of the impact of the latter two on the Patriot war effort will highlight their strategic consequence.[9]

For its military supplies and stores of food, the Continental Army was greatly dependent on New England. Huge magazines were established in Connecticut and Massachusetts to funnel provisions and equipment to the area of operations. Beef and pork moved westward while flour flowed eastward from New York. Uniforms came from Eastern mills to clothe the rebel army. In one six-month period, a single Massachusetts firm shipped 18,000 uniforms. Privateering and regular shipping poured uncounted quantities of goods into northeast ports. Those were then transshipped across the Hudson to Washington. It also proved impossible for the British to blockade the New England coast. "Massachusetts," Alexander Hamilton ventured, "is in a different situation from any other [state]. Its position has made it impossible for the enemy to intercept its trade. . . . It has become in consequence the mart of the states northward of Pennsylvania. . . ." But Massachusetts was not alone. Other New England States shared in this high-seas trade. Thousands of muskets and scores of cannon entered America through Yankee ports. Washington became exultant at one point, claiming so many arms were at Portsmouth "we shall have no further complaint for the want of them." Moreover, in the first two and a half years of the war, 90 percent of all gunpowder used by the United States was imported—and not a small portion of this all-important item landed in New England. Almost as critical as meat and gunpowder to the armies of that age was rum. For much of its supply of this valuable commodity, the Continental Army looked east of the Hudson.[10]

In addition to impeding the flow of supplies from New England, loss of the Hudson would have cancelled the considerable resources the Commander-in-Chief drew from the Hudson River Valley itself. Flour, lumber, and grain were major exports from lands bordering the river, while the region around Albany was a primary source of draft horses for the Patriot cause. Further, as supplies of meat continued to dwindle, Washington contracted for appreciable amounts of Hudson River fish to supplement the diet of his soldiers. It should pass undisputed to say the Americans deemed it quite necessary to block any British attempt to interdict the supply routes over the Hudson.

A look at the sources of manpower in Revolutionary America is illuminating. The four eastern states provided virtually half the men who fought under Continental colors. This is particularly amazing when it is remembered the army was rarely in New England after the British left Boston. (For example, only 800 men in the pay of Congress were to be found east of the Hudson in 1779.) By the crucial year of 1781, the year the campaign of Yorktown was fought, the total Continental Army had shrunk to 13,000. Of those, over 7,000 were New Englanders. The United States did not dare risk having the source of such considerable support dry up behind a British-owned Hudson River.

Now, one must ask what would have been the impact on the Continental Army if the British had succeeded in blocking its crossing sites over the Hudson? How would the disruption of supplies and manpower have affected Washington's war effort?

Tribulations for want of provisions can be traced throughout the war. The horrors of winter cantonments hardly need further exploration. The lament of the wretched soldiers—"no pay, no clothes, no provisions, no

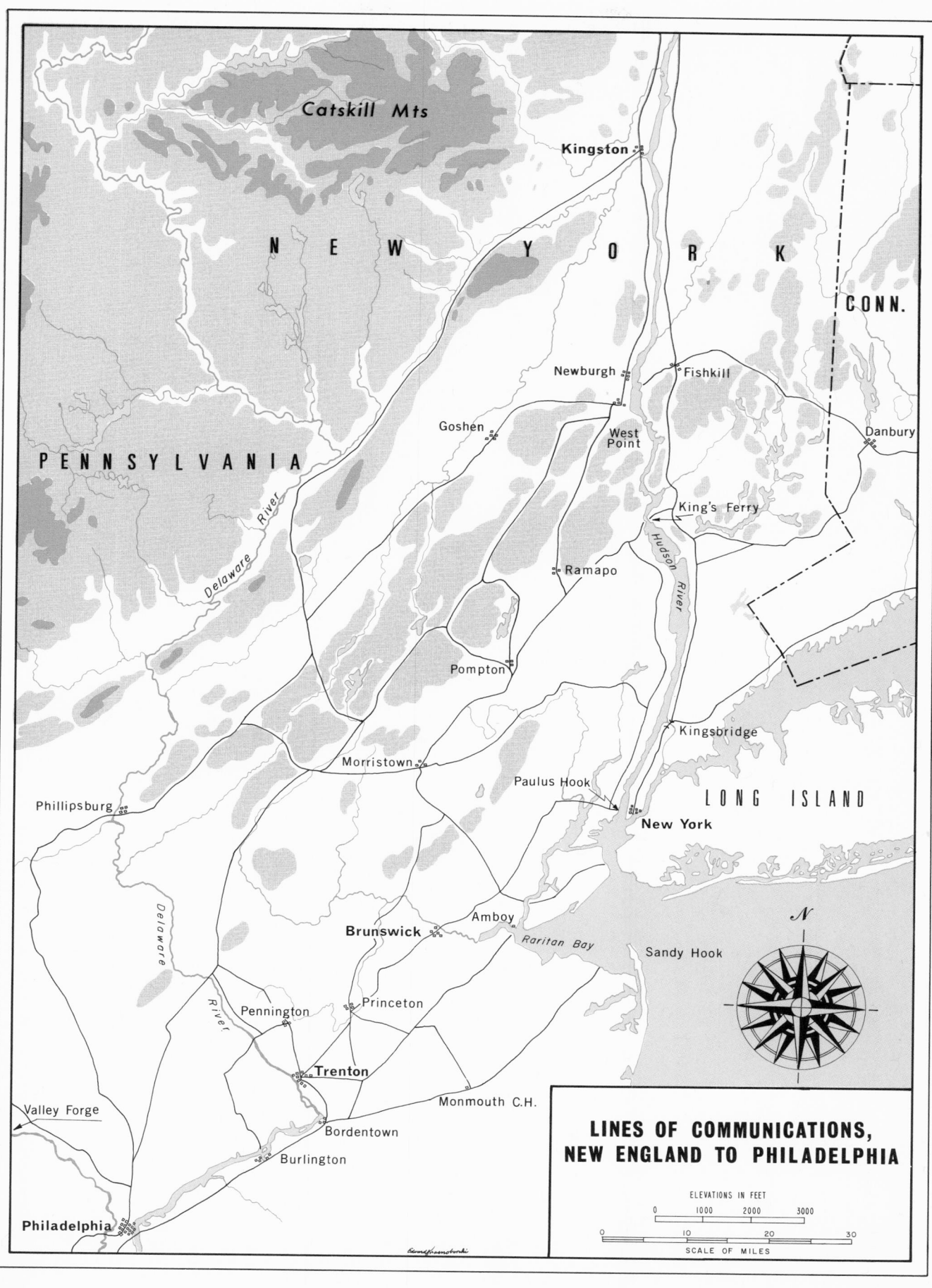

Catskill Mts

N E W   Y O R K

CONN.

Kingston

Newburgh   Fishkill

Goshen   West Point   Danbury

PENNSYLVANIA

King's Ferry

Delaware River

Hudson River

Ramapo

Pompton

Kingsbridge

Morristown

Paulus Hook

LONG ISLAND

Phillipsburg

New York

Delaware River

Amboy

Brunswick   Raritan Bay   Sandy Hook

Princeton

Pennington

Trenton

Valley Forge

Monmouth C.H.

Bordentown

Burlington

Philadelphia

Edward Krasnoborski

**LINES OF COMMUNICATIONS,
NEW ENGLAND TO PHILADELPHIA**

ELEVATIONS IN FEET

0   1000   2000   3000

0   10   20   30

SCALE OF MILES

rum"—was not exaggerated. At Valley Forge, just before Christmas, the despairing Commander-in-Chief informed Congress that his men could not defend themselves, so weak were they from hunger. He darkly estimated another few days' bad weather would destroy the army. By January, nearly four thousand men were unfit for duty simply from lack of clothing. Then, in the nick of time, New England supplies rescued the pitiable rabble. Cattle from the East made the difference between life and death, while great quantities of Yankee clothing eventually relieved the nakedness of the soldiers. Washington stated he could not have operated without the supplies that passed over the Hudson.[11]

The anguish of Valley Forge was not unique. By the middle of December 1779, the situation in the Continental camp at Morristown was even worse. Washington vowed the army was in the worst straits ever and would be forced to disband within a fortnight if food and clothing did not materialize. As the New Year arrived, severe cold and want of food placed the destitute horde in a critical state. Helplessly, Washington watched as his troops, who had been four or five days without meat, began to ravage the country. Living from day to day, the Patriots barely lasted the terrible winter; one wonders whether they could have survived without food from east of the Hudson. Furthermore, the precarious situation did not abate with the coming of spring. In April the faithful band was reduced to four days' supply of meat with no more in sight. Officers feared, with reason, the dissolution of the army. Two droves of New England cattle arrived and Washington credited them with relieving the explosive situation.[12]

Not only did food and clothing from the east maintain the army, those supplies made it possible for Washington to employ his force. Prior to the decisive Yorktown campaign, the Americans were "distressed beyond expression" for want of meat. Washington, as a last resort, sent General Heath to New England in search of rum and beef. The success of the campaign of 1781, Heath was told, depended upon the results of his mission. Heath was able to forward so many cattle to the army on its march to Yorktown that Washington, in what must have been a novel experience for him, finally had to order the shipments stopped. If an army truly marches on its stomach, New England beef had a leading role in Cornwallis' downfall. The Continental Army was also reinforced prior to its move to Virginia by most of the cannon, mortars, powder, shot, shells, and other military stores in Massachusetts and Rhode Island. Had the British controlled the Hudson, such a transfer of equipment would not have been possible. For that matter, neither could the French Army have crossed to march with the Americans.

Washington quite likely could not have held his forlorn followers together had the flow of supplies from New England been stopped. At the very least, one conclusion must lie beyond all argument: without those supplies the sufferings, and hence the casualties, would have been greatly increased.

As mentioned earlier, the four states east of New York furnished nearly half the men for the Continental Army. By virtue of the center of military operations having shifted away from New England, very few of the

Eastern draftees fought near their homes. The psychological blow of New England's being separated from the remaining colonies would have produced several unfortunate side effects. In the first place, the Yankees would have been somewhat more loathe to send their men to fight in other colonies. The danger facing their own state would have appeared much magnified, a fact which would have made the men more prone to desert the Continental service in favor of home defense. It would have been difficult for them to have comprehended a supreme loyalty to America while their families were stranded, vulnerable and unprotected, beyond the Hudson. The actual extent to which Washington's strength would have been reduced defies assumption, but we can say the army would have been noticeably weakened by a loss of manpower.

In sum, then, Patriot concern with retaining those crucial supply lines across the Hudson River does indeed seem to have been well founded. British occupation of the waterway would have dealt a traumatic blow to Washington's supply and personnel systems, and both were at best tenuous to begin with.

Just as scholars have tended to slough off as unimportant the British interest in Indians, too few historians have recognized the major place held by the savages in American minds. Most vividly do documents of the Revolution dramatize the Americans' anxiety over the Indian problem. It could be argued that no other single factor, in relation to its effect on the people, has been so underplayed in the various accounts of the Revolution. Beyond debate is the very real concern felt by all Patriot leaders and the constant fear experienced by those citizens unfortunate enough to live within reach of marauding war parties. Such fears were perpetuated by actual events—which were awful enough—as well as by an exaggerated manner of reporting Indian atrocities. One poem, for instance, written to relate the wanton murder of a young woman, depicts the Indians slinking through the forest "like beasts of prey, in quest of human blood" to slaughter an aged man, a mother with suckling child, and a girl on her way to be married.

Not yet ten days in office as Commander-in-Chief, Washington admonished against permitting the British to draw Indians into the conflict. Hopes for winning tribal neutrality continued through 1775. Desperate efforts were launched to convince the chiefs of the wisdom in avoiding the struggle. Washington personally received Indian delegations, passed out presents, and strove to impress all the tribes with the strength of Continental forces. However, by 1776 it became more and more obvious that the Indians would not observe neutrality, but would probably fight for the side which appeared stronger.

In 1777, the question was brought into the open when Burgoyne utilized Indians to assist his expedition. Some tribes remained loyal to the Americans and a few maintained neutrality, but most of the ferocious northern and northwestern nations, particularly the feared Iroquois, sided with the British. Each succeeding year through 1783 saw frontier areas ablaze with burning settlements as raid followed raid, massacre succeeded massacre. The United States had failed to keep the Indians aloof and, largely, had failed to gain their support against the King. The only alternative for Washington was to fight them.

To hold the redskins at bay, forts were constructed and manned on the frontiers, and several expeditions were mounted against the marauders' bases. Partly to counteract the English use of Indians, Washington ordered Colonel Daniel Morgan to organize a picked corps of riflemen. These men were trained to operate as braves against the British. As Continental forces in New York in 1777 showed evidence of buckling under the pressure of Burgoyne's advance, Washington committed Morgan's Corps. "The people in the Northern Army seem so intimidated by the Indians," he wrote, "[that I am sending Morgan's Riflemen] who will fight them in their own way."[13]

All these attempts to cope with the Indian threat amply portray the colonists' dread of the red man. To have permitted the tribes an unimpeded access to the Hudson Valley would have been unthinkable. Yet, British control over the Hudson would have accomplished that very thing. Standing alone, the Indian situation would have made the Hudson loom high on the list of places to defend.

Washington appears to have been correct in his evaluation of the river's worth. It was undoubtedly vitally important for all the reasons he mentioned. But one must look farther yet. There are other factors to consider, factors, perhaps, which Washington sensed rather than reasoned, felt rather than articulated. To understand them, one must comprehend two phenomena that colored George Washington's view of his world and his war; namely, the colonial heritage which had shaped him, and the very nature of revolutionary warfare itself.

First, it is a too common oversimplification to picture enraged Americans rushing to defend their seashores from British despotism. On more careful consideration, it should become rather evident that the people inhabiting America in that day would have been quite concerned with their more traditional enemy to the west and north—the hostile frontier itself. Within the lifetime of all—and in the vivid memory of the leaders—had occurred the French and Indian War and numerous Indian atrocities. The constant, cold, harsh reality of the frontier was a fact of life. Danger had heretofore lurked in the inland forests; the Atlantic Ocean had been the source of friendship and succor. Historically, the link to England had been the maternal tie, while the north and west had been the source of sudden terror and violent death. It is hardly plausible, therefore, to expect the colonists, even in their most violent opposition to the British, to have lost an older fear of an older enemy. The feud with Parliament was, after all, a relatively recent one which had become intransigent only after undergoing a "test by fire." Dislike of the British was a new emotion; it did not supplant fear of the frontier. Rather, it was superimposed on the older dread.

This contention is not intended to belittle the threat posed by British control of the Atlantic; it is to place in better perspective the frontier as the historical direction of danger. Washington's army could not simply "square off" at an enemy from the east; he was, in essence, surrounded before he began to fight. And, by reason of their personal, bitter experiences, Americans of that era must surely have ascribed a more sinister aspect to the frontier than we normally attribute to it. To be better aware of this facet of their outlook is to be better prepared to probe the colonists' comprehension of the Hudson's strategic value.

Secondly, in a gross oversimplification of an awesomely complex subject, revolutionary warfare can be classed as offensive warfare. On the one side is a fixed or established order. On the other are ranged forces intent on overthrowing or displacing that establishment. To be successful, these revolutionary forces must attack the set order. Whether this be by riot, subversion, or open warfare is beside the point. By definition, the rebel cause must seek the initiative. The all-permeating theme, from the first conscious decision to revolt to the final planning for the climactic battle, is the insurgents' desire to seize the initiative.

With those two factors in mind, let us survey the situation as the American Revolutionary War was triggered by bloody skirmishes in April of 1775.

Practically by default, revolutionary leaders found themselves in control of thirteen colonies. This was a great and fortunate stroke, for it meant they would not have to win over any of those colonies by force. The single lodgment of British troops was almost immediately besieged in Boston. Elsewhere, royal forces held the vast region of Canada, a few strong points in Florida, some scattered forts along the frontier, the province of Nova Scotia, several islands in the West Indies, and the Lake Champlain forts in northern New York.

The almost instinctive offensive bent of the insurgents is nowhere better evidenced than in their rapid strike at Fort Ticonderoga. By the time the Continental Congress had reconvened—only a fortnight after the eruption of fighting in Massachusetts—Ethan Allen and Benedict Arnold had seized Ticonderoga and all its stores of military equipment. Perusal of the Commander-in-Chief's writings in the six months following his appointment provides evidence of a burning impulse to maintain the initiative gained by Allen and Arnold. In June Washington ordered preparations begun to "facilitate any future operation" into Canada. He exhorted General Schuyler, in July, to "expedite every movement" aimed at bringing Canadians into the Continental fold. During August he conferred with the Massachusetts Legislature on the advisability of attacking Nova Scotia. That same month found him completing plans for Arnold's invasion of Canada by way of the Kennebec River. As September opened, the General wrote to the people of Bermuda pleading for their support. By late September he was chafing under the unwelcome stalemate at Boston. He informed Congress: "The state of inactivity in which this army has lain for some time past by no means corresponds with my wishes, by some decisive stroke, to relieve my country from the heavy expences its subsistence must create." In November he was investigating once more the possibilities of invading Nova Scotia, and, a day before Christmas, he recommended an attack of the British base at St. Augustine, Florida.[14]

For the duration of the conflict, the leaders of the Revolution nurtured a permanent ambition to gain and retain the initiative. Numerous plans were laid for excursions into Canada, and several expeditions were actually launched against British and Indian forces in the west and northwest. Nova Scotia and Florida continued to receive consideration, while Bermuda was mentioned as a possible objective as late as 1782. Washington never failed to probe for opportunities to smash the various coastal enclaves held by his opponents; each English seizure, from Boston to Savannah, was met by American efforts to forge a counterattack, while the recovery of New York City was constantly in the forefront of the Commander-in-Chief's thinking. Even in the midst of the despair of Valley Forge, Patriots debated a plan to attack Howe in Philadelphia. Although mostly stillborn, those persistent plans for hitting British lodgments on American soil add substance to the picture of American insurgents seeking the initiative, behaving aggressively. Often forced by circumstances to act defensively, they were, in truth, markedly offensive-minded.[15]

A direct relationship between the Hudson River and the Revolutionaries' need to grasp the initiative becomes starkly obvious when geography and seapower are considered. The United States was unable to contest seriously British naval superiority. That primary reality prohibited effective attacks on Bermuda and the West Indies, made impractical any earnest effort to invade Nova Scotia or Florida, and invalidated most plans to eliminate coastal strong points. Lacking naval means to operate against any of those areas, Washington was therefore limited to Canada and the frontier posts. The possession of the Hudson was absolutely necessary for the prosecution of an advance toward either objective. The Hudson–Lake Champlain portage was the primary route into Canada while the Hudson–Mohawk axis led into Indian country. British ownership of the Hudson, coupled with the virtual impregnability of their fleet-protected possessions, would have reduced the American offensive threat to little more than harassment. By seizing the river, royal forces would have taken a very large step toward rendering impotent the rebels' initiative.

Introduction of the French fleet in American waters failed at first to alter the situation. Assuredly, it aided the American cause as it reduced British advantage, but changes wrought were relative rather than absolute. For example, the odds for a successful invasion of Nova Scotia would have been improved by support from the French fleet. However, such an attack remained impractical because the communication lines would have depended upon long-term French superiority on the ocean. Given the presence of the powerful British fleet and the absence of allied unity of command, such dependence simply was not feasible. Witness the failures of the French naval arm in 1778, 1779, and 1780.

In addition to the Patriot requirement to assert the initiative, there was an enduring interest—almost a preoccupation—in lands to the north and west, with Canada and the frontier.

The peculiar position of Canada in the colonial mind deserves closer investigation. To be sure, Canada was a candidate for invasion by the Continental Army. It was also a constantly threatening source of English irruption into the United States. But Canada assumed an aspect of importance that was much more than purely military.

The natural enmity between the colonists—particularly the Yankees and Yorkers—and the Canadians can be traced from the long French occupation of Canada, through the bitterness of the French and Indian War, down to the Quebec Act of 1774. That act raised impassioned outcries in the thirteen colonies to the South. It permitted a Catholic hierarchy to occupy a favored position in Canada and compounded that insult by extending the borders of the province southward to the Ohio River. A Catholic Quebec was anathema to Protestants in New England, while the thought of losing their claims to the western lands raised the nettle of most of the colonists.[16]

The First Continental Congress angrily resolved that the Quebec Act violated the colonists' rights. Establishing French law and the Catholic religion in Quebec was "to the great danger of the neighboring British Colonies." The delegates feared an extension of Quebec to the western borders of their own lands would discourage future settlement and create an antagonistic country in the west "whenever a wicked ministry shall choose to direct."[17]

Canada, then, was much more than a desirable military objective. As one of the political causes which helped ignite the Revolution, it remained a political objective of the war. Much has been written of the efforts to take Canada in 1775–1776, but relatively little has been said of the residual, even habitual, nature of the rebels' passion to annex, by guile or by force, their northern neighbor.

Following its October 1774 denouncements of the Quebec Act, the First Continental Congress dispatched a long letter to the inhabitants of Canada exhorting them to join in the common cause against King and Parliament. That letter failed; but, after redcoats and militia tangled in the spring of 1775, the Second Continental Congress resolved to plead again with the Canadians for a linking of arms against Great Britain. Initially it was decided to launch no invasion of Canada, but, fearing attack from the north and perhaps growing dubious of winning support by persuasion, Congress abruptly changed its position and authorized an expedition. The courageous but vain efforts of Richard Montgomery and Benedict Arnold ensued. A letter urging the people to rise against British rule accompanied the army into Canada. Washington, hoping to avoid alienating the Canadians, imposed severe standards of discipline to preclude any adverse incidents in the wake of the invasion. He even went so far as to suggest to Arnold that the first soldier caught injuring a Canadian or an Indian should be summarily executed as an example to others.[18]

As forebodings of repulse darkened the beginning of 1776, Washington rushed reinforcements to the north. With Canada in British hands, he wrote, the outcome of the war would be doubtful, whereas England, without Canada, could not win. To improve his communications, the General then issued funds to begin construction of a road leading from New England into Canada. Meanwhile, Congress had not forsaken dreams of drawing the "Fourteenth Colony" into an alliance against the Crown. In mid-February it appointed a committee, headed by Benjamin Franklin, to represent the aims of the United States to the Canadians. The committee was instructed to "Inform [the Canadians], that in our judgement, their interests and ours are inseparably united. . . ." The mission reached Canada too late.

Frustrated in every attempt to win Canada, the colonists nonetheless never turned their backs on the vision. Washington strove throughout the war to protect, improve, and increase his invasion routes to the St. Lawrence; and each succeeding year witnessed some version of a Canadian expedition seriously debated in councils of war. Congress proposed an invasion in 1777; Washington recommended and prepared for a winter campaign northward in 1778. Feeling it to be impossible early in 1779 to expel the British from their bases on the Atlantic, the Commander-in-Chief leaned toward the second choice: an expedition against Niagara to secure the frontier and "open a door into Canada." He had earlier suggested a major campaign by way of Lake Ontario should the British evacuate the coast. Early in 1780 he urged Philip Schuyler to initiate actions against enemy forces in the north, and Canada was among the three objectives broached in a conference with the French at Hartford that year. Congress once again pushed for a Canadian invasion in 1781, but the aborted attempt on New York City and the successful campaign of Yorktown intervened. Nor did jubilation over the decisive victory at Yorktown still the desire to operate against Canada; Washington's proposals to Congress in May 1782 placed New York City and Canada at the top of the list of that year's possible objectives.[19]

From his early remonstrance that "the Security of Canada is [of] the [greatest] importance to the well being of these Colonies" to his final choice in 1782 of Canada as a proper objective for the Continental Army, Washington left little doubt of the special significance of Canada in his mind. Congress also seemed possessed of a peculiar attachment to that province. For their part, the English were not unaware of American designs northward. One of the major objectives behind Sir Henry Clinton's stroke in 1779 against Stony Point and Verplanck's Point was prevention of the United States "from pursuing any scheme they might have meditated for the annoyance of Canada." Implicit in Clinton's reasoning was an understanding that possession of the Hudson River was necessary to execute an invasion of Canada.[20]

Although it approaches triteness to attribute vision to the founding fathers, we are perpetually reminded of the wisdom they displayed in shaping our nation. Not so often, though, do we discuss their prescience as it existed during the actual conduct of the fighting. It is logical to assume, however, that some sense of the future must have been present before the war ended. The foresight that helped to forge America could not have burst into being merely at the signing of an armistice. And what, if not a view of tomorrow, could have sustained the will to fight for eight trying years? Obviously, some concept of the country they were going to have did exist among the Patriots. Obviously, too, the western frontier was the direction of the future in their eyes. And the Hudson River was an integral part of that mental picture. Henry Knox, visiting Albany in December of the first year of the struggle, noted the town's strategic location with respect to the western lands, and predicted it "must one day be, if not the capital of America, yet nearly to it."[21]

Seven of the thirteen states professed ownership of lands in the west. Citing original charters or subsequent agreements, these "landed" states claimed borders running from sea to sea—or at least to the Mississippi River. Sentiment ran strong on the subject. The future disposition of those vast lands was a matter of most urgent concern to the founding fathers. Indeed, arguments between "landed" and "landless" states delayed for five years ratification of the Articles of Confederation. But, if there was animosity between Americans over lands beyond the Appalachians, there was unanimity among them that England should have no portion of the area. The ideal, of course, would have been complete evacuation of North America by all European powers. Short of that, the United States wanted to verify its claim to the western lands and to extend its border toward the St. Lawrence in the north. Rebel strategy was colored by adherence to those expansive goals.

America's earliest expressed rebellious thoughts dealt with eliminating Quebec's claims in the west. The future strategic vulnerability of the United States, should Great Britain have retained those lands, was evident. The St. Lawrence, Ohio, and Mississippi Rivers would have provided England a complete circuit of the original united colonies and their lands. Under weight of that threat, it became necessary for Americans to remove the hostile frontier posts before the larger struggle was terminated. The immediate goal was to reduce the Indian menace, but the long-term ambition was to possess physically the western lands. This idea was admirably explained in a detailed study of the Sullivan-Clinton Campaign of 1779:

> Washington and other leaders saw that independence with a mere fringe of land along the seacoast would scarcely be worth the cost of the struggle if the rest of the continent to the westward and northward remained in the hands of the motherland. Washington knew by actual experience the potential wealth of the fertile regions of the interior of the continent. He realized that when the time came to discuss terms of peace that rich area could be secured for the young nation only if it was in possession of the Americans. The conquest of western New York, the capture of Oswego and Niagara and the seizure of posts farther west would assure American possession at the end of the war. Hence in the Sullivan-Clinton Expedition *an inland empire was the stake for which Washington was playing* and not merely the punishment of dusky foes on our border.[22]

The constant desire of Americans to displace English authority in Canada has already been explained, in part, but there is yet another reason behind their predilection for that northern province: the future. In 1782, Washington put to pen this view of the future with a Canada in American hands:

> I shall say nothing of the benefits which America would derive, and the injury Great Britain must sustain, by the fur and other trade of Canada shifting hands. Nor of the immense importance it must be to the future peace and quiet of these States; especially the western parts of them, to annihilate the British interest in that country; thereby putting a stop to

their intriguing after peace shall be established. These are too obvious to stand in need of illustration, they will speak for themselves.[23]

If it was considered bad to have Britain remain in Canada after the war, it was unthinkable to have any semblance of French influence reasserted there. When Congress proposed a joint American–French venture against Canada in 1779, Washington marshaled all the power and persuasion of his position to head it off. He feared King Louis XVI would embrace the opportunity to reclaim his old domain. It would be better, he heatedly argued, to await a chance to invade Canada alone than to risk giving the French a toehold. It would have been an embarrassing situation indeed had their allies claimed the very area coveted so ardently by the colonists.[24]

That incident serves to reinforce the belief that visions of the future —a future with the united colonies supreme on the continent—were firm long before hostilities ceased. And those visions instrumentally affected American strategic operations. Had the British held the Hudson, the dream of pushing Patriot influence north and west would have been, at the very least, severely dimmed—and quite probably extinguished. Without the Hudson, neither an advance into Canada nor an expedition against Niagara could have been successful. In fact, just the opposite result would have occurred; hostile elements from the north and west would have spilled into the colonies.

As became obvious during the prolonged peace negotiations, the English enemy was not alone in hoping to limit the United States to a strip of land east of the Appalachians. Spain and even the French "allies" were in accord with George III's ministers on that matter. Had Americans been unable physically to conquer and control the area west of the mountains, it is highly doubtful whether the Old Northwest would have become a part of the new nation.[25]

The initiative, the "Fourteenth Colony," and the future; though each had its own importance, all were related. Snatching the initiative meant operating offensively against the British, especially the British in Canada. Taking that vast land situated to the north and northwest of the United States would pave the way for a future free of foreign influence. Two factors link all three points. First, all are primarily aggressive and offensive actions. Second, the Hudson River is very nearly if not entirely indispensable to the attainment of any one of the three. Finally, there was one more strategic reason why General Washington needed to retain the Hudson: without control of the river, he would have lost the great advantage of operating on interior lines.

Enjoying the benefits of naval superiority, the British had the capability of striking anywhere along the coast they chose. The small Continental Army could not protect every likely objective. The ability to operate on interior lines—that is, the ability to concentrate at a central location in order to react to any enemy threat on the periphery of the defenses—was Washington's only counter to superior British seaborne mobility. So long as the Hudson remained in American hands, Washington could station his army on the river above New York City and enjoy interior lines. This is his own explanation of that strategy:

Shou'd the enemy's design be to penetrate the country up the North River, [we] are well posted to oppose them; shou'd they attempt to penetrate into New England, [we] are well stationed to cover them; if they move westward [we] can easily form a junction; and besides, it will oblige the enemy to leave a much stronger garrison at New York.[26]

Sir Henry Clinton was painfully aware of this trump card the Hudson handed his opponent. As an immediate result of his intended purchase of the Highlands forts from Benedict Arnold, for example, Clinton anticipated separating Rochambeau, then based in New England, from any prospect of assistance from the Americans. He then hoped to defeat the isolated French. Moreover, by controlling the Hudson, Washington not only facilitated his own communications, but he forced the English to rely upon a sea voyage from New York, around Nova Scotia, and up the St. Lawrence River to effect coordination between theater commanders or to transfer troops from one theater to another.

A recapitulation of American strategic motives for retaining the Hudson now shows: (1) a junction of British forces was prevented; (2) communications to the east were held intact; (3) hostile Indians were kept at arm's length; (4) the resources of interior New York and western New England were denied to the enemy; (5) flexibility in maneuvering the Continental Army was obtained; (6) ability to grasp the initiative was improved; (7) the capability for invading Canada was protected; and (8) revolutionary aspirations for a United States supreme on the continent were enhanced. It was a river of many eddies. It was much more than merely a convenient line to be defended (or occupied) to protect (or cut) communications to New England. It was everything Washington and his opponents attributed to it—and much more. Strategically, possession of the waterway was fully as vital as contemporary leaders on both sides proclaimed. Indeed, it was in all likelihood even more crucial than they themselves realized.

22

. . . AND TACTICS

WITH THE strategic importance of the Hudson thus established, an intriguing question comes immediately to mind. If New England had been isolated from the other colonies, what would have been the actual impact on the War of Independence? In other words, would England's "line of the Hudson" strategy have worked? Could it have won the war for George III?

Even before addressing that question, however, one must recognize and evaluate certain tactical assumptions that would have been prerequisites to the strategy. It is almost too obvious to broach, but before the "line of the Hudson" theory could have had any opportunity of operating—either successfully or unsuccessfully—the British must first have been able to seize the river. Furthermore, it ought also to have been within their capability to have retained it. Finally, it had to be actually within their power to have choked off American east-west traffic. If any of those three assumptions should have proven unsound or impractical, the strategy itself would have failed for lack of a solid tactical underpinning. Therefore, prior to examining what the strategic results of isolating New England might have been, it is necessary to consider the tactical aspects to determine whether the "line of the Hudson" concept was valid theory or royal pipe dream.

It is not really necessary to assume the British could have wrested the Hudson from its American defenders. They could have. A determined effort probably would have broken through in 1776. Sir Henry Clinton did conquer the crucial Highlands defenses and control most of the river for a fortnight in 1777 just as Burgoyne's army was tasting defeat at Saratoga. He might have repeated in 1779 had reserves from Europe arrived in time. A year later, but for a stroke of fortune, Arnold's efforts to surrender West

Point would probably have succeeded. At almost any time prior to the erection of West Point, English generals could have seized the crucial Highlands choke point—and, hence, the river—if they had pursued that objective vigorously. Their chances diminished sharply after 1778, but even then it was far from being an impossible task. General Duportail, Washington's Chief of Engineers, stated flatly that "they could have done it anytime" prior to May 1779. West Point, and the Hudson, *could* have been taken.[1]

An accepted military truism states that any defensive position can be overrun if the attacker is willing to accept the price in both blood and money. The question, then, of whether or not the British could have held the Hudson devolves to asking what cost the Americans would have been forced to pay to extricate them. Should that price have been higher than the Continental Army's moral or material capability to meet, the King's troops would have retained the Hudson.

The Hudson Highlands afforded the only location where the river was narrow enough for effective obstructions to be covered by fire. Therefore, as was amply demonstrated in 1777, by holding only the Highlands, the British would have been unchecked from New York City to Albany. Royal officers would not have found defense of the Highlands a simple task. For that matter, neither did the Americans. But the problems to be overcome were different. Americans had to block a water avenue to their forts as well as land approaches. Blessed with a fleet to control the river itself, the English would have had only to contend with an assault from the land side. Also, with shipping available to provide supplies, a siege could not have evicted the scarlet-coated squatters. All factors considered, it would probably have been somewhat easier for the British to have retained the Hudson than it was for the Patriots to do so. Therefore, by examining American commitments to the mountain stronghold we can obtain a feeling for the number of English soldiers which would have been required to defend the forts against Patriot counterattacks. When Clinton successfully stormed the Hudson forts in 1777, West Point had not yet been built. Even so, Clinton himself admitted that had the weaker forts been properly defended he could not have captured them with twice the troops. When the much stronger position at West Point was finished, General Washington estimated that a force of 100 men could adequately block an overland approach through the mountainous country beyond the main defenses. The minimum number of soldiers considered necessary to defend all the positions was 2,000. Even at their weakest, the English could have spared that many.[2]

A strong British garrison, backed by complete naval freedom on the wide river and burrowed deep into the natural fastness of the Hudson Highlands, would have constituted a most formidable foe. The cost of rooting out the "lobsterbacks" would have been very dear indeed. One can justly wonder if the Americans were either willing or able to pay it. Too, whether or not a sufficiently large American force could have been employed solely by land in the treacherously broken Highlands is itself quite doubtful. Logistical and maneuver limitations would have been staggering.

What is more, by concentrating a large army in a restricted area so near the river at a time when the enemy could turn him by rushing shipborne reserves north of the Highlands, Washington might have precipitated the decisive, pitched battle the British were seeking. All in all, it is difficult to see Americans ejecting a determined British garrison.

Investigating the practicability of isolating New England by commanding the Hudson is a relatively simple task—but one must first understand what was contemplated. It can never be supposed that all intercourse between the east and west banks could have been canceled. The mission of policing the entire length of the waterway from New York City to Albany would have been an impossible one. Individuals, perhaps even small groups, could have infiltrated across the river with relative impunity, while selected items of military equipment could have been slipped over the river almost at will. The proper question, obviously, is whether or not militarily significant crossings could have been conducted by the Patriots.

By the purposeful destruction of boats and rafts, coupled with raids against suspected staging areas, the British would have methodically reduced the rebel capability to transfer units or supplies. And, by aggressive patrolling of the waters, the fleet would have made hazardous all such attempted crossings. The Provincial Congress of New York, as a matter of fact, believed the British could have prevented all movements whatsoever south of Albany. As the British themselves envisioned accomplishing their purpose, they would have commanded the Hudson "with a number of small men-of-war, and cutters, stationed in different parts of it so as to cut off all communication by water . . . except for the King's service." The eminent American naval historian Alfred Thayer Mahan wrote, "The difficulties in the way of moving up and down [the Hudson] were doubtless much greater to sailing vessels than they now are to steamers; yet it seems impossible to doubt that active and capable men, wielding the great sea power of England, could so have held that river . . . with ships-of-war at intervals and accompanying galleys as to have supported a sufficient army . . . while themselves preventing any intercourse by water between New England and the states west of the river."[3]

Using interior lines provided by the Hudson, vessel-transported forces of the Crown would have enjoyed a marked mobility advantage over the landbound Continental Army. Should Washington have chanced throwing a strong body of men over the Hudson, he would have been dangerously vulnerable to defeat in detail. The Virginian was quite cognizant of that danger. Even with the Highlands forts in friendly hands, he feared a division of his army by the great river. "For should the enemy find us disjointed," he reasoned in 1778, "they may throw the whole of theirs upon a part of ours, and, by their shipping, keep us from making a junction." The Americans could not, then, without courting disaster, have moved any appreciable bodies of men or significant amounts of material across a Hudson in English hands. From time to time, surprise crossings could have been carried out. Perhaps an occasional herd of cattle might have been slipped past the King's patrols. In winter, advantage could have been taken of ice on the river to smuggle equipment to the rebel camp. But such efforts would have been undependable and sporadic, while prospects of suffering a complete loss would have been rather high. Furthermore, the difficult land passage north of Albany could have been used only for the movement of limited numbers of men and small amounts of supplies. It is safe to say that east-west traffic could and would have been effectively interdicted by his Majesty's forces if they had held the Hudson.[4]

A modern British historian has succinctly summarized the entire question: "Permanent control of the whole length of the river was unnecessary, for if the British held the Highlands they could use the waterway beyond at any time, and cut the last link in Washington's lateral communications."[5]

All things considered, British ability to implement the "line of the Hudson" strategy must be conceded. Now it is proper to return to the original question: Would the rebellion have been defeated by a vigorous and successful pursuit of that plan?

We turn, at this point, from the relatively secure ground of recorded history to the ephemeral realm of conjectural history. At the outset, it must be frankly recognized that second guessing the facts of the past is a risky business. Events are often predictable, but the unsuspected is more than a casual visitor in the affairs of man. Especially is this true during the traumatic times of war and revolution. Results which might have been, had some particular course been followed, are obscured forever in the dust of real results from the actual course. No matter how clear the situation appears in the light of hindsight, one can never be sure what accidents of fate would have acted along a path which was never followed. This is not to say no good can be obtained from historical hypothesizing. With a respectful appreciation of the limitations inherent in the method and a firm grasp of actual events to provide a yardstick, conjecture on what-might-have-been can provide some valuable insights to the past. Two facets deserving scrutiny are the amount and type of foreign assistance and that will-o'-the-wisp known as the will to fight. Both were essential ingredients of Washington's recipe for victory. What would have been the impact on each if the British had held the Hudson?

Although it is patently impossible to say how European powers would have reacted should the British have succeeded in halving the colonies, there are indications that their support might not have been so rapidly or so fully given. Certain French ministers began agitating as early as 1775 for French assistance to the American insurgents, but Louis XVI was far from sure he approved of a rebellion against a fellow monarch, even if that monarch did happen to be George III. Accordingly, he only agreed to aid the rebels surreptitiously. Silas Deane, an agent sent to obtain assistance, wrote glowingly from France on 1 December 1776 of the excellent environment favoring his negotiating large loans. Just two days later, reports of Guy Carleton's victories in Canada reached Paris, immediately reversing French readiness to extend financial support. Deane was forced to report dejectedly his inability to obtain credit with Carleton "on the frontiers of the colonies." France did continue to prime the Revolutionary pump, but not openly. Spain was pleased to see the English king in trouble, but, weak and cautious, wanted to be sure of backing the eventual winner; Prussia declined to help until France made an overt move. All Europe was poised in the wings awaiting a cue to enter the fray—or to stay in the wings.[6]

The failure of Burgoyne to seize the line of the Hudson in 1777 crystallized support beyond the Atlantic. "All France is joyous," elatedly wrote Benjamin Franklin, Silas Deane, and Arthur Lee from Paris. The unexpected American victory at Saratoga precipitated a decision by Louis XVI to recognize the United States. Straightway, Prussia began to cooperate, and Spain and Holland eventually entered the war against England. The impact of European support was a key—some would say the primary —factor in the Revolutionary War. How rapid and how profuse would that support have been had Burgoyne achieved his goal? One cannot suppress the suspicion that it would have been less and later.

The American will to fight was never the united, zealous, self-sacrificing ideal portrayed in all too many history books. Washington, himself a Southerner, was early critical of the "unaccountable kind of stupidity" prevailing in the men and officers from New England. Yankees reciprocated with open disdain for their comrades from the south. Four years after the war began French envoys still detected a severe lack of unity between southern, center, and eastern states. As for the American will and capability to continue the struggle, Rochambeau's opinion was recorded in his blunt request to France: "Send us troops, ships, and money, but do not depend upon these people, nor upon their means." Thomas Paine authored "The Crisis Extraordinary" in 1780 as a desperate plea to laggard states to support their commitments. The slothfulness of Congress and selfishness of the states forced Hamilton's bitter pen to cry, ". . . our countrymen have all the folly of the ass and all the passiveness of the sheep in their compositions. They are determined not to be free. . . . If we are saved France and Spain must save us." The Continental Congress had no real power over any state, so there was no central discipline. Neither was there complete cohesion or unity within the army. John Adams, disgusted with the petty bickerings amongst generals, wrote scathingly of their scrambling for rank and pay "like apes for nuts." The very existence of the army was seriously threatened by numerous mutinies of the men and several mutterings from the officers. Holes and chinks aplenty existed in the tarnished armor of American unity.[7]

Trying to analyze the damage that would have been done to the Patriots' will to resist by a British seizure of the Hudson is a difficult exercise. No one can predict the manner in which a people will react to adversity. Throughout the Revolution, Americans became strongest just when danger was greatest. However, seeds of disunity were always present and might well have found fertile ground in a physical separation of the colonies.

The nearest analogy to the loss of the Hudson that can be drawn was the British occupation of Philadelphia and subsequent control of the Delaware River in 1777. To an extent, the southernmost states—Delaware, Maryland, Virginia, North Carolina, South Carolina and Georgia—were then separated from the other seven. There occurred at that time no apparent lessening of the will to fight among Americans. However, the analogy is not a valid one. North-south commerce was conducted west of Philadelphia with far greater ease than east-west trade could have been north of Albany. In the wilderness west of Philadelphia lurked no counterpart to the strong British army in Canada. The states south of the Delaware in no wise matched those east of the Hudson in wealth of supplies for the war effort. Moreover, New England states constantly provided around half of all Continental soldiers, whereas those south of Philadelphia never fielded more than 40 percent in any year and usually turned out only 20 or 30 percent of the total. Significantly, English control of the Delaware did not open the Pennsylvania countryside to the ravages of the red man. And, finally, Patriot propaganda had not billed the fall of Philadelphia as being synonymous with the loss of the war. West Point became known as the "American Gibraltar"; it was an accepted cliché to say the loss of the Hudson would prove ruinous to the American cause. Psychologically, inhabitants of the United States were better prepared to accept the surrender of Philadelphia than the undoing of the Highlands defenses.

A will to win must be based on at least a sliver of hope. The Hudson was the center pole of Patriot offensive actions; it was a finger pointing toward the archenemy, Catholic Quebec; and it was the road to a future America existing then only in dreams. With the Hudson in British hands, hope would have been severely dimmed, maybe extinguished.

Napoleon believed that in war the value of the morale is to the physical as three is to one. The division of the continent at the Hudson would have provoked several drastic conditions, all direly affecting the always delicate morale of Americans. The numerical strength of Washington's army would have dwindled. Critical shipments of food and military supplies would have been withheld. Succor from friendly European nations might have been lessened or delayed. Indian atrocities would have multiplied as the tribes advanced into more populated areas. The always present threat of a political breach between the various states would have been increased by the physical wedge. Psychologically, the loss of West Point, a post regarded as absolutely essential to the war effort, would have been an extremely telling blow. Hope for future expansion westward and northward would have been dashed. The colonists' will to resist might have been stiffened by such somber events, but it might also have succumbed to the cumulative shock. Assuredly, the actual capability to fight on would have been severely impaired. For America to have continued to resist, her moral mainspring must necessarily have grown much stronger. From our vantage point, removed by nearly two centuries, there is reason to wonder if that would have been the likely result.

In brief, if there was a way the British could have won the war, it was through capturing and keeping the Hudson River.

23

THE TWO LONGEST YEARS

FREDERICK the Great, the renowned Prussian warrior-king, closely followed the American Revolutionary War, openly applauding each time Great Britain was embarrassed by her upstart colonists. When information of Yorktown reached Berlin, the aged monarch considered for a moment the impact of such a loss and quickly forecast the war's end. England, he proclaimed, would have to "get off her high horse" and admit defeat. He chortled to an advisor, "Superb Albion will be forced to put some water in its wine."

As it turned out, Frederick was entirely correct. Unfortunately, neither Great Britain nor America realized it so rapidly. It is a sad commentary on human nature that wars always prove easier to get into than out of; men invariably leap to arms but creep to peace. When victorious Continentals returned to the Hudson Highlands in November and December of 1781, they had won a war as well as a battle; except for numerous and nameless outpost squabbles and forage raids, the War of Independence was over. But not until December of 1783 could General Washington finally sheathe his sword. From Yorktown to peace stretched two long years of disease and hunger and poverty, two freezing winters and two idle summers, month upon month of continued sacrifice to a cause already won, more than a hundred weeks of nigh unbearable waiting. They were the Revolution's two longest years—and, in a sense, the two most rife with danger for America.

Heath had the great chain taken up on 11 November. At the same time, energetically and uncharacteristically, he launched into a major construction program on the Point. From Yorktown, Washington had sent word to prepare the Highlands to receive the bulk of the Continental Army, cautioning Heath to assure "that the army should be so disposed of and accommodated in their winter quarters as to render them fit for early, vigorous, and decisive action in the spring." Among the more ambitious projects, a huge hospital was designed, workers began a new guardhouse, and masons laid the foundation for "a grand house of stone for the artillery." Doctor Adams surveyed the activity approvingly, especially the new hospital, and told his diary the construction "ought to have been done years since." Apart from their apparent need, he felt, the "great works carrying on here" would also serve notice to the British that Americans were still in earnest about continuing the war.[1]

For once, troops tramping into West Point found adequate facilities. There was no frenzied, last-minute scramble for shelter or food. Though bread was in short supply, meat was actually plentiful. There was cloth for uniforms. Huts, built in past years, were numerous enough to permit the quartermaster to assign separate structures to men with families on the basis of about three or four families per hut. Furloughs were granted liberally to officers and men alike. Morale, sky-high after Yorktown, remained up as winter closed in. Congress designated 12 December as a day of thanksgiving in honor of the Yorktown victory. The men at West Point were delighted to have official sanction to celebrate again. Heath entertained "a large company of the officers of the army" at Beverley Robinson's house, while everyone in the garrison enjoyed a day of rest, an extra half pound of meat, and a gill of rum. The men had much to be thankful for, not the least of which was the prospect of being warm and well-fed during the forthcoming winter.[2]

But somewhere in that happy band there might have been a cynic, a soldier who had wintered at West Point before. He might have looked pessimistically for the catch, for the dark lining to the silver cloud, for the evil lurking beneath the surface. He would not have been disappointed. Nor would he have had far to look. A smallpox epidemic was building even as the troops rejoiced in their good fortune.

Watching the columns of self-satisfied soldiers swinging gaily back from Virginia, Heath had noticed some who had "brought the smallpox with them." Immediately, special huts were set aside to quarantine all those afflicted, but it was already too late. By Christmas the disease had spread alarmingly; it reached epidemic proportions by New Year's Day. Nine men died in the first week of 1782. Smallpox was a terrible scourge in army camps of that day. Many a time entire armies had been decimated by the pestilence. Heath had to stop it or lose his garrison. He reacted promptly and forcefully.[3]

Surgeons quickly inoculated everyone who had neither had the disease nor been previously inoculated. Women and children, too, underwent the dangerous procedure as well as men. All told, over two thousand submitted to "the operation of inoculation." (In many cases the prevention was worse than the disease, for "a considerable number were seized with putrid fever" and died.) Quarantine regulations were stiffened and enforced. All duties were pulled by those men already immune; everyone else remained inside. Officers insisted upon a fastidious standard of camp and personal hygiene. Garrison orders spelled out, "No soldier is to come on the parade . . . with his face or hands dirty." In an age when perfume was used more lavishly than soap, such an order had meaning. New latrines were opened daily and everyone caught not using them received thirty lashes on the spot without benefit of court-martial. Carpenters erected smokehouses and tacked up pertinent instructions: "No persons [are] allowed to go from infected quarters until they are properly smoked." Floors of the huts, being considered "naucious," were removed and burned; occupants even scraped away the top few inches of soil. Troops changed or cleaned bunk straw. Gradually, all those measures succeeded. The epidemic abated. Gravediggers got some rest. By March the danger had passed, but the graveyard on the far southwest corner of the plain was no longer small.[4]

The winter had been different from others only in the form of its misery. Death and disease had mercilessly stalked the Highlands fastness. In addition to those men struck down by illness, several deserters had died by execution, while accidents had claimed still others. The garrison's once bright optimism changed to despondency. Men argued and grumbled, even at the top level. Heath and McDougall crossed verbal lances, resulting in the arrest and subsequent court-martial of the hot-headed Scot—an event which does not seem to have hurt McDougall's reputation or standing. Spring brought relief from contagion and closeness, but it also heralded a new (but oh so very old) crisis over provisions.* Once more subsisting under the familiar "system of starving," the men became withdrawn and sullen.

After an unhappy winter of his own, during which he buried his step-son who had died of camp fever contacted in the Yorktown Campaign, George Washington returned to the Hudson Highlands. He selected for his headquarters a sturdy Dutch house built by Jonathan Hasbrouck in 1750. The house, standing on a hill in Newburgh, commanded a lovely sweep of the Hudson River. It served the Commander-in-Chief as home and head-quarters from then until the end of the war.

West Point was on the General's mind. He had not seen the fortress since conducting Rochambeau on that hurried tour over seven months before. As soon as he was established in the Hasbrouck House, he invited Heath up for dinner and an informal briefing on the status of the strong-hold. Then on 6 April he inspected some troops at the great bastion and checked the defenses. He repeated that procedure in ensuing days until he had seen every unit and had looked at all the positions. At first the works appeared little changed. Several new projects, of course, were in various stages of completion, but the defenses themselves seemed to be in good shape, showing only the wear and tear of exposure to another winter. Then, the longer he looked and questioned, the deeper he probed, the more uneasy he became. By all rights, the positions should have been *improved* in his absence. However, he eventually discovered several disconcerting signs of neglect. Perhaps Washington then recalled that Heath had never

---

* It had been decided to turn to private contractors in an attempt better to provide the army with necessary supplies. On 1 January 1782, Comfort Sands and Company undertook to supply the Continental Army in and around the Highlands. Mr. Sands proved to be, if anything, even more inept than the army quartermasters.

displayed the slightest interest or talent in performing what were basically engineering responsibilities. Displeased, he instructed Villefranche to provide him a complete report on the state of the works and an estimate of the men and equipment needed to make "the most essential repairs . . . before the army shall take the field." Returning to Newburgh, he ordered sappers and miners to march to West Point to begin what he fully expected to be a major job of refurbishing.[5]

Villefranche's report verified Washington's suspicions. He found fascines at Fort Clinton to be so dry a spark would "set the fort in a blaze." In fact, the rampart walls were too dry to permit the firing of the fort's own cannon. The half-bastion facing the river had never been completed. It should be finished, the engineer believed, and the bombproof should be made larger. Fort Putnam needed a cistern, and "good masonry" ought to replace the dry stonework. Fort Webb, already abandoned, need not be rebuilt. Fort Wyllys should have higher walls. Around the numbered redoubts, the Frenchman recommended placing even more batteries. Sherburne Redoubt had been allowed to pass into disuse and, like Webb, need not be repaired. Between Redoubts 3 and 4 was a weak spot which required a blockhouse—Gouvion's similar recommendation over a year earlier had been ignored. Redoubts on Constitution Island needed abatis. Batteries to cover the eastern side of the island would strengthen the complex on that side of the river. North and South Redoubts were satisfactory. Apparently, Sugarloaf Redoubt had been entirely discontinued. To accomplish all that construction, Villefranche asked for two months and 200 men. Washington concurred. General Orders on 18 April specified, "The repairs most necessary at the post of West Point (agreeably to the report of Major Villefranche . . .) are to be set about immediately and executed with the greatest dispatch." Once again West Point owed a debt to the direct intervention of the Commander-in-Chief.[6]

Gorgeous northern lights, "the most extraordinary aurora borealis ever before seen by those who observed it," lit up the evening of 4 May. Next day, General Guy Carleton, who had commanded throughout the war in Canada, replaced Sir Henry Clinton as commander of his Majesty's forces in America. Sir Henry and Mrs. Baddeley sailed home. George Washington had outlasted all three of the British generals who had arrived in Boston Harbor so full of hope so long ago: Howe, Clinton, and Burgoyne. That should have been a satisfying moment; but the very next day the specter of mutiny struck again at West Point.

Fortunately, late on the 5th, Colonel Heman Swift had learned from a servant that men in his Connecticut line planned to revolt at reveille next morning and march home to demand justice from the state assembly at Hartford. Swift was able to arrest the ringleaders during the night, thereby snipping the mutiny in its embryonic stage. Two sergeants of the 3rd Connecticut and Lud Gaylord, a soldier from the 1st Connecticut, were court-martialed. The court acquitted both sergeants for lack of evidence, but convicted Gaylord. One week after he had planned to carry his complaints to Hartford he was hanged in Execution Hollow. An attending surgeon probably caught the mood of the army, saying it was "very hard to

Blockhouse at West Point. Sketched by Archibald Robertson about 1796. Courtesy of the West Point Museum.

take the life of a soldier while their reasons for complaining are so great." The mutiny had been aborted, but its causes remained.[7]

For more than seven years the Continental Army had endured a hell born of the inefficiency and inadequacy of Congress. That body had assumed for itself in the beginning the power to wage war, but it had failed to acquire the essential corollary, the power to raise monies to pay for that war. Consequently, the soldiers went unpaid, unfed, unclothed. With some justice, the Continentals felt forsaken. Sacrificing the most, they got the least. Lazy or cowardly cousins grew fat; fighting men starved. While officers and troops alike wallowed in abject poverty, many civilians became rich. It did not escape the army's notice that all too many officials, unable to find a way to pay the men, had scant trouble amassing and managing personal fortunes. Influence often led to affluence. So far, although the bitterness had bubbled over a few times (including a recent attempt in the Southern Army which Greene crushed in April 1782), Washington had been able to control his army. Patriotism and discipline had been the carrot and the stick, but in the final analysis an officer corps dedicated and obedient to the Commander-in-Chief had been the instrument through which he had kept the mutinous soldiers relatively quiescent. But now even the formerly loyal officers were beginning to turn defiant. The first concrete sign of that unrest appeared right after Gaylord's body was cut down.

Lewis Nicola, the sixty-five-year-old commander of the Corps of Invalids, had listened with some interest to discussions among the officers —discussions becoming more and more prevalent—comparing and contrasting various forms of government. Born in France and educated in Ireland, he had no inbred love of republicanism to begin with and, like a great many other officers, he quite feared democracy as something akin to anarchy. Surveying the scene in America, he foresaw the thirteen states growing progressively weaker and splintered until they should dissolve or be gobbled up by European nations. In his view, nothing but a strong central authority, a monarchy, could save the country. Looking around, he saw only one man Americans could accept as king—George Washington. On 22 May Nicola sent the General a seven-page document which traced the plight of the army, discussed forms of government, blasted the inefficiency of Congress, and proposed a scheme to make Washington king. Although he was saying what many of his contemporaries believed, Nicola was making no pretext to be speaking for them.

Washington read the proposal "with a mixture of great surprise and astonishment." Having just thrown off the shackles of George III, he had no inclination to become George I. Curtly and bitingly he responded to Nicola, telling him "to banish these thoughts from your mind, and never communicate . . . a sentiment of the like nature." Lest someone in the future think he had ever encouraged Nicola, the Virginian carefully had two aides attest to the accuracy of a copy of his letter that was retained at headquarters. Washington, who could have overthrown the weak central government with a wave of his hand, would not. A Frenchman, traveling then through America and knowing nothing of the exchange between Nicola and Washington, said of the General: "This is the seventh year that he has commanded the army, and that he has obeyed Congress; more need not be said, especially in America, where they know how to appreciate this simple fact." Nonetheless, trouble was brewing. The men had been on the verge of mutiny for years—and now the officers were veering. Washington's past mission had been to defeat the British; after Yorktown, it was to hold his army together until peace should be declared. In some respects the first task had been the easier. And one could argue that the second was more important. For, if the Continental Army dissolved, England would win the war after all; if the army revolted, the American Revolution, like so many others, would devour itself. Either way, the Patriot cause would be lost.[8]

Being a keen observer of human nature, Washington knew that the best medicine for a person feeling sorry for himself is some diversion in which he can participate. Armies are just an accumulation of people; the same cure, in a collective sense, holds true. Fortunately, a ready-made answer arrived just then. Queen Marie Antoinette had given birth to a son the previous autumn, a dauphin slated to become France's next king. Official American policy was to celebrate with France the happy event. Washington, seizing upon that pretext, began right away to lay plans to throw the grandest, flashiest party West Point had ever seen.

Scheduling the celebration for Thursday, 30 May, the General assigned Villefranche the prodigious mission of decorating the entire parade ground. The French engineer outdid even Washington's most expansive thoughts. Taking a thousand men, he put them to work cutting and hauling logs, gathering evergreen boughs, carving planks, preparing signs, and polishing weapons. An amazed officer described the "curious edifice" raised on the plain:

> It is about six hundred feet in length and thirty feet wide, supported by a grand colonnade of one hundred and eighteen pillars, made of the trunks of trees. The covering of the roof consists of boughs, or branches of trees curiously interwoven, and the same materials form the walls, leaving the ends entirely open. On the inside, every pillar was encircled with muskets and bayonets, bound round in a fanciful and handsome manner, and the whole interior was decorated with evergreens, with American and French military colors, and a variety of emblems and devices, all adjusted in such style as to beautify the whole interior of the fabric. This superb structure in symmetry of proportion, neatness of workmanship, and elegance of arrangement, has seldom perhaps been surpassed on any temporary occasion. . . . Several appropriate mottos decorated the grand edifice, pronouncing benedictions on the dauphin and happiness to the two allied nations.[9]

Rain delayed the construction somewhat, forcing postponement of the festival for a day, but only whetting everyone's curiosity to see the glittering open-air ball.

Shortly after noon on the appointed day, all troops encamped in the vicinity of West Point "having previously cooked their provisions," assembled under command of their officers and marched to predesignated locations. Each regiment was formed in a long line of two ranks, facing inward toward the plain, but remaining out of sight. The 1st and 2nd Massachusetts Brigades stretched from the hill above the Red House (where the post cemetery is now located), behind the plain, and part way to the bluffs overlooking the river (near where the present post headquarters stands). Completing the other half of that great circuit across the waterway, were two Connecticut brigades and two more from Massachusetts. They formed a curving line beginning on the heights behind Constitution Island, running down the ridge crest past North and Middle (by then called South) Redoubts, and cutting back to the high ground above Nelson's Point (near the present village of Garrison). Formed on the plain itself, at the hub of that huge wheel, was the artillery regiment. Washington's guard had the post of honor, standing proudly inside the vast colonnade. With the hills denuded of trees, every unit had an unobstructed field of vision to witness the entire ceremony. At four o'clock, three cannon fired, declaring in blast and echo the official opening of the celebration. That was also the signal for the regiments "to advance and display in full view of the Point, and stack their arms." Then all "general, regimental, and staff officers of the army" left the troops in charge of lower-ranking officers and made their way to the plain. The soldiers stood by to observe the spectacle.

Nearly five hundred officers and ladies had assembled in the colonnade when, sharply at five o'clock, trumpets and drums sounded a fanfare. The artillerymen had formed a double line leading from McDougall's quarters to the arbor. Between those twin ranks of stiffly saluting gunners passed the dignitaries, headed by General and Mrs. Washington. Governor and Mrs. George Clinton were there, the Governor reflecting, no doubt, on the early years of the war when he and his brother had been so intimately involved in the defenses along the Hudson. Gigantic Henry Knox was accompanied by his equally fat wife, Lucy, who, as usual, sported an outlandishly garish hat. Most of the "principle officers of the army and their ladies," as well as "respectable characters from the States of New York and New Jersey" were there. They partook of an elegant dinner while, as one participant described it, "a martial band charmed our senses with music." The majority of the men and women were as interested in gazing "with admiration on the illustrious guests and the novel spectacle" as they were in eating. After the meal, "thirteen appropriate toasts were drunk, each one being announced by the discharge of thirteen cannon and accompanied by music." For emphasis and effect, the first toast was also *followed* by thirteen guns firing at water level beneath the plain. At seven o'clock the elaborate if noisy dinner was over. Regimental officers returned to their waiting men.

To begin the evening phase, thirteen cannon rattled the hills. Immediately after the reverberating echoes died out, a rippling *feu de joie* began near the shore south of the plain, proceeded down the line of troops past Fort Putnam and toward the Red House, and jumped the river to race southward along the heights on the east side until it again reached the river bank opposite its starting point. By that time the first man to fire had reloaded. A cannon from South Redoubt boomed out the word that one circuit was complete. In answer, artillery began all over again. Three times a thirteen-gun salute and the musketry began all over again. Three times a chain of retorts and flame from thousands of muskets, firing rapidly one after another with machine-gunlike effect, circled West Point. Each time it was preceded by thirteen cannon on the plain and punctuated by a single gun in South Redoubt. To some, at a loss for adequate words, it "had a pleasing appearance to the eye as well as the ear." To others it "could be compared only to the most vivid flashes of lightning from the clouds." To all it was manifestly magnificent. When the huge smoke ring had dispersed, "the united voices of the whole army on all sides" raised three resounding cheers for the dauphin.

The arbor was then "illuminated by a vast number of lights which, being arranged in regular and tasteful order, exhibited a scene vying in brilliancy with the starry firmament." Washington, who was "unusually cheerful," grabbed Lucy Knox around what passed for her waist and opened the ball. Gay couples followed, dancing on the grass underneath the lighted arbor until half-past eleven. Lights were then extinguished and everyone turned toward the southwest. From Redoubt Webb erupted the most artistic and lovely display of fireworks ever seen at the Point. When dark descended once more, three cannon on the plain barked a final salute and the grand party was over. No one who participated would ever forget it.[10]

Militarily, 1782 was expected to be a quiet year, and in America it was. With peace talks underway, neither side was likely to risk a reverse on the battlefield. For his part, Washington did not like the arrangement. He doubted Great Britain's sincerity, thinking the English planned only to delay at the peace table while awaiting some opportunity to gain a victory. Then, too, idleness was as much a danger to his army as combat. But he accepted the unwritten moratorium on major clashes—partly, at least, because the Continental Army, even when reinforced by the 4,000 French troops still in America under Rochambeau, was too weak to attack the English enclaves. The Commander-in-Chief moved his forces out of the Highlands toward New York City, but the major purpose was to provide a change of scenery and a fresh place to bivouac. Washington himself took advantage of the lull in hostilities to make an excursion into northern New York in order to become familiarized with the geography of avenues leading to Canada or the frontier over which he might soon commit his army. Also in July, the English abandoned Savannah. Charleston and New York City were then their sole remaining bases in the United States. Rumors were abundant all summer of a pending evacuation of New York City; instead, redcoats vacated Charleston in December. There were small clashes where outpost lines touched, and a sort of civil warfare continued between Americans in contested areas, but all in all, 1782 was a peaceful year. The officers and men had ample time—too much, as it turned out—to think about the future and to dwell on the injustice of their situation.

To be sure, the larger war had not ended. Fighting continued in other theatres. English and French forces clashed bitterly throughout the year in the West Indies. Admiral de Grasse, a hero of Yorktown, was captured with his huge flagship, the 110-gun *Ville de Paris*, in April. A Spanish armada took the Bahamas shortly afterward, leaving all three European powers rather scrambled with regard to the sunny Caribbean Isles. The English continued to maintain their base at Gibraltar in spite of a determined if ineffective Spanish blockade. In September a combined French and Spanish fleet made an attempt to seize the rock but was beaten back. The vigor of the allied effort can be imagined when it is considered that the Spanish admiral, Cordoba, was eighty, "an age when one is no more fit for war than for love." The siege was resumed. In a more exotic portion of the world, a French fleet under the able Admiral Suffren generally bested the English in a series of sprawling sea battles off India. But little of note happened in North America. The conflict had moved away from the Thirteen Colonies. West Point was in a backwater of the war.

The summer of 1782 was cold and rainy in France, ruining that year's wine crop. Along the Hudson, though, the season was unusually arid and hot. Sources of water dried up, making it difficult for the army to obtain enough fresh water. So too were the springs and wells of manpower drying up. After seven years of war, few young men viewed service in the army as romantic or exciting. Furthermore, with peace expected at any moment, there was no longer much motivation to bear arms in order to protect home and hearth. Recruiters found it a dismal summer. In an effort to meet quotas, they had to reach way down into the manpower basket. They resorted to operating with their eyes half shut, signing men up who were obviously unfit. Thomas Machin was one of many found guilty of "a breach of his recruiting instructions" that summer. He was sentenced "to be reprimanded by the Commander-in-Chief" and to pay a fine for enlisting a soldier from a nearby unit and accepting another man "unfit for service." A New England officer was court-martialed for even more gross irregularities: he had enlisted four deserters, two from the French army and another pair from the English, a Negro who was "lame in the ankle," two immigrants who remained only long enough to collect their bonus, four boys considered "undersized" as well as too young, and even one man described as "an idiot." Observing the lack of quality in the new soldiers, one officer, Lieutenant Colonel Ebenezer Huntington, claiming females were more spirited than these dregs improperly called men, suggested hiring several women to do the recruiting. Huntington revealed in an afterthought the bonus that he envisioned would be offered by the lady recruiters to induce virile young men to volunteer: "I would recommend that tall girls be procured that the offspring may be five feet six inches high." As a matter of fact, Huntington's idea was not all fantasy. The army, desperate for new conscripts, was taking almost anyone willing to sign up and healthy enough to march. At least one girl enlisted and served as a soldier.[11]

Deborah Sampson, a lanky, horse-faced young woman, bored with farming and school teaching, cropped her hair, donned men's clothes, and volunteered in the spring of 1782. For a time that summer she was a part of the West Point garrison. Fighting Tories below the Highlands she sustained a saber slash on the side of her head and later a musket wound in the thigh. One gets the impression that she was a better "man" than most of the recruits reporting to Washington's army in the twilight years of the War of Independence.

At West Point, construction was the major preoccupation. On 4 July, the Board of War decreed that the Point would become a vast depository for gunpowder, ordering to be erected there a cavernous powder magazine. Complying with the Board's directive, Washington selected for the site a hollow on the plain some distance west of Execution Hollow and issued instructions to begin building the magazine. Sappers and miners went to Constitution Island to quarry rock. Sand was transported from New Windsor. Masons assembled and readied their tools. By early August everything was set to begin when, in a scene reminiscent of the early days in the Highlands, the engineer balked. Villefranche disagreed with the location Washington had chosen. However, unlike Romans and Radière, he was able to persuade his American superiors to change. On 12 August, "a large stone magazine, capable of containing 1,000 barrels of gunpowder," was begun to be erected on Constitution Island. The massive storage facility was built upon the principles of Monsieur Vauban." At long last, the French engineers were able to apply their trade as they had learned it. Not surprisingly, the powder house was not finished that year. A shortage "both in point of masons and materials" prevented its completion prior to winter. But the magazine, and other ambitious efforts to improve the existing works, served to keep the men busy and relatively happy.[12]

Henry Knox, the bookseller from Boston, who served throughout the Revolution as Washington's Chief of Artillery, became commander of West Point in August, 1782. He held that position for the remainder of the war, seventeen months all told. Washington, by no means a small man, was dwarfed by the artilleryman. Stepping on a set of scales at West Point, the Commander-in-Chief balanced at 209, Knox at 280. Knox's corpulence masked but did not hinder a mind both sharp and agile. The role he was fated to play in shaping the future American army made it most appropriate that he should be West Point's last wartime commander.

Autumn's months paraded by. Rochambeau marched his men back to Rhode Island, crossing the Hudson in September amid elaborate pomp and pageantry performed by both allied armies. American and British generals discussed prisoner exchanges as the trees took on fall hues. The Corps of Invalids made plans in October to move to Constitution Island where they would have "comfortable barracks and fuel at hand" and where there were requirements for "very few sentries, and those may be under cover." In November the chain was removed from the river. By December, workers had finished a handsome barracks large enough "to accommodate two or three regiments," on Constitution Island. "They were two stories high with wings at each end, brick chimneys, and a gallery in front the whole length of the building, with large flights of steps to ascend to the gallery and the upper room." The Corps of Invalids, half a regiment of artillerymen, and the Corps of Sappers and Miners moved in. That month also, George III announced to Parliament that Great Britain had recognized the independence of the United States. The war was over, but in that age of slow communications the Continental Army had to endure one more winter before learning it—and the Commander-in-Chief had to weather yet another serious threat to the freedom of his fledgling nation.[13]

With all parts of the Thirteen Colonies save the enemy enclave in New York firmly in Patriot hands, the bulk of the Continental Army bedded down for the winter at New Windsor and West Point. Great numbers of men were discharged in anticipation of a general peace—but the "discharge" papers cautiously carried a proviso on the reverse side making the individual eligible for recall should fighting flare up again. Except that no one seriously anticipated a spring campaign, the final winter was no better than its predecessors. Food and clothing and fuel were scarce. "I lived half the winter upon tripe and cowheels, and the other half upon what I could get," one veteran sergeant recalled. All over again was reenacted the familiar scene of a plentiful countryside seeming heartlessly to stand aloof from destitute, starving soldiers. The players were tired of the role; that last winter at New Windsor was one too many. The officers broke.

Having spent the better part of a decade fighting for independence while, in most cases, losing business and home and savings, the officers wanted some sort of decent restitution from the new government, a step Congress was woefully unprepared to take. "The expectations of the army," Knox warned, "from the drummer to the highest officers, are so keen for pay that I shudder at the idea of their not receiving it." A committee was chosen to draft a petition to Congress. Alexander McDougall carried the recorded complaints to Philadelphia. A young officer at West Point put into words what many were thinking: McDougall's efforts must be successful, "or I dread the consequences." But the Scot had no success—Congress would not ("could not" might be a fairer phrase) take action to appease the army. When word of the rebuff reached the Highlands, officers bristled. Talk of turning the army against the civilian government, never uncommon in those days, increased. Pointedly, Knox wrote from West Point, "I consider the reputation of the American army as one of the most immaculate things on earth, and that we should even suffer wrongs and injuries to the utmost verge of toleration rather than sully it in the least degree. But, there is a point beyond which there is no sufferance." A mounting if not formalized drive, aimed at convincing George Washington to wield his angry army in a crusade to right all of the obvious political wrongs in America, was coming out into the open. The sword forged by the Virginian could easily cut down an impotent government and establish—what? The agitators were not sure, but they felt they could trust Washington to stop short of becoming a complete dictator, and they knew that no other man could do as he pleased with the army. Knox and McDougall and Alexander Hamilton (then a member of Congress) were the prime movers, while virtually every other officer either supported them or was neutral. The future of America hung on a precarious balance. Dictatorship or democracy? The answer rested with General Washington.[14]

Washington, bothered by failing eyesight and rotting teeth, passed the long winter weeks in Newburgh uneasily aware of the ferment among his officers but apparently not apprised of the extent of their restlessness nor of the place he held in their plans. Then in February a letter arrived from his ex-aide, Alexander Hamilton. Congress, the Congressman wrote, was not "governed by reason or foresight but by circumstances." That body would be unable to help its highly deserving army. The young New Yorker urged the General "to take the direction" of the army's move to redress its

General Henry Knox. Courtesy of the West Point Museum. 345

grievances. In words scarcely subtle, Hamilton predicted that once the soldiers "lay down their arms, they will part with the means of obtaining justice." Other feelers crossed Washington's desk. The picture of intrigue came slowly into sharp focus. His Excellency found himself in an incredibly awkward situation. On one hand he sympathized with his suffering officers and men, on the other he had no intention of leading a military revolt. After much mental anguish, he informed Hamilton unequivocally that he would not participate in any move to intimidate the states or Congress.[15]

The plotters then decided to proceed without the General. An unauthorized meeting was set for 11 March in the Temple, a large assembly hall standing on a hill in the center of the cantonment at New Windsor. When Washington learned of the projected meeting and read an anonymous tract which compellingly outlined the conspirators' viewpoint, he issued a statement prohibiting the meeting and calling one of his own for four days later. The day set was Saturday, 15 March 1783. It might have been the day America was saved from itself.

At noon the spacious building was crowded with officers. Washington was not expected to attend so Horatio Gates approached the podium to open the proceedings. At that moment, the Commander-in-Chief rode up, dismounted, and wedged his way through the packed men to the small dais. There, with more emotion than was his wont, he delivered a prepared address designed to stem the malign movement which he believed would "open the flood gates of civil discord and deluge our rising empire in blood." His speech failed in its purpose. When he finished, he had changed no minds, shifted no stands. The officers remained sullen; they wanted action, not rhetoric. He looked sadly out over the jumble of faces. Reaching into a pocket he withdrew a sheet of paper, a letter from a member of Congress. He would read it to them, he said.

An impatient murmur was audible from the rear of the long room. The seditious officers had already heard more than they could stomach from Congress. Then, slowly, a stark silence enshrouded the assemblage as Washington fumbled strangely with the letter. The General, looking uncomfortable, was unable to read it. He paused a moment, a little disconcerted. Then, from his waistcoat, he pulled something his officers had never seen him wear—a pair of reading glasses. In a subdued voice echoing the terrible burden he had carried for nearly eight years, he explained, "Gentlemen, you will permit me to put on my spectacles, for I have not only grown gray but almost blind in the service of my country." He read the letter, but no one heard him. It no longer mattered. By that one simple statement he had won them over. Quietly, he walked out and rode away. There was not a dry eye in the Temple. The officers of the Continental Army would continue to obey their Commander-in-Chief. The backlash had been averted.

The men at West Point constantly heard rumors, growing more emphatic every day, of an armistice. They also heard reports of plans to place the chain across the river on this day or that. They watched closely the pile of rusty links next to the Red House, "for the putting down or keeping up of the chain was the criterion by which we were to judge of peace or war." When mid-April passed and the chain still remained undisturbed on shore, they began to believe peace really had arrived. Then, seeing a merchandise-laden schooner from Nantucket sail past the fort, the first American vessel to come up the river since the summer of 1776, they *knew* peace was at hand. When Washington received official word of the cessation of hostilities, he waited a few days to announce it. With a fine sense of the dramatic, he ordered the announcement "to be publicly proclaimed" at noon on 19 April, the eighth anniversary of the fighting at Lexington and Concord which had opened the war. He issued every man "an extra ration of liquor," requesting them to join him in a toast wishing "perpetual peace, independence, and happiness to the United States of America." The victory celebration at West Point was anticlimactic and comparatively reserved, but the men felt it all the more deeply. They had waited a long, long time.

With peace a certainty, General Washington turned his mind to thoughts of a peacetime establishment for the army. The very first thing that must be provided, he wrote, was "a regular and standing force for garrisoning West Point and such other posts upon our northern, western and southern frontiers . . . to awe the Indians, protect our trade, prevent the encroachment of our neighbors of Canada and the Florida's, and guard us at least from surprises." West Point, the future, Indians, and the frontiers were still inextricably intermingled in his mind. The importance of West Point, he continued, "is so great as justly to have been considered the key of America; it has been so pre-eminently advantageous to the defence of the United States, and is still so necessary in that view, . . . that the loss of it might be productive of the most ruinous consequences." Also, he felt it essential to establish one or more academies "for the instruction of the art military; particularly those branches of it which respect engineering and artillery, which are highly essential, and the knowledge of which is most difficult to obtain." Never again did he want the United States to be dependent upon foreign military advisors.[16]

Although victory loosed in the nation a sincere wave of elation and relief, the summer and autumn of 1783 was a period of mixed jubilation and irritation, of mingled happiness and bitterness. Until the British should finally evacuate New York, the army's job would not be over, although most of the men were conditionally released. Those remaining under arms were consolidated at West Point. When the discharged soldiers reached home they found a seething populace. Debt, always endemic, was now epidemic. Inflation had reached ludicrous proportions. Paper money bought nothing. In New England some incensed men had already resorted to violence, and more seemed unavoidable. In Philadelphia, "a body of armed soldiers" forced Congress to test one last time its tactical mobility. The lawmakers fled to Princeton. Washington dispatched Continental troops under Robert Howe to quell the disturbance in the City of Brotherly Love. Many people looked upon the recently returned Continentals with resentment rather than with the reverence the soldiers had expected. Some veterans were even mobbed. From West Point, outspoken Ebenezer Huntington acidly protested against "ungrateful countrymen" who considered soldiers to be "the harpies and locusts of the country." God grant us a strong government, he cried, "or give us a king; even tyranny is better than anarchy." With that climate of unrest prevailing across the land, Washington dared not leave his post until the last Britisher was gone.[17]

Nor were the final months especially enjoyable at the familiar rock on the Hudson. The drought continued; forest fires were common in the Highlands. An epidemic of measles prostrated the garrison in June. Men were kept hard at work maintaining the buildings, cleaning the enormous number of weapons being deposited at the Point, and building a huge, two-story arsenal to cover the stack of muskets and cannon. Gradually, the size of the army was reduced to around two thousand, including the sappers and invalids. Departing men were asked to cut two cords of wood before leaving. When he had chopped and stacked his pile of firewood—an unusual legacy—the beaming soldier obtained discharge papers and became a civilian.

Money was never far from the minds of Americans of that era. Many saw an opportunity to turn a profit from the demise of the Continental Army. Old cannon were selling for $20 a ton and "useless shot and shell" brought £12 a ton. It was even proposed to sell the great chain in one-ton portions for the same price commanded by new bar iron.* Congress, however, put a stop to such thoughts by forbidding its sale. At West Point, the Long Barracks, empty huts, unfinished structures, and those buildings inside the redoubts were put up for sale. Left standing, it was alleged, the huts would "serve only for harbors to troublesome inmates." Nearly everything except the Long Barracks was sold, mostly for firewood. By November, West Point was virtually a ghost town of stripped, skeletonlike stone forts and batteries.[18]

On 14 November General Washington established his final headquarters at West Point. He remained there a week waiting for Sir Guy Carleton completely to evacuate New York City. To while away a few of the heavy hours, he rode around the strangely quiet redoubt trails. Dismounting in Redoubt 4, from where he could see all the various works, he gazed for a last time on the bastion that bore so much of his own stamp. The days in Congress when he had first recommended closing the river seemed now to belong to a different world. Memories of the difficulties and debates over selecting the site and building the defenses might have reinforced his ideas about the need for a military academy to produce professional soldiers. He smiled, recalling those happy days in 1779. The smile probably faded to a scowl as he glanced across the river to Beverley Robinson's house and remembered Arnold. Maybe it struck him then, as all the old memories tumbled one after another through his mind, that the story of fortress West Point was, in microcosm, the history of the Revolutionary War. Surveying the stair-stepped system of defense, perhaps he wondered whether or not it

---

* By this time the boom was gone. After the decision to discontinue using it (perhaps in 1779), the obstacle had been left in a stack on the eastern shore. An unknown number of the great logs, with attached metal parts, had been lost in the river at one time or another. There is evidence indicating that a portion of the iron was sold as scrap in the spring of 1781. During the winter of 1781–1782 some of the iron was beaten into axes and the rest reforged.

really would have turned back a determined British attack. A realist, not given to dwelling overly long in the realm of what might have been, he most likely answered the hypothetical question to his own satisfaction by reflecting that West Point had fulfilled its mission of blocking the Hudson River by deterring an English effort. And, after all, deterrence is the cheapest form of defense. Remounting, he descended slowly to the plain.

When Carleton sailed away, George Washington entered the city which he had lost over seven years before. After an emotional farewell to his officers in Fraunces' Tavern, he continued to Philadelphia to resign his commission. As Mr. Washington, he returned to Mount Vernon in time for Christmas.

Henry Knox journeyed back to West Point when Washington set out from New York City. There he closed out the last of America's wartime army and organized the new nation's peacetime force, consisting of "one battalion of infantry of 500 rank and file and about 100 artillery." On 3 January 1784 he wrote Washington, "Having brought the affairs here nearly to a close, I shall soon depart for Boston." The next day he left. The role of West Point in shaping the destiny of America had just begun.

FROM MILITARY FORTRESS
TO MILITARY
ACADEMY

TO BE prepared for war," George Washington stoutly declared, "is one of the most effectual means of preserving peace." No man ever had more reason than he to appreciate the profound wisdom in that simple sentence. America prior to the Revolution had been pitifully unprepared for hostilities. She had possessed enough substance for an army, but none of the machinery to convert the raw material into an instrument of war. General Washington was forced to shape a fighting organization in the very midst of conflict. How much easier his task would have been if, like Alexander or Hannibal or Caesar or Gustavus or Frederick or, indeed, any of the great captains to precede him, he had inherited a strong, trained throng of soldiers, a roster of professional officers, and a carefully developed body of doctrine. Most of the blunders and miseries of the War of Independence could have been avoided. The Continental Army would not have consumed three whole years simply waiting for a German to teach it to form line from column and to wield a bayonet; nor would Patriots have wasted more than thirty months in determining the proper location for a fortress to close the Hudson. The extreme tribulations they were obliged to undergo and overcome convinced Washington and his lieutenants of the absolute necessity for establishing a military system to insure that the nation they had won would never again be a military beggar.

Such ideas led eventually to the founding of the United States Military Academy at West Point. But, just as the steps toward erecting a military fortress at that peculiar hook in the Hudson had been halting and pained, so was the path to a military academy narrow and tortuous. Another war would be at hand before the United States would finally recognize the requirement for professional soldiers—and many of the old Continentals who would have so roundly applauded the Academy's birth never lived to see it.

The first mention of a military academy occurred quite early in the war with England. In times of need, the need itself is always seen and comprehended particularly clearly. Not many weeks into the second year of fighting, Congress dispatched a committee to discover what was the cause of its army's woes. The committee quickly found out: amateur officers. Big, blunt Henry Knox, himself an amateur doing his best to become a professional, quite plainly explained that "officers can never act with confidence until they are masters of their profession." He most strongly urged the Congressmen to provide for an "academy . . . where the whole theory and practice of fortification and gunnery should be taught." At the same time, back in Philadelphia, plump John Adams, who never was a soldier and always mistrusted them, concluded that there must be "a military academy in the army" if the United States was ever going to have a fighting force "to be confided in." Hit almost simultaneously by Knox's suggestion, Adams' proposal, and a letter from Washington urging the organization of a corps of trained engineers, Congress, in October of 1776, directed a committee "to prepare a plan for establishing a continental laboratory and a military academy." Perhaps Congress meant well, but the committee system was not especially efficient. Nothing more was heard of that proposal for an institution to train officers.

A year later Congress did establish the Corps of Invalids. Designed primarily as an organization to care for and utilize disabled veterans, the Corps was also expected to function as "a military school for young gentlemen." More specifically, it was "a school for propagating military knowledge and discipline." For four years the cripples guarded facilities in such metropolitan areas as Philadelphia and Boston. Historians have so far failed to discover how many "young gentlemen" were trained in matters military, probably for the very good reason that the Corps did not in fact serve as a school. When the handicapped troops marched to their permanent home at West Point in 1781, they represented America's total academic faculty for the propagation of the military art.

By then, however, not much was expected of them. Steuben had provided the Continental Army with a set of modified Prussian regulations, Frenchmen had filled the void in engineering expertise, and Lady Luck had combined with British blunders to give Washington time to train his officers at the costly school of experience. For that particular war a military academy was no longer a need; by borrowing professional help from Europe, the Americans had muddled through. In the future, however, the new nation could not afford to rely upon handouts from the Old World. America must have its own military system, its own traditions, its own professionals. Its security and destiny could not again be laid subserviently into foreign hands.

Near the end of the war, Congress appointed Alexander Hamilton to chair a committee charged with investigating the nation's requirements for a peacetime military establishment. Hamilton asked Washington's opinion. The General in turn requested the ideas of several ranking officers. Many mentioned both West Point and a military academy.

General Jedediah Huntington most strongly pressed for the continuation of a post at the Point even during peace. "The British," he averred, "will keep their eye upon it as long as they regret the loss of the country or have a passion for power and conquest." One inexpensive means of providing a garrison, Huntington felt, would be to establish at the fort on the Hudson an academy "for instruction in all the branches of the military art." Governor George Clinton emphatically espoused the maintenance of a strong army—even recommending that it continue to be called the Continental Army—and pleaded for a system which would assure "a succession of officers well versed in the tactics of war." However, he believed a "seminary of learning" in each state would be less costly than a single academy. Timothy Pickering also thought "it might be expedient to establish a military school, or academy, at West Point." The curriculum the Quartermaster envisioned would be comprised of "what is usually called military discipline, tactics, and the theory and practice of fortification and gunnery." To save money, Pickering proposed selecting faculty members from among those officers normally assigned to the garrison. General von Steuben submitted the most elaborate and detailed report. He thought three military academies, one in each section of the country, would be about the right number. The one for the middle states would, of course, be at West Point.

Of all, the Baron proved to be the most far-seeing. He wanted a course of study to broaden and educate the military officer rather than merely to produce a narrow technician. Cadets should study "natural and experimental philosophy, eloquence and belles lettres, civil law and the law of nations, history and geography, mathematics, civil architecture, drawing, the French language, horsemanship, fencing, dancing, and music," not to mention specialized training in artillery and fortifications. To help defray expenses, Steuben thought a tuition of $300 a year would not be too much to ask. Reviewing the various papers, Washington saw three threads common in all: a method of perpetuating military professionalism was essential; West Point must be retained; and funding by a bankrupt government was expected to be an obstacle.

On 2 May 1783 the Commander-in-Chief forwarded to Hamilton a thick document entitled, "Sentiments on a Peace Establishment." In it he listed four military requirements that the United States should support after peace arrived: a regular army "for garrisoning West Point" and other posts; a carefully organized militia, standardized among the states; arsenals to make and store military supplies; and "academies, one or more, for the instruction of the art military." Enlarging on that latter subject, he said it was beyond question "that an institution calculated to keep alive and diffuse the knowledge of the military art would be highly expedient."

Acknowledging that "great and expensive arrangements" were not within reach or reason, given the poverty of the government, he nonetheless insisted:

> I must, however, mention some things which I think cannot be dispensed with under the present or any other circumstances; until a more perfect system of education can be adopted, I would propose that provision should be made at some post or posts . . . for instructing a certain number of young gentlemen in the theory of the art of war, particularly in . . . the artillery and engineering departments. . . .
>
> Of so great importance is it to preserve the knowledge which has been acquired thro' the various stages of a long and arduous service that I cannot conclude without repeating the necessity of the proposed Institution, unless we intend to let the science become extinct and to depend entirely upon the foreigners for their friendly aid if ever we should again be involved in hostility.

As the war dragged slowly on to its conclusion in those waning months of its ninth year, Washington realized that, much as he wanted to be rid of foreign influence, the proposed military school would at first need outside help. The General reckoned it would be necessary "for us to retain some of the French engineers in America," at least until the institution should be formed. Duportail himself was not willing to stay, but he thought some of his comrades might. On the subject of a military academy, the foreign chief of engineers was abrupt and adamant: "The necessity of an academy . . . is too obvious to be insisted upon."

Hamilton's committee, fortified with all of that compelling testimony justifying the establishment of a military academy, promptly reported a bill which *rejected* the founding of such an institution. Instead, claiming somewhat lamely "that military knowledge is best acquired in the service," the committee proposed merely attaching five professors to the corps of engineers. These instructors would have been expected to circulate from post to post, teaching as they passed through. The committee was apparently influenced by Congress' inability to pay for an academy. It didn't really matter; Congress felt itself unable even to provide the roving professors. No action was taken to set up any form of military education at all. As a matter of fact, there was in being at that time hardly any kind of military establishment worthy of the name. One fine day in June 1784, 3 million or more Americans were guarded by the grand total of eighty privates commanded by a captain. And those eighty men were split between West Point and Fort Pitt. It should not be surprising that legislators spurned a school which would have produced officers for an all but nonexistent army.

For several years, West Point slept. The garrison, such as it was, guarded stores of supplies, cleaned and recleaned stacks of weapons, and swapped war stories. The chain rusted. Stones tumbled from untended walls. The invalids were available to teach, but they had neither ability nor students. If "Captain Molly," the name by which Margaret Corbin became widely known, is a fair example of the soldiers, the Corps of Invalids was nothing more than a hard-drinking group of wizened individuals willing enough to spin a yarn over a mug, but otherwise rather unproductive. Molly, a shrill wench who insisted upon salutes from the privates, was as loud and vile as the roughest man. A hearty drinker as well, and apt at any time to form an improper though temporary liaison with one of her fellow old soldiers, she was a most "disagreeable object to take care of." Captain Molly was boarded from time to time with different families, but for some reason she never captured their hearts. Perhaps her continual complaining grated on her hosts' nerves. The old veteran's clamors for new dresses were the cause of several letters between West Point's commandant and the Secretary of War. A profane and colorful fixture at West Point, she produced whatever excitement might have occurred in those somnolent years.

But America was as noisy as West Point was quiet. Great Britain refused to vacate several small posts in the Old Northwest and the United States was powerless to do anything about it but complain. Internally, in 1786, Daniel Shays organized and led a revolt in Massachusetts which neither the state nor the federal government was economically able to suppress. Raising $20,000 by private subscription, General Benjamin Lincoln scattered the insurgents, capturing Shays in the process. When frontier Indians acted up, America's shameful response was to dispatch unprepared and undersized detachments to quell them. General Josiah Harman was disgracefully routed by the red men. Arthur St. Clair took over only to walk into a massacre. Not until "Mad" Anthony Wayne was handed the command and given the necessary support were the Indians vanquished—and that was in 1794, the time of the Whiskey Rebellion in Pennsylvania and a year when Europe was ablaze with the holocaust of the Wars of the French Revolution. By then a new Constitution had been written and President George Washington was well into his second term. That year was also an important one at the army post in the Highlands.

West Point had returned to the public eye in 1790 when it became legally a part of the public domain. Stephen Moore, the actual owner of the rocky fortress on the Hudson, had petitioned the government in 1786 to be reimbursed for his lost lands. Henry Knox, the Secretary of War, recommended purchasing the site. Congress readily agreed—but could not raise enough money. Four years later Alexander Hamilton, as Secretary of the Treasury, renewed the request. This time Congress found the funds. For the price of $11,085, West Point became federal property on 10 September 1790.

There was reason behind obtaining a clear deed to the land: Washington, as President, still wanted to establish a military academy. He was backed strongly by Knox and Hamilton. Knox introduced a bill in 1790 which included a clause "to establish a military school." Congress at once pruned that provision. Three years later, with the prospect of becoming involved in the conflagration in Europe a distinct possibility, Washington tried again. Thomas Jefferson, Secretary of State, spoke out against an academy, believing it to be unconstitutional. Jefferson was the lone dissenter in the President's Cabinet, however, so Washington submitted the recommendation. (Jefferson, ironically enough, would ultimately be the President to sign into law a bill establishing the Military Academy.)

Congress, fearing a standing army more than foreign domination, refused to found the school the Chief Executive wanted. But the representatives did make a slight concession by providing books and instruments and by establishing vacancies for a number of cadets within existing regular army companies. No formal creation of an academy was involved, but there were students, texts, equipment, and instructors in the persons of three French engineers. All that was lacking was a site. Only one federal post was available, West Point. Thus by default it became an academic center. Beginning in 1794, cadets were educated in buildings on the plain. Nonetheless, for political reasons the United States steadfastly disclaimed ownership of a military academy. Steuben, whose concept of a broad education would be realized in another century, died the same year in which cadets came to West Point.

In that manner, on a bootleg basis, the academy began to operate, holding classes initially in the abandoned Revolutionary War jail house. Lieutenant Colonel Stephen Rochefontaine, commandant of West Point, designed a curriculum comprising the study of fortifications, military maneuvers (using Steuben's *Blue Book* as a text), and drawing. Officers as well as cadets attended classes. Unfortunately, academic endeavors received a setback in 1796 when all books and apparatus were lost in a fire which destroyed the old prison—a blaze touched off, many thought, by a disgruntled cadet. Rochefontaine thereupon transformed several private quarters into study rooms. The academy that was not an academy functioned on a reduced and cramped scale, but it functioned.

Along with a revised interest in the academy came a parallel concern with the fortress. Engineers initiated reconstruction of Forts Putnam and Clinton in 1794. Walls were made higher and stronger, magazines deeper and sturdier. Troops cleared brush from long unused trails and roads. Once again artificers swarmed around the works. The dormant stronghold began to come to life. Then, in the middle of the project, Congress cut off the money. Repairs halted. Workers were dismissed. Two of the Point's citadels stood half demolished, half rebuilt. The others were piles of stone fast disappearing beneath more than a decade of vegetation. To show his cadet and officer students what a fort should look like, Rochefontaine had to construct a wooden model near the cemetery. Studying fortifications from a mock-up at West Point was something akin to taking a hot dog to a banquet.

In 1798, with war against their old ally France staring them in the face, Congressmen passed two measures, not without bitter opposition, moving the academy toward a more regular footing. The first bill doubled the number of cadets, while the second authorized the President, then John Adams, to appoint "four teachers of the arts and sciencies." Adams, who had been one of the staunchest supporters for establishing a military academy back in 1776, waited some three years to take any action, and then he appointed only one instructor, a mathematician.

But pressure was building for a more comprehensive school. In 1799, Alexander Hamilton drafted plans for an academy with a two-year curriculum offering "all the sciences necessary to a perfect knowledge of the different branches of the military art." Those included mathematics, geography, drawing, natural philosophy, and chemistry. Washington, who had tried unsuccessfully to found an academy during his eight years in the

Presidency, fervently backed his ex-aide's proposal. On 12 December 1799, in the last letter he ever penned on public business, George Washington affirmed his feelings on the subject of a military academy: "The establishment of an institution of this kind, upon a respectable and extensive basis, has ever been considered by me as an object of primary importance to this country; and while I was in the Chair of Government I omitted no proper opportunity of recommending it . . . to the attention of the Legislature." Two days later the great man was dead.

Early in 1800, Hamilton's scheme was submitted to Congress, but the lawmakers adjourned in April without reaching a decision. In the autumn session that year the matter was debated. A strong faction, dead set against a military academy, urged abolishing even the semblance of a school already at West Point. "Light-Horse Harry" Lee, then a Congressman from Virginia, made an impassioned plea for saving "the only military school we have left." He narrowly carried the argument, giving renewed life to the little academy on the Hudson. (His son, Robert E. Lee, would one day be superintendent of the United States Military Academy.)

Thomas Jefferson succeeded John Adams in 1801. Adams, an early proponent of a military academy, had failed to act upon such powers as Congress had given him; Jefferson, a longtime opponent of a federal academy to produce professional officers, wasted no time in founding one. (Perhaps the puzzling practice of politics in America has not changed so much over the years after all.) Jefferson promptly appointed a second professor to instruct "such officers and cadets as may be at West Point." Then, deciding "in favor of the immediate establishment of a military school at West Point," the new President appointed Major Jonathan Williams as inspector of fortifications and made him commandant of the proposed institution. A survey of the Point was made to determine what was necessary "for the inspectors, teachers, cadets, etc., whom it is in contemplation to station at that post." Finally, orders went to all cadets in the army, except one, telling them "to repair to West Point by the first of September next."

In December 1801 the Senate confirmed Williams' appointment. Immediately, a disciplinary problem faced him. The first superintendent discovered a three-sided dispute between the cadets, the mathematics instructor, and the officer commanding the garrison. He fired the teacher.

The dozen or so cadets in attendance at any one time might or might not have been learning anything. When a young man became a cadet, one of them wrote in later life, "all order and regulation, either moral or religious, gave way to idleness, dissipation, and irreligion." At least once an angry student turned on a teacher, forcing him to fly to safety behind locked doors. Williams brought some order and discipline to the school, although he still headed an ill-defined institution designed to train both officers and cadets. But the final step, placing the academy on a proper and permanent basis, followed within months.

In an act passed on 16 March 1802, Congress authorized the President to organize a Corps of Engineers which would include ten cadets, with provisions to add ten more. The bill stipulated that the Corps "shall be stationed at West Point, in the State of New York, and shall constitute a military academy." Williams opened operations of the United States Military Academy on an appropriate date: 4 July 1802. Three months later the first class graduated. It consisted of two men.

After the school had been operating for a handful of years Williams wrote, "The Military Academy, as it now stands, is like a foundling, barely existing among the mountains, and nurtured at a distance out of sight and almost unknown to its legitimate parents." Nevertheless, the foundling had survived a most trying birth and was living. Placed in the same stony cradle which had provided security to the infant United States, the tiny school flourished. Rocked gently by ghosts of Revolutionary soldiers, soothed by the softly rolling waves of the grand river, watched over by towering mountains of granite, it developed into the finest military academy the world has known. The fortress had secured the colonies; the academy would protect the nation.

NOTES

CHAPTER 1 DECISION IN MAY

1. Worthington C. Ford (ed.), *Journals of the Continental Congress* (Washington, D.C., 1904–1937), II,* p. 52.

2. *Ibid.*, p. 54.

3. John C. Fitzpatrick (ed.), *The Diaries of George Washington* (New York, 1925), II, pp. 195–196.

4. John C. Fitzpatrick (ed.), *The Writings of George Washington* (Washington, D.C., 1931–1944), III, p. 292.

5. *Journals of Congress*, II, pp. 59–61, 64.

6. *Diaries of George Washington*, II, pp. 196–197.

CHAPTER 2 CONSTRUCTION BY COMMITTEE

1. Peter Force (ed.), *American Archives* (Washington, D.C., 1837–1853), Fourth Series, II, pp. 1259–1261. See also *Journals of Congress*, II, pp. 73–74.

2. *American Archives*, Fourth Series, II, pp. 1261–1266.

3. *Ibid.*, pp. 1291, 1295–1296. The map that accompanied their report is printed in *American Archives*, Fourth Series, III, opposite p. 736.

4. *Journals of Congress*, II, p. 95.

5. *American Archives*, Fourth Series, III, p. 535.

6. *Ibid.*, pp. 542, 558, 559, 656, 880.

7. *Ibid.* pp. 893, 897, 902, 1323. See also Berthold Fernow (ed.), *New York in the Revolution*, I, "New York State Archives," (XV Albany, 1887), p. 40.

*Roman numeral refers to volume number.

8. *American Archives*, Fourth Series, III, pp. 733–736 and maps following p. 736.

9. Letter, Berrien to Commissioners, 21 September 1775. The letter is presently in the possession of the Constitution Island Association.

10. *American Archives*, Fourth Series, III, pp. 902, 1274.

11. *Ibid.*, pp. 914–915.

12. *Ibid.*

13. *Ibid.*, pp. 914–915, 917, 919–920.

14. *Ibid.*, p. 1268.

15. For the various letters concerning the controversy over rendering honors while passing the forts, see *American Archives*, Fourth Series, III, pp. 1290–1291, 1293, 1295–1297.

16. *Journals of Congress*, III, pp. 280–282, 485–487.

17. *American Archives*, Fourth Series, III, pp. 1293–1294.

18. *American Archives*, Fourth Series, III, pp. 1284, 1299, 1301, 1311; IV, pp. 388, 390; VI, p. 1405; and Fifth Series, II, p. 666.

19. *Ibid.*, Fourth Series, III, pp. 1354–1367.

20. *Journals of Congress*, III, p. 341.

21. *American Archives*, Fourth Series, III, pp. 1657–1658.

22. *Ibid.*, IV, pp. 387–388, 420–422, 425.

23. Romans' map and the explanatory notes used to convince Congressmen are now a part of the collection of the West Point Museum. See also *Journals of Congress*, IV, pp. 34, 53, 152–153; *American Archives*, Fourth Series, IV, pp. 875, 1051, 1064, 1097, 1155.

CHAPTER 3 THE SCENE OF WAR SHIFTS

1. A strategic study can be seen in Collections of the New-York Historical Society, *The Letters and Papers of Cadwallader Colden, 1765–1775* ("The Cadwallader Colden Papers" [New York, 1923]), VII, pp. 197–198. See also Dartmouth to Gage, 15 April 1775, Whitehall, in Public Record Office, *America and the West Indies and Military Correspondence, 1773–1783*, C.O. 5/92, p. 103.

2. Sir Henry Clinton, *The American Rebellion*, William B. Willcox, ed., (New Haven, 1954), pp. 11–12.

3. Sir John Fortescue, *A History of the British Army* (London, 1911), III, p. 168.

4. *Writings of Washington*, IV, pp. 217–226.

5. *Ibid.*, p. 222.

6. *American Archives*, Fourth Series, IV, pp. 1062–1063. See also John Alden, *General Charles Lee* (Baton Rouge, 1951), pp. 95–103.

7. *American Archives*, Fourth Series, IV, pp. 427, 1051, 1064.

8. William B. Willcox, *Portrait of a General* (New York, 1964), pp. 69–76.

9. *American Archives*, Fourth Series, IV, pp. 1155–1156; V, pp. 297–299.

10. Peter J. Guthorn, *American Maps and Mapmakers of the Revolution* (Monmouth Beach, N.J., 1966), p. 33. See also *American Archives*, Fourth Series, V, pp. 316, 321–322, 325–326.

11. *American Archives*, Fourth Series, V, pp. 1416–1417.

12. *Ibid.*, pp. 811–812, 1435.

13. *Writings of Washington*, V, pp. 10–11; and *American Archives*, Fourth Series, V, p. 1493; VI, p. 673.

14. *American Archives*, Fourth Series, VI, pp. 445–446.

15. *Writings of Washington*, V, p. 69.

16. *American Archives*, Fourth Series, VI, p. 673.

17. *Ibid.*, pp. 792–793, 818; *Writings of Washington*, V, pp. 138–139.

CHAPTER 4 RETREAT AND PANIC

1. *Writings of Washington*, V, pp. 265, 313.

2. *American Archives*, Fifth Series, I, p. 1409.

3. *Ibid.*, p. 1411.

4. Hugh Hastings (ed.), *Public Papers of George Clinton* (New York, 1899–1914), I, pp. 247–253.

5. *Minutes of the Secret Committee*, manuscript in Washington's Headquarters Museum, Newburgh, New York. See Minutes for 19, 20, 22 July 1776.

6. *Public Papers of George Clinton*, I, pp. 273–275.

7. *Writings of Washington*, V, pp. 318–319.

8. No full-length biography of Machin exists. For a brief account of his life, see Paul B. Mattice, "Captain Thomas Machin," *Schoharie County Historical Review* (October 1955), pp. 5–13.

9. From a letter of Lord Rawdon to the Earl of Huntington, 5 August 1775, in George F. Scheer and Hugh F. Rankin, *Rebels and Redcoats* (New York, 1957), p. 159.

10. *American Archives*, Fifth Series, I, pp. 751–752, 762, 766–767. See also *Writings of Washington*, V, pp. 454, 458–459.

11. *Writings of Washington*, VI, p. 184.

12. *American Archives*, Fifth Series, I, pp. 557, 1562; II, pp. 662, 666–667, 670.

13. *Minutes of the Secret Committee*, 25 July–15 September 1776. See also *American Archives*, Fifth Series, I, pp. 112–113.

14. Rawdon to Huntington, *loc. cit.*

15. *Minutes of the Secret Committee*, 9 October and 11 October 1776.

16. *Public Papers of George Clinton*, I, pp. 404–405.

17. *American Archives*, Fifth Series, III, pp. 316, 331–334, 371, 1140.

18. *Writings of Washington*, VI, pp. 271–298. See also *American Archives*, Fifth Series, III, pp. 679–680.

19. *American Archives*, Fifth Series, III, p. 302.

20. *Ibid.*, pp. 283, 316, 332, 327–328, 361, 1043.

21. *Ibid.*, pp. 338–342, 348, 1169–1170, 1366–1367, 1450, 1467.

CHAPTER 5 FIVE LANGUID MONTHS

1. *Public Papers of George Clinton*, I, pp. 487–488.

2. William Heath, *Heath's Memoirs of the American War* (New York, 1904), pp. 62,

114–118. See also *Public Papers of George Clinton*, I, pp. 509–529. Some statistics are in Fernow, *New York in the Revolution*, I, p. 145. A manuscript letter, William Duer to McDougall, 25 February 1777, in the *Alexander McDougall Papers* (manuscript in the New-York Historical Society, New York), provides further information.

3. *American Archives*, Fifth Series, III, pp. 338–339.

4. *Public Papers of George Clinton*, I, pp. 529–583.

5. Letter, George Clinton to Thomas Machin, 31 January 1777 (Sterling Manuscript Collection, New York State Library), pp. 608–609.

6. *Writings of Washington*, VII, p. 77.

7. *Public Papers of George Clinton*, I, pp. 619–620.

8. *Ibid.*, I, pp. 640–642, 662, 666, 671, 679.

9. John E. Wilmot, *Journals of the Provincial Congress, Provincial Convention, Committee of Safety and Council of the State of New York, 1775–1777* (Albany, 1842), I, p. 842.

10. Erastus C. Knight (compiler), *New York in the Revolution*, Supplement, "New York State Archives" (Albany, 1901), p. 49.

11. *Public Papers of George Clinton*, I, pp. 677–682.

12. *Writings of Washington*, VII, pp. 317–319.

13. *Alexander McDougall Papers*. See items relating to the court-martial of Colonel Henry B. Livingston, June 1777.

14. *Public Papers of George Clinton*, I, pp. 682–683, 688–689, 725–728, 821.

15. See *McDougall Papers*, especially April 1777. See also *Public Papers of George Clinton*, I, p. 802.

16. Letter, McDougall to James Clinton, 27 April 1777, and Minutes of a "Council of Warr" held 28 April 1777, both in *McDougall Papers*.

17. Jared Sparks (ed.), *Correspondence of the American Revolution* (Cambridge, 1853), I, p. 373.

18. *Writings of Washington*, VII, pp. 445, 474; VIII, p. 25.

19. *Ibid.*, VIII, pp. 34, 39.

20. *Correspondence of the American Revolution*, I, p. 377.

CHAPTER 6 AN UNCERTAIN SUMMER

1. *Writings of Washington*, VIII, p. 116.

2. Fernow, *New York in the Revolution*, I, pp. 153–155; *Writings of Washington*, VII, pp. 291–294; VIII, p. 95; *American Archives*, Fifth Series, III, pp. 355–357, 1192; *Public Papers of George Clinton*, II, pp. 5–6, 8, 28, 73–74; Letters, McDougall to New York Provincial Convention, 22 March 1777, and McDougall to Continental Navy Board of War, 16 May 1777, in *McDougall Papers*; *Public Papers of George Clinton*, II, p. 8.

3. *Writings of Washington*, VIII, pp. 234, 257, 276, 283, 309, 324.

4. *Ibid.*, pp. 324, 326, 328–331.

5. *Public Papers of George Clinton*, II, pp. 73–75.

6. *Ibid.*, pp. 93, 103.

7. Charles F. Adams (ed.), *Familiar Letters of John Adams and His Wife Abigail Adams, During the Revolution* (New York, 1876), p. 283.

8. *Public Papers of George Clinton*, II, p. 122; *Writings of Washington*, VIII, pp. 376, 409, 414; *Familiar Letters of John Adams*, p. 282.

9. Randolph G. Adams (ed.), *The Headquarters Papers of the British Army in North America* (Ann Arbor, 1926), opposite p. 12. The message is contained in the body of a covering message and can be read only with the aid of a special mask. The mask is included in the papers left by Clinton.

10. This account was gleaned from Joseph B. Turner (ed.), *The Journal and Orderly Book of Captain Robert Kirkwood* (Wilmington, Del., 1910), pp. 95–130.

11. Worthington C. Ford (ed.), *Putnam's General Orders, 1777* (Brooklyn, 1893), pp. 34, 38.

12. *Writings of Washington*, VIII, p. 491; IX, pp. 1–3.

13. *Public Papers of George Clinton*, II, pp. 140, 183–187, 195–197.

14. Quoted in *Putnam's General Orders, 1777*, p. 49. Information relating to this incident is also in New York Secretary of State, *Calendar of Historical Manuscripts Relating to the War of the Revolution* (Albany, 1868), II, pp. 258–260.

15. *Writings of Washington*, VIII, pp. 32, 40, 43, 71, 107, 111, 117.

16. E. Wilder Spaulding, *His Excellency George Clinton* (New York, 1964), p. 74; "Report of the Court of Enquiry," 5 April 1778, in *McDougall Papers*; *Public Papers of George Clinton*, II, p. 133. See Letters, Colonel John Lamb to Machin, 2, 8, and 19 September 1777, in H. G. Babcock (compiler), *The Great Chain* (in Manuscript Collection, United States Military Academy, West Point, New York). See also miscellaneous manuscript receipts, summer 1777, in *The Great Chain*. Machin's expense account is printed in part in Knight, *New York in the Revolution*, Supplement, p. 49.

17. Testimony of Captain Machin, "Report of The Court of Enquiry," *McDougall Papers*; also *Public Papers of George Clinton*, II, p. 270.

18. *Putnam's General Orders, 1777*, pp. 43, 49–50, 60–61, 70.

19. Letter, Clinton to Burgoyne, 10 September 1777, in Revolutionary War Manuscript Collection, Duke University.

20. *Writings of Washington*, IX, p. 218; *Public Papers of George Clinton*, II, pp. 322–323; Spaulding, *Clinton*, pp. 74–75.

21. Letter, Putnam to President of Congress, 29 September 1777, in *McDougall Papers*.

CHAPTER 7 THE BATTLE OF FORT MONTGOMERY

1. Clinton, *The American Rebellion*, pp. 67–72; Willcox, *Portrait of a General*, pp. 174–177.

2. Willcox, *Portrait of a General*, pp. 178–180.

3. *Beverley Robinson's Orderly Books*, covering the period May 1777 to November 1779, with some omissions, are a part of the Manuscript Collection of the USMA Library. The entry quoted here is dated 5 May 1777. See also Carl Van Doren, *Secret History of the American Revolution* (New York, 1941), pp. 3–4; Testimony of Colonel Lamb, "Court of Enquiry," *McDougall Papers*.

4. In his report of the battle, Henry Clinton commended Robinson, "by whose knowledge of the country I was much aided in forming my plan." See Letter, Clinton to Howe, 9 October 1777, in Donald F. Clark, *Fort Montgomery and Fort Clinton* (Highlands, N.Y., 1952), pp. 11–12.

5. Letter, Hotham to Lord Howe, 9 October 1777, in Clark, *Fort Montgomery and Fort Clinton*, pp. 13–14; Testimony of Captain Hoo, "Court of Enquiry," *McDougall Papers*.

6. *Public Papers of George Clinton*, II, pp. 348–350, 360.

7. *Ibid.*, pp. 362–363.

8. *Ibid.*, p. 364.

9. Testimony of Captain Buchannan, "Court of Enquiry," *McDougall Papers;* Letters, Hotham to Lord Howe and Clinton to Howe, 9 October 1777, in Clark, *Fort Montgomery and Fort Clinton*, pp. 11–14.

10. *Public Papers of George Clinton*, II, p. 391; Testimony of General Putnam, "Court of Enquiry," *McDougall Papers.*

11. Testimony of Captain Rosecrans, Lieutenant English, Colonel Dubois, and George Clinton, "Court of Enquiry," *McDougall Papers.*

12. Testimony of Colonel Hughes, Colonel Lamb, Brigadier General Parsons, and Mr. George Leonard, "Court of Enquiry," *McDougall Papers.*

13. *Public Papers of George Clinton*, II, pp. 391–392; Testimony of Thomas Machin and Colonel Dubois, "Court of Enquiry," *McDougall Papers;* William Carr and Richard Koke, *Twin Forts of the Popolopen* (Bear Mountain Trailsides Museum Historical Bulletin Number 1, 1937), p. 33.

14. Charles Stedman, *History of the Origin, Progress, and Termination of the American War* (Dublin, 1794), I, pp. 400–401.

15. Testimony of General Putnam, "Court of Enquiry," *McDougall Papers.*

16. *Public Papers of George Clinton*, II, pp. 391–392; Testimony of Colonel Dubois, "Court of Enquiry," *McDougall Papers.*

17. *Public Papers of George Clinton*, III, pp. 311–312.

18. Testimony of Thomas Machin, George Clinton, Major Newkirk, and Colonel Dubois, "Court of Enquiry," *McDougall Papers.*

19. Testimony of Captain Moody, General James Clinton, and Captain Faulkner, "Court of Enquiry," *McDougall Papers.*

20. Stedman, *History of the American War*, I, p. 403; Testimony of Captain Hodge and Captain Moody, "Court of Enquiry," *McDougall Papers;* Clinton, *The American Rebellion*, p. 76.

21. "Extracts from the Log of *Dependence Galley*," *Year Book* (Dutchess County Historical Society, 1935), XX, p. 96; Testimony of Captain Hodge, "Court of Enquiry," *McDougall Papers.*

22. *Public Papers of George Clinton*, II, p. 393; Testimony of Thomas Machin, "Court of Enquiry," *McDougall Papers.*

23. Letter, Oswald to Lamb, 6 October 1777, in *Lamb Papers* (Manuscript Collection, New-York Historical Society); Testimony of Colonel Meigs and General Parsons, "Court of Enquiry," *McDougall Papers.*

24. Stedman, *History of the American War*, I, p. 462; Clinton, *The American Rebellion*, p. 76; Testimony of General James Clinton and Major Newkirk, "Court of Enquiry," *McDougall Papers.*

25. Testimony of James Clinton and Captain Faulkner, "Court of Enquiry," *McDougall Papers.*

26. Testimony of Thomas Machin, Colonel Dubois, Captain Rosecrans, and Major Newkirk, "Court of Enquiry," *McDougall Papers;* Clinton, *The American Rebellion*, p. 76; *Public Papers of George Clinton*, II, pp. 393–394.

27. Testimony of General James Clinton, "Court of Enquiry," *McDougall Papers;* *Public Papers of George Clinton*, II, pp. 393–394.

28. Stedman, *History of the American War*, I, pp. 405–406; "Log of *Dependence*

Galley," p. 96; Testimony of Captain Hodge, "Court of Enquiry," *McDougall Papers.*

CHAPTER 8 A FORTNIGHT OF DEFEAT

1. *Public Papers of George Clinton,* II, pp. 382, 388.

2. Letter, Hotham to Lord Howe, 9 October 1777, in Clark, *Fort Montgomery and Fort Clinton,* pp. 13–14. See also "Log of *Dependence Galley,*" 6, 7, 8 October 1777.

3. Timothy Dwight, *Travels in New England and New York* (New Haven, 1822), III, pp. 435–436; United States Military Academy, *The Centennial of the United States Military Academy at West Point, New York* (Washington, D.C., 1904), I, p. 156. The question of burials is also discussed in Carr and Koke, *Twin Forts of the Popolopen,* pp. 48–52.

4. Letter, Hotham to Lord Howe, 9 October 1777, in Clark, *Fort Montgomery and Fort Clinton,* pp. 13–14. See also "Log of *Dependence Galley,*" 6, 7, 8 October 1777.

5. "Court of Enquiry," *McDougall Papers; Public Papers of George Clinton,* II, pp. 382, 394; Letters, Hotham to Lord Howe, 9 October 1777, and Henry Clinton to William Howe, 9 October 1777, in Clark, *Fort Montgomery and Fort Clinton,* pp. 11–14.

6. Letter, Clinton to Burgoyne, 8 October 1777, in Revolutionary War Collection, Duke University.

7. Letters, Clinton to General Howe, 9 October 1777, and Hotham to Lord Howe, 9 October 1777, in Clark, *Fort Montgomery and Fort Clinton,* pp. 11–15.

8. Quoted in Mrs. James C. Cross, *The Moores of West Point* (unpublished manuscript in the USMA Library, 1966). Other information relating to the Moores and the Moore House can be found in Agnes Miller, "Owner of West Point," *New York History,* XXXIII (July 1952), pp. 303–312.

9. Clinton, *The American Rebellion,* p. 79; Letter, Clinton to Burgoyne, 10 October 1777, in Revolutionary War Collection, Duke University; also Carr and Koke, *Twin Forts of the Popolopen,* p. 43.

10. *Public Papers of George Clinton,* II, pp. 385, 388.

11. *Ibid.,* pp. 387–395.

12. *Ibid.,* pp. 402–403.

13. Accounts of the spy with the silver bullet, most quite fanciful, can be found in many sources. This account relies on contemporary documents. See *Public Papers of George Clinton,* II, pp. 398, 403, 413, 443–444; James Thacher, *Military Journal of the American Revolution* (Hartford, 1862), p. 106.

14. *Public Papers of George Clinton,* II, 423–426; Carr and Koke, *Twin Forts of the Popolopen,* p. 43; "Log of *Dependence Galley,*" 11 October 1777.

15. *Public Papers of George Clinton,* II, pp. 405, 417, 419.

16. Clinton's Orders and Instructions, 11 October 1777, Revolutionary War Collection, Duke University; Clinton, *The American Rebellion,* p. 79; Willcox, *Portrait of a General,* pp. 187–188; "Log of *Dependence Galley,*" 15 October 1777.

17. Letters, Vaughan and Wallace to Hotham, 17 October 1777, in *Public Papers of George Clinton,* II, p. 458; "Log of *Dependence Galley,*" entries 16 and 17 October 1777. See also Clinton to Gates, 16 October 1777, in *Public Papers of George Clinton,* II, pp. 444–445.

18. Testimony of Colonel Lamb, "Court of Enquiry," *McDougall Papers.*

19. Van Doren, *Secret History of the American Revolution,* pp. 3–6.

20. Letter, Howe to Clinton, 9 October 1777, in Revolutionary War Collection, Duke University; Clinton, *The American Rebellion,* pp. 80–81; Collections of the New-York Historical Society, *The Kemble Papers* (New York, 1884), I, p. 139.

21. "Log of *Dependence Galley,*" entries 23 October 1777. See also Letter, Hotham to Lord Howe, 15 October 1777, in *Year Book,* XX, p. 93.

22. "Extracts from the Log of *Preston,*" *Year Book,* entry of 28 October 1777.

CHAPTER 9 FIVE LOST MONTHS

1. The complete return of items captured and destroyed is printed in Clark, *Fort Montgomery and Fort Clinton,* p. 15.

2. *Journals of Congress,* IX, p. 774; *Writings of Washington,* IX, pp. 325, 339.

3. Elizabeth S. Kite, *Brigadier General Louis Le Bègue Duportail* (Baltimore, 1933), pp. 1–34.

4. *Writings of Washington,* X, p. 35.

5. *Correspondence of the American Revolution,* II, p. 30.

6. Harold C. Syrett (ed.), *The Papers of Alexander Hamilton* (New York, 1961), I, pp. 347–360.

7. *Journals of Congress,* IX, pp. 864–868; *Writings of Washington,* X, p. 40.

8. *Familiar Letters of John Adams,* pp. 322–323.

9. *Journals of Congress,* IX, pp. 971–972; *Public Papers of George Clinton,* II, pp. 586–589.

10. *Writings of Washington,* X, pp. 129–133.

11. *Ibid.,* pp. 135–136.

12. Kite, *Duportail,* pp. 34, 79–85.

13. *Public Papers of George Clinton,* II, pp. 586–589.

14. *Ibid.,* pp. 589–594.

15. *Writings of Washington,* X, pp. 212–213; *Public Papers of George Clinton,* II, pp. 607–608.

16. Kite, *Duportail,* pp. 82–87.

17. *Public Papers of George Clinton,* II, p. 712.

18. *Ibid.,* p. 679.

19. Kite, *Duportail,* pp. 85–88.

20. *Centennial of the United States Military Academy,* I, pp. 154–155.

21. *Writings of Washington,* X, pp. 307, 348–349.

22. Letter, Putnam to Washington, 13 February 1778, quoted in Charles S. Hall, *Life and Letters of Samuel Holden Parsons* (Binghamton, N.Y., 1905), p. 142; Edward C. Boynton, *History of West Point* (New York, 1863), pp. 59–60; Parsons to George Clinton, 15 February 1778, in Hall, *Parsons,* p. 143.

23. *Writings of Washington,* XI, p. 69; *Public Papers of George Clinton,* II, pp. 690–691, 724–729.

24. *Journals of Congress,* X, pp. 180–181; Hall, *Parsons,* pp. 153–155.

25. *Writings of Washington,* X, pp. 469–470; *Public Papers of George Clinton,* II,

pp. 859–860; Frank Moore, *Diary of the American Revolution* (New York, 1860), I, entry of 31 December 1777.

26. Kite, *Duportail*, pp. 85, 87.

27. *Journals of Congress*, X, pp. 221–222; Letter, Gates to Putnam, 5 March 1778, in *McDougall Papers*.

28. Letter, Parsons to Washington, 7 March 1778, in Hall, *Parsons*, pp. 153–155.

29. Hall, *Parsons*, pp. 161–162.

30. *Public Papers of George Clinton*, II, p. 820; Hall, *Parsons*, p. 161.

CHAPTER 10 THE GREAT CHAIN

1. *Public Papers of George Clinton*, II, p. 679.

2. *Ibid.*, pp. 651, 679–680, 690–691.

3. Knight, *New York in the Revolution*, Supplement, p. 49.

4. *Journals of Congress*, X, 180–181; *Writings of Washington*, X, p. 349; *Public Papers of George Clinton*, II, pp. 687–688, 711–712; Knight, *New York in the Revolution*, Supplement, p. 153; Edward M. Ruttenber, *Obstructions to the Navigation of Hudson's River* (Albany, 1860), p. 141.

5. The entire agreement is printed in *Public Papers of George Clinton*, II, 708–709. A photograph of the manuscript copy (lost in a fire in Albany) can be seen in the frontispiece of William M. Horner, *Obstructions of the Hudson River during the Revolution* (Privately printed: New Jersey, 1927); Ruttenber, *Obstructions to the Navigation of Hudson's River*, p. 141.

6. Knight, *New York in the Revolution*, Supplement, p. 49; *Public Papers of George Clinton*, II, pp. 729, 848; Ruttenber, *Obstructions to the Navigation of Hudson's River*, p. 141.

7. Knight, *New York in the Revolution*, Supplement, p. 49; *Public Papers of George Clinton*, III, p. 21.

8. Letter, Hughes to Machin, 11 March 1778, in Babcock, *The Great Chain*, p. 2.

9. *Writings of Washington*, XI, pp. 95–96; McDougall's Diary entries, 21 March–8 April 1778, *McDougall Papers*.

10. McDougall's Diary, 10 April 1778, *McDougall Papers*; Ruttenber, *Obstructions to the Navigation of Hudson's River*, p. 142.

11. A contemporary description of the chain can be found in Thacher, *Journal*, p. 216. A modern but superficial study of the chain is Major Andrew Mansinne, Jr., "The West Point Chain and Hudson River Obstructions in the Revolutionary War," *Constitution Island Association Annual Report*, 1967. A book-length treatment of the subject, now in preparation, is Edward Hermann, *Thirteen Links* (tentative title).

12. McDougall's Diary, 30 April 1778, *McDougall Papers*; Knight, *New York in the Revolution*, Supplement, p. 49; *Public Papers of George Clinton*, III, p. 246; Letter, George Clinton to Thomas Machin, 3 May 1778, in Sterling Manuscript Collection, New York State Library, p. 633; Ruttenber, *Obstructions to the Navigation of Hudson's River*, p. 142.

CHAPTER 11 AN ENGINEER FROM POLAND

1. Hall, *Parsons*, pp. 149–150, 157.

2. *Public Papers of George Clinton*, III, p. 29; Hall, *Parsons*, pp. 156–157.

3. *Writings of Washington,* XI, pp. 95–97, 103–104; *Journals of Congress,* X, pp. 275–276.

4. *Public Papers of George Clinton,* II, p. 848.

5. *Ibid.,* III, pp. 85–86.

6. *Writings of Washington,* XI, p. 119.

7. Letter, Parsons to McDougall, 28 March 1778, in *McDougall Papers.*

8. McDougall's Diary, 29 March 1778, *McDougall Papers.*

9. *Writings of Washington,* XI, pp. 222, 298; McDougall's Diary, month of April 1778, *McDougall Papers;* Kite, *Duportail,* pp. 91–95.

10. *Public Papers of George Clinton,* III, pp. 72–73, 117; McDougall's Diary, 3 and 4 April 1778, *McDougall Papers.*

11. *Public Papers of George Clinton,* II, p. 803; III, p. 151.

12. Letters, McDougall to Parsons, 2 April 1778, McDougall to George Clinton, 3 April 1778, Parsons to McDougall, 3 and 4 April 1778, in *McDougall Papers.*

13. McDougall's Diary, 8–11 April 1778, *McDougall Papers;* Miecislaus Haiman, *Kosciuszko in the American Revolution* (New York, 1943), p. 48.

14. Rufus Putnam, *The Memoirs of Rufus Putnam* (Cambridge, 1903), p. 75.

15. *Centennial of the United States Military Academy,* I, pp. 161–163.

16. *Public Papers of George Clinton,* III, pp. 180, 195; Haiman, *Kosciuszko,* p. 48.

17. Hall, *Parsons,* p. 175; Haiman, *Kosciuszko,* pp. 49–50; Thacher, *Journal,* pp. 324–325.

18. *Writings of Washington,* XI, pp. 351–352.

19. *Public Papers of George Clinton,* III, pp. 294, 312.

20. *Journals of Congress,* X, pp. 354–355; *Public Papers of George Clinton,* III, p. 310.

21. McDougall's Diary, 11–13 May 1778, *McDougall Papers.* See one of the earliest uses of "Fort Arnold" in *Public Papers of George Clinton,* III, p. 311.

22. McDougall's Diary, 11–26 May 1778, *McDougall Papers; Public Papers of George Clinton,* III, p. 294.

23. Thacher, *Journal,* p. 133.

24. *Ibid.,* pp. 133–134.

25. *General John Glover's Orderly Books* (Collection in United States Military Academy Library, typescript copies), III, pp. 365, 369–370, 372.

26. *Writings of Washington,* XII, p. 343.

27. *Public Papers of George Clinton,* III, p. 496; *Writings of Washington,* XII, p. 129; Haiman, *Kosciuszko,* p. 51.

28. *Glover's Orderly Books,* III, p. 366; Knight, *New York in the Revolution,* Supplement, p. 49; Mansinne, "The West Point Chain . . ."; Ruttenber, *Obstructions to the Navigation of Hudson's River,* pp. 138–146.

29. Thacher, *Journal,* p. 139; *Writings of Washington,* XII, pp. 167, 188, 197; Miscellaneous manuscript document, "Return of Ordnance in Fort Arnold and the Several Redoubts, and Batteries," 28 June 1778, West Point Library Collection.

30. Letter, Malcolm to Lamb, 2 August 1778, quoted in Isaac Q. Leake, *Memoir of General John Lamb* (Albany, 1850), p. 207; Thacher, *Journal,* p. 140; *Glover's Orderly Books,* III, p. 384.

1. Thacher, *Journal*, p. 216.

2. Quoted in Hall, *Parsons*, p. 185.

3. *Writings of Washington*, XII, pp. 282, 302–303, 314–315, 332–333, 363, 366–367, 372–373; XIII, p. 218; XV, p. 340.

4. *Orderly Book of Lieutenant Joshua Drake* (Orderly Book Collection, New-York Historical Society), entries 5 and 11 August 1778 and 7 October 1778; *Writings of Washington*, XII, pp. 282, 320; *Miscellaneous Revolutionary War Documents*, National Archives, No. 21053, p. 17.

5. *Miscellaneous Revolutionary War Documents*, National Archives, No. 31621; *Public Papers of George Clinton*, III, pp. 667–668, 674.

6. *Writings of Washington*, XII, pp. 314–315; XIII, p. 360.

7. *Writings of Washington*, XII, pp. 363, 408–409.

8. Duportail's entire report is quoted in Kite, *Duportail*, pp. 96–101.

9. *Writings of Washington*, XII, pp. 376–377; Kite, *Duportail*, pp. 111–113.

10. *Writings of Washington*, XII, pp. 419–420.

11. Haiman, *Kosciuszko*, pp. 70–73.

12. *Writings of Washington*, XII, p. 469; Haiman, *Kosciuszko*, pp. 54–55.

13. *Writings of Washington*, XII, pp. 480, 526–527.

14. *Writings of Washington*, XIII, p. 13; *Public Papers of George Clinton*, III, pp. 651–652.

15. *Public Papers of George Clinton*, IV, pp. 301–302.

16. *Joshua Drake's Orderly Book*, 25 August 1778, 29 August 1778, 4 September 1778, 25 September 1778, and 4 October 1778.

17. *Journals of Congress*, XII, p. 1018.

18. *Writings of Washington*, XIII, pp. 320–321, 375, 399; *Public Papers of George Clinton*, IV, pp. 353, 357, 362–363; Letter, McDougall to Paterson, 7 December 1778, in *McDougall Papers*.

19. Letters, McDougall to Washington, 9 and 10 December 1778, in *McDougall Papers*; *Writings of Washington*, XIII, p. 400.

20. Haiman, *Kosciuszko*, pp. 74–78; Letter, Kosciuszko to McDougall, 6 February 1779, and Returns made by General Paterson, 22 January 1779, in *McDougall Papers*.

21. Letter, McDougall to George Clinton, 4 December 1778, in *McDougall Papers*.

22. Letter, McDougall to Washington, 10 December 1778, in *McDougall Papers*.

23. Instructions to Gouvion, 17 December 1778, and Letter, McDougall to Gouvion, 20 December 1778, in *McDougall Papers*.

24. "Estimate of Barracks Room at West Point," 1779, *McDougall Papers*.

25. *Writings of Washington*, XIII, p. 218; Letter, McDougall to Major Dobbs, 22 December 1778, in *McDougall Papers*.

26. Letters, Paterson to McDougall, 21 and 24 December 1778, in *McDougall Papers*.

27. Letter, Paterson to McDougall, 25 December 1778, in *McDougall Papers*.

28. Letters, McDougall to Paterson, 27 December 1778, Kosciuszko to McDougall, 28 December 1778, Paterson to McDougall, 29 December 1778, Kosciuszko to McDougall, 2 January 1779, in *McDougall Papers*.

29. Letters, Paterson to McDougall, 5 and 6 January 1778, McDougall to Washington, 6 November 1779, in *McDougall Papers*.

30. *Public Papers of George Clinton*, IV, pp. 383–387; Letter, McDougall to Paterson, 21 February 1779, in *McDougall Papers;* Letter, E. Huntington to A. Huntington, 3 June 1778, in Charles F. Heartman (ed.), *Letters Written by Ebenezer Huntington* (New York, 1914), p. 70.

CHAPTER 13 STEUBEN AND STONY POINT

1. An excellent brief sketch of Steuben's career in America is Jay Luvaas, " 'Baron' von Steuben: Washington's Drillmaster," *American History Illustrated*, II (April 1967), pp. 4–11 and 55–58. The best biography is John M. Palmer, *General von Steuben* (New Haven, 1937). An up-to-date biography is needed.

2. *Writings of Washington*, XIV, pp. 411–412; Letter, Timothy Whiting to John Fisher, 2 April 1779, in Babcock, *The Great Chain*.

3. *Writings of Washington*, XXIV, p. 125.

4. Letters, Timothy Whiting to John Fisher, 7 and 9 May 1779, in Babcock, *The Great Chain;* Letter, Duportail to Jay, 11 May 1779, in *Washington Papers*, Library of Congress.

5. See Clinton's explanation of his scheme in Clinton, *The American Rebellion*, pp. 121–124.

6. *Writings of Washington*, XV, pp. 141, 167.

7. Clinton, *The American Rebellion*, pp. 124–125.

8. *Writings of Washington*, XV, pp. 213, 219, 225, 228–229; Hall, *Parsons*, p. 247; *Miscellaneous Revolutionary War Records*, "Rations Issued at Fort Arnold," 10 June 1779, National Archives, No. 22104.

9. Clinton, *The American Rebellion*, pp. 125–126; *Writings of Washington*, XV, p. 319.

10. Letters, Bauman to Lamb, 7 and 30 June 1779, in *Lamb Papers*.

11. *McDougall's Orderly Book*, "Highlands and West Point," 6 June–21 August 1779 (Orderly Book Collection, New-York Historical Society), entry of 27 June 1779.

12. Thomas E. Griess, "Washington's Commandant of Engineers: The Service of Louis Le Bègue Duportail, 1777–1783" (Unpublished Duke University Study, 1965), pp. 21–22; Kite, *Duportail*, p. 139; *Writings of Washington*, XV, pp. 213–214, 255.

13. Heath, *Memoirs*, p. 218; *Writings of Washington*, XV, pp. 354–356; *McDougall's Orderly Book*, 30 June 1779.

14. *Writings of Washington*, XV, pp. 364, 366–367.

15. Putnam, *Memoirs*, pp. 80–81; *Writings of Washington*, XV, pp. 380, 386.

16. Heath, *Memoirs*, p. 221; *Writings of Washington*, XV, p. 373; *McDougall's Orderly Book*, 13 July 1779.

17. The route has recently been most accurately plotted by Mr. John H. Mead, an archeologist and historian, by the technique of projecting Erskine's maps to the same scale as modern topographical maps of the area, superimposing the two, and validating the results by personal examinations of the ground.

18. I. W. Sklarsky, *The Revolution's Boldest Venture* (Port Washington, N.Y., 1965), pp. 74–77; Henry P. Johnson, *The Storming of Stony Point* (New York, 1900), pp. 76–77; Christopher Ward, *The War of the Revolution* (New York, 1952), II, p. 599.

19. Wayne's Letter is reproduced in Sklarsky, *The Revolution's Boldest Venture*, p. 90.

20. *Writings of Washington*, XV, pp. 426–431.

21. *Ibid.*, pp. 433–434.

22. Phillips Russell, *North Carolina in the Revolutionary War* (Charlotte, 1965), pp. 4–7.

23. *Writings of Washington*, XV, p. 434 and note, p. 439.

24. Letter, McDougall to Washington, 17 July 1779, in *Washington Papers*.

25. Scheer and Rankin, *Rebels and Redcoats*, pp. 363–364.

CHAPTER 14 WASHINGTON AT WEST POINT

1. *Writings of Washington*, XV, pp. 436–437, 443–444.

2. Elijah Fisher, *Elijah Fisher's Journal*, W. B. Lapham, ed. (Augusta, Ga., 1880), p. 12.

3. *Writings of Washington*, XV, pp. 341–342, 465.

4. *Ibid.*, p. 442.

5. *Ibid.*, pp. 442, 446.

6. McDougall's Diary, 24 and 27 July 1779, *McDougall's Papers; Writings of Washington*, XV, p. 475; XVII, frontispiece.

7. John H. Mead, *Archeological Survey of Fort Putnam and Other Revolutionary Fortifications at West Point, N.Y., 1967–1968* (Unpublished study, USMA Museum, 1968), pp. 76–80.

8. The original manuscript of Duportail's report, dated 20 August 1779, is preserved in Paris in the French *Archives Historiques* in the *Dépôt de la Guerre* under title *"Mémoire sur la défense de Wes[t]point."* A reproduction with a translation by Lieutenant Colonel Donald T. Dunne is in the West Point Library's Revolutionary War Collection.

9. *Writings of Washington*, XV, pp. 489–490, 501–502; XVI, pp. 17–18.

10. *Ibid.*, XVI, pp. 72, 137–138, 163, 230–231.

11. Willcox, *Portrait of a General*, pp. 283–284 and footnote, p. 284.

12. *Writings of Washington*, XVI, p. 70.

13. *Ibid.*, XVI, pp. 116–117.

14. Marquis de Chastellux, *Travels in North America* (Great American Historical Classics Series [Bowling Green, Ohio, 1919]), pp. 370–371.

15. *Ibid.*, p. 371; Receipts made by Caleb Gibbs, 14 August and 19 September 1779, *Washington Papers*, Library of Congress.

16. James T. Flexner, *George Washington in the American Revolution* (Boston, 1968), p. 203; Scheer and Rankin, *Rebels and Redcoats*, p. 369; *Writings of Washington*, XVI, p. 425.

17. *Public Papers of George Clinton*, V, pp. 203–204.

18. James R. Case, "Nominal Role, American Union Lodge, 1776–1783," *Transactions, the American Lodge of Research*, Vol. VI, No. 3 (30 January–27 December 1956), pamphlet.

19. *Writings of Washington*, XVI, p. 13.

20. *Ibid.*, p. 56; *McDougall's Orderly Book*, 17 August 1779.

21. Letter, Bauman to Lamb, 3 September 1779, in *Lamb Papers*.

22. Eugene P. Chase (ed. and trans.), *Our Revolutionary Forefathers; The Letters of François, Marquis de Barbe-Marbois* (New York, 1929), pp. 113–119.

23. *Writings of Washington*, XVI, pp. 294–299.

24. Letter, Knox to Lamb, 13 September 1779, in *Lamb Papers; Writings of Washington*, XVI, pp. 272–275, 453–454.

25. *Writings of Washington*, XVII, p. 31.

26. *Correspondence of the American Revolution*, II, p. 353.

27. Letter, McDougall to Washington, 6 November 1779, in *McDougall Papers;* Letter, Knox to Lamb, 23 November 1779, in *Lamb Papers; Writings of Washington*, XVII, pp. 100–102, 154.

28. *McDougall's Orderly Book*, 19 November 1779.

29. *Writings of Washington*, XVII, pp. 191–196, 202.

CHAPTER 15 THE TERRIBLE WINTER

1. *Diary of Doctor Samuel Adams* (manuscript in New York Public Library), entries 2–5 January 1780; Heath, *Memoirs*, p. 239.

2. *Orderly Book of McDougall's Brigade, 20 November–5 December 1779* (Orderly Book Collection, New-York Historical Society), entries 21 November, 1 December 1779; *Diary of Dr. Adams*, entry 2 December 1779.

3. *Orderly Book of McDougall's Brigade*, 4–5 December 1779.

4. *Diary of Dr. Adams*, 5 December 1779–1 January 1780; *Heath Papers, Collections of the Massachusetts Historical Society* (Boston, 1898–1905), Fifth Series, IV, pp. 332–334.

5. Heath, *Memoirs*, p. 239; *Orderly Book of Colonel Gamaliel Bradford, 1 January–27 May 1780* (Orderly Book Collection, New-York Historical Society), entry 1 January 1780; *Diary of Dr. Adams*, 1 January 1780; *Writings of Washington*, XVII, pp. 397–398.

6. *Writings of Washington*, XVII, pp. 396–397; Scheer and Rankin, *Rebels and Redcoats*, p. 367; *Heath Papers*, Fifth Series, IV, pp. 338–340.

7. Heath, *Memoirs*, pp. 240–243; *Diary of Dr. Adams*, 9 and 26 January 1780; *Bradford's Orderly Book*, 9 and 26 January, and 1 and 2 February 1780.

8. *Writings of Washington*, XVIII, p. 17; *Bradford's Orderly Book*, 1 March 1780.

9. Joseph Plumb Martin, *Private Yankee Doodle*, George F. Scheer, ed. (Boston, 1962), p. 172.

10. *Bradford's Orderly Book*, 14 January and 12 February 1780.

11. *Writings of Washington*, XVII, pp. 478–479; *Bradford's Orderly Book*, 7 February 1780.

12. *Writings of Washington*, XVIII, pp. 237, 332, 350, 355–356; *Bradford's Orderly Book*, 5 February 1780; Letter, James to Lamb, 9 December 1778, in *Lamb Papers*.

13. *Diary of Dr. Adams*, 23 January 1780, 3 March 1780; *Bradford's Orderly Book*, 26 January 1780; Scheer and Rankin, *Rebels and Redcoats*, pp. 367–368.

14. *Public Papers of George Clinton*, V, pp. 464–466.

15. *Bradford's Orderly Book*, 21 February 1780; Heath, *Memoirs*, p. 246; *Diary of Dr. Adams*, 5 March 1780.

CHAPTER 16 DARK DAYS AND PRUSSIAN ADVICE

1. *Diary of Dr. Adams*, 24 March, 5 April 1780; *Bradford's Orderly Book*, 15 and 31 March 1780; *Writings of Washington*, XVIII, pp. 131–132.

2. Haiman, *Kosciuszko*, pp. 86–89; *Writings of Washington*, XVIII, p. 182.

3. *Bradford's Orderly Book*, 29 February, 6 April, 8 April, 9 April, 11 April, 1 May 1780.

4. *Diary of Dr. Adams*, 27 December 1779, 13 March, 12 April 1780; *Bradford's Orderly Book*, 25–26 April 1780; *Writings of Washington*, XVIII, pp. 350–351.

5. *Writings of Washington*, XVIII, pp. 413, 428–429, 434; Thacher, *Journal*, p. 197.

6. *Diary of Dr. Adams*, 19 May 1780; Howard P. Nash, "New England's Darkest Day," *American History Illustrated*, I (June 1966), p. 27; Martin, *Private Yankee Doodle*, pp. 181–182.

7. Martin, *Private Yankee Doodle*, pp. 182–187; *Writings of Washington*, XVIII, pp. 424–425, 428.

8. Sir John Fortescue (ed.), *The Correspondence of King George the Third* (London, 1928), V, p. 57.

9. *Papers of Alexander Hamilton*, II, pp. 347–348.

10. *Writings of Washington*, XVII, pp. 463–466, 477, 494–496.

11. Van Doren, *Secret History of the American Revolution*, pp. 258–259, 264–266; *Writings of Washington*, XIX, pp. 12–13.

12. Van Doren, *Secret History of the American Revolution*, pp. 266–267.

13. *Bradford's Orderly Book*, 22 and 25 May 1780; *Florence Crowley's Orderly Book, 1 June–14 July 1780* (Orderly Book Collection, New-York Historical Society), 14 June 1780; *Writings of Washington*, XIX, pp. 42, 90–91.

14. *Papers of Alexander Hamilton*, II, pp. 344–345.

15. *Writings of Washington*, XVIII, p. 333; *Bradford's Orderly Book*, 10 May, 22 May, 25 May 1780; *Crowley's Orderly Book*, 1–22 June 1780.

16. *Writings of Washington*, XIX, pp. 14–16, 24, 40–41, 52–54, 58–59.

17. *Ibid.*, pp. 90–92; Flexner, *George Washington in the American Revolution*, pp. 364–365.

18. John M. Palmer, *General von Steuben*, pp. 230–232; Inventories dated 30 June 1780, *Miscellaneous Revolutionary War Records*, National Archives, No. 21087; *Captain V. D. Burgh's Orderly Book, July–August 1780* (Collection of USMA Library), 8, 9, 10, 13, 14, 15, 19, 22, 27 July 1780; *Writings of Washington*, XIX, p. 239; Letters, Steuben to Washington, 18, 21, 28 July 1780, and Howe to Washington, 28 July 1780, in *Washington Papers*, Library of Congress.

19. *Burgh's Orderly Book*, 9 July 1780.

20. *Bradford's Orderly Book*, 16 April 1780; *Writings of Washington*, XIX, p. 370.

21. *Burgh's Orderly Book*, 25, 27 June and 3 July 1780.

22. *Burgh's Orderly Book*, 8, 11, 16, 22, 26 July 1780, 2 August 1780; Letter, Steuben to Washington, 28 July 1780, in *Washington Papers*, Library of Congress.

23. *Writings of Washington,* XIX, pp. 202, 231, 239; *Papers of Alexander Hamilton,* II, pp. 349, 366.

24. *Writings of Washington,* XIX, pp. 270, 278–289; Flexner, *George Washington in the American Revolution,* p. 365.

CHAPTER 17 THE DARK EAGLE

1. Quoted in Willard M. Wallace, *Traitorous Hero* (New York, 1954), p. vii. To that work I am indebted for much of the information contained in this chapter.

2. John Pell, *Ethan Allen* (Cambridge, 1929), pp. 80–86.

3. *Writings of Washington,* VII, pp. 251–252; Leake, *Lamb,* pp. 152–153.

4. *Familiar Letters of John Adams,* p. 276.

5. Dwight D. Eisenhower, *Crusade in Europe* (New York, 1955), p. 224; *Writings of Washington,* VIII, p. 377.

6. *Writings of Washington,* XIV, pp. 420, 428.

7. *Ibid.,* XVIII, p. 225.

8. Letter, André to Arnold, late July 1779, in Van Doren, *Secret History of the American Revolution,* pp. 452–453.

9. Letter, Arnold to André, 15 June 1780, in Van Doren, *Secret History of the American Revolution,* p. 460.

10. Letter, Arnold to André, 16 June 1780, in Van Doren, *Secret History of the American Revolution,* pp. 460–461.

11. Letter, Livingston to Washington, 22 June 1780, in *Correspondence of the American Revolution,* III, pp. 1–2.

12. Letter, Arnold to André, 15 July 1780, in Van Doren, *Secret History of the American Revolution,* pp. 464–465.

13. See correspondence between Arnold and André, 11 to 24 July 1780, in Van Doren, *Secret History of the American Revolution,* pp. 462–466.

14. Flexner, *George Washington in the American Revolution,* pp. 381–382.

15. *Writings of Washington,* XIX, pp. 302, 313; Flexner, *George Washington in the American Revolution,* pp. 382–383.

CHAPTER 18 RENDEZVOUS WITH THE "VULTURE"

1. *Miscellaneous Revolutionary War Documents,* National Archives, No. 29469; *Burgh's Orderly Book,* 4 and 5 August 1780.

2. Van Doren, *Secret History of the American Revolution,* pp. 287–289.

3. Letter, Howe to Arnold, 5 August 1780, in *Washington Papers,* Library of Congress.

4. *Benjamin Peabody's Orderly Book* (Orderly Book Collection, USMA Library, West Point, N.Y.), 6 and 7 August 1780; Letter, Arnold to Washington, 8 August 1780, in *Washington Papers,* Library of Congress.

5. *Writings of Washington,* XIX, pp. 331–332; Letter, Howe to Arnold, 5 August 1780, in *Washington Papers,* Library of Congress.

6. Letters, Arnold to Washington, 8 August 1780, and Villefranche to Franks, 19 August 1780, in *Washington Papers,* Library of Congress; *Peabody's Orderly Book,* entries of 8–16 August 1780.

7. Van Doren, *Secret History of the American Revolution*, p. 291; *Peabody's Orderly Book*, 25 August 1780.

8. *Centennial of the United States Military Academy*, I, p. 181.

9. Villefranche's Estimate, 12 August 1780, *Miscellaneous Revolutionary War Documents*, National Archives, No. 035439; *Peabody's Orderly Book*, 9, 14, 15, 16, 23, 24 August 1780; Leake, *Lamb*, p. 251.

10. *Papers of Alexander Hamilton*, II, pp. 376–378; Albert B. Hart (ed.), *Proceedings of the Varick Court of Inquiry* (Boston, 1907), testimony of Richard Varick, Henry D. Tripp, Mrs. Catherine Martin, Colonel John Lamb, Major David Franks; *Public Papers of George Clinton*, VI, pp. 138–139.

11. *Papers of Alexander Hamilton*, II, p. 377; *Diary of Dr. Adams*, 23 and 24 August 1780; *Peabody's Orderly Book*, 16, 25, 31 August 1780.

12. *Diary of Dr. Adams*, 24 August 1780; *Peabody's Orderly Book*, 24 August 1780.

13. Hall, *Parsons*, pp. 307–309; Van Doren, *Secret History of the American Revolution*, pp. 296–299.

14. Van Doren, *Secret History of the American Revolution*, pp. 300–302.

15. *Papers of Alexander Hamilton*, II, p. 421.

16. Van Doren, *Secret History of the American Revolution*, pp. 360, 384–385, 479; Clinton, *The American Rebellion*, pp. 220–221.

17. Letter, Arnold to Howe, 12 September 1780, in *Washington Papers*, Library of Congress.

18. Van Doren, *Secret History of the American Revolution*, pp. 302–306.

19. Letters, André to Sheldon, 7 September 1780, and Arnold to André, 10 September 1780, in Van Doren, *Secret History of the American Revolution*, pp. 471–472.

20. Letters, Arnold to Lamb, 13 and 16 September 1780, and Bauman to Lamb, 18 September 1780, in *Lamb Papers*.

21. Villefranche's Estimate and Bauman's Report are in *Miscellaneous Revolutionary War Documents*, National Archives, Nos. 20957 and 22120. See also *Centennial of the United States Military Academy*, I, pp. 179–183; Van Doren, *Secret History of the American Revolution*, pp. 311–313.

22. Letter, Arnold to André, 15 September 1780, in Van Doren, *Secret History of the American Revolution*, p. 472.

23. *Writings of Washington*, XX, p. 48; Van Doren, *Secret History of the American Revolution*, pp. 314 and opposite.

24. Log of H.M.S. *Vulture*, 1 July 1780–7 November 1780, from "Journal of the Proceedings of His Majesty's Sloop *Vulture* . . ." (Manuscript, National Maritime Museum, London), entry of 17 September 1780.

25. *Writings of Washington*, XXXVII, p. 551.

26. *Peabody's Orderly Book*, 18 September 1780.

27. Letter, Robinson to Clinton, 24 September 1780, in Van Doren, *Secret History of the American Revolution*, pp. 474–475.

CHAPTER 19 "TREASON OF THE BLACKEST DYE!"

1. Letter, Lamb to Livingston, 20 September 1780, in Leake, *Lamb*, p. 258; Log of *Vulture*, 22 September 1780; Letter, Robinson to Clinton, 24 September 1780, in Van Doren, *Secret History of the American Revolution*, pp. 474–475.

2. *Peabody's Orderly Book,* 24 September 1780; Clinton, *The American Rebellion,* p. 214; *Diary of Dr. Adams,* 23 September 1780; Bernhard A. Uhlendorf (ed. and trans.), *Revolution in America* (New Brunswick, 1957), pp. 374–375. The last reference is a compilation of letters written by Adjutant General Carl Leopold von Baurmeister. Baurmeister wrote on 6 October 1780 that "the 28th [of September] was set as the day of embarkation."

3. Wallace, *Traitorous Hero,* p. 245.

4. Letter, Jameson to Washington, 22 September 1780. This letter was discovered in 1968 and is at this writing at Union College, Schenectady, N.Y.

5. Van Doren, *Secret History of the American Revolution,* pp. 342–344.

6. Wallace, *Traitorous Hero,* pp. 248–249.

7. Log of *Vulture,* 25 September 1780.

8. *Diary of Dr. Adams,* 25 September 1780; Letter, Daniel McCarthy to Varick, 23 August 1780, in *Washington Papers,* Library of Congress.

9. Letter, Varick to his sister Jane, 1 October 1780, quoted in part in Van Doren, *Secret History of the American Revolution,* pp. 346–348.

10. *Papers of Alexander Hamilton,* II, p. 441; Flexner, *George Washington in the American Revolution,* p. 388.

11. *Papers of Alexander Hamilton,* II, pp. 438–441.

12. *Ibid.,* pp. 439–440.

13. *Writings of Washington,* XX, p. 85.

14. *Ibid.,* pp. 84–88.

15. *Ibid.,* pp. 86–87.

16. *Diary of Dr. Adams,* 25 September 1780.

17. *Writings of Washington,* XX, p. 89; *Peabody's Orderly Book,* 26 September 1780; *Diary of Dr. Adams,* 25 September 1780.

18. *Peabody's Orderly Book,* 28 and 30 September 1780; *Writings of Washington,* XX, p. 99.

19. *Writings of Washington,* XX, p. 101.

20. *Ibid.,* p. 110.

21. Thacher, *Journal,* p. 228.

22. *Journals of Congress,* XVIII, p. 899; *Writings of Washington,* XX, p. 95.

23. *Writings of Washington,* XX, pp. 95–96; *Journals of Congress,* XVIII, p. 950; *Diary of Dr. Adams,* 25 September 1780.

CHAPTER 20 FROM MUTINY TO VICTORY

1. *Peabody's Orderly Book,* 4 and 9 October 1780; *Writings of Washington,* XX, pp. 99, 106, 125–128.

2. *Peabody's Orderly Book,* 6 and 7 October 1780; *Samuel Frost's Orderly Book* (Manuscript copy in USMA Collection, West Point, N.Y.), 4 and 5 December 1780; *Public Papers of George Clinton,* VI, pp. 273, 286; Heath, *Memoirs,* 275; *Diary of Dr. Adams,* 7 October 1780; Thacher, *Journal,* p. 242.

3. Heath, *Memoirs,* p. 275; *Diary of Dr. Adams,* entries in December 1780; *Writings of Washington,* XX, pp. 457–459; Chastellux, *Travels,* p. 346.

4. *Writings of Washington*, XX, pp. 457–459; *Diary of Dr. Adams*, 1 January 1781; *Frost's Orderly Book*, 12 December 1780.

5. *Diary of Dr. Adams*, 1, 11, 21 January 1781.

6. A full treatment of the mutinies is in Carl Van Doren, *Mutiny in January* (New York, 1943).

7. *Writings of Washington*, XXI, pp. 55–57.

8. Thacher, *Journal*, p. 242; *Writings of Washington*, XXI, pp. 58–59.

9. Van Doren, *Mutiny in January*, pp. 164–165.

10. *Writings of Washington*, XXI, pp. 60–61, 65–66, 80; *Public Papers of George Clinton*, VI, p. 551; Thacher, *Journal*, p. 246.

11. *Writings of Washington*, XXI, pp. 80–81, 90, 92; Heath, *Memoirs*, p. 284.

12. *Writings of Washington*, XXI, pp. 88, 96, 99, 116, 121, 129.

13. The petition is quoted in Van Doren, *Mutiny in January*, pp. 205–206; *Writings of Washington*, XXI, p. 154.

14. *Diary of Dr. Adams*, 21 January 1781.

15. *Writings of Washington*, XXI, pp. 123–128.

16. *Ibid.*, p. 128.

17. Van Doren, *Mutiny in January*, pp. 218–220; *Writings of Washington*, XXI, p. 149.

18. Thacher, *Journal*, p. 252.

19. Van Doren, *Mutiny in January*, p. 221.

20. *Writings of Washington*, XXI, pp. 6, 167, 210, 306, 380; *Papers of Alexander Hamilton*, II, pp. 478, 559–560; "A Report of the State of the Works at West Point," Jean Baptiste Gouvion, 2 November 1780, *Washington Papers*, Library of Congress.

21. *Writings of Washington*, XXI, pp. 228, 255.

22. *Journals of Congress*, XX, pp. 488–489; *Writings of Washington*, XXII, p. 22; Chastellux, *Travels*, p. 353.

23. Heath, *Memoirs*, pp. 295–297; *Writings of Washington*, XXII, pp. 58–59.

24. *Writings of Washington*, XXII, pp. 51, 151, 203, 240–241, 250, 386, 405–406.

25. *Writings of Washington*, XXII, pp. 241–242.

26. *Journals of Congress*, VIII, p. 485.

27. *Writings of Washington*, XXIII, pp. 19–23.

28. *Diary of Dr. Adams*, 27 and 30 August, 1 and 28 September, 17 and 18 October 1781.

29. Heath, *Memoirs*, pp. 336–337; *Diary of Dr. Adams*, 24, 28, 30, 31 October 1781; *Glover's Orderly Books*, V, pp. 683–684.

CHAPTER 21 STRATEGY . . .

1. *Writings of Washington*, VII, p. 334; John Richard Alden, *The American Revolution, 1775–1783* (New York, 1962), pp. 9, 116; Ward, *The War of the Revolution*, I, p. 400.

2. See Dave R. Palmer, "West Point: The Key to the Continent?" (Unpublished thesis, Duke University, 1966), for an investigation of the role of the Hudson. Much of this chapter and the following one is taken from that study.

3. *The Letters and Papers of Cadwallader Colden, 1765–1775*, pp. 197–198.

4. Fortescue, *A History of the British Army*, III, p. 169. Emphasis added.

5. *The Correspondence of King George the Third*, III, p. 443; IV, p. 544.

6. *Ibid.*, IV, pp. 250–253; Quoted in J. F. C. Fuller, *Decisive Battles of the U.S.A.* (New York, 1942), p. 74.

7. Fortescue, *History of the British Army*, III, p. 338.

8. Piers Mackesy, *The War for America, 1775–1783* (Cambridge, 1964), p. 143.

9. That list of six reasons is recorded in Fernow, *New York in the Revolution*, p. 154.

10. Robert A. East, *Business Enterprise in the American Revolutionary Era* (New York, 1938), pp. 52–55; *Papers of Alexander Hamilton*, II, p. 612; Orlando W. Stephenson, "The Supply of Gunpowder in 1776," *American Historical Review*, XXX (1924–1925), p. 277.

11. *Writings of Washington*, X, pp. 193, 334, 423–424, 459, 515.

12. *Ibid.*, XVII, pp. 272–274, 287, 357; XVIII, pp. 229, 327, 428–432.

13. *Ibid.*, VIII, pp. 236–237.

14. *Ibid.*, III, pp. 302–303, 374, 415, 437–438, 475–476, 511; IV, pp. 112, 172.

15. *Ibid.*, IV, p. 401, 437; VIII, pp. 297–299, 343; X, pp. 202–205; XXIV, pp. 194–215.

16. *American Archives*, Fourth Series, I, pp. 216–220.

17. *Journals of Congress*, I, pp. 35, 73, 77.

18. *Ibid.*, pp. 105–113; *Writings of Washington*, III, pp. 478–480, 491–492.

19. *Writings of Washington*, IV, pp. 532–533; V, p. 162; VIII, pp. 356–357, 487; XII, pp. 261–266, 421–422, 434–436; XIII, pp. 297–305; XIV, pp. 6–11; XVII, p. 464; XX, pp. 79–81; XXII, p. 278; XXIV, pp. 107–110, 194, 215.

20. Clinton, *The American Rebellion*, p. 126.

21. North Callahan, *Henry Knox, General Washington's General* (New York, 1958), p. 39.

22. *The Sullivan-Clinton Campaign of 1779*, prepared by the Division of Archives and History of the University of the State of New York (Albany, 1929), p. 10. Emphasis added.

23. *Writings of Washington*, XXIV, p. 199.

24. *Ibid.*, XIII, pp. 223–244, 254–257.

25. Richard B. Morris, *The Peacemakers* (New York, 1965), p. 308.

26. *Writings of Washington*, XII, pp. 272–276.

CHAPTER 22 . . . AND TACTICS

1. Duportail's analysis of the ability of the West Point defenses to withstand attack is in a manuscript report, in French, "*Mémoire sur la Defense de Wes[t]point*," dated 20 August 1779. A copy and a translation are in the West Point Library's Revolutionary War Collection.

2. Clinton, *The American Rebellion*, p. 83; *Writings of Washington*, XI, p. 186; XII, pp. 526–527.

3. *Papers of Alexander Hamilton*, I, 217; Horner, *Obstructions of the Hudson River*

during the Revolution, p. 2; A. T. Mahan, *The Influence of Sea Power Upon History* (Boston, 1908), p. 342.

4. *Writings of Washington,* XII, pp. 169–171.

5. Mackesy, *The War for America,* p. 143.

6. John Durand (ed.), *Documents on the American Revolution* (Translated from documents in the French archives [New York, 1889]), p. 31; Jared Sparks (ed.), *The Diplomatic Correspondence of the American Revolution* (Washington, D.C., 1857), I, pp. 63–66, 455; Henri Doniol, *Histoire de la participation de la France a l'établissement des Étas-Unis d'Amérique* (Paris, 1888), I, pp. 1–30.

7. Doniol, *Histoire,* IV, p. 226; *Papers of Alexander Hamilton,* II, p. 347; *Familiar Letters of John Adams,* p. 276.

CHAPTER 23 THE TWO LONGEST YEARS

1. *Writings of Washington,* XXIII, p. 291; *Diary of Dr. Adams,* 11, 15, 20 November 1781; "Estimate of the Principal Materials in Building an Hospital on West Point . . . ," *Miscellaneous Revolutionary War Records,* National Archives, No. 28543.

2. *Captain Christopher Marshall's Orderly Book, 4 September 1781–24 February 1782* (Orderly Book Collection, New-York Historical Society), December entries, 1781; Heath, *Memoirs,* pp. 339–340.

3. Heath, *Memoirs,* pp. 340–341.

4. *Marshall's Orderly Book,* January and February entries; Heath, *Memoirs,* pp. 341–343; Thacher, *Journal,* pp. 307–308.

5. *Writings of Washington,* XXIV, pp. 115, 117.

6. Report, Villefranche to Washington, 15 and 16 April 1782, *Washington Papers,* Library of Congress; *Writings of Washington,* XXIV, p. 133.

7. *Writings of Washington,* XXIV, pp. 227, 249; *Diary of Dr. Adams,* 13 May 1782; Heath, *Memoirs,* pp. 360–361.

8. *Writings of Washington,* XXIV, pp. 272–273 and footnote, p. 273; Chastellux, *Travels,* p. 376.

9. Thacher, *Journal,* pp. 310–311.

10. *Writings of Washington,* XXIV, pp. 299, 302, 308; *Diary of Dr. Adams,* 24–27 May 1782; Thacher, *Journal,* pp. 310–312; Heath, *Memoirs,* pp. 362–363; *Centennial of the United States Military Academy,* I, pp. 196–197; Boynton, *West Point,* pp. 155–163. A picture of the arbor appears opposite p. 161 in Boynton.

11. Flexner, *George Washington in the American Revolution,* p. 476; Letter, Huntington to Webb, 20 June 1782, in *Correspondence and Journals of Samuel Blachley Webb* (Lancaster, Pa., 1893), II, p. 405; *Writings of Washington,* XXV, pp. 173, 219–220.

12. *Miscellaneous Revolutionary War Documents,* 4 July 1782, No. 25455, and 31 July 1782, No. 24628, National Archives; *Writings of Washington,* XXVI, p. 478; XXV, pp. 172, 179; Heath, *Memoirs,* p. 366; Martin, *Private Yankee Doodle,* p. 262.

13. *Writings of Washington,* XXV, p. 255; Martin, *Private Yankee Doodle,* pp. 267, 272.

14. Letters, Knox to Lincoln, 20 December 1782, and Knox to McDougall, 21 February 1783, in Francis S. Drake (ed.), *The Life and Correspondence of Henry Knox* (Boston, 1783), pp. 77–78; Flexner, *George Washington in the American Revolu-*

tion, pp. 492–495; Letter, E. Huntington to A. Huntington, 9 December 1782, in Heartman, *Letters written by Ebenezer Huntington,* p. 102.

15. *Papers of Alexander Hamilton,* III, pp. 253–255; *Writings of Washington,* XXVI, pp. 185–188.

16. *Writings of Washington,* XXVI, pp. 374–398.

17. Letter, E. Huntington to A. Huntington, 12 August 1783, in Heartman, *Letters Written by Ebenezer Huntington,* p. 106; *Writings of Washington,* XXVII, p. 35.

18. *Miscellaneous Revolutionary War Documents,* No. 24415, No. 24232, and unnumbered document titled "Buildings to be Sold at West Point," National Archives.

SELECTED
BIBLIOGRAPHY

THIS history of Revolutionary War West Point is more than
the story of a fortress. West Point was a hub from which the spokes of war
radiated. The interrelationship between the Highlands stronghold and the
War of Independence—the impact of one upon the other—is too powerful
to ignore. Therefore, the history of the fort is, in miniature, a history of the
war; and this bibliography, to be complete, would be too extensive for the
present volume. It has accordingly been confined to a listing of those documents and works that were most useful in the preparation of the manuscript.
The reader or researcher who wants a more comprehensive listing should
consult the bibliographies contained in John R. Alden, *The American Revolution* (New York, 1954), and Mark M. Boatner, *Encyclopedia of the American Revolution* (New York, 1966).

MANUSCRIPT SOURCES

Alexander McDougall Papers. New-York Historical Society, New York, N.Y. This large
and valuable collection contains letters to and from McDougall, as well as maps, drawings, returns, and reports. No study of the Revolution in New York can afford to
ignore it. Available on microfilm.

BABCOCK, H. G. (compiler). *The Great Chain.* USMA Library, West Point, N.Y. A
scrapbook containing original documents relating to the chain at West Point, mostly
bills and receipts.

Beverley Robinson's Orderly Books, USMA Library, West Point, N.Y. These books cover
the activities of Robinson's Loyalist regiment from its founding in May 1777 to
November 1779, although there are some gaps. Unfortunately, one of the gaps occurs
during the period of the regiment's attack of the Highlands in 1777.

Diary of Doctor Samuel Adams. New York Public Library, New York, N.Y. Adams made a diary entry practically every day of his life. Because he was stationed for much of the war at West Point, his diary is invaluable for local color, weather, day-to-day happenings, and a personal account of major events.

HAACKER COLLECTION. New-York Historical Society, New York, N.Y. The product of years of research and assembling by Frederick Haacker, this collection contains hundreds of obscure documents—articles, excerpts, letters, reports, etc.—pertaining to the history of the Hudson River Valley. It is organized topically, making it a most important research source.

Lamb Papers. New-York Historical Society, New York, N.Y. The correspondence and reports of John Lamb, mostly letters to him. Available on microfilm.

Minutes of the Secret Committee. Washington's Headquarters Museum, Newburgh, N.Y. A valuable and relatively unknown collection. Letters, reports, receipts, sketches. Copies are also available in the USMA Library.

MISCELLANEOUS REVOLUTIONARY WAR DOCUMENTS. National Archives, Washington, D.C. These documents are all that survived a fire in the record storage area many years ago. Generally, they consist of returns, receipts, and records of inspections. But some surprises await a patient researcher willing to wade through the uncatalogued collection.

ORDERLY BOOK COLLECTION. USMA Library, West Point, N.Y. Original manuscript books as well as typed copies constitute this collection of daily orders issued by units stationed at West Point.

ORDERLY BOOK COLLECTION. New-York Historical Society, New York, N.Y. This large and mostly untapped collection of orderly books covers several shelves in the NYHS Library. Excellent for obtaining day-to-day coverage of the war at unit level.

REVOLUTIONARY WAR COLLECTION. USMA, West Point, N.Y. No single collection as such exists at USMA, but in both the Library and the Museum at West Point there is a treasure cache of prints, maps, sketches, letters, documents, artifacts, photographs, special studies, paintings, and rare books. Included in that grouping would be such things as relics of the great chain and ruins of the old forts and redoubts. Jointly, all of those items represent a collection which has been invaluable to me in the research and writing of this book. Many of the individual items have been listed by title in the footnotes.

REVOLUTIONARY WAR COLLECTION. Cornell University. The most useful items for this work were the maps of the Highlands, of New York, and of West Point.

REVOLUTIONARY WAR MANUSCRIPT COLLECTION. Duke University. Like the West Point Library, the Duke Library has acquired a considerable body of material on the Revolution. Mostly reproductions of documents by various means including microfilm. Especially useful were the Public Record Office papers of military correspondence from America and the West Indies between 1773 and 1803.

STERLING MANUSCRIPT COLLECTION. New York State Library, Albany, N.Y. Documents relating mostly to the chain and other iron products made for West Point by Sterling Furnace.

WASHINGTON PAPERS. Library of Congress, Washington, D.C. This vast collection contains many letters written to Washington by men stationed at West Point. One can only insecurely write about any facet of the Revolutionary War without examining this collection.

PRINTED PRIMARY SOURCES

ADAMS, CHARLES F. (ed.). *Familiar Letters of John Adams and His Wife Abigail, During the Revolution.* New York, 1876.

ADAMS, RANDOLPH G. (ed.). *The Headquarters Papers of the British Army in North America*. Ann Arbor, 1926. Gleaned from the vast and valuable Clements Collection at the University of Michigan.

————. *The Papers of Lord George Germain*. Ann Arbor, 1928.

BOYNTON, EDWARD C. *History of West Point*. New York, 1863. For a century, this book has served as the most complete work on West Point in the Revolutionary War. It is the direct forebear of the present volume, for which Boynton has paved the way.

BURGOYNE, JOHN. *A State of the Expedition from Canada*. London, 1780.

CHASTELLUX, FRANCOIS JEAN, Marquis de. *Travels in North America*. Reprinted from the original; Bowling Green, Ohio, 1919. Chastellux visited and described fortress West Point. He also provides a Frenchman's views on other facets of America in the 1780's.

CLARK, DONALD F. (ed.). *Fort Montgomery and Fort Clinton*. Highlands, N.Y., 1952. A brief compilation of documents relating to the British attack in 1777.

DRAKE, FRANCIS S. (ed.). *The Life and Correspondence of Henry Knox*. Boston, 1893.

DURAND, JOHN (ed. and trans.). *Documents on the American Revolution*. New York, 1889. Documents gleaned from the French Archives.

DWIGHT, TIMOTHY. *Travels in New England and New York*. 4 vols. New Haven, 1822. A chaplain in the war, Dwight spent many months in and around West Point. He was later President of Yale University.

FERNOW, BERTHOLD (ed.). *New York in the Revolution*, Vol. I ("New York State Archives," Vol. XV). Albany, N.Y., 1887. Miscellaneous records relating to New York's efforts and activities in the War of Independence.

FITZPATRICK, JOHN C. (ed.). *The Diaries of George Washington*. 4 vols. New York, 1925.

————. *The Writings of George Washington*. 39 vols. Washington, D.C., 1931–1944.

FORCE, PETER (ed.). *American Archives*. Fourth and fifth series. Washington, D.C., 1837–1853. An especially comprehensive collection of correspondence and minutes of state and federal governments in the early years of the war.

FORD, WORTHINGTON C. (ed.). *Journals of the Continental Congress*. 34 vols. Washington, D.C.: 1904–1937. The minutes of the Continental Congress. The editor's footnotes and comments greatly enhance the worth of these volumes to the researcher.

————. *Putnam's General Orders, 1777*. Brooklyn, N.Y., 1893. General Israel Putnam's orders in the critical weeks prior to and during the British attack up the Hudson in 1777.

FORTESCUE, SIR JOHN (ed.). *The Correspondence of King George the Third*. 6 vols. London, 1928.

General John Glover's Orderly Books. 5 vols. Typescript copies in the USMA Library, West Point. Glover was stationed at West Point on several occasions and was once Commandant.

HALL, CHARLES S. *Life and Letters of Samuel Holden Parsons*. New York, 1905. Of questionable value as a biography, this work redeems itself by printing much of Parsons' correspondence, especially during the periods he was at West Point.

HART, ALBERT B. (ed.). *Proceedings of the Varick Court of Inquiry*. Boston, 1907. The court cleared Varick of complicity in the Arnold conspiracy. Colorful and interesting information on the treason.

HASTINGS, HUGH (ed.). *Public Papers of George Clinton*. 10 vols. New York, 1899–1914. Entirely indispensable to anyone researching any subject having to do with New York in the Revolutionary War. Consists of letters, reports, returns, and orders pertaining to New York militia, state government, and activities within the state.

Heath Papers, Collections of the Massachusetts Historical Society. Boston, 1898–1905. Heath was commander of the Highlands on several occasions, making this collection an important source of information. Unfortunately, Heath's interests were generally focused elsewhere even when his body was at West Point.

HEATH, WILLIAM. *Heath's Memoirs of the American War.* New York, 1904. A cryptic account of the war as Heath saw it. A good source of color and corroborative material, though not substantive.

HISTORICAL MANUSCRIPTS COMMISSION. *Report on American Manuscripts.* 4 vols. London, 1904. An asset to the scholar as a printed source of documents across the Atlantic. Photostats of many of these documents can be seen at Colonial Williamsburg.

———. *Report on the Manuscripts of Mrs. Stopford-Sackville.* 2 vols. London, 1910. Lord George Sackville was known during the war as Lord George Germain.

HORNER, WILLIAM M. *Obstructions of the Hudson River During the Revolution.* Metuchen, N.J., privately printed, limited edition, 1927. Of value for the letters it reprints.

KITE, ELIZABETH S. *Brigadier General Louis Le Bègue Duportail.* Baltimore, 1933. An account of the French engineers in Washington's army. Although biased, incomplete, and inaccurate, the book is nonetheless beneficial because it offers so many letters and documents.

KNIGHT, ERASTUS C. (compiler). *New York in the Revolution,* Supplement. Edited by Frederick G. Mather. Albany, N.Y., 1901. Additional material on New York. See Berthold Fernow, above.

LAPHAM, W. B. (ed.). *Elijah Fisher's Journal.* Augusta, Ga., 1880. A soldier of the Revolution who served in Washington's guard. Good for local color, details, and a picture of war as a common soldier saw it from day to day.

MARTIN, JOSEPH P. *Private Yankee Doodle.* Edited by George F. Scheer. Boston, 1962. An entertaining and sometimes hilarious account of a continental soldier. He was at West Point during much of the war.

MOORE, FRANK. *Diary of the American Revolution.* 2 vols. New York, 1860. Contemporary publications, largely newspapers, printed during the revolution.

NEW YORK SECRETARY OF STATE. *Calendar of Historical Manuscripts Relating to the War of the Revolution.* Albany, N.Y., 1868. Miscellaneous records, minutes of proceedings, court-martial transcripts, etc. Its lack of organization reduces its value unless the researcher is willing to concentrate on every page.

PAINE, THOMAS. *The Complete Writings of Thomas Paine.* Edited by Philip S. Foner. 2 vols. New York, 1945.

PUTNAM, RUFUS. *The Memoirs of Rufus Putnam.* Cambridge, Mass., 1903. Putnam's regiment was at West Point during the fort's construction and later served there as a part of the garrison.

SCHEER, GEORGE F. and HUGH F. RANKIN. *Rebels and Redcoats.* New York, 1957. Superb for anecdotes and flavor. The story of the Revolution in the words of participants.

SPARKS, JARED (ed.). *Correspondence of the American Revolution.* 4 vols. Cambridge, Mass., 1853.

———. *The Diplomatic Correspondence of the American Revolution.* 6 vols. Washington, D.C., 1857.

SYRETT, HAROLD C. (ed.). *The Papers of Alexander Hamilton.* 13 vols. to date. New York, 1961–1968.

THACHER, JAMES. *Military Journal of the American Revolution.* Hartford, Conn., 1862. Surgeon Thacher was an accomplished observer and a splendid writer. He lived in or near the fortress for many months. His account of events is generally quite accurate and always enjoyable reading.

TURNER, JOSEPH B. (ed.). *The Journal and Orderly Book of Captain Robert Kirkwood.* Wilmington, Del., 1910. Kirkwood commanded a company of the Delaware line.

UHLENDORF, BERNHARD A. (ed. and trans.). *Revolution in America.* New Brunswick, N.J., 1957. A compilation of letters written by Adjutant General Carl Leopold von Baurmeister, a German officer serving under the British in America.

UNITED STATES MILITARY ACADEMY. *The Centennial of the United States Military Academy at West Point, New York.* 2 vols. Washington, D.C., 1904. The section on West Point in the Revolution, written by Captain Horace M. Reeve, includes many printed documents and helpful leads to locating and researching others.

VAN DOREN, CARL. *Secret History of the American Revolution.* New York, 1941. This books prints in full most of the correspondence relating to the Arnold conspiracy. It is also an excellent secondary source on matters pertaining to the affair.

WILMOT, JOHN E. (ed.). *Journals of the Provincial Congress of New York, 1775–1777.* 2 vols. Albany, N.Y., 1842. Much of this material is also printed in American Archives. See Peter Force, above.

Year Book, Dutchess County Historical Society, XX (1935). This excellent pamphlet devotes a section to the British movements on the Hudson in 1777, including extracts from the logbooks of some of the raiding vessels.

SECONDARY SOURCES

ALBION, ROBERT and JENNIE B. POPE. *Sea Lanes in Wartime.* New York, 1942.

ALDEN, JOHN R. *The American Revolution.* New York, 1954. This book will long be a standard work on the Revolution. Accurate, brilliantly written, concise yet affording broad coverage, it is a must for anyone really wanting to understand the war.

ANDERSON, TROYER S. *Command of the Howe Brothers During the American Revolution.* New York, 1936. Especially good for its coverage of the year 1777. Anderson's interpretation of the Burgoyne-Howe controversy is questionable, however.

BOATNER, MARK M., III. *Encyclopedia of the American Revolution.* New York, 1966. This work is an absolute requirement for any student of the Revolution so long as the user understands that Boatner has condensed secondary sources and is, therefore, liable to the errors of his selected authors. A handy compendium when precise accuracy is not important.

CALLAHAN, NORTH. *Henry Knox, General Washington's General.* New York, 1958.

CARMER, CARL. *The Hudson.* New York, 1939. A readable history of events along the river.

CARR, WILLIAM and RICHARD KOKE. *Twin Forts of the Popolopen.* Bear Mountain, N.Y., 1937. A carefully researched booklet on Forts Montgomery and Clinton.

CLINTON, SIR HENRY. *The American Rebellion.* Edited by William B. Willcox. New Haven, Conn., 1954.

CONSTITUTION ISLAND ASSOCIATION. *Constitution Island and West Point in the Revolutionary War.* Annual report: 1966. Contains articles on Constitution Island by Alexander C. Flick and Adam E. Potts, the Secret Committee by Dorothy C. Barck, and West Point during the Revolution by John R. Elting.

————. *Fifty-first Annual Report.* 1967. The report includes an article on the Great Chain and other river obstructions by Andrew Mansinne and another on the history of the river prior to the Revolutionary War by Dave R. Palmer.

CROSS, MRS. JAMES C. *The Moores of West Point.* Unpublished manuscript, USMA

Library, West Point, 1966. A study done by a descendant of the man who once owned the West Point lands.

DENTON, EDGAR, III. *The Formative Years of the United States Military Academy, 1775–1833.* Unpublished Syracuse University dissertation, 1964. A well-researched work on the efforts to forge a military academy in America. Only the first 26 pages are devoted to the period 1775–1802.

DONIOL, HENRI. *Histoire de la participation de la France a l'établissement des États-Unis d'Amérique.* 5 vols. Paris, 1888. A storehouse of information too often neglected because it has not been translated.

EAST, ROBERT A. *Business Enterprise in the American Revolutionary Era.* New York, 1938.

FLEXNER, JAMES T. *George Washington in the American Revolution.* Boston, 1968. The second of a projected trilogy on Washington, this is an excellent study of the man during the war years. Unfortunately, the book is considerably shaky—in fact, not to be trusted—in the realm of military matters. The definitive work on the General has yet to be done.

FORTESCUE, SIR JOHN. *A History of the British Army.* 13 vols. London, 1911. Only Vol. III bears directly on the War of Independence.

GREENE, NELSON (ed.). *History of the Valley of the Hudson.* 2 vols. Chicago, 1931.

HAIMAN, MIECISLAUS. *Kosciuszko in the American Revolution.* New York, 1943. Biased in favor of the Pole, but fairly reliable.

HUSTON, JAMES A. *The Sinews of War: Army Logistics, 1775–1953.* Washington, D.C., Office of the Chief of Military History, 1966. The first hundred pages of this work deal with Revolutionary efforts and failures to forge an adequate supply system.

IRVING, WASHINGTON. *A Book of the Hudson.* New York, 1849.

JOHNSON, VICTOR LEROY. *The Administration of the American Commissariat During the Revolutionary War.* Philadelphia, 1941.

LEAKE, ISAAC Q. *Memoir of General John Lamb.* Albany, N.Y., 1850.

LUVAAS, JAY. "'Baron' von Steuben: Washington's Drillmaster," *American History Illustrated*, II (April 1967), pp. 4–11, 55–58.

MACKESY, PIERS. *The War for America, 1775–1783.* Cambridge, Mass., 1964. A good study of the war by a modern British scholar. Presents the other side of the coin.

MAHAN, ALFRED THAYER. *The Influence of Seapower Upon History, 1660–1783.* Fifth ed. New York, 1964. Mahan has quite definite ideas on the role of navies in the War of Independence.

MATTICE, PAUL B. "Captain Thomas Machin," *Schoharie County Historical Review* (October 1955). A very incomplete biographical sketch of West Point's unsung engineer.

PALMER, DAVE R. *West Point: The Key to the Continent?* Unpublished Duke University thesis, 1966. A detailed study of the strategic role of the Hudson and the tactical value of West Point.

PALMER, JOHN M. *General von Steuben.* New Haven, Conn., 1937.

PHILLIPS, P. LEE. *Notes on the Life and Works of Bernard Romans.* Deland, Fla., 1924.

RUTTENBER, EDWARD M. *Obstructions to the Navigation of Hudson's River.* Albany, N.Y., 1860. A pioneering work, rather inaccurate, but still in use.

SPAULDING, E. WILDER. *His Excellency George Clinton.* New York, 1964. Not really thorough or accurate regarding Clinton's wartime years, but the best source available.

STEDMAN, CHARLES. *History of the Origin, Progress, and Termination of the American War.* 2 vols. Dublin, Ireland, 1794. History written by a Britisher who participated in the war. Worth reading to gain a contemporary English view of the American rebellion. Stedman was actually a Loyalist.

STOWE, GERALD C. and JAC WELLER. "Revolutionary West Point: 'The Key to the Continent,'" *Military Affairs*, XIX (July 1955), pp. 81–98.

VAN DOREN, CARL. *Mutiny in January*. New York, 1943. The story of the mutinies in January 1781.

WALLACE, WILLARD M. *Traitorous Hero*. New York, 1954. A biography of Benedict Arnold.

WARD, CHRISTOPHER. *The War of the Revolution*. 2 vols. New York, 1952. A study of all the battles and some of the skirmishes.

WILLCOX, WILLIAM B. *Portrait of a General*. New York, 1964. A biography of Henry Clinton, with emphasis on the Briton's psychological makeup.

WILSTACH, PAUL. *Hudson River Landings*. Indianapolis, Ind., 1933.

INDEX

Bushnell, David, 64–65, 300
Buttermilk Falls, 27

Cabot, John, 7
Cahoon, Samuel, 268–269
Camden, warship, 112, 115
Campbell, Col. Mungo, 107–109, 111–113
Canada, abortive invasion of, 146, 321–323, 325
Carleton, Gen. Guy, 47, 63, 67–68, 76, 91, 245–247, 336, 348
Carroll, John, 54
Carroll of Carrollton, Charles, 53–54
Carter, John, 174
Cerberus, frigate, 23, 37, 45, 126
chain barrier, 61, 66–69, 78–79, 150, 152, 228–229; cutting of by British, 118–119; earliest concept of, 30; removal and refloating of, 184–185; successful stretching of, 84–86, 139, 153, 163; *illus.*, 87, 149; *see also* Great Chain
Champlain, Lake, 11, 19, 37, 63, 76, 240, 242, 246, 248, 313; as "highroad of war," 13, 25
Chase, Samuel, 21, 53–54
Chesapeake Bay, 6
chevaux-de-frise, 79, 83, 99, 117, 120–124, 127, 135, 141, 150, 155, 174, 207
Clement's Sawmill, 197
Clinton, Gov. George, 20, 50, 59–60, 62, 66, 70, 78–80, 83, 85–86, 91, 93, 96–97, 99–100, 103–106, 108–118, 122–125, 134–139, 143, 147–150, 152–154, 157, 159–160, 164, 171, 179–181, 212, 226, 234, 259, 292, 340, 353
Clinton, Gen. Sir Henry, 23, 37, 47, 49–50, 63, 76, 94, 98, 100–104, 107–111, 115, 118, 120–123, 125, 127, 146, 166, 174, 188, 190, 192, 194, 200, 207, 231, 235, 249, 251, 283, 286, 294, 302, 314, 326–327, 336; Arnold and, 251ff.; at Battle of Monmouth, 167; disengagement of, 131, 134; plan to attack West Point, 190–191; returns to New York, 232.
Clinton, Col. James, 25, 27, 30, 50, 54, 57, 59–62, 66–67, 77–78, 80, 86, 89, 96, 104, 106, 109, 111, 113–115, 122, 131, 134, 139, 152, 160–162, 164, 232–234, 286, 291; *illus.*, 26, 29
clothing, shortage of, 214, 293, 296, 337
Clove, headquarters in, 94–95
colonial congress, Albany, 14
Columbus, Christopher, 7
Committee of Safety, New York, 31–34, 36, 39, 43, 48, 54, 78, 122
Concord, Battle of, 15, 19–20
Congress, frigate, 91, 106, 119
Congress, U.S., 352, 356; *see also* Continental Congress
Constantinople, chain at, 30
Constitution Island, 4, 8, 27, 33–34, 37–39, 50, 59, 77, 84, 115, 127, 139, 162, 167, 174–175, 178, 183, 196, 301, 343; *illus.*, 35, 55; *see also* Fort Constitution
Continental Army, 30, 240, 247, 351; Baron von Steuben and, 187–202; clothing of, 214, 293, 296, 317, 337; demise of, 347–348; disease in, 209, 334; "divided and separated," 192; food of, 190, 315–317, 337; and Hudson River, 315–316; mass mutiny in, 292ff.; morale in, 230, 299; retreat of, 76; at Valley Forge, 138, 140–141, 143, 155, 159, 166, 188, 195–196, 313, 317, 321; at West Point, 159
Continental Congress, 19–21, 24, 29, 30–31, 40, 43–44, 53–54, 58, 75–76, 88, 91, 100, 244, 248, 322
Continental Navy, 91
Continental Village, Peekskill, 84, 88, 120
Convention Army, 181
Conway Cabal, 135, 159
Conway, Thomas, 159
Coote, Richard, 12
Corbin, Margaret (Molly), 307, 354
Cornwallis, Charles, Marquis of, 76, 291, 302; surrender of, 309–310
Corps of Engineers, 357
Corps of Invalids, 304–305, 309, 343, 352
Crane, frigate, 119, 123, 127
Crane, Col. John, 310
Croton River, 68
Crown Hill, 161
Crown Point, 22, 24, 42, 63, 160–161, 247
Crow's Nest Mountain, 28, 119, 127

Dartmouth, Lord (William Legge), 45, 47, 82
Dawes, William, 124
Declaration of Independence, 33, 42, 58, 157
de Grasse. *See* Grasse
Delaware River, 7, 10, 157; Washington's crossing of, 76
Dependence, frigate, 118–119, 125
deserters, 171, 230, 238, 251
De Witt, Col. Charles, 68
Dickinson, John, 20–21
discipline, 171, 217, 229–230, 236–238, 299
disease, in Continental Army, 209, 334
Dobb's Ferry, 265
Doodletown, N.Y., 102, 106–108, 118, 197
Dorchester Heights, Boston, 53, 56
Drake, Joseph, 43
drunkenness, 40, 77, 166, 171, 180, 310
Dubois, Maj. Lewis, 104, 119
Duchess of Gordon, sloop, 50
Dunderberg Mountain, 107
Duportail, Louis Le Bègue de Presle, 132–133, 137, 145, 168, 172, 175, 178, 182, 190, 193–194, 204, 206–207, 214, 216, 328, 354
Dutch, clash with English, 10–11
Dutchess County, militia from, 85
Dwight, Timothy, 14, 186

Eisenhower, Gen. Dwight D., 248 n.
Enfant, Pierre L', *illus.*, 257
engineers, scarcity of, 32; *see also* Corps of Engineers
English: clash with Dutch, 10–11; migration of to Hudson Valley, 12; rule established by, 11
English, Lt. Sam, 105
Ennis, Richard, 96
Erskine, Robert, 79
Esopus (Kingston), 10; *see also* Kingston
Estaing, Adm. Jean Baptiste D', 168, 178, 215
European wars, "importing" of, 13

Eustis, Dr. William, 280
Execution Hollow, 217, 230, 234, 238

Fenno, Capt. Ephraim, 110
Ferguson, Maj. Patrick, 292
Fishbourne, Capt. Benjamin, 200
Fishkill, N.Y., 65, 69, 78, 95, 117, 139,
  151, 158, 163–164, 187, 214, 252
Fletcher, Gen. Benjamin, 12
Flirtation Walk, 152
food and food supplies, 226, 259, 292–
  294, 313; Hudson River as key to, 313–
  318
forest fires, 231
Forest of Dean, 107, 109, 298
Fort Arnold, 164, 168, 171–172, 175,
  178, 180, 182, 186, 208, 222, 291
Fort Clinton, 66, 99, 106, 111–113, 118,
  121, 132, 138, 151, 161–162, 249, 291,
  309; see also Fort Vaughan
Fort Constitution, 34, 40, 42, 44, 49, 51,
  82, 119, 249; British attack on, 104–
  105; building of, 48–50; chain barrier
  and, 61; "deplorable condition" of, 56;
  fall of, 119–120; fatal flaw in, 43; garrison of, 78; see also Constitution Island
Fortescue, J. W., 313
Fort Independence, 82, 104–105, 127
Fort Lee, 65, 70
Fort Montgomery, 54, 56–57, 59–60, 62,
  68, 70, 77–78, 82, 84, 93, 99, 102, 112,
  132–133, 141, 148, 151–152, 163, 195,
  249; British attack on, 106–107; burial
  of dead in, 118; defenseless nature
  of, 109–110; taken by British, 112–115;
  illus., 87
Fort Orange (Albany), 10–11
Fort Putnam, 162, 168, 172, 204, 208,
  222, 256, 269, 301
Fort Ticonderoga, 14, 19, 25, 33, 43, 53,
  63, 68, 146, 157, 161, 168, 173–174,
  205, 242, 320; British defeat at, 21–22;
  British victory at, 92–93
Fort Vaughan, 121, 124, 126–127
Fort Washington, 65, 70
Fort Webb, 208, 336
Fort Wyllys, 208, 234, 309, 336
Franklin, Benjamin, 14, 54, 132, 188, 251
Franks, Maj. David, 255, 257, 275, 280
Fraunces' Tavern, 349
Frederick the Great, 187, 333
Freemasonry, 213, 230
French, expulsion from America, 14
French and Indian War, 13–14, 54
French engineers, appointment of, 132
French fleet, assistance from, 215
French Huguenots, 12
Friendship, warship, 124

Gage, Gen. Thomas, 21, 37, 45, 47
Gardiner's Island, 12
Gates, Maj. Gen. Horatio, 101, 120, 126,
  134, 137–138, 144, 157, 162, 164–165,
  174–176, 217, 249, 262
gauntlet, running of, 237–238
Gaylord, Lud, 336
George, Lake, 19, 22, 24, 313
George III, 15, 23, 33, 45, 82, 92, 127,
  163, 231, 325, 338, 343
George Washington Bridge, 65
Germain, Lord George, 82, 127, 262, 314

Germans, migration of to America, 12
Germantown, Battle of, 122, 127
Gibbons, Lt., 202
glaciers, in Hudson Valley, 4–6
Glover, Brig. Gen. John, 166–168, 286,
  296
Gomez, Estevan, 7
Gouvion, Jean Baptiste de, 132–133, 145,
  181, 183, 204, 229, 282, 300
Gowdy, John, 171
Grabouski, Count, 109, 114
graft, 41
granary, of colonies, 313
"Grand Bastion," 34, 42
Grant, Maj. Alexander, 107
Grasse, François Joseph Paul de, 302, 341
Great Chain, 147–153, 171, 208, 228,
  303, 346; boom for, 165, 167; ice
  danger and, 184–185; inspection of by
  Washington, 178; refloating of, 188–
  190; illus., 87, 149; see also boom;
  chain barrier
Great Lakes, 6, 313
Greene, Kitty (Mrs. Nathanael), 212
Greene, Maj. Gen. Nathanael, 89, 165,
  200, 212, 216, 267, 282, 286–288, 291–
  292
Green Mountain Boys, 19, 243
Green Mountains, 3
Grenell, John, 33
Grenell, Thomas, 32, 41, 49

Half Moon, 6–9, 12
Hamilton, Alexander, 134, 215–216, 232,
  234, 280–282, 297, 316, 344, 353–357
Hammill, Maj. Daniel, 106, 118
Hancock, John, 20–21, 23, 37
Hand, Brig. Gen. Edward, 286
Hannover, N.Y., 96
Hanson, John, 31, 36–38, 42
Harlem Heights, Battle of, 67
Harvey, Gen. Edward, 315
Hasbrouck, Jonathan, 335
Haverstraw, N.Y., 27, 36, 183, 266
Heath, Brig. Gen. William, 69, 77, 201,
  204, 217, 222, 227, 292, 295–296, 301,
  303, 307, 310, 334
"Hellcats," 214 n.
Hell Hole, 110
Heron, William, 260
Hessian Lake, 111, 118
Hessian troops, 63, 75; defeat of at Tren-
  ton, 76–77; forced labor by, 172
Highlands. See Hudson Highlands
Highlands Fortifications Commission, 59
High Tor, 1
Hitchcock, Rev. Enos, 213
Hodge, Capt. John, 112, 115
Holland, settlements by, 9–10
Hotham, Commo. William, 103, 118, 120,
  126
Howe, Lord Richard, 63
Howe, Maj. Gen. Robert, 200, 209, 228–
  229, 232–234, 252, 256, 260, 296, 298,
  303
Howe, Gen. William, 37, 47, 53, 63, 67,
  76, 86, 92, 94, 99–100, 121, 126–127,
  246, 248, 315; attack on Ticonderoga,
  92; disengagement of, 95–97
Hudson Gorge, birth of, 2
Hudson, Henry, 6–8
Hudson Highlands, 1, 178–180; colonial
  home sites on, 14; defenses in, 25, 30–

31, 36; geology of, 2–3; as obstacle to British, 51, 313–315, 328; trade in, 14–15; *see also* Hudson River; Hudson Valley

Hudson River: British strategy and, 46, 313–315, 328; commercial shipping on, 38; food supply and, 313–318; fresh water in, 6; as highroad of war, 13, 27; as "Key to Continent," 15; as New York–Canada link, 47; path of, 1–2; pirates on, 12; strategic importance of, 22, 187–188, 311–315, 319, 326–332; *illus.*, 5

Hudson River sloop, 15

Hudson Valley: British attacks in, 82; Dutch and Mohican relations in, 10; English settlements and rule in, 10–11; as highroad of war, 13, 27; ice ages in, 4; Indians of, 6–7; *see also* Hudson River

Hughes, Hugh, 147, 150, 160

Huguenots, in America, 12

Hull, Lt. Col. William, 196, 199, 300

Humphreys, David, 297

Huntington, Col. Ebenezer, 185, 342

Huntington, Brig. Gen. Jedidiah, 286

Independence. *See* Declaration of Independence

Indians: Asiatic origins of, 6; campaigns against, 215–216; early relations with, 10; early skirmishes with, 9, 13; enslavement of, 12; in Revolutionary War, 318

inflation, 230, 293

Iroquois Indians, campaign against, 215

Irving, Washington, 2

Jackson, Lt. Paton, 107–108, 118

Jameson, Lt. Col. John, 265, 273, 275, 280, 282–283

Jamestown, Va., settlement at, 6

Jay, James, 172, 225, 230, 263

Jay, John, 59, 70, 172, 212

Jefferson, Thomas, 357

Johnson, Lt. Col. Henry, 197–200

Juet, Robert, 8–9

Kennebec River, 239

Kennedy, Dennis, 135

Kidd, Capt. William, 12

Kieft, William, 10

King George's War, 13

Kingsbridge, N.Y., 23, 25, 134, 238

King's Ferry, 184, 229

King's Mountain, 292

Kingston, N.Y., 10, 83, 97, 122, 124–125

King William's War, 13

Kirkwood, Capt. Robert, 95

Knox, Lt. George, 199, 202

Knox, Col. Henry, 43–44, 53, 56, 58, 80, 89, 158, 215–216, 235, 275, 281, 286, 323, 343–344, 349, 352, 355; *illus.*, 345

Knox, Lucy (Mrs. Henry), 212, 341

Kosciuszko, Col. Thaddeus, 133, 152, 157–159, 162–163, 165, 171–172, 174, 176, 181, 188, 193, 204, 222, 228–229, 234, 249, 256; dispute with Duportail, 178; plan for Redoubt 4 (*illus.*), 173; West Point's debt to, 207; as West Point's new engineer, 157; *illus.*, 156

Lady Washington, warship, 64, 91, 112, 115, 119, 125, 179, 192, 202

Lafayette, Marquis de, 159, 275–277, 281, 286, 298

Lake George, 19, 22, 24, 313

Lakeman, John, 230

Lamb, Col. John, 104, 106, 119, 125, 172, 247–248, 259, 266, 271–272, 278, 283

Langdon, John, 42

latrines, open, 225

Laumoy, Jean Baptiste Joseph de, 132–133

Lauzun, Duc de, 302

Lawrence, Augustine, 61

Lawrence, Jonathan, 41, 51–52

Lawrence, Lt. Oliver, 111

Ledyard, Benjamin, 33

Lee, Maj. Gen. Charles, 47, 50, 63, 75

Lee, Gen. Henry ("Light-Horse Harry"), 197, 199, 209, 357

Lee, Richard Henry, 21, 247

Leisler, Jacob, 11

Lexington, Battle of, 15, 19–20

lightning rods, 234

Lincoln, Maj. Gen. Benjamin, 215, 231

links, in early chains, 79; *see also* chain barrier; Great Chain

Livingston, Gilbert, 52, 56–57, 59, 61

Livingston, Col. Henry Beekman, 54

Livingston, Robert R., 20, 39, 42, 59, 61, 66, 142, 163–164, 235, 256, 271

Livingston, Col. William S., 109, 113, 118

Livingston, Mrs. William, 211, 282

Logan, Maj. Samuel, 105–107, 118

Long Island: Battle of, 50, 64–65; British sympathizers in, 48

Long Island Sound, 94, 103

Loring, Joshua, 37

Loring, Sir William, 94

Loring, Mrs. William, 53, 94

Louis XVI, 325

Lovett, John, 85

Lush, Maj. Stephen, 118

Lusk Reservoir, 161

Luzerne, Chevalier de La, 214

Lynch, Thomas, 21–22

McCarthy, Mrs. Mary, 261, 263

McClaughry, Lt. Col. James, 107, 109, 111, 114–115, 118

McDougall, Brig. Gen. Alexander, 24, 80–82, 84–86, 88–90, 151–152, 155, 158, 160, 162–163, 165, 181–186, 191–193, 203, 206, 216, 222, 233–234, 292, 302, 304, 307, 310, 335, 340

McHenry, Maj. James, 276

Machin, Capt.-lt. Thomas, 62, 67–69, 78, 83–86, 107, 110–111, 120, 123, 148, 150–154, 163, 165, 167, 179, 300

McKenney, Mathew, 61

Mackesy, Piers, 315

McTheil (Mekeel), Uriah, 217

Malcolm, Col. William, 168, 170, 172, 179–181, 184–185

Malta, Great Chain of, 30

Manhattan Island: abandoned by Washington, 67; exploration of, 8; population of, 10; purchase of, 10; in Revolutionary War, 23, 26, 58, 65; Royal Navy and, 50

Marie Antoinette, 302, 339

Martalear's Rock (Constitution Island), 27–28, 33, 44

The River and the Rock *was composed in Linotype Caledonia, with Baskerville and Bulmer display type, by Kingsport Press, Inc., Kingsport, Tennessee. The entire book was printed by offset lithography. Typography and binding design by Joan Stoliar.*

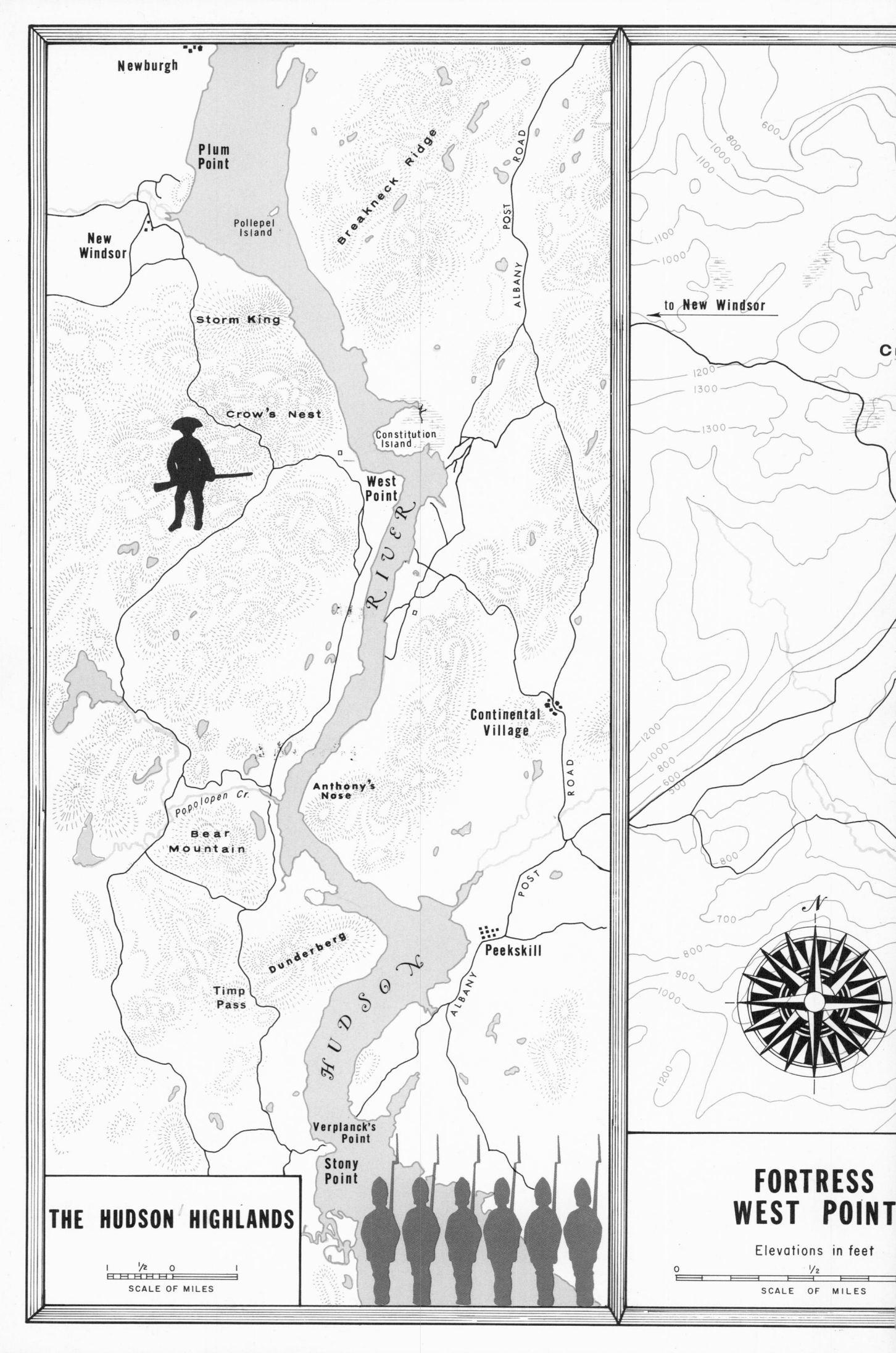

Newburgh

Plum
Point

Pollepel
Island

New
Windsor

Breakneck Ridge

ALBANY POST ROAD

Storm King

Crow's Nest

Constitution
Island

West
Point

HUDSON RIVER

Continental
Village

Anthony's
Nose

Popolopen Cr.

Bear
Mountain

ROAD

Dunderberg

Peekskill

ALBANY POST

Timp
Pass

HUDSON

Verplanck's
Point

Stony
Point

THE HUDSON HIGHLANDS

1   ½   0   1

SCALE OF MILES

to New Windsor

600

1000

1100

1000

1200

1300

1300

C

1200

800

600

700

800

900

1000

1200

N

FORTRESS
WEST POINT

Elevations in feet

0   ½

SCALE   OF   MILES

Essentials of Criminal Justice

FOURTH EDITION

Larry J. Siegel
University of Massachusetts–Lowell

Joseph J. Senna
Northeastern University

THOMSON

WADSWORTH   Australia • Canada • Mexico • Singapore • Spain • United Kingdom • United States

THOMSON

WADSWORTH

Senior Acquistions Editor, Criminal Justice: Jay Whitney
Development Editor: Shelley Murphy
Assistant Editor: Dawn Mesa
Editorial Assistant: Paul Massicotte
Technology Project Manager: Susan DeVanna
Marketing Manager: Dory Schaeffer
Marketing Assistant: Neena Chandra
Advertising Project Manager: Stacey Purviance
Project Manager, Editorial Production: Jennie Redwitz
Print/Media Buyer: Karen Hunt
Permissions Editor: Kiely Sexton
Production Service: Linda Jupiter, Jupiter Productions

Text Designer: Jennifer Dunn
Photo Researcher: Linda Rill
Copy Editor: Sandra Beriss
Proofreader: M. Kate St.Clair
Illustrator: Scientific Illustrators
Indexer: Do Mi Stauber
Cover Designer: Yvo Riezebos
Cover Image: *Divisidero Night* by Veerakeat Tongpaiboon.
    Courtesy of NextMonet
Compositor: R&S Book Composition
Text and Cover Printer: Transcontinental Printing/Interglobe

Printed in Canada
1 2 3 4 5 6 7   07 06 05 04 03

For more information about our products, contact us at:
Thomson Learning Academic Resource Center
1-800-423-0563

For permission to use material from this text, contact us by:
Phone: 1-800-730-2214
Fax: 1-800-730-2215
Web: http://www.thomsonrights.com

Library of Congress Control Number: 2002117049

Student Edition: ISBN 0-534-61641-0
Instructor Edition: ISBN 0-534-61648-8

Wadsworth/Thomson Learning
10 Davis Drive
Belmont, CA 94002-3098
USA

Asia
Thomson Learning
5 Shenton Way, #01-01
UIC Building
Singapore 068808

Australia/New Zealand
Thomson Learning
102 Dodds Street
Southbank, Victoria 3006
Australia

Canada
Nelson
1120 Birchmount Road
Toronto, Ontario M1K 5G4
Canada

Europe/Middle East/Africa
Thomson Learning
High Holborn House
50/51 Bedford Row
London WC1R 4LR
United Kingdom

Latin America
Thomson Learning
Seneca, 53
Colonia Polanco
11560 Mexico D.F.
Mexico

Spain/Portugal
Paraninfo
Calle/Magallanes, 25
28015 Madrid, Spain

Dedication

To my children, Eric, Andrew, Julie, and Rachel; to my son-in-law, Jason Macy; to my new grandson, Jack Macy; and as always, to my wife, Therese J. Libby.

    Larry J. Siegel

To my wife, Janet, and to my wonderful children, Joseph, Peter, Stephen, and Christian.

    Joseph J. Senna

About the Authors

LARRY J. SIEGEL was born in the Bronx in 1947. While attending City College of New York in the 1960s he was introduced to the study of crime and justice in courses taught by sociologist Charles Winick. After graduation he attended the newly opened program in criminal justice at the State University of New York at Albany, where he earned both his M.A. and Ph.D. and studied with famed scholars such as Michael Hindelang, Gilbert Geis, and Donald Newman. After completing his graduate work, Dr. Siegel began his teaching career at Northeastern University, where he worked closely with colleague Joseph Senna on a number of texts and research projects. After leaving Northeastern, he held teaching positions at the University of Nebraska–Omaha and Saint Anselm College in New Hampshire. He is currently a professor at the University of Massachusetts–Lowell.

Dr. Siegel has written extensively in the area of crime and justice, including books on juvenile law, delinquency, criminology, and criminal procedure. He is a court-certified expert on police conduct and has testified in numerous legal cases. He resides in Bedford, New Hampshire, with his wife, Therese J. Libby, Esq., and their children.

JOSEPH J. SENNA was born in Brooklyn, New York. He graduated from Brooklyn College, Fordham University Graduate School of Social Service, and Suffolk University Law School. Mr. Senna has spent over sixteen years teaching law and justice courses at Northeastern University. In addition, he has served as an assistant district attorney, director of Harvard Law School Prosecutorial Program, and consultant to numerous criminal justice organizations. His academic specialties include areas of criminal law, Constitutional due process, criminal justice, and juvenile law.

Mr. Senna lives with his wife and sons outside of Boston.

Brief Contents

Contents

Preface

David and Clara Harris personified the modern, successful, happy couple. They operated a dental corporation, owned a Mercedes, had young twin sons and lived in a palatial Houston-area home. The couple also owned a summer home and a ski chalet. However, behind this façade the couple was experiencing marital problems. David was having an affair with a coworker named Gail Bridges. Clara hired a private investigator to follow the couple; on July 24, 2002, the investigators told Clara that her husband and Bridges were together in a local motel. She sped to the scene to confront her unfaithful husband. While investigators were secretly filming David and his paramour, Clara arrived with her stepdaughter Lindsey at her side. Lindsey, who had initially been sympathetic toward Clara's plight, testified at the trial that as her dad had led his girlfriend Gail Bridges toward her Lincoln Navigator in the parking lot, Clara Harris climbed into her Mercedes and "stomped on the accelerator" of the car, lurching toward her husband who was standing at the driver's side of the Navigator. David Harris was thrown about 25 feet by the impact, and as Lindsey screamed at her stepmother to stop, Clara and ran over the body again and again.

On February 13, 2003, a jury of nine women and three men found that Clara Harris intentionally and repeatedly ran over her husband, causing his death. Dr. Harris did not face the death penalty because the case did not meet any of the special circumstances the state of Texas requires for capital punishment. However, if the jury found she had killed because of a "sudden passion," they could recommend probation as a sole sentence. David Harris' father, mother, and brother testified in favor of probation: "We feel like a member of our family has erred and we forgive that," his father told the jury.

The Harris case received widespread publicity in 2003. Clara, the "Mercedes Murderer," was described as a wealthy and vengeful woman who took the law into her own hands. She became the poster child for women scorned. Yet the jury found that her anguish did not justify the taking of a human life. During her attorney's argument to the jury, he painted a picture of his client as a model citizen who was "respected by her neighbors, loved by her neighbors, loved by the colleagues she employed, loved by the family that was closest to David." He added, "She worked hard. She was a good mother, a good wife. She has requested and she will be able to abide by terms of probation." Despite, however, the fact that the jury decided she had acted in "sudden passion," they also noted Clara had used her sedan as a deadly weapon, a finding which meant she will have to serve at least 10 years behind bars.

The Harris case raises a number of critical criminal justice issues. It shows how perception and discretion play a role in some of the most important justice decisions. David Harris was dead. If a jury were convinced his wife had planned to kill him or intended his death, she might have faced the death penalty; instead, they found she acted out of passion and she received a 20-year sentence. She might even have walked away with probation. Is it fair and just to give one person the death penalty and another probation for committing the same crime simply because of how a jury interprets their motives and feelings? Should so much discretion be placed in the hands of ordinary citizens? The Harris case also shows that criminals rarely serve their entire sentence behind bars. While David Harris will never again walk the streets of Houston, Clara will be out in 10 years assuming good behavior. Is that outcome fair to the victim? The case also received widespread publicity. Is it possible to receive a fair trial and a just sentence in a case that becomes a media circus? Should we allow cameras in the courtroom?

The Harris case is by no means unique. Events of the past few years remind us of the great impact crime, law, and justice have had on the American psyche. Each year the criminal justice system routinely processes millions of cases involving theft, violence, drug trafficking, and other crimes. How does this vast enterprise costing billions of dollars and involving millions of people operate? What are its most recent trends and policies? How effective are its efforts to control crime? What efforts are being made to improve its efficiency? We have written *Essentials of Criminal Justice* in an attempt to help answer these questions in a concise, forthright, and objective manner.

Because the study of criminal justice is a dynamic, ever-changing field of scientific inquiry and the concepts and processes of justice are constantly changing and evolving, we have updated *Essentials of Criminal Justice* to reflect the most critical legal cases, research studies, and policy initiatives that have taken place during the past few years. *Essentials* lays a groundwork for the study of criminal justice by analyzing and describing the agencies of justice and the procedures they use to identify and treat criminal offenders. It covers what most experts believe are the critical issues in criminal justice and analyzes their impact on the justice system. This edition focuses on critical policy issues in the criminal justice system, including efforts to control and contain terrorism.

Our primary goals in writing this fourth edition remain, as they have been for the previous three:

1. To provide students with a thorough knowledge of the criminal justice system.
2. To be as readable and interesting as possible.
3. To be objective and unbiased.
4. To describe the most current methods of social control and analyze their strengths and weaknesses.

Every attempt has been made to make the presentation of material interesting, balanced, and objective. No single political or theoretical position dominates the text; instead, the many diverse views that are contained within criminal justice and characterize its interdisciplinary nature are presented. The text includes topical information on recent cases and events that enliven the presentation.

We have tried to provide a text that is informative, comprehensive, interesting, well organized, and objective, yet provocative and thought provoking.

ORGANIZATION OF THE TEXT

This new edition has been thoroughly revised and the chapter organization streamlined. The material that was contained in Chapter 7 of the previous edition on Police and the Rule of Law has been incorporated into Chapter 6, Issues in Policing. We hope this reorganization will make the text more appropriate for the Introduction to Criminal Justice course.

Part One gives the student a basic introduction to crime, law, and justice. Chapter 1 covers the agencies of justice, the formal justice process, and introduces students to the concept of the informal justice system, which involves discretion, deal making, and plea bargains. This chapter discusses the major perspectives on justice and shows how they shape justice policy. Chapter 2 reviews the nature and extent of crime and victimization: How is crime measured? Where and when does it occur? Who commits crime? Who are its victims? What social factors influence the crime rate? Chapter 3 provides a discussion of the criminal law and its relationship to criminal justice. It covers the legal definition of crime, the defenses to crime, and issues in Constitutional procedural law.

Part Two provides an overview of law enforcement. Three chapters cover the history and development of police departments, the functions of police in modern society, issues in policing, and the police and the rule of law. There is an emphasis on community policing and community crime prevention, technology and policing, changes in police procedure, and other current issues.

Part Three is devoted to the adjudication process, from pretrial indictment to the sentencing of criminal offenders. In this section, individual chapters focus on organization of the court system, pretrial procedures, the criminal trial, and sentencing. Topics included are bail, court reorganization, sentencing, and capital punishment.

Part Four focuses on the correctional system, including probation and the intermediate sanctions of house arrest, intensive supervision, and electronic monitoring. While the traditional correctional system of jails, prisons, community-based corrections, and parole are also discussed at length, there is a new section on restorative justice programs. Such issues as the prison and jail overcrowding crisis, house arrest, correctional workers, super-maximum-security prisons, and parole effectiveness are discussed.

Part Five explores the juvenile justice system. There is information on the development of juvenile justice, waiving youths to the adult court, and the death penalty for children.

Great care has been taken to organize the text to reflect the structure and process of justice. Each chapter attempts to be comprehensive, self contained, and orderly.

WHAT'S NEW IN THIS EDITION

New Features

Boxed Features To keep up with the changes in the criminal justice system the fourth edition of *Essentials of Criminal Justice* has been thoroughly revised and renewed. The evolution of crime control policy has been followed by updating the discussion of the criminal justice system with recent court decisions, legislative changes, and theoretical concepts that reflect the changing orientation of the field. To meet this goal, the text now contains six different kinds of boxed features that help students analyze material in greater depth:

- **Policy, Programs, and Issues in Criminal Justice** helps students think critically about current justice issues, policies, and practices. For example, in Chapter 2, a feature entitled "Teens and Guns" discusses how sharp swings in the murder rate can be linked to teenage gun ownership.
- **Criminal Justice and the Media** shows how the criminal justice system is portrayed in films and TV shows and also how the media influences crime and justice. In Chapter 1, "*The Red Dragon*" discusses how popular films help shape our image of criminals.
- **Law in Review** gives the facts, decision, and significance of critical legal cases. For example, in Chapter 6, "*United States v. Bin Laden*" answers the provocative question "Do terrorists captured overseas enjoy the same rights as criminal suspects apprehended in the United States?"
- **Race, Culture, Gender and in Criminal Justice** helps students better understand diversity issues and the justice system. In Chapter 6, "Racial Profiling: Does Race Influence the Police Use of Discretion?" examines this controversial issue in detail.

- **Criminal Justice and Technology** reviews some of the more recent scientific advances that can aid the justice system. For example, in Chapter 4, a feature on "Crime Mapping" shows how computer-generated crime maps give the police the power to create immediate, detailed visuals of crime patterns.
- All-new **Careers in Criminal Justice** reviews specific criminal justice careers and gives information on how to prepare for and obtain jobs in the criminal justice system. For example, Chapter 11 has a feature describing careers in probation.

Criminal Justice Confronts Terrorism   There is no more important topic today than how the criminal justice system is being called on to confront terrorism. To keep up with this evolving issue, there are now Part-ending features that describe how the criminal justice system is adapting to our post-9-11 world. These essays include:

Who Is the Terrorist?

The Law Enforcement Response to Terrorism

Courts and Terrorism

Corrections and Terrorism

Internet/InfoTrac College Edition Research Links   Throughout the book there are a variety of links so students can do further research and reading on the Internet. Some are links to Web sites containing information that can enrich the textual material; others guide students to articles and keyword searches on InfoTrac College Edition. Each feature now has InfoTrac College Edition research links, designed to guide students who wish to supplement the textual material. Chapters end with InfoTrac College Edition exercises, which help students learn to research critical criminal justice issues.

New Content

Each chapter has been thoroughly updated and revised. We have made the text more concise and "leaner." The book also contains many new graphs, figures, charts, and tables, which make the presentation easier to understand and conceptualize.

- Chapter 1 **Crime and Criminal Justice** has been totally revised and now includes perspectives on justice. It covers the case of Samantha Runnion, a 5-year-old girl who was kidnapped in 2002, while playing in front of her California home, and killed. There are features on Careers in Criminal Justice and the movie *Red Dragon* as a media event. Data on criminal justice expenditures and the number of people in the correctional system has been updated. Recent research on the effect of imprisonment on recidivism rates of felony offenders is reviewed.
- Chapter 2 **The Nature of Crime and Victimization** begins with the Elizabeth Smart case, the Utah teen taken from her home while her family was asleep and found nine months later. There are updated sections on international crime trends and the factors that influence crime rates. Recent research on gender and crime, TV watching and crime, biosocial influences on antisocial and violent behavior in children and adults, and how exposure to community violence, traumatic victimization, and other stressful life events affects people's lives are discussed. A new Policy, Programs, and Issues feature explores teens and guns.
- Chapter 3 **Criminal Law: Substance and Procedure** examines the Andrea Yates case, in which a young mother killed her five children while suffering postpartum depression. A number of new statutes are discussed including one on "creating a hazard." There is analysis of research on sex offender registration laws. A new Law in Review feature reviews the *Chicago v. Morales* case, and

a new Policy, Programs, and Issues feature on criminal law and terrorism covers the U.S.A. Patriot Act.

- Chapter 4 **Police in Society: History and Organization** begins with the investigation into the spread of the deadly anthrax virus. There is a new feature on careers in law enforcement. The Criminal Justice and Technology feature updates crime mapping. Another new technology topic, data mining, shows how it can help identify crime patterns and link them to suspects. The Communications Assistance for Law Enforcement Act (CALEA) is also reviewed.

- Chapter 5 **The Police: Role and Function** examines the Chandra Levy disappearance investigation. It reviews current community- and problem-oriented policing programs. New Policy, Programs, and Issues features look at the Indianapolis Gun Control Program and the role of civilian review boards. A new Criminal Justice and the Media box reviews the *CSI* shows and how they impact the public's perception of the police. New research includes studies showing that increased police presence may actually reduce crime levels.

- Chapter 6 **Issues in Policing: Professional, Social, and Legal** begins with a review of the D.C. sniper case, which shows how law enforcement cooperation can help solve even the most challenging cases. There are new features—Race, Culture, and Gender on racial profiling and a Law in Review on *United States v. Bin Laden*. The chapter now contains new sections on the police and the rule of law, including the recent *Kirk v. Louisiana* (2002) case in which the Supreme Court ruled that police officers need either a warrant or probable cause plus exigent circumstances in order to make a lawful entry into a suspect's home.

- Chapter 7 **Courts, Prosecution, and the Defense** reviews the Knoller dog murder case in which a San Francisco couple was convicted of manslaughter because their dog killed a neighbor. A federal initiative to allow Internet access to criminal case files is examined. A Criminal Justice and Technology feature looks at technology and court management.

- Chapter 8 **Pretrial Procedures** analyzes the case of John Walker Lindh, the "American Taliban." The role of prosecutors in plea bargaining is updated. Efforts to reduce plea negotiations in serious felonies are discussed. A new Policy, Programs, and Issues feature looks at pretrial service programs. There is a review of recent research on grand juries.

- Chapter 9 **The Criminal Trial** begins with the Sarah Jane Olson case, a former radical who was tried after more than twenty years in hiding. There is a new Criminal Justice and the Media feature on televising criminal trials, as well as a new Law In Review box: "The Danielle van Dam Case: Should Defense Lawyers Tell the Truth?" The recent *Alabama v. Shelton* (2002) case—in which the Supreme Court ruled that a person cannot receive a probation sentence in which a prison or jail term is suspended, or any other type of sentence containing a threat of future incarceration, unless they are afforded the right to counsel at trial—is reviewed.

- Chapter 10 **Punishment and Sentencing** begins with the story of Willie Ervin Fisher, described as "an easygoing, sweet person," who was put to death in 2001 for killing his girlfriend, Angela Johnson. It also updates three-strikes sentencing information and reviews the "truth in sentencing" movement. The Race, Culture, and Gender feature "The Death Penalty Abroad" has been updated, and includes material on the case of Amina Lawal, a Nigerian woman who was convicted and sentenced to death by stoning by an Islamic Shariah court after giving birth to a baby girl more than nine months after divorcing her husband. The 2002 cases of *Atkins v. Virginia* in which the Supreme Court ruled that executions of mentally retarded criminals are "cruel and unusual punishments," and *Ring v. Arizona,* in which the Supreme Court ruled that juries, not judges, must make the critical findings that send convicted killers to death row are reviewed.

- Chapter 11 **Community Sentences: Probation, Intermediate Sanctions, and Restorative Justice** begins with the Winona Ryder case and how the court handled her treatment after she was convicted of shoplifting. There is recent material on felony sentencing in state courts. This chapter looks at the explosive growth of restorative justice techniques in alternative sanctions. A new Careers in Criminal Justice feature focuses on probation officers. The *United States v. Knights* (2001) case, in which the Supreme Court upheld the legality of a warrantless search of a probationer's home for the purposes of gathering criminal evidence, is analyzed. A Race, Gender, and Culture feature discusses alternatives to incarceration abroad. There is new information on available electronic monitoring systems. A Policy, Programs, and Issues feature covers the classic work by John Braithwaite on reintegrative shaming; a new Policy, Programs, and Issues feature looks at restorative justice in the community.

- Chapter 12 **Corrections: History, Institutions, and Populations** updates trends in correctional populations and shows how changes in sentencing policy have influenced corrections. The case of *Correctional Services Corp. v. Malesko* (2001), which defines the rights and protections of inmates in private correctional facilities, is reviewed.

- Chapter 13 **Prison Life** has new features, including a Criminal Justice and the Media discussion of the book *Newjack;* a Criminal Justice and Technology analysis called "Technocorrections: Contemporary Correctional Technology"; and a Law in Review look at *Hope v. Pelzer* (2002), in which the Supreme Court reviewed the case of an Alabama prison inmate who was twice handcuffed to a hitching post for disruptive conduct. A Policy, Programs, and Issues feature examines the problems of reentry. There are reviews of research on serious mental disorder in prisoners; HIV- and AIDS-risk behaviors among female jail detainees; and the prevalence of substance abuse and dependence disorders among prison inmates. Data from the latest report on *Recidivism of Prisoners* (2002) is included.

- Chapter 14 **The Juvenile Justice System** begins with a discussion of the King case, which involved two teens who killed their father. It reviews the changing view of juvenile justice in the new millennium, including new "get tough" laws and trends in juvenile waiver to adult court. A new Policy, Programs, and Issues feature looks at teen courts and another reviews Operation Ceasefire, a successful police-inspired delinquency prevention program in Boston, Massachusetts, that is aimed at reducing youth homicide victimization and youth gun violence. Another new Policy, Programs, and Issues feature asks the provocative question "Should we abolish the juvenile court?" The chapter reviews the 2002 case of *Pottawatomie County v. Earls* in which the Supreme Court ruled that it is permissible to allow a school drug testing policy that established random, suspicionless urinalysis testing of any students participating in extracurricular competitive activities.

Ancillary Material

To help instructors use *Essentials of Criminal Justice* in their courses and to aid students in preparing for exams, Wadsworth provides several pedagogic supplements.

These materials are available to qualified adopters. Please consult your local sales representative for details.

For the Instructor

Instructor's Edition At the center of the book's linked system of instructor resources, this information-packed *Instructor's Edition* helps you effectively utilize all the resources available with the text. We've provided a key teaching tool, the *Resource Integration Guide.* The guide provides grids that link each chapter's outline—topic by topic—to instructional ideas and corresponding supplement resources.

***Instructor's Resource Manual* by Lynn Newhart** This revised and updated *Instructor's Resource Manual* includes the following for every text chapter: learning objectives, key terms, detailed chapter outlines, discussion topics/student activities, Internet connections, media resources, and a test bank. The completely new test bank features the following for each text chapter: 35 multiple-choice, 15 true/false, 20 fill-in-the-blank, and five essay questions.

***ExamView*®** Create, deliver, and customize printed and online tests and study guides in minutes with this easy-to-use assessment and tutorial system. *ExamView* includes a Quick Test Wizard and an Online Test Wizard to guide instructors step-by-step through the process of creating tests. The test appears onscreen exactly as it will print or display online. Using *ExamView*'s complete word processing capabilities, you can enter an unlimited number of new questions or edit questions that are included. *ExamView* offers flexible delivery and the ability to test and grade online.

Multimedia Manager for Criminal Justice 2004: A Microsoft*® *PowerPoint*® *Link Tool This one-stop digital library and presentation tool not only provides complete *PowerPoint*® lectures with text images and video, it also lets you easily assemble, edit, publish, and present your own custom lectures for your introductory course—bringing together art from this CD-ROM, the Web, and your own material. The *Manager* includes:

- Hundreds of images (art, figures, and tables) from this book and other Wadsworth criminal justice textbooks
- Text images organized for your convenience by topic
- Exciting, relevant *CNN*® *Today* video clips
- Topic-specific *PowerPoint*® presentations
- A very simple wizard that guides you in publishing your lectures online for student reference and distance learning

***CNN*® *Today: Video Series, Introduction to Criminal Justice* (formerly *CJ in the News*), Vols. I–VI** Now you can integrate the up-to-the-minute programming power of CNN and its affiliate networks right into your course. These videos feature short, high-interest clips perfect for launching your lectures. A current new volume is available to adopters each year. Ask your Thomson/Wadsworth representative about our video policy by adoption size.

The Wadsworth Criminal Justice Video Library So many exciting, new videos... so many great ways to enrich your lectures and spark discussion of the material in this text! Your Thomson/Wadsworth representative will be happy to provide details on our video policy by adoption size. The library includes these selections and many others:

- *Court TV Videos*—one-hour videos presenting seminal and high-profile court cases
- Videos from the *A&E American Justice Series, Films for the Humanities,* and the *National Institute of Justice Crime File Videos*

Customized Criminal Justice Videos Produced by Wadsworth and *Films for the Humanities,* these videos include short 5- to 10-minute segments that encourage classroom discussion. Topics include: white collar crime, domestic violence, forensics, suicide and the police officer, the court process, the history of corrections, prison society, and juvenile justice. Now available: Volume I and Volume II.

For the Student

***Study Guide* by William Smith**   This helpful guide contains learning objectives, chapter summaries, key terms and concepts, Internet connections, and a self-test bank with a variety of test questions, including 25 multiple choice, 20 true/false, 20 fill-in-the-blank, and five essay questions for each chapter in the text.

The Criminal Justice Resource Center's Companion Web Site for* Essentials of Criminal Justice, *Fourth Edition

http://cj.wadsworth.com

Once you're at the Criminal Justice Resource Center, click on "Student or Instructor Companion Web Sites" from the left navigation bar and select your book cover to go to the text's companion Web site. There, you will find many useful learning resources for your course. Some of those resources include:

- CNN videos
- Chapter outlines
- Chapter reviews/summaries
- Glossary
- Crossword
- Flashcards
- Tutorial quizzing (10 multiple-choice, 5 true/false, 5 matching, 1 discussion)
- Final exam
- Internet activities
- InfoTrac College Edition exercises
- Web references (related Web sites)
- Discussion forum
- Multimedia Manager demo
- Instructor's Manual
- Career Resource Center (book specific, with links to Resume Writing and Career Links Web sites)
- MicroCase exercises
- Group projects with a discussion forum
- Topical discussion forum
- "Concept Builder," which consists of these parts:
  —Concept
  —Application
  —Exercise: Student responds to a question, or scenario, keying in his/her answer into a text window and e-mailing to instructor

InfoTrac® College Edition   With every new copy of this text, adopters and their students automatically receive four months of FREE access to InfoTrac College Edition, a world-class, online university library that offers complete articles (not just abstracts) from thousands of scholarly and popular publications. Updated daily and going back as far as 22 years, InfoTrac College Edition is a great way to expand your course beyond the pages of this text. It is available only to colleges and universities.

Additional Useful Material

InfoTrac College Edition Student Guide for Criminal Justice   This booklet provides detailed user guidelines for students, illustrating how to use the InfoTrac College Edition database. Special features include log-in help, a complete search-tips worksheet, and a topic list of suggested keyword search terms for criminal justice.

***The Criminal Justice Internet Investigator*, Third Edition**   This colorful trifold brochure lists some of the most popular Internet addresses for criminal justice–related Web sites.

***Internet Activities for Criminal Justice*, Second Edition**   This completely updated booklet shows how to best utilize the Internet for research through fun and informative exercises, searches, and activities.

***Internet Guide for Criminal Justice*, Second Edition**   Intended for the less-experienced Internet user, the first part of this completely revised booklet explains the background and vocabulary necessary for navigating the Internet; the second part focuses on Internet applications in criminal justice, doing criminal justice research online, and criminal justice career information on the Web.

***Wadsworth's Guide to Careers in Criminal Justice*, Second Edition**   Fully updated, this comprehensive guide includes information on careers in law enforcement, courts, and corrections. It includes job descriptions and requirements, training and salary/benefits information, and contact details for many of the top employers and associations in criminal justice.

***Terrorism: An Interdisciplinary Perspective*, Second Edition**   This 80-page booklet (with companion Web site) discusses terrorism in general and the issues surrounding the events of September 11, 2001. Information-packed, it examines the origins of terrorism in the Middle East, focusing on Osama bin Laden in particular, as well as issues involving bioterrorism; the specific role played by religion in Middle Eastern terrorism; globalization as it relates to terrorism; and the reactions and repercussions of terrorist attacks.

The Criminal Justice Resource Center   http://cj.wadsworth.com
This Web site provides instructors and students alike a wealth of FREE information and resources, such as:

- The Terrorism: An Interdisciplinary Perspective page
- The NEW Criminal Justice lecture series
- The NEW Crime and Technology page
- What Americans Think polls
- The Criminal Justice Timeline, highlighting significant events and developments from before 601 C.E. to the present

And so much more!

Careers in Criminal Justice 2.0 Interactive CD-ROM   Completely updated with many new career profile videos, this CD-ROM is designed to help students focus on the criminal justice career choices right for them. This engaging self-exploration provides an interactive discovery of careers in criminal justice with such exciting features as FREE online access to the Holland Personalized Self-Assessment Test, video profiles of practicing professionals, and information and references to assist students in learning more about various jobs, and effective job-search strategies and practices as well.

***Mind of a Killer* CD-ROM**   Voted one of the top 100 CD-ROMs by an annual *PC Magazine* survey, *Mind of a Killer* gives students a chilling glimpse into the realm of serial killers with over 80 minutes of video, 3D simulations, an extensive mapping system, a library, and much more.

***Crime Scenes: An Interactive Criminal Justice* CD-ROM**   Awarded the gold medal in higher education and silver medal for video interface by *New Media Magazine*'s

Invision Awards, this interactive CD-ROM features six vignettes that allow students to adopt various roles as they explore all aspects of the criminal justice system, such as policing/investigation, courts, sentencing, and corrections.

***Seeking Employment in Criminal Justice and Related Fields,* Fourth Edition**
Written by J. Scott Harr and Kären M. Hess, this completely updated book provides students with extensive information on the wide range of criminal justice professions. It also helps students develop a job-search strategy, and provides information on resumes and interviewing techniques.

ACKNOWLEDGMENTS

Many people helped make this book possible. Those who reviewed the fourth edition, some of whom also reviewed previous editions, and made suggestions that I attempted to follow to the best of my ability include Kelly Asmussen, Peru State College; E. Elaine Bartgis, Fairmont State College; Stephen M. Cox, Central Connecticut State University; Jacqueline Fitzgerald, Temple University; and Mark Jones, East Carolina University.

I also thank my colleagues who reviewed the previous editions: Kelly Asmussen, E. Elaine Bartgis, Stephen M. Cox, Jacqueline Fitzgerald, and Mark Jones; Ronald R. Brooks, Clinton Community College; Tom Fields, Cape Fear Community College; Kathrine Johnson, Kentucky State University; William Kelly, Auburn University; Daniel A. Klotz, Los Angeles Valley College; Cecilia Tubbs, Jefferson State Community College; and Ellen F. Van Valkenburgh, Jamestown Community College.

Special thanks must also go to Kathleen Maguire and Ann Pastore, editors of the *Sourcebook of Criminal Justice;* the staff at the Institute for Social Research at the University of Michigan; and the National Criminal Justice Reference Service, who are always there when I need them the most.

The form and content of this new edition were directed by Sabra Horne, executive editor, aka Wonderwoman. It has been a pleasure working with Sabra and my other colleagues at Wadsworth: Jay Whitney—our kind and patient editor, the incomparable developmental editor Shelley Murphy, the fabulous production manager Jennie Redwitz, my production editor and confidante Linda Jupiter, photo editor and friend Linda Rill, the highly talented assistant editor Dawn Mesa, technology project manager nonpareil Susan DeVanna, our fantastic marketing manager Dory Schaeffer, and Joy Westberg, who has that knack of describing the essence of things so nicely. Special thanks to Sandra Beris, the diligent copyeditor, and M. Kate St.Clair, the professional proofreader, who help me compensate for all the time I spent dozing in my high school English classes.

Larry Siegel
Bedford, NH

The Nature of Crime, Law, and Criminal Justice

On October 22, 2001, a New Jersey jury found Augustin Garcia, forty-nine, a successful businessman and neighborhood leader, guilty of murder. There was no question that Garcia had committed the crime. During his trial, the jury was shown a home videotape in which he could be seen shooting former girlfriend Gladys Ricart, thirty-nine, in her living room in Ridgefield, New Jersey, as she presented bouquets to her bridesmaids on the day of her wedding. The question the jury was forced to decide was Garcia's degree of criminal responsibility.

During the trial, Garcia argued that the shock of suddenly learning that his longtime girlfriend was marrying someone else induced a temporary mental illness known as acute adjustment disorder. His altered mental state made it impossible for him to control his emotions and behavior. He claimed that he believed that Ricart still had feelings for him, and he was shocked to walk in on her wedding! The defense produced videotape evidence from a security camera showing Garcia and Ricart embracing at a supermarket early on the morning of the killing. They claimed that the two remained romantically linked right up to her wedding day. Garcia testified that he drove by Ricart's house on the way to an art show opening and was puzzled to see signs of a celebration. At first he left the scene, but then returned an hour later. When he entered the home he was assaulted by her relatives. Overcome with shock, confusion, and fear, he drew his gun, which fired during the struggle.

To be found guilty of manslaughter, which he had hoped, rather than murder, the jurors would have to conclude that, among other things, Garcia had reasonable provocation to kill Ricart. The jury rejected this vision. "Even if she did have a relationship with him, it made no difference in him killing her," said the jury forewoman. "He saw the love of his life slipping away and he couldn't deal with it. You know, 'If I can't have her, nobody will.'" Some jury members felt that Garcia must have known a wedding was under way because there were limousines parked in front of the house and people in formal wear. Others were swayed by the fact that Garcia had an hour to think about the crime before he shot Ricart.

Garcia's actions illustrate the complex nature of crime and justice in America. Here a jury was asked not to decide whether the defendant had committed a crime, but what was going through his mind as he assaulted his victim. Could they really be sure whether the motive was vengeance, jealousy, or an irrational urge that might mitigate the defendant's guilt? The case also raises other questions: How can such crimes be explained? Are they a product of an abnormal mind, or the result of social and economic factors? Finally, the case shows how, under criminal law, merely committing an illegal act is not enough for conviction. The law demands that various physical and mental elements must be proven before a person may be convicted of crime.

The first section of *Essentials of Criminal Justice* deals with these issues in some detail. The first chapter reviews the criminal justice process, the second analyzes the nature and extent of crime, while chapter 3 looks at the criminal law and its processes. ■

1 Crime and Criminal Justice

Chapter Outline

Criminal Justice Links

Criminal Justice Viewpoints

ON JULY 15, 2002, Samantha Runnion, age five, was kidnapped while playing in front of her California home.[1] Within a day, the local police received a phone tip from someone who had stumbled upon her body; she had been raped and murdered. A playmate of Samantha gave the police a good description of her attacker, and they soon arrested Alejandro Avila and charged him with four felonies—one of kidnapping, two of forcible lewd acts on a child, and one of murder. Avila had been charged in a previous child molestation case but had not been convicted. After Avila's arrest prosecutors cited "special circumstances" in the killing, kidnapping, and sexual assault on a minor, a standard that would allow them to seek the death penalty. Tony Ruckauckas, the Orange County district attorney, told reporters that he would consult with the victim's family and members of his staff before coming to a decision whether Avila, if convicted, would be put to death. But, he said, "Anyone who commits this kind of crime in Orange County will either die in prison of natural causes or will be executed." The DA's office also let it be known that DNA evidence found at the crime scene linked Avila to the crime. Ruckauckas told reporters that the evidence was "very, very compelling, and we are satisfied that we have the right person." ▪

 *To view the CNN video clip of this story, go to the book-specific Web site at* http://cj.wadsworth.com/siegel_essen4e.

This tragic case made national headlines in July 2002. And although such terrible incidents are relatively rare, the Runnion case raises important issues for the **criminal justice** system. First, the suspect's name and picture were broadcast almost instantly after his arrest, along with statements testifying to the incriminating evidence that had been gathered at the crime scene. Does such pretrial publicity make it virtually impossible for a suspect in a high-profile murder case to get a fair trial? Does invasive and persistent media exposure make a fair trial impossible? Should limits be placed on press coverage? Or would that violate the Constitution's guarantee of free speech and press? And can the media's constant barrage of violent event coverage actually increase the nation's violence rate?

The Runnion case also illustrates the system's growing dependence on technology to solve crimes. How did the DA conclude that Avila was the real culprit? Because of DNA matches found at the crime scene. Is it fair to convict someone of a crime based on relatively new technologies that have not been proven over years

criminal justice The decision-making points from the initial investigation or arrest by police to the eventual release of the offender and his or her reentry into society; the various sequential criminal justice stages through which the offender passes.

Though media exposure may be harmful to some, the media may also play a beneficial role in reducing crime. Go to Info-Trac College Edition and access William DeJong, "The Role of Mass Media campaigns in Reducing High-Risk Drinking Among College Students," *Journal of Studies on Alcohol,* March 2002 v63 i2 pS182(11).

of use? Avila may face the death penalty in the case. Should a person be executed based solely on a DNA match?

Finally, the Runnion case shows the complex issues that surround the use of capital punishment in the United States. The DA told the press he would consult with the family before making the decision to seek the death penalty. Should family and relatives, justifiably emotional soon after their loss, be part of the decision to take a defendant's life? Would the outcome be different if the victim did not have any living family members with whom the DA could consult? What role does public opinion play in the distribution of the death penalty? Samantha Runnion was an adorable five-year-old girl. Her death caused understandable public outrage. But should her killer be treated more harshly than another person who killed someone less vulnerable and less attractive? Are not all people and crime victims created equal? And finally, should the death penalty be employed if Samantha's killer suffers from some mental defect that causes him to have uncontrollable violent sexual urges? The Supreme Court has ruled that the death penalty cannot be used with people who are insane at the time they committed their offense. But what about people who are not legally insane but still suffer from severe psychological problems? Skeptics might suggest that all criminals suffer from psychological deficits or else they would not have committed their crimes. Should they all be immune from punishments?

The public relies on the agencies of the criminal justice system to provide solutions to the crime problem and to shape the direction of crime policy. This loosely organized collection of agencies is charged with, among other matters, protecting the public, maintaining order, enforcing the law, identifying transgressors, bringing the guilty to justice, and treating criminal behavior. The public depends on this vast system, employing more than two million people and costing taxpayers about $150 billion a year, to protect them from evil-doers and to bring justice to their lives.

This text serves as an introduction to the study of criminal justice. This chapter introduces some basic issues, beginning with a discussion of the concept and the study of criminal justice. The major processes of the criminal justice system are then introduced so that you can develop an overview of how the system functions. Because there is no single view of the underlying goals that help shape criminal justice, the varying perspectives on what criminal justice really is or should be are set out in some detail.

Is Crime a Recent Development?

We often hear older people say, "crime is getting worse every day" and "I can remember when it was safe to walk the streets at night," but their memories may be colored by wishful thinking. Crime and violence have existed in the United States for more than two hundred years. In fact, the crime rate may actually have been much higher in the nineteenth and early twentieth centuries than it is today.

Crime and violence have been common since the nation was first formed.[2] Guerilla activity was frequent before, during, and after the revolutionary war. Bands supporting the British—the Tories—and the American revolutionaries engaged in savage attacks on each other, using hit-and-run tactics, burning, and looting.

The struggle over slavery during the mid-nineteenth century generated decades of conflict, crimes, and violence, including a civil war. After the war, night riders and the Ku Klux Klan were active in the South, using vigilante methods to maintain the status quo and terrorize former slaves. The violence spilled over into bloody local feuds in the hill country of southern Appalachia. Factional hatreds, magnified by the lack of formal law enforcement and grinding poverty, gave rise to violent attacks and family feuding. Some former Union and Confederate soldiers, heading west with the dream of finding gold or starting a cattle ranch, resorted to theft and robbery.

Crime in the Old West

Some western lawmen developed reputations that have persisted for over a century. Of these men, none is more famous than Wyatt Earp. In 1876 he became chief deputy marshal of Dodge City, Kansas, a lawless frontier town, and later moved on to Deadwood in the Dakota Territory. In 1879 Earp and his brothers Morgan and Virgil journeyed to Tombstone, Arizona, where he eventually was appointed deputy U.S. marshal for the Arizona Territory. The Earps, along with their gun-slinging dentist friend Doc Holliday, participated in the famous OK Corral gunfight in 1881, during which they killed several members of a rustler gang known as the Cowboys, which was led by Curly Bill Brocius and Johnny Ringo.

The Cowboys were not the only gang to ply their trade in the Old West. Train robbery was popularized by the Reno brothers of Indiana and bank robbery by the James-Younger gang of Missouri.

Although the Civil War generated criminal gangs, it also produced widespread business crime. The great robber barons bribed government officials and intrigued to corner markets and obtain concessions for railroads, favorable land deals, and mining and mineral rights on government land. The administration of President Ulysses Grant was tainted by numerous corruption scandals.

To read more about Wyatt Earp's fascinating life, go to InfoTrac College Edition and read Allen Barra's "Who Was Wyatt Earp?" *American Heritage,* December 1998 p76(1).

Crime at the Turn of the Twentieth Century

From 1900 to 1935, the nation experienced a sustained increase in criminal activity. This period was dominated by Depression-era outlaws who later became mythic figures. Charles "Pretty Boy" Floyd was a folk hero among the sharecroppers of eastern Oklahoma, and the entire nation eagerly followed the exploits of its premier bank robber, John Dillinger, until he was killed in front of a Chicago movie house. The infamous "Ma" Barker and her sons Lloyd, Herman, Fred, and Arthur are credited with killing more than ten people, and Bonnie Parker and Clyde Barrow killed more than thirteen before they were slain in a shootout with federal agents.

While these relatively small and mobile outlaw gangs were operating in the Midwest, more organized gangs flourished in the nation's largest cities. The first criminal gangs formed before the Civil War in urban slums, such as the Five Points and Bowery neighborhoods in New York City. Though they sported colorful names, such as the Plug Uglies, the Hudson Dusters, and the Dead Rabbits, they engaged in mayhem, murder, and extortion. These gangs were the forerunners of the organized crime families that developed in New York and then spread to Philadelphia, Chicago, New Orleans, and other major urban areas.

The crime problem in the United States has been evolving along with the nation itself. Crime has provided a mechanism for the frustrated to vent their anger, for business leaders to maintain their position of wealth and power, and for those outside the economic mainstream to take a shortcut to the American dream. To protect itself from this ongoing assault, the public has supported the development of a great array of government agencies whose stated purpose is to control and prevent crime; identify, apprehend, and bring to trial those who choose to violate the law; and devise effective methods of criminal correction. These agencies make up what is commonly referred to today as the criminal justice system, and it is to their nature and development we now turn our attention.

Bonnie and Clyde remain subjects of fascination almost seventy years after their death. Read more about them at InfoTrac College Edition: Gary Cartwright, "The Whole Shootin' Match," *Texas Monthly,* February 2001 v29 i2 p74.

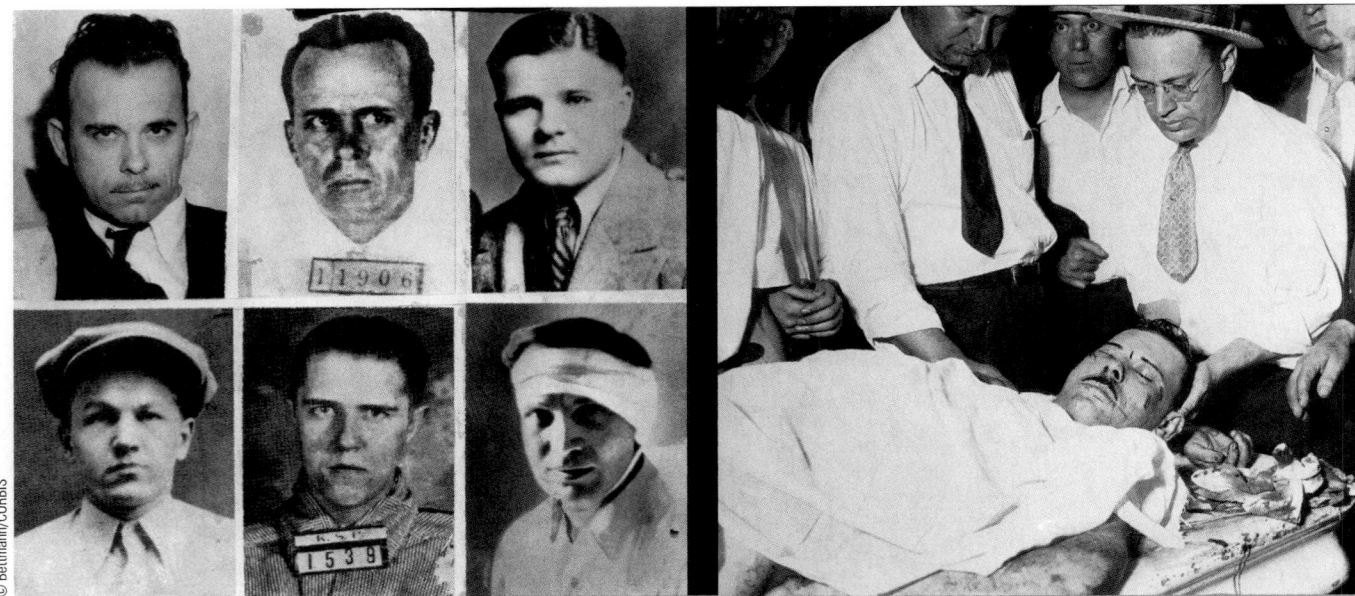

© Bettmann/CORBIS

At the turn of the last century, rural outlaws became mythic figures. At left are photos of the FBI's six most wanted men in 1934. Charles "Pretty Boy" Floyd (left photo, top right) was a folk hero among the sharecroppers of eastern Oklahoma. Floyd robbed as many as thirty banks, filing a notch in his pocket watch for each of the ten men he killed. Floyd was shot dead by police on October 19, 1934. John Dillinger (left photo, top left and right photo) became the nation's premier bank robber until he was killed in front of a Chicago movie house on July 22, 1934. After his death, his body was put on view at the morgue. Hordes of people came to view America's most notorious criminal.

Developing the
Criminal Justice System

To learn more about Beccaria's views, go to InfoTrac College Edition and access Richard Bellamy, "Crime and Punishment," *History Review*, September 1997 n28 p24(2).

The debate over the proper course for effective crime control can be traced back to the publication in 1764 of Cesare Beccaria's famous treatise *On Crime and Punishment*. Beccaria, an Italian social philosopher, made a convincing argument against the use of torture and capital punishment, which were common practices in the eighteenth century. He persuasively argued that only the minimum amount of punishment was needed to control crime if criminals could be convinced that their law violations were certain to be discovered and swiftly punished.[3]

In 1829 the first police agency, the London Metropolitan Police, was developed to keep the peace and identify criminal suspects. In the United States, police agencies began to appear during the mid-nineteenth century. The penitentiary, or prison, was created to provide nonphysical correctional treatment for convicted offenders; these were considered "liberal" innovations that replaced corporal or capital punishment.

To learn more about the history of the London Metropolitan Police, go to its Web page:
www.met.police.uk/police/mps/history/index.htm

Although significant and far-reaching, these changes were rather isolated developments. As criminal justice developed over the next century, these fledgling agencies of justice rarely worked together in a systematic fashion. It was not until 1919—when the Chicago Crime Commission, a professional association funded by private contributions, was created—that the work of the criminal justice system began to be recognized.[4] This organization acted as a citizen's advocate group and kept track of the activities of local justice agencies. The commission still carries out its work today.

In 1931 President Herbert Hoover appointed the National Commission of Law Observance and Enforcement, which is commonly known today as the Wickersham Commission. This national study group made a detailed analysis of the U.S. justice system and helped usher in the era of treatment and rehabilitation. The final report found that thousands of rules and regulations governed the system and made it difficult for justice personnel to keep track of the system's legal and administrative complexity.[5]

The Modern Era of Justice

The modern era of criminal justice can be traced to a series of research projects, first begun in the 1950s, under the sponsorship of the American Bar Foundation.[6] Originally designed to provide in-depth analysis of the organization, administration, and operation of criminal justice agencies, the ABF project discovered that the justice system contained many procedures that heretofore had been kept hidden from the public view. The research focus then shifted to an examination of these previously obscure processes and their interrelationship—investigation, arrest, prosecution, and plea negotiations. It became apparent that justice professionals used a great deal of personal choice in decision making, and showing how this discretion was used became a prime focus of the research effort. For the first time, the term *criminal justice system* began to be used, a view that justice agencies could be connected in an intricate yet often unobserved network of decision-making processes.

The American Bar Foundation is a nonprofit, independent national research institute committed to basic empirical research on law and legal institutions. For more than forty years, its research products have served to expand knowledge of the theory and functioning of law, legal institutions, and the legal profession. Visit the Web site at www.abf-sociolegal.org/

Federal Involvement in Criminal Justice

In 1967 the President's Commission on Law Enforcement and Administration of Justice (the Crime Commission), which had been appointed by President Lyndon Johnson, published its final report entitled *The Challenge of Crime in a Free Society.*[7] This group of practitioners, educators, and attorneys was given the charge of creating a comprehensive view of the criminal justice process and recommending reforms. Concomitantly, Congress passed the Safe Streets and Crime Control Act of 1968, providing for the expenditure of federal funds for state and local crime control efforts.[8] This act helped launch a massive campaign to restructure the justice system. It funded the National Institute of Law Enforcement and Criminal Justice (NILECJ), which encouraged research and development in criminal justice. Renamed the National Institute of Justice (NIJ) in 1979, it has continued its mission as a major source of funding for the implementation and evaluation of innovative experimental and demonstration projects in the criminal justice system.[9]

The Safe Streets Act provided funding for the **Law Enforcement Assistance Administration (LEAA)**, which granted hundreds of millions of dollars in aid to local and state justice agencies. Throughout its fourteen-year history, the LEAA provided the majority of federal funds to states for criminal justice activities. On April 15, 1982, the program came to an end when Congress ceased funding it. Although the LEAA suffered its share of criticism, it supported many worthwhile programs, including the development of a vast number of criminal justice departments in colleges and universities and the use of technology in the criminal justice system.

The federal government continues to fund the National Institute of Justice (NIJ), the Office of Juvenile Justice and Delinquency Prevention (OJJDP), and the Bureau of Justice Statistics (BJS). These agencies have a more limited role in supporting criminal justice research and development, and publish extremely valuable data and research findings.

Law Enforcement Assistance Administration (LEAA) Funded by the federal government's Safe Streets Act, this agency provided technical assistance and hundreds of millions of dollars in aid to local and state justice agencies between 1969 and 1982.

The National Institute of Justice, or NIJ, is the research and development agency of the U.S. Department of Justice. It is the only federal agency dedicated solely to researching crime control and justice issues. Visit the Web site and access online publications: www.ojp.usdoj.gov/nij/welcome.html

The Criminal Justice System Today

social control The ability of society and its institutions to control, manage, restrain, or direct human behavior.

Use the term "criminal justice, administration of" as a subject guide on InfoTrac College Edition to find out more about this engrossing subject.

The National Center for State Courts is an independent nonprofit organization dedicated to the improvement of justice. NCSC activities include developing policies to enhance state courts, advancing state courts' interests within the federal government, fostering state-court adaptation to future changes, securing sufficient resources for state courts, strengthening state court leadership, facilitating state court collaboration, and providing a model for organizational administration.
Go to
www.ncsc.dni.us

The criminal justice system is society's instrument of **social control:** some behaviors are considered so dangerous that they must either be strictly controlled or outlawed outright; some people are so destructive that they must be monitored or even confined. It is the task of the agencies of justice to prevent or deter outlawed behavior by apprehending, adjudicating, and sanctioning lawbreakers. Society maintains other forms of informal social control, such as parental and school discipline, but these are designed to deal with moral, not legal misbehavior. Only the criminal justice system maintains the power to control crime and punish outlawed behavior through the arm of the criminal law.

Agencies of the Criminal Justice System

The contemporary criminal justice system in the United States is monumental in size. It consists of over fifty-five thousand public agencies and now costs federal, state, and local governments about $150 billion per year for civil and criminal justice, increasing more than 300 percent since 1982 (see Exhibit 1.1).

Today the system can be divided into three main components: *law enforcement agencies,* which are charged with investigating crimes and apprehending suspects; the *court system,* where a determination is made whether a criminal suspect is guilty as charged; and the *correctional system,* which is charged with both treating and rehabilitating offenders and with incarcerating them so that they may not repeat their crimes (see Exhibit 1.2).

One reason why the justice system is so expensive to run is because it employs over two million people, including about nine hundred thousand in law enforcement. It consists of over fifty-five thousand public agencies, including seventeen thousand police agencies, nearly seventeen thousand courts, over eight thousand prosecutorial agencies, about six thousand correctional institutions, and over thirty-five hundred probation and parole departments. There are also capital costs.

Exhibit 1.1   Justice system expenditures

- Federal, state, and local governments in the United States spent $147 billion in fiscal year 1999 on criminal and civil justice.
- In 1999 the federal government alone spent $27 billion on the justice system. Between 1982 and 1999, expenditures by the federal government grew 514 percent!
- State governments spent $57 billion on criminal and civil justice in 1999. At nearly $35 billion, 60 percent of state spending was for corrections. State justice expenditures have grown approximately 9 percent each year since 1982.
- Local governments contributed the most—51 percent—to the criminal and civil justice system, almost $75 billion. By far the largest component of local expenditures was police protection, at nearly $46 billion.
- Federal, state, and local governments had 2.2 million justice-related employees in 1999.

- Local governments employed the greatest number of people for justice functions, about 1.3 million.
- The total number of justice employees grew 72 percent between 1982 and 1999, with the greatest growth in state governments (107 percent).
- From 1977 to 1999, total state and local expenditures for all justice functions increased 401 percent: police protection rose 411 percent, corrections rose 946 percent, and judicial and legal expenditures rose 1,518 percent.
- For comparison purposes, here's a look at some other government functions during the same period: education expenditures increased 370 percent, hospitals and health care increased 418 percent, interest on debt increased 490 percent, and public welfare increased 510 percent.
- The three levels of government together spend about $440 for each U.S. resident.

Source: Sidra Lea Gifford, *Justice Expenditure and Employment in the United States, 1999* (Washington, D.C.: Bureau of Justice Statistics, 2002).

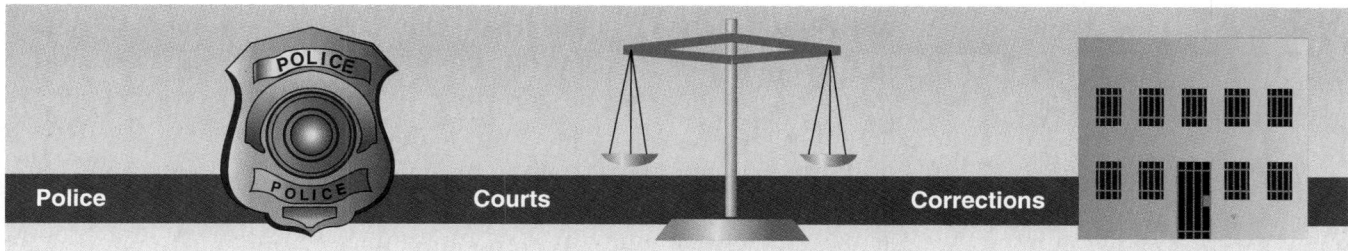

Exhibit 1.2 Components of the criminal justice system

Police

Courts

Corrections

Police departments are those public agencies created to maintain order, enforce the criminal law, provide emergency services, keep traffic on streets and highways moving freely, and create a sense of community safety. Police officers work actively with the community to prevent criminal behavior, they help divert members of special needs populations, such as juveniles, alcoholics, and drug addicts, from the criminal justice system; they participate in specialized units such as a drug prevention task force or anti-rape unit; they cooperate with public prosecutors to initiate investigations into organized crime and drug trafficking; they resolve neighborhood and family conflicts; and they provide emergency services, such as preserving civil order during strikes and political demonstrations.

The criminal courthouse is the scene of the trial process. Here the criminal responsibility of defendants accused of violating the law is determined. Ideally, the court is expected to convict and sentence those found guilty of crimes while ensuring that the innocent are freed without any consequence or burden. The court system is formally required to seek the truth, to obtain justice for the individual brought before its tribunals, and to maintain the integrity of the government's rule of law. The main actors in the court process are the judge, whose responsibilities include overseeing the legality of the trial process, and the prosecutor and the defense attorney, who are the opponents in what is known as the adversary system. These two parties oppose each other in a hotly disputed contest—the criminal trial—in accordance with rules of law and procedure.

In the broadest sense, correctional agencies include community supervision or probation, various types of incarceration (including jails, houses of correction, and state prisons), and parole programs for both juvenile and adult offenders. These programs range from the lowest security, such as probation in the community with minimum supervision, to the highest security, such as 24-hour lockdown in an ultra-maximum security prison. Corrections ordinarily represent the post-adjudicatory care given to offenders when a sentence is imposed by the court and the offender is placed in the hands of the correctional agency.

State jurisdictions are now conducting a massive correctional building campaign, adding tens of thousands of prison cells. It costs about $70,000 to build a prison cell, and about $22,000 per year is needed to keep an inmate in prison; juvenile institutions cost about $30,000 per year per resident.

The system is so big because it must process, treat, and care for millions of people each year. Although the crime rate has declined substantially, about 14 million people are still being arrested each year, including more than 2 million for serious felony offenses.[10] In addition, about 1.5 million juveniles are handled by the juvenile courts.[11] Today state and federal courts convict a combined total of over 1 million adults on felony charges.[12]

Considering the enormous number of people processed each year, the correctional system population is at an all-time high. As Table 1.1 shows, about 6.5 million people are under the control of the correctional system, including about 2 million behind bars and another 4 million under some form of community supervision. There has been a 50 percent increase in the correctional population despite a decade-long drop in the crime rate.

As a student of criminal justice, you may be gratified to know that there are many career opportunities in this vast and complex organization. The following Careers in Criminal Justice feature can help you get started in finding the right one for you.

Information on federal job opportunities is available at www.usajobs.opm.gov

| Table 1.1 | Number of people under correctional supervision, 1990–2001 |

	Total	Probation	Parole	Jail	Prison
1990	4,350,300	2,670,234	531,407	405,320	743,382
1995	5,342,900	3,077,861	679,421	507,044	1,078,542
2000	6,445,100*	3,826,209	723,898	621,149	1,316,333
2001	6,592,800*	3,932,751	731,147	631,240	1,330,980

*Excludes probationers in jail or prison.

Source: Bureau of Justice Statistics Correctional Surveys, www.ojp.usdoj.gov/bjs/glance/tables/ corr2tab.htm. Washington, D.C.: Bureau of Justice Statistics, 2002.

The Formal Criminal Justice Process

Another way of understanding criminal justice is to view it as a process that takes an offender through a series of decision points beginning with arrest and concluding with reentry into society. During this process, key decision makers resolve whether to maintain the offender in the system or to discharge the suspect without further action. This decision making is often a matter of individual discretion, based on a variety of factors and perceptions. Legal factors, including the seriousness of the charges, available evidence, and the suspect's prior record, are usually considered legitimate influences on decision making. Troubling is the fact that such extralegal factors as the suspect's race, gender, class, and age may also influence decision outcomes. There is a significant and ongoing debate over the impact of extralegal factors in the decision to arrest, convict, and sentence suspects: critics believe a suspect's race, class, and gender can often determine the direction a case will take, whereas supporters argue that the system is relatively fair and unbiased.[13]

In reality, few cases actually are processed through the entire formal justice system. Most are handled informally and with dispatch. The system of justice has been roundly criticized for its "backroom deals" and bargain justice. Although informality and deal making are in fact the rule, the concept of the formal justice process is important because it implies every criminal defendant charged with a serious crime is entitled to a full range of rights under law. Central to the American concept of liberty is that every individual is entitled to his or her day in court, to be represented by competent counsel in a fair trial before an impartial jury, with trial procedures subject to review by a higher authority. Secret and hidden kangaroo courts and summary punishment are elements of political systems that most Americans fear and despise. The fact that most criminal suspects are actually treated informally may be less important than the fact that all criminal defendants are entitled to a full range of legal rights and constitutional protections.

A comprehensive view of the formal criminal process would normally include the following:

1. *Initial contact.* In most instances, the initial contact with the criminal justice system takes place as a result of a police action. For example, patrol officers observe a person acting suspiciously, conclude the suspect is under the influence of drugs, and take her into custody. In another instance, police officers are contacted by a victim who reports a robbery; they respond by going to the scene of the crime and apprehend a suspect. In a third case, an informer tells police about some ongoing criminal activity in order to receive favorable treatment. Initial contact may also be launched by the police department's re-

Careers in Criminal Justice

Finding a Career in the Criminal Justice System

Employment in criminal justice fields can be found in government, the private sector, educational institutions, and nonprofit organizations. Criminal justice fields are evolving to include some specialization in areas of technology and computer security and to explore new approaches to treatment and rehabilitation of offenders. Over the past decades, the employment possibilities in the traditional police, courts, and corrections areas have been expanding.

Criminal justice careers can include a variety of jobs and professions. They do not always require that the applicant major in criminal justice, but may also welcome people with backgrounds in criminology, sociology, political science, psychology, social work, and other social science or human services disciplines. So although a criminal justice degree may be preferred, if you are majoring in another discipline the door will not be closed to you.

There are a number of ways to get started in searching for the right career in the criminal justice system. First off, you must decide where your personal interests lie, or at least form a general idea of your career goals: law enforcement, human services, research, teaching, and so on. Once you have decided which general area of criminal justice best suits you, one method of starting on a career path is to contact the campus career services program. Career services programs can assist students with resume writing and developing interviewing skills.

There are also many Web sites that help students find out about the many different types and titles of criminal justice jobs. Although it is difficult to keep current with job openings around the country, a number of sites have fairly up-to-date listings:

- The govjobs.com Web site concentrates on public sector jobs (cities, counties, and states) and can be searched by job type. You can sign up to receive an e-mail when job listings change. Govjobs.com seeks to provide cost-efficient, user-friendly ways of sharing employment information to worldwide job seekers and all government and commercial employers.
- The College of Criminal Justice (University of South Carolina) offers a listing of key sites in general but is

especially helpful in identifying career-related sites. *GovtJob.net* has a section on public safety and criminal justice employment that lists current openings around the country.

In addition to these generalized sites, many others provide more specific information. For example:

- *Wackenhut's Recruitment Center* offers detailed information about employment opportunities with this worldwide enterprise.
- The *Corrections Corporation of America* provides an employment page with information about careers with this leading private sector provider of detention and corrections services to all government levels.
- *Cornell Corrections,* a leading provider of privatized institutional, pre-release and juvenile services in the United States, offers information about career opportunities via a link from the company's homepage.

You can also contact the various agencies in your local area to find out about their hiring programs, needs, and requirements. For example, state police agencies offer regularly scheduled hiring tests that typically include psychological, physical, and intellectual components. Those scoring high will be invited to the police academy for further training.

Critical Thinking
A career in criminal justice can provide numerous personal benefits, not the least of which is knowing that the career you have chosen provides a valuable community service and affords you the opportunity to make a meaningful contribution to society. Are there other reasons for you to consider a career in criminal justice?

InfoTrac College Edition Research
Use "criminal justice personnel" as a subject guide to find out more about possible careers in criminal justice.

To find out more about careers in criminal justice, go to the book-specific Web site at http://cj.wadsworth.com/siegel_essen4e.

sponding to the request of the mayor or other political figures to control an ongoing social problem. The police chief may then initiate an undercover investigation into such corrupt practices as gambling, prostitution, or drug trafficking.

2. *Investigation.* The purpose of the investigatory stage of justice is to gather sufficient evidence to identify a suspect and support a legal arrest. An investigation can take but a few minutes, as in the case where a police officer sees a crime in progress and can apprehend the suspect within minutes. Or it can

Go to InfoTrac College Edition and use "criminal investigation" as a key term.

take many months and involve hundreds of law enforcement agents, such as the FBI's pursuit of the so-called Unabomber, which led to the eventual arrest of Ted Kaczynski. Investigations may be conducted at the local, state, or federal level and involve coordinated teams of law enforcement agents, prosecutors, and other justice officials.

3. *Arrest.* An arrest is considered legal when all of the following conditions exist: (a) the police officer believes there is sufficient evidence, referred to as *probable cause,* that a crime is being or has been committed and the suspect is the person who committed it; (b) the officer deprives the individual of freedom; and (c) the suspect believes that he is now in the custody of the police and has lost his *liberty.* The police officer is not required to use the word "arrest" or any similar term to initiate an arrest, nor does the officer have to bring the suspect to the police station. To make an arrest in a misdemeanor, the officer must have witnessed the crime personally, known as the *in-presence requirement;* a felony arrest can be made based upon the statement of a witness or victim. Arrests can also be made when a magistrate, presented with sufficient evidence by police and prosecutors, issues a warrant authorizing the arrest of the suspect.

4. *Custody.* The moment after an arrest is made, the detained suspect is considered in police custody. At this juncture, the police may wish to search the suspect for weapons or contraband, interrogate her in order to gain more information, find out if she had any accomplices, or even encourage the suspect to confess to the crime. The police may wish to enter the suspect's home, car, or office to look for further evidence. Similarly, the police may want to bring witnesses to view the suspect in a lineup or in a one-on-one confrontation. Personal information will also be taken from the suspect, including name, address, fingerprints, and photo. Because these procedures are so crucial and can have a great impact at trial, the U.S. Supreme Court has granted suspects in police custody protection from the unconstitutional abuse of police power, such as illegal searches and intimidating interrogations.

5. *Charging.* If the arresting officers or their superiors believe that sufficient evidence exists to charge a person with a crime, the case will be turned over to the prosecutor's office. Minor crimes—that is, misdemeanors—are generally handled with a complaint being filed before the court that will try the case. For serious crimes—that is, felonies—the prosecutor must decide whether to bring the case to either a grand jury or a preliminary hearing (depending on the procedures used in the jurisdiction; see item 6, next). In either event, the decision to charge the suspect with a specific criminal act involves many factors, including evidence sufficiency, crime seriousness, case pressure, and political issues, as well as personal factors such as a prosecutor's own specific interests and biases. For example, in some jurisdictions obscenity charges may be vigorously pursued, while in another they are all but ignored. After conducting a preliminary investigation of its legal merits, prosecutors may decide to take no further action in a case; this is referred to as a **nolle prosequi.**

nolle prosequi   The term used when a prosecutor decides to drop a case after a complaint has been formally made. Reasons for a nolle prosequi include evidence insufficiency, reluctance of witnesses to testify, police error, and office policy.

6. *Preliminary hearing/grand jury.* Because a criminal suspect faces great financial and personal costs when forced to stand trial for a felony, the U.S. Constitution mandates that before a trial can take place, the government must first prove probable cause that the accused committed the crime for which he is being charged. In about half the states and the federal system, this decision is rendered by a group of citizens brought together to form a grand jury; they consider the merits of the case in a closed hearing at which only the prosecutor presents evidence. If the evidence is sufficient, the grand jury will issue a bill of indictment, which specifies the exact charges on which the accused must stand trial. In the remaining states, the grand jury has been replaced with a preliminary hearing. In these jurisdictions, a charging document called an *information* is filed before a lower trial court, which then conducts an open

hearing on the merits of the case. During this procedure, sometimes referred to as a *probable cause hearing,* the defendant and the defendant's attorney may appear and dispute the prosecutor's charges. The suspect will be called to stand trial if the presiding magistrate or judge accepts the prosecutor's evidence as factual and sufficient.

7. *Arraignment.* Before the trial begins, the defendant will be arraigned, or brought before the court that will hear the case. Formal charges are read, the defendant informed of his constitutional rights (for example, the right to be represented by legal counsel), an initial plea entered in the case (not guilty or guilty), a trial date set, and bail issues considered.

8. *Bail/detention.* Bail is a money bond levied to ensure the return of a criminal defendant for trial, while allowing the person pretrial freedom to prepare a defense. Defendants who do not show up for trial forfeit their bail. Those people who cannot afford to put up bail or who cannot borrow sufficient funds for it will remain in state custody prior to trial. In most instances, this means an extended stay in a county jail or house of correction. Most jurisdictions allow defendants awaiting trial to be released on their own recognizance (promise to the court), without bail, if they are stable members of the community and have committed nonviolent crimes.

9. *Plea bargaining.* Soon after an arraignment, if not before, defense counsel will meet with the prosecution to see if the case can be brought to a conclusion without a trial. In some instances, this can involve filing the case while the defendant participates in a community-based treatment program for substance abuse or psychiatric care. Most commonly, the defense and prosecution will discuss a possible guilty plea in exchange for reducing or dropping some of the charges or agreeing to a request for a more lenient sentence. It is generally accepted that almost 90 percent of all cases end in a plea bargain, rather than a criminal trial.

10. *Trial/adjudication.* If an agreement cannot be reached or if the prosecution does not wish to arrange a negotiated settlement of the case, a criminal trial will be held before a judge or jury, who will decide whether the prosecution's evidence against the defendant is sufficient beyond a reasonable doubt to prove guilt. If a jury cannot reach a decision—that is, if it is deadlocked—the case is left unresolved, leaving the prosecution to decide whether it should be retried at a later date.

© Getty Images

Alejandro Avila, shown here attending a hearing behind bulletproof glass, was charged with four felonies in the Samantha Runnion case: one of kidnapping, two of forcible lewd acts on a child, and one of murder. Prosecutors cited "special circumstances" in the killing, kidnapping, and sexual assault on a minor, a standard that would allow them to seek the death penalty.

11. *Sentencing/disposition.* If after a criminal trial the accused has been found guilty as charged, he will be returned to court for sentencing. Possible dispositions may include a fine, probation, a period of incarceration in a penal institution, or some combination of these. In cases involving first-degree murder, more than thirty-five states and the federal government now allow the death penalty.

Sentencing is a key decision point in the criminal justice system because, in many jurisdictions, judicial discretion can result in people receiving vastly different sentences even though they have committed the same crime. Some may be released on community supervision, whereas others committing the same crime can receive long prison sentences.

12. *Appeal/postconviction remedies.* After conviction, the defense can ask the trial judge to set aside the jury's verdict because she believes there has been a mistake of law. For example, in 1997 Louise Woodward, a young British nanny, was convicted on the charge of second-degree murder when a Massachusetts jury found her responsible for the death of Matthew Eappen, an infant boy placed in her care. Woodward allegedly violently shook Matthew, causing his death. The verdict was soon set aside by the trial judge, Hiller Zobel, because he believed that the facts of the case did not substantiate the charge of second-degree murder; he instead reduced the charge to manslaughter and sentenced Woodward to time already served while she was awaiting trial.[14] An appeal may be filed if after conviction the defendant believes that he has not received fair treatment or that his constitutional rights were violated. Appellate courts review such issues as whether evidence was used properly, a judge conducted the trial in an approved fashion, jury selection was properly done, and the attorneys in the case acted appropriately. If the court rules that the appeal has merit, it can hold that the defendant be given a new trial or, in some instances, order his outright release. For example, outright release can be ordered when the state prosecutes the case in violation of the double jeopardy clause (Fifth Amendment) or when it violates the defendant's right to a speedy trial (Sixth Amendment).

13. *Correctional treatment.* After sentencing, the offender is placed within the jurisdiction of state or federal correctional authorities. The offender may serve a probationary term, be placed in a community correctional facility, serve a term in a county jail, or be housed in a prison. During this stage of the criminal justice process, the offender may be asked to participate in rehabilitation programs designed to help her make a successful readjustment to society.

14. *Release.* Upon completion of the sentence and period of correction, the offender will be free to return to society. Most inmates do not serve the full term of their sentence but are freed through an early-release mechanism, such as parole or pardon or by earning time off for good behavior. Offenders sentenced to community supervision simply finish their term and resume their lives in the community.

15. *Postrelease.* After termination of their correctional treatment, offenders may be asked to spend some time in a community correctional center, which acts as a bridge between a secure treatment facility and absolute freedom. Offenders may find that their conviction has cost them some personal privileges, such as the right to hold certain kinds of employment. These may be returned by court order once the offenders have proven their trustworthiness and willingness to adjust to society's rules.

The Criminal Justice Assembly Line

The image that comes to mind is an assembly line conveyor belt down which moves an endless stream of cases, never stopping, carrying them to workers who stand at fixed stations and who perform on each case as it comes by the same small but essential operation that brings it one step closer to being a finished product, or to exchange the metaphor for the reality, a closed file. The criminal process is seen as a screening process in which each successive stage—pre-arrest investigation, arrest, post-arrest investigation, preparation for trial or entry of plea, conviction, disposition—involves a series of routinized operations whose success is gauged primarily by their tendency to pass the case along to a successful conclusion.[15]

This is how Herbert Packer describes the criminal justice process. According to this view, each of the preceding fifteen stages is actually a decision point through which cases flow (see Figure 1.1). For example, at the investigatory stage, police must decide whether to pursue the case or terminate involvement because there is insufficient evidence to identify a suspect, the case is considered trivial, the victim

Figure 1.1
The critical stages in the justice process

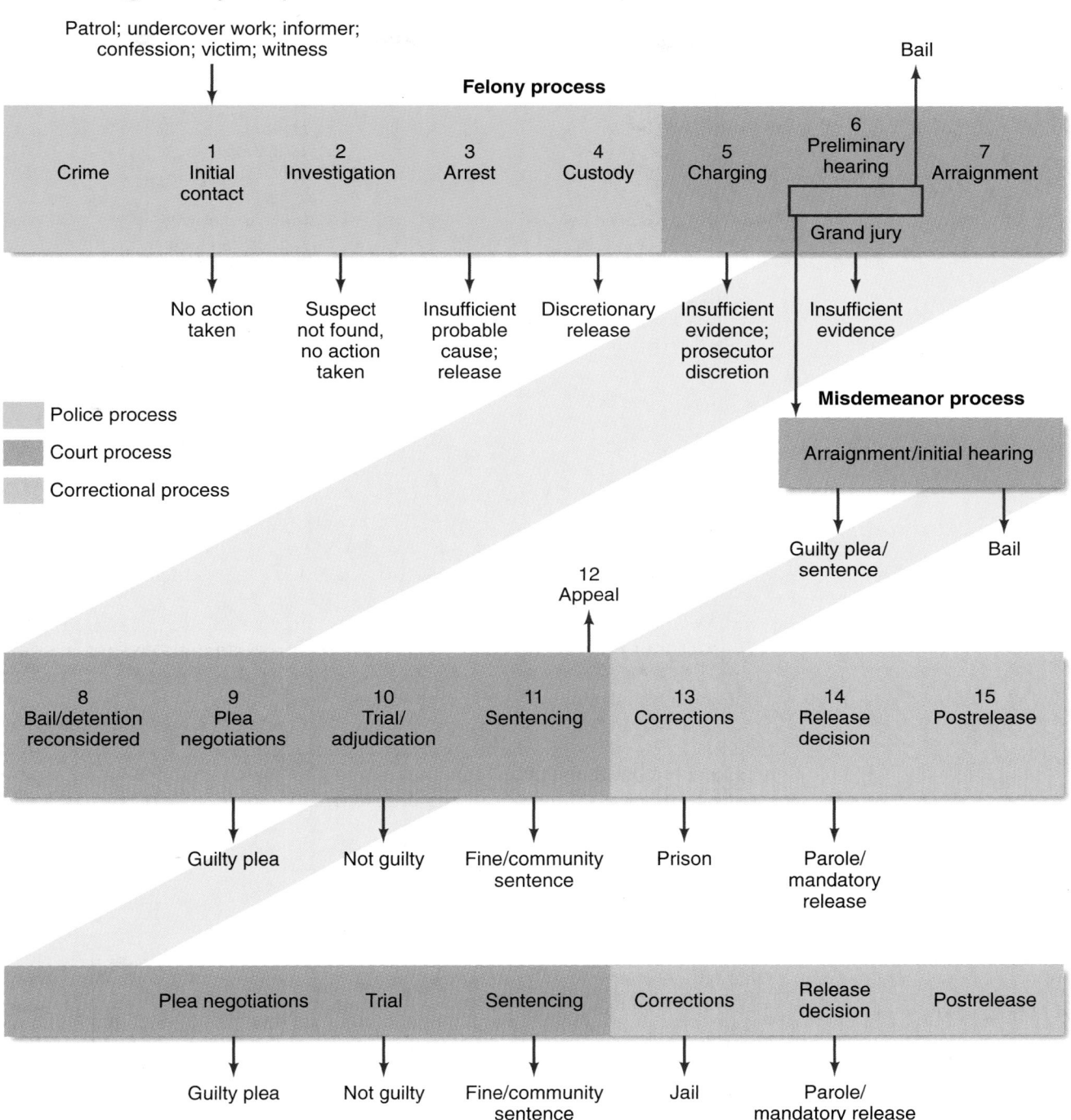

decides not to press charges, and so on. At the bail stage, a decision must be made whether to set so high a bail that the defendant remains in custody, set a reasonable bail, or release the defendant on his or her own recognizance without requiring any bail at all. Each of these decisions can have a critical effect on the defendant, the justice system, and society. If an error is made, an innocent person may suffer or a dangerous individual may be released to continue to prey upon society.

Exhibit 1.3	The interrelationship of the criminal justice system and the criminal justice process

The System: Agencies of Crime Control	The Process
1. Police	1. Contact
	2. Investigation
	3. Arrest
	4. Custody
2. Prosecution and defense	5. Complaint/charging
	6. Grand jury/preliminary hearing
	7. Arraignment
	8. Bail/detention
	9. Plea negotiations
3. Court	10. Adjudication
	11. Disposition
	12. Appeal/postconviction remedies
4. Corrections	13. Correction
	14. Release
	15. Postrelease

Figure 1.2 illustrates the approximate number of offenders removed from the criminal justice system at each stage of the process. As the figure shows, most people who commit crime escape detection, and of those who do not, relatively few are bound over for trial, convicted, and eventually sentenced to prison. About 70 percent of people arrested on felony charges are eventually convicted in criminal court; however, about 25 percent of those convicted are released back into the community without doing time in prison.[16]

In actual practice, many suspects are released before trial because of a procedural error, evidence problems, or other reasons that result in a case dismissal by the prosecutor, or nolle prosequi. Though most cases that go to trial wind up in a conviction, others are dismissed by the presiding judge because of a witness or a complainant's failure to appear or procedural irregularities. So the justice process can be viewed as a funnel that holds many cases at its mouth and relatively few at its end.

Theoretically, nearly every part of the process requires that individual cases be disposed of as quickly as possible. However, the criminal justice process is slower and more tedious than desired because of congestion, inadequate facilities, limited resources, inefficiency, and the nature of governmental bureaucracy. When defendants are not processed smoothly—often because of the large caseloads and inadequate facilities that exist in many urban jurisdictions—the procedure breaks down, the process within the system fails, and the ultimate goal of a fair and efficient justice system cannot be achieved. Exhibit 1.3 shows the interrelationship of the component agencies of the criminal justice system and the criminal justice process.

The Informal Criminal Justice System

The traditional model of the criminal justice system depicts the legal process as a series of decision points through which cases flow. Each stage of the system, beginning with investigation and arrest and ending after a sentence has been served,

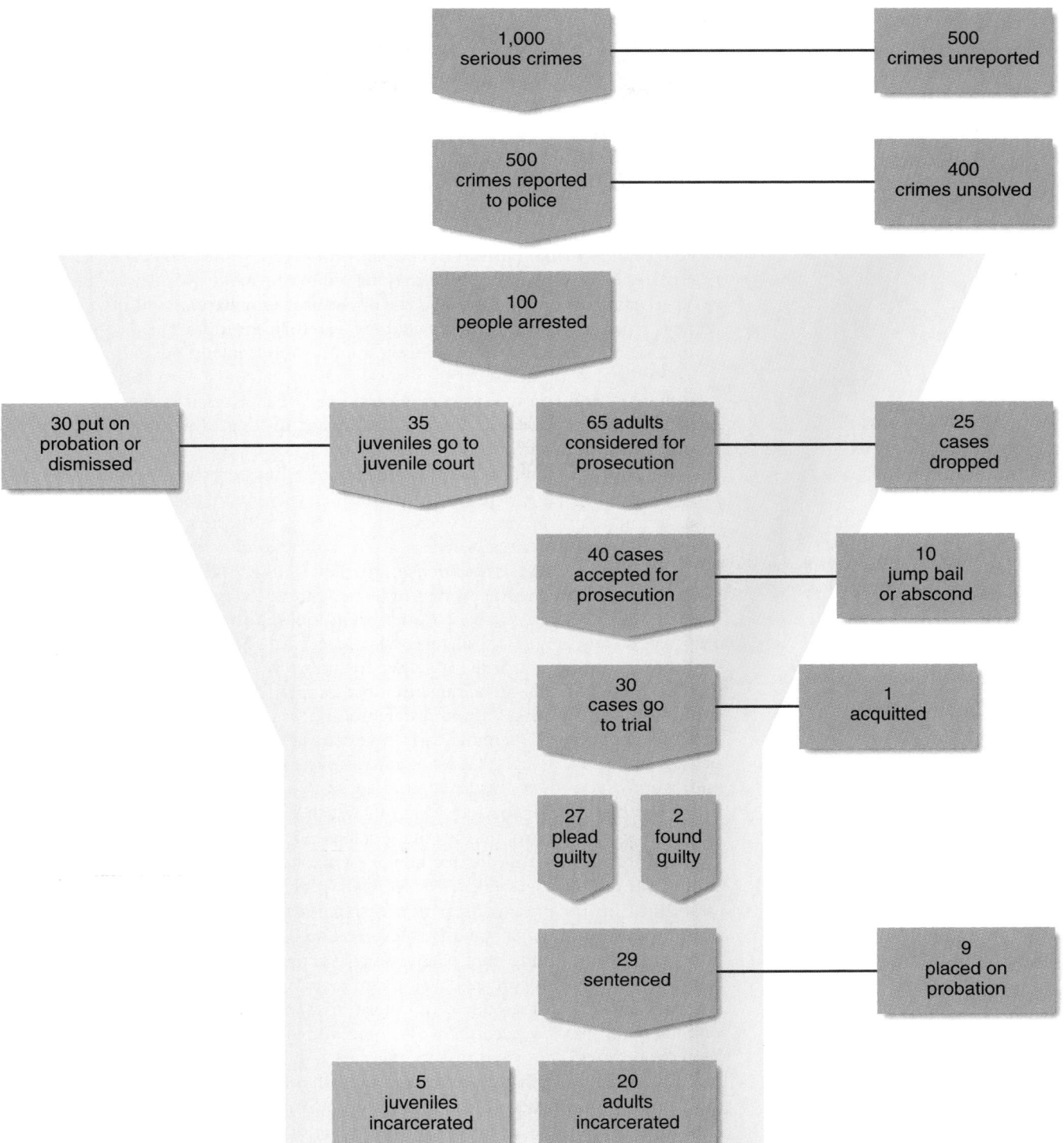

Figure 1.2
The criminal justice funnel

Source: Brian Reaves, *Felony Defendants in Large Urban Counties, 1998* (Washington, D.C.: Bureau of Justice Statistics, 2001).

is defined by time-honored administrative procedures and controlled by the rule of law. The public's perception of the system, which is fueled by the media, is that it is composed of daredevil, crime-fighting police officers who never ask for over-time or sick leave, crusading district attorneys who stop at nothing to send the mob boss up the river, wily defense attorneys who neither ask clients for up-front cash nor cut office visits to play golf, no-nonsense judges who are never inept po-litical appointees, and tough wardens who rule the yard with an iron hand. Though this "ideal" model of justice still merits concern and attention, it would be overly simplistic to assume that the system works this way for every case. Al-though a few cases receive a full measure of rights and procedures, many are settled in an informal pattern of cooperation between the major actors in the jus-tice process. For example, police may be willing to make a deal with a suspect in order to gain his cooperation, and the prosecutor may bargain with the defense at-torney to gain a plea of guilty as charged in return for a promise of leniency. Law enforcement agents and court officers are allowed tremendous discretion in their decision to make an arrest, bring formal charges, handle a case informally, substi-tute charges, and so on. Crowded courts operate in a spirit of getting the matter settled quickly and cleanly, rather than engage in long, drawn-out criminal pro-ceedings with an uncertain outcome.

Whereas the traditional model regards the justice process as an adversarial proceeding in which the prosecution and defense are combatants, most criminal cases are actually cooperative ventures in which all parties get together to work out a deal; this is often referred to as the **courtroom work group**.[17] This group, made up of the prosecutor, defense attorney, judge, and other court personnel, functions to streamline the process of justice through the extensive use of plea bar-gaining and other alternatives. Rather than looking to provide a spirited defense or prosecution, these legal agents, who often attended the same schools, know each other, and have worked together for many years, try to work out a case to their own professional advantage. In most criminal cases, cooperation rather than conflict between prosecution and defense appears to be the norm. It is only in a few widely publicized criminal cases involving rape or murder that the adversarial process is called into play. Consequently, upward of 80 percent of all felony cases and over 90 percent of misdemeanors are settled without trial.

What has developed is a system in which criminal court experiences can be viewed as a training ground for young defense attorneys looking for seasoning and practice. It provides a means for newly established lawyers to receive government compensation for cases taken to get their practice going or an arena in which established firms can place their new associates for experience before they are as-signed to paying clients. Similarly, successful prosecutors can look forward to a po-litical career or a highly paid partnership in a private firm. To further their career aspirations, prosecutors must develop and maintain a winning track record in crim-inal cases. Although the courtroom work group limits the constitutional rights of defendants, it may be essential for keeping our overburdened justice system afloat. Moreover, though informal justice exists, it is not absolutely certain that it is in-herently unfair to both the victim and the offender. Research evidence shows that the defendants who benefit the most from informal court procedures commit the least serious crimes, whereas the more chronic offender gains relatively little.[18]

The "Wedding Cake" Model of Justice

Samuel Walker, a justice historian and scholar, has come up with a rather dramatic way of describing this informal justice process: he compares it to a four-layer cake, as depicted in Figure 1.3.[19]

courtroom work group   The phrase used to denote that all parties in the ad-versary process work together in a coop-erative effort to settle cases with the least amount of effort and conflict.

[handwritten note: sense and nonsense about crime]

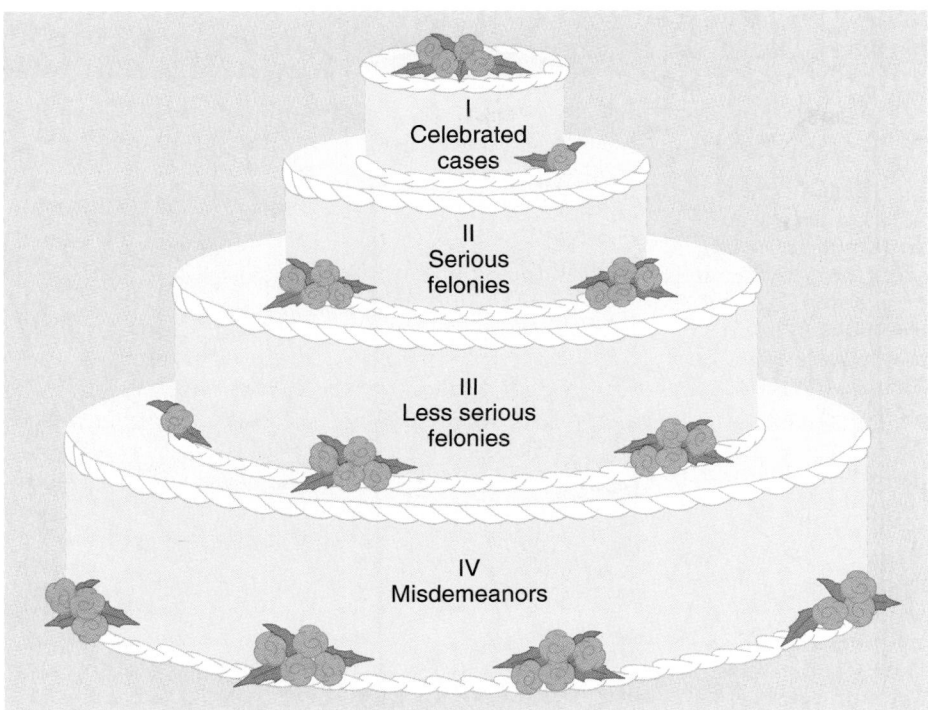

Figure 1.3
The criminal justice "wedding cake"

Source: Based on Samuel Walker, *Sense and Nonsense About Crime* (Belmont, Calif.: Wadsworth, 2001).

- *Level I.* The first layer of Walker's model is made up of the celebrated cases involving the wealthy and famous, such as O. J. Simpson or Wall Street financier Michael Milken, or the not-so-powerful who victimize a famous person—for example, John Hinckley Jr., who shot President Ronald Reagan. Other cases fall into the first layer because they are widely reported in the media and become the subject of a TV investigation. The media usually focus on hideous or unusual cases, such as the murder of JonBenet Ramsey or the disappearance of congressional intern Chandra Levy.

  Cases in the first layer of the criminal justice wedding cake usually receive the full array of criminal justice procedures, including competent defense attorneys, expert witnesses, jury trials, and elaborate appeals. Because of the media focus on Level I cases and the Hollywood treatment of them, the public is given the impression that most criminals are sober, intelligent people and most victims are members of the upper classes, a patently false impression (see the Criminal Justice and the Media feature).

- *Level II.* In the second layer are the serious felonies—rapes, robberies, and burglaries—which have become all too routine in U.S. society. They are in the second layer because they are serious crimes committed by experienced offenders. Burglaries are included if the amount stolen is quite high and the techniques used indicate the suspect is a real pro. Violent crimes, such as rape and assault, are vicious incidents against an innocent victim and may involve a weapon and extreme violence. Robberies involve large amounts of money and suspects who brandish handguns or other weapons and are considered career criminals. Police, prosecutors, and judges all agree that these are serious cases,

There are many different "models of justice." To find out more, use the phrase as a key term on InfoTrac College Edition.

Criminal Justice and the Media

Red Dragon

Agents of the criminal justice system routinely confront calculating, intelligent criminals who use guile and cunning to carry out their fiendish plots. Crime victims are wealthy, attractive, and glamorous, highly intelligent, and well educated...even if they are cannibals. These are the themes of the film series that focuses on the exploits of the media's most infamous criminal, Hannibal "The Cannibal" Lecter, played by the distinguished British actor Anthony Hopkins.

Lecter is a unique character. While undeniably murderous and violent (he eats his victims), he is also urbane, witty, and brilliant. In the 1991 movie *Silence of the Lambs,* the incarcerated Lecter locks horns with FBI agent Clarice Starling (Jodie Foster) and helps her identify and capture a serial killer, all the while masterminding his own escape. In the 2001 hit *Hannibal,* Lecter is now free, finding employment as an art curator in Italy. (Why should being the most wanted man in the world stop him from getting a high-paid job that usually requires impeccable references and impressive credentials?) He is able to foil police detectives and take revenge against an old nemesis while lending a hand to his beloved Clarice (this time played by Julianne Moore). In the 2002 release *Red Dragon,* a prequel to the first two stories, Lecter aids FBI agent Will Graham (Edward Norton), the man who originally tracked him down and brought him to justice. Graham has come out of retirement to identify a serial killer who police call the "Tooth Fairy" because he bites, maims, and murders entire families in hideous ways. The police

Anthony Hopkins' vivid portrayal of serial killer Hannibal "The Cannibal" Lecter has turned the character into one of the most notorious and memorable bad guys in film history. Lecter has been featured in *The Silence of the Lambs* (1991), *Hannibal* (2001), and *Red Dragon* (2002).

have no leads, and that is why Graham turns to Lecter for inside information—in other words, it takes one to know one. Asking the imprisoned killer for help in solving a case may seem like a clever idea, but it places Graham and his family in great danger when the killer, Francis Dolarhyde (Ralph Fiennes), who calls himself "Red Dragon," teams up with Lecter for revenge.

worthy of the full attention of the justice system. Offenders in such Level II cases receive a full jury trial and, if convicted, can look forward to a prison sentence.

- *Level III.* Though they can also be felonies, crimes that fall in the third layer of the wedding cake are either less serious offenses, committed by young or first-time offenders, or involve people who knew each other or were otherwise related: an inebriated teenager committed a burglary and netted $50; the rape victim had gone on a few dates with her assailant before he attacked her; the robbery involved members of rival gangs and no weapons; the assault was the result of a personal dispute and there is some question of who hit whom first. Agents of the criminal justice system relegate these cases to the third level because they see them as less important and less deserving of attention. Level III crimes may be dealt with by an outright dismissal, a plea bargain, reduction in charges, or most typically, a probationary sentence or intermediate sanction, such as victim restitution.
- *Level IV.* The fourth layer of the cake is made up of the millions of misdemeanors, such as disorderly conduct, shoplifting, public drunkenness, and

In this exciting action-adventure film series, Hannibal and his cohorts are typical of the media's romanticized vision of criminals and the criminal justice system. According to Hollywood, most cases fall into the top layer of the criminal justice wedding cake. The stakes are high, the law enforcement agents dedicated, street battles and shootouts common, lots of people die, and in the end the case is always solved. Because the victims, police, and criminals are all attractive, articulate, and well educated (after all, they are Hollywood actors) they often form close bonds or friendships and can even become romantically involved with one another. Other films of this type include *Jagged Edge,* in which an attorney (Glenn Close) and the client she is defending on murder charges (Jeff Bridges) become romantically involved; *Basic Instinct,* where an accused killer (Sharon Stone) and the detective investigating the case (Michael Douglas) hook up; and *The Fugitive,* in which a prison escapee (Harrison Ford), a well-known physician, and pursuing U.S. marshal Samuel Gerard (Tommy Lee Jones) form a bond. Everyone seems wealthy and articulate, as in *Ransom,* in which a billionaire's (Mel Gibson) son is kidnapped, and *A Perfect Murder,* in which a multimillionaire banker (Michael Douglas) plots to kill his beautiful wife (Gwyneth Paltrow). Sometimes these formulas are so successful that they breed a score of sequels with almost identical plots. For example, *The Fugitive* was recycled as *U.S. Marshals.*

These films give the public a distorted view of both criminals and the criminal justice system. Although it is true that some cases do involve the wealthy and glamorous, these are actually few and far between. Most victims and criminals come from the lower end of the socio-

economic scale and live in very poor neighborhoods, not penthouses. In fact, few people are murdered on their yachts, as was the case in the film *Double Jeopardy* with Ashley Judd. Very few crimes involve millions of dollars; most criminals "earn" far less than the minimum wage for their efforts. Rather than being intelligent and articulate, they are more likely to be drug-abusing and desperate.

So although *Hannibal* makes an exciting film, it is far from the social reality of criminal justice. It also does little to enhance the reputation of federal law enforcement agents, whom Lecter seems to outwit without much effort—they cannot even catch a criminal without being advised by one. On the other hand, it does give the impression that an FBI career is exciting and glamorous, which, of course, does not hurt recruiting efforts.

Critical Thinking
Can you think of other films that portray criminals as glamorous, intelligent, and sophisticated? What about those who take the opposite tack and show them as seedy, uneducated, and impoverished?

InfoTrac College Edition Research
There is a long history of crime films in the American movie industry. Use "crime film" to search InfoTrac College Edition and read more about them.

minor assault. These are handled by the lower criminal courts in assembly-line fashion. Few defendants insist on exercising their constitutional rights because the delay would cost them valuable time and money. Because the typical penalty is a small fine, everyone wants to get the case over with.[20]

The wedding cake model of informal justice is an intriguing alternative to the traditional criminal justice flowchart. Criminal justice officials handle individual cases quite differently, yet there is a high degree of consistency with which particular types or classes of cases are dealt in every legal jurisdiction. For example, police and prosecutors in Los Angeles and Boston will each handle the murder of a prominent citizen in similar fashion. They will also deal with the death of an unemployed street person killed in a brawl in a similar manner. Yet, in each jurisdiction, the two cases will be handled very differently. The bigwig's killer will receive a full-blown jury trial (with details on the six o'clock news); the drifter's killer will get a quick plea bargain. The model is useful because it helps us realize that public opinion about criminal justice is often formed on the basis of what happened in an atypical case.

Perspectives on Justice

Though it has been more than thirty-five years since the field of criminal justice began to be the subject of both serious academic study and attempts at unified policy formation, significant debate continues over the actual meaning of *criminal justice* and how the problem of crime control should be approached. After decades of effort in research and policy analysis, it is clear that criminal justice is far from a unified field. Practitioners, academics, and commentators alike have expressed irreconcilable differences concerning its goals, purpose, and direction. Some conservatives see the solution to the crime problem to be increasing the number of police, apprehending more criminals, and giving them long sentences to maximum-security prisons. In contrast, liberals call for increased spending on social services and community organization. Others worry about giving the government too much power to regulate and control behavior and to interfere with individual liberty and freedom.

This lack of consensus is particularly vexing when we consider the multitude of problems facing the justice system. The agencies of justice must attempt to eradicate such seemingly diverse social problems as substance abuse, gang violence, pornography, price fixing, and environmental contamination while respecting individual liberties and civil rights. It is also assumed that the agencies of the justice system have adequate resources and knowledge to carry out their complex tasks in an efficient and effective manner, something that so far seems to be wishful thinking. Experts are still searching for the right combination of policies and actions that will significantly reduce crime and increase public safety while maintaining individual freedoms and social justice.

Considering the complexity of criminal justice, it is not surprising that no single view, perspective, or philosophy dominates the field. What are the dominant views of the criminal justice system today? What is the role of the justice system, and how should it approach its tasks? The different perspectives on criminal justice are discussed next.

Crime Control Perspective

More than twenty years ago political scientist James Q. Wilson made the persuasive argument that most criminals are not poor unfortunates who commit crime to survive but are greedy people who choose theft or drug dealing for quick and easy profits.[21] Criminals, he argued, lack inhibition against misconduct, value the excitement and thrills of breaking the law, have a low stake in conformity, and are willing to take greater chances than the average person. If they could be convinced that their actions will bring severe punishment, then only the totally irrational would be willing to engage in crime. Restraining offenders and preventing their future misdeeds, he argued, is a much more practical goal for the criminal justice system than trying to eradicate the root causes of crime: poverty, poor schools, racism, and family breakup. He made this famous observation:

> *Wicked people exist. Nothing avails except to set them apart from innocent people. And many people, neither wicked nor innocent, but watchful, dissembling, and calculating of their chances, ponder our reaction to wickedness as a clue to what they might profitably do.*[22]

crime control perspective A model of criminal justice that emphasizes the control of dangerous offenders and the protection of society. Its advocates call for harsh punishments as a deterrent to crime, such as the death penalty.

Wilson's views helped define the **crime control perspective** of criminal justice. According to this view, the proper role of the justice system is to prevent crime through the judicious use of criminal sanctions. Because the public is outraged by such crimes as mass shootings, such as the one at Columbine High School, it demands an efficient justice system that hands out tough sanctions to those who choose to violate the law.[23] If the justice system operated in an effective manner, potential criminals would be deterred from committing law violations, while those who did commit a crime would be apprehended, tried, and punished so that they would never dare risk committing a crime again. Crime rates trend upward, the argument goes, when criminals do not sufficiently fear apprehension and punishment. If the efficiency of the system could be increased and the criminal law could be toughened, crime rates would eventually decline. Effective law enforcement, strict mandatory punishment, and expanding use of prison are the keys to reduce crime rates. Though crime control may be expensive, reducing the pains of criminal activity is well worth the price.

Focus on the Victim   According to the crime control perspective, so that innocent people can be protected from the ravages of crime, the focus of justice should be on the victim of crime, not the criminal. This objective can be achieved through more effective police protection, tough sentences (including liberal use of the death penalty), and the construction of prisons designed to safely incapacitate hardened criminals. If punishment was both certain and severe, few would be tempted to break the law.

Crime control advocates do not want legal technicalities to help the guilty go free and tie the hands of justice. They lobby for the abolition of legal restrictions that control a police officer's ability to search for evidence and interrogate suspects. For example, they want law enforcement officers to be able to profile people at an airport in order to identify terrorists, even if it means singling out people because of their gender, race, or ethnic origin. "Isn't this a violation of the Constitution?" critics might ask. Crime control advocates might reply that we are in the midst of a national emergency and the ends justify the means. "We are not worried about middle-aged Norwegian woman, so why bother to search them?" they

© 2002 AP/Wide World Photos

According to the crime control model, the focus of justice should be on the victim, not the criminal. Here, family and friends of Michael Costin listen as a verdict of guilty of involuntary manslaughter is read at Thomas Junta's trial in Cambridge, Massachusetts, January 11, 2002. Junta was sentenced for the beating death of Costin following their sons' hockey practice in July 2000.

Drug Abuse Resistance Education (DARE)   A school-based antidrug program initiated by the Los Angeles Police Department and now adopted around the United States.

rehabilitation perspective   A model of criminal justice that views its primary purpose as helping to care for people who cannot manage themselves. Crime is an expression of frustration and anger created by social inequality that can be controlled by giving people the means to improve their lifestyle through conventional endeavors.

due process perspective   Due process is the basic constitutional principle based on the concept of the privacy of the individual and the complementary concept of limitation on governmental power; a safeguard against arbitrary and unfair state procedures in judicial or administrative proceedings. Embodied in the due process concept are the basic rights of a defendant in criminal proceedings and the requisites for a fair trial. These rights and requirements have been expanded by appellate court decisions and include (1) timely notice of a hearing or trial that informs the accused of the charges against him or her; (2) the opportunity to confront accusers and to present evidence on one's own behalf before an impartial jury or judge; (3) the presumption of innocence under which guilt must be proven by legally obtained evidence and the verdict must be supported by the evidence presented; (4) the right of an accused to be warned of constitutional rights at the earliest stage of the criminal process; (5) protection against self-incrimination; (6) assistance of counsel at every critical stage of the criminal process; and (7) the guarantee that an individual will not be tried more than once for the same offense (double jeopardy).

might retort. They are angry at judges who let obviously guilty people go free because a law enforcement officer made an unintentional procedural error.

Crime control advocates also question the criminal justice system's ability to rehabilitate offenders. Most treatment programs are ineffective because the justice system is simply not equipped to treat people who have a long history of antisocial behavior. Even when agents of the system attempt to prevent crime by working with young people, the results are unsatisfactory. For example, evaluations of the highly touted **Drug Abuse Resistance Education (DARE)** antidrug program indicate that it has had little impact on students.[24] From both a moral and a practical standpoint, the role of criminal justice should be the control of antisocial people. If not to the justice system, then where can the average citizen turn for protection from society's criminal elements?

Rehabilitation Perspective

If the crime control perspective views the justice system in terms of protecting the public and controlling criminal elements, then advocates of the **rehabilitation perspective** may be said to see the justice system as a means of caring for and treating people who cannot manage themselves. They view crime as an expression of frustration and anger created by social inequality. Crime can be controlled by giving people the means to improve their lifestyle through conventional endeavors.

The rehabilitation concept assumes that people are at the mercy of social, economic, and interpersonal conditions and interactions. Criminals themselves are the victims of racism, poverty, strain, blocked opportunities, alienation, family disruption, and other social problems. They live in socially disorganized neighborhoods that are incapable of providing proper education, health care, or civil services. Society must help them in order to compensate for their social problems.

Alternatives to Crime   Rehabilitation advocates believe that government programs can help reduce crime on both a societal (macro-) and individual (micro-) level. For example, on the macro-, or societal, level, research shows that as the number of legitimate opportunities to succeed declines, people are more likely to turn to criminal behaviors, such as drug dealing, in order to survive. Increasing economic opportunities through job training, family counseling, educational services, and crisis intervention are more effective crime reducers than prisons and jails. As legitimate opportunities increase, violence rates decline.[25]

On a micro level, rehabilitation programs can help at-risk kids avoid entry into criminal careers by providing them with legitimate alternatives to crime. Even those who find themselves in trouble with the law can avoid recidivism if they are placed in effective, well-designed treatment efforts that can reduce repeat offending. For example, counseling programs, which help offenders develop interpersonal skills, induce a prosocial change in attitudes and improve cognitive thinking patterns, both of which have been shown to significantly reduce recidivism rates.[26]

Clearly, punishing offenders and placing them in prison does not seem to deter future criminality. Society has a choice: pay now, by funding treatment and educational programs, or pay later, when troubled youths enter costly correctional facilities over and over again. This view is certainly not lost on the public. Although the public may want to "get tough" on crime, many are willing to make exceptions, for example, by advocating leniency for younger offenders.[27]

Due Process Perspective

Advocates of the **due process perspective** argue that the greatest concern of the justice system should be providing fair and equitable treatment to those accused of crime.[28] This means providing impartial hearings, competent legal counsel, equitable treatment, and reasonable sanctions. The use of discretion in the justice system should be strictly monitored to ensure that no one suffers from racial, religious, or ethnic discrimination. Though there are many views of what the true goals of justice should be, there is no question that the system must operate in a fair and unbiased manner.

Those who advocate the due process orientation are quick to point out that the justice system remains an adversarial process that pits the forces of an all-powerful state against those of a solitary individual accused of a crime. If concern for justice and fairness did not exist, the defendant who lacked resources could easily be overwhelmed; miscarriages of justice are common. Numerous criminal convictions have been overturned because newly developed DNA evidence later shows that the accused could not have committed the crimes; many of the falsely convicted spend years in prison before their release.[29] Evidence also shows that many innocent people have been executed for crimes they did not commit. For example, during a single period ranging from 1976 to 1999, 566 people were executed. During that same period of time, 82 convicts awaiting execution were exonerated—a ratio of 1 freed for every 7 put to death.[30] Because such mistakes can happen, even the most apparently guilty offender deserves all the protection the justice system can offer.

Those who question the due process perspective claim that the legal privileges afforded criminal suspects have gone too far and that the effort to protect individual rights now interferes with public safety. Is it fair, they argue, for evidence to be suppressed if it was obtained in violation of the constitutional right to be free from illegal search and seizure, even if suppressing it means that a dangerous person will go free? Is it better to free a guilty person than trample on the civil rights of citizens, even those who commit criminal acts? And what about the rights of actual or potential victims of crime? Should the needs of the victim take precedence over those of criminal offenders? Those who advocate for the due process perspective believe firmly that legal principles of fairness and due process must be upheld even if it means that on occasion we must free a patently guilty person. Preserving the democratic ideals of American society takes precedence over the need to punish the guilty.

Nonintervention Perspective

Supporters of the **nonintervention perspective** believe that justice agencies should limit their involvement with criminal defendants. Regardless of whether intervention is designed to punish or treat people, the ultimate effect of any involvement is harmful. Whatever their goals or design, programs that involve people with a social control agency—such as the police, a mental health department, the correctional system, or a criminal court—will have long-term negative effects. Once involved with such an agency, criminal defendants may be watched, people might consider them dangerous and untrustworthy, and they can develop a lasting record that has negative connotations. Bearing an official label disrupts their personal and family life and harms parent-child relationships. Eventually, they may even come to believe what their official record suggests; they may view themselves as bad, evil, outcasts, troublemakers, or crazy. Thus, official labels promote rather than reduce the continuity in antisocial activities.[31]

Noninterventionists are concerned about the effect of the stigma that criminal suspects bear when they are given negative labels such as "rapist" or "child abuser." These labels will stick with them forever; once labeled, these people may find it difficult ever to be accepted back into society, even after they have completed their sentence. It is not surprising, considering these effects of stigma and labeling, that recidivism rates are so high. When people are given less stigmatized forms of punishment, such as probation, they are less likely to become repeat offenders.[32]

Fearing the harmful effects of stigma and labels, noninterventionists have tried to place limitations on the government's ability to control people's lives.

To read about such critical due process issues as defending judicial independence, controversial judicial opinions, federal judicial selection, state judicial elections, judicial appointments in the states, impeachment and disciplining of judges, judicial reform, and other similar issues, go to the homepage of the Brennan Judicial Center at New York University:

http://brennancenter.org/

nonintervention perspective   A justice philosophy that emphasizes the least intrusive treatment possible. Among its central policies are decarceration, diversion, and decriminalization. In other words, less is better.

decriminalization Reducing the penalty for a criminal act but not actually legalizing it.

legalization The removal of all criminal penalties from a previously outlawed act.

victimless crime An act that is in violation of society's moral code and therefore has been outlawed—for example, drug abuse, gambling, and prostitution. These acts are linked together because, although they have no external victim, they are considered harmful to the social fabric.

deinstitutionalization The movement to remove as many offenders as possible from secure confinement and treat them in the community.

pretrial diversion A program that provides nonpunitive, community-based alternatives to more intrusive forms of punishment such as jail or prison.

widening the net of justice The charge that programs designed to divert offenders from the justice system actually enmesh them further in the process by substituting more intrusive treatment programs for less intrusive punishment-oriented outcomes.

Read about the movement to decriminalize marijuana in Canada on InfoTrac College Edition, "Politics: Washington Fumes as Canada Moves to Decriminalize Pot," *Inter Press Service*, July 27, 2002.

restorative justice perspective A view of criminal justice that advocates peaceful solutions and mediation rather than coercive punishments.

They have called for the **decriminalization** (reduction of penalties) and **legalization** of nonserious **victimless crimes,** such as the possession of small amounts of marijuana, public drunkenness, and vagrancy. They demand the removal of nonviolent offenders from the nation's correctional system, a policy referred to as **deinstitutionalization.** First offenders who commit minor crimes should instead be placed in informal, community-based treatment programs, a process referred to as **pretrial diversion.**

Sometimes the passage of new criminal laws designed to help or treat offenders actually helps stigmatize them beyond the scope of their actual offense; this is referred to as **widening the net of justice.** For example, a person who purchases pornography on the Internet is labeled a dangerous sex offender, or someone caught for a second time with marijuana is considered a habitual drug abuser. Noninterventionists have fought implementation of community notification–type laws that require that convicted sex offenders register with state law enforcement officials and allow officials to publicly disclose when a registrant moves into a community. Their efforts have resulted in rulings stating that these laws can be damaging to the reputation and the future of offenders who have not been given an opportunity to defend themselves from the charge that they are chronic criminal sex offenders.[33] As a group, noninterventionist initiatives have been implemented to help people avoid the stigma associated with contact with the criminal justice system.

Justice Perspective

The core of the justice perspective is that all people should receive the same treatment under the law. Any effort to distinguish between criminal offenders will create a sense of unfairness that can interfere with readjustment to society. It is frustrating when two people commit the same crime but receive different sentences or punishments. The resulting anger and a sense of unfairness will increase the likelihood of recidivism.

To remedy this situation, the criminal justice system must reduce discretion and unequal treatment. Law violators should be evaluated on the basis of their current behavior, not on what they have done in the past (they have already paid for that behavior) nor on what they may do in the future (since future behavior cannot be accurately predicted). The treatment of criminal offenders must be based solely on present behavior: punishment must be equitably administered and based on "just desert."

The justice perspective has had considerable influence in molding the nation's sentencing policy. There has been an ongoing effort to reduce discretion and guarantee that every offender convicted of a particular crime receives equal punishment. There have been a number of initiatives designed to achieve this result, including mandatory sentences requiring that all people convicted of a crime receive the same prison sentence. *Truth-in-sentencing laws* now require offenders to serve a substantial portion of their prison sentence behind bars, limiting their eligibility for early release on parole.[34]

Restorative Justice Perspective

According to the concept of restorative justice, the true purpose of the criminal justice system is to promote a peaceful and just society; the justice system should aim for peacemaking, not punishment.[35]

The **restorative justice perspective** draws its inspiration from religious and philosophical teachings ranging from Quakerism to Zen. Advocates of restorative justice view the efforts of the state to punish and control as encouraging crime rather than discouraging crime. The violent, punishing acts of the state, they claim, are not dissimilar from the violent acts of individuals.[36] Therefore, mutual aid rather than coercive punishment is the key to a harmonious society. Without

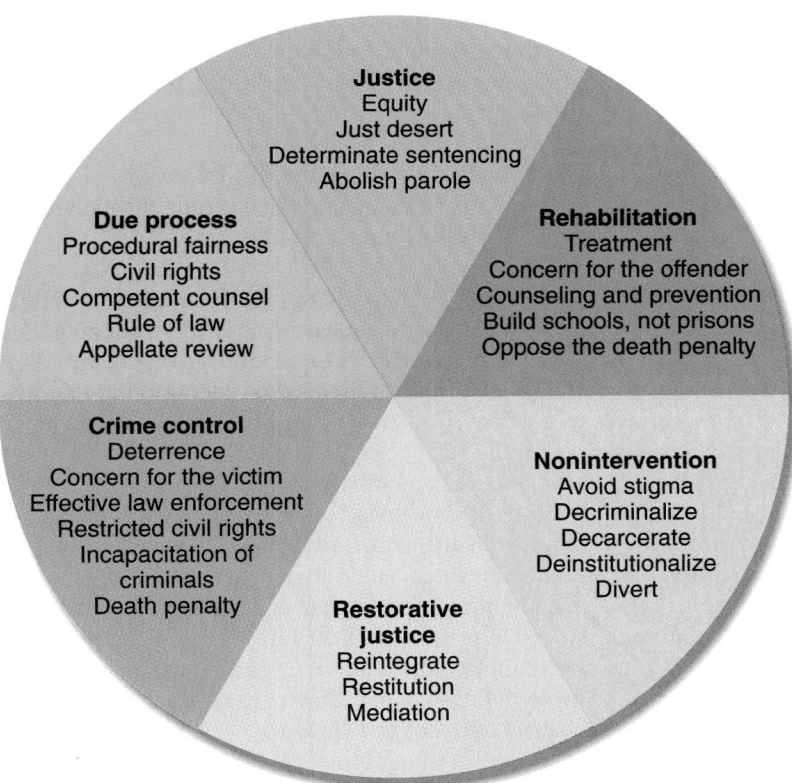

Figure 1.4
Perspectives on justice: Key concerns and concepts

the capacity to restore damaged social relations, society's response to crime has been almost exclusively punitive.

According to restorative justice, resolution of the conflict between criminal and victim should take place in the community in which it originated and not in some far-off prison. The victim should be given a chance to voice his story, and the offender can directly communicate his need for social reintegration and treatment. The goal is to enable the offender to appreciate the damage he has caused, to make amends, and to be reintegrated back into society.

Restorative justice programs are now being geared to these principles. Police officers, as elements of community policing programs, are beginning to use mediation techniques to settle disputes rather than resort to formal arrest.[37] Mediation and conflict resolution programs are common features in many communities. Financial and community service restitution programs as an alternative to imprisonment have been in operation for more than two decades.

The various perspectives are summarized in Figure 1.4.

Perspectives in Action: Controlling the Drug Trade

The fact that multiple perspectives of justice exist can nowhere be seen better than in the so-called war on drugs. Reducing drug abuse is a top priority, considering its social costs.

Because of their importance and costs, agencies of the criminal justice system have used a number of strategies to reduce drug trafficking and use. Some have re-

Are we fighting a war on drugs? Are we winning it? Use "war on drugs" as a key term on InfoTrac College Edition.

lied on a strict crime control orientation, whereas others feature nonintervention, justice, and rehabilitation strategies. The following sections illustrate how each perspective influences criminal justice efforts to control or reduce the drug trade.

Crime Control Strategies

There have been a number of efforts to control the drug trade through strict crime control efforts. These include the following:

Source Control A major effort has been made to cut off supplies of drugs by destroying crops and arresting members of drug cartels in drug-producing countries; this approach is known as **source control**. The federal government's Drug Enforcement Administration has been in the vanguard of encouraging exporting nations to step up efforts to destroy drug crops and prosecute dealers. Translating words into deeds is a formidable task. Drug lords are willing and able to fight back through intimidation, violence, and corruption. The drug cartels in Colombia and Mexico do not hesitate to use violence and assassination to protect their interests. Enforcement efforts in Peru and Bolivia have been so successful that drug crops have been significantly reduced. Rather than inhibit drug shipments, Colombia soon became the premier coca-cultivating country. When the Colombian government mounted an effective eradication campaign in the traditional growing areas, the drug cartel linked up with rebel groups in remote parts of the country for their drug supply.[38] Enforcement efforts in Colombia have promoted the emergence of Mexican drug cartels.

source control Eradicating the drug problem through a policy of destroying crops and manufacturing plants located in source countries before the drugs can be shipped to the United States.

Border Control Another crime control approach to the drug problem has been to interdict drug supplies as they enter the country. Border patrols and military personnel using sophisticated hardware have been involved in massive interdiction efforts; many impressive multimillion-dollar seizures have been made. Yet U.S. borders are so vast and unprotected that meaningful interdiction is difficult. To aid law enforcement agencies, the U.S. military has become involved in stemming the flow of drugs across the border. The cost of staffing listening posts and patrolling borders is growing rapidly; today interdiction and eradication strategies costs billions of dollars, yet they do little to reduce drug supplies.

Police Crackdowns Local, state, and federal law enforcement agents have also been actively fighting drug dealers. One approach is to direct efforts at large-scale drug rings. However, this effort has merely served to decentralize drug dealing. Law enforcement efforts have significantly reduced the strength of traditional organized syndicates. Rather than reducing the inflow of drugs, their place has been taken by Asian, Latino, and Jamaican groups, motorcycle clubs, and local gangs. Colombian syndicates have established cocaine distribution centers on every continent, and Mexican organizations are responsible for large methamphetamine shipments to the United States. Russian, Turkish, Italian, Nigerian, Chinese, Lebanese, and Pakistani heroin-trafficking syndicates are now competing for dominance.

In terms of weight and availability, no commodity is more lucrative than illegal drugs. They cost relatively little to produce and provide large profit margins to dealers and traffickers. At an average street price of $100 per gram in the United States, a metric ton of pure cocaine is worth $100 million; cutting it and reducing purity can double or triple the value. It is difficult for law enforcement agencies to counteract the inducement of drug profits. When large-scale drug busts are made, supplies become scarce and market values increase, encouraging more people to enter the drug trade.

Aiming efforts at low-level dealers is also problematic. Some street-level enforcement efforts have been successful, but others are considered failures. Drug sweeps have clogged courts and correctional facilities with petty offenders while proving a costly drain on police resources. A displacement effect is also suspected: stepped-up efforts to curb drug dealing in one area or city simply encourage dealers to seek out friendlier territory.

Justice Model Strategies

According to the justice model, if drug violations were to be punished with criminal sentences commensurate with their harm, then the "rational" drug trafficker would look for a new line of employment. The cornerstone of this antidrug model is the adoption of mandatory minimum sentences for drug crimes, which ensure that all offenders receive similar punishments for their acts. The justice model advocates lobby for sentencing policies that will standardize punishments. The Federal Anti-Drug Abuse Act of 1988 provides minimum mandatory prison sentences for serious drug crimes, with especially punitive sentences for anyone caught distributing drugs within one thousand feet of a school playground, youth center, or other areas where minors congregate.[39] Once convicted, drug dealers are subject to very long sentences and the seizure of their homes, automobiles, boats, and other assets bought with drug-trafficking profits.

Rehabilitation Strategies

Advocates of the rehabilitation model criticize punitive efforts to control the drug trade. They suggest that law enforcement efforts such as source and border control are doomed to failure because even if they were effective they would drive up the price of illegal drugs and encourage more people to enter the drug trade. Moreover, severely punishing users with long prison sentences may have little deterrent effect. They point to research such as that conducted by Cassia Spohn and David Holleran, which shows drug-involved offenders are the ones most likely to recidivate after serving a prison sentence.[40] Instead, rehabilitation advocates suggest that the only effective way to reduce drug use is to create strategies aimed at reducing the desire to use drugs and increasing incentives for users to eliminate substance abuse. What strategies have been tried?

Rehabilitation advocates believe that at-risk youngsters will forgo criminal behavior if they are provided with adequate alternatives to crime. Here, a police officer works with schoolchildren at a community-run, summer gang-resistance program in Boston.

Drug Prevention   One approach relies on drug prevention—convincing nonusers not to start using drugs. This effort relies heavily on educational programs that teach children to "say no" to drugs. The most well known is DARE, mentioned earlier, an elementary school program designed to give students the skills they need to resist peer pressure to experiment with tobacco, drugs, and alcohol. Evaluations of the program have been disappointing, indicating that it does increase knowledge about dangerous substances but has been insignificant in shaping attitudes toward drug abuse and law enforcement, increasing self-esteem, or reducing student drug use.[41]

Offender Treatment   The rehabilitation model suggests that it is possible to treat known users, get them clean of drugs and alcohol, and help them reenter conventional society.

There has been an active effort to identify drug abusers in order to get them into treatment. Drug testing of arrestees is common. Public and private institutions now regularly test employees and clients in order to determine if they are drug abusers.

Once users have been identified, a number of treatment strategies have been implemented. One approach rests on the assumption that users have low self-esteem and holds that treatment efforts must focus on building a sense of self. In this approach, users participate in outdoor activities and wilderness training in order to create self-reliance and a sense of accomplishment.[42]

More intensive efforts use group therapy approaches relying on group leaders who once were substance abusers. Group sessions try to give users the skills and support that can help them reject the social pressure to use drugs. These programs are based on the Alcoholics Anonymous approach: users must find within themselves the strength to stay clean, and peer support from those who understand the users' experiences can help them achieve a drug-free life.

methadone A synthetic narcotic used as a substitute for heroin in drug-control efforts.

Residential programs have been established for the heavily involved users, and a large network of drug treatment centers has been developed. Some are detoxification units that use medical procedures to wean patients from the most addicting drugs to those such as **methadone,** whose use can be more easily regulated. Methadone, a drug similar to heroin, is given under controlled conditions to addicts at clinics. Methadone programs have been undermined because some users sell their methadone on the black market, and others supplement their dosages with illegally obtained heroin.

Despite their good intentions, little evidence exists that these treatment programs can efficiently end substance abuse. A stay can help stigmatize residents as "addicts" even if they have never used hard drugs, and while in treatment they may be introduced to hard-core users with whom they may associate after release. Users often do not enter these programs voluntarily and have little motivation to change.[43] Even for those who could be helped, there are simply more users who need treatment than there are beds in treatment facilities. Many programs are restricted to users whose health insurance will pay for short-term residential care; when the insurance coverage ends, the patients are often released before their treatment program is completed. Simply put, if treatment strategies are to be successful, far more funding and programs are needed.

Restorative Justice Strategies

Numerous restorative justice–based programs are currently in operation. Mediation and conflict resolution programs are now common. Financial and community service restitution programs as an alternative to imprisonment have been in operation for more than two decades. These serve as an alternative to traditional criminal justice prosecution for drug-related offenses and work to tailor nonpunitive, effective, and appropriate responses to drug offenders. One restorative effort involves the use of specialized drug courts as an alternative to more punitive criminal processing. Defendants eligible for the drug court program are identified as soon as possible and if accepted into the program, are referred immediately to multiphased outpatient treatment. Treatment entails multiple weekly (often daily) contacts with the treatment provider for counseling, therapy, education, and a rehabilitation program that includes vocational, educational, family, medical, and other support services.[44]

Nonintervention Strategies

Despite the massive effort to control drug use through both crime control and rehabilitation strategies, the fight has not been successful. Getting people out of the drug trade is difficult because drug trafficking involves enormous profits, and both dealers and users lack meaningful economic alternatives. Controlling drugs by convincing known users to quit is equally hard; few treatment efforts have proven successful.

Considering these problems, some commentators, relying on a noninterventionist strategy, have called for the legalization of drugs. If drugs were legalized, the argument goes, then distribution could be controlled by the government. Price and the distribution method could be regulated, reducing the addict's cash requirements. Crime rates would be cut because drug users would no longer need the same cash flow to support their habit. Drug-related deaths would decrease because government control would reduce the sharing of needles and thus the spread of AIDS. Legalization would also destroy the drug-importing cartels and gangs. Since drugs would be bought and sold openly, the government would reap a windfall from taxes on both the sale of drugs and the income of drug dealers, which now is untaxed as part of the hidden economy. Drug distribution would be regulated, keeping narcotics out of the hands of adolescents. Those who favor legalization point to The Netherlands as a country that has legalized drugs and remains relatively crime-free.[45] Advocates of legalization suggest that, like it or not, drug use is here to stay because using mood-altering substances is customary in almost all human societies. No matter how hard we try to stop them, people will find ways of obtaining psychoactive drugs.[46] Banning drugs serves to create networks of manufacturers and distributors, many of whom use violence as part of their standard operating procedures. Though some may charge that drug use is immoral, is it any worse than using alcohol and cigarettes, both of which are addicting and unhealthy? Far more people die each year because they abuse these legal substances than the numbers who are killed in drug wars or from illegal substances (an estimated 100,000 people die each year from alcohol-related causes and another 320,000 from tobacco).[47]

Despite what some critics imply, not all those who advocate legalization are pie-in-the-sky liberals. Judge James P. Gray, a political conservative, is an outspoken critic of America's antidrug policies. In his book *Why Our Drug Laws Have Failed and What We Can Do About It* (2001) he decries the program of massive imprisonment and demonization of drug users that has flowed from making drugs illegal. Illegality is futile because it amounts to an attempt to repeal the law of supply and demand, which is an impossible task. Criminalizing drugs raises the price of the goods, which encourages growers, while dealers risk their lives to sell drugs for huge profits. Gray also argues that antidrug efforts have eroded civil liberties and due process, giving police too much power to seize assets and confiscate property or money from criminals in order to obstruct further criminal activity. Few of those whose assets have been seized are later charged with crime. Some form of legalization would help reduce these problems. However, rather than condone drug use he calls for a program of drug maintenance (allowing addicts a monitored drug intake) and controlled distribution (in which government-regulated drugs are sold in a controlled fashion). Gray goes so far as to suggest that generically packaged drugs such as marijuana could be sold by pharmacists, with a steep tax that would fund rehabilitation programs and drug education.[48]

Debating Legalization Although legalization can have the short-term effect of reducing crime, critics are wary of its social consequences. Legalization may harm the well-being of the community by creating health and social damage. Individuals do not have the right to harm society, even if it means curbing their freedom and personal choices—that is, the right to use drugs. If injured by their drug use, individuals would have to be cared for by the community at a very substantial cost to non–drug users.[49] Legalization would result in an increase in the nation's rate of drug usage, creating an even larger group of nonproductive, drug-dependent people who must be cared for by the rest of society.[50] If drugs were legalized and freely available, users might significantly increase their daily intake. In countries like Iran and Thailand, where drugs are cheap and readily available, narcotics use rates are high.

Others argue that the problems of alcoholism should serve as a warning of what can happen when controlled substances are made readily available. The number of drug-dependent babies could begin to match or exceed the number who are delivered with fetal alcohol syndrome.[51] Drunk-driving fatalities, which today number about twenty-five thousand per year, could be matched by deaths caused by driving under the influence of pot or crack. And though distribution would be regulated, adolescents likely would have the same opportunity to obtain potent drugs as they now have with beer and other forms of alcohol.

Perspectives in Perspective

The variety of tactics being used in the war on drugs aptly illustrates the impact of these various perspectives on the actual operations of the criminal justice system (Figure 1.5). Advocates of each view have attempted to promote their vision of what justice is all about and how it should be enforced. During the past decade, the crime control and justice models have dominated. Laws have been toughened and the rights of the accused curtailed, the prison population has grown, and the death penalty has been employed against convicted murderers. Because the crime rate has been dropping, these policies seem to be effective; they may be questioned if crime rates once again begin to rise. At the same time, efforts to rehabilitate offenders, to provide them with elements of due process, and to give them the least intrusive treatment have not been abandoned. Police, courts, and correctional agencies supply a wide range of treatment and rehabilitation programs to offenders in all stages of the criminal justice system. Whenever possible, those accused of crime are

Figure 1.5
Strategies for controlling drugs

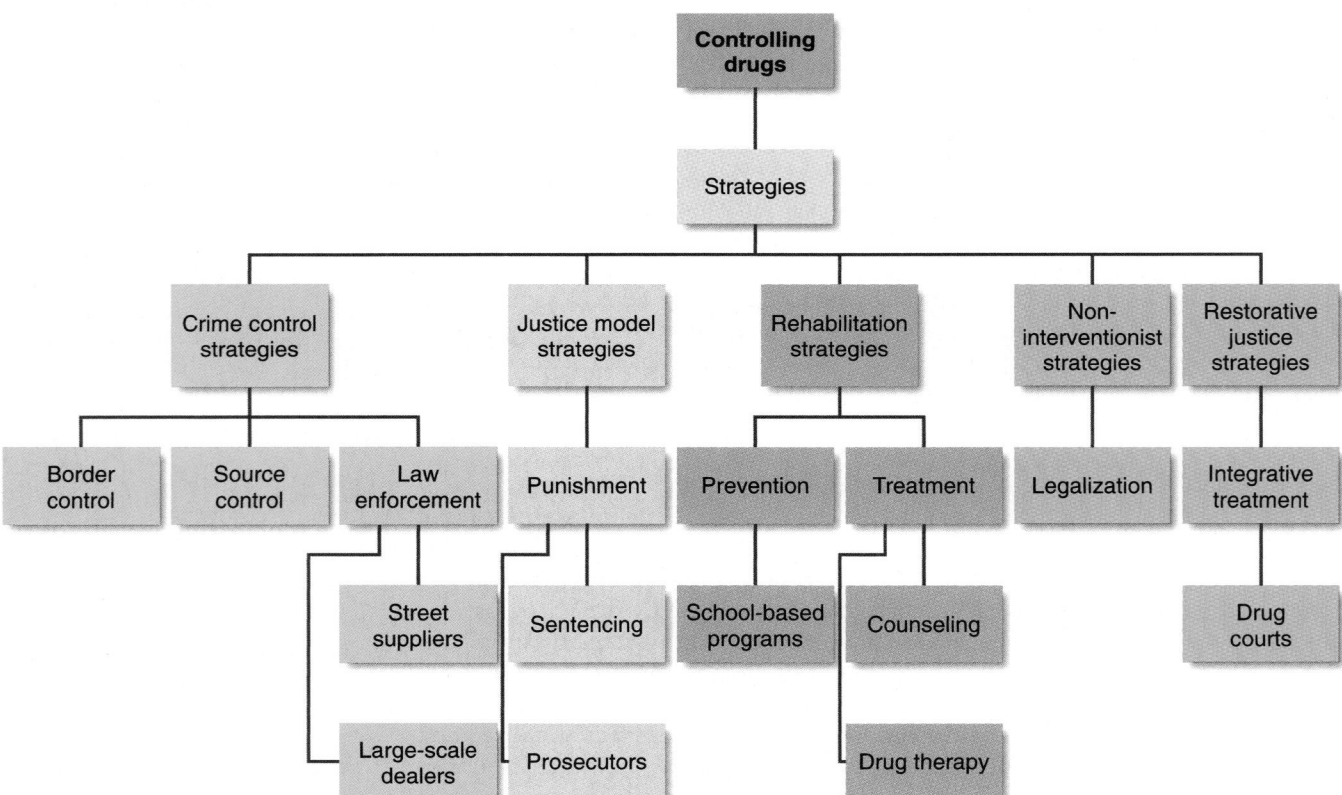

treated informally in nonrestrictive, community-based programs, and the effects of stigma are guarded against. Although the legal rights of offenders are being closely scrutinized by the courts, the basic constitutional rights of the accused remain inviolate. Guardians of the process have made sure that defendants are allowed the maximum protection possible under the law. For example, criminal defendants have been awarded the right to competent legal counsel at trial; merely having a lawyer to defend them is not considered sufficient legal protection.

In sum, understanding the justice system today requires analyzing a variety of occupational roles, institutional processes, legal rules, and administrative doctrines. Each predominant view of criminal justice provides a vantage point for understanding and interpreting these rather complex issues. No single view is the right or correct one. Each individual must choose the perspective that best fits his or her own ideas and judgment—or they can all be discarded and the individual's own view substituted. ■

SUMMARY

America has experienced crime throughout most of its history. In the Old West justice was administered by legendary lawmen like Wyatt Earp. There was little in the way of a formal criminal justice system. The term *criminal justice* became prominent around 1967, when the President's Commission on Law Enforcement and the Administration of Justice began a nationwide study of the nation's crime problem. Since then, a field of study has emerged that uses knowledge from various disciplines in an attempt to understand what causes people to commit crimes and how to deal with the crime problem. Criminal justice, therefore, consists of the study of crime and of the agencies concerned with its prevention and control.

Criminal justice is both a system and a process. As a system, it ideally functions as a cooperative effort among the primary agencies—police, courts, and corrections. The process, on the other hand, consists of the actual steps the offender takes from the initial investigation through trial, sentencing, and appeal.

In many instances, the criminal justice system works informally in order to expedite the disposal of cases. Criminal acts that are very serious or notorious may receive the full complement of criminal justice processes, from arrest to trial. However, less serious cases are often settled when a bargain is reached between the prosecution and the defense.

The role of criminal justice can be interpreted in many ways. People who study the field or work in its agencies bring their own ideas and feelings to bear when they try to decide on the right course of action to take or recommend. There are a number of different perspectives on criminal justice today. The crime control perspective is oriented toward deterring criminal behavior and incapacitating serious criminal offenders. In contrast, the rehabilitation model views the justice system as a treatment agency focused on helping offenders. Counseling programs are stressed over punishment and deterrence strategies. Those who hold the due process perspective see the justice system as a legal process. Their concern is that every defendant receives the full share of legal rights granted under law.

In addition to these views, the nonintervention model is concerned about stigma and helping defendants avoid the net of justice; these advocates call for the least intrusive methods possible. Those who advocate the justice model are concerned with making the system equitable. The arrest, sentencing, and correctional process should be structured so that every person is treated equally. Finally, the restorative justice model focuses on finding peaceful and humanitarian solutions to crime.

The various perspectives on justice are visible in the way the nation has sought to control substance abuse. Some programs rely on a strict crime control policy featuring the detection and arrest of drug traffickers, whereas others seek the rehabilitation of known offenders. The justice model has influenced development of sentencing policies that emphasize mandatory punishments. Another approach is to legalize drugs, thereby reducing abusers incentive to commit crimes, a policy that reflects nonintervention policies.

For an up-to-date list of Web links, go to
http://cj.wadsworth.com/siegel_essen4e.

KEY TERMS

criminal justice   3

Law Enforcement Assistance
   Administration (LEAA)
   7

social control   8

nolle prosequi   12

courtroom work group   18

crime control perspective
   22

Drug Abuse Resistance
   Education (DARE)   24

rehabilitation perspective
   24

due process perspective   24

nonintervention perspective
   25

decriminalization   26

legalization   26

victimless crime   26

deinstitutionalization   26

pretrial diversion   26

widening the net of justice
   26

restorative justice perspective
   26

source control   28

methadone   30

INFOTRAC COLLEGE EDITION EXERCISES

THE ISSUE OF DRUG LEGALIZATION has been the subject of endless debate. To get more information using InfoTrac College Edition, do a search using the following terms: "drug legalization" and "decriminalization."

FOR AN OVERVIEW of all sides of the issue, read Erich Goode, "Strange Bedfellows: Ideology, Politics, and Drug Legalization," *Society,* 1998 v35 i1 p18.

FOR A MORE SUBJECTIVE VIEW, see Charles B. Rangel, "Why Drug Legalization Should Be Opposed," *Criminal Justice Ethics,* 1998 v17 i2 p2.

QUESTIONS

1. Which criminal behavior patterns pose the greatest threat to the public? Should the justice system devote greater resources to combating these crimes? If so, which crime patterns should be deemphasized?

2. Describe the differences between the formal and informal justice systems. Is it fair to treat some offenders informally?

3. What are the layers of the criminal justice "wedding cake"? Give an example of a crime for each layer.

4. What are the basic elements of each model or perspective on justice? Which best represents your own point of view?

5. How would each perspective on criminal justice consider the use of the death penalty as a sanction for first-degree murder?

NOTES

1. Nick Madigan, "Man Accused of Killing Girl in California Postpones Plea," *New York Times,* 22 July 2002, 1.

2. This section leans heavily on Ted Robert Gurr, "Historical Trends in Violent Crime: A Critical Review of the Evidence," in *Crime and Justice: An Annual Review of Research,* vol. 3, eds. Michael Tonry and Norval Morris (Chicago: University of Chicago Press, 1981); Richard Maxwell Brown, "Historical Patterns of American Violence," in *Violence in America: Historical and Comparative Perspectives,* eds. Hugh Davis Graham and Ted Robert Gurr (Beverly Hills, Calif.: Sage, 1979), 18–29.

3. Cesare Beccaria, *On Crimes and Punishments* (1764; reprint, Indianapolis: Bobbs-Merrill, 1963).

4. Samuel Walker, *Popular Justice* (New York: Oxford University Press, 1980).

5. Ibid.

6. For an insightful analysis of this effort, see Samuel Walker, "Origins of the Contemporary Criminal Justice Paradigm: The American Bar Foundation Survey, 1953–1969," *Justice Quarterly* 9 (1992): 47–76.

7. President's Commission on Law Enforcement and the Administration of Justice, *The Challenge of Crime in a Free Society* (Washington, D.C.: Government Printing Office, 1967).

8. See Public Law No. 90-351, *Title I—Omnibus Crime Control Safe Streets Act of 1968,* 90th Congress, 19 June 1968.

9. For a review, see Kevin Wright, "Twenty-Two Years of Federal Investment in Criminal Justice Research: The National Institute of Justice, 1968–1989," *Journal of Criminal Justice* 22 (1994): 27–40.

10. Federal Bureau of Investigation, *Crime in the United States, 2001* (Washington, D.C.: Government Printing Office, 2002), 208.

11. Jeffrey Butts, *Offenders in Juvenile Court, 1994* (Washington, D.C.: Office of Juvenile Justice and Delinquency Prevention, 1996).

12. Jodi M. Brown and Patrick A. Langan, *Felony Sentences in the United States, 1996* (Washington, D.C.: Bureau of Justice Statistics, 1999).

13. For an analysis of this issue, see William Wilbanks, *The Myth of a Racist Criminal Justice System* (Monterey, Calif.: Brooks/Cole, 1987); Stephen Klein, Joan Petersilia, and Susan Turner, "Race and Imprisonment Decisions in California," *Science* 247 (1990): 812–816; Alfred Blumstein, "On the Racial Disproportionality of the United States Prison Population," *Journal of Criminal Law and Criminology* 73 (1982): 1259–1281; Darnell Hawkins, "Race, Crime Type, and Imprisonment," *Justice Quarterly* 3 (1986): 251–269.

14. Middlesex SS Superior Court Criminal No. 97-0433, *Commonwealth Memorandum and Order v. Louise Woodward,* 1997.

15. Herbert L. Packer, *The Limits of the Criminal Sanction* (Stanford, Calif.: Stanford University Press, 1975), 21.

16. Jacob Perez, *Tracking Offenders, 1990* (Washington, D.C.: Bureau of Justice Statistics, 1994), 2.

17. James Eisenstein and Herbert Jacob, *Felony Justice* (Boston: Little, Brown, 1977); Peter Nardulli, *The Courtroom Elite* (Cambridge, Mass.: Ballinger, 1978); Paul Wice, *Chaos in the Courthouse* (New York: Praeger, 1985); Marcia Lipetz, *Routine Justice: Processing Cases in Women's Court* (New Brunswick, N.J.: Transaction Books, 1983).

18. Douglas Smith, "The Plea Bargaining Controversy," *Journal of Criminal Law and Criminology* 77 (1986): 949–967.

19. Samuel Walker, *Sense and Nonsense About Crime* (Belmont, Calif.: Wadsworth, 1985).

20. Malcolm Feeley, *The Process Is the Punishment* (New York: Russell Sage, 1979).

21. James Q. Wilson, *Thinking about Crime* (New York: Vintage Books, 1983).

22. Ibid., 128.

23. John DiLulio, *No Escape: The Future of American Corrections* (New York: Basic Books, 1991).

24. Dennis Rosenbaum and Gordon Hanson, "Assessing the Effects of School-Based Drug Education: A Six-Year Multilevel Analysis of Project D.A.R.E.," *Journal of Research in Crime and Delinquency* 35 (1998): 381–412.

25. Karen Parker and Patricia McCall, "Structural Conditions and Racial Homicide Patterns: A Look at the Multiple Disadvantages in Urban Areas," *Criminology* 37 (1999): 447–448.

26. Francis Cullen, John Paul Wright, and Mitchell Chamlin, "Social Support and Social Reform: A Progressive Crime Control Agenda," *Crime and Delinquency* 45 (1999): 188–207.

27. Jane Sprott, "Are Members of the Public Tough on Crime? The Dimensions of Public 'Punitiveness,'" *Journal of Criminal Justice* 27 (1999): 467–474.

28. Packer, *The Limits of the Criminal Sanction,* 175.

29. "DNA Testing Has Exonerated 28 Prison Inmates, Study Finds," *Criminal Justice Newsletter,* 17 June 1996, 2.

30. Caitlin Lovinger, "Death Row's Living Alumni," *New York Times,* 22 August 1999, 1.

31. Eric Stewart, Ronald Simons, Rand Conger, and Laura Scaramella, "Beyond the Interactional Relationship Between Delinquency and Parenting Practices: The Contribution of Legal Sanctions," *Journal of Research in Crime and Delinquency* 39 (2002): 36–60.

32. Cassia Spohn and David Holleran, "The Effect of Imprisonment on Recidivism Rates of Felony Offenders: A Focus on Drug Offenders," *Criminology* 40 (2002): 329–359.

33. *Doe v. Pryor M.D. Ala,* Civ.No. 99-T-730-N, Thompson, J. 8/16/99.

34. This section is based on Paula M. Ditton and Doris James Wilson, *Truth in Sentencing in State Prisons* (Washington, D.C.: Bureau of Justice Statistics, 1999).

35. Herbert Bianchi, *Justice as Sanctuary* (Bloomington: Indiana University Press, 1994); Nils Christie, "Conflicts as Property," *British Journal of Criminology* 17 (1977): 1–15; L. Hulsman, "Critical Criminology and the Concept of Crime," *Contemporary Crises* 10 (1986): 63–80.

36. Larry Tifft, foreword to *The Mask of Love,* by Dennis Sullivan (Port Washington, N.Y.: Kennikat Press, 1980), 6.

37. Christopher Cooper, "Patrol Police Officer Conflict Resolution Processes," *Journal of Criminal Justice* 25 (1997): 87–101.

38. U.S. Department of State, *1998 International Narcotics Control Strategy Report* (February 1999).

39. *Anti-Drug Abuse Act of 1988,* Public Law No. 100-6901 21 U.S. Ct. 1501; Subtitle A—*Death Penalty, Sec. 001, Amending the Controlled Substances Abuse Act,* 21 USC 848.

40. Spohn and Holleran, "The Effect of Imprisonment on Recidivism Rates of Felony Offenders."

41. Dennis Rosenbaum, Robert Flewelling, Susan Bailey, Chris Ringwalt, and Deanna Wilkinson, "Cops in the Classroom: A Longitudinal Evaluation," *Journal of Research in Crime and Delinquency* 31 (1994): 3–31.

42. See, generally, Peter Greenwood and Franklin Zimring, *One More Chance* (Santa Monica, Calif.: Rand, 1985).

43. Eli Ginzberg, Howard Berliner, and Miriam Ostrow, *Young People at Risk: Is Prevention Possible?* (Boulder, Colo.: Westview Press, 1988), 99.

44. Drug Court Clearinghouse and Technical Assistance Project, *Looking at a Decade of Drug Courts* (Washington, D.C.: Government Printing Office, 1999).

45. See, generally, Ralph Weisheit, *Drugs, Crime, and the Criminal Justice System* (Cincinnati, Ohio: Anderson, 1990).

46. Ethan Nadelmann, "America's Drug Problem," *Bulletin of the American Academy of Arts and Sciences* 65 (1991): 24–40.

47. Ethan Nadelmann, "Should We Legalize Drugs? History Answers Yes," *American Heritage* (February/March 1993): 41–56.

48. James P. Gray, *Why Our Drug Laws Have Failed and What We Can Do About It: A Judicial Indictment of the War on Drugs* (Philadelphia: Temple University Press, 2001).

49. This and other arguments are presented in Erich Goode, *Between Politics and Reason: The Drug Legalization Debate* (New York: St. Martin's Press, 1997).

50. David Courtwright, "Should We Legalize Drugs? History Answers No," *American Heritage* (February/March 1993): 43–56.

51. James Inciardi and Duane McBride, "Legalizing Drugs: A Gormless, Naive Idea," *The Criminologist* 15 (1990): 1–4.

2 The Nature of Crime and Victimization

Chapter Outline

Criminal Justice Links

Criminal Justice Viewpoints

Courtesy of CNN

ON JUNE 5, 2002, Elizabeth Smart was kidnapped at gunpoint from the bedroom of her house in Salt Lake City, Utah. An unknown male allegedly entered the residence and, after having the fourteen-year-old Elizabeth put on her shoes, abducted her from the home. The police suspected former handyman Richard Ricci in the case, but he denied any involvement. While the investigation was ongoing Ricci died suddenly, so his involvement could not be determined. On March 12, 2003, Elizabeth was found alive thanks to her younger sister who remembered that the abductor looked a lot like Emmanuel, a one-time Smart family handyman. The information was included on the television program *America's* *Most Wanted* and Elizabeth was found walking down the street with Brian David Mitchell (aka Emmanuel) and his wife, after police received calls from two couples who recognized Mitchell from television reports.

(CNN) *To view the CNN video clip of this story, go to the book-specific Web site at* http://cj.wadsworth.com/siegel_essen4e.

The Elizabeth Smart case was one of a rash of child abductions that made headlines in 2002. Incidents such as these are the subject of daily newspaper stories and the six o'clock news. They help give the public the impression that violent crime is a daily feature of American life. At the time, some commentators argued that these cases are quite unique and that the media hype had given people the misleading impression that a child abduction plague was occurring. But justice experts cannot rely on such media stories either to make policy decisions or to evaluate program effectiveness. Administrators and policymakers must have up-to-date, accurate information about the nature and extent of crime in order to make effective choices about crime and its control.

Unless we have accurate information about crime, we cannot be sure whether a particular policy, process, or procedure has the effect its creators envisioned. For example, a state may enact a new law requiring that anyone who uses a firearm to commit a crime serve a mandatory prison term. The new statute is aimed directly at reducing the incidence of such violent crimes as murder, armed robbery, and assault. The effectiveness of this statutory change cannot be demonstrated without hard evidence that the use of firearms actually declines after the law is instituted and that the use of knives or other weapons does not increase. Without being able to measure crime accurately, it would be impossible either to understand its cause or to plan its elimination.

Exhibit 2.1 **Child abductions**

- During the study year, there were an estimated 115 *stereotypical kidnappings,* defined as abductions perpetrated by a stranger or slight acquaintance involving a child who was transported fifty or more miles, detained overnight, held for ransom or with the intent to keep the child permanently, or killed.
- In 40 percent of stereotypical kidnappings, the child was killed, and in another 4 percent, the child was not recovered.
- There were an estimated 58,200 child victims of *nonfamily abduction,* defined more broadly to include all nonfamily perpetrators (friends and acquaintances as well as strangers) and crimes involving lesser amounts of forced movement or detention in addition to the more serious crimes entailed in stereotypical kidnappings.
- Of children abducted by a nonfamily perpetrator, 57 percent were missing from caretakers for at least one hour before police were contacted; police were contacted to help locate 21 percent of all abducted children.
- Teenagers were by far the most frequent victims of both stereotypical kidnappings and nonfamily abductions.
- Nearly half of all child victims of stereotypical kidnappings and nonfamily abductions were sexually assaulted by the perpetrator.

Source: David Finkelhor, Heather Hammer, and Andrea Sedlak, *Nonfamily Abducted Children: National Estimates and Characteristics,* National Incidence Studies of Missing, Abducted, Runaway, and Thrownaway Children Series Bulletin (Washington, D.C.: U.S. Department of Justice, Office of Justice Programs, Office of Juvenile Justice and Delinquency Prevention, 2002).

In the case of child abductions, there has been ongoing federally sponsored research that charts the national incidence of missing, abducted, runaway, and thrownaway children. The national incidence study found that about 115 kids are abducted by strangers each year, or about 2 per week (see Exhibit 2.1); in 40 percent of these cases the victim is killed. The study also found that more than 58,000 children are abducted by people known to the family as either friends or acquaintances. These findings indicate that although stranger abduction is a relatively rare event child abduction certainly is not, and the justice system should create effective policies to prevent its occurrence.

Another goal of criminal justice study is to develop an understanding of the nature and cause of crime and victimization. Without knowing why crime occurs or the factors that influence the crime rate, creating effective crime reduction programs would be difficult. Policymakers would never be sure whether efforts were being aimed at the proper audience, or if they were, whether these efforts were likely to produce positive change. For example, a crime prevention program based on providing jobs for unemployed teenagers would only be effective if in fact crime is linked to unemployment. Similarly, a plan to reduce prison riots by eliminating the sugar intake of inmates is feasible only if research shows there is a link between diet and violence.

In addition to understanding the nature and cause of criminal behavior, it is important for criminal justice policymakers to study and understand the role of victims in the crime process. Such knowledge is essential for developing strategies to reduce the probability of predatory crime while providing information that people can use to decrease their likelihood of becoming a target of predatory criminals.

This chapter discusses some of the basic questions in the study of crime and justice: How is crime defined? How is crime measured? How much crime is there, and what are its trends and patterns? Why do people commit crime? How many people become victims of crime, and under what circumstances does victimization take place?

How Is Crime Defined?

consensus view of crime The belief that the majority of citizens in a society share common ideals and work toward a common good and that crimes are acts that are outlawed because they conflict with the rules of the majority and are harmful to society.

How can we understand the concept of crime? According to what is known as the **consensus view of crime,** crimes are behaviors that (1) are essentially harmful to a majority of citizens living in society and (2) have been controlled or prohibited by the existing criminal law. The criminal law is a set of rules that express the norms, goals, and values of a majority of society. Consequently, the criminal law has a social control function—restraining those who would take advantage of others' weakness for their own personal gain and thereby endanger the social framework. Although differences in behavior can be tolerated within a properly functioning social system, behaviors that are considered inherently destructive and dangerous are outlawed to maintain the social fabric and ensure the peaceful functioning of society. The consensus view is so named because it infers that the great majority of citizens agree that certain behaviors must be outlawed or controlled and that the criminal law is designed to protect citizens from social harm.

According to a second and opposing viewpoint, referred to as the **conflict view of crime,** crime is the outcome of a class struggle between the rich and poor, the have's and have-not's. Conflict works to promote crime by creating a social atmosphere in which the criminal law is a mechanism for controlling dissatisfied, have-not members of society while the wealthy maintain their position of power. Groups able to assert their political and economic power use the law and the criminal justice system to advance their own causes and to control the behavior of those who oppose their ideas and values.[1] For example, property crimes are punished heavily in order to protect the wealth of the affluent; drug laws ensure that workers will be productive, clearheaded, and sober. In contrast, business and white-collar crimes receive relatively lenient punishments.

Despite these differences, there is general agreement that the criminal law defines crime, that this definition is constantly changing and evolving, that social forces mold the definition of crimes, and that the criminal law has a social control function. Therefore, as used here, the term **crime** is defined as follows:

> *Crime is a violation of social rules of conduct, interpreted and expressed by a written criminal code, created by people holding social and political power. Its content may be influenced by prevailing public sentiments, historically developed moral beliefs, and the need to protect public safety. Individuals who violate these rules may be subject to sanctions administered by state authority, which include social stigma and loss of status, freedom, and on occasion, their lives.*

conflict view of crime (or *critical view of crime*) The belief that the law is controlled by the rich and powerful who shape its content to ensure their continued economic domination of society. The criminal justice system is an instrument of social and economic repression.

crime A violation of societal rules of behavior as interpreted and expressed by a criminal legal code created by people holding social and political power. Individuals who violate these rules are subject to sanctions by state authority, social stigma, and loss of status.

How Is Crime Measured?

Criminal justice scholars use a variety of techniques to study crime and its consequences. The following sections review in some detail some of the most important of these methods.

Survey Data

You may have read newspaper reports that teenage drug use has been on the rise (or is falling). How can the daily substance abuse of American teenagers possibly be calculated? Drug use is something that teens rarely talk freely about with strangers, especially those who work in the criminal justice system! The answer to this dilemma can be found in the use of anonymous surveys that ask teens about their substance abuse. A drug use survey can provide information on the percentage of students who use drugs and the type of adolescent who becomes a drug user. Conducted annually, these surveys can provide information on long-term trends in alcohol and drug usage.[2]

Most survey data come from samples in which a limited number of subjects are randomly selected from a larger population. If the sample is carefully drawn, every individual in the population has an equal chance of being selected for the study. Complex statistical analysis can then be used to make estimates about behavior in the general population. For example, a sample of ten thousand high school seniors can be selected at random and asked about the frequency of their use of alcohol and drugs. From this relatively small sample, estimates can be made of drug use among the millions of high school seniors in the United States.

Survey data typically include information on people's behaviors, attitudes, beliefs, and abilities; surveys provide information on the background and personal characteristics of offenders that otherwise would remain unknown. Surveys also provide a valuable source of information on particular crime problems—like drug use—that are rarely reported to police and may therefore go undetected.

Surveys can be used to measure the nature and extent of criminal victimization as well. The **National Crime Victimization Survey (NCVS),** conducted by the

National Crime Victimization Survey (NCVS) The ongoing victimization study conducted jointly by the Justice Department and the U.S. Census Bureau that surveys victims about their experiences with law violation.

U.S. Department of Justice, uses a large, carefully drawn sample of citizens who are queried about their experiences with criminal activity during the past year. The NCVS enables crime experts to estimate the total number of criminal incidents that occur each year, including those that are never reported to police; it is one of the most important sources of crime data.[3]

Record Data

I L state police homepage

A significant proportion of criminal justice data comes from the compilation and evaluation of official records. The records may be acquired from a variety of sources, including schools, courts, police departments, social service centers, and correctional agencies.

Records can be used for a number of purposes. Prisoners' files can be analyzed in an effort to determine what types of inmates adjust to prison and what types tend to become disciplinary problems or suicidal. Educational records are important indicators of intelligence, academic achievement, school behavior, and other information that can be related to criminal behavior patterns. However, records compiled by police departments and annually collected and analyzed by the Federal Bureau of Investigation are the most important source of crime data; these are referred to as the **official crime statistics.**

The FBI compiles the official crime statistics in a yearly publication referred to as the **Uniform Crime Report (UCR),** which is a compendium of data on where, when, and how much crime occurred during the prior year.[4]

official crime statistics Compiled by the FBI in its Uniform Crime Reports, these are a tally of serious crimes reported to police agencies each year.

Uniform Crime Report (UCR) The FBI's yearly publication of where, when, and how much serious crime occurred in the prior year.

Alternative Data Sources

In addition to these primary data sources, there are a number of alternative methods used by criminal justice researchers:

Observation The systematic observation, recording, and deciphering of behavior types within a sample or population is a common method of criminal justice data collection. Some observation studies are conducted in the field, where the researcher observes subjects in their natural environments; other observations take place in a contrived, artificial setting or a laboratory. For example, children will watch a violent TV program in a university psychology lab, and researchers will record their behavior to determine whether it undergoes a discernible change.

Still another type of observation study is called *participant observation.* In this type of research, the criminologist joins the group being studied and behaves like a member of the group. It is believed that participation enables the scientist to better understand the motives that the subjects may have for their behavior and attitudes. Participation also enables the researcher to develop a frame of reference similar to that of the subjects and to understand how the subjects interact with the rest of the world. Participant observation studies allow the researcher to gain insights into behavior that might never be available otherwise.

Interviews Some criminal justice researchers conduct in-depth interviews with a small sample of offenders. This kind of study provides insights into the causes of crime that surveys and records cannot capture. For example, a 2002 study of delinquent girls sent to adult prisons conducted by Emily Gaarder and Joanne Belknap found that many of these young women had troubled lives that set them on a criminal career path.[5] One girl told them how her father had attacked her, yet her mother shortly let him return home:

I told her I'd leave if he came back, but she let him anyway. I was thinking, you know, she should be worrying about me. I left and went to my cousin's house. Nobody even called me. Mom didn't talk to me for two weeks, and

Dad said to me, "Don't call." It was like they didn't care. I started smoking weed a lot then, drinking, skipping school, and shoplifting.... I had no (delinquency) record before this happened.

Such interviews help us understand that many young people in trouble with the law have themselves been the victims of abuse, neglect, and social disadvantage.

Life Histories   Another technique of criminal justice data collection is the **life history**. This method uses personal accounts of individuals who have had experience in crime, deviance, and other related areas. Diaries or autobiographies can be used; sometimes an account is given to an interested second party to record "as told to."[6] Life histories provide insights into the human condition that other, less personal research methods cannot hope to duplicate.

life history A research method that uses the experiences of an individual as the unit of analysis, such as using the life experience of an individual gang member to understand the natural history of gang membership.

Measuring Crime Trends

Each source of data collection helps criminal justice experts understand the nature and extent of criminal behavior in the United States and measure crime trends and patterns. Typically, crime rates, patterns, and trends rely on the two primary methods of data collection—official records and surveys. More specifically, researchers rely on the FBI's Uniform Crime Reports, the NCVS, and a variety of national **self-report surveys** to know about crime patterns and trends. Each source can be used independently, but taken together they provide a detailed picture of the crime problem. The data provided by these sources diverge in many key areas, but they have enough similarities to enable crime experts to draw some conclusions about crime in the United States. Each method is discussed in detail in the following sections.

self-report survey A research approach that requires subjects to reveal their own participation in delinquent or criminal acts.

Official Crime Data: The Uniform Crime Reports

The Federal Bureau of Investigation's UCR is the best known and most widely cited source of aggregate criminal statistics.[7] The FBI receives and compiles records from over seventeen thousand police departments serving a majority of the U.S. population. Its main unit of analysis involves **index (Part I) crimes**: criminal homicide, forcible rape, robbery, aggravated assault, burglary, larceny/theft, motor vehicle theft, and arson. Exhibit 2.2 defines these crimes. The FBI tallies and annually publishes the number of reported offenses by city, county, standard metropolitan statistical area, and geographical divisions of the United States. Besides these statistics, the UCR shows the number and characteristics (age, race, and gender) of individuals who have been arrested for these and all other crimes—**nonindex (Part II) crimes**—except traffic violations.

index (Part I) crimes The eight crimes that, because of their seriousness and frequency, the FBI reports the incidence of in the annual Uniform Crime Reports. Index crimes include murder, rape, assault, robbery, burglary, arson, larceny, and motor vehicle theft.

nonindex (Part II) crimes All other crimes except the eight index crimes recorded by the FBI. The FBI records all arrests made by police of Part II crimes.

Data on the number of clearances involving the arrest of only juvenile offenders, data on the value of property stolen and recovered in connection with Part I offenses, and detailed information pertaining to criminal homicide are also reported.

Traditionally, slightly more than 20 percent of all reported index crimes are cleared by arrest each year. Violent crimes are more likely to be solved than property crimes because police devote more resources to the more serious acts. For these types of crimes, witnesses (including the victim) are frequently available to identify offenders, and in many instances the victim and offender were previously acquainted.

The UCR uses three methods to express crime data. First, the number of crimes reported to the police and arrests made are expressed as raw figures (for example, 15,980 murders occurred in 2001). Second, crime rates per one hundred thousand people are computed. That is, when the UCR indicates that the murder

Exhibit 2.2   FBI index crimes

Criminal homicide

Murder and nonnegligent manslaughter. The willful (non-negligent) killing of one human being by another. Deaths caused by negligence, attempts to kill, assaults to kill, suicides, accidental deaths, and justifiable homicides are excluded. Justifiable homicides are limited to: (1) the killing of a felon by a law enforcement officer in the line of duty; and (2) the killing of a felon by a private citizen.

Manslaughter by negligence. The killing of another person through gross negligence. Traffic fatalities are excluded. While manslaughter by negligence is a Part I crime, it is not included in the crime index.

Forcible rape

The carnal knowledge of a female forcibly and against her will. Included are rapes by force and attempts or assaults to rape. Statutory offenses (no force used—victim under age of consent) are excluded.

Robbery

The taking or attempting to take anything of value from the care, custody, or control of a person or persons by force or threat of force or violence and/or by putting the victim in fear.

Aggravated assault

An unlawful attack by one person on another for the purpose of inflicting severe or aggravated bodily injury. This type of assault is usually accompanied by the use of a weapon or by means likely to produce death or great bodily harm. Simple assaults are excluded.

Burglary

Breaking or entering. The unlawful entry of a structure to commit a felony or a theft. Attempted forcible entry is included.

Larceny/theft *(except motor vehicle theft)*

The unlawful taking, carrying, leading, or riding away of property from the possession or constructive possession of another. Examples are thefts of bicycles or automobile accessories, shoplifting, pocket picking, or the stealing of any property or article which is not taken by force and violence or by fraud. Attempted larcenies are included. Embezzlement, "con" games, forgery, worthless checks, etc., are excluded.

Motor vehicle theft

The theft or attempted theft of a motor vehicle. A motor vehicle is self-propelled and runs on the surface and not on rails. Specifically excluded from this category are motorboats, construction equipment, airplanes, and farming equipment.

Arson

Any willful or malicious burning or attempt to burn, with or without intent to defraud, a dwelling, house, public building, motor vehicle or aircraft, personal property of another, etc.

Source: Federal Bureau of Investigation, *Crime in the United States, 2001* (Washington, D.C.: U.S. Government Printing Office, 2002).

---

rate was 5.6 in 2001, it means that almost six people in every one hundred thousand were murdered between January 1 and December 31, 2001. This is the equation used:

$$\frac{\text{Number of reported crimes}}{\text{Total U.S. population}} \times 100,000 = \text{Rate per } 100,000$$

Third, the FBI computes changes in the number and rate of crime over time. For example, murder rates increased 1.3 percent between 2000 and 2001.

How Accurate Is the UCR?   Despite criminologists' continued reliance on the UCR, its accuracy has been suspect. Some criminologists claim that victims of many serious crimes do not report these incidents to police; therefore, these crimes do not become part of the UCR. The reasons for not reporting vary. Some victims—for example, those living in disadvantaged neighborhoods—do not trust the police or have confidence in their ability to solve crimes. Others do not have property insurance and therefore believe it is useless to report theft. In other cases, victims fear reprisals from an offender's friends or family. According to surveys of crime victims, fewer than 40 percent of all criminal incidents are reported to the police. The way police departments record and report criminal and delinquent activity also affects the validity of UCR statistics. Some departments may define crimes loosely—for example, reporting a trespass as a burglary or an assault on a woman as an attempted rape—whereas others pay strict attention to FBI guidelines. These reporting practices may help explain interjurisdictional differences in crime.[8]

Some local police departments make systematic errors in UCR reporting. Some count an arrest only after a formal booking procedure, although the UCR

You can access the UCR at the FBI Web site at
www.fbi.gov/

requires arrests to be counted if the suspect is released without a formal charge. Exhibit 2.3 lists other issues that have been raised about the UCR's validity.[9]

Although these criticisms are troubling, the UCR continues to be one of the most widely used sources of criminal statistics.

Victim Surveys: The National Crime Victimization Survey (NCVS)

Surveys that ask crime victims about their encounters with criminals are the second primary source of crime data. Because many victims do not report their experiences to the police, victim surveys are considered a method of getting at the unknown figures of crime.

The most important and widely used victim survey, the NCVS, sponsored by the Bureau of Justice Statistics of the U.S. Department of Justice, is a national survey. Samples of housing units are selected using a complex, multistage sampling technique. Each year, data are obtained from a large nationally representative sample; in 2001, 43,680 households and 79,950 people age twelve or older were interviewed.[10] Those contacted are asked to report on the frequency, characteristics, and consequences of criminal victimization for such crimes as rape, sexual assault, robbery, assault, theft, household burglary, and motor vehicle theft.

Is the NCVS Valid? Because of the care with which the samples are drawn and the high completion rate, NCVS data are considered a relatively unbiased, valid estimate of all victimizations for the target crimes included in the survey. Yet, like the UCR, the NCVS may also suffer from some methodological problems. As a result, its findings must be interpreted with caution. Some of the potential problems are listed in Exhibit 2.4.

Self-Report Surveys

The problems associated with official statistics have led many criminologists to seek alternative sources of information in assessing the true crime patterns. In addition, official statistics do not say much about the personality, attitudes, and behavior of individual criminals. And they are of little value in charting the extent of substance abuse in the population because relatively few abusers are arrested. Criminologists have therefore sought additional sources to supplement and expand official data. Self-report surveys are one frequently employed alternative to official statistics. These surveys allow participants to reveal information about their violations. Most often, self-report surveys are administered to groups of subjects through a mass distribution of questionnaires. Although the surveys might ask for the subjects' names, more commonly the responses remain anonymous. The basic assumption of self-report surveys is that anonymity and confidentiality will be ensured, which encourages people to accurately describe their illegal activities. Self-reports are viewed as a mechanism to get at the "dark figures of crime," the numbers missed by official statistics. Figure 2.1 illustrates some typical self-report items.

Exhibit 2.3 **Validity issues in the UCR**

- No federal crimes are reported.
- Reports are voluntary and vary in accuracy and completeness.
- Not all police departments submit reports.
- The FBI uses estimates in its total crime projections.
- If an offender commits multiple crimes, only the most serious is recorded. Thus if a narcotics addict rapes, robs, and murders a victim, only the murder is recorded. Consequently, many lesser crimes go unreported.
- Each act is listed as a single offense for some crimes but not for others. If a man robbed six people in a bar, the offense is listed as one robbery; but if he assaulted or murdered them, it would be listed as six assaults or six murders.
- Incomplete acts are lumped together with completed ones.
- Important differences exist between the FBI's definition of certain crimes and those used in a number of states.

To read more about the administration of victim surveys, use "victims of crime surveys" as a subject guide on InfoTrac College Edition.

To access the most recent NCVS data, go to www.ojp.usdoj.gov/bjs/abstract/cv01.htm

---

Exhibit 2.4 **Validity issues in the NCVS**

- Victims may overreport due to their misinterpretation of events; for example, a lost wallet may be reported as stolen, or an open door may be viewed as a burglary attempt.
- Victims may underreport because they are embarrassed about reporting crime to interviewers, afraid of getting in trouble, or simply forget an incident.
- There may be an inability to record the personal criminal activity of those interviewed, such as drug use or gambling; murder is not included for obvious reasons.
- Sampling errors may produce a group of respondents that does not represent the nation as a whole.
- An inadequate question format may invalidate responses; some groups, such as adolescents, may be particularly susceptible to error because of question format.

PLEASE INDICATE HOW OFTEN IN THE PAST 12 MONTHS YOU DID EACH ACT. (CHECK THE BEST ANSWER.)

	Never did act	1 time	2–5 times	6–9 times	10+ times
Stole something worth less than $50					
Stole something worth more than $50					
Used cocaine					
Been in a fistfight					
Carried a weapon such as a gun or knife					
Fought someone using a weapon					

Figure 2.1
Self-report survey questions

chronic offender A delinquent offender who is arrested five or more times before he or she is eighteen and who stands a good chance of becoming an adult criminal; these offenders are responsible for more than half of all serious crimes.

Most self-report studies have focused on juvenile delinquency and youth crime, for two reasons.[11] First, the school setting makes it convenient to test thousands of subjects simultaneously because they all have the means to respond to a research questionnaire (pens, desks, and time). Second, because school attendance is universal, a school-based self-report survey represents a cross section of the community. However, self-reports are not restricted to youth crime. They are also used to examine the offense histories of prison inmates, drug users, and other segments of the population. They can be used to estimate the number of criminal offenders who have previously been unknown to the police. These respondents represent many criminals who have never figured in official crime statistics, some of whom may even be serious or **chronic offenders.**[12] In sum, self-reports provide an appreciable amount of information about offenders that cannot be found in official statistics.

In general, self-reports indicate that the number of people who break the law is far greater than the number projected by official statistics. Almost everyone questioned is found to have violated some law.[13] Furthermore, self-reports dispute the notion that criminals and delinquents specialize in one type of crime or another; offenders seem to engage in a "mixed bag" of crime and deviance.[14]

Self-report surveys indicate that the most common offenses are truancy, alcohol abuse, use of a false ID, shoplifting or larceny under $50, fighting, marijuana use, and damage to the property of others. It is not unusual for self-reports to find combined substance abuse, theft, violence, and damage rates of more than 50 percent among suburban, rural, and urban high school youths. What is surprising is the consistency of these findings in samples taken around the United States.

Table 2.1 contains data from a self-report survey called *Monitoring the Future,* which researchers at the University of Michigan Institute for Social Research (ISR) conduct annually. This national survey of thousands of high school seniors, one of the most important sources of self-report data, shows a widespread yet stable pattern of youth crime since 1978.[15] As Table 2.1 shows, young people self-report a great deal of crime: about 31 percent of high school seniors reported stealing something worth less than $50 and 11 percent admitted stealing something worth more than $50 in the last twelve months, almost 20 percent said they were involved in a gang fight, about 13 percent injured someone so badly that the victim had to see a doctor, about 30 percent admitted shoplifting, and almost 25 percent engaged in breaking and entering. The fact that so many—at least 33 percent—of all U.S. high school students engaged in theft and almost 19 percent committed a serious violent act during the past year shows that criminal activity is widespread and is not restricted to a few "bad apples."

Table 2.1	Self-reported delinquent activity during the past 12 months among high school seniors, 2001		
Type of Crime	**Never (%)**	**Once (%)**	**More Than Once (%)**
Set fire on purpose	97	2	1
Damaged school property	86	7	7
Damaged work property	93	3	4
Committed auto theft	93	4	3
Committed auto part theft	95	2	3
Broke and entered	76	12	12
Stole less than $50	69	13	18
Stole more than $50	88	5	6
Shoplifted	69	12	18
Got into gang fight	80	12	8
Hurt someone bad	87	8	5
Used force to steal	97	1	2
Hit teacher or supervisor	97	2	1
Got into serious fight	84	9	7

Source: Monitoring the Future, 2001 (Ann Arbor, Mich.: Institute for Social Research, 2002).

Are Self-Reports Valid?   Although self-report data have profoundly affected criminological inquiry, some important methodological issues have been raised about their accuracy too. Critics of self-report studies frequently suggest that it is unreasonable to expect people to candidly admit illegal acts. They have nothing to gain, and the ones taking the greatest risk are the ones with official records who may be engaging in the most criminality. On the other hand, some people may exaggerate their criminal acts, forget some of them, or be confused about what is being asked. Some surveys contain an overabundance of trivial offenses, such as shoplifting small amounts of items or using false identification, often lumped together with serious crimes, to form a total crime index. Consequently, comparisons between groups can be highly misleading.

Although many criminologists believe in the reliability of self-reports, nagging questions remain about their validity.[16] Even if 90 percent of a school population voluntarily participates in a self-report survey, researchers can never be sure whether the few who refuse to participate or are absent that day account for a significant portion of the school's population of persistent, high-rate offenders.[17] It is also unlikely that the most serious chronic offenders in the teenage population are the most willing to cooperate with university-based criminologists administering self-report tests.[18] For example, persistent substance abusers tend to underreport the frequency of their drug use.[19]

The Institute of Social Research Web site:

http://monitoringthefuture.org/

To read a study using a self-report instrument with a sample of incarcerated youth, go to InfoTrac College Edition and access David C. May, Lesa Rae Vartanian, and Keri Virgo, "The Impact of Parental Attachment and Supervision on Fear of Crime Among Adolescent Males," *Adolescence,* Summer 2002 v37 i146 p267(21).

Are the Sources of Crime Statistics Compatible?

Are the various sources of crime statistics compatible? Each has strengths and weaknesses. The FBI survey is carefully tallied and contains data on the number of murders and people arrested, information that the other data sources lack. However, this survey omits the many crimes that victims choose not to report to police, and it is subject to the reporting caprices of individual police departments.

The NCVS contains unreported crime and important information on the personal characteristics of victims but the data consist of estimates made from relatively limited samples of the total U.S. population, so that even narrow fluctuations in the rates of some crimes can have a major impact on findings. It also relies on personal recollections that may be inaccurate. Furthermore, the NCVS does not include data on important crime patterns, including murder and drug abuse.

Self-report surveys can provide information on the personal characteristics of offenders—such as their attitudes, values, beliefs, and psychological profiles—that is unavailable from any other source. Yet, at their core, self-reports rely on the honesty of criminal offenders and drug abusers, a population not generally known for accuracy and integrity.

Despite these differences, the data sources seem more compatible than was first believed. Although their tallies of crimes are certainly not in sync, the crime patterns and trends they record are often similar.[20] For example, all three sources generally agree about the personal characteristics of serious criminals (such as age and gender) and where and when crime occurs (such as urban areas, nighttime, and summer months).

Crime Trends

Use the term "crime trends" as a subject guide on InfoTrac College Edition to learn more about developments in the crime rate.

As we have seen in Chapter 1, crime is not new to this century.[21] Studies have indicated that a gradual increase in the crime rate, especially in violent crime, occurred from 1830 to 1860. Following the Civil War, this rate increased significantly for about fifteen years. Then, from 1880 up to the time of World War I—with the possible exception of the years immediately preceding and following the war—the number of reported crimes decreased. After a period of readjustment, the crime rate steadily declined until the Depression (about 1930), when another crime wave was recorded. Crime rates increased gradually following the 1930s until the 1960s, when the growth rate became much greater. The homicide rate, which had actually declined from the 1930s to the 1960s, also began a sharp increase that continued through the 1970s.

In 1981 the number of index crimes peaked at about 13.4 million and then began a consistent decline until 1984, when police recorded 11.1 million crimes. By the following year, however, the crime rate once again began an upward trend, so that by 1991 police recorded about 14.6 million crimes. Both the number of crimes and the rate of crime declined for the remainder of the decade. Even the teen murder rate, which had remained stubbornly high, underwent a significant decline.[22] (See Figure 2.2.) Then in 2001, the official crime rate ticked slightly upward, increasing about 2 percent.[23]

The factors that help explain the upward and downward movement in crime rates are discussed in the following Policy, Programs, and Issues feature.

© 2002 AP/Wide World Photos

Though crime is not new to this century, high-profile cases give the impression that our society is particularly crime-prone. Here, Vermont teenager Robert Tullock leaves the Grafton County Jail in Haverhill, New Hampshire, April 4, 2002, on his way to court. Tullock pleaded guilty to the first-degree murder of two Dartmouth College professors in 2001 and was sentenced to two terms of life without parole. These killings and similar cases give the public the impression that violence is increasing, although the official statistics tell a different tale.

Trends in Official Violent Crime

The violent crimes reported by the FBI include murder, rape, assault, and robbery.

According to the UCR, the violent crime rate trended downward for most of the 1990s. Particularly encouraging in the 1990s was the decrease in the number and rate of murders. Figure 2.3 illustrates homicide rate trends since 1900. Note how the rate peaked around 1930, then fell, began to rise dramatically around 1960, and peaked once again in 1991, when the number of murders topped twenty-four thousand for the first time in U.S. history. Between 1993 and 2001, the U.S. homicide rate dropped by

Rate per 1,000 population

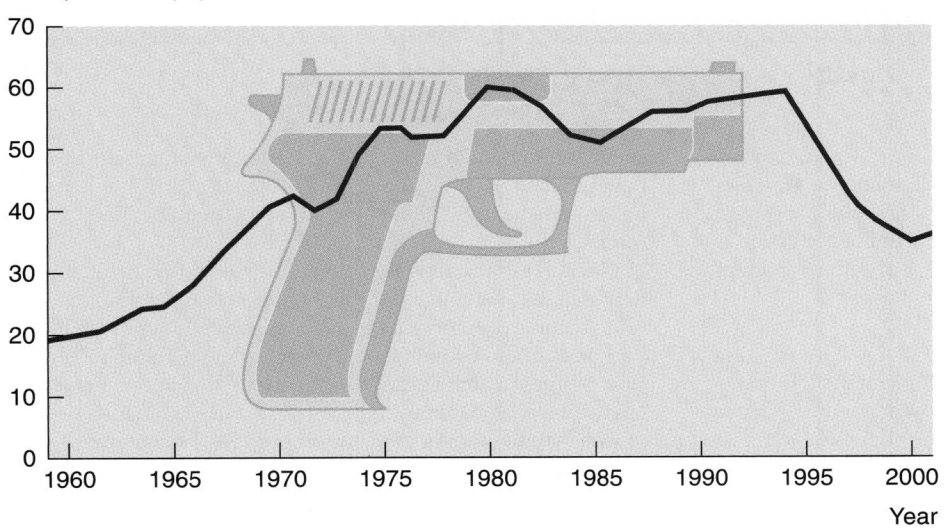

Figure 2.2
Crime rate trends
After years of steady increase, crime rates declined from 1993 through 2000, then
increased in 2001.

Source: FBI, Uniform Crime Report, 2000; updated June 2002.

Rate per 100,000 population

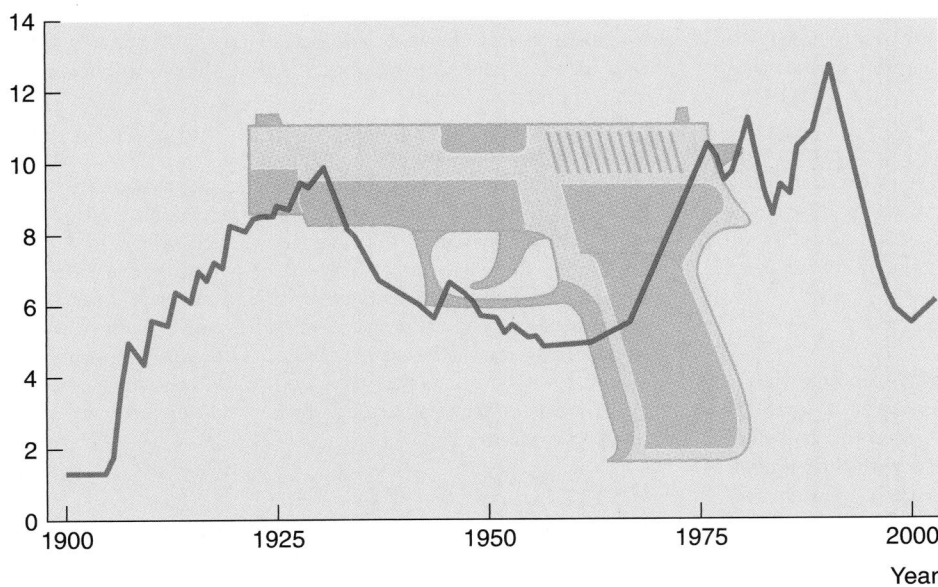

Figure 2.3
Homicide rate trends, 1900–2000

Source: FBI, Uniform Crime Report, 2000; updated June 2002.

Factors That Have an Impact on Crime Rates

What are the most important influences on fluctuations in the crime rate? Criminologists have identified a variety of social, economic, personal, and demographic factors that influence crime rate trends. Some of the most important factors are discussed here.

Age
Because the teenage population has extremely high crime rates, a change in the general population age distribution may have a significant influence on crime trends: when the number of young males increases, so too do crime rates. With the "graying" of society in the 1980s and a decline in the birthrate, it is not surprising that the overall crime rate declined between 1991 and 2000. The number of juveniles should be increasing over the next decade, and some criminologists fear that this will signal a return to escalating crime rates. However, the number of senior citizens is also expanding and their presence in the population may have a moderating effect on crime rates (seniors do not commit much crime), offsetting the effect of teens.

Economy
There is debate over the effects the economy has on crime rates. Some criminologists believe that a poor economy actually helps lower crime rates because unemployed parents are at home to supervise children and guard their possessions. Because there is less money to spend, a poor economy reduces the number of valuables worth stealing. Also, it seems unlikely that law-abiding, middle-aged workers will suddenly turn to a life of crime if they are laid off during an economic downturn. Recent research by Gary Kleck and Ted Chiricos confirms that the unemployment-crime rate relationship is modest.

Although a poor economy may lower crime rates in the short run, long-term periods of sustained economic weakness and unemployment in a particular area can eventually increase crime rates when measured at the local or neighborhood level. It is also possible that a long-term sustained economic recession may produce increases in the crime rate.

Social Malaise
As the level of social problems increases—such as the number of single-parent families, dropout rates, level of racial conflict, and teen pregnancies—so too do crime rates. For example, crime rates are correlated with the number of unwed mothers in the population. It is possible that children of unwed mothers need more social services than children in two-parent families. As the number of kids born to single mothers increases, the child welfare system will be taxed and services depleted. As the teenage birthrate began to drop in the late 1980s and 1990s, so too did crime rates.

Racial conflict may also increase crime rates. Areas undergoing racial change, especially those experiencing an in-migration of minorities into predominantly white neighborhoods, seem prone to significant increases in their crime rate. Whites in these areas may be using violence to protect what they view as their home turf. Racially motivated crimes actually diminish as neighborhoods become more integrated and power struggles diminish.

Abortion
In a controversial work, John J. Donohue III and Steven D. Levitt found empirical evidence that the recent drop in the crime rate can be attributed to the availability of legalized abortion. Donohue and Levitt suggested that the crime rate drop began approximately eighteen years after *Roe v. Wade* legalized abortions. They found that states that legalized abortion before the rest of the nation were the first to experience decreasing crime and that states with high abortion rates have seen a greater fall in crime since 1985. It is possible that the link between crime rates and abortion is the result of two mechanisms: (1) selective abortion on the part of women most at risk to have children who will later engage in criminal activity, and (2) improved child-rearing or environmental circumstances caused by better maternal, familial, or fetal circumstances because women are having fewer children. If abortion were illegal, the authors found, crime rates might be 10 to 20 percent higher than they currently are. If their estimates are correct, legalized abortion can explain about half of the recent fall in crime.

Guns and Teens
The availability of firearms may influence the crime rate, especially the proliferation of weapons in the hands of teens. There is evidence that more guns than ever before are finding their way into the hands of young people. Surveys of high school students indicate that between 6 and 10 percent carry guns at least some of the time. Guns also cause escalation in the seriousness of crime. As the number of gun-toting students increases, so too does the seriousness of violent crime as, for example, a schoolyard fight turns into murder.

Gangs
Another factor that affects crime rates is the explosive growth in teenage gangs. Surveys indicate that there are

more than 850,000 gang members in the United States. Boys who are members of gangs are far more likely to possess guns than non–gang members; criminal activity increases when kids join gangs. According to Alfred Blumstein, gangs involved in the urban drug trade recruit juveniles because they work cheaply, are immune from heavy criminal penalties, and are "daring and willing to take risks." Arming themselves for protection, these drug-dealing children present a menace to their communities, which persuade non-gang-affiliated neighborhood adolescents to arm themselves for protection. The result is an arms race that produces an increasing spiral of violence.

The recent decline in the crime rate may be tied to changing gang values. Some streetwise kids have told researchers that they now avoid gangs because of the "younger brother syndrome"—they have watched their older siblings or parents caught in gangs or drugs and want to avoid the same fate.

Drug Use

Some experts tie increases in the violent crime rate between 1980 and 1990 to the crack cocaine epidemic, which swept the nation's largest cities, and drug-trafficking gangs, which fought over drug turf. These well-armed gangs did not hesitate to use violence to control territory, intimidate rivals, and increase market share. As the crack epidemic has subsided, so too has the violence in cities such as New York and in other metropolitan areas where the crack epidemic was rampant.

Justice Policy

Some law enforcement experts have suggested that a reduction in crime rates may be attributed to aggressive police practices that target "quality of life" crimes such as panhandling, graffiti, petty drug dealing, and loitering. By showing that even the smallest infractions will be dealt with seriously, aggressive police departments may be able to discourage potential criminals from committing more serious crimes.

It is also possible that tough laws targeting drug dealing and repeat offenders with lengthy prison terms can affect crime rates. The fear of punishment may inhibit some would-be criminals. Lengthy sentences also help boost the nation's prison population. Placing a significant number of potentially high-rate offenders behind bars may help stabilize crime rates. Some ex-criminals have told researchers that they stopped committing crimes because they perceived higher levels of street enforcement and incarceration rates.

Crime Opportunities

Crime rates may drop when (1) market conditions change and (2) an alternative criminal opportunity develops. For example, the decline in the burglary rate over the past two decades may be explained in part by the abundance and subsequent decline in price of commonly stolen merchandise such as VCRs, TVs, and cameras. Improving home and commercial security devices may also deter would-be burglars, convincing them to turn to other forms of theft, such as from motor vehicles. These are nonindex crimes and do not contribute to the national crime rate.

Critical Thinking

1. Do you agree that the factors listed here contribute to fluctuations in the crime rate? If not, why?
2. What other factors then may increase or reduce crime rates?

InfoTrac College Edition Research

Can fear of gangs and their contribution to the crime rate lead to an overzealous response by police? To find out, read Diane Schaefer, "Police Gang Intelligence Infiltrates a Small City," *Social Science Journal*, January 2002 v39 i1 p95(14).

Sources: Steven Messner, Lawrence Raffalovich, and Richard McMillan, "Economic Deprivation and Changes in Homicide Arrest Rates for White and Black Youths, 1967–1998: A National Time Series-Analysis," *Criminology* 39 (2001): 591–614; John Laub, "Review of the Crime Drop in America," *American Journal of Sociology* 106 (2001): 1820–1822; John J. Donohue III and Steven D. Levitt, "Legalized Abortion and Crime" (June 24, 1999, unpublished paper, University of Chicago); Donald Green, Dara Strolovitch, and Janelle Wong, "Defended Neighborhoods, Integration, and Racially Motivated Crime," *American Journal of Sociology* 104 (1998): 372–403; Robert O'Brien, Jean Stockard, and Lynne Isaacson, "The Enduring Effects of Cohort Characteristics on Age-Specific Homicide Rates, 1960–1995," *American Journal of Sociology* 104 (1999): 1061–1095; Darrell Steffensmeier and Miles Harer, "Making Sense of Recent U.S. Crime Trends, 1980 to 1996/1998: Age Composition Effects and Other Explanations," *Journal of Research in Crime and Delinquency* 36 (1999): 235–274; Desmond Ellis and Lori Wright, "Estrangement, Interventions, and Male Violence Toward Female Partners," *Violence and Victims* 12 (1997): 51–68; Richard Rosenfeld, "Changing Relationships Between Men and Women: A Note on the Decline in Intimate Partner Homicide," *Homicide Studies* 1 (1997): 72–83; Bruce Johnson, Andrew Golub, and Jeffrey Fagan, "Careers in Crack, Drug Use, Drug Distribution, and Nondrug Criminality," *Crime and Delinquency* 41 (1995): 275–295; Alfred Blumstein, "Violence by Young People: Why the Deadly Nexus," *National Institute of Justice Journal* 229 (1995): 2–9; Alan Lizotte, Gregory Howard, Marvin Krohn, and Terence Thornberry, "Patterns of Illegal Gun Carrying Among Young Urban Males," *Valparaiso University Law Review* 31 (1997): 376–394; Gary Kleck and Ted Chiricos, "Unemployment and Property Crime: A Target-Specific Assessment of Opportunity and Motivation as Mediating Factors," *Criminology* 40 (2002): 649–680.

40 percent to a level of less than six per one hundred thousand population—a rate not seen since 1966.

In 2001, the volume of violent crime offenses remained relatively unchanged—a 0.3 percent increase—when compared with 2000. Robbery showed the greatest increase, 3.9 percent, and forcible rape showed a minimal increase of 0.2 percent. Aggravated assault, which is the most frequently occurring violent crime in the index, was the only violent offense to show a decrease from the 2000 volume—down by 1.4 percent.[24] But, disturbingly, there was a 3.1 percent increase in the number of murders.

Trends in Official Property Crime

The property crimes reported in the UCR include larceny, motor vehicle theft, and arson. Property crime rates declined during the 1990s, though the drop was not as dramatic as that experienced in violent crimes. Then, in 2001, the volume of property crime offenses rose by 2.2 percent. In the property crime category, motor vehicle theft increased 5.9 percent, and burglary rose 2.6 percent. Arson and larceny/theft increased 2.0 percent and 1.4 percent, respectively.

The recent uptick in the official crime rate, and especially in the homicide rate, is perplexing. It is possible that it is a one-year aberration or portends an upward trend in crime. While it is impossible to predict the future, there is little question that crime rates will always undergo an ebb and flow.

Victimization Trends

According to the NCVS, Americans age twelve and older experienced approximately 24.2 million violent and property victimizations in 2001, a decrease from 25.9 million victimizations in 2000. This downward trend in reported victimizations began in 1994 and resulted in the lowest number of criminal victimizations recorded since 1973, when an estimated 44 million victimizations were recorded. In 2001, the violent crime rate fell 10 percent from 28 to 25 violent victimizations per 1,000 persons; the personal theft rate fell 33 percent; and the property crime rate fell 6 percent, from 178 to 167 victimizations per 1,000 households. The drop in the violent crime rate was due primarily to a significant decrease in the rate of simple assault (see Figure 2.4).

So although the official crime statistics indicate a slight uptick in the crime rate, the victim data continue to show a drop in the rate and number of crimes. However, the increase in the official crime rate was rather small, so that taken as a whole both sources show little evidence of a significantly increasing crime rate.

Go to InfoTrac College Edition and use "victimization" as a key term to find out more about these trends.

Self-Report Trends

As previously noted, self-report studies indicate that most youth engage in law-violating behavior on a regular basis. Yet the incidence of self-reported criminality has been relatively stable. While a self-reported crime wave has not occurred, neither has there been a sharp decline in reported behavior.

One of the most important features of self-report studies is that they allow criminologists to record changes in teen drug use.[25] The *Monitoring the Future* study has found that drug use declined from a high point around 1980 until 1990, when it began once again to increase until 1996; since then teenage drug use has either stabilized or declined. Marijuana, the most widely used of the illicit drugs, accounted for most of the increase in overall illicit drug use during the 1990s and it now accounts for much of the observed decrease. Kids in the eighth, tenth, and twelfth grades showed a gradual decrease in marijuana use in the prior twelve months. Even though marijuana use is decreasing, more than one-third of all seniors said they smoked pot at least once during the prior twelve months. The *Mon-*

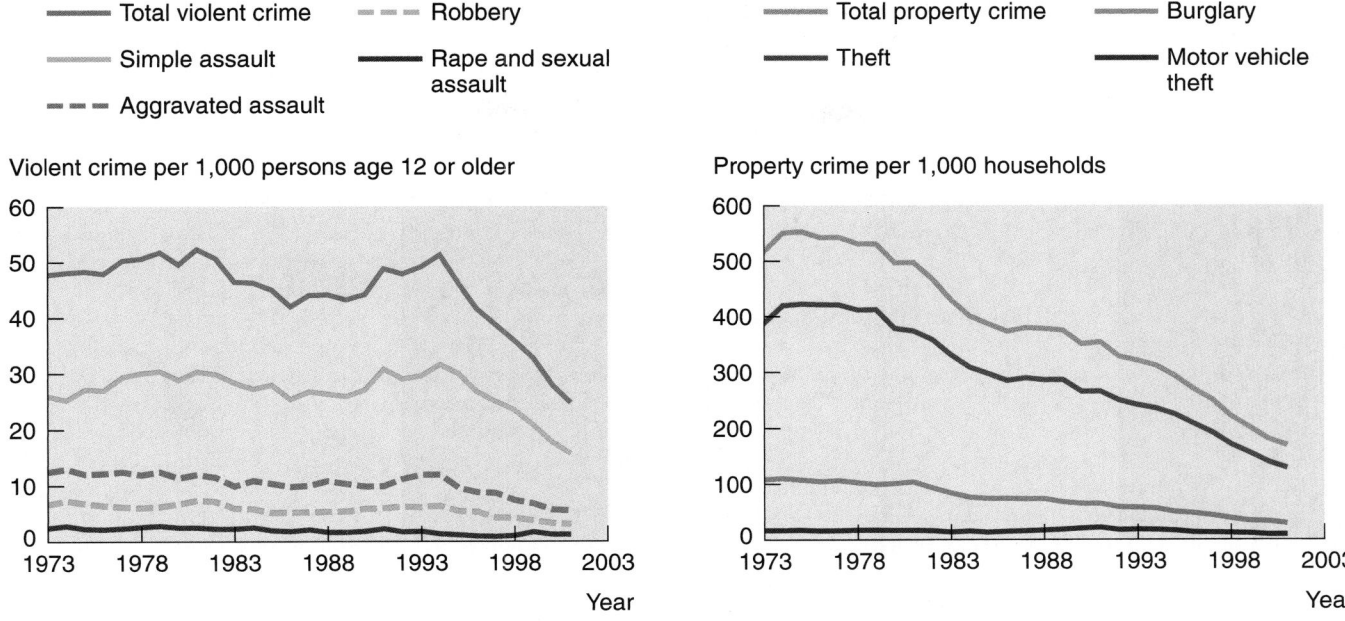

Total violent crime	Robbery	Total property crime	Burglary
Simple assault	Rape and sexual assault	Theft	Motor vehicle theft
Aggravated assault			

Figure 2.4
Victimization rate per 1,000 persons age twelve or older, 1973–2001

Source: Callie Marie Rennison, *Criminal Victimization 2001: Changes 2000–2001 with Trends 1993–2001* (Washington, D.C.: Bureau of Justice Statistics, 2002), 2.

itoring the Future survey shows that the drug Ecstasy has been increasing in popularity among the nation's youth; about 8 percent of seniors report using that drug, making it now more popular than cocaine. The most recent data indicate that the rapid increase in the use of Ecstasy may now be slowing. Though alcohol use has stabilized, nearly one-quarter of eighth-graders and half of all seniors reported drinking in the past month.[26]

What the Future Holds

Speculating about the future of crime trends is always risky because current conditions can change rapidly. But some criminologists have tried to predict future patterns. Criminologist James Fox predicts a significant increase in teen violence if current trends persist. There are approximately fifty million school-age children in the United States, many are under age ten; this is more than we have had for decades. Though many come from stable homes, others lack stable families and adequate supervision; these are some of the children who will soon enter their prime crime-committing years. As a result, Fox predicts a wave of youth violence that will be even worse than that of the 1980s. If current trends persist, the number of juvenile homicides should grow from fewer than four thousand today to about nine thousand in the next few years.[27] Such predictions are based on population trends and other factors discussed earlier.

Fox's warnings are persuasive, but some experts dispute the fact that we are in for a big upswing in the crime rate. Even if teens commit more crime in the future, their contribution may be offset by the growing senior citizen and elderly population, a group with a relatively low crime rate. [28]

It is also possible that economic, technological, and social factors could help moderate the crime rate.[29] Technological developments such as the rapid expansion of e-commerce on the Internet have created new classes of crime. Concern about the environment may produce an increase in environmentally motivated

Race, Culture, and Gender in Criminal Justice

International Crime Trends

How do crime rates in the United States compare with those in other nations? While we sometimes think that the crime rate in the United States is extremely high, the fact is that crime rates here have been trending downward, a development that has allowed the rest of the world to catch up or even surpass us. At one time we were the "world leader" in violence, but evidence now shows we are only in the middle of the pack. Table A shows data from a United Nations sponsored survey on homicide. If nations are grouped together by income, the United States homicide rate compares favorably with the homicide rate of nations with a similar income structure. However, it is significantly lower than the homicide rate of less economically developed nations.

Table A   Top rates of homicide per 100,000 population, internationally, by income

High income:	
Argentina	9.3
U.S.	5.7
Portugal	3.8
Middle income:	
South Africa	60.4
Colombia	57.9
Kazakhstan	16.4
Low income:	
Albania	52.6
Latvia	11.0
Sri Lanka	10.1

Source: Sixth United Nations Survey on Crime Trends and the Operations of Criminal Justice Systems, 1995–1997 (Vienna: United Nations Crime and Justice Information Network, 2000).

In fact, while the United States underwent a downward trend in crime between 1990 and 2000, there was a sharp increase in the murder rate in England, Germany, and Sweden. Racial assaults and hate crimes have increased dramatically in Germany and England. Russia and the former Soviet republics have seen the rise of large-scale organized crime gangs that commonly use violence and intimidation. One of the most alarming developments has been the involvement of children in the international sex trade. Russia has been plagued with Internet sex rings that involve pornographic pictures of youths. In May 2001, more than eight hundred tapes and videos were seized in Moscow during Operation Blue Orchid, a joint operation conducted by Russian police and U.S. Customs agents. Operation Blue Orchid led to criminal investigations of people who ordered child pornography in more than twenty nations. Even more disturbing has been the involvement of European youths in global prostitution rings. Desperate young girls and boys in war-torn areas such as the former Yugoslavia and in impoverished areas such as Eastern Europe have gotten involved with gangs that ship them around the world. In one case, an organized crime group that was involved in wildlife smuggling—particularly tiger bones and skins—to Asian markets began a sideline of supplying sex clubs with young Russian women.

Fueling the rise in European violence has been a dramatic growth in the number of illegal guns smuggled in from the former Soviet republics. Also, unrestrictive immigration has brought newcomers who face cultural differences, lack of job prospects, racism, and social and economic pressures, including unemployment and cutbacks in the social welfare system.

There have also been reports of increased criminal activity in Asia. Japanese youth gangs have started to carry

crimes, ranging from vandalism to violence against violators and polluters and those accused of being part of the globalization movement.[30] Furthermore, while the crime rate has declined during the past decade in the United States, it seems to be increasing abroad, as the following Race, Culture, and Gender feature shows.

Crime Patterns

Crime experts look for stable crime rate patterns, to gain insight into the nature of crime. If crime rates are consistently higher at certain times, in certain areas, and among certain groups, this knowledge might help explain the onset or cause of crime. For example, if criminal statistics showed that crime rates were consistently higher in poor neighborhoods in large urban areas, then crime may be a function of poverty and neighborhood decline. If, in contrast, crime rates were spread evenly across the social structure, this would provide little evidence that

out what they call "uncle hunting," where four or five gang members single out a lone businessman walking home and beat him to the ground. Victim reports claim that gangs are not only doing this for the money but also for the thrill of inflicting pain on others.

Authorities in Vietnam report a troubling increase in street crimes such as burglary and theft. Many crimes are drug-related: there are an estimated two hundred thousand opium addicts in the country, and almost fifty thousand acres of land are now being cultivated for growing the poppy from which heroin is produced.

Although it is difficult to obtain accurate crime data from China, the world's largest nation seems to be cracking down on criminal offending. Chinese courts annually hand down more than one thousand death sentences and many thousands more are given sentences of life in prison. The current wave of punishment is a response to a significant increase in street crimes, including robberies and drug trafficking. According to the most recent (and, admittedly, limited and incomplete) Amnesty International records, China executed 2,468 people in 2001; the true figure is believed to have been much higher.

What factors predict high crime and violence rates around the world? A number of national characteristics are predictive of violence. These include a high level of social disorganization, economic stress (rather than support), high child-abuse rates, approval of violence by the government, political corruption, and an inefficient justice system. Children in high-violence nations are likely to be economically deprived and socially isolated, exposed to constant violence, and lacking in hope and respect for the law. Guns are common in these nations because, without an efficient justice system, people arm themselves or hire private security forces for protection.

Thus, although crime rates are still comparably low overseas, these trends indicate that international crime rates may yet converge.

Critical Thinking

1. What policies can be developed to bring the crime rate down in the United States? Is it feasible to tackle the social sources of crime by making families more cohesive, ending poverty, or reducing drug use?
2. Regardless of why crime rates are so high, might it not be possible to reduce them through aggressive law enforcement policies and the incarceration of known criminals?

InfoTrac College Edition Research

During the past decade, transnational crime has become a problem as offenders move from city to city and continent to continent to commit their crimes, with no regard for national boundaries. Read about this phenomenon by going to InfoTrac College Edition and accessing Marvene O'Rourke, "Transnational Crime: A New Health Threat for Corrections," *Corrections Today,* February 2002 v64 i1 p86(4).

Sources: The United Nations Crime and Justice Information Network can be accessed at www.uncjin.org; Sarah Shannon, "The Global Sex Trade: Humans as the Ultimate Commodity," *Crime and Justice International* 17 (2001): 5–7; "Pornography Cartel Broken," *Crime and Justice International* 17 (2001): 13; Calvin Sims, "Shaken Japan Tries to Face Aftermath of School Attack," *New York Times,* New England ed., 10 June 2001; Erika Fairchild and Harry R. Dammer, *Comparative Criminal Justice Systems,* second edition (Belmont, Calif.: Wadsworth, 2001); Doug Struck, "Surge in Violent Crime Worries Japan," *Washington Post,* 10 February 2000. Data from Amnesty International available at www.amnesty.org/.

---

crime has an economic basis; instead, crime might be linked to **socialization,** personality, intelligence, or some other trait unrelated to class position or income. In this section we examine traits and patterns that may influence the crime rate.

socialization The process in which a person learns to adapt to the cultural and social institutions in society.

Ecological and Seasonal Differences

A distinct relationship exists between crime rates and urbanization. Areas with rural and suburban populations are likely to have much lower crime rates than large urban areas. This finding, consistent over many years, suggests that the crime problem is linked to the social forces operating in the nation's largest cities—overcrowding, poverty, social inequality, narcotics use, and racial conflict.

UCR data also show that crime rates are highest in the summer months, most likely because (1) people spend so much time outdoors and are less likely to secure their homes and (2) schools are closed and young people have greater opportunity for criminal activity. Crime rates are also related to the region of the country. The

© 2000 AP/Wide World Photos

Crimes are more common in urban areas in the West and South. Here, a police helicopter hovers over a Target store in Culver City, California, after gunmen invaded the closed discount store and ordered employees to the floor in a botched robbery attempt. Other police and sheriffs' forces can be seen on the ground outside the store. Two people were arrested, no shots were fired, and no one was injured.

West and South usually have significantly higher rates than the Midwest and New England.

Gender and Crime

There are many explanations for the gender differences in the crime rate. To research this topic on InfoTrac College Edition, use "gender" and "crime" as key words.

UCR arrest data consistently show that males have a much higher crime rate than females. The UCR arrest statistics indicate that the overall male-female arrest ratio is about 3.5 male offenders to 1 female offender; for serious violent crimes, the ratio is closer to 4 males to 1 female; murder arrests, 8.1 males to 1 female. Self-report studies show that males commit more serious crimes, such as robbery, assault, and burglary, than females. However, although the patterns in self-reports parallel official data, the ratios seem smaller. In other words, males self-report more criminal behavior than females, but not to the degree suggested by official data.

Explaining Gender Differences Traditionally, gender differences in the crime rate were explained by the biological differences between the sexes (males are stronger, there are hormonal differences, and so on) or by the fact that girls were socialized to be less aggressive than boys and consequently developed moral values that strongly discouraged antisocial behavior. These values helped shield females from pro-crime influences, such as the behavior of delinquent peers, an influence to which males are decidedly more vulnerable.[31]

These views, however, are now being challenged by the rapid rise in the female crime rate. Some experts attribute this to the emergence of a "new female criminal" whose criminal activity mirrors the changing role of women in modern society.[32] As women's roles in the workplace have become more similar to men's, it is not surprising that their crime rates are converging. As a result, there has been a rise in female participation in traditionally male-oriented forms of criminality such as juvenile gang membership.[33]

Race and Crime

Official crime data indicate that minority group members are involved in a disproportionate share of criminal activity. According to UCR reports, African Americans make up about 12 percent of the general population, yet they account for about 38 percent of Part I violent crime arrests and 31 percent of property crime arrests. They also are responsible for a disproportionate number of Part II arrests (except for alcohol-related arrests, which detain primarily white offenders). African Americans are arrested for murder, rape, and robbery at a rate higher than their relative representation in the population; an absolute majority of people arrested for murder and robbery are African Americans.

These data have proven to be controversial. Some criminologists argue that racial differences in the crime rate are caused by law enforcement practices that discriminate against African Americans. In contrast, other experts view the official crime statistics as being an accurate reflection of the African-American crime rate. Their view is that racism, differential opportunity, powerlessness, and other social problems in the United States have resulted in a higher African-American crime rate as an expression of anger and frustration. For example, as economic competition between the races grows, interracial homicides do likewise; economic and political rivalries lead to greater levels of interracial violence.[34]

Many young black males believe they are unfairly targeted by biased police officers. In some jurisdictions, such as Washington, D.C., almost half of the young African-American men are under control of the justice system on any given day. Is it possible that this reflects racism and discrimination and a violation of their civil rights?[35] African Americans also have a significantly greater chance of being the target of violence. Nonwhites at birth are more than five times as likely to become murder victims as whites. Yet, when African Americans are the victims of crime, their plight receives less public concern and media attention than that afforded white victims.[36] These data indicate why the crime problem is of special significance for the black community.

To read more about race and crime, go to InfoTrac College Edition and read Maya Bell, "Census Data Show Race, Crime Inextricably Linked," *Knight-Ridder/Tribune News Service,* July 25, 2001 pK5871.

Social Class and Crime

Researchers have used UCR data in conjunction with census data to determine whether crime is associated with poverty, unemployment, and lower-class status.[37] Official data seem to indicate that crime rates are highest in deprived, inner-city slum areas and that the level of poverty in an area can predict its crime rate.

A number of explanations have been offered for the association between social class and official crime rates. One view is that the social forces in a high-risk, socially disorganized neighborhood—poverty, dilapidated housing, poor schools, broken families, drugs, and street gangs—significantly increase the likelihood that residents will engage in criminality. Another view is that crime rates are high in deteriorated areas where the disadvantaged and the affluent live side by side. In these neighborhoods, social differences are magnified, and less affluent residents perceive a feeling of relative deprivation and social inequality that results in a higher crime rate.[38]

Age and Crime

Official statistics tell us that young people are arrested at a disproportionate rate to their numbers in the population; victim surveys generate similar findings for

Arrest rate per 100,000 persons

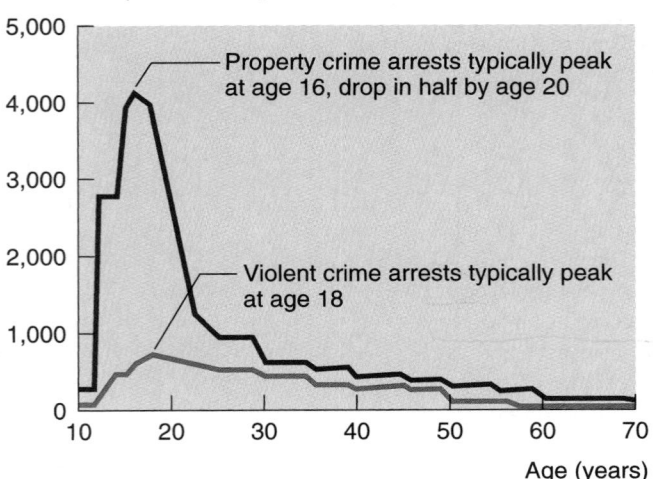

Figure 2.5
The relationship between age and serious crime arrests

Source: FBI, Uniform Crime Report, 2001, p. 226.

crimes in which assailant age can be determined. As a general rule, the peak age for property crime is believed to be sixteen and for violence, eighteen (Figure 2.5). In contrast, the elderly are particularly resistant to the temptations of crime; elderly males ages sixty-five and over are predominantly arrested for alcohol-related matters (public drunkenness and drunk driving) and elderly females for larceny (shoplifting). The elderly crime rate has remained stable for the past twenty years.

When violence rates surged in the 1980s, the increase was due almost entirely to young people; the adult violence rate remained rather stable. How can the age-crime relationship be explained? One factor is lifestyle; many young people are part of a youth culture that favors risk taking, short-run hedonism, and other behaviors that may involve them in law violation. Youths have limited financial resources and may resort to theft and drug dealing for income. The high-risk lifestyle of most youths ends as they mature and become involved in forming a family and a career.[39] Some adolescents may desist from crime when they begin to understand that the chances of winning friends, happiness, and wealth via crime are limited. Another explanation is biological: young people have the energy, strength, and physical skill needed to commit crime, all of which erode with age.[40] Some experts believe that social and legal forces influence the association between crime and age. The upsurge in teen crime in the 1980s may be attributed to the easy availability of guns in the hands of immature teens. This relationship is examined in the following Policy, Programs, and Issues in Criminal Justice feature.

Persistence and Crime: Career Criminals Criminologists now recognize that there are people who enter into a life of crime early in their adolescence and maintain a high rate of criminal violations throughout their lifetime. These chronic offenders are immune to both the ravages of age and the punishments of the justice system. More important, this small group may be responsible for a significant portion of all serious criminal behavior.

Chronic offenders can be distinguished from conventional criminals. The latter category contains law violators who may commit and be apprehended for a single instance of criminal behavior, usually of relatively minor seriousness—shoplifting, simple assault, petty larceny, and so on. The chronic offender is one who has serious and persistent brushes with the law, who is building a career in crime, and whose behavior may be excessively violent and destructive.

The concept of the chronic offender is most closely associated with the research efforts of Marvin Wolfgang and his associates at the University of Pennsylvania. In 1972 Wolfgang, Robert Figlio, and Thorsten Sellin published a landmark study entitled *Delinquency in a Birth Cohort.*[41] Wolfgang, Figlio, and Sellin used official records to follow the criminal careers of a cohort of 9,945 boys born in Philadelphia in 1945 until they reached age eighteen in 1963. About two-thirds of the cohort (6,470) never had contact with police authorities, while the remaining 3,475 had at least one contact with the police during their minority. Of these, a relatively small group of 627 boys were arrested fives times or more. These chronic offenders were responsible for 5,305 arrests, or 51.9 percent of the total. Even more striking was the involvement of chronic offenders in serious criminal acts. Of the entire sample, they committed 71 percent of the homicides, 73 percent of the rapes, 82 percent of the robberies, and 69 percent of the aggravated assaults. Arrest and punishment did little to deter them. In fact, punishment was inversely related to chronicity—the stricter the sanctions they received, the more likely they were to engage in repeated criminal behavior.

Policy, Programs, and Issues in Criminal Justice

Teens and Guns

Alfred Blumstein, one of the nation's leading experts on crime rates, finds that the sharp swings in the homicide rate can be linked to the association between children and guns. His meticulous analysis stands in contrast to the dire warnings that were issued when the teen murder rates skyrocketed in the 1980s. Some experts then warned that the nation was breeding a new generation of "superpredators," highly violent, amoral youth. These chronic offenders were responsible for the upsurge in violent crime.

Blumstein's analysis of existing data showed that in the 1980s handgun homicides committed by juveniles younger than eighteen quadrupled, and the number of long-gun (rifle and shotgun) homicides doubled; in contrast, the number of non-gun homicides declined about 20 percent. Why the sudden shift in the means used to commit murder? A major change occurred after 1985: young people were acquiring handguns in alarming numbers. Older people may have had more handguns during this period, but they appear to have exercised greater restraint in their use.

Why did gun possession translate into increased teen murder rates? Blumstein argues that it is widely recognized that teenage males are poor dispute resolvers; they have always fought to settle their disputes. When they fight with fists, the conflict evolves relatively slowly; the loser will eventually find a way to withdraw, or a third party, observing the incident, will have time to intervene. The dynamics are extremely different when a handgun is present; the conflict escalates well before anyone can retreat or intervene. Once handguns become prevalent in a neighborhood, each person who carries one has an incentive to make a preemptive strike before his adversary does.

Between 1985 and 1993, the weapons involved in settling young people's disputes changed from fists and knives to handguns—and more recently, to semiautomatic pistols, which have much greater firepower and lethality.

Blumstein's observations suggest that the growth in homicide committed by young people during the 1980s was attributable more to the weapons they used than to the emergence of inadequately socialized cohorts of "superpredators." If American youth were truly becoming more vicious, then one would expect to see a growth in homicides by all forms of weaponry rather than by only handguns. Blumstein finds that teenagers had disputes as they always had, but that the availability and lethality of

handguns, and later semiautomatic pistols, resulted in an increase in homicides.

Why did teen murder rates decline after 1993? A number of social and legal changes resulted in a decline in possessing and carrying weapons. Police became more concerned about weapons, especially in the hands of young people, and began to increase the number of arrests made for carrying weapons. They adopted aggressive stop-and-frisk tactics to search for concealed weapons. Community groups in many cities also took an active role in negotiating truces among gangs and seeking to establish norms that precluded the carrying of guns.

Important federal initiatives also are likely to have contributed to the decline. The Brady Handgun Violence Prevention Act (P.L. 103-159) became effective in 1994, the first year of the decline. There are also approaches by the Bureau of Alcohol, Tobacco and Firearms (ATF) to identify dealers and individuals disproportionately involved in the sale or purchase of "crime guns." ATF tries to trace back to the original dealers guns seized by law enforcement. Such efforts may lead not only to deterring inappropriate handgun transactions but to making guns harder to obtain.

All these efforts have a mutually reinforcing effect. A reduction in the carrying of handguns, because of either the threat of confiscation or the difficulty in acquiring them, would lead to a reduced incentive for others to carry, thereby reducing the likelihood of handgun homicides, especially among the young people for whom it is so deadly.

Critical Thinking

Considering the danger, should all handguns be banned? Is there a purpose for carrying a handgun aside from shooting someone else? Do you own a handgun and if so why? If not, why not?

InfoTrac College Edition Research

The InfoTrac College Edition has numerous articles dealing with the issue of teens and guns. Use "teens" and "guns" as a subject to access the most recent ones.

Source: Alfred Blumstein, "Why Is Crime Falling—or Is It?" in *Perspectives on Crime and Justice: 2000–2001* (Washington, D.C.: National Institute of Justice, 2002).

Since the Philadelphia survey was carried out, a number of other independent studies, including one of a larger Philadelphia cohort of children born in 1958, have also confirmed the existence of a repeat offender.[42]

The chronic offender research indicates that young persistent offenders grow up to become adult repeat offenders. This phenomenon is referred to as *persistence* or continuity of crime. Chronic delinquents who commit the most serious violent acts as youngsters have the greatest chance of later becoming adult offenders.[43] Youthful offenders who persist are more likely to abuse alcohol, get into trouble while in military service, become economically dependent, have lower aspirations, get divorced or separated, and have a weak employment record.

A number of criminologists have suggested that chronic offending is caused by some individual trait, genetic condition, or physical characteristic.[44] These conditions may exist before birth or may be a function of birth complications—factors that for all practical purposes are uncontrollable. Some preliminary research efforts indicate that such factors as limited intelligence (as measured by IQ tests) and impulsive personality predict chronic offending.[45]

The chronic offender concept has had a great impact on the criminal justice system. If a small group of offenders commits almost all of the serious crime, then it stands to reason that their incarceration might have an appreciable influence on the crime rate. This thought pattern has been responsible for the recent spate of "get-tough" laws designed to put habitual offenders behind bars for long periods of time. As a consequence of these get-tough sentences, the prison population has trended upward as crime rates have fallen.

Crime Victims

Whereas the UCR and self-report surveys help us determine the characteristics of criminals, the NCVS data provide a snapshot of the social and demographic characteristics of its victims. What are these characteristics?

Gender   Gender affects victimization risk. Men are much more likely than women to be victims of robbery and aggravated assault; they are also more likely to experience theft, but the differences are less pronounced. Although females are far more likely to be the victim of sexual assault, the NCVS estimates that 0.2 males are assaulted per 1,000 population; assuming a male population of 140 million, that means that more than 28,000 males are raped or sexually assaulted each year. About 1.9 women are raped or sexually assaulted per 1,000 population.

When men are the victims of violent crime, the perpetrator is usually described as a stranger. Women are much more likely to be attacked by a relative than men are; about two-thirds of all attacks against women are committed by a husband or boyfriend, family member, or acquaintance. In two-thirds of sexual assaults as well, the victim knows the attacker.

Age   Young people face a much greater victimization risk than older persons do. Victim risk diminishes rapidly after age twenty-five. The elderly, who are thought of as being the helpless targets of predatory criminals, are actually much safer than their grandchildren. People over age sixty-five, who make up 14 percent of the population, account for 1 percent of violent victimizations; teens ages twelve to nineteen, who also make up 14 percent of the population, account for more than 30 percent of crime victims.

The association between age and victimization may be bound up in the lifestyle shared by young people. Adolescents often stay out late at night, go to public places, and hang out with other teens who have a high risk of criminal involvement. Most adolescents ages twelve to nineteen are attacked by offenders in the same age category, while a great majority of adults are victimized by adult criminals. Teens face a high victimization risk because they spend a great deal of time in the most dangerous building in the community: the local schoolhouse!

Income   The poorest Americans might be expected to be the most likely victims of crime, since they live in areas that are crime-prone: inner-city, urban neighborhoods. The NCVS does in fact show that the least affluent (annual incomes of less than $7,500) are by far the most likely to be victims of violent crimes, and this association occurs across all gender, racial, and age groups. Whereas the poor are al-

The victim data tell us that men are much more likely than women to be victims of violent crime, but females are more likely to be victims of sexual assault. The Reverend Don Kimball, left, and his attorney, Chris Andrian, sit in front of molestation victim Ellen Brem while listening to the testimony of others allegedly molested by Kimball, June 7, 2002, in Sonoma County Superior Court in Santa Rosa, California. Convicted of molesting Brem twenty years earlier when she was thirteen, Kimball, an inactive minister, was sentenced to seven years in prison.

most twice as likely to be the victims of burglary, the wealthy are more likely to be the target of theft crimes, such as pocket picking and purse snatching. Perhaps the affluent, who sport more expensive attire and drive better-make cars, earn the attention of thieves looking for attractive targets.

Marital Status Marital status also influences victimization risk. The unmarried or never married are victimized more often than married people or widows and widowers. These relationships are probably influenced by age, gender, and lifestyle. Many of the young people who have the highest victim risk are actually too young to have been married. Younger unmarried people also go out in public more often and interact with high-risk peers, increasing their exposure to victimization. In contrast, widows, who are more likely to be older women, suffer much lower victimization rates because they interact with older people, are more likely to stay home at night, and avoid public places. These data are further evidence of the relationship between lifestyle and victimization risk.

Race One of the most important distinctions found in the NCVS data is the racial difference in the victim rate. African Americans experience violent crimes at a higher rate than other groups. NCVS data show that African Americans have strikingly higher rates of violent personal crimes than do whites. Although the race-specific risk of theft victimization is more similar, African Americans are still more likely to be victimized than whites.

Crimes committed against African Americans tend to be more serious than those committed against whites. For example, African Americans experience higher rates of aggravated assault, whereas whites are more often the victims of simple assault. The most striking difference recorded by the NCVS is in the incidence of robberies: African Americans are about three times as likely to become robbery victims as whites.

Young African-American males are also at great risk for homicide victimization. They face a murder risk four or five times greater than that of young African-American females, five to eight times higher than that of young white males, and sixteen to twenty-two times higher than that of young white females.[46]

Why do these discrepancies exist? One clear reason is that young black males tend to live in the largest U.S. cities, in areas beset by alcohol and drug abuse, poverty, racial discrimination, and violence. Forced to live in the most dangerous areas, their lifestyle places them in the highest at-risk population group.

Ecological Factors   The NCVS data parallel the crime patterns found in the UCR. Most victimizations occur in large urban areas; rural and suburban victim rates are far lower. Most incidents occur during the evening hours (6 P.M. to 6 A.M.). Generally, more serious crimes take place after 6 P.M.; less serious, before 6 P.M. For example, aggravated assaults occur at night, whereas simple assaults are more likely to take place during the daytime. It seems that the best way to avoid victimization is to stay home at night with doors and windows locked! The most likely site for a victimization—especially a violent crime such as rape, robbery, and aggravated assault—is an open, public area such as a street, park, or field. Sadly, one of the most dangerous public places is a public school building. About 10 percent of all U.S. youth ages twelve to nineteen (approximately two million) are crime victims while on school grounds each year.

An overwhelming number of victimizations involve a single person. Most victims report that their assailant was not armed (except for the crime of robbery, where about half the offenders carry weapons). In the robberies and assaults involving injury, however, a majority of the assailants are reported as armed. The use of guns and knives is about equal, and there does not seem to be a pattern of a particular weapon being used for a particular crime.

Victim-Offender Relationships   The NCVS can tell us something about the characteristics of people who commit crime. This information is available only on criminals who actually came in contact with the victim through such crimes as rape, assault, or robbery.

About 50 percent of all violent crimes are committed by strangers. The other half of violent crimes are committed by people who were known to the victim, including family members, spouses, parents, children, and siblings. Women seem much more likely than men to be victimized by acquaintances; a majority of female assault victims know their assailants.

A majority of victims report that the crime was committed by a single offender over the age of twenty. About 25 percent of victims indicate that their assailant was a young person twelve to twenty years of age. This may reflect the criminal activities of youth gangs and groups in the United States.

Whites are the offenders in a majority of single-offender rapes and assaults; there is no racial pattern in single-offender robberies. However, multiple-offender robberies are more likely to be committed by African Americans.

Repeat Victimization   Does prior victimization enhance or reduce the chances of future victimization? Stable patterns of behavior may encourage victimization, and a few people who maintain them may become "chronic victims," constantly the target of predatory crimes.

Most research does in fact show that individuals who have had prior victimization experiences have a significantly higher chance of repeat victimization than do people who have been nonvictims.[47] Research also shows that households that have experienced victimization are the ones most likely to experience it again.[48] Repeat victimizations are most likely to occur in areas with high crime rates; one study found that during a four-year period, 40 percent of all trauma patients in an urban medical center in Ohio were repeat victims.[49]

What factors predict chronic victimizations? Some combination of personal and social factors may possibly encourage victimization risk. Most revictimizations happen soon after a previous crime, suggesting that repeat victims share some personal characteristics that make them a magnet for predators.[50]

Causes of Crime and Victimization

Although the various sources of criminal statistics can tell us about the nature of crime patterns and trends, knowing why an individual commits crime in the first place is also important. Such knowledge is critical if programs are to be devised to deter or prevent crime. If, for example, people commit crime because they are poor and desperate, the key to crime prevention might be a job program and government economic aid. If, however, the root cause of crime is a poor family life marked by conflict and abuse, then providing jobs will not help lower the crime rate; family counseling and parenting skills courses would prove to be more effective.

There is still a great deal of uncertainty about the "real" cause of crime. Some of the more popular explanations are discussed in the following sections.

Choice Theory: Because They Want To

One prominent view of criminality is that people choose to commit crime after weighing the potential benefits and consequences of their criminal acts. According to **choice theory,** people commit crime if they believe it will provide immediate benefits without the threat of long-term risks. For example, before concluding a drug sale, experienced traffickers will mentally balance the chances of making a large profit with the consequences of being apprehended and punished for drug dealing. They know that most drug deals are not detected and that the potential for enormous, untaxed profits is great. They evaluate their lifestyle and determine how much cash they need to maintain their standard of living, which is usually extravagant. They may have borrowed to finance the drug deal, and their creditors are not usually reasonable if loans cannot be repaid promptly. They also realize that they could be the target of a "sting" operation by undercover agents and, if caught, will get a long mandatory sentence in a forbidding federal penitentiary. If they conclude that the potential for profits is great enough, their need for cash urgent, and the chances of apprehension minimal, they will carry out the deal. If, however, they believe that the transaction will bring them only a small profit and a large risk of apprehension and punishment, they may forgo the deal as too risky. Crime, then, is a matter of personal choice.

In sum, according to this view, crimes are events that occur when offenders decide to risk crime after considering personal needs (a desire for money, excitement, experience, or revenge), situational factors (how well a target is protected, the risk of apprehension, the chance for hurting bystanders), and legal factors (the efficiency of police, the threat of legal punishment, the effect of a prior criminal record on future punishment). The decision to commit a specific crime is thus a matter of personal decision making based on a weighing of available information.[51]

The main principles of choice theory are the following:

1. All people of their own free will can choose between conventional or criminal behaviors.
2. For some people, criminal solutions are more attractive because they require less effort for greater gain.
3. People will refrain from antisocial acts if they believe that the punishment or pain they will receive for their actions will be greater than any potential gain.
4. The punishments threatened by the existing criminal law are the primary deterrent to crime.

Sociobiological Theory: It's in Their Blood

In recent years, there has been interest in finding a biological basis of crime. Modern **biosocial theories** believe that elements of the environment—family life, community

choice theory The school of thought holding that people will engage in delinquent and criminal behavior after weighing the consequences and benefits of their actions. Delinquent behavior is a rational choice made by a motivated offender who perceives the chances of gain outweigh any perceived punishment or loss.

The principles of choice theory can be traced to the work of eighteenth-century criminologist Cesare Beccaria. To read about Beccaria's life history and the formulation of his ideas, go to www.criminology.fsu.edu/crimtheory/beccaria.htm

biosocial theory The school of thought holding that human behavior is a function of the interaction of biochemical, neurological, and genetic factors with environmental stimulus.

To read about the early history of biological criminology and its "founding father" Cesare Lombroso, go to www.tld.jcu.edu.au/hist/stats/lomb/

factors—interact with biological factors—neurological makeup—to control and influence behavior. For example, children who suffer deficits caused by birth complications will be predisposed to committing violent acts as they mature if they also are forced to grow up in a dysfunctional and negative home environment.[52]

Sociobiological theories can be divided into three broad areas of focus: biochemical factors, neurological problems, and genetic abnormalities.

Biochemical Factors   Crime and violence are possibly functions of biochemical abnormality. Such biochemical factors as vitamin and mineral deficiencies, improper diet, environmental contaminants, and allergies have been linked to antisocial behavior. Some of the most important research on diet and crime has been conducted by Stephen Schoenthaler. In one study of 803 New York City public schools, Schoenthaler found academic performance of 1.1 million schoolchildren rose 16 percent and the number of "learning-disabled" children fell from 125,000 to 74,000 in one year after school diets were modified.[53] In a similar experiment conducted in a correctional institution, violent and nonviolent antisocial behavior fell on average 48 percent among 8,047 offenders after dietary changes were implemented.

A great deal of research has linked hormonal activity to aggressive behavior. Some criminologists argue that gender differences in the crime rate can be linked to the male hormone testosterone and its assumed effect on behavior.[54]

Biochemical studies also suggest that some criminal offenders have abnormal levels of organic or inorganic substances in their bodies that influence their behavior and in some way make them prone to antisocial behavior. When criminologists Paul Stretesky and Michael Lynch examined air lead concentrations across counties in the United States they found that areas with the highest concentrations of lead also reported the highest level of homicide.[55]

Neurological Problems   Another area of interest to biocriminologists is the relationship of brain activity to behavior. Biocriminologists have used the electroencephalogram to record the electrical impulses given off by the brain. Preliminary studies indicate that 50 to 60 percent of those with behavior disorders display abnormal recordings.[56]

People with an abnormal cerebral structure, referred to as *minimal brain dysfunction,* may experience periods of explosive rage that can lead to violent episodes.[57] Brain dysfunction is sometimes manifested as an attention deficit disorder, another suspected cause of antisocial behavior. About 3 percent of all U.S. children, primarily boys, are believed to suffer from this disorder, and it is the most common reason children are referred to mental health clinics. The condition usually results in poor school performance, bullying, stubbornness, and a lack of response to discipline.[58]

Genetic Abnormalities   Violent behavior is possibly inherited and a function of a person's genetic makeup. One approach has been to evaluate the behavior of adopted children. If an adopted child's behavior patterns run parallel to those of his or her biological parents, it would be strong evidence to support a genetic basis for crime. Studies conducted in Europe have indicated that the criminality of the biological father is a strong predictor of a child's antisocial behavior.[59] The probability that a youth will engage in crime is significantly enhanced when both biological and adoptive parents exhibit criminal tendencies.

One method of studying the genetic nature of crime is to compare the behavior of twins. Using twin pairs, it has been found that genetic effects are a significant predictor of problem behaviors in children as young as three years old.[60] Whereas the behavior of some twin pairs seems to be influenced by their environment—that is, the twins are raised in similar circumstances and therefore equally influenced by their environment—others display behavior disturbances that can only be explained by their genetic similarity.[61] Analyzing the effect of the environment on twin behavior is the goal of the famous Minnesota Study of Twins Reared Apart. This research compares the behavior of twin pairs that were raised together with others who were separated at birth and in some cases did not even know of each other's existence. The study shows some striking similarities in behavior and ability for twin pairs raised apart. An identical twin reared away from a co-twin has about as good a chance of being similar to the co-twin in terms of personality, interests, and attitudes as one who has been reared with the co-twin. The conclusion: similarities between twins are due to genes, not the environment.[62]

Criminologist David Rowe has reviewed the available research and concludes that individuals who share genes are alike in personality regardless of how they are reared; in contrast, environment induces little or no personality resemblance in twin pairs.[63] There is evidence, then, that the onset of criminal behavior patterns is at least partly genetic.[64]

However, as critics warn, it is probably too early to accept a genetic basis of crime. The Minnesota study uses relatively small samples, so findings are not conclusive. It is therefore possible that what appears to be a genetic effect picked up by various attempts to research the behavior of twins is actually the effect of sibling influence on criminality, referred to as the contagion effect: it is possible that if one twin is crime-oriented that behavior will be learned or copied by the co-twin. It is possible that having an antisocial sibling in the household influences the onset of criminality, even if there is no direct genetic linkage.[65]

Psychological Theory: It's in Their Heads

Sometimes when we hear of a particularly gruesome crime, we say of the criminal, "That guy must be crazy." It comes as no surprise, then, that some experts believe that criminality is caused by psychological factors.

There are actually a number of views on this subject.

Psychoanalytic Theory   According to the **psychoanalytic view**, some people encounter problems during their early development that cause an imbalance in their personality.

The most deeply disturbed are referred to as psychotics who cannot restrain their impulsive behavior. One type of psychosis is schizophrenia, a condition marked by incoherent thought processes, a lack of insight, hallucinations, feelings of persecution, and so on. Schizophrenics may suffer delusions and feel persecuted, worthless, and alienated.[66] Other offenders may suffer from a garden variety of mood and behavior disorders that render them histrionic, depressed, antisocial, or narcissistic.[67] They may suffer from conduct disorders, which include long histories of antisocial behavior or mood disorders characterized by disturbance in expressed emotions. Among the latter is *bipolar disorder*, in which moods alternate between periods of wild elation and deep depression.[68] Some offenders are driven by an unconscious desire to be punished for prior sins, either real or imaginary. As a result, they may violate the law or even harm their parents to gain attention.

According to the psychoanalytic view, crime is a manifestation of feelings of oppression and people's inability to develop the proper psychological defenses and rationales to keep these feelings under control. Criminality may allow these troubled people to survive by producing positive psychic results: it helps them to feel free and independent, it gives them the possibility of excitement and the chance to use their skills and imagination. It also provides them with the promise of positive gain; it allows them to blame others for their predicament (for example, the police), and it gives them a chance to rationalize their sense of failure ("If I hadn't gotten into trouble, I could have been a success").[69]

Social Learning   Another psychological view is that criminal behavior is learned through interactions with others. One assumption is that people act aggressively

Findings from the Minnesota Study of Twins Raised Apart can be accessed at www.psych.umn.edu/psylabs/mtfs/special.htm

psychoanalytic view   This position holds that criminals are driven by unconscious thought patterns, developed in early childhood, that control behaviors over the life course.

Psychoanalytic theory was founded by famed psychiatrist Sigmund Freud. For a collection of links to libraries, museums, and biographical materials related to Sigmund Freud and his works, go to http://users.rcn.com/brill/freudarc.html

Criminal Justice and the Media

The Media and Violence

Does the media influence behavior? Does broadcast violence cause aggressive behavior in viewers? What about music? This has become a hot topic because of the persistent violence in television and films and the violent lyrics in popular songs. Critics have called for drastic measures, ranging from banning TV violence to putting warning labels on heavy metal albums because of a fear that listening to the words produces delinquency.

If there is in fact a TV-violence link, the problem is indeed alarming. Systematic viewing of TV begins at two-and-a-half years of age and continues at a high level during the preschool and early school years. It has been estimated that children ages two to five watch TV for 27.8 hours each week; children ages six to eleven, 24.3 hours per week; and teens, 23 hours per week. Market research indicates that adolescents ages eleven to fourteen rent violent horror movies at a higher rate than any other age group. Children this age use older peers and siblings and apathetic parents to gain access to R-rated films. More than 40 percent of U.S. households now have cable TV, which features violent films and shows. Even children's programming is saturated with violence.

The fact that children watch so much violent TV is not surprising, considering the findings of a well-publicized study conducted by UCLA researchers that found that at least 10 shows broadcast on network TV make heavy use of violence. Of the 161 television movies monitored (every one that aired that season), 23 raised concerns about their use of violence, violent theme, violent title, or inappropriate portrayals of a scene. Of the 118 theatrical films monitored (every one that aired that season), 50 raised concerns about their use of violence. A University of Pennsylvania study also found that children's programming contained an average of 32 violent acts per hour, that 56 percent had violent characters, and that 74 percent had characters who became the victims of violence (though "only 3.3 percent had characters who were actually killed"). In all, the average child views eight thousand TV murders before finishing elementary school.

What is the connection between watching violent media and violent behavior?

- Violent media can provide aggressive "scripts" that children store in memory. Repeated exposure to these scripts can increase their retention and lead to changes in attitudes.

- Children learn from what they observe. In the same way they learn cognitive and social skills from their parents and friends, children learn to be violent from television.

- Television violence increases the arousal levels of viewers and makes them more prone to act aggressively. Studies measuring the galvanic skin response of subjects—a physical indication of arousal based on the amount of electricity conducted across the palm of the hand—have shown that viewing violent television programs leads to increased arousal levels in young children.

- Watching television violence promotes such negative attitudes as suspiciousness and the expectation that the viewer will become involved in violence. Those who watch television frequently come to view aggression and violence as common and socially acceptable behavior.

- Television violence allows aggressive youths to justify their behavior. It is possible that, instead of causing violence, television helps violent youths rationalize their behavior as a socially acceptable and common activity.

- Television violence may disinhibit aggressive behavior, which is normally controlled by other learning processes. Disinhibition takes place when adults are viewed as being rewarded for violence and when violence is seen as socially acceptable. This contradicts previous learning experiences in which violent behavior was viewed as wrong.

Such distinguished bodies as the American Psychological Association, the National Institute of Mental Health, and

because as children they experienced violence firsthand, either observing it at home or being its target from parents. Children model their behavior after the violent acts of adults. Observed and experienced violence may have an interactive effect: kids who live in high-crime neighborhoods and witness violence in the community and at home, who are the direct victims of domestic and community-based violence, are the ones most likely to commit crime.[70]

One area of particular interest to **social learning** is whether the media can influence violence. Studies have shown that youths exposed to aggressive, antisocial behavior on television and in movies are likely to copy that violent behavior. Laboratory studies generally conclude that violence on television can lead to aggres-

social learning The view that behavior patterns are modeled and learned in interactions with others.

the National Research Council support the TV-violence link. They base their conclusions on research efforts such as a recent one (2002) conducted by Jeffrey Johnson and his associates at Columbia University. This study found that fourteen-year-old boys who watched less than one hour of TV per a day later got into an average of nine fights resulting in injury; in contrast, adolescent males watching one to three hours of TV per day got into an average of twenty-eight fights as they grew, and those watching more than three hours got into an average of forty-two fights. Of those watching one to three hours per day, 22.5 percent later showed aggression or engaged in violence, such as assaults or robbery, in their adulthood; in contrast, 28.8 percent of kids who regularly watched more than three hours of TV in a twenty-four-hour period engaged in violent acts as adults.

According to a recent analysis of all scientific data since 1975, Brad Bushman and Craig Anderson found that the weight of the evidence is that watching violence on TV does correlate to aggressive behaviors and that the newest most methodologically sophisticated works show the greatest amount of association. The weight of the experimental results, then, indicates that violent media has an immediate impact on people with a preexisting tendency toward crime and violence.

Although this research is quite persuasive, not all criminologists accept that watching TV or movies and listening to heavy metal music eventually leads to violent and antisocial behavior. There is also little evidence that areas that experience the highest levels of violent TV viewing also have rates of violent crime that are above the norm. Millions of children watch violence every night but do not become violent criminals. In fact, despite the prevalence of violent TV shows, films, and video games, which have become a universal norm, the violence rate among teens was in a significant decline during the 1990s. If violent TV shows did, indeed, cause interpersonal violence, then there should be few ecological and regional patterns in the crime rate, yet there are many. Put another way, how can regional differences in the violence rate be explained considering the fact that people all across the nation watch the same TV shows and films?

Critical Thinking

1. Should the government control the content of TV shows and limit the amount of weekly violence? How could the national news be shown if violence were omitted? What about boxing matches or hockey games?
2. How can we explain the fact that millions of kids watch violent TV shows and remain nonviolent? If there is a TV-violence link, how can we explain the fact that violence rates may have been higher in the Old West than they are today? Do you think kids who belong to violent gangs stay home and watch TV shows?

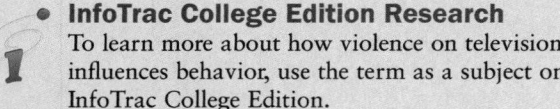

InfoTrac College Edition Research

To learn more about how violence on television influences behavior, use the term as a subject on InfoTrac College Edition.

Sources: Jeffrey Johnson, Patricia Cohen, Elizabeth Smailes, Stephanie Kasen, and Judith Brook "Television Viewing and Aggressive Behavior During Adolescence and Adulthood" *Science* 295 (2002): 2468–2471; Brad Bushman and Craig Anderson, "Media Violence and the American Public," *American Psychologist* 56 (2001): 477–489; UCLA Center for Communication Policy, Television Violence Monitoring Project (Los Angeles, Calif., 1995); "Hollywood Is Blamed in Token Booth Attack," *Boston Globe,* 28 November 1995, 30; Garland White, Janet Katz, and Kathryn Scarborough, "The Impact of Professional Football Games upon Violent Assaults on Women," *Violence and Victims* 7 (1992): 157–171; Simon Singer, "Rethinking Subcultural Theories of Delinquency and the Cultural Resources of Youth" (Paper presented at the annual meeting of the American Society of Criminology, Phoenix, Arizona, November 1993); Albert Reiss and Jeffrey Roth, eds., *Understanding and Preventing Violence* (Washington, D.C.: National Academy Press, 1993); "Seventy-Nine Percent in Survey Link Violence on TV and Crime," *Boston Globe,* 19 December 1993, 17; Scott Snyder, "Movies and Juvenile Delinquency: An Overview," *Adolescence* 26 (1991): 121–131; Steven Messner, "Television Violence and Violent Crime: An Aggregate Analysis," *Social Problems* 33 (1986): 218–235; Candace Kruttschnitt, Linda Heath, and David Ward, "Family Violence, Television Viewing Habits, and Other Adolescent Experiences Related to Violent Criminal Behavior," *Criminology* 243 (1986): 235–267; Jonathan Freedman, "Television Violence and Aggression: A Rejoinder," *Psychological Bulletin* 100 (1986): 372–378; Wendy Wood, Frank Wong, and J. Gregory Chachere, "Effects of Media Violence on Viewers' Aggression in Unconstrained Social Interaction," *Psychological Bulletin* 109 (1991): 371–383.

sive behavior by children and teenagers who watch such programs.[71] Whether the evidence obtained in controlled laboratory studies can be applied to the real world is still being debated.[72] Considering that the average child watches more than twenty hours of TV a week, any link between TV violence and criminal behavior is important. This issue is discussed further in the Criminal Justice and the Media feature.

Psychopathic Personality   Psychologists have explored the link between personality and crime. Evidence shows that aggressive youth have unstable personality structures often marked by hyperactivity, impulsiveness, and instability.

© AP/Wide World Photos

Michael McDermott killed seven co-workers at Edgewater Technology on December 26, 2000. At his trial McDermott, forty-three, calmly told the court that he had been given a mission from the Archangel Michael to prevent the Holocaust. He said he had heard Hitler's thoughts, and he sent family members of the victims fleeing from the courtroom in tears when he methodically described killing the "Nazis" one by one. The jury rejected his insanity defense and found him guilty of seven counts of first-degree murder.

psychopathic (antisocial, sociopathic) personality Psychopaths are chronically antisocial individuals who are always in trouble, and who do not learn from either experience or punishment They are loners who engage in frequent callous and hedonistic behaviors, are emotionally immature, and lack responsibility, judgment, and empathy.

One area of particular interest to criminology is the identification of the **psychopathic** (sometimes referred to as the **antisocial** or **sociopathic**) **personality**. Psychopaths are believed to be dangerous, aggressive, antisocial individuals who act in a callous manner. They neither learn from their mistakes nor are deterred by punishment.[73] Although they may appear charming and have at least average intelligence, psychopaths lack emotional depth, are incapable of caring for others, and maintain an abnormally low level of anxiety. They are likely to be persistent alcohol and drug abusers.[74]

The concept of the psychopathic personality is important for criminology, because it has been estimated that somewhere between 10 and 30 percent of all prison inmates can be classified as psychopaths or sociopaths or as having similar character disorders.[75] Psychopathy has also been linked to the phenomenon of serial murder.[76]

Although psychologists are still not certain of its cause, a number of factors are believed to contribute to the development of a psychopathic personality. They include having a psychopathic parent, parental rejection and lack of love during childhood, and inconsistent discipline.[77] Some psychologists suspect that psychopathy is a function of physical abnormality, especially the activity of the autonomic nervous system. Studies measuring the physical makeup of clinically diagnosed psychopaths indicate that such persons react differently to pain and have lower arousal levels to noise and environmental stimuli than do control subjects.[78] Another view is that the psychopathic personality is imprinted at birth and is relatively unaffected by socialization.[79] These people are among the most disturbed offenders who may be at risk for chronic offending.

Social Structure Theory: Because They're Poor

There seems to be an economic bias in the crime rate: prisons are filled with the poor and hopeless, not the rich and famous. Because crime patterns have a decidedly social orientation, sociological explanations of crime have predominated in criminology.

According to **social structure theory**, the United States is a stratified society. The contrast between the lifestyles of the wealthiest members of the upper class and the poorest segment of the lower class is striking. The gap between the richest and the poorest Americans seems to be growing wider; the number of families living in poverty doubled in the past decade. About twenty million high school dropouts face dead-end jobs, unemployment, and social failure. Because of their meager economic resources, lower-class citizens are often forced to live in poor areas marked by substandard housing, inadequate health care, renters rather than homeowners, poor educational opportunities, underemployment, and despair. These indicators of neighborhood disorder are highly predictive of crime rates.[80]

The problems of lower-class culture are particularly acute for racial and ethnic minorities who have an income level significantly below that of whites and an unemployment rate almost twice as high. In addition, they face the burden of racism and racial stereotyping. Research shows that whites are averse to living in or visiting black neighborhoods because they consider them crime-ridden even if these neighborhoods actually have relatively low crime rates.[81] Fear and suspicion may keep the races apart.

The crushing burden of urban poverty results in the development of a **culture of poverty**.[82] This culture is marked by apathy, cynicism, helplessness, and distrust. The culture is passed from one generation to another so that slum dwellers become part of a permanent underclass, "the truly disadvantaged."[83] Considering the social disability suffered by the impoverished, it is not surprising that they turn to crime as a means of support and survival. Forced to endure substandard housing and schools in deteriorated inner-city, socially disorganized neighborhoods, and cut off from conventional society, the urban poor are faced with a constant assault on their self-image and sense of worth. Criminal acts and drug dealing provide a means of survival in an otherwise bleak existence. In these areas the forces of social control have broken down; this is referred to as *social disorganization*.

social structure theory The view that a person's position in the social structure controls behavior. Those in the lowest socioeconomic tier are more likely to succumb to crime-promoting elements in their environment, whereas those in the highest tier enjoy social and economic advantages that insulate them from crime-producing forces.

Why does social class have such a great impact on individual behavior? To find out, go to InfoTrac College Edition and use the term as a subject guide.

culture of poverty The crushing lifestyle of slum areas produces a culture of poverty, passed from one generation to the next, marked by apathy, cynicism, feelings of helplessness, and mistrust of social institutions, such as schools, government agencies, and the police.

Robert
Hare

Social Process Theory: Socialized to Crime

Not all criminologists agree that the cause of crime can be found solely within the culture of poverty. Some argue that people commit crime as a result of the experiences they have while they are being socialized by the various organizations, institutions, and processes of society. People are most strongly influenced toward criminal behavior by poor family relationships, destructive peer-group relations, educational failure, and labeling by agents of the justice system. Although lower-class citizens have the added burdens of poverty and strain, even middle-class or upper-class citizens may turn to crime if their socialization is poor or destructive.

Social process theory points to research efforts linking family problems to crime as evidence that socialization, not social structure, is the key to understanding the onset of criminality. Family problems linked to criminality include inconsistent discipline, poor supervision, and the lack of a warm, loving, supportive parent-child relationship.[84] Parents who are supportive and effectively control their children in a noncoercive fashion—parental efficacy—are more likely to raise children who refrain from delinquency.[85] In contrast, the likelihood of delinquency increases if parents are unable to provide the type of family structure that gives children the ability to assert their individuality and regulate their own behavior.[86]

social process theory The view that an individual's interactions with key social institutions—family, school, peer group—shapes behavior.

Washington, D.C., sniper suspect John Lee Malvo, left, was seventeen at the time of his arrest. Social process theorists might argue that he learned his criminal ways from his stepfather, John Allen Muhammad, right, before participating in their murderous rampage, which left ten dead.

Educational experience has also been found to have a significant impact on behavioral choices. Youths who fail at school and eventually drop out are the ones most likely to engage in criminal behavior; academic performance is a significant predictor of crime and delinquency.[87] Children who fail in school have been found to offend more frequently than those who are successful in school. These children commit more serious and violent offenses, and persist in their offending into adulthood.[88] In a similar fashion, socialization within the peer group is also a significant influence on behavior. Children who maintain ties with a deviant peer group are the ones most likely to persist in criminal behavior into their adulthood.[89]

The social process approach has several independent branches. The first branch, *social learning theory,* suggests that people learn the techniques and attitudes of crime from close and intimate relationships with criminal peers; crime is a learned behavior. The second, *social control theory,* maintains that everyone has the potential to become a criminal but that most people are controlled by their bond to society. Crime occurs when the forces that bind people to society are weakened or broken. The third branch, *social reaction (labeling) theory,* says people become criminals when significant members of society label them as such and they accept those labels as a personal identity.

Put another way, social learning theory assumes people are born "good" and learn to be "bad"; social control theory assumes people are born "bad" and must be controlled in order to be "good"; social reaction theory assumes that whether "good" or "bad," people are controlled by the reactions of others.

Conflict Theory: It's a "Dog-Eat-Dog" World

Conflict theory views the economic and political forces operating in society as the fundamental causes of criminality. The criminal law and criminal justice systems are viewed as vehicles for controlling the poor members of society. The criminal justice system is believed to help the powerful and rich impose their particular morality and standards of good behavior on the entire society, while it protects their property and physical safety from the have-nots, even though the cost may be the legal rights of the lower class. Those in power control the content and direction of the law and legal system.

Crimes are defined in a way that meets the needs of the ruling classes. The theft of property worth $5 by a poor person can be punished much more severely than the misappropriation of millions by a large corporation. Those in the middle class are drawn into this pattern of control because they are led to believe that they too have a stake in maintaining the status quo and should support the views of the upper-class owners of production.[90]

An important aspect of conflict theory, radical feminist theory, tries to explain how capitalism places particular stress on women and to explicate the role of male dominance in female criminality.[91] Radical feminists view female crime as originating with the onset of male supremacy (patriarchy), the subsequent subordination of women, male aggression, and efforts of men to control women sexually.[92] They focus on the social forces that shape women's lives and experiences to explain female criminality. For example, they attempt to show how the sexual victimization of females is a function of male socialization because so many young males learn to be aggressive and exploitative of women. Exploited at home, female victims try to cope by running away and by engaging in premarital sex and substance abuse. The double standard means that female adolescents still have a much narrower range of acceptable behavior than male adolescents. Any sign of misbehavior is viewed as a substantial challenge to authority that requires immediate control. Feminist scholars view the female criminal as a victim of gender inequality.

conflict theory The view that human behavior is shaped by interpersonal conflict and that those who maintain social power will use it to further their own needs.

To learn more about a popular theory of crime that takes a feminist perspective read Brenda Sims Blackwell, Christine S. Sellers, and Sheila M. Schlaupitz, "A Power-Control Theory of Vulnerability to Crime and Adolescent Role Exits—Revisited," *Canadian Review of Sociology and Anthropology,* May 2002 v39 i2 p199(20), on InfoTrac College Edition.

Developmental Theory: Things Change

According to **developmental theory**, even as toddlers, people begin relationships and behaviors that will determine their adult life course.[93] These transitions are expected to take place in order—beginning with completing school, entering the workforce, getting married, and having children. Some individuals, however, are incapable of maturing in a reasonable and timely fashion because of family, environmental, or personal problems. In some cases, transitions can occur too early—for example, when adolescents engage in precocious sex. In other cases, transitions may occur too late, such as when a student fails to graduate on time because of bad grades. Sometimes disruption of one trajectory can harm another. For example, teenage childbirth will most likely disrupt educational and career development. Because developmental theories focus on the associations between life events and deviant behaviors, they are sometimes referred to as life-course theories.

Disruptions in life's major transitions can be destructive and ultimately can promote criminality. Those who are already at risk because of socioeconomic problems or family dysfunction are the most susceptible to these awkward transitions. The cumulative impact of these disruptions sustains criminality from childhood into adulthood.

Because a transition from one stage of life to another can be a bumpy ride, the propensity to commit crimes is neither stable nor constant; it is a developmental process. A positive life experience may help some criminals desist from crime for a while, whereas a negative one may cause them to resume their activities. Criminal

developmental theory The view that social interactions developed over the life course shape behavior. Some interactions, such as involvement with deviant peers, encourage law violations, whereas others, such as marriage and military service, may help people desist from crime.

Exhibit 2.5

Concepts and theories of criminology: A review

Theory	Major Premise
Choice theory	People commit crime when they perceive that the benefits of law violation outweigh the threat and pain of punishment.
Biosocial theory	
Biochemical	Crime, especially violence, is a function of diet, vitamin intake, hormonal imbalance, or food allergies.
Neurological	Criminals and delinquents often suffer brain impairment. Attention deficit disorder and minimum brain dysfunction are related to antisocial behavior.
Genetic	Delinquent traits and predispositions are inherited. The criminality of parents can predict the delinquency of children.
Psychological theory	
Psychoanalytic	The development of personality early in childhood influences behavior for the rest of a person's life. Criminals have weak egos and damaged personalities.
Social learning	People commit crime when they model their behavior after others whom they see being rewarded for the same acts. Behavior is enforced by rewards and extinguished by punishment.
Social structure theory	
Social disorganization	The conflicts and problems of urban social life and communities control the crime rate. Crime is a product of transitional neighborhoods that manifest social disorganization and value conflict.
Strain	People who adopt the goals of society but lack the means to attain them seek alternatives, such as crime.
Social process theory	
Learning theory	People learn to commit crime from exposure to antisocial behaviors. Criminal behavior depends on the person's experiences with rewards for conventional behaviors and punishments for deviant ones. Being rewarded for deviance leads to crime.
Social control theory	A person's bond to society prevents him or her from violating social rules. If the bond weakens, the person is free to commit crime.
Self-control theory	Crime and criminality are separate concepts. People choose to commit crime when they lack self-control. People lacking self-control will seize criminal opportunities.
Conflict theory	
Conflict theory	People commit crime when the law, controlled by the rich and powerful, defines their behavior as illegal. The immoral actions of the powerful go unpunished.
Radical feminist theory	The capital system creates patriarchy, which oppresses women. Male dominance explains gender bias, violence against women, and repression.
Developmental theory	
Developmental theory	Early in life people begin relationships that determine their behavior through their life course. Life transitions control the probability of offending.

careers are said to be developmental because people are influenced by the behavior of those around them and in turn influence others' behavior. For example, a youth's antisocial behavior may turn his more conventional friends against him; their rejection solidifies and escalates his antisocial behavior.

Developmental theory also recognizes that, as people mature, the factors that influence their behavior change.[94] At first, family relations may be most influential; in later adolescence, school and peer relations predominate; in adulthood, vocational achievement and marital relations may be the most critical influences.[95] For example, some antisocial children who are in trouble throughout their adolescence may manage to find stable work and maintain intact marriages as adults; these life events help them desist from crime. In contrast, the less fortunate adolescents who develop arrest records and get involved with the wrong crowd may find themselves limited to menial jobs and at risk for criminal careers.[96]

A Final Word

There are probably so many views of crime causation because there are so many types of crimes. It is possible that all explanations are partially correct: some people commit crime because they are poorly socialized; some succumb to the obstacles placed in their path by lower-class life; others have psychological or biological problems; some are victims of class conflict. The various forms of crime theory are summarized in Exhibit 2.5. ■

SUMMARY

We get our information on crime from a number of sources. One of the most important is the Uniform Crime Report compiled by the FBI. This national survey of serious criminal acts reported to local police departments indicates that almost twelve million index (Part I) crimes (murder, rape, burglary, robbery, assault, larceny-theft, and motor vehicle theft) occurred in 2001. Questioning the validity of the UCR, critics point out that many people fail to report crime to police because of fear, apathy, or lack of respect for law enforcement. Many crime victims also do not report criminal incidents to the police because they believe that nothing can be done or that they should not get involved. However, evidence indicates that the crimes not reported to the police are less serious than reported crimes.

Questions have also been raised about the accuracy of police records and reporting practices. To remedy this situation, the federal government sponsors a massive victim survey designed to uncover the true amount of annual crime. The National Crime Victimization Survey (NCVS) reveals that about twenty-four million serious personal crimes are committed every year and that the great majority are not reported to police. A third form of information is self-report surveys, which ask offenders themselves to tell about their criminal behaviors.

The various sources of criminal statistics tell us much about the nature and patterns of crime. Rate increases have been attributed to the influence of drugs, the economy, the age structure, social decay, and other factors. All three data sources indicate that crime rates have been in decline during the past decade, although the most recent UCR data indicate that the declines may be abating.

The crime patterns found in all three data sources may be more similar than some critics believe. Crime occurs more often in large cities during the summer and at night. Some geographic areas (the South and the West) have higher crime rates than others (the Midwest and New England). Arrest and victim data indicate that males, minorities, the poor, and the young have relatively high rates of criminality. Victims of crime have many of the same demographic characteristics as criminals. They tend to be poor, young, male, and members of a minority group.

Unfortunately, the police cannot do much about crime; only about 20 percent of all reported crimes are solved by police. However, a positive relationship exists between crime seriousness and the probability of a successful clearance; that is, murders and rapes are much more often solved than car thefts or larcenies.

Diverse schools of criminological theory approach the understanding of the cause of crime and its consequences. Some focus on the individual, whereas others view social factors as the most important element in producing crime.

For an up-to-date list of Web links, go to
http://cj.wadsworth.com/siegel_essen4e.

KEY TERMS

consensus view of crime   38

conflict view of crime   39

crime   39

National Crime
 Victimization Survey
 (NCVS)   39

official crime statistics   40

Uniform Crime Report
 (UCR)   40

life history   41

self-report survey   41

index (Part I) crimes   41

nonindex (Part II) crimes   41

chronic offender   44

socialization   53

choice theory   61

biosocial theory   61

psychoanalytic view   63

social learning   64

psychopathic (antisocial,
 sociopathic) personality
 66

social structure theory   67

culture of poverty   67

social process theory   67

conflict theory   69

developmental theory   69

INFOTRAC COLLEGE EDITION EXERCISES

DO EARLY-CHILDHOOD FACTORS predetermine one's chances of becoming a victim? Some researchers believe that behavior problems appear to play an important role in determining victimization within the peer group later in life. For more on this provocative concept, read the following article, using InfoTrac College Edition: David Schwartz, Steven McFayden-Ketchum, Kenneth A. Dodge, Gregory S. Pettit, and John E. Bates, "Early Behavior Problems as a Predictor of Later Peer Group Victimization: Moderators and Mediators in the Pathways of Social Risk," *Journal of Abnormal Child Psychology 27* (1999): 191.

VICTIMS NEED a great deal of support from family and friends after their traumatic experiences. Without support they may begin to suffer depression and low self-esteem. To find out more about this topic, read Adriaan Denkers, "Factors Affecting Support after Criminal Victimization: Needed and Received Support from the Partner, the Social Network, and Distant Support Providers," *Journal of Social Psychology 139* (1999): 191.

SOME PEOPLE may be at greater risk for victimization than others. To find out about the concept of "victimization risk," search that term on InfoTrac College Edition.

QUESTIONS

1. Why are crime rates higher in the summer than during other seasons?

2. What factors account for crime rate trends?

3. What factors are present in poverty-stricken urban areas that produce high crime rates?

4. It seems logical that biological and psychological factors might explain why some people commit crime. How would a biologist or a psychologist explain the fact that crime rates are higher in the West than in the Midwest? Or that there is more crime in the summer than in the winter?

5. If crime is a routine activity, what steps should you take to avoid becoming a crime victim?

NOTES

1. For a general discussion of Marxist thought on the criminal law, see Michael Lynch, Raymond Michalowski, and W. Byron Groves, *The New Primer in Radical Criminology: Critical Perspectives on Crime, Power, and Identity,* 3rd ed. (Monsey, N.Y.: Criminal Justice Press, 2000).

2. See, for example, Lloyd Bachman, Patrick O'Malley, and Jerald Bachman, *Monitoring the Future, 2001* (Ann Arbor: University of Michigan, Institute for Social Research, 2002).

3. Callie Marie Rennison, *Criminal Victimization 2001: Changes 2000–2001 with Trends 1993–2001* (Washington, D.C.: Bureau of Justice Statistics, 2002). Hereinafter cited as *Criminal Victimization, 2001.*

4. The data used in this chapter come from Federal Bureau of Investigation, *Crime in the United States, 2000* (Washington,

D.C.: Government Printing Office, 2001); this has been updated with 2001 preliminary data released on June 24, 2002.

5. Emily Gaarder and Joanne Belknap, "Tenuous Borders: Girls Transferred to Adult Court," *Criminology 40* (2002): 481–517.

6. Carl Klockars, *The Professional Fence* (New York: Free Press, 1976); Darrell Steffensmeier, *The Fence: In the Shadow of Two Worlds* (Totowa, N.J.: Rowman and Littlefield, 1986).

7. Federal Bureau of Investigation, *Crime in the United States, 2000* (Washington, D.C.: Government Printing Office, 2001), updated with 2001 preliminary data released 2002. Hereinafter cited in notes as FBI, Uniform Crime Report, and referred to in text as Uniform Crime Report, or UCR.

8. Duncan Chappell, Gilbert Geis, Stephen Schafer, and Larry Siegel, "Forcible Rape: A Comparative Study of Offenses Known to the Police in Boston and Los Angeles," in *Studies in the Sociology of Sex,* eds. James Henslin (New York: Appleton-Century-Crofts, 1971), 169–193.

9. Leonard Savitz, "Official Statistics," in *Contemporary Criminology,* eds. Leonard Savitz and Norman Johnston (New York: Wiley, 1982), pp. 3–15.

10. *Criminal Victimization, 2001.* Data in this section come from this report.

11. A pioneering effort in self-report research is A. L. Porterfield, *Youth in Trouble* (Fort Worth, Tex.: Leo Potishman Foundation, 1946); for a review, see Robert Hardt and George Bodine, *Development of Self-Report Instruments in Delinquency Research: A Conference Report* (Syracuse, N.Y.: Syracuse University Youth Development Center, 1965). See also Fred Murphy, Mary Shirley, and Helen Witner, "The Incidence of Hidden Delinquency," *American Journal of Orthopsychology* 16 (1946): 686–696.

12. Franklyn Dunford and Delbert Elliott, "Identifying Career Criminals Using Self-Reported Data," *Journal of Research in Crime and Delinquency* 21 (1983): 57–86.

13. For example, the following studies have noted the great discrepancy between official statistics and self-report studies: Martin Gold, "Undetected Delinquent Behavior," *Journal of Research in Crime and Delinquency* 3 (1966): 27–46; James Short and F. Ivan Nye, "Extent of Undetected Delinquency, Tentative Conclusions," *Journal of Criminal Law, Criminology and Police Science* 49 (1958): 296–302; Michael Hindelang, "Causes of Delinquency: A Partial Replication and Extension," *Social Problems* 20 (1973): 471–487.

14. D. Wayne Osgood, Lloyd Johnston, Patrick O'Malley, and Jerald Bachman, "The Generality of Deviance in Late Adolescence and Early Adulthood," *American Sociological Review* 53 (1988): 81–93. See also the three works cited in previous note.

15. Lloyd Johnston, Patrick O'Malley, and Jerald Bachman, *Monitoring the Future, 2000* (Ann Arbor: University of Michigan, Institute for Social Research, 2001).

16. Michael Hindelang, Travis Hirschi, and Joseph Weis, *Measuring Delinquency* (Beverly Hills, Calif.: Sage, 1981).

17. Leonore Simon, "Validity and Reliability of Violent Juveniles: A Comparison of Juvenile Self-Reports with Adult Self-Reports" (Paper presented at the meeting of the American Society of Criminology, Boston, November 1995), 26.

18. Stephen Cernkovich, Peggy Giordano, and Meredith Pugh, "Chronic Offenders: The Missing Cases in Self-Report Delinquency," *Criminology* 76 (1985): 705–732.

19. Eric Wish, Thomas Gray, and Eliot Levine, *Recent Drug Use in Female Juvenile Detainees: Estimates from Interviews, Urinalysis, and Hair Analysis* (College Park, Md.: Center for Substance Abuse Research, 1996); Thomas Gray and Eric Wish, *Maryland Youth at Risk: A Study of Drug Use in Juvenile Detainees* (College Park, Md.: Center for Substance Abuse Research, 1993).

20. Alfred Blumstein, Jacqueline Cohen, and Richard Rosenfeld, "Trend and Deviation in Crime Rates: A Comparison of UCR and NCVS Data for Burglary and Robbery," *Criminology* 29 (1991): 237–248. See also Hindelang, Hirschi, and Weis, *Measuring Delinquency.*

21. Clarence Schrag, *Crime and Justice: American Style* (Washington, D.C.: Government Printing Office, 1971), 17.

22. Thomas Bernard, "Juvenile Crime and the Transformation of Juvenile Justice: Is There a Juvenile Crime Wave?" *Justice Quarterly* 16 (1999): 336–356.

23. The 2001 crime rate was affected by the tragic events of September 11. If the number of those murdered and injured in the attack are included, it obviously skews the crime rate upward. These data are eliminated from the analysis here to make yearly comparisons meaningful.

24. Again, these data do not reflect casualties suffered on September 11.

25. Lloyd Johnston, Patrick O'Malley, and Jerald Bachman, "Rise in Ecstasy Use Among American Teens Begins to Slow," national press release, 19 December 2001.

26. Ibid.

27. James A. Fox, *Trends in Juvenile Violence: A Report to the United States Attorney General on Current and Future Rates of Juvenile Offending* (Boston: Northeastern University, 1996).

28. Steven Levitt, "The Limited Role of Changing Age Structure in Explaining Aggregate Crime Rates," *Criminology* 37 (1999): 581–599.

29. Darrell Steffensmeier and Miles Harer, "Making Sense of Recent U.S. Crime Trend Composition Effects and Other Explanations," *Journal of Research in Crime and Delinquency* 36 (1999): 235–274.

30. Ralph Weisheit and L. Edward Wells, "The Future of Crime in Rural America," *Journal of Criminal Justice* 22 (1999): 1–22.

31. Daniel Mears, Matthew Ploeger, and Mark Warr, "Explaining the Gender Gap in Delinquency: Peer Influence and Moral Evaluations of Behavior," *Journal of Research in Crime and Delinquency* 35 (1998): 251–266.

32. Freda Adler, *Sisters in Crime* (New York: McGraw-Hill, 1975); Rita James Simon, *The Contemporary Woman and Crime* (Washington, D.C.: Government Printing Office, 1975).

33. Finn-Aage Esbensen and Elizabeth Piper Deschenes, "A Multisite Examination of Youth Gang Membership: Does Gender Matter?" *Criminology* 36 (1998): 799–828.

34. David Jacobs and Katherine Woods, "Interracial Conflict and Interracial Homicide: Do Political and Economic Rivalries Explain White Killings of Blacks and Black Killings of Whites?" *American Journal of Sociology* 105 (1999): 157–190.

35. Eric Lotke, "Hobbling a Generation: Young African-American Men in Washington, D.C.'s, Criminal Justice System—Five Years Later," *Crime and Delinquency* 44 (1998): 355–366.

36. Alexander Weiss and Steven Chermak, "The News Value of African-American Victims: An Examination of the Media's Presentation of Homicide," *Journal of Crime and Justice* 21 (1998): 71–84.

37. Emilie Andersen Allan and Darrell Steffensmeier, "Youth, Underemployment, and Property Crime: Differential Effects of Job Availability and Job Quality on Juvenile and Young Adult Arrest Rates," *American Sociological Review* 54 (1989): 107–123.

38. Judith Blau and Peter Blau, "The Cost of Inequality: Metropolitan Structure and Violent Crime," *American Sociological Review* 47 (1982): 114–129.

39. Herman Schwendinger and Julia Schwendinger, "The Paradigmatic Crisis in Delinquency Theory," *Crime and Social Justice* 18 (1982): 70–78.

40. Michael Gottfredson and Travis Hirschi, "The True Value of Lambda Would Appear to Be Zero: An Essay on Career Criminals, Criminal Careers, Selective Incapacitation, Cohort Studies and Related Topics," *Criminology* 24 (1986): 213–234; further support for their position can be found in Lawrence Cohen and Kenneth Land, "Age Structure and Crime," *American Sociological Review* 52 (1987): 170–183.

41. Marvin Wolfgang, Robert Figlio, and Thorsten Sellin, *Delinquency in a Birth Cohort* (Chicago: University of Chicago Press, 1972).

42. Marvin Wolfgang, Terence Thornberry, and Robert Figlio, *From Boy to Man, from Delinquency to Crime* (Chicago: University of Chicago Press, 1996).

43. Kimberly Kempf-Leonard, Paul Tracy, and James Howell, "Serious, Violent, and Chronic Juvenile Offenders: The Relationship of Delinquency Career Types to Adult Criminality," *Justice Quarterly* 18 (2001): 449–478.

44. Michael Schumacher and Gwen Kurz, *The 8% Solution: Preventing Serious Repeat Juvenile Crime* (Thousand Oaks, Calif.: Sage, 1999); Peter Jones, Philip Harris, James Fader, and Lori Grubstein, "Identifying Chronic Juvenile Offenders," *Justice Quarterly* 18 (2001): 478–507.

45. Deborah Gorman-Smith, Patrick H. Tolan, Rolf Loeber, and David B. Henry, "Relation of Family Problems to Patterns of Delinquent Involvement among Urban Youth," *Journal of Abnormal Child Psychology* 26 (1998): 319.

46. Centers for Disease Control, "Homicide Among Young Black Males—United States, 1978–1987," *Morbidity and Mortality Weekly Report* 39 (1990): 869–873.

47. Janet Lauritsen and Kenna Davis Quinet, "Repeat Victimizations Among Adolescents and Young Adults," *Journal of Quantitative Criminology* 11 (1995): 143–163.

48. Denise Osborn, Dan Ellingworth, Tim Hope, and Alan Trickett, "Are Repeatedly Victimized Households Different?" *Journal of Quantitative Criminology* 12 (1996): 223–245.

49. Terry Buss and Rashid Abdu, "Repeat Victims of Violence in an Urban Trauma Center," *Violence and Victims* 10 (1995): 183–187.

50. Graham Farrell, "Predicting and Preventing Revictimization," in *Crime and Justice: An Annual Review of Research*, vol. 20, eds. Michael Tonry and David Farrington (Chicago: University of Chicago Press, 1995), 61–126.

51. Lawrence Cohen and Richard Machalek, "A General Theory of Expropriative Crime: An Evolutionary Ecological Approach," *American Journal of Sociology* 94 (1988): 465–501.

52. Adrian Raine, "Biosocial Studies of Antisocial and Violent Behavior in Children and Adults: A Review," *Journal of Abnormal Child Psychology* 30 (2002): 311–327.

53. Stephen Schoenthaler, *Intelligence, Academic Performance, and Brain Function* (Turlock: California State University Stanislaus, 2000); see also, Stephen Schoenthaler and Ian Bier, "The Effect of Vitamin-Mineral Supplementation on Juvenile Delinquency Among American Schoolchildren: A Randomized Double-Blind Placebo-Controlled Trial," *Journal of Alternative and Complementary Medicine: Research on Paradigm, Practice, and Policy* 6 (2000): 7–18.

54. Alan Booth and D. Wayne Osgood, "The Influence of Testosterone on Deviance in Adulthood: Assessing and Explaining the Relationship," *Criminology* 31 (1993): 93–118.

55. Paul Stretesky and Michael Lynch, "The Relationship Between Lead Exposure and Homicide," *Archives of Pediatric Adolescent Medicine* 155 (2001): 579–582.

56. Nathaniel Pallone and James Hennessy, "Brain Dysfunction and Criminal Violence," *Society* 35 (1998).

57. Adrian Raine, Monte Buchsbaum, and Lori LaCasse, "Brain Abnormalities in Murderers Indicated by Positron Emission Tomography," *Biological Psychiatry* 42 (1997): 495–508.

58. Leonore Simon, "Does Criminal Offender Treatment Work?" *Applied and Preventive Psychology* (Summer, 1998); Stephen Faraone, et al., "Intellectual Performance and School Failure in Children with Attention Deficit Hyperactivity Disorder and in Their Siblings," *Journal of Abnormal Psychology* 102 (1993): 616–623.

59. B. Hutchings and S. A. Mednick, "Criminality in Adoptees and Their Adoptive and Biological Parents: A Pilot Study," in *Biosocial Bases of Criminal Behavior,* eds. S. A. Mednick and Karl O. Christiansen (New York: Gardner Press, 1977).

60. Edwin J.C.G. van den Oord, Frank Verhulst, and Dorret Boomsma, "A Genetic Study of Maternal and Paternal Ratings of Problem Behaviors in Three-Year-Old Twins," *Journal of Abnormal Psychology* 105 (1996): 349–357.

61. Michael Lyons, "A Twin Study of Self-Reported Criminal Behavior," 61–75; Judy Silberg, Joanne Meyer, Andrew Pickles, Emily Simonoff, Lindon Eaves, John Hewitt, Hermine Maes, and Michael Rutter, "Heterogeneity Among Juvenile Antisocial Behaviors: Findings from the Virginia Twin Study of Adolescent Behavioral Development," both articles in *Genetics of Criminal and Antisocial Behavior,* Ciba Foundation Symposium, eds. Gregory Bock, Jamie Goode, and Michael Rutter (Chichester, England: Wiley, 1995), 128–156.

62. Thomas Bouchard, "Genetic and Environmental Influences on Intelligence and Special Mental Abilities," *American Journal of Human Biology* 70 (1998): 253–275.

63. David Rowe, *The Limits of Family Influence: Genes, Experiences, and Behavior* (New York: Guilford Press, 1995), 64.

64. David Rowe and David Farrington, "The Familial Transmission of Criminal Convictions," *Criminology* 35 (1997): 177–201.

65. Marshall Jones and Donald Jones, "The Contagious Nature of Antisocial Behavior," *Criminology* 38 (2000): 25–46.

66. August Aichorn, *Wayward Youth* (New York: Viking Press, 1965).

67. Paige Crosby Ouimette, "Psychopathology and Sexual Aggression in Nonincarcerated Men," *Violence and Victimization* 12 (1997): 389–397.

68. Robert Krueger, Avshalom Caspi, Phil Silva, and Rob McGee, "Personality Traits Are Differentially Linked to Mental Disorders: A Multitrait-Multidiagnosis Study of an Adolescent Birth Cohort," *Journal of Abnormal Psychology* 105 (1996): 299–312.

69. Seymour Halleck, *Psychiatry and the Dilemmas of Crime* (Berkeley: University of California Press, 1971).

70. David Eitle and R. Jay Turner, "Exposure to Community Violence and Young Adult Crime: The Effects of Witnessing Violence, Traumatic Victimization, and Other Stressful Life Events," *Journal of Research in Crime and Delinquency* 39 (2002): 214–238. See also Albert Bandura, *Aggression: A Social Learning Analysis* (Englewood Cliffs, N.J.: Prentice-Hall, 1973); idem, *Social Learning Theory* (Englewood Cliffs, N.J.: Prentice-Hall, 1977).

71. U.S. Department of Health and Human Services, *Television and Behavior* (Washington, D.C.: Government Printing Office, 1982).

72. Richard Kania, "TV Crime and Real Crime: Questioning the Link" (Paper presented at the annual meeting of the American Society of Criminology, Chicago, November 1988).

73. David Lykken, "Psychopathy, Sociopathy, and Crime," *Society* 34 (1996): 30–38.

74. Steven Smith and Joseph Newman, "Alcohol and Drug Abuse–Dependence Disorders in Psychopathic and Nonpsychopathic Criminal Offenders," *Journal of Abnormal Psychology* 99 (1990): 430–439.

75. Ibid.

76. Jack Levin and James Alan Fox, *Mass Murder* (New York: Plenum, 1985).

77. Spencer Rathus and Jeffrey Nevid, *Abnormal Psychology* (Englewood Cliffs, N.J.: Prentice-Hall, 1991), 310–316.

78. Ibid.

79. Samuel Yochelson and Stanton Samenow, *The Criminal Personality* (New York: Jason Aronson, 1977).

80. Ralph Taylor, *Breaking Away from Broken Windows: Baltimore Neighborhoods and the Nationwide Fight against Crime, Grime, Fear, and Decline* (Boulder, Colo.: Westview Press, 2001).

81. Lincoln Quillian and Devah Pager, "Black Neighbors, Higher Crime? The Role of Racial Stereotypes in Evaluations of Neighborhood Crime," *American Journal of Sociology, 107* (2001): 717–769.

82. Oscar Lewis, "The Culture of Poverty," *Scientific American* 215 (1966): 19–25.

83. William Julius Wilson, *The Truly Disadvantaged* (Chicago: University of Chicago Press, 1987).

84. Joseph Rankin and L. Edward Wells, "The Effect of Parental Attachments and Direct Controls on Delinquency," *Journal of Research in Crime and Delinquency* 27 (1990): 140–165.

85. John Paul Wright and Francis Cullen, "Parental Efficacy and Delinquent Behavior: Do Control and Support Matter?" *Criminology* 39 (2001): 677–706.

86. Carter Hay, "Parenting, Self-Control, and Delinquency: A Test of Self-Control Theory," *Criminology* 39 (2001): 707–736

87. Eugene Maguin and Rolf Loeber, "Academic Performance and Delinquency," in *Crime and Justice: An Annual Review of Research*, vol. 20, eds. Michael Tonry and David Farrington (Chicago: University of Chicago Press, 1996), 145–264.

88. Ibid.

89. David Fergusson, Nicola Swain-Campbell, L. John Horwood, "Deviant Peer Affiliations, Crime, and Substance Use: A Fixed Effects Regression Analysis," *Journal of Abnormal Child Psychology* 30 (2002): 419–431.

90. W. Byron Groves and Robert Sampson, "Critical Theory and Criminology," *Social Problems* 33 (1986): 58–80.

91. Susan Ehrlich Martin and Nancy Jurik, *Doing Justice, Doing Gender* (Thousand Oaks, Calif.: Sage, 1996).

92. For a general review of this issue, see Sally Simpson, "Feminist Theory, Crime, and Justice," *Criminology* 27 (1989): 605–632; James Messerschmidt, *Capitalism, Patriarchy, and Crime* (Totawa, N.J.: Rowman & Littlefield, 1986).

93. Marvin Krohn, Alan Lizotte, and Cynthia Perez, "The Interrelationship Between Substance Use and Precocious Transitions to Adult Sexuality," *Journal of Health and Social Behavior* 38 (1997): 88.

94. G. R. Patterson, Barbara DeBaryshe, and Elizabeth Ramsey, "A Developmental Perspective on Antisocial Behavior," *American Psychologist* 44 (1989): 329–335.

95. Alex R. Piquero and He Len Chung, "On the Relationships Between Gender, Early Onset, and the Seriousness of Offending," *Journal of Criminal Justice* 29 (2001): 189–206.

96. Rolf Loeber and David Farrington, "Young Children Who Commit Crime: Epidemiology, Developmental Origins, Risk Factors, Early Interventions, and Policy Implications," *Development and Psychopathology* 12 (2000): 737–762.

3 Criminal Law: Substance and Procedure

Chapter Outline

Criminal Justice Links

Criminal Justice Viewpoints

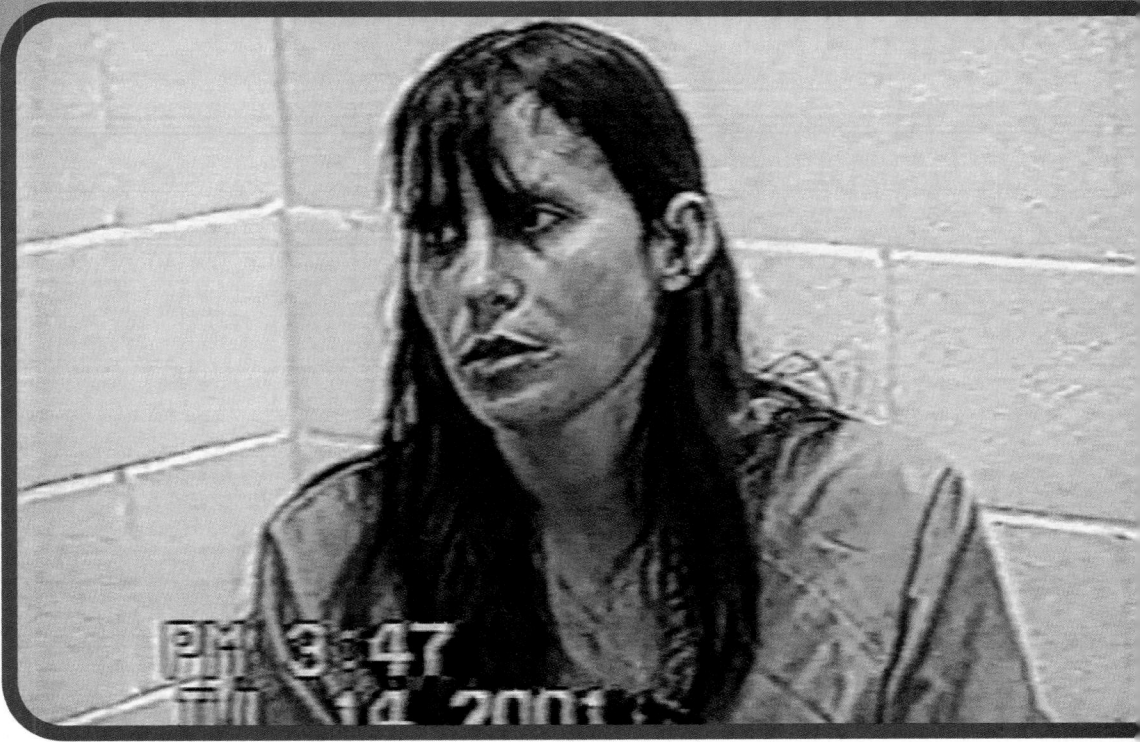

ON JUNE 20, 2001, Andrea Yates called 911 and told police she had drowned her children. When the police arrived they found Yates soaking wet. She had turned on the bathroom faucet, filled the tub, moved aside the mat to give herself traction for kneeling on the floor, and then methodically drowned her five children. She had to chase down the last one, and they scuffled in the family room. After drowning the children, she took them from the tub to her bedroom, where she placed them in bed and straightened the blankets around the kids in their pajamas. She also called her husband and told him, "It's time. I finally did it," before hanging up. He called back to ask what happened and she said, "It's the kids." He asked which of the five.

"All of them," she replied.

Andrea Yates, thirty-seven, pleaded not guilty by reason of insanity to multiple counts of capital murder. Her attorneys argued that the killings were brought on by psychotic delusions, exacerbated by repeated episodes of postpartum depression. Prosecutors disputed the extent of her psychosis and told the jury of how she had plotted the crime; they asked for the death penalty. The jury found her guilty as charged and recommended a sentence of life in prison.

There is little doubt that a person such as Andrea Yates is suffering from a significant personality defect. Should her mental state insulate her from legal punishments? If so, should all murderers be spared? Couldn't it be argued that anyone who intentionally takes another person's life is suffering from some sort of mental disturbance? Can a truly rational person kill? These are some of the issues that are dealt with by the criminal law. ■

 *To view the CNN video clip of this story, go to the book-specific Web site at* http://cj.wadsworth.com/siegel_essen4e.

The **substantive criminal law** defines crime and punishment in U.S. society. It involves such issues as the mental and physical elements of crime, crime categories, and criminal defenses. Each state government and the federal government has its own criminal code, developed over many generations and incorporating moral beliefs, social values, and political, economic, and other societal concerns. The substantive criminal law is a living document, constantly evolving to keep pace with society and its needs.

substantive criminal law A body of specific rules that declare what conduct is criminal and prescribe the punishment to be imposed for such conduct.

criminal procedure The rules and laws that define the operation of the criminal proceedings. Procedural law describes the methods that must be followed in obtaining warrants, investigating offenses, effecting lawful arrests, conducting trials, introducing evidence, sentencing convicted offenders, and reviewing cases by appellate courts.

civil law All law that is not criminal, including torts (personal wrongs), contract, property, maritime, and commercial law.

The rules designed to implement the substantive law are known as procedural law. Procedural law involves the basic rights people have when they come into contact with the justice system because they are suspected of violating the substantive law. It is concerned with the criminal process—the legal steps through which an offender passes—commencing with the initial criminal investigation and concluding with release of the offender. Some elements of the law of **criminal procedure** are the rules of evidence, the law of arrest, the law of search and seizure, questions of appeal, and the right to counsel. Many of the rights that have been extended to offenders over the past two decades lie within procedural law.

A working knowledge of the law is critical for the criminal justice practitioner. In our modern society, the rule of law governs almost all phases of human enterprise, including commerce, family life, property transfer, and the regulation of interpersonal conflict. It contains elements that control personal relationships between individuals and public relationships between individuals and the government. The former is known as **civil law,** while the latter is called criminal law; both concepts are distinguished later in this chapter. Because the law defines crime, punishment, and procedure, which are the basic concerns of the criminal justice system, it is essential for students to know something of the nature, purpose, and content of the substantive and procedural criminal law.

This chapter focuses on the basic principles of the substantive criminal law. In addition, the chapter discusses constitutional criminal procedure, showing how the rules of procedure, laid out in the U.S. Constitution and interpreted over time by the Supreme Court, control the operations of the justice system.

The Historical
Development of the Criminal Law

The roots of the criminal codes used in the United States can be traced back to such early legal charters as the Babylonian Code of Hammurabi (2000 B.C.), the Mosaic Code of the Israelites (1200 B.C.), and the Roman Twelve Tables (451 B.C.), which were formulated by a special commission of ten noble Roman men in response to pressure from the lower classes, who complained that the existing, unwritten legal code gave arbitrary and unlimited power to the wealthy classes. The original code was written on bronze plaques, which have been lost, but records of sections, which were memorized by every Roman male, survive.

During the sixth century, under the leadership of Byzantine Emperor Justinian, the first great codification of law in the Western world was prepared. Justinian's *Corpus Juris Civilis,* or body of civil law, summarized the system of Roman law that had developed over a thousand years. Rules and regulations to ensure the safety of the state and the individual were organized into a code and served as the basis for future civil and criminal legal classifications. Centuries later, French Emperor Napoleon I created the French civil code, using Justinian's code as a model. France and the other countries that have modeled their legal systems on French and Roman law have what are known as civil law systems.[1]

Though most of the early formal legal codes were lost during the Dark Ages, early German and Anglo-Saxon societies developed legal systems featuring monetary compensation, called *wergild* (*wer* means "worth" and refers to what the person, and therefore the crime, was worth), for criminal violations. Guilt was determined by two methods: *compurgation,* which involved having the accused person swear an oath of innocence while being backed up by a group of twelve to twenty-five oath-helpers, who would attest to his or her character and claims of

To read some of the original elements of the Roman Twelve Tables, go to http://members.aol.com/pilgrimjon/private/LEX/12tables.html

To read some of the statutes in the Justinian code, go to www.fordham.edu/halsall/basis/535institutes.html

innocence, and *ordeal,* which was based on the principle that divine forces would not allow an innocent person to be harmed.

Determining guilt by ordeal involved such measures as having the accused place his or her hand in boiling water or hold a hot iron. If the wound healed, the person was found innocent; conversely, if the wound did not heal, the accused was deemed guilty. Another ordeal, trial by combat, allowed the accused to challenge his accuser to a duel, with the outcome determining the legitimacy of the accusation. Punishments included public flogging, branding, beheading, and burning.

Common Law and the Principle of Stare Decisis

After the Normans conquered England in 1066, royal judges began to travel throughout the land, holding court in each county several times a year. When court was in session, the royal administrator, or judge, would summon a number of citizens who would, on their oath, tell of the crimes and serious breaches of the peace that had occurred since the judge's last visit. The royal judge then would decide what to do in each case, using local custom and rules of conduct as his guide in a system known as **stare decisis** (Latin for "to stand by decided cases").

Courts were bound to follow the law established in previous cases unless a higher authority, such as the king or the pope, overruled it.

The present English system of law came into existence during the reign of Henry II (1154–1189), when royal judges began to publish their decisions in local cases. This allowed judicial precedents to be established, and a national law to be established. Judges began to use these written decisions as a basis for their decision making, and eventually a fixed body of legal rules and principles was produced. If the new rules were successfully applied in a number of different cases they would become precedents, which would then be commonly applied in all similar cases— hence the term **common law.** Crimes such as murder, burglary, arson, and rape are common law crimes whose elements were initially defined by judges. They are referred to as **mala in se,** inherently evil and depraved. When the situation required it, the English Parliament enacted legislation to supplement the judge-made common law. These were referred to as statutory or *mala prohibitum* crimes, which reflected existing social conditions.

English common law evolved constantly to fit incidents that the judges encountered. In fact, legal scholars have identified specific cases in which judges created new crimes, some of which exist today. For example, in the *Carriers* case (1473), an English court ruled that a merchant who had been hired to transport merchandise was guilty of larceny (theft) if he kept the goods for his own purposes.[2] Before the *Carriers* case, the common law had not recognized a crime when people kept something that was voluntarily placed in their possession, even if the rightful owner had only given them temporary custody of the merchandise. Breaking with legal tradition, the court recognized that the commercial system could not be maintained unless the laws of theft were changed. Thus, larcenies defined by separate and unique criminal laws—such as embezzlement, extortion, and false pretenses—came into existence.

Before the American Revolution, the colonies, then under British rule, were subject to the common law. After the colonies acquired their independence, state legislatures standardized common law crimes such as murder, burglary, arson, and rape by putting them into statutory form in criminal codes. As in England, whenever common law proved inadequate to deal with changing social and moral issues, the states and Congress supplemented it with legislative statutes, creating new elements in the various state and federal legal codes. Similarly,

To read more about life in the barbarian tribes, use "Germanic tribes" as a subject guide on InfoTrac College Edition.

Need to look up legal terms such as "stare decisis"? Here is a link to a good online legal dictionary: www.duhaime.org/diction.htm

stare decisis   To stand by decided cases. The legal principle by which the decision or holding in an earlier case becomes the standard by which subsequent similar cases are judged.

common law   Early English law, developed by judges, that incorporated Anglo-Saxon tribal custom, feudal rules and practices, and the everyday rules of behavior of local villages. Common law became the standardized law of the land in England and eventually formed the basis of the criminal law in the United States.

mala in se   A term that refers to acts that society considers inherently evil, such as murder or rape, and that violate the basic principles of Judeo-Christian morality.

***Carriers* case**   A fifteenth-century case that defined the law of theft and reformulated the concept of taking the possession of another.

Use "stare decisis" as a key term on InfoTrac College Edition to learn more about this common-law concept.

For a site with numerous links to important historical legal documents and codes, go to www.wagonerlaw.com/DKmilestones.html

"Wager of Battel" from *Le Coutume de Normandie*, an illuminated manuscript (1450–1470)

Before the trial by jury, legal disputes could be settled by a duel in which the survivor was considered the "innocent" party. It was believed that God intervened on behalf of the victor. The *wager of battel* was introduced in England by the Normans and was used in both civil and criminal disputes.

statutes prohibiting such offenses as the sale and possession of narcotics or the pirating of videotapes have been passed to control human behavior unknown at the time the common law was formulated. Today, criminal behavior is defined primarily by statute. With few exceptions, crimes are removed, added, or modified by the legislature of a particular jurisdiction.

Criminal Law and Civil Law

Over time, law came to be divided into two broad categories: criminal law and civil law. Criminal law is the law of crimes and their punishments. Civil law, in contrast, includes **tort** law (personal wrongs and damages), property law (the law governing the transfer and ownership of property), and contract law (the law of personal agreements).

The differences between criminal law and civil law are significant, because in the U.S. legal system criminal proceedings are completely separate from civil actions.

The main objective of the criminal law is to protect the public against harm by preventing criminal offenses. The primary concern of the civil law is the control and regulation of human interaction. It regulates agreements and contracts, ownership of property, inheritance, and personal relationships such as marriage and child custody. However, it is in the area of private wrongs, or torts, that the criminal and civil law are most similar. A tort typically involves some harm, such as an injury that occurs due to the negligence of a motor vehicle operator. It can also involve injury caused by malicious **intent,** such as when a person strikes another causing injury. A tort action is a lawsuit aimed at collecting damages for harm done. Although similar to a crime because a victim has been injured, the two actions are somewhat different. When a crime is committed, the state initiates the legal process and imposes a punishment in the form of a criminal sanction. Furthermore, in criminal law, the emphasis is on the intent of the individual committing the crime. In contrast, a civil proceeding gives primary attention to affixing the blame each party deserves for producing the damage or conflict.

Despite these important differences, criminal and civil law share certain features. Both seek to control people's behavior by preventing them from acting in an undesirable manner, and both impose sanctions on those who commit violations of the law. The payment of damages to the victim in a tort case, for example, serves some of the same purposes as the payment of a fine in a criminal case. In addition, many actions, such as assault and battery, various forms of larceny, and negligence, are the basis for criminal as well as civil actions. Table 3.1 summarizes the main similarities and differences between criminal law and tort law.

The O. J. Simpson Case   The widely publicized case of O. J. Simpson provides a good example of the similarities and differences between tort and criminal law. In the so-called Trial of the Century—Part I, the famous athlete was tried by the state of California and acquitted of the murder of his ex-wife, Nicole, and her friend, Ron Goldman, in a criminal prosecution. As a defendant, Simpson was required to be in court but did not have to testify

tort   The law of personal wrongs and damage. Tort-type actions include negligence, libel, slander, assault, and trespass.

intent   An action that on its face indicates a criminal purpose—for example, breaking into a locked building or trespassing on someone's property; a guilty mind.

© AP/Wide World Photos

Civil law may involve both interpersonal agreements and conflicts. Here, Regina Lewis, daughter of former Boston Celtics star Reggie Lewis, rests in her mother's arms during closing arguments in the Reggie Lewis medical malpractice trial. Donna Harris-Lewis sued her late husband's primary cardiologist, Gilbert Mudge, for damages after Lewis's tragic death. The jury found for Mudge, even though the basketball star died while in his care.

Table 3.1	A comparison of criminal and tort law

Similarities

- Goal of controlling behavior
- Imposition of sanctions
- Some common areas of legal action—for example, personal assault, control of white-collar offenses such as environmental pollution

Differences

Criminal Law	*Tort Law*
Crime is a public offense.	Tort is a civil or private wrong.
The sanction associated with criminal law is incarceration or death.	The sanction associated with tort law is monetary damages.
The right of enforcement belongs to the state.	The individual brings the action.
The government ordinarily does not appeal.	Both parties can appeal.
Fines go to the state.	The individual receives damages as compensation for harm done.

How is the concept of negligence interpreted? To find out, go to www.duhaime.org/Tort/ca-negl.htm

Want to read more about the O. J. Simpson case? There are numerous Web sites devoted to the "Trial of the Century." Here is one maintained by CNN:

www.cnn.com/US/OJ/

during the trial. The standard of proof "beyond a reasonable doubt" was used to assess the evidence, and the verdict had to be unanimous. A conviction would have brought a sentence of life in prison.

In the Trial of the Century—Part II, the estate of Nicole Simpson and the family of Ron Goldman sued O. J. Simpson for the wrongful deaths of his ex-wife and her friend in a civil trial. This was a lawsuit brought by the families of the deceased against the person believed to have caused the deaths. Simpson was not required to be in court, but when called by either side he had to provide testimony. No television cameras were allowed in the courtroom, whereas the criminal trial was televised on network TV. The burden of proof in the civil case was "preponderance of the evidence," or which side had the most convincing case before the jury. In addition, only nine of the twelve jurors had to agree on a general verdict, and any judgment involved money, not imprisonment. Although he was found not guilty at his criminal trial, Simpson was required to pay significant damages at his civil case.

Sources of the Criminal Law

The three main sources of the criminal law are (1) common law, statutes, and case decisions; (2) administrative rules and regulations; and (3) constitutional laws.[3]

Common Law, Statutes, and Case Decisions

The common law crimes adopted into state codes form one major source of the substantive criminal law today. As common law, crimes had a general meaning, and everyone basically understood the definition of such actions as murder, larceny, and rape. Today, statutes enacted by state and federal legislative bodies have built on these common law meanings and often contain more detailed and specific definitions of the crimes. Statutes are thus a way in which the criminal law is created, modified, or expunged. They reflect existing social conditions and deal with issues of morality, such as gambling and sexual activity, as well as traditional common law crimes, such as murder, burglary, and arson.

Case law and judicial decision making also change and influence laws. For example, a statute may define murder as the "unlawful killing of one human being by another with malice." Court decisions might help explain the meaning of the term *malice* or clarify whether *human being* may refer to a fetus. A judge may rule that a statute is vague, deals with an act no longer of interest to the public, or is an unfair exercise of state control over an individual. Conversely, some judges may interpret the law so that behaviors that were previously acceptable become outlawed. For example, judges in a particular jurisdiction might find all people who sell magazines depicting nude men and women guilty of the crime of selling obscene material, whereas in the past obscenity was interpreted much more narrowly. Or some courts might consider drunken driving a petty crime, whereas others might interpret the statute on driving under the influence more severely.

Administrative Rule Making

Administrative agencies with rule-making authority also develop measures to control conduct in our society.[4] Some agencies regulate taxation, health, environment, and other public functions; others control drugs, illegal gambling, or pornographic material. Administrative laws also control the operations of the justice system. Parole boards are administrative agencies that implement the thousands of regulations governing the conduct of criminal offenders after their release from prison. Such rules are called *administrative rules with criminal sanctions,* and agency decisions about these rules have the force and authority of law.

Constitutional Law and Its Limits

Regardless of its source, all criminal law in the United States must conform to the rules and dictates of the U.S. Constitution.[5] In other words, any criminal law that conflicts with the various provisions and articles of the Constitution will eventually be challenged in the appellate courts and stricken from the legal code by judicial order (or modified to adhere to constitutional principles). As Chief Justice John Marshall's opinion in *Marbury v. Madison* indicated, "If the courts are to regard the Constitution...as superior to any ordinary act of the legislature, the Constitution and not such ordinary act must govern the case to which they [both] apply."[6] This landmark case of 1803 established the concept of judicial review. All laws, including criminal statutes, must therefore meet constitutional standards or be declared invalid.

Among the general limitations set by the Constitution are those that forbid the government to pass ex post facto laws. Such laws make an action a crime that was not a crime at the time it was done; they create penalties that are enforced retroactively (see Exhibit 3.1 for more on ex post facto laws).

The Constitution also forbids *bills of attainder*: legislative acts that inflict punishment without a judicial trial. In addition, criminal laws have been interpreted as violating constitutional principles if they are too vague or overly broad to give clear meaning of their intent. For example, a law forbidding adults to engage in "immoral behavior" could not be enforced because it does not use clear and precise language or give adequate notice as to which conduct is forbidden. The following Law in Review feature concerns an important case that dealt with the concept of vagueness.[7]

Exhibit 3.1 Ex post facto laws

Is it possible for the state to pass laws to retroactively punish people? No, but states may pass laws that apply retroactive treatment. In the 1997 case *Kansas v. Hendricks*, the Supreme Court upheld the use of the Kansas Sexually Violent Predator Act, which allows for indefinite civil confinement for sexual predators after their criminal term has concluded. Hendricks, a habitual offender, was serving a prison term for sexual misconduct when the law was implemented. He appealed on the grounds that his ex post facto rights were violated because he now could be confined under a law that did not exist when he was first convicted. But the Supreme Court upheld his confinement, concluding the act was nonpunitive in nature and designed to treat rather than harm offenders. Therefore, it did not violate ex post facto laws against retroactive punishment.

Source: Kansas v. Hendricks, 117 S. Ct. 2072, 2078 (1997).

Law in Review

Chicago v. Morales

Facts

Because of an epidemic of gang violence, the city of Chicago passed the Gang Congregation Ordinance in 1997, which prohibited "criminal street gang members" from loitering in public places.

Under the ordinance, if a police officer observed a person whom he or she believed to be a gang member loitering in a public place with one or more persons, the officer could order them all to disperse; failure to do so was a violation of the ordinance and grounds for arrest. The police department's General Order 92-4 attempted to limit officers' enforcement discretion by confining arrest authority to designated officers, establishing detailed criteria for defining street gangs and membership, and providing for designated, but publicly undisclosed, enforcement areas.

In 1998, after a number of arrests of gang members by the police, the Illinois Supreme Court found that the statute violated due process of law because it was vague and an arbitrary restriction on personal liberty. An appeal was filed before the U.S. Supreme Court.

Decision

In 1999, in a six-to-three decision, the U.S. Supreme Court affirmed the Illinois Supreme Court and ruled that the ordinance's broad sweep violated the requirement that the legislature establish minimal guidelines to govern law enforcement activities. The Court said the ordinance criminalized too much behavior that would otherwise be considered harmless. For example, persons in the company of a gang member could be ordered by police to disperse even if they were committing no offensive or illegal act. More importantly, the state courts had interpreted the statutory language of loitering as being "to remain in any one place with no apparent purpose." This vague language gave police officers enormous discretion to determine what activities constituted loitering. The Supreme Court ruled the three features of the ordinance that limited an officer's discretion (it did not permit issuance of a dispersal order to anyone who was moving along or had an apparent purpose; it did not permit an arrest if individuals obeyed a dispersal order; and no order could be issued unless the officer reasonably believed that one of the loiterers was a gang member) were insufficient to limit police discretion. Ironically, the Court noted that the ordinance was also "under-inclusive"; it did not cover loitering with an apparent purpose even if the purpose was to conceal drug trafficking or claim territory for a gang.

Significance of the Case

This case reinforces the constitutional principle that criminal laws with unlimited discretion and vagueness will be struck down. The problem with this statute was that it covered a broad range of innocent conduct and delegated too much discretion to the police. On the other hand, the Court said that the statute could be "made constitutional by requiring that loiterers have some harmful purpose before being arrested, or making it clear that only gang members could be arrested rather than people standing nearby." This language has been taken by legal scholars as a cue that a properly drafted ordinance could be constitutional. Chicago intended to try this approach to gang control again.

Critical Thinking

Considering the current threat of terrorism, should we give greater powers to law enforcement agencies to stop, question, detain, and arrest suspicious people under statutes that are loosely worded and vague? For example, should police be allowed to question people if they "seem suspicious" or be allowed to make arrests for "suspicious behavior"?

InfoTrac College Edition Research

For a more detailed analysis of *Chicago v. Morales,* go to Kim Strosnider, "Anti-Gang Ordinances After *City of Chicago v. Morales*: The Intersection of Race, Vagueness Doctrine, and Equal Protection in the Criminal Law," *American Criminal Law Review,* Winter 2002 v39 i1 p101(46).

The Constitution also forbids laws that make a person's status a crime. For example, addiction to narcotics cannot be made a crime, though laws can forbid the sale, possession, and manufacture of dangerous drugs.

In general, the Constitution has been interpreted to forbid any criminal law that violates a person's right to be treated fairly and equally; this principle is referred to as substantive due process. Usually, this means that before a new law can be created, the state must show that there is a compelling need to protect public safety or morals.[8]

Crimes and Classifications

The decision of how a crime should be classified rests with the individual jurisdiction. Each state has developed its own body of criminal law and consequently determines its own penalties for the various crimes. Thus, the criminal law of a given state defines and grades offenses, sets levels of punishment, and classifies crimes into categories. Over the years, crimes have been generally grouped into (1) felonies, misdemeanors, and violations and (2) other statutory classifications, such as juvenile delinquency, sex-offender categories, and multiple- or first-offender classifications. In general terms, *felonies* are considered serious crimes, *misdemeanors* are seen as less serious crimes, and *violations* may be noncriminal offenses such as traffic offenses and public drunkenness. Some states consider violations civil matters, whereas others classify them as crimes.

Felonies and Misdemeanors

The most common classification in the United States is the division between felonies and misdemeanors.[9] This distinction is based primarily on the degree of seriousness of the crime. Distinguishing between a **felony** and a **misdemeanor** is sometimes difficult. Simply put, a felony is a serious offense, and a misdemeanor is a less serious one. *Black's Law Dictionary* defines the two terms as follows:

> *A felony is a crime of a graver or more atrocious nature than those designated as misdemeanors. Generally it is an offense punishable by death or imprisonment in a penitentiary. A misdemeanor is lower than a felony and is generally punishable by fine or imprisonment otherwise than in a penitentiary.*[10]

Each jurisdiction in the United States determines by statute what types of conduct constitute felonies or misdemeanors. The most common definition of a felony is that it is a crime punishable in the statute by death or by imprisonment in a state or federal prison. In Massachusetts, for example, any crime that a statute punishes by imprisonment in the state prison system is considered a felony, and all other crimes are misdemeanors.[11] Another way of determining what category an offense falls into is by providing in the statute that a felony is any crime punishable by imprisonment for more than one year. In the former method, the place of imprisonment is critical; in the latter, the length of the prison sentence distinguishes a felony from a misdemeanor.

In the United States today, felonies include serious crimes against the person, such as criminal homicide, robbery, and rape, as well as such crimes against property as burglary and larceny. Misdemeanors include petit (or petty) larceny, assault and battery, and the unlawful possession of marijuana. The least serious, or petty, offenses, which often involve traffic violations and are called violations, may also be called *infractions.*

The felony-misdemeanor classification has a direct effect on the offender charged with the crime. A person convicted of a felony may be barred from certain fields of employment or some professions, such as law and medicine. A felony offender's status as an alien in the United States might also be affected, or the offender might be denied the right to hold public office, vote, or serve on a jury.[12] These and other civil liabilities exist only when a person is convicted of a felony offense, not a misdemeanor.

Whether the offender is charged with a felony or a misdemeanor also makes a difference at the time of arrest. Normally, the law of arrest requires that if the crime is a misdemeanor and has not been committed in the presence of a police officer, the officer cannot make an arrest. This is known as the

felony A more serious offense that carries a penalty of incarceration in a state prison, usually for one year or more. Persons convicted of felony offenses lose such rights as the rights to vote, hold elective office, or maintain certain licenses.

misdemeanor A minor crime usually punished by less than one year's imprisonment in a local institution, such as a county jail.

© 2002 AP/Wide World Photos

Each state has developed its own body of criminal law and consequently determines its own penalties for the various crimes. However, even if a state legalizes an act, people who engage in it may still be law violators under federal law. Here, Robert Anton Wilson, right, who suffers from post-polio syndrome, receives marijuana from Jeremy Griffey, left, and Kathy Nicholson, second from left, both with the Wo/Men's Alliance for Medical Marijuana, at City Hall in Santa Cruz, California, September 17, 2002. Calling Santa Cruz a "sanctuary" from federal authorities, medical marijuana advocates joined by city leaders passed out pot to about a dozen sick and dying patients at City Hall.

in-presence requirement. However, the police officer does have the legal authority to arrest a suspect for a misdemeanor at a subsequent time by the use of a validly obtained arrest warrant. In contrast, an arrest for a felony may be made regardless of whether the crime was committed in the officer's presence, as long as the officer has reasonable grounds to believe that the person has committed the felony. There are some specific crimes for which states have passed legislation allowing police to make misdemeanor arrests without the need for witnessing the crimes firsthand. For example, a number of jurisdictions have passed domestic violence prevention acts, which allow such arrests, in an effort to protect the target of the abuse from further attacks. Exhibit 3.2 contains provisions from the Massachusetts abuse prevention law. Note how it gives police the specific right to make arrests in nonfelonies if they have probable cause that abuse occurred.

Other Statutory Classifications

In addition to the felony-misdemeanor classifications, crimes may be classified according to the characteristics of the offender. All states, for example, have juvenile delinquency statutes that classify children under a certain age as juvenile delinquents if they commit acts that would constitute crimes if committed by adults. Some states have special statutory classifications for sex offenders, multiple offenders, youthful offenders, and first offenders. Generally, no special statutory classification exists for white-collar crimes, such as embezzlement, fraud, and income tax violation, which usually involve nonviolent conduct.

Exhibit 3.2	Massachusetts Domestic Abuse Prevention Act

Chapter 209A: Definitions.

Section 1. As used in this chapter the following words shall have the following meanings:

"Abuse," the occurrence of one or more of the following acts between family or household members:

(a) Attempting to cause or causing physical harm
(b) Placing another in fear of imminent serious physical harm
(c) Causing another to engage involuntarily in sexual relations by force, threat, or duress

Chapter 209A: Section 6. Powers of police; civil liability; victim's right to copy of incident report; notice of release of arrested persons; no-contact orders.

Arrest any person a law officer witnesses or has probable cause to believe has violated a temporary or permanent vacate, restraining, or no-contact order or judgment issued pursuant to sections 18, 34B or 34C of chapter 208; section 32 of chapter 209; sections 3, 3B, 3C, 4, or 5 of this chapter; or sections 15 or 20 of chapter 209C or similar protection order issued by another jurisdiction. When there are no vacate, restraining, or no-contact orders or judgments in effect, arrest shall be the preferred response whenever an officer witnesses or has probable cause to believe that a person:

(a) Has committed a felony
(b) Has committed a misdemeanor involving abuse as defined in section 1 of this chapter
(c) Has committed an assault and battery in violation of section 13A of chapter 265

The safety of the victim and any involved children shall be paramount in any decision to arrest. Any officer arresting both parties must submit a detailed, written report in addition to an incident report, setting forth the grounds for dual arrest.

No law officer investigating an incident of domestic violence shall threaten, suggest, or otherwise indicate the arrest of all parties for the purpose of discouraging requests for law enforcement intervention by any party.

No law officer shall be held liable in any civil action regarding personal injury or injury to property brought by any party to a domestic violence incident for an arrest based on probable cause when such officer acted reasonably and in good faith and in compliance with this chapter and the statewide policy as established by the Secretary of Public Safety.

Source: General Laws of Massachusetts, Part II: Real and Personal Property and Domestic Relations. Title III. Domestic Relations, Section 209 (June 30, 2002).

The Legal Definition of a Crime

In the media, we occasionally hear about people who admit at trial that they committed the act of which they are accused, yet they are not found guilty of the crime. For example, there was little question that John Hinckley attempted to assassinate President Ronald Reagan in 1981; the act was shown on national TV. Yet Hinckley was not found guilty of a crime because he lacked one of the legal requirements needed to prove his guilt: mental competency. The jury concluded he was not mentally competent at the time of the crime. In most instances, this occurs because state or federal prosecutors have not proven that the defendant's behavior falls within the legal definition of a crime. To fulfill the legal definition, all elements of the crime must be proven. For example, in Alabama, the common law crime of burglary in the first degree is defined as shown in Exhibit 3.3.

> **Exhibit 3.3** Alabama definition of burglary in the first degree
>
> **Section 13A-7-5. Burglary in the first degree.**
>
> A person commits the crime of burglary in the first degree if he knowingly and unlawfully enters or remains unlawfully in a dwelling with intent to commit a crime therein, and if, in effecting entry or while in dwelling or in immediate flight therefrom, he or another participant in the crime:
>
> (1) Is armed with explosives or a deadly weapon, or
> (2) Causes physical injury to any person who is not a participant in the crime, or
> (3) Uses or threatens the immediate use of a dangerous instrument
>
> Burglary in the first degree is a Class A felony.
>
> *Source:* Alabama Criminal Code, Acts 1977, No. 607, p. 812, and sec. 2610; Acts 1979, No. 79-471, p. 862, and sec. 1; www.legislature.state.al.us/CodeofAlabama/1975/13A-7-5.htm.

Note that armed burglary has the following elements:

- It involves breaking, entering, or both.
- It happens at a dwelling house.
- The accused is armed or arms himself after entering the house, or commits an actual assault on a person who is lawfully in the house.
- The accused intends to commit a felony.

For the state to prove a crime occurred, and that the defendant committed it, the prosecutor must show that the accused engaged in the guilty act (**actus reus**) and had the intent to commit the act (**mens rea**). Under common law, both the actus reus and the mens rea must be present for the act to be considered a crime. Thoughts of committing an act do not alone constitute a crime; there must also be an illegal act. Let us now look more closely at these issues.

Actus Reus

The actus reus is an aggressive act, such as taking someone's money, burning a building, or shooting someone. The act must be voluntary for it to be considered illegal; an accident or involuntary act would not be considered criminal. For example, if while walking down the street a person has a seizure and as a result strikes another person in the face, he cannot be held criminally liable for assault. But if he knew beforehand that he might have a seizure and unreasonably put himself in a position where he was likely to harm others—for instance, by driving a car—he could be criminally liable for his behavior.

In addition, there are occasions when the failure or omission to act can be considered a crime:

1. *Failure to perform a legally required duty that is based on relationship or status.* These relationships include parent and child and husband and wife. If a husband finds his wife unconscious because she took an overdose of sleeping pills, he is obligated to save her life by seeking medical aid. If he fails to do so and she dies, he can be held responsible for her death. Parents are required to look after the welfare of their children; failure to provide adequate care can be a criminal offense.
2. *Imposition by statute.* Some states have passed laws that require a person who observes an automobile accident to stop and help the other parties involved.
3. *Contractual relationship.* These relationships include lifeguard and swimmer, doctor and patient, and babysitter or au pair and child. Because lifeguards have been hired to ensure the safety of swimmers, they have a legal duty to

actus reus An illegal act. The actus reus can be an affirmative act, such as taking money or shooting someone, or a failure to act, such as failing to take proper precautions while driving a car.

mens rea Guilty mind. The mental element of a crime or the intent to commit a criminal act.

come to the aid of drowning persons. If a lifeguard knows a swimmer is in danger and does nothing about it and the swimmer drowns, the lifeguard can be held legally responsible for the swimmer's death.

The duty to act is a legal and not a moral duty. The obligation arises from the relationship between the parties or from explicit legal requirements. For example, a private citizen who sees a person drowning is under no legal obligation to save that person. Although we may find it morally reprehensible, the private citizen could walk away and let the swimmer drown without facing legal sanctions.

Mens Rea

In most situations, for an act to constitute a crime, it must be done with criminal intent. A person who enters a store with a gun with the intention of stealing money indicates by his actions his intent to commit a robbery. However, the definition also encompasses situations in which recklessness or negligence establishes the required criminal intent. For example, a drunk driver may not have intended to kill her victim, yet her negligent and reckless behavior—driving while drunk— creates a condition that a reasonable person can assume may lead to injury.

Criminal intent is implied if the results of an action, though originally unintended, are certain to occur. For example, when Mohammed Atta and his terrorist band crashed aircraft into the World Trade Center on September 11, 2001, they did not intend to kill any particular person in the building. Yet the law would hold that Atta, or any other person, would be substantially certain that people in the building would be killed in the blast and that he therefore had the criminal intent to commit the crime of murder.

To read more about the concept of mens rea, go to InfoTrac College Edition and read Claire Finkelstein, "The Inefficiency of Mens Rea (The Morality of Criminal Law: A Symposium in Honor of Professor Sanford Kadish)," *California Law Review,* May 2000 v88 i3 p895.

To be found guilty of a crime, a person must commit the guilty act (actus reus) and at the same time have sufficient intent (mens rea) as required by law. Here, British au pair Louise Woodward, on trial for the death of Matthew Eappen, the baby left in her care, reacts to the jury's verdict of guilty of second-degree murder. The guilty verdict was later overturned by the trial judge, who ruled that the prosecution had not adequately proved all the elements of the crime.

Exhibit 3.4   Common law crimes

	Crime	Definition	Example
Crimes against the person	First-degree murder	Unlawful killing of another human being with malice aforethought and with premeditation and deliberation.	A woman buys some poison and pours it into a cup of coffee her husband is drinking, intending to kill him. The motive—to get the insurance benefits of the victim.
	Voluntary manslaughter	Intentional killing committed under extenuating circumstances that mitigate the killing, such as killing in the heat of passion after being provoked.	A husband coming home early from work finds his wife in bed with another man. The husband goes into a rage and shoots and kills both lovers with a gun he keeps by his bedside.
	Battery	Unlawful touching of another with intent to cause injury.	A man seeing a stranger sitting in his favorite seat in the cafeteria goes up to that person and pushes him out of the seat.
	Assault	Intentional placing of another in fear of receiving an immediate battery.	A student aims an unloaded gun at her professor who believes the gun is loaded. The student says she is going to shoot.
	Rape	Unlawful sexual intercourse with a female without her consent.	After a party, a man offers to drive a young female acquaintance home. He takes her to a wooded area and, despite her protests, forces her to have sexual relations with him.
	Robbery	Wrongful taking and carrying away of personal property from a person by violence or intimidation.	A man armed with a loaded gun approaches another man on a deserted street and demands his wallet.
Inchoate (incomplete) offenses	Attempt	An intentional act for the purpose of committing a crime that is more than mere preparation or planning of the crime. The crime is not completed, however.	A person intending to kill another places a bomb in the second person's car, so that it will detonate when the ignition key is used. The bomb is discovered before the car is started. Attempted murder has been committed.
	Conspiracy	Voluntary agreement between two or more persons to achieve an unlawful object or to achieve a lawful object using means forbidden by law.	A drug company sells larger-than-normal quantities of drugs to a doctor, knowing that the doctor is distributing the drugs illegally. The drug company is guilty of conspiracy.
Crimes against property	Burglary	Breaking and entering of a dwelling house of another with the intent to commit a felony.	Intending to steal some jewelry and silver, a young man breaks a window and enters another's house.
	Arson	Intentional burning of a dwelling house of another.	A secretary, angry that her boss did not give her a raise, goes to her boss's house and sets fire to it.
	Larceny	Taking and carrying away the personal property of another with the intent to steal the property.	While a woman is shopping, she sees a diamond ring displayed at the jewelry counter. When no one is looking, the woman takes the ring and walks out of the store.

The Relationship of Mens Rea and Actus Reus

The third element needed to prove a crime was committed is the immediate relationship of the act to the criminal intent or result. The law requires that the offender's conduct be the approximate cause of any injury resulting from the criminal act. If, for example, a man chases a victim into the street intending to assault him and the victim is struck and killed by a car, the accused could be convicted of murder if the court felt that his actions made him responsible for the victim's death. If, however, a victim dies from a completely unrelated illness after being assaulted, the court must determine whether the death was a probable consequence of the defendant's illegal conduct or whether it would have resulted even if the assault had not occurred. Exhibit 3.4 sets out common law crimes and their definitions.

Strict Liability

Certain statutory offenses exist in which mens rea is not essential. These offenses fall in a category known as public safety or **strict liability crimes.** A person can be held responsible for such a violation independent of the existence of intent to commit the offense. Strict liability criminal statutes generally include narcotics control laws, traffic laws, health and safety regulations, sanitation laws, and other regulatory statutes. For example, a driver could not defend herself against a speeding ticket by claiming that she was unaware of how fast she was going and did not intend to speed; nor could a bartender claim that a juvenile to whom he sold liquor looked quite a bit older. No state of mind is generally required where a strict liability statute is violated.[13] For example, consider the New York State law S 270.10: Creating a hazard, which is laid out in Exhibit 3.5.[14] Notice that the intent to commit this crime is not required for a conviction on charges of creating a hazardous condition.

strict liability crime Illegal act whose elements do not contain the need for intent or mens rea; usually, acts that endanger the public welfare, such as illegal dumping of toxic wastes.

To access the public safety statutes in New York, go to http://assembly.state.ny.us/leg/?cl=82&a=69

Criminal Defenses

When people defend themselves against criminal charges, they must refute one or more of the elements of the crime of which they have been accused. Defendants may deny the actus reus by arguing that they were falsely accused and the real culprit has yet to be identified. Defendants may also claim that while they did engage in the criminal act they are accused of, they lacked the mens rea, or mental intent, needed to be found guilty of the crime. If a person whose mental state is impaired commits a criminal act, it is possible for the person to excuse his criminal actions by claiming he lacked the capacity to form sufficient intent to be held criminally responsible. **Insanity,** intoxication, and ignorance are also among the types of excuse defenses.

Another type of defense is justification. Here, the individual usually admits committing the criminal act, but maintains that the act was justified and that he or she, therefore, should not be held criminally liable. Among the justification defenses are necessity, duress, **self-defense,** and **entrapment.** Thus, persons standing trial for criminal offenses may defend themselves by claiming either that their actions were justified under the circumstances or that their behavior can be excused by their lack of mens rea. If either the physical or mental elements of a crime cannot be proven, then the defendant cannot be convicted. We will now examine some of these defenses and justifications in greater detail.

insanity A legal defense that maintains a defendant was incapable of forming criminal intent because he or she suffers from a defect of reason or mental illness.

self-defense A legal defense in which defendants claim that their behavior was legally justified by the necessity to protect their own life and property or that of another victim from potential harm.

entrapment A criminal defense that maintains the police originated the criminal idea or initiated the criminal action.

Ignorance or Mistake

Ignorance or mistake can be an excuse if it negates an element of a crime. As a general rule, however, ignorance of the law is no excuse. Some courts have had to

---

Exhibit 3.5   **New York State law: Section 270.10: Creating a hazard**

A person is guilty of creating a hazard when:

1. Having discarded in any place where it might attract children, a container which has a compartment of more than one and one-half cubic feet capacity and a door or lid which locks or fastens automatically when closed and which cannot easily be opened from the inside, he fails to remove the door, lid, locking or fastening device; or
2. Being the owner or otherwise having possession of property upon which an abandoned well or cesspool is located, he fails to cover the same with suitable protective construction.

Creating a hazard is a class B misdemeanor.

Source: New York State Consolidated Laws, Article 270: Other Offenses Relating to Public Safety, Section 270.10: Creating a hazard (2002).

accept this excuse in cases where the government failed to make enactment of a new law public. It is also a viable justification when the offender relies on an official statement of the law that is later deemed incorrect. Barring that, even immigrants and other new arrivals to the United States are required to be aware of the content of the law. For example, on October 7, 1998, Chris Ahamefule Iheduru, a Nigerian immigrant, was convicted of sexual assault on the grounds that he had intimate relations with his fourteen-year-old stepdaughter after signing a contract with the girl to bear him a son (she gave birth to a daughter in September 1998).[15] At trial, Iheduru testified that it is not illegal in his native country to have sex with a juvenile and that he did not know it was against the law in the United States. His ignorance of American law did not shield him from conviction.

Insanity

Insanity is a defense to criminal prosecution in which the defendant's state of mind negates his or her criminal responsibility. A successful insanity defense results in a verdict of "not guilty by reason of insanity." Insanity, in this case, is a legal category. As used in U.S. courts, it does not necessarily mean that everyone who suffers from a form of mental illness can be excused from legal responsibility. Many people who are depressed, suffer mood disorders, or have a psychopathic personality can be found legally sane. Instead, insanity means that the defendant's state of mind at the time the crime was committed made it impossible for that person to have the necessary mens rea to satisfy the legal definition of a crime. Thus, a person can be undergoing treatment for a psychological disorder but still be judged legally sane if it can be proven that at the time he committed the crime he had the capacity to understand the wrongfulness of his actions

Defense attorney George Parnham presents his opening arguments, February 18, 2002, during the first day of the trial of Andrea Yates for the killing of her five children. Most states define insanity by requiring that defendants prove that they lacked the ability to understand the wrongfulness of their acts. Though Yates suffered from severe depression she knew that killing her children was wrong. A jury found her guilty of murder.

Exhibit 3.6	Various insanity defense standards		
Test	**Legal Standard of Mental Illness**	**Final Burden of Proof**	**Who Bears Burden of Proof**
M'Naghten	"didn't know what he was doing or didn't know it was wrong"	Balance of probabilities	Defense
Irresistible impulse	"could not control his conduct"	Beyond reasonable doubt	Prosecutor
Substantial capacity	"lacks substantial capacity to appreciate the wrongfulness of his conduct or to control it"	Beyond reasonable doubt	Prosecutor
Present federal law	"lacks capacity to appreciate the wrongfulness of his conduct"	Clear and convincing evidence	Defense

Source: National Institute of Justice, Crime Study Guide: Insanity Defense, by Norval Morris (Washington, DC: U.S. Department of Justice, 1986), p. 3.

If a defendant uses the insanity plea, it is usually left to psychiatric testimony to prove that the person understood the wrongfulness of his actions and was therefore legally sane, or conversely, was mentally incapable of forming intent. The jury then must weigh the evidence in light of the test for sanity currently used in the jurisdiction.

Such tests vary throughout the United States; the commonly used tests are listed in Exhibit 3.6.

Because the issue of insanity is so controversial, it is discussed further in the following Law in Review feature.

Use "the insanity defense" as a subject guide on InfoTrac College Edition to learn more about this controversial criminal defense.

Intoxication

As a general rule, intoxication, which may include drunkenness or being under the influence of drugs, is not considered a defense. However, a defendant who becomes involuntarily intoxicated under duress or by mistake may be excused for crimes committed. Involuntary intoxication may also lessen the degree of the crime; a judgment may be decreased from first- to second-degree murder because the defendant uses intoxication to prove the lack of the critical element of mens rea. Thus, the effect of intoxication on criminal liability depends on whether the defendant uses alcohol or drugs voluntarily. For example, a defendant who enters a bar for a few drinks, becomes intoxicated, and strikes someone can be convicted of assault and battery. On the other hand, if the defendant ordered a nonalcoholic drink that was spiked by someone else, the defendant may have a legitimate legal defense.

The American Psychiatric Association is a medical specialty society dedicated to the humane care and effective treatment for all persons with mental disorders, including mental retardation and substance-related disorders. To read their take on the insanity plea, go to www.psych.org/public_info/insanity.cfm

Because of the frequency of crime-related offenses involving drugs and alcohol, the impact of intoxication on criminal liability is a persistent issue in the criminal justice system. The connection between drug use, alcoholism, and violent street crime has been well documented. Although those in law enforcement and the judiciary tend to emphasize the use of the penal process in dealing with problems of chronic alcoholism and drug use, others in corrections and crime prevention favor approaches that depend more on behavioral theories and the social sciences. For example, in the case of *Robinson v. California,* the U.S. Supreme Court struck down a California statute making addiction to narcotics a crime, on the ground that it violated the defendant's rights under the Eighth and Fourteenth Amendments to the Constitution.[16] On the other hand, the landmark decision in *Powell v. Texas* placed severe limitations on the behavioral science approach in *Robinson* when it rejected the defense of chronic alcoholism of a defendant charged with the crime of public drunkenness.[17]

The Insanity Defense

Facts

The insanity defense has been the source of debate and controversy. Many critics of the defense maintain that inquiry into a defendant's psychological makeup is inappropriate at the trial stage; they would prefer that the issue be raised at the sentencing stage, after guilt has been determined. Opponents also charge that criminal responsibility is separate from mental illness and that the two should not be equated. It is a serious mistake, they argue, to consider criminal responsibility as a trait or quality that can be detected by a psychiatric evaluation. Moreover, some criminals avoid punishment because they are erroneously judged by psychiatrists to be mentally ill. Conversely, some people who are found not guilty by reason of insanity because they suffer from a mild personality disturbance are then incarcerated in mental health facilities far longer than they would have been imprisoned if they had been convicted of a criminal offense.

Advocates of the insanity defense say that it serves a unique purpose. Most successful insanity verdicts result in the defendant's being committed to a mental institution until he or she has recovered. The general assumption is that the insanity defense makes it possible to single out for special treatment certain persons who would otherwise be subjected to further penal sanctions following conviction.

The insanity plea was thrust into the spotlight when John Hinckley's unsuccessful attempt to kill President Ronald Reagan was captured by news cameras. Hinckley was found not guilty by reason of insanity. Public outcry against this seeming miscarriage of justice prompted some states to revise their insanity statutes. New Mexico, Georgia, Alaska, Delaware, Michigan, Illinois, and Indiana, among other states, have created the plea of *guilty but insane,* in which the defendant is required to serve the first part of his or her sentence in a hospital and, once "cured," to be then sent to prison.

Decisions

In 1984, the federal government revised its criminal code to restrict insanity as a defense solely to individuals who are unable to understand the nature and wrongfulness of their acts. The burden of proof has made an important shift from the prosecutor's need to prove sanity to the defendant's need to prove insanity. About eleven states have followed the federal government's lead and made significant changes in their insanity defenses, such as shifting the burden of proof from prosecution to defense; three states (Idaho, Montana, and Utah) no longer use evidence of mental illness as a defense in court, though psychological factors can influence sentencing. On March 28, 1994, the U.S. Supreme Court failed to overturn the Montana law (*Cowan v. Montana,* 93-1264), thereby giving the states the right to abolish the insanity defense if they so choose.

Although this backlash against the insanity plea is intended to close supposed legal loopholes allowing dangerous criminals to go free, the public's fear may be misplaced. It is estimated that the insanity plea is used in fewer than 1 percent of all cases. Moreover, evidence shows that relatively few insanity defense pleas are successful.

Even if the insanity defense is successful, the offender must be placed in a secure psychiatric hospital or the psychiatric ward of a state prison. Since many defendants who successfully plead insanity are nonviolent offenders, it is certainly possible that their hospital stay will be longer than the prison term they would have received if they had been convicted of the crimes of which they were originally accused.

Despite efforts to ban its use, the insanity plea is probably here to stay. Most crimes require mens rea, and unless we are willing to forgo that standard of law, we will be forced to find not guilty those people whose mental state makes it impossible for them to rationally control their behavior.

Critical Thinking

1. Is it fair to excuse the criminal responsibility of someone who acted under an "irresistible impulse?"
2. Couldn't we argue that all criminals are impulsive people who lack the capacity to control their behavior?
3. If that is not true, why would they commit crime in the first place? Is it possible that child molesters, for example, are rational people who do not have "irresistible impulses?"

InfoTrac College Edition Research

To research the impact of the insanity plea on criminal defenses check out the following article: Richard J. Bonnie, Norman G. Poythress, Steven K. Hoge, John Monahan, and Marlene Eisenberg, "Decision-Making in Criminal Defense: An Empirical Study of Insanity Pleas and the Impact of Doubted Client Competence," *Journal of Criminal Law and Criminology,* Fall 1996 v87 i1 p48–62.

Sources: Richard Moran, *Knowing Right from Wrong: The Insanity Defense of Daniel McNaughtan* (New York: Free Press, 2000); Daniel N. Robinson, *Wild Beasts & Idle Humours: The Insanity Defense from Antiquity to the Present* (Cambridge, Mass.: Harvard University Press, 1998); Ralph Slovenko, *Psychiatry and Criminal Culpability* (New York: Wiley, 1995).

Age

The law holds that a child is not criminally responsible for actions committed at an age that precludes a full realization of the gravity of certain types of behavior. Under common law, there is generally a conclusive presumption of incapacity for a child under age seven, a reliable presumption for a child between the ages of seven and fourteen, and no presumption for a child over the age of fourteen. This generally means that a child under age seven who commits a crime will not be held criminally responsible for these actions and that a child between ages seven and fourteen may be held responsible. These common law rules have been changed by statute in most jurisdictions. Today, the maximum age of criminal responsibility for children ranges from age fourteen to seventeen or eighteen, while the minimum age may be set by statute at age seven or under age fourteen.[18] In addition, every jurisdiction has established a juvenile court system to deal with juvenile offenders and children in need of court and societal supervision. Thus, the mandate of the juvenile justice system is to provide for the care and protection of children under a given age, established by state statute. In certain situations, a juvenile court may transfer a more serious chronic youthful offender to the adult criminal court.

Justification and Excuse

In 1884 two British sailors, desperate after being shipwrecked for days, made the decision to kill and eat a suffering cabin boy. Four days later, they were rescued by a passing ship and returned to England. English authorities, wanting to end the practice of shipwreck cannibalism, tried and convicted the two men for murder. Clemency was considered and a reluctant Queen Victoria commuted the death sentences to six months.[19] Were the seamen justified in killing a shipmate to save their lives? If they had not done so it is likely they all would have died. Can there ever be a good reason to take a life? Can we ever justify killing another? Before you answer, remember that we can kill in self-defense, to prevent lethal crimes, or in times of war. The passengers aboard United Airlines Flight 93 are considered heroes for overcoming and (probably) killing the hijackers on September 11. Few would condemn their acts even though they may have resulted in the death of others without trial. Often, it is not the quality of the act that is most important but the way society defines and reacts to it that determines whether it is a crime.

Criminal defenses may be based on the concepts of justification or excuse. In these instances, defendants normally acknowledge that they committed the act but claim that they cannot be prosecuted because they were justified in doing so. The following major types of criminal defenses involving justification or excuse are explained in this section: *consent, self-defense, entrapment,* and *mistake, compulsion, and necessity.*

Consent   As a general rule, the victim's consent to a crime does not justify or excuse the defendant who commits the action. The type of crime involved generally

© 2002 AP/Wide World Photos

Age may be an excuse for crime and it is rare that a child under seven be prosecuted. On February 29, 2000, Kayla Rolland, a first-grader, was killed by a six-year-old classmate who had taken a gun from his home. Though the boy could not be prosecuted, a grand jury indicted one man for stealing and two others for buying the gun that he used to shoot the girl in her classroom. This photo, a tribute to Kayla, now hangs in her elementary school.

determines the validity of consent as an appropriate legal defense. Such crimes as common law rape and larceny require lack of consent on the part of the victim. In other words, a rape does not occur if the victim consents to sexual relations. In the same way, a larceny cannot occur if the owner voluntarily consents to the taking of property. Consequently, in such crimes consent is an essential element of the crime, and it is a valid defense where it can be proven or shown that it existed at the time the crime was committed. In statutory rape, however, consent is not an element of the crime and is considered irrelevant because the state presumes that young people are not capable of providing consent.

Self-Defense   In certain instances, the defendant who admits to the acts that constitute a crime may claim to be not guilty because of an affirmative self-defense. To establish the necessary elements to constitute self-defense, the defendant must have acted under a reasonable belief that he was in danger of death or great harm and had no means of escape from the assailant.

As a general legal rule, however, a person defending herself may use only such force as is reasonably necessary to prevent personal harm. A person who is assaulted by another with no weapon is ordinarily not justified in hitting the assailant with a baseball bat. A person verbally threatened by another is not justified in striking the other party. If a woman hits a larger man, generally speaking the man would not be justified in striking the woman and causing her physical harm. In other words, to exercise the self-defense privilege, the danger to the defendant must be immediate. In addition, the defendant is obligated to look for alternative means of avoiding the danger, such as escape, retreat, or assistance from others.

Today, there is a good deal of debate over the application of self-defense to a battered woman who kills her abusive husband. This is known as *battered-wife syndrome* (or in cases involving child abuse, *battered-child syndrome*). A finding of self-defense most often requires the presence of imminent danger and the inability of the accused to escape from the assailant.

Should people be allowed to carry handguns for self-defense? Go to InfoTrac College Edition and read Linda Gorman and David Kopel, "Self-Defense: The Equalizer," *Forum for Applied Research and Public Policy*, Winter 2000 v15 i4 p92.

Entrapment   The term *entrapment* refers to an affirmative defense in the criminal law that excuses a defendant from criminal liability when law enforcement agents use traps, decoys, and deception to induce criminal action. It is generally legitimate for law enforcement officers to set traps for criminals by getting information about crimes from informers, undercover agents, and codefendants. Police officers are allowed to use ordinary opportunities for defendants to commit crime and to create these opportunities without excessive inducement and solicitation to commit and involve a defendant in a crime. However, when the police instigate the crime, implant criminal ideas, and coerce individuals into bringing about crime, defendants have the defense of entrapment available to them. Entrapment is not a constitutional defense but has been created by court decision and statute in most jurisdictions.

The degree of government involvement in a criminal act leading to the entrapment defense has been defined in a number of Supreme Court decisions beginning in 1932. The majority view of what constitutes entrapment can be seen in the 1932 case of *Sorrells v. United States*.[20] During Prohibition, a federal officer passed himself off as a tourist while gaining the defendant's confidence. The federal agent eventually enticed the defendant to buy illegal liquor for him. The defendant was then arrested and prosecuted for violating the National Prohibition Act. The Court held that the officer used improper inducements that amounted to entrapment. In deciding this case, the Court settled on the subjective view of entrapment, which means that the predisposition of the defendant to commit the offense is the determining factor in entrapment. Following the *Sorrells* case, the Court stated in *Sherman v. United States* that the function of law enforcement is to prevent crime and to apprehend criminals, not to implant a criminal design originating with officials of the government in the mind of an innocent person.[21]

Mistake, Compulsion, and Necessity   Mistake or ignorance of the law is generally no defense to a crime. According to the great legal scholar William Blackstone, "Ignorance of the law, which everyone is bound to know, excuses no man."[22] Consequently, a defendant cannot present a legitimate defense by saying he was unaware of a criminal law, had misinterpreted the law, or believed the law to be unconstitutional.

On the other hand, mistakes of fact, such as taking someone else's coat that is similar to your own, may be a valid defense. If the jury or judge as trier of fact determines that criminal intent was absent, such an honest mistake may remove the defendant's criminal responsibility.

Compulsion or duress may also be a criminal defense under certain conditions. In these cases, the defendant has been forced into committing a crime. For this defense to be upheld, a defendant must show that the actions were the only means of preventing death or serious harm to self or others. For example, a bank employee might be excused from taking bank funds if she can prove that her family was being threatened and that consequently she was acting under duress. But there is widespread general agreement that duress is no defense for an intentional killing.

Closely connected to the defense of compulsion is that of necessity. According to the Model Penal Code (a substantive model of the criminal code used as a guide by states), "Necessity may be an acceptable defense, provided the harm to be avoided is greater than the offense charged."[23] In other words, the defense of necessity is justified when the crime was committed because the circumstances could not be avoided. For example, a husband steals a car to bring his pregnant wife to the hospital for an emergency delivery, or a hunter shoots an animal of an endangered species that was about to attack her child. The defense has been found inapplicable, however, in cases where defendants sought to shut down nuclear power plants or abortion clinics or to destroy missile components under the belief that the action was necessary to save lives or prevent a nuclear war.

Reforming the Criminal Law

In recent years, many states and the federal government have been examining their substantive criminal law. Since the law, in part, reflects public opinion and morality regarding various forms of behavior, what was considered criminal forty years ago may not be considered so today. In some states, crimes such as possession of marijuana have been decriminalized—that is, given reduced penalties. Such crimes may be punishable by a fine instead of a prison sentence. Other former criminal offenses, such as vagrancy, have been legalized—all criminal penalties have been removed. And in some jurisdictions, penalties have been toughened, especially for violent crimes, such as rape and spousal assault.

In some instances, new criminal laws have been created to conform to emerging social issues. For example, physician-assisted suicide became the subject of a national debate when Dr. Jack Kevorkian began practicing what he calls *obitiatry*—helping people take their lives.[24] In an attempt to stop Kevorkian, Michigan passed a statutory ban on assisted suicide, reflecting what lawmakers believed to be prevailing public opinion.[25] Kevorkian was convicted on this law and is currently serving a long prison sentence.

Assisted suicide is but one of many emerging social issues that has prompted change in the criminal law. More than twenty-five states have enacted stalking statutes, which prohibit and punish acts described typically as "the willful, malicious, and repeated following and harassing of another person."[26] Stalking laws

Can community notification laws stand the test of legal scrutiny by the Supreme Court or do they unfairly single out sex offenders and deprive them of due process? To find out, go to InfoTrac College Edition and read Wayne A. Logan, "Liberty Interests in the Preventive State: Procedural Due Process and Sex Offender Community Notification Laws," *Journal of Criminal Law and Criminology,* Summer 1999 v89 i4 p1167.

were originally formulated to protect women terrorized by former husbands and boyfriends, although celebrities often are plagued by stalkers as well. In celebrity cases, these laws often apply to stalkers who are strangers or casual acquaintances of their victims.

Community notification laws are a response to concern about sexual predators moving into neighborhoods. These are usually referred to as "Megan's Laws," named after seven-year-old Megan Kanka of Hamilton Township, New Jersey, who was killed in 1994. Charged with the crime was a convicted sex offender who the Kankas were unaware lived across the street from them. The New Jersey law requires that neighbors in the community be notified if an offender is living near them. In 1996, the federal government passed legislation requiring that the general public be informed of local *pedophiles,* sexual offenders who target children. It was left up to the officials to determine how much public warning was necessary, based on the danger posed by the offender.[27]

Similarly, new laws have been passed to keep the sexually dangerous under control. California's sexual predator law allows authorities to keep some criminals in custody even after their sentences are served. The law, which took effect January 1, 1996, allows people convicted of sexually violent crimes against two or more victims to be tried on civil charges and committed to a treatment facility upon completion of their criminal sentence.[28] (See Exhibit 3.1 for the Supreme Court's response to these laws.)

Changing technology and the ever-increasing role of technology in our daily lives will require modification in the criminal law. For example, such technologies as automatic teller machines and cellular phones have already spawned a new generation of criminal acts involving "theft" of access numbers and cards and software piracy. As the "information highway" sprawls toward new expanses, the nation's computer network advances, and biotechnology produces new substances, the criminal law will be forced to address threats to the public safety that are today unknown.

Changing Defenses

Criminal defenses are also undergoing rapid change. As society becomes more aware of existing social problems that may in part produce crime, it has become commonplace for defense counsels to defend their clients by raising a variety of new defenses based on preexisting conditions or syndromes with which their clients were afflicted. Examples might include "battered woman syndrome," "Vietnam syndrome," "child sexual abuse syndrome," "Holocaust survivor syndrome," and "adopted child syndrome." In using these defenses, attorneys are asking judges either to recognize a new excuse for crime or to fit these conditions into preexisting defenses. For example, a person who used lethal violence in self-defense may argue that the trauma of serving in the Vietnam War caused him to overreact to provocation. Or a victim of child abuse may use her experiences to mitigate her culpability in a crime, asking a jury, for example, to consider her background when making a death penalty decision. In some cases these defenses have been successful. For example, in the widely publicized Menendez case, two brothers tried for killing their parents claimed that their actions were the product of earlier sexual and physical abuse. This defense tactic led to a hung jury, although the brothers were later convicted after a second trial. In some instances, exotic criminal defenses have been gender-specific. Attorneys have argued that their female clients' behavior was a result of their premenstrual syndrome (PMS) and that male clients were aggressive because of an imbalance in their testosterone levels. These defenses have achieved relatively little success in the United States.[29] Others contend that attorneys can turn the tables and use these defenses against the defendant. For example, some commentators have suggested that courts will ultimately view PMS as an aggravating condition in a crime prompting harsher penalties.

While criminal law reform may be guided by good intentions it is sometimes difficult to put the changes into actual operation. Law reform may require new enforcement agencies to be created or severely tax existing ones. As a result the system becomes strained, and cases are backlogged. A case in point occurred in Massachusetts, which recently passed a community notification law that created a sex offender registry designed to warn neighbors and police about past offenders living in their midst. After a particularly brutal murder was committed in 2002 by a known sex offender, the state revealed that only one thousand out of eighteen thousand past offenders were actually registered because of a lengthy injunction and a staff of only eleven hearing examiners to process cases.[30]

The criminal law has also undergone extensive change in both substance and procedure in the aftermath of the September 11 terrorist attacks. This change is addressed in the following Policy, Programs, and Issues feature.

Constitutional Criminal Procedure

Whereas substantive criminal law primarily defines crimes, the law of criminal procedure consists of the rules and procedures that govern the pretrial processing of criminal suspects and the conduct of criminal trials. The principles that govern criminal procedure flow from the relationship between the individual and the state and include (1) a belief in the presumption of innocence, (2) the right to a defense against criminal charges, and (3) the requirement that the government act in a lawful manner. In general, these policies are mandated by the provisions of state constitutions. A sound understanding of criminal procedure requires an awareness of constitutional law.

The U.S. Constitution

The U.S. Constitution has played and continues to play a critical role in the development of the criminal law used in the criminal justice system. A document called the Articles of Confederation, which was adopted by the Continental Congress in 1781, was the forerunner to the Constitution. This document was found to be generally inadequate as the foundation for effective government because it did not create a proper balance of power between the states and the central government. As a result, in 1787 the Congress of the Confederation adopted a resolution calling for a convention of delegates from the original states. Meeting in Philadelphia, the delegates' express purpose was to revise the Articles of Confederation. The work of that convention culminated in the drafting of the Constitution; it was ratified by the states in 1788 and put into effect in 1789. In its original form, the Constitution consisted of a preamble and seven articles. The Constitution divided the powers of government into three independent but equal parts: the executive, the legislative, and the judicial branches. The purpose of the separation of powers was to ensure that no single branch of government could usurp power for itself and institute a dictatorship. The measures and procedures initiated by the framers of the Constitution have developed over time into our present form of government.

How does the Constitution, with its formal set of rights and privileges, affect the operations of the criminal justice system? One way is to guarantee that no one branch of government can in and of itself determine the fate of those accused of crimes. The workings of the criminal justice process illustrate this principle. A police officer, who represents the executive branch of government, makes an arrest on the basis of laws passed by the legislative branch, and the accused is subsequently tried by the judiciary. In this way, citizens are protected from the arbitrary abuse of power by any single element of the law.

The Criminal Law and Terrorism

Soon after the September 11 terrorist attacks, the U.S. government enacted several laws focused on preventing further acts of violence against the United States. Most importantly, Congress passed the USA Patriot Act (USAPA) on October 26, 2001. The bill is over 342 pages long, creates new laws, and makes changes to over fifteen different existing statutes. Its aim is to give sweeping new powers to domestic law enforcement and international intelligence agencies in an effort to fight terrorism, to expand the definition of terrorist activities, and to alter sanctions for violent terrorism. While it is impossible here to discuss every provision of this sweeping legislation, a few of its more important elements will be examined.

Among its provisions, USAPA expands all four traditional tools of surveillance—wiretaps, search warrants, pen/trap orders (installing devices that record phone calls), and subpoenas. The Foreign Intelligence Surveillance Act (FISA) that allows domestic operations by intelligence agencies are also expanded. USAPA gives greater power to the FBI to check and monitor phone, Internet, and computer records without first needing to demonstrate that they were being used by a suspect or target of a court order.

The government may now serve a single wiretap, or pen/trap order, on any person regardless of whether that person or entity is named in a court order. Prior to this act, telephone companies could be ordered to install pen/trap devices on their networks that would monitor calls coming to a surveillance target and to whom the surveillance target made calls; the USAPA extends this monitoring to the Internet. Law enforcement agencies may now also obtain the e-mail addresses and Web sites visited by a target, and e-mails of the people with whom they communicate. It is possible to require that an Internet service provider install a device that records e-mail and other electronic communications on its servers, looking for communications initiated or received by the target of an investigation. Under USAPA, the government does not need to show a court that the information or communication is relevant to a criminal investigation, nor does it have to report where it served the order or what information it received.

The act also allows enforcement agencies to monitor cable operators and obtain access to their records and systems. Before the act, a cable company had to give prior notice to the customer, even if that person was a target of an investigation. Information can now be obtained on people with whom the cable subscriber communicates, the content of the person's communications, and the person's subscription records; prior notice is still required if law enforcement agencies want to learn what television programming a subscriber purchases.

The act also expands the definition of "terrorism" and enables the government to monitor more closely those people suspected of "harboring" and giving "material support" to terrorists (sections 803, 805). It increases the authority of the U.S. attorney general to detain and deport noncitizens with little or no judicial review. The attorney general may certify that he has "reasonable grounds to believe" that a noncitizen endangers national security and is therefore eligible for deportation. The attorney general and secretary of state are also given the authority to designate domestic groups as terrorist organizations, and deport any noncitizen who is a member.

Although law enforcement agencies may applaud these new laws, civil libertarians are troubled because they view the act as eroding civil rights. Political commentator Morton Halperin, for one, complains that there are provisions that permit the government to share information from grand jury proceedings and from criminal wiretaps with intelligence agencies. He also argues that First Amendment–protected activities of American citizens—watching TV, for example—may be violated. He is concerned that this new and sweeping authority is not limited to true terrorism investigations but covers a much broader range of activity involving reasonable political dissent.

Critical Thinking

1. Does the war on terrorism mean that Americans will be sacrificing rights that they have long cherished, such as political dissent and privacy? Is it worth sacrificing some civil rights if it means that law enforcement agencies can be more effective in the fight against terrorism? If not, are you afraid that once these rights are taken away they are not easily returned?

2. What additional powers should the government have to fight the war on terrorism? For example, should all foreign nationals be forced to report on a regular basis to the Department of Homeland Security?

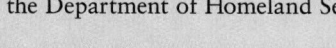

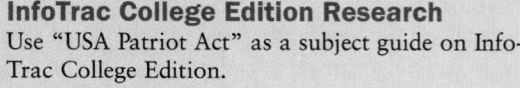

InfoTrac College Edition Research

Use "USA Patriot Act" as a subject guide on InfoTrac College Edition.

Sources: Douglas A. Kash, "Hunting Terrorists Using Confidential Informant Reward Programs," *FBI Law Enforcement Bulletin,* 71 (2002): 26–28; Sara Sun Beale and James Felman, "The Consequences of Enlisting Federal Grand Juries in the War on Terrorism: Assessing the USA Patriot Act's Changes to Grand Jury Secrecy," *Harvard Journal of Law & Public Policy* 25 (2002): 699–721; Morton Halperin, "Less Secure, Less Free: Striking Terror at Civil Liberty," *American Prospect, 12* (November 19, 2001): 1013.

The Bill of Rights

Besides providing protection by ensuring a separation of powers within the government, the Constitution controls the operations of the criminal justice system. It does so by guaranteeing individual freedoms in the ten amendments added to it on December 15, 1791, collectively known as the **Bill of Rights**.[31]

The Bill of Rights was added to the Constitution to prevent government from usurping the personal freedoms of citizens. In its original form, the Constitution contained few specific guarantees of individual rights. The founding fathers, aware of the past abuses perpetrated by the British government, wanted to ensure that the rights of U.S. citizens would be safe. The Bill of Rights was adopted to protect individual liberties from being abused by the national government alone, however, and did not apply to the actions of state or local officials. This oversight resulted in abuses that have been rectified only with great difficulty and even today remain the subject of court action.

The principles that govern criminal procedure are required by the Constitution and the Bill of Rights. Of primary concern are the Fourth, Fifth, Sixth, and Eighth Amendments, which limit and control the manner in which the federal government operates the justice system. In addition, the due process clause of the Fourteenth Amendment, which is discussed in the next section, has helped define the nature and limits of governmental action against the accused on a state level.

- The *Fourth Amendment* is especially important for the criminal justice system because it establishes that police officers cannot indiscriminately use their authority to investigate a possible crime or arrest a suspect unless either or both actions are justified by the law and the facts of the case. Stopping, questioning, or searching an individual without legal justification represents a serious violation of the Fourth Amendment right to personal privacy.
- Limiting the admissibility of confessions that have been obtained unfairly is another method of controlling police behavior. The right against **self-incrimination** is frequently asserted by a defendant in an effort to exclude confessions or admissions that might be vital to the government's case. In such instances, the application of the *Fifth Amendment* to the Constitution is critical to the criminal justice system. The Fifth Amendment has, in fact, had a tremendous impact on the criminal justice system. In 1966 in the landmark case of *Miranda v. Arizona*, the Supreme Court held that a person accused of a crime has the right to refuse to answer questions when placed in police custody.[32]
- The *Sixth Amendment* guarantees the defendant the right to a speedy and public trial by an impartial jury, the right to be informed of the nature of the charges, and the right to confront any prosecution witnesses. This amendment has had a profound effect on the treatment of persons accused of crimes and has been the basis for numerous significant Supreme Court decisions that have increased the rights of criminal defendants. Many Court decisions regarding the Sixth Amendment have also concerned the individual's right to counsel. The right of a defendant to be represented by an attorney has been extended to numerous stages of the criminal justice process, including pretrial custody, identification and lineup procedures, preliminary hearing, submission of a guilty plea, trial, sentencing, and postconviction appeal.
- According to the *Eighth Amendment,* "Excessive bail shall not be required, nor excessive fines imposed, nor cruel and unusual punishments inflicted." *Bail* is a money bond put up by the accused to attain freedom between arrest and trial. Bail is meant to ensure a trial appearance, since the bail money is forfeited if the defendant misses the trial date. The Eighth Amendment does not guarantee a constitutional right to bail but rather prohibits the exactment of excessive bail. Nevertheless, since many state statutes place no precise limit on the amount of bail a judge may impose, many defendants who

Bill of Rights The first ten amendments to the U.S. Constitution.

self-incrimination Personal utterances or statements that can be used as evidence in a criminal matter. The Fifth Amendment prohibits law enforcement officials from using force or coercion to obtain incriminating statements from suspects in criminal cases.

cannot make bail are often placed in detention while awaiting trial. Another goal of the framers of the Constitution was to curtail the use of torture and excessive physical punishment. Consequently, the prohibition against cruel and unusual punishment was added to the Eighth Amendment. This prohibition has affected the imposition of the death penalty and other criminal dispositions and has become a guarantee that serves to protect both the accused and convicted offenders from actions regarded as unacceptable by a civilized society.

These key amendments furnish the basis of our system of criminal procedure.

The Fourteenth Amendment

The Fourteenth Amendment has been the vehicle most often used to apply the protection of the Bill of Rights to the states. The most important aspect of this amendment is the clause that says no state shall "deprive any person of life, liberty, or property, without due process of law." This meant that the same general constitutional restrictions previously applicable to the federal government were to be imposed on the states. It is essential to keep the following constitutional principles in mind:

1. The first ten amendments—the Bill of Rights—originally applied to the federal government only; they were designed to protect citizens against injustices inflicted by federal authorities. The Bill of Rights restricts the actions of the federal government and does not apply to the states.
2. The Fourteenth Amendment's due process clause applies to state governments. It has been used to provide individuals in all states with the basic liberties guaranteed by the Bill of Rights.
3. The U.S. Supreme Court has expanded the rights of defendants in the criminal justice system by interpreting the due process clause to mean that the states must be held to standards similar to those applicable to the federal government by the Bill of Rights.

Through a long series of court decisions, the Supreme Court has held that the guarantees of the First, Fourth, Fifth, Sixth, and Eighth Amendments apply to the states as well as to the federal government. These decisions were based on the theory of *selective incorporation,* which states that the Bill of Rights does apply to the states through the due process clause of the Fourteenth Amendment, but only on a case-by-case basis. Advocates of this theory believe that some of the provisions of the Bill of Rights may be binding on the states—such as the right to a jury trial or the right to be free from self-incrimination—but that these should apply only after a careful consideration of the facts, or merits, of each case.

Using this formula, the incorporation of the provisions of the Bill of Rights into the Fourteenth Amendment moved forward slowly, accelerating in 1953 when Earl Warren became chief justice of the Supreme Court. Under his leadership, the due process movement reached its peak. The Court decided numerous landmark cases focusing on the rights of the accused and brought about a revolution in the area of constitutional criminal procedure. The Warren Court of the 1960s granted many new rights to those accused of crimes and went so far as to impose specific guidelines on the policies of police, courts, and correctional services that ensured that due process of law would be maintained.

Today, the Fourteenth Amendment's due process clause has been interpreted by the Supreme Court to mean that an accused in a state criminal case is virtually entitled to the same protections available under the federal Bill of Rights.

To read more about these issues, use "constitutional law" as a subject guide on InfoTrac College Edition.

Procedural Due Process of Law

The concept of due process has been used as a basis for incorporating the Bill of Rights into the Fourteenth Amendment. Due process has also been used to evaluate the constitutionality of legal statutes and to set standards and guidelines for fair procedures in the criminal justice system.

In seeking to define the meaning of the term, most legal experts believe that it refers to the essential elements of fairness under law.[33] *Black's Law Dictionary* presents an elaborate and complex definition of due process:

> *Due process of law in each particular case means such an exercise of the powers of government as the settled maxims of law permit and sanction, and under such safeguards for the protection of individual rights as those maxims prescribe for the class of cases to which the one in question belongs.*[34]

This definition refers to the legal system's need for rules and regulations that protect individual rights. Due process seeks to ensure that no person will be deprived of life, liberty, or property without notice of charges, assistance from legal counsel, a hearing, and an opportunity to confront those making the accusations. Basically, due process is intended to guarantee that fundamental fairness exists in each individual case. This doctrine of fairness as expressed in due process of law is guaranteed under both the Fifth and Fourteenth Amendments.[35] Abstract definitions are only one aspect of due process. Much more significant are the procedures that give meaning to due process in the everyday practices of the criminal justice system. In this regard, due process provides numerous procedural safeguards for the offender. The specific due process procedures are listed here:

1. Notices of charges
2. A formal hearing
3. The right to counsel or some other representation
4. The opportunity to respond to charges
5. The opportunity to confront and cross-examine witnesses and accusers
6. The privilege to be free from self-incrimination
7. The opportunity to present one's own witnesses
8. A decision made on the basis of substantial evidence and facts produced at the hearing
9. A written statement of the reasons for the decision
10. An appellate review procedure

Exactly what constitutes due process in a specific case depends on the facts of the case, the federal and state constitutional and statutory provisions, previous court decisions, and the ideas and principles that society considers important at a given time and in a given place.[36] Justice Felix Frankfurter emphasized this point in *Rochin v. California* (1952):

> *Due process of law requires an evaluation based on a disinterested inquiry pursued in the spirit of science on a balanced order of facts, exactly and clearly stated, on the detached consideration of conflicting claims...on a judgment not ad hoc and episodic but duly mindful of reconciling the needs both of continuity and of change in a progressive society.*[37]

The interpretations of due process of law are not fixed but rather reflect what society deems fair and just at a particular time and place. The degree of loss suffered by the individual (victim or offender) balanced against the state's interests also determines which and how many due process requirements are ordinarily applied.

SUMMARY

The criminal justice system is basically a legal system. Its foundation is the criminal law, which is concerned with people's conduct. The purpose of criminal law is to regulate behavior and maintain order in society. What constitutes a crime is defined primarily by the state and federal legislatures and reviewed by the courts.

What is considered criminal conduct changes from one period to another. Social norms, values, and community beliefs play major roles in determining what conduct is antisocial. Crimes are generally classified as felonies or misdemeanors, depending on their seriousness. Since a crime is a public wrong against the state, the criminal law imposes sanctions in the form of fines, probation, or imprisonment on a guilty defendant.

Under the criminal law, all adults are presumed to be aware of the consequences of their actions, but the law does not hold an individual blameworthy unless that person is capable of intending to commit the crime of which he is accused. Such factors as insanity, a mental defect, and age mitigate a person's criminal responsibility.

States periodically revise and update the substantive criminal law. The definition of crime and criminal defense change to reflect existing social and cultural change. For example, recent changes in laws controlling terrorism reflect the public condemnation of the September 11 terrorist attacks.

Procedural laws set out the rules for processing the offender from arrest through trial, sentencing, and release. An accused must be provided with the guarantees of due process under the Fifth and Fourteenth Amendments to the U.S. Constitution.

For an up-to-date list of Web links, go to http://cj.wadsworth.com/siegel_essen4e.

KEY TERMS

substantive criminal law 78	common law 79	felony 85	insanity 91
criminal procedure 78	mala in se 79	misdemeanor 85	self-defense 91
civil law 78	*Carriers* case 79	actus reus 88	entrapment 91
stare decisis 79	tort 81	mens rea 88	Bill of Rights 101
	intent 81	strict liability crime 91	self-incrimination 101

INFOTRAC COLLEGE EDITION EXERCISES

THE JURY in the 1997 Massachusetts murder trial of British au pair Louise Woodward, who was accused of killing the baby she was caring for, had four choices:

1. *First-degree murder:* There was intent to kill, cause harm or injury or atrocity, and extreme cruelty

2. *Second-degree murder:* Woodward acted with malice

3. *Acquittal:* Woodward is innocent because the prosecution failed to prove her guilt beyond a reasonable doubt

4. *Hung jury:* The jury is divided between Woodward's guilt and innocence.

After the jury found her guilty of second-degree murder, the judge reduced Woodward's sentence to manslaughter because the intent to do bodily harm or act with malice was not present. *Involuntary manslaughter* is a killing with no intention to cause serious bodily harm, such as acting without proper caution.

Suppose you work in the prosecutor's office and you have been assigned the task of coming up with information on criminal homicide to assist the government in its appeal. Search for articles using InfoTrac College Edition regarding the distinction between murder and manslaughter. Use key words such as "malice," "intent to kill," and "provocation."

To read a critique of the decision by conservative columnist William Buckley, look up William F. Buckley Jr., "Scrambled Justice," *National Review,* December 8, 1997 v49 i23 p62(1).

QUESTIONS

1. What are the specific aims and purposes of the criminal law? To what extent does the criminal law control behavior?

2. What kinds of activities should be labeled criminal in contemporary society? Why?

3. What is a criminal act? What is a criminal state of mind? When are individuals liable for their actions?

4. Discuss the various kinds of crime classifications. To what extent or degree are they distinguishable?

5. Numerous states are revising their penal codes. Which major categories of substantive crimes do you think should be revised?

6. Entrapment is a defense when the defendant was entrapped into committing the crime. To what extent should law enforcement personnel induce the commission of an offense?

7. What legal principles can be used to justify self-defense? As the law seeks to prevent, not promote, crime, are such principles sound?

8. What are the minimum standards of criminal procedure required in the criminal justice system?

NOTES

1. Some of the historical criminal law concepts discussed here are a synthesis of those contained in Peter Stein, *Roman Law in European History* (London: Cambridge University Press, 1999); Norman Cantor, *Imagining the Law: Common Law and the Foundations of the American Legal System* (New York: Harper Collins, 1999); Jerome Hall, *General Principles of Criminal Law* (Charlottesville, Va.: Michie, 1961).

2. Carriers *Case Yearbook,* 13 Edward IV 9.pL.5 (1473).

3. See, generally, Wayne R. LaFave and Austin W. Scott, *Criminal Law* (St. Paul, Minn.: West Publishing Horn Book Series, 1986).

4. E. Gellhorn, *Administrative Law and Process* (St. Paul, Minn.: West Publishing Nutshell Series, 1981).

5. See John Weaver, *Warren—The Man, the Court, the Era* (Boston: Little, Brown, 1967); see also "We the People," *Time,* 6 July 1987, 6.

6. *Marbury v. Madison,* 5 U.S. (1 Cranch) 137, 2 L.Ed. 60 (1803).

7. *City of Chicago v. Morales et al.* 527 U.S. 41 (1999).

8. *Kansas v. Hendricks,* 117 S.Ct. 2072 (1997); *Chicago v. Morales,* 119 S.Ct. 246 (1999).

9. See American Law Institute, Model Penal Code, sec. 104.

10. Henry Black, *Black's Law Dictionary,* 5th ed. (St. Paul, Minn.: West, 1979), 744, 1150.

11. Mass. Gen. Laws, chap. 274, sec. 1.

12. Sheldon Krantz, *Law of Corrections and Prisoners' Rights, Cases and Materials,* 3d ed. (St. Paul, Minn.: West, 1986), 702; Barbara Knight and Stephen Early Jr., *Prisoners' Rights in America* (Chicago: Nelson-Hall, 1986), Chap 1; see also Fred Cohen, "The Law of Prisoners' Rights—An Overview," *Criminal Law Bulletin* 24 (188): 321–349.

13. See *United States v. Balint,* 258 U.S. 250, 42 S.Ct. 301, 66 L.Ed. 604 (1922); see also *Morissette v. United States,* 342 U.S. 246, 72 S.Ct. 240, 96 L.Ed. 288 (1952).

14. New York State Consolidated Laws, Article 270: Other Offenses Relating to Public Safety, Section 270.10: Creating a hazard (2002).

15. "Nigerian Used Stepdaughter, Fourteen, for a Son, Jury Finds," *Boston Globe,* 8 October 1998, 9.

16. 370 U.S. 660, 82 S.Ct. 1417, 8 L.Ed.2d 758 (1962).

17. 392 U.S. 514, 88 S.Ct. 2145, 20 L.Ed.2d 1254 (1968).

18. Samuel M. Davis, *Rights of Juveniles: The Juvenile Justice System* (New York: Boardman, 1974; updated 1993), chap. 2; Larry Siegel and Joseph Senna, *Juvenile Delinquency: Theory, Practice, and Law* (St. Paul, Minn.: West, 1996).

19. *Regina v. Dudley and Stephens,* 14 Q.B.D. 273 (1884).

20. 287 U.S. 435, 53 S.Ct. 210, 77 L.Ed. 413 (1932).

21. 356 U.S. 369, 78 S.Ct. 819, 2 L.Ed.2d 848 (1958); see also *Jacobson v. United States,* 503 U.S. 540, 112 S.Ct. 1535, 118 L.Ed.2d 174 (1992).

22. William Blackstone, *Commentaries on the Law of England,* vol. 1, ed. Thomas Cooley (Chicago: Callaghan, 1899), 4, 26. Blackstone was an English barrister who lectured on the English common law at Oxford University in 1753.

23. American Law Institute, Model Penal Code, sec. 2.04.

24. Marvin Zalman, John Strate, Denis Hunter, and James Sellars, "Michigan Assisted Suicide Three Ring Circus: The Intersection of Law and Politics," *Ohio Northern Law Review* 23 (1997): 218–247.

25. 1992 P.A.270 as amended by 1993 P.A.3, M.C. L. Sections 752.1021 to 752.1027.

26. National Institute of Justice, *Project to Develop a Model Antistalking Statute* (Washington, D.C.: National Institute of Justice, 1994).

27. "Clinton Signs Tougher 'Megan's Law,'" CNN News Service, 17 May 1996.

28. "Judge Upholds State's Sexual Predator Law," *Bakersfield Californian,* 2 October 1996, 1.

29. Deborah W. Denno, "Gender, Crime, and the Criminal Law Defenses," *Journal of Criminal Law and Criminology 85* (Summer 1994): 80–180.

30. Michele Kurtz, "Predator Laws Hit by Rulings, Backlogs," *Boston Globe,* 20 July 2002, 1.

31. For a real-world application and the impact of the Bill of Rights on criminal justice in particular, see Ellen Alderman and Caroline Kennedy, *In Our Defense—The Bill of Rights in Action* (New York: Morrow, 1991).

32. 384 U.S. 436, 86 S.Ct. 1602, 16 L.Ed.2d 694 (1966).

33. See "Essay," *Time,* 26 February 1973, 95; also, for a tribute to the Bill of Rights and due process, see James MacGregor Burns and Steward Burns, *The Pursuit of Rights in America* (New York: Knopf, 1991).

34. Black, *Black's Law Dictionary,* 449.

35. See, generally, Joseph J. Senna, "Changes in Due Process of Law," *Social Work 19* (1974): 319; see also the interesting student rights case *Goss v. Lopez,* 419 U.S. 565, 95 S.Ct. 729, 42 L.Ed.2d 725 (1975).

36. 342 U.S. 165, 72 S.Ct. 205, 95 L.Ed. 183 (1952).

37. Ibid. at 172, 72 S.Ct. at 209.

Who Is the Terrorist?

There have been a number of competing visions of why terrorists engage in criminal activities such as bombings, shootings, and kidnappings to achieve a political end. One view is that terrorists begin as members of disenfranchised groups angered by their positions of helplessness and feelings of oppression. They believe that they are being victimized by some group or government. Once these potential terrorists recognize that these conditions can be changed by an active governmental reform effort that has not happened, they conclude that they must resort to violence to encourage change. The violence need not be aimed at a specific goal. Rather, terror tactics must help set in motion a series of events that enlist others in the cause and lead to long-term change. "Successful" terrorists believe that their "self-sacrifice" outweighs the guilt created by harming innocent people. Terrorism, therefore, requires violence without guilt; the cause justifies the violence.

Another view is that terrorists may be motivated by feelings of alienation and failure to comprehend post-technological society. For example, in a recent book, Haruki Murakami, a Japanese novelist, interviewed members of the Aum Shinrikyo, a radical religious group that set off poison gas in a Tokyo subway in 1995, killing twelve and injuring five thousand. Murakami found that the terrorist fanatics lived in what they considered to be a perfect world, where there were easy answers to even the most complex questions. The terrorists found modern society too complex to understand, with few clear-cut goals and values. Surprisingly, the cult members he interviewed were relatively "ordinary" people; some were school dropouts with few prospects, but others were highly educated professionals. All seemed alienated from modern society, and some felt that a suicide mission would cleanse them from the corruption of the modern world.

Some experts believe that terrorists are emotionally disturbed individuals who act out their psychoses within the confines of violent groups. According to this view, terrorist violence is not so much a political instrument as an end in itself; it is the result of compulsion or psychopathology. Terrorists do what they do because of a garden variety of emotional problems, including but not limited to self-destructive urges, disturbed emotions combined with problems with authority, and inconsistent and troubled parenting.

The Postmodern Terrorist

"Today, international terrorists likely to target the United States are individuals," and the "greatest threat to the security of the United States in the next millennium will come from the hands of the freelancer." These prophetic words were written by terrorism expert Harvey Kushner in 1998, several years before the September 11 attack on the World Trade Center. Kushner correctly recognized that the traditional image of the armed professional terrorist group with a clear-cut goal such as nationalism or independence was giving way to a new breed of terrorists with diverse motives and sponsors. It is now generally recognized that the new breed of terrorist may have different backgrounds and motivations. After all, terrorist leader Osama bin Laden is a multi-millionaire who has never personally suffered at the hands of the United States. The postmodern terrorist motivation may combine feelings of religious and political oppression, personal alienation, and psychological deficits.

Osama bin Laden is a striking example of this phenomenon. On the surface, it appears that he was the favored son of a wealthy Saudi family. The fortune he has used to finance his terrorist activities derives from an inheritance of over $300 million. Rather than poverty and helplessness, his violent aggression may be motivated by some deep-rooted psychological deficits. Bin Laden is the only son of his late father's least favorite wife, who was a Syrian and not a Saudi. Though bin Laden may have been close to his mother, he may have felt driven to achieve stature in the eyes of his father and the rest of the family. He may have been willing to do anything to gain power and eclipse his father, who died when bin Laden was ten years old.

In other words, the impulse for his murderous actions may stem from bin Laden's unconscious efforts to gain his father's approval. He modeled his behavior after his father in many ways, including working with the Saudi royal family on construction projects. Bin Laden once told an interviewer of his desire to please his father: "My father was very keen that one of his sons should fight against the enemies of Islam. So I am the one son who is acting according to the wishes of his father." Perhaps this need for acceptance explains bin Laden's religious zeal, which is in excess of anyone else in his large extended family.

After his father's death, bin Laden was mentored by a Jordanian named Abdullah Azzam, whose motto was "Jihad and the rifle alone: no negotiations, no conferences, and no dialogues." When Azzam was killed in 1989 by a car bomb in Pakistan, bin Laden vowed to carry on Azzam's "holy war" against the West. He threw himself into the Afghan conflict against the Soviet Union, and when the Russians withdrew, was convinced that the West was vulnerable. "The myth of the superpower was destroyed not only in my mind but also in the minds of all Muslims," bin Laden has told interviewers.

Bin Laden's personal issues became cloaked in religious fervor that drew adherents to his al Qaeda organization, which grew sixfold from 1980 to 1992, and has continued to increase steadily ever since. His religiously inspired terrorist attacks are more likely to result in high casualties because they are motivated not by efforts to obtain political freedom or a national homeland but by cultural and religious beliefs. Because they are on a holy mission, his followers can justify in their minds the deaths of large numbers of people; after all, the violence is a divine duty justified by scripture.

Osama bin Laden and the al Qaeda group are the paradigm of the new value-oriented terrorist organization. Bin Laden's masterminding of the September 11, 2001, attacks was not designed to restore his homeland or bring about a new political state but rather to have his personal value structure adopted by Muslim nations. His attack may have been designed to create the military invasion of Afghanistan, which he hoped to exploit for his particular brand of revolution. Some experts believe that bin Laden hoped that his acts would ignite the *umma,* or universal Islamic community. The media would show the Americans killing innocent civilians in Afghanistan and the umma would find it shocking that Americans nonchalantly caused Muslims to suffer and die. The ensuing outrage would open a chasm between the Moslem population of the Middle East and the ruling governments in states such as Saudi Arabia that have been allied with the West. On October 7, 2001, bin Laden made a broadcast in which he said that the Americans and the British "have divided the entire world into two regions—one of faith, where there is no hypocrisy, and another of infidelity, from which we hope God will protect us."

C. Sherburne/PhotoLink/Getty Images

It is possible that bin Laden's true aim for the September 11 attacks was to cause an Islamic revolution within the Muslim world itself, in Saudi Arabia especially, and not to win a war with the United States. Bin Laden views the leaders of the Arab and Islamic worlds as hypocrites and idol worshipers, propped up by American military might. His attack was designed to force those governments to choose: you are either with the idol-worshiping enemies of God or you are with the true believers. The attack on the United States was merely an instrument designed to help his brand of extremist Islam survive and flourish among the believers who could bring down these corrupt governments. Americans, in short, were drawn into somebody else's civil war.

These new-generation terrorists, represented by bin Laden, are especially frightening because they feel no need to live to enjoy the fruits of victory. Because they do not hope to regain a homeland or a political victory, they are willing to engage in suicide missions to achieve their goals. The devoted members of al Qaeda are willing to martyr themselves because they believe they are locked in a life-or-death struggle with the forces of nonbelievers. They consider themselves true believers surrounded by blasphemers and have concluded that the future of religion itself, and therefore the world, depends on them and their battle against idol worship. They believe that victory and salvation can be achieved in a martyr's death. Rather than a unified central command, postmodern terrorists are organized in far-flung nets. Not located in any particular nation or area, they have no identifiable address. They are capable of attacking anyone at any time with great destructive force. They may employ an arsenal of weapons of mass destruction—chemical, biological, nuclear—without fear of contaminating their own homeland, because in reality they may not have one. ■

Sources: Haruki Murakami, *Underground* (New York: Vintage Books, 2001); Peter L. Bergen, *Holy War, Inc.: Inside the Secret World of Osama bin Laden* (New York: Free Press, 2001), 41–50; Yonah Alexander and Michael S. Swetnam, *Usama bin Laden's al-Qaida: Profile of a Terrorist Network* (New York: Transnational Publishers, 2001); Michael Scott Doran, "Somebody Else's Civil War," *Foreign Affairs 81* (January-February 2002): 22–25; Bruce Hoffman, "Change and Continuity in Terrorism," *Studies in Conflict and Terrorism 24* (2001); Harvey Kushner, *Terrorism in America: A Structured Approach to Understanding the Terrorist Threat* (Springfield: Charles C. Thomas, 1998), 87, 92; Ian Lesser, Bruce Hoffman, John Arquilla, David Ronfeldt, and Michele Zanini, *Countering the New Terrorism* (Washington, D.C.: RAND, 1999); Jessica Stern, *The Ultimate Terrorists* (Cambridge, Mass.: Harvard University Press, 1999); Mark Jurgensmeyer, *Terror in the Mind of God* (Berkeley and Los Angeles: University of California Press, 2000); Jerrold M. Post, "Terrorist Psycho-Logic: Terrorist Behavior as a Product of Psychological Forces," in Walter Reich (ed.), *Origins of Terrorism: Psychologies, Ideologies, Theologies, States of Mind* (Cambridge: Cambridge University Press, 1990), 12; Reuel Marc Gerecht, "The Counterterroist Myth," *Atlantic Monthly 288* (July-August 2001): 288–293.

To find out more about terrorism, go to http://cj.wadsworth.com and click on "Terrorism Update."

The Police and Law Enforcement

A few years ago, the Richmond, Virginia, homicide rate was the second highest in the nation; gun toting had become a way of life. Then the local police, in cooperation with the U.S. Bureau of Alcohol, Tobacco and Firearms, created Project Exile. This innovative program was designed to combat gun crime in a simple and direct fashion. Any time Richmond police found a gun on a drug dealer, user, convicted felon, or suspect in a violent crime, the case would be tried under federal statutes that carry mandatory sentences of at least five years without parole—and longer for repeated or aggravated offenses. To publicize the program, its slogan—*An Illegal Gun Gets You Five Years in Prison*—was splashed across billboards in high-crime neighborhoods and on city buses. A TV campaign spread the word over the airwaves. Since the program began, hundreds of gun offenders have been sent to prison and hundreds of guns have been removed from the street. Much to the program creators' delight, murders and armed robberies in Richmond dropped sharply after the program was instituted. Because of its success, Project Exile–type programs are being adopted in Atlanta, Georgia; Birmingham, Alabama; Fort Worth, Texas; New Orleans; Norfolk, Virginia; Philadelphia; Rochester, New York; and San Francisco. In Texas, the program's motto is "Gun crime means hard time," while in Rochester billboards on the side of city buses read: "You + illegal gun = federal prison."

Programs such as Project Exile typify the effort of modern police agencies to take an aggressive stance against crime. Rather than simply react after a crime occurs, local police are now cooperating with other governmental agencies and working in partnership with the general public to reduce area crime rates. Cracking down on gun crimes, patrolling crime-ridden schools, and acting as community change agents are but a few of the roles of the modern police. In the following three chapters the history, role, and police profession will be discussed in some detail. We will be looking at legal, social, and professional issues in depth. ∎

4 Police in Society: History and Organization

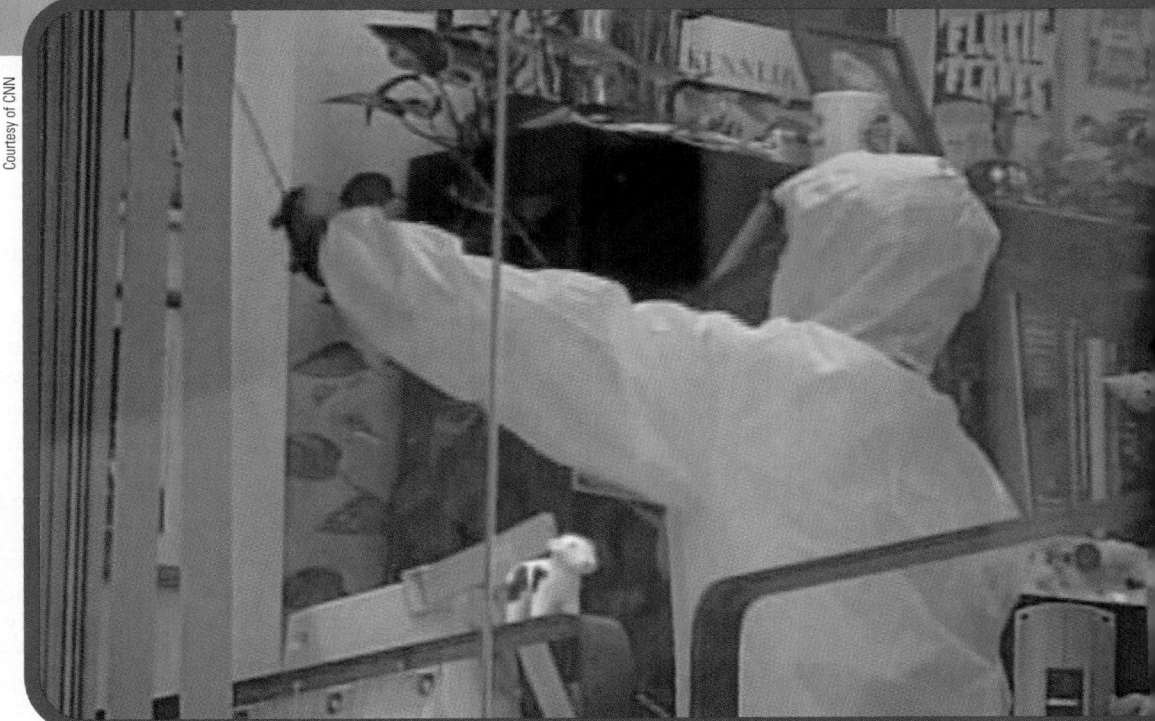

IN THE FALL OF 2001, soon after the September 11 attack, two employees of American Media Company in Florida contracted the deadly disease anthrax; one later died. Soon people were reported ill with the disease in New York and Washington, D.C. A New Jersey postal worker and an employee of CBS News in New York both tested positive for skin anthrax. At the same time, the Kenyan government said that four people had been exposed to the bacteria in a letter posted from America.

A letter addressed to Senator Tom Daschle was discovered to contain anthrax. After the FBI and Environmental Protection Agency (EPA) agents checked letters in 280 barrels of unopened mail collected from Capitol Hill, they discovered a second contaminated letter addressed to Senator Patrick Leahy. The discovery of the Leahy letter was accomplished by teams of hazardous materials (hazmat) workers from the FBI and the EPA Criminal Investigative Division. An innovative protocol was developed by scientific and forensic experts in these agencies to analyze these congressional mailbags for anthrax contamination. The new method eliminated the need for hazardous materials teams to sift through each piece of mail to find additional contaminated mail. The mail was sampled and sorted in a containment facility constructed inside a large warehouse. For a while the capitol building was shut down. In the following months, the FBI responded to more than twenty-three hundred incidents or suspected incidents involving anthrax or other dangerous agents. Thankfully, the overwhelming majority of these incidents turned out not to be real cases of anthrax; they were false alarms or practical jokes. ■

To view the CNN video clip of this story, *go to the book-specific Web site at* http://cj.wadsworth.com/siegel_essen4e.

The anthrax alert galvanized the nation. And although the actual cause of the problem is still under investigation, how the situation was handled in the weeks following the discovery of the tainted mail illustrates the complex tasks that are carried out by the nation's law enforcement agencies. The responsibility for tracking down suspect letters was given to a variety of federal agencies that make up a significant part of the nation's law enforcement community. The anthrax case also shows the complex and evolving nature of police work and law enforcement in postmodern society.

The changing police role is of critical importance to the criminal justice system. The police are the gatekeepers of the criminal justice process. They initiate contact with law violators and decide whether to arrest them formally and start their journey through the criminal justice system, to settle the issue in an informal way (such as by issuing a warning), or to take no action at all. The strategic position of law enforcement officers, their visibility and contact with the public, and their use of weapons and arrest power kept them in the forefront of public thought for most of the twentieth century.

The public may applaud police efforts that have brought the crime rate down, but they are also concerned by media reports of police officers who abuse their power by either using unnecessary force and brutality or routinely violating the civil rights of suspects. Even when community members believe police officers are competent and dependable, many question their priorities and often consider them disrespectful.[1] For example, some critics charge that police officers routinely induce or force confessions from criminal suspects. Later at trial, these false confessions may influence jurors even if they seem inconsistent with the facts of the case.[2] Another concern is that police are racially and ethnically biased and use racial profiling to routinely stop African Americans and search their cars. Some cynics suggest that police have created a new form of crime: *DWB*, "driving while black."[3] In the post–September 11 age, police are focusing their attention on suspected Middle Eastern terrorists. For example, on September 13, 2002, three men of Middle Eastern descent were detained along a South Florida highway, their possessions searched, and a backpack blown up because they were suspected of plotting a terrorist attack. The police were alerted by a woman who claimed to have overheard them planning a terror attack while eating in a restaurant.[4] Should cars containing Arab males be searched with less than probable cause, or is this a violation of their civil rights?

Despite such concerns, the majority of citizens give their local police force high marks.[5] Citizens are especially likely to give police high marks if they view their neighborhood as safe and believe that police efficiency is a key to its protection.[6] Metropolitan police departments are attracting applicants who value an exciting, well-paid job that also holds the opportunity to provide valuable community service. So, although police agencies are still trying to define their role and effectively marshal their resources, they continue to be held in high esteem by the public they serve. Those of you reading this book who are planning a career in law enforcement may want to read the following boxed feature.

In this and the following three chapters, we will evaluate the history, role, organizational issues, and procedures of police agents and agencies and discuss the legal rules that control police behavior.

The History of Police

What was the life of an English constable like? Read Robert D. Storch, "The Old English Constabulary," *History Today*, November 1999 v49 i11 p43, on InfoTrac College Edition.

The origin of U.S. police agencies, like the origins of criminal law, can be traced to early English society.[7] Before the Norman Conquest, no regular English police force existed. Every person living in the villages scattered throughout the countryside was responsible for aiding neighbors and protecting the settlement from thieves and marauders. This was known as the *pledge system*. People were grouped in collectives of ten families, called **tithings,** and were entrusted with policing their own minor problems. When trouble occurred, the citizen was expected to make a **hue and cry.** Ten tithings were grouped into a **hundred,** whose affairs were supervised by a **constable** appointed by the local nobleman. The constable, who might be considered the first real police officer, dealt with more serious breaches of the law.[8]

Shires, which resembled the counties of today, were controlled by the **shire reeve,** who was appointed by the Crown or local landowner to supervise the territory and ensure that order would be kept. The shire reeve, a forerunner of today's **sheriff,** soon began to pursue and apprehend law violators as part of his duties.

In the thirteenth century, the **watch system** was created to help protect property in England's larger cities and towns. Watchmen patrolled at night and helped protect against robberies, fires, and disturbances. They reported to the area constable, who became the primary metropolitan law enforcement agent. In larger cities, such as London, the watchmen were organized within church parishes and were usually members of the parish they protected.

In 1326 the office of **justice of the peace** was created to assist the shire reeve in controlling the county. Eventually, these justices took on judicial functions in addition to their primary role as peacekeepers. The local constable became the operational assistant to the justice of the peace, supervising the night watchmen, investigating offenses, serving summonses, executing warrants, and securing prisoners. This system helped delineate the relationship between police and the judiciary, which has continued for more than 670 years.

Eighteenth-Century Developments

As the eighteenth century began, rising crime rates encouraged a new form of private, monied police, who were able to profit both legally and criminally from the lack of formal police departments. These private police agents, referred to as *thief takers,* were universally corrupt, taking profits not only from catching and informing on criminals but also from receiving stolen property, theft, intimidation, perjury, and blackmail. They often relieved their prisoners of money and stolen goods and made more income by accepting hush money, giving perjured evidence, swearing false oaths, and operating extortion rackets. Petty debtors were especially easy targets for those who combined thief taking with the keeping of alehouses and taverns. While incarcerated, the health and safety of prisoners were entirely at the whim of the keepers, or thief takers, who were virtually free to charge what they wanted for board and other necessities. Court bailiffs who also acted as thief takers were the most passionately detested legal profiteers. They seized debtors and held them in small lockups where they forced their victims to pay exorbitant prices for food and lodging.

The thief takers' use of violence was notorious. They went armed and were prepared to maim or kill in order to gain their objectives. Before he was hanged in 1725, Jack Wild, the most notorious thief taker, "had two fractures in his skull and his bald head was covered with silver plates. He had seventeen wounds in various parts of his body from swords, daggers, and gunshots, [and] . . . his throat had been cut in the course of his duties."[9]

Henry Fielding, famed author of *Tom Jones,* along with Saunders Welch and Sir John Fielding, sought to clean up the thief-taking system. Appointed a city magistrate in 1748, Fielding operated his own group of monied police out of Bow Street in London, directing and deploying them throughout the city and its environs, deciding which cases to investigate and what streets to protect. His agents were carefully instructed on their legitimate powers and duties. Fielding's Bow Street Runners were a marked improvement over the earlier monied police because they actually had an administrative structure that improved record-keeping

tithing In medieval England, a group of ten families who collectively dealt with minor disturbances and breaches of the peace.

hue and cry A call for assistance in medieval England. The policy of self-help used in villages demanded that everyone respond if a citizen raised a hue and cry to get their aid.

hundred In medieval England, a group of one hundred families that had the responsibility to maintain the order and try minor offenses.

constable In medieval England, an appointed official who administered and supervised the legal affairs of a small community.

shire reeve In medieval England, the senior law enforcement figure in a county; the forerunner of today's sheriff.

sheriff The chief law enforcement officer in a county.

watch system During the Middle Ages in England, men were organized in church parishes to guard at night against disturbances and breaches of the peace under the direction of the local constable.

justice of the peace Established in 1326 England, the office was created to help the shire reeve in controlling the county and later took on judicial functions.

Careers in Criminal Justice

Law Enforcement

The majority of people in law enforcement work for city police departments. The work of the patrol officer, traffic cop, and detective is familiar to anyone who watches television or goes to movies (although the accuracy of the portrayal by those entertainment vehicles is highly suspect). Besides these familiar roles, however, police work also includes a great many administrative and service jobs, such as officer training, communications, records management, purchasing, and so on. Salaries in municipal police agencies are competitive, and entry-level officers in some departments may earn in excess of $35,000. Larger cities may offer higher starting salaries and provide a full range of benefits. For example, the Dallas Police Department has the following pay scales and benefits programs:

Police officer
Trainee: $33,382–$34,582
Apprentice: $33,716, plus $1,000 bonus on academy graduation
Probationary: $34,053
Start: $36,002
Two year: $37,802
Three year: $39,692
Five year: $41,677
Seven year: $43,760
Nine year: $45,948
Eleven year: $48,246
Thirteen year: $50,658
Fifteen year: $53,191

Senior corporal
Start: $37,022
Fourteen year: $58,643
Subsequent years: 5 percent step increases at the two, four, six, eight, ten, twelve, and fourteen year anniversaries

Sergeant
Start: $42,528
Ten year: $64,225
Subsequent years: 5 percent step increases at the one, two, four, six, eight, and ten year anniversaries

Lieutenant
Start: $46,672
Eight year: $70,349
Subsequent years: 5 percent step increases at the one, two, four, six, eight year anniversaries

Benefits

Health insurance: On the date you are hired, you become eligible for one of the City of Dallas's major medical insurance programs. The city offers several separate insurance packages, each providing coverage for hospital room and medical expenses, outpatient care and maternity care. The packages offer different supplemental dental and vision plans and varying coverage for dependents. Noncity health coverage plans also are available.

Life insurance: Once you are hired, you are enrolled in the City of Dallas group life insurance program. You can choose from three plans: option 1 is paid by the City of Dallas, and options 2 and 3 are available at a reduced rate premium.
• Option 1: $40,000 basic insurance policy
• Option 2: pays the equivalent of your annual salary plus $40,000
• Option 3: pays the amount of double your annual salary plus $40,000

Retirement: You become eligible for retirement benefits after twenty years of service or on your forty-fifth birthday after five years of service. The retirement plan pays up to a maximum of 96 percent of the average of your best thirty-six consecutive months of computation pay. Officers who remain more than twenty years are eligible for additional benefits.

and investigative procedures. Although an improvement, Fielding's forces were not adequate, and by the nineteenth century state police officers were needed.

In 1829 Sir Robert Peel, England's home secretary, guided through Parliament an "Act for Improving the Police in and near the Metropolis." The Metropolitan Police Act established the first organized police force in London. Composed of over one thousand men, the London police force was structured along military lines; its members would be known from then on as *bobbies,* after their creator. They wore a distinctive uniform and were led by two magistrates, who were later given the title of commissioner. However, the ultimate responsibility for the police fell to the home secretary and consequently to the Parliament.

In addition, officers can get salary increases for completing college courses and becoming language specialists. In Massachusetts, salaries start at about $30,000 a year. However, under state legislation known as the Quinn Bill, if police officers earn an undergraduate degree, they get an extra 20 percent on their base pay; a master's or law degree increases their starting pay by 25 percent. Overtime and special detail pay can add to this sum. It is not uncommon for uniformed police officers to top $100,000 in a single year.

Civilian Employees

In addition to sworn personnel, many police agencies hire civilian employees who bring special skills to the department. For example, it is common in the computer age for departments to employ information resource managers who are charged with improving data processing, integrating the department's computer information database with others in the state, operating computer-based fingerprint identification systems and other high-tech investigation devices, and linking with national computer systems such as that of the FBI's National Crime Information Center, which holds the records of millions of criminal offenders.

State and County Law Enforcement

State and county governments also provide career opportunities in law enforcement. The state police and county sheriff's department do much the same work as city police agencies—traffic, patrol, and investigation—depending on their area of jurisdiction. These agencies commonly take on a greater law enforcement role in more rural areas and provide ancillary services, such as running the local jail or controlling traffic, in urban centers. State agencies also hire investigators as part of their enforcement mandate. For example, the California Department of Insurance employs fraud investigators to conduct felony investigations of insurance fraud and related statutes. It also employs property controllers to handle property seized in investigations of insurance fraud. Similarly, the California Division of Consumer Affairs employs investigators to enforce rules and regulations relating to consumer protection. State investigators carry out many of the tasks of other law enforcement officers, including serving warrants, making arrests, and conducting undercover investigations.

Federal Law Enforcement

The federal government employs thousands of law enforcement personnel in such agencies as the Federal Bureau of Investigation, the Drug Enforcement Agency, the Secret Service, and so on. These agencies are often considered the elite of the law enforcement profession, and standards for entry are quite high. The duties of these federal agencies include upholding federal laws controlling counterfeiting, terrorism, espionage, bank robbery, and importation and distribution of controlled substances, among others.

Private Security

The field of private security also offers many career opportunities. Some positions are in large security companies, such as Pinkerton or Wackenhut. Others are in company security forces, such as those maintained by large retail chains, manufacturing companies, and railroads. Public institutions such as hospitals, airports, and port facilities also have security teams. For example, large retail chains usually employ so-called loss prevention agents, who are responsible for the protection of company assets.

Other private companies maintain their own enforcement branches. Insurance firms hire field investigators to determine the origin and cause of accidents, fires, and other events for which the company is liable. Insurance investigators also handle claims in which client fraud is suspected.

To find out more about careers in criminal justice, go to the book-specific Web site at http://cj.wadsworth.com/siegel_essen4e.

Critical Thinking

1. What factors would shape your decision to enter a law enforcement career? Are you more interested in the financial reward, lifestyle, or public service?
2. Are you pleasantly surprised or somewhat disappointed in the financial remuneration given to the typical law enforcement officer?

 InfoTrac College Edition Research
To learn more about careers in law enforcement, use the phase as a subject guide on InfoTrac College Edition.

The early bobbies suffered from many of the same ills as their forebears. Many were corrupt, they were unsuccessful at stopping crime, and they were influenced by the wealthy. Owners of houses of ill repute who in the past had guaranteed their undisturbed operations by bribing watchmen now turned their attention to the bobbies. Metropolitan police administrators fought constantly to terminate cowardly, corrupt, and alcoholic officers, dismissing in the beginning about one-third of the bobbies each year.

Despite its recognized shortcomings, the London experiment proved a vast improvement over what had come before. It was considered so successful that the London Metropolitan Police soon began providing law enforcement assistance to

To read about Sir Robert Peel's life and political career, go to
www.spartacus.schoolnet.co.uk/PRpeel.htm

© Bettmann/CORBIS

One of the few policemen who stayed at work during the Boston police strike of 1919. Police earned about twenty-five cents an hour and were expected to work up to ninety-eight hours a week!

To read a detailed account of the creation of the first police forces, go to InfoTrac College Edition and read Clive Emsley, "The Origins of the Modern Police," *History Today,* April 1999 v49 i4 p8(1).

vigilantes   A citizen group who tracked down wanted criminals in the Old West.

Vigilantes are still with us today. To read about the modern versions, use "vigilante" as a key word on InfoTrac College Edition.

outlying areas that requested it. Another act of Parliament allowed justices of the peace to establish local police forces, and by 1856 every borough and county in England was required to form its own police force.

Law Enforcement in Colonial America

Law enforcement in colonial America paralleled the British model. In the colonies, the county sheriff became the most important law enforcement agent. In addition to keeping the peace and fighting crime, sheriffs collected taxes, supervised elections, and handled a great deal of other legal business.

The colonial sheriff did not patrol or seek out crime. Instead, he reacted to citizens' complaints and investigated crimes that had occurred. His salary, related to his effectiveness, was paid on a fee system. Sheriffs received a fixed amount for every arrest made. Unfortunately, their tax-collecting chores were more lucrative than fighting crime, so law enforcement was not one of their primary concerns. In the cities, law enforcement was the province of the town marshal, who was aided, often unwillingly, by a variety of constables, night watchmen, police justices, and city council members. However, local governments had little power of administration, and enforcement of the criminal law was largely an individual or community responsibility. After the American Revolution larger cities relied on elected or appointed agents to serve warrants and recover stolen property, sometimes in cooperation with the thieves themselves. Night watchmen, referred to as "leatherheads" because of the leather helmets they wore, patrolled the streets calling the hour, equipped with a rattle to summon help and a nightstick to ward off lawbreakers. Watchmen were not widely respected: rowdy young men enjoyed tipping over the watch houses with the leatherhead inside, and a favorite saying in New York was "While the city sleeps the watchmen do too."[10]

In rural areas in the South, slave patrols charged with recapturing escaped slaves were an early, if loathsome, form of law enforcement.[11] In the western territories, individual initiative was encouraged by the practice of offering rewards for the capture of felons. If trouble arose, the town vigilance committee might form a posse to chase offenders. These **vigilantes** were called on to eradicate such social problems as theft of livestock through force or intimidation; the San Francisco Vigilance Committee actively pursued criminals in the mid-nineteenth century.

As cities grew, it became exceedingly difficult for local leaders to organize ad hoc citizen vigilante groups. Moreover, the early nineteenth century was an era of widespread urban unrest and mob violence. Local leaders began to realize that a more structured police function was needed to control demonstrators and keep the peace.

Early Police Agencies

The modern police department was born out of urban mob violence that wracked the nation's cities in the nineteenth century. Boston created the first formal U.S. police department in 1838. New York formed its police department in 1844; Philadelphia in 1854. The new police departments replaced the night-watch system and relegated constables and sheriffs to serving court orders and running jails.

At first, the urban police departments inherited the functions of the institutions they replaced. For example, Boston police were charged with maintaining public health until 1853, and in New York the police were responsible for street sweeping until 1881. Politics dominated the departments and determined the recruitment of new officers and promotion of supervisors. An individual with the right connections could be hired despite a lack of qualifications. Early police agencies were corrupt, brutal, and inefficient.[12]

In the late nineteenth century, police work was highly desirable because it paid more than most other blue-collar jobs. By 1880 the average factory worker earned $450 a year, while a metropolitan police officer made $900 annually. For immigrant groups, having enough political clout to be appointed to the police department was an important step up the social ladder.[13] However, job security was uncertain because it depended on the local political machine's staying in power.

Police work itself was primitive. There were few of even the simplest technological innovations common today, such as centralized record keeping. Most officers patrolled on foot, without backup or the ability to call for help. Officers were commonly taunted by local toughs and responded with force and brutality. The long-standing conflict between police and the public was born in the difficulty that untrained, unprofessional officers had in patrolling the streets of nineteenth-century U.S. cities and in breaking up and controlling labor disputes. Police were not crime fighters as we know them today. Their main role was maintaining order, and their power was almost unchecked. The average officer had little training, no education in the law, and a minimum of supervision, yet the police became virtual judges of law and fact with the ability to exercise unlimited discretion.[14]

At mid-nineteenth century, the detective bureau was set up as part of the Boston police. Until then, thief taking had been the province of amateur bounty hunters, who hired themselves out to victims for a price. When professional police departments replaced bounty hunters, the close working relationships that developed between police detectives and their underworld informants produced many scandals, and consequently, high personnel turnover.

Police during the nineteenth century were regarded as incompetent and corrupt and were disliked by the people they served. The police role was only minimally directed at law enforcement. Its primary function was serving as the enforcement arm of the reigning political power, protecting private property, and keeping control of the ever-rising numbers of foreign immigrants.

Police agencies evolved slowly through the second half of the nineteenth century. Uniforms were introduced in 1853 in New York. The first technological breakthroughs in police operations came in the area of communications. The linking of precincts to central headquarters by telegraph began in the 1850s. In 1867 the first telegraph police boxes were installed; an officer could turn a key in a box, and his location and number would automatically register at headquarters. Additional technological advances were made in transportation. The Detroit Police Department outfitted some of its patrol officers with bicycles in 1897. By 1913 the motorcycle was being used by departments in the eastern part of the nation. The first police car was used in Akron, Ohio, in 1910, and the police wagon became popular in Cincinnati in 1912.[15] Nonpolice functions, such as care of the streets, had already begun to be abandoned after the Civil War.

However, big-city police were still not respected by the public, unsuccessful in their role as crime stoppers, and uninvolved in progressive activities. The control of police departments by local politicians impeded effective law enforcement and fostered an atmosphere of graft and corruption.

To read about the operations of an early police department, go to InfoTrac College Edition, and read L. Wayne Hicks, "1927: A Police Force Stands Ready," *Denver Business Journal,* November 12, 1999 v51 i12 p24.

Twentieth-Century Reform

In an effort to reduce police corruption, civic leaders in a number of jurisdictions created police administrative boards to reduce local officials' control over the

What effect did the Boston police strike have on police labor unions? To find out go to www.geocities.com/fcpa.geo/ no1union.htm

police. These tribunals were responsible for appointing police administrators and controlling police affairs. In many instances, these measures failed because the private citizens appointed to the review boards lacked expertise in the intricacies of police work.

Another reform movement was the takeover of some big-city police agencies by state legislators. Although police budgets were financed through local taxes, control of police was usurped by rural politicians in the state capitals. New York City temporarily lost authority over its police force in 1857. It was not until the first decades of the twentieth century that cities regained control of their police forces.

The Boston police strike of 1919 heightened interest in police reform. The strike came about basically because police officers were dissatisfied with their status in society. Other professions were unionizing and increasing their standards of living, but police salaries lagged behind. The Boston police officers' organization, the Boston Social Club, voted to become a union affiliated with the American Federation of Labor. The officers went out on strike on September 9, 1919. Rioting and looting broke out, resulting in Governor Calvin Coolidge's mobilization of the state militia to take over the city. Public support turned against the police, and the strike was broken. Eventually, all the striking officers were fired and replaced by new recruits. The Boston police strike ended police unionism for decades and solidified power in the hands of reactionary, autocratic police administrators. In the aftermath of the strike, various local, state, and federal crime commissions began to investigate the extent of crime and the ability of the justice system to deal with it effectively, and made recommendations to improve police effectiveness.[16] However, with the onset of the Depression, justice reform became a less important issue than economic revival, and for many years little changed in the nature of policing.

The Emergence of Professionalism

Around the turn of the twentieth century, a number of nationally recognized leaders called for measures to help improve and professionalize the police. In 1893 the International Association of Chiefs of Police (IACP), a professional society, was formed. Under the direction of its first president, District of Columbia Chief of Police Richard Sylvester, the IACP became the leading voice for police reform during the first two decades of the twentieth century. The IACP called for creating a civil service police force and for removing political influence and control. It also advocated centralized organizational structure and record keeping to curb the power of politically aligned precinct captains. Still another professional reform the IACP fostered was the creation of specialized units, such as delinquency control squads.

The most famous police reformer of the time was August Vollmer. While serving as police chief of Berkeley, California, Vollmer instituted university training for young officers. He also helped develop the School of Criminology at the University of California at Berkeley, which became the model for justice-related programs around the United States. Vollmer's disciples included O. W. Wilson, who pioneered the use of advanced training for officers when he took over and reformed the Wichita (Kansas) Police Department in 1928. Wilson was also instrumental in applying modern management and administrative techniques to policing. His text, *Police Administration*, became the single most influential work on the subject.

During this period, police professionalism was equated with an incorruptible, tough, highly trained, rule-oriented department organized along militaristic lines. The most respected department was that of Los Angeles, which emphasized police as incorruptible crime fighters who would not question the authority of the central command.

The Modern Era of Policing: 1960–2003

The modern era of policing can be traced from 1960 to the present time. What are the major events that occurred during this period?

Policing in the 1960s

Turmoil and crisis were the hallmarks of policing during the 1960s. Throughout this decade, the Supreme Court handed down a number of decisions designed to control police operations and procedures. Police officers were now required to obey strict legal guidelines when questioning suspects, conducting searches and wiretapping, and so on. As the civil rights of suspects were significantly expanded, police complained they were being "handcuffed by the courts."

Also during this time, civil unrest produced a growing tension between police and the public. African Americans, who were battling for increased rights and freedoms in the civil rights movement, found themselves confronting police lines. When riots broke out in New York, Detroit, Los Angeles, and other cities between 1964 and 1968, the spark that ignited conflict often involved the police. When students across the nation began marching in anti–Vietnam War demonstrations, local police departments were called on to keep order. Police forces were ill equipped and poorly trained to deal with these social problems; it is not surprising that the 1960s were marked by a number of bloody confrontations between the police and the public.

Confounding these problems was a rapidly growing crime rate. The number of violent and property crimes increased dramatically. Drug addiction and abuse grew to be national concerns, common among all social classes. Urban police departments could not control the crime rate, and police officers resented the demands placed on them by dissatisfied citizens.

Policing in the 1970s

The 1970s witnessed many structural changes in police agencies themselves. The end of the Vietnam War significantly reduced tensions between students and police. However, the relationship between police and minorities was still rocky. Local fears and distrust, combined with conservative federal policies, encouraged police departments to control what was perceived as an emerging minority group "threat."[17]

Increased federal government support for criminal justice greatly influenced police operations. During the decade, the Law Enforcement Assistance Administration (LEAA) devoted a significant portion of its funds to police agencies. Although a number of police departments used this money to purchase little-used hardware, such as antiriot gear, most of it went to supporting innovative research on police work and advanced training of police officers. Perhaps most significant, LEAA's Law Enforcement Education Program helped thousands of officers further their college education. Hundreds of criminal justice programs were developed on college campuses around the country, providing a pool of highly educated police recruits. LEAA funds were also used to import or transfer technology originally developed in other fields into law enforcement. Technological innovations involving computers transformed the way police kept records, investigated crimes, and communicated with one another. State training academies improved the way police learned to deal with such issues as job stress, community conflict, and interpersonal relations.

More women and minorities were recruited into police work. Affirmative action programs helped, albeit slowly, alter the ethnic, racial, and gender composition of U.S. policing.

Policing in the 1980s

As the 1980s began, the police role seemed to be changing significantly. A number of experts acknowledged that the police were not simply crime fighters and called for police to develop a greater awareness of community issues, which resulted in the emergence of the *community policing concept.*[18]

Police unions, which began to grow in the late 1960s, continued to have a great impact on departmental administration in the 1980s. Unions fought for and won increased salaries and benefits for their members; starting salaries of more than $30,000 became more common in metropolitan police agencies. In many instances, unions eroded the power of the police chief to make unquestioned policy and personnel decisions. During the decade, chiefs of police commonly consulted with union leaders before making significant decisions concerning departmental operations.

Although police operations improved markedly during this time, police departments were also beset by problems that impeded their effectiveness. State and local budgets were cut back during the Reagan administration, while federal support for innovative police programs was severely curtailed with the demise of the LEAA.

Police-community relations continued to be a major problem. Riots and incidents of urban conflict occurred in some of the nation's largest cities.[19] They triggered continual concern about what the police role should be, especially in inner-city neighborhoods.

Go to InfoTrac College Edition and use the term "police unions" as a subject guide to learn more about them in the United States and around the world.

Policing in the 1990s

The 1990s began on a sour note and ended with an air of optimism. The incident that helped change the face of American policing occurred on March 3, 1991, when Rodney King and friend Bryant Allen were driving in Los Angeles, California. They refused to stop when signaled by a police car behind them but instead increased their speed; King, the driver, was apparently drunk or on drugs. When police finally stopped the car, they delivered fifty-six baton blows and six kicks to King in a period of two minutes, producing eleven skull fractures, brain damage, and kidney damage. They did not realize that their actions were being videotaped by an observer who later gave the tape to the media. The officers involved were eventually tried and acquitted in a suburban court by an all-white jury. The acquittal set off six days of rioting in South Central Los Angeles that was brought under control by the California National Guard, who were mobilized to quell the riots. When it was all over 54 people had been killed, 2,383 were known to have been injured, and more than 12,000 people were arrested.[20]

The King case prompted an era of reform. Several police experts decreed that the nation's police forces should be evaluated not on their crime-fighting ability but on their courteousness, deportment, and helpfulness. Interest renewed in reviving an earlier style of police work featuring foot patrols and increased citizen contact. Police departments began to embrace new forms of policing that stressed cooperation with the community and problem solving. Ironically, urban police departments

Abner Louima, the victim of a vicious attack by rogue New York City police officers, stands with Reverend Al Sharpton (left). Justin Volpe, the New York City police officer found guilty of sodomizing Louima, received a 30-year sentence. The Louima case was a shocking reminder that the nation's police forces must work closely with the community to end violence and brutality.

Exhibit 4.1	**The most notable achievements of contemporary American police**

- The intellectual caliber of the police has risen dramatically. American police today at all ranks are smarter, better informed, and more sophisticated than police in the 1960s.
- Senior police managers are more ambitious for their organizations than they used to be. Chiefs and their deputies want to leave their own distinctive stamp on their organizations. Many recognize that management is a specialized skill that must be developed.
- An explicit scientific mind-set has taken hold in American policing that involves an appreciation of the importance of evaluation and the timely availability of information.
- The standards of police conduct have risen. Despite recent well-publicized incidents of brutality and corruption, American police today treat the public more fairly, more equitably, and less venally than police did 30 years ago.

- Police are remarkably more diverse in terms of race and gender than a generation ago. This amounts to a revolution in American policing, changing both its appearance and, more slowly, its behavior.
- The work of the police has become intellectually more demanding, requiring an array of new specialized knowledge about technology, forensic analysis, and crime. This has had profound effects on recruitment—notably, civilianization—organizational structure, career patterns, and operational coordination.
- Civilian review of police discipline has gradually become accepted by police. Although the struggle is not yet over, expansion is inevitable as more and more senior police executives see that civilian review reassures the public and validates their own favorable opinion of the overall quality of police performance.

Source: David H. Bayley, "Policing in America," *Society* 36 (December 1998): 16–20.

---

began to shift their focus to becoming community organizers at a time when technological improvements increased the ability to identify suspects. An ongoing effort was made to make departments more diverse, and African Americans began to be hired as chiefs of police, most notably in Los Angeles. Exhibit 4.1 lists some of the most notable achievements of the decade.

To read more about the infamous L.A. incident, use "Rodney King case" as a subject guide on InfoTrac College Edition.

Policing and Law Enforcement Today

Policing and law enforcement today are divided into four broad categories: federal, state, county, and local policing agencies (and many subcategories within). There is no real hierarchy, and each branch has its own sphere of operations, though overlap may exist.

Federal Law Enforcement Agencies

The federal government has a number of law enforcement agencies designed to protect the rights and privileges of U.S. citizens; no single agency has unlimited jurisdiction, and each has been created to enforce specific laws and cope with particular situations. Federal police agencies have no particular rank order or hierarchy of command or responsibility, and each reports to a specific department or bureau.

The Justice Department/Federal Bureau of Investigation
The U.S. Department of Justice is the legal arm of the federal government. Headed by the attorney general, it is empowered to (1) enforce all federal laws, (2) represent the United States when it is party to court action, and (3) conduct independent investigations through its law enforcement services.

The Department of Justice maintains several separate divisions that are responsible for enforcing federal laws and protecting U.S. citizens. The Civil Rights Division proceeds legally against violations of federal civil rights laws that protect citizens from discrimination on the basis of their race, creed, ethnic background, age, or sex. Areas of greatest concern include discrimination in education, housing, and employment, including affirmative action cases. The Tax Division brings legal actions against tax violators. The Criminal Division prosecutes violations of the federal criminal code. Its responsibility includes enforcing statutes relating to bank robbery (since bank deposits are federally insured), kidnapping, mail fraud, interstate transportation of stolen vehicles, and narcotics and drug trafficking.

The Justice Department first became involved in law enforcement when the attorney general hired investigators to enforce the Mann Act (forbidding the transportation of women between states for immoral purposes). These investigators were formalized in 1908 into a distinct branch of the government, the Bureau of Investigation, and the agency was later reorganized into the **Federal Bureau of Investigation (FBI)**, under the direction of J. Edgar Hoover (1924–1972).

Today's FBI is not a police agency but an investigative agency with jurisdiction over all matters in which the United States is or may be an interested party. It limits its jurisdiction, however, to federal laws, including all federal statutes not specifically assigned to other agencies. Areas covered by these laws include espionage, sabotage, treason, civil rights violations, murder and assault of federal officers, mail fraud, robbery and burglary of federally insured banks, kidnapping, and interstate transportation of stolen vehicles and property. The FBI headquarters in Washington, D.C., oversees fifty-six field offices, approximately four hundred satellite offices known as resident agencies, four specialized field installations, and more than forty foreign liaison posts. The foreign liaison offices, each of which is headed by a legal attaché or legal liaison officer, work abroad with American and local authorities on criminal matters within FBI jurisdiction. In all, the FBI has approximately 11,400 special agents and over 16,400 other employees who perform professional, administrative, technical, clerical, craft, trade, or maintenance operations. About 9,800 employees are assigned to FBIHQ; nearly 18,000 are assigned to field installations.

The FBI offers a number of important services to local law enforcement agencies. Its Identification Division, established in 1924, collects and maintains a vast fingerprint file that can be used by local police agencies. Its sophisticated crime laboratory, established in 1932, aids local police in testing and identifying such evidence as hairs, fibers, blood, tire tracks, and drugs. The Uniform Crime Reports (UCR) is another service of the FBI. The UCR is an annual compilation of crimes reported to local police agencies, arrests, police killed or wounded in action, and other information. Finally, the FBI's National Crime Information Center is a computerized network linked to local police departments that provides ready information on stolen vehicles, wanted persons, stolen guns, and so on. The major activities of the FBI are described in Exhibit 4.2.

The FBI mission has been evolving to keep pace with world events. With the end of the cold war and the reduction in East-West tensions, the FBI's counterintelligence mission has diminished. In some offices, agents have been reassigned to antigang and drug control efforts.[21] Since September 11, the FBI has dedicated itself to combating terrorism. This effort will be discussed more fully in the feature on law enforcement and terrorism that can be found at the end of Part Two of this book.

Federal Bureau of Investigation (FBI) The arm of the U.S. Justice Department that investigates violations of federal law, gathers crime statistics, runs a comprehensive crime laboratory, and helps train local law enforcement officers.

© AP/Wide World Photos

Police agencies are learning from the mistakes of the past, but racial and ethnic conflict and charges of police brutality are still common. Here, police speak to protesters rallying against racial profiling and police brutality in front of the Ramparts police station in downtown Los Angeles. Some of the protesters, who urged police to arrest them, were later arrested peacefully.

Exhibit 4.2   Special programs and divisions of the Federal Bureau of Investigation

- *The Criminal Justice Information Services (CJIS) Division.* Located in Clarksburg, West Virginia, the CJIS centralizes criminal justice information. It serves as the national repository for fingerprint information and criminal record data and also manages Law Enforcement On-Line (LEO), a law enforcement intranet that provides secure communications, distance learning, and information services to the law enforcement community. It operates the National Instant Check System (NICS), mandated by the Brady bill, to check on the backgrounds of people desiring to purchase firearms. It is currently developing the Integrated Automated Fingerprint Identification System (IAFIS).
- *The Crime Laboratory.* The FBI laboratory, one of the largest and most comprehensive forensic laboratories in the world, examines evidence free of charge for federal, state, and local law enforcement agencies. Among its activities are the following:
  - Scientific analysis of physical evidence submitted for examination followed by expert testimony in court
  - Operational and technical support to investigations
  - Research and development of forensic techniques and procedures
  - Development and deployment of new forensic technologies

- Training programs and symposia for U.S. and international crime laboratory practitioners and law enforcement personnel
- *The Child Abduction and Serial Killer Unit (CASKU),* created in 1994, responds upon request from local law enforcement agencies to kidnappings and to serial killer cases.
- *Combined DNA Index System (CODIS)* is a national database of DNA profiles from convicted offenders, unsolved crime scenes, and missing persons. CODIS allows state and local law enforcement crime labs to exchange and compare DNA profiles electronically.
- *The Critical Incident Response Group (CIRG)* is ready to assist law enforcement agencies in hostage-taking and barricade situations, terrorist activities, and other critical incidents.
- *The Uniform Crime Report (UCR)* is an annual compilation of crimes reported to local police agencies, arrests, police killed or wounded in action, and other information.
- *The National Crime Information Center (NCIC)* is a computerized network linked to local police departments that provides ready information on stolen vehicles, wanted persons, stolen guns, and other crime related materials.

Source: FBI Facts and Figures (Washington, D.C.: Federal Bureau of Investigation, 2001).

Drug Enforcement Administration   Government interest in drug trafficking can be traced back to 1914, when the Harrison Act established federal jurisdiction over the supply and use of narcotics. A number of drug enforcement units, including the Bureau of Narcotics and Dangerous Drugs, were charged with enforcing drug laws. In 1973 these agencies were combined to form the **Drug Enforcement Administration (DEA).**

DEA agents assist local and state authorities in investigating illegal drug use and carrying out independent surveillance and enforcement activities to control the importation of narcotics. For example, DEA agents work with foreign governments in cooperative efforts aimed at destroying opium and marijuana crops at their source—hard-to-find fields tucked away in the interiors of Latin America, Asia, Europe, and Africa. Undercover DEA agents infiltrate drug rings and simulate buying narcotics to arrest drug dealers.

Treasury Department   The U.S. Treasury Department maintains the following enforcement branches:

1. *Bureau of Alcohol, Tobacco and Firearms.* The ATF helps control sales of untaxed liquor and cigarettes, and through the Gun Control Act of 1968 and the Organized Crime Control Act of 1970, has jurisdiction over the illegal sales, importation, and criminal misuse of firearms and explosives.
2. *Internal Revenue Service.* The IRS, established in 1862, enforces violations of income, excise, stamp, and other tax laws. Its Intelligence Division actively pursues gamblers, narcotics dealers, and other violators who do not report their illegal financial gains as taxable income. For example, the career of Al Capone, the famous 1920s gangster, was brought to an end by the efforts of IRS agents.
3. *Customs Service.* The Customs Service guards points of entry into the United States and prevents smuggling of contraband into (or out of) the country. It

Drug Enforcement Administration (DEA)   The federal agency that enforces federal drug control laws.

Use "FBI and terrorism" as a key words on InfoTrac College Edition to find out what the Bureau is doing to counter terrorist acts.

The homepage of the Drug Enforcement Administration (DEA) is located at www.usdoj.gov/dea/

ensures that taxes and tariffs are paid on imported goods and helps control the flow of narcotics into the country.

4. *Secret Service.* The Secret Service was originally charged with enforcing laws against counterfeiting. Today it is also accountable for the protection of the president and the vice-president and their families, presidential candidates, and former presidents. The Secret Service maintains the White House Police Force, which is responsible for protecting the executive mansion, and the Treasury Guard, which protects the mint.

Other Justice Department Agencies Other federal law enforcement agencies under the direction of the Justice Department include the U.S. Marshals, the Immigration and Naturalization Service, and the Organized Crime and Racketeering Unit. The U.S. Marshals are court officers who help implement federal court rulings, transport prisoners, and enforce court orders. The Immigration and Naturalization Service is responsible for the administration of immigration laws governing the exclusion and deportation of illegal aliens and the naturalization of aliens lawfully present in the United States. This service also maintains border patrols to prevent illegal aliens from entering the United States. The Organized Crime and Racketeering Unit, under the direction of the U.S. attorney general, coordinates federal efforts to curtail organized crime primarily through the use of federal racketeering laws.

State Law Enforcement Agencies

Unlike municipal police departments, state police were legislatively created to deal with the growing incidence of crime in nonurban areas, a consequence of the increase in population mobility and the advent of personalized mass transportation in the form of the automobile. County sheriffs—elected officials with occasionally corrupt or questionable motives—had proven to be ineffective in dealing with the wide-ranging criminal activities that developed during the latter half of the nineteenth century. In addition, most local police agencies were unable to protect effectively against highly mobile lawbreakers who randomly struck at cities and towns throughout a state. In response to citizens' demands for effective and efficient law enforcement, state governors began to develop plans for police agencies that would be responsible to the state, instead of being tied to local politics and possible corruption.

The Texas Rangers, created in 1835, was one of the first state police agencies formed. Essentially a military outfit that patrolled the Mexican border, it was followed by the Massachusetts State Constables in 1865 and the Arizona Rangers in 1901. Pennsylvania formed the first truly modern state police in 1905.[22]

Today about twenty-three state police agencies have the same general police powers as municipal police and are territorially limited in their exercise of law enforcement regulations only by the state's boundaries. The remaining state police agencies are primarily responsible for highway patrol and traffic law enforcement. Some state police, such as those in California, direct most of their attention to the enforcement of traffic laws. Most state police organizations are restricted by legislation from becoming involved in the enforcement of certain areas of the law. For example, in some jurisdictions, state police are prohibited from becoming involved in strikes or other labor disputes, unless violence erupts.

The nation's eighty thousand state police employees (fifty-five thousand officers and twenty-five thousand civilians) carry out a variety of functions besides law enforcement and highway safety, including maintaining a training academy and providing emergency medical services. State police crime laboratories aid local departments in investigating crime scenes and analyzing evidence. State police also provide special services and technical expertise in such areas as bomb-site analysis and homicide investigation. Some state police departments, such as California's, are involved in highly sophisticated traffic and highway safety programs, including the use of helicopters for patrol and rescue, the testing of safety devices for cars, and the conducting of postmortem examinations to determine the causes of fatal accidents.

County Law Enforcement Agencies

The county sheriff's role has evolved from that of the early English shire reeve, whose primary duty was to assist the royal judges in trying prisoners and enforcing sentences. From the time of the westward expansion in the United States until municipal departments were developed, the sheriff was often the sole legal authority over vast territories.

Today, there are nearly thirty-one hundred county sheriffs' offices operating nationwide, employing more than 290,000 full-time employees, including about 186,000 sworn personnel.[23] The duties of a sheriff's department vary according to the size and degree of development of the county. Nearly all sheriffs' offices provide basic law enforcement services such as routine patrol (97 percent), responding to citizen calls for service (95 percent), and investigating crimes (92 percent).

Other standard tasks of a typical sheriff's department are serving civil process (summons and court orders), providing court security, and operating the county jail. Less commonly, sheriffs' departments may serve as coroners, tax collectors, overseers of highways and bridges, custodians of the county treasury, and providers of fire, animal control, and emergency medical services; in years past, sheriffs' offices also conducted executions. Typically, a sheriff's department's law enforcement functions are restricted to unincorporated areas of a county, unless a city or town police department requests its help.

Some sheriffs' departments are exclusively law enforcement oriented; some carry out court-related duties only; some are involved solely in correctional and judicial matters and not in law enforcement. However, a majority are full-service programs that carry out judicial, correctional, and law enforcement activities. As a rule, agencies serving large population areas (over one million) are devoted to maintaining county correctional facilities, whereas those in smaller population areas are focused on law enforcement.

In the past, sheriffs' salaries were almost always based on the fees they received for the performance of official acts. They received fees for every summons, warrant, subpoena, writ, or other process they served; they were also compensated for summoning juries or locking prisoners in cells. Today, sheriffs are salaried to avoid conflict of interest.

Metropolitan Law Enforcement Agencies

Local police form the majority of the nation's authorized law enforcement personnel. Metropolitan police departments range in size from the New York City Police Department with almost 40,000 full time-officers and 10,000 civilian employees, to rural police departments, which may have a single officer. At last count, the more than thirteen thousand local police departments nationwide had an estimated 556,631 full-time employees, including about 436,000 sworn personnel.[24]

Most TV police shows feature the trials of big-city police officers, but the overwhelming number of departments actually have fewer than fifty officers and serve a population of under twenty-five thousand. Recent data indicated that seventy law enforcement agencies employed one thousand or more full-time sworn personnel, including forty-six local police departments with one thousand or more officers; these agencies accounted for about a third of all local police officers. In contrast, nearly eight hundred departments employed just one officer.

Regardless of their size, most individual metropolitan police departments perform a standard set of functions and tasks and provide similar services to the community. These include the following:

Traffic enforcement	Narcotics and vice control
Accident investigation	Radio communications
Patrol and peacekeeping	Crime prevention
Property and violent crime investigation	Fingerprint processing
Death investigation	Search and rescue

The police role is expanding, so procedures must be developed to help with special-needs populations, including AIDS-infected suspects, the homeless, and victims of domestic and child abuse.

These are only a few examples of the multiplicity of roles and duties assumed today by some of the larger urban police agencies around the nation. Smaller agencies can have trouble effectively carrying out these tasks; the hundreds of small police agencies in each state often provide duplicative services. Whether unifying smaller police agencies into "superagencies" would improve services is often debated among police experts. Smaller municipal agencies can provide important specialized services that might have to be relinquished if they were combined and incorporated into larger departments. Another approach has been to maintain smaller departments but to link them via computerized information-sharing and resource management networks.[25]

Technology and Law Enforcement

Policing is relying more and more frequently on modern technology to increase effectiveness, and there is little doubt that the influence of technology on policing will continue to grow. Police officers now trained to prevent burglaries may someday have to learn to create high-tech forensic labs that can identify suspects involved in theft of genetically engineered cultures from biomedical labs.[26] Criminal investigation will be enhanced by the application of sophisticated electronic gadgetry: computers, cellular phones, and digital communication devices.

Police are becoming more sophisticated in their use of computer software to identify and convict criminals. For example, some have begun to use computer software to conduct analysis of behavior patterns, a process called *data mining*, in an effort to identify crime patterns and link them to suspects.[27] By discovering patterns in burglaries, especially those involving multiple offenders, computer programs can be programmed to recognize a particular way of working at crime and thereby identify suspects most likely to fit the working profile. Advanced computer software has helped in the investigations of Internet crime. For example, in one recent case that occurred in England, police used forensic software to show in court that a defendant had used a particular Internet search engine to find Web pages that contained information about child pornography and then followed links to sites that he used to obtain and view such pornography. The Internet evidence was used to obtain his conviction.[28]

It is now recognized that there are geographic "hot spots" where a majority of predatory crimes are concentrated. Computer mapping programs that can translate addresses into map coordinates allow departments to identify problem areas for particular crimes, such as drug dealing. Computer maps allow police to identify the location, time of day, and linkage among criminal events and to concentrate their forces accordingly. Crime mapping is discussed in the following Criminal Justice and Technology feature.

For news about police technology and related issues, go to the Police Officer Internet Directory, at www.officer.com/

Information Technology

Crime mapping is not the only way technology can be used to improve the effectiveness of police resources. Budget realities demand that police leaders make the most effective use of their forces, and technology seems to be an important method of increasing productivity at a relatively low cost. The introduction of technology has already been explosive. In 1964, for example, only one city, St. Louis, had a police computer system; by 1968, ten states and fifty cities had state-level criminal justice information systems; today, almost every city of more than fifty thousand people has some sort of computer-support services.[29] The most recent federally sponsored survey of the nation's police forces found that most have embraced technology. Some of the advances are described in Exhibit 4.3.

One of the most important computer-aided tasks is the identification of criminal suspects. Computers now link neighboring agencies so they can share information on cases, suspects, and warrants. On a broader jurisdictional level, the FBI implemented the National Crime Information Center in 1967. This system provides rapid collection and retrieval of data about persons wanted for crimes anywhere in the fifty states.

Some police departments are using computerized imaging systems to replace mug books. Photos or sketches are stored in computer memory and easily retrieved for viewing. Several software companies have developed identification programs that help witnesses create a composite picture of the perpetrator (Figure 4.1 on page 130). A vast library of photographed or drawn facial features can be stored in computer files and accessed on a terminal screen. Witnesses can scan through thousands of noses, eyes, and lips until they find those that match the suspect's. Eyeglasses, mustaches, and beards can be added; skin tones can be altered. When the composite is created, an attached camera prints a hard copy for distribution.

Are police entering the age of "Big Brother"? Here, a bicyclist pulls his shopping cart of scavenged recyclables past an alley where a new motion-sensor camera, mounted on a power pole, keeps watch over potential illegal dumpers and taggers, August 2, 2002, in South Los Angeles. The camera is designed to photograph anyone who lingers, broadcasting the warning "Stop! This is the LAPD. We have just taken your photograph. We will use this photograph to prosecute you. Leave now!" It is the first of eleven such cameras that will be installed in alleys and near abandoned buildings throughout South Los Angeles.

Exhibit 4.3 The use of technology in the nation's police departments

- All departments serving twenty-five thousand or more residents now use computers. Just 1 percent of all local police officers work for a department not using computers.
- More than half of local police dispatch systems are now computer-aided, including nearly all departments serving fifty thousand or more residents
- During the past decade, the percent of officers employed by a department with computerized arrest records increased from 81 percent to 95 percent. Increases were also observed for criminal histories (60 to 79 percent), warrants (68 to 78 percent), and summonses (28 to 52 percent).
- About a third of departments now use computers for crime analysis (38 percent) and crime mapping (32 percent). Most departments serving a population of ten thousand or more use some form of computerized crime analysis.
- The percent of local police officers working for a department using in-field computers or terminals increased from 31 percent to 73 percent during the 1990s. Local police departments now have about twenty in-field computers or terminals per one hundred officers.
- More than half of local police officers work in a department where at least some officers in the field could use in-field computers to access information on wanted suspects (62 percent) or driving records (54 percent). About two in five officers are in departments where calls for service (41 percent) or criminal history (39 percent) records can be accessed.

Source: Matthew Hickman and Brian Reaves, *Local Police Departments 1999* (Washington, D.C.: Bureau of Justice Statistics, 2001).

Criminal Justice and Technology

Crime Mapping

Crime maps offer police administrators graphic representations of where crimes are occurring in their jurisdiction. Computerized crime mapping gives the police the power to analyze and correlate a wide array of data to create immediate, detailed visuals of crime patterns. The most simple maps (see Figure A, which shows the occurrence of Part I crimes in Tempe, Arizona, during the month of August 1999) display crime locations or concentrations and can be used to help direct patrols to the places they are most needed. More complex maps can be used to chart trends in criminal activity, and some have even proven valuable in solving individual criminal cases. For example, a serial rapist may be caught by observing and understanding the patterns of his crime so that detectives may predict where he will strike next and stake out the area with police decoys.

Crime mapping makes use of new computer technology. Instead of archaic pin maps, computerized crime mappings let the police detect crime patterns and pathologies of related problems. It enables them to work with multiple layers of information and scenarios, and thus identify emerging hot spots of criminal activity far more successfully and target resources accordingly.

A survey conducted by the National Institute of Justice found that 36 percent of agencies with one hundred or more sworn officers are now using some form of computerized crime mapping.

A number of the nation's largest departments are now using mapping techniques. The New York City Police Department's CompStat process relies on computerized crime mapping to identify crime hot spots and hold officers accountable for crime reduction along the department's chain of command. The department credits CompStat for dramatic and continuing reductions in crime in New York City. The Chicago Police Department has developed ICAM (Information Collection for Automated Mapping), designed to help police officers in analyzing and solving neighborhood crime problems. ICAM, operational in all of the department's twenty-five police districts, lets beat officers and other police personnel quickly and easily generate maps of timely, accurate crime data for their beats and

larger units. The police use the information they develop to support the department's community policing philosophy.

Some mapping efforts cross jurisdictional boundaries. Examples of this approach include the Regional Crime Analysis System in the greater Baltimore-Washington area and the multijurisdictional efforts of the Greater Atlanta PACT Data Center. The Charlotte-Mecklenburg Police Department (North Carolina) uses data collected by other city and county agencies in its crime mapping efforts. By coordinating the tax assessor's, public works, planning, and sanitation departments, these police department analysts have made links between disorder and crime that have been instrumental in supporting the department's community policing philosophy.

Critical Thinking

1. Crime mapping represents one of the latest technological advances in the allocation of police resources to fight crime effectively. Is it possible that recent downturns in the crime rate reflect this emphasis on technology?

2. Does a growing police technology capability present a danger to personal privacy? How far should the police go in order to keep tabs on potentially dangerous people? For example, should DNA samples be taken at birth from all people and kept on file to match with genetic materials collected at crime scenes?

InfoTrac College Edition Research

To read more about developments in police technology, read Christina Couret, "Police and Technology: The Silent Partnership," *American City & County*, August 1999 v114 i9 p31.

Sources: William W. Bratton and Peter Knobler, *Turnaround: How America's Top Cop Reversed the Crime Epidemic* (New York: Random House, 1998), 289; Jeremy Travis, "Computerized Crime Mapping," *NIJ News* (National Institute of Justice), January 1999.

Criminal Identification

Computer systems now used in the booking process can also help in the suspect identification process. During booking, a visual image of the suspect is stored in a computer's memory, along with other relevant information. By calling up color photos on the computer monitor, police can then easily create a "photo lineup" of all suspects having a particular characteristic described by a witness.

New techniques are constantly being developed. Soon, through the use of genetic algorithms (mathematical models), a computerized composite image of a

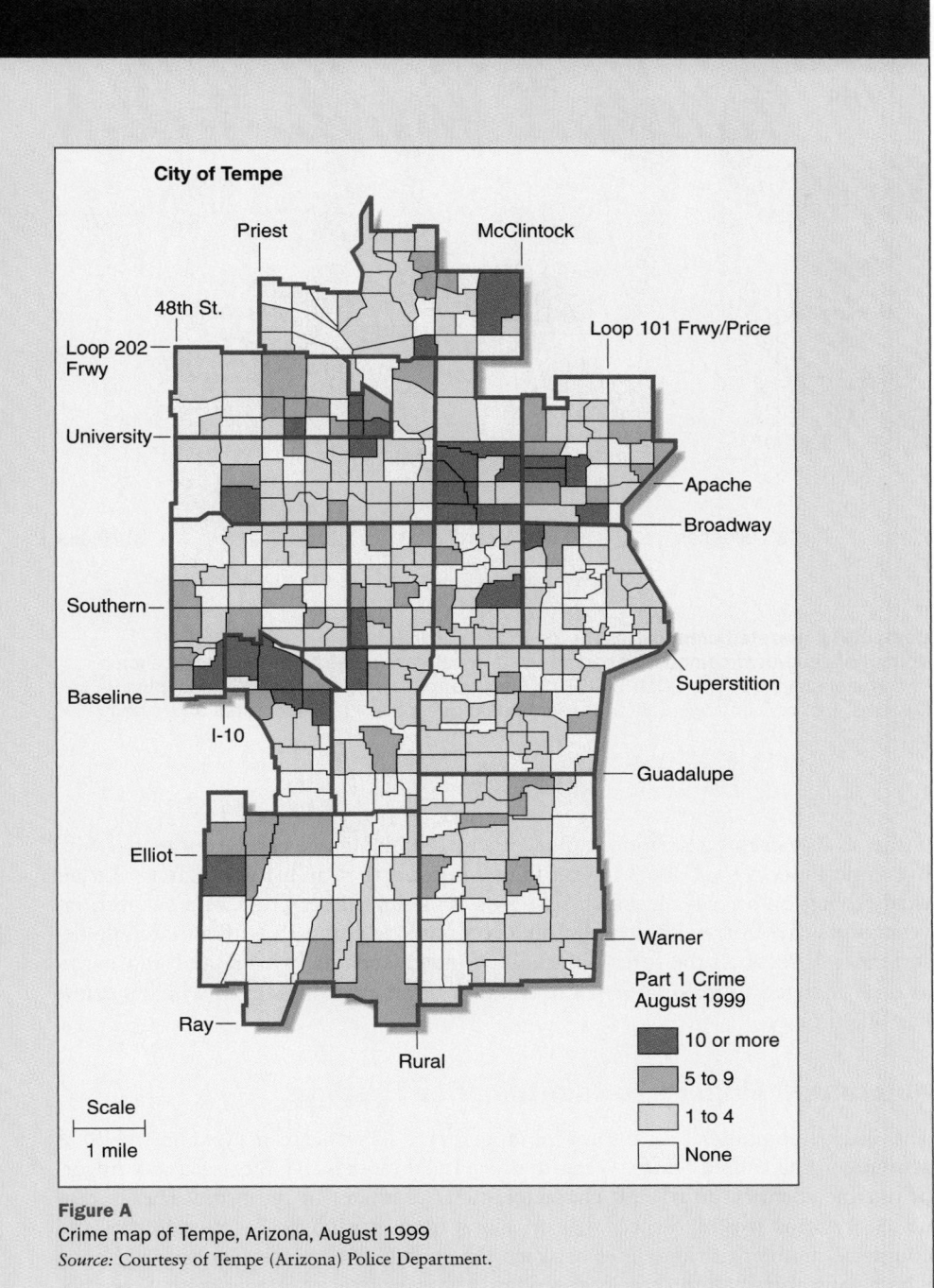

Figure A
Crime map of Tempe, Arizona, August 1999
Source: Courtesy of Tempe (Arizona) Police Department.

suspect's face will be constructed from relatively little information. Digitization of photographs will enable the reconstruction of blurred images. Videotapes of bank robbers or blurred photos of license plates—even bite marks—can be digitized using highly advanced mathematical models.

New computer software is being created that allows two-dimensional mug shots to be re-created on a three-dimensional basis. This technology has the human face divided into 64 features. For each of the 64 features, such as noses, mouths, and chins, there are 256 different types of each to choose from in the program. The result is that virtually anyone's face can be re-created according to a

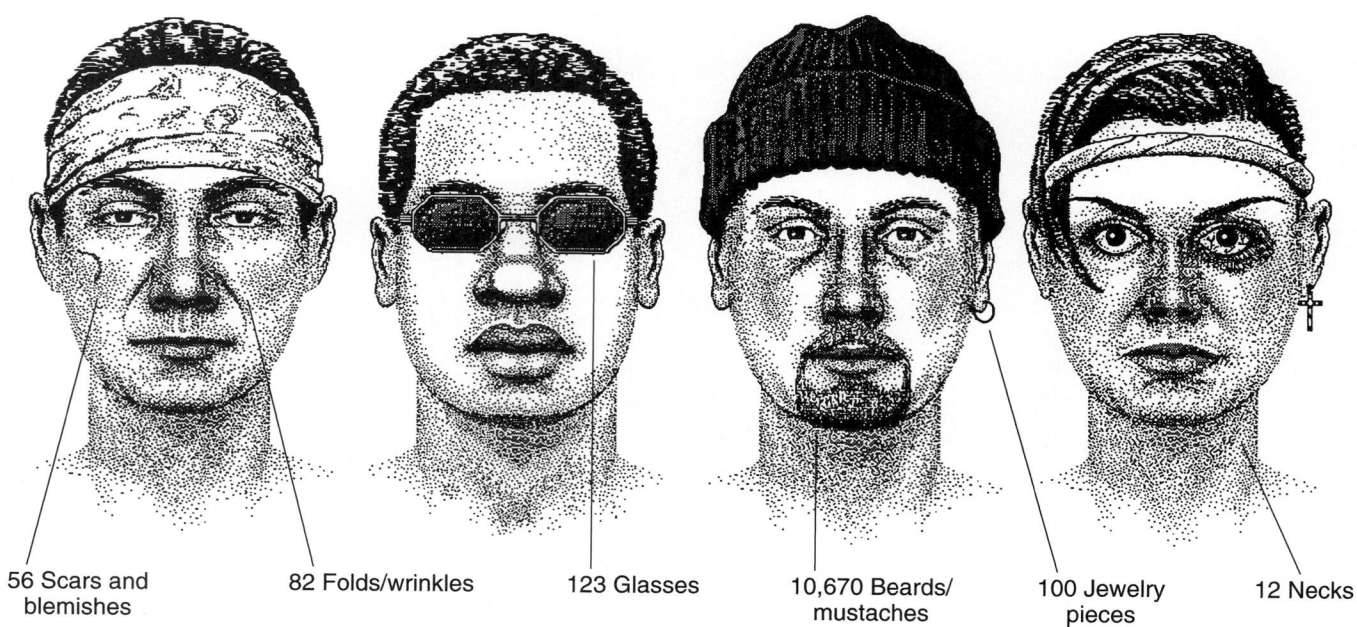

| 56 Scars and blemishes | 82 Folds/wrinkles | 123 Glasses | 10,670 Beards/ mustaches | 100 Jewelry pieces | 12 Necks |

Figure 4.1

Computer-generated composites for identifying suspects

Computer-generated composites can be used to help a witness create a precise sketch of criminal suspects. The COMPU-SKETCH® program developed by Digital Descriptor Systems, Inc. of Campbell, California, contains thousands of facial features and details.

witness's or victim's description. Once re-created, the image can be compared with over one million mug shots in less than a second to search for a match. Rather than relying on an artist's sketch based on a victim's description of a suspect, investigators can work with a victim on a computer to come up with a matching description. Effects on the three-dimensional image such as lighting and angles can also be changed to make a better re-creation of an environment in which a crime has taken place.[30]

Automated Fingerprint Identification Systems

The use of computerized automated fingerprint identification systems (AFIS) is growing in the United States. Using mathematical models, AFIS can classify fingerprints and identify up to 250 characteristics (minutiae) of the print. These automated systems use high-speed silicon chips to plot each point of minutiae and count the number of ridge lines between that point and its four nearest neighbors, which substantially improves its speed and accuracy over earlier systems. Some police departments report that computerized fingerprint systems are allowing them to make over one hundred identifications a month from fingerprints taken at crime scenes. AFIS files have been regionalized. For example, the Western Identification Network (WIN) consists of eight central site members (Alaska, Idaho, Montana, Nevada, Oregon, Utah, Wyoming, and Portland Police Bureau), two interface members (California and Washington), multiple local members, and six federal members (Drug Enforcement Administration, Federal Bureau of Investigation, Immigration and Naturalization Service, Internal Revenue Service, Postal Inspection Service, and Secret Service).[31] When it first began, the system had a centralized automated database of nine hundred thousand fingerprint records; today with the ad-

The Western Identification Network (WIN) Web site is at www.winid.org/history.htm

New breakthroughs in fingerprint identification have revolutionized suspect identification. Here, Jeffrey Graham reviews an enlargement of the latent fingerprint taken from the motor home of David Westerfield, during Westerfield's murder trial, June 19, 2002, in San Diego. Graham is employed by the San Diego Police Department as a latent print examiner. His fingerprint analysis helped prosecutors convict Westerfield of the death of seven-year-old Danielle van Dam.

dition of new jurisdictions (Alaska, California, and Washington) the system's number of searchable fingerprint records increased to more than fourteen million.

If these computerized fingerprint files become standardized and a national database is formed, it will be possible to check records in all fifty states to determine whether a suspect's fingerprints match those taken at the crime scene of previously unsolved cases. A national fingerprint identification system should become an even more effective tool because laser technology is likely to vastly improve fingerprint analysis. Investigators will soon be able to recover prints that in the past were too damaged to be used as evidence. Other new breeds of fingerprint analysis will also soon be available. The FBI plans to create an integrated AFIS that will allow local departments to scan fingerprints, send them electronically to a national depository, and receive back identification and criminal history of suspects.

Want to work with **AFIS files**? Go to this Web site for a job description: www.ci.mesa.az.us/police/identification/fptech_job.htm

DNA Testing

Advanced technology is also spurring new forensic methods of identification and analysis.[32] The most prominent technique is **DNA profiling,** a procedure that has gained national attention because of the O. J. Simpson trial. This technique allows suspects to be identified on the basis of the genetic material found in hair, blood, and other bodily tissues and fluids. When DNA is used as evidence in a rape trial, DNA segments are taken from the victim, the suspect, and blood and semen found on the victim. A DNA match indicates a four-billion-to-one likelihood that the suspect is the offender.

Two methods of DNA matching are used. The most popular technique, known as *RFLP* (restriction fragment length polymorphism), uses radioactive material to produce a DNA image on an X-ray film. The second method, *PCR* (polymerase chain reaction), amplifies DNA samples through molecular photocopying.[33]

DNA fingerprinting is now used as evidence in criminal trials in more than twenty states.[34] The use of DNA evidence to gain convictions has also been upheld

DNA profiling   The identification of criminal suspects by matching DNA samples taken from their person with specimens found at the crime scene.

on appeal.[35] Its use in criminal trials received a boost in 1997 when the FBI announced that the evidence has become so precise that experts no longer have to supply a statistical estimate of accuracy while testifying at trial ("The odds are a billion to one that this is the culprit"); they can now state in court that there exists "a reasonable degree of scientific certainty" that evidence came from a single suspect.[36]

Leading the way in the development of the most advanced forensic techniques is the Forensic Science Research and Training Center, operated by the FBI in Washington, D.C., and Quantico, Virginia. The lab provides information and services to hundreds of crime labs throughout the United States. The National Institute of Justice is also sponsoring research to identify a wider variety of DNA segments for testing and is involved in developing a PCR-based DNA-profiling examination using fluorescent detection that will reduce the time required for DNA profiling. The FBI is now operating the DNA Index System (NDIS), a computerized database that will allow DNA taken at a crime scene to be searched electronically to find matches against samples taken from convicted offenders and from other crime scenes. The first database will allow suspects to be identified, and the second will allow investigators to establish links between crimes, such as those involving serial killers or rapists. In 1999 the FBI announced the system made its first "cold hit" by linking evidence taken from crime scenes in Jacksonville, Florida, to ones in Washington, D.C., thereby tying nine crimes to a single offender.[37] When Timothy Spence was executed in Virginia on April 27, 1994, he was the first person convicted and executed almost entirely on the basis of DNA evidence.[38]

Although DNA is a very useful tool there are still some ethical and practical questions concerning its use. Some crime experts such as Paul Tracy and Vincent Morgan find that the cost of maintaining a national DNA database is significant, rising into the hundreds of millions of dollars, while the number of criminals identified using DNA is relatively small.[39] They argue that DNA databases cannot be used to solve the vast majority of serious crimes and few if any nonserious ones. Even if crime scenes contain DNA evidence, local law enforcement agencies do not have the necessary resources to collect evidence and identify criminals. Tracy and Morgan also warn that having DNA evidence on file poses a serious threat to civil liberties. Should a person who is arrested for placing a bet on a football game have his DNA kept on file with convicted rapists and child molesters?

Want to read more about the science of DNA testing? Go to http://arbl.cvmbs.colostate.edu/hbooks/genetics/medgen/dnatesting/

Communications

Computer technology will enhance communications and information dissemination. Many larger departments have equipped officers with portable computers, which significantly cuts down the time needed to write and duplicate reports.[40] Police can now use terminals to draw accident diagrams, communicate with city traffic engineers, and merge their incident reports into other databases. Pen computing, in which officers write directly on a computer screen, eliminates paperwork and increases the accuracy of reports.[41] To make this material more accessible to the officer on patrol, head-up display (HUD) units now project information onto screens located on patrol car windshields; police officers can now access computer readouts without taking their eyes off the road![42]

Future police technology will involve more efficient communications systems. Officers are now using cellular phones in their cars to facilitate communications with victims and witnesses.[43] Departments that cover wide geographical areas and maintain independent precincts and substations are experimenting with **teleconferencing** systems that provide both audio and video linkages. Police agencies may use advanced communications gear to track stolen vehicles. Car owners will be able to buy transmitters that give off a signal to a satellite or other listening device

teleconferencing Using audio and video linkups to allow people to communicate from distant locations.

that can then be monitored and tracked by the specially equipped patrol cars; this system is being tested.[44] Some departments are linking advanced communications systems with computers, making use of electronic bulletin boards that link officers in an active on-line system, enabling them to communicate faster and more easily.

Combating Terrorism with Communications   Communication technology has become even more important now that police agencies are involved in a war on terrorism. Keeping surveillance on suspected terrorist groups is not an easy task. However, when Congress passed the Communications Assistance for Law Enforcement Act (CALEA) in 1994, it aided law enforcement's ability to monitor suspects. The act required that communication equipment manufacturers and carriers design equipment, facilities, and services that are compatible with electronic surveillance needs.[45] Under the law, telecommunications carriers must ensure that equipment has the capability to facilitate the isolation and interception of communications content and call-identifying information and make it easy to deliver these data to law enforcement agencies.[46] CALEA allows that upon issue of a court order or other lawful authorization, communication carriers must be able to: (1) expeditiously isolate all wire and electronic communications of a target transmitted by the carrier within its service area; (2) expeditiously isolate call-identifying information of a target; (3) provide intercepted communications and call-identifying information to law enforcement; and (4) carry out intercepts unobtrusively, so targets are not made aware of the electronic surveillance, and in a manner that does not compromise the privacy and security of other communications. Under CALEA the government reimburses telecommunications carriers for the costs of developing software to intercept communications. ■

SUMMARY

U.S. police agencies are modeled after their British counterparts. Early in British history, law enforcement was a personal matter. Later, constables were appointed to keep peace among groups of one hundred families. This rudimentary beginning was the seed of today's police departments. In 1838 the first true U.S. police department was formed in Boston.

The earliest U.S. police departments were created because of the need to control mob violence, which was common during the nineteenth century. The police were viewed as being dominated by political bosses who controlled their hiring practices and policies.

Reform movements begun in the 1920s culminated in the concept of professionalism in the 1950s and 1960s. Police professionalism was interpreted to mean tough, rule-oriented police work featuring advanced technology and hardware. However, the view that these measures would quickly reduce crime proved incorrect.

There are several major law enforcement agencies. On the federal level, the FBI is the premier law enforcement

organization. Other agencies include the Drug Enforcement Administration, the U.S. Marshals, and the Secret Service. County-level law enforcement is provided by sheriff's departments, and most states maintain state police agencies. However, most law enforcement activities are carried out by local police agencies, which perform patrol, investigative, and traffic functions, as well as many support activities.

Today, most police departments have begun to rely on advanced computer-based technology to identify suspects and collate evidence. Automated fingerprint systems and computerized identification systems will have become widespread. There is danger that technology may make police overly intrusive and interfere with civil liberties.

For an up-to-date list of Web links, go to http://cj.wadsworth.com/siegel_essen4e.

KEY TERMS

tithing   113

hue and cry   113

hundred   113

constable   113

shire reeve   113

sheriff   113

watch system   113

justice of the peace   113

vigilantes   116

Federal Bureau of Investigation (FBI)   122

Drug Enforcement Administration (DEA)   123

DNA profiling   131

teleconferencing   132

INFOTRAC COLLEGE EDITION EXERCISES

SUPPLEMENTING LOCAL POLICE forces has been a burgeoning private security industry. InfoTrac College Edition provides some important research on the private security industry. Do a search using the key words "private security" and "private police."

Private security service has become a multibillion-dollar industry with ten thousand firms and 1.5 million employees. Even federal police services have been privatized to cut expenses, a move that was opposed by the American Federation of Government Employees. To learn more about this growth, see Gayle M. B. Hanson, "Private Protection Is Secure Industry," *Insight on the News* 13 (1997): 19.

THERE WILL BE MORE legal scrutiny as the private security business blossoms. For example, are security guards subject to the same search-and-seizure standards as police officers? The Supreme Court has repeatedly stated that purely private search activities do not violate the Fourth Amendment's prohibitions. Might security guards be subject to Fourth Amendment requirements if they are performing services that are traditionally reserved for the police, such as guarding communities? To find out, read John B. Owens, "Westec Story: Gated Communities and the Fourth Amendment," *American Criminal Law Review* 34 (1997): 127–160.

QUESTIONS

1. List the problems faced by today's police departments that were also present during the early days of policing.

2. Distinguish between the duties of the state police, sheriffs' departments, and local police departments.

3. Do you believe that the general public has greater respect for the police today than in the past? If so, why? If not, why?

4. What are some of the technological advances that should help the police solve more crimes? What are the dangers of these advances?

5. Discuss the trends that will influence policing during the coming decade. What other social factors may affect police?

NOTES

1. Sara Stoutland, "The Multiple Dimensions of Trust in Resident/Police Relations in Boston," *Journal of Research in Crime and Delinquency* 38 (2001), 226–256.

2. Richard A. Leo and Richard J. Ofshe, "The Consequences of False Confessions: Deprivations of Liberty and Miscarriages of Justice in the Age of Psychological Interrogation," *Journal of Criminal Law and Criminology* 88 (1998): 429–496.

3. "Law Enforcement Seeks Answers to 'Racial Profiling' Complaints," *Criminal Justice Newsletter* 29 (1998): 5.

4. "Three Men Detained in Security Check in Florida," *New York Times,* 13 September 2002, A1.

5. Liqun Cao, James Frank, and Francis Cullen, "Race, Community Context, and Confidence in the Police," *American Journal of Police* 15 (1996): 3–15.

6. Thomas Priest and Deborah Brown Carter, "Evaluations of Police Performance in an African American Sample," *Journal of Criminal Justice* 27 (1999): 457–465.

7. This section relies heavily on such sources as Malcolm Sparrow, Mark Moore, and David Kennedy, *Beyond 9-11, A New Era for Policing* (New York: Basic Books, 1990); Daniel Devlin, *Police Procedure, Administration, and Organization* (London: Butterworth, 1966); Robert Fogelson, *Big City Police* (Cambridge, Mass.: Harvard University Press, 1977); Roger Lane, *Policing the City, Boston 1822–1885* (Cambridge, Mass.: Harvard University Press, 1967); J. J. Tobias, *Crime and Industrial Society in the Nineteenth Century* (New York: Schocken Books, 1967); Samuel Walker, *A Critical History of Police Reform: The Emergence of Professionalism* (Lexington, Mass.: Lexington Books, 1977); Samuel Walker, *Popular Justice* (New York: Oxford University Press, 1980); John McMullan, "The New Improved Monied Police: Reform Crime Control and Commodification of Policing in London, *British Journal of Criminology* 36 (1996): 85–108.

8. Devlin, *Police Procedure, Administration, and Organization,* 3.

9. John L. McMullan, "The New Improved Monied Police: Reform, Crime Control, and the Commodification of Policing in London," *British Journal of Criminology* 36 (1996): 92.

10. Wilbur Miller, "The Good, the Bad & the Ugly: Policing America," *History Today,* 50 (2000): 29–32.

11. Phillip Reichel, "Southern Slave Patrols as a Transitional Type," *American Journal of Police 7* (1988): 51–78.

12. Walker, *Popular Justice,* 61.

13. Ibid., 8.

14. Dennis Rousey, "Cops and Guns: Police Use of Deadly Force in Nineteenth-Century New Orleans," *American Journal of Legal History 28* (1984): 41–66.

15. Law Enforcement Assistance Administration, *Two Hundred Years of American Criminal Justice* (Washington, D.C.: Government Printing Office, 1976).

16. National Commission on Law Observance and Enforcement, *Report on the Police* (Washington, D.C.: Government Printing Office, 1931), 5–7.

17. Pamela Irving Jackson, *Minority Group Threat, Crime, and Policing* (New York: Praeger, 1989).

18. James Q. Wilson and George Kelling, "Broken Windows," *Atlantic Monthly 249* (1982): 29–38.

19. Frank Tippett, "It Looks Just Like a War Zone," *Time,* 27 May 1985, 16–22; "San Francisco, New York Police Troubled by Series of Scandals," *Criminal Justice Newsletter 16* (1985): 2–4; Karen Polk, "New York Police: Caught in the Middle and Losing Faith," *Boston Globe,* 28 December 1988, 3.

20. Staff of the *Los Angeles Times, Understanding the Riots: Los Angeles Before and After the Rodney King Case* (Los Angeles: *Los Angeles Times,* 1992).

21. Kathleen Grubb, "Cold War to Gang War," *Boston Globe,* 22 January 1992, 1.

22. Bruce Smith, *Police Systems in the United States* (New York: Harper & Row, 1960).

23. Brian A. Reaves and Matthew Hickman, *Sheriffs' Office 1999* (Washington, D.C.: Bureau of Justice Statistics, 2001).

24. Data in this section come from Matthew Hickman and Brian A. Reaves, *Local Police Departments 1999* (Washington, D.C.: Bureau of Justice Statistics, 2001).

25. See, for example, Robert Keppel and Joseph Weis, *Improving the Investigation of Violent Crime: The Homicide Investigation and Tracking System* (Washington, D.C.: National Institute of Justice, 1993).

26. Larry Coutorie, "The Future of High-Technology Crime: A Parallel Delphi Study," *Journal of Criminal Justice 23* (1995): 13–27.

27. Bill Goodwin, "Burglars Captured by Police Data Mining Kit," *Computer Weekly,* 8 August 2002, 3.

28. "Forensic Computing Expert Warns Interpol About Computer Crime," *Information Systems Auditor,* August 2002, 2.

29. Lois Pliant, "Information Management," *Police Chief 61* (1994): 31–35.

30. "Spotlight on Computer Imaging," *Police Chief 66* (1999): 6–8.

31. See, generally, Laura Moriarty and David Carter, *Criminal Justice Technology in the Twenty-First Century* (Springfield, Ill.: Charles C. Thomas, 1998).

32. See, generally, Ryan McDonald, "Juries and Crime Labs: Correcting the Weak Links in the DNA Chain," *American Journal of Law and Medicine 24* (1998): 345–363; "DNA Profiling Advancement," *FBI Law Enforcement Bulletin 67* (1998): 24.

33. Ronald Reinstein, *Postconviction DNA Testing: Recommendations for Handling Requests* (Philadelphia: Diane Publishing Co., 1999).

34. "California Attorney General Endorses DNA Fingerprinting," *Criminal Justice Newsletter 1* (1989): 1.

35. *State v. Ford,* 301 S.C. 485, 392 S.E.2d 781 (1990).

36. "Under New Policy, FBI Examiners Testify to Absolute DNA Matches," *Criminal Justice Newsletter 28* (1997): 1–2.

37. "FBI's DNA Profile Clearinghouse Announce First 'Cold Hit,'" *Criminal Justice Newsletter 16* (1999): 5.

38. "South Side Strangler's Execution Cited as DNA Evidence Landmark," *Criminal Justice Newsletter 2* (1994): 3.

39. Paul Tracy and Vincent Morgan, "Big Brother and His Science Kit: DNA Databases for 21st-Century Crime Control?" *Journal of Criminal Law and Criminology 90* (2000): 635–690.

40. Brewer Stone, "The High-Tech Beat in St. Pete," *Police Chief 55* (1988): 23–28.

41. "Pen Computing: The Natural 'Next Step' for Field Personnel," *Law and Order 43* (1995): 37.

42. Miller McMillan, "High Tech Enters the Field of View," *Police Chief 62* (1994): 29.

43. Ibid., 24.

44. Mark Thompson, "Police Seeking Radio Channel for Stolen Auto Tracking System," *Criminal Justice Newsletter 15* (1989): 1.

45. Communications Assistance for Law Enforcement Act of 1994, Pub. L. No. 103-414, 108 Stat. 4279.

46. Michael P. Clifford, "Communications Assistance for Law Enforcement Act (CALEA)," *FBI Law Enforcement Bulletin 71* (2002): 11–14.

5 The Police: Role and Function

Chapter Outline

Criminal Justice Links

Criminal Justice Viewpoints

Courtesy of CNN

ON APRIL 30, 2001, Chandra Levy, twenty-four, a Washington, D.C.–based intern, was last seen at her health club, where she cancelled her membership. She had just completed an internship with the federal Bureau of Prisons and was due to fly home to Modesto, California. Her packed bags were found at her apartment. As the search for her commenced, Linda Zamsky, her aunt, told the *Washington Post* that her niece had admitted to having an affair with married congressman Gary Condit. On July 8, 2001, Condit admitted to the police that he had had an affair with Levy but denied any knowledge of her whereabouts or the circumstances of her disappearance. With a cloud of suspicion hanging over him, Condit lost his reelection bid. Then, on May 22, 2002, Levy's skeletal remains were discovered in Rock Creek Park in Washington, D.C.; forensic examination indicated that her death had been caused by homicide although the condition of the remains did not allow police experts to determine how she had died or whether she had died in the park or if her body been moved there from somewhere else. There were rumors that she had been sexually assaulted before her death, or had been tied up. But despite diligent efforts by the police her murderer has so far escaped detection. ■

 *To view the CNN video clip of this story, go to the book-specific Web site at* http://cj.wadsworth.com/siegel_essen4e.

Although the Chandra Levy case was certainly one of the most notorious of recent years, it is not unique. Every day, police are called in to solve cases long after a crime has been committed. In addition, they are asked to prevent crimes before they occur. The police are expected to be enforcers of the law.

They are told to be enforcers of the law in some of the toughest areas in urban America, yet they are criticized or even jailed when their tactics become too aggressive. Is it unrealistic to expect police officers to fulfill society's demand for order while maintaining a tight grip on their behavior and emotions?

This chapter describes the organization of police departments and their various operating branches: patrol, investigation, service, and administration. It discusses the realities and ambiguities of the police role and how the concept of the police mission has been changing radically. The chapter concludes with a brief overview of some of the most important administrative issues confronting today's U.S. law enforcement agencies.

The Police Organization

The Chicago Police Department maintains a Web site designed to provide basic information about it and its Alternative Policing Strategy (CAPS): www.ci.chi.il.us/CommunityPolicing/

police chief The top administrator of the police department, who sets policy and has general control over all operating branches.

time-in-rank system For police officers to advance in rank they must spend an appropriate amount of time, usually years, in the preceding rank; that is, to become a captain an officer must first spend time as a lieutenant.

Copsonline provides information about how to become a police officer, recent books on the subject, training, and jobs: www.copsonline.com/

Most municipal police departments in the United States are independent agencies within the executive branch of government, operating without specific administrative control from any higher governmental authority.

On occasion, police agencies will cooperate and participate in mutually beneficial enterprises, such as sharing information on known criminals, or they may help federal agencies investigate interstate criminal cases. Aside from such cooperative efforts, police departments tend to be functionally independent organizations with unique sets of rules, policies, procedures, norms, budgets, and so on. The unique structure of police agencies greatly influences their function and effectiveness.

Although many police agencies are rethinking their organization and goals, the majority are still organized in a militaristic, hierarchical manner, as illustrated in Figure 5.1. Within this organizational model, each element of the department normally has its own chain of command. For example, in a large municipal department, the detective bureau might have a captain who serves as the director of a particular division (such as homicide), a lieutenant who oversees individual cases and acts as liaison with other police agencies, and sergeants and inspectors who carry out the actual fieldwork. Smaller departments may have a captain as head of all detectives, while lieutenants supervise individual subsystems, such as robbery or homicide. At the head of the organization is the **police chief,** who sets policy and has general administrative control over all the department's various operating branches.

The organizational structure of the typical police department has several problems. First, citizens often have difficulty in determining who is actually responsible for the department's policies and operations. Second, the large number of operating divisions and the lack of any clear relationship between them almost guarantee that the decision-making practices of one branch will be unknown to another; two divisions may compete with each other over jurisdiction on a particular case.

Most departments also follow a military-like system in promoting personnel within the ranks; at an appropriate time, a promotion test may be given, and based on his scores and recommendations, an officer may be advanced in rank. This organizational style frustrates some police officers from furthering their education, because a college or advanced degree may have little direct impact on their promotion potential or responsibilities. Furthermore, some otherwise competent police officers cannot increase their rank because of their inability to take tests well.

Most police departments employ a **time-in-rank system** for determining promotion eligibility. This means that before moving up the administrative ladder, an officer must spend a certain amount of time in the next lowest rank; a sergeant cannot become a captain without serving an appropriate amount of time as a lieutenant. Although this system is designed to promote fairness and limit favoritism, it also restricts administrative flexibility. Unlike in the private sector, where talented people can be pushed ahead in the best interests of the company, the time-in-rank system prohibits rapid advancement. A police agency would probably not be able to hire a computer systems expert with a Ph.D. and give her a command position in charge of its data-analysis section. The department would be forced to hire the expert as a civilian employee under the command of a ranking senior officer who may not be as technically proficient.

Under this rank system, a title can rarely be taken away or changed once it is earned. Police administrators become frustrated when qualified junior officers cannot be promoted or reassigned to appropriate positions because they lack time in rank or because less qualified officers have more seniority. Inability to advance through the ranks convinces numerous educated and ambitious officers to seek private employment. The rank system also means that talented police officers can-

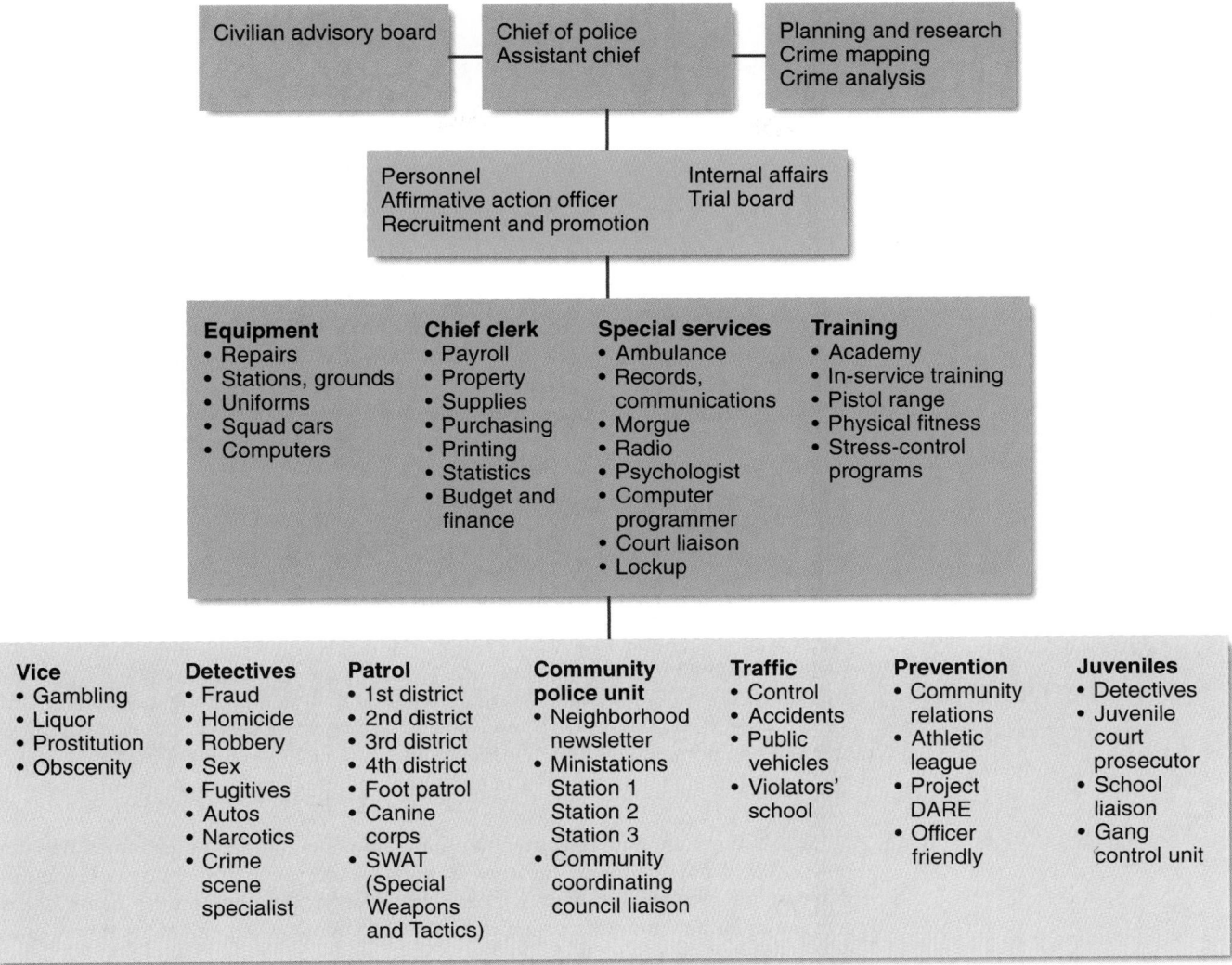

Figure 5.1
Organization of a traditional metropolitan police department

not transfer to other departments or sell their services to the highest bidder. Time in rank ensures the stability—for better or worse—of police agencies.

The Police Role

In countless books, movies, and TV shows, the public has been presented with a view of policing that romanticizes police officers as fearless crime fighters who think little of their own safety as they engage in daily shootouts with Uzi-toting drug runners, psychopathic serial killers, and organized-crime hit men. Occasionally, but not often, fictional patrol officers and detectives seem aware of departmental rules, legal decisions, citizen groups, civil suits, or physical danger. They are rarely faced with the economic necessity of moonlighting as security guards, caring about an annual pay raise, or griping when someone less deserving gets promoted ahead of them for political reasons.

How close is this portrayal of a selfless crime fighter to real life? Not very close, according to most research efforts.

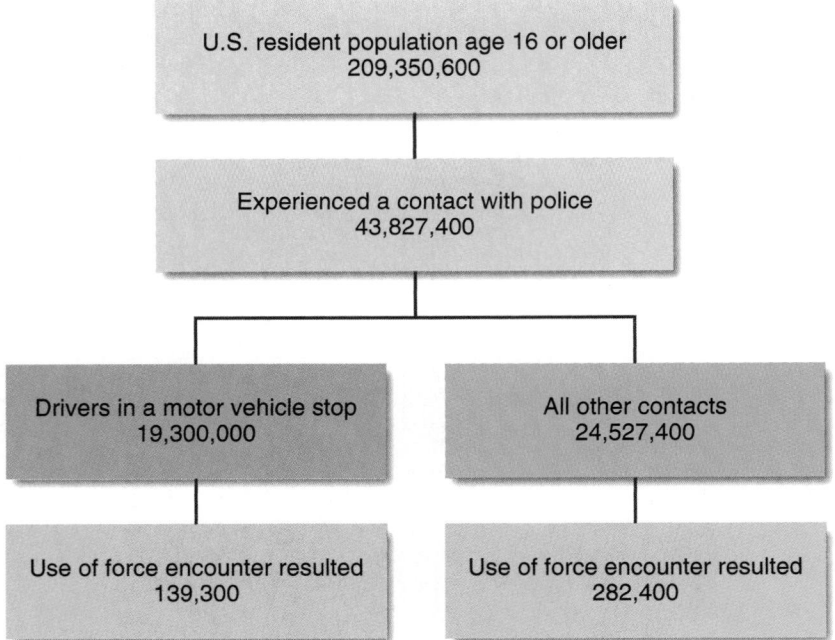

Figure 5.2
Police encounters with citizens

Source: Patrick A. Langan, Lawrence A. Greenfeld, Steven K. Smith, Matthew R. Durose, and David J. Levin, *Contacts Between Police and the Public: Findings from the 1999 National Survey* (Washington, D.C.: Bureau of Justice Statistics, 2001).

Most research efforts show that a police officer's crime-fighting efforts are only a small part of his or her overall activities. Studies of police work indicate that a significant portion of an officer's time is spent handling minor disturbances, service calls, and administrative duties. Police work, then, involves much more than catching criminals. Figure 5.2 shows the results of a national survey of police behavior. About forty-four million Americans have contacts with the police each year.[1] Most involve some form of motor vehicle or traffic-related issues. About five million annual contacts involve citizens asking for assistance—for example, responding to a neighbor's complaint about music being too loud during a party, or warning kids not to shoot fireworks. This survey indicates that the police role is both varied and complex.[2] Force is rarely used.

These results are not surprising when Uniform Crime Report (UCR) arrest data are considered. Each year, about seven hundred thousand local, county, and state police officers make about 14 million arrests, or about 20 each. Of these, about 2.2 million are for serious index crimes (Part I), or about 3 per officer. Given an even distribution of arrests, it is evident that the average police officer makes less than 2 arrests per month and less than 1 felony arrest every four months.

These figures should be interpreted with caution because not all police officers are engaged in activities that allow them to make arrests, such as patrol or detective work. About one-third of all sworn officers in the nation's largest police departments are in such units as communications, antiterrorism, administration, and personnel, and are therefore unlikely to make arrests. Even if the number of arrests per officer were adjusted by one-third, it would still amount to only nine or ten serious crime arrests per officer per year. So though police handle thousands of calls each year, relatively few result in an arrest for a serious crime such as a robbery and burglary; in suburban and rural areas, years may go by before a police officer arrests someone for a serious crime.

The evidence, then, shows that the police role involves many non-crime-related activities. While TV and movies show police officers busting criminals and engaging in high-speed chases, the true police role is much more complex. Police officers function in a variety of roles ranging from dispensers of emergency medical care to keepers of the peace on school grounds. Although officers in large urban departments may be called on to handle more felony cases than those in small towns, they too will probably find that most of their daily activities are not crime-related. What are some of the most important functions of police?

The Patrol Function

Regardless of style of policing, uniformed patrol officers are the backbone of the police department, usually accounting for about two-thirds of a department's personnel.[3] Patrol officers are the most highly visible components of the entire criminal justice system. They are charged with supervising specific areas of their jurisdiction, called **beats,** whether on foot, bicycle, in a patrol car, or by motor-cycle, horse, helicopter, or even boat. Each beat, or patrol area, is covered twenty-four hours a day by different shifts. The major purposes of patrol are to

beat A defined patrol area.

1. Deter crime by maintaining a visible police presence.
2. Maintain public order (peacekeeping) within the patrol area.
3. Enable the police department to respond quickly to law violations or other emergencies.
4. Identify and apprehend law violators.

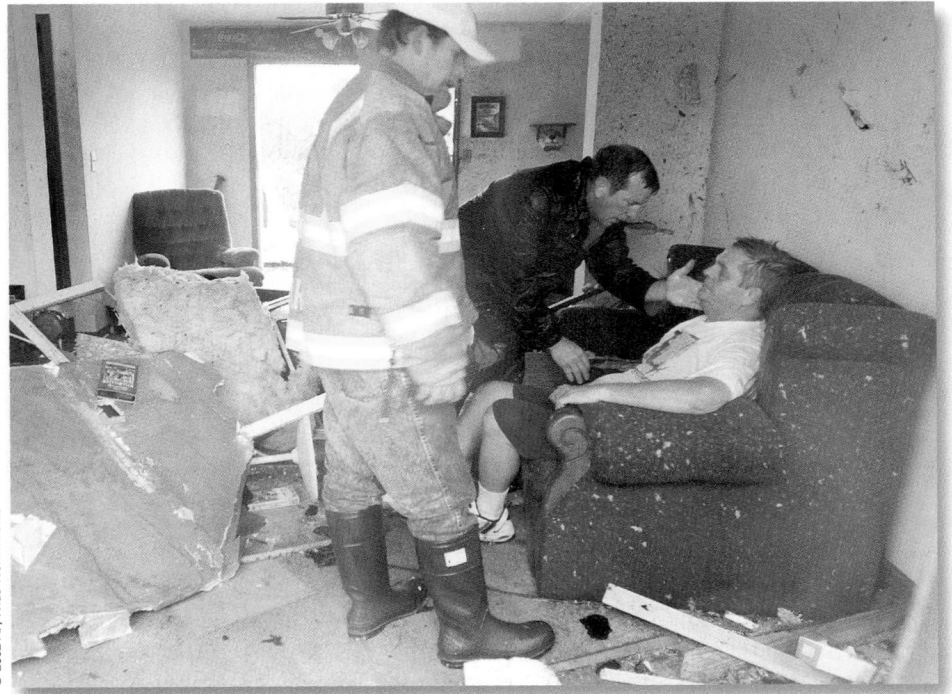

© 2002 AP/Wide World Photos

Police patrol means more than fighting crime. Here, Indiana State Police officer J. D. Maxwell checks Terry Martin of Ellettsville, fifty miles south of Indianapolis, on September 20, 2002, after Martin survived a tornado that ripped the roof off his home. He said he got through the ordeal by lying in fetal position next to his entertainment center after he failed to reach a closet in his bedroom in time. Some twelve houses were destroyed and an apartment complex was damaged in Ellettsville.

© 2002 AP/Wide World Photos

Maintaining order and keeping the peace are important duties in the patrol function. Here, Philadelphia police patrol South Street during Mardi Gras festivities, February 12, 2002. One year after drunken revelers threw bottles, smashed windows, and looted stores on South Street, a popular stretch of bars and shops downtown, police presence outnumbered partiers.

5. Aid individuals and care for those who cannot help themselves.
6. Facilitate the movement of traffic and people.
7. Create a feeling of security in the community.[4]

Patrol officers' responsibilities are immense; they may suddenly be faced with an angry mob, an armed felon, or a suicidal teenager and be forced to make split-second decisions on what action to take. At the same time, they must be sensitive to the needs of citizens who are often of diverse racial and ethnic backgrounds.

Patrol Activities

order maintenance (peacekeeping)
The order-maintenance aspect of the police role involves peacekeeping, maintaining order and authority without the need for formal arrest, "handling the situation," and keeping things under control by using threats, persuasion, and understanding.

Most experts agree that the great bulk of patrol efforts are devoted to what has been described as **order maintenance,** or **peacekeeping:** maintaining order and civility in their assigned jurisdiction.[5] Order-maintenance functions fall on the border between criminal and noncriminal behavior. The patrol officer's discretion often determines whether a noisy neighborhood dispute involves the crime of disturbing the peace or whether it can be controlled with street-corner diplomacy, and sending the combatants on their way. Similarly, teenagers milling around in the shopping center parking lot may be brought in and turned over to the juvenile authorities or handled in a less formal and often more efficient manner.

The primary role of police seems to be "handling the situation." Police encounter many troubling incidents that need some sort of "fixing up."[6] Enforcing the law might be one tool a patrol officer uses; threat, coercion, sympathy, and understanding might be others. Most important is keeping things under control so that there are no complaints that the officer is doing nothing at all or doing too much. The real police role, then, may be as a community problem solver.

Police officers actually practice a policy of selective enforcement, concentrating on some crimes but handling the majority in an informal manner. A police officer is supposed to know when to take action and when not to, whom to arrest and whom to deal with by issuing a warning or some other informal action. If a mistake is made, the officer can come under fire from peers and superiors, as well as the general public. Consequently, the patrol officer's job is extremely demanding and often unrewarding and unappreciated. It is not surprising that the attitudes of police officers toward the public are sometimes characterized as ambivalent and cynical.[7]

To find out more about "police patrol," use it as a subject guide on InfoTrac College Edition.

Does Patrol Deter Crime?

For many years, preventive police patrol has been considered one of the greatest deterrents to criminal behavior. The visible presence of patrol cars on the street and the rapid deployment of police officers to the scene of the crime were viewed as particularly effective law enforcement techniques. However, research efforts have questioned the basic assumptions of patrol. The most widely heralded attempt at measuring patrol effectiveness was undertaken during the early 1970s in Kansas City, Missouri, under sponsorship of the Police Foundation, a private institute that studies police behavior.[8]

To evaluate the effectiveness of patrol, the researchers divided fifteen separate police districts into three groups: one group retained normal patrol; the second (proactive) set of districts were supplied with two to three times the normal amount of patrol forces; and the third (reactive) group had its preventive patrol eliminated, with police officers responding only when summoned by citizens to the scene of a particular crime.

Data from the Kansas City study indicated that these variations in patrol techniques had little effect on the crime patterns in the fifteen districts. The presence or absence of patrol did not seem to affect residential or business burglaries, motor vehicle thefts, larceny involving auto accessories, robberies, vandalism, or other criminal behavior.[9] Moreover, variations in patrol techniques appeared to have little influence on citizens' attitudes toward the police, their satisfaction with police, or their fear of future criminal behavior.[10]

Although the Kansas City study found little evidence that police patrol could deter crime, police in a number of jurisdictions have attempted to test the effectiveness of patrol by targeting areas for increased police presence. For example, a police task force might target street-level narcotics dealers by using undercover agents and surveillance cameras in known drug-dealing locales. Or they may actively enforce public nuisance laws in an effort to demonstrate the department's crime-fighting resolve. These efforts have not proven to be successful mechanisms for lowering crime rates.[11] In addition, there is the problem of **displacement:** criminals move from an area targeted for increased police presence to another that is less well protected; when the police leave, they return to "business as usual."

© Tom Carter/Photo Edit

Though police detectives play an important role in investigations, research indicates that most arrests are made by patrol officers soon after a crime is committed. Here a police officer questions a witness at a crime scene.

displacement   The process by which the presence of police officers in one area causes criminals to move to another, less well guarded neighborhood.

Proactive Patrol

The Kansas City study, although subject to criticism because of its research design, greatly influenced the way police experts viewed the effectiveness of patrol. Its rather lukewarm findings set the stage for community and problem-oriented

© 2002 AP/Wide World Photos

To be more effective police may want to target specific crimes using aggressive tactics. Sometimes their efforts step over the boundaries of the Fourth Amendment's protection against illegal searches and seizures. Indianapolis Police Department officer Mark Fagan and his partner, Raider, a Dutch Sheppard, examine a car during a 1998 roadblock set up in an effort to find illegal drugs. Lawyers for motorists delayed by the roadblock asked the Supreme Court to ban the practice, calling it risky and heavy-handed. The city of Indianapolis argued that such roadblocks were a simple, effective way to stem drug trafficking in high-crime neighborhoods and were no more intrusive than random checks for drunk drivers or illegal immigrants. The Supreme Court disagreed, and in the case of *Indianapolis v. Edmond* (2000) it ruled the practice unlawful.

policing models, which stress social service over crime deterrence. However, it may be too soon to dismiss police patrol as a crime-fighting technique. Although the mere presence of police may not be sufficient to deter crime, the manner in which they approach their task may make a difference. Evidence shows that cities with larger police departments that have more officers per capita than the norm also experience lower levels of violent crimes.[12]

Police departments that use a proactive, aggressive law enforcement style may help reduce crime rates. Jurisdictions that encourage patrol officers to stop motor vehicles to issue citations and to aggressively arrest and detain suspicious persons also experience lower crime rates than jurisdictions that do not follow such proactive policies.[13] Departments that more actively enforce minor regulations, such as disorderly conduct and traffic laws, are also more likely to experience lower felony rates.[14]

Pinpointing why **proactive policing** works so effectively is difficult. It may have a **deterrent effect:** aggressive policing increases community perception that police arrest many criminals and that most violators get caught; criminals are scared to commit crimes in a town that has such an active police force! Proactive policing may also help control crime because it results in conviction of more criminals. Because aggressive police arrest more suspects, there are fewer left on the street to commit crime; fewer criminals produce lower crime rates.

Aggressive police patrol efforts have been a critical success. The downturn in the New York City violent crime rate during the 1990s has been attributed to aggressive police work aimed at lifestyle crimes: vandalism, panhandling, and graffiti.[15] See the following Policy, Programs, and Issues in Criminal Justice feature.

proactive policing A police department policy emphasizing stopping crimes before they occur rather than reacting to crimes that have already occurred.

deterrent effect Stopping or reducing crime by convincing would-be criminals that they stand a significant risk of being apprehended and punished for their crimes.

Policy, Programs, and Issues in Criminal Justice

The Indianapolis Gun Control Program

During the mid-1990s, Indianapolis found itself in an unusual situation. Although the local economy was strong, the city also was experiencing record-setting levels of homicide at a time when homicide was declining in many comparable cities.

Local officials took several steps to address the problem. For example, they used data to identify where and when homicides were occurring. To produce the data, the Indianapolis Police Department (IPD) created the Indianapolis Management Accountability Program, or IMAP, an adaptation of the New York City Police Department's computer comparison statistics (CompStat) program.

IPD then applied directed patrol tactics in two areas of the city that had high concentrations of violent crime. *Directed patrol* involves assigning officers to a particular area to proactively investigate suspicious activities and to enforce existing gun, drug, traffic, and related laws. Officers assigned to directed patrol areas are freed from having to respond to calls for service. The most common approach in a directed patrol effort is to make traffic stops. The strategy generally includes increasing the number of police officers in a given location and the number of contacts with citizens.

IPD applied directed patrol tactics in two police districts in two different ways. Put in the simplest terms, the east district followed a *general deterrence strategy,* whereby it assigned many police officers who stopped many people, issued many citations, and made one felony arrest for every one hundred traffic stops. The north district, employing a *targeted deterrence strategy,* assigned fewer officers who stopped fewer people and issued fewer citations but made almost three times as many arrests for every one hundred stops. Officers in the north district were more likely to stop and arrest felons because they focused on specific suspicious behaviors and individuals.

Homicide went down in both districts, but the north district also reduced gun crime overall—and used fewer resources.

Directed patrol in the north target area reduced gun crime, homicide, aggravated assault with a gun, and armed robbery. In contrast, in the east target area it had no effect on gun-related crime, except for a possible effect on homicide. Why? The north district's targeted deterrence approach probably sent a message of increased surveillance to those individuals most likely to commit violent gun-related crimes.

The results of the Indianapolis directed patrol program are consistent with a growing body of research that shows that when police identify a specific problem and focus their attention on it, they can reduce crime and violence. Directed police patrol led to sizable reductions in gun crime here. In addition, it did not shift crime to surrounding areas or harm police-community relations.

The finding that the community generally accepted the program supports the idea that crime control benefits need not generate police-citizen conflict. However, the lack of impact in Indianapolis's east target area, which used a more general deterrence model, and the potential strain that these types of police initiatives could have on police-community relations, suggest the need for continued research on both the benefits and the potential costs of such strategies.

Critical Thinking

1. Would you abandon traditional police patrol in favor of more directed, aggressive patrol tactics aimed at specific crimes? What are the advantages, if any, of the more traditional forms of patrol?
2. What other reforms might you make if you were the chief of police in a larger city?

InfoTrac College Edition Research

To learn more about new forms of police patrol, use the phrase as a subject guide on InfoTrac College Edition.

Source: Edmund McGarrell, Steven Chermak, and Alexander Weiss, *Reducing Gun Violence: Evaluation of the Indianapolis Police Department's Directed Patrol* (Washington, D.C.: National Institute of Justice, 2002).

Targeting Crimes Evidence also shows that targeting specific crimes can be successful. One aggressive patrol program, known as the Kansas City Gun Experiment, was directed at restricting the carrying of guns in high-risk places at high-risk times. Working with academics from the University of Maryland, the Kansas City Police Department focused extra patrol attention on a "hot spot" high-crime area identified by computer analysis of all gun crimes. Over a twenty-nine-week period, the gun patrol officers made thousands of car and pedestrian checks and traffic stops and made over six hundred arrests. Using frisks and searches, they found twenty-nine guns; an additional forty-seven weapons were seized by other officers in the experimental area. There were 169 gun crimes in the target beat in the twenty-nine weeks prior to the gun patrol but only 86 while the experiment was under way, a decrease of 49 percent. Drive-by shootings dropped significantly, as did homicides, without any displacement to other areas of the city. It is possible that the weapons seized were taken from high-rate offenders who were among the most likely perpetrators of gun-related crimes; their "lost opportunity" to commit violent crimes may have resulted in an overall rate decrease. It is also possible that the gun sweeps caused some of the most violent criminals to be taken off the streets. And as word of the patrol got out, there may have been a general deterrent effect: people contemplating violent crime may have been convinced that apprehension risks were unacceptably high.[16]

Making Arrests   Is it possible that more formal police action, such as an arrest, can reduce crime? A number of experts have expressed doubt that formal police action can have any general deterrent effect, or if it does, that it would be anything but short-lived and temporary.[17] Research studies do show, however, that contact with the police may cause some offenders to forgo repeat criminal behavior; formal police action, such as arrest, may in fact deter future criminality. For example, an arrest for drunk driving reduces the likelihood of further driving while intoxicated. An arrest apparently increases people's belief that they will be rearrested if they drink and drive and heightens their perception of the unpleasantness associated with an arrest.[18] Evidence also points out that many first offenders will forgo criminal activity after arrest.[19] Research conducted in Florida indicates that arrest activity may have an immediate impact on the crime rate; that is, as the number of arrests increase, the number of crimes reported to authorities decreases substantially the following day.[20] It is possible that news of increased and aggressive police activity is rapidly diffused through the population and has an immediate impact that erodes over time. Studies using data collected annually may miss this immediate deterrent effect.

However, even if formal action does deter crime, police chiefs may find it difficult to convince patrol officers to make more arrests. Despite a departmental policy requiring officers to be more active, police officers may be reluctant to change their style and tactics. Research efforts indicate that departmental directives to make more arrests may have relatively little effect on police behavior.[21] Influencing actual police activities in the field may prove to be a difficult task.

Adding Patrol Officers

One reason why patrol activity may be less effective than desired is the lack of adequate resources. Does adding more police help bring down the crime rate? Comparisons of police expenditures in U.S. cities indicate that cities with the highest crime rates also spend the most on police services.[22] At one time critics questioned whether adding police was effective because reviews of the existing research found that the actual number of law enforcement officers in a jurisdiction seemed to have little effect on area crimes.[23] However, a number of recent studies, using different methodologies, have found that police presence may actually reduce crime levels and that adding police may bring crime levels down.[24]

Although it now looks as if adding police officers in communities can lower crime rates, increasing the size of the patrol force might have utility even if it did not produce a deterrent effect on crime. For example, increasing resources may improve the overall effectiveness of the justice system. Communities with relatively high crime rates that devote fewer financial resources to police work find that many cases that result in arrest are dropped before they ever get to trial.[25] It is possible that overworked police in high-crime areas may be processing cases with little hope of prosecution to give the public the message that they are trying to "do something." Inadequate resources make it difficult to gather sufficient evidence to ensure a conviction, and prosecutors are likely to drop these cases. Adding resources, in this instance, could possibly improve the quality of police arrests.

The Investigation Function

Since the first independent detective bureau was established by the London Metropolitan Police in 1841,[26] criminal investigators have been romantic figures vividly portrayed in novels, in movies such as *Beverly Hills Cop,* with Eddie Murphy playing Axel Foley, and Clint Eastwood's *Dirty Harry* series, and in television shows such as *CSI, NYPD Blue,* and *Law & Order.* The fictional police detective is usually depicted as a loner, willing to break departmental rules, and perhaps even violate the law, to capture the suspect. The average fictional detective views departmental policies and U.S. Supreme Court decisions as unfortunate roadblocks to police efficiency. Civil rights are either ignored or actively scorned.[27]

Although every police department probably has a few "hell-bent for leather" detectives who take matters into their own hands at the expense of citizens' rights, the modern criminal investigator is most likely an experienced civil servant, trained in investigatory techniques, knowledgeable about legal rules of evidence and procedure, and at least somewhat cautious about the legal and administrative consequences of his or her actions.[28] The character of Gil Grissom—played by actor William Peterson—head of the *Crime Scene Investigation* team, may be a more realistic portrayal of the modern investigator than Dirty Harry or Axel Foley. Although detectives are often handicapped by limited time, money, and resources, they are certainly aware of how their actions will one day be interpreted in a court of law.

Criminal investigation is a key element of police work. Here police officers scour a crime scene for evidence during the Washington, D.C., sniper investigation, October 19, 2002.

Detectives are probably the elite of the police force: they are usually paid more than patrol officers, engage in more interesting tasks, wear civilian clothes, and are subject to less stringent departmental control than patrol officers.[29] Detectives investigate the causes of crime and attempt to identify the individuals or groups responsible for committing particular offenses. They may enter a case after patrol officers have made the initial contact, such as when a patrol car interrupts a crime in progress and the offenders flee before they can be apprehended. They can investigate a case entirely on their own, sometimes by following up on leads provided by informants.

Detective divisions are typically organized into sections or bureaus, such as homicide, robbery, or rape. Some jurisdictions maintain **vice squads,** which are usually staffed by plainclothes officers or detectives specializing in victimless crimes, such as prostitution or gambling. Vice squad officers may set themselves up as customers for illicit activities to make arrests. For example, male undercover detectives may frequent public men's rooms and wait for advances by entering men; those who respond are arrested for homosexual soliciting. In other instances, female police officers may pose as prostitutes. These covert police activities have often been criticized as violating the personal rights of citizens, and their appropriateness and fairness have been questioned.

vice squad Police officers assigned to enforce morality-based laws, such as those on prostitution, gambling, and pornography.

Sting Operations

sting operation An undercover police operation in which police pose as criminals to trap law violators.

Another approach to detective work, commonly referred to as a **sting operation,** involves organized groups of detectives who deceive criminals into openly committing illegal acts or conspiring to engage in criminal activity. Numerous sting operations have been aimed at capturing professional thieves and seizing stolen merchandise. Undercover detectives pose as "fences," set up ongoing fencing operations, and encourage thieves interested in selling stolen merchandise. Transactions are videotaped to provide prosecutors with strong cases. Sting operations have netted millions of dollars in recovered property and resulted in the arrests of many criminals. These results seem impressive, but sting operations have drawbacks.[30] By its very nature, a sting involves deceit by police agents that often comes close to entrapment. Sting operations may encourage criminals to commit new crimes because they have a new source for fencing stolen goods. Innocent people may hurt their reputations by buying merchandise from a sting operation when they had no idea the items had been stolen. By putting the government into the fencing business, such operations blur the line between law enforcement and criminal activity.

Undercover Work

Sometimes detectives go undercover in order to investigate crime.[31] Undercover work can take a number of forms. A lone agent can infiltrate a criminal group or organization to gather information on future criminal activity. For example, a DEA (Drug Enforcement Administration) agent may go undercover to gather intelligence on drug smugglers. Undercover officers can also pose as victims to capture predatory criminals who have been conducting street robberies and muggings.

Undercover work is considered a necessary element of police work, although it can prove dangerous for the agent. Police officers may be forced to engage in illegal or immoral behavior to maintain their cover. They also face significant physical danger in playing the role of a criminal and dealing with mobsters, terrorists, and drug dealers. In far too many cases, undercover officers are mistaken for real criminals and are injured by other law enforcement officers or private citizens trying to stop a crime. Arrest situations involving undercover officers may also provoke violence when suspects do not realize they are in the presence of police and therefore violently resist arrest.

Undercover officers may also experience psychological problems. Being away from home, keeping late hours, and always worrying that their identity will be uncovered all create enormous stress. Officers have experienced *postundercover stress,* resulting in trouble at work, and in many instances, ruined marriages and botched prosecutions. Hanging around with criminals for a long period of time, making friends, and earning their trust can also have a damaging psychological impact.

Use the term "undercover operations" as a subject guide on InfoTrac College Edition to learn more about this form of investigation.

Evaluating Investigations

Serious criticism has been leveled at the nation's detective forces for being bogged down in paperwork and relatively inefficient in clearing cases. One famous study of 153 detective bureaus found that a great deal of a detective's time was spent in unproductive work and that investigative expertise did little to solve cases; half of all detectives could be replaced without negatively influencing crime clearance rates.[32]

Although some question remains about the effectiveness of investigations, police detectives do make a valuable contribution to police work because their skilled interrogation and case-processing techniques are essential to eventual criminal conviction.[33] Nonetheless, a majority of cases that are solved are done so when the perpetrator is identified at the scene of the crime by patrol officers. Research shows that if a crime is reported while in progress, the police have about a 33 percent chance of making an arrest; the arrest probability declines to about 10 percent if the crime is reported one minute later, and to 5 percent if more than fifteen minutes have elapsed. As the time between the crime and the arrest grows, the chances of a conviction are also reduced, probably because the ability to recover evidence is lost. Put another way, once a crime has been completed and the investigation is put in the hands of detectives, the chances of identifying and arresting the perpetrator diminish rapidly.[34]

Improving Investigations

A number of efforts have been made to revamp and improve investigation procedures. One practice has been to give patrol officers greater responsibility for conducting preliminary investigations at the scene of the crime. In addition, the old-fashioned precinct detective has been replaced by specialized units, such as homicide or burglary squads, that operate over larger areas and can bring specific expertise to bear. Technological advances in DNA and fingerprint identification have also aided investigation effectiveness. The following Criminal Justice and the Media feature highlights how advances are being portrayed on one popular TV series, *CSI.*

One reason for investigation ineffectiveness is that detectives often lack sufficient resources to carry out a lengthy ongoing probe of any but the most serious cases. Research shows the following:

1. *Unsolved cases.* Almost 50 percent of burglary cases are screened out by supervisors before assignment to a detective for a follow-up investigation. Of those assigned, 75 percent are dropped after the first day of the follow-up investigation. Although robbery cases are more likely to be assigned to detectives, 75 percent of them are also dropped after one day of investigation.
2. *Length of investigation.* The vast majority of cases are investigated for no more than four hours stretching over three days. An average of eleven days elapses between the initial report of a crime and the suspension of the investigation.
3. *Sources of information.* Early in an investigation, the focus is on the victim; as the investigation is pursued, emphasis shifts to the suspect. The most critical information for determining case outcome is the name and description of the

Crime Scene Investigation: CSI

Crime Scene Investigation is a surprise television hit. Rather than relying on shootouts and car chases, it depicts a dedicated team of forensic scientists who work for the Las Vegas, Nevada, PD, and use their forensic skill to trap the most wily criminal offenders. Rather than using their brawn, the CSI investigators rely on their wits and scientific training.

The team is led by Gil Grissom, played by experienced character actor William Peterson, the level-three head CSI investigator. He is a trained scientist whose specialty is forensic entomology, the study of insects found on or near a crime scene. He uses his expertise to search for clues within victims' bodies, outside of their bodies, or in any other way that can provide evidence to identify the suspect or solve the crime. For example, he can test the waste products from an insect found in the body of the deceased to determine the time of death, whether the body has been moved, and so on. Rather than a hard-drinking, two-fisted crime fighter, Grissom is a shy, quiet guy who when not working can be found doing crossword puzzles.

Although not all CSI members were trained as scientists, most have the skills and education that make them formidable forensic specialists. For example, Sara Sidle, played by Jorja Fox, holds a B.S. degree in physics from Harvard; she was brought in specifically by Grissom. She is completely dedicated to her work and seems to spend her free time studying forensics.

Each show revolves around a seemingly unsolvable crime. In some instances, a leading suspect is exonerated when the team uses its skills to show that despite appearances that person could not have committed the crime. For example, in one episode—"Sex, Lies, and Larvae"—which first aired on December 22, 2000, the team investigates the shooting death of a young woman whose bloodied and bug-infested body is found on a nearby mountain. At first glance, it seems that the woman's abusive husband is the killer. But Grissom's analysis of the bugs found on the woman's body indicates that the victim was killed three days earlier, a time when her husband was out of town. The *CSI* series has proven so popular that a second version set in Miami premiered in 2002.

The *CSI* series draws attention to the developing field of forensics in police work. *Forensic* means "pertaining to the law," and forensic scientists perform comprehensive chemical and physical analyses on evidence submitted by law enforcement agencies. Although most forensic scientists focus on criminal cases (they are sometimes referred to as *criminalists*), others work in the civil justice system—for example, performing handwriting comparisons to determine the validity of a signature on a will. When working on crimes, their analyses involve a variety of sciences, mathematical principles, and problem-solving methods, including use of complex instruments and chemical, physical, and microscopic examining techniques. In addition to ana-

lyzing crime scene investigations, forensic scientists provide testimony in a court of law when the case is brought to trial. Although some forensic scientists are generalists, others like Gil Grissom specialize is a particular scientific area. What are some of these specialties?

- *Controlled substances and toxicology.* Crime lab professionals specializing in this area examine blood and other body fluids and tissues for the presence of alcohol, drugs, and poisons.
- *Biology.* Crime lab professionals compare body fluids and hair for typing factors, including DNA analysis. Analysis of a hair found at a crime scene can determine factors such as whether the hair belongs to a human or animal, the body area a hair came from, diseases the person or animal has, and, sometimes, race.
- *Chemistry.* Forensic scientists analyze trace physical evidence such as blood spatters, paint, soil, and glass. For example, blood spatters help reconstruct a crime scene: the pattern of spatters and the shape of blood droplets tell how the crime was committed.
- *Document examination.* Document examination includes many areas of expertise, including forgery, document dating, and analysis of handwriting, typewriting, computer printing, and photocopying.
- *Firearms and toolmark identification.* Firearms examination involves matching identifying characteristics between a firearm and projectile and between a projectile and target. Typically, this includes matching bullets to the gun that fired them. Toolmark identification involves matching some identifying characteristics of a tool, such as a pry bar, to the object on which it was used, such as a door frame. It also includes explosives and imprint evidence.

Critical Thinking

They say that life imitates art. As the popularity of the *CSI* series continues to grow, it is likely that more students will be drawn into forensics and more police and law enforcement agencies will employ forensic specialists in their daily operations. Do you think that crime is better solved in the lab or on the beat?

InfoTrac College Edition Research

How accurate is *CSI?* Read Michael Lipton and Lorenzo Benet, "Getting Dead Right: Forensics Expert Elizabeth Devine Makes Sure *CSI's* Corpses Are Ready for Their Close-Ups," *People Weekly,* April 22, 2002 v57 i15 p77.

Use "crime scene investigation" as a subject guide on InfoTrac College Edition to learn more about the show.

Source: Information on forensics used here comes from Hall Dillon, "Forensic Scientists: A Career in the Crime Lab," *Occupational Outlook Quarterly* 43 (1999): 2–5.

suspect and related crime information. Victims are most often the source of information; unfortunately, witnesses, informants, and members of the police department are consulted far less often. However, when these sources are tapped, they are likely to produce useful information.

4. *Effectiveness*. Preliminary investigations by patrol officers are critical. In situations where the suspect's identity is not known immediately after the crime is committed, detectives make an arrest in less than 10 percent of all cases.[35]

Considering these findings, detective work may be improved if greater emphasis is placed on collecting physical evidence at the scene of the crime, identifying witnesses, checking departmental records, and using informants. The probability of successfully settling a case is improved if patrol officers gather evidence at the scene of a crime and effectively communicate it to detectives working the case. Police managers should pay more attention to screening cases, monitoring case flow and activity, and creating productivity measures to make sure that individual detectives and detective units are meeting their goals. Also recommended is the use of targeted investigations that direct attention at a few individuals, such as career criminals, who are known to have engaged in the behavior under investigation.

Community Policing

Many police officers feel unappreciated by the public they serve, a perception that may be due to the underlying conflicts inherent in the police role. Police may want to be proactive crime fighters who initiate actions against law violators, yet most remain reactive, responding when a citizen calls for service. The desire for direct action is often blunted because police are expected to perform many civic duties that in earlier times were the responsibility of every citizen: keeping the peace, performing emergency medical care, dealing with family problems, and helping during civil emergencies.

Most of us agree that a neighborhood brawl must be stopped, that shelter must be found for the homeless, and that the inebriate must be taken safely home, but few of us want to jump into the fray personally; we would rather "call the cops." The police officer has become a "social handyman" called in to fix up problems that the average citizen wishes would simply go away. Police officers are viewed as the "fire it takes to fight fire."[36] The public needs the police to perform those duties that the average citizen finds distasteful or dangerous, such as breaking up a domestic quarrel. At the same time, the public resents the power the police have to use force, arrest people, and deny people their vices. Put another way, the average citizen wants the police to crack down on undesirable members of society while excluding her own behavior from legal scrutiny.

Because of these natural role conflicts, the relationship between the police and the public has been the subject of a great deal of concern. As you may recall, the respect Americans have for police effectiveness, courtesy, honesty, and conduct seems to be problematic. Citizens may be less likely to go to police for help, to report crimes, to step forward as witnesses, or to cooperate with and aid police. Victim surveys indicate that many citizens have so little faith in the police that they will not report even serious crimes, such as rape or burglary. In some communities, citizen self-help groups have sprung up to supplement police protection.[37] In return, police officers often feel ambivalent and uncertain about the public they are sworn to protect.

Because of this ambivalence and role conflict, more communities are adapting new models of policing that reflect the changing role of the police. Some administrators now recognize that police officers are better equipped to be civic problem solvers than effective crime fighters. Rather than ignore, deny, or fight this reality, police departments are being reorganized to maximize their strengths and minimize their weaknesses. What has emerged is the *community policing movement,* a

Albert Fanning/The Image Works

Community policing efforts employ a variety of innovative techniques to reach out to the public. Here, two Syracuse, New York, police officers ride twenty-one-speed bicycles, providing high visibility to store owners and citizens.

new concept of policing designed to bridge the gulf between police agencies and the communities they serve.

Broken Windows: The Development of Community Policing

As author George Kelling put it: "A quiet revolution is reshaping American policing."[38]

Police agencies have been trying to gain the cooperation and respect of the communities they serve for more than thirty years. At first, efforts at improving the relationships between police departments and the public involved programs with the general title of **police-community relations (PCR)**. Developed at the station-house and departmental levels, these initial PCR programs were designed to make citizens more aware of police activities, alert them to methods of self-protection, and improve general attitudes toward policing.

Though PCR efforts showed a willingness for police agencies to cooperate with the public, some experts believed that law enforcement agencies must undergo a significant transformation in order to create meaningful partnerships with the public. These views were articulated in a critical 1982 paper by two justice policy experts, George Kelling and James Q. Wilson, who espoused a new approach to improving police relations in the community that has come to be known as the **broken windows model**.[39] Kelling and Wilson made three points:

1. *Neighborhood disorder creates fear.* Urban areas filled with street people, youth gangs, prostitutes, and the mentally disturbed are the ones most likely to maintain a high degree of crime.
2. *Neighborhoods give out crime-promoting signals.* A neighborhood filled with deteriorated housing, unrepaired broken windows, and untended disorderly behavior gives out crime-promoting signals. Honest citizens live in fear in these areas, and predatory criminals are attracted to them.
3. *Police need citizen cooperation.* If police are to reduce fear and successfully combat crime in these urban areas, they must have the cooperation, support, and assistance of the citizens.

police-community relations (PCR) Programs developed by police departments to improve relations with the community and develop cooperation with citizens. The forerunner of the community policing model.

broken windows model The term used to describe the role of the police as maintainers of community order and safety.

According to the broken windows approach, community relations and crime control effectiveness cannot be the province of a few specialized units housed within a traditional police department. Instead, the core police role must be altered if community involvement is to be won and maintained. To accomplish this goal, urban police departments should return to the earlier style of policing, in which officers on the beat had intimate contact with the people they served. Modern police departments generally rely on motorized patrol to cover wide areas, to maintain a visible police presence, and to ensure rapid response time. Although effective and economical, the patrol car removes officers from the mainstream of the community, alienating people who might otherwise be potential sources of information and help to the police.

The broken windows approach holds that police administrators would be well served by deploying their forces where they can encourage public confidence, strengthen feelings of safety, and elicit cooperation from citizens. Community preservation, public safety, and order maintenance—not crime fighting—should become the primary focus of patrol. Put another way, just as physicians and dentists practice preventive medicine and dentistry, police should help maintain an intact community structure rather than simply fight crime.

Implementing Community Policing The community policing concept was originally implemented through a number of innovative demonstration projects.[40] Among the most publicized were experiments in **foot patrol**, which took officers out of cars and set them to walking beats in the neighborhood. Foot patrol efforts were aimed at forming a bond with community residents by acquainting them with the individual officers who patrolled their neighborhood, letting them know that police were caring and available. The first foot patrol experiments were conducted in cities in Michigan and New Jersey. An evaluation of foot patrol indicated that, although it did not bring down the crime rate, residents in areas where foot patrol was added perceived greater safety and were less afraid of crime.[41]

Since the advent of these programs, hundreds of communities have adopted innovative forms of decentralized, neighborhood-based community policing models. Recent surveys indicate that there has been a significant increase in community policing activities in recent years and that certain core programs, such as crime prevention activities, have become embedded in the police role.[42]

Community-oriented policing (COP) programs have been implemented in large cities, suburban areas, and rural communities.[43] The most successful programs give officers the time to meet with local residents to talk about crime in the neighborhood and to use personal initiative to solve problems.

Although not all programs work (police-community newsletters and cleanup campaigns do not seem to do much good), the overall impression has been that patrol officers can actually reduce the level of fear in the community. Some COP programs assign officers to neighborhoods, organize training programs for community leaders, and feature a bottom-up approach to deal with community problems: decision making involves the officer on the scene, not a directive from central headquarters. Others have created programs for juveniles who might ordinarily have little to do other than get involved in gangs but are now directed at such activities as neighborhood cleanup efforts.[44] In Spokane, Washington, for example, the community-police effort created a program called COPY Kids, a summer outreach program for disadvantaged youths that promotes a positive work ethic, emphasizes the values of community involvement, and helps create a positive image of the police department.[45] Washington, D.C.'s, Howard University Violence Prevention Project aims to create a safety net that protects youths against social risk factors. The project relies on a team approach that involves parents, teachers, mental health professionals, business owners, and local police. The police component of the project, called the Youth Trauma Team, requires that police officers, along with psychologists, respond to violent incidents that occur at night. They talk to children who have been a part of or have witnessed violence and

Use "broken windows" as a subject guide on InfoTrac College Edition to learn more about this concept.

The School of Criminal Justice at Michigan State University maintains a comprehensive Web site devoted to community policing that contains an extensive collection of full-text papers on all aspects of community policing: www.ssc.msu.edu/~cj/cp/cptoc.html

foot patrol Police patrols that take officers out of cars and put them on a walking beat in order to strengthen ties with the community.

The Community Policing Consortium was created and funded in 1993 by the U.S. Department of Justice, Bureau of Justice Assistance (BJA), to deliver community policing training and technical assistance to police departments and sheriff's offices that receive federal grant money. Access its Web site at

www.communitypolicing.org/

neighborhood-oriented policing (NOP)
Community policing efforts aimed at individual neighborhoods.

What needs to be done to involve the community in community policing? Go to InfoTrac College Edition and read David Thacher, "Equity and Community Policing: A New View of Community Partnerships," *Criminal Justice Ethics*, Winter-Spring 2001 v20 i1 p3(14).

afterward link them with services as needed. Police officers involved in the project receive training in conflict resolution, cultural sensitivity, and crisis deescalation. They also have networked or partnered extensively with existing social service providers in the community in a multidisciplinary team effort to provide comprehensive care.[46]

Neighborhood Policing   Community policing means more than implementing direct-action programs. It also refers to a philosophy of policing that requires departments to reconsider their recruitment, organization, and operating procedures. What are some of the most important community policing concepts? First, community policing emphasizes results, not bureaucratic process. Rather than react to problems in the community, police departments take the initiative in identifying issues and actively treating their cause. Problem-solving and analysis techniques replace emphasis on bureaucratic detail. There is less concern with "playing it by the book" and more with getting the job done.

To achieve the goals of COP, some agencies have tried to decentralize, an approach sometimes referred to as innovative **neighborhood-oriented policing (NOP)**.[47] Problem solving is best done at the neighborhood level where issues originate, not at a far-off central headquarters. Because each neighborhood has its own particular needs, police decision making must be flexible and adaptive. For example, neighborhoods undergoing change in racial composition all experience high levels of racially motivated violence.[48] Police must be able to distinguish these neighborhood characteristics and allocate resources to meet their needs.

Changing the Police Role   Community policing also stresses sharing power with local groups and individuals. A key element of the community policing philosophy is that citizens must actively participate with police to fight crime.[49] This participation might involve providing information in areawide crime investigations or helping police reach out to troubled youths.

True to its name, neighborhood policing emphasizes helping citizens at the neighborhood level. Here, Merced police officer Joe Deliman chats with Amanda Flores, eleven, and Krystin Beatty, twelve (middle), during a police community outreach on August 28, 2002, in Merced, California. Officers handed out coloring books, safety booklets, candy, and balloons, and gave neighborhood kids tours of a mobile command unit on-site to promote trust between the police and the community.

Community policing philosophy

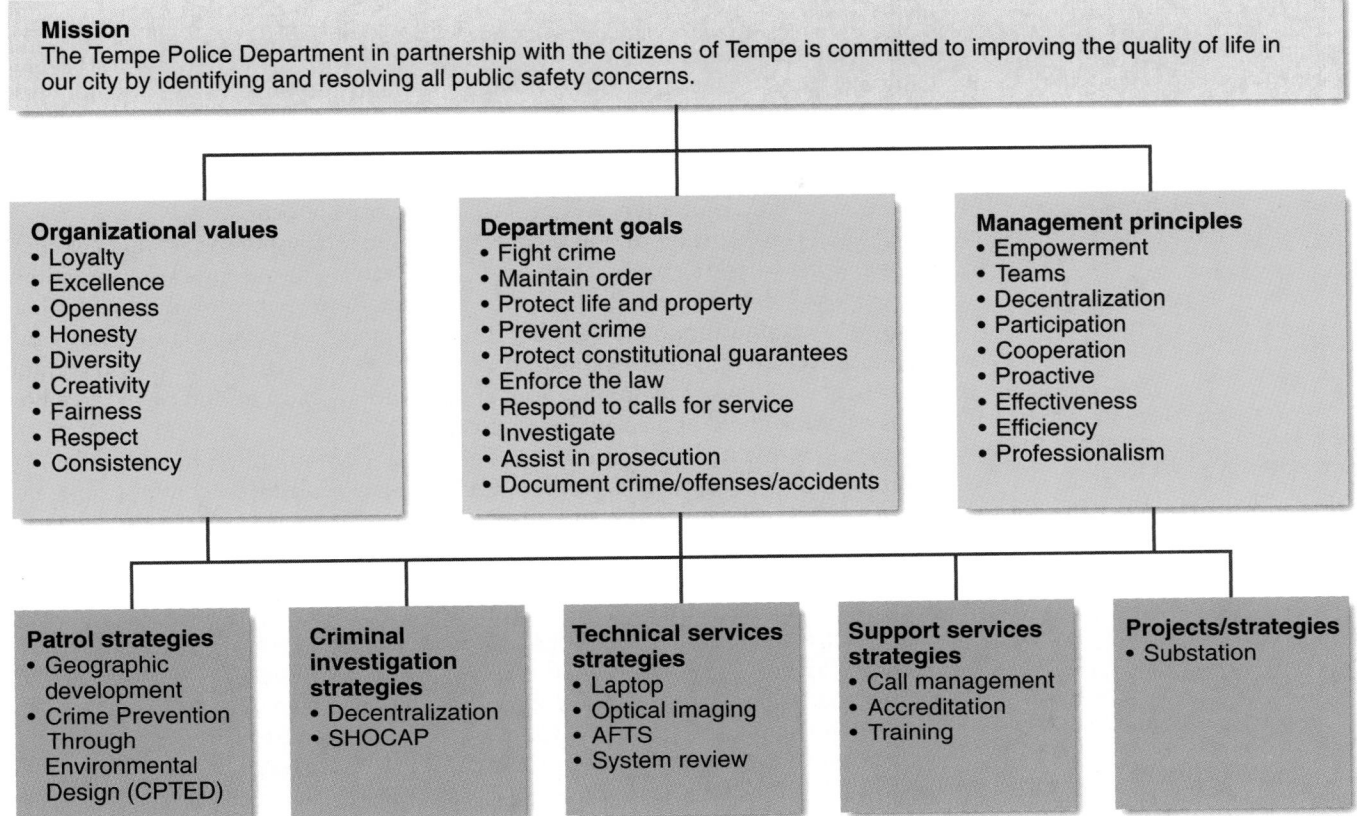

Mission
The Tempe Police Department in partnership with the citizens of Tempe is committed to improving the quality of life in our city by identifying and resolving all public safety concerns.

Organizational values
- Loyalty
- Excellence
- Openness
- Honesty
- Diversity
- Creativity
- Fairness
- Respect
- Consistency

Department goals
- Fight crime
- Maintain order
- Protect life and property
- Prevent crime
- Protect constitutional guarantees
- Enforce the law
- Respond to calls for service
- Investigate
- Assist in prosecution
- Document crime/offenses/accidents

Management principles
- Empowerment
- Teams
- Decentralization
- Participation
- Cooperation
- Proactive
- Effectiveness
- Efficiency
- Professionalism

Patrol strategies
- Geographic development
- Crime Prevention Through Environmental Design (CPTED)

Criminal investigation strategies
- Decentralization
- SHOCAP

Technical services strategies
- Laptop
- Optical imaging
- AFTS
- System review

Support services strategies
- Call management
- Accreditation
- Training

Projects/strategies
- Substation

Figure 5.3
Tempe (Arizona) Police Department planning model

Source: Temple (Arizona) Police Department, 2002.

Community policing also means the eventual redesign of police departments. Management's role must be reordered to focus on the problems of the community, not on the needs of the police department. The traditional vertical police organizational chart must be altered so that top-down management gives way to bottom-up decision making. The patrol officer becomes the manager of his beat and a key decision maker. Figure 5.3 shows how one police department's goals and missions reflect the new era of community policing.

Community policing requires that police departments alter their recruitment and training requirements. Future officers must develop community-organizing and problem-solving skills, along with traditional police skills. Their training must prepare them to succeed less on their ability to make arrests or issue citations and more on their ability to solve problems effectively.

The community policing concept is not only catching on in the United States; it has captured the interest of police departments around the world.[50] Community policing is being used in numerous countries, including Denmark, Finland, and Great Britain.

Problem-Oriented Policing

Closely associated with yet independent from the community policing concept are **problem-oriented policing** strategies. Traditional police models focus on responding to calls for help in the fastest possible time, dealing with the situation, and then

problem-oriented policing   A style of police operations that stresses proactive problem solving, rather than reactive crime fighting.

getting on the street again as soon as possible.[51] In contrast, problem-oriented policing is proactive.

Problem-oriented policing strategies require police agencies to identify particular long-term community problems—street-level drug dealers, prostitution rings, gang hangouts—and to develop strategies to eliminate them.[52] As with community policing, police departments must rely on local residents and private resources in order to be problem solvers. This means that police managers must learn how to develop community resources, design cost-efficient and effective solutions to problems, and become advocates as well as agents of reform.[53]

A significant portion of police departments are now using special units to confront specific social problems. Problem-oriented policing models are supported by the evidence that a great deal of urban crime is concentrated in a few "hot spots."[54] A significant portion of all police calls in metropolitan areas typically radiate from a relatively few locations: bars, malls, the bus depot, hotels, and certain apartment buildings.[55] By implication, concentrating police resources on these **hot spots of crime** could appreciably reduce crime.[56]

Problem-oriented strategies can also be developed within traditional police organizations.[57] For example Operation Ceasefire is a problem-oriented policing intervention aimed at reducing youth homicide and youth firearms violence in Boston. The Ceasefire plan assumed that a relatively small number of chronically offending gang-involved youth were responsible for much of the shooting incidents in the area and focused police attention on these persistent offenders. Evaluations of the program found Ceasefire produced significant reductions in youth homicide victimization, shots-fired calls for service, and gun assault incidents in Boston that were not experienced in other communities in New England or elsewhere in the nation.[58] The Jersey City (New Jersey) police recently applied a variety of aggressive crime-reducing techniques in some of the city's highest crime areas. Evaluations of the program show that crime rates were reduced when police officers used aggressive problem-solving (for example, drug enforcement) and community-improvement (for example, increased lighting and cleaned vacant lots) techniques in high-crime areas.[59] Another recent initiative by the Dallas Police Department assigned officers to aggressively pursue truancy and curfew enforcement, a tactic that resulted in lower rates of gang violence.[60]

Although programs such as these seem successful, the effectiveness of any street-level problem-solving effort must be interpreted with caution.[61] It is possible that the criminals will be displaced to other, "safer" areas of the city and will return shortly after the program is called a success and the additional police forces have been pulled from the area.[62] Nonetheless, evidence shows that merely saturating an area with police may not deter crime, but focusing efforts on a particular problem may have a crime-reducing effect.

The Challenges of Community Policing

The core concepts of police work are changing as administrators recognize the limitations and realities of police work in modern society. If they are to be successful, community policing strategies must be able to react effectively to some significant administrative problems:

1. *Defining community.* Police administrators must be able to define the concept of community as an ecological area defined by common norms, shared values, and interpersonal bonds.[63] After all, the main focus of community policing is to activate the community norms that make neighborhoods more crime-resistant. If, in contrast, community policing projects cross the boundaries of many different neighborhoods, any hope of learning and accessing community norms, strengths, and standards will be lost.[64] And even if natural community structures can be identified, it will be necessary for policing agencies to continually monitor the changing norms, values, and attitudes of the community

hot spots of crime   Places from which a significant portion of all police calls originate. These hot spots include taverns and housing projects.

Though community policing advocates would object, most police administrators still consider law enforcement their top priority; providing community and social services is not considered a significant role. Rather than retraining and reorienting police from their traditional roles into a more social service orientation, many departments rely on older methods, such as training dogs to subdue criminals, as the officer is doing here.

they serve, a process that has the side effect of creating positive interactions between the community and the police.[65]

2. *Defining roles.* Police administrators must also establish the exact role of community police agents. How should they integrate their activities with those of regular patrol forces? For example, should foot patrols have primary responsibility for policing in an area, or should they coordinate their activities with officers assigned to patrol cars? Should community police officers be solely problem identifiers and neighborhood organizers, or should they also be expected to be law enforcement agents who get to the crime scene rapidly and later do investigative work? Can community police teams and regular patrols work together, or must a department abandon traditional police roles and become purely community policing–oriented?

3. *Changing the command structure.* Some supervisors are wary of community policing because it supports a decentralized command structure. This would

mean fewer supervisors, and consequently, less chance for promotion and a potential loss of authority.[66]

4. *Reorienting police values.* Research shows that police officers who have a traditional crime control orientation are less satisfied with community policing efforts than those who are public service–oriented.[67] Although this finding comes as no surprise, it is indicative of the difficulty police managers will face in convincing experienced officers, many of whom hold traditional law-and-order values, to embrace community policing models.

5. *Revise training.* Because the community policing model calls for a revision of the police role from law enforcer to community organizer, police training must be revised to reflect this new mandate. If community policing is to be adopted on a wide scale, a whole new type of police officer must be recruited and trained in a whole new way. Retraining and reorienting police from their traditional roles into a more social service orientation may also be difficult. Most police officers do not have the social service skills required of effective community agents. Thus, community policing requires that police departments alter their training requirements. Future officers must develop community-organizing and problem-solving skills, along with traditional police skills. Their training must prepare them to succeed less on their ability to make arrests or issue citations and more on their ability to solve problems, prevent crime effectively, and deal with neighborhood diversity and cultural values.[68]

6. *Reorient recruitment.* To make community policing successful, midlevel managers must be recruited and trained who are receptive to and can implement community-change strategies.[69] The selection of new recruits must be guided by a desire to find individuals with the skills and attitudes that support community policing. They must be open to the fact that community policing will help them gain knowledge of the community, give them opportunities to gain skill and experience, and help them engage in proactive problem solving.[70] Selecting people who find these values attractive and then providing training that accentuates the community vision of policing is essential to the success of the COP model.

To find a Web site dedicated to providing the latest information, training, advice, and discussion on community policing go to www.policing.com

The view here is that community policing is a philosophy based on the recognition that nothing can outperform dedicated people working together to make their communities better and safer places in which to live, work, and raise children.

Overcoming Obstacles   Although these are formidable obstacles to overcome, there is growing evidence that community and problem-oriented policing can work and fit well with traditional forms of policing.[71] Many police experts and administrators have embraced the community and problem-oriented policing concepts as revolutionary revisions of the basic police role. Community policing efforts have been credited with helping reduce crime rates in large cities such as New York and Boston. The most professional and highly motivated officers are the ones most likely to support community policing efforts.[72]

These results are encouraging, but there is no clear-cut evidence that community policing is highly successful at reducing crime or changing the traditional values and attitudes of police officers involved in the programs.[73] Crime rate reductions in cities that have used COP may be the result of an overall downturn in the nation's crime rate or some other factor, such as an improved economy.

National surveys find that police administrators still consider law enforcement their top priority; providing community and social services is not considered a significant police role.[74] Rather than reflect community policing needs, most police agencies still value crime control and improving professional standards as their top priorities.[75]

Despite these professional obstacles, community policing has become a stable part of municipal police departments. Even critics, such as Ralph Taylor, recognize the usefulness of community policing. In his book *Breaking Away from Broken Windows: Baltimore Neighborhoods and the Nationwide Fight Against Crime, Grime, Fear, and Decline,* Taylor argues that the policing policies based on the broken windows model are not a panacea for crime control. Although efforts by policing programs to improve levels of physical decay and disorder are helpful, in the long term, neighborhood economic decline is a more important crime-producing factor. He concludes that community policing programs can provide some relief, but that for crime rates to remain low, politicians, businesses, and community leaders must work together to improve the economic climate in high-crime areas.[76]

Support Functions

As the model of a typical police department indicates (see again Figure 5.1), not all members of a department engage in what the general public regards as "real police work"—patrol, detection, and traffic control. Even in departments that are embracing community and problem-oriented policing, a great deal of police resources are actually devoted to support and administrative functions. There are too many tasks to mention in detail, but the most important include those discussed next.

Many police departments maintain their own personnel service, which carries out such functions as recruiting new police officers, creating exams to determine the most qualified applicants, and handling promotions and transfers. Innovative selection techniques are constantly being developed and tested. For example, the Behavioral-Personnel Assessment Device (B-PAD) requires police applicants to view videotaped scenarios and respond as if they were officers handling the situation; reviews indicate that this procedure may be a reliable and unbiased method of choosing new recruits.[77]

Larger police departments often maintain an **internal affairs** branch that is charged with policing the police. Internal affairs units process citizen complaints of police corruption, investigate what may be the unnecessary use of force by police officers, and even probe police participation in actual criminal activity, such as burglaries or narcotics violations. In addition, internal affairs divisions may assist police managers when disciplinary action is brought against individual officers. Internal affairs is a controversial function since investigators are feared and distrusted by fellow police officers. Nonetheless, rigorous self-scrutiny is the only way police departments can earn the respect of citizens. Because of these concerns it has become commonplace for police departments to institute citizen oversight over police practices and put in place civilian review boards that have the power to listen to complaints and conduct investigations. Civilian oversight is the subject of the following Policy, Programs, and Issues in Criminal Justice feature.

Most police departments are responsible for the administration and control of their own budgets. This task includes administering payroll, purchasing equipment

© 2002 AP/Wide World Photos

A Kansas City, Missouri, police officer directs rush hour traffic at a darkened intersection. Freezing rain left a heavy coat of ice on trees and power lines, resulting in a loss of power to large parts of the metropolitan area in January 2002. Traffic control remains a significant part of the police role.

internal affairs The branch of the police department that investigates charges of corruption or misconduct made against police officers.

Police Oversight: Civilian Review Boards

Two Rochester, New York, police officers arrest two young males allegedly for dealing drugs, and during the melee one youth is pushed through a plate glass window. The mother of one claims that these innocent young men were the victims of police brutality; they had merely been walking along the street when the officers approached.

At a hearing, the city's citizen review finds out that the arrestees had drugs in their possession, that the officers had remained polite and professional during the encounter, and that it was actually one of the boys who started the confrontation. The officers were exonerated by the review board.

Citizen oversight of police conduct can be a critical method of improving community relations, but it is also one that has caused conflict with police officers. Nonetheless, there has been a considerable increase in citizen oversight of police in the United States.

Typically, there are four models of oversight systems:

1. Citizens investigate allegations of police misconduct and recommend a finding to the head of the agency.
2. Officers investigate allegations and develop findings. Then, citizens review and recommend that the head of the agency approve or reject the findings.
3. Complainants may appeal findings established by the agency to citizens who review them and make recommendations to the head of the agency.
4. An auditor investigates the process the agency uses to accept and investigate complaints and reports to the agency and the community the thoroughness and fairness of the process.

There are many variations on these basic models. For example, the Minneapolis, Minnesota, civilian police review operates in two stages. First, paid, professional investigators and a director examine citizen complaints to determine if there is reasonable evidence that police misconduct occurred. Then, volunteer board members conduct closed-door hearings to decide whether they should support the allegations that came from the initial screening process in probable cause cases. And in Orange County, Florida, a nine-volunteer citizen review board holds hearings, open to the public and the media, on all cases involving the alleged use of excessive force and abuse of power after the sheriff's department has conducted an investigation.

Although police agencies in some communities have embraced citizen review, others find them troublesome. Departmental opposition is most likely when oversight procedures represent outside interference, oversight staff lack experience with and understanding of police work, and oversight processes are unfair. Most police administrators believe that their agencies should have the final say in matters of discipline, policies and procedures, and training, and some bridle at the hint of outside interference by nonprofessionals. In some communities local governments have established oversight bodies that act only in an advisory capacity and make nonbinding recommendations to law enforcement agencies.

Another familiar complaint is that civilians are unable to understand the complexities of police work. To compensate, candidates for the review board in Rochester, New York, attend a condensed version of a police academy run by the police department. The forty-eight-hour course involves three hours per evening for two weeks and two all-day Saturday sessions. The members use a shoot/don't shoot simulator, practice handcuffing, and learn about department policies and procedures, including the use-of-force continuum.

Many officers believe that review members hold them accountable for minor infractions, such as placing the wrong offense code on a citation or failing to record the end mileage on a vehicle transport. There is also the belief that the review process is often lengthy and that delays both harm the credibility of the oversight process and cause officers considerable stress as they wait for their cases to be decided. To overcome these problems, some police administrators have taken the initiative by helping to set up a citizen oversight system before being required to do so and then becoming involved in the planning process.

Despite serious reservations about citizen oversight, many law enforcement administrators have identified positive outcomes from having a review board in place. These include improving community relations, enhancing an agency's ability to police itself, and most important, improving an agency's policies and procedures. Citizen oversight bodies can recommend changes in the way the department conducts its internal investigation into alleged misconduct and also to improve department policies governing officer behavior.

Critical Thinking

1. This research, conducted by Liqun Cao and Bu Huang, shows that having a civilian review board is not a panacea that eliminates or significantly reduces citizen complaints. One reason is police resistance to civilian oversight. If you were the chief of police, would you want civilians to oversee how you ran your department or handled citizen complaints?
2. If you were the head of a civilian review board, how would you get the local police to accept your authority?

InfoTrac College Edition Research

Should there be civilian oversight over police? For one viewpoint, read Sidney L. Harring, "The Diallo Verdict: Another Tragic Accident in New York's War on Street Crime?" *Social Justice* 27 (2000): 9.

Sources: Liqun Cao and Bu Huang, "Determinants of Citizen Complaints Against Police Abuse of Power: *Journal of Criminal Justice* 28 (2000): 203–213; Peter Finn, "Getting Along with Citizen Oversight," *FBI Law Enforcement Bulletin,* 69 (2000): 22–27.

and services, planning budgets for future expenditures, and auditing departmental financial records.

Police departments include separate units that are charged with maintaining and disseminating information on wanted offenders, stolen merchandise, traffic violators, and so on. Modern data management systems enable police to use their records in a highly sophisticated fashion. For example, officers in a patrol car who spot a suspicious-looking vehicle can instantly receive a computerized rundown on whether it has been stolen. Or, if property is recovered during an arrest, police using this sort of system can determine who reported the loss of the merchandise and arrange for its return.

Another important function of police communication is the effective and efficient dispatching of patrol cars. Again, modern computer technologies have been used to make the most of available resources.[78]

In many departments, training is continuous throughout an officer's career. Training usually begins at a police academy, which may be run exclusively for larger departments or may be part of a regional training center servicing smaller and varied governmental units. More than 90 percent of all police departments require preservice training, including almost all departments in larger cities (population over one hundred thousand). The average officer receives more than five hundred hours of preservice training, including four hundred hours in the classroom and the rest in field training. Police in large cities receive over one thousand hours of instruction divided almost evenly between classroom and field instruction.[79] Among the topics usually covered are law and civil rights, firearms handling, emergency medical care, and restraint techniques.[80]

After assuming their police duties, new recruits are assigned to field-training officers who break them in on the job. However, training does not stop here. On-the-job training is a continuous process in the modern police department and covers such areas as weapons skills, first aid, crowd control, and community relations. Some departments use roll call training, in which superior officers or outside experts address police officers at the beginning of the workday. Other departments allow police officers time off to attend annual training sessions to sharpen their skills and learn new policing techniques.

To learn more about police training, use the term as a subject guide on InfoTrac College Edition.

Police departments provide emergency aid to the ill, counsel youngsters, speak to school and community agencies on safety and drug abuse, and provide countless other services designed to improve citizen-police interactions.

Larger police departments maintain specialized units that help citizens protect themselves from criminal activity. For example, they advise citizens on effective home security techniques or conduct Project ID campaigns—engraving valuables with an identifying number so that they can be returned if recovered after a burglary; police also work in schools teaching kids how to avoid drug use.[81]

Police agencies maintain (or have access to) forensic laboratories that enable them to identify substances to be used as evidence and to classify fingerprints.

Planning and research functions include designing programs to increase police efficiency and strategies to test program effectiveness. Police planners monitor recent technological developments and institute programs to adapt them to police services. ■

SUMMARY

Today's police departments operate in a military-like fashion; policy generally emanates from the top of the hierarchy. Most police officers therefore use a great deal of discretion when making on-the-job decisions.

The most common law enforcement agencies are local police departments, which carry out patrol and investigative functions as well as many support activities. Many questions have been raised about the effectiveness of police work, and some research efforts seem to indicate that police are not effective crime fighters. However, there are indications that aggressive police work, the threat of formal action, and cooperation between departments can have a measurable impact on crime. To improve effectiveness, police departments have developed new methods of policing that stress community involvement and problem solving.

For an up-to-date list of Web links, go to
http://cj.wadsworth.com/siegel_essen4e.

KEY TERMS

police chief 138	displacement 143	police-community relations 152	neighborhood-oriented policing (NOP) 154
time-in-rank system 138	proactive policing 144	broken windows model 152	problem-oriented policing 155
beat 141	deterrent effect 144	foot patrol 153	hot spots of crime 156
order maintenance (peacekeeping) 142	vice squad 148		internal affairs 159
	sting operation 148		

INFOTRAC COLLEGE EDITION EXERCISES

THERE ARE NUMEROUS SOURCES in InfoTrac College Edition to research the topic of community-oriented policing (COP). First, do a search on the term "problem-oriented policing." Then, to find out what COP means to various police departments in terms of strategies, philosophy, and officer skills, check out Michael G. Breci and Timothy E. Erickson, "Community Policing: The Process of Transitional Change," *FBI Law Enforcement Bulletin 67* (1998): 16.

TO CHECK OUT the effectiveness of citizen participation in community policing, read Eli Lehrer, "Communities and Cops Join Forces," *Insight on the News 15* (1999): 16. This paper finds that communities in which the residents watch out for one another and take active steps in crime prevention have a crime rate that is 40 percent lower than equivalent communities that do not take such measures.

FINALLY, TO SEE HOW community policing strategies can be applied in other milieus, read Stephen Doherty, "How Can Workplace Violence Be Deterred? The Community Policing Model Has Been Successfully Applied to the Problem of Domestic Violence. The Same Model Can Be Used to Address Workplace Violence," *Security Management,* April 2002 v46 i4 p134(3).

QUESTIONS

1. Should the primary police role be law enforcement or community service? Explain.

2. Should a police chief be permitted to promote an officer with special skills to a supervisory position, or should all officers be forced to spend "time in rank?" Why or why not?

3. Do the advantages of proactive policing outweigh the disadvantages? Explain.

4. Should all police recruits take the same physical tests, or are different requirements permissible for male and female applicants? Explain.

5. Can the police and the community ever form a partnership to fight crime? Why or why not? Does the community policing model remind you of early forms of policing? Explain.

NOTES

1. Patrick A. Langan, Lawrence A. Greenfeld, Steven K. Smith, Matthew R. Durose, and David J. Levin, *Contacts Between Police and the Public: Findings from the 1999 National Survey* (Washington, D.C.: Bureau of Justice Statistics, 2001).

2. Lawrence A. Greenfeld, Patrick A. Langan, and Steven K. Smith, *Police Use of Force: Collection of National Data* (Washington, D.C.: Bureau of Justice Statistics, 1997).

3. Brian A. Reaves and Pheny Smith, *Law Enforcement Management and Administrative Statistics, 1993: Data for Individual State and Local Agencies with 100 or More Officers* (Washington, D.C.: Bureau of Justice Statistics, 1995).

4. American Bar Association, *Standards Relating to Urban Police Function* (New York: Institute of Judicial Administration, 1974), standard 2.2.

5. Albert J. Reiss, *The Police and the Public* (New Haven, Conn.: Yale University Press, 1971), 19.

6. James Q. Wilson, *Varieties of Police Behavior: The Management of Law and Order in Eight Communities* (Cambridge, Mass.: Harvard University Press, 1968).

7. See Harlan Hahn, "A Profile of Urban Police," in *The Ambivalent Force,* eds. A. Niederhoffer and A. Blumberg (Hinsdale, Ill.: Dryden Press, 1976), 59.

8. George Kelling, Tony Pate, Duane Dieckman, and Charles Brown, *The Kansas City Preventive Patrol Experiment: A Summary Report* (Washington, D.C.: Police Foundation, 1974).

9. Ibid., 3–4.

10. Ibid.

11. Kenneth Novak, Jennifer Hartman, Alexander Holsinger, and Michael Turner, "The Effects of Aggressive Policing of Disorder on Serious Crime," *Policing 22* (1999): 171–190.

12. David Jacobs and Katherine Woods, "Interracial Conflict and Interracial Homicide: Do Political and Economic Rivalries Explain White Killings of Blacks or Black Killings of Whites?" *American Journal of Sociology 105* (1999): 157–190.

13. James Q. Wilson and Barbara Boland, "The Effect of Police on Crime," *Law and Society Review 12* (1978): 367–384.

14. Robert Sampson, "Deterrent Effects of the Police on Crime: A Replication and Theoretical Extension," *Law and Society Review 22* (1988): 163–191.

15. For a thorough review of this issue, see Andrew Karmen, *Why Is New York City's Murder Rate Dropping So Sharply?* (New York: John Jay College, 1996).

16. Lawrence Sherman, James Shaw, and Dennis Rogan, *The Kansas City Gun Experiment* (Washington, D.C.: National Institute of Justice, 1994).

17. H. Lawrence Ross, *Deterring the Drunk Driver: Legal Policy and Social Control* (Lexington, Mass.: Heath, 1982); Samuel Walker, *Sense and Nonsense About Crime* (Belmont, Calif.: Wadsworth, 1985), 82–85.

18. Perry Shapiro and Harold Votey, "Deterrence and Subjective Probabilities of Arrest: Modeling Individual Decisions to Drink and Drive in Sweden," *Law and Society Review 18* (1984): 111–149.

19. Mitchell Chamlin, "Crime and Arrests: An Autoregressive Integrated Moving Average (ARIMA) Approach," *Journal of Quantitative Criminology 4* (1988): 247–255.

20. Stewart D'Alessio and Lisa Stolzenberg, "Crime, Arrests, and Pretrial Jail Incarceration: An Examination of the Deterrence Thesis," *Criminology 36* (1998): 735–761.

21. Frances Lawrenz, James Lembo, and Thomas Schade, "Time Series Analysis of the Effect of a Domestic Violence Directive on the Number of Arrests per Day," *Journal of Criminal Justice 17* (1989): 493–499; Kathleen Ferraro, "Policing Woman Battering," *Social Problems 36* (1989): 61–74.

22. Craig Uchida and Robert Goldberg, *Police Employment and Expenditure Trends* (Washington, D.C.: Bureau of Justice Statistics, 1986).

23. Thomas Marvell and Carlysle Moody, "Specification Problems, Police Levels, and Crime Rates," *Criminology 34* (1996): 609–646; Colin Loftin and David McDowall, "The Police, Crime, and Economic Theory: An Assessment," *American Sociological Review 47* (1982): 393–401.

24. Tomislav V. Kovandzic and John J. Sloan, "Police Levels and Crime Rates Revisited: A County-Level Analysis from Florida (1980–1998)," *Journal of Criminal Justice 30* (2002): 65–76; Steven Levitt, "Using Electoral Cycles in Police Hiring to Estimate the Effect of Police on Crime," *American Economic Review 87* (1997): 270–291.

25. Joan Petersilia, Allan Abrahamse, and James Q. Wilson, "A Summary of Rand's Research on Police Performance, Community Characteristics, and Case Attrition," *Journal of Police Science and Administration 17* (1990): 219–229.

26. See Belton Cobb, *The First Detectives* (London: Faber & Faber, 1957).

27. See, for example, James Q. Wilson, "Movie Cops: Romantic vs. Real," *New York Magazine,* 19 August 1968, 38–41.

28. For a view of the modern detective, see William Sanders, *Detective Work: A Study of Criminal Investigations* (New York: Free Press, 1977).

29. James Ahern, *Police in Trouble* (New York: Hawthorn Books, 1972), 83–85.

30. Robert Langworthy, "Do Stings Control Crime? An Evaluation of a Police Fencing Operation," *Justice Quarterly 6* (1989): 27–45.

31. Mark Pogrebin and Eric Poole, "Vice Isn't Nice: A Look at the Effects of Working Undercover," *Journal of Criminal Justice 21* (1993): 385–396; Gary Marx, *Undercover: Police Surveillance in America* (Berkeley: University of California Press, 1988).

32. Peter Greenwood and Joan Petersilia, *Summary and Policy Implications,* vol. 1, *The Criminal Investigation Process* (Santa Monica, Calif.: Rand, 1975).

33. Mark Willman and John Snortum, "Detective Work: The Criminal Investigation Process in a Medium-Size Police Department," *Criminal Justice Review 9* (1984): 33–39.

34. Police Executive Research Forum, *Calling the Police: Citizen Reporting of Serious Crime* (Washington, D.C.: Police Executive Research Forum, 1981).

35. John Eck, *Solving Crimes: The Investigation of Burglary and Robbery* (Washington, D.C.: Police Executive Research Forum, 1984).

36. Egon Bittner, *The Functions of Police in Modern Society* (Cambridge, Mass.: Oelgeschlager, Gunn & Hain, 1980), 8; see also James Q. Wilson, "The Police in the Ghetto," in *The Police and the Community,* ed. Robert F. Steadman (Baltimore: Johns Hopkins University Press, 1974), 68.

37. George Kelling, *Police and Communities: The Quiet Revolution* (Washington, D.C.: National Institute of Justice, 1988).

38. Ibid.

39. George Kelling and James Q. Wilson, "Broken Windows: The Police and Neighborhood Safety," *Atlantic Monthly 249* (1982): 29–38.

40. For a general review, see Robert Trojanowicz and Bonnie Bucqueroux, *Community Policing: A Contemporary Perspective* (Cincinnati, Ohio: Anderson, 1990).

41. Police Foundation, *The Newark Foot Patrol Experiment* (Washington, D.C.: Police Foundation, 1981).

42. Jihong Zhao, Nicholas Lovrich, and Quint Thurman, "The Status of Community Policing American Cities," *Policing* 22 (1999): 74–92.

43. Albert Cardarelli, Jack McDevitt, and Katrina Baum, "The Rhetoric and Reality of Community Policing in Small and Medium-Sized Cities and Towns," *Policing* 21 (1998): 397–415.

44. Quint Thurman, Andrew Giacomazzi, and Phil Bogen, "Research Note: Cops, Kids, and Community Policing: An Assessment of a Community Policing Demonstration Project," *Crime and Delinquency* 39 (1993): 554–564.

45. Quint Thurman and Phil Bogen, "Research Note: Spokane Community Policing Officers Revisited," *American Journal of Police* 15 (1996): 97–114.

46. Diana Fishbein, "The Comprehensive Care Model," *FBI Law Enforcement Bulletin* 67 (1998): 1–5.

47. Susan Sadd and Randolph Grinc, *Implementation Challenges in Community Policing* (Washington, D.C.: National Institute of Justice, 1996).

48. Donald Green, Dara Strolovitch, and Janelle Wong, "Defended Neighborhoods: Integration and Racially Motivated Crime," *American Journal of Sociology* 104 (1998): 372–403.

49. Walter Baranyk, "Making a Difference in a Public Housing Project," *Police Chief* 61 (1994): 31–35.

50. Jerome Skolnick and David Bayley, *Community Policing: Issues and Practices Around the World* (Washington, D.C.: National Institute of Justice, 1988).

51. Ibid., 17.

52. Herman Goldstein, "Improving Policing: A Problem-Oriented Approach," *Crime and Delinquency* 25 (1979): 236–258.

53. Skolnick and Bayley, *Community Policing*, 12.

54. Lawrence Sherman, Patrick Gartin, and Michael Buerger, "Hot Spots of Predatory Crime: Routine Activities and the Criminology of Place," *Criminology* 27 (1989): 27–55.

55. Ibid., 45.

56. Dennis Roncek and Pamela Maier, "Bars, Blocks, and Crimes Revisited: Linking the Theory of Routine Activities to the Empiricism of 'Hot Spots,'" *Criminology* 29 (1991): 725–753.

57. Herman Goldstein, "Toward Community-Oriented Policing: Potential Basic Requirements, and Threshold Questions," *Crime and Delinquency* 33 (1987): 6–30.

58. Anthony A. Braga, David M. Kennedy, Elin J. Waring, and Anne Morrison Piehl, "Problem-Oriented Policing, Deterrence, and Youth Violence: An Evaluation of Boston's Operation Ceasefire," *Journal of Research in Crime and Delinquency*, 38 (2001): 195–225.

59. Anthony A. Braga, David Weisburd, Elin J. Waring, Lorraine Green Mazerolle, William Spelman, and Francis Gajewski, "Problem-Oriented Policing in Violent Crime Places: A Randomized Controlled Experiment," *Criminology* 37 (1999): 541–580.

60. Eric Fritsch, Tory Caeti, and Robert Taylor, "Gang Suppression Through Saturation Patrol, Aggressive Curfew, and Tru-

61. Bureau of Justice Assistance, *Problem-Oriented Drug Enforcement: A Community-Based Approach for Effective Policing* (Washington, D.C.: National Institute of Justice, 1993).

62. Ibid., 64–65.

63. Jack R. Greene, "The Effects of Community Policing on American Law Enforcement: A Look at the Evidence" (Paper presented at the International Congress on Criminology, Hamburg, Germany, September 1988), 19.

64. Roger Dunham and Geoffrey Alpert, "Neighborhood Differences in Attitudes Toward Policing: Evidence for a Mixed-Strategy Model of Policing in a Multi-Ethnic Setting," *Journal of Criminal Law and Criminology* 79 (1988): 504–522.

65. Mark E. Correia, "The Conceptual Ambiguity of Community in Community Policing: Filtering the Muddy Waters," *Policing: An International Journal of Police Strategies & Management* 23 (2000): 218–233.

66. Scott Lewis, Helen Rosenberg, and Robert Sigler, "Acceptance of Community Policing Among Police Officers and Police Administrators," *Policing: An International Journal of Police Strategies & Management* 22 (1999): 567–588.

67. Amy Halsted, Max Bromley, and John Cochran, "The Effects of Work Orientations on Job Satisfaction Among Sheriffs' Deputies Practicing Community-Oriented Policing," *Policing: An International Journal of Police Strategies & Management* 23 (2000): 82–104.

68. Michael Palmiotto, Michael Birzer, and N. Prabha Unnithan, "Training in Community Policing: A Suggested Curriculum," *Policing: An International Journal of Police Strategies & Management* 23 (2000): 8–21

69. Lisa Riechers and Roy Roberg, "Community Policing: A Critical Review of Underlying Assumptions," *Journal of Police Science and Administration* 17 (1990): 112–113.

70. John Riley, "Community-Policing: Utilizing the Knowledge of Organizational Personnel," *Policing: An International Journal of Police Strategies & Management* 22 (1999): 618–633.

71. David Kessler, "Integrating Calls for Service with Community- and Problem-Oriented Policing: A Case Study," *Crime and Delinquency* 39 (1993): 485–508.

72. L. Thomas Winfree, Gregory Bartku, and George Seibel, "Support for Community Policing Versus Traditional Policing Among Nonmetropolitan Police Officers: A Survey of Four New Mexico Police Departments," *American Journal of Police* 15 (1996): 23–47.

73. Jihong Zhao, Ni He, and Nicholas Lovrich, "Value Change Among Police Officers at a Time of Organizational Reform: A Follow-up Study of Rokeach Values," *Policing* 22 (1999): 152–170.

74. Jihong Zhao and Quint Thurman, "Community Policing: Where Are We Now?" *Crime and Delinquency* 43 (1997): 345–357.

75. Jihong Zhao, Nicholas Lovrich, and T. Hank Robinson, "Community Policing: Is It Changing the Basic Functions of Policing? Findings from a Longitudinal Study of 200+ Municipal Police Agencies," *Journal of Criminal Justice* 29 (2001): 365–377.

76. Ralph B. Taylor, *Breaking Away from Broken Windows: Baltimore Neighborhoods and the Nationwide Fight Against*

ancy Enforcement: A Quasi-Experimental Test of the Dallas Anti-Gang Initiative," *Crime and Delinquency* 45 (1999): 122–139.

Crime, Grime, Fear, and Decline (Boulder, Colo.: Westview Press, 2000).

77. William Doerner and Terry Nowell, "The Reliability of the Behavioral-Personnel Assessment Device (BPAD) in Selecting Police Recruits," *Policing 22* (1999): 343–352.

78. See, for example, Richard Larson, *Urban Police Patrol Analysis* (Cambridge, Mass.: MIT Press, 1972).

79. Brian A. Reaves, *State and Local Police Departments, 1990* (Washington, D.C.: Bureau of Justice Statistics, 1992), 6.

80. Philip Ash, Karen Slora, and Cynthia Britton, "Police Agency Officer Selection Practices," *Journal of Police Science and Administration 17* (1990): 258–269.

81. Dennis Rosenbaum, Robert Flewelling, Susan Bailey, Chris Ringwalt, and Deanna Wilkinson, "Cops in the Classroom: A Longitudinal Evaluation of Drug Abuse Resistance Education (DARE)," *Journal of Research in Crime and Delinquency 31* (1994): 3–31.

6 Issues in Policing: Professional, Social, and Legal

Chapter Outline

Criminal Justice Links

Criminal Justice Viewpoints

DURING THE TWO-DAY period from October 2 to October 3, 2002 in the Washington, D.C., area, a mysterious and deadly sniper killed six people, each with a single shot. Afterward, the sniper circled through areas to the east, south, and west of the original shootings, cutting down individuals as they went about their daily business, shopping, working, and going to school. At a shooting scene on October 7, the sniper reportedly left a tarot death card inscribed, "Dear Policeman, I am God." As the investigation proceeded rumors were rampant: the sniper was part of a terrorist cell; he was a psychopath. The sniper attacks seemed unique. Unlike most mass murderers, he did not kill his victims in a single violent outburst; unlike most serial killers, he did not touch, interact, or get close to his victims. Nor did the sniper seek out a specific class of victims; his casualties included the young and the old, African Americans and Caucasians, men and women.

When the sniper contacted police his crime spree began to unravel. Clearly, he felt his early calls were not being given the proper attention. In order to give himself more credibility, the man called a local priest and bragged about a robbery and killing in Montgomery, Alabama; he hoped that the priest would act as a go-between. Instead, the priest told authorities about the strange phone call. When authorities investigated the Alabama case, they were able to obtain a crime scene fingerprint and identify John Lee Malvo, seventeen, a Jamaican citizen. Malvo was known as the unofficial stepson and traveling companion of John Allen Muhammad, forty-one, a U.S. Army veteran with an expert's rating in marksmanship. Authorities then put out a bulletin describing Muhammad's car, and an alert traveler identified the car in a rest stop parking lot and called police. Inside the car, police found the sleeping Muhammad and Malvo, as well as a Bushmaster XM-15 .223-caliber rifle with scope and bipod; ballistic testing later confirmed it to be the murder weapon. Modifications had been made to the car's backseat and trunk area so that it could be used as a sniper's perch, with the gunman hidden flat in the car and firing through a hole bored in the trunk lid. Clearly the sniper shootings were well thought-out and planned attacks. ▨

 *To view the CNN video clip of this story,* go to the book-specific Web site at http://cj.wadsworth.com/siegel_essen4e.

The sniper case was one among a number of highly publicized incidents of violence that reinforced the critical role played by police and law enforcement agencies. These incidents highlight the critical and controversial role police play in the justice system and the need for developing a professional, competent police force. The police are the gatekeepers of the criminal justice process. They initiate contact with law violators and decide whether to formally arrest them and start their journey through the criminal justice system, settle the issue in an informal way (such as by issuing a warning), or simply take no action at all. The strategic position of law enforcement officers, their visibility and contact with the public, and their use of weapons and arrest power have kept them in the forefront of public thought for most of the twentieth century.

In the late 1960s and early 1970s, great issue was taken with the political and social roles of the police. Critics viewed police agencies as biased organizations that harassed minority citizens, controlled political dissidents, and generally seemed out of touch with the changing times. The main issues appeared to be controlling the abuse of police power and making police agencies more responsible to the public. During this period, major efforts were undertaken in the nation's largest cities to curb police power.

Since the mid-1970s, the relationship between police and the public has changed. Police departments have become more sensitive to their public image. Programs have been created to improve relations between police and community—to help police officers on the beat be more sensitive to the needs of the public and cope more effectively with the stress of their jobs.

For the past three decades, much public interest has focused on the function of the police. The U.S. public seems genuinely concerned today about the quality and effectiveness of local police. Most citizens seem to approve of their local law enforcement agents; about 60 percent say they have a "great deal of confidence" in the police.[1] Although this is encouraging, approval is often skewed along racial lines: police procedures have been questioned because overenforcement may be present in minority communities.[2] Minority citizens also seem to be affected more adversely than whites when well-publicized incidents of police misconduct occur.[3] It may not be surprising then that 28 percent of African-American citizens report having little confidence in the police, compared with 6 percent of whites.[4]

The general public is not the only group concerned about police attitudes and behavior. Police administrators and other law enforcement experts have focused their attention on issues that may influence the effectiveness and efficiency of police performance in the field. Some of their concerns are outgrowths of the development of policing as a profession: Does an independent police culture exist, and what are its characteristics? Do police officers develop a unique working personality, and if so, does it influence their job performance? Are there **police officer styles** that make some police officers too aggressive and others inert and passive? Is policing too stressful an occupation?

Another area of concern is the social composition of police departments: Who should be recruited as police officers? Are minorities and women being attracted to police work, and what have their experiences been on the force? Should police officers have a college education?

There are also important issues concerning legal controls over police. Should the courts closely monitor their behavior and limit their power to investigate and arrest suspects? Or, conversely, should the police be given a free hand to carry out their investigative duties?

Important questions are also being raised about the problems police departments face interacting with the society they are entrusted to supervise: Are police officers too forceful and brutal, and do they discriminate in their use of **deadly force**? Are police officers corrupt, and how can police deviance be controlled?

How does the general public view the police in England? Are perceptions different from in the United States, and are they influenced by race? To find out, read one study's findings on InfoTrac College Edition: Ellis Cashmore, "Behind the Window Dressing: Ethnic Minority Police Perspectives on Cultural Diversity," *Journal of Ethnic and Migration Studies,* April 2002 v28 i2 p327(15).

police officer styles The belief that the bulk of police officers can be classified into four personality types. Popular types include crime fighters, who desire to enforce only serious crimes, such as robbery and rape; law enforcers, who emphasize the professional elements of police work; social agents, who see their job as a helping profession; and watchmen, whose priority is maintaining public order. The actual existence of these police officer types has been much debated.

deadly force The ability of the police to kill suspects if they resist arrest or present a danger to the officer or the community. The police cannot use deadly force against an unarmed fleeing felon.

The Police Profession

All professions have unique characteristics that distinguish them from other occupations and institutions. Policing is no exception. Police experts have long sought to understand the unique nature of the police experience and to determine how the challenges of police work shape the field and its employees. In this section, some of the factors that make policing unique are discussed in detail.

The Police Culture

Police experts have found that the experience of becoming a police officer and the nature of the job itself cause most officers to band together in a police subculture, characterized by **cynicism,** clannishness, secrecy, and insulation from others in society—the so-called **blue curtain.** Police officers tend to socialize with one another and believe that their occupation cuts them off from relationships with civilians. Joining the police subculture means always having to stick up for fellow officers against outsiders, maintaining a tough, macho exterior personality, and distrusting the motives and behavior of outsiders.[5] Six core beliefs are viewed as being the heart of the police culture today:

1. *Police are the only real crime fighters.* The public wants the police officer to fight crime; other agencies, both public and private, only play at crime fighting.
2. *No one else understands the real nature of police work.* Lawyers, academics, politicians, and the public in general have little concept of what it means to be a police officer.
3. *Loyalty to colleagues counts above everything else.* Police officers have to stick together because everyone is out to get the police and make the job more difficult.

The Police Foundation is a nonprofit organization dedicated to conducting research on law enforcement. To check out its activities and publications, go to the Web site:
www.policefoundation.org/

cynicism   The belief that most people's actions are motivated solely by personal needs and selfishness.

blue curtain   The secretive, insulated police culture that isolates officers from the rest of society.

Some experts believe there is a police subculture, referred to as the *blue curtain,* characterized by cynicism, clannishness, secrecy, and insulation from others in society. Members of the police subculture stick up for fellow officers against outsiders and distrust outsiders' motives and behavior.

4. *It is impossible to win the war against crime without bending the rules.* Courts have awarded criminal defendants too many civil rights.
5. *Members of the public are basically unsupportive and unreasonably demanding.* People are quick to criticize police unless they need police help themselves.
6. *Patrol work is the pits.* Detective work is glamorous and exciting.[6]

Is there a police culture in other nations? To find out, read Janet Chan, "Changing Police Culture," *British Journal of Criminology,* Winter 1996 v36 i1 p109–134, on InfoTrac College Edition.

The forces that support a police culture generally are believed to develop out of on-the-job experiences. Most officers, both male and female, originally join police forces because they want to help people, fight crime, and have an interesting, exciting, prestigious career with a high degree of job security.[7] Recruits often find that the social reality of police work does not mesh with their original career goals. They are unprepared for the emotional turmoil and conflict that accompany police work today.

Membership in the police culture helps recruits adjust to the rigors of police work and provides the emotional support needed for survival.[8] The culture encourages decisiveness in the face of uncertainty and the ability to make split-second judgments that may later be subject to extreme criticism. Officers who view themselves as crime fighters are the ones most likely to value solidarity and depend on the support and camaraderie of their fellow officers.[9] The police subculture encourages its members to draw a sharp distinction between good and evil. Officers, more than mere enforcers of the law, are warriors in the age-old battle between right and wrong.[10] In contrast, criminals are referred to as "terrorists" and "predators," terms that convey the fact that they are evil individuals ready to prey upon the poor and vulnerable. Because predators represent a real danger, the police culture demands that its members be both competent and concerned with the safety of their peers and partners. Competence often translates into respect and authority, and citizens must obey or face "payback."[11]

In sum, the police culture has developed in response to the insulated, dangerous lifestyle of police officers. Policing is a dangerous occupation, and the unquestioned support and loyalty of their peers is not something officers could readily do without.[12]

The Police Personality

One of the most enduring questions in the criminal justice literature is whether police officers develop a unique set of personality traits that distinguishes them from the average citizen.[13] To some commentators, the typical police personality can be described as dogmatic, authoritarian, and suspicious.[14] Cynicism has been found at all levels of policing, including chiefs of police, and throughout all stages of a police career.[15] These negative values and attitudes are believed to cause police officers to be secretive and isolated from the rest of society, producing the blue curtain.[16]

The police officer's working personality is shaped by constant exposure to danger and the need to use force and authority to reduce and control threatening situations.[17] Police feel suspicious of the public they serve and defensive about the actions of their fellow officers. There are two opposing viewpoints on the cause of this phenomenon. One position holds that police departments attract recruits who are by nature cynical, authoritarian, secretive, and so on.[18] Other experts maintain that socialization and experience on the police force itself cause these character traits to develop in officers.

Since the first research measuring police personality was published, numerous efforts have been made to determine whether the typical police recruit does indeed possess a unique personality that sets him or her apart from the average citizen. The results have been mixed.[19] Although some research concludes that police values are different from those of the general adult population, other efforts reach an opposite conclusion; some have found that police officers are actually more psychologically healthy than the general population, less depressed and anxious, and more social and assertive.[20] Still other research on police personality has found that police officers highly value such personality traits as warmth, flexibility, and emotion; these traits are far removed from rigidity and cynicism.[21] Since research has found evidence supportive of both viewpoints, no one position dominates on the issue of how the police personality develops, or even if one actually exists.

In his classic study of police personality, *Behind the Shield* (1967), Arthur Neiderhoffer examined the assumption that most police officers develop into cynics as a function of their daily duties.[22] Among his most important findings were that police cynicism did increase with length of service and that military-like police academy training caused new recruits to quickly become cynical about themselves.[23]

Policing Style

Policing encompasses a multitude of diverse tasks, including peacekeeping, criminal investigation, traffic control, and providing emergency medical service. Part of the socialization as a police officer is developing a working attitude, or style, through which to approach policing. For example, some police officers may view the job as a well-paid civil service position that stresses careful compliance with written departmental rules and procedures. Other officers may see themselves as part of the "thin blue line" that protects the public from wrongdoers. They will use any means to get the culprit, even if it involves such cheating as planting evidence on an obviously guilty person who has so far escaped arrest. Should the police bend the rules to protect the public? This has been referred to as the "Dirty Harry problem," after the popular Clint Eastwood movie character who routinely (and successfully) violated all known standards of police work.[24]

Several studies have attempted to define and classify police styles into behavioral clusters. These classifications, called *typologies,* attempt to categorize law enforcement agents by groups, each with a unique approach to police work. The purpose of such classifications is to demonstrate that the police are not a cohesive, homogeneous group, as many believe, but rather are individuals with differing approaches to their work.[25] The way police approach their task and their attitude toward the police role, as well as toward their peers and superior officers, have been shown to affect police work.[26]

An examination of the literature suggests that four styles of police work seem to fit the current behavior patterns of most police agents: the crime fighter, the social agent, the law enforcer, and the watchman. These are described in Exhibit 6.1.

Do Police Styles Actually Exist?   Although officers who embrace a particular style of policing may emphasize one area of law enforcement over another, their daily activities will likely require them to engage in police duties they consider to be trivial or unimportant. Although some pure types exist, an officer probably cannot specialize in one area of policing while ignoring the others.[27]

It is possible that today's police officer is more of a generalist than ever before and that future police recruits will be required to engage in a great variety of police tasks.

Exhibit 6.1 The four basic styles of policing

The crime fighter
To the crime fighter, the most important aspect of police work is investigating serious crimes and apprehending criminals. Crime fighters focus on the victim and view effective police work as the only force that can keep society's "dangerous classes" in check. They are the "thin blue line" protecting society from murderers and rapists. They consider property crimes to be less significant, and believe that such matters as misdemeanors, traffic control, and social service functions would be better handled by other agencies of government. The ability to investigate criminal behavior that poses a serious threat to life and safety, combined with the power to arrest criminals, separates a police department from other municipal agencies. Crime fighters see diluting these functions with minor social service and nonenforcement duties as harmful to police efforts to create a secure society.

The social agent
The social agent believes that police should be involved in a wide range of activities without regard for their connection to law enforcement. Rather than viewing themselves as "criminal catchers," the social agents consider themselves as community problem solvers. They are troubleshooters who patch the holes that appear where the social fabric wears thin. They are happy to work with special-needs populations, such as the homeless, schoolkids, and those in need of emergency services. The social agent fits well in a community policing unit.

The law enforcer
According to this officer's view, duty is clearly set out in law. The law enforcer stresses playing it "by the book." Since the police are specifically charged with apprehending all types of lawbreakers, they see themselves as generalized law enforcement agents. Although law enforcers may prefer working on serious crimes—because they are more intriguing and rewarding in terms of achievement, prestige, and status—they see the police role as one of enforcing all statutes and ordinances. They perceive themselves neither as community social workers nor vengeance-seeking vigilantes; quite simply, they are professional law enforcement officers who perform the functions of detecting violations, identifying culprits, and taking the lawbreakers before a court. The law enforcer is devoted to the profession of police work and is the officer most likely to aspire to command rank.

The watchman
The watchman style is characterized by an emphasis on maintaining public order as the police goal, rather than law enforcement or general service. Watchmen choose to ignore many infractions and requests for service unless they believe that the social or political order is jeopardized. Juveniles are "expected" to misbehave and are best ignored or treated informally. Motorists will often be left alone if their driving does not endanger or annoy others. Vice and gambling are problems only when the currently accepted standards of public order are violated. Like the watchman of old, this officer only takes action when and if a problem arises. The watchman is the most passive officer, more concerned with retirement benefits than crime rates.

Sources: William Muir, *Police: Streetcorner Politicians* (Chicago: University of Chicago Press, 1977); James Q. Wilson, *Varieties of Police Behavior* (Cambridge, Mass.: Harvard University Press, 1968).

Police Discretion

discretion The use of personal decision making and choice in carrying out operations in the criminal justice system. For example, police discretion can involve the decision to make an arrest; prosecutorial discretion can involve the decision to accept a plea bargain.

Style and role orientation may influence how police officers carry out their duties and the way they may use their **discretion.**[28] Police have the ability to deprive people of their liberty, arrest them and take them away in handcuffs, and even use deadly force to subdue them. A critical aspect of this professional responsibility is the personal discretion each officer has in carrying out his daily activities. Discretion can involve the selective enforcement of the law—as when a vice squad plainclothes officer decides not to take action against a tavern that is serving drinks after hours. Patrol officers use discretion when they decide to arrest one suspect for disorderly conduct but escort another home.

The majority of police officers use a high degree of personal discretion in carrying out daily tasks, sometimes referred to as *low-visibility decision making* in criminal justice.[29] This terminology suggests that, unlike members of almost every other criminal justice agency, police are neither regulated in their daily procedures by administrative scrutiny nor subject to judicial review (except when their behavior clearly violates an offender's constitutional rights). As a result, the exercise of discretion by police may sometimes deteriorate into discrimination, violence, and other abusive practices. The following sections describe the factors that influence police discretion and review suggestions for its control.

Legal Factors

Police discretion is inversely related to the severity of the offense. There is far less personal discretion available when police confront a suspect in a case involving murder or rape than there is with a simple assault or trespass. The likelihood of a police officer taking legal action then may depend on how the individual views the severity of the offense.

The perception of offense seriousness may be influenced by the relationship between the parties involved. An altercation between two friends or relatives may be handled differently than an assault on a stranger. A case in point is policing domestic violence cases. Research indicates that police are reluctant even to respond to these kinds of cases because they are a constant source of frustration and futility.[30] Evidence shows that police intentionally delay responding to domestic disputes, hoping that by the time they get there the problem will be settled.[31] Victims, they believe, often fail to get help or change their abusive situation.[32] Even when they are summoned, police are likely to treat domestic violence cases more casually than other assault cases. If, however, domestic abuse involves extreme violence, especially if a weapon is brandished or used, police are much more likely to respond with a formal arrest.[33] Police, therefore, use their discretion to separate what they consider nuisance cases from those serious enough to demand police action.

Environmental Factors

The degree of discretion an officer will exercise is at least partially defined by the officer's living and working environment.[34] Police officers may work or dwell in a community culture that either tolerates eccentricities and personal freedoms or expects extremely conservative, professional, no-nonsense behavior on the part of its civil servants. Communities that are proactive and contain progressive governmental institutions also may influence a police officer's discretion. For example, police officers in communities that provide training in domestic violence prevention and maintain local shelters for battered women are more likely to take action in cases involving spousal abuse.[35]

An officer who lives in the community he or she serves is probably strongly influenced by and shares a large part of the community's beliefs and values and is likely to be sensitive to and respect the wishes of neighbors, friends, and relatives. Conflict may arise, however, when the police officer commutes to an assigned area

How do police use discretion and what can be done to control behaviors that violate community standards? The answer to these questions may be found in a publication of the National Institute of Justice entitled *"Broken Windows" and Police Discretion*, by criminologist George Kelling: www.ncjrs.org/pdffiles1/nij/178259.pdf

© Richard Hutchings/Photo Edit

Police enjoy significant discretion in their daily activities. Unlike members of almost every other criminal justice agency, police are neither regulated in their daily procedures by administrative scrutiny nor subject to judicial review. They are given the discretion to decide when conduct becomes disorderly or whether a person is inebriated.

of jurisdiction, which is often the case in inner-city precincts. The officer who holds personal values in opposition to those of the community can exercise discretion in ways that conflict with the community's values and result in ineffective law enforcement.[36]

A police officer's perception of community alternatives to police intervention may also influence discretion. A police officer may exercise discretion to arrest an individual in a particular circumstance if it seems that nothing else can be done, even if the officer does not believe that an arrest is the best possible example of good police work. In an environment that has a proliferation of social agencies—detoxification units, drug control centers, and child-care services, for example—a police officer will obviously have more alternatives to choose from in deciding whether to make an arrest. In fact, referring cases to these alternative agencies saves the officer both time and effort—records do not have to be made out and court appearances can be avoided. Thus, social agencies provide greater latitude in police decision making.

Departmental Factors

The policies, practices, and customs of the local police department are another influence on discretion. These conditions vary from department to department and strongly depend on the judgment of the chief and others in the organizational hierarchy. For example, departments can issue directives aimed at influencing police conduct. Patrol officers may be asked to issue more tickets and make more arrests or to refrain from arresting under certain circumstances. Occasionally, a directive will instruct officers to be particularly alert for certain types of violations or to make some sort of interagency referral when specific events occur. For example, the department may order patrol officers to crack down on street panhandlers or to take formal action in domestic violence cases.[37]

The ratio of supervisory personnel to subordinates may also influence discretion: departments with a high ratio of sergeants to patrol officers may experience fewer officer-initiated actions than those in which fewer eyes are observing the action in the streets. It is also possible that supervisory style may influence how police use discretion. For example, Robin Shepard Engel found that patrol officers supervised by sergeants who are "take-charge" types, and like to participate in high levels of activity in the field themselves, spend significantly more time per shift engaging in self-initiated and community-policing or problem-solving activities than they do in administrative activities. In contrast, officers with supervisors who spend time mentoring and coaching subordinates are more likely to devote significantly more time engaging in administrative tasks.[38] The size of the department may also determine officer discretion. In larger departments, looser control by supervisors seems to encourage a level of discretion unknown in smaller, more tightly run police agencies.

Peer Influence   Police discretion is also subject to peer influence.[39] Police officers suffer a degree of social isolation because the job involves strange working conditions and hours, including being on twenty-four-hour call, and their authority and responsibility to enforce the law may cause embarrassment during social encounters. At the same time, officers must handle irregular and emotionally demanding encounters involving the most personal and private aspects of people's lives. As a result, police officers turn to their peers for both on-the-job advice and off-the-job companionship, essentially forming a subculture to provide a source of status, prestige, and reward.

The peer group affects how police officers exercise discretion on two distinct levels. In an obvious, direct manner, other police officers dictate acceptable responses to street-level problems by providing or withholding approval in office discussions. Second, officers who take their job seriously and desire the respect and friendship of others will take their advice, abide by their norms, and seek out the most experienced and most influential patrol officers on the force and follow their behavior models.

Situational Factors

The situational factors attached to a particular crime are another extremely important influence on police actions and behavior. Regardless of departmental or community influences, the officer's immediate interaction with a criminal act, offender, citizen, or victim will weigh heavily on the use of discretionary powers. Some early research efforts found that police officers rely on **demeanor** (the attitude and appearance of the offender) in making decisions. If an offender is surly, talks back, or otherwise challenges the officer's authority, formal action is more likely to be taken.[40] More recent studies have also shown that a negative demeanor will result in formal police action.[41]

demeanor The way in which a person outwardly manifests his or her personality.

However, in a series of research studies, David Klinger has challenged the long-held believe that bad demeanor has a significant influence on police decision making. Klinger, a police officer turned criminologist, suggests that it is criminal behavior and actions that occur during police detention, and not negative attitude, that influences the police decision to take formal action.[42] For example, a person who struggles or touches police during a confrontation is a likely candidate for arrest; merely having a "bad attitude" is not enough to generate police retaliation. Klinger's research suggests that experienced police officers are unimpressed by a bad attitude; they have seen it all before.

Another set of situational influences on police discretion is the manner in which a crime or situation is encountered. If, for example, a police officer stumbles on an altercation or break-in, the discretionary response may be different than if the officer is summoned by police radio. If an act has received official police recognition, such as the dispatch of a patrol car, police action must be taken or an explanation made as to why it was not. Or if a matter is brought to an officer's attention by a citizen observer, the officer can ignore the request and risk a complaint or take discretionary action. In contrast, when an officer chooses to become involved in a situation, without benefit of a summons or complaint, maximum discretion can be used. Even in this circumstance, however, the presence of a crowd or of witnesses may influence the officer's decision making.

And, of course, the officer who acts alone is also affected by personal matters—physical condition, mental state, police style, and whether he or she has other duties to perform.

Other factors that might influence police are the use of a weapon, seriousness of injury, and the presence of alcohol or drugs.

Extralegal Factors

One often-debated issue is whether police take race, class, and gender into account when making arrest decisions. For example, research shows that police are less likely to make arrests in cases of elder mistreatment than in other assaults; the age of the victim influences their decision making.[43] The question then is whether police discretion is shaped by such extralegal factors as age, gender, income, and race. Because this issue is so important, it is the topic of the Race, Culture, and Gender feature on pages 178–179.

Police discretion is one of the most frequently debated issues in criminal justice (see Figure 6.1). On its face, unequal enforcement of the law smacks of unfairness and violates the Constitution's doctrines of due process and equal protection. Yet if some discretion were not exercised, police would be forced to function as robots, merely following the book. Administrators have sought to control discretion so that its exercise may be both beneficial to citizens and nondiscriminatory.[44]

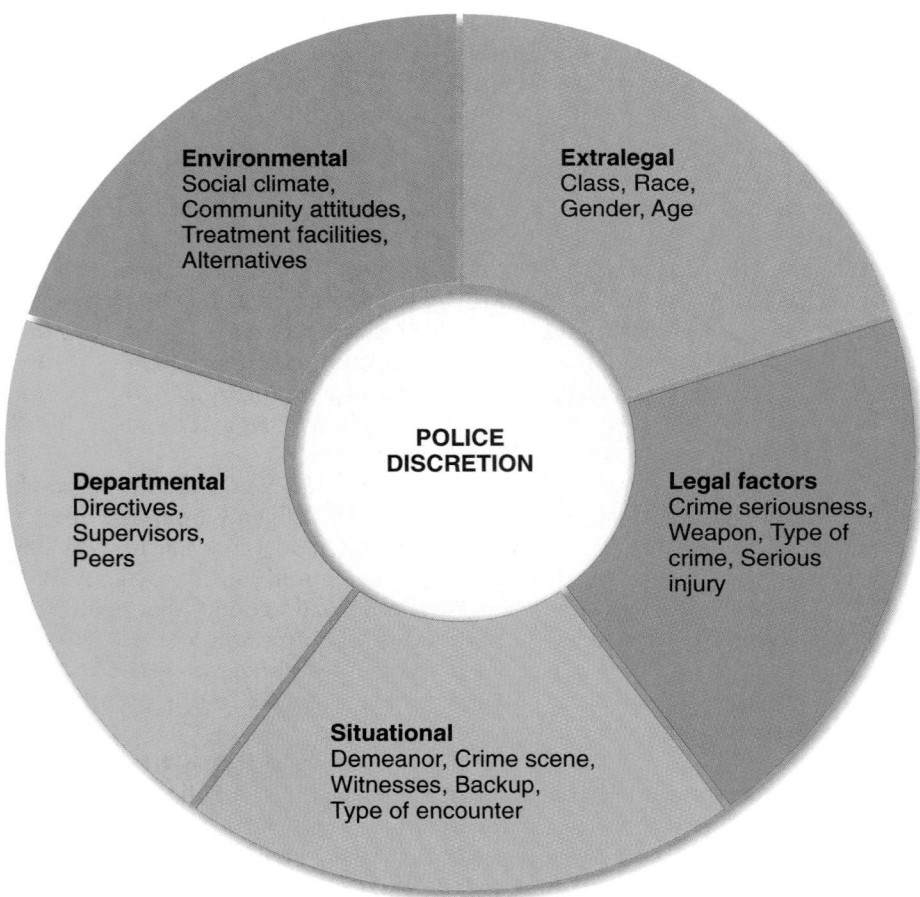

Figure 6.1
Influences on police discretion

Source: Brian Reeves & Andrew Goldberg, *Local Police Departments 1997* (Washington, DC: Bureau of Justice Statistics, 2000).

Who Are the Police?

The composition of the nation's police forces is changing. Traditionally, police agencies were composed of white males with a high school education who viewed policing as a secure position that brought them the respect of family and friends and took them a step up the social ladder. It was not uncommon to see police families in which one member of each new generation would enter the force. This picture has been changing and will continue to change. As criminal justice programs turn out thousands of graduates every year, an increasing number of police officers have at least some college education. In addition, affirmative action programs have slowly helped change the racial and gender composition of police departments to reflect community makeup. The following sections explore these changes in detail.

Police Education

In recent years, many police experts have argued that police recruits should have a college education. This development is not unexpected, considering that higher education for police officers has been recommended by national commissions since 1931.[45]

Though most law enforcement agencies still do not require recruits to have a college degree, the number requiring advanced education in the hiring and promotion process is growing. A recent national survey of larger police departments found that during the past decade the percentage of departments requiring new officers to have at least some college rose from 19 percent to 37 percent, and the percent requiring a two-year or four-year degree grew from 6 percent to 14 percent.[46] About half the surveyed departments expressed a preference for criminal justice majors, most often because of their enhanced knowledge of the entire criminal justice system and issues in policing. Another promising trend was this: although not requiring college credits for promotion, 82 percent of the departments recognized that college education is an important element in promotion decisions.

What are the benefits of higher education for police officers? Better communication with the public, especially minority and ethnic groups, is believed to be one benefit. Educated officers write better and more clearly and are more likely to be promoted. Police administrators believe that education enables officers to perform more effectively, generate fewer citizen complaints, show more initiative in performing police tasks, and generally act more professionally.[47] In addition, educated officers are less likely to have disciplinary problems and are viewed as better decision makers.[48] Studies have similarly shown that college-educated police officers generate fewer citizen complaints and have better behavioral and performance characteristics than their less-educated peers. Research indicates that educated officers are more likely to rate themselves higher on most performance indicators, indicating that if nothing else higher education is associated with greater self-confidence and assurance.[49]

Though education has its benefits, there is little conclusive evidence that educated officers are more effective crime fighters.[50] The diversity of the police role, the need for split-second decision making, and the often boring and mundane

You can access some data from this survey on InfoTrac College Edition: "Education and Training Requirements for Big City Police Officers Increase, Starting Salaries Remain Flat," *M2 Presswire*, May 13, 2002.

© 2002 AP/Wide World Photos

The number of minority police officers is increasing, and so is their presence in command authority. No law enforcement officer has played a more prominent role in the media than Charles Moose, chief of the Montgomery County, Maryland, Police, who led the D.C. sniper investigation in 2002.

Race, Culture, and Gender in Criminal Justice

Racial Profiling: Does Race Influence the Police Use of Discretion?

In the late summer of 1997 New Yorkers were shocked as an astounding case of police brutality began to unfold in the daily newspapers. Abner Louima, age thirty-three, a Haitian immigrant, had been arrested outside Club Rendez-vous, a Brooklyn nightclub, on August 9, 1997, after a fight had broken out. Louima later claimed that the arresting officers had become furious when he protested his arrest, twice stopping the patrol car to beat him with their fists. When they arrived at the station house, two officers, apparently angry because some of the clubgoers had fought with the police, led Louima to the men's room, removed his trousers and attacked him with the handle of a toilet plunger, first shoving it into his rectum and then into his mouth, breaking teeth while Louima screamed: "Why are you doing this to me? Why? Why?" The officers also shouted racial slurs at Louima, who was rushed to a hospital for emergency surgery to repair a puncture in his small intestine and injuries to his bladder. Louima, who witnesses said had no bruises or injuries when officers took him into custody, arrived at the hospital three hours later bleeding profusely.

In the aftermath of the case, NYPD investigators granted departmental immunity to nearly one hundred officers in order to gain information. Because the blue curtain of silence was cracked open, a number of police officers were given long prison sentences on charges of sexual abuse and first-degree assault.

The Louima case and other incidents involving the police and the minority community has reignited the long debate over whether police use race as a factor when making decisions such as stopping and questioning a suspect or making an arrest; this practice is referred to as *racial profiling.*

Profiling Remains a Problem

Many experts remain concerned about the police use of profiling and discrimination. After thoroughly reviewing the literature on police bias, Samuel Walker, Cassia Spohn, and Miriam DeLone concluded that police discriminate against racial minorities and that significant problems persist between the police and racial and ethnic communities in the United States. Similarly, in *No Equal Justice: Race and Class in the American Criminal Justice System,* constitutional scholar David Cole argued that, despite efforts to create racial neutrality, a race-based double standard operates in virtually every aspect of criminal justice. These disparities allow the privileged to enjoy constitutional protections from police power without extending these protections across the board to minorities and the poor.

Ronald Weitzer and Steven Tuch used data from a national survey of two thousand people to gauge the prevalence of racial profiling. They found that about 40 percent of African-American respondents believed they were stopped by police because of their race compared with just 5 percent of Caucasians. Almost three-quarters of young African-American men ages eighteen to thirty-four believed they had been a victim of profiling. Interestingly, African Americans who were better educated and wealthier were more likely to report being the victim of profiling than their lower-class, less-educated peers. Weitzer and Tuch speculated that more affluent minority group members have greater mobility and therefore are more likely to encounter police suspicious of them because they are "out of place" as they travel to different neighborhoods. It is also possible that middle-class African Americans drive a better type of car, which may suggest to police officers who use racial profiling that the driver is involved in the drug trade or some other form of criminal activity.

Is the Tide Turning?

Efforts to control racial profiling and discrimination are now ongoing in most major police departments, and there is some evidence that these programs and policies are paying off. For example, a recent national study of police con-

tasks police are required to do are all considered reasons why formal education may not improve performance on the street.[51] Nonetheless, because police administrators value educated officers and citizens find them to be exceptional in the use of good judgment and problem solving, it is likely that the trend toward having a more educated police force will continue.[52]

Minorities in Policing

For the past two decades, U.S. police departments have made a concerted effort to attract minority police officers, and there have been some impressive gains. As

tact with civilians found that most drivers regardless of race who experienced a traffic stop said they felt the officer had a legitimate reason for making the stop. Nearly nine out of ten white drivers and three out of four African-American drivers described the officer as having a legitimate reason for the stop. Both African-American and Caucasian drivers maintained these perceptions regardless of the race of the officer involved. Even though more African Americans than Caucasians felt the stop was illegitimate, the survey found that a clear majority of members of both racial groups believed the police acted in a forthright fashion, that they were not the victims of profiling, and that the race of the police officer had no influence on their performance.

According to legal experts Dan Kahan and Tracey Meares, racial discrimination may be on the decline because minorities now possess sufficient political status to protect them from abuses in the justice system. Community policing efforts may also be helping police officers become more sensitive to issues that concern the public, such as profiling.

Although racial profiling is a significant issue, there is evidence that as a group, minority citizens still value the police and believe they contribute to a community's wellbeing. Ronald Weitzer's (2000) study of three Washington, D.C., neighborhoods found that African Americans valued racially integrated police services and welcomed the presence of both white and African-American police officers; such a finding would seem improbable if they believed that most white officers were racially biased. Similarly, Thomas Priest and Deborah Brown Carter found that the African-American community is generally supportive of the local police, especially when officers respond quickly to calls for service. It is unlikely that African Americans would appreciate rapid responses from racist police. Harvard University law professor Randall Kennedy forcefully argues that it should come as no surprise that the African-American community desires police protection: they are more likely to become crime victims than Caucasians and therefore are the group most likely to benefit from aggressive law enforcement efforts.

Critical Thinking

1. What, if anything, can be done to reduce racial bias on the part of police? Would adding minority officers help? Would it be a form of racism to assign minority officers to minority neighborhoods?

2. Would research showing that police are more likely to make arrests in interracial incidents than in intraracial incidents constitute evidence of racism?

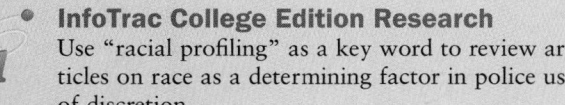

InfoTrac College Edition Research

Use "racial profiling" as a key word to review articles on race as a determining factor in police use of discretion.

Sources: Ronald Weitzer and Steven Tuch, "Perceptions of Racial Profiling: Race, Class and Personal Experience," *Criminology* 40 (2002): 451; Patrick A. Langan, Lawrence A. Greenfeld, Steven K. Smith, Matthew R. Durose, and David J. Levin, *Contacts Between Police and the Public: Findings from the 1999 National Survey* (Washington, D.C.: Bureau of Justice Statistics, 2001); Richard Felson and Jeff Ackerman, "Arrest for Domestic and Other Assaults," *Criminology* 39 (2001): 655–676; Ronald Weitzer, "White, African-American, or Blue Cops? Race and Citizen Assessments of Police Officers," *Journal of Criminal Justice* 28 (2000): 313–324; Sidney L. Harring, "The Diallo Verdict: Another 'Tragic Accident' in New York's War on Street Crime?" *Social Justice* 27 (2000): 9–14; Robert Worden and Robin Shepard, "Demeanor, Crime, and Police Behavior: A Reexamination of the Police Services Study Data," *Criminology* 34 (1996): 83–105; Stephen Mastrofski, Robert Worden, and Jeffrey Snipes, "Law Enforcement in a Time of Community Policing," *Criminology* 33 (1995): 539–563; Thomas Priest and Deborah Brown Carter, "Evaluations of Police Performance in an African-American Sample," *Journal of Criminal Justice* 27 (1999): 457–465; Matt De Lisi and Bob Regoli, "Race, Conventional Crime, and Criminal Justice: The Declining Importance of Skin Color," *Journal of Criminal Justice* 27 (1999): 549–557; David Cole, *No Equal Justice: Race and Class in the American Criminal Justice System* (New York: New Press, 2000); Randall Kennedy, *Race, Crime, and the Law* (New York: Vintage Books, 1998); Dan M. Kahan and Tracey L. Meares, "The Coming Crisis of Criminal Procedure," *Georgetown Law Journal* 86 (1998): 1153–1184; David Kocieniewski, "Man Says Officers Tortured Him After Arrest," *New York Times,* 13 August 1997, 1; Ronald Weitzer, "Racial Discrimination in the Criminal Justice System: Findings and Problems in the Literature," *Journal of Criminal Justice* 24 (1996): 309–322; Samuel Walker, Cassia Spohn, and Miriam DeLone, *The Color of Justice, Race, Ethnicity and Crime in America* (Belmont, Calif.: Wadsworth, 1996), 115; Sandra Lee Browning, Francis Cullen, Liqun Cao, Renee Kopache, and Thomas Stevenson, "Race and Getting Hassled by the Police: A Research Note," *Police Studies* 17 (1994): 1–10.

might be expected, cities with large minority populations are the ones with a higher proportion of minority officers in their police departments.[53]

The reasons behind this effort are varied. Viewed in its most positive light, police departments recruit minority citizens to field a more balanced force that truly represents the communities they serve. African Americans generally have less confidence in the police than whites and are skeptical of their ability to protect them from harm.[54] African Americans also seem to be more adversely affected than whites when well-publicized incidents of police misconduct occur.[55] It comes as no surprise then that public opinion polls and research surveys show that African-American citizens report having less confidence in the police when compared to both Hispanics and Caucasians.[56] African-American juveniles seem particularly suspicious of police, even when they deny having a negative encounter with a police officer.[57]

A heterogeneous police force can be instrumental in gaining the confidence of the minority community by helping dispel the view that police departments are generally bigoted or biased organizations. Furthermore, minority police officers possess special qualities that can serve to improve police performance. For example, Spanish-speaking officers can help with investigations in Hispanic neighborhoods, while Asian officers are essential for undercover or surveillance work with Asian gangs and drug importers.

The earliest known date of when an African American was hired as a police officer was 1861 in Washington, D.C.; Chicago hired its first African-American officer in 1872.[58] By 1890 an estimated two thousand minority police officers were employed in the United States. At first, African-American officers suffered a great deal of discrimination. Their work assignments were restricted, as were their chances for promotion. Minority officers were often assigned solely to the patrol of African-American neighborhoods, and in some cities they were required to call a white officer to make an arrest. White officers held highly prejudicial attitudes, and as late as the 1950s some refused to ride with African Americans in patrol cars.[59]

The experience of African-American police officers has not been an easy one. In his classic 1969 book, *African American in Blue*, Nicholas Alex pointed out that African-American officers of the time suffered from what he called **double marginality**.[60] On the one hand, African-American officers had to deal with the expectation that they would give members of their own race a break. On the other hand, they often experienced overt racism from their police colleagues. Alex found that African-American officers adapted to these pressures in a range of ways, from denying that African-American suspects should be treated differently from whites to treating African-American offenders more harshly than white offenders do in order to prove their lack of bias. Alex offered several reasons why some African-American officers are tougher on African-American offenders: they desire acceptance from their white colleagues; they are particularly sensitive to any disrespect given them by African-American teenagers; and they view themselves as protectors of the African-American community. Ironically, minority citizens may actually be more likely to accuse a minority officer of misconduct than white officers, a circumstance that underscores the difficult position of the minority officer in contemporary society.[61]

However, these issues have become more muted as the number of minority officers has increased. For example, between 1990 and 2000 in larger cities (with populations over 250,000) Hispanic representation among officers increased from 9 percent to 14 percent, and African American representation rose from 18 percent to 20 percent.[62] As Figure 6.2 shows, the ratio of minority police officers to minority population has been increasing over the past decade.

Minority police officers now seem more aggressive and self-assured, less willing to accept any discriminatory practices by the police department.[63] They appear to be experiencing some of the same problems and issues encountered by white officers.[64] For example, minority officers report feeling similar if somewhat higher rates of job-related stress and strain than white officers.[65] However, they may deal with stress in a different fashion. Minority officers are more likely to deal with stress by seeking aid from fellow minority officers, whereas white officers are more likely to try to express their feelings to others, form social bonds, and try to get others to like them better.[66]

African-American and white police officers share similar attitudes toward community policing, although minority officers report being even more favorable to it than white officers.[67] African-American officers may today be far less detached and alienated from the local community than white or Hispanic officers.[68]

double marginality The social burden African-American police officers carry by being both minority group members and law enforcement officers (see Nicholas Alex, *African American in Blue*, 1969).

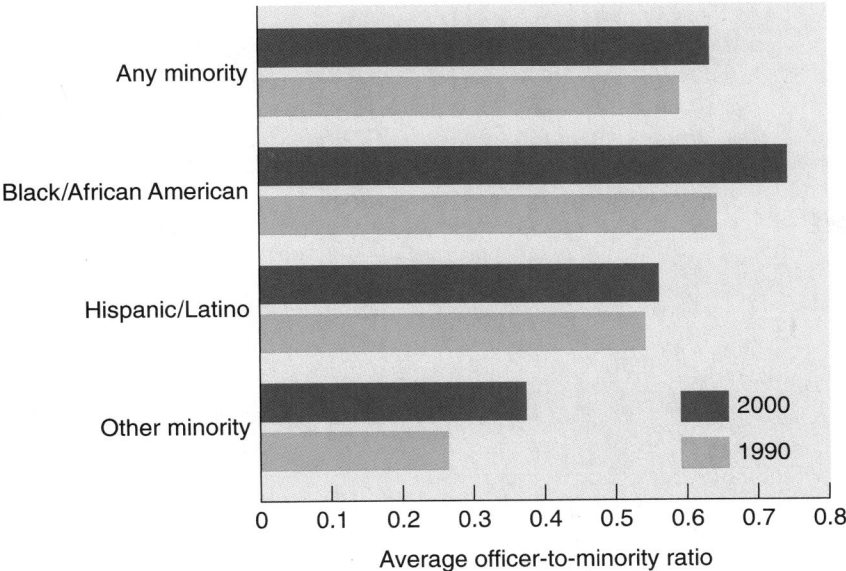

Figure 6.2
Ratio of minority officers to the minority population, 1990–2000

Source: Brian A. Reaves and Matthew J. Hickman, *Police Departments in Large Cities, 1990–2000* (Washington, D.C.: Bureau of Justice Statistics, 2002).

Also helping to overcome the problem of double marginality is the fact that the number of African-American officers in some of the nation's largest cities is now proportionate to minority representation in the population.[69]

When affirmative action was first instituted, white police officers viewed it as a threat to their job security.[70] But as more minorities join U.S. police forces, the situation appears to be changing. Caucasian officers are now more likely to appreciate the contribution of minority officers. For example, when Charles Katz examined the formation of a police gang unit in a midwestern city he found that commanders chose minority officers so that the unit could be representative of the community it served.[71] One Hispanic officer told Katz, "When you talk to Hispanics, you have to know and be familiar with their culture.... You always talk to the man of the house, never presenting your position to the kid or to the mother."[72]

Women in Policing

In 1910 Alice Stebbins Wells became the first woman to hold the title of police officer (in Los Angeles) and to have arrest powers.[73] For more than half a century, female officers endured separate criteria for selection, were given menial tasks, and were denied the opportunity for advancement.[74] Some relief was gained with the passage of the 1964 Civil Rights Act and its subsequent amendments. Courts have consistently supported the addition of women to police forces by striking down entrance requirements that eliminated almost all female candidates but could not be proven to predict job performance, such as height and upper-body strength.[75] Women do not do as well as men on strength tests and are much more likely to fail the entrance physical than male recruits; critics contend that many of these tests do not reflect the actual tasks of police on the job.[76] Nonetheless, the role of women in police work is still restricted by social and administrative barriers that have been difficult to remove. Today, about 16 percent of all sworn officers

About 16 percent of all sworn officers in larger cities (population over 250,000) are women; in all, about 11 percent of sworn officers are female. Despite their increased presence, policewomen still struggle for acceptance in some departments and many report that they do not receive equal credit for their job performance.

in larger cities (with populations over 250,000) are women; in all, about 11 percent of sworn officers are female.[77]

Studies of policewomen indicate that they are still struggling for acceptance, believe that they do not receive equal credit for their job performance, and report that it is common for them to be sexually harassed by their co-workers.[78] One reason for this may be that many male police officers tend to view policing as an overtly masculine profession that is not appropriate for women. For example, officers in the LAPD make an important distinction between two models of officers—"hard chargers" and "station queens." The former display such characteristics as courage and aggressiveness; they are willing to place themselves in danger and handle the most hazardous calls.[79] In contrast, the station queens like to work in the station house doing paperwork or other administrative tasks. Note the term *queen,* which is designed to be a pejorative to indicate that these officers are effeminate.[80]

Female police officers may also be targeted for more disciplinary action by administrators and, if cited, are more likely to receive harsher punishments than male officers—that is, a greater percentage receive punishments more severe than a reprimand.[81] Considering the sometimes hostile reception they get from male colleagues and supervisors, it may not come as a surprise that female officers report significantly higher levels of job-related stress than male officers.[82]

Job Performance   Gender bias is certainly not supported by existing research, which indicates that female officers are highly successful police officers.[83] In an important study of recruits in the Metropolitan Police Department of Washington, D.C., policewomen were found to have extremely satisfactory work performances.[84] Compared with male officers, women were found to respond to similar types of calls, and the arrests they made were just as likely to result in conviction. Women were more likely than their male colleagues to receive support from the community and less likely to be charged with improper conduct. Because female officers seem to have the ability to avoid violent encounters with citizens and to

Do male and female police officers differ in their reactions to domestic violence situations? To find out, go to InfoTrac College Edition and read "Police Officers' Judgments of Blame in Family Violence: The Impact of Gender and Alcohol," by Anna Stewart and Kelly Maddren, in *Sex Roles: A Journal of Research,* December 1997 v37 i11–12 p921(13).

deescalate potentially violent arrest situations they are typically the target of fewer citizen complaints.[85]

Gender Conflicts   Despite the overwhelming evidence supporting their performance, policewomen still face many problems.[86] Surveys of male officers show that only one-third actually accept a woman on patrol and that more than half do not think that women can handle the physical requirements of the job as well as men can.[87] This form of bias is not unique to the United States. Research shows that policewomen working in northern England report being excluded from full membership in the force based on gender inequality. Though policewomen in England are enthusiastic for crime-related work, their aspirations are frequently frustrated in favor of male officers.[88]

Women working in this male-dominated culture can experience stress and anxiety.[89] Furthermore, significantly more female than male officers report being the victim of discrimination on the job. The male officers who claim to have experienced gender-based discrimination suggest that it comes at the hands of policewomen who use their "sexuality" for job-related benefits.[90]

Female officers are frequently caught in the classic catch-22 dilemma: if they are physically weak, male partners view them as a risk in street confrontations; if they are actually more powerful and aggressive than their male partners, they are regarded as an affront to the male officer's manhood.

Minority Women   African-American women, who account for less than 5 percent of police officers, occupy a unique status. In a study of African-American policewomen serving in five large municipal departments, Susan Martin found that they do in fact perceive significantly more racial discrimination than both other female officers and African-American male officers.[91] However, white policewomen were significantly more likely to perceive sexual discrimination than African-American policewomen were.

Martin found that African-American policewomen often incur the hostility of both white women and African-American men, who feel threatened that they will take their place. On patrol, African-American policewomen are treated differently than are white policewomen by male officers. Neither group of women are viewed as equals: white policewomen are more likely to be seen as protected and coddled, whereas African-American policewomen are more likely to be viewed as passive, lazy, and unequal. In the station house, male officers show little respect for African-American women, who face "widespread racial stereotypes as well as outright racial harassment."[92] African-American women also report having difficult relationships with African-American male officers; their relationships are strained by tensions and dilemmas "associated with sexuality and competition for desirable assignments and promotions."[93] Surprisingly, there was little unity among the female officers. Martin concludes: "Despite changes in the past two decades, the idealized image of the representative of the forces of 'law and order' and protector who maintains 'the thin blue line' between 'them' and 'us' remains white and male."[94]

Nevertheless, the future of women in policing grows brighter every year.[95] Female officers want to remain in policing because it pays a good salary, offers job security, and is a challenging and exciting occupation.[96] These factors should continue to bring women to policing for years to come.

Legal Control of Policing

An important issue surrounding police work is the practice of the judicial system to scrutinize police conduct and issue rulings that define how police officers may act when they conduct investigations, arrest suspects, and interrogate those in police custody. Court control over police conduct is sometimes vexing to police administrators. The police are charged with protecting the public and upholding the law. They want a free hand to enforce the law as they see fit, unencumbered by outside interference. The courts are charged with protecting the civil liberties of all citizens, even those accused of committing heinous crimes. The courts must balance the needs of efficient law enforcement with the constitutional rights of citizens.

In recent years, a more conservative U.S. Supreme Court has given police officers greater leeway to interrogate suspects, stop cars, detain drivers and their passengers, and search vehicles—often with the intent of finding illegal drugs or other contraband. However, although the balance may have tipped, the courts have by no means revoked the basic rights of American citizens to be protected from overzealous police work. Yet the question remains: Should personal rights have supremacy over public safety? Should guilty people be freed because the police made an error while carrying out their stated duties? Should a criminal be set free because the police officer failed to "read him his rights" or conducted a search that went beyond what is allowed by the law? This section addresses these questions by reviewing the relationship between the police and the courts and discussing in some depth the legal cases that define the scope of police conduct—that is, what police can do and what they are prevented from doing.

The Police and the Courts

The police are charged with preventing crime and, failing to do so, investigating the case, gathering evidence, identifying the culprit, and making an arrest, all the while gathering sufficient evidence to convict the culprit at trial. To carry out these tasks, police officers need to be able to search for evidence, to seize items such as guns and drugs, and to question suspects, witnesses, and victims, because at trial, they need to provide prosecutors with sufficient evidence to prove guilt "beyond a reasonable doubt." This requirement means that soon after a crime is committed, they must make every effort to gather physical evidence, obtain confessions, and take witness statements that will stand up in court. Police officers also realize that evidence such as the testimony of a witness or a co-conspirator may evaporate before the trial begins. Then the case outcome may depend on some piece of physical evidence or a suspect's statement taken early during the investigation.

The need for police officers to gather evidence can conflict with the constitutional rights of citizens. For example, although police might prefer a free hand to search homes and cars for evidence, the Fourth Amendment restricts police activities by limiting searches and seizures only to those deemed "reasonable." When police wish to vigorously interrogate a suspect, they must honor the Fifth Amendment's prohibition against forcing people to incriminate themselves. The following sections address some of the key areas in which police operations have been restricted or curtailed by the courts.

Custodial Interrogation

After an arrest is made, police want to interrogate suspects, hoping they will confess to a crime, name co-conspirators, or make incriminating statements that can be used against them in court. But the Fifth Amendment guarantees people the right to be free from self-incrimination. The courts have used this phrase to prohibit law enforcement agents from using physical or psychological coercion while interrogating suspects under their control to get them to confess or give information. Confessions obtained from defendants through coercion, force, trickery, or promises of leniency are inadmissible because their trustworthiness is questionable.

The Miranda Rule In 1966, in the case of *Miranda v. Arizona,* the Supreme Court created objective standards for questioning by police after a defendant has been taken into custody.[97] Custody occurs when a person is not free to walk away,

© 2002 AP/Wide World Photos

In their daily routines, police officers face many situations in which they may want to interrogate suspects. Here, Nathaniel Negron-Gonzalez, twenty-two, center, one of two murder suspects who escaped in broad daylight from the Lebanon County Prison, is escorted from an apartment where he was recaptured July 21, 2002, one day later, in Lebanon, Pennsylvania. Negron-Gonzalez and Jose Rivera-Encanasion, the second escapee, were charged with killing a Lebanon man by setting him on fire. The victim, Anthony Mingledough, forty-nine, died of complications 103 days later. After they are taken into custody, suspects must be given the Miranda warning before they may be questioned.

as when an individual is arrested. The Court maintained that before the police can question a person who has been arrested or is in custody, they must inform the individual of the Fifth Amendment right to be free from self-incrimination. This is accomplished by the police issuing what is known as the **Miranda warning,** which informs the suspect that

- He has the right to remain silent.
- If he makes a statement, it can be used against him in court.
- He has the right to consult an attorney and to have the attorney present at the time of the interrogation.
- If he cannot afford an attorney, one will be appointed by the state.

If the defendant is not given the Miranda warning before the investigation, the evidence obtained from the interrogation cannot be admitted at trial. An accused person can waive his or her Miranda rights at any time. However, for the waiver to be effective, the state must first show that the defendant was aware of all the Miranda rights and must then prove that the waiver was made with the full knowledge of constitutional rights. People who cannot understand the Miranda warning because of their age, mental handicaps, or language problems, cannot be legally questioned absent an attorney; if they can understand their rights, they may be questioned.[98]

Miranda warning The result of two U.S. Supreme Court decisions (*Escobedo v. Illinois* and *Miranda v. Arizona*) that require police officers to inform individuals under arrest that they have a constitutional right to remain silent, that their statements can later be used against them in court, that they can have an attorney present to help them, and that the state will pay for an attorney if they cannot afford to hire one. Although aimed at protecting an individual during in-custody interrogation, the warning must also be given when the investigation shifts from the investigatory to the accusatory stage—that is, when suspicion begins to focus on an individual.

Once the suspect asks for an attorney, all questioning must stop unless the attorney is present. And if the criminal suspect has invoked his or her Miranda rights, police officials cannot reinitiate interrogation in the absence of counsel even if the accused has consulted with an attorney in the meantime.[99]

The Miranda Rule Today The Supreme Court has used case law to define the boundaries of the Miranda warning since its inception. Although statements made by suspects who were not given the Miranda warning or received it improperly cannot be used against them in a court of law it is possible to use illegally gained statements and the evidence they produce in some well-defined instances:

1. Evidence obtained in violation of the Miranda warning can be used by the government to impeach defendants' testimony during trial, if they perjure themselves.[100]
2. At trial, the testimony of a witness is permissible even though his or her identity was revealed by the defendant in violation of the Miranda rule.[101]
3. It is permissable to use information provided by a suspect who has not been given the Miranda warning that leads to the seizure of incriminating evidence if the evidence would have been obtained anyway by other means or sources; this is now referred to as the **inevitable discovery rule.**[102]
4. Initial errors by police in getting statements do not make subsequent statements inadmissible; a subsequent Miranda warning that is properly given can "cure the condition" that made the initial statements inadmissible.[103]
5. The admissions of mentally impaired defendants can be admitted in evidence as long as the police acted properly and there is a "preponderance of the evidence" that they understood the meaning of Miranda.[104]
6. The erroneous admission of a coerced confession at trial can be ruled a "harmless error" and therefore not automatically result in overturning a conviction.[105]

The Supreme Court has also ruled that in some instances the Miranda warning may not have to be given before a suspect is questioned and it has also narrowed the scope of Miranda, for example by restricting the people with whom a suspect may ask to consult:

1. The Miranda warning applies only to the right to have an attorney present; the suspect cannot demand to speak to a priest, probation officer, or any other official.[106]
2. A suspect can be questioned in the field without a Miranda warning if the information the police seek is needed to protect public safety; for example, in an emergency, suspects can be asked where they hid their weapons.[107] This is known as the **public safety doctrine.**
3. Suspects need not be aware of all the possible outcomes of waiving their rights for the Miranda warning to be considered properly given.[108]
4. An attorney's request to see the defendant does not affect the validity of the defendant's waiver of the right to counsel; police misinformation to an attorney does not affect waiver of Miranda rights.[109] For example, a suspect's statements may be used if they are given voluntarily even though the suspect's family has hired an attorney and the statements were made before the attorney arrived. Only the suspect can request an attorney, not friends or family.
5. A suspect who makes an ambiguous reference to an attorney during questioning, such as "Maybe I should talk to an attorney," is not protected under Miranda; the police may continue their questioning.[110]

Debate about the Miranda warnings has been ongoing since the *Miranda* case was decided over three decades ago. Although it appears that recent case law has narrowed the scope of *Miranda* and given police greater leeway in their actions, in the critical case of *Dickerson v. United States,* the Supreme Court made it clear that

inevitable discovery rule Evidence seized in violation of the Fifth Amendment's self-incrimination clause may be used in a court of law if a judge rules that it would have been found or discovered even if the incriminating statements had never been made.

public safety doctrine Statements elicited by police violation of the Fifth Amendment's self-incrimination clause may be used in a court of law if a judge rules that the questioning was justified in order to maintain public safety. So, for example, it would be permissible for police to ask a suspected terrorist where he planted a bomb and then use his statement in a criminal trial even though he had never been apprised of his Fifth Amendment (Miranda) rights.

the Miranda ruling is here to stay and has become enmeshed in the prevailing legal system.[111] It is not surprising that today police administrators who in the past might have been wary of the restrictions forced by Miranda now actually favor its use.[112] One survey found that nearly 60 percent of police chiefs believe that the Miranda warning should be retained and the same number report that abolishing it would change the way the police function.[113]

With the war on terrorism ongoing, law enforcement officers may find themselves in unique situations involving national security and forced to make an immediate decision as to whether the Miranda rule applies. For example, the following Law in Review case looks at whether Miranda applies to noncitizens arrested outside the United States.

The Library of Congress contains more than 121 million items, some of them designated "treasures." One of the treasures is Chief Justice Earl Warren's handwritten notes on the *Miranda* case. You can view them at www.loc.gov/exhibits/treasures/trr038.html

Search and Seizure

When conducting investigations, police officers want to collect evidence, seize it, and carry it away. For example, they may wish to enter a suspect's home, look for evidence of a crime such as bloody clothes, drugs, the missing money, or a weapon, seize the evidence, and store it in the evidence room so it can later be used at trial.

But the manner in which police may seize evidence is governed by the search-and-seizure requirements of the Fourth Amendment of the U.S. Constitution, which was designed by the framers to protect a criminal suspect against unreasonable searches and seizures. Under normal circumstances, no search or seizure undertaken without a **search warrant** is lawful.

A search warrant is a court order authorizing and directing the police to search a designated place for evidence of a crime. To obtain a search warrant, the following procedural requirements must be met: (1) the police officer must request the warrant from the court; (2) the officer must submit an affidavit establishing the proper grounds for the warrant; and (3) the affidavit must state the place to be searched and the property to be seized. A warrant cannot be issued unless the presiding magistrate is presented with sufficient evidence to conclude that an offense has been or is being committed and the suspect is the one who committed the offense; this is referred to as the **probable cause** requirement. In other words, the presiding judge must conclude from the facts presented by the police that there is probable cause a crime has been committed and the person or place to be searched

search warrant An order issued by a judge, directing officers to conduct a search of specified premises for specified objects or persons and bring them before the court.

probable cause The evidentiary criterion necessary to sustain an arrest or the issuance of an arrest or search warrant; less than absolute certainty or "beyond a reasonable doubt" but greater than mere suspicion or "hunch." Probable cause consists of a set of facts, information, circumstances, or conditions that would lead a reasonable person to believe that an offense was committed and that the accused committed that offense. An arrest made without probable cause may be susceptible to prosecution as an illegal arrest under "false imprisonment" statutes.

© 2002 AP/Wide World Photos

Police execute a search warrant in Miami, Florida. The Fourth Amendment requires that a search warrant be particular, specifying the place to be searched and the reasons for the search.

Law in Review

United States v. Bin Laden

The war against terrorism presents many challenges for law enforcement agencies, especially when they are working under extreme circumstances abroad. The case of *United States v. Bin Laden,* decided in a federal appeals court, is an example of this problem.

Facts

Bin Laden involved the prosecution of several members of the al Qaeda network who were thought to be responsible for the terrorist attacks on American embassies in Kenya and Tanzania on August 7, 1998. Following the bombing, a team of FBI agents and other American law enforcement officers were assigned to Nairobi, Kenya, to investigate the crime. On August 12, 1998, FBI agents received a tip that led them to Mohamed Rashed Daoud al-'Owhali. The Kenyan National Police, who had accompanied the FBI agents, arrested al-'Owhali without a warrant because he did not have identification papers. Under Kenyan law, the absence of identification papers is a valid basis for arrest.

Al-'Owhali was administered the following Miranda warning by FBI agents, which had been modified from the standard Miranda warning because the interrogation was taking place in Kenya and in accordance with Kenyan law:

We are representatives of the United States government. Under our laws, you have certain rights. Before we ask you any questions, we want to be sure that you understand those rights.

You do not have to speak to us or answer any questions. Even if you have already spoken to the Kenyan authorities, you do not have to speak to us now.

If you do speak with us, anything that you say may be used against you in a court in the United States or elsewhere.

In the United States, you would have the right to talk to a lawyer to get advice before we ask you any questions and you could have a lawyer with you during

questioning. In the United States, if you could not afford a lawyer, one would be appointed for you, if you wish, before any questioning.

Because we are not in the United States, we cannot ensure that you will have a lawyer appointed for you before any questioning.

If you decide to speak with us now, without a lawyer present, you will still have the right to stop answering questions at any time.

You should also understand that if you decide not to speak with us, that fact cannot be used as evidence against you in a court in the United States.

I have read this statement of my rights and I understand what my rights are. I am willing to make a statement and answer questions. I do not want a lawyer at this time. I understand and know what I am doing. No promises or threats have been made to me and no pressure or coercion of any kind has been used against me.

After indicating that he understood these rights, al-'Owhali agreed to speak to the investigators and continually denied his involvement in the bombing. On August 21, however, FBI agents confronted al-'Owhali with all the evidence they had collected linking him to the Kenyan bombing. Acknowledging that the agents "knew everything," al-'Owhali stated that he would tell the truth about his role in the bombing if he could be tried in the United States rather than in Kenya. At that moment, an assistant United States attorney, who was assisting the FBI in its questioning of al-'Owhali, administered from memory the standard domestic Miranda warning—without making reference to the modified Kenyan version of the warnings that had been administered to him previously. al-'Owhali proceeded to implicate himself in the Kenyan bombing in detail.

After being brought to the United States for trial, al-'Owhali moved to suppress all the statements he had made to the American investigators in Kenya on the ground that the modified Miranda warning that had been administered

is materially involved in that crime; there must be solid evidence of criminal involvement. Similarly, the courts have ruled that police officers may not enter a person's home without a warrant unless emergency or exigent circumstances are present. In *Kirk v. Louisiana* (2002), police officers acting on an anonymous tip observed a suspect engaging in what they considered to be drug deals. Without a warrant, they entered his home, arrested him, frisked him, found a drug vial in his underwear, and observed contraband in plain view in the apartment. Only after these actions did the officers obtain a warrant. The Supreme Court ruled against the police officers in this case. It held that police officers need either a warrant or probable cause plus exigent circumstances in order to make a lawful entry into a home. Although the Court left unclear the factors that define "exigent circumstances," the facts of the *Kirk* case indicate that merely observing a suspect com-to him when he was first taken into Kenyan custody were deficient under American law. He argued that the modified warning advised him of the limited right to counsel in light of the uncertainties of Kenyan law rather than the explicit American right to counsel as required by the Miranda decision. The government responded that, as a non-American whose only connection to America was hostile, al-'Owhali was not protected by the Fifth Amendment's privilege against self-incrimination, and thus, he was not entitled to Miranda warnings in the first place. As a result, the government contended that the failure to give correct Miranda warnings could not be a basis for suppression. The government argued alternatively that even if the court were to rule that the Fifth Amendment attached to al-'Owhali, the modified warning that he received was sufficient to satisfy Miranda under the circumstances.

Decision

The *Bin Laden* court disagreed with the government on both points. First, the court held that the Fifth Amendment's privilege against self-incrimination did in fact apply to al-'Owhali. Second, the court held that Miranda's requirements must be satisfied in overseas interrogations just as they must be satisfied in domestic interrogations. According to the decision, a suspect must be told the following: he has the right to remain silent and anything that he does say may be used against him in a court of law; if he were in the United States, he would have an absolute right to counsel before and during any questioning; because he is not in the United States his right to an attorney depends on foreign law, but the United States government will do its best to help him obtain retained or appointed counsel, if the suspect desires, by making that request of the host country; and if the foreign authorities will not provide him with a lawyer, he does not have to speak with United States authorities, and if he does choose to speak, he may stop at any time. The *Bin Laden* court also required FBI agents abroad to make "a detailed inquiry into a specific nation's law" regarding what Miranda-type rights are available to the suspect, and to speak to local authorities

to determine whether they will allow the suspect to consult with an attorney. Because the modified Miranda warnings did not accomplish all of these things, the court suppressed the statements made by al-'Owhali following these warnings. The court further ruled that the statements made by al-'Owhali after the assistant United States attorney later recited the full domestic warnings to him could be admitted into evidence, because these warnings cured the deficiencies in the previously administered modified version of the Miranda warnings.

According to legal scholar Mark A. Godsey, the *Bin Laden* court was correct in holding that the privilege against self-incrimination protects non-Americans interrogated abroad but tried in the United States. The court's analysis of the warnings required pursuant to *Miranda* was flawed, however. In creating the way the warnings were required in the international context, the court did not analyze the competing interests and established a rule that is unworkable in an international context. It remains to be seen whether the *Bin Laden* decision will be considered by the United States Supreme Court. But as it stands it shows how the rule of law enjoyed by American citizens is also available to noncitizens, event those bent on terrorism and destruction.

Critical Thinking

Do you believe that suspected terrorists apprehended abroad should receive the same civil rights as American citizens involved in the legal process at home? Does it matter that they will be tried in American courts?

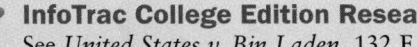
InfoTrac College Edition Research

See *United States v. Bin Laden,* 132 F. Supp. 2d 168, 181 (S.D.N.Y. 2001); also see Mark A. Godsey, "*Miranda*'s Final Frontier, the International Arena: A Critical Analysis of *United States v. Bin Laden,* and a Proposal for a New *Miranda* Exception Abroad," *Duke Law Journal* 51 (2002): 1703–1782.

mitting what appears to be a nonviolent crime is not enough to justify a warrantless entry of a person's home.[114]

Searches must also be reasonable under the circumstances of the crime. For example, police would not be able to get a warrant to search a suspect's desk drawer for a missing piano! Nor could a police officer obtain a warrant that allows them to tear down the walls of a person's house because it is suspected that they contain drugs. A search is considered unreasonable when it exceeds the scope of police authority or is highly invasive of personal privacy, even if it reveals incriminating evidence.

The Fourth Amendment also requires that a search warrant be particular, specifying the place to be searched and the reasons for the search. The courts frown on issuing generalized or open-ended warrants that allow police to search every aspect of a person's private possessions unless there is overwhelming evidence of criminal involvement.

Use of Informers In order to obtain a warrant, police must present specific and verified knowledge of the suspect's criminal involvement. How can they possibly know that a suspect keeps drugs in the downstairs closet, or has a garage filled with stolen merchandise? In many instances, the information comes from an informer, who provides detailed information on another person's criminal activities. The informer may have been caught red-handed committing a crime and, wishing to get the charges dismissed or reduced, is willing to cooperate with the police. For many years, the Supreme Court ruled that in order to use such *hearsay evidence* to get a warrant, the police were required to prove that the informer had (1) firsthand knowledge of the crime and (2) was a reliable and trustworthy source of information. In 1983 the Supreme Court made it easier to use informers when, in the case of *Illinois v. Gates* (1983), it established what is known as the "totality of the circumstances" test.[115] In this case, the police were sent an anonymous letter detailing the drug trafficking of Lance and Sue Gates. They began an investigation into the couple's activities and used the information to obtain a search warrant. The Gateses were arrested and the evidence seized with the warrant was used during their trial. The couple then appealed their conviction, arguing that because the police relied on an anonymous tip, there was no way of proving that the informer was "reliable." However, the Supreme Court allowed the search because the letter, even though it was unverifiable, indicated that the informer did have detailed knowledge of the drug activity, and the police backed up the information with surveillance and other hard evidence. In its ruling, the Court held that a warrant can be legally issued when the presiding judge, considering the totality of the circumstances of the case, believes that the evidence is sufficient to show probable cause to justify the issuance of a search warrant. Loosely interpreted, if judges are presented with sufficient, knowledgeable evidence for issuing a warrant, they may do so even if the source of the information is anonymous or unknown. The *Gates* doctrine makes it significantly easier for police to obtain valid search warrants.

Warrantless Searches To make it easier for police to conduct investigations and to protect public safety, the Court has ruled that under certain circumstances a valid search may be conducted without a search warrant. The six major exceptions are search incident to a valid arrest, threshold inquiry (**stop and frisk**), automobile search, consent search, plain-sight search, and seizure of nonphysical evidence.

stop and frisk The situation when police officers who are suspicious of an individual run their hands lightly over the suspect's outer garments, to determine whether the person is carrying a concealed weapon. Also called a patdown or threshold inquiry, a stop and frisk is intended to stop short of any activity that could be considered a violation of Fourth Amendment rights.

1. *Search incident to a valid arrest.* A warrantless search is valid if it is made incident to a lawful arrest. The reason for this exception is that the arresting officer must have the power to disarm the accused, protect himself or herself, preserve the evidence of the crime, and prevent the accused from escaping from custody. Because the search is lawful, the officer retains what he or she finds if it is connected with a crime. The officer is permitted to search only the defendant's person and the areas in the defendant's immediate physical surroundings that are under his or her control.[116]

2. *Threshold inquiry (stop and frisk).* Threshold inquiry deals with the situation where although the officer does not have probable cause to arrest, his or her suspicions are raised concerning the behavior of an individual. For example, the individual is found lurking behind a closed store. In such a case, the officer has a right to stop and question the individual, and if the officer has reason to believe that the person is carrying a concealed weapon, may frisk the subject—that is, pat-down the person's outer clothing for the purpose of finding a concealed weapon. If an illegal weapon is found, then an arrest can be

made and a search incident to the arrest performed.[117] Would it be legal to pat down a person merely because that person is standing in a high-crime neighborhood? Probably not. The High Court suggests that an officer would need more suspicion—for example, if the person ran away when he spotted the police approaching.[118]

3. *Automobile search.* An automobile may be searched without a warrant if there is probable cause to believe that the car was involved in a crime.[119] Because automobiles are inherently mobile there is a significant chance that the evidence will be lost if the search is not conducted immediately; also, people should not expect as much privacy in their cars as in their homes.[120] Police officers who have legitimately stopped an automobile and who have probable cause to believe that contraband is concealed somewhere inside it may conduct a warrantless search of the vehicle that is as thorough as a magistrate could authorize by warrant. The Supreme Court has also ruled that police who have stopped a motorist for a routine traffic violation can conduct a search if they find probable cause that the vehicle has been involved in a crime—for example, after stopping a car for an illegal U-turn, they spot drug paraphernalia in the front seat.[121]

 Because traffic stops can be dangerous, the Court has ruled that if a police officer perceives danger during routine a routine traffic stop he can order drivers and passengers from the car without suspicion and conduct a limited search of their persons to ensure police officer safety.[122] However, sometimes people believe that the police use the pretext of a traffic violation in order to gain access to their vehicles. For example, police officers may believe that the driver is acting in a suspicious fashion and may be a drug trafficker. They stop the car for a minor motor vehicle violation and search the driver and the interior. The legality of these so-called pretext stops was challenged in *Whren v. United States* (1996). Two African-American defendants claimed that plainclothes police officers used traffic violations as an exercise to stop their vehicle because the officers lacked objective evidence that they were drug couriers. The Court said, however, that if probable cause exists to stop a person for a traffic violation, the motivation of the officers is irrelevant. However, in *Knowles v. Iowa* (1998), the Court ruled that it is a Fourth Amendment violation if a police officer stops a defendant for speeding and then searches the car from top to bottom without probable cause or consent. The search is not justified on either of the two bases relied on by the Court in past decisions— the protection of the officer or the need to discover or preserve evidence. So, police officers can search car and passengers after a traffic stop as long as the search is reasonable and related to officer safety.[123]

4. *Consent search.* In a consent search, individuals waive their constitutional rights; therefore, neither a warrant nor probable cause need exist. For example, a police officer stops a car because the driver has an outstanding traffic ticket that has never been paid. He asks if he can search the trunk and the driver gives consent. Any illegal contraband found in the trunk can be seized. However, for the search to be legal, the consent must be given voluntarily; threat or compulsion invalidates the search.[124] Although it has been held that voluntary consent is required, it has also been maintained that the police are under no obligation to inform individuals of their right to refuse the search. For example, police do not have to tell motorists they have stopped for a traffic violation that they are actually free to go before asking permission to search the car.[125]

5. *Plain-sight search.* Even when an object is in a house or other areas involving an expectation of privacy, the object can be freely inspected if it can be seen by the general public. For example, if a police officer looks through a fence and sees marijuana growing in a suspect's fields, no search warrant is needed

for the property to be seized. The articles are considered to be in plain view, and therefore a search warrant need not be obtained to seize.[126]

6. *Seizure of nonphysical evidence.* Police can seize nonphysical evidence, such as a conversation, if the suspects had no reason to expect privacy—for example, it would be legal for a police officer who overhears a conversation in which two people conspire to kill a third party to record the conversation and use the recording in a court of law. In *Katz v. United States,* the Supreme Court addressed the issue that the Fourth Amendment protects people and not property.[127] In *Katz,* the FBI attached an electronic recording device to a public telephone booth for the purpose of obtaining evidence that the defendant was transmitting wagering information in violation of a federal statute. The Court held that the FBI's action constituted an unreasonable search and seizure because it was reasonable for the defendant to expect that he would have privacy in a phone booth.

Exhibit 6.2 summarizes the notable Fourth and Fifth Amendment case doctrines and holdings.

The Exclusionary Rule

The most controversial issue revolving around the Court's control of police behavior is what is commonly known as the **exclusionary rule,** which provides that all evidence obtained by unreasonable searches and seizures is inadmissible in criminal trials. Similarly, it excludes the use of illegal confessions under Fifth Amendment prohibitions.

After police agencies were created in the mid-nineteenth century, evidence obtained by unreasonable searches and seizures was admitted by state and federal governments in criminal trials. The only criteria for admissibility were whether the evidence was incriminating and whether it would assist the judge or jury in reaching a verdict. Then, in 1914, the U.S. Supreme Court established the exclusionary rule in the case of *Weeks v. United States,* when it ruled that evidence obtained by unreasonable search and seizure must be excluded in a federal criminal trial.[128]

In 1961 the Supreme Court made the exclusionary rule applicable to state courts in the landmark decision of *Mapp v. Ohio.*[129]

Current Status and Controversy   The U.S. Supreme Court, with its conservative bent of recent years, has been diminishing the scope of the exclusionary rule. In a critical case, *United States v. Leon* (1984), the Court ruled that evidence seized by police relying on a warrant issued by a detached and neutral magistrate can be used in a court proceeding even if the judge who issued the warrant relied on less than sufficient evidence or made a mistake in issuing the warrant.[130] In this case, the Court articulated a **good faith exception** to the exclusionary rule: evidence obtained with less than an adequate search warrant may be admissible in court if the police officers acted in good faith by obtaining court approval for their search and there was no police misconduct. However, deliberately misleading a judge or using a warrant that the police know is deficient would be grounds to invoke the exclusionary rule.

Police administrators have long decried the exclusionary rule because it means that valuable evidence may not be usable at trial because the police made an error or failed to obtain a proper warrant. The most widely voiced criticism of the exclusionary rule, however, is that it allows guilty defendants to go free. Because courts frequently decide in many types of cases (particularly those involving victimless offenses, such as gambling and drug use) that certain evidence should be excluded, the rule is believed to result in excessive court delays and to affect plea-bargaining negotiations negatively. In fact, however, the rule appears to result in

---

exclusionary rule   The principle that prohibits using evidence illegally obtained in a trial. Based on the Fourth Amendment "right of the people to be secure in their persons, houses, papers, and effects, against unreasonable searches and seizures," the rule is not a bar to prosecution because legally obtained evidence may be available that may be used in a trial.

To learn more about the exclusionary rule, use the term as a subject guide on InfoTrac College Edition.

good faith exception   The principle of law holding that evidence may be used in a criminal trial, even though the search warrant used to obtain it is technically faulty, if the police acted in good faith and to the best of their ability when they sought to obtain it from a judge.

Exhibit 6.2	Notable case doctrines and exceptions to the Fourth Amendment (search and seizure) and Fifth Amendment (self-incrimination) clauses	

	Case Decision	Holding
Fourth Amendment Doctrine		
Expectation of privacy	*Katz v. United States* (1968)	Electronic eavesdropping is a search.
Plain view	*Arizona v. Hicks* (1967)	Fourth Amendment may not apply when the object is in plain view.
Open fields	*Oliver v. United States* (1984)	To what extent can police search a field and curtilage?
Stop and frisk	*Terry v. Ohio* (1967)	Police are authorized to stop and frisk suspicious persons.
Consent	*Schneckloth v. Bustamonte* (1973)	Consent to search must be voluntarily given.
Bus sweep	*Florida v. Bostick* (1991)	Police, after obtaining consent, may conduct a search of luggage without a search warrant or probable cause.
Warrant Requirements		
Probable cause	*Illinois v. Gates* (1983)	Probable cause to issue a warrant is based on a "totality of circumstances."
Home entry	*Kirk v. Louisiana* (2002)	Police need a warrant to enter a home absent probable cause and exigent circumstances.
Exceptions to the Warrant Requirement		
Federal requirement of exclusionary rule	*Weeks v. United States* (1914)	U.S. Supreme Court applied the exclusionary rule to federal prosecutions.
State application	*Mapp v. Ohio* (1961)	U.S. Supreme Court applied the exclusionary rule to state prosecutions.
Automobile search	*United States v. Ross* (1982)	Warrantless search of an auto is permissible when it is based on probable cause.
Search incident to arrest	*Chimel v. California* (1969)	Permissible scope for a search is the area "within the arrestee's immediate control."
Traffic stop	*Whren v. United States* (1996)	Traffic violation can be used as a pretext to stop suspicious vehicles.
Exceptions to the Exclusionary Rule		
Good faith	*United States v. Leon* (1984)	When police rely on "good faith" in a warrant, the evidence seized is admissible even if the warrant is subsequently deemed defective.
Good faith	*Arizona v. Evans* (1995)	Even though police arrested a man based on an erroneous warrant that resulted from a court employee's computer error, the evidence they found in a subsequent search is admissible.
Fifth Amendment Doctrine		
Self-incrimination	*Miranda v. Arizona* (1966)	Defendant must be given the *Miranda* warning before questioning begins.
Miranda warning	*Dickerson v. United States* (2000)	Congress cannot overrule the requirements that *Miranda* rights be read to criminal suspects.

relatively few case dismissals. Research efforts show that prosecutions are lost because of suppression rulings less than 1 percent of the time.[131]

Suggested approaches to dealing with violations of the exclusionary rule include (1) criminal prosecution of police officers who violate constitutional rights, (2) internal police control, (3) civil lawsuits against state or municipal

contingent exclusionary rule   A plan that would allow evidence seized in violation of the Fourth Amendment to be used in a court of law. It would apply when a judge finds police testimony questionable, but also concludes that the release of the guilty would be unpleasant and unwarranted. Rather than simply excluding the evidence, the judge could request that the prosecution or police pay a fee, similar to a fine, in order to use the evidence in court. Exclusion of the evidence would be contingent on the failure to pay the damages set by the court.

To learn more about the exclusionary rule, go to
http://caselaw.lp.findlaw.com/data/constitution/amendment04/06.html

police officers, and (4) federal lawsuits against the government under the Federal Tort Claims Act (FTCA). Law professor Donald Dripps has derived a novel approach for modifying the exclusionary rule. His approach, which he labels the **contingent exclusionary rule,** would apply when a judge finds police testimony questionable but also concludes that the release of the guilty would be unpleasant and unwarranted. Rather than simply excluding the evidence, the judge could request that the prosecution or police pay a fee, similar in form to a fine, in order to use the evidence in court. Exclusion of the evidence would be contingent on the failure of the police department to pay the damages set by the court. The judge thereby could uphold the Constitution without freeing the guilty. The contingent exclusionary rule would force the prosecution to decide whether justice was worth the damages.[132]

Problems of Policing

Law enforcement is not an easy job. The role ambiguity, social isolation, and threat of danger present in "working the street" are the police officer's constant companions. What effects do these strains have on police? This section discusses three of the most significant problems: job stress, violence, and corruption.

Job Stress

The complexity of their role, the need to exercise prudent discretion, the threat of using violence and having violence used against them, and isolation from the rest of society all take a toll on law enforcement officers. It is not surprising, then, that police officers experience tremendous stress, a factor that leads to alcoholism, depression, and even suicide. There is evidence that police officers are all too often involved in marital disputes and even incidents of domestic violence that may be linked to stress.[133] Stress may not be constant, but at some time during their career (usually the middle years) most officers will feel the effects of stress.[134]

Causes of Stress   A number of factors have been associated with job stress.[135] The pressure of being on duty twenty-four hours a day leads to stress and emotional detachment from both work and public needs. Policing is a dangerous profession and officers are at risk for many forms of job-related accidental deaths. (See Table 6.1.)

Stress has been related to internal conflict with administrative policies that deny officers support and a meaningful role in decision making. For example, of-

Table 6.1   Circumstances of accidental deaths, 1996–2000

Circumstances	Total	1996	1997	1998	1999	2000
Total	344	51	63	81	65	84
Automobile accidents	197	33	33	48	41	42
Motorcycle accidents	23	4	4	3	6	6
Aircraft accidents	19	0	4	4	4	7
Struck by vehicles	59	7	15	14	9	14
Traffic stops/roadblocks	22	4	4	4	3	7
Directing traffic/assisting motorists	37	3	11	10	6	7
Accidental shootings	12	2	1	3	3	3
Other (drownings, falls, and so on)	34	5	6	9	2	12

Source: U.S. Department of Justice, *Federal Bureau of Investigation, Law Enforcement Officers Killed and Assaulted, 2000* (Washington, D.C.: U.S. Department of Justice, 2001), 64.

ficers may become stressed when they are forced to adapt to a department's new methods of policing, such as community-oriented policing, but are skeptical about the change in policy.[136] In addition, police suffer stress in their personal lives when they "bring the job home" or when their work hours are shifted, causing family disruptions.[137] Other stressors include poor training, substandard equipment, inadequate pay, lack of opportunity, job dissatisfaction, role conflict, exposure to brutality, and fears about competence, success, and safety.[138] Some officers may feel stress because they believe that the court system favors the rights of the criminal and handcuffs the police; others might be sensitive to a perceived lack of support from governmental officials and the general public.[139] Some officers believe that their superiors care little about their welfare.[140]

Police psychologists have divided these stressors into four distinct categories:[141]

1. *External stressors* include verbal abuse from the public, justice system inefficiency, and liberal court decisions that favor the criminal. What are perceived to be antipolice judicial decisions may alienate police and reduce their perceptions of their own competence.
2. *Organizational stressors* include low pay, excessive paperwork, arbitrary rules, and limited opportunity for advancement.
3. *Duty stressors* include rotating shifts, work overload, boredom, fear, and danger.
4. *Individual stressors* include discrimination, marital difficulties, and personality problems.

The effects of stress can be shocking. Police work has been related to both physical and psychological ailments.[142] Police have a high rate of premature death caused by such conditions as heart disease and diabetes. They also experience a disproportionate number of divorces and other marital problems. Research indicates that police officers in some departments, but not all, have higher suicide rates than the general public.[143] Police who feel stress may not be open to adopting new ideas and programs such as community policing.[144]

Combating Stress Research efforts have shown that the more support police officers get in the workplace, the lower their feelings of stress and anxiety.[145] Consequently, departments have attempted to fight job-related stress by training officers to cope with its effects. Today, stress training includes diet information, biofeedback, relaxation and meditation, and exercise. Many departments include stress management as part of an overall wellness program also designed to promote physical and mental health, fitness, and good nutrition.[146] Some programs have included family members: they may be better able to help the officer cope if they have more knowledge about the difficulties of police work. Total wellness programming enhances the physical and emotional well-being of officers by emphasizing preventive physical and psychological measures.[147] Research also shows that because police perceive many benefits of their job and enjoy the quality of life it provides,

© 2002 AP/Wide World Photos

Because police are called on to handle difficult interactions and situations, stress is a routine aspect of their work. Here, Tory Kennedy, ten, is comforted by Little Rock, Arkansas, police officers after being held hostage in a Little Rock neighborhood, March 12, 2002. The child, one of four, escaped through a window before the three others were released by a man police identified as Allen Lewis.

stress reduction programs can help officers focus on the positive aspects of police work.[148]

Because stress is a critically important aspect of police work, further research is needed to create valid methods of identifying police officers under considerable stress and to devise effective stress reduction programs.[149]

Violence

Anthony Baez was playing touch football in the street with his brothers in December 1994 when an errantly thrown ball struck New York City police officer Francis Livoti's patrol car. The officer tried to stop the game, and Baez, twenty-nine, of Orlando, Florida, died in the ensuing struggle.

A police department investigation found that Livoti had used an illegal choke hold to subdue Baez. Although Livoti was acquitted in 1996 of negligent homicide, he was fired from the force and in June 1998 was convicted of violating Baez's civil rights in federal court. On October 1, 1998, the city agreed to pay nearly $3 million to settle lawsuits filed by the family of the man who had been choked to death by a police officer.[150]

The Baez case illustrates the persistent problems police departments have in regulating violent contacts with citizens. Police officers are empowered to use force and violence in pursuit of their daily tasks. Some scholars argue that the use of violent measures is the core of the police role.[151]

Since their creation, U.S. police departments have wrestled with the charge that they are brutal, physically violent organizations. Early police officers resorted to violence and intimidation to gain the respect that was not freely given by citizens. In the 1920s, the Wickersham Commission detailed numerous instances of **police brutality,** including the use of the third degree to extract confessions.

police brutality Usually involves such actions as the use of abusive language, unnecessary use of force or coercion, threats, prodding with nightsticks, stopping and searching people to harass them, and so on.

Today, police brutality continues to be a concern, especially when police use excessive violence against members of the minority community. The nation looked on in disgust when a videotape was aired on network newscasts showing members of the Los Angeles Police Department beating, kicking, and using electric stun guns on Rodney King. Earlier, Los Angeles police stopped using a restraining choke hold, which cuts off blood circulation to the brain, after minority citizens complained that it caused permanent damage and may have killed as many as seventeen people. It is not surprising that three-quarters of all complaints filed against the police for misconduct tend to be by nonwhite males under the age of thirty.[152]

How Common Is the Use of Force Today? How much force is being used by the police today?[153] Despite some highly publicized incidents that get a lot of media attention, the research data show that the use of force is not a very common event. A recent survey on police contacts with civilians found that in a single year, 1999, out of an estimated 43 million police-citizen interactions, approximately 1 percent, or 422,000, involved the use or threatened use of force. Of these, an estimated 2 in 10 involved the threat of force only. When force was used, it usually involved the citizen being pushed or grabbed: less than 20 percent of those experiencing force reported an injury.[154] The least intrusive types of force, like handcuffing, are used much more often than the most intrusive, like lethal violence. The use of weapons is quite rare: for everyone thousand police officers there are about four incidents in which an officer shoots at a civilian.[155]

Race and Force The routine use of force may be diminishing, but there is still debate over whether police are more likely to get rough with minority suspects. The survey on police contacts with civilians found that African Americans (2 percent) and Hispanics (2 percent) were more likely than whites (just under 1 percent) to experience police threat or use of force as a consequence of police contact.[156] Although these differences may not be conclusive evidence that police unfairly use more force against minorities, minority citizens are much more likely to perceive that police are more likely to "hassle them"—stop them or watch them closely when they have done nothing wrong. They are also more likely to know someone who has been "hassled" by police. Perceptions of "hassling" may erode an individual's future relations with police and affect police-community relations as a whole.[157]

Who Are the Problem Cops? There is evidence that only a small proportion of officers are continually involved in use-of-force incidents.[158] What kind of police officer gets involved in problem behavior? Are some officers "chronic offenders?" Research conducted in a southeastern city by Kim Michelle Lersch and Tom Mieczkowski found that a few officers (7 percent) were in fact chronic offenders who accounted for a significant portion of all citizen complaints (33 percent). Those officers receiving the bulk of the complaints tended to be younger and less experienced and had been accused of harassment or violence after a proactive encounter that they had initiated. Although repeat offenders were more likely to be accused of misconduct by minority citizens, there was little evidence that attacks were racially motivated.[159] Efforts to deal with these "problem cops" are now being undertaken in police departments around the nation. The following Policy, Programs, and Issues feature describes these efforts in some detail.

© 2002 AP/Wide World Photos

Incidents of police violence have made headlines, and when captured on videotape, repeatedly shown on the local news. In this image taken from an amateur video allegedly recorded in Oklahoma City on July 8, 2002, a police officer raises his baton as he and his colleague apprehend a man who the two officers claimed was refusing to comply with their orders to remain lying down. The video came to light just two days after the suspension of police officers in California for alleged use of excessive force, also recorded by a witness on videotape.

Curbing Brutality   Because incidents of brutality undermine efforts to build a bridge between police and the public, police departments around the United States have instituted specialized training programs to reduce them. Urban police departments are now implementing or considering implementing neighborhood and community policing models to improve relations with the public. In addition, detailed rules of engagement that limit the use of force are now common in major cities. However, the creation of departmental rules limiting behavior is often haphazard and is usually a reaction to a crisis situation (for example, a citizen is seriously injured) rather than part of a systematic effort to improve police-citizen interactions.[160] Some departments have developed administrative policies that stress limiting the use of deadly force and containing armed offenders until specially trained backup teams are sent to take charge of the situation. Administrative policies have been found to be an effective control on use of deadly force, and their influence can be enhanced if given the proper support by the chief of police.[161]

Some cities are taking an aggressive, proactive stance to curb violent cops. Since 1977 the New York City Police Department has been operating a Force-Related Integrity Testing program in which undercover officers pose as angry citizens in elaborate sting operations intended to weed out officers with a propensity for violence. In a typical encounter, officers responding to a radio call on a domestic dispute confront an aggressive husband who spews hatred at everyone around, including the police. The "husband" is actually an undercover officer

Policy, Programs, and Issues in Criminal Justice

Working with the Problem Cops: Early Intervention Programs

Research indicates about 10 percent of all police officers account for 90 percent of the problems experienced by the department. In some departments as few as 2 percent of all officers are responsible for 50 percent of all citizen complaints. In 1981, the U.S. Commission on Civil Rights recommended that all police departments create an early warning system to identify problem officers—those who are frequently the subject of complaints or who demonstrate identifiable patterns of inappropriate behavior. During the past two decades, a number of police departments have set up early warning systems to identify officers whose behavior is problematic and provide a form of intervention to correct that performance.

An early response system enables police departments to intervene with potentially problem police before an officer is in a situation that requires formal disciplinary action. The system alerts the department to these individuals and warns the officers while providing counseling or training to help them change their problem behavior. A recent (2001) survey by police experts Samuel Walker, Geoffrey Alpert, and Dennis J. Kenney found that in 1999, 39 percent of all municipal and county law enforcement agencies that serve populations greater than fifty thousand people either had an early warning system in place or were planning to implement one.

Although these systems are becoming prevalent, Walker and his associates found that there are still questions about their effectiveness and about the various program elements that are associated with effectiveness.

Walker and his colleagues found that early warning systems have three basic phases: selection, intervention, and postintervention monitoring.

Selecting Officers for the Program

No standards have been established for identifying officers for early warning programs, but there is general agreement about the criteria that should influence their selection. Performance indicators that can help identify officers with problematic behavior include citizen complaints, firearm-discharge and use-of-force reports, civil litigation, resisting-arrest incidents, and high-speed pursuits and vehicular damage. Most departments use a combination of these indicators to select officers for help. Of those that rely solely on citizen complaints, most (67 percent) require three complaints in a given time frame (76 percent specify a twelve-month period) to identify an officer.

Intervening with the Officer

The primary goal of early warning systems is to change the behavior of individual officers who have been identified as having performance problems. The basic intervention strategy involves a combination of deterrence and education. According to the deterrence strategy:

- Officers who are subject to intervention will change their behavior in response to a perceived threat of punishment.
- Those officers not subject to the early warning system will also change their behavior to avoid potential punishment.

from the Internal Affairs Bureau, who is testing whether the officers, some of whom have a history of civilian complaints, will respond to verbal abuse with threats or violence. The NYPD conducts about six hundred sting operations each year to test the integrity of its officers; several dozen are devoted to evaluating the conduct of officers with a history of abuse complaints.[162]

Perhaps the greatest single factors in controlling the use of police brutality are the threat of civil judgments against individual officers who use excessive force, police chiefs who ignore or condone violent behavior, and the cities and towns in which they are employed.

Deadly Force   As it is commonly used, the term *deadly force* refers to the actions of a police officer who shoots and kills a suspect who is fleeing from arrest, assaulting a victim, or attacking an officer.[163] The justification for the use of deadly force can be traced to English common law, where almost every criminal offense was a felony and bore the death penalty. The use of deadly force in the course of arresting a felon was considered expedient, saving the state the burden of trial (the *fleeing felon rule*).[164]

Early warning systems also operate on the assumption that training, as part of the intervention, can help officers improve their performance.

In most systems, the initial intervention generally consists of a review by the officer's immediate supervisor. Almost half of the responding agencies involve other command officers in counseling the officer. Also, these systems frequently include a training class for groups of officers identified by the system.

Monitoring the Officer's Subsequent Performance

Nearly all the agencies that have an early warning system in place report that they monitor an officer's performance after the initial intervention. Such monitoring is generally informal and conducted by the officer's immediate supervisor, but some departments have developed a formal process of observation, evaluation, and reporting. Almost half of the agencies monitor the officer's performance for thirty-six months after the initial intervention. Half of the agencies indicate that the follow-up period is not specified and that officers are monitored either continuously or on a case-by-case basis.

Do the Early Warning Systems Work?

Walker and associates made detailed evaluations of the early warning systems in three cities—Minneapolis, Miami, and New Orleans—in order to assess the impact of such systems on officers' performance. They found that these systems appear to have a dramatic effect on reducing citizen complaints and other indicators of problematic police performance among those officers subject to intervention. In Minneapolis, the average number of citizen com-

plaints received by officers subject to early intervention dropped by 67 percent one year after the intervention. In New Orleans, that number dropped by 62 percent one year after intervention. In Miami-Dade, 96 percent of the officers sent to early intervention had experienced complaints about excessive use of force. Following the intervention, that number had dropped to 50 percent.

Critical Thinking

Although early intervention systems alone may not be capable of neutralizing the inappropriate behavior of problem officers, they are emerging as an important tool that can be used along with other techniques to reduce unacceptable behaviors. Could they be used as an intervention to combat racial profiling? For example, would it be appropriate to identify officers who make disproportionate number of traffic stops of racial or ethnic minorities (relative to other officers with the same assignment) and place them in an early intervention program? Or is this a violation of their civil rights—labeling them without a hearing or trial?

InfoTrac College Edition Research

To read an article on psychologists who work with problem cops, see Alan W. Benner, "Cop Docs," *Psychology Today*, November 2000 v33 i6 p36, on InfoTrac College Edition.

Source: Samuel Walker, Geoffrey P. Alpert, and Dennis J. Kenney, *Early Warning Systems: Responding to the Problem Police Officer, Research in Brief* (Washington, D.C.: National Institute of Justice, 2001).

Although the media depict hero cops in a constant stream of deadly shootouts in which scores of "bad guys" are killed, the actual number of people killed by the police each year is most likely between 250 and 300.[165] Although these data are encouraging, some researchers believe that the actual number of police shootings is far greater and may be hidden or masked by a number of factors. For example, coroners may be intentionally or accidentally underreporting police homicides by almost half.[166]

Factors Related to Police Shootings   Is police use of deadly force a random occurrence, or are there social, legal, and environmental factors associated with it? The following patterns have been related to police shootings.

1. *Exposure to violence.* Most police shootings involve suspects who are armed and either attack the officer or are engaged in violent crimes. A number of studies have found that fatal police shootings were closely related to reported violent crime rates and criminal homicide rates; police officers kill civilians at a higher rate in years when the general level of violence in the nation is

A relationship exists between police violence and the number of police on the street, the number of calls for service, the number and nature of police dispatches, the number of arrests made in a given jurisdiction, and police exposure to stressful situations. Here a Massillon, Ohio, police officer sits after a shootout, August 9, 2002, that left two people dead. Killed were fellow officer Eric Taylor, not shown, and the man, on ground at left, who had led police on a chase. State Highway Patrol Sergeant Rick Zwayer said the chase began on State Route 21 in Wayne County, when a vehicle failed to stop for a trooper. The chase continued into Massillon, and Massillon police assisted. The chased vehicle stopped in a parking lot and the driver got out with a gun. Zwayer said shots were then fired.

higher.[167] The perception of danger may contribute to the use of violent means for self-protection.[168]

Police officers may also be exposed to violence when they are forced to confront the emotionally disturbed. Some distraught people attack police as a form of suicide.[169] This tragic event has become so common that the term *suicide by cop* has been coined to denote victim-precipitated killings by police. For example, over the past decade more than 10 percent of the shootings by police officers in Los Angeles involved suicidal people intentionally provoking police.[170]

2. *Workload.* A relationship exists between police violence and the number of police officers on the street, the number of calls for service, the number and nature of police dispatches, the number of arrests made in a given jurisdiction, and police exposure to stressful situations.

3. *Firearms availability.* Cities that experience a large number of crimes committed with firearms are likely to have high police-violence rates. A strong association has been found between police use of force and "gun density" (the proportion of suicides and murders committed with a gun).[171]

4. *Social variables.* The greatest number of police shootings occur in areas that have significant disparities in economic opportunity and high levels of income inequality.[172] One reason for this may be that residents in these deprived areas are the ones who are most likely to direct violence toward the police themselves. According to David Jacobs and Jason Carmichael, cities that have the greatest economic and political subordination of minority group members are also the location of the highest number of officers killed and wounded.[173] Interestingly, the presence of an African-American mayor significantly reduces the likelihood of police being killed in the line of duty. Jacobs and Carmichael conclude that economic disadvantage in the minority community coupled with political alienation fosters a climate where conflict is sharpened. Politically excluded groups may turn to violence to gain ends that the unexcluded can acquire with conventional tactics. In contrast, the presence of an African-

American mayor may reduce African-American feelings of powerlessness and consequently result in less anger against the state, of which the police are the most visible officials.

5. *Administrative policies.* The philosophy, policies, and practices of individual police chiefs and departments significantly influence the police use of deadly force.[174] Departments that stress restrictive policies on the use of force generally have lower shooting rates than those that favor tough law enforcement and encourage officers to shoot when necessary. Poorly written or ambivalent policies encourage shootings because they allow the officer at the scene to decide when deadly force is warranted, often under conditions of high stress and tension.

6. *Race and police shootings.* No other issue is as important to the study of the police use of deadly force as racial discrimination. A number of critics have claimed that police are more likely to shoot and kill minority offenders than whites. In a famous statement, Paul Takagi charged that police have "one trigger finger for whites and another for African Americans."[175] Takagi's complaint was supported by a number of research studies that showed that a disproportionate number of police killings involved minority citizens—almost 80 percent in some of the cities surveyed.[176]

Do these findings alone indicate that police discriminate in the use of deadly force? Some pioneering research by James Fyfe helps provide an answer to this question. In his study of New York City shootings over a five-year period, Fyfe found that police officers were most likely to shoot suspects who were armed and with whom they became involved in violent confrontations. Once such factors as being armed with a weapon, being involved in a violent crime, and attacking an officer were considered, the racial differences in the police use of force ceased to be significant. In fact, Fyfe found that African-American officers were almost twice as likely as white officers to have shot citizens. Fyfe attributes this finding to the fact that (1) African-American officers work and live in high-crime, high-violence areas where shootings are more common and (2) African-American officers hold proportionately more line positions and fewer administrative posts than white officers, which would place them more often on the street and less often behind a desk.[177]

InfoTrac College Edition has numerous articles on the police use of force. Use the term "police shootings" as a subject guide to locate the most recent ones.

Controlling Deadly Force   Because the police use of deadly force is such a serious problem, ongoing efforts have been made to control it.

One of the most difficult issues in controlling the problem was the continued use of the fleeing felon rule in a number of states. However, in 1985 the Supreme Court outlawed the indiscriminate use of deadly force with its decision in *Tennessee v. Garner.* In this case, the Court ruled that the use of deadly force against apparently unarmed and nondangerous fleeing felons is an illegal seizure of their person under the Fourth Amendment. Deadly force may not be used unless it is necessary to prevent the escape and the officer has probable cause to believe that the suspect poses a significant threat of death or serious injury to the officer or others. The majority opinion stated that where the suspect poses no immediate threat to the officer and no threat to others, the harm resulting from failing to apprehend the suspect does not justify the use of deadly force to do so: "A police officer may not seize an unarmed, nondangerous suspect by shooting him dead."[178]

With *Garner,* the Supreme Court effectively put an end to any local police policy that allowed officers to shoot unarmed or otherwise nondangerous offenders if they resisted arrest or attempted to flee from police custody. However, the Court did not ban the use of deadly force or otherwise control police shooting policy. Consequently, in *Graham v. Connor,* the Court created a reasonableness standard for the use of force: force is excessive when, considering all the circumstances known to the officer at the time he acted, the force used was unreasonable.[179] For example, an officer is approached in a threatening manner by someone wielding a

Reasonable officer's perception	Enforcement electives	Reasonable officer's response
Assaultive (serious bodily harm/death)	V	Deadly force
Assaultive (bodily harm)	IV	Defensive tactics
Resistant (active)	III	Compliance techniques
Resistant (passive)	II	Contact controls
Compliant (cooperative)	I	Verbal commands

Figure 6.3
The Federal Law Enforcement Training Center's use-of-force model

Source: Franklin Graves and Gregory Connor, Federal Law Enforcement Training Center, Glynco, Georgia.

knife. The assailant fails to stop when warned and is killed by the officer, but it turns out later that the shooting victim was deaf and could not hear the officer's command. The officer would not be held liable if at the time of the incident he had no way of knowing the person's disability.

Individual state jurisdictions still control police shooting policy. Some states have adopted statutory policies that restrict the police use of violence. Others have upgraded training in the use of force. The Federal Law Enforcement Training Center has developed the FLETC use-of-force model, illustrated in Figure 6.3, to teach officers the proper method to escalate force in response to the threat they face. As the figure shows, resistance ranges from compliant and cooperative to assaultive with the threat of serious bodily harm or death. Officers are taught via lecture, demonstration, computer-based instruction, and training scenarios to assess the suspect's behavior and apply an appropriate and corresponding amount of force.[180]

Another way to control police shootings is through internal review and policy-making by police administrative review boards. For example, New York's Firearm Discharge Review Board was established to investigate and adjudicate all police firearm discharges. Among the dispositions available to the board are the following:

1. The discharge was in accordance with law and departmental policy.
2. The discharge was justifiable, but the officer should be given additional training in the use of firearms or in the law and departmental policy.
3. The shooting was justifiable under law but violated departmental policy and warrants departmental disciplinary action.
4. The shooting was in apparent violation of law and should be referred to the appropriate prosecutor if criminal charges have not already been filed.
5. The officer involved should be transferred (or offered the opportunity to transfer) to a less sensitive assignment.
6. The officer involved should receive testing or alcoholism counseling.[181]

The review board approach is controversial because it can mean that the department recommends that one of its own officers be turned over for criminal prosecution.[182]

Nonlethal Weapons   In the last few years, about a thousand local police forces have started using some sort of less-than-lethal weapon designed to subdue suspects. The most widely used nonlethal weapons are wood, rubber, or polyurethane bullets shot out of modified 37-mm pistols or 12-gauge shotguns. At short distances, officers use pepper spray and tasers, which deliver electric shocks with long wire tentacles, producing intense muscle spasms. Other technologies still in development include guns that shoot giant nets, guns that squirt sticky glue, and lights that can temporarily blind a suspect. New weapons are being developed that shoot bags filled with lead pellets; the weapons have a range of one hundred feet and pack the wallop of a pro boxer's punch.[183]

Recent research efforts indicate that nonlethal weapons may help reduce police use of force.[184] Greater effort must be made to regulate these nonlethal weapons and create effective policies for their use.[185]

Police as Victims   Police use of force continues to be an important issue, but there is little question that control measures seem to be working. Fewer people are being killed by police, and fewer officers are being killed in the line of duty than ever before: about 50 each year. The number rose dramatically in 2001 because 23 officers were killed in the September 11 attack along, with 343 firefighters.

Before this increase, the number of officers slain in the line of duty has been trending downward for the past decade.[186] About half of the officers were killed while making arrests or conducting a traffic stop. A long-held belief has been that police officers who answer domestic violence calls are at risk of violence against themselves; when confronted, one of the two battling parties turns on the outsider who dares to interfere in a "private matter." Research conducted in Charlotte, North Carolina, however, indicates that domestic violence calls may be no more dangerous than many other routine police interactions.[187] So while police officers should be on their guard when investigating a call for assistance from an abused spouse, the risk of violence against them may be no greater than when they answer a call for a burglary or car theft.

Corruption

In July 1996 the elite antigang unit from the Los Angeles Police Department's Rampart Division raided gang-infested apartments at Shatto Place; their target was the notorious 18th Street Gang, one of Los Angeles's most violent gangs. During the raid, police officers killed one gang member and wounded another. A departmental investigation found nothing wrong and exonerated the police involved. Then in 1999, Rafael A. Perez, an officer who took part in the raid, was caught stealing eight pounds of cocaine from police evidence lockers. After pleading guilty in September 1999, he bargained for a lighter sentence by telling departmental investigators about police brutality, perjury, planted evidence, drug corruption, and attempted murder within the Rampart Division and its antigang unit, known as CRASH (Community Resources Against Street Hoodlums). Perez told authorities that during the Shatto raid the victims may have been unarmed, so that the raiding officers resorted to a "throwdown"—slang for a weapon being planted to make a shooting legally justifiable. Perez's testimony resulted in at least twelve Rampart cops being fired or relieved from duty. But Perez was not done. He also said that he and his partner, Officer Nino Durden, shot an unarmed 18th Street Gang member named Javier Ovando, then planted a semiautomatic rifle on the unconscious suspect and claimed that Ovando had tried to shoot them during a stakeout. Their testimony had helped get Ovando, confined to a wheelchair for life because of the shooting, a twenty-three-year sentence for assault. Now Ovando has been freed from prison and is suing the city for more than $20 million.[188]

From their creation, U.S. police departments have wrestled with the problem of controlling illegal and unprofessional behavior by their officers. Corruption pervaded the American police when the early departments were first formed. In the nineteenth century, police officers systematically ignored violations of laws related to drinking, gambling, and prostitution in return for regular payoffs. Some actually entered into relationships with professional criminals, especially pickpockets. Illegal behavior was tolerated in return for goods or information. Police officers helped politicians gain office by allowing electoral fraud to flourish; some senior officers sold promotions to higher rank in the department.[189]

Since the early nineteenth century, scandals involving police abuse of power have occurred in many cities, and elaborate methods have been devised to control or eliminate the problem. Although most police officers are not corrupt, the few who are dishonest bring discredit to the entire profession.

Varieties of Corruption   Police deviance can include a number of activities. In a general sense, it involves misuse of authority by police officers in a manner designed to produce personal gain for themselves or others.[190] However, debate continues over whether a desire for personal gain is an essential part of corruption. Some experts argue that police misconduct also involves such issues as the unnecessary use of force, unreasonable searches, or an immoral personal life and that these should be considered as serious as corruption devoted to economic gain.

Scholars have attempted to create typologies categorizing the forms that the abuse of police powers can take. For example, when investigating corruption among police officers in New York, the **Knapp Commission** classified abusers into two categories: **meat eaters** and **grass eaters**.[191] Meat eaters aggressively misuse police power for personal gain by demanding bribes, threatening legal action, or cooperating with criminals. Across the country, police officers have been accused, indicted, and convicted of shaking down club owners and other businesspeople.[192] In contrast, grass eaters accept payoffs when their everyday duties place them in a position to be solicited by the public. For example, police officers have been investigated for taking bribes to look the other way while neighborhood bookmakers ply their trade.[193] The Knapp Commission concluded that the vast majority of police officers on the take are grass eaters, although the few meat eaters who are caught capture all the headlines. In 1993 another police scandal prompted formation of the **Mollen Commission,** which found that some New York cops were actively involved in violence and drug dealing.

Other police experts have attempted to create models to better understand police corruption. It may be possible to divide police corruption into four major categories:[194]

1. *Internal corruption.* This corruption takes place among police officers themselves, involving both the bending of departmental rules and the outright performance of illegal acts. For example, Chicago police officers conspired to sell relatively new police cars to other officers at cut-rate prices, forcing the department to purchase new cars unnecessarily. In Boston a major scandal hit the police department when a captain was indicted in an exam-tampering-and-selling scheme. Numerous officers bought promotion exams from the captain, while others had him lower the scores of rivals who were competing for the same job.[195]

2. *Selective enforcement or nonenforcement.* This form occurs when police abuse or exploit their discretion. If an officer frees a drug dealer in return for

Knapp Commission   A public body that led an investigation into police corruption in New York and uncovered a widespread network of payoffs and bribes.

meat eaters   A term used to describe police officers who actively solicit bribes and vigorously engage in corrupt practices.

grass eaters   A term to describe police officers who accept payoffs when everyday duties place them in a position to be solicited by the public.

Mollen Commission   An investigatory body formed in New York City in 1993 to scrutinize police misconduct.

valuable information, that is considered a legitimate use of discretion; if the officer does so for money, that is an abuse of police power.

3. *Active criminality.* This is participation by police in serious criminal behavior. Police may use their positions of trust and power to commit the very crimes they are entrusted with controlling. For example, a police burglary ring in Denver was so large that it prompted one commentator to coin the phrase "burglars in blue." During the past twenty years, police burglary rings have been uncovered in Chicago, Reno, Nashville, Cleveland, and Burlington, Vermont, among other cities.[196] Another disturbing trend has been police use of drugs and alcohol. Police departments have been active in referring officers to treatment programs when substance abuse problems are detected.[197]

4. *Bribery and extortion.* This includes practices in which law enforcement roles are exploited specifically to raise money. Bribery is initiated by the citizen; extortion is initiated by the officer. Bribery or extortion can be a one-shot transaction, as when a traffic violator offers a police officer $100 to forget about issuing a summons. Or the relationship can be an ongoing one, in which the officer solicits (or is offered) regular payoffs to ignore criminal activities, such as gambling or narcotics dealing. This is known as "being on the pad."

   Sometimes police officers accept routine bribes and engage in petty extortion without considering themselves corrupt; they consider these payments as some of the unwritten "benefits" of police work. For example, *mooching* involves receiving free gifts of coffee, cigarettes, meals, and so on in exchange for possible future acts of favoritism. *Chiseling* occurs when officers demand admission to entertainment events or price discounts; *shopping* involves taking small items, such as cigarettes, from a store whose door was accidentally left unlocked after business hours.[198]

Corrupt Departments   It has also been suggested that entire police departments can be categorized on the basis of the level and type of corruption existing within them.[199] Three types of departments may exist:

1. *"Rotten apples" and "rotten pockets."* This type of police department has a few corrupt officers ("rotten apples") who use their position for personal gain. When these corrupt officers band together, they form a "rotten pocket." Robert Daley described the activities of such a group in his book *Prince of the City.*[200] Agents of New York City's Special Investigations Unit kept money they confiscated during narcotics raids and used illegal drugs to pay off informers. *Prince of the City* tells the story of New York detective Frank Leuci, whose testimony against his partners before investigating committees made him an outcast in the police department. Rotten pockets help institutionalize corruption because their members expect newcomers to conform to their illegal practices and to a code of secrecy.

2. *Pervasive unorganized corruption.* This type of department contains a majority of personnel who are corrupt but have little relationship to one another. Though many officers are involved in taking bribes and extortion, they are not cooperating with one another for personal gain.

3. *Pervasive organized corruption.* This describes a department in which almost all members are involved in systematic and organized corruption. The Knapp Commission found this type of relationship in New York City's vice divisions, where payoffs and bribes were an organized and accepted way of police life.

The Causes and Control of Corruption   No single explanation satisfactorily accounts for the various forms the abuse of power takes. One view puts the blame on the type of person who becomes a police officer. This position holds that policing

How do police feel about the abuse of power themselves? To find out, read the findings of a national survey on police attitudes toward abuse of authority:
www.ncjrs.org/pdffiles1/nij/181312.pdf

tends to attract lower-class individuals who do not have the financial means to maintain a coveted middle-class lifestyle. As they develop the cynical, authoritarian police personality, accepting graft seems an all-too-easy method of achieving financial security.

A second view is that the wide discretion police enjoy, coupled with low visibility among the public and their own supervisors, makes them likely candidates for corruption. In addition, the code of secrecy maintained by the police subculture helps insulate corrupt officers from the law. Similarly, police managers, most of whom have risen through the ranks, are reluctant to investigate corruption or punish wrongdoers. Thus, corruption may also be viewed as a function of police institutions and practices.[201]

A third position holds that corruption is a function of society's ambivalence toward many forms of vice-related criminal behavior that police officers are sworn to control. Unenforceable laws governing moral standards promote corruption because they create large groups with an interest in undermining law enforcement. These include consumers—people who gamble, wish to drink after the legal closing hour, or patronize a prostitute—who do not want to be deprived of their chosen form of recreation. Even though the consumers may not actively corrupt police officers, their existence creates a climate that tolerates active corruption by others.[202] Since vice cannot be controlled and the public apparently wants it to continue, the officer may have little resistance to inducements for monetary gain offered by law violators.

How can police misconduct be controlled? One approach is to strengthen the internal administrative review process in police departments. A strong and well-supported internal affairs division has been linked to lowered corruption rates.[203] However, asking police to police themselves is not a simple task. Officers are often reluctant to discipline their peers. For example, a 1999 review of disciplinary files found that hundreds of New York City police officers escaped punishment when their cases were summarily dismissed by the police department without ever interviewing victims or witnesses or making any other efforts to examine the strength of the evidence.[204]

Another approach, instituted by then New York Commissioner Patrick Murphy in the wake of the Knapp Commission, is the accountability system. This holds that supervisors at each level are directly accountable for the illegal behaviors of the officers under them. Consequently, a commander can be demoted or forced to resign if one under his or her command is found guilty of corruption.[205] Close scrutiny by a department, however, can lower officer morale and create the suspicion that the officers' own supervisors distrust them.

Some departments have set up guidelines to help reduce corruption. In 1996 the city of Philadelphia agreed to implement a set of reforms to combat corruption in order to settle a lawsuit brought by civil rights organizations. The following were among the measures taken to reduce corruption:

- A policy mandating that all citizens' complaints be forwarded for investigation by the internal affairs division
- Development of computer files that contain all types of complaints and suits against individual officers that could be easily accessed during investigations
- A policy requiring that internal affairs give a high priority to any officer's claim that another officer was corrupt or used excessive force
- Mandatory reporting and recording of all incidents in which an officer used more than incidental force
- Training of officers to treat citizens without racial bias; assigning a deputy commissioner to monitor charges of race discrimination
- Reviewing all policies and practices to ensure they do not involve or have the potential for race bias[206]

Another approach is to create outside review boards or special prosecutors, such as the Mollen Commission in New York and the Christopher Commission in Los Angeles, to investigate reported incidents of corruption. However, outside investigators and special prosecutors are often limited by their lack of intimate knowledge of day-to-day operations. As a result, they depend on the testimony of a few officers who are willing to cooperate, either to save themselves from prosecution or because they have a compelling moral commitment. Outside evaluators also face the problem of the blue curtain, which is quickly closed when police officers feel their department is under scrutiny.

A more realistic solution to corruption, albeit a difficult one, might be to change the social context of policing. Police operations must be made more visible, and the public must be given freer access to controlling police operations. All too often, the public finds out about police problems only when a scandal hits the newspaper. Some of the vice-related crimes the police now deal with might be decriminalized or referred to other agencies. Although decriminalization of vice cannot in itself end the problem, it could lower the pressure placed on individual police officers and help eliminate their moral dilemmas. ■

SUMMARY

Police departments today are faced with many critical problems in their development and relationship with the public. Police are believed to be insulated from the rest of society. Some experts hold that police officers have distinct personality characteristics marked by authoritarianism and cynicism. It is also alleged that police maintain a separate culture with distinct rules and loyalties. A police personality also influences their working style. Four distinct police styles have been identified, and each influences the officer's decision making. The complexity and danger of the police role produce an enormous amount of stress that harms police effectiveness.

Social concerns also affect police operations. Today, many police officers seek higher education. The jury is still out on whether educated officers are actually more effective. Women and minorities are now being recruited into the police in increasing numbers. Research indicates that, with few exceptions, they perform as well or even better than other officers. The percentage of minorities on police forces reflects their representation in the general population, but the number of female officers still lags behind. Of greater importance is increasing the number of women and minorities in supervisory positions.

Police officers are subject to control by the courts while conducting their daily activities. The Supreme Court has handed down numerous decisions that set the rules on how police are to conduct interrogations and search for evidence. If the police violate these Court-ordered parameters then the evidence may be excluded from trial. The Court issued these decisions in an effort to protect the civil rights of criminal suspects. Although at first police officers were dismayed about these legal controls and viewed them as an attempt to handcuff the police, they have now become part of standard operating procedure. In addition, conservative Supreme Court justices have created many exceptions that allow police greater leeway to conduct their investigations.

Police departments have also been concerned about limiting police stress and improving police-community relations. One critical concern is the police use of deadly force. Research indicates that antishooting policies can limit deaths resulting from police action. Another effort has been to identify and eliminate police corruption, which still mars the reputation of police forces.

For an up-to-date list of Web links, go to http://cj.wadsworth.com/siegel_essen4e.

KEY TERMS

police officer styles 168	cynicism 169	discretion 172	double marginality 180
deadly force 168	blue curtain 169	demeanor 175	Miranda warning 185

INFOTRAC COLLEGE EDITION EXERCISES

IN ORDER TO CONTROL POLICE USE OF FORCE, a number of force continuums such as the FLETC model have been created. However, there is some question about whether this is a wise move. Should law enforcement abide by force continuums, and should police agencies continue to require their officers to start at the lowest level of force and escalate to higher levels without considering the effectiveness such action has in serving the law enforcement mission? To find out more about this important topic, go to InfoTrac College Edition and read George T. Williams, "Force Continuums: A Liability to Law Enforcement?" *FBI Law Enforcement Bulletin*, June 2002 v71 i6 p14(6).

QUESTIONS

1. Should male and female officers have exactly the same duties in a police department? Explain your reasoning.

2. Do you think that an officer's working the street will eventually produce a cynical personality and distrust for civilians? Explain.

3. How can education help police officers?

4. Should a police officer who accepts a free meal from a restaurant owner be dismissed from the force? Why or why not?

5. A police officer orders an unarmed person running away from a burglary to stop; the suspect keeps running and is shot and killed by the officer. Has the officer committed murder? Explain.

6. Would you like to live in a society that abolished police discretion and used a full enforcement policy? Why or why not?

7. Should illegally seized evidence be excluded from trial, even though it is conclusive proof of a person's criminal acts? Might there be another way to deal with police violation of the Fourth Amendment—for example, making them pay a fine?

8. Have criminals been given too many rights by the courts? Should courts be more concerned with the rights of victims or the rights of offenders? Have the police been "handcuffed" and prevented from doing their job in the most efficient manner?

NOTES

1. Kathleen Maguire and Ann Pastore, eds., *Sourcebook of Criminal Justice Statistics;* www.albany.edu/sourcebook/1995/pdf/t216.pdf

2. John Klofas, "Drugs and Justice: The Impact of Drugs on Criminal Justice in a Metropolitan Community," *Crime and Delinquency* 39 (1993): 204–224.

3. Steven Tuch and Ronald Weitzer, "The Polls-Trends: Racial Differences in Attitudes Toward the Police," *Public Opinion Quarterly* 61 (1997): 642–663.

4. Maguire and Pastore, eds., *Sourcebook of Criminal Justice Statistics.*

5. See, for example, Richard Harris, *The Police Academy: An Inside View* (New York: Wiley, 1973); John Van Maanen, "Observations on the Making of a Policeman," in *Order Under Law,* eds. R. Culbertson and M. Tezak (Prospect Heights, Ill.: Waveland Press, 1981), 111–126; Jonathan Rubenstein, *City Police* (New York: Ballantine Books, 1973); John Broderick, *Police in a Time of Change* (Morristown, N.J.: General Learning Press, 1977).

6. Malcolm Sparrow, Mark Moore, and David Kennedy, *Beyond 911: A New Era for Policing* (New York: Basic Books, 1992), 51.

7. M. Steven Meagher and Nancy Yentes, "Choosing a Career in Policing: A Comparison of Male and Female Perceptions," *Journal of Police Science and Administration* 16 (1986): 320–327.

8. Michael K. Brown, *Working the Street* (New York: Russell Sage, 1981), 82.

9. Stan Shernock, "An Empirical Examination of the Relationship Between Police Solidarity and Community Orientation,"

Journal of Police Science and Administration 18 (1988): 182–198.

10. Ibid., 360.

11. Ibid., 359.

12. Egon Bittner, *The Functions of Police in Modern Society* (Cambridge, Mass.: Oelgeschlager, Gunn & Hain, 1980), 63.

13. Wallace Graves, "Police Cynicism: Causes and Cures," *FBI Law Enforcement Bulletin* 65 (1996): 16–21.

14. Richard Lundman, *Police and Policing* (New York: Holt, Rinehart & Winston, 1980); see also Jerome Skolnick, *Justice Without Trial* (New York: Wiley, 1966).

15. Robert Regoli, Robert Culbertson, John Crank, and James Powell, "Career Stage and Cynicism Among Police Chiefs," *Justice Quarterly* 7 (1990): 592–614.

16. William Westly, *Violence and the Police: A Sociological Study of Law, Custom, and Morality* (Cambridge, Mass.: MIT Press, 1970).

17. Skolnick, *Justice without Trial*, 42–68.

18. Milton Rokeach, Martin Miller, and John Snyder, "The Value Gap Between Police and Policed," *Journal of Social Issues* 27 (1971): 155–171.

19. Bruce Carpenter and Susan Raza, "Personality Characteristics of Police Applicants: Comparisons Across Subgroups and with Other Populations," *Journal of Police Science and Administration* 15 (1987): 10–17.

20. Larry Tifft, "The 'Cop Personality' Reconsidered," *Journal of Police Science and Administration* 2 (1974): 268; David Bayley and Harold Mendelsohn, *Minorities and the Police* (New York: Free Press, 1969); Robert Balch, "The Police Personality: Fact or Fiction?" *Journal of Criminal Law, Criminology, and Police Science* 63 (1972): 117.

21. Lowell Storms, Nolan Penn, and James Tenzell, "Policemen's Perception of Real and Ideal Policemen," *Journal of Police Science and Administration* 17 (1990): 40–43.

22. Arthur Niederhoffer, *Behind the Shield: The Police in Urban Society* (Garden City, N.Y.: Doubleday, 1967).

23. Ibid., 216–220.

24. Carl Klockars, "The Dirty Harry Problem," *Annals* 452 (1980): 33–47.

25. Jack Kuykendall and Roy Roberg, "Police Manager's Perceptions of Employee Types: A Conceptual Model," *Journal of Criminal Justice* 16 (1988): 131–135.

26. Stephen Matrofski, R. Richard Ritti, and Jeffrey Snipes, "Expectancy Theory and Police Productivity in DUI Enforcement," *Law and Society Review* 28 (1994): 113–138.

27. Ellen Hochstedler, "Testing Types: A Review and Test of Police Types," *Journal of Criminal Justice* 9 (1981): 451–66.

28. For a thorough review, see Eric Riksheim and Steven Chermak, "Causes of Police Behavior Revisited," *Journal of Criminal Justice* 21 (1993): 353–383.

29. Skolnick, *Justice Without Trial.*

30. Helen Eigenberg, Kathryn Scarborough, and Victor Kappeler, "Contributory Factors Affecting Arrest in Domestic and Nondomestic Assaults," *American Journal of Police* 15 (1996): 27–51.

31. Leonore Simon, "A Therapeutic Jurisprudence Approach to the Legal Processing of Domestic Violence Cases," *Psychology, Public Policy and Law* 1 (1995): 43–79.

32. Peter Sinden and B. Joyce Stephens, "Police Perceptions of Domestic Violence: The Nexus of Victim, Perpetrator, Event, Self, and Law," *Policing* 22 (1999): 313–326.

33. Robert Kane, "Patterns of Arrest in Domestic Violence Encounters: Identifying a Police Decision-Making Model," *Journal of Criminal Justice* 27 (1999): 65–79.

34. Gregory Howard Williams, *The Law and Politics of Police Discretion* (Westport, Conn.: Greenwood Press, 1984).

35. Dana Jones and Joanne Belknap, "Police Responses to Battering in a Progressive Pro-Arrest Jurisdiction," *Justice Quarterly* 16 (1999): 249–273.

36. Douglas Smith and Jody Klein, "Police Control of Interpersonal Disputes," *Social Problems* 31 (1984): 468–481.

37. Jones and Belknap, "Police Responses to Battering," 249–273.

38. Robin Shepard Engel, "Patrol Officer Supervision in the Community Policing Era," *Journal of Criminal Justice* 30 (2002): 51–64.

39. Westly, *Violence and the Police.*

40. Nathan Goldman, *The Differential Selection of Juvenile Offenders for Court Appearance* (New York: National Council on Crime and Delinquency, 1963).

41. Richard Lundman, "Demeanor or Crime? The Midwest City Police–Citizen Encounters Study," *Criminology* 32 (1994): 631–653; Robert Worden and Robin Shepard, "On the Meaning, Measurement, and Estimated Effects of Suspects' Demeanor Toward the Police" (Paper presented at the American Society of Criminology meeting, Miami, November 1994).

42. David Klinger, "Bringing Crime Back In: Toward a Better Understanding of Police Arrest Decisions," *Journal of Research in Crime and Delinquency* 33 (1996): 333–336; "More on Demeanor and Arrest in Dade County," *Criminology* 34 (1996): 61–79; "Demeanor or Crime? Why 'Hostile' Citizens Are More Likely to Be Arrested," *Criminology* 32 (1994): 475–493.

43. R. Steven Daniels, Lorin Baumhover, William Formby, and Carolyn Clark-Daniels, "Police Discretion and Elder Mistreatment: A Nested Model of Observation, Reporting, and Satisfaction," *Journal of Criminal Justice* 27 (1999): 209–225.

44. Brown, *Working the Street*, 290.

45. See Larry Hoover, *Police Educational Characteristics and Curricula* (Washington, D.C.: Government Printing Office, 1975).

46. Brian A. Reaves and Matthew Hickman, *Police Departments in Large Cities, 1990–2000* (Washington, D.C: Bureau of Justice Statistics, 2002).

47. Bruce Berg, "Who Should Teach Police: A Typology and Assessment of Police Academy Instructors," *American Journal of Police* 9 (1990): 79–100.

48. David Carter and Allen Sapp, *The State of Police Education: Critical Findings* (Washington, D.C.: Police Executive Research Forum, 1988), 6.

49. John Krimmel, "The Performance of College-Educated Police: A Study of Self-Rated Police Performance Measures," *American Journal of Police* 15 (1996): 85–95.

50. Robert Worden, "A Badge and a Baccalaureate: Policies, Hypotheses, and Further Evidence," *Justice Quarterly* 7 (1990): 565–592.

51. See Lawrence Sherman and Warren Bennis, "Higher Education for Police Officers: The Central Issues," *Police Chief 44* (1977): 32.

52. Worden, "A Badge and a Baccalaureate," 587–589.

53. Jihong Zhao and Nicholas Lovrich, "Determinants of Minority Employment in American Municipal Police Agencies: The Representation of African-American Officers," *Journal of Criminal Justice 26* (1998): 267–278.

54. David Murphy and John Worrall, "Residency Requirements and Public Perceptions of the Police in Large Municipalities," *Policing 22* (1999): 327–342.

55. Tuch and Weitzer, "The Polls-Trends: Racial Differences in Attitudes Toward the Police," 642–663.

56. Sutham Cheurprakobkit, "Police-Citizen Contact and Police Performance: Attitudinal Differences Between Hispanics and Non-Hispanics," *Journal of Criminal Justice 28* (2000) 325–336; Maguire and Pastore, eds., *Sourcebook of Criminal Justice Statistics.*

57. Yolander G. Hurst, James Frank, and Sandra Lee Browning, "The Attitudes of Juveniles Toward the Police: A Comparison of African-American and White Youth," *Policing: An International Journal of Police Strategies & Management 23* (2000): 37–53.

58. Jack Kuykendall and David Burns, "The African-American Police Officer: An Historical Perspective," *Journal of Contemporary Criminal Justice 1* (1980): 4–13.

59. Ibid.

60. Nicholas Alex, *African American in Blue: A Study of the Negro Policeman* (New York: Appleton-Century-Crofts, 1969).

61. Kim Michelle Lersch, "Predicting Citizen's Race in Allegations of Misconduct Against the Police," *Journal of Criminal Justice 26* (1998): 87–99.

62. Brian A. Reaves and Matthew J. Hickman, *Police Departments in Large Cities, 1990–2000* (Washington, D.C.: Bureau of Justice Statistics, 2002).

63. Nicholas Alex, *New York Cops Talk Back* (New York: Wiley, 1976).

64. Stephen Leinen, *African-American Police, White Society* (New York: New York University Press, 1984).

65. Donald Yates and Vijayan Pillai, "Frustration and Strain Among Fort Worth Police Officers," *Sociology and Social Research 76* (1992): 145–149.

66. Robin Haarr and Merry Morash, "Gender, Race, and Strategies of Coping with Occupational Stress in Policing," *Justice Quarterly 16* (1999): 303–336.

67. Donald Yates and Vijayan Pillai, "Race and Police Commitment to Community Policing," *Journal of Intergroup Relations 19* (1993): 14–23.

68. Bruce Berg, Edmond True, and Marc Gertz, "Police, Riots, and Alienation," *Journal of Police Science and Administration 12* (1984): 186–190.

69. Yates and Pillai, "Frustration and Strain Among Fort Worth Police Officers."

70. James Jacobs and Jay Cohen, "The Impact of Racial Integration on the Police," *Journal of Police Science and Administration 6* (1978): 182.

71. Charles Katz, "The Establishment of a Police Gang Unit: An Examination of organizational and Environmental Factors," *Criminology 39* (2001): 37–73.

72. Ibid., 61.

73. For a review of the history of women in policing, see Dorothy Moses Schulz, "From Policewoman to Police Officer: An Unfinished Revolution," *Police Studies 16* (1993): 90–99; Cathryn House, "The Changing Role of Women in Law Enforcement," *Police Chief 60* (1993): 139–144.

74. Susan Martin, "Female Officers on the Move? A Status Report on Women in Policing," in *Critical Issues in Policing*, eds. Roger Dunham and Geoffery Alpert (Grove Park, Ill.: Waveland Press, 1988), 312–31.

75. *Le Bouef v. Ramsey,* 26 FEP Cases 884 (9/16/80).

76. Michael Birzer and Delores Craig, "Gender Differences in Police Physical Ability Test Performance," *American Journal of Police 15* (1996): 93–106.

77. Reaves and Hickman, *Police Departments in Large Cities, 1990–2000.*

78. James Daum and Cindy Johns, "Police Work from a Woman's Perspective," *Police Chief 61* (1994): 46–49.

79. Steve Herbert, *'Hard Charger' or 'Station Queen'? Policing and the Masculinist State, Gender Place & Culture: A Journal of Feminist Geography 8* (2001): 55–72.

80. Ibid., 58.

81. Matthew Hickman, Alex Piquero, and Jack Greene, "Discretion and Gender Disproportionality in Police Disciplinary Systems," *Policing: An International Journal of Police Strategies & Management 23* (2000): 105–116.

82. Robin Haarr and Merry Morash, "Gender, Race, and Strategies of Coping with Occupational Stress in Policing," *Justice Quarterly 16* (1999): 303–336.

83. Merry Morash and Jack Greene, "Evaluating Women on Patrol: A Critique of Contemporary Wisdom," *Evaluation Review 10* (1986): 230–255.

84. Peter Bloch and Deborah Anderson, *Policewomen on Patrol: Final Report* (Washington, D.C.: Police Foundation, 1974).

85. Steven Brandl, Meghan Stroshine, and James Frank, "Who Are the Complaint-Prone Officers? An Examination of the Relationship Between Police Officers' Attributes, Arrest Activity, Assignment, and Citizens' Complaints About Excessive Force," *Journal of Criminal Justice 29* (2001): 521–529.

86. Daum and Johns, "Police Work from a Woman's Perspective," 46–49.

87. Mary Brown, "The Plight of Female Police: A Survey of NW Patrolmen," *Police Chief 61* (1994): 50–53.

88. Simon Holdaway and Sharon K. Parker, "Policing Women Police: Uniform Patrol, Promotion and Representation in the CID," *British Journal of Criminology 38* (1998): 40–48.

89. Curt Bartol, George Bergen, Julie Seager Volckens, and Kathleen Knoras, "Women in Small-Town Policing: Job Performance and Stress," *Criminal Justice and Behavior 19* (1992): 245–259.

90. Susan Martin, "Outsider Within the Station House: The Impact of Race and Gender on African-American Women Police," *Social Problems 41* (1994): 383–400.

91. Martin, "Outsider Within the Station House," 387.

92. Ibid., 392.

93. Ibid., 394.

94. Ibid., 397.

95. Ibid.

96. Eric Poole and Mark Pogrebin, "Factors Affecting the Decision to Remain in Policing: A Study of Women Officers," *Journal of Police Science and Administration* 16 (1988): 49–55

97. *Miranda v. Arizona*, 384 U.S. 436 (1966).

98. *Colorado v. Connelly*, 107 S.Ct. 515 (1986).

99. *Minnick v. Miss.*, 498 U.S. 46; 111 S.Ct. 486; 112 L.Ed.2d. 489 (1990).

100. *Harris v. New York*, 401 U.S. 222 (1971).

101. *Michigan v. Tucker*, 417 U.S. 433 (1974).

102. *Nix v. Williams*, 104 S.Ct. 2501 (1984).

103. *Oregon v. Elstad*, 105 S.Ct. 1285 (1985).

104. *Colorado v. Connelly*, 107 S.Ct. 515 (1986).

105. *Arizona v. Fulminante*, 499 U.S. 279, 111 S.Ct. 1246; 113 L.Ed.2d. 302 (1991).

106. *Moran v. Burbine*, 106 S.Ct. 1135 (1986); *Michigan v. Mosley*, 423 U.S. 96 (1975); *Fare v. Michael C.*, 442 U.S. 23 (1979).

107. *New York v. Quarles*, 104 S.Ct. 2626 (1984).

108. *Colorado v. Spring*, 107 S.Ct. 851 (1987).

109. *Moran v. Burbine*, 106 S.Ct. 1135 (1986).

110. *Davis v. United States*, 114 S.Ct. 2350 (1994).

111. *Dickerson v. United States*, 530 U.S. 428 (2000)

112. Victoria Time and Brian Payne, "Police Chiefs' Perceptions About *Miranda*: An Analysis of Survey Data," *Journal of Criminal Justice* 30 (2002): 77–86.

113. Ibid.

114. *Kirk v. Louisiana*, No. 01-8419; U.S. Supreme Court; per curiam opinion; decided June 24, 2002.

115. *Illinois v. Gates*, 462 U.S. 213, 103 S.Ct. 2317, 76 L.Ed.2d 527 (1983).

116. *Chimel v. California*, 395 U.S. 752 (1969).

117. *Terry v. Ohio*, 392 U.S. 1 (1968).

118. *Illinois v. Wardlow*, 528 U.S. 119 (2000).

119. *Carroll v. United States*, 267 U.S. 132 (1925).

120. *United States v. Ross*, 102 S.Ct. 2147 (1982).

121. *Whren v. United States*, 116 S.Ct. 1769 (1996).

122. Drivers, *Pennsylvania v. Mimms*, 434 U.S. 106 (1977); passengers, *Maryland v. Wilson*, 117 U.S. 882 (1997).

123. Mark Hansen, "Rousting Miss Daisy?" *American Bar Association Journal* 83 (1997): 22; *Knowles v. Iowa*, 119 S.Ct. 507 (1998); *Wyoming v. Houghton*, 119 S.Ct. 1297 (1999).

124. *Bumper v. North Carolina*, 391 U.S. 543 (1960).

125. *Ohio v. Robinette*, 117 S. Ct. 417 (1996).

126. Limitations on the plain view doctrine have been defined in *Arizona v. Hicks*, 107 S.Ct. 1149 (1987); the recording of serial numbers from stereo components in a suspect's apartment could not be justified as being in plain view.

127. *Katz v. United States*, 389 U.S. 347 (1967).

128. *Weeks v. United States*, 232 U.S. 383, 34 S.Ct. 341, 58 L.Ed. 652 (1914).

129. *Mapp v. Ohio*, 367 U.S. 643, 81 S.Ct. 1684, 6 L.Ed.2d 1081 (1961).

130. *United States v. Leon*, 468 U.S. 897, 104 S.Ct. 3405, 82 L.Ed.2d 677 (1984).

131. William Greenhalgh, *The Fourth Amendment Handbook: A Chronological Survey of Supreme Court Decisions* (Chicago: American Bar Association Section on Criminal Justice, 1995).

132. Donald Dripps, "The Case for the Contingent Exclusionary Rule," *American Criminal Law Review* 38 (2001): 1–47.

133. Karen Kruger and Nicholas Valltos, "Dealing with Domestic Violence in Law Enforcement Relationships," *FBI Law Enforcement Bulletin* 71 (2002): 1–7.

134. Yates and Pillai, "Frustration and Strain Among Fort Worth Police Officers."

135. For an impressive review, see Richard Farmer, "Clinical and Managerial Implication of Stress Research on the Police," *Journal of Police Science and Administration* 17 (1990): 205–217.

136. Lawrence Travis III and Craig Winston, "Dissension in the Ranks: Officer Resistance to Community Policing and Support for the Organization," *Journal of Crime and Justice* 21 (1998): 139–155.

137. Francis Cullen, Terrence Lemming, Bruce Link, and John Wozniak, "The Impact of Social Supports on Police Stress," *Criminology* 23 (1985): 503–522.

138. Farmer, "Clinical and Managerial Implications"; Nancy Norvell, Dale Belles, and Holly Hills, "Perceived Stress Levels and Physical Symptoms in Supervisory Law Enforcement Personnel," *Journal of Police Science and Administration* 16 (1988): 75–79.

139. Donald Yates and Vijayan Pillai, "Attitudes Toward Community Policing: A Causal Analysis," *Social Science Journal* 33 (1996): 193–209.

140. Harvey McMurray, "Attitudes of Assaulted Police Officers and Their Policy Implications," *Journal of Police Science and Administration* 17 (1990): 44–48.

141. Robert Ankony and Thomas Kelly, "The Impact of Perceived Alienation of Police Officers' Sense of Mastery and Subsequent Motivation for Proactive Enforcement," *Policing* 22 (1999): 120–132.

142. Lawrence Blum, *Force Under Pressure: How Cops Live and Why They Die* (New York: Lantern Books, 2000).

143. Rose Lee Josephson and Martin Reiser, "Officer Suicide in the Los Angeles Police Department: A Twelve-Year Follow-Up," *Journal of Police Science and Administration* 17 (1990): 227–230.

144. Yates and Pillai, "Attitudes Toward Community Policing," 205–206.

145. Ibid.

146. Rosanna Church and Naomi Robertson, "How State Police Agencies Are Addressing the Issue of Wellness," *Policing* 22 (1999): 304–312.

147. Farmer, "Clinical and Managerial Implications," 215.

148. Peter Hart, Alexander Wearing, and Bruce Headey, "Assessing Police Work Experiences: Development of the Police Daily Hassles and Uplifts Scales," *Journal of Criminal Justice* 21 (1993): 553–573.

149. Vivian Lord, Denis Gray, and Samuel Pond, "The Police Stress Inventory: Does It Measure Stress?" *Journal of Criminal Justice* 19 (1991): 139–49.

150. "New York Pays $3M to Police Victim Kin," *New York Times*, 2 October 1998, A1.

151. Bittner, *The Functions of Police in Modern Society*, 46.

152. Richard R. Johnson, "Citizen Complaints: What the Police Should Know," *FBI Law Enforcement Bulletin 67* (1998): 1–6.

153. For a general review, see Tom McEwen, *National Data Collection on Police Use of Force* (Washington, D.C.: National Institute of Justice, 1996).

154. Patrick A. Langan, Lawrence A. Greenfeld, Steven K. Smith, Matthew R. Durose, and David J. Levin, *Contacts Between Police and the Public Findings from the 1999 National Survey* (Washington, D.C.: Bureau of Justice Statistics, 2001).

155. Antony Pate and Lorie Fridell, *Police Use of Force: Official Reports, Citizen Complaints, and Legal Consequences* (Washington, D.C.: Police Foundation, 1993).

156. Langan, Greenfeld, Smith, Durose, and Levin, *Contacts Between Police and the Public Findings from the 1999 National Survey.*

157. Sandra Lee Browning, Francis Cullen, Liqun Cao, Renee Kopache, and Thomas Stevenson, "Race and Getting Hassled by the Police: A Research Note," *Police Studies 17* (1994): 1–11.

158. Ibid.

159. Kim Michelle Lersch and Tom Mieczkowski, "Who Are the Problem-Prone Officers? An Analysis of Citizen Complaints," *American Journal of Police 15* (1996): 23–42.

160. Samuel Walker, "The Rule Revolution: Reflections on the Transformation of American Criminal Justice, 1950–1988," Working Papers, Series 3 (Madison: Institute for Legal Studies, University of Wisconsin Law School, December 1988).

161. Michael D. White, "Controlling Police Decisions to Use Deadly Force: Reexamining the Importance of Administrative Policy," *Crime and Delinquency 47* (2001): 131.

162. Kevin Flynn, "New York Police Sting Tries to Weed Out Brutal Officers," *New York Times,* 24 September 1999, 2.

163. Lawrence Sherman and Robert Langworthy, "Measuring Homicide by Police Officers," *Journal of Criminal Law and Criminology 4* (1979): 546–560.

164. Ibid.

165. James Fyfe, "Police Use of Deadly Force: Research and Reform," *Justice Quarterly 5* (1988): 165–205.

166. Sherman and Langworthy, "Measuring Homicide by Police Officers."

167. Richard Kania and Wade Mackey, "Police Violence as a Function of Community Characteristics," *Criminology 15* (1977): 27–48.

168. John MacDonald, Geoffrey Alpert, and Abraham Tennenbaum, "Justifiable Homicide by Police and Criminal Homicide: A Research Note," *Journal of Crime and Justice 22* (1999): 153–164.

169. Richard Parent and Simon Verdun-Jones, "Victim-Precipitated Homicide: Police Use of Deadly Force in British Columbia," *Policing 21* (1998): 432–449.

170. "10 Percent of Police Shootings Found to Be 'Suicide by Cop,'" *Criminal Justice Newsletter 29* (1998): 1.

171. Sherman and Langworthy, "Measuring Homicide by Police Officers."

172. Jonathan Sorenson, James Marquart, and Deon Brock, "Factors Related to Killings of Felons by Police Officers: A Test of the Community Violence and Conflict Hypotheses," *Justice Quarterly 10* (1993): 417–440; David Jacobs and David Britt, "Inequality and Police Use of Deadly Force: An Empiri-

cal Assessment of a Conflict Hypotheses," *Social Problems 26* (1979): 403–412.

173. David Jacobs and Jason Carmichael, "Subordination and Violence Against State Control Agents: Testing Political Explanations for Lethal Assaults Against the Police," *Social Forces 80* (2002): 1223–1252.

174. Fyfe, "Police Use of Deadly Force," 181.

175. Paul Takagi, "A Garrison State in a 'Democratic' Society," *Crime and Social Justice 5* (1974): 34–43.

176. Mark Blumberg, "Race and Police Shootings: An Analysis in Two Cities," in *Contemporary Issues in Law Enforcement,* ed. James Fyfe (Beverly Hills, Calif.: Sage, 1981), 152–166.

177. James Fyfe, "Shots Fired" (Ph.D. diss., State University of New York, Albany, 1978).

178. *Tennessee v. Garner,* 471 U.S. 1, 105 S.Ct. 1694, 85 L.Ed.2d 889 (1985).

179. *Graham v. Connor,* 490 U.S. 386, 109 S.Ct. 1865, 104 L.Ed.2d 443 (1989).

180. Franklin Graves and Gregory Connor, "The FLETC Use-of-Force Model," *Police Chief 59* (1992): 56–58.

181. See James Fyfe, "Administrative Interventions on Police Shooting Discretion: An Empirical Examination," *Journal of Criminal Justice 7* (1979): 313–325.

182. Frank Zarb, "Police Liability for Creating the Need to Use Deadly Force in Self-Defense," *Michigan Law Review 86* (1988): 1982–2009.

183. Warren Cohen, "When Lethal Force Won't Do," *U.S. News & World Report 122* (23 June 1997): 12.

184. Richard Lumb and Paul Friday, "Impact of Pepper Spray Availability on Police Officer Use-of-Force Decisions," *Policing 20* (1997): 136–149.

185. Tom McEwen, "Policies on Less-than-Lethal Force in Law Enforcement Agencies," *Policing 20* (1997): 39–60.

186. FBI, "Law Enforcement Officers Killed and Assaulted, 2000," press release, 26 October 2001.

187. J. David Hirschel, Charles Dean, and Richard Lumb, "The Relative Contribution of Domestic Violence to Assault and Injury of Police Officers," *Justice Quarterly 11* (1994): 99–118.

188. John Cloud, "L.A. Confidential, for Real: Street Cops Accused of Frame-Ups in Widening Scandal," *Time,* 27 September 1999, 44; "L.A.'s Dirty War on Gangs: A Trail of Corruption Leads to Some of the City's Toughest Cops," *Newsweek,* 11 October 1999, 72.

189. Walker, *Popular Justice,* 64.

190. Herman Goldstein, *Police Corruption* (Washington, D.C.: Police Foundation, 1975), 3.

191. Knapp Commission, *Report on Police Corruption* (New York: Braziller, 1973), 1–34.

192. Elizabeth Neuffer, "Seven Additional Detectives Linked to Extortion Scheme," *Boston Globe,* 25 October 1988, 60.

193. Kevin Cullen, "U.S. Probe Eyes Bookie Protection," *Boston Globe,* 25 October 1988.

194. Michael Johnston, *Political Corruption and Public Policy in America* (Monterey, Calif.: Brooks/Cole, 1982), 75.

195. William Doherty, "Ex-Sergeant Says He Aided Bid to Sell Exam," *Boston Globe,* 26 February 1987, 61.

196. Anthony Simpson, *The Literature of Police Corruption,* vol. 1 (New York: John Jay Press, 1977), 53.

197. Peter Kraska and Victor Kappeler, "Police On-Duty Drug Use: A Theoretical and Descriptive Examination," *American Journal of Police* 7 (1988): 1–28.

198. Ellwyn Stoddard, "Blue Coat Crime," in *Thinking About Police,* ed. Carl Klockars (New York: McGraw-Hill, 1983), 338–349.

199. Lawrence Sherman, *Police Corruption: A Sociological Perspective* (Garden City, N.Y.: Doubleday, 1974).

200. Robert Daley, *Prince of the City* (New York: Houghton Mifflin, 1978).

201. Sherman, *Police Corruption,* 40–41.

202. Samuel Walker, *Police in Society* (New York: McGraw-Hill, 1983), 181.

203. Sherman, *Police Corruption,* 194.

204. Kevin Flynn, "Police Department Routinely Drops Cases of Officer Misconduct, Report Says," *New York Times,* 15 September 1999, 1.

205. Barbara Gelb, *Tarnished Brass: The Decade After Serpico* (New York: Putnam, 1983); Candace McCoy, "Lawsuits Against Police: What Impact Do They Have?" *Criminal Law Bulletin* 20 (1984): 49–56.

206. "Philadelphia Police Corruption Brings Major Reform Initiative," *Criminal Justice Newsletter* 27 (1996): 4–5.

The Law Enforcement Response to Terrorism

In the aftermath of the September 11, 2001, attacks it became obvious that the nation was not prepared to deal adequately with the threat of terrorism. One reason is the very nature of American society. Because we live in a free and open nation, it is extremely difficult to seal the borders and prevent the entry of terrorist groups. For example, terrorism expert Stephen E. Flynn notes that even with the assistance of new high-tech sensors it takes five customs inspectors three hours to conduct a thorough physical inspection of a loaded forty-foot container or an eighteen-wheel truck. Every day, nearly five thousand trucks enter the United States on the Ambassador Bridge between Detroit, Michigan, and Windsor, Ontario. With only eight primary inspection lanes and a parking lot that can hold just ninety tractor-trailers at a time, U.S. Customs officers must average no more than two minutes per truck. If they fall behind, the parking lot fills, trucks back up onto the bridge, and chaos occurs on the roadways throughout metropolitan Windsor and Detroit.

Sensing this problem, law enforcement agencies around the country began to realign their resources to combat future terrorist attacks. In some instances, proposed changes are in the planning or approval stage while in others change has already been completed.

Federal Law Enforcement

One of the most significant proposals has been a realignment of the Federal Bureau of Investigation. The FBI has already announced a reformulation of its priorities, as shown in Exhibit A.1, making protecting the United States from terrorist attack its Number One commitment.

To carry out its newly formulated mission, the FBI is expanding its force of agents, hiring approximately one thousand more between 2002 and 2003. In addition to recruiting candidates with the traditional background in law enforcement, law, and accounting, the Bureau is concentrating on hiring agents with scientific and technological skills as well as foreign-language proficiency in priority areas such as Arabic, Farsi, Pashtun, Urdu, all dialects of Chinese, Japanese, Korean, Russian, Spanish, and Vietnamese, and with other priority backgrounds such as foreign counterintelligence, counterterrorism, and military intelligence. Besides helping in counterterrorism activities, these agents will staff the new Cyber Division, which was created in 2001 to coordinate, oversee, and fa-

Exhibit A.1	Reformulated FBI priorities

1. Protect the United States from terrorist attack.
2. Protect the United States against foreign intelligence operations and espionage.
3. Protect the United States against cyber-based attacks and high-technology crimes.
4. Combat public corruption at all levels.
5. Protect civil rights.
6. Combat transnational and national criminal organizations and enterprises.
7. Combat major white-collar crime.
8. Combat significant violent crime.
9. Support federal, state, local, and international partners.
10. Upgrade technology to successfully perform the FBI's mission.

cilitate FBI investigations in which the Internet, online services, and computer systems and networks are the principal instruments or targets of terrorists. Exhibit A.2 describes some of the other actions the FBI has undertaken to combat terrorist activities.

Department of Homeland Security

Soon after the 2001 attack, President George W. Bush proposed the creation of a new cabinet-level agency called the Department of Homeland Security and assigned it the following mission:

- Preventing terrorist attacks within the United States
- Reducing America's vulnerability to terrorism
- Minimizing the damage and recovering from attacks that do occur

On November 19, 2002, Congress passed legislation authorizing the creation of a new cabinet-level Department of Homeland Security "providing for intelligence analysis and infrastructure protection, strengthening our borders, improving the use of science and technology to counter weapons of mass destruction, and creating a comprehensive response and recovery division." While the agency's final form is still being shaped, under the legislation signed by President Bush on November 25, 2002, the of-

C. Sherburne/PhotoLink/Getty Images

Exhibit A.2 **Key near-term actions to combat counterterrorism**

1. Restructure the Counterterrorism Division at FBI headquarters (redefine relationship between HQ and field; shift from reactive to proactive orientation).
2. Establish "flying squads" to coordinate national and international investigations.
3. Establish a national Joint Terrorism Task Force.
4. Substantially enhance analytical capabilities with personnel and technology (expand use of data mining, financial record analysis, and communications analysis to combat terrorism; establish Office of Intelligence).
5. Build a national terrorism response capability that is more mobile, agile, and flexible.
6. Permanently shift additional resources to counterterrorism.
7. Augment overseas capabilities and partnerships.
8. Target recruitment to acquire agents, analysts, translators, and others with specialized skills and backgrounds.
9. Enhance counterterrorism training for FBI and law enforcement partners.

fice would fold existing agencies within its framework to create a superagency with four divisions:

Border and Transportation Security. The Department of Homeland Security would be responsible for securing our nation's borders and transportation systems, which include 350 ports of entry. The department would manage who and what enters our the country, and work to prevent the entry of terrorists and the instruments of terrorism while simultaneously ensuring the speedy flow of legitimate traffic. The border security mission would incorporate the customs service (currently part of the Department of Treasury), the Immigration and Naturalization Service and Border Patrol (Department of Justice), the Animal and Plant Health Inspection Service (Department of Agriculture), and the Transportation Security Administration (Department of Transportation). The department would also incorporate the Federal Protective Service (General Services Administration) to perform the additional function of protecting government buildings, a task closely related to the department's infrastructure protection responsibilities. In order to secure territorial waters, including ports and waterways, the department would assume authority over the United States Coast Guard.

Emergency Preparedness and Response. The Department of Homeland Security would ensure the pre-

paredness of emergency response professionals, provide the federal government's response, and aid America's recovery from terrorist attacks and natural disasters. To fulfill these missions, the department would incorporate within its structure the Federal Emergency Management Agency (FEMA). The department would be responsible for reducing the loss of life and property and protecting institutions from all types of hazards through an emergency management program of preparedness, mitigation, response, and recovery. It would lead our national response to a biological attack, direct the Nuclear Emergency Search Teams, Radiological Emergency Response Team, Radiological Assistance Program, Domestic Emergency Support Team, National Pharmaceutical Stockpile, and the National Disaster Medical System, and it would manage the Metropolitan Medical Response System. The department would also coordinate the involvement of other federal response assets such as the National Guard in the event of a major incident.

Chemical, Biological, Radiological, and Nuclear Countermeasures. The Department of Homeland Security would lead the federal government's efforts in preparing for and responding to the full range of terrorist threats involving weapons of mass destruction. To do this, the department would set national policy and establish guidelines for state and local governments. It would direct exercises and drills for federal, state, and local chemical, biological, radiological, and nuclear (CBRN) response teams and plans. The department would also work to prevent the importation of nuclear weapons and material. It would focus on better detection of illicit nuclear material transport on the open seas, at U.S. ports of entry, and throughout the national transportation system. It would also develop, deploy, manage, and maintain a national system for detecting the use of biological agents within the United States. This system would consist of a national public health data surveillance system to monitor public and private databases for indications that a bioterrorist attack has occurred, as well as a sensor network to detect and report the release of bioterrorist pathogens in densely populated areas.

Information Analysis and Infrastructure Protection. In this capacity the department would analyze legally accessible information from multiple available sources, including foreign intelligence, the CIA, FBI, the National Security Agency, and local law enforcement information. By obtaining and analyzing this information, the department would have the ability to view the dangers facing the nation comprehensively, ensure that the President is briefed on relevant information, and take necessary protective action. The Department of Homeland Security would complement the FBI's enhanced emphasis on counterterrorism law enforcement by ensuring that information from the FBI is analyzed side by side with all other intelligence. In addition to analyzing law enforcement and intelligence information, the Department of Homeland Security would protect the nation's cyber infrastructure from terrorist attack by unifying and focusing the key cybersecurity activities performed by the Critical Infrastructure Assurance Office (currently part of the Department of Commerce) and the National Infrastructure Protection Center (FBI). The department would augment those capabilities with the response functions of the federal Computer Incident Response Center (General Services Administration).

Local Law Enforcement

Federal law enforcement agencies are not alone in responding to the threat of terrorism. And, of course, nowhere is the threat of terrorism being taken more seriously than in New York City, which has established a new Counterterrorism Bureau. Teams within the bureau have been trained to examine potential targets in the city and are now attempting to insulate them from possible attack. Viewed as prime targets are the city's bridges, the Empire State Building, Rockefeller Center, and the United Nations. Bureau detectives will be assigned overseas to work with the police in several foreign cities, including cities in Canada and Israel. Detectives have been assigned as liaisons with Interpol, in Lyon, France, and with the FBI. The city is now recruiting detectives with language skills from Pashtun and Urdu to Arabic, Fujianese, and other dialects. The existing New York City Police Intelligence Division has been revamped, and agents are examining foreign newspapers and monitoring Internet sites. The department is also setting up several backup command centers in different parts of the city in case a terror attack puts headquarters out of operation. Several backup senior command teams have been created so that if people at the highest levels of the department are killed, individuals will already have been tapped to step into their jobs.

The Counterterrorism Bureau has assigned more than one hundred city police detectives to work with FBI agents as part of a Joint Terrorist Task Force. In addition, the Intelligence Division's seven hundred investigators now devote 35 to 40 percent of their resources to counterterrorism, up from about 2 percent before January 2002. The department is also drawing on the expertise of other institutions around the city. For example, medical specialists have been enlisted to monitor daily developments in the city's hospitals to detect any suspicious outbreaks of illness that might reflect a biological attack. And the police are now conducting joint drills with the New York Fire Department to avoid the problems in communication and coordination that marked the emergency response on September 11. ■

Sources: William K. Rashbaum, "Terror Makes All the World a Beat for New York Police," *New York Times,* 15 July 2002, B1; Al Baker, "Leader Sees New York Police in Vanguard of Terror Fight," *New York Times,* 6 August 2002, A2; Stephen Flynn, "America the Vulnerable," *Foreign Affairs 81* (January-February 2002): 60; White House press release, 11 November 2002, www.whitehouse.gov/news/releases/2002/11/20021119-4.html. The section on homeland security relies heavily on "The Department of Homeland Security," www.whitehouse.gov/deptofhomeland/.

 To find out more about terrorism, go to http://cj.wadsworth.com and click on "Terrorism Update."

Courts
and
Adjudication

The nation's court system is the location of some of the most critical decisions in the criminal justice system. Take, for instance, the recent decision by the Supreme Court in *Pottawatomie County et al. v. Earls* (2002). In its decision, the Court decided to uphold the student activities drug testing policy adopted by the Tecumseh, Oklahoma, School District. The policy requires all middle and high school students to consent to urinalysis testing for drugs if they wish to participate in any extracurricular activity. A federal appellate court had previously overruled the policy, holding that it violated the Fourth Amendment right to privacy.

The Supreme Court disagreed. It ruled that a search of schoolchildren may be reasonable when supported by "special needs" beyond the normal need for law enforcement; making sure that kids who participate in extracurricular activities are drug-free is one of those needs. The Court concluded that the students affected by this policy have a limited expectation of privacy and that the policy does not interfere with their personal lives. Under the policy, a faculty monitor waits outside the closed rest room stall for the student to produce a sample and must listen for the normal sounds of urination to guard against tampered specimens and ensure an accurate chain of custody. The Court did not see this as particularly intrusive or as an invasion of privacy. Furthermore, the only consequence of a failed drug test is to limit the student's privilege of participating in extracurricular activities. The Court ruled that this drug-testing policy is valid because preventing drug use by schoolchildren is an important governmental concern. Given the nationwide epidemic of drug use, and the evidence of drug use in Tecumseh schools that was presented, the Court concluded that the

conditions necessary to allow such a testing policy were amply met by the school district.

Pottawatomie County et al. v. Earls is a case that illustrates the delicate balance between individual freedom and governmental concerns, which is reviewed by the court system every day. Kids who have never been in trouble and who are not suspected of taking drugs must hand over urine samples in order to get a part in the school play or go on a field trip. Is this a violation of their right to privacy? The Supreme Court said "No!" What do you think?

This section reviews the workings of the court system. Four chapters cover the structure of the courts: court personnel, early court processes, the criminal trial, and sentencing. ■

7 Courts, Prosecution, and the Defense

Chapter Outline

Criminal Justice Links

Criminal Justice Viewpoints

Courtesy of CNN

ON JANUARY 26, 2001, Diane Whipple, a San Francisco woman, died after two large Presa Canario dogs attacked her in the hallway of her apartment building. The dogs' owners and keepers, Marjorie Knoller and her husband, Robert Noel, were charged with second-degree murder and involuntary manslaughter, respectively. During the trial it was revealed that the couple was involved with prison inmates Paul Schneider and Dale Bretches, members of the white supremacist Aryan Brotherhood who are serving life sentences without parole. The inmates were selling the lawyers' services as part of a business training dogs for fighting and for guarding illegal drug labs.

After the couple's conviction on March 21, 2002, and to the chagrin of Whipple's friends and family, Judge James Warren used his discretion to overturn the conviction. He concluded that the evidence overwhelmingly proved manslaughter but did not show Knoller knew her two dogs would fatally attack her neighbor Diane Whipple, and therefore did not support the charge of second-degree murder. He qualified his decision when he stated, "This does not in any way excuse or change the horror of what happened.... This does not minimize or excuse the despicable conduct of the defendants. I don't believe there is anybody in San Francisco who would rather not see Ms. Knoller go to prison for second-degree murder." Warren called Noel and Knoller "the most despised couple in San Francisco." ■

To view the CNN video clip of this story, go to the book-specific Web site at http://cj.wadsworth.com/siegel_essen4e.

The Knoller case illustrates the powerful role that the judge, along with the prosecutor and defense attorney, play in the criminal trial. In this case, a judge used his discretion and interpretation of the law to overturn a jury verdict.

The criminal court is the setting in which many of the most important decisions in the criminal justice system are made: eyewitness identification, bail, trial, plea negotiations, and sentencing all involve court-made decisions. Within the confines of the court, those accused of crime (defendants) call on the tools of the legal system to provide them with a fair and just hearing, with the burden of proof resting on the state; crime victims ask the government to provide them with justice for the wrongs done them and the injuries they have suffered; and agents of the criminal justice system attempt to find solutions that benefit the victim, the defendant, and society in general. The court process is designed to provide an open and impartial forum for deciding the truth of the matter and reaching a solution that, although punitive, is fairly arrived at and satisfies the rule of law.

It must render fair, impartial justice in deciding the outcome of a conflict between criminal and victim, law enforcement agents and violators of the law, parent and child, federal government and violators of governmental regulations, or other parties. Regardless of the issues involved, the parties' presence in a courtroom should guarantee that they will have a hearing conducted under rules of procedure in an atmosphere of fair play and objectivity and that the outcome of the hearing will be clear. If a party believes that the ground rules have been violated, he or she may take the case to a higher court, where the procedures of the original trial will be reexamined. If it finds that a violation of legal rights has occurred, the appellate court may deem the findings of the original trial improper and either order a new hearing or hold that some other measure must be carried out; for example, the court may dismiss the charge outright.

The court is a complex social agency with many independent but interrelated subsystems—clerk, prosecutor, defense attorney, judge, and probation department—each having a role in the court's operation. Ideally, the judicatory process operates with absolute fairness and equality. The entire process—from filing the initial complaint to final sentencing of the defendant—is governed by precise rules of law designed to ensure fairness. No defendant tried before a U.S. court should suffer or benefit because of his or her personal characteristics, beliefs, or affiliations. However, in today's crowded court system, such abstract goals are often impossible to achieve. The nation's court system is chronically underbudgeted and recent economic downturns have not helped matters. In Alabama, funds were so low in 2002 that the state's senior justice called for a five-month moratorium on most jury trials; in Massachusetts, the trial court system, paralyzed by budget cuts, stopped conducting civil trials in twenty-five superior courtrooms in early May 2002; Kentucky's judicial system was in crisis in 2002 after the legislature failed to pass a budget.[1]

These constraints have a significant impact on the way courts carry out justice. Quite often, the U.S. court system is the scene of accommodation and "working things out," rather than an arena for a vigorous criminal defense. Plea negotiations and other nonjudicial alternatives, such as diversion, are far more common than the formal trial process. Consequently, U.S. criminal justice can be selective. Discretion accompanies defendants through every step of the process, determining what will happen to them and how their cases will be resolved. *Discretion* means that two people committing similar crimes will receive highly dissimilar treatment; for example, most people convicted of homicide receive a prison sentence, but about 4 percent receive probation as a sole sentence; indeed, more murderers get probation than the death penalty.[2]

In this chapter, we examine the structure and function of the court system. We begin by looking at the nature of the court process and its major players: judge, prosecutor, and defense attorney.

Use the term "court crowding" as a subject guide on InfoTrac College Edition to learn more about this social problem.

The Criminal Court Process

The U.S. court system has evolved over the years into an intricately balanced legal process, which has recently come under siege because of the sheer number of cases it must consider and the ways in which it is forced to handle such overcrowding. Overloaded court dockets have given rise to charges of "assembly-line justice," in which a majority of defendants are induced to plead guilty, jury trials are rare, and the speedy trial is highly desired but unattainable.

Overcrowding causes the poor to languish in detention while the wealthier go free on bail. It is possible that an innocent person may be frightened into pleading guilty and, conversely, a guilty person released because a trial has been delayed too long.[3] Whether providing more judges or new or larger courts will solve the problem of overcrowding remains to be seen. Meanwhile, diversion programs, decriminalization of certain offenses, and bail reform provide other avenues of possible relief. More efficient court management and administration is also seen as a step that might ease the congestion of the courts. The introduction of professional trial court managers—administrators, clerks, and judges with management skills—is one of the more significant waves of change in the nation's courts in recent decades.

To house this rather complex process, each state maintains its own state court organization and structure. American courts basically have two systems: state and federal. There are fifty state trial and appellate systems and separate courts for the District of Columbia and the Commonwealth of Puerto Rico. Usually three (or more) separate court systems exist within each state jurisdiction. These are described next.

Use "criminal court process" as a subject guide on InfoTrac College Edition to learn more about court conditions in the United States and abroad.

State Courts

The state court system alone handled about ninety-two million new cases in 2000 (the last data available).[4] That total included about twenty million civil and domestic cases, over fourteen million criminal cases, two million juvenile cases, and fifty-six million traffic and ordinance violations. Significant growth has characterized the states' criminal caseloads, which rose about 46 percent from 1984 to 2000 (see Figure 7.1). Although criminal case filings rose significantly, traffic cases actually declined, probably because the number of driving while intoxicated (DWI) cases dropped by about 5 percent. The decline in DWI filings probably reflects stricter law enforcement, media attention to the problem, and alcohol awareness programs. The recent uptick, however—between 1997 and 2000—shows that the DWI problem remains a national concern.

The National Center for State Courts is an independent, nonprofit organization dedicated to the improvement of justice. NCSC activities include developing policies to enhance state courts, advancing state courts' interests in the federal government, fostering state-court adaptation to future changes, securing sufficient resources for state courts, strengthening state court leadership, facilitating state court collaboration, and providing a model for organizational administration. To access its Web site, go to www.ncsc.dni.us

Courts of Limited Jurisdiction

There are approximately fourteen thousand courts of limited jurisdiction in the United States. Most are organized along town, municipal, and county lines of government; the rest are controlled by state governments. Limited jurisdiction courts outnumber general jurisdiction courts approximately five to one (fourteen thousand to three thousand).[5]

Courts of limited jurisdiction (sometimes called municipal courts, or **lower courts**) are restricted in the types of cases they may hear. Usually, they will handle misdemeanor criminal infractions, violations of municipal ordinances, traffic violations, and civil suits where the damages involve less than a certain amount of money (usually $10,000). These courts also conduct preliminary hearings for felony criminal cases.

The lower criminal courts are restricted in the criminal penalties they can impose. Most can levy a fine of $1,000 or less and incarcerate a person for twelve months or less in the local jail.

Included in the category of courts of limited jurisdiction are special courts, such as juvenile, family, and probate (divorce, estate issues, and custody) courts.

lower court A generic term referring to a court that has jurisdiction over misdemeanors and conducts preliminary investigations of felony charges.

Cases filed in state courts, 1984–2000 (in millions)

Juvenile

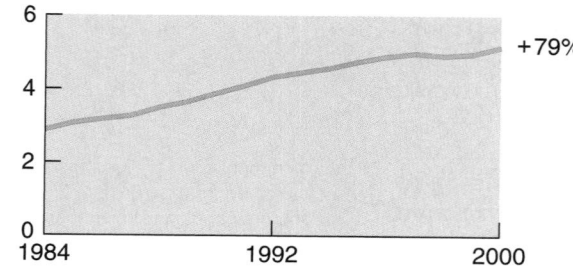

+66%

Domestic

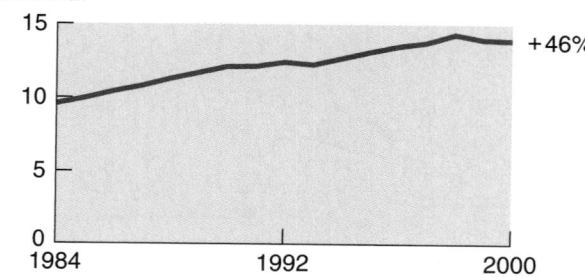

+79%

Criminal

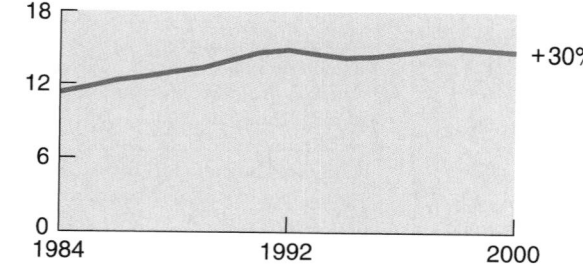

+46%

Civil

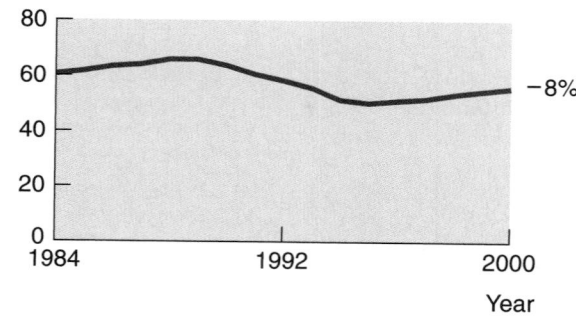

+30%

Traffic

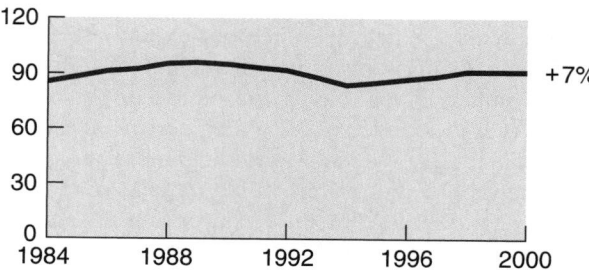

−8%

Year

Total state court caseloads, 1984–2000 (in millions)

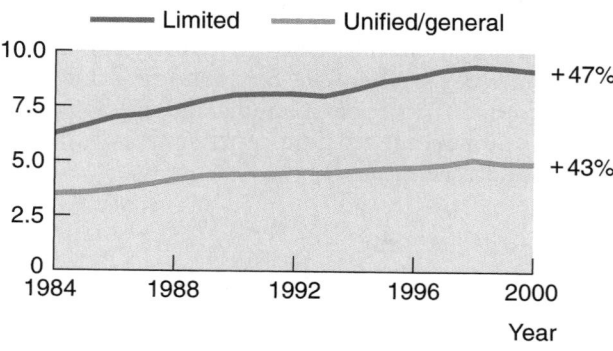

+7%

Criminal cases filed in state courts by court jurisdiction, 1984–2000 (in millions)

Limited — Unified/general

+47%

+43%

Year

Figure 7.1
State court cases, 1984–2000

Source: Brian Ostrom, Neal Kauder, and Robert LaFountain, *Examining the Work of State Courts* (Williamsburg, Va.: National Center for State Courts, 2001). Used with permission.

© 2002 AP/Wide World Photos

There are currently more than 450 tribal justice forums among the 556 federally recognized tribes in the United States. Sometimes they claim jurisdiction over cases that regularly go to state courts. Kirk Douglas Billie, a Miccosukee Seminole Indian charged with murder in the deaths of his two young sons, sits with his attorneys, Diane Ward, left, and Ed O'Donnell, right, February 6, 2001, in Miami-Dade County Court. In opening arguments, the defense maintained that Billie did not know the two boys were asleep in the back seat of the sport utility vehicle he drove into a canal near the reservation; the state argued that he did. Billie's tribe said it had already meted out punishment for the crime and that Billie should be set free. Billie was found guilty of second-degree murder but planned to appeal on the grounds that he had already been tried by the tribal courts.

Some states separate limited courts into those that handle civil cases only and those that settle criminal cases. A particular problem, such as drug use, may cause states even to create specialized juvenile and adult drug courts. These newest types of specialty courts are discussed in the Policy, Programs, and Issues in Criminal Justice feature.

The nation's lower courts are the ones most often accused of providing assembly-line justice. Because the matters they decide involve minor personal confrontations and conflicts—family disputes, divorces, landlord-tenant conflicts, barroom brawls—the rule of the day is "handling the situation" and resolving the dispute.

Courts of General Jurisdiction

Approximately three thousand courts of general jurisdiction, or **felony courts,** exist in the United States. They process about five million felony cases each year, a number that has doubled since 1984 (see again Figure 7.1). Courts of general jurisdiction handle the more serious felony cases (for example, murder, rape, robbery), whereas courts of limited jurisdiction handle misdemeanors (for example, simple assault, shoplifting, bad checks). About 90 percent of the general courts are state-administered, and the remainder are controlled by counties or municipalities.

felony court   A state or federal court that has jurisdiction over felony offenses—serious crimes that carry a penalty of incarceration in a state or federal prison for one year or more.

Policy, Programs, and Issues in Criminal Justice

Specialized Courts

A growing phenomenon in the United States is the creation of specialty courts that focus on one type of criminal act—for example, drug courts and gun courts. All cases within the jurisdiction that involve this particular type of crime are funneled to the specialty court, where presumably they will get prompt resolution.

Gun and Drug Courts

One well-known example is the Gun Court in Providence, Rhode Island. All felony cases in Bristol and Providence counties are automatically routed to Gun Court, where once a preliminary hearing has begun the cases must be heard within sixty days. The purpose is to make sure that violent felons are not lost in the shuffle of crowded urban courts, where witnesses disappear and offenders are free to abscond.

Another specialty court is the drug court, which has jurisdiction over the burgeoning number of cases involving substance abuse and trafficking. The aim is to place nonviolent first offenders into intensive treatment programs rather than in jail or prison. One such court, the Drug Night Court program in Cook County, Illinois, was set up in 1975 as an emergency measure to deal with the rapidly expanding number of narcotics cases being filed. Today there are 327 drug courts across forty-three states, the District of Columbia, and Puerto Rico. Drug courts address the overlap between the public health threats of drug abuse and crime: crimes are often drug-related; drug abusers are frequently involved with the criminal justice system. Drug courts provide an ideal setting to address these problems by linking the justice system with health services and drug

treatment providers while easing the burden on the already overtaxed correctional system.

Some early evaluations have praised the drug court program, indicating that it is an efficient method for processing cases, dramatically reducing the processing time of drug cases. However, recent research finds that drug courts may not be as effective as originally believed and that recidivism for drug court participants is significantly higher than for similar offenders who are processed in traditional courts. It is possible that drug courts stigmatize defendants as substance abusers, and consequently impede their rehabilitation.

Other Specialized Courts

Today most states have family courts that serve some number of counties or districts or have statewide jurisdiction. These courts usually have jurisdiction over domestic and marital matters such as divorce, child custody and support, and domestic violence. There are also juvenile courts, which specialize in cases of underage minors who violate the criminal law (called *juvenile delinquents*), who are uncontrollable or unmanageable (called *status offenders,* who may be truants and runaways), or who are not provided with adequate care by their parents (called *neglected children*).

There has been a movement to merge juvenile courts with domestic relations court caseloads and other case types that are family-related. In some instances, this has been accomplished by statewide statute, as in Michigan. In Nevada and elsewhere the merger of family-related matters into a single court has been mandated by law for several judicial districts but made optional for the rest of the state.

The overwhelming majority of general courts hear both serious civil and criminal matters (felonies). A general jurisdiction trial court is the highest state trial court where felony criminal cases are adjudicated.

Courts of general jurisdiction may also be responsible for reviewing cases on appeal from courts of limited jurisdiction. In some instances they will base their decision on a review of the transcript of the case, whereas in others they can actually grant a new trial; this latter procedure is known as the *trial de novo process*. Changes in the courts of general jurisdiction, such as increases in felony filing rates, are watched closely because serious crime is of great public concern.

Appellate Courts

If defendants believe that the procedures used in their case were in violation of their constitutional rights, they may appeal the outcome of their case. For example, defendants can file an appeal if they believe that the law they were tried under violates constitutional standards (for example, it was too vague) or if the procedures

Still others have been made fully optional while allowing for any judicial district to submit a family court proposal for approval by a chief justice, as in Oregon.

To relieve overcrowding and provide an alternative to traditional forms of juvenile courts, more than three hundred jurisdictions are now experimenting with teen courts. These differ from other juvenile justice programs because young people rather than adults determine the disposition in a case. Cases handled in these courts typically involve young juveniles (ages ten to fifteen) with no prior arrest records who have been charged with minor law violations, such as shoplifting, vandalism, and disorderly conduct. Usually, young offenders are asked to volunteer to have their case heard in a teen court instead of the more formal court of the traditional juvenile justice system. Though decisions are made by juveniles, adults are involved in teen courts as well. They often administer the programs, and they are usually responsible for essential functions such as budgeting, planning, and personnel. In many programs, adults supervise the courtroom activities, and they often coordinate the community service placements, where youths work to fulfill the terms of their dispositions. In some programs, adults act as the judges while teens serve as attorneys and jurors.

There are currently over 450 tribal justice forums among the 556 federally recognized tribes in the United States. Sixteen states have assumed mandatory or optional jurisdiction over tribal lands, pursuant to Public Law 280.

Although the specialized court movement holds the promise of bringing efficiency and expertise to the justice system, not all evaluations have proven that they are more effective than traditional court models. In addition to the problems uncovered in the drug courts, evaluation of teen courts indicate that recidivism levels range from 25 to 30 percent. Considering that these cases usually involve offenses of only moderate seriousness, the findings do not suggest that the program can play a significant role in reducing teenage crime rates. It remains to be seen whether specialized courts are simply a fad or a significant contribution to crime prevention and treatment.

Critical Thinking

1. Do you believe that specialized courts are needed for other crime types, such as sex offenses or domestic violence?
2. Should a judge preside over a specialized court or should it be administered by treatment personnel?

• InfoTrac College Edition Research

To learn more about the drug court movement, use the term as a subject guide on InfoTrac College Edition.

Sources: Bureau of Justice Assistance, *Drug Night Courts: The Cook County Experience* (Washington, D.C.: National Institute of Justice, 1994); Terance Miethe, Hong Lu, and Eric Reese, "Reintegrative Shaming and Recidivism Risks in Drug Court: Explanations for Some Unexpected Findings," *Crime and Delinquency* 46 (2000): 522–541; Jeffrey A. Butts and Janeen Buck, "Teen Courts: A Focus on Research," *Juvenile Justice Bulletin, October 2000* (Washington, D.C.: Office of Juvenile Justice and Delinquency Prevention, 2000); Kevin Minor, James Wells, Irinia Soderstrom, Rachel Bingham, and Deborah Williamson, "Sentence Completion and Recidivism Among Juveniles Referred to Teen Courts," *Crime and Delinquency* 45 (1999): 467–480; Paige Harrison, James R. Maupin, and G. Larry Mays, "Teen Court: An Examination of Processes and Outcomes," *Crime and Delinquency* 47 (2001): 243–264; Suzanne Wenzel, Douglas Longshore, Susan Turner, and Susan Ridgely, "Drug Courts: A Bridge Between Criminal Justice and Health Services," *Journal of Criminal Justice* 29 (2001): 241–253.

used in the case contravened principles of due process and equal protection or were in direct opposition to a constitutional guarantee (for example, defendants were denied the right to have competent legal representation). **Appellate courts** do not try cases; they review the procedures of the case to determine whether an error was made by judicial authorities. Judicial error can include admitting into evidence illegally seized material, improperly charging a jury, allowing a prosecutor to ask witnesses improper questions, and so on. The appellate court can order a new trial, allow the defendant to go free, or uphold the original verdict.

Most criminal appeals are limited to trial convictions, sentences, and guilty plea convictions. The most basic feature of the appellate system is the distinction between mandated appeals by right and discretionary review of certain cases. For example, appeals of trial convictions are ordinarily under the courts' mandatory jurisdiction. The most famous appellate court with discretionary jurisdiction is the U.S. Supreme Court, the nation's highest court.

State criminal appeals are heard in one of the appellate courts in the fifty states and the District of Columbia. Each state has at least one **court of last resort,**

appellate court A court that reconsiders a case that has already been tried in order to determine whether the measures used complied with accepted rules of criminal procedure and were in line with constitutional doctrines.

court of last resort A court that handles the final appeal on a matter. The U.S. Supreme Court is the official court of last resort for criminal matters.

usually called a state supreme court, which reviews issues of law and fact appealed from the trial courts; a few states have two high courts, one for civil appeals and the other for criminal cases. In addition, many states have established intermediate appellate courts (IAC) to review decisions by trial courts and administrative agencies before they reach the supreme court stage. Currently, thirty-nine states have at least one permanent IAC. Mississippi was the last state to create an IAC; it began operations in 1995.

Many people believe that criminal appeals clog the nation's court system because so many convicted criminals try to "beat the rap" on a technicality. Actually, criminal appeals represent a small percentage of the total number of cases processed by the nation's appellate courts. All types of appeals, including criminal ones, continue to inundate the courts, so most courts are having problems processing cases expeditiously.

State courts have witnessed an increase in the number of appellate cases each year. In the meantime, the number of judges and support staff has not kept pace. The resulting imbalance has led to the increased use of intermediate courts to screen cases.

Figure 7.2 illustrates the interrelationship of appellate and trial courts in a model state court structure. Each state's court organization, of course, varies from this standard pattern. All states have a tiered court organization (lower, upper, and appellate courts), but they vary somewhat in the way they have delegated responsibility to a particular court system.

In sum, most states have at least two trial courts and two appellate courts, but they differ about where jurisdiction over such matters as juvenile cases and felony versus misdemeanor offenses is found. These matters vary from state to state and between the state courts and the federal system.

Use "appellate court" as a subject guide on InfoTrac College Edition to learn more about how these courts operate.

Federal Courts

The legal basis for the federal court system is contained in ARTICLE 3, SECTION 1, of the U.S. Constitution, which provides that "the judicial power of the United States shall be vested in one Supreme Court, and in such inferior courts as Congress may from time to time ordain and establish." The important clauses in ARTICLE 3 indicate that the federal courts have jurisdiction over the laws of the United States and treaties and cases involving admiralty and maritime jurisdiction, as well as over controversies between two or more states and citizens of different states.[6] This complex language generally means that state courts have jurisdiction over all legal matters, unless they involve a violation of a federal criminal statute or a civil suit between citizens of different states or between a citizen and an agency of the federal government.

Within this authority, the federal government has established a three-tiered hierarchy of court jurisdiction that, in order of ascendancy, consists of the (1) U.S. district courts, (2) U.S. courts of appeals (circuit courts), and (3) the U.S. Supreme Court (Figure 7.3).

U.S. District Courts

U.S. district courts are the trial courts of the federal system. They have jurisdiction over cases involving violations of federal laws, including civil rights abuses, interstate transportation of stolen vehicles, and kidnappings. They may also hear cases on questions involving citizenship and the rights of aliens. The jurisdiction of the U.S. district court will occasionally overlap that of state courts. For example, citizens who reside in separate states and are involved in litigation of an amount in excess of $10,000 may choose to have their cases heard in either of the states or in

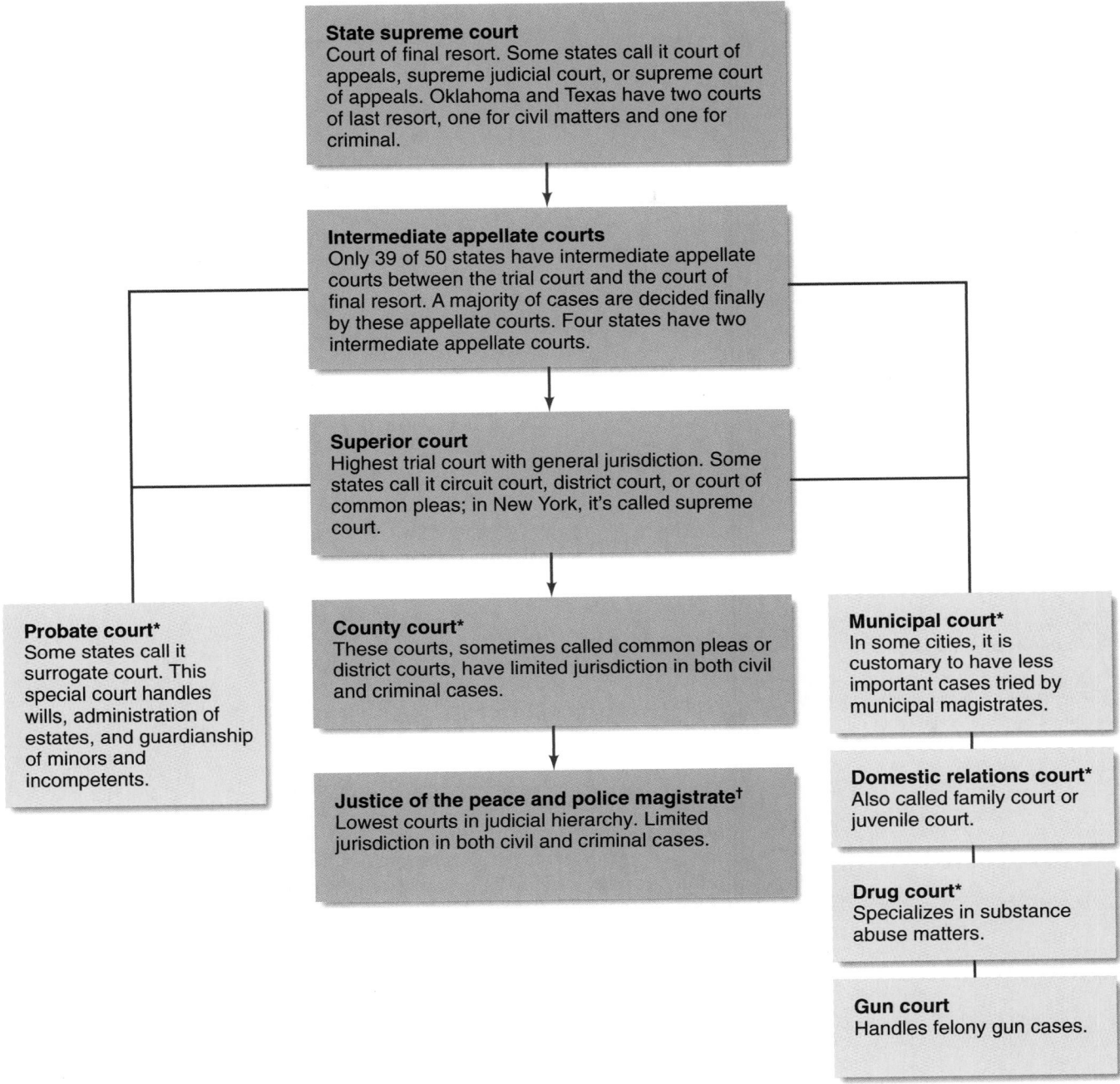

State supreme court
Court of final resort. Some states call it court of appeals, supreme judicial court, or supreme court of appeals. Oklahoma and Texas have two courts of last resort, one for civil matters and one for criminal.

Intermediate appellate courts
Only 39 of 50 states have intermediate appellate courts between the trial court and the court of final resort. A majority of cases are decided finally by these appellate courts. Four states have two intermediate appellate courts.

Superior court
Highest trial court with general jurisdiction. Some states call it circuit court, district court, or court of common pleas; in New York, it's called supreme court.

Probate court*
Some states call it surrogate court. This special court handles wills, administration of estates, and guardianship of minors and incompetents.

County court*
These courts, sometimes called common pleas or district courts, have limited jurisdiction in both civil and criminal cases.

Municipal court*
In some cities, it is customary to have less important cases tried by municipal magistrates.

Justice of the peace and police magistrate†
Lowest courts in judicial hierarchy. Limited jurisdiction in both civil and criminal cases.

Domestic relations court*
Also called family court or juvenile court.

Drug court*
Specializes in substance abuse matters.

Gun court
Handles felony gun cases.

Figure 7.2
A model of a state judicial system

* Courts of special jurisdiction, such as probate, family, or juvenile courts, and the so-called inferior courts, such as common pleas or municipal courts, may be separate courts or part of the trial court of general jurisdiction.

† Justices of the peace do not exist in all states. Where they do exist, their jurisdictions vary greatly from state to state.

Sources: American Bar Association, *Law and the Courts* (Chicago: ABA, 1974), 20; Bureau of Justice Statistics, *State Court Organization—1998* (Washington, D.C.: Department of Justice, 2000).

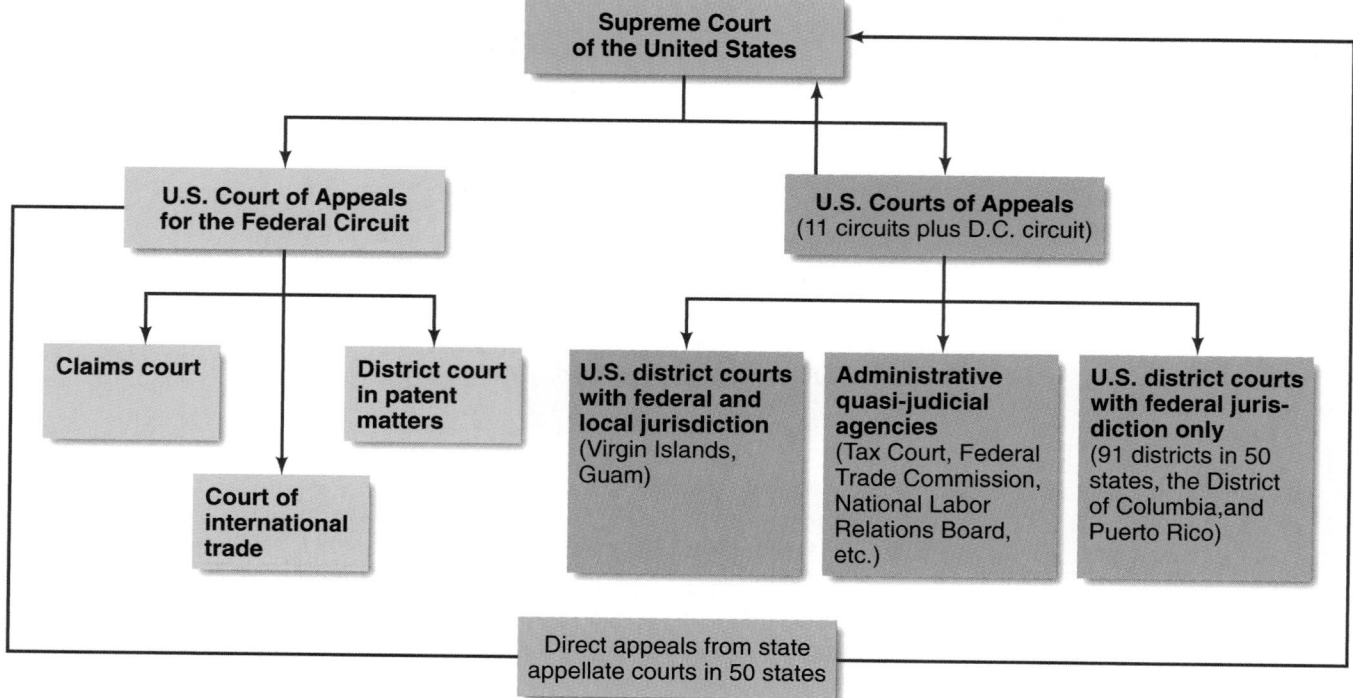

Figure 7.3
The federal judicial system

Sources: American Bar Association, *Law and the Courts* (Chicago: ABA, 1974), 21; updated information provided by the Federal Courts Improvement Act of 1982 and West Publishing Company, St. Paul, Minnesota.

the federal district court. Finally, federal district courts hear cases in which one state sues a resident (or firm) in another state, where one state sues another, or where the federal government is a party in a suit. A single judge ordinarily presides over criminal trials; a defendant may also request a jury trial.

Federal district courts were organized by Congress in the Judicial Act of 1789, and today ninety-four independent courts are in operation. Originally, each state was allowed one court; as the population grew, however, so did the need for courts. Now each state has one or more district courts, and the District of Columbia has one for itself.

U.S. Courts of Appeals

Approximately forty thousand appeals from the district courts are heard each year in the twelve federal courts of appeals, sometimes referred to as *U.S. circuit courts.* This name is derived from the historical practice of having judges ride the circuit and regularly hear cases in the judicial seats of their various jurisdictions. Today, appellate judges are not required to travel (although some may sit in more than one court), and each federal appellate court jurisdiction contains a number of associate justices who share the caseload. Circuit court offices are usually located in major cities, such as San Francisco and New York, and cases to be heard must be brought to these locations by attorneys.

The circuit court is empowered to review federal and state appellate court cases on substantive and procedural issues involving rights guaranteed by the Constitution. Circuit courts do not actually retry cases, nor do they determine whether the facts brought out during trial support conviction or dismissal. Instead, they

Sketch by Jane Collins © AFP/CORBIS

Richard Reid, the "Shoe Bomber," shown here in a courtroom drawing rendered in federal court. Reid pleaded guilty to all eight counts against him—including attempted use of a weapon of mass destruction, attempted homicide, and placing an explosive device on an aircraft—and was sentenced to a possible sixty years in prison.

analyze judicial interpretations of the law, such as the charge (or instructions) to the jury, and reflect on the constitutional issues involved in each case they hear.

Although federal court criminal cases make up only a small percentage of appellate cases, they are still of concern to the judiciary. Steps have been taken to make appealing more difficult. For example, the U.S. Supreme Court has tried to limit the number of appeals being filed by prison inmates, which often represent a significant number of cases appealed in the federal criminal justice system.

The U.S. Supreme Court

The U.S. Supreme Court is the nation's highest appellate body and the court of last resort for all cases tried in the various federal and state courts.

The Supreme Court is composed of nine members appointed for lifetime terms by the president, with the approval of Congress. The Court has discretion over most of the cases it will consider and may choose to hear only those it deems important, appropriate, and worthy of its attention. The Court chooses some three hundred of the five thousand cases that are appealed each year, and only about one hundred of these receive full opinions (Figure 7.4).

When the Supreme Court decides to hear a case, it grants a **writ of certiorari,** requesting a transcript of the proceedings of the case for review. However, the Court must grant jurisdiction in a few instances, such as decisions from a three-judge federal district court on reapportionment or cases involving the Voting Rights Act.

When the Supreme Court rules on a case, usually by majority decision (at least five votes), its rule becomes a precedent that must be honored by all lower courts. For example, if the Court grants a particular litigant the right to counsel at a police lineup, all similarly situated clients must be given the same right. This type of ruling is usually referred to as a **landmark decision.** The use of precedent in the legal system gives the Supreme Court power to influence and mold the everyday operating procedures of the police, trial courts, and corrections agencies. This influence became particularly pronounced during the tenure of Chief Justices Earl Warren and Warren Burger, who greatly amplified and extended the power of

writ of certiorari An order of superior court requesting that the record of an inferior court (or administrative body) be brought forward for review or inspection.

landmark decision A decision handed down by the U.S. Supreme Court that becomes the law of the land and serves as a precedent for similar legal issues.

© 2002 AP/Wide World Photos

Supreme Court rulings set precedents that guide the administration of justice. For example, in the 2002 case *Atkins v. Virginia,* the Court ruled that executions of mentally retarded criminals are "cruel and unusual punishments" prohibited by the Eighth Amendment. The Court noted that a significant number of states have concluded that death is not a suitable punishment for a mentally retarded criminal and the direction states have taken is to prohibit executing such offenders. Here Daryl Renard Atkins, who has an IQ of fifty-nine, sits in a Virginia courtroom during his trial in 1998.

the Court to influence criminal justice policies. Under current Chief Justice William Rehnquist, the Court has continued to influence criminal justice matters, ranging from the investigation of crimes to the execution of criminals. The personal legal philosophy of the justices and their orientation toward the civil and personal rights of victims and criminals significantly affect the daily operations of the justice system.

How a Case Gets to the Supreme Court   The Supreme Court is unique in several ways. First, it is the only court established by constitutional mandate rather than federal legislation. Second, it decides basic social and political issues of grave consequence and importance to the nation. Third, the Court's nine justices shape the future meaning of the U.S. Constitution. Their decisions identify the rights and liberties of citizens throughout the United States.

When the nation was first established, the Supreme Court did not review state court decisions involving issues of federal law. Even though Congress had given the Supreme Court jurisdiction to review state decisions, much resistance and controversy surrounded the relationship between the states and the federal government. However, in a famous decision, *Martin v. Hunter's Lessee* (1816), the Court reaffirmed the legitimacy of its jurisdiction over state court decisions when such courts handled issues of federal or constitutional law.[7] This decision allowed the Court to actively review actions by states and their courts and reinforced the Court's power to make the supreme law of the land. Since that time, a defendant who indicates that governmental action—whether state or federal—violates a constitutional law is in a position to have the Court review such action.

To carry out its responsibilities, the Supreme Court had to develop a method for dealing with the large volume of cases coming from the state and federal courts for final review. In the early years of its history, the Court sought to review every case brought before it. Since the middle of the twentieth century, however, the Court has used the writ of certiorari to decide what cases it should hear. (*Certiorari* is a Latin term meaning "to bring the record of a case from a lower court up to a higher court for immediate review.") When applied, it means that an accused in a criminal case is requesting the U.S. Supreme Court to hear the case. More than 90 percent of the cases heard by the Court are brought by petition for a writ of certiorari. Under this procedure, the justices have discretion to select the cases they will review for a decision. Four of the nine justices sitting on the Court must vote to hear a case brought by a writ of certiorari for review. Generally, these votes are cast in a secret meeting attended only by the justices.

After the Supreme Court decides to hear a case, it reviews written and oral arguments. The written materials are referred to as *legal briefs,* and oral arguments are normally presented to the justices at the Supreme Court in Washington, D.C.

After the material is reviewed and the oral arguments heard, the justices normally meet in what is known as a *case conference.* At the case conference, they

The Supreme Court maintains a Web site that has a wealth of information on its history, judges, procedures, cases filings, rules, opinions, and other Court-related material. To access the site, go to
www.supremecourtus.gov/

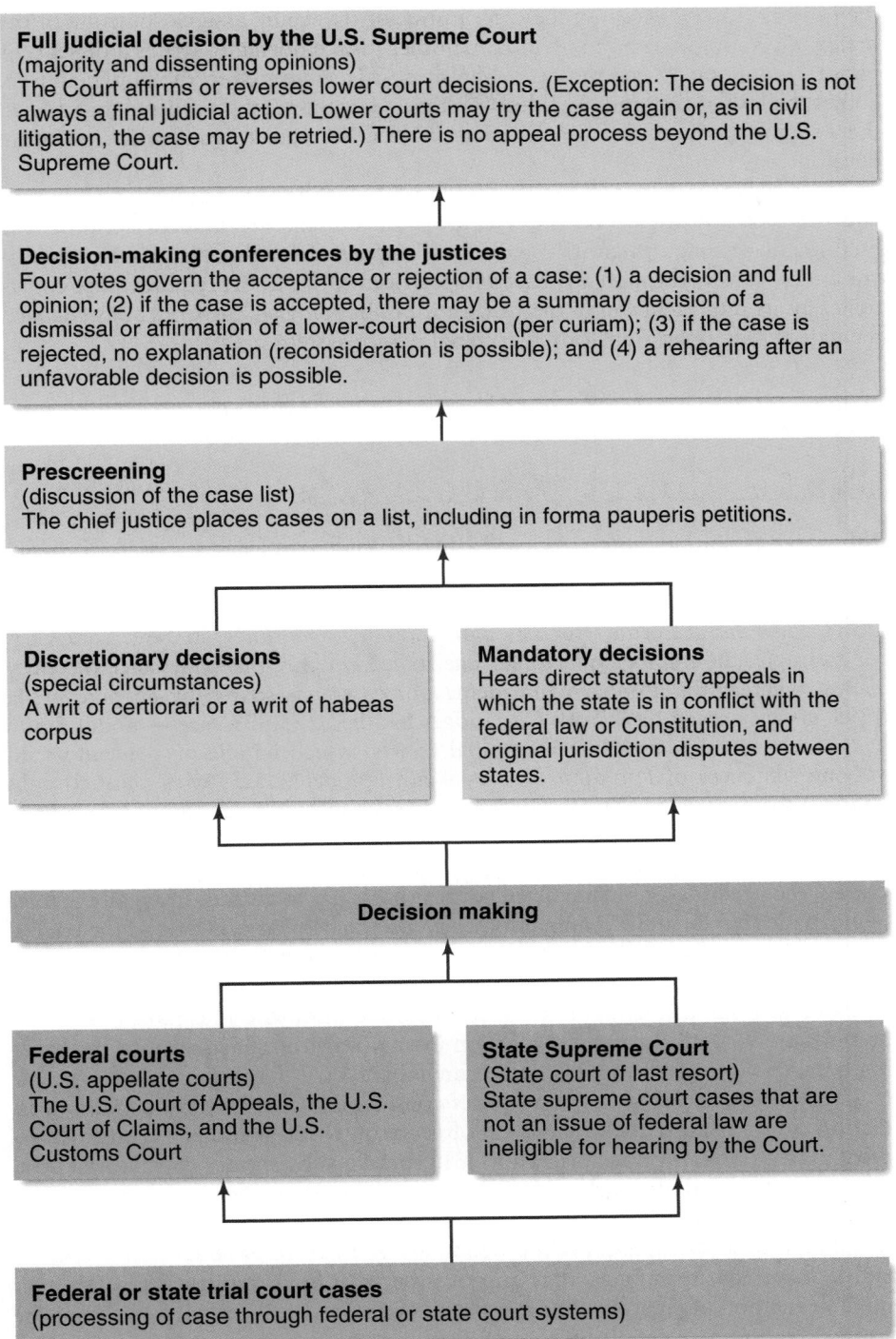

Figure 7.4
Tracing the course of a case to the U.S. Supreme Court

discuss the case and vote to reach a decision. The cases voted on by the Court generally come from the judicial systems of the various states or the U.S. courts of appeals, and they represent the entire spectrum of law.

In reaching a decision, the Supreme Court reevaluates and reinterprets state statutes, the U.S. Constitution, and previous case decisions. Based on a review of the case, the Court either affirms or reverses the decision of the lower court. When the justices reach a decision, the chief justice of the Court assigns someone of the majority group to write the opinion. Another justice normally writes a dissent, or minority, opinion. When the case is finished, it is submitted to the public and becomes the law of the land. The decision represents the legal precedents that add to the existing body of law on a given subject, change it, and guide its future development.

In the area of criminal justice, the decisions of the U.S. Supreme Court have had the broadest impact on the reform of the system. The Court's action is the final step in settling constitutional criminal disputes throughout the nation. By discretionary review through a petition for certiorari, the Court requires state courts to accept its interpretation of the Constitution. In doing so, the Court has changed the day-by-day operations of the criminal justice system.

Federal and State Court Caseloads

This vast system has been overloaded by the millions of cases that are brought each year. One reason for the increase in court caseloads is the recent attempt in some communities to lower the crime rate by aggressively prosecuting petty offenses and nuisance crimes such as panhandling or vagrancy. In New York City, for example, the number of felonies has stayed roughly the same since the early 1990s, whereas the number of misdemeanor cases has soared by 85 percent. In 1998, seventy-seven New York City judges handled 275,379 cases—about 3,500 cases each—in the city's lower criminal courts, which handle misdemeanors involving sentences of less than a year in jail. For defendants who want to fight charges, the average waiting time for a misdemeanor trial was 284 days, up from 208 days in 1991.[8]

As the law becomes more complex and involves such issues as computer crimes, the need for a more involved court process has escalated. Ironically, efforts being made to reform the criminal law may also be helping to overload the courts. For example, the increase of mandatory prison sentences for some crimes may reduce the use of plea bargaining and increase the number of jury trials because defendants fear that a conviction will lead to incarceration and thus must be avoided at all costs. Second, the recent explosion in civil litigation has added to the backlog because most courts handle both criminal and civil matters.

The processing of felony cases poses considerable problems for general jurisdiction courts because the offenses (1) often involve violent or drug crimes, (2) receive a great deal of public attention, (3) generate substantial prosecutorial cost, (4) impose tremendous burdens on the victims, and (5) involve serious evidentiary issues, such as DNA or blood analysis.

If relief is to be found, it will probably be in the form of better administrative and management techniques that improve the use of existing resources. Another possible method of creating a more efficient court system is to unify existing state courts into a single administrative structure using modern management principles.

The Judiciary

The judge is the senior officer in a court of criminal law. His duties are quite varied and far more extensive than might be expected. During trials, the judge rules on the appropriateness of conduct, settles questions of evidence and procedure, and guides the questioning of witnesses. In a **jury trial** the judge must instruct jurors on which evidence is proper to examine and which should be ignored. The judge also formally charges the jury by instructing its members on what points of

jury trial The process of deciding a case by a group of persons selected and sworn in to serve as jurors at a criminal trial, often as a six- or twelve-person jury.

law and evidence they must consider to reach a decision of either guilty or not guilty. When a jury trial is waived, the judge must decide whether to hold for the complainant or the defendant. Finally, if a defendant is found guilty, the judge must decide on the sentence (in some cases, this is legislatively determined), which includes choosing the type of sentence, its length, and in the case of probation, the conditions under which it may be revoked.

Judicial Functions

Beyond these stated duties, the trial judge has extensive control and influence over the other agencies of the court: probation, the court clerk, the police, and the district attorney's office. Probation and the clerk may be under the judge's explicit control. In some courts, the operations, philosophy, and procedures of these agencies are within the magistrate's administrative domain. In others—for example, where a state agency controls the probation department—the attitudes of the county or district court judge greatly influence the way a probation department is run and how its decisions are made. Judges often consult with probation staff on treatment decisions, and many judges are interested in providing the most innovative and up-to-date care possible.

Police and **prosecutors** are also directly influenced by the judge, whose sentencing discretion affects the arrest and charging processes. For example, if a judge usually chooses minimal sentences—such as a fine for a particular offense—the police may be reluctant to arrest offenders for that crime, knowing that doing so will basically be a waste of time. Similarly, if a judge is known to have a liberal attitude toward police discretion, the local department may be more inclined to engage in practices that border on entrapment or to pursue cases through easily obtained wiretaps. However, a magistrate oriented toward strict use of due-process guarantees would stifle such activities by dismissing all cases involving apparent police abuses of personal freedoms. The district attorney's office may also be sensitive to judicial attitudes. The district attorney might forgo indictments in cases that the presiding magistrate expressly considers trivial or quasi-criminal and in which the judge has been known to take only token action, such as the prosecution of pornographers.

Finally, the judge considers requests by police and prosecutors for leniency (or severity) in sentencing. The judge's reaction to these requests is important if the police and the district attorney are to honor the bargains they may have made with defendants to secure information, cooperation, or guilty pleas. For example, when police tell informers that they will try to convince the judge to go easy on them to secure required information, they will often discuss the terms of the promised leniency with representatives of the court. If a judge ignores police demands, the department's bargaining power is severely diminished, and communication within the criminal justice system is impaired.

Judicial Qualifications

The qualifications for appointment to one of the existing thirty thousand judgeships vary from state to state and court to court. Most typically the potential judge must be a resident of the state, licensed to practice law, a member of the state bar association, and at least twenty-five years and less than seventy years of age. However, a significant degree of diversity exists in the basic qualification, depending on the level of court jurisdiction. Although almost every state requires judges to have a law degree if they are to serve on appellate courts or courts of general jurisdiction, it is not uncommon for municipal or town court judges to lack a legal background, even though they maintain the power to incarcerate criminal defendants.

Many methods are used to select judges, depending on the level of court jurisdiction. In some jurisdictions, the governor simply appoints judges. In others, the

The purposes of the American Judges Association are to improve the effective and impartial administration of justice, to enhance the independence and status of the judiciary, to provide for continuing education of its members, and to promote the interchange of ideas of a judicial nature among judges, the court organization, and the public. Go to its Web site at http://aja.ncsc.dni.us/

prosecutor   Representative of the state (executive branch) in criminal proceedings; advocate for the state's case—the charge—in the adversary trial, for example, the attorney general of the United States, U.S. attorneys, attorneys general of the states, district attorneys, and police prosecutors. The prosecutor participates in investigations both before and after arrest, prepares legal documents, participates in obtaining arrest or search warrants, decides whether to charge a suspect and, if so, with which offense. The prosecutor argues the state's case at trial, advises the police, participates in plea negotiations, and makes sentencing recommendations.

The National Summit on Improving Judicial Selection was convened on January 25, 2001 under the leadership of Texas Supreme Court Chief Justice Thomas R. Phillips and Texas Senator Rodney Ellis for the purpose of discussing how best to improve judicial selection processes. They focused on those states in which judicial selection is subject to popular election. Read about their findings at www.ncsconline.org/WC/Publications/Res_JudSel_CallToActionPub.pdf

What are the problems involved in electing judges? Go to InfoTrac College Edition and read Michael Scherer, "State Judges for Sale: In the Thirty-Nine States That Elect Appellate Judges, Politicization of the Bench Is Growing," *The Nation,* September 2, 2002 v275 i7 p20.

Missouri Plan A way of picking judges through nonpartisan elections as a means of ensuring judicial performance standards.

Do research on the role of the "trial judge" by using the term as a subject guide on InfoTrac College Edition.

governor's recommendations must be confirmed by (1) the state senate, (2) the governor's council, (3) a special confirmation committee, (4) an executive council elected by the state assembly, or (5) an elected review board. Some states employ a judicial nominating commission that submits names to the governor for approval.

Another form of judicial selection is popular election. In some jurisdictions, judges run as members of the Republican, Democratic, or other parties, whereas in others they run without party affiliation. In thirteen states, partisan elections are used for selecting judges in courts of general jurisdiction; in seventeen states, nonpartisan elections are used; and in the remainder, upper-trial court judges are appointed by the governor or the legislature.

Many states have adopted some form of what is known as the **Missouri Plan** to select appellate court judges, and six states also use it to select trial court judges. This plan consists of three parts: (1) a judicial nominating commission to nominate candidates for the bench, (2) an elected official (usually from the executive branch) to make appointments from the list submitted by the commission, and (3) subsequent nonpartisan and noncompetitive elections in which incumbent judges run on their records and voters can choose either their retention or dismissal.[9]

The quality of the judiciary is a concern. Although merit plans, screening committees, and popular elections are designed to ensure a competent judiciary, it has often been charged that many judicial appointments are made to pay off political debts or to reward cronies and loyal friends. Also not uncommon are charges that those desiring to be nominated for judgeships are required to make significant political contributions.

Judicial Overload There has been great concern about stress placed on judges by the size of their assigned caseloads. In most states, people appointed to the bench have had little or no training in the role of judge. Others may have held administrative posts and may not have appeared before a court in years. Once they are appointed to the bench, judges are given an overwhelming amount of work that has risen dramatically over the years. The number of civil and criminal filings per state court judge has increased significantly since 1985. Annually there are about 1,500 civil and criminal case filings per state court judge, and 450 per federal judge.[10] State court judges deal with far more cases, but federal cases may be more complex and demand more judicial time. In any event, the number of civil and criminal cases, especially in state courts, seems to be outstripping the ability of states to create new judgeships.

The Prosecutor

There are about twenty-four hundred state court prosecutors' offices, which employ about sixty-five thousand attorneys, investigators, and support staff to handle felony cases in the state trial courts. Hundreds of municipal and county attorneys prosecute criminal cases in courts of limited jurisdiction, while others work in the federal court system. The personnel and workload of prosecutors' offices (county, state, and federal) have increased by 20 percent since 1996.[11] Usually, the most active prosecutors are employed in larger counties with populations of over five hundred thousand. Exhibit 7.1 gives a profile of these attorneys.

Depending on the level of government and the jurisdiction in which she functions, the prosecutor may be known as a *district attorney, county attorney, state's attorney,* or *U.S. attorney.* Whatever the title, the prosecutor is ordinarily a member of the practicing bar who has been appointed or elected as a public prosecutor.

Although the prosecutor participates with the judge and defense attorney in the adversary process, the prosecutor is responsible for bringing the state's case against the accused. She focuses the power of the state on those who are accused

Exhibit 7.1	Prosecutors in large courts (population 500,000+)

- Over fourteen thousand assistant prosecutors and supervisory attorneys who litigated cases were employed by prosecutors' offices in large districts.
- Large district offices had combined total budgets of $2.9 billion for prosecutorial functions in 2001. The median office budget was $14 million.
- Annually, prosecutors' offices in large districts closed over one million felony cases, with a median conviction rate of 85 percent.
- Sixty-five percent of prosecutors' offices in large districts reported a threat or assault against an assistant prosecutor, 41 percent against the chief prosecutor, and 22 percent against a staff investigator.
- During the previous twelve months, prosecutors' offices in large districts processed almost eleven thousand juvenile cases.

Source: Carol J. DeFrances, *State Court Prosecutors in Large Districts, 2001* (Washington, D.C.: Bureau of Justice Statistics, 2001).

of disobeying the law by charging them with a crime, releasing them from prosecution, or eventually bringing them to trial.

Although the prosecutor's primary duty is to enforce the criminal law, her fundamental obligation as an attorney is to seek justice, as well as to convict those who are guilty. For example, if the prosecutor discovers facts suggesting that the accused is innocent, she must bring this information to the attention of the court.

The senior prosecutor must make policy decisions on the exercise of prosecutorial enforcement powers in a wide range of cases in criminal law, consumer protection, housing, and other areas of the law. In so doing, the prosecutor determines and ultimately shapes the manner in which justice is exercised in society.

Many individual prosecutors are caught between being compelled by their supervisors to do everything possible to obtain a guilty verdict and acting as concerned public officials to ensure that justice is done. Sometimes this conflict can lead to *prosecutorial misconduct.* According to some legal authorities, unethical prosecutorial behavior is often motivated by the desire to obtain a conviction and by the fact that such misbehavior is rarely punished by the courts.[12] Some prosecutors may conceal evidence or misrepresent it, or influence juries by impugning the character of opposing witnesses. Even where a court may instruct a jury to ignore certain evidence, a prosecutor may attempt to sway the jury or the judge by simply mentioning the tainted evidence. Because appellate courts generally uphold convictions in cases where such misconduct is not considered serious (the *harmless error doctrine*), prosecutors are not penalized for their misbehavior; nor are they personally liable for their conduct. Overzealous, excessive, and even cruel prosecutors, motivated by a desire for political gain or notoriety, produce wrongful convictions, thereby abusing their office and the public trust.[13] According to legal expert Stanley Fisher, prosecutorial excesses appear when the government (1) always seeks the highest charges, (2) interprets the criminal law expansively, (3) wins as many convictions as possible, and (4) obtains the severest penalties.[14]

Duties of the Prosecutor

The prosecutor is the chief law enforcement officer of a particular jurisdiction. Her participation spans the entire gamut of the justice system, from the time search and arrest warrants are issued or a grand jury is empaneled to the final sentencing decision and appeal. The general duties of a prosecutor include (1) enforcing the law, (2) representing the government, (3) maintaining proper standards of conduct as an attorney and court officer, (4) developing programs and legislation for law and criminal justice reform, and (5) being a public spokesperson for

The prosecutor is responsible for bringing the state's case against the accused. Here, prosecutor Jeff Dusek holds a photo of Twin Peaks Cleaners, where David Westerfield dropped off clothes to be cleaned. Store employee Julie Mills points to where Westerfield's motor home was parked when he dropped off the clothes, as she testifies June 17, 2002, at his murder trial in San Diego. Westerfield was later convicted of killing his neighbor, seven-year-old Danielle van Dam, and sentenced to death.

The Office of Research and Evaluation of the American Prosecutors Research Institute conducts cutting-edge studies to ensure that state and local prosecutors have access to the most up-to-date and needed research about prosecution and criminal justice policies and programs. Visit its Web site: www.ndaa.org/research/apri_index.html

the field of law. Of these, representing the government while presenting the state's case to the court is the prosecutor's most frequent task.

In addition to these duties, local jurisdictions may create teams or task forces that involve prosecutors in some form of priority prosecution. For example, career criminal prosecution programs are popular in many jurisdictions. This involves identifying dangerous adult and juvenile offenders who commit a high number of crimes, so that prosecutors can target them for swift prosecution. In 1999 the NDAA developed a National Traffic Law Center to focus on improving the quality of justice in traffic safety prosecutions.[15]

Types of Prosecutors

In the federal system, prosecutors are known as U.S. attorneys and are appointed by the president. They are responsible for representing the government in federal district courts. The chief prosecutor is usually an administrator, and assistants normally handle the actual preparation and trial work. Federal prosecutors are professional civil service employees with reasonable salaries and job security.

On the state and county levels, the attorney general and the district attorney, respectively, are the chief prosecutorial officers. Again, the bulk of the criminal prosecution and staff work is performed by scores of full- and part-time attorneys, police investigators, and clerical personnel. Most attorneys who work for prosecutors at the state and county levels are political appointees who earn low salaries, handle many cases, and in some jurisdictions, maintain private law practices. Many young lawyers take these staff positions to gain the trial experience that will qualify them for better opportunities. In most state, county, and municipal jurisdictions, however, the office of the prosecutor can be described as having the highest standards of professional skill, personal integrity, and working conditions.

In urban jurisdictions, the structure of the district attorney's office is often specialized, with separate divisions for felonies, misdemeanors, and trial and appeal assignments. In rural offices, chief prosecutors handle many of the criminal cases themselves. Where assistant prosecutors are employed, they often work part-time, have limited professional opportunities, and depend on the political patronage of chief prosecutors for their positions.

The personnel practices, organizational structures, and political atmosphere of many prosecutors' offices often restrict the effectiveness of individuals in investigating and prosecuting criminal offenses. For many years, prosecutors have been criticized for bargaining justice away, using their positions as stepping-stones to higher political office, and often failing to investigate or simply dismissing criminal cases. Lately, however, the prosecutor's public image has improved. Violations of federal laws, such as white-collar crime, drug peddling, and corruption, are being more aggressively investigated by the ninety-four U.S. attorneys and the nearly two thousand assistant U.S. attorneys. Aggressive federal prosecutors have also made extraordinary progress in the war against insider trading and security fraud on Wall Street. There have been a number of highly publicized indictments alleging that some corporate managers abused their power to loot company assets.

State crimes ranging from murder to larceny are prosecuted in state courts by district attorneys, who are stepping up their efforts against career criminals, shortening the time it takes to bring serious cases to trial, and addressing the long-neglected problems of victims and witnesses. With such actions, the prosecutor will continue to be one of the most powerful and visible professionals in the justice system.

Prosecutorial Discretion

One might expect that after the police arrest and bring a suspect to court, the entire criminal court process would be mobilized. This is often not what happens, however. For a variety of reasons, a substantial percentage of defendants are never brought to trial. The prosecutor decides whether to bring a case to trial or to dismiss it outright. Even if the prosecutor decides to pursue a case, the charges may later be dropped if conditions are not favorable for a conviction, in a process called *nolle prosequi.*

Even in felony cases, the prosecutor ordinarily exercises much discretion in deciding whether to charge the accused with a crime.[16] After a police investigation, the prosecutor may be asked to review the sufficiency of the evidence to determine whether a criminal complaint should be filed. In some jurisdictions, this may involve presenting the evidence at a preliminary hearing. In other cases, the prosecutor may decide to seek a criminal complaint through the grand jury or other information procedure.

There is little question that prosecutors exercise a great deal of discretion in even the most serious cases. In one classic study, Barbara Boland examined the flow of felony cases through three jurisdictions in the United States: Golden, Colorado; the borough of Manhattan in New York City; and Salt Lake City, Utah.[17] Although procedures were different in the three districts, prosecutors used their discretion to dismiss a high percentage of the cases before trial. When cases were forwarded for trial, very few defendants were actually acquitted, indicating that the prosecutorial discretion was exercised to screen out the weakest cases. In addition, of those cases accepted for prosecution, a high percentage ended with the defendant pleading guilty. All the evidence here points to the conclusion that prosecutorial discretion is used to reduce potential trial cases to a minimum.

The prosecutor may also play a limited role in exercising discretion in minor offenses. This role may consist of simply consulting with the police after their investigation results in a complaint being filed against the accused. In such instances, the decision to charge a person with a crime may be left primarily to the discretion of the law enforcement agency. The prosecutor may decide to enter this type of case after an arrest has been made and a complaint has been filed with the court, and she may subsequently determine whether to adjust the matter or proceed to trial.

The power to institute formal charges against the defendant is the key to the prosecutorial function. The ability to initiate or discontinue charges against a defendant is the control and power the prosecutor has over an individual's liberty. Almost seventy years ago, Newman Baker commented on the problems of prosecutorial decision making:

> *"To prosecute or not to prosecute?" is a question which comes to mind of this official scores of times each day. A law has been contravened and the statute says he is bound to commence proceedings. His legal duty is clear. But what will be the result? Will it be a waste of time? Will it be expensive to the state? Will it be unfair to the defendant (the prosecutor applying his own ideas of justice)? Will it serve any good purpose to society in general? Will it have good publicity value? Will it cause a political squabble? Will it prevent the prosecutor from carrying the offender's home precinct when he, the prosecutor, runs for Congress after his term as prosecutor? Was the law violated a foolish piece of legislation? If the offender is a friend, is it the square thing to do to reward friendship by initiating criminal proceedings? These and many similar considerations are bound to come to the mind of the man responsible for setting the wheels of criminal justice in motion.*[18]

Factors Influencing Decision Making

Research indicates that widely varied factors influence prosecutorial discretion in invoking criminal sanction. In general they can be divided into legal, extralegal, and resource issues.

Legal issues can include the characteristics of the justice system, crime, the criminal, and the victim. The quality of police work and the amount and relevance of the evidence the police gather is a critical legal variable in deciding whether a proscutor will bring a case forward to trial.[19] A defendant who is a known drug user, who has a long history of criminal offending, and who causes the victim extensive physical injuries will more likely be prosecuted than one who is a first offender, does not use drugs, and does not seriously injure a victim.[20] In some instances, the victim's behavior may influence charging decisions. When Myrna Dawson and Ronit Dinovitzer examined the prosecution of domestic violence cases they found that victim cooperation is a key factor in the decision to prosecute cases; the odds of a case being prosecuted is seven times greater when victims are considered "cooperative." Ironically, Dawson and Dinovitzer found that victim cooperation was linked to prosecutorial sensitivity. Prosecutors were able to gain the cooperation of victims and proceed to trial when they showed interest in the victim's plight—by, for example, allowing victims to videotape their statements—or provided victim/witness assistance.[21]

Extralegal factors include the offender's race, gender, or ethnic background. Of course, due process considerations demand that these personal characteristics have no bearing on the use of prosecutorial discretion. Nonetheless, their effect on prosecutorial decision making is uncertain. For example, while some research efforts have found that the race of the offender or victim influences prosecutorial discretion, others show that decisions are relatively unbiased.[22] Proving racial influence is difficult. In order to establish bias, a defendant must produce credible evidence that similarly situated defendants of other races could have been prosecuted, but were not.

Resource issues that influence prosecutorial discretion include the availability of treatment and detention facilities, the size of caseloads, and the number of prosecutors available. Some research efforts have concluded that the availability of resources may be a more critical factor in shaping prosecutorial discretion than either legal or extralegal factors.

The Role of Prosecutorial Discretion

Regardless of its source, the proper exercise of prosecutorial discretion can improve the criminal justice process. For example, its use can prevent unnecessarily rigid implementation of the criminal law. Discretion allows the prosecutor to consider alternative decisions and humanize the operation of the criminal justice system. If prosecutors had little or no discretion, they would be forced to prosecute all cases brought to their attention. Judge Charles Breitel has stated, "If every policeman, every prosecutor, every court, and every postsentence agency performed his or its responsibility in strict accordance with rules of law, precisely and narrowly laid down, the criminal law would be ordered but intolerable."[23]

On the other hand, too much discretion can lead to abuses that result in the abandonment of law. Prosecutors are political creatures. Although they are charged with serving the people, they also must be wary of their reputations; losing too many high-profile cases may jeopardize their chances of reelection. They therefore may be unwilling to prosecute cases where the odds of conviction are low; they are worried about *convictability.*[24]

Legal Restraints

The courts have reviewed such prosecutorial behavior issues as (1) disciplining a prosecutor for making disruptive statements in court, (2) the failure of a prosecutor to adhere to sentence recommendations pursuant to a plea bargain, (3) disqualifying a prosecutor who represented a criminal defendant currently under indictment, (4) removing a prosecutor for making public statements harmful to the office of the district attorney that are not constitutionally protected under the First Amendment, and (5) removing a prosecutor for withholding evidence that might exonerate a defendant.

Courts have also been more concerned about prosecutors who use their discretion in a vindictive manner to punish defendants who exercise their legal rights. For example, in *North Carolina v. Pearce,* the U.S. Supreme Court held that a judge in a retrial cannot impose a sentence more severe than that originally imposed. In other words, a prosecutor cannot seek a stricter sentence for a defendant who succeeds in getting her first conviction set aside.[25] In *Blackledge v. Perry,* the Court found that imposing a penalty on a defendant for having successfully pursued a statutory right of appeal is a violation of due process of law and amounts to prosecutorial vindictiveness.[26] But in *Bordenkircher v. Hayes,* the Court allowed the prosecutor to carry out threats of increased charges made during plea negotiations when the defendant refused to plead guilty to the original charge.[27]

These decisions provide the framework for the "prosecutorial vindictiveness" doctrine: due process of law may be violated if the prosecutor retaliates against a defendant and there is proof of actual vindictiveness. The prosecutor's legitimate exercise of discretion must be balanced against the defendant's legal rights.

The Defense Attorney

The defense attorney is the counterpart of the prosecuting attorney in the criminal process. The accused has a constitutional right to counsel, and when the defendant cannot afford an attorney, the state must provide one. The accused may ob-

© 2002 AP/Wide World Photos

Defense attorneys represent their clients' interests during pretrial hearings, during the trial and sentencing, and in cases where their client has been convicted, may also be called on to draft an appeal. Here, Providence, Rhode Island, Mayor Vincent A. Cianci, Jr., right, stands with his attorney Richard Egbert, left, as they are surrounded by media during a news conference about the verdict in the federal trial dubbed "Operation Plunder Dome," June 24, 2002. Cianci was convicted of one count of racketeering conspiracy.

public defender An attorney generally employed by the government to represent poor persons accused of a crime at no cost to the accused.

tain counsel from the private bar if he can afford to do so; if the defendant is indigent, private counsel or a **public defender** may be assigned by the court (see the discussion on the defense of the indigent later in this chapter).

The Role of the Criminal Defense Attorney

The defense counsel is an attorney as well as an officer of the court. As an attorney, the defense counsel is obligated to uphold the integrity of the legal profession and to observe the requirements of the ABA's Code of Professional Responsibility in the defense of a client. In the code, the duties of the lawyer to the adversary system of justice are stated as follows:

adversarial procedure The procedure used to determine truth in the adjudication of guilt or innocence in which the defense (advocate for the accused) is pitted against the prosecution (advocate for the state), with the judge acting as arbiter of the legal rules. Under the adversary system, the burden is on the state to prove the charges beyond a reasonable doubt. This system of having the two parties publicly debate has proved to be the most effective method of achieving the truth regarding a set of circumstances. (Under the accusatory, or inquisitorial, system, which is used in continental Europe, the charge is evidence of guilt that the accused must disprove; the judge takes an active part in the proceedings.)

> *Our legal system provides for the adjudication of disputes governed by the rules of substantive, evidentiary, and procedural law. An adversary presentation counters the natural human tendency to judge too swiftly in terms of the familiar that which is not yet fully known; the advocate, by his zealous preparation of facts and law, enables the tribunal to come to the hearing with an open and neutral mind and to render impartial judgments. The duty of a lawyer to his client and his duty to the legal system are the same: to represent his client zealously within the boundaries of the law.*[28]

Because of the way the U.S. system of justice operates today, criminal defense attorneys face many role conflicts. They are viewed as the prime movers in what is essentially an **adversarial procedure**: the prosecution and the defense engage in conflict over the facts of the case at hand, with the prosecutor arguing the case for the state and the defense counsel using all the means at his disposal to aid the client.

However, as members of the legal profession, defense counsels must be aware of their role as officers of the court. As an attorney, the defense counsel is obligated to uphold the integrity of the legal profession and to rely on constitutional ideals of fair play and professional ethics (discussed next) to provide adequate representation for a client.

Ethical Issues

As an officer of the court, along with the judge, prosecutors, and other trial participants, the defense attorney seeks to uncover the basic facts and elements of the criminal act. In this dual capacity of being both a defensive advocate and an officer of the court, the attorney is often confronted with conflicting obligations to his client and profession. Monroe Freedman identifies three of the most difficult problems involving the professional responsibility of the criminal defense lawyer:

1. Is it proper to cross-examine for the purpose of discrediting the reliability or credibility of an adverse witness whom you know to be telling the truth?
2. Is it proper to put a witness on the stand when you know she will commit perjury?
3. Is it proper to give your client legal advice when you have reason to believe that the knowledge you give him will tempt him to commit perjury?[29]

There are other, equally important issues with respect to a lawyer's ethical responsibilities. Suppose, for example, a client confides that she is planning to commit a crime. What are the defense attorney's ethical responsibilities in this case? Obviously, the lawyer would have to counsel the client to obey the law; if the lawyer assisted the client in engaging in illegal behavior, the lawyer would be subject to charges of unprofessional conduct and even criminal liability. In another area, suppose the defense attorney is aware that the police made a procedural error and that the guilty client could be let off on a technicality. What are the attorney's ethical responsibilities in this case? The criminal lawyer needs to be aware of these troublesome situations to properly balance the duties of being an attorney with those of being an officer of the court.

Because the defense attorney and the prosecutor have different roles, their ethical dilemmas may also vary. The defense attorney must maintain confidentiality and advise his client of the constitutional requirements of counsel, the privilege against self-incrimination, and the right to trial. Conversely, the prosecutor represents the public and is not required to abide by such restrictions in the same way. In some cases, the defense counsel may even be justified in withholding evidence by keeping the defendant from testifying at the trial. In addition, although prosecutors are prohibited from expressing a personal opinion as to the defendant's guilt on summation of the case, defense attorneys are not altogether barred from expressing their belief about a client's innocence.

The Right to Counsel

Over the past decade, the rules and procedures of criminal justice administration have become extremely complex. Bringing a case to court involves a detailed investigation of a crime, knowledge of court procedures, the use of rules of evidence, and skills in criminal advocacy. Both the state and the defense must have this specialized expertise, particularly when an individual's freedom is at stake. Consequently, the right to the assistance of counsel in the criminal justice system is essential if the defendant is to have a fair chance of presenting a case in the adversary process.

One of the most critical issues in the criminal justice system has been whether an **indigent** defendant has the right to counsel. Can the accused who is poor and cannot afford an attorney have a fair trial without the assistance of counsel? Is

The Association of Federal Defense Attorneys (AFDA) has a commitment to provide attorneys with the educational resources and support that are essential to represent defendants effectively in federal district and appellate courts. You can go to AFDA's Web site:
www.afda.org/afda/overview/o-index.htm

indigent Person who is needy and poor or who lacks the means to hire an attorney.

The United States Supreme Court has ruled that all criminal defendants facing jail or prison time are entitled to a lawyer. If they cannot afford one, the state must provide counsel free of charge. Most often, that means a public defender. Here, public defender Kathryn Benson talks with Richard Allen Williams following his arraignment July 22, 2002, in Boone County, Missouri, Circuit Court. Williams, thirty-six, pleaded innocent to ten counts of first-degree murder for allegedly killing patients a decade ago while working as a nurse at the Truman Memorial Veterans Hospital in Columbia, Missouri. Boone County prosecutor Kevin Crane told the court he would seek the death penalty.

Sixth Amendment The U.S. constitutional amendment containing various criminal trial rights, such as the right to public trial, right to trial by jury, and the right to confrontation of witnesses.

Gideon v. Wainwright The 1963 U.S. Supreme Court case that granted counsel to indigent defendants in felony prosecutions.

counsel required at preliminary hearings? Should the convicted indigent offender be given counsel at state expense in appeals of the case? Questions such as these have arisen constantly in recent years. The federal court system has long provided counsel to the indigent defendant on the basis of the **Sixth Amendment** to the U.S. Constitution, unless that defendant waived this right.[30] This constitutional mandate clearly applies to the federal courts, but its application to state criminal proceedings has been less certain.

In the 1963 landmark case of ***Gideon v. Wainwright,*** the U.S. Supreme Court took the first major step on the issue of right to counsel by holding that state courts must provide counsel to indigent defendants in felony prosecutions.[31] Almost ten years later, in the 1972 case of *Argersinger v. Hamlin,* the Court extended the obligation to provide counsel to all criminal cases where the penalty includes imprisonment—regardless of whether the offense is a felony or misdemeanor.[32] These two major decisions relate to the Sixth Amendment right to counsel as it applies to the presentation of a defense at the trial stages of the criminal justice system.

In numerous Supreme Court decisions since *Gideon v. Wainwright,* the states have been required to provide counsel for indigent defendants at virtually all other stages of the criminal process, beginning with arrest and concluding with the defendant's release from the system. Today, the Sixth Amendment right to counsel and the Fifth and Fourteenth Amendment guarantee of due process of law have been judicially interpreted together to provide the defendant with counsel by the state in all types of criminal proceedings.

In addition to guaranteeing the right of counsel at the earliest stages of the justice system, as well as at trials, the Supreme Court has moved to extend the right to counsel to postconviction and other collateral proceedings, such as probation and parole revocation and appeal. When, for example, the court intends to revoke a defendant's probation and impose a sentence, the probationer has a right to counsel at the deferred sentence hearing.[33] Where the state provides for an appellate review of the criminal conviction, the defendant is entitled to the assistance of counsel for this initial appeal.[34] The defendant does not have the right to counsel for an appellate review beyond the original appeal or for a discretionary review to the U.S. Supreme Court. The Supreme Court has also required the states to provide counsel in other proceedings that involve the loss of personal liberty, such as juvenile delinquency hearings[35] and mental health commitments.[36]

Areas still remain in the criminal justice system where the courts have not required assistance of counsel for the accused. These include (1) preindictment lineups; (2) booking procedures, including the taking of fingerprints and other forms of identification; (3) grand jury investigations; (4) appeals beyond the first review; (5) disciplinary proceedings in correctional institutions; and (6) postrelease revocation hearings. Nevertheless, the general rule of thumb is that no person can be deprived of freedom or lose a "liberty interest" without representation by counsel.

The right to counsel can also be spelled out in particular federal or state statutes. For example, beyond abiding by current constitutional requirements, a state may provide counsel by statute at all stages of juvenile proceedings, in dealing with inmate prison infractions or pretrial release hearings, or when considering temporary confinement of drug or sex offenders for psychiatric examination.

Today the scope of representation for the indigent defendant is believed to cover virtually all areas of the criminal process and most certainly those critical points at which a person's liberty is at stake.

The Private Bar

Today, the lawyer whose practice involves a substantial proportion of criminal cases is often considered a specialist in the field. Since most lawyers are not prepared in law school for criminal work, their skill often results from their experience in the trial courts. Such famous lawyers as Alan Dershowitz and John Cochran are the elite of the private criminal bar; they are nationally known criminal defense attorneys who often represent defendants for large fees in celebrated and widely publicized cases. Attorneys like these are relatively few in number and do not regularly handle the ordinary criminal defendant.

Besides this limited group of well-known criminal lawyers, some lawyers and law firms serve as house counsel for such professional criminals as narcotics dealers, gamblers, prostitutes, and even big-time burglars. These lawyers, however, constitute a very small percentage of the private bar practicing criminal law.

A large number of criminal defendants are represented by lawyers who often accept many cases for small fees. These lawyers may belong to small law firms or work alone, but a sizable portion of their practice involves representing those accused of crime. Other private practitioners occasionally take on criminal matters as part of their general practice.

Associated with the private practice of criminal law is the fact that the fee system can create a conflict of interest. Because private attorneys are usually paid in advance and do not expect additional funds if their client is convicted and because many are aware of the guilt of their clients before the trial begins, they earn the greatest profit if they get the case settled as quickly as possible. This usually means bargaining with the prosecutor rather than going to trial. Even if attorneys win the case at trial, they may lose personally, since the time expended will not be compensated by more than the gratitude of their client. And, of course, many criminal defendants cannot afford even a modest legal fee and therefore cannot avail themselves of the services of a private attorney. For these reasons, an elaborate, publicly funded legal system has developed.

Legal Services for the Indigent

To satisfy the constitutional requirements that indigent defendants be provided with the assistance of counsel at various stages of the criminal process, the federal government and the states have had to evaluate and expand criminal defense services. Today, about three thousand state and local agencies are providing indigent legal services in the United States.

Providing legal services for the indigent offender is a huge and costly undertaking. And although most states have a formal set of rules to signify who is an indigent and many require indigents to repay the state for at least part of their legal services (known as *recoupment*), indigent legal services still cost over $1.5 billion annually.

Programs providing counsel assistance to indigent defendants can be divided into three major categories: public defender systems, **assigned counsel** systems, and **contract systems** (see Exhibit 7.2). In addition, other approaches to the delivery of legal services include the use of mixed systems, such as representation by both the public defender and the private bar, law school clinical programs, and prepaid legal services. Although many jurisdictions have a combination of these programs, statewide public defender programs seem to be on the increase.[37]

These three systems can be used independently or in combination. For example, in Maine the majority of its indigent criminal defense services are through an assigned counsel program; Oregon primarily uses a system of awarded contracts; Minnesota and New Mexico do not have assigned counsel programs but instead relied on statewide public defender programs and contract attorney programs.[38]

In general, the attorney list/assigned counsel system is used in less populated areas, where case flow is minimal and a full-time public defender is not needed. Public defenders are usually found in larger urban areas with high case flow rates. So although a proportionately larger area of the country is served by the assigned counsel system, a significant proportion of criminal defendants receive public defenders.

assigned counsel   A lawyer appointed by the court to represent a defendant in a criminal case because the person is too poor to hire counsel.

contract system (attorney)   Providing counsel to indigent offenders by having attorneys under contract to the county handle all (or some) such cases.

Want to read about the mission and organization of a typical public defender's office? Go to the site maintained by the Wisconsin Office of the State Public Defender: www.wisspd.org/

Exhibit 7.2   The principal forms of indigent defense

- *Public defender:* A salaried staff of full-time or part-time attorneys that renders indigent criminal defense services through a public or private nonprofit organization, or as direct government-paid employees. The first public defender program in the United States opened in 1913 in Los Angeles. Public defenders can be part of a statewide agency, county government, the judiciary, or an independent nonprofit organization or other institution.

- *Assigned counsel:* The appointment, from a list of private bar members, who accept cases on a judge-by-judge, court-by-court, or case-by-case basis. This may include an administrative component and a set of rules and guidelines governing the appointment and processing of cases handled by the private bar members. There are two main types of assigned counsel systems. In the first, which makes up about 75 percent of all assigned counsel systems, the presiding judge appoints attorneys on a case-by-case basis; this is referred to as an *ad hoc assigned counsel system.* The second type is referred to as a *coordinated assigned counsel system,* in which an administrator oversees the appointment of counsel and sets up guidelines for the administration of indigent legal services. The fees awarded to assigned counsels can vary widely, ranging from a low of $10 per hour for handling a misdemeanor out of court to over $100 per hour for a serious felony handled in court. Some jurisdictions may establish a maximum allowance per case of $750 for a misdemeanor and $1,500 for a felony. Average rates seem to be between $40 and $80 per hour, depending on the nature of the case. Restructuring the attorney fee system is undoubtedly needed to maintain fair standards for the payment of such legal services.

- *Contract:* Nonsalaried private attorneys, bar associations, law firms, consortiums or groups of attorneys, or nonprofit corporations that contract with a funding source to provide court-appointed representation in a jurisdiction. In some instances, an attorney is given a set amount of money and is required to handle all cases assigned. In other jurisdictions, contract lawyers agree to provide legal representation for a set number of cases at a fixed fee. A third system involves representation at an estimated cost per case until the dollar amount of the contract is reached. At that point, the contract may be renegotiated, but the lawyers are not obligated to take new cases.

Source: Carol J. DeFrances, *State-Funded Indigent Defense Services, 1999* (Washington, D.C.: Bureau of Justice Statistics, 2001).

Costs of Defending the Poor   Over the past decade, the justice system has been faced with extreme pressure to provide counsel for all indigent criminal defendants. Inadequate funding has made implementation of this Sixth Amendment right an impossible task. The chief reasons for underfunded defender programs are (1) caseload problems, (2) lack of available attorneys, and (3) legislative restraints. Increasing numbers of drug cases, mandatory sentencing, and even overcharging have put tremendous stress on defender services. The system is also overloaded with appeals by indigent defendants convicted at the trial level whose representation involves filing complex briefs and making oral arguments. Such postconviction actions often consume a great deal of time and result in additional backlog problems. Death penalty litigation is another area where legal resources for the poor are strained.

In some jurisdictions, attorneys are just not available to provide defense work. Burnout due to heavy caseloads, low salaries, and poor working conditions are generally the main causes for the limited supply of attorneys interested in representing the indigent defendant. Some attorneys even refuse to accept appointments in criminal cases because the fees are too low.

Lack of government funding is the most significant problem today. Although the entire justice system is often underfunded, the prosecutor-defense system is usually in the worst shape. Ordinarily, providing funding for indigent criminal defendants is not the most politically popular thing to do.

Obviously, the Sixth Amendment means little without counsel. The constitutional mandate that calls for legal representation requires adequate funding for these services. The National Center for State Courts, the National Legal Aid and Defenders Association, the American Bar Association, and many other legal and citizen groups believe that the public defender system is losing the battle for funding because of the enormous increase in drug cases.

Funding for defender programs is ordinarily the responsibility of state and local government. As a result of an amendment to the Crime Control Act of 1990, however, federal funds are also available through the Drug Control Act of 1988.[39] According to most experts on defense funding, jurisdictions whose legislatures have been relatively generous in funding such programs in the past have continued to do so, while underfunded programs have become more seriously hampered. The Anti-Terrorism Act of 1996 authorizes over $300 million to improve the federal judiciary's defender program.[40]

The Competence of Defense Attorneys

The presence of competent and effective counsel has long been a basic principle of the adversary system. With the Sixth Amendment guarantee of counsel for virtually all defendants, the performance of today's attorneys has come into question.

Inadequacy of counsel may occur in a variety of instances. The attorney may refuse to meet regularly with the client, fail to cross-examine key government witnesses, or fail to investigate the case properly. A defendant's plea of guilty may be based on poor advice, where the attorney may misjudge the admissibility of evidence. When codefendants have separate counsel, conflicts of interest between the defense attorneys may arise. On an appellate level, the lawyer may decline to file a brief, instead relying on a brief submitted for one of the coappellants. Such problems as these are being raised with increasing frequency.

The concept of attorney competence was defined by the U.S. Supreme Court in the 1984 case of *Strickland v. Washington*.[41] Strickland had been arrested for committing a string of extremely serious crimes, including murder, torture, and kidnapping. Against his lawyer's advice, he pleaded guilty and threw himself on the mercy of the trial judge at a capital sentencing hearing. He also ignored his attorney's recommendation that he exercise his right to have an advisory jury at his sentencing hearing.

Strickland v. Washington   The 1984 U.S. Supreme Court decision upholding that defendants have the right to reasonably effective assistance of counsel (that is, competent representation).

In preparing for the hearing, the lawyer spoke with Strickland's wife and mother but did not otherwise seek character witnesses. Nor was a psychiatric examination requested since, in the attorney's opinion, Strickland did not have psychological problems. The attorney also did not ask for a presentence investigation because he felt such a report would contain information damaging to his client.

Although the presiding judge had a reputation for leniency in cases where the defendant confessed, he sentenced Strickland to death. Strickland appealed on the grounds that his attorney had rendered ineffective counsel, citing his failure to seek psychiatric testimony and present character witnesses.

The case eventually went to the Supreme Court, which upheld Strickland's sentence. The justices found that a defendant's claim of attorney incompetence must have two components. First, the defendant must show that the counsel's performance was deficient and that such serious errors were made as to essentially eliminate the presence of counsel guaranteed by the Sixth Amendment. Second, the defendant must also show that the deficient performance prejudiced the case to an extent that the defendant was deprived of a fair trial. In the case at hand, the Court found insufficient evidence that the attorney had acted beyond the boundaries of professional competence. The Strickland case established the two-pronged test for determining effectiveness of counsel.

The U.S. Supreme Court dealt with the issue of conflict of interest between defense lawyers in ***Burger v. Kemp*** (1987).[42] Two defendants charged with murder were represented by law partners. Each defendant was tried separately, but the attorneys conferred and assisted each other in the trial process. One defendant, who was found guilty and sentenced to death, claimed ineffective legal representation because he believed his attorney failed to present mitigating circumstances to show that he was less culpable than the codefendant. But the Supreme Court said this view was unfounded because the defendant claiming the conflict of interest actually perpetrated the crime. The Court also said it is not per se a violation of constitutional guarantees of effective assistance of counsel when a single attorney represents two defendants or when two partners supplement each other in the trial defense.

The key issue is the level of competence that should be required of defense counsel in criminal cases. This question concerns appointed counsel, as well as counsel chosen by the accused. Some appellate court decisions have overturned lower-court convictions when it was judged that the performance of counsel had reduced the trial to a farce or a mockery. Other appellate courts have held that there was ineffective counsel where gross incompetence had the effect of eliminating the basis for a substantial defense.

Sentencing Stage The right to competent counsel also applies during the sentencing stage of the trial. Defense attorneys must provide reasonable representation when the issue of punishment is being considered. Attorney competence is particularly critical in capital punishment cases where an attorney's performance during the sentencing phase of trial can determine the life or death of his client. There have been horror stories of incompetent attorneys who fell asleep during a hearing or did not raise critical issues or present important evidence.

One suggested remedy to ensure attorney competence at the sentencing stage is to expand the definition of unreasonable attorney performance and include more lapses of professional duties that are considered prejudicial to a defendant. For example, it would be considered incompetence if an attorney failed to introduce mitigating evidence, such as history of child abuse, that might convince a judge or jury not to apply the death penalty. Similarly, an attorney who failed to object when the prosecution presented inadmissible evidence during the sentencing hearing might be considered legally incompetent.[43] It may also be advisable to shift the burden of proof in such cases, so that attorneys accused of being ineffective would have to prove that they took the necessary steps to provide effective legal advice.[44]

Burger v. Kemp The 1987 U.S. Supreme Court decision upholding that no conflict of interest results when a defense attorney represents two defendants charged with the same crime as long as counsel acts competently and effectively.

© 2002 AP/Wide World Photos

The right to competent counsel also applies during the sentencing stage of the trial. Defense attorneys must provide reasonable representation when the issue of punishment is being considered. In this photo, former Macomb County Sheriff William Hackel, left, is comforted by his attorney James Howarth, May 15, 2000, as Chief Isabella County Court Judge Paul H. Chamberlain sentences him to a three- to fifteen-year prison term for raping an acquaintance. Hackel, fifty-eight, was convicted of two counts of third-degree criminal sexual conduct in the sexual attack of a twenty-five-year-old woman at the Soaring Eagle Casino & Resort in Mount Pleasant, Michigan.

Court Administration

In addition to qualified personnel, there is a need for efficient management of the judiciary system. The need for efficient management techniques in an ever-expanding criminal court system has led to the recognition of improved court administration as a way to relieve court congestion. Management goals include improving organization and scheduling of cases, devising methods to allocate court resources efficiently, administering fines and monies due the court, preparing budgets, and overseeing personnel.

The federal courts have led the way in creating and organizing court administration. In 1939 Congress passed the Administrative Office Act, which established the Administrative Office of the United States Courts. Its director was charged with gathering statistics on the work of the federal courts and preparing the judicial budget for approval by the Conference of Senior Circuit Judges. One clause of the act created a judicial council with general supervisory responsibilities for the district and circuit courts.

Unlike the federal government, the states have experienced slow and uneven growth in the development and application of court management principles. The first state to establish an administrative office was North Dakota in 1927. Today, all states employ some form of central administration.

The federal government has encouraged the development of state court management through funding assistance to court managers. In addition, the federal judiciary has provided the philosophical impetus for better and more effective court management.

Despite the multitude of problems in reforming court management, some progress is being made. In most jurisdictions today, centralized court administrative services perform numerous functions with the help of sophisticated computers that free the judiciary to fulfill their roles as arbiters of justice.

The following Criminal Justice and Technology feature illustrates how the use of technology is reforming court administration. ■

Use "court administration" as a subject guide on InfoTrac College Edition.

Technology and Court Management

As trial reconvenes, the participants blink into existence on the computer monitors that supply the only commonality applicable to them. Judge, counsel, parties, witnesses, and jury appear in virtual form on each person's monitor. Necessary evidentiary foundations are laid by witnesses with distant counsel's questions; documentary evidence is not seen by the jury until received by the court. A real-time, multimedia record (transcript with digital audio, video, and evidence) is available instantly. Sidebar conferences are accomplished simply by switching the jury out of circuit. During the interim, the jurors can head for their kitchens or for rest room breaks. The public can follow the proceedings on the Internet. Should critical interlocutory motions be argued, the appellate court can directly monitor the proceedings.

This is how court technology expert Fredric I. Lederer foresees the court of the future. His projections may not be too far off. Computers are becoming an important aid in the administration and management of courts. Rapid retrieval and organization of data are now being used for such functions as these:

- Maintaining case histories and statistical reporting
- Monitoring and scheduling cases
- Preparing documents
- Indexing cases
- Issuing summonses
- Notifying witnesses, attorneys, and others of required appearances
- Selecting and notifying jurors
- Preparing and administering budgets and payrolls

The federal government has encouraged the states to experiment with computerized information systems. Federal funds were used to begin a fifty-state consortium for the purpose of establishing a standardized crime-reporting system called SEARCH (Systems for the Electronic Analysis and Retrieval of Criminal Histories).

Computer technology is also being applied in the courts in such areas as videotaped testimonies, new court-reporting devices, information systems, and data-processing systems to handle such functions as court docketing and jury management. In 1968, only ten states had state-level automated information systems; today, all states employ such systems for a mix of tasks and duties. A survey of Georgia courts found that 84 percent used computers for three or more court administration applications.

Developing Areas of Court Technology

What are some other developing areas of court technology?

Communications

Court jurisdictions are also cooperating with police departments in the installation of communications gear that allows defendants to be arraigned over closed-circuit television while they are in police custody. Closed-circuit television has been used for judicial conferences and scheduling meetings. Some courts are using voice-activated cameras to record all testimony during trials; these are the sole means of keeping trial records.

Other communication methods being used include these:

Videoconferencing

About 400 courts across the country have videoconferencing capability. It is now being employed for juvenile-detention hearings, expert witness, testimony at trial, oral arguments on appeal, and parole hearings. More than

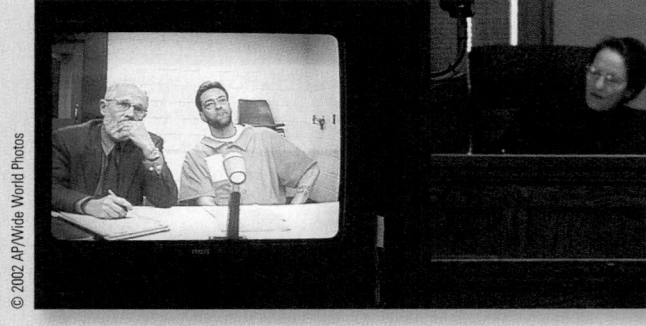

© 2002 AP/Wide World Photos

About four hundred courts across the country have videoconferencing capability, and it is now being used for juvenile detention hearings, testimony at trial, oral arguments on appeal, and parole hearings. Here, Sixth Judicial District Associate Judge Sylvia Lewis, right, reads charges of first-degree murder and kidnapping to Richard Dodd, center, and Johnson County public defender Dick Klausner, left, in Johnson County District Court on February 1, 2002, in Iowa City, Iowa. Dodd, who is currently serving a life sentence at the Iowa State Penitentiary for a 1984 kidnapping and rape conviction, is charged with the 1981 murder of Vicki Klotzbach. Dodd appeared via closed circuit television from the Johnson County Jail.

150 courts use two-way live, televised remote link-ups for first appearance and arraignment. In the usual arrangement, defendants appear from a special location in the jail where they are able to see and hear and be seen and heard by the presiding magistrate. Such appearances are now being authorized by state statute—for example, Virginia Code § 19.2-3. 1. Televising appearances minimizes delays in prisoner transfer, effects large cost savings through the elimination of transportation and security costs, and reduces escape and assault risks.

Evidence Presentation

More than fifty high-tech courtrooms are now equipped for real-time transcription and translation, audio-video preservation of the court record, remote witness participation, computer graphics displays, television monitors for jurors, and computers for counsel and judge. In one interesting development, attorneys in the case of *Yukiyo v. Watanabe,* 114 F.3d 1207 (9th Cir. 1997) filed an appellate brief on a CD-ROM containing hot links to the entire trial transcript, the deposition record, the full opinions of all cases cited by the attorneys, and replications of all exhibits used by expert witnesses during trial. Although the CD-ROM brief was dismissed after opposing counsel objected to its use, it provides a glimpse of how technology may be changing the court process.

Case Management

Case management will soon be upgraded. In the 1970s, municipal courts installed tracking systems, which used databases to manage court data. These older systems were limited and could not process the complex interrelationships of information pertaining to persons, cases, time, and financial matters that occur in court cases.

Contemporary relational databases now provide the flexibility to handle complex case management. To help programmers define the multiplicity of relationships that occur in a court setting, the National Center for State Courts in Williamsburg, Virginia, has developed a methodology for structuring a case management system that tracks a person to the case or cases in which he or she is a defendant, the scheduling of cases to avoid any conflicts, and of increasing importance, the fines that have been levied and the accounts to which the money goes.

The Internet

The Internet has begun finding its way into the court system. For example, in the federal system, "J-Net," is the Judiciary's intranet Web site. It makes it easier for judges and court personnel to find important information in a timely fashion. The federal court's Administrative Office has begun sending official correspondence by e-mail, which provides instantaneous communication of important information. In 1999, an automated library management system was developed, which meant that judges could access a Web-based virtual law library. A Web-based electronic public access network providing the public with access to court records and other information via the Internet was also implemented. In 2002, eleven federal courts announced that they would allow Internet access to criminal case files as part of a pilot program adopted by the Judicial Conference of the United States (a panel of twenty-seven federal judges responsible for crafting policy in the federal court system). This was the first time the public could gain access to criminal case files.

Future Importance

The computer cannot replace the judge, but it can be used as an ally to help speed the trial process by identifying backlogs and bottlenecks that can be eradicated with intelligent managerial techniques. Just as a manager must know the type and quantity of goods on hand in a warehouse, so an administrative judge must have available information about those entering the judge's domain, what happens to them once they are in it, and how they fare after judgment has been rendered.

Critical Thinking

Does the advent of technology in the courtroom spell the eventual demise of the trial system as we know it? Can you foresee people sitting in their homes and participating in cases over the Internet? What are the advantages of such a system and what are its drawbacks?

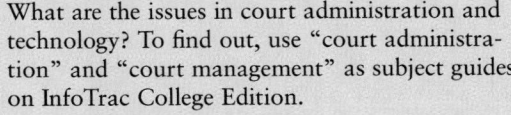

InfoTrac College Edition Research

What are the issues in court administration and technology? To find out, use "court administration" and "court management" as subject guides on InfoTrac College Edition.

Sources: Fredric I. Lederer, "The Road to the Virtual Courtroom? Consideration of Today's—and Tomorrow's—High-Technology Courtrooms," *South Carolina Law Review 50* (1999): 799; "Criminal Court Records Go Online," *The Quill 90* (2002), 39; Donald C. Dilworth, "New Court Technology Will Affect How Attorneys Present Trials," *Trial 33* (1997): 100–114.

SUMMARY

The U.S. court system is a complex social institution. There is no set pattern of court organization. Courts are organized on federal, state, county, and local levels of government. The judge, the prosecutor, and the defense attorney are the main officers of justice in the judicial system. The judge approves plea bargains, tries cases, and determines the sentence that is given to the offender. The prosecutor, who is the people's attorney, has discretion to decide the criminal charge and disposition. The prosecutor's daily decisions significantly affect police and court operations.

The role of the defense attorney in the criminal justice system has expanded dramatically over the past thirty years. Today, providing defense services to the indigent criminal defendant is an everyday practice. Under landmark decisions of the U.S. Supreme Court, particularly *Gideon v. Wainwright* and *Argersinger v. Hamlin*, all defendants who may be imprisoned for any offense must be afforded counsel at trials. Methods of providing

counsel include systems for assigned counsel, where an attorney is selected by the court to represent the accused, and public defender programs, where public employees provide legal services. Lawyers doing criminal defense work have discovered an increasing need for their services, not only at trial but also at the pre- and postjudicial stages of the criminal justice system.

The trial process is undergoing significant change through the introduction of technology and court management. Caseloads are being more effectively managed, and modern communications allow many aspects of the court process to be conducted in cyberspace. Some experts believe that we are on the threshold of a new form of trial in which the courthouse of old will be supplanted by the computer, the Internet, and wireless communications.

For an up-to-date list of Web links, go to
http://cj.wadsworth.com/siegel_essen4e.

KEY TERMS

lower court 221	landmark decision 229	adversarial procedure 240	contract system (attorney) 244
felony court 223	jury trial 232	indigent 241	*Strickland v. Washington* 245
appellate court 225	prosecutor 233	Sixth Amendment 242	*Burger v. Kemp* 246
court of last resort 225	Missouri Plan 234	*Gideon v. Wainwright* 242	
writ of certiorari 229	public defender 240	assigned counsel 244	

INFOTRAC COLLEGE EDITION EXERCISES

THE ROLE OF COUNSEL for the accused is complex, involving multiple obligations. Toward the client, the defense lawyer is a counselor and advocate; toward the prosecutor, the lawyer is a professional adversary; and toward the court, the lawyer is both advocate for the client and officer of the court. The defense attorney advocates the use of the due process perspective because it provides fair and equitable treatment to those accused of a

crime. Public defenders use hearings, notices, motions, and other legal devices in gaining outcomes for their clients (acquittals, charge reductions, and short sentences to prison).

Using InfoTrac College Edition, search for articles on the role of the criminal defense attorney in the justice system. Use such key terms as "public defenders," "indigency," and "right to counsel."

QUESTIONS

1. Should attorneys disclose information given them by their clients concerning participation in an earlier unsolved crime? Explain.

2. Should defense attorneys cooperate with a prosecutor if it means that their clients will go to jail? Explain.

3. Should a prosecutor have absolute discretion over which cases to proceed on and which to drop? Explain.

4. Should clients be made aware of an attorney's track record in court? Explain.

5. Does the assigned counsel system present an inherent conflict of interest, since attorneys are hired and paid by the institution they are to oppose? Explain.

6. Do you believe prosecutors have a great deal of discretion? Why or why not?

7. Was independent counsel Ken Starr's pursuit of President Bill Clinton an example of prosecutorial abuse? Explain.

NOTES

1. "Courts Hit by Budget Cuts," *State Government News 45* (June-July 2002): 6.

2. Matthew Durose and Patrick A. Langan, *State Court Sentencing of Convicted Felons, 1998* (Washington, D.C.: Bureau of Justice Statistics, February 2001).

3. Thomas Henderson, *The Significance of Judicial Structure: The Effect of Unification on Trial Court Operations* (Washington, D.C.: National Institute of Justice, 1984).

4. The court data used here and in the following sections relies heavily on Brian Ostrom, Neal Kauder, and Robert LaFountain, *Examining the Work of State Courts, 2001* (Williamsburg, Va.: National Center for State Courts, 2001). Hereinafter cited as State Court Statistics, 2001.

5. State Court Statistics, 2001.

6. U.S. Constitution, Art. 3, Secs. 1 and 2.

7. 1 Wharton 304, 4 L.Ed. 97 (1816).

8. David Rohde, "Arrests Soar in Giuliani Crackdown," *New York Times*, 2 February 1999.

9. Sari Escovitz with Fred Kurland and Nan Gold, *Judicial Selection and Tenure* (Chicago: American Judicature Society, 1974), 3–16.

10. State Court Statistics, 2001.

11. Bureau of Justice Statistics Bulletin, "Prosecutors in State Courts, 1996" (Washington, D.C.: Office of Justice Programs, 1999).

12. "Prosecutor Conduct," editorial, *USA Today*, 1 April 1999, 14A.

13. American Bar Association, *Model Rules of Professional Conduct* (Chicago: ABA, 1983), rule 3.8; see also Stanley Fisher, "In Search of the Virtuous Prosecutor: A Conceptual Framework," *American Journal of Criminal Law 15* (1988): 197.

14. Stanley Fisher, "Zealousness and Overzealousness: Making Sense of the Prosecutor's Duty to Seek Justice," *Prosecutor 22* (1989): 9; see also Bruce Green, "The Ethical Prosecutor and the Adversary System," *Criminal Law Bulletin 24* (1988): 126–145.

15. Marcia Chaiken and Jan Chaiken, *Priority Prosecutors of High-Rate Dangerous Offenders* (Washington, D.C.: National Institute of Justice, 1991).

16. Kenneth C. Davis, *Discretionary Justice* (Baton Rouge: Louisiana State University Press, 1969), 180; see also James B. Stewart, *The Prosecutor* (New York: Simon & Schuster, 1987).

17. Barbara Boland, *The Prosecution of Felony Arrests* (Washington, D.C.: Government Printing Office, 1983).

18. Newman Baker, "The Prosecutor—Initiation of Prosecution," *Journal of Criminal Law, Criminology, and Police Science 23* (1993): 770–771; see also Joan Jacoby, *The American Prosecutor: A Search for Identity* (Lexington, Mass.: Lexington Books, 1980).

19. Jeffrey Spears and Cassia Spohn, "The Effect of Evidence Factors and Victim Characteristics on Prosecutors' Charging Decisions in Sexual Assault Cases," *Justice Quarterly 14* (1997): 501–524.

20. Janell Schmidt and Ellen Hochstedler Steury, "Prosecutorial Discretion in Filing Charges in Domestic Violence Cases," *Criminology 27* (1989): 487–510.

21. Myrna Dawson and Ronit Dinovitzer, "Victim Cooperation and the Prosecution of Domestic Violence in a Specialized Court," *Justice Quarterly 18* (2001): 593–622.

22. Rodney Kingsworth, John Lopez, Jennifer Wentworth, and Debra Cummings, "Adult Sexual Assault: The Role of Racial/Ethnic Composition in Prosecution and Sentencing," *Journal of Criminal Justice 26* (1998): 359–372; *United States v. Armstrong* 517 U.S. 456 (1996).

23. Charles D. Breitel, "Controls in Criminal Law Enforcement," *University of Chicago Law Review 27* (1960): 427.

24. Cassia Spohn, Dawn Beichner, and Erika Davis-Frenzel, "Prosecutorial Justificiations for Sexual Assault Case Rejection: Guarding the 'Gateway to Justice,'" *Social Problems 48* (2001): 206–235.

25. *North Carolina v. Pearce*, 395 U.S. 711, 89 S.Ct. 2072, 23 L.Ed.2d 656 (1969).

26. *Blackledge v. Perry*, 417 U.S. 21, 94 S.Ct. 2098, 40 L.Ed.2d 628 (1974).

27. *Bordenkircher v. Hayes*, 434 U.S. 357, 98 S.Ct. 663, 54 L.Ed.2d 604 (1978).

28. American Bar Association, *Model Code of Professional Responsibility and Judicial Conduct* (Chicago: ABA, 1980), rule 3.8.

29. Monroe H. Freedman, "Professional Responsibility of the Criminal Defense Lawyer: The Three Hardest Questions," *Michigan Law Review 64* (1966): 1468.

30. The Sixth Amendment provides: "In all criminal prosecutions, the accused shall enjoy the right . . . to have the assistance of counsel for his defense."

31. *Gideon v. Wainwright*, 372 U.S. 335, 83 S.Ct. 792, 9 L.Ed.2d 799 (1963).

32. *Argersinger v. Hamlin*, 407 U.S. 25, 92 S.Ct. 2006, 32 L.Ed.2d 530 (1972).

33. *Mempa v. Rhay*, 389 U.S. 128, 88 S.Ct. 254, 19 L.Ed.2d 336 (1967).

34. *Douglas v. California*, 372 U.S. 353, 83 S.Ct. 814, 9 L.Ed.2d 811 (1963).

35. *In re Gault*, 387 U.S. 1, 875 S.Ct. 1428, 18 L.Ed.2d 527 (1967).

36. *Specht v. Patterson*, 386 U.S. 605, 87 S.Ct. 1209, 18 L.Ed.2d 326 (1967).

37. Carol J. DeFrances, *State-Funded Indigent Defense Services, 1999* (Washington, D.C.: Bureau of Justice Statistics, 2001).

38. Ibid.

39. See Drug Control Act of 1988, 42 U.S.C., sec. 375(G)(10).

40. Anti-Terrorism Act of 1996, Public Law No. 104-132 (1996).

41. *Strickland v. Washington*, 466 U.S. 668, 104 S.Ct. 2052, 80 L.Ed.2d 674 (1984).

42. *Burger v. Kemp*, 483 U.S. 776, 107 S.Ct. 3114, 97 L.Ed.2d 638 (1987).

43. Jeffrey Levinson, "Don't Let Sleeping Lawyers Lie: Raising the Standard for Effective Assistance of Counsel," *American Criminal Law Review 38* (2001): 147–179.

44. Ibid.

8 Pretrial Procedures

Chapter Outline

Criminal Justice Links

Criminal Justice Viewpoints

**Policy, Programs, and Issues
in Criminal Justice**
Pretrial Service Programs   256

Law in Review
United States v. Salerno   264

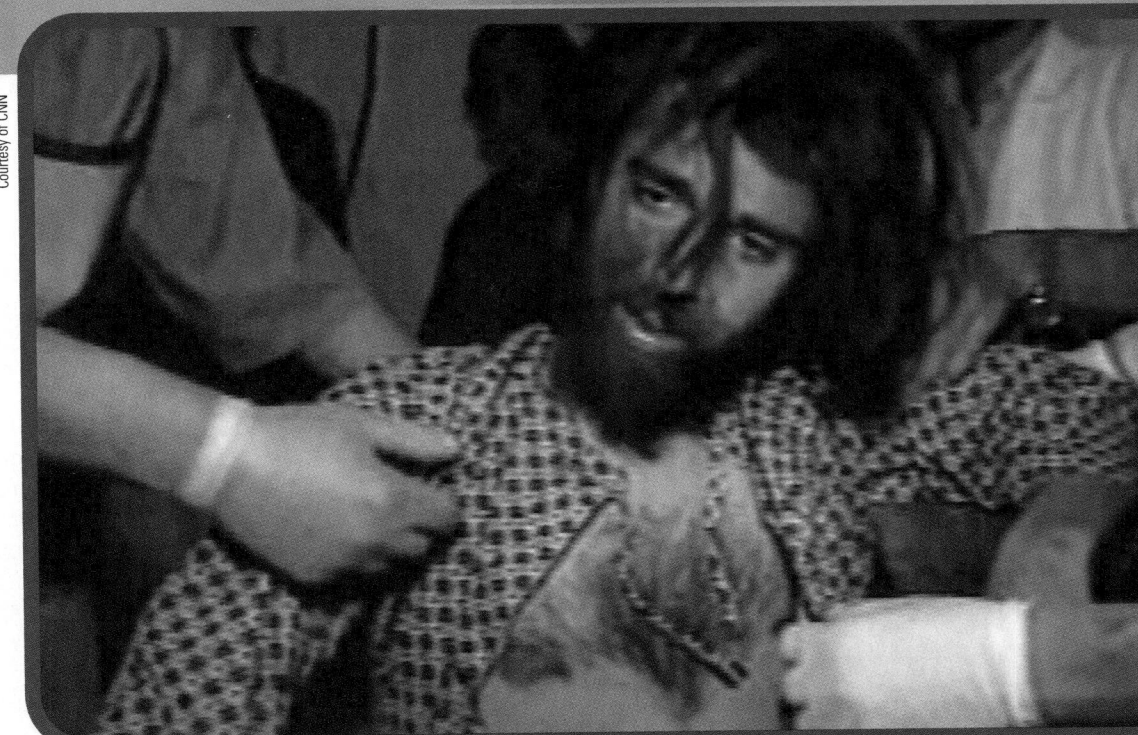

ONE OF THE MOST unexpected stories in the war on terrorism is that of John Walker Lindh, also known as the "American Taliban." Lindh was captured in Afghanistan during November 2001, fighting alongside Taliban and Al Qaeda forces. After his capture, he participated in a prison uprising during which American CIA agent Johnny "Mike" Spann was killed. Lindh was charged with treason and conspiracy to kill U.S. military forces in Afghanistan.

Lindh's story was quite unusual. He had grown up in a wealthy suburb of San Francisco, where he became interested in religion. Born a Catholic, at age fifteen he began to communicate with Muslims and attend mosques in the San Francisco area. Later Lindh decided to convert to Islam. After graduating high school he moved to Yemen to attend an Islamic school. He returned to California for a while, but left again in 2000, reportedly feeling lonely and unsettled. Walker returned to Yemen for additional studies and then moved to Pakistan, where he met and joined the Taliban.

Rather than being treated as a POW, Lindh was indicted under criminal law and was to be tried in an American criminal court on the charges of treason. To convict on treason, the U.S. Constitution requires "confession in open court" or testimony by two witnesses to the same treasonous act. Lindh could have been found guilty if he had any substantial knowledge of the September 11, 2001, attacks or if he took up arms against American troops after the U.S. began military strikes. Less than thirty treason convictions have ever happened in United States history; since World War II, no successful prosecution has occurred. Rather than go to trial under these circumstances, a plea bargain was hammered out in July 2002 in which Lindh was spared a possible life prison sentence and all terrorism charges against him were dropped. In exchange, he pleaded guilty to two charges of aiding the Taliban and carrying explosives and received a twenty-year sentence. ▪

To view the CNN video clip of this story, go to the book-specific Web site at http://cj.wadsworth.com/siegel_essen4e.

pretrial procedure A proceeding held before an official trial, such as a pretrial hearing, bail review, and pretrial diversion to a noncriminal program.

Cases like Lindh's show that many cases, even the most notorious ones, are settled at the pretrial stage of justice. The plea bargain is just one of a series of events that are critical links in the chain of justice. These include arraignments, grand jury investigations, bail hearings, plea-bargaining negotiations, and predisposition treatment efforts. These **pretrial procedures** are critically important components of the justice process because the great majority of all criminal cases are resolved informally at this stage and never come before the courts. Although the media like to focus on the elaborate jury trial with its dramatic elements and impressive setting, formal criminal trials are relatively infrequent. Consequently, understanding the events that take place during the pretrial period is essential in grasping the reality of criminal justice policy.

Cases are settled during the pretrial stage in a number of ways. Prosecutors can use their discretion to drop cases before formal charges are filed, because of insufficient evidence, office policy, witness conflicts, or similar problems. Even if charges are filed, the prosecutor can decide not to proceed against the defendant (*nolle prosequi*) because of a change in the circumstances of the case.

In addition, the prosecution and the defense almost always meet to try to arrange a nonjudicial settlement for the case. Plea bargaining, in which the defendant exchanges a guilty plea for some consideration, such as a reduced sentence, is commonly used to terminate the formal processing of the case. The prosecution or the defense may believe, for example, that a trial is not in the best interests of the victim, the defendant, or society because the defendant is incapable of understanding the charges or controlling her behavior. In this instance, the defendant may have a competency hearing before a judge and be placed in a secure treatment facility until ready to stand trial. Or the prosecutor may waive further action so that the defendant can be placed in a special treatment program, such as a detoxification unit at a local hospital.

booking process The administrative record of an arrest, listing the offender's name, address, physical description, date of birth, and employer; the time of arrest; the offense; and the name of the arresting officer. Photographing and fingerprinting of the offender are also part of the booking process.

Procedures Following Arrest

After arrest, the accused is ordinarily taken to the police station, where the police list the possible criminal charges against him and obtain other information for the **booking process.** This may include recording a description of the suspect and the circumstances of the offense. The suspect may then be fingerprinted, photographed, and required to participate in a lineup.

complaint A sworn allegation made in writing to a court or judge that an individual is guilty of some designated (complained of) offense. This is often the first legal document filed regarding a criminal offense. The complaint may be "taken out" by the victim, the police officer, the district attorney, or another interested party. Although the complaint charges an offense, an indictment or information may be the formal charging document.

Individuals arrested on a misdemeanor charge are ordinarily released from the police station on their own recognizance to answer the criminal charge before the court at a later date. They are usually detained by the police until it is decided whether a criminal complaint will be filed. The **complaint** is the formal written document identifying the criminal charge, the date and place where the crime occurred, and the circumstances of the arrest. The complaint is sworn to and signed under oath by the complainant, usually a police officer. The complaint will request that the defendant be present at an **initial hearing** held soon after the arrest is made; in some jurisdictions, this may be referred to by other names, such as **arraignment.** The defendant may plead guilty at the initial hearing, and the case may be disposed of immediately. Defendants who plead not guilty to a minor offense have been informed of the formal charge, provided with counsel if they are unable to afford a private attorney, and asked to plead guilty or not guilty as charged. A date in the near future is set for trial, and the defendant is generally released on bail or on her own recognizance to await trial.

initial hearing The stage in the justice process during which the suspect is brought before a magistrate for consideration of bail. The suspect must be taken for an initial hearing within a "reasonable time" after arrest. For petty offenses, this step often serves as the final criminal proceedings, either by adjudication by a judge or the offering of a guilty plea.

arraignment The step at which accused offenders are read the charges against them and are asked how they plead. In addition, the accused are advised of their rights. Possible pleas are guilty, not guilty, nolo contendere, and not guilty by reason of insanity.

Where a felony or a more serious crime is involved, the U.S. Constitution requires an intermediate step before a person can be tried. This involves proving to an objective body that there is probable cause to believe that a crime has taken place and that the accused should be tried on the matter. This step of the formal charging process is ordinarily an **indictment** from a **grand jury** or an **information** issued by a lower court.

An indictment is a written accusation charging a person with a crime; it is drawn up by a prosecutor and submitted to a grand jury, which—after considering the evidence presented by the prosecutor—votes to endorse or deny the indictment. An information is a charging document drawn up by a prosecutor in jurisdictions that do not use the grand jury system. The information is brought before a lower-court judge in a **preliminary hearing** (sometimes called a **probable cause hearing**). The purpose of this hearing is to require the prosecutor to present the case so that the judge can determine whether the defendant should be held to answer for the charge in a felony court.

After an indictment or information is filed, the accused is brought before the trial court for arraignment, during which the judge informs the defendant of the charge, ensures that the accused is properly represented by counsel, and determines whether he should be released on bail or some other form of release pending a hearing or trial.

The defendant who is arraigned on an indictment or information can ordinarily plead *guilty, not guilty,* or *nolo contendere,* which is equivalent to a guilty plea but cannot be used as evidence against the defendant in a civil case on the same matter. In cases where a guilty plea is entered, the defendant admits to all elements of the crime, and the court begins a review of the person's background for sentencing purposes. A not-guilty plea sets the stage for a trial on the merits or for negotiations, known as **plea bargaining,** between the prosecutor and the defense attorney.

Before discussing these issues, it is important to address the question of pretrial release and bail, which may arise at the police station, at the initial court appearance in a misdemeanor, or at the arraignment in most felony cases.

Pretrial Services

Many jurisdictions today are faced with significant increases in the number of criminal cases, particularly those involving drugs. The police have responded with an unprecedented number of arrests, clogging an already overburdened jail system. Of these arrestees, the justice system must determine which can safely be released pending trial. Pretrial services help courts deal with this problem. At the pretrial stage, the system is required to balance the often conflicting goals of ensuring community safety and respecting the rights of the arrestee.

Virtually all larger jurisdictions in the United States have pretrial release in one form or another. Court-administered programs make up the greatest percentage of pretrial programs, and probation-administered programs constitute the next largest segment. The general criteria used to assess eligibility for release center on the defendant's community ties and prior criminal justice involvement. Many jurisdictions have conditional and supervised release and third-party custody release, in addition to release on a person's own recognizance.

In recent years, many states have also begun to rely on pretrial programs to help manage defendants. The aim is to provide a judge with an objective measure of a defendant's behavior and suitability for pretrial release and later to serve as a tool for controlling possible misconduct during the pretrial release period. One key area of concern is drug abuse, and judges and magistrates generally believe that pretrial drug testing is a valuable tool in implementing the statutory requirements of any pretrial release program.[1]

The following Policy, Programs, and Issues feature examines the pretrial services mechanism in greater detail.

indictment A written accusation returned by a grand jury charging an individual with a specified crime after determination of probable cause; the prosecutor presents enough evidence (a prima facie case) to establish probable cause.

grand jury A group (usually consisting of twenty-three citizens) chosen to hear testimony in secret and to issue formal criminal accusations (indictments). It also serves an investigatory function.

information Like the indictment, a formal charging document. The prosecuting attorney makes out the information and files it in court. Probable cause is determined at the preliminary hearing, which, unlike grand jury proceedings, is public and attended by the accused and his or her attorney.

preliminary hearing (probable cause hearing) The step at which criminal charges initiated by an information are tested for probable cause; the prosecution presents enough evidence to establish probable cause—that is, a prima facie case. The hearing is public and may be attended by the accused and his or her attorney.

nolo contendere A plea of "no contest"; the defendant submits to sentencing without any formal admission of guilt that could be used against him or her in a subsequent civil suit.

plea bargaining The discussion between the defense counsel and the prosecution by which the accused agrees to plead guilty for certain considerations. The advantage to the defendant may be a reduction of the charges, a lenient sentence, or (in the case of multiple charges) dropped charges. The advantage to the prosecution is that a conviction is obtained without the time and expense of lengthy trial proceedings.

To read how nolo pleas are taken, go to www.almd.uscourts.gov/ Web%20Orders%20&%20Info/ Guilty%20Plea%20Colloquy.PDF

The Pretrial Services Resource Center is an independent nonprofit clearinghouse for information on pretrial issues and a technical assistance provider for pretrial practitioners, criminal justice officials, academicians, and community leaders nationwide: www.pretrial.org/

Policy, Programs, and Issues in Criminal Justice

Pretrial Service Programs

Pretrial service programs, now operating in more than three hundred counties and in all ninety-four districts in the federal court system, first began operations in the 1960s. They were part of the effort to improve the release/detention decision-making process by improving the breadth and quality of information available to judges at the point of initial decision making. Personnel gathered information on such factors as the defendant's housing arrangements, family ties, and employment. When the federal government passed the Federal Bail Reform Act of 1966, it encouraged judges to consider factors other than the seriousness of the charge in setting conditions of release and to use conditions other than the setting of a money bond amount, further encouraging the development of pretrial service programs. A "second generation" of pretrial service programs developed during the 1980s and 1990s focused primarily on trying to identify defendants who were unable to make bail but who would be acceptable risks for release either on their own recognizance or under supervision.

Today pretrial service programs perform two critically important functions in the effective administration of criminal justice:

• They gather and present information about newly arrested defendants and about available release options for use by judicial officers in deciding what (if any) conditions are to be set for defendants' release prior to trial.
• They supervise the defendants released from custody during the pretrial period by monitoring their compliance with release conditions and by helping to ensure they appear for scheduled court events.

These tasks are designed to minimize the use of unnecessary pretrial detention, reduce jail crowding, increase public safety, ensure that released defendants appear for scheduled court events, and lessen discrimination between the rich and the poor in the pretrial process.

To carry out these stated goals, pretrial service programs have at their core the collection, verification, and analysis of information about newly arrested defendants

and available supervisory options. Pretrial programs should collect and provide to the court at least the following defendant information:

• Identity, including date of birth and gender
• Community ties, including residence, employment, and family status
• Physical and mental condition, including alcohol or drug abuse
• Criminal record, including history of adjudication of delinquency
• Prior record of compliance with conditions of release, including record of appearing for scheduled court dates

Most pretrial services use the information they collect to develop recommendations or identify options for the judicial officer who makes the release/detention decision.

In addition, pretrial programs monitor offenders and help them avoid missing court dates and manage their behavior in the community. Defendants who miss a court appearance generally return to court when contacted, but a missed appearance nevertheless disrupts the court schedule, inconveniences victims and other witnesses, delays case disposition, and wastes valuable time. Pretrial service programs use a variety of monitoring and reminder techniques to anticipate and avoid possible nonappearance problems. When a defendant does miss a court appearance, the programs seek to contact the defendant immediately to resolve the problem. The following program activities can play an important role, however, in managing the risks that released defendants pose to public safety:

• Monitoring released defendants' compliance with conditions of release designed to minimize pretrial crime, including curfews, orders restricting contact with alleged victims and possible witnesses, home confinement, and drug and alcohol testing
• Providing direct "intensive" supervision for some categories of defendants by using program staff and collaborating with the police, other agencies, and community organizations

In the following section, one state's pretrial service function is discussed in some detail.

Bail

bail The monetary amount for or condition of pretrial release, normally set by a judge at the initial appearance. The purpose of bail is to ensure the return of the accused at subsequent proceedings.

Bail is money or some other security provided to the court to ensure the appearance of the defendant at every subsequent stage of the criminal justice process. Its purpose is to obtain the release from custody of a person charged with a crime. Once the amount of bail is set by the court, the defendant is required to deposit all or a percentage of the entire amount in cash or security (or to pay a professional bonding agent to submit a bond). If the defendant is released on bail but fails to

Kentucky: A Statewide Pretrial Services Agency

The Kentucky state legislature established the Pretrial Services and Court Security Agency in 1976 to replace the commercial bail bonding system. The new agency immediately assumed responsibility for implementing the pretrial release process, and the enabling act made it a crime to post a bond for profit in Kentucky.

The agency now has 220 staff members located in sixty offices serving a state population of approximately four million. The agency operates within the judicial branch as part of Kentucky's Administrative Office of the Courts. Staff members interview about 180,000 defendants each year, or approximately 84 percent of all arrestees. They conduct interviews around the clock in the state's population centers of Louisville, Lexington, and the Kentucky sector of the Cincinnati metropolitan area. Interviewers are on duty sixteen to twenty hours per day in smaller cities and on call at all times in rural regions. A pretrial officer interviews all arrestees except those who decline to be interviewed or who post bail immediately. The officer's top interview priority is obtaining background information for use by the judge at the defendant's first court appearance. Increasingly, the agency is able to draw on information in its own records system.

Interview information is treated as confidential—only the judge is given access to the report, and neither the interview nor the report can be subpoenaed. The information goes into the agency's records system for future reference in subsequent cases involving the defendant and also may be used by the agency's failure-to-appear unit.

Pretrial officers in Kentucky must be prepared to present information to the judge at the court appearance and to provide—or renew the search for—information the judge may request at that time. Using a point-scoring system that accounts for current charges, prior record, and family and community ties, the agency recommends release on recognizance (ROR) for defendants who score above the cutoff line. Judges are required by law to consider ROR and to identify in writing issues regarding risk of flight or community safety, although this does not always happen in practice. In making the release/detention decision, judges can use a variety of methods in addition to ROR, including placing the defendant in the custody of a person or organization, placing restrictions on the defendant's travel or residence, and requiring the defendant to post a cash bond with the court.

The agency supervises defendants principally through a tracking and notification system, using the system to remind defendants of upcoming court appearances. More intensive supervision is reserved for major felony cases and court requests. Drug testing is done at court request.

The failure to appear (FTA) rate for defendants under the agency's supervision is 8 percent. Most FTAs occur in cases involving minor offenses, such as public intoxication. In most FTA cases, a warrant is issued and the agency's FTA unit draws on all the information the agency has collected to locate and return the defendant. The agency has an active in-service training program and is working to broaden officer skills related to domestic violence, cultural diversity, victim advocacy, and driving while intoxicated.

Critical Thinking

Let's say an effective technology is developed that could be installed in a wearable device that monitors an offender's physical and emotional processes. The device would measure heartbeat, skin conductivity, and so on and alert authorities if the wearer was having an emotional crisis or even contemplating some forbidden activity such as committing crime. Would you be inclined to increase the number of offenders given pretrial release if such a device actually existed?

InfoTrac College Edition Research

What would happen if the jails were so crowded that all arrestees were given immediate pretrial release? To find out, go to InfoTrac College Edition and read Sarah B. Vandenbraak, "Bail, Humbug! Why Criminals Would Rather Be in Philadelphia," *Policy Review,* Summer 1995 v73 p73(4).

Source: Barry Mahoney, Bruce D. Beaudin, John A. Carver III, Daniel B. Ryan, and Richard B. Hoffman, "Pretrial Services Programs: Responsibilities and Potential," *Issues and Practices, A Publication of the National Institute of Justice* (March 2001): 1–122.

---

appear in court at the stipulated time, the bail deposit is forfeited. A defendant who fails to make bail is confined in jail until the court appearance.

Bail Today

The most recent national data available indicate that most defendants (64 percent) made bail; an estimated 36 percent of all defendants were detained until the courts disposed of their cases, including 7 percent who were denied bail. Murder

Use "bail" for a keyword search on InfoTrac College Edition.

Most serious arrest charge

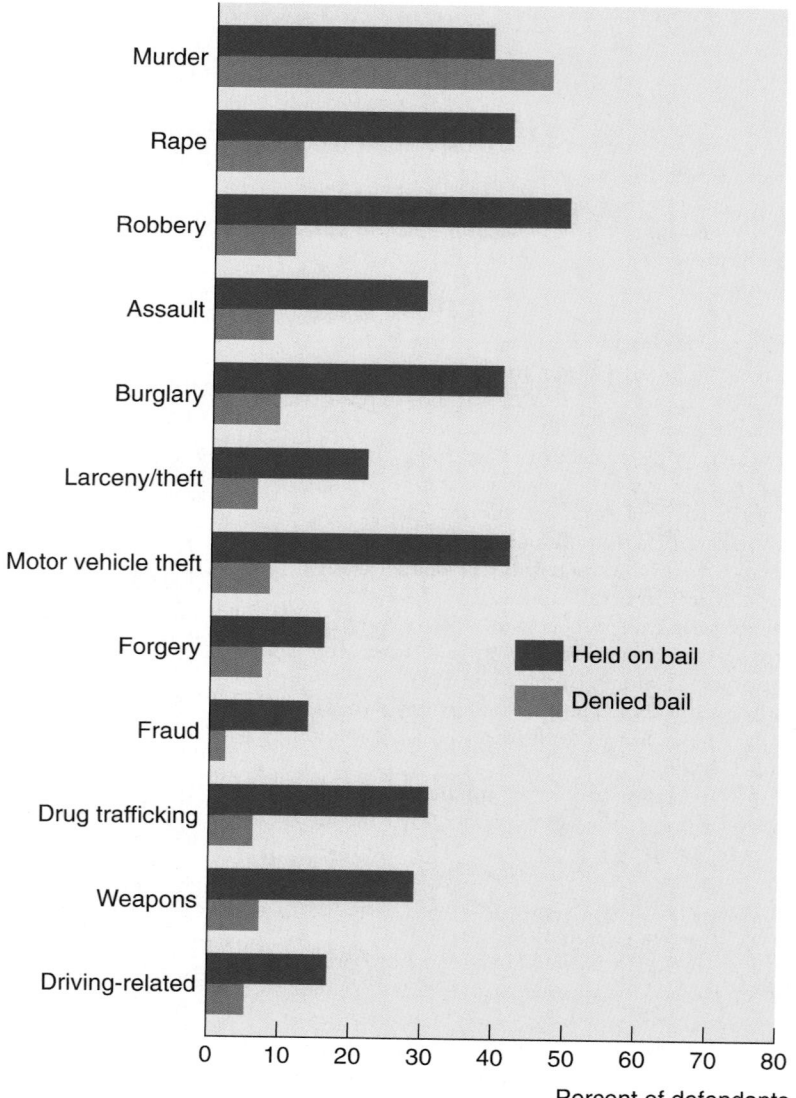

Figure 8.1

Pretrial detention of felony defendants in the seventy-five largest counties, by most serious arrest charge

Source: Brian A. Reaves, *Felony Defendants in Large Urban Counties, 1998* (Washington, D.C.: Bureau of Justice Statistics, 2001), 16.

defendants were the least likely to be released prior to case disposition (only 13 percent of them), followed by defendants whose most serious arrest charge was robbery (38 percent), rape (47 percent), burglary (50 percent), or motor vehicle theft (50 percent).[2] (See Figure 8.1.) About a third of released defendants were either rearrested for a new offense, failed to appear in court as scheduled, or committed some other violation that resulted in the revocation of their pretrial release. Those rearrested tended to (1) be on bail longer (nine months or more), (2) have a serious prior record, (3) abuse drugs, and (4) have a poor work record. They were also disproportionately young, male, and minority group members.

Receiving Bail

Whether a defendant can be expected to appear at the next stage of the criminal proceedings is a key issue in determining bail.[3] Bail cannot be used to punish an accused, nor can it be denied or revoked at the indulgence of the court. Critics argue that money bail is one of the most unacceptable aspects of the criminal justice system: it is discriminatory because it works against the poor; it is costly because the government must pay to detain those offenders who are unable to make bail but who would otherwise remain in the community; it is unfair because a higher proportion of detainees receive longer sentences than people released on bail; and it is dehumanizing because innocent people who cannot make bail suffer in the nation's deteriorated jail system.

The Legal Right to Bail

The Eighth Amendment to the U.S. Constitution does not guarantee a right to bail but rather prohibits "excessive bail." Since many state statutes place no precise limit on the amount of bail a judge may impose, many defendants who cannot make bail are placed in detention while awaiting trial. It has become apparent over the years that the bail system is discriminatory because defendants who are financially well-off can make bail, whereas indigent defendants languish in **pretrial detention** in the county jail. In addition, keeping a person in jail imposes serious financial burdens on local and state governments—and, in turn, on taxpayers—who must pay for the cost of confinement. These factors have given rise to bail reform programs that depend on the defendant's personal promise to appear in court for trial (*recognizance*), rather than on financial ability to meet bail. These

pretrial detention Holding an offender in secure confinement before trial.

© 2002 AP/Wide World Photos

Actor Robert Blake, right, was arrested on suspicion that he killed his wife Bonny Bakley, on May 4, 2001, outside a San Fernando Valley restaurant. He also faced charges of conspiracy, solicitation to murder, and the special circumstance of lying in wait. Here, he is at a bail hearing at which a Los Angeles judge denied him bail. On March 14, 2003, Blake was allowed to post $1.5 million bail to set him free from jail for the first time in 11 months.

reforms have enabled many deserving but indigent offenders to go free, but another trend has been to deny people bail on the grounds that they are a danger to themselves or to others in the community.

The Eighth Amendment restriction on excessive bail may also be interpreted to mean that the sole purpose of bail is to ensure that the defendant returns for trial; bail may not be used as a form of punishment, nor may it be used to coerce or threaten a defendant. In most cases, a defendant has the right to be released on reasonable bail. Many jurisdictions also require a bail review hearing by a higher court in cases in which the initial judge set what might be considered excessive bail.

The U.S. Supreme Court's interpretation of the Eighth Amendment's provisions on bail was set out in the 1951 case of *Stack v. Boyle*.[4] In that case, the Supreme Court found bail to be a traditional right to freedom before trial that permits unhampered preparation of a defense and prevents the criminal defendant from being punished prior to conviction. The Court held that bail is excessive when it exceeds an amount reasonably calculated to ensure that the defendant will return for trial. The Court indicated that bail should be in the amount that is generally set for similar offenses. Higher bail can be imposed when evidence supporting the increase is presented at a hearing at which the defendant's constitutional rights can be protected. Although *Stack* did not mandate an absolute right to bail, it did set guidelines for state courts to follow: if a crime is bailable, the amount set should not be frivolous, unusual, or beyond a person's ability to pay.

Making Bail

Bail is usually considered at a hearing that is conducted shortly after a person has been taken into custody. At the hearing such issues as crime type, flight risk, and dangerousness will be considered before a bail amount is set. Some jurisdictions have developed bail schedules to make amounts uniform based on crime and criminal history.

As Exhibit 8.1 shows, there are numerous other junctures during which bail is considered.

Because many criminal defendants are indigent, making bail is a financial challenge that if not met can result in a long stay in a county jail. In desperation, indigent defendants may turn to bail bondsmen. For a fee, bonding agents lend money to people who cannot make bail on their own. Typically, they charge a percentage of the bail amount. For example, a person who is asked to put up $10,000 will be asked to contribute $2,000 of his own and the bondsman covers the remaining $8,000. After trial, the bondsman keeps the $2,000 as his fee.

Powerful ties often exist between bonding agents and the court, with the result that defendants are steered toward particular bonding agents. Charges of kickbacks and cooperation accompany such arrangements. Consequently, efforts have been made to reform and even eliminate money bail and reduce the importance of bonding agents. Until the early 1960s, the justice system relied primarily on money bonds as the principal form of pretrial release. Many states now allow defendants to be released on their own recognizance without any money bail. **Release on recognizance (ROR)** was pioneered by the Vera Institute of Justice in an experiment called the **Manhattan Bail Project**, which began in 1961 with the cooperation of the New York City criminal courts and local law students.[5] It came about because defendants with financial means were able to post bail to secure pretrial release, while indigent defendants remained in custody. The project found that if the court had sufficient background information about the defendant, it could make a reasonably good judgment about whether the accused would return to court. When release decisions were based on such information as the nature of the offense, family ties, and employment record, most defendants returned to court when released on their own recognizance. The results of the Vera Institute's initial operation showed a default rate of less than 0.7 percent. The bail project's

If you want to understand how a bail bond agency operates, go to Action Bail Bond's homepage:
www.actionbail.com

The Web site of the Professional Bail Agents of the United States is designed to help bail bondspersons to be more competent and effective. You can visit the site:
www.pbus.com/pba2.htm

release on recognizance (ROR) A nonmonetary condition for the pretrial release of an accused individual; an alternative to monetary bail that is granted after the court determines that the accused has ties in the community, has no prior record of default, and is likely to appear at subsequent proceedings.

Manhattan Bail Project The innovative experiment in bail reform that introduced and successfully tested the concept of release on recognizance.

Exhibit 8.1	Pretrial release alternatives

Stage	Release Mechanism
1. Police	**Field citation release:** An arresting officer releases the arrestee on a written promise to appear in court, made at or near the actual time and location of the arrest. This procedure is commonly used for misdemeanor charges and is similar to issuing a traffic ticket.
2. Police	**Station house citation release:** The determination of an arrestee's eligibility and suitability for release and her actual release are deferred until after she has been removed from the scene of an arrest and brought to the station house or police headquarters.
3. Police/ pretrial	**Jail citation release:** The determination of an arrestee's eligibility and suitability for citation release and his actual release are deferred until after he has been delivered by the arresting department to a jail or other pretrial detention facility for screening, booking, and admission.
4. Pretrial/court	**Direct release authority by pretrial program:** To streamline release court processes and reduce the length of stay in detention, courts may authorize pretrial programs to release arrestees without direct judicial involvement. Where court rule delegates such authority, the practice is generally limited to misdemeanor charges, but felony release authority has been granted in some jurisdictions.
5. Police/court	**Bail schedule:** An arrestee can post bail at the station house or jail, according to amounts specified in a bail schedule. The schedule is a list of all bailable charges and a corresponding dollar amount for each. Schedules may vary widely from jurisdiction to jurisdiction.
6. Court	**Judicial release:** Arrestees who have not been released by either the police or the jailer and who have not posted bail appear at the hearing before a judge, magistrate, or bail commissioner within a set period of time. In jurisdictions with pretrial release programs, program staff often interview arrestees detained at the jail prior to the first hearing, verify the background information, and present recommendations to the court at arraignment.

experience suggested that releasing a person on the basis of verified information more effectively guaranteed appearance in court than did money bail. Highly successful ROR projects were set up in major cities around the country, including Philadelphia and San Francisco. By 1980 more than 120 formal programs were in operation, and today they exist in almost every major jurisdiction.[6]

The success of ROR programs in the early 1960s resulted in bail reforms that culminated with the enactment of the federal Bail Reform Act of 1966, the first change in federal bail laws since 1789.[7] This legislation sought to ensure that release would be granted in all noncapital cases in which there was sufficient reason to believe that the defendant would return to court. The law clearly established the presumption of ROR that must be overcome before money bail is required, authorized 10 percent **deposit bail,** introduced the concept of conditional release, and stressed the philosophy that release should be under the least restrictive method necessary to ensure court appearance.

During the 1970s and early 1980s, the pretrial release movement was hampered by public pressure over pretrial increases in crime. As a result, the more recent federal legislation, the **Bail Reform Act of 1984,** mandated that no defendants shall be kept in pretrial detention simply because they cannot afford money bail, established the presumption for ROR in all cases in which a person is bailable, and formalized restrictive preventive detention provisions, which are explained later in this chapter. The 1984 act required that community safety, as well as the risk of flight, be considered in the release decision. Consequently, such criminal justice

To see the provisions of the Bail Reform Act of 1984, 18 U.S.C. §§ 3141–3150, 3156, go to www.law.ukans.edu/research/bailrfrm.htm

deposit bail   The monetary amount set by a judge at a hearing as a condition of pretrial release, ordering a percentage of the total bond required to be paid by the defendant.

Bail Reform Act of 1984   Federal legislation that provides for both greater emphasis on release on recognizance for nondangerous offenders and preventive detention for those who present a menace to the community.

factors as the seriousness of the charged offense, the weight of the evidence, the sentence that may be imposed upon conviction, court appearance history, and prior convictions are likely to influence the release decisions of the federal court.

Bail reform is considered one of the most successful programs in the recent history of the criminal justice system. Yet it is not without critics, who suggest that emphasis should be put on controlling the behavior of serious criminals rather than on making sure that nondangerous defendants are released before their trials. Criminal defendants released without bail and those who commit crimes awaiting trial fuel the constant debate over pretrial release versus community protection. Although some experts believe that all people, even noncitizens accused of crimes, enjoy the right to bail, others view it as a license to abscond or commit more crimes.[8]

A number of innovative alternative bail programs are described in Exhibit 8.2. The most often used are personal recognizance, unsecured or personal bond,

To find out which factors influence the ROR decision, read Thomas A. Petee, "Recommended for Release on Recognizance: Factors Affecting Pretrial Release Recommendations," *Journal of Social Psychology*, June 1994 v134 i3 p375(8), on InfoTrac College Edition.

Exhibit 8.2 Innovative bail systems	
Program	**Description**
NONFINANCIAL RELEASE	
Release on recognizance (ROR)	The defendant is released on a promise to appear, without any requirement of money bond. This form of release is unconditional—i.e., without imposition of special conditions, supervision, or specially provided services.
Conditional release	The defendant is released on a promise to fulfill some stated requirements that go beyond those associated with ROR. Four types of conditions are placed on defendants: (1) status quo conditions, such as requiring that the defendant retain residence or employment status; (2) restrictive conditions, such as requiring that the defendant remain in the jurisdiction; (3) contact conditions, such as requiring that the defendant report by telephone or in person to the release program; and (4) problem-oriented conditions, such as requiring that the defendant participate in drug or alchohol treatment programs.
FINANCIAL RELEASE	
Unsecured bail	The defendant is released with no immediate requirement of payment. However, if the defendant fails to appear, he or she is liable for the full amount.
Privately secured bail	A private organization or individual posts the bail amount, which is returned when the defendant appears in court.
Property bail	The defendant may post evidence of real property in lieu of money.
Deposit bail	The defendant deposits a percentage of the bail amount, typically 10%, with the court. When the defendant appears in court, the deposit is returned, sometimes minus an administrative fee. If the defendant fails to appear, he or she is liable for the full amount of the bail.
Surety bail	The defendant pays a percentage of the bond, usually 10%, to a bonding agent who posts the full bail. The fee paid to the bonding agent is not returned to the defendant if he or she appears in court. The bonding agent is liable for the full amount of the bond should the defendant fail to appear. Bonding agents often require posting collateral to cover the full bail amount.
Cash bail	The defendant pays the entire amount of bail set by the judge to secure release. The bail is returned to the defendant when he or she appears in court.

Source: Adapted from Andy Hall, *Pretrial Release Program Options* (Washington, D.C.: National Institute of Justice, 1984), 32–33.

surety or cash bond, and percentage or deposit bail. As Exhibit 8.2 shows, most bailees receive surety bond; next most common is ROR.

Preventive Detention

Figure 8.2 shows the percentage of people receiving bail for common criminal acts. More than half of all violent criminals are now released on bail, including people on trial for committing murder (13 percent). However, as we noted previously, numerous people granted pretrial release re-offend. The presumption of bail is challenged by those who believe that releasing dangerous criminals before trial poses a threat to public safety. They point to evidence showing that many people released on bail commit new crimes while at large and often fail to appear for trial. One response to the alleged failure of the bail system to protect citizens is the adoption of **preventive detention** statutes. These laws require that certain dangerous defendants be confined before trial for their own protection and that of the community. Preventive detention is an important manifestation of the crime control perspective on justice, because it favors the use of incapacitation to control the future behavior of suspected criminals. Often, the key question is whether preventive detention is punishment before trial.

The most striking use of preventive detention can be found in the federal Bail Reform Act of 1984, which contrasted sharply with previous law.[9] Although the act does contain provisions for ROR, it also allows judges to order preventive detention if they determine "that no condition or combination of conditions will reasonably assure the appearance of the person as required and the safety of any other person and the community."[10]

A number of state jurisdictions have incorporated elements of preventive detention into their bail systems. Although most of the restrictions do not constitute outright preventive detention, they serve to narrow the scope of bail eligibility. These provisions include (1) exclusion of certain crimes from bail eligibility;

preventive detention   The practice of holding dangerous suspects before trial without bail.

is it a punishment

Use "preventive detention" as a subject guide on InfoTrac College Edition to find out about the various forms it can take.

Figure 8.2
Pretrial release of felony defendants in the seventy-five largest counties, by type of release

Source: Brian A. Reaves, *Felony Defendants in Large Urban Counties, 1998* (Washington, D.C.: Bureau of Justice Statistics, 2001), 17.

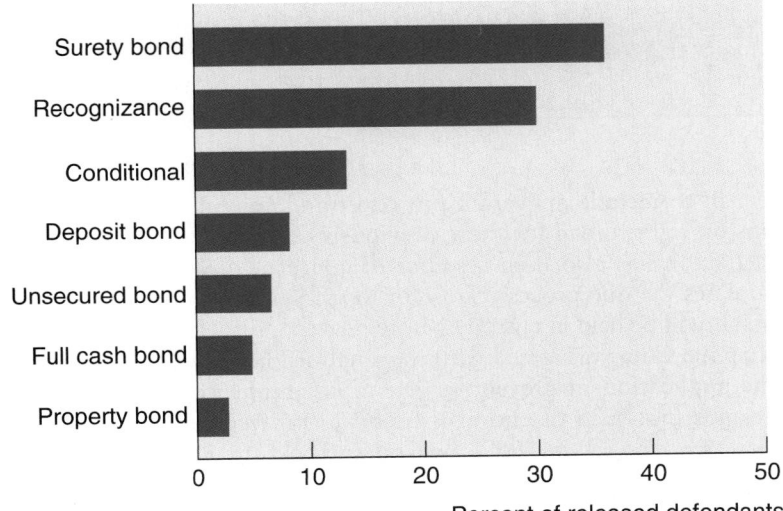

Law in Review

United States v. Salerno

In this case, the U.S. Supreme Court held that the use of preventive detention is constitutionally permissible.

Facts

On March 21, 1986, Anthony Salerno and co-defendant Vincent Cafaro were charged in a twenty-nine-count indictment alleging various racketeering violations, including gambling, wire fraud, extortion, and conspiracy to commit murder. At their arraignment, the government moved to have them detained on the grounds that no condition of release could ensure community safety. At a detention hearing, the prosecution presented evidence that Salerno was the "boss" of the Genovese crime family and that Cafaro was a "captain." Wiretap evidence indicated that the two men had participated in criminal conspiracies, including murder. The court heard testimony from two witnesses who had personally participated in the murder conspiracies. In rebuttal, Salerno provided character statements, presented evidence that he had a heart condition, and challenged the veracity of the government's witnesses. Cafaro claimed the wiretaps had merely recorded "tough talk." The trial court allowed the detention on the grounds that the defendants wanted to use their pretrial freedom to continue their "family" business and "when business as usual involves threats, beatings, and murder, the present danger such people pose to the community is self-evident."

On appeal, the U.S. Court of Appeals for the Second Circuit agreed with the defendants' claim that the government could not detain suspects simply because they were thought to represent a danger to the community. The circuit court found that the criminal law system holds people accountable for their past deeds, not their anticipated future actions. The government then reappealed the case to the U.S. Supreme Court.

Decision

The Supreme Court held that the preventive detention act had a legitimate and compelling regulatory purpose and did not violate the due process clause. Preventive detention was not designed to punish dangerous individuals but to find a solution for the social problem of people committing crimes while on bail; preventing danger to the community is a legitimate societal goal.

The Court also stated that society's need for protection can outweigh an individual's liberty interest: under some circumstances, individuals can be held without bail. The act provides that only the most serious criminals can be held and mandates careful procedures to ensure that the judgment of future dangerousness is made after careful deliberation. Finally, the Court found that the Eighth Amendment does not limit the setting (or denial) of bail simply to prohibit defendants' flight to avoid trial and held that considerations of dangerousness are a valid reason to deny pretrial release.

Significance of the Case

Salerno (1987) legitimizes the use of preventive detention as a crime control method. It permits the limitations on bail already in place in many state jurisdictions to continue. *Salerno* further illustrates the concern for community protection that has developed in the past decades. It is a good example of the recent efforts by the Court to give the justice system greater control over criminal defendants. At this time, it is still unclear how often judges will rely on preventive detention statutes that require a hearing on the facts or whether they will simply continue to set extremely high bail for defendants whom they wish to remain in pretrial custody.

Critical Thinking

Do you believe that some dangerous offenders, such as rapists and child molesters, should never be granted pretrial release? Does preventive detention violate the basic right that a person is "innocent until proven guilty?"

InfoTrac College Edition Research

Use InfoTrac College Edition to access articles that compare the use of preventive detention programs for adult offenders with those used to detain juvenile offenders.

(2) definition of bail to include appearance in court and community safety; and (3) the limitations on right to bail for those previously convicted.

Preventive detention has also been a source of concern for civil libertarians, who believe it violates the due process clause of the U.S. Constitution because it means that a person will be held in custody before proven guilty. In two important cases the U.S. Supreme Court disagreed with this analysis. In *Schall v. Martin*, the Court upheld the application of preventive detention statutes to juvenile defendants on the grounds that such detention is useful to protect the welfare of the minor and society as a whole.[11] In 1987, the Court upheld the Bail Reform Act's provision on preventive detention as it applied to adults in the case of *United States v. Salerno*, which is set out in the Law in Review feature above.[12]

Pretrial Detention

The criminal defendant who is not eligible for bail or ROR is subject to pretrial detention in the local county jail.

In terms of the number of persons affected each year, pretrial custody accounts for more incarceration in the United States than does imprisonment after sentencing. On any given day in the United States, more than six hundred thousand people were held in more than thirty-five hundred local jails. Over the course of a year, many times that number pass through the jailhouse door. More than 50 percent of those held in local jails have been accused of crimes but not convicted; they are *pretrial detainees*. In the United States, people are detained at a rate twice that of neighboring Canada and three times that of Great Britain. Hundreds of jails are overcrowded, and many are under court orders to reduce their populations and improve conditions. The national jail-crowding crisis has worsened over the years.

Jails are often considered the weakest link in the criminal justice process: they are frequently dangerous, harmful, decrepit, and filled with the poor and friendless. The costs of holding a person in jail range up to more than $100 per day and $36,000 per year. In addition, detainees are often confined with those convicted of crimes and those who have been transferred from other institutions because of overcrowding. Many felons are transferred to jails from state prisons to ease crowding. It is possible to have in close quarters a convicted rapist, a father jailed for nonpayment of child support, and a person awaiting trial for a crime that he did not actually commit. Thus, jails contain a mix of inmates, and this can lead to violence, brutality, and suicide.

The Effects of Detention

What happens to people who do not get bail or who cannot afford to put up bail money? Traditionally, they find themselves more likely to be convicted and then get a longer prison sentence than those who commit similar crimes but who were released on bail. A federally sponsored study of case processing in the nation's

© Alon Reininger/Contact Press Images

People who cannot make bail not only are subject to incarceration before they are tried but also suffer higher rates of conviction and incarceration than defendants who are released on bail. Bail reform has attempted to remedy this problem by reducing the number of detained defendants. Here are inmates in the Los Angeles County Jail.

largest counties found that about 63 percent of all defendants granted bail were convicted; in contrast, 78 percent of detainees were convicted.[13] Detainees are also more likely to be convicted of a felony offense than releasees, and therefore are eligible for a long prison sentence rather than the much shorter term of incarceration given misdemeanants. People being held in jails are in a less attractive bargaining position than those released on bail, and prosecutors, knowing their predicament, may be less generous in their negotiations.

Charging the Defendant

Charging a defendant with a crime is a process that varies somewhat, depending on whether it occurs via a *grand jury* or a *preliminary hearing*.

The Indictment Process—The Grand Jury

The grand jury was an early development of the English common law. Under the Magna Carta (1215), no freeman could be seized and imprisoned unless he had been judged by his peers. To determine fairly who was eligible to be tried, a group of freemen from the district where the crime was committed would be brought together to examine the facts of the case and determine whether the charges had merit. Thus, the grand jury was created as a check against arbitrary prosecution by a judge who might be a puppet of the government.

The concept of the grand jury was brought to the American colonies by early settlers and later incorporated into the Fifth Amendment of the U.S. Constitution, which states that "no person shall be held to answer for a capital, or otherwise infamous crime, unless on presentment or indictment of a grand jury."

What is the role of the grand jury today? First, the grand jury has the power to act as an independent investigating body. In this capacity, it examines the possibility of criminal activity within its jurisdiction. These investigative efforts may be directed toward general rather than individual criminal conduct—for example, looking at organized crime or insider trading. After an investigation is completed, a report called a **presentment** is issued. The presentment contains not only information concerning the findings of the grand jury but also, usually, a recommendation of indictment.

The grand jury's second and better known role is accusatory in nature. In this capacity, the grand jury acts as the community's conscience in determining whether the accusation of the state (the prosecution) justifies a trial. The grand jury relies on the testimony of witnesses called by the prosecution through its subpoena power. After examining the evidence and the testimony of witnesses, the grand jury decides whether probable cause exists for prosecution. If it does, an indictment, or **true bill,** is affirmed. If the grand jury fails to find probable cause, a **no bill** (meaning that the indictment is ignored) is passed. In some states, a prosecutor can present evidence to a different grand jury if a no bill is returned; in other states, this action is prohibited by statute.

Critiquing the Grand Jury The grand jury usually meets at the request of the prosecution, and hearings are closed and secret. Neither the defense attorney, the defendant, nor the general public are allowed to attend. The prosecuting attorney presents the charges and calls witnesses who testify under oath to support the indictment. This process has been criticized as being a "rubber stamp" for the prosecution because the presentation of the evidence is shaped by the district attorney who is not required by law to reveal information that might exonerate the accused.[14] In the case of *United States v. Williams* (1992), the Supreme Court ruled that that there is no supervisory power in the federal courts to require presentation of *exculpatory evidence* (evidence that can clear a defendant from blame or

---

presentment The report of a grand jury investigation, which usually includes a recommendation of indictment.

true bill The action by a grand jury when it votes to indict an accused suspect.

no bill The action by a grand jury when it votes not to indict an accused suspect.

To get the latest news on grand juries, go to
www.udayton.edu/~grandjur/

fault).[15] Some legal scholars find that the *Williams* decision conflicted with the grand jury's historical purpose of shielding criminal defendants from unwarranted and unfair prosecution and overrode the mandate that it be both informed and independent. An alternative might be to change the rule of criminal procedure so that prosecutors would be obliged to present exculpatory evidence to the grand jury even if it might result in the issuance of a no bill or indictment.[16] Another alternative put forth by defense lawyers is to open the grand jury room to the defense and hold the government to the same types of constitutional safeguards required to protect defendants that are now used at trial.[17]

To read more about grand juries, use the term as a subject guide on InfoTrac College Edition.

The Indictment Process—The Preliminary Hearing

The preliminary hearing is used in about half the states as an alternative to the grand jury. Although the purpose of the preliminary hearing and the grand jury hearing is the same—to establish whether probable cause is sufficient to merit a trial—the procedures differ significantly.

The preliminary hearing is conducted before a magistrate or lower court judge, and unlike the grand jury hearing, is open to the public unless the defendant requests otherwise. Present at the preliminary hearing are the prosecuting attorney, the defendant, and the defendant's counsel, if already retained. The prosecution presents its evidence and witnesses to the judge. The defendant or the defense counsel then has the right to cross-examine witnesses and to challenge the prosecutor's evidence.

© 2002 AP/Wide World Photos

In 2002 Adelphia Communications Corporation founder John J. Rigas; his three sons, Timothy J. Rigas, Michael J. Rigas, and James P. Rigas; and two senior executives at Adelphia, James R. Brown and Michael C. Mulcahey, were indicted in one of the most extensive financial frauds ever to take place at a public company. They were charged with fraudulently excluding billions of dollars in liabilities from the company's consolidated financial statements by hiding them in off-balance-sheet affiliates, falsifying operations statistics and inflating Adelphia's earnings to meet Wall Street's expectations, and concealing rampant self-dealing by the Rigas family, including the undisclosed use of corporate funds for family stock purchases and the acquisition of luxury condominiums in New York and elsewhere. Michael Rigas, left, is shown here leaving a Manhattan federal court hearing.

After hearing the evidence, the judge decides whether there is sufficient probable cause to believe that the defendant committed the alleged crime. If so, the defendant is bound over for trial, and the prosecuting attorney's information (described earlier, similar to an indictment) is filed with the superior court, usually within fifteen days. When the judge does not find sufficient probable cause, the charges are dismissed and the defendant is released from custody.

A unique aspect of the preliminary hearing is the defendant's right to waive the proceeding. In most states, the prosecutor and the judge must agree to this waiver. A waiver has advantages and disadvantages for both the prosecutor and the defendant. In most situations, a prosecutor will agree to a waiver because it avoids revealing evidence to the defense before trial. However, if the state believes it is necessary to obtain a record of witness testimony because of the possibility that a witness or witnesses may be unavailable for the trial or unable to remember the facts clearly, the prosecutor might override the waiver. In this situation, the record of the preliminary hearing can be used at the trial.

The defendant will most likely waive the preliminary hearing for one of three reasons: (1) he has already decided to plead guilty; (2) he wants to speed the criminal justice process; or (3) he hopes to avoid the negative publicity that might result from the hearing. On the other hand, the preliminary hearing is of obvious advantage to the defendant who believes that it will result in a dismissal of the charges. In addition, the preliminary hearing gives the defense the opportunity to learn what evidence the prosecution has. Figure 8.3 outlines the significant differences between the grand jury and the preliminary hearing processes.

Arraignment

Use the word "arraignment" as a key term on InfoTrac College Edition.

After an indictment or information is filed following a grand jury or preliminary hearing, an arraignment takes place before the court that will try the case. At the arraignment, the judge informs the defendant of the charges against her and appoints counsel if one has not yet been retained. According to the Sixth Amendment of the U.S. Constitution, the accused has the right to be informed of the nature and cause of the accusation; thus, the judge at the arraignment must make sure that the defendant clearly understands the charges.

After the charges are read and explained, the defendant is asked to enter a plea. If a plea of not guilty or not guilty by reason of insanity is entered, a trial date is set. When the defendant pleads guilty or nolo contendere, a date for sentencing is arranged. The magistrate then either sets bail or releases the defendant on personal recognizance.

© AP/Wide World Photos

Sometimes arraignments don't go as planned. Here, handcuffed murder suspect Alfred Gaynor, thirty-one, left, lies slumped over a railing in a Springfield district courtroom, April 30, 1998, in Springfield, Massachusetts, after being struck with a chair by a man at the start of his pretrial hearing in connection with the murder of two Springfield women. Gaynor's assailant was Eric Downs, son of one of the victims.

The Plea

Ordinarily, a defendant in a criminal trial will enter one of three pleas: guilty, not guilty, or nolo contendere.

Guilty   On July 7, 2001, Lizzie Grubman, a New York publicist with a dazzling roster of clients, was asked her to move her Mercedes SUV from a fire lane in front of a trendy nightclub in the Hamptons. She angrily slammed

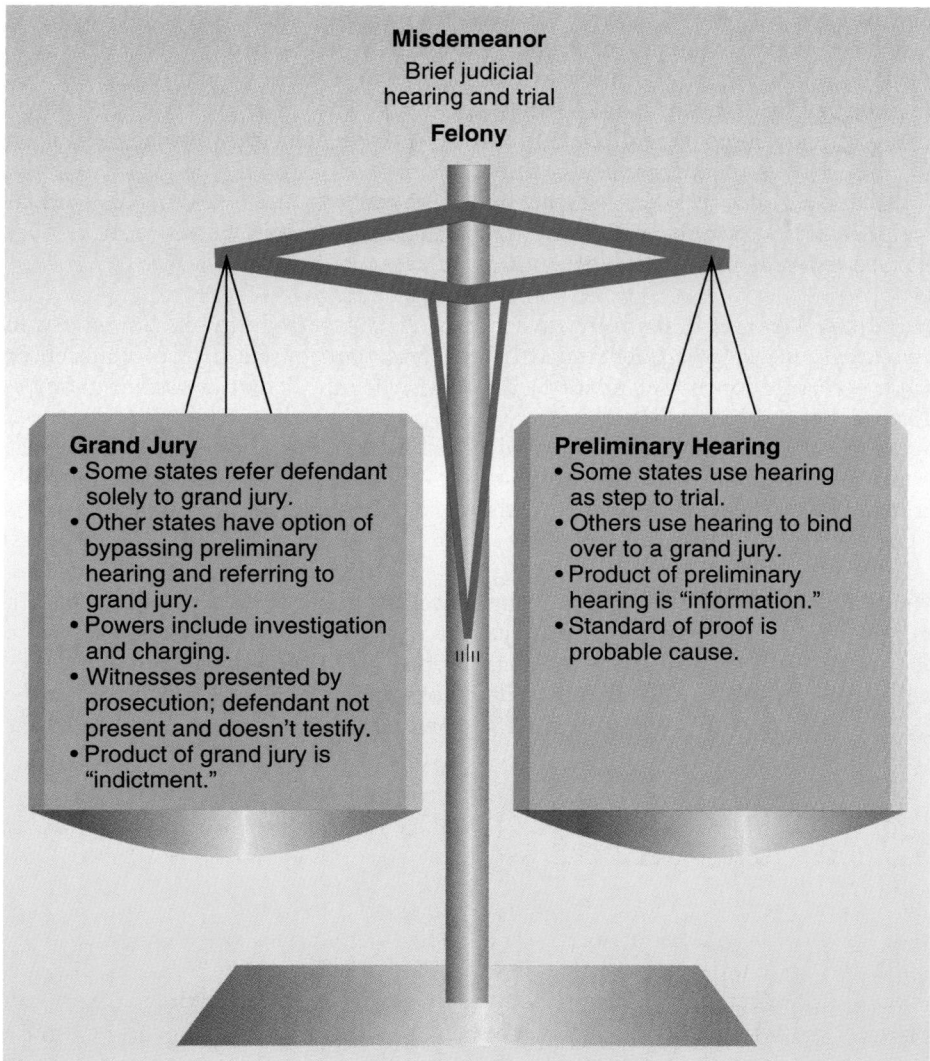

Misdemeanor
Brief judicial
hearing and trial
Felony

Grand Jury
• Some states refer defendant solely to grand jury.
• Other states have option of bypassing preliminary hearing and referring to grand jury.
• Powers include investigation and charging.
• Witnesses presented by prosecution; defendant not present and doesn't testify.
• Product of grand jury is "indictment."

Preliminary Hearing
• Some states use hearing as step to trial.
• Others use hearing to bind over to a grand jury.
• Product of preliminary hearing is "information."
• Standard of proof is probable cause.

Figure 8.3
Charging the defendant with a crime
Note the differences between the grand jury and preliminary hearing.

her SUV into reverse and drove into a crowd of onlookers, injuring sixteen people before she drove away. On August 23, 2002, she pled guilty to third-degree assault and leaving the scene of an accident in exchange for a sentence of two months in jail, 280 hours of community service, and five years' probation. She could have faced up to seven years behind bars if convicted at trial.[18]

The Grubman case is certainly not unique. More than 90 percent of defendants appearing before the courts plead guilty prior to the trial stage. A guilty plea has several consequences. It functions not only as an admission of guilt but also as a surrender of the entire array of constitutional rights designed to protect a criminal defendant against unjustified conviction, including the right to remain silent, the right to confront witnesses against him or her, the right to a trial by jury, and the right to be proven guilty by proof beyond a reasonable doubt. Once a plea is made it cannot be rescinded or withdrawn after sentencing even if there is a change in the law that might have made conviction more problematic.[19]

As a result, judges must take certain procedures when accepting a plea of guilty. First, the judge must clearly state to the defendant the constitutional guarantees that are automatically waived by this plea. Second, the judge must believe that the facts of the case establish a basis for the plea and that the plea is made voluntarily. Third, the defendant must be informed of the right to counsel during the pleading process. In many felony cases, the judge will insist on the presence of defense counsel. Finally, the judge must inform the defendant of the possible sentencing outcomes, including the maximum sentence that can be imposed.

After a guilty plea has been entered, a sentencing date is arranged. In a majority of states, a guilty plea may be withdrawn and replaced with a not-guilty plea at any time prior to sentencing if good cause is shown.

Not Guilty At the arraignment or before the trial, a not-guilty plea is entered in two ways: (1) it is verbally stated by the defendant or the defense counsel, or (2) it is entered for the defendant by the court when the defendant stands mute before the bench.

Once a plea of not guilty is recorded, a trial date is set. In misdemeanor cases, trials take place in the lower court system, whereas felony cases are normally transferred to the superior court. At this time, a continuance or issuance of bail is once again considered.

Nolo Contendere The plea *nolo contendere* ("no contest") is essentially a plea of guilty. This plea has the same consequences as a guilty plea, with one exception: it may not be held against the defendant as proof in a subsequent civil matter because technically there has been no admission of guilt. This plea is accepted at the discretion of the trial court and must be voluntarily and intelligently made by the defendant.

Plea Bargaining

Plea bargaining is one of the most common practices in the criminal justice system today and a cornerstone of the informal justice system. Plea bargaining is actually a relatively recent development, taking hold late in the nineteenth century. At first, judges were reluctant to accept pleas, preferring trials to sharing their power with prosecutors (who make the deal). However, plea bargaining became more attractive at the turn of the twentieth century when the mechanization of manufacture and transportation prompted a flood of complex civil cases; this event persuaded judges that criminal cases had to be settled quickly lest the court system break down.[20] Today more than 90 percent of criminal convictions are estimated to result from negotiated pleas of guilty. Even in serious felony cases, some jurisdictions will have several plea-bargaining arrangements for every trial.

Plea bargaining is the exchange of prosecutorial and judicial concessions for pleas of guilty. Normally, a bargain can be made between the prosecutor and the defense attorney in four ways: (1) the initial charges may be reduced to those of a lesser offense, thus automatically reducing the sentence imposed; (2) in cases where many counts are charged, the prosecutor may reduce the number of counts; (3) the prosecutor may promise to recommend a lenient sentence, such as probation; and (4) when the charge imposed has a negative label attached (for example, child molester), the prosecutor may alter the charge to a more "socially acceptable" one (such as assault) in exchange for a plea of guilty. In a jurisdiction where sentencing disparities exist between judges, the prosecutor may even agree to arrange for a defendant to appear before a lenient judge in exchange for a plea; this practice is known as *judge shopping*.

Because of excessive criminal court caseloads and the personal and professional needs of the prosecution and the defense (to get the case over with in the shortest amount of time), plea bargaining has become an essential yet controver-

To gain some more insight into plea bargaining, go to
www.lawsguide.com/mylawyer/
guideview.asp?layer=2&article=147

© 2002 AP/Wide World Photos

Plea bargains are commonly used in even the most notorious cases that make media headlines. Here, Robert Iler, center, the teenage star of the HBO series *The Sopranos,* returns to court surrounded by friends and family after pleading guilty to misdemeanor petty larceny in return for a sentence of three years' probation, April 23, 2002, outside New York State Supreme Court. Iler, seventeen, agreed to a plea bargain for his role in a robbery on July 2001 on New York City's Upper East Side.

sial part of the administration of justice. Proponents contend that plea bargaining actually benefits both the state and the defendant in the following ways:

1. The overall costs of the criminal prosecution are reduced.
2. The administrative efficiency of the courts is greatly improved.
3. The prosecution can devote more time to more serious cases.
4. The defendant avoids possible detention and an extended trial and may receive a reduced sentence.
5. Resources can be devoted more efficiently to cases that need greater attention.[21]

Those who favor plea bargaining believe it is appropriate to enter into plea discussions when the interests of the state in the effective administration of justice will be served. Opponents of the plea-bargaining process believe that the negotiated plea should be eliminated. Some argue that plea bargaining is objectionable because it encourages defendants to waive their constitutional right to trial. In addition, some experts suggest that sentences tend to be less severe when a defendant enters a guilty plea than in actual trials and that plea bargains result in even greater sentencing disparity. Particularly in the eyes of the general public, this allows the defendant to beat the system and further tarnishes the criminal process. Plea bargaining also raises the danger that an innocent person will be convicted of a crime if he is convinced that the lighter treatment from a guilty plea is preferable to the risk of conviction with a harsher sentence following a formal trial.

It is unlikely that plea negotiations will be eliminated or severely curtailed in the near future. Supporters of the total abolition of plea bargaining are in the minority. As a result of abuses, however, efforts are being made to improve plea-bargaining operations. Such reforms include development of uniform plea practices, representation of counsel during plea negotiations, and establishment of time limits on plea negotiations.

Legal Issues in Plea Bargaining

The U.S. Supreme Court has reviewed the propriety of plea bargaining in several decisions, particularly in regard to the voluntariness of guilty pleas. Defendants are entitled to the effective assistance of counsel to protect them from pressure and influence. The Court ruled in *Hill v. Lockhart* (1985) that to prove ineffectiveness the defendant must show a "reasonable probability that, but for counsel's errors, he would not have pleaded guilty and would have insisted on going to trial."[22]

In *Boykin v. Alabama* (1969), the Court held that an affirmative action (such as a verbal statement) that the plea was made voluntarily must exist on the record before a trial judge may accept a guilty plea.[23] This is essential, because a guilty plea basically constitutes a waiver of the defendant's Fifth Amendment privilege against self-incrimination and Sixth Amendment right to a jury trial. Subsequent to *Boykin,* the Court ruled in *Brady v. United States* (1970) that a guilty plea is not invalid because it is entered merely to avoid the possibility of the death penalty.[24]

When the question arose about whether a guilty plea may be accepted by a defendant maintaining his or her innocence, the Supreme Court, in *North Carolina v. Alford* (1970), said that such action was appropriate where a defendant was seeking a lesser sentence. In other words, a defendant could plead guilty without admitting guilt.[25]

In *Santobello v. New York* (1971), the Court held that the promise of the prosecutor must be kept and that a prosecutor's breaking of a plea-bargaining agreement required a reversal for the defendant.[26]

Not only must the prosecutor keep her word in a plea bargain agreement, so too must the defendant. In *Ricketts v. Adamson* (1987), the Court ruled that defendants must also keep their side of the bargain to receive the promised offer of leniency.[27] An example of defendant cooperation can be observed in the recent New York appellate case *People v. Hicks* (2002).[28] In *Hicks*, a defendant pleaded guilty to sex-related crimes in exchange for a promised lenient sentence. A condition of the plea included that he truthfully answer all questions asked by probation officers when they investigated the case. After he told the investigators that he was not really guilty and that the children initiated sexual contact with him, the trial judge imposed a more severe sentence. On appeal, the Supreme Court upheld the sentence, maintaining that by lying to the probation officers, Hicks violated his promise to be truthful, thereby negating the plea bargain agreement.

How far can prosecutors go to convince a defendant to plead guilty? The Supreme Court ruled in the 1978 case of *Bordenkircher v. Hayes* that a defendant's due process rights are not violated when a prosecutor threatens to reindict the accused on more serious charges if the defendant does not plead guilty to the original offense.[29]

In 1995, the U.S. Supreme Court decided the case of *United States v. Mezzanatto,* which may cause the plea-bargaining process to change in state courts. In *Mezzanatto,* the Court declared that statements made by the defendant during plea bargaining can be used at trial for impeachment purposes. This means that a prosecutor can refuse to plea-bargain with a defendant unless the defendant agrees that any statements made during the negotiations can be used to impeach him at trial. The Court narrowly interpreted Rule 410 of the Federal Rules of Evidence, which says that statements made during plea bargaining are inadmissible at trial.

Exhibit 8.3	Notable U.S. Supreme Court cases on the regulation of plea bargaining

Case	Ruling
Boykin v. Alabama (1969)	A defendant must make an affirmative statement that the plea is voluntary before the judge can accept it.
Brady v. United States (1970)	Avoiding the possibility of the death penalty is not grounds to invalidate a guilty plea.
North Carolina v. Alford (1970)	Accepting a guilty plea from a defendant who maintains his or her innocence is valid.
Santobello v. New York (1971)	The promise of a prosecutor that rests on a guilty plea must be kept in a plea-bargaining agreement.
Bordenkircher v. Hayes (1978)	A defendant's constitutional rights are not violated when a prosecutor threatens to reindict the accused on more serious charges if he or she is not willing to plead guilty to the original offense.
Hill v. Lockhart (1985)	To prove ineffectiveness of defense counsel, a defendant needs to show a reasonable probability that, except for counsel's errors, the defendant would not have pleaded guilty.
Ricketts v. Adamson (1987)	A defendant is required to keep his or her side of the bargain to receive the promised offer of leniency, since plea bargaining rests on an agreement between the parties.
United States v. Mezzanatto (1995)	A defendant who wants to plea-bargain in federal court can be required to agree that, if he testifies at trial, his statements during the plea-bargain negotiations can be used against him.

Although the ruling applies only to federal trials, it is likely to be adopted by many state court systems that watch Supreme Court decisions and follow suit.[30]

Based on repeated actions by the Supreme Court, we realize that plea bargaining is a constitutionally accepted practice in the United States. Exhibit 8.3 summarizes the major Supreme Court decisions regulating plea-bargaining practices.

Plea-Bargaining Decision Making

Because the plea-bargaining process is largely informal, lacking in guidelines, and discretionary, some effort has been made to determine what kinds of information and how much information is used by the prosecutor to make plea-bargaining decisions. Research has found that certain information weighs heavily in the prosecutorial decision to accept a plea negotiation.[31] Such factors as the offense; the defendant's prior record and age; and the type, strength, and admissibility of evidence are considered important in the plea-bargaining decision. The attitude of the complainant is also an important factor in the decision-making process; for example, in victimless cases, such as heroin possession, the police attitude is most often considered, whereas in victim-related crimes, such as rape, the attitude of the victim is a primary concern. The study also revealed that prosecutors in low-population or rural jurisdictions not only use more information while making their decisions but also seem more likely than their urban counterparts to accept bargains. It was suggested that "this finding tends to dispute the notion that plea bargaining is a response to overcrowding in large urban courts."[32] It appears that where caseload pressures are less, the acceptance of a plea bargain is actually more probable.

The Role of the Prosecutor

The prosecutor in the U.S. system of criminal justice has broad discretion in the exercise of his responsibilities. Such discretion includes deciding whether to initiate a criminal prosecution, determining the nature and number of the criminal charges, and choosing whether to plea-bargain a case and under what conditions. Plea bargaining is one of the most significant tools the prosecutor uses to control and influence the criminal justice system (the other two are the decision to initiate a charge and the ability to take the case to trial). Few states have placed limits on the discretion of prosecutors in plea-bargaining situations. Instead, in making a plea-bargaining decision, the prosecutor is generally free to weigh competing alternatives and factors, such as the seriousness of the crime, the attitude of the victim, the police report of the incident, and applicable sentencing provisions. Plea bargaining frequently occurs in cases where the government believes the evidence is weak, as when a key witness seems unreliable or unwilling to testify. Bargaining permits a compromise settlement in a weak case where the criminal trial outcome is in doubt.

On a case-by-case basis, the prosecutor determines the concessions to be offered in the plea bargain and seeks to dispose of each case quickly and efficiently. On the broader scale, however, the role of the chief prosecutor as an administrator also affects plea bargaining. Whereas the assistant prosecutor evaluates and moves individual cases, the chief prosecutor must establish plea-bargaining guidelines for the entire office. In this regard, the prosecutor may be acting as an administrator.[33] Guidelines cover such aspects as avoiding overindictment and controlling nonprovable indictments, reducing felonies to misdemeanors, and bargaining with defendants.

Some jurisdictions have established guidelines to provide consistency in plea-bargaining cases. For instance, a given office may be required to define the kinds and types of cases and offenders that may be suitable for plea bargaining. In other jurisdictions, approval to plea-bargain may be required. Other controls might include procedures for internally reviewing decisions by the chief prosecutor and the use of written memorandums to document the need and acceptability for a plea bargain in a given case. For example, pleas may be offered on a "take it or leave it" basis. In each case, a special prosecutor, whose job it is to screen cases, sets the bargaining terms. If the defense counsel cannot accept the agreement, there is no negotiation, and the case must go to trial. Only if complications arise in the case, such as witnesses changing their testimony, can negotiations be reopened.[34]

The prosecutor's role in plea bargaining is also important on a statewide or systemwide basis because it involves exercising leadership in setting policy. The most extreme example of a chief prosecutor influencing the plea-negotiation process has occurred where the prosecutor has attempted to eliminate plea bargaining. In Alaska such efforts met with resistance from assistant prosecutors and others in the system, particularly judges and defense attorneys.[35]

The Role of the Defense Counsel

Both the U.S. Supreme Court and such organizations as the American Bar Association (ABA) have established guidelines for the court receiving a guilty plea and for the defense counsel representing the accused in plea negotiations.[36] No court should accept a guilty plea unless the defendant has been properly advised by counsel and the court has determined that the plea is voluntary and has a factual basis; the court has the discretion to reject a plea if it is inappropriately offered. The defense counsel—a public defender or a private attorney—is required to play an advisory role in plea negotiations. The defendant's counsel is expected to be aware of the facts of the case and of the law and to advise the defendant of the alternatives available. The defense attorney is basically responsible for making certain that the accused understands the nature of the plea-bargaining process and the guilty plea. This means that the defense counsel should explain to the defendant that by pleading guilty, he is waiving certain rights that would be available on going to trial. In addition, the defense attorney has the duty to keep the defendant informed of developments and discussions with the prosecutor regarding plea bargaining. While doing so, the attorney for the accused cannot misrepresent evidence or mislead the client into making a detrimental agreement. The defense counsel is not only ethically but also constitutionally required to communicate all plea-bargaining offers to a client even if counsel believes the offers to be unacceptable.[37]

In reality, most plea negotiations occur in the chambers of the judge, in the prosecutor's office, or in the courthouse hallway. Under these conditions, it is often difficult to assess the actual roles played by the prosecutor and the defense attorney. Even so, it is fundamental that a defendant not be required to plead guilty until advised by counsel and that a guilty plea should not be made unless it is done with the consent of the accused.

The Role of the Judge

One of the most confusing issues in the plea-bargaining process has been the proper role of the judge. Should the judge act only in a supervisory capacity or actually enter into the negotiation process? The leading national legal organization, the ABA, is opposed to judicial participation in plea negotiations.[38] According to ABA standards, judges should not be a party to arrangements for the determination of a sentence, whether as a result of a guilty plea or a finding of guilty based on proof. Furthermore, judicial participation in plea negotiations (1) creates the impression in the mind of the defendant that he could not receive a fair trial, (2) lessens the ability of the judge to make an objective determination of the voluntariness of the plea, (3) is inconsistent with the theory behind the use of presentence investigation reports, and (4) may induce an innocent defendant to plead guilty because he is afraid to reject the disposition desired by the judge.[39]

In addition to the ABA, the Federal Rules of Criminal Procedure prohibit federal judges from participating in plea negotiations.[40] A few states disallow any form of judicial involvement in plea bargaining, but others permit the judge to participate.

On the other hand, those who suggest that the judge should participate directly in plea bargaining argue that such an approach would make sentencing more uniform and ensure that the plea-bargaining process would be fairer and more efficient.

The Victim

What role should victims play in plea bargaining? Some suggest that the system today is too "victim-driven" and that prosecutors too frequently seek approval for the plea from a victim or family member. Others maintain that the victim plays an almost secondary role in the process.

In reality, the victim is not "empowered" at the pretrial stage of the criminal process. Statutes do not require that the prosecutor defer to the victim's wishes, and there are no legal consequences for ignoring the victim in a plea-bargaining decision. Even the ABA's Model Uniform Victims of Crime Act only suggests that the prosecutor "confer" with the victim.[41]

Victims are certainly not in a position to veto a plea bargain. Most of the work of the victims' rights movement in the justice system is devoted to securing financial compensation from the state and some restitution when possible from the defendant. At the current time, it is at the trial stage that the victim has the greatest influence. Here, the victim often has the right to offer a victim-impact statement after a guilty determination and before the court imposes a sentence.

There is no question that the prosecutor should consider the impact that a plea bargain may have on the victim or victim's family. Some victims' groups even suggest that the victim's family have statutory authority to approve or disapprove any plea bargain between the prosecutor and defense attorney in criminal homicide cases. Given the volume of plea bargains, it appears that the victim should have greater control and participation.

Plea-Bargaining Reform

Plea bargaining is an inevitable result and essential to the continued functioning of the criminal justice process.[42] Yet, despite its prevalence, its merits are hotly debated. Those opposed to the widespread use of plea bargaining assert that it is coercive in its inducement of guilty pleas, that it encourages the unequal exercise of prosecutorial discretion, and that it complicates sentencing as well as the job of correctional authorities. Others argue that it is unconstitutional and results in cynicism and disrespect for the entire system.

On the other hand, its proponents contend that the practice ensures the flow of guilty pleas essential to administration efficiency. It allows the system the flexibility to individualize justice and inspires respect for the system because it is associated with certain and prompt punishment.[43]

In recent years, efforts have been made to convert plea bargaining into a more visible, understandable, and fair dispositional process. Many jurisdictions have developed safeguards and guidelines to prevent violations of due process and to ensure that innocent defendants do not plead guilty under coercion. Such safeguards include the following: (1) the judge questions the defendant about the facts of the guilty plea before accepting the plea; (2) the defense counsel is present and can advise the defendant of his or her rights; (3) the prosecutor and the defense attorney openly discuss the plea; and (4) full and frank information about the defendant and the offenses is made available at this stage of the process. In addition, judicial supervision ensures that plea bargaining is conducted in a fair manner.

What would happen if plea bargaining were banned outright, as its critics advocate? Numerous jurisdictions throughout the United States have experimented with bans on plea bargaining. In 1975 Alaska eliminated the practice. Honolulu has also attempted to abolish plea bargaining. Other jurisdictions, including Iowa, Arizona, Delaware, and the District of Columbia, have sought to limit the use of plea bargaining.[44] In theory, eliminating plea bargains means that prosecutors in these jurisdictions give no consideration or concessions to a defendant in exchange for a guilty plea.

In reality, however, in these and most jurisdictions, sentence-related concessions, charge-reduction concessions, and alternative methods for prosecution continue to be used in one fashion or another.[45] Where plea bargaining is limited or abolished, the number of trials may increase, the sentence severity may change, and more questions regarding the right to a speedy trial may arise. Discretion may also be shifted further up the system. Instead of spending countless hours preparing for and conducting a trial, prosecutors may dismiss more cases outright or decide not to prosecute them after initial action has been taken.

Reform can be difficult. Candace McCoy's study of plea reform in California investigated legislative efforts to eliminate the state's plea-bargaining process. Instead of achieving a ban on plea bargaining, the process shifted from the superior to the municipal courts. McCoy found that the majority of defendants pled guilty after some negotiations and that the new law actually accelerated the guilty plea process. McCoy's alternative model of plea bargaining reform includes emphasizing public scrutiny of plea bargaining, adhering to standards of professionalism, and making a greater commitment to due process procedures.[46]

Pretrial Diversion

Another important feature in the early court process is placing offenders into non-criminal **diversion** programs before their formal trial or conviction. Pretrial diversion programs were first established in the late 1960s and early 1970s, when it became apparent that a viable alternative to the highly stigmatized criminal sentence was needed. In diversion programs, formal criminal proceedings against an accused are suspended while that person participates in a community treatment program under court supervision. Diversion helps the offender avoid the stigma of a criminal conviction and enables the justice system to reduce costs and alleviate prison crowding.

Many diversion programs exist throughout the United States. These programs vary in size and emphasis but generally pursue the same goal: to constructively bypass criminal prosecution by providing a reasonable alternative in the form of treatment, counseling, or employment programs.

The prosecutor often plays the central role in the diversion process. Decisions about nondispositional alternatives are based on (1) the nature of the crime, (2) special characteristics of the offender, (3) whether the defendant is a first-time offender, (4) whether the defendant will cooperate with a diversion program, (5) the impact of diversion on the community, and (6) consideration for the opinion of the victim.[47]

Diversion programs can take many forms. Some are separate, independent agencies that were originally set up with federal funds but are now being continued with county or state assistance. Others are organized as part of a police, prosecutor, or probation department's internal structure. Still others are a joint venture between the county government and a private, nonprofit organization that actually carries out the treatment process.

First viewed as a panacea that could reduce court congestion and help treat minor offenders, diversion programs have come under fire for their alleged failures. Some national evaluations have concluded that diversion programs are no more successful at avoiding stigma and reducing recidivism than traditional justice processing.[48] The most prominent criticism is that they help *widen the net of the justice system.* By this, critics mean that the people placed in diversion programs are the ones most likely to have otherwise been dismissed after a brief hearing with a warning or small fine.[49]

Those who would have ordinarily received a more serious sentence are not eligible for diversion anyway. Thus, rather than limiting contact with the system, the diversion programs actually increase it. Of course, not all justice experts agree with this charge, and some have championed diversion as a worthwhile exercise of the criminal justice system's rehabilitation responsibility. Although diversion may not be a cure-all for criminal behavior, it is an important effort that continues to be made in most jurisdictions across the United States. Originally proposed by the well-known President's Commission on Law Enforcement in 1967 and supported by federal funds, most existing programs are now underwritten with state funds.[50] ■

diversion   A noncriminal alternative to trial, usually featuring counseling, job training, and educational opportunities.

Read about the federal government's pretrial diversion program at www.usdoj.gov/usao/eousa/ foia_reading_room/usam/ title9/22mcrm.htm

SUMMARY

Many important decisions about what happens to a defendant are made prior to trial. Hearings, such as before the grand jury and the preliminary hearing, are held to determine if probable cause exists to charge the accused with a crime. If so, the defendant is arraigned, enters a plea, is informed of his constitutional rights, particularly the right to the assistance of counsel, and is considered for pretrial diversion. The use of money bail and other alternatives, such as release on recognizance, allows most defendants to be free pending their trial. Bail provisions are beginning to be toughened, resulting in the preventive detention of people awaiting trial. Preventive detention has been implemented because many believe that significant numbers of criminals violate their bail and commit further crimes while on pretrial release.

The issue of discretion plays a major role at this stage of the criminal process. Since only a small percentage of criminal cases eventually go to trial, many defendants agree to plea bargains or are placed in diversion programs. Not enough judges, prosecutors, defense attorneys, and courts exist to try every defendant accused of a crime. As a result, such subsystems as plea bargaining and diversion are essential elements in the administration of the criminal justice system. Research indicates that most cases never go to trial but are bargained out of the system. Although plea bargaining has been criticized, efforts to control it have not met with success. Similarly, diversion programs have not been overly successful, yet they continue to be used throughout the United States.

For an up-to-date list of Web links, go to http://cj.wadsworth.com/siegel_essen4e.

KEY TERMS

pretrial procedure 254	grand jury 255	bail 256	Bail Reform Act of 1984 261
booking process 254	information 255	pretrial detention 259	preventive detention 263
complaint 254	preliminary hearing (probable cause hearing) 255	release on recognizance (ROR) 260	presentment 266
initial hearing 254		Manhattan Bail Project 260	true bill 266
arraignment 254	nolo contendere 255		no bill 266
indictment 255	plea bargaining 255	deposit bail 261	diversion 277

INFOTRAC COLLEGE EDITION EXERCISES

DOESN'T PREVENTIVE DETENTION punish an individual who has not been found guilty of the allegations made by the state? At the same time, aren't justice officials required to protect the community? A preventive detention statute is an example of the crime control perspective and the judicious use of a serious criminal sanction: jail. Denying defendants the right to bail because they are dangerous is the basis of the preventive detention law. Merely accusing a person of a crime and keeping that person incarcerated has caused critics to question the legality of such a practice. Yet the U.S. Supreme Court upheld the constitutionality of the preventive detention statute in *United States v. Salerno* (1987).

Using InfoTrac College Edition, search for articles that argue against the use of preventive detention. Use key words such as "bail," "detention," and "pretrial release."

QUESTIONS

1. Should criminal defendants be allowed to bargain for a reduced sentence in exchange for a guilty plea? Should the victim always be included in the plea-bargaining process?

2. Should those accused of violent acts be subjected to preventive detention instead of bail, even though they have not been convicted of a crime? Is it fair to the victim to have his alleged attacker running around loose?

3. What purpose does a grand jury or preliminary hearing serve in adjudicating felony offenses? Should one of these methods be abandoned and if so, which one?

4. Why should we provide pretrial services for defendants?

5. Should suspects in a terrorist case be allowed bail? If so, wouldn't that give them a license to carry out their plot?

NOTES

1. U.S. Department of Justice, *Predicting Pretrial Misconduct with Drug Tests of Arrestees* (Washington, D.C.: National Institute of Justice Research in Brief, 1996), 1; William Rhodes, Raymond Hyatt, and Paul Scheiman, "Predicting Pretrial Misconduct with Drug Tests of Arrestees: Evidence from Eight Settings," *Journal of Quantitative Criminology* 12 (1996): 315–347; D. Alan Henry and John Clark, *Pretrial Drug Testing—An Overview* (Washington, D.C.: Bureau of Justice Assistance, 1999).

2. Brian A. Reaves, *Felony Defendants in Large Urban Counties, 1998* (Washington, D.C.: Bureau of Justice Statistics, 2001).

3. Christopher Stephens, "Bail" section of the Criminal Procedure project, *Georgetown Law Journal 90* (2002) 1395–1416.

4. *Stack v. Boyle,* 342 U.S. 1, 72 S.Ct. 1, 96 L.Ed. 3 (1951).

5. Vera Institute of Justice, *1961–1971: Programs in Criminal Justice* (New York: Vera Institute of Justice, 1972).

6. Chris Eskridge, *Pretrial Release Programming* (New York: Clark Boardman, 1983), 27.

7. Public Law No. 89-465, 18 U.S.C., sec. 3146 (1966).

8. Ellis M. Johnston, "Once a Criminal, Always a Criminal? Unconstitutional Presumptions for Mandatory Detention of Criminal Aliens," *Georgetown Law Journal 89* (2001): 2593–2636.

9. 18 U.S.C., sec. 3142 (1984).

10. See, generally, Fred Cohen, "The New Federal Crime Control Act," *Criminal Law Bulletin 21* (1985): 330–337.

11. *Schall v. Martin,* 467 U.S. 253, 104 S.Ct. 2403, 81 L.Ed.2d 207 (1984).

12. *United States v. Salerno,* 481 U.S. 739, 107 S.Ct. 2095, 95 L.Ed.2d 697 (1987).

13. Reaves, *Felony Defendants in Large Urban Counties, 1998.*

14. Ric Simmons, "Reexamining the Grand Jury: Is There Room for Democracy in the Criminal Justice System?" *Boston University Law Review 82* (2002): 1–76.

15. *United States v. Williams,* 504 U.S. 36, 38 (1992).

16. Suzanne Roe Neely, "Preserving Justice and Preventing Prejudice: Requiring Disclosure of Substantial Exculpatory Evidence to the Grand Jury," *American Criminal Law Review 39* (2002): 171–200.

17. John Gibeaut, "Indictment of a System," *ABA Journal 87* (2001): 34.

18. "Grubman Pleads Guilty in Hamptons Crash," *New York Times,* 23 August 2002, A3.

19. Kirke D. Weaver, "A Change of Heart or a Change of Law? Withdrawing a Guilty Plea Under Federal Rule of Criminal Procedure 32(e)," *Journal of Criminal Law and Criminology 92* (2001): 273–306.

20. George Fisher, "Plea Bargaining's Triumph," *Yale Law Journal 109* (2000): 857–1058.

21. Fred Zacharis, "Justice in Plea Bargaining," *William and Mary Law Review 39* (1998): 1211–1140.

22. *Hill v. Lockhart,* 474 U.S. 52, 106 S.Ct. 366, 88 L.Ed.2d 203 (1985).

23. *Boykin v. Alabama,* 395 U.S. 238, 89 S.Ct. 1709, 23 L.Ed.2d 274 (1969).

24. *Brady v. United States,* 397 U.S. 742, 90 S.Ct. 1463, 25 L.Ed.2d 747 (1970).

25. *North Carolina v. Alford,* 400 U.S. 25, 91 S.Ct. 160, 27 L.Ed.2d 162 (1970).

26. *Santobello v. New York,* 404 U.S. 257, 92 S.Ct. 495, 30 L.Ed.2d 427 (1971).

27. *Ricketts v. Adamson,* 483 U.S. 1, 107 S.Ct. 2680, 97 L.Ed.2d 1 (1987).

28. *People v. Hicks,* 2002 NY Int. 84 (7/1/02).

29. *Bordenkircher v. Hayes,* 434 U.S. 357, 98 S.Ct. 663, 54 L.Ed.2d 604 (1978).

30. *United States v. Mezzanatto,* 116 S.Ct. 1480, 134 L.Ed.2d 687 (1995).

31. Stephen P. Lagoy, Joseph J. Senna, and Larry J. Siegel, "An Empirical Study on Information Usage for Prosecutorial Decision Making in Plea Negotiations," *American Criminal Law Review 13* (1976): 435–471.

32. Ibid., 462.

33. Alan Alschuler, "The Prosecutor's Role in Plea Bargaining," *University of Chicago Law Review 36* (1968): 50–112.

34. Barbara Boland and Brian Forst, *The Prevalence of Guilty Pleas* (Washington, D.C.: Bureau of Justice Statistics, 1984), 3; see also Gary Hengstler, "The Troubled Justice System," *American Bar Association Journal 80* (1994): 44.

35. National Institute of Law Enforcement and Criminal Justice, *Plea Bargaining in the United States* (Washington, D.C.: Georgetown University, 1978), 8.

36. See American Bar Association, *Standards Relating to Pleas of Guilty,* 2d ed. (Chicago: ABA, 1988); see also *North Carolina v. Alford,* 400 U.S. 25, 91 S.Ct. 160, 27 L.Ed.2d 162 (1970).

37. Keith Bystrom, "Communicating Plea Offers to the Client," in *Ethical Problems Facing the Criminal Defense Lawyer,* ed. Rodney Uphoff (Chicago: American Bar Association Section on Criminal Justice, 1995), 84.

38. American Bar Association, *Standards Relating to Pleas of Guilty,* standard 3.3; National Advisory Commission on Criminal Justice Standards and Goals, *Task Force Report on Courts* (Washington, D.C.: Government Printing Office, 1973), 42.

39. American Bar Association, *Standards Relating to Pleas of Guilty,* 73; see also Alan Alschuler, "The Trial Judge's Role in Plea Bargaining," *Columbia Law Review 76* (1976): 1059.

40. Federal Rules of Criminal Procedure, rule 11.

41. American Bar Association, *Model Uniform Victims of Crime Act* (Chicago: ABA, 1992).

42. George P. Fletcher, *With Justice for Some—Victims' Rights in Criminal Trials* (New York: Addison-Wesley, 1995), 190–193.

43. *Santobello v. New York,* 404 U.S. 257, 92 S.Ct. 495, 30 L.Ed.2d 427 (1971).

44. National Institute of Law Enforcement and Criminal Justice, *Plea Bargaining in the United States,* 37–40.

45. For a discussion of this issue, see Michael Tonry, "Plea Bargaining Bans and Rules," in *Sentencing Reform Impacts* (Washington, D.C.: Government Printing Office, 1987).

46. Candace McCoy, *Politics and Plea Bargaining: Victims' Rights in California* (Philadelphia: University of Pennsylvania Press, 1993).

47. National District Attorneys Association, *National Prosecution Standards,* 2d ed. (Alexandria, Va.: NDAA, 1991), 130.

48. Franklyn Dunford, D. Wayne Osgood, and Hart Weichselbaum, *National Evaluation of Diversion Programs* (Washington, D.C.: Government Printing Office, 1982).

49. Sharla Rausch and Charles Logan, "Diversion from Juvenile Court: Panacea or Pandora's Box?" in *Evaluating Juvenile Justice,* ed. James Kleugel (Beverly Hills, Calif.: Sage, 1983), 19–30.

50. See Malcolm Feeley, *Court Reform on Trial* (New York: Basic Books, 1983).

9 The Criminal Trial

Chapter Outline

Criminal Justice Links

Criminal Justice Viewpoints

Criminal Justice and the Media
TV or Not TV? Should Criminal Trials
Be Televised?   288

Law in Review
The Danielle van Dam Case:
Should Defense Lawyers Tell the Truth?   297

ON JANUARY 18, 2002, Sarah Jane Olson was sentenced to twenty years to life in prison for her role in a failed bomb plot to kill Los Angeles police officers in 1975. Then known as Kathy Soliah, a member of the radical Symbionese Liberation Army (SLA), Olson escaped capture and fled to Minnesota, where she led a quiet life. She married a doctor, raised a family, and became an upstanding member of the community, engaging in many charitable works. Then, in a segment of the television show *America's Most Wanted,* pictures of Soliah and another SLA fugitive, James Kilgore, were broadcast. The FBI offered a $20,000 reward for information leading to Soliah's capture. Identified by someone who watched the show, on June 16, 1999, she peacefully surrendered to the police after being pulled over a few blocks from her home in St. Paul, Minnesota.

During trial, Olson's defense attorneys suffered one setback after another. They argued she could not hope to get a fair hearing in light of the events of September 11; the motion was denied by the judge who sided with the prosecutor's argument that international acts of terrorism have no bearing on any case in the court system, even one that involves domestic terrorism. Her defense also suffered a blow when the judge ruled that prosecutors could present evidence of the Symbionese Liberation Army's criminal history during her trial. Even though Olson was not accused of committing them, the judge ruled that all the acts were relevant because they showed the deadly intentions of the group. ■

To view the CNN video clip of this story, go to the book-specific Web site at http://cj.wadsworth.com/siegel_essen4e.

The Olson case illustrates the difficulty of getting a fair trial in a highly charged political environment. Might she have been found not guilty if the 2001 terrorist acts had never taken place? Can such high-profile cases ever hope to get fair and unbiased juries? The Olson case aptly illustrates the moral and legal dilemmas that are raised when we consider such issues as pretrial publicity and televised trials. It also raises issues on the purpose of prosecuting and

On November 6, 2002, Sarah Jane Olson, along with three other former members of the SLA, agreed to plead guilty to murder in the shotgun slaying of a bank customer during a 1975 holdup. They were charged with first-degree murder but agreed to plead guilty to second-degree murder in a deal with prosecutors to avoid a possible sentence of life in prison. Olson received a six-year sentence for the crime, which she will have to serve after completing her earlier sentence for the bomb plot. To read more about the Olson case, go to the Court TV site at www.courttv.com/trials/soliah/

bench trial The trial of a criminal matter by a judge only. The accused waives any constitutional right to trial by jury.

verdict A finding of a jury or a judge on questions of fact at a trial.

adjudication The determination of guilt or innocence; a judgment concerning criminal charges. The majority of offenders charged plead guilty; of the remainder, some cases are adjudicated by a judge and a jury, some are adjudicated by a judge without a jury, and others are dismissed.

confrontation clause The constitutional right of a criminal defendant to see and cross-examine all the witnesses against him or her.

punishing criminal defendants. This middle-aged mother hardly presented a danger to society. Since Sarah Jane Olson had rehabilitated herself, was her prosecution and trial merely a cruel afterthought? On the other hand, should she be rewarded with lenient treatment because she was able to escape capture and elude the authorities for twenty-five years? Her sterling record as a wife and mother could only have been accomplished because she evaded the grasp of the law at the time her crimes were committed. Should we free a rapist merely because he escaped capture for twenty years?

The center point of the adjudicatory process is the criminal trial, an open and public hearing designed to examine the facts of the case brought by the state against the accused. Though trials are relatively rare events and most cases are settled by a plea bargain, the trial is an important and enduring fixture in the criminal justice system. By its very nature, it is a symbol of the moral authority of the state. The criminal trial is the symbol of the administration of objective and impartial justice. Regardless of the issues involved, the defendant's presence in a courtroom is designed to guarantee that she will have a hearing conducted under rules of procedure in an atmosphere of fair play and objectivity and that the outcome of the hearing will be clear and definitive. If the defendant believes that her constitutional rights and privileges have been violated, she may appeal the case to a higher court, where the procedures of the original trial will be examined. If after examining the trial transcript, the appellate court rules that that the original trial employed improper and unconstitutional procedures, it may order a new hearing be held or even that the charges against the defendant be dismissed.

Most formal trials are heard by a jury, though some defendants waive their constitutional right to a jury trial and request a **bench trial,** in which the judge alone renders a **verdict.** In this situation, which occurs daily in the lower criminal courts, the judge may initiate a number of formal or informal dispositions, including dismissing the case, finding the defendant not guilty, finding the defendant guilty and imposing a sentence, or even continuing the case indefinitely. The decision the judge makes often depends on the seriousness of the offense, the background and previous record of the defendant, and the judgment of the court about whether the case can be properly dealt with in the criminal process. The judge may simply continue the case without a finding, in which case the verdict is withheld without a finding of guilt to induce the accused to improve her behavior in the community; if the defendant's behavior does improve, the case is ordinarily closed within a specific amount of time.

This chapter reviews some of the institutions and processes involved in **adjudication** and trial. We begin with a discussion of the legal rights that structure the trial process.

Legal Rights During Trial

Underlying every trial are constitutional principles, complex legal procedures, rules of court, and interpretations of statutes, all designed to ensure that the accused will receive a fair trial. This section discusses the most important constitutional rights of the accused at the trial stage of the criminal justice system and reviews the legal nature of the trial process. We examine the major legal decisions and statutes involving the right to confront witnesses and the rights to a jury trial, counsel, self-representation, and a speedy and public trial.

The Right to Confront Witnesses

The Sixth Amendment states, "In all criminal prosecutions, the accused shall enjoy the right . . . to be confronted with the witnesses against him."[1] The **confrontation** clause is essential to a fair criminal trial because it restricts and controls the admissibility of hearsay, or secondhand evidence. Under normal circumstances, evidence can only be presented by witnesses who are in court and testify under oath. They must attest to their personal knowledge of the crime and not repeat what others told them, known as **hearsay evidence.** Let's say, for example, that Joe hears from Steve about an incident in which someone was injured. Steve witnessed it, but Joe did not. If Joe attempts to repeat Steve's version in court, the testimony would be objected to as "hearsay." A witness is, however, permitted to repeat a rumor or testify that someone told them a story. Under the hearsay rule, the testimony would not be evidence of the actual facts of the story, but only that this person heard those words spoken by others.

Under the confrontation clause, the accused has the right to confront the witnesses and challenge their assertions and perceptions: Did they really see what they believe? Are they biased? Can they be trusted? What about the veracity of their testimony? The confrontation clause also applies to documents that someone wrote implicating a defendant, or even a taped confession given by an accomplice to police that contains some statements implicating the accused. The author of the documents or confession must be in court to testify to their accuracy.[2]

In general, Supreme Court rulings have been nearly unanimous that the right of confrontation and cross-examination is an essential requirement for a fair trial.[3] The most significant exception to the rule was articulated in the case of *Maryland v. Craig* (1990). Here the Supreme Court ruled that in cases of child abuse it would be permissible to cross-examine young victims via closed-circuit TV if the judge believed that their being in the courtroom in the presence of their attackers would be too traumatic.[4] In allowing the states to take testimony via closed-circuit TV, the Court ruled that circumstances exist in child sex abuse cases that override the defendant's right of confrontation.

Maryland v. Craig is important because it shows that the confrontation clause does not guarantee criminal defendants the absolute right to a face-to-face meeting with witnesses at their trial. This right may be denied when necessary to further an important public policy, such as protecting a child from trauma in a criminal trial.

The Right to a Jury Trial

The Sixth Amendment to the U.S. Constitution guarantees the right to a jury trial; however, the Constitution is silent on whether all offenders, both misdemeanants and felons, have an absolute right to a jury trial. In *Duncan v. Louisiana* (1968), the Supreme Court held that the Sixth Amendment right to a jury trial applies to all defendants accused of serious crimes.[5] In *Duncan,* the Court based its holding on the premise that a jury trial for a serious offense is a fundamental right, essential for preventing miscarriages of justice and for ensuring that fair trials are provided for all defendants.[6] The *Duncan* decision did not settle whether all defendants charged with crimes in state courts are constitutionally entitled to jury trials.

Then in *Baldwin v. New York* the Supreme Court decided that a defendant has a constitutional right to

hearsay evidence Testimony that is not firsthand but related information told by a second party.

To read more about *Maryland v. Craig* and similar cases, go to www.ipt-forensics.com/journal/volume2/j2_3_7.htm

According to the Sixth Amendment's confrontation clause, evidence can only be presented by witnesses who are in court, testify under oath, and attest to their personal knowledge of the crime. Here, Debbie Rivera testifies in the trial of four New York City officers charged in the shooting of Amadou Diallo.

a jury trial when facing a prison sentence of six months or more, regardless of whether the crime committed was a felony or a misdemeanor.[7] Where the possible sentence is six months or less, the accused is not entitled to a jury trial unless it is authorized by state statute.

The Supreme Court has held to this standard ever since. In the 1989 case of *Blanton v. North Las Vegas,* the Court ruled unanimously that there is no right to jury trials in drunk driving cases when state law defines them as a petty offense. If, however, a state treats driving under the influence as a serious crime, a jury trial would be required.[8] Here we can see that how states interpret and define particular crimes determines whether defendants will be entitled to a trial by jury.

The latest Supreme Court decision on jury trials occurred in the 1996 case of *Lewis v. United States.*[9] The defendant Lewis had been charged with committing numerous petty offenses. If convicted on all counts he would have faced more than six months in prison; he argued that he was constitutionally entitled to a jury trial because his potential penalties exceeded the Court's standard line of six months in prison. But the Court said there was no Sixth Amendment right to a jury trial for a string of petty offenses tried together, even where the potential aggregate sentence could exceed six months. The reasons were (1) the Court believed the legislature is responsible for the design of an offense with a maximum possible penalty, and (2) the prosecutor has the right to exercise discretion to join different offenses in one trial without defeating the legislative intent to distinguish between petty and serious offenses.

Jury Size   The actual size of the jury has been a matter of great concern. Can a defendant be tried and convicted of a crime by a jury of fewer than twelve persons? Traditionally, twelve jurors have deliberated as the triers of fact in criminal cases involving misdemeanors or felonies. However, the U.S. Constitution does not specifically require a jury of twelve persons. As a result, in *Williams v. Florida* in 1970, the U.S. Supreme Court held that a **six-person jury** in a criminal trial does not deprive a defendant of the constitutional right to a jury trial.[10] The Court made clear that the twelve-person panel is not a necessary ingredient of a trial by jury, and it upheld a Florida statute permitting the use of a six-person jury in a robbery trial.

Justice Byron White, writing for the majority, said, "In short, while sometime in the fourteenth century the size of the jury came to be fixed generally at twelve, that particular feature of the jury system appears to have been a historical accident, unrelated to the great purpose which gave rise to the jury in the first place."[11] *Williams v. Florida* has offered a welcome measure of relief to an overburdened crime control system. Today, jury size may be reduced for all but the most serious criminal cases.

Unanimous Verdict   Besides the convention of twelve-person juries in criminal trials, tradition also had been that the jurors' decision must be unanimous. However, in the 1972 case of *Apodica v. Oregon,* the U.S. Supreme Court held that the Sixth and Fourteenth Amendments do not prohibit criminal convictions by less than unanimous jury verdicts in noncapital cases.[12] In the *Apodica* case, the Court upheld an Oregon statute requiring only ten of twelve jurors to convict the defendant of assault with a deadly weapon, burglary, and grand larceny. Such verdicts are not unusual in civil matters, but much controversy remains regarding their place in the criminal process.

The Right to Counsel at Trial

Recall from previous chapters that the defendant has a right to counsel at numerous points in the criminal justice system. Today, state courts must provide counsel at trial to indigent defendants who face the possibility of incarceration. In *Scott v.*

How important are juries? To find out go to Zakaria Erzinclioglu, "The Role of Juries in the Justice System," *Contemporary Review,* June 1999 v274 i1601 p297(6), on InfoTrac College Edition.

six-person jury   The criminal trial of a defendant before a jury of six persons as opposed to a traditional jury of twelve persons.

Here's a site with links to famous trials in world history, from Joan of Arc to O. J.:
www.law.umkc.edu/faculty/projects/FTrials/WorldTrial_all.html

Illinois in 1979, that was limited to cases where the defendant has the potential to be incarcerated.[13] In its most recent ruling on the matter, *Alabama v. Shelton,* the Court ruled that a person cannot receive a probation sentence in which a prison or jail term is suspended, or any other type of sentence containing a threat of future incarceration, unless that person is afforded the right to counsel at trial. Moreover, *Shelton* prohibits incarceration of any person whose probation is revoked unless that person was represented by counsel at trial or plea.[14] "We hold that a suspended sentence that may 'end up in the actual deprivation of a person's liberty' may not be imposed unless the defendant was accorded 'the guiding hand of counsel' in the prosecution for the crime charged."[15] *Shelton* may be interpreted as saying that any person who is currently in jail on the basis of a probation violation stemming from a misdemeanor conviction without a valid waiver of counsel is being held unconstitutionally.

The Right to Self-Representation

Another important question regarding the right to counsel is whether criminal defendants are guaranteed the right to represent themselves—that is, to act as their own lawyers. Before the 1975 U.S. Supreme Court decision in *Faretta v. California,*[16] defendants in most state courts and in the federal system claimed the right to proceed **pro se,** or for themselves, by reason of federal and state statutes and on state constitutional grounds. This permitted defendants to choose between hiring counsel or conducting their own defense. Whether a constitutional right to represent oneself in a criminal prosecution existed remained an open question until the *Faretta* decision.

pro se The defense of self-representation.

The defendant, Anthony Faretta, was charged with grand theft in Los Angeles County. Before his trial, he requested that he be permitted to represent himself. The judge told Faretta that he believed this would be a mistake, but accepted his waiver of counsel. The judge then held a hearing to inquire into Faretta's ability to conduct his own defense and subsequently ruled that Faretta had not made an intelligent and knowing waiver of his right to the assistance of counsel. As a result, the judge appointed a public defender to represent Faretta, who was brought to trial, found guilty, and sentenced to prison. He appealed, claiming that he had a constitutional right to self-representation.

Upon review, the U.S. Supreme Court recognized Faretta's pro se right on a constitutional basis, while making it conditional on a showing that the defendant could competently, knowingly, and intelligently waive his right to counsel. The Court's decision was based on the belief that the right of self-representation finds support in the structure of the Sixth Amendment, as well as in English and colonial jurisprudence from which the amendment emerged. Thus, in forcing Faretta to accept counsel against his will, the California trial court deprived him of his constitutional right to conduct his own defense.

It is important to recognize that the *Faretta* case dealt only with the constitutional right of

Sketch by Andrea Shepard © AFP/CORBIS

The U.S. Supreme Court has ruled that defendants can proceed pro se, or defend themselves at trial, if they can prove to the presiding judge that they can provide a competent defense and that the waiver was knowing and intelligent. This court drawing shows the trial of Zacarias Moussaoui, the so-called "twentieth hijacker," presided by Judge Barbara Jones. On June 13, 2002, federal judge Leonie Brinkema ruled that Moussaoui was competent to defend himself, but assigned him "standby" lawyers who would step in if she decided he was no longer capable.

Does self-representation ever make sense? To find out go to
www.nolo.com/lawcenter/ency/
article.cfm/objectID/980A3D6F-2C3F-
43B5-A4AEC4EDD8151BEF/
catID/7BBA11EC-A686-4A81-
8C6A1E017A20FE13

self-representation at trial. It did not provide guidelines for administering the right during other elements of the criminal process. In *Martinez v. Court of Appeal of California* (2000), the Court ruled that neither *Faretta*'s holding nor its reasoning requires a state to recognize a constitutional right to self-representation on appeal of a criminal conviction. In its decision, the Court noted that there are significant distinctions between trial and appeal; for example, the Sixth Amendment deals strictly with trial rights and does not include any right to appeal. The Court left it up to the states to recognize a constitutional right to appellate self-representation under their own constitutions.[17]

The Right to a Speedy Trial

The requirement of the right to counsel at trial in virtually all criminal cases often causes delays in the formal processing of defendants through the court system. Counsel usually seeks to safeguard the interests of the accused and in so doing may employ a variety of legal devices—pretrial motions, plea negotiations, trial procedures, and appeals—that require time and extend the decision-making period in a particular case. The involvement of counsel, along with inefficiencies in the court process—such as the frequent granting of continuances, poor scheduling procedures, and the abuse of time by court personnel—has made the problem of delay in criminal cases a serious and constitutional issue. As the American Bar Association states in the *Standards Relating to Speedy Trial*: "Congestion in the trial courts of this country, particularly in urban centers, is currently one of the major problems of judicial administration."[18]

The Sixth Amendment guarantees a criminal defendant the right to a speedy trial in federal prosecutions. This right has been made applicable to the states by the 1967 decision in *Klopfer v. North Carolina*.[19] In this case, the defendant Klopfer was charged with criminal trespass. His original trial ended in a mistrial, and he sought to determine whether and when the government intended to retry him. The prosecutor asked the court to take a "nolle prosequi with leave"—a legal device discharging the defendant but allowing the government to prosecute him in the future. The U.S. Supreme Court held that the effort by the government to postpone Klopfer's trial indefinitely without reason denied him the right to a speedy trial guaranteed by the Sixth and Fourteenth Amendments.

In *Klopfer,* the Supreme Court emphasized the importance of the speedy trial in the criminal process by stating that this right was "as fundamental as any of the rights secured by the Sixth Amendment."[20] Its primary purposes are to

1. Improve the credibility of the trial by seeking to have witnesses available for testimony as early as possible.
2. Reduce the anxiety for the defendant in awaiting trial, as well as to avoid pretrial detention.
3. Avoid extensive pretrial publicity and questionable conduct of public officials that would influence the defendant's right to a fair trial.
4. Avoid any delay that could affect the defendant's ability to defend herself.

To access the Federal Criminal Code rules on speedy trial, go to
http://www4.law.cornell.edu/uscode/18/
pIIch208.html

Since the 1967 *Klopfer* case, the Supreme Court has dealt with the speedy trial guarantee on numerous occasions. One such example is the 1992 case of *Doggett v. United States,* in which the Court found that a delay of eight and a half years between indictment and arrest was prejudicial to the defendant and required a dismissal of the charges against the defendant.[21]

The Right to a Fair Trial

Every person charged with a crime also has a fundamental right to a fair trial. What does it mean to have a fair trial in the criminal justice system? A fair trial is one that takes place before an impartial judge and jury, in an environment of judicial restraint, orderliness, and fair decision making. Although it is not expressly stated in the U.S. Constitution, the right of the accused to a fair trial is guaranteed by the due process clauses of the Fifth and Fourteenth Amendments. This fair trial right may be violated in a number of ways. A hostile courtroom crowd, improper pressure on witnesses, or any behavior that produces prejudice toward the accused, among other things, can preclude a fair trial. When, for example, a defendant was required to go to trial in prison clothing, the U.S. Supreme Court found a violation of the due process clause of the Fourteenth Amendment.[22]

To learn more about the concept of "fair trial," use the term as a subject guide on InfoTrac College Edition.

Pretrial Publicity   Adverse pretrial publicity can also deny a defendant a fair trial. The release of premature evidence by the prosecutor, extensive and critical reporting by the news media, and vivid and uncalled-for details in indictments can all prejudice a defendant's case. Press coverage can begin early in a criminal case and help bias the outcome. The Supreme Court seemed to sense the danger in the 1999 case *Wilson et al. v. Layne,* in which it ruled that it was an unconstitutional invasion of privacy for law enforcement agents to invite a newspaper reporter and a photographer to accompany them as they served a warrant.[23]

Judges involved in newsworthy criminal cases have attempted to place restraints on media coverage to preserve the defendant's right to a fair trial; at the same time, it is generally believed that the media have a constitutional right to provide news coverage. The U.S. Supreme Court dealt with the fair trial–free press issue in the 1976 case of *Nebraska Press Association v. Stuart.*[24] The Court ruled unconstitutional a trial judge's order prohibiting the press from reporting the confessions implicating the defendant in the crime. The Court's decision was based primarily on the fact that "prior restraints on speech and publication are the most serious and least tolerable infringement on First Amendment rights."[25]

In *Gannett Co. v. DePasquale* (1979), the Court was asked to decide whether the press and public had an independent constitutional right of access to a pretrial judicial hearing, even though all the parties had agreed that to guarantee a fair trial the courtroom should be closed.[26] The Court ruled that the press had a right of access of constitutional dimensions but that this right was outweighed by the defendant's right to a fair trial.[27] In other words, the Court balanced competing social interests and found that denial of access by the public did not violate the First, Sixth, or Fourteenth Amendment rights of the defendant. The interest of justice requires that the defendant's case not be jeopardized, and the desire for a fair trial far outweighs the public's right of access to a pretrial suppression hearing. However, the *Gannett* decision applied to hearings and not full-blown trials. In the 1986 case *Press-Enterprise Co. v. Superior Court,* the Supreme Court further defined this concept when it ruled that closing a hearing is permissible under the **First Amendment** only if there is substantial probability that the defendant's right to a fair trial would be prejudiced by publicity that closed proceedings would prevent. According to the Court, preliminary hearings have traditionally been open to the public and should remain so.[28]

First Amendment   The U.S. constitutional amendment that guarantees freedom of speech, religion, press, and assembly and the right of the people to petition the government for a redress of grievances.

The Right to a Public Trial

The familiar language of the Sixth Amendment clearly states that "the accused shall enjoy the right to a speedy and public trial." Underlying this provision is the belief that a trial in the criminal justice system must be a public activity. The amendment is rooted in the principle that justice cannot survive behind walls of silence.[29] It was enacted because the framers of the U.S. Constitution distrusted secret trials and arbitrary proceedings. In the 1948 case of *In re Oliver,* for instance, the Supreme Court held that the secrecy of a criminal contempt trial violated the right of the defendant to a public trial under the Fourteenth Amendment.[30] In *Oliver,* the Court recognized the constitutional guarantee of a public trial for the defendant in state and federal courts.

Use "pretrial publicity" as a subject guide on InfoTrac College Edition.

Criminal Justice and the Media

TV or Not TV? Should Criminal Trials Be Televised?

On January 18, 2002, a federal judge refused to allow TV cameras into the trial of Zacarias Moussaoui, alleged to be one of the September 11 terrorists. Judge Leonie N. Brinkema, in a thirteen-page ruling, denied the request of the Court TV cable network to broadcast the trial of Moussaoui, who was charged with six terrorism conspiracy counts. In her ruling, Brinkema wrote that she had no authority to reject a federal court ban on cameras in courtrooms. Even if she did, she would not, she wrote, because, "given the issues raised in this indictment, any societal benefits from photographing and broadcasting these proceedings are heavily outweighed by the significant dangers worldwide [that] broadcasting of this trial would pose to the orderly and secure administration of justice." Her ruling embraced concerns raised by prosecutors that broadcasting the trial would intimidate witnesses, endanger court officers, and provide Moussaoui with a platform to vent his political beliefs. In contrast, Moussaoui's lawyers favored televising the trial, with restrictions. They argued that the broadcasts would give their client an added layer of protection in getting a fair trial on charges that could result in the death penalty. The judge's decision outraged some commentators who felt the American people were cheated by the decision.

In *Newsweek* magazine, Anna Quindlen wrote: "The events of September 11 have left a nation of victims, and the number who bear witness should not be determined by the square footage of a courtroom. Let the world see how well the American justice system works. The point of public trials in the first place was to let the people in. In the twenty-first century, letting the people in means letting the cameras in."

The Supreme Court has upheld the public's right of access to the judicial system, but has stopped short of saying the right to a public trial means the right to a televised trial. Justice David Souter testified in 1996 before a Senate subcommittee: "The day you see [a] camera come into our courtroom, it's going to roll over my dead body." Until recently, the justices did not even allow the live audio broadcasting of arguments, though they did permit archival audiotaping. In the landmark case of *Bush v. Gore*—the case that awarded Bush the presidency after the 2000 election—the justices finally relented and permitted the real-time audio transmission of the final arguments. As Court TV expert Hedieh Nasheri points out, *Bush v. Gore* was a good first step, but many Americans wondered why the justices were prepared to be heard but not seen. Today's television cameras require no special lighting, she argues in her new book, *Crime and Justice in the Age of Court TV*, and can be placed discreetly behind walls so as not to interfere with courtroom proceedings. *Bush v. Gore* was a wonderful civics lesson, but it was somewhat incomplete because the television cameras were excluded. One option, she notes, is the Sunshine in the Courtroom Act, which is still pending before Congress as this book goes to press. This bill would give judges in federal trial and appeals courts discretion to permit cameras in their courtrooms, but it would require them to afford witnesses the option of having their faces and voices obscured.

Although federal court rules specifically prohibit the televising of any federal criminal trial, state courts are more flexible; all states now allow some judicial proceedings to be broadcast and thirty-eight states permit the showing of state criminal trials.

What are the pros and cons of televising criminal trials? Lawyers who represent the news media often point out valid arguments for using cameras in the courtroom:

1. Public trials would encourage participants to do a better job.
2. In a democratic society, the public should have access to all trials, even those of a scandalous nature.
3. TV coverage can contribute to educating the public about the justice system.

Press Coverage of Trials   Not only does the public have the right to attend trials, so too does the press. In the landmark case *Richmond Newspapers, Inc. v. Virginia* (1980), the Supreme Court clearly established that criminal trials must remain open to the press.[31] The Court extended the right of the press to attend trials involving even highly sensitive, sexually related matters in which the victim is under eighteen years of age.[32]

More recently the issue of press coverage has focused on bringing TV cameras into the courtroom. Because of the public interest in high-profile criminal cases, whether jury trials should be televised is one of the most controversial questions in the criminal justice system. The legal community is divided over the use of TV cameras in the courtroom. Today, many state courts permit such coverage, often

Conversely, some defense lawyers and judges believe that televised trials should be restricted because they serve only as a form of entertainment and suppress the search for truth. Others question whether public interest outweighs the defendant's ability to obtain a fair trial. Still, resistance to the idea remains firm. The U.S. Judicial Conference, the policymaking body for the federal courts, says cameras in courtrooms raise privacy concerns for witnesses in sensitive cases and put traditionally low-profile, but powerful, federal judges at risk.

One advocate of cameras in the courtroom is lawyer Ronald Goldfarb, who in his book *TV or Not TV* argued that the proper line between entertainment and education, between exploitation and information, between the negative consequences of televised and nontelevised trials, is not clear; nor can it be measured with scientific objectivity. So even though visibility on TV may be a yet-unmeasured risk to trial fairness, it is a risk worth taking. Televising trials keeps the legal system in the "sunlight" and assures that judges, lawyers, and even witnesses act honestly. Allowing cameras in the courtroom helps the public's perception of the trial as a fair process. The public is more suspicious of the outcome if the trial is held behind closed doors. He dismisses critics by stating that "much of the current criticism of televised trials amounts to killing the messenger while ignoring the message." It is not the media's fault for showing that trials are sometimes unfair and boring, or that lawyers may be bullies or incompetent; that is the nature of the trial process and not the media coverage. Rather, he argues, live and inconspicuous television might improve on some shortcomings of ordinary press coverage of the courts. "One can bribe a reporter, but not a camera."

Goldfarb proposes a regulated system of total media coverage. He foresees cameras in every courtroom, with the broadcast of every trial available for viewing on a publicly run TV station or through the Internet. However, he would also allow for the right to oppose broadcast by a number of people involved in the trial.

Critical Thinking

Three major concerns arise in televising criminal trials: (1) Jurors and potential jurors are exposed to media coverage that may cause prejudgment; (2) in-court media coverage, especially cameras and TV, can increase community and political pressure on participants and even cause grandstanding by participants; (3) media coverage can erode the dignity and decorum of the courtroom. Yet, in a democratic society, shouldn't the public have access to all trials through the TV medium, regardless of these concerns?

● InfoTrac College Edition Research

Televising courtroom dramas in criminal trials has resulted in an explosion of lawyer-centered talk shows, including *Burden of Proof* on CNN, *Cochran & Co.* on Court TV, and *Rivera Live* on CNBC. Does the public actually debate the legal, political, and social issues through these trials? Use InfoTrac College Edition to do research on high profile criminal trials such as the O. J. Simpson case. Focus on such issues as a defendant's right to a public trial and the rights of the press under the First Amendment.

Sources: Hedieh Nasheri, *Crime and Justice in the Age of Court TV* (New York: LFB Scholarly Publishing, 2002); Ronald Goldfarb, *TV or Not TV: Television, Justice, and the Courts* (New York: New York University Press, 1998): 164, 172; Anna Quindlen "Lights, Camera, Justice for All," *Newsweek* (21 January 2002): 64; "Judge Won't Allow Televising Terror Trial" *Quill 90* (March 2002): 8.

at the judge's discretion, but federal courts prohibit TV coverage altogether. In 1981, the U.S. Supreme Court in *Chandler v. Florida* removed any constitutional obstacles to the use of electronic media coverage and still photography of public criminal proceedings over the objections of a criminal defendant.[33] To be certain, the defendant has a constitutional right to a public trial, but it is equally imperative that the media be allowed to exercise its First Amendment rights.

In sum, the defendant's right to an impartial trial and jury under the Fifth and Sixth Amendments often runs into direct conflict with the First Amendment's guarantee of freedom of the press and public access. In the Criminal Justice and the Media feature above, the matter of televising criminal trials is reviewed.

The Court TV Web site can be found at www.courttv.com/

© 2002 AP/Wide World Photos

The issue of press coverage in the courtroom is of critical importance because of public interest in high-profile criminal cases. How much freedom should the press be allowed to televise or film jury trials? Should they be allowed in the jury deliberation room itself? Here, members of the media are allowed to photograph the evidence jury members will review during the 2002 murder trial of Jonathan and Reginald Carr in Wichita, Kansas. The two brothers were convicted of five murders, including the slayings of four friends who were forced to engage in sexual acts with each other before they were taken to a snowy soccer field and shot.

The Trial Process

The trial of a criminal case is a formal process conducted in a specific and orderly fashion in accordance with rules of criminal law, procedure, and evidence. Unlike what transpires in popular TV programs involving lawyers—where witnesses are often asked leading and prejudicial questions and where judges go far beyond their supervisory role—the modern criminal trial is a complicated and often time-consuming, technical affair. It is a structured adversary proceeding in which both the prosecution and defense follow specific procedures and argue the merits of their cases before the judge and jury. Each side seeks to present its case in the most favorable light. When possible, the prosecutor and the defense attorney will object to evidence they consider damaging to their positions. The prosecutor will use direct testimony, physical evidence, and a confession, if available, to convince the jury that the accused is guilty beyond a reasonable doubt. The defense attorney will rebut the government's case with her own evidence, make certain that the rights of the criminal defendant under the federal and state constitutions are considered during all phases of the trial, and determine whether an appeal is appropriate if the client is found guilty.

Although each jurisdiction in the United States has its own trial procedures, all jurisdictions conduct criminal trials in a generally similar fashion. The basic steps of the criminal trial, which proceed in an established order, are described in this section and outlined in Figure 9.1.

Jury Selection

In both civil and criminal cases, jurors are selected randomly from licensing or voter registration lists within each court's jurisdiction.

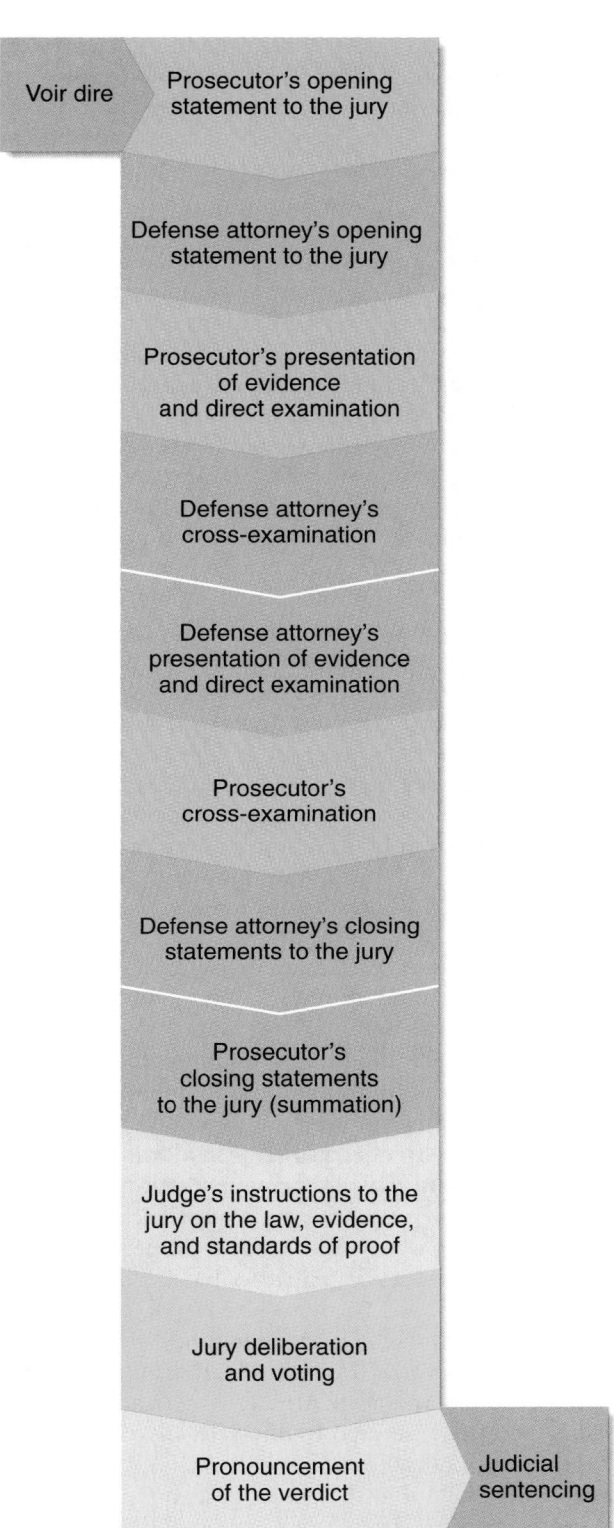

Voir dire

Prosecutor's opening
statement to the jury

Defense attorney's opening
statement to the jury

Prosecutor's presentation
of evidence
and direct examination

Defense attorney's
cross-examination

Defense attorney's
presentation of evidence
and direct examination

Prosecutor's
cross-examination

Defense attorney's closing
statements to the jury

Prosecutor's
closing statements
to the jury (summation)

Judge's instructions to the
jury on the law, evidence,
and standards of proof

Jury deliberation
and voting

Pronouncement
of the verdict

Judicial
sentencing

Figure 9.1
The steps in a jury trial

Source: Marvin Zalman and Larry Siegel, *Criminal Procedure: Constitution and Society* (St. Paul, Minn.: West, 1991), 655.

Few states impose qualifications on those called for jury service, though most mandate a residency requirement.[34] There is also little uniformity in the amount of time served by jurors, with the term ranging from one day to months, depending on the nature of the trial. In addition, most jurisdictions prohibit convicted felons from serving on juries, as well as others exempted by statute, such as public officials, physicians, and attorneys.

The initial list of persons chosen, which is called **venire**, or jury array, provides the state with a group of potentially capable citizens able to serve on a jury. Many states, by rule of law, review the venire to eliminate unqualified persons and to exempt those who by reason of their professions are not allowed to be jurors. The actual jury selection process begins with those remaining on the list.

The court clerk, who handles the administrative affairs of the trial—including the processing of the complaint, evidence, and other documents—randomly selects enough names to fill what she believes will be the required number of places on the jury. After reporting to a courtroom, the prospective jurors are first required to swear that they will truthfully answer all questions asked about their qualifications to serve. A group of twelve will be asked to sit in the jury box while the remaining group stands by.

Voir Dire Once twelve prospective jurors are chosen, the lengthy process of **voir dire** (from the French for "to tell the truth") starts. To determine their appropriateness to sit on the jury, prospective jurors are examined under oath by the government, the defense, and sometimes the judge, about their backgrounds, occupations, residences, and possible knowledge of or interest in the case. A juror who acknowledges any bias for or prejudice against the defendant—if the defendant is a friend or relative, for example, or if the juror has already formed an opinion about the case—may be removed by either the prosecution or defense with a **challenge for cause** asking the judge to dismiss the biased juror. If the judge accepts the challenge, the juror is removed for cause and replaced with another from the remaining panel. Because normally no limit is placed on the number of challenges for cause that can be exercised, it often takes considerable time to select a jury for controversial and highly publicized criminal cases.

Peremptory Challenges Besides challenges for cause, both the prosecution and the defense are allowed **peremptory challenges**, which enable the attorneys to excuse jurors for no particular reason or for undisclosed reasons. For example, a prosecutor might not want a bartender as a juror in a drunk-driving case, believing that a person with that occupation would be sympathetic to the accused. Or the defense attorney might excuse a prospective male juror because the attorney prefers to have a predominantly female jury. The number of peremptory challenges permitted is limited by state statute and often varies by case and jurisdiction.

The peremptory challenge has been criticized by legal experts who question the fairness and propriety with which it has been used.[35] Historically, the most significant criticism was that it was used to exclude African Americans from hearing cases in which the defendant was also African American, a policy that was extremely troublesome because it seemed to allow legally condoned discrimination against minority group members. Then in the landmark 1986 case *Batson v. Kentucky,* the Supreme Court held that the use of peremptory challenges against potential jurors by prosecutors in criminal cases violated the U.S. Constitution if the challenges were based solely on race.[36] Since that decision, the issue of race discrimination in the use of peremptory challenges has been raised by defendants in numerous cases. In the 1991 case of *Powers v. Ohio,* the Supreme Court held that it is unconstitutional to exclude juries based on race even if they are not the same race as the defendant. In other words, the equal protection clause prohibits a prosecutor from using the peremptory challenge to exclude qualified and unbiased persons from a jury solely by reason of race, regardless of the race of the parties in-

---

venire The group called for jury duty from which jury panels are selected.

voir dire The process in which a potential jury panel is questioned by the prosecution and the defense in order to select jurors who are unbiased and objective.

challenge for cause Removing a juror because he or she is biased or has prior knowledge about a case, or for other reasons that demonstrate the individual's inability to render a fair and impartial judgment in a case.

peremptory challenge The dismissal of a potential juror by either the prosecution or the defense for unexplained, discretionary reasons.

To read about juror selection in California, go to
www.courtinfo.ca.gov/jury/step1.htm

| Exhibit 9.1 | Evolution of *Batson v. Kentucky* and its progeny |

Case	Ruling
Batson v. Kentucky (1986)	Under the Fourteenth Amendment, the Supreme Court ruled that prosecutors were barred from using peremptory challenges to remove black jurors because of their race.
Powers v. Ohio (1991)	The Court concluded that a defendant has the standing to object to the race-based exclusion by the use of peremptory challenges of jurors on the grounds of equal protection, even if not of the same race as the challenged jurors.
Edmonson v. Leesville Concrete Co. (1991)	The Batson ruling applies to attorneys in civil lawsuits. In other words, a private party in a civil action may not raise peremptory challenges to exclude jurors on the basis of race.
Georgia v. McCollum (1992)	On the basis of *Batson,* the Georgia decision prohibited the exercise of peremptory challenges on the basis of race by defense attorneys in criminal cases.
J.E.B. v. Alabama (1994)	The Court held that the equal protection clause of the Fourteenth Amendment bars discrimination in jury selection on the basis of sex. Discrimination in jury selection, whether based on race or gender, causes harm to the litigants, the community, and the individual jurors who are wrongfully excluded from participation in the judicial process.

volved.[37] In 1994 the Court applied the *Batson* doctrine to gender-based peremptory challenges, ruling that attorneys must provide a nondiscriminatory reason for removing a large number of prospective male or female jurors (*J.E.B. v. Alabama*).[38] Exhibit 9.1 summarizes these decisions.

Batson strikes down a legal procedure that was "out of sync" with modern ideas of justice and fairness. It prevents an element of racial discrimination from entering into the trial stage of justice, which is one of the cornerstones of American freedom. Yet it preserves, under controlled circumstances, the use of the peremptory challenge, which is an integral part of the jury selection process. However, as legal expert Charles Ogletree points out, the seemingly neutral explanations of prosecutors for using peremptory challenges sometimes still undermine the protection against jury discrimination established by the *Batson* case. Ogletree suggests that the following procedural protections be implemented: (1) the dismissal of a criminal case where a prosecutor violates *Batson* and (2) the elimination of prosecution peremptory challenges.[39] However, it seems unlikely that such rules would be established by a state court or legislature.

Opening Statements

Once the jury has been selected and the criminal complaint has been read to the jurors by the court clerk, the prosecutor and the defense attorney may each make an opening statement about the case. The purpose of the prosecutor's statement is to introduce the judge and the jury to the particular criminal charges, to outline the facts, and to describe how the government will prove the defendant guilty beyond a reasonable doubt. The defense attorney reviews the case and indicates how the defense intends to show that the accused is not guilty.

Usually, the defense attorney makes an opening statement after the government reads its case. In some jurisdictions, the court in its discretion can permit the defense to make opening remarks before any evidence is introduced. But, for the most part, current rules dictate that the prosecutor is entitled to offer an opening statement first.

The opening statement gives the jury a concise overview of the evidence that is to follow. In the opening statement, neither attorney is allowed to make prejudicial remarks or inflammatory statements or mention irrelevant facts. Both are free, however, to identify what they will eventually prove by way of evidence, which includes witnesses, physical evidence, and the use of expert testimony. As a general rule, the opening statements used in jury trials are important because they provide the fact finders (the jury) with an initial summary of the case. They are infrequently used and less effective in bench trials, however, where juries are not used. Most lower-court judges have handled hundreds of similar cases and do not need the benefit of an opening statement.

Witness Testimony

direct examination The questioning of one's own (prosecution or defense) witness during a trial.

Following the opening statements, the government begins its case by presenting evidence to the court through its witnesses. Those called as witnesses—such as police officers, victims, or experts—provide testimony via **direct examination.** During direct examination, the prosecutor questions the witness to reveal the facts believed pertinent to the government's case. Testimony involves what the witness actually saw, heard, or touched, and does not include opinions. However, a witness's opinion can be given in certain situations, such as when describing the motion of a vehicle or indicating whether a defendant appeared to act intoxicated or insane. Witnesses may also qualify to give opinions because they are experts on a particular subject relevant to the case; for example, a psychiatrist may testify about a defendant's mental capacity at the time of the crime.

© 2002 AP/Wide World Photos

Wichita, Kansas, police crime scene investigator Barbara Siwek testifies in the murder trial of Jonathan and Reginald Carr. The prosecutor used direct testimony and physical evidence to convince the jury that the accused were guilty beyond a reasonable doubt.

Upon completion of the prosecutor's questioning, the defense usually conducts a **cross-examination** of the witness. During this exchange, the defense attorney may challenge elements of the testimony, such as their accuracy in reporting what they saw or heard. The right to cross-examine witnesses is an essential part of a trial, and unless extremely unusual circumstances exist (such as a person's being hospitalized), witness statements will not be considered unless they are made in court and open for question. If desired, the prosecutor may seek a second direct examination after the defense attorney has completed cross-examination; this allows the prosecutor to ask additional questions about information brought out during cross-examination. Finally, the defense attorney may then question, or re-cross-examine, the witness once again. All witnesses for the trial are sworn in and questioned in the same basic manner.

Types of Evidence at a Criminal Trial   Besides testimonial evidence given by police officers, citizens, and experts, the court also acts on real, or nonverbal, evidence.[40] **Real evidence** often consists of the exhibits taken into the jury room for review by the jury. A revolver that may have been in the defendant's control at the time of a murder, tools in the possession of a suspect charged with a burglary, and a bottle allegedly holding narcotics are all examples of real, or physical, evidence. Photographs, maps, diagrams, and crime scene displays are further types of real evidence. The criminal court judge will also review documentary evidence, such as writings, government reports, public records, business or hospital records, fingerprint identification, and DNA profiling.

In general, the primary test for the admissibility of evidence in a criminal proceeding is its relevance; that is, the court must consider whether the gun, tool, or bottle, for example, has relevant evidentiary value in determining the issues in the case. Ordinarily, evidence that establishes an element of the crime is acceptable to the court. For example, in a prosecution for possession of drugs, evidence that shows the defendant to be a known drug user might be relevant. In a prosecution for bribery, photos of the defendant receiving a package from a co-conspirator would clearly be found relevant to the case.

Circumstantial (indirect) evidence is also often used in trial proceedings. Such evidence is often inferred or indirectly used to prove a fact in question. For example, in a murder case, evidence that carpet fibers found on the body match the carpet in the defendant's home may be used at trial to link the two, even though they do not provide direct evidence that the suspect actually killed the victim.

Motion for a Directed Verdict

Once the prosecution has provided all the government's evidence against a defendant, it will inform the court that it rests the people's case. The defense attorney at this point may enter a motion for a **directed verdict**. This is a procedural device in which the defense attorney asks the judge to order the jury to return a verdict of not guilty. Depending on the weight of the prosecution's case, the judge may either sustain it or overrule the motion. In essence, the defense attorney argues in the directed verdict that the prosecutor's case against the defendant is insufficient to support the legal elements needed to prove the defendant guilty beyond a reasonable doubt. If the motion is sustained, the trial is terminated. If it is rejected by the court, the case continues with the defense portion of the trial.

Presentation of the Defense Attorney's Evidence

The defense attorney has the option of presenting many, some, or no witnesses on behalf of the defendant. The burden of guilt is on the prosecution, and if the defense team believes that the burden has not been met they may feel there is no need

cross-examination   The process in which the defense and the prosecution interrogate witnesses during a trial.

Can psychiatrists be held liable for civil actions because of their appearance as expert witnesses? To find out, read Barbara Boughton, "Immunity for Expert Witnesses Dwindling Due to Case Law: Psychiatrists Can Sometimes Be Held Liable," *Clinical Psychiatry News*, August 2002 v30 i8 p37(1), on InfoTrac College Edition.

real evidence   Any object produced for inspection at the trial (weapon, photograph).

circumstantial (indirect) evidence   Evidence not bearing on the fact in dispute but on various indirect circumstances from which the judge or jury might infer the existence of the fact (for example, if the defendant was seen in the house with wet clothing, that is circumstantial evidence that the person had walked in the rain).

directed verdict   The right of a judge to direct a jury to acquit a defendant because the state has not proven the elements of the crime or otherwise has not established guilt according to law.

How can lawyers use technology to present evidence at trial? Go to InfoTrac College Edition and read Brian Panish and Christine Spagnoli, "Take Technology to Trial: Jurors Remember Best What They See and Hear, So Use Visual Technology to Make Your Message Stick," *Trial*, July 2002 v38 i7 p39(7).

to present witnesses of their own. In addition, the defense attorney must decide whether the defendant should take the stand and testify in his own behalf. In a criminal trial, the defendant is protected by the Fifth Amendment right to be free from self-incrimination, which means that a person cannot be forced by the state to testify against himself. However, defendants who choose voluntarily to tell their side of the story can be subject to cross-examination by the prosecutor.

The defense attorney is charged with putting on a vigorous defense in the adversary system of justice. How far can defense attorneys go and how far should they go? That is the topic of the following Law in Review feature.

After the defense concludes its case, the government may then present rebuttal evidence. This normally involves bringing evidence forward that was not used when the prosecution initially presented the case. The defense may examine the rebuttal witnesses and introduce new witnesses in a process called a *surrebuttal.* After all evidence has been presented to the court, the defense attorney may again submit a motion for a directed verdict. If the motion is denied, both the prosecution and the defense prepare to make closing arguments, and the case on the evidence is ready for consideration by the jury.

Closing Arguments

Closing arguments are used by the attorneys to review the facts and evidence of the case in a manner favorable to each of their positions. At this stage of the trial, both prosecution and defense are permitted to draw reasonable inferences and to show how the facts prove or refute the defendant's guilt. Often both attorneys have a free hand in arguing about the facts, issues, and evidence, including the applicable law. They cannot comment on matters not in evidence, however, or on the defendant's failure to testify in a criminal case. Normally, the defense attorney will make a closing statement first, followed by the prosecutor. Either party can elect to forgo the right to make a final summation to the jury.

Instructions to the Jury

charge In a criminal case, the judge's instruction to the jurors before deliberation.

In a criminal trial, the judge will instruct, or **charge,** the jury members on the principles of law that ought to guide and control their decision on the defendant's innocence or guilt. Included in the charge will be information about the elements of the alleged offense, the type of evidence needed to prove each element, and the burden of proof required to obtain a guilty verdict. Although the judge commonly provides the instruction, he or she may ask the prosecutor and the defense attorney to submit instructions for consideration; the judge will then use discretion in determining whether to use any of their instructions. The instructions that cover the law applicable to the case are extremely important because they may serve as the basis for a subsequent appeal. Procedurally, in highly publicized and celebrated cases, the judge may have sequestered the jury overnight to prevent them from having contact with the outside world. This process, called *sequestration,* is discretionary with the trial judge, and most courts believe that "locking up a jury" is needed only in sensational cases.

The Verdict

Once the charge is given to the jury members, they retire to deliberate on a verdict. As previously mentioned, the verdict in a criminal case—regardless of whether the trial involves a six- or twelve-person jury—is usually required to be unanimous. Unanimity of twelve is not required by the U.S. Constitution in state

The Danielle van Dam Case: Should Defense Lawyers Tell the Truth?

Facts

One of the most highly publicized criminal cases of the past few years was the Danielle van Dam murder case. The pretty seven-year-old California girl was abducted from her bedroom and later found dead in a wooded area. Suspicion was soon directed at neighbor David Westerfield, who was arrested and charged with the crime.

During the trial, Westerfield's attorneys, Steven Feldman and Robert Boyce, put on a vigorous defense. They pointed a finger at the lifestyle of the seven-year-old's parents, Brenda and Damon van Dam, who were forced to admit on the stand that they engaged in partner swapping and group sex. The defense lawyers told jurors that the couple's sex life brought them in contact with sleazy characters who were much more likely to have harmed Danielle than Westerfield, who had no felony record. The defense also told jurors that scientific evidence proved Westerfield could not have dumped Danielle's body by a remote roadside. Forensic entomologists testified that the insects in her decaying body indicated her death occurred during a period during which Westerfield could account for his activities. Despite their efforts, physical evidence found in Westerfield's home proved very damaging in court and he was convicted of the murder and sentenced to death.

Significance of the Case

After the trial was over, the *San Diego Union-Tribune* broke the story that Westerfield's lawyers had tried to broker a deal before trial in which Westerfield would reveal the location of Danielle's body in exchange for a guarantee that he would not face the death penalty but only life without parole. Both sides were about to make the deal when volunteer searchers found the girl's body. Talk show host Bill O'Reilly (*The O'Reilly Factor*) revealed the contents of the *Union-Tribune* article on national TV. He was disgusted to learn that Westerfield's attorneys thus actually knew their client was guilty before the trial began, yet put on a defense in which they claimed he was innocent:

Would these two men have allowed Westerfield to walk out of the courtroom a free man if he had been acquitted? Remember, these guys knew he killed Danielle and were willing to lead authorities to her body, according to the *Trib*.

So forget all the smears they made up. Forget about the fact they consciously misled the jury. Would these two men have allowed Westerfield to walk free, knowing he was a child-killer?

He added, "No American should ever talk to these two people again—that's how sleazy they are." He filed a formal complaint with the state bar of California.

While O'Reilly was expressing his disgust, members of the legal community in San Diego defended the trial tactics of Feldman and Boyce. Defense lawyers and former prosecutors pointed out that plea discussions are never admissible during trial, and Feldman and Boyce would have been accused of incompetence if they did not try to raise reasonable doubt in the case. The defense attorney's job is not to decide whether the client committed the offense but to provide the client with a vigorous defense and ensure that the client isn't convicted, unless the prosecution can prove its case beyond a reasonable doubt. And it's impossible to make the prosecution meet its burden without aggressively challenging the evidence, even if the defender believes the client committed the crime. One San Diego defense lawyer, Bill Nimmo, defended the lawyers' decision to raise the parents' swinging lifestyle and the bug evidence. "You [as a defense lawyer] are not personally vouching for everything. You are arguing what the evidence shows, not what you personally know," said Nimmo. "If the evidence is good enough, if the prosecution has strong enough evidence, what do you care what the defense lawyer knows? He'll get convicted." If Westerfield had attempted to take the stand and lie about his involvement in the murder, then Feldman and Boyce would have been required to tell the judge, but Westerfield did not testify.

Critical Thinking

Do you agree that defense attorneys should put on a vigorous defense, casting doubt on their client's guilt, even if they know beyond doubt that their client is guilty? If witnesses are not allowed to lie in court, why should attorneys maintain that privilege? Attorneys are compelled by professional oath to defend their client to the best of their ability. But does that mean misleading the jury?

InfoTrac College Edition Research

Use "Danielle van Dam" and "David Westerfield" as subject guides on InfoTrac College Edition to learn more about this case.

Sources: Harriet Ryan, "Fox Talk Show Host Calls for Disbarment of Westerfield Lawyers," Court TV (www.courttv.com/trials/westerfield/091902_ctv.html), 19 September 2002; Alex Roth, "Experts Make Case for Defense Attorneys," *San Diego Union Tribune,* 22 September 2002; Alex Roth, "Story of Plea Attempt Raises Ire of Many," *San Diego Union Tribune,* 18 September 2002; "Did Westerfield's Attorneys Mislead the Jury?" Fox News (www.foxnews.com/story/0,2933,63596,00.html).

© AP/Wide World Photos

At the completion of a trial, the jury verdict is publicly announced. Here, a packed courtroom in Las Vegas listens as guilty verdicts on all charges for the murder of casino heir Ted Binion are read, May 19, 2000. From left, defense attorney John Momot, defendants Sandy Murphy and Rick Tabish, Tabish's attorney Louis Palazzo, attorney Rob Murdock, and Linda Norvell show little emotion. Prosecutors said Binion was forced to ingest a lethal dose of heroin and the prescription antianxiety drug, Xanax, then was suffocated by Murphy, Binion's live-in girfriend, and Tabish, her lover.

cases but is the rule in federal criminal trials. Unanimity is required with six-person juries. A review of the case by the jury may take hours or even days. The jurors are always sequestered during their deliberations, and in certain lengthy and highly publicized cases, they are kept overnight in a hotel until the verdict is reached. In less sensational cases, the jurors may be allowed to go home, but they are cautioned not to discuss the case with anyone.

If a verdict cannot be reached, the trial may result in a *hung jury,* after which the prosecutor must bring the defendant to trial again if the prosecution desires a conviction. If found not guilty, the defendant is released from the criminal process. If the defendant is convicted, the judge will normally order a presentence investigation by the probation department before imposing a sentence. Before sentencing, the defense attorney will probably submit a motion for a new trial, alleging that legal errors occurred in the trial proceedings. The judge may deny the motion and impose a sentence immediately, a practice quite common in most misdemeanor offenses. In felony cases, however, the judge will set a date for sentencing, and the defendant will either be placed on bail or held in custody until that time.

The Sentence

The imposition of the criminal sentence is normally the responsibility of the trial judge. In some jurisdictions, the jury may determine the sentence or make recommendations involving leniency for certain offenses. Often, the sentencing decision is based on information and recommendations given to the court by the probation department after a presentence investigation of the defendant. The sentence itself is determined by the statutory requirements for the particular crime as established by the legislature; in addition, the judge ordinarily has a great deal of discretion in reaching a sentencing decision. The different criminal sanctions available include fines, probation, imprisonment, and even commitment to a state hospital. The sentence may be a combination of all these. (Sentencing is discussed in detail in Chapter 10.)

The Appeal

Defendants have as many as three possible avenues of appeal: *the direct appeal, postconviction remedy,* and *federal court review.* Both the direct appeal and federal court review provide the convicted person with the opportunity to appeal to a higher state or federal court on the basis of an error that affected the conviction in the trial court. Extraordinary trial court errors, such as the denial of the right to counsel or the inability to provide a fair trial, are subject to the plain error rule of the federal courts.[41] Harmless errors, such as the use of innocuous identification procedures or the denial of counsel at a noncritical stage of the proceeding, would not necessarily result in the overturning of a criminal conviction. A postconviction appeal (or remedy), on the other hand, or what is often referred to as *collateral attack,* takes the form of a legal petition, such as habeas corpus, and is the primary means by which state prisoners have their convictions or sentences reviewed in the federal court. A **writ of habeas corpus** (meaning "you have the body") seeks to determine the validity of a detention by asking the court to release the person or give legal reasons for the incarceration.

In most jurisdictions, direct criminal appeal to an appellate court is a matter of right. This means that the defendant has an automatic right to appeal a conviction based on errors that may have occurred during the trial proceedings. A substantial number of criminal appeals are the result of disputes over points of law, such as the introduction at the trial of illegal evidence detrimental to the defendant or statements made during the trial that were prejudicial to the defendant. Through objections made at the pretrial and trial stages of the criminal process, the defense counsel will reserve specific legal issues on the record as the basis for appeal. A copy of the transcript of these proceedings will serve as the basis on which the appellate court will review any errors that may have occurred during the lower-court proceedings.

Because an appeal is an expensive, time-consuming, and technical process involving a review of the lower-court record, the research and drafting of briefs, and the presentation of oral arguments to the appellate court, the defendant has been granted the right to counsel at this stage of the criminal process. In the 1963 case of *Douglas v. California,* the U.S. Supreme Court held that an indigent defendant has a constitutional right to the assistance of counsel on a direct first appeal.[42] If the defendant appeals to a higher court, the defendant must have private counsel or apply for permission to proceed **in forma pauperis** (meaning "in the manner of a pauper")—that is, the defendant may be granted counsel at public expense if the court believes the appeal has merit. There is no constitutional right to free counsel beyond the first appeal.[43]

After an appeal has been fully heard, the appeals court renders an opinion on the procedures used in the case. If an error of law is found—such as an improper introduction of evidence or an improper statement by the prosecutor that was prejudicial to the defendant—the appeals court may reverse the decision of the trial court and order a new trial. If the lower-court decision is upheld, the case is finished, unless the defendant seeks a discretionary appeal to a higher state or federal court.

writ of habeas corpus A judicial order requesting that a person detaining another produce the body of the prisoner and give reasons for his or her capture and detention. Habeas corpus is a legal device used to request that a judicial body review the reasons for a person's confinement and the conditions of confinement. Habeas corpus is known as "the great writ."

in forma pauperis "In the manner of a pauper." A criminal defendant granted permission to proceed in forma pauperis is entitled to assistance of counsel at state expense.

Over the last decade, criminal appeals have increased significantly in almost every state and the federal courts. Criminal case appeals make up close to 50 percent of the state appellate caseload and over 35 percent of the total federal caseload, which includes prisoner petitions and ordinary criminal appeals. Today, a substantial number of these appeals involve drug-related cases and appeals of sentences where the offender was institutionalized. Most appeals occur after final trial court decisions on convictions and sentencing of the defendant.

Evidentiary Standards

proof beyond a reasonable doubt   The standard of proof needed to convict in a criminal case. The evidence offered in court does not have to amount to absolute certainty, but it should leave no reasonable doubt that the defendant committed the alleged crime.

Proof beyond a reasonable doubt is the standard required to convict a defendant charged with a crime at the adjudicatory stage of the criminal process. This requirement dates back to early American history and over the years has become the accepted measure of persuasion needed by the prosecutor to convince the judge or jury of the defendant's guilt. Many twentieth-century U.S. Supreme Court decisions have reinforced this standard by making "beyond a reasonable doubt a due process and constitutional requirement."[44] In *Brinegar v. United States* (1949), for instance, the Supreme Court stated:

> Guilt in a criminal case must be proven beyond a reasonable doubt and by evidence confined to that which long experience in the common-law tradition, to some extent embodied in the Constitution, has crystallized into rules of evidence consistent with that standard. These rules are historically grounded rights of our system, developed to safeguard men from dubious and unjust convictions with resulting forfeitures of life, liberty, and property.[45]

The reasonable doubt standard is an essential ingredient of the criminal justice process. It is the prime instrument for reducing the risk of convictions based on

---

Exhibit 9.2   Evidentiary standards of proof: Degrees of certainty

Standard	Definition	Ruling
Absolute certainty	No possibility of error; 100% certainty	Not used in civil or criminal law
Beyond reasonable doubt; moral certainty	Conclusive and complete proof, while leaving any reasonable doubt about the innocence or guilt of the defendant; allows the defendant the benefit of any possibility of innocence.	Criminal trial
Clear and convincing evidence	Prevailing and persuasive to the trier of fact	Civil commitments, insanity defense
Preponderance of evidence	Greater weight of evidence in terms of credibility; more convincing than an opposite point of view	Civil trial
Probable cause	U.S. constitutional standard for arrest and search warrants, requiring existence of facts sufficient to warrant that a crime has been committed	Arrest, preliminary hearing, motions
Sufficient evidence	Adequate evidence to reverse a trial court	Appellate review
Reasonable suspicion	Rational, reasonable belief that facts warrant investigations of a crime on less than probable cause	Police investigations
Less than probable cause	Mere suspicion; less than reasonable belief to conclude criminal activity exists	Prudent police investigation where safety of an officer or others is endangered

factual errors.[46] The underlying premise of this standard is that it is better to release a guilty person than to convict someone who is innocent. Since the defendant is presumed innocent until proven guilty, this standard forces the prosecution to overcome this presumption with the highest standard of proof. Unlike the civil law, where a mere **preponderance of the evidence** is the standard, the criminal process requires proof beyond a reasonable doubt for each element of the offense. As the Supreme Court pointed out in *In re Winship* (1970), where the reasonable doubt standard was applied to juvenile trials, "If the standard of proof for a criminal trial were a preponderance of the evidence rather than proof beyond a reasonable doubt, there would be a smaller risk of factual errors that result in freeing guilty persons, but a far greater risk of factual errors that result in convicting the innocent."[47] The various evidentiary standards of proof are analyzed and compared in Exhibit 9.2. ■

preponderance of the evidence The level of proof in civil cases; more than half the evidence supports the allegations of one side.

SUMMARY

The number of cases disposed of by trials is relatively small in comparison with the total number that enter the criminal justice system. Nevertheless, the criminal trial provides the defendant with an important option. Unlike other steps in the system, the U.S. criminal trial allows the accused to assert the right to a day in court. The defendant may choose between a trial before a judge alone or a trial by jury. In either case, the purpose of the trial is to adjudicate the facts, ascertain the truth, and determine the guilt or innocence of the accused.

Criminal trials represent the adversary system at work. The state uses its authority to seek a conviction, and the defendant is protected by constitutional rights, particularly those under the Fifth and Sixth Amendments. When they involve serious crimes, criminal trials are complex legal affairs. Each jurisdiction relies on rules and procedures that have developed over many years to resolve legal issues. As the U.S. Supreme Court has extended the rights of the accused, the procedures have un-

doubtedly contributed to the system's complexities and delays. Some solutions have included smaller juries, more efficient control of police misconduct, and reduced time delays between arrest, indictment, and trial. But the right to a fair trial, trial by jury, and the due process rights to counsel and confrontation also need to be guarded and protected in the twenty-first century.

An established order of steps is followed throughout a criminal trial, beginning with the selection of a jury, proceeding through opening statements and the introduction of evidence, and concluding with closing arguments and a verdict. The criminal trial serves both a symbolic and a pragmatic function for defendants who require a forum of last resort to adjudicate their differences with the state. The trial is the central test of the facts and law involved in a criminal case.

For an up-to-date list of Web links, go to http://cj.wadsworth.com/siegel_essen4e.

KEY TERMS

bench trial 282
verdict 282
adjudication 282
confrontation clause 283
hearsay evidence 283
six-person jury 284

pro se 285
First Amendment 287
venire 292
voir dire 292
challenge for cause 292
peremptory challenge 292

direct examination 294
cross-examination 295
real evidence 295
circumstantial (indirect) evidence 295
directed verdict 295

charge 296
writ of habeas corpus 299
in forma pauperis 299
proof beyond a reasonable doubt 300
preponderance of the evidence 300

INFOTRAC COLLEGE EDITION EXERCISES

G. K. CHESTERTON, the great English author, said this on the issue of juries: "Our civilization has decided that determining the guilt or innocence of men is a thing too important to be trusted to trained men. When it wants a library catalogued, or the solar system discovered, or any trifle of that kind, it uses wise specialists. But when it wishes anything done which is really serious, it collects twelve of the ordinary men standing around."

What is the meaning of Chesterton's statement? Should the justice system employ professional jurors? Use InfoTrac College Edition to find articles about juries that would help you understand Chesterton's statement. Use key words such as "jury trial," "jury selection," and "peremptory challenge."

QUESTIONS

1. What are the steps involved in the criminal trial?

2. What are the pros and cons of a jury trial versus a bench trial?

3. What are the legal rights of the defendant in a trial process?

4. Should people be denied the right to serve as jurors without explanation or cause? In other words, should the peremptory challenge be maintained?

5. "In the adversary system of criminal justice, the burden of proof in a criminal trial to show that the defendant is guilty beyond a reasonable doubt is on the government." Explain the meaning of this statement.

NOTES

1. U.S. Constitution, Sixth Amendment.
2. *Lilly v. Virginia,* 98-5881 (1999).
3. *Pointer v. State of Texas,* 380 U.S. 400, 85 S.Ct. 1065, 13 L.Ed.2d 923 (1965).
4. *Maryland v. Craig,* 497 U.S. 836, 110 S.Ct. 3157, 111 L.Ed.2d 666 (1990).
5. *Duncan v. Louisiana,* 391 U.S. 145, 88 S.Ct. 1444, 20 L.Ed.2d 491 (1968).
6. Ibid., at S.Ct. at 1451–1452.
7. *Baldwin v. New York,* 399 U.S. 66, 90 S.Ct. 1886, 26 L.Ed.2d 437 (1970).
8. *Blanton v. North Las Vegas,* 489 U.S. 538, 109 S.Ct. 1289, 103 L.Ed.2d 550 (1989).
9. *Lewis v. United States,* 116 S.Ct. 2163 (1996).
10. *Williams v. Florida,* 399 U.S. 78, 90 S.Ct. 1893, 26 L.Ed.2d 446 (1970).
11. Ibid., at 101, 90 S.Ct. at 1906.
12. *Apodica v. Oregon,* 406 U.S. 404, 92 S.Ct. 1628, 32 L.Ed.2d 184 (1972).
13. *Scott v. Illinois,* 440 U.S. 367, 99 S.Ct. 1158, 59 L.Ed.2d 383 (1979).
14. *Shelton v. Alabama,* 122 U.S. 1764 (2002).
15. *Shelton* (quoting *Argersinger v. Hamlin,* 407 U.S. 25, 40 [1972]).
16. *Faretta v. California,* 422 U.S. 806, 95 S.Ct. 2525, 45 L.Ed.2d 562 (1975).
17. *Martinez v. Court of Appeal of California,* 120 S.Ct. 684 (2000).
18. See American Bar Association, *Standards Relating to Speedy Trial* (Chicago: ABA, 1995).
19. *Klopfer v. North Carolina,* 386 U.S. 213, 87 S.Ct. 988, 18 L.Ed.2d 1 (1967).
20. Ibid., at 223, 87 S.Ct. at 993.
21. *Doggett v. United States,* 505 U.S. 162, 112 S.Ct. 2686, 120 L.Ed.2d 520 (1992).
22. *Estelle v. Williams,* 425 U.S. 501, 96 S.Ct. 1691, 48 L.Ed.2d 126 (1976); see also American Bar Association, "Fair Trial and Free Press," in *Standards for Criminal Justice* (Washington, D.C.: ABA, 1993).
23. *Wilson et al. v. Layne,* Public Law No. 98-83 (1999).
24. *Nebraska Press Association v. Stuart,* 427 U.S. 539, 96 S.Ct. 2791, 49 L.Ed.2d 683 (1976).
25. Ibid., at 547, 96 S.Ct. at 2797.
26. *Gannett Co. v. DePasquale,* 443 U.S. 368, 99 S.Ct. 2898, 61 L.Ed.2d 608 (1979).
27. Ibid., at 370, 99 S.Ct at 2900.
28. *Press-Enterprise Co. v. Superior Court,* 478 U.S. 1, 106 S.Ct. 2735, 92 L.Ed.2d 1 (1986).
29. Nicholas A. Pellegrini, "Extension of Criminal Defendant's Right to Public Trial," *St. John's University Law Review 611* (1987): 277–289.
30. *In re Oliver,* 333 U.S. 257, 68 S.Ct. 499, 92 L.Ed. 682 (1948).
31. *Richmond Newspapers, Inc. v. Virginia,* 448 U.S. 555, 100 S.Ct. 2814, 65 L.Ed.2d 973 (1980).
32. *Globe Newspaper Co. v. Superior Court for County of Norfolk,* 457 U.S. 596, 102 S.Ct. 2613, 73 L.Ed.2d 248 (1982).
33. *Chandler v. Florida,* 449 U.S. 560 (1981); see also American Bar Association, *Criminal Justice Standards, Fair Trial, and Free Press* (Washington, D.C.: ABA, 1992).

34. Conference of State Court Administrators, *State Court Organization, 1987* (Williamsburg, Va.: National Center for State Courts, 1988), 10.

35. George Hayden, Joseph Senna, and Larry Siegel, "Prosecutorial Discretion in Peremptory Challenges: An Empirical Investigation of Information Use in the Massachusetts Jury Selection Process," *New England Law Review 13* (1978): 768.

36. *Batson v. Kentucky,* 476 U.S. 79, 106 S.Ct. 1712, 90 L.Ed.2d 69 (1986); see also Alan Alschuler and Randall Kennedy, "Equal Justice—Would Color-Conscious Jury Selection Help?" *American Bar Association Journal 81* (1995): 36–37.

37. *Powers v. Ohio,* 479 U.S. 400, 111 S.Ct. 1364, 113 L.Ed.2d 411 (1991).

38. *J.E.B. v. Alabama,* 511 U.S. 114 S.Ct. 1419, 128 L.Ed.2d 89 (1994).

39. Charles Ogletree, "Just Say No! A Proposal to Eliminate Racially Discriminatory Uses of Peremptory Challenges," *American Criminal Law Review 31* (1994): 1099–1151; see also Hiroshi Fukurai, "Race, Social Class, and Jury Participation: New Dimensions for Evaluating Discrimination in Jury Service," *Journal of Criminal Justice 24* (1996): 71–78.

40. See Charles McCormick, Frank Elliott, and John Sutton Jr., *Evidence—Cases and Materials* (St. Paul, Minn.: West, 1981), chap. 1.

41. *Chapman v. California,* 386 U.S. 18, 87 S.Ct. 824, 17 L.Ed.2d 705 (1967).

42. *Douglas v. California,* 372 U.S. 353, 83 S.Ct. 814, 9 L.Ed.2d 811 (1963).

43. *Ross v. Moffitt,* 417 U.S. 600, 94 S.Ct. 2437, 41 L.Ed.2d 341 (1974).

44. See *Brinegar v. United States,* 338 U.S. 160, 69 S.Ct. 1302, 93 L.Ed. 1879 (1949); *In re Winship,* 397 U.S. 358, 90 S.Ct. 1068, 25 L.Ed.2d 368 (1970).

45. Ibid., at 174.

46. See *In re Winship,* at 397.

47. Ibid., at 371, 90 S.Ct. at 1076.

10 Punishment and Sentencing

Criminal Justice Links

Criminal Justice Viewpoints

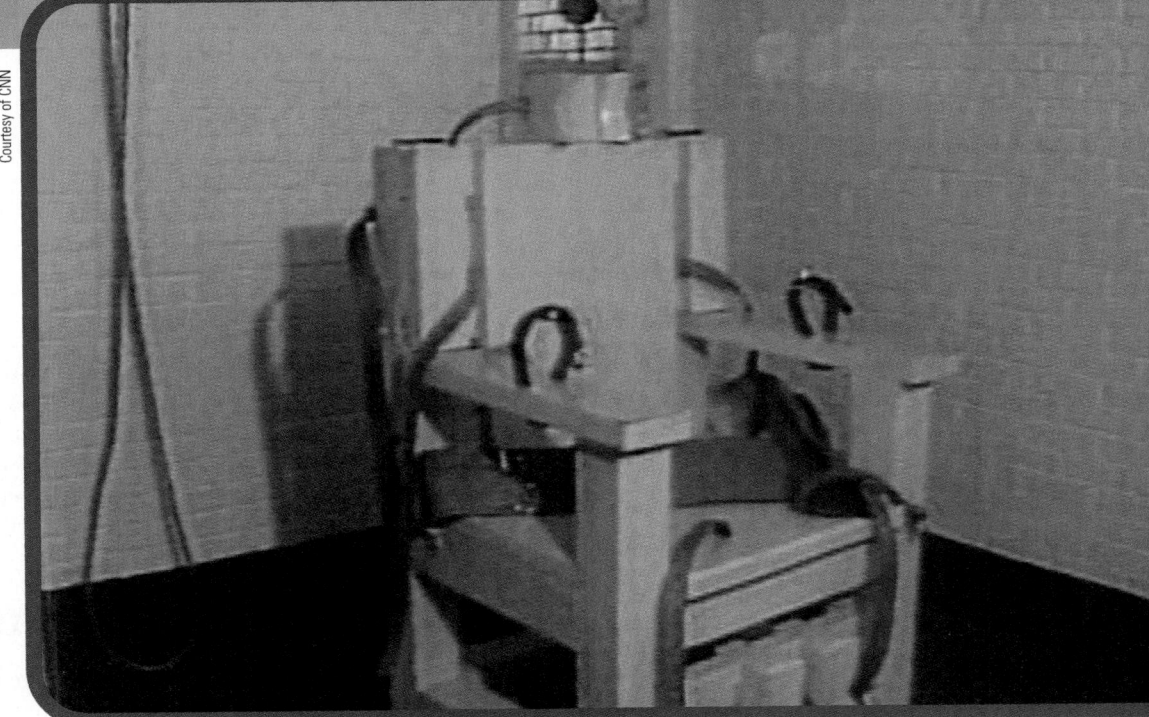

Courtesy of CNN

THE YEARS ON DEATH ROW had brought peace to Willie Ervin Fisher. In the hours before his execution on March 9, 2001, Fisher spent his time comforting his sister, Sally Fisher-Ervin, and his niece, Regina Fisher, who had come to visit him at Raleigh's Central Prison, that he wasn't worried about dying. "He's not ready to leave," Sally said her brother told her, "but if he has to, he's in God's hands, and he'll be fine." Willie Fisher, convicted of killing his girlfriend Angela Johnson, was able to face death at age thirty-nine with faith-filled confidence. "He didn't cry at all," Regina said. The murder of Johnson happened after Fisher, the youngest of nine children, had abused alcohol and crack cocaine. All who knew Fisher claimed he had never been violent prior to the day of the murder. Sally said her brother was always "an easygoing, sweet person. He was a mama's boy."[1]

(CNN) *To view the CNN video clip of this story, go to the book-specific Web site at* http://cj.wadsworth.com/siegel_essen4e.

Should someone like Willie Fisher be executed for committing a single violent act in an otherwise nonviolent life? Should the fact that he was a substance abuser be taken into account? Would your answer be different if you knew that his attorney was disbarred soon after his trial? Yet the story of Willie Fisher is not unique and thousands of people remain on death row today. How may are innocent? How many deserve to be put to death? Should the death penalty be retained as a common criminal punishment?

Historically, a full range of punishments has been inflicted on criminal defendants, including physical torture, branding, whipping, and for most felony offenses, death. During the Middle Ages, the philosophy of punishment was to "torment the body for the sins of the soul."[2] People who violated the law were considered morally corrupt and in need of strong discipline. If punishment was harsh enough, it was assumed, they would never repeat their mistakes. Punishment was also viewed as a spectacle that taught a moral lesson. The more gruesome and public the sentence, the greater the impact it would have on the local

Is torture still being used today? To find out, use "torture" as a subject guide on InfoTrac College Edition.

populace.[3] Harsh physical punishments would control any thoughts of rebellion and dissent against the central government and those who held political and economic control. Such barbaric use of state power is, of course, not tolerated in the United States today.

The controversy over punishment involves both its nature and extent: Are too many people being sent to prison?[4] Do people get widely different sentences for very similar crimes?[5] Is there discrimination in sentencing based on race, gender, or social class?[6] These are but a few of the most significant issues in the sentencing process.

This chapter first examines the history of punishment and then focuses on incarceration and capital punishment, the two most traditional and punitive forms of criminal sanctions used today. Chapter 11 reviews alternative sentences that have been developed to reduce the strain on the overburdened correctional system; these sentences provide intermediate sanctions designed to control people whose behavior and personality make incarceration unnecessary. Such sanctions include probation and other forms of community correction.

The History of Punishment

The punishment and correction of criminals has changed considerably through the ages, reflecting custom, economic conditions, and religious and political ideals.[7]

From Exile to Fines, Torture to Forfeiture

In early Greece and Rome, the most common state-administered punishment was banishment, or exile. Only slaves were commonly subjected to harsh physical punishment for their misdeeds. Interpersonal violence, even attacks that resulted in death, were viewed as a private matter. These ancient peoples typically used eco-

The Granger Collection, New York

In earlier times, punishment was quite severe. Even kings, such as Charles I of England, were not immune from death by beheading.

nomic punishments, such as fines, for such crimes as assault on a slave, arson, or housebreaking.

During the Middle Ages (the fifth to thirteenth centuries), there was little law or governmental control. Offenses were settled by blood feuds carried out by the families of the injured parties. When possible, the Roman custom of settling disputes by fine or an exchange of property was adopted as a means of resolving interpersonal conflicts with a minimum of bloodshed. After the eleventh century, during the feudal period, forfeiture of land and property was common punishment for persons who violated law and custom or who failed to fulfill their feudal obligations to their lord. The word *felony* actually has its origins in the twelfth century, when the term *felonia* referred to a breach of faith with one's feudal lord.

During this period the main emphasis of criminal law and punishment was on maintaining public order. If in the heat of passion or while intoxicated a person severely injured or killed his neighbor, freemen in the area would gather to pronounce a judgment and make the culprit do penance or pay compensation called **wergild**. The purpose of the fine was to pacify the injured party and ensure that the conflict would not develop into a blood feud and anarchy. The inability of the peasantry to pay a fine led to the use of corporal punishment, such as whipping or branding, as a substitute penalty.

The development of the common law in the eleventh century brought some standardization to penal practices. However, corrections remained an amalgam of fines and brutal physical punishments. The criminal wealthy could buy their way out of punishment and into exile, but capital and corporal punishment were used to control the criminal poor, who were executed and mutilated at ever-increasing rates. Execution, banishment, mutilation, branding, and flogging were used on a whole range of offenders, from murderers and robbers to vagrants and Gypsies. Punishments became unmatched in their cruelty, featuring a gruesome variety of physical tortures, often part of a public spectacle, presumably so that the sadistic sanctions would act as deterrents. But the variety and imagination of the tortures inflicted on even minor criminals before their death suggest that retribution, sadism, and spectacle were more important than any presumed deterrent effect.

wergild Under medieval law, the money paid by the offender to compensate the victim and the state for a criminal offense.

The trial and execution of William Wallace was popularized by Mel Gibson in the film *Braveheart*. The actual execution was a textbook case of medieval punishment. Read about it at www.lawbuzz.com/justice/braveheart/betrayed.htm

Public Work and Transportation to the Colonies

By the end of the sixteenth century, the rise of the city and overseas colonization provided tremendous markets for manufactured goods and spurred the need for labor. Punishment of criminals changed to meet the demands created by these social conditions. Instead of being tortured or executed, many offenders were made to do hard labor for their crimes. *Poor laws*, developed at the end of the sixteenth century, required that the poor, vagrants, and vagabonds be put to work in public or private enterprises. Houses of correction were developed to make it convenient to assign petty law violators to work details. In London a workhouse was developed at Brideswell in 1557; its use became so popular that by 1576 Parliament ordered a Brideswell-type workhouse to be built in every county in England. Many convicted offenders were pressed into sea duty as galley slaves. Galley slavery was considered a fate so loathsome that many convicts mutilated themselves rather than submit to servitude on the high seas.

The constant shortage of labor in the European colonies also prompted authorities to transport convicts overseas. In England, an Order in Council of 1617 granted a reprieve and stay of execution to people convicted of robbery and other felonies who were strong enough to be employed overseas. Similar measures were used in France and Italy to recruit galley slaves and workers.

Transporting convicts to the colonies became popular: it supplied labor, cost little, and was actually profitable for the government, since manufacturers and plantation owners paid for the convicts' services. The Old Bailey Court in London supplied at least ten thousand convicts between 1717 and 1775. Convicts would serve a period as workers and then become free again.

The American Revolution ended the transportation of felons to North America, but it continued in Australia and New Zealand. Between 1787 and 1875, when the practice was finally abandoned, over 135,000 felons were transported to Australia.

Although transportation in lieu of a death sentence may at first glance seem advantageous, transported prisoners endured enormous hardships. Those who were sent to Australia suffered incredible physical abuse, including severe whippings and mutilation. Many of the British prison officials placed in charge of the Australian penal colonies could best be described as sociopaths, or sadists.

The Rise of the Prison

Between the American Revolution in 1776 and the first decades of the nineteenth century, the European and U.S. populations increased rapidly. Transportation of convicts to North America was no longer an option. The increased use of machinery made industry capital-intensive, not labor-intensive. As a result, there was less need for unskilled laborers in England, and many workers could not find suitable employment.

The gulf between poor workers and wealthy landowners and merchants widened. The crime rate rose significantly, prompting a return to physical punishment and increased use of the death penalty. During the later part of the eighteenth century, 350 types of crime in England were punishable by death. Although many people sentenced to death for trivial offenses were spared the gallows, the use of capital punishment was extremely common in England during the mid-eighteenth century. Prompted by the excessive use of physical and capital punishment, legal philosophers argued that physical punishment should be replaced by periods of confinement and incapacitation. Jails and workhouses were thus used to hold petty offenders, vagabonds, the homeless, and debtors. However, these institutions were not meant for hard-core criminals. One solution to imprisoning a growing criminal population was to keep prisoners in abandoned ships anchored in rivers and harbors throughout England. In 1777, the degradation under which prisoners lived in these ships inspired John Howard, the sheriff of Bedfordshire, to write *The State of the Prisons in England and Wales,* which led to Parliament's passage of legislation mandating the construction of secure and sanitary structures to house prisoners.

penitentiary A state or federal correctional institution for incarceration of felony offenders for terms of one year or more.

By 1820 long periods of incarceration in walled institutions called reformatories or **penitentiaries** began to replace physical punishment in England and the United States. These institutions were considered liberal reforms during a time when harsh physical punishment and incarceration in filthy holding facilities were the norm. The history of correctional institutions will be discussed further in Chapter 12. Incarceration has remained the primary mode of punishment for serious offenses in the United States since it was introduced in the early nineteenth century. Ironically in our high-tech society, some of the institutions developed soon after the Revolutionary War are still in use today. In recent times, prison as a method of punishment has been supplemented by a sentence to community supervision for less serious offenders, and the death penalty is reserved for those considered to be the most serious and dangerous.

The Goals of Modern Sentencing

When we hear about a notorious criminal—such as serial killers Jeffrey Dahmer and Ted Bundy—receiving a long prison sentence or the death penalty for a particularly heinous crime, each of us has a distinct reaction. Some of us are gratified that a truly evil person "got just what he deserved"; many people feel safer because a dangerous person is now "where he can't harm any other innocent victims"; others hope the punishment serves as a warning to potential criminals that "everyone gets caught in the end"; some may actually feel sorry for the defendant—"He got a raw deal, he needs help, not punishment"; and still others hope that "when he gets out, he'll have learned his lesson." And when an offender is forced to pay a large fine, we say, "What goes around comes around."

Each of these sentiments may be at work when criminal sentences are formulated. After all, sentences are devised and implemented by judges, many of whom are elected officials and share the general public's sentiments and fears. The objectives of criminal sentencing today can usually be grouped into six distinct areas: *general deterrence, incapacitation, specific deterrence, retribution/just desert, rehabilitation,* and *equity/restitution.*

General Deterrence

What is the impact on the community when a criminal offender is punished? By punishing an offender severely, the state can demonstrate its determination to control crime and deter potential offenders. Too lenient a sentence might encourage criminal conduct; too severe a sentence might reduce the system's ability to dispense fair and impartial justice and may actually encourage criminality. For example, if the crime of rape were punished by death, rapists might be encouraged to kill their victims to dispose of the one person who could identify them; since they would already be facing the death penalty for rape, they would have nothing more to lose. Maintaining a balance between fear and justice is an ongoing quest in the justice system.

Sentencing for the purposes of **general deterrence,** then, is designed to give a signal to the community at large: *crime does not pay!* Some justice experts attribute the recent decline in the crime rate to the fact that criminal penalties have been toughened for many crimes; once arrested, people have a greater chance of being convicted now than they did in the past. This is referred to as "expected punishment," which is defined as the number of days in prison a typical criminal can expect to serve per crime, as determined by the probabilities of being apprehended, prosecuted, convicted, and going to prison, and the median months served for each crime.[8] According to the National Center for Policy Analysis (NCPA), a conservative think tank, crime rates dropped dramatically between 1980 and 1997 because expected punishment rose:

- For murder, punishment nearly tripled, from fourteen months to forty-one months.
- For rape it tripled to 128 days.
- For robbery it increased by 70 percent to 59 days.
- For serious assault it more than doubled to 18 days.
- For burglary it more than doubled from 4 days to 9 days.

Despite these increases, expected punishment is still quite low because most criminals are never apprehended and many that are have their cases dropped; still others are given probationary rather than prison sentences. For example, NCPA figures indicate that for every one hundred burglaries, only about seven are cleared by arrest and less than two convicted burglars are sentenced to prison.[9] Such inefficiency limits the deterrent effect of punishment. Other people may be too desperate or psychologically impaired by drugs and alcohol to be deterred by the threat of distant criminal punishment, or their economic circumstances may be too dire for the threat of punishment to have an effect. Nonetheless, some experts believe that severe and draconian sentences can eventually bring down crime rates. They call for a get-tough policy featuring long, mandatory prison terms with little chance for early release.

general deterrence A crime control policy that depends on the fear of criminal penalties. General deterrence measures, such as long prison sentences for violent crimes, are aimed at convincing the potential law violator that the pains associated with the crime outweigh the benefits.

Would increasing the severity of punishment deter more crimes? To find out, read Silvia M. Mendes and Michael D. McDonald, "Putting Severity of Punishment Back in the Deterrence Package," *Policy Studies Journal,* Winter 2001 v29 i4 p588(23), on InfoTrac College Edition.

incapacitation   The policy of keeping dangerous criminals in confinement to eliminate the risk of their repeating their offense in society.

Which has a greater crime-reducing effect, deterrence or incapacitation? Read Steven D. Lewitt, "Why Do Increased Arrest Rates Appear to Reduce Crime: Deterrence, Incapacitation, or Measurement Error?" *Economic Inquiry,* July 1998 v36 i3 p353(20), on InfoTrac College Edition.

recidivism   Repetition of criminal behavior; habitual criminality. Recidivism is measured by (1) criminal acts that resulted in conviction by a court when committed by individuals who are under correctional supervision or who had been released from correctional supervision within the previous three years and (2) technical violations of probation or parole in which a sentencing or paroling authority took action that resulted in an adverse change in the offender's legal status.

specific deterrence   A crime control policy suggesting that punishment should be severe enough to convince convicted offenders never to repeat their criminal activity.

blameworthy   The culpability or guilt a person maintains for participating in a particular criminal offense.

just desert   The philosophy of justice asserting that those who violate the rights of others deserve to be punished. The severity of punishment should be commensurate with the seriousness of the crime.

Incapacitation

If an offender is a risk to society, he may be sentenced to a period of secure confinement. **Incapacitation** of criminals is a justifiable goal of sentencing because inmates will not be able to repeat their criminal acts while they are under state control. For some offenders, this means a period in a high-security state prison where behavior is closely monitored. Fixing sentence length involves determining how long a particular offender needs to be incarcerated to ensure that society is protected.

To some critics, incapacitation strategies seem of questionable utility because little association seems to exist between the number of criminals behind bars and the crime rate. Although the prison population jumped between 1980 and 1990, the crime rate also increased. This indicates that crime rates have little to do with incarceration trends and that reductions in crime are related to other factors, such as population makeup, police effectiveness, declining drug use, a strong economy, and other unrelated factors.

In contrast, those who favor an incapacitation policy claim that the crime-reducing effect of putting people in prison has just taken a little longer than expected. The number of people and percentage of the general population behind bars escalated rapidly between 1990 and 2001, and the crime rate fell. This correlation is not a mere coincidence but a true incapacitation effect.

Specific Deterrence

Experiencing harsh criminal punishments should convince convicted offenders that crime does not pay and **recidivism** is not in their best interests. The suffering caused by punishment should inhibit future law violations. A few research efforts have found that punishment can have significant specific deterrence on future criminality, but they are balanced by research that has failed to find specific deterrence effects. For example, in their study of the effect of punishment on spousal abusers, Robert Davis and his associates also found little association between severity of punishment for past spousal abuse and rearrest on subsequent charges. Men were just as likely to recidivate if their case was dismissed, if they were given probation, or even if they were sent to jail.[10] A similar analysis conducted by Christopher Maxwell and his associates found that arresting batterers had only a modest effect on reducing subsequent aggression against female intimate partners.[11] The effect of **specific deterrence** is further undermined by data showing that most inmates (more than 80 percent) who are released from prison have had prior convictions, and the great majority (68 percent) will re-offend soon after their release. A prison stay seems to have little effect on their re-offending.[12]

Retribution/Just Desert

According to the retributive goal of sentencing, the essential purpose of the criminal process is to punish deserving offenders—fairly and justly—in a manner that is proportionate to the gravity of their crimes.[13]

Offenders are punished simply and solely because they deserve to be disciplined for what they have done; "the punishment should fit the crime."[14] It would be wrong to punish people to set an example for others or to deter would-be criminals, as the general deterrence goal demands. Punishment should be no more or less than the offender's actions deserve; it must be based on how **blameworthy** the person is. This is referred to as the concept of **just desert**.[15]

According to this view, punishments must be equally and fairly distributed to all people who commit similar illegal acts. Determining just punishments can be difficult because there is generally little consensus about the treatment of criminals, the seriousness of crimes, and the proper response to criminal acts. Nonetheless, there has been an ongoing effort to calculate fair and just sentences by creating guidelines to control judicial decision making. This effort will be discussed in greater detail later in the chapter.

Rehabilitation

Can criminal offenders be effectively treated so that they can eventually readjust to society? It may be fairer to offer offenders an opportunity for rehabilitation rather than harsh criminal punishments. In a sense, society has failed criminal offenders, many of whom have grown up in disorganized neighborhoods and dysfunctional families. They may have been the target of biased police officers; and once arrested and labeled, the offender is placed at a disadvantage at home, at school, and in the job market.[16] Society is therefore obligated to help these unfortunate people who, through no fault of their own, experience social and emotional problems that are often the root of their criminal behavior.

The rehabilitation aspect of sentencing is based on a prediction of the future needs of the offender, not on the gravity of the current offense. For example, if a judge sentences a person convicted of a felony to a period of community supervision, the judge's actions reflect her belief that the offender can be successfully treated and presents no future threat to society. This faith is supported by studies showing that under the right circumstances rehabilitation efforts can be effective.[17]

© AP/Wide World Photos

Should a person's age or gender affect sentencing decisions? Faye Copeland, the nation's oldest woman on death row, is now seventy-eight. Copeland's death sentence was commuted to life in prison by a federal judge on August 10, 1999. She was convicted with her husband, Ray, of the murder of five men in a livestock swindle deal.

The rehabilitation goal of sentencing has also been criticized by those who find little conclusive evidence exists that correctional treatment programs can prevent future criminality.[18] Although the rehabilitative ideal has been undermined by such attacks, surveys indicate that the general public still supports the treatment goal of sentencing.[19] Many people express preferences for programs that are treatment-oriented, such as early childhood intervention and services for at-risk children, rather than those that espouse strict punishment and incarceration policies.[20]

Equity/Restitution

Because criminals gain from their misdeeds, it seems both fair and just to demand that they reimburse society for its loss caused by their crimes. In the early common law, wergild and fines represented the concept of creating an equitable solution to crime by requiring the convicted offender to make restitution to both the victim and the state. Today, judges continue to require that offenders pay victims for their losses.

The **equity** goal of punishment means that convicted criminals must pay back their victims for their loss, the justice system for the costs of processing their case, and society for any disruption they may have caused. In a so-called victimless crime such as drug trafficking, the social costs might include the expense of drug enforcement efforts, drug treatment centers, and care for infants born to drug-addicted mothers. In predatory crimes, the costs might include the services of emergency room doctors, lost workdays and productivity, and treatment for long-term psychological problems. To help defray these costs, convicted offenders might be required to pay a fine, forfeit the property they acquired through illegal gain, do community service work, make financial restitution to their victim, and

equity The action or practice of awarding each person his or her just due; sanctions based on equity seek to compensate individual victims and the general society for their losses due to crime.

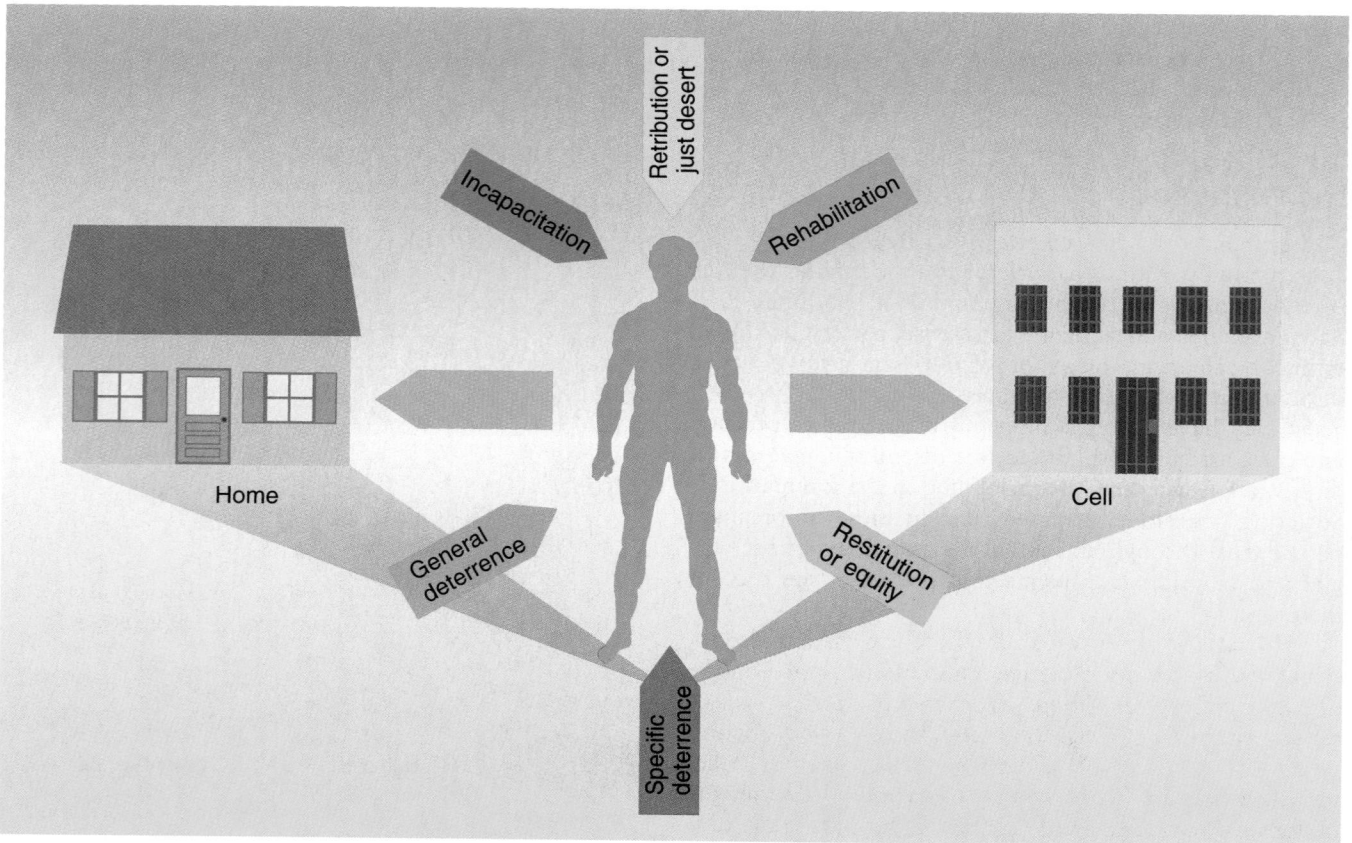

Figure 10.1
The goals behind sentencing decisions

reimburse the state for the costs of the criminal process. Because the criminals' actions helped expand their personal gains, rights, and privileges at society's expense, justice demands that they lose rights and privileges to restore the social balance.

Each factor that influences sentencing decisions is illustrated in Figure 10.1.

Imposing the Sentence

Regardless of the factors that influence the sentence, it is generally imposed by the judge, and sentencing is one of the most crucial functions of judgeship. Sentencing authority may also be exercised by the jury, or it may be mandated by statute (for example, a mandatory prison sentence for a certain crime).

In most felony cases, except where the law provides for mandatory prison terms, sentencing is usually based on a variety of information available to the judge. Some jurisdictions allow victims to make impact statements that are considered at sentencing hearings. Most judges also consider a presentence investigation report by the probation department in making a sentencing decision. This report is a social and personal history, as well as an evaluation of the defendant's chances for rehabilitation within the community. Some judges give the presentence investigation report great weight; others may dismiss it completely or rely on only certain portions.

When an accused is convicted of two or more charges, he must be sentenced on each charge. If the sentences are concurrent, they begin the same day and are

Example: In state X	Consecutive sentence	Concurrent sentence
1. Rape is punishable by 10 years in prison	Rape + possession of a handgun + possession of heroin	Rape + possession of a handgun + possession of heroin
2. Possession of a handgun by 3 years	10 + 3 + 4 = 17 years (each sentence must be served)	10 years (all sentences served simultaneously)
3. Possession of heroin by 4 years		

Figure 10.2
Consecutive versus concurrent sentences

completed when the longest term has been served. For example, a defendant is convicted of burglarizing an apartment and assaulting its occupant; he is sentenced to three years on a charge of assault and ten years for burglary, with the sentences to be served concurrently. After ten years in prison, the sentences would be completed.

In contrast, receiving a **consecutive sentence** means that on completion of the sentence for one crime the offender begins serving time for the second of multiple crimes. If the defendant in the previous example had been sentenced consecutively, he would serve three years on the assault charge and then ten years for the burglary. Therefore, the total term on the two charges would be thirteen years. **Concurrent sentences** are the norm; consecutive sentences are requested for the most serious criminals and for those who are unwilling to cooperate with authorities. Figure 10.2 shows the difference between a consecutive and concurrent sentence.

consecutive sentence A prison sentence for two or more criminal acts that are served one after the other, or that follow one another.

concurrent sentence A prison sentence for two or more criminal acts that are served simultaneously, and run together.

Sentencing Models

When a convicted offender is sentenced to prison, the statutes of the jurisdiction in which the crime was committed determine the penalties that may be imposed by the court. Over the years, a variety of sentencing structures have been used in the United States. They include indeterminate sentences, determinate sentences, and mandatory sentences.

Indeterminate Sentences

In the 1870s, prison reformers such as Enoch Wines and Zebulon Brockway, called for creation of **indeterminate sentences,** tailored to fit individual needs. Offenders, the argument went, should only be placed in confinement until they are rehabilitated and then released on parole. Criminals were believed to be "sick" rather than bad; they could be successfully treated in prison. Rather than holding that "the punishment should fit the crime," reformers believed "the treatment should fit the offender."

The indeterminate sentence is still the most widely used type of sentence in the United States. Convicted offenders are typically given a "light" minimum sentence that must be served and a lengthy maximum sentence that is the outer boundary of the time that can be served. For example, the legislature might set a sentence of a minimum of three years and a maximum of twenty years for burglary; the convicted offender must be sentenced to no less than three years but no more than twenty years in prison. Under this scheme, the actual length of time served by the offender is controlled by both the judge and the correctional agency. A judge could sentence a burglar to between three and twenty years. The inmate could then be paroled from confinement soon after serving the minimum sentence if the correctional authorities believe that she is ready to live in the community. If the inmate

indeterminate sentence A term of incarceration with a stated minimum and maximum length, such as a sentence to prison for a period of from three to ten years. The prisoner would be eligible for parole after the minimum sentence has been served. Based on the belief that sentences should fit the criminal, indeterminate sentences allow individualized sentences and provide for sentencing flexibility. Judges can set a high minimum to override the purpose of the indeterminate sentence.

© 2002 AP/Wide World Photos

The indeterminate sentence is considered the heart of the rehabilitation/treatment model of justice. Even those who commit the most heinous crimes may one day be released from prison if they can prove they have rehabilitated themselves. Here, Michael Skakel, center, is escorted by court officials as he departs the Norwalk, Connecticut, courthouse, August 29, 2002, at the conclusion of the second day of his sentencing hearing. Skakel, a nephew of Ethel Kennedy, was convicted in June 2002 of beating Martha Moxley to death with a golf club when they were fifteen years old. He was sentenced to twenty years to life for the crime.

accumulates good time, she could be released in eighteen months; a troublesome inmate would be forced to do all twenty years.

The basic purpose of the indeterminate sentence is to individualize each sentence in the interests of rehabilitating the offender. This type of sentencing allows for flexibility not only in the type of sentence to be imposed but also in the length of time to be served.

Most jurisdictions that use indeterminate sentences employ statutes that specify minimum and maximum terms but allow judicial discretion to fix the actual sentence within those limits. The typical minimum sentence is at least one year; a few state jurisdictions require at least a two-year minimum sentence for felons.[21]

Determinate Sentences

The indeterminate sentence has come under attack in recent years for a variety of reasons. It is alleged to produce great disparity in the way people are treated in the correctional system. For example, one offender may serve one year and another may serve twenty years, both for the same crime. Further, the indeterminate sentence is believed to take control of sentencing out of the hands of the judiciary and place it within the framework of corrections, especially when the minimum sentence is quite short. Every time an inmate who is granted early release via discretionary parole commits a violent crime, the call goes up to get tough on prison inmates. In contrast, many inmates feel cheated by the system when they are denied parole despite having a good prison record. The protections of due process maintained in the courtroom are absent in the correctional setting. Dissatisfaction with the disparity and uncertainty of indeterminate sentencing has prompted some states and the federal government to abandon it in favor of *determinate sentencing models* or *structured sentencing models* (discussed in the next section).

Determinate sentences, actually the first kind used in the United States, are today employed in about ten jurisdictions. As originally conceived, a determinate sentence was a fixed term of years, the maximum set in law by the legislature, to be served by the offender sentenced to prison for a particular crime. For example, if the law provided for a sentence of up to twenty years for robbery, the judge might sentence a repeat offender to a fifteen-year term; another less-experienced felon might receive a more lenient sentence of five years.

Although determinate sentences provide a single term of years to be served without benefit of parole, the actual time spent in prison is reduced by the implementation of "time off for good behavior." This concept was first used in 1817 in New York, and it was quickly adopted in most other jurisdictions. Good time is still in use today; inmates can accrue *standard good time* at a rate ranging from ten to fifteen days per month. In addition, some correctional authorities grant *earned sentence reductions* to inmates who participate in treatment programs, such as educational and vocational training, or who volunteer for experimental medical testing programs. More than half of a determinate sentence can be erased by accumulating both standard and earned good time.

Good-time laws allow inmates to calculate their release date at the time they enter prison by subtracting the expected good time from their sentence. However, good time can be lost if inmates break prison rules, get into fights, or disobey correctional officers. In some jurisdictions, former inmates can be returned to prison to serve the balance of their unexpired sentence when their good time is revoked for failing to conform to conditions set down for their release (for example, not reporting to a postrelease supervisor or abusing drugs).

determinate sentence　A fixed term of incarceration, such as three years' imprisonment. Determinate sentences are felt by many to be too restrictive for rehabilitative purposes; the advantage is that offenders know how much time they have to serve—that is, when they will be released.

Structural Sentences

Coinciding with the development of determinate sentencing has been the development of sentencing guidelines to control and structure the process and make it more rational. Guidelines are usually based on the seriousness of a crime and the background of an offender: The more serious the crime and the more extensive the offender's criminal background, the longer the prison term recommended by the guidelines. For example, guidelines might require that all people convicted of robbery who had no prior offense record and who did not use excessive force or violence be given an average of a five-year sentence; those who used force and had a prior record will have three years added to their sentence. By eliminating judicial discretion, they are designed to reduce racial and gender disparity.[22] Exhibit 10.1 lists some of the goals of sentencing guidelines.

Exhibit 10.1 **The goals of sentencing guidelines**

- Reduce judicial disparity in sentencing.
- Promote more uniform and consistent sentencing.
- Project the amount of correctional resources needed.
- Prioritize and allocate correctional resources.
- Increase punishments for certain categories of offenders and offenses.
- Decrease punishment for certain categories of offenders and offenses.
- Establish truth in sentencing.

- Make the sentencing process more open and understandable.
- Encourage the use of particular sanctions for particular categories of offenders.
- Encourage increased use of nonincarceration sanctions (intermediate and community-based).
- Reduce prison crowding.
- Provide a rational basis for sentencing.
- Increase judicial accountability.

Source: Robin Lubitz and Thomas Ross, *Sentencing Guidelines: Reflections on the Future* (Washington, D.C.: National Institute of Justice, June 2001).

How Are Guidelines Used?   Today, about eighteen states use some form of structured sentencing. About seven states employ *voluntary/advisory sentencing guidelines* (sometimes called descriptive guidelines), which merely suggest rather than mandate sentencing. In the other states, *presumptive sentencing guidelines* (sometimes called prescriptive guidelines) are used. These require judges to use the guidelines to shape their sentencing decisions, and their sentencing decisions may be open to appellate review if they stray from the mandated sentences. Michigan, Washington, Oregon, Pennsylvania, Minnesota, North Carolina, and the federal government mandate that judges follow a set of comprehensive presumptive guidelines.[23] Presumptive guidelines are created by appointed sentencing commissions. The commission members determine what an "ideal" sentence would be for a particular crime and offender. There is, however, a great deal of variation within presumptive sentencing.[24]

Within this basic framework there are many different approaches to using guidelines. Some coexist with discretionary parole release, while others replace parole with mandatory release from prison once the statutory guideline sentence has been fulfilled. Some deal with all crimes and others only with felonies. Some set narrow sentencing ranges, and some set broad ones.[25] Some states provide for a wide range of sentences while others prescribe a very narrow range. Some states link use of guidelines to the availability of correctional resources, whereas others do not take resources into account. There are states that address only confinement and those that incorporate a range of intermediate sentencing options, such as probation and community service. Finally, there are states whose guidelines incorporate an appellate review process for all sentences and those with no appellate review.[26]

The Minnesota Guidelines   There are a number of ways to formulate guidelines. One method is to create a grid with prior record and current offense as the two coordinates and set out specific punishments. Table 10.1 shows Minnesota's guidelines. Note that as prior record and offense severity increase, so does recommended sentence length. After a certain point, probation is no longer an option, and the defendant must do prison time. A burglar with no prior convictions can expect to receive probation or an eighteen-month sentence for a house break-in; an experienced burglar with six or more prior convictions can get four years for the same crime, and probation is not an option.

Minnesota judges do retain some discretion and are allowed to depart from the guidelines when substantial and compelling aggravating (or mitigating) circumstances exist. If they depart from the guidelines, the judge must provide written reasons that articulate the substantial and compelling circumstances and that demonstrate why the sentence given is more appropriate or fair than the presumptive sentence.[27] The prosecution or defense may appeal the sentence if the judge departs from the guidelines. If an offender is sent to prison, the sentence consists of two parts: a *term of imprisonment* equal to two-thirds of the total executed sentence and a *supervised release* term equal to the remaining one-third. The amount of time the offender actually serves in prison may be extended by the commissioner of corrections if the offender violates disciplinary rules while in prison or violates conditions of supervised release. This extension period could result in the offender serving the entire sentence in prison.[28]

Federal Guidelines   The federal guidelines use a somewhat different "cookbook" approach to determine sentences. A magistrate must first determine the base penalty that a particular charge is given in the guidelines. For example, the federal guidelines give a base score (twenty) and mitigation factors for robbery. The base level can be adjusted upward if the crime was particularly serious or violent. Seven points could be added to the robbery base if a firearm was discharged during the crime; five points if the weapon was simply in the offender's possession. Similarly,

To access the Minnesota Sentencing Guidelines Commission homepage, go to
www.msgc.state.mn.us/

Table 10.1 Sentencing guidelines grid (presumptive sentence lengths in months)

Severity Level of Conviction Offense		Criminal History Score						
		0	1	2	3	4	5	6 or More
Murder, 2nd degree (intentional murder; drive-by shootings)	XI	306 *299–313*	326 *319–333*	346 *339–353*	366 *359–373*	386 *379–393*	406 *399–413*	426 *419–433*
Murder, 3rd degree Murder, 2nd degree (unintentional murder)	X	150 *144–156*	165 *159–171*	180 *174–186*	195 *189–201*	210 *204–216*	225 *219–231*	240 *234–246*
Criminal sexual conduct, 1st degree* Assault, 1st degree	IX	86 *81–91*	98 *93–103*	110 *105–115*	122 *117–127*	134 *129–139*	146 *141–151*	158 *153–163*
Aggravated robbery, 1st degree	VIII	48 *44–52*	58 *54–62*	68 *64–72*	78 *74–82*	88 *84–92*	98 *94–102*	108 *104–112*
Felony DWI	VII	36	42	48	54 *51–57*	60 *57–63*	66 *63–69*	72 *69–75*
Criminal sexual conduct, 2nd degree (a) & (b)	VI	21	27	33	39 *37–41*	45 *43–47*	51 *49–53*	57 *55–59*
Residential burglary Simple robbery	V	18	23	28	33 *31–35*	38 *36–40*	43 *41–45*	48 *46–50*
Nonresidential burglary	IV	12†	15	18	21	24 *23–25*	27 *26–28*	30 *29–31*
Theft crimes (over $2,500)	III	12†	13	15	17	19 *18–20*	21 *20–22*	23 *22–24*
Theft crimes ($2,500 or less) Check forgery ($200–$2,500)	II	12†	12†	13	15	17	19	21 *20–22*
Sale of simulated controlled substance	I	12†	12†	12†	13	15	17	19 *18–20*

☐ Presumptive commitment to state imprisonment. First Degree Murder is excluded from the guidelines by law and continues to have a mandatory life sentence. See section **II.E. Mandatory Sentences** for policy regarding those sentences controlled by law, including minimum periods of supervision for sex offenders released from prison.

▨ Presumptive stayed sentence; at the discretion of the judge, up to a year in jail and/or other non-jail sanctions can be imposed as conditions of probation. However, certain offenses in this section of the grid always carry a presumptive commitment to state prison. These offenses include Third Degree Controlled Substance Crimes when the offender has a prior felony drug conviction, Burglary of an Occupied Dwelling when the offender has a prior felony burglary conviction, second and subsequent Criminal Sexual Conduct offenses and offenses carrying a mandatory minimum prison term due to the use of a dangerous weapon (e.g., Second Degree Assault). See sections **II.C. Presumptive Sentence** and **II.E. Mandatory Sentences.**

* Pursuant to M.S. § 609.342, subd. 2, the presumptive sentence for Criminal Sexual Conduct in the First Degree is a minimum of 144 months (see **II.C. Presumptive Sentence** and **II.G. Convictions for Attempts, Conspiracies, and Other Sentence Modifiers**).

† One year and one day.

Note: Italicized numbers within the grid denote the range within which a judge may sentence without the sentence being deemed a departure. Offenders with nonimprisonment felony sentences are subject to jail time according to law.

Source: Minnesota Sentencing Guidelines Commission, August 1, 2002.

points can be added to a robbery if a large amount of money was taken, a victim was injured, a person was abducted or restrained in order to facilitate an escape, or the object of the robbery was to steal weapons or drugs. Upward adjustments can also be made if the defendant was a ringleader in the crime, obstructed justice, or used a professional skill or position of trust (such as doctor, lawyer, or politician) to commit the crime. Offenders designated as career criminals by a court can likewise receive longer sentences.

Once the base score is computed, judges determine the sentence by consulting a sentencing table that converts scores into months to be served. Offense levels are set out in the vertical column, and the criminal history (ranging from one to six prior offenses) is displayed in a horizontal column, forming a grid that contains the various sentencing ranges (similar to the Minnesota guidelines grid). By matching the applicable offense level and the criminal history, the judge can determine the sentence that applies to the particular offender.

How Effective Are Guidelines? Despite the widespread acceptance of guidelines, some nagging problems remain. A number of critics, including sentencing expert Michael Tonry, argue that they are rigid, harsh, overly complex, and disliked by the judiciary, and should be substantially revised or totally eliminated.[29] One important criticism is that guidelines are biased against African Americans despite their stated goal of removing discrimination from the sentencing process. For example, possession of crack cocaine is punished far more severely by the federal guidelines than possession of powdered cocaine. Critics charge that this amounts to racial bias because African Americans are much more likely to possess crack cocaine, whereas white offenders usually possess powdered cocaine.[30] Some jurisdictions give enhanced sentences if defendants have a prior juvenile conviction or if they were on juvenile probation or parole at the time of an arrest. African-American offenders are more likely than white offenders to have a prior record as a juvenile and therefore receive harsher sentences for their current crime.[31]

Some defense attorneys oppose the use of guidelines because they result in longer prison terms, prevent judges from considering mitigating circumstances, and reduce the use of probation. Even the widely heralded federal guidelines have had and will continue to have some dubious effects. The use of probation has diminished and the size of the federal prison population is increasing because guideline sentences are tougher and defendants have very little incentive to plea-bargain. They require incarceration sentences for minor offenders who in preguideline days would have been given community release; many of these petty offenders might be better served with cheaper alternative sanctions.[32] Because of these problems, Michael Tonry calls them "the most controversial and disliked sentencing reform initiative in United States history."[33]

In his important book *Sentencing Matters,* Tonry offers a prescription to improve structured sentencing guidelines that calls in part for the creation of ongoing sentencing commissions, creation of realistic guidelines, reliance on alternative sanctions, and a sentencing philosophy that stresses the "least punitive and intrusive appropriate sentence."[34]

Mandatory Sentences

Another effort to limit judicial discretion and at the same time get tough on crime has been the development of the **mandatory sentence.** Some states, for example, prohibit people convicted of certain offenses, such as violent crimes, and chronic offenders (recidivists) from being placed on probation; they must serve at least some time in prison. Other statutes bar certain offenders from being considered for parole. Mandatory sentencing legislation may impose minimum and maximum terms, but usually it requires a fixed prison sentence.

The federal sentencing Web site is located at
www.ussc.gov/

To read about the use of sentencing guidelines abroad, go to InfoTrac College Edition and read Martin Wasik, "Sentencing Guidelines: The Problem of Conditional Sentences," *Criminal Justice Ethics,* Winter-Spring 1994 v13 i1 p50.

mandatory sentence A statutory requirement that a certain penalty shall be set and carried out in all cases on conviction for a specified offense or series of offenses.

Mandatory sentencing generally limits the judge's discretionary power to impose any disposition but that authorized by the legislature; as a result, it limits individualized sentencing and restricts sentencing disparity. Mandatory sentencing provides equal treatment for all offenders who commit the same crime, regardless of age, sex, or other individual characteristics.

More than thirty-five states have already replaced discretionary sentencing with fixed-term mandatory sentences for such crimes as the sale of hard drugs, kidnapping, gun possession, and arson. The results have been mixed. Mandatory sentences have helped increase the size of the correctional population to record levels. Because of mandatory sentences, many offenders who in the past might have received probation are being incarcerated. They have also failed to eliminate racial disparity from the sentencing process.[35] Some state courts have ruled such practices unconstitutional.

The use of mandatory sentencing is discussed in the following Policy, Programs, and Issues feature, which describes a recent development in mandatory sentencing: three-strikes laws.

For more on mandatory sentencing, the Sentencing Project has news publications and a search engine. Go to www.sentencingproject.org/

Truth in Sentencing

Truth-in-sentencing laws, another get-tough measure designed to fight a rising crime rate, require offenders to serve a substantial portion of their prison sentence behind bars.[36] Parole eligibility and good-time credits are restricted or eliminated. The movement was encouraged by the Violent Offender Incarceration and Truth-in-Sentencing Incentive Grants Program, part of the federal government's 1994 crime act, which offered funds to support the state costs involved with creating longer sentences. To quality for federal funds, states must require persons convicted of a violent felony crime to serve not less than 85 percent of the prison sentence. The provision is already having an effect. Violent offenders released from prison in 1996 were sentenced to serve an average of eighty-five months in prison. Prior to release, they served about half of their prison sentence, or forty-five months. Under truth-in-sentencing laws requiring 85 percent of the sentence, violent offenders would serve an average of eighty-eight months in prison, based on the average sentence for violent offenders admitted to prison in 1996. Today, more than half the states and the District of Columbia met the federal Truth-in-Sentencing Incentive Grants Program eligibility criteria. Eleven states adopted truth-in-sentencing laws in 1995, one year after the 1994 crime act.

truth in sentencing A new sentencing scheme which requires that offenders serve at least 85 percent of their original sentence before being eligible for parole or other forms of early release.

How People Are Sentenced

How are people sentenced? Some of the most important information comes from national studies sponsored by the Bureau of Justice Statistics.[37] In 1998 (the last data available), state courts convicted a combined total of nearly 930,000 adults of felonies (federal courts convicted another 50,000 felons). As Table 10.2A shows, 68 percent of all felons convicted in state courts were sentenced to a period of confinement (44 percent to state prisons and 24 percent to local jails); 32 percent of convicted felons were given straight probation with no jail or prison time to serve. Those convicted felons sentenced to a state prison had an average sentence of five years but were likely to serve less than half (47 percent) of that sentence—or just over two years—before release; the average sentence to local jail was six months.

Though the crime rate has dropped during the past decade, the correctional population has not followed suit. One reason is that the amount of time spent behind bars before release has been increasing. In 1988 the typical felon received a 6-year sentence and served about 2 years or a third of that sentence before being released. By contrast, in 1998 the typical felon received a 5-year sentence and served

Let's Get Tough: Three-Strikes Laws

During his lifetime, Michael Riggs had been convicted eight times in California for such offenses as car theft and robbery. In 1996 he was once again in trouble, this time for shoplifting a $20 bottle of vitamins. Riggs was sentenced to a term of twenty-five years to life under California's "three-strikes" law, which mandates a life sentence for anyone convicted of a third offense. The law enables a trial judge to treat a defendant's third offense, even a petty crime such as shoplifting, as if it were a felony for purposes of applying the law's mandatory sentencing provisions. Riggs must serve a minimum of 20.8 years before parole eligibility. Without the three-strikes law, he would ordinarily have earned a maximum sentence of six months; if he had been convicted of murder he would have had to serve only 17 years. Riggs appealed his conviction to the Supreme Court in 1999, but the justices refused to rule on the case, letting his sentence stand.

Although the punishment given Michael Riggs seems excessive, public concern over crime has convinced lawmakers to toughen sentences for repeat offenders and those who commit serious crimes.

Three-Strikes Laws

Three-strikes (and-you're-out) laws provide these lengthy terms for any person convicted of three felony offenses, even if the third crime is relatively trivial. California's three-strikes law is aimed at getting habitual criminals off the street. Anyone convicted of a third felony must do a minimum term of twenty-five years to life; the third felony does not have to be serious or violent. The federal Crime Act of 1994 also adopted a three-strikes provision, requiring a mandatory life sentence for any offender convicted of three felony offenses; twenty-six states have so far followed suit and passed some form of the three-strikes law.

Although welcomed by conservatives looking for a remedy for violent crime, the three-strikes policy is controversial because a person convicted of a minor felony can receive a life sentence. There are reports that some judges are defying three-strikes provisions because they consider them unduly harsh. Much to the chagrin of three-strikes advocates, two California court decisions, *People v. Romero* (1996) and *People v. Garcia* (1999), allows judges to disregard an earlier conviction if the judge believes a life term is unjustified.

The Costs Are High

Three-strikes laws have undeniable political appeal to legislators being pressured by their constituents to "do something about crime." Yet even if possibly effective against crime, any effort to deter criminal behavior through tough laws is not without costs. In California alone the three-strikes law is estimated to increase correctional spending by $4.5 to $6.5 billion per year.

Three-strikes laws may in fact help put some chronic offenders behind bars, but can they realistically be expected to lower the crime rate?

Criminologist Marc Mauer, a leading opponent of the three-strikes law, finds that the approach may satisfy the public's hunger for retribution but makes little practical sense. First, "three-time losers" are on the brink of aging out of crime; locking them up for life should have little effect on the crime rate. In addition, current sentences for chronic violent offenders are already severe, yet their punishment seems to have had little influence on reducing national violence rates. A three-strikes policy also suffers because criminals typically underestimate their risk of apprehension while overestimating the rewards of crime. Given their inflated view of the benefits of crime, coupled with a seeming disregard of the risks of apprehension and punishment, it is unlikely a three-strikes policy can have a measurable deterrent effect on the crime rate.

Even if such a policy could reduce the number of career offenders on the street, the drain in economic resources that might have gone for education and social welfare ensures that a new generation of young criminals will fill the offending shoes of their incarcerated brethren. Mauer also suggests that a three-strikes policy will enlarge an already overburdened prison system, driving up costs, and, presumably, reducing resources available to house non-three-strikes inmates. Mauer warns too that African Americans face an increased risk of being sentenced under three-strikes statutes, expanding the racial disparity in sentencing. More ominous is the fact that police officers may be put at risk because two-time offenders would violently resist arrest, knowing that they face a life sentence.

Legal Controls

Because of its use with petty offenders, there are ongoing legal challenges to the use of three-strikes laws, and their future is still uncertain. However, on March 6, 2003, the U.S. Supreme Court in *Lockyer v. Andrade* (01-1127) upheld the three-strike sentence of Leandro Andrade, a man sentenced to prison in California for fifty years for stealing $153 worth of videotapes. It also upheld the conviction of Gary Ewing, who appealed a prior twenty-five-year sentence for stealing a set of golf clubs (*Ewing v. California*, 2002, 01-6978). In both cases the Court ruled that the challenged sentences were not so grossly disproportionate as to violate the Eighth Amendment's prohibition against

ity had been met. Writing in the *Andrade* case, Justice Souter said, "If Andrade's sentence is not grossly disproportionate the principle has no meaning."

These cases are not unique. At the time of the ruling, more than six thousand people were serving twenty-five-years-to-life terms in California and of these 340 had been convicted of petty theft. The *Andrade* and *Ewing* cases indicate that the Court is unlikely to overturn three-strikes laws on the grounds that they provide sentences that are disproportionate to the criminal behavior involved.

Critical Thinking

Is a policy that calls for spending billions on incarceration throwing money into the wind? Why or why not? After all, the number of people in prison already exceeds one million, and little conclusive evidence shows that incarceration alone can reduce crime rates. Might the funds earmarked for prison construction be used elsewhere with greater effect? Explain.

A large portion of the prison population consists of drug offenders. Although the number of people incarcerated for violent and property crimes has actually decreased in recent years, the number of incarcerated drug offenders has skyrocketed. Are the nation's interests best served by giving a life sentence to someone convicted of a third drug-trafficking charge, even if the crime involves selling a small amount of cocaine? Explain.

InfoTrac College Edition Research

To learn more about three-strikes laws, read Kelly McMurry, "Three-Strikes Laws Proving More Show Than Go," *Trial 33* (1997): 12; and Chi Chi Sileo, "Are Three-Strikes Laws Handcuffing the Courts?" *Insight on the News 11* (1995): 14.

Sources: Henry Weinstein, "Long Terms Voided in Two Petty Thefts Justice: Court Did Not Reject Three-Strikes Law, But Ruling in Two Cases Will Affect Many Others," *Los Angeles Times,* 8 February 2002, 1; *Riggs v. California,* No. 98-5021 (1999); "California Supreme Court Undercuts Three-Strikes Law," *Criminal Justice Newsletter,* 1 July 1996, 2; "Three-Strikes Laws Rarely Used, Except California's, Study Finds," *Criminal Justice Newsletter,* 17 September 1996, 4; "California Passes a Tough Three-Strikes-You're-Out Law," *Criminal Justice Newsletter,* 4 April 1993, 6; Rand Research Brief, *California's New Three-Strikes Law: Benefits, Costs, and Alternatives* (Santa Monica, Calif.: RAND, 1994); Marc Mauer, testimony before the U.S. Congress House Judiciary Committee on "Three Strikes and You're Out," 1 March 1994 (Washington, D.C.: The Sentencing Project, 1994); Lois Forer, *A Rage to Punish: The Unintended Consequences of Mandatory Sentencing* (New York: Norton, 1994).

Some critics believe that three-strikes laws are "cruel and unusual" because they provide extremely long sentences for relatively minor crimes. Joanna Verduzco, ten, of Riverside, California, whose father, Pedro Verduzco, seen in photo, is in jail for twenty-nine years to life for possession of 0.6 grams of methamphetamine, pauses during a protest against California's three-stikes law, March 9, 2002, at the federal building in the Westwood area of Los Angeles. The event was organized by Families to Amend California's Three Strikes (FACTS) and other groups.

cruel and unusual punishment. In her majority decision, Justice Sandra Day O'Connor added that any criticism of the law "is appropriately directed at the Legislature" and was not a judicial matter. Four judges dissented in the case arguing that the Court's test for sentence disproportional-

Table 10.2A Types of felony sentences imposed by state courts, by offense

Most Serious Conviction Offense	Percent of Felons Sentenced to Incarceration				
	Total	Total	Prison	Jail	Probation
All offenses	100%	68%	44%	24%	32%
Violent offenses	100%	78%	59%	19%	22%
Murder[a]	100	96	94	2	4
Sexual assault[b]	100	82	67	15	18
Rape	100	84	70	14	16
Other sexual assault	100	80	64	16	20
Robbery	100	88	76	12	12
Aggravated assault	100	72	46	26	28
Other violent[c]	100	67	41	26	33
Property offenses	100%	65%	43%	22%	35%
Burglary	100	75	54	21	25
Larceny[d]	100	64	40	24	36
Motor vehicle theft	100	76	43	33	24
Fraud[e]	100	55	35	20	45
Drug offenses	100%	68%	42%	26%	32%
Possession	100	65	36	29	35
Trafficking	100	71	45	26	29
Weapon offenses	100%	66%	42%	24%	34%
Other offenses[f]	100%	63%	35%	28%	37%

Note: For persons receiving a combination of sentences, the sentence designation came from the most severe penalty imposed—prison being the most severe, followed by jail, then probation. Prison includes death sentences. Felons receiving a sentence other than incarceration or probation are classified under "probation." This table is based on an estimated 921,328 cases.

[a] Includes nonnegligent manslaughter.

[b] Includes rape.

[c] Includes offenses such as negligent manslaughter and kidnaping.

[d] Includes motor vehicle theft.

[e] Includes forgery and embezzlement.

[f] Composed of nonviolent offenses such as receiving stolen property and vandalism.

Source: Brian A. Reaves, *Felony Sentences in State Courts, 1998* (Washington, D.C.: Bureau of Justice Statistics, 2002).

about half of that, or 2.5 years, before being released. In 1988 the average murderer spent 79 months in prison, while by 1998 the average was 136. The increased time spent behind bars is due to the passage of tough sentencing laws, which require offenders to spend a considerable portion of their sentence behind bars (see Table 10.2B).

What Factors Affect Sentencing?

What factors influence judges when they decide on criminal sentences? As already mentioned, crime seriousness and the offender's prior record are certainly considered. State sentencing codes usually include various factors that can legitimately influence the length of prison sentences, including the following:

- The severity of the offense
- The offender's prior criminal record
- Whether the offender used violence
- Whether the offender used weapons
- Whether the crime was committed for money

Table 10.2B Estimated time to be served
in state prison, by offense

Most Serious Conviction Offense	Mean Prison Sentence	To Be Served in Prison, Estimated	
		Percent of Sentence[a]	Time[b]
All offenses	57 mo	47%	27 mo
Violent offenses	100 mo	54%	54 mo
Murder[c]	263	52	136
Sexual assault[d]	111	56	62
Rape	147	58	81
Other sexual assault	88	55	45
Robbery	106	51	54
Aggravated assault	66	57	38
Other violent[e]	56	55	31
Property offenses	44 mo	45%	20 mo
Burglary	52	45	24
Larceny[f]	37	45	17
Motor vehicle theft	35	43	15
Fraud[g]	40	42	17
Drug offenses	47 mo	41%	19 mo
Possession	35	40	14
Trafficking	54	41	22
Weapon offenses	42 mo	60%	25 mo
Other offenses[h]	40 mo	51%	20 mo

[a] Percentages are based on data from 237,443 persons released from State prisons in 1998 (National Corrections Reporting Program, 1998 tables 2-8 and 2-12). These percentages included credited jail time.

[b] Derived by multiplying the percentage of sentence to be served by the mean sentence imposed.

[c] Includes nonnegligent manslaughter.

[d] Includes rape.

[e] Includes offenses such as negligent manslaughter and kidnaping.

[f] Includes motor vehicle theft.

[g] Includes forgery and embezzlement.

[h] Composed of nonviolent offenses such as receiving stolen property and vandalism.

Source: Brian A. Reaves, *Felony Sentences in State Courts, 1998* (Washington, D.C.: Bureau of Justice Statistics, 2002).

Research does in fact show a strong correlation between these legal variables and the type and length of sentence received. For example, judges seem less willing to use discretion in cases involving the most serious criminal charges such as terrorism, while employing greater control in low-severity cases.[38]

Besides these legally appropriate factors, sentencing experts suspect that judges may also be influenced by the defendant's age, race, gender, and income. Considerations of such variables would be a direct violation of constitutional due process and equal protection, as well as of federal statutes, such as the civil rights act. Limiting judicial bias is one of the reasons why states have adopted determinate and mandatory sentencing statutes. Do extralegal factors actually influence judges when they make sentencing decisions?

Social Class   Evidence supports an association between social class and sentencing outcomes: members of the lower class may expect to get longer prison sentences than more affluent defendants. One reason is that poor defendants may be unable to obtain quality legal representation or to make bail, factors that influence sentencing.[39] Race may also influence the association between incomes and sentence length. At least in some jurisdictions, minorities receive longer sentences than Caucasians if they are currently indigent or unemployed. Judges may possibly view their status as "social dynamite," considering them more dangerous and likely to recidivate than white offenders.[40]

Not all research efforts have found a consistent class-crime relationship, however, and the relationship may be more robust for some crime patterns than others.[41]

Gender   Does a defendant's gender influence how he or she is sentenced? Some theorists believe that women benefit from sentence disparity because the criminal justice system is dominated by men who have a paternalistic or protective attitude toward women; this is referred to as the **chivalry hypothesis.** Others argue that female criminals can be the victim of bias because their behavior violates what men believe is "proper" female behavior.[42]

chivalry hypothesis   The view that the low female crime and delinquency rates are a reflection of the leniency with which police treat female offenders.

Most research indicates that women receive more favorable outcomes the further they go in the criminal justice system: they are more likely to receive preferential treatment from a judge at sentencing than they are from the police officer making the arrest or the prosecutor seeking the indictment.[43] Favoritism crosses both racial and ethnic lines, benefiting African-American, white, and Hispanic women.[44] Gender bias may be present because judges perceive women as better risks than men. Women have been granted more lenient pretrial release conditions and lower bail amounts than men; women are also more likely to spend less time in pretrial detention.[45]

Age   Another extralegal factor that may play a role in sentencing is age. Judges may be more lenient with elderly defendants and more punitive toward younger ones.[46] Although sentencing leniency may be a result of judges' perception that the elderly pose little risk to society, such practices are a violation of the civil rights of younger defendants.[47] On the other hand, judges may also wish to protect the youngest defendants, sparing them the pains of a prison experience.[48]

Victim Characteristics   Victim characteristics may also influence sentencing. They may be asked to make a **victim impact statement** before the sentencing judge. This gives victims an opportunity to tell of their experiences and describe their ordeal; in the case of a murder trial, the surviving family can recount the effect the crime has had on their lives and well-being.[49] The effect of victim and witness statements on sentencing has been the topic of some debate. Some research finds that victim statements result in a higher rate of incarceration, but other efforts find that the effects of victim and witness statements are insignificant.[50]

A victim's personal characteristics may influence sentencing. Sentences may be reduced when victims have "negative" personal characteristics or qualities. For example, rapists whose victims are de-

© 2002 AP/Wide World Photos

Although most research shows that there is a gender gap in sentencing, there are some crimes that are considered inappropriate for women and for which they may receive relatively harsh punishments. Here, defense attorney David Allen speaks to his client Susan G. Lemery at her sentencing hearing in Snohomish County Superior Court in Everett, Washington, July 26, 2002. Lemery, a second-grade teacher convicted of sexually abusing two fourteen-year-old boys, was sentenced to five years in prison, the maximum sentence for three counts of third-degree child rape and two counts of third-degree child molestation.

scribed as prostitutes or substance abusers or who have engaged in risky behaviors, such as hitchhiking or going to bars alone, receive much shorter sentences than those who assault women without these negative characteristics.[51]

victim impact statement   A postconviction statement by the victim of crime that may be used to guide sentencing decisions.

Race   No issue concerning personal factors in sentencing is more important than the suspicion that race influences sentencing outcomes. Racial disparity in sentencing has been suspected because a disproportionate number of African-American inmates are in state prisons and on death row. The war on drugs has been centered in African-American communities, and politically motivated punitive sentencing policies aimed at crack cocaine have had a devastating effect on young African-American men. If, charges Michael Tonry, such punitive measures are allowed to continue or are even expanded, an entire cohort of young African Americans may be placed in jeopardy.[52] Because this issue is so important, it is the focus of the following Race, Culture, and Gender feature.

Capital Punishment

The most severe sentence used in the United States is capital punishment, or execution. More than 14,500 confirmed executions have been carried out in America under civil authority, starting with the execution of Captain George Kendall in 1608. Most of these executions have been for murder and rape. However, federal, state, and military laws have conferred the death penalty for other crimes, including robbery, kidnapping, treason (offenses against the federal government), espionage, and desertion from military service.

InfoTrac College Edition has more than one thousand articles on capital punishment. Use the term as a subject guide to access to InfoTrac College Edition's library.

In recent years, the U.S. Supreme Court has limited the death penalty to first-degree murder and only then when aggravating circumstances, such as murder for profit or murder using extreme cruelty, are present.[53] The federal government still has provisions for granting the death penalty for espionage by a member of the armed forces, treason, and killing during a criminal conspiracy, such as drug trafficking. Some states still have laws assessing capital punishment for such crimes as aircraft piracy, ransom kidnapping, and the aggravated rape of a child, but it remains to be seen whether the courts will allow criminals to be executed today for any crime less than aggravated first-degree murder.

Today, the death penalty for murder is used in thirty-eight states and by the federal government. After many years of abolition, New York reinstated the use of the death penalty in 1995 and expanded its use to cover numerous acts, including serial murder, contract killing, and the use of torture.[54]

There are currently more than thirty-five hundred people on death row.[55] Between seventy-five and one hundred people are now executed each year, most having served ten years on death row before their execution. California actually has the most people on death row while Texas executes the most (around forty per year, or almost half the total executions in the United States). In 2000, about fourteen states carried out at least one execution (eighty-five in all); almost all of these occurred in southern and western states; in 2001, sixty-six inmates were executed (see Figure 10.3 on page 328). In 2002, seventy-one persons in thirteen states were executed: thirty-three in Texas; seven in Oklahoma; six in Missouri; four each in Georgia and Virginia; three each in Florida, South Carolina, and

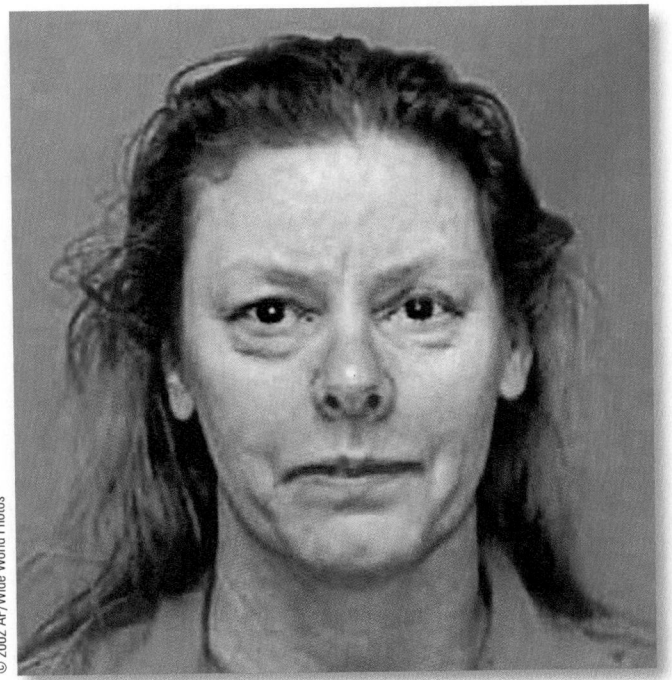

© 2002 AP/Wide World Photos

Aileen Wuornos killed seven men in Florida. A prostitute, she gave a shocking, detailed confession of her crimes and was executed on October 9, 2002. Was her execution justified?

Race, Culture, and Gender in Criminal Justice

Race and Sentencing

Although critics of American race relations may think otherwise, research on sentencing has failed to show a definitive pattern of racial discrimination. While some works do indicate that a defendant's race has a direct impact on sentencing outcomes, other efforts show that the influence of race on sentencing is less clear-cut than anticipated. It is possible that the disproportionate number of minority group members in prison inmates is a result of crime and arrest patterns and not racial bias by judges when they hand out criminal sentences; racial and ethnic minorities commit more crime, the argument goes, and therefore they are more likely to wind up in prison.

Despite the inconclusive evidence, racial disparity in sentencing has been suspected because a disproportionate number of minority inmates are in state prisons and on death row. If there is racial disparity in sentencing its cause may lie outside of judicial sentencing practices. For example, research efforts show that minority defendants suffer discrimination in a variety of court actions: They are more likely to be detained before trial than whites and, upon conviction, are more likely to receive jail sentences rather than fines. Prosecutors are less likely to divert minorities from the legal system than whites who commit the same crimes; minorities are less likely to win appeals than white appellants.

The relationship between race and sentencing may be difficult to establish because their association may not be linear: while minority defendants may be punished more severely for some crimes, and under some circumstances, they are treated more leniently for others. The most recent sentencing data indicates that minorities do in fact receive longer and harsher sentences for some crimes (robberies) while Caucasians actually receive longer sentences for other criminal offenses (drug trafficking).

Sociologist Darnell Hawkins explains this phenomenon as a matter of "appropriateness":

> Certain crime types are considered less "appropriate" for blacks than for whites. Blacks who are charged with committing these offenses will be treated more severely than blacks who commit crimes that are considered more "appropriate." Included in the former category are various white-collar offenses and crimes against political and social structures of authority. The latter group of offenses would include various forms of

victimless crimes associated with lower social status (for example, prostitution, minor drug use, or drunkenness). This may also include various crimes against the person, especially those involving black victims.

Race may have an impact on sentencing because some race-specific crimes are punished more harshly than others. African Americans receive longer sentences for drug crimes than whites because (1) they are more likely to be arrested for crack possession and sale and (2) crack dealing is more severely punished by state and federal laws than other drug crimes. Because Caucasians are more likely to use marijuana and methamphetamines, prosecutors are more willing to plea-bargain and offer shorter jail terms.

Racial bias has also been linked to the victim-offender status. Minority defendants are sanctioned more severely if their victim is white than if their target is a fellow minority-group member; minorities who kill whites are more likely to get the death penalty than those who kill other minorities. Judges may base sentencing decisions on the race of the victim and not the race of the defendant. For example, Charles Crawford, Ted Chiricos, and Gary Kleck found that African-American defendants are more likely to be prosecuted under habitual offender statutes if they commit crimes where there is a greater likelihood of a white victim—for example, larceny and burglary—than if they commit violent crimes that are largely intraracial. Where there is a perceived "racial threat" (from African Americans to Caucasians), punishments are enhanced.

System Effects

Sentencing disparity may also reflect race-based differences in criminal justice practices and policies associated with sentencing outcome. Probation presentence reports may favor white over minority defendants, causing judges to award whites probation more often than minorities. Caucasians are more likely to receive probation in jurisdictions where African Americans and Caucasians receive prison sentences of similar duration; this is referred to as the "in-out" decision.

Defendants who can afford bail receive more lenient sentences than those who remain in pretrial detention; minority defendants are less likely to make bail because they suffer a higher degree of income inequality. That is, minorities earn less on average and therefore are less likely to be able to make bail. Sentencing outcome is also affected

Ohio; two each in Alabama, Mississippi, and North Carolina; and one each in Louisiana and California.

In addition to the drop in executions in 2001 (the last year for which full data are available), for the first time in more than twenty years the number of inmates on death row also declined (down 20 to about 3,581), and the number of inmates sentenced to death row was the lowest since 1973. The decline in executions and

by the defendant's ability to afford a private attorney and put on a vigorous legal defense that makes use of high-paid expert witnesses. These factors place the poor and minority-group members at a disadvantage in the sentencing process and result in sentencing disparity. And while considerations of prior record may be legitimate in forming sentencing decisions, there is evidence that minorities are more likely to have prior records because of organizational and individual bias on the part of police.

Are Sentencing Practices Changing?

If in fact racial discrepancies exist, new sentencing laws featuring determinate and mandatory sentences may be helping to reduce disparity. For example, Jon'a Meyer and Tara Gray found that jurisdictions in California that use mandatory sentences for crimes such as drunk driving also show little racial disparity in sentences between Caucasians and minority group members. Similarly, a national survey of sentencing practices conducted by the Bureau of Justice Statistics found that while white defendants are somewhat more likely to receive probation and other nonincarceration sentences than black defendants (34 percent versus 31 percent), there was little racial disparity in the length of prison sentences.

These results are encouraging, but it is also possible that some studies miss a racial effect because they combine white and Hispanic cases into a single category of "white" defendants and then compare them with the sentencing of black defendants. Darrell Steffensmeier and Stephen Demuth's analysis of sentencing in Pennsylvania found that Hispanics are punished considerably more severely than non-Hispanic Caucasians and that combining the two groups masks the ethnic differences in sentencing. Steffensmeier and Demuth also found that federal court judges in Pennsylvania were less likely to consider race and ethnic origin in their sentencing decisions than state court judges. This outcome suggests that federal judges, insulated from community pressures and values and holding a lifetime appointment, are better able to render objective decisions. By implication, justice may become more objective if judges held life tenure and were selected from a pool of qualified applicants who reside outside the county in which they serve.

Critical Thinking

Do you feel that sentences should be influenced by the fact that one ethnic or racial group is more likely to commit that crime? For example, critics have called for change in the way federal sentencing guidelines are designed, asking that the provisions that punish crack possession more heavily than powdered cocaine possession be repealed because African Americans are more likely to use crack and Caucasians powdered cocaine. Do you approve of such a change? Because of the lingering problem of racial and class bias in the sentencing process, one primary goal of the criminal justice system in the 1990s was to reduce disparity by creating new forms of criminal sentences that limit judicial discretion and are aimed at uniformity and fairness.

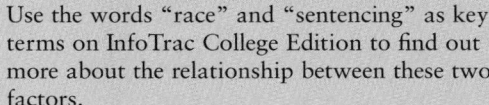

InfoTrac College Edition Research
Use the words "race" and "sentencing" as key terms on InfoTrac College Edition to find out more about the relationship between these two factors.

Sources: Marian R. Williams and Jefferson E. Holcomb, "Racial Disparity and Death Sentences in Ohio," *Journal of Criminal Justice* 29 (2001): 207–218; Rodney Engen and Randy Gainey, "Modeling the Effects of Legally Relevant and Extralegal Factors Under Sentencing Guidelines: The Rules Have Changed," *Criminology* 38 (2000): 1207–1230; Darrell Steffensmeier and Stephen Demuth, "Ethnicity and Judges' Sentencing Decisions: Hispanic-Black-White Comparisons," *Criminology* 39 (2001): 145–178; Travis Pratt, "Race and Sentencing: A Meta-Analysis of Conflicting Empirical Research Results," *Journal of Criminal Justice* 26 (1998): 513–525; Charles Crawford, Ted Chiricos, and Gary Kleck, "Race, Racial Threat, and Sentencing of Habitual Offenders," *Criminology* 36 (1998): 481–511; Jon'a Meyer and Tara Gray, "Drunk Drivers in the Courts: Legal and Extra-Legal Factors Affecting Pleas and Sentences," *Journal of Criminal Justice* 25 (1997): 155–163; Alexander Alvarez and Ronet Bachman, "American Indians and Sentencing Disparity: An Arizona Test," *Journal of Criminal Justice* 24 (1996): 549–561; Carole Wolff Barnes and Rodney Kingsnorth, "Race, Drug, and Criminal Sentencing: Hidden Effects of the Criminal Law," *Journal of Criminal Justice* 24 (1996): 39–55; Samuel Walker, Cassia Spohn, and Miriam DeLone, *The Color of Justice: Race, Ethnicity, and Crime in America* (Belmont, Calif.: Wadsworth, 1996), 145–146; Jo Dixon, "The Organizational Context of Sentencing" *American Journal of Sociology* 100 (1995): 1157–1198; Alfred Blumstein, "On the Racial Disproportionality of the United States Prison Population," *Journal of Criminal Law and Criminology* 73 (1982); Celesta Albonetti and John Hepburn, "Prosecutorial Discretion to Defer Criminalization: The Effects of Defendant's Ascribed and Achieved Status Characteristics," *Journal of Quantitative Criminology* 12 (1996): 63–81; Darnell Hawkins, "Race, Crime Type, and Imprisonment," *Justice Quarterly* 3 (1986): 251–269.

death row admissions may be a product of several factors, including a lower murder rate. However, there seems to be growing unease with the administration of the death penalty, and the recent use of scientific evidence based on DNA has resulted in numerous exonerations of death row inmates. Even though the general public continues to support capital sentences, those in political power have become concerned about charges of racial bias and sloppy investigations.

Number of executions

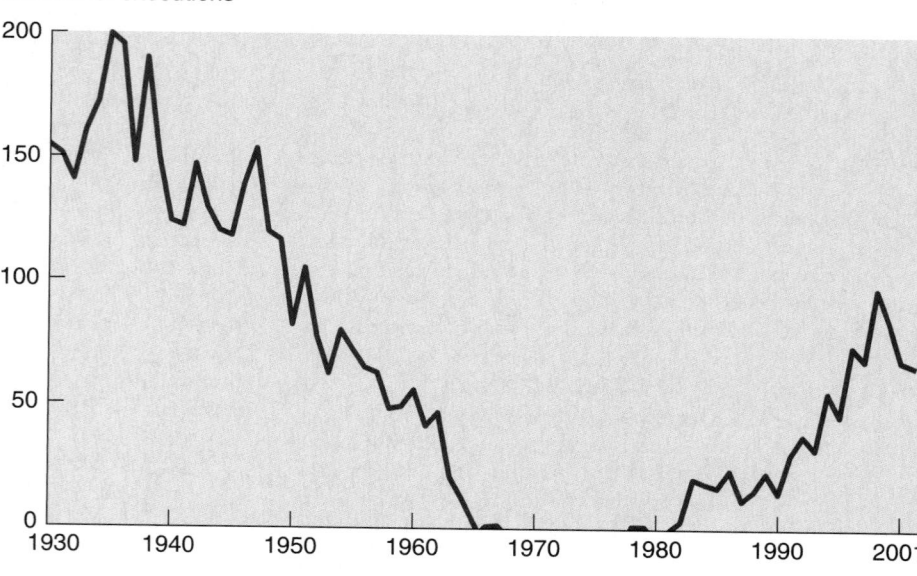

Figure 10.3
Executions, 1930–2001

Source: Tracy Snell, *Capital Punishment 2000* (Washington, D.C.: Bureau of Justice Statistics, 2002).

The number of executions increased slightly in 2002, but it is possible that use of the death penalty will continue to decline. Especially significant is the January 11, 2003, decision of Illinois Governor George Ryan to commute all Illinois death sentences—a gesture that spared the lives of 163 men and 4 women who have served a collective two thousand years for the murders of more than 250 people.

Lethal injection is the predominant method of death, though a number of states maintain the gas chamber and the electric chair. In 1999 the U.S. Supreme Court refused to hear a case concerning Florida's use of the electric chair as the sole means of execution. Even though the chair has malfunctioned several times, sending up smoke and flames, the Court refused to consider whether this amounted to cruel and unusual punishment. Of the thirty-eight death penalty states, only Alabama, Georgia, Nebraska, and Florida still use the electric chair as the sole means of execution.[56] Although the death penalty is generally approved of in the United States, it fares less well abroad. See the Race, Culture, and Gender feature that follows.

No issue in the criminal justice system is more controversial or emotional than the implementation of the death penalty. Opponents and proponents have formulated a number of powerful arguments in support of their positions; these arguments are reviewed in the following sections.

Arguments for the Death Penalty

Let's look at some of the most common arguments for retaining the death penalty in the United States.

Incapacitation   Supporters argue that death is the "ultimate incapacitation" and the only one that can ensure that convicted killers can never be pardoned, be paroled, or escape. Most states that do not have capital punishment provide the sentence of "life in prison without the chance of parole." However, forty-eight states

The Death Penalty Abroad

In March 2002, a Nigerian woman Amina Lawal, thirty, was convicted and sentenced to death by stoning by an Islamic Shariah court after giving birth to a baby girl more than nine months after divorcing her husband. The sentence was suspended until the baby finished breastfeeding, sometime in 2004! Two Saudi brothers, Saud and Musaid bin Abdul-Rahman al-Aulian, were beheaded for kidnapping, raping, and robbing a woman whom they had lured to a secluded area. The Saudis behead about 125 people each year for such crimes as murder, rape, drug trafficking, and armed robbery. But not all Saudi executions concern violent crime: on February 28, 2001 Hassan bin Awad al-Zubair, a Sudanese national, was beheaded after he was convicted on charges of "sorcery"; al-Zubair claimed the power to heal the sick and to "separate married couples."

The United States is not alone in using the death penalty. According to the latest data from watchdog group Amnesty International, about seventy-five nations have abolished the death penalty for ordinary crimes and another thirty-six retain it but have abolished it in practice. Another eighty-four nations retain the death penalty.

Most non-U.S. executions take place in China, Iran, Saudi Arabia, and the Democratic Republic of Congo. During 2001, Amnesty International estimates that at least 3,048 prisoners were executed in thirty-one countries and 5,265 people were sentenced to death in sixty-nine countries. These figures include only cases known to Amnesty International; the true figures are certainly higher. The 2001 figures are much higher than 2000, when 1,457 people were executed, indicating a rapid increase in the use of the death penalty. One reason for the increase is that China has instituted a "strike hard" campaign against crime. It alone executed about 2,500 people in 2001. In addition to violent crimes, executions were carried out for crimes such as stealing gasoline, bribery, pimping, embezzlement, tax fraud, drug offenses, and selling harmful foodstuffs.

Although opposition to executions is growing in many areas, there are some nations where the public still demands the use of the death penalty.

In addition to China, nations that operate under Islamic law routinely employ the death penalty. At least 79 executions were carried out in Saudi Arabia during 2001 and 139 in Iran, but the real numbers may be higher. The governments of Jamaica, Guyana, and Barbados have all expressed interest in speeding the use of the death penalty and more than 250 prisoners are currently on death row across the English-speaking Caribbean.

Japan, a nation that prides itself on nonviolence, routinely uses the death penalty. Prisoners are told less than two hours before execution, and the families and lawyers are never told of the decision to carry out the death penalty.

Executions of Juveniles

International human rights treaties prohibit anyone under eighteen years old at the time of the crime being sentenced to death. The International Covenant on Civil and Political Rights, the American Convention on Human Rights and the U.N. Convention on the Rights of the Child all have provisions to this effect. More than one hundred countries have laws specifically excluding the execution of juvenile offenders or may be presumed to exclude such executions by being parties to one or another of the named treaties. A small number of countries, however, continue to execute juvenile offenders. Six countries since 1990 are known to have executed prisoners who were under eighteen years old at the time of the crime—Iran, Nigeria, Pakistan, Saudi Arabia, the United States, and Yemen. Between 1997 and 2001 there were twelve executions of juvenile offenders worldwide: three in Iran, one in the Democratic Republic of Congo, and eight in the United States.

Critical Thinking

1. The movement toward abolition in the United States is encouraged by the fact that so many nations have abandoned the death penalty. Should we model our own system of punishment after other nations or is our crime problem so unique that it requires the use of capital punishment?

2. Do you believe that people who join a terrorist group and train to kill Americans deserve the death penalty even if they have never actually killed anyone?

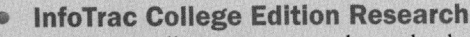

InfoTrac College Edition Research

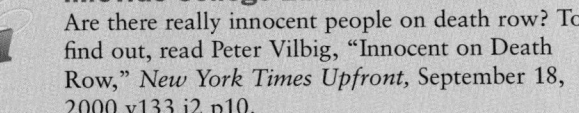

Are there really innocent people on death row? To find out, read Peter Vilbig, "Innocent on Death Row," *New York Times Upfront,* September 18, 2000 v133 i2 p10.

The death penalty remains a controversial issue around the world. To learn more, read Stefanie Grant, "A Dialogue of the Deaf? New International Attitudes and the Death Penalty in America," *Criminal Justice Ethics 17* (1998): 19.

Sources: Amnesty International's most recent data on the death penalty can be accessed at http://web.amnesty.org/rmp/dplibrary.nsf/index?openview; "Nigeria: Stoning Sentence Stands," *New York Times,* 10 September 2002, A6; *Death Penalty News,* "Saudi Arabia Executes Man for Sorcery," Amnesty International news release, 15 March 2000; "USA Set to Break a Global Consensus—Execution of Child Offender Due," Amnesty International news release, 22 October 2001; China 'Striking Harder' Than Ever Before," Amnesty International news release, 7 June 2001; "Saudi Brothers Beheaded for Raping," *New York Times,* 20 July 2001, 3; Larry Rohter, "In Caribbean, Support Growing for Death Penalty," *New York Times,* 4 October 1998; "Chechen Pair Executed in Public," *Boston Globe,* 19 September 1997, 9; "Saudi Beheadings Over One Hundred for 1997," *Boston Globe,* 28 September 1997, A29.

grant their chief executive the right to grant clemency and commute a life sentence and may give "lifers" eligibility for various furlough and release programs.

Death penalty advocates believe that the potential for recidivism is a serious enough threat to require that murderers be denied further access to the public. Stephen Markman and Paul Cassell analyzed the records of 52,000 state prison inmates serving time for murder and found that 810 had previously been convicted of homicide and that these recidivists had killed 821 people following their first convictions.[57] More than 250 inmates on death row today had prior homicide convictions; if they had been executed for their first offense, 250 innocent people would still be alive.[58]

Deterrence   Proponents of capital punishment argue that executions serve as a strong deterrent for serious crimes. Although capital punishment would probably not deter the few mentally unstable criminals, it could have an effect on the cold, calculating murderer, such as the hired killer or someone who kills for profit; the fear of death may also convince felons not to risk using handguns during armed robberies.

Proponents argue that the deterrent effect of an execution can produce a substantial decline in the murder rate.[59] Some supporters use a commonsense approach, not relying on scientific analysis. They argue, for example, that homicide rates *increased* dramatically in the 1960s and 1970s when executions were halted by the courts and death penalty laws were subsequently abolished. Proponents also maintain that even if homicide rates increase after the death penalty is adopted in a state, murder rates may actually have been much higher if capital punishment had never been legislated.[60]

Other proponents rely on more scientific analysis of data. In one assessment of sixteen well-publicized executions, Steven Stack found that they may have saved 480 lives by immediately deterring potential murderers.[61] In a more recent survey, he concluded that well-publicized executions of criminals in California reduced the homicide rate 12 percent during the month of the execution.[62]

Moral Correctness   Advocates of capital punishment justify its use on the grounds that it is morally correct because it is mentioned in the Bible and other religious works. Although the U.S. Constitution forbids "cruel and unusual punishments," this prohibition would not include the death penalty since capital punishment was widely used at the time the Constitution was drafted. The "original intent" of the founding fathers was to allow the states to use the death penalty; capital punishment may be cruel, but it is not unusual.

The death penalty is morally correct because it provides the greatest justice for the victim and helps alleviate the psychic pain of the victim's family and friends. It has even been accepted by criminal justice experts who consider themselves humanists, people who are concerned with the value and dignity of human beings. As the noted humanist David Friedrichs argues, a civilized society has no choice but to hold responsible those who commit horrendous crimes. The death penalty makes a moral statement: There is behavior that is so unacceptable to a community of human beings that one who engages in such behavior forfeits his right to live.[63]

Proportional to the Crime   Putting dangerous criminals to death also conforms to the requirement that the punishment must be proportional to the seriousness of the crime. Since we use a system of escalating punishments, it follows that the most serious punishment should be used to sanction the most serious crime. Before the brutality of the death penalty is considered, the cruelty with which the victim was treated should not be forgotten.

Reflects Public Opinion   Those who favor capital punishment charge that a majority of the public believes that criminals who kill innocent victims should forfeit their own lives. Public opinion polls show that up to 67 percent of the public favors the death penalty, almost double the percentage of twenty years ago (though the percentages have declined somewhat in the last five years from a high of 75 percent).[64] Public approval is based on the rational belief that the death penalty is an important instrument of social control, can deter crime, and is less costly than maintaining a murderer in prison for life.[65] It is also possible that the 67 percent approval rating may underestimate public opinion. Research by Alexis Durham and his associates found that almost everyone (95 percent) would give criminals the death penalty under some circumstances, and the most heinous crimes are those for which the public is most likely to approve capital punishment.[66]

Unlikely Chance of Error   The many legal controls and appeals currently in use make it almost impossible for an innocent person to be executed or for the death penalty to be used in a racist or capricious manner. Although some unfortunate mistakes may have been made in the past, the current system makes it virtually impossible to execute an innocent person. Federal courts closely scrutinize all death penalty cases and rule for the defendant in an estimated 60 percent to 70 percent of the appeals. Such judicial care should ensure that only those who are both truly guilty and deserving of death are executed.

In sum, those who favor the death penalty find it to be traditional punishment for serious crimes and one that can help prevent criminality; in keeping with the traditional moral values of fairness and equity; and highly favored by the public.

Arguments Against the Death Penalty

Arguments for the death penalty are matched by those that support its abolition.

Possibility of Error   Critics of the death penalty believe capital punishment has no place in a mature democratic society.[67] They point to the finality of the act and the real possibility that innocent persons can be executed. Examples of people wrongfully convicted of murder abound. Critics point to miscarriages of justice such as the case of Rolando Cruz and Alejandro Hernandez, who, wrongfully convicted of murder, were released in 1995 after spending more than a decade on death row in the Illinois prison system; three former prosecutors and four deputy sheriffs who worked on the case were charged with fabricating evidence against the pair.[68] Cruz and Hernandez are certainly not alone. Jeffrey Blake went to prison for a double murder in 1991 and spent seven years behind bars before his conviction was overturned in 1998. It seems that the prosecution's star witness conceded that he lied on the stand, forcing Blake to spend a quarter of his life in prison for a crime he did not commit.[69] These wrongful convictions would have been even more tragic if the men had been executed for their alleged crimes. A congressional report cited forty-eight cases in the past two decades in which people who served time on death row were released because of new evidence proving their innocence; one Maryland man served nine years on death row before DNA testing proved that he could not have committed the crime.[70] These findings show that even with the best intentions there is grave risk that an innocent person can be executed.[71] Some states have placed a moratorium on executions until the possibility of error can be investigated. In Illinois thirteen men on death row have been exonerated over the past two decades, causing then Governor George Ryan to commute the sentences of death row inmates there because of the high number of mistaken convictions.[72]

According to classic research by Michael Radelet and Hugo Bedeau, there have been about 350 wrongful murder convictions this century, of which 23 led to executions. They estimate that about three death sentences are returned every two years in cases where the defendant has been falsely accused. More than half the errors stem from perjured testimony, false identifications, coerced confessions, and suppression of evidence. In addition to the 23 who were executed, 128 of the

Does capital punishment present ethical problems that make its use morally dubious? Read what the American Civil Liberties Union has to say at
www.aclu.org/death-penalty/

© 2002 AP/Wide World Photos

Those who oppose the death penalty argue that it is possible that mistakes can be made and innocent people executed. Juan Melendez, left, spent eighteen years on death row before being exonerated.

falsely convicted served more than six years in prison, 39 served more than sixteen years in confinement, and 8 died while serving their sentence.[73] It is their view that even though the system attempts to be especially cautious in capital cases, unacceptable mistakes can occur. Although there is careful review of death penalty sentences, relatively few stays of execution are actually granted (about two out of fifty); obviously, there is room for judicial error.[74]

Unfair Use of Discretion   Critics also frown on the tremendous discretion used in seeking the death penalty and the arbitrary manner in which it is imposed. Of the approximately 10,000 persons convicted each year on homicide charges, only 250 to 300 are sentenced to death, while an equal number receive a sentence of probation or community supervision only. It is true that many convicted murderers do not commit first-degree murder and therefore are ineligible for execution, but it is also likely that many serious criminals who could have received the death penalty are not sentenced to death because of prosecutorial discretion. Some escape death by cooperating or giving testimony against their partners in the crime. A person who commits a particularly heinous crime and knows full well that he will receive the death penalty if convicted may be the one most likely to plea-bargain to avoid capital punishment. Is it fair to spare the life of a dangerous killer who cooperates with the prosecutor while executing another who does not?

Abolitionists also argue that juries use inappropriate discretion when they make capital punishment recommendations. The ongoing Capital Jury Project has been interviewing members of juries involved in making death penalty decisions and finds that many are motivated by ignorance and error (see Exhibit 10.2).

To read more about the Capital Jury Project, go to
www.lawschool.cornell.edu/lawlibrary/death/cjp_publ.htm

Vicious Criminals Often Go Free   Some vicious criminals who grievously injure victims during murder attempts are spared the death penalty because a physician's skill saved the victim. Some notable cases come to mind. Lawrence Singleton used

Exhibit 10.2   The Capital Jury Project (CJP)

The Capital Jury Project (CJP), begun by sociologist William Bowers in 1990, has sent research teams to fifteen states to interview jurors in death penalty cases. The three-hour-plus interviews are taped and coded for analysis.

CJP findings show that the decision making in capital cases often strays from legal and moral guidelines. Some express overwhelming racial prejudice in making their decisions. Others say that they have decided on the punishment before the trial is completed and the defendant found guilty!

Others are confused about the law and influenced by factual misconceptions. For example, many believe that prison terms are far shorter than they really are and many underestimate the time served for murder by ten years or more. Many jurors mistakenly believe that the death penalty is mandatory in cases when it is not, while others reject capital punishment in situations in which the law clearly mandates its use. The greater the factual errors, the most likely the juror will vote for death.

Many capital jurors are unwilling to accept primary responsibility for their punishment decisions. They vote for the death penalty in the mistaken belief that most defendants will never be executed, absolving them of responsibility. They often place responsibility for the defendant's punishment elsewhere, such as with the judge or other jurors. For example, one female juror who had recommended death told CJP interviewers that she had voted only to go along with the other jurors and that she had never believed the man should be executed. "I really had no thought about it," she said. "It wasn't my choice to make. It was a judgment call. It really doesn't mean a whole lot what I say because it's ultimately up to the judge." These feelings were most often expressed in states where the law allows judges to override a jury's decisions and either impose or reject a capital sentence.

The CJP findings indicate that jurors often rely on faulty information and use extralegal criteria in making a decision that is truly "life or death."

Sources: William J. Bowers, "The Capital Jury Project: Rationale, Design, and Preview of Early Findings," *Indiana Law Journal 70* (1995): 1043–1102; William J. Bowers, Marla Sandys, and Benjamin Steiner, "Foreclosed Impartiality in Capital Sentencing: Jurors' Predispositions, Trial Experience, and Premature Decision Making," *Cornell Law Review 83* (1998): 1476–1556; Margaret Vandiver, "Race in the Jury Room: A Preliminary Analysis of Cases from the Capital Jury Project," unpublished paper presented to the American Academy of Criminal Justice Sciences, March 1997.

an axe to cut off the arms of a woman he raped, yet he served only eight years in prison because the victim's life was saved by prompt medical care (after being released from prison, Singleton killed a female companion in 1997). "David," a boy severely burned in a murder attempt, lives in fear because his assailant, his father, Charles Rothenberg, was paroled from prison after serving a short sentence.[75] Although these horrific crimes received national attention and the intent to kill the victim was present, the death penalty could not be applied because of the availability of effective medical treatment. Areas that have superior medical resources actually have lower murder rates than less well-equipped areas; for example, ambulance response time can reduce the death rate by expeditiously transporting victims to an appropriate treatment center.[76] It makes little sense to punish someone for an impulsive murder while sparing the life of those who intentionally maim and torture victims who happen by chance to live because of prompt medical care.

Misplaced Vengeance   Although critics acknowledge that the general public approves of the death penalty, they maintain that prevailing attitudes reflect a primitive desire for revenge and not "just desert." Public acceptance of capital punishment has been compared to the approval of human sacrifices practiced by the Aztecs in Mexico five hundred years ago.[77] It is ironic that many death penalty advocates also oppose abortion on the grounds that it is the taking of human life.[78] The desire to be vengeful and punitive outweighs their concern about taking life.

Even if the majority of the general public favors the death penalty, support has been associated with prejudice against racial minorities and the approval of revenge as a rationale for punishment.[79] Public support is not as strong as death penalty advocates believe: When surveys ask about a choice of punishments, such as life without parole, support for the death penalty declines from 80 percent to 50 percent.[80] Public opinion is influenced by such factors as the personal characteristics of the offender and the circumstances of the offense. Therefore, the public does not support death in many cases of first-degree murder.[81] It is possible that politicians favor the death penalty in the mistaken belief that the public favors such harsh punishment for criminal offenders.[82]

No Deterrent Effect   Those opposed to the death penalty also find little merit in the argument that capital punishment deters crime. They charge that insufficient evidence exists that the threat of a death sentence can convince potential murderers to forgo their criminal activity. Most murders involve people who knew each other, very often friends and family members. Since murderers are often under the influence of alcohol or drugs or are suffering severe psychological turmoil, no penalty will likely be a deterrent. Most research concludes that the death penalty is not an effective deterrent.[83] For example, Keith Harries and Derral Cheatwood studied differences in homicide rates in 293 contingent counties in the United States and found that there were actually higher violent crime rates in counties that routinely employed the death penalty than in those in which the use of the death penalty was quite rare.[84]

Hope of Rehabilitation   The death sentence also rules out any hope of offender rehabilitation. There is evidence that convicted killers actually make good parole risks; convicted murderers are actually model inmates, and once released, commit fewer crimes than other parolees. It is possible that the general public, including people who sit on juries, overestimate the dangerousness of people who commit murder. One recent study found that capital jurors estimated that there was an 85 percent likelihood that the defendant would commit a future violent crime and a 50 percent likelihood that the defendant would commit a new homicide if they were given a sentence of life imprisonment. In reality, those people given a life sentence for capital murder have a *less than 1 percent* (0.2 percent) chance of committing another homicide over a forty-year term; the risk of their committing an assault is about 16 percent.[85]

Racial, Gender, and Other Bias   Capital punishment may be tarnished by gender, racial, and ethnic and other biases. There is evidence that homicides with male offenders and female victims are more likely to result in a death sentence than homicides involving female offenders and male victims.[86] Homicides involving strangers are more likely to result in a death sentence than homicides involving nonstrangers and acquaintances. Prosecutors are more likely to recommend the death sentence for people who kill white victims than they are in any other racial combination of victim and criminal—for example, whites who kill blacks.[87] It is not surprising, then, that since the death penalty was first instituted in the United States, disproportionate numbers of minorities have been executed. Charges of racial bias are supported by the disproportionate numbers of African Americans who have received the death sentence, are currently on death row, and who have been executed (53.5 percent of all executions). Racism was particularly blatant when the death penalty was invoked in rape cases: of those receiving the death penalty for rape, 90 percent in the South and 63 percent in the North and West were African American.[88] Today, about 40 percent of the inmates on death row are African American, a number disproportionate to the minority representation in the population.

White criminals arrested for homicide actually have a slightly greater chance of getting the death penalty than African Americans do, and a majority of murderers executed since 1980 have also been white.[89] Does this statistical anomaly mean that discrimination in the use of the death penalty has either ended or that it never actually existed? The answer may be that simply calculating the relative proportion of each racial group sentenced to death may not tell the whole story. A number of researchers have found that the death penalty is associated with the race of the victim rather than the race of the offender. In most instances, as mentioned before, prosecutors are more likely to ask for the death penalty if the victim was white. The fact that most murders involving a white victim also involve a white attacker (86 percent) accounts for the higher death sentence rate for white murderers.[90] With few exceptions, the relatively infrequent interracial murder cases involving a black criminal and a white victim (14 percent) are the most likely to result in the death penalty.[91] In contrast, since 1976 only two white criminals have been executed for murdering a black victim, the most recent being Kermit Smith, who was executed on January 24, 1995, in North Carolina for the kidnap, rape, and murder of a twenty-year-old college cheerleader.[92]

Causes More Crime Than It Deters Some critics fear that the introduction of capital punishment will encourage criminals to escalate their violent behavior, consequently putting police officers at risk. For example, a suspect who kills someone during a botched robbery may be inclined to "fire away" upon encountering police rather than surrender peacefully; the killer faces the death penalty already, what does he have to lose? Geoffrey Rapp studied the effect of capital punishment on the killings of police and found that, all other things being equal, the greater the number of new inmates on death row, the greater the number of police officers killed by citizens.[93] Rapp concluded that what the death penalty seems to do is create an extremely dangerous environment for law enforcement officers because it does not deter criminals and may lull officers into a false sense of security, because officers believe that the death penalty will deter violence directed against them and will cause them to let their guard down.

It Is Brutal Abolitionists believe that executions are unnecessarily cruel and inhuman and come at a high moral and social cost. Our society does not punish criminals by subjecting them to the same acts they themselves committed. Rapists are not sexually assaulted, and arsonists do not have their houses burned down; why, then, should murderers be killed?

Robert Johnson has described the execution process as a form of torture in which the condemned are first tormented psychologically by being made to feel powerless and alone while on death row; suicide is a constant problem among those on death row.[94] The execution itself is a barbaric affair marked by the smell of burning flesh and stiffened bodies. The executioners suffer from delayed stress reactions, including anxiety and a dehumanized personal identity.

The brutality of the death penalty may actually produce more violence than it prevents—the so-called **brutalization effect**.[95] Executions may increase murder rates because they raise the general violence level in society and because violence-prone people actually identify with the executioner, not with the target of the death penalty. When someone gets in a conflict with such individuals or challenges their authority, they execute them in the same manner the state executes people who violate its rules.[96] The brutalization effect was encountered by John Cochran and his associates when they studied the influence of a well-publicized execution in Oklahoma: after the execution, murders of strangers actually increased by one per month.[97] Follow-up research by William Bailey finds that (1) the brutalization effect extends to other types of murder (for example, nonstranger murder) and (2) a vicarious brutalization effect may occur where people in a state that does not practice capital punishment are influenced by news reports of executions in death penalty states.[98]

Because of its brutality, many enlightened nations have abandoned the death penalty with few ill effects. Abolitionists point out that such nations as Denmark and Sweden have long abandoned the death penalty and that 40 percent of the countries with a death penalty have active abolitionist movements.[99] It is ironic that citizens of countries that have eliminated the death penalty sometimes

brutalization effect The belief that capital punishment creates an atmosphere of brutality that enhances, rather than deters, the level of violence in society. The death penalty reinforces the view that violence is an appropriate response to provocation.

find themselves on death row in the United States. For example, a Paraguayan citizen, Angel Francisco Breard, age thirty-two, was executed on April 14, 1998, in Virginia, for murder and attempted rape, despite a plea from the International Court of Justice that he be spared and intense efforts by the Paraguayan government to stay the execution.[100]

It Is Expensive   Some people complain that they do not want to support "some killer in prison for thirty years." Abolitionists counter that legal appeals drive the cost of executions far higher than the cost of years of incarceration. If the money spent on the judicial process were invested, the interest would more than pay for the lifetime upkeep of death row inmates. For example, in 1998 there were 508 men and 9 women on death row in California. Because of numerous appeals, the median time between conviction by a jury, sentencing by a judge, and execution averaged fourteen years. The cost of processing appeals is extremely costly, and the annual budget for the state's public defender staff of forty-five lawyers who represent inmates in death cases is $5 million.[101]

At least thirty states now have a sentence of life in prison without parole, and this can more than make up for an execution. Being locked up in a hellish prison without any chance of release (barring a rare executive reprieve) may be a worse punishment than a painless death by lethal injection. If vengeance is the goal, life without parole may eliminate the need for capital punishment.

Legal Issues

The constitutionality of the death penalty has been a major concern to both the nation's courts and its social scientists. In 1972 the U.S. Supreme Court in *Furman v. Georgia*[102] decided that the discretionary imposition of the death penalty was cruel and unusual punishment under the Eighth and Fourteenth Amendments of the U.S. Constitution. This case not only questioned whether capital punishment is a more effective deterrent than life imprisonment but also challenged the very existence of the death penalty on the grounds of its brutality and finality. The Supreme Court did not completely rule out the use of capital punishment as a penalty; rather, it objected to the arbitrary and capricious manner in which it was imposed. After *Furman*, many states changed statutes that had allowed jury discretion in imposing the death penalty. In some states this was accomplished by enacting statutory guidelines for jury decisions; in others the death penalty was made mandatory for certain crimes only. Despite these changes in statutory law, no further executions were carried out while the Court pondered additional cases concerning the death penalty.

Then, in July 1976, the Supreme Court ruled on the constitutionality of five state death penalty statutes. In the first case, *Gregg v. Georgia*,[103] the Court found valid the Georgia statute holding that a finding by the jury of at least one "aggravating circumstance" out of ten is required in pronouncing the death penalty in murder cases. In the *Gregg* case, for example, the jury imposed the death penalty after finding beyond a reasonable doubt two aggravating circumstances: (1) the offender was engaged in the commission of two other capital felonies, and (2) the offender committed the offense of murder for the purpose of receiving money and other financial gains (for example, an automobile).[104]

In probably one of the most important death penalty cases, *McLesky v. Kemp,* the Court upheld the conviction of a black defendant in Georgia, despite social science evidence that black criminals who kill white victims have a significantly greater chance of receiving the death penalty than white offenders who kill black victims. The Court ruled that the evidence of racial patterns in capital sentencing was not persuasive without a finding of racial bias in the immediate case.[105] Many observers believe that *McLesky* presented the last significant legal

In the 2002 ruling *Ring v. Arizona,* the U.S. Supreme Court ruled that juries, not judges, must make the critical findings that send convicted killers to death row. However, Timothy Ring, shown here, a former state corrections officer, was sentenced to death by a judge for killing a guard in an armored truck robbery in 1994. Ring hoped to have his sentence overturned by the U.S. Supreme Court, but it affirmed the death sentence.

obstacle that death penalty advocates had to overcome and that, as a result, capital punishment will be a sentence in the United States for years to come (McLesky was executed in 1991).

Although the Court has generally supported the death penalty, it has also placed some limitations on its use. Rulings have promoted procedural fairness in the capital sentencing process. For example, the Court has limited the death penalty sentence to capital murder cases, ruling that it is not permissible to punish rapists with death.[106] It has prohibited prosecutors from presenting damaging evidence about the defendant's background unless it is directly relevant to the case.[107]

The Court has also reinforced the idea that mental and physical conditions such as age, though not excusing criminal behavior, can be considered as mitigating factors in capital sentencing decisions. In *Wilkins v. Missouri* and *Stanford v. Kentucky,* the Court set a limit of sixteen years as the age of defendants who could be sentenced to death.[108] These rulings effectively barred the use of capital punishment for minors under the age of sixteen who have been waived or transferred from the juvenile to the adult court system. And in a 2002 case, *Atkins v. Virginia,* the Court ruled that execution of mentally retarded criminals is "cruel and unusual punishment" prohibited by the Eighth Amendment. The Court noted that a significant number of states have concluded that death is not a suitable punishment for a mentally retarded criminal and the direction states have taken is to prohibit executing retarded offenders.[109]

Jury Issues

The role of the jury has become an important legal issue in the debate over capital punishment. One area of interest is the **death-qualified jury,** in which any person opposed in concept to capital punishment has been removed during voir dire.

death-qualified jury   The process during jury selection of removing any juror in a capital case who acknowledges that he or she will not convict knowing that there is a potential for the death penalty being applied. The U.S. Supreme Court has ruled that prosecutors have the right to discharge those jurors who would not consider the death penalty under any circumstances.

Defense attorneys are opposed to death qualification because it bars from serving on juries those citizens who oppose the death penalty and who may be more liberal and less likely to convict defendants. Death qualification creates juries that are nonrepresentative of the 20 percent of the public that opposes capital punishment.

In *Witherspoon v. Illinois* (1968), the Supreme Court upheld the practice of excusing jurors who are opposed to the death penalty.[110] The Court has made it easier to convict people in death penalty cases by ruling that any jurors can be excused if their views on capital punishment are deemed by a trial judge to "prevent or substantially impair the performance of their duties."[111] The Court has also ruled that jurors can be removed because of their opposition to the death penalty at the guilt phase of a trial, even though they would not have to consider the issue of capital punishment until a separate sentencing hearing. In *Lockhart v. McCree* (1986), the Court also ruled that removing anti-capital-punishment jurors does not violate the Sixth Amendment provision that juries represent a fair cross section of the community, nor does it unfairly tip the scale toward juries who are prone to convict people in capital cases.[112] So, it appears that for the present, prosecutors will be able to excuse jurors who feel that the death penalty is wrong or immoral.

A second jury issue is whether it is the judge or jury who makes the decision to use the death penalty. Some states had left this critical decision to the judge alone. However, in a 2002 ruling, *Ring v. Arizona,* the U.S. Supreme Court ruled that juries, not judges, must make the critical findings that send convicted killers to death row. The seven-to-two ruling should force states that allow judge-only decisions, such as Arizona, Colorado, Idaho, Montana, and Nebraska, to redo their death penalty statutes, and it should also affect states such Florida, Alabama, Indiana, and Delaware, which allow a judge to impose a death sentence despite a jury's recommendation of life in prison; many people now on death row may have to have their sentence reconsidered or reduced. The Court reasoned that the Sixth Amendment's right to a jury trial would be "senselessly diminished" if it did not allow jurors to decide whether a person deserves the death penalty.[113]

Does the Death Penalty Deter Murder?

The key issue in the capital punishment debate is whether it can actually lower the murder rate and save lives. Despite its inherent cruelty, capital punishment might be justified if it proved to be an effective crime deterrent that could save many innocent lives. Abolitionists claim it has no real deterrent value; advocates claim it does. Who is correct?

Considerable empirical research has been carried out on the effectiveness of capital punishment as a deterrent. In particular, studies have tried to discover whether the death sentence serves as a more effective deterrent than life imprisonment for capital crimes such as homicide. Three methods have been used:

- *Immediate-impact studies,* which calculate the effect a well-publicized execution has on the short-term murder rate
- *Time-series analysis,* which compares long-term trends in murder and capital punishment rates
- *Contiguous-state analysis,* which compares murder rates in states that have the death penalty with a similar state that has abolished capital punishment

Using these three methods over a sixty-year period, most researchers have failed to show any deterrent effect of capital punishment.[114] These studies show that murder rates do not seem to rise when a state abolishes capital punishment any more so than they decrease when the death penalty is adopted. The murder rate is also quite similar both in states that use the death penalty and neighboring states that have abolished capital punishment. Finally, little evidence shows that executions can lower the murder rate. For example, a test of the deterrent effect of the death penalty in Texas found no association between the frequency of execution during the years 1984 to 1997 and murder rates.[115]

Only a few studies have found that the long-term application of capital punishment may actually reduce the murder rate.[116] However, these have been disputed by researchers who have questioned the methodology used and indicate that the deterrent effects the studies uncover are an artifact of the statistical techniques used in the research.[117]

The general consensus among death penalty researchers today is that the threat of capital punishment has little effect on murder rates. It is still unknown why capital punishment fails as a deterrent, but the cause may lie in the nature of homicide. As noted earlier, murder is often a crime of passion involving people who know each other, and many murders are committed by people under the influence of drugs and alcohol—more than 50 percent of all people arrested for murder test positively for drug use. People involved in interpersonal conflict with friends, acquaintances, and family members and who may be under the influence of drugs and alcohol are not likely to be capable of considering the threat of the death penalty.

Murder rates have also been linked to the burdens of poverty and income inequality. Desperate adolescents who get caught up in the cycle of urban violence and become members of criminal groups and gangs may find that their life situation gives them little choice except to engage in violent and deadly behavior; they have few chances to ponder the deterrent impact of the death penalty.

The failure of the "ultimate deterrent" to deter the "ultimate crime" has been used by critics to question the value of capital punishment.

Despite the less-than-conclusive empirical evidence, many people still hold to the efficacy of the death penalty as a crime deterrent, and recent U.S. Supreme Court decisions seem to justify its use. Of course, even if the death penalty were no greater a deterrent than a life sentence, some people would still advocate its use on the grounds that it is the only way to permanently rid society of dangerous criminals who deserve to die. ■

SUMMARY

Punishment and sentencing have gone through various phases throughout the history of Western civilization. Initially, punishment was characterized by retribution and the need to fix sentences for convicted offenders. Throughout the middle years of the twentieth century, individualized sentencing was widely accepted, and the concept of rehabilitation was used in sentencing and penal codes. During the 1960s, however, experts began to become disenchanted with rehabilitation and concepts related to treating the individual offender. There was less emphasis on treatment and more on the legal rights of offenders. A number of states returned to the concept of punishment in terms of mandatory and fixed sentences.

Theorists suggest that the philosophy of sentencing has thus changed from a concentration on rehabilitation to a focus on incapacitation and deterrence, where the goal is to achieve equality of punishment and justice in the law and to lock up dangerous criminals for as long as possible.

Sentencing in today's criminal justice system is based on deterrence, incapacitation, and rehabilitation. Traditional dispositions include fines, probation, and incarceration, with probation being the most common choice.

A number of states have developed determinate sentences that eliminate parole and attempt to restrict judicial discretion. Methods for making dispositions more uniform include the institution of sentencing guidelines that create uniform sentences based on offender background and crime characteristics. Despite these changes, most states continue to use indeterminate sentences, which give convicted offenders a short minimum sentence after which they can be released on parole if they are considered "rehabilitated." Jurisdictions that use either determinate or indeterminate sentences allow inmates to be released early on good behavior.

The death penalty continues to be the most controversial sentence, with over half the states reinstituting capital punishment laws since the *Furman v. Georgia* decision of 1972. Although there is little evidence that the death penalty deters murder, supporters still view it as necessary in terms of incapacitation and retribution and cite the public's support for the death penalty and the low

chance of error in its application. Opponents point out that mistakes can be made, that capital sentences are apportioned in a racially biased manner, and that the practice is cruel and barbaric. Nonetheless, the courts have generally supported the legality of capital punishment, and it has been used more frequently in recent years.

For an up-to-date list of Web links, go to
http://cj.wadsworth.com/siegel_essen4e.

KEY TERMS

wergild 307	specific deterrence 310	concurrent sentence 313	chivalry hypothesis 324
penitentiary 308	blameworthy 310	indeterminate sentence 313	victim impact statement 325
general deterrence 309	just desert 310	determinate sentence 315	
incapacitation 310	equity 311	mandatory sentence 318	brutalization effect 335
recidivism 310	consecutive sentence 313	truth in sentencing 319	death-qualified jury 337

INFOTRAC COLLEGE EDITION EXERCISES

CAPITAL PUNISHMENT provokes more debate than almost any other criminal justice issue. Some oppose the death penalty on moral and religious grounds. They argue, for example, that many innocent people are on death row. Read about this issue in Ramesh Ponnuru, "Bad List: A Suspect Roll of Death Row 'Innocents,'" *National Review,* September 16, 2002 v54 i17.

ANOTHER CRITICISM is that the United States is one of the few nations that executes people who committed crimes while they were juveniles. Read more about this provocative topic in Allyssa D. Wheaton-Rodriguez, "The United States' Choice to

Violate International Law by Allowing the Juvenile Death Penalty," *Houston Journal of International Law,* Fall 2001 v24 i1 p209(18).

ALTHOUGH MOST ACADEMICS are opposed to the death penalty for these and other reasons, some still believe it is a valuable criminal justice policy. Use the "death penalty" as a subject guide on InfoTrac College Edition to research the utility and benefits of the death penalty. Do you agree with those who advocate its use?

QUESTIONS

1. Discuss the sentencing dispositions in your jurisdiction. What are the pros and cons of each?

2. Compare the various types of incarceration sentences. What are the similarities and differences? Why are many jurisdictions considering the passage of mandatory sentencing laws?

3. Discuss the issue of capital punishment. In your opinion, does it serve as a deterrent? What new rulings has the U.S. Supreme Court made on the legality of the death penalty?

4. Why does the problem of sentencing disparity exist? Do programs exist that can reduce disparate sentences? If so, what are they? Should all people who commit the same crime receive the same sentence? Explain.

5. Should convicted criminals be released from prison when correctional authorities are convinced they are rehabilitated? Why or why not?

NOTES

1. Patrick O'Neill, "The Business of Killing," *Independent Weekly,* 14 March 2001.
2. Michel Foucault, *Discipline and Punishment* (New York: Vintage Books, 1978).
3. Graeme Newman, *The Punishment Response* (Philadelphia: Lippincott, 1978), 13.
4. Peter Greenwood with Allan Abrahamse, *Selective Incapacitation* (Santa Monica, Calif.: Rand, 1982).

5. Kathleen Auerhahn, "Selective Incapacitation and the Problem of Prediction," *Criminology* 37 (1999): 703–734.

6. Kathleen Daly, "Neither Conflict nor Labeling nor Paternalism Will Suffice: Intersections of Race, Ethnicity, Gender, and Family in Criminal Court Decisions," *Crime and Delinquency* 35 (1989): 136–168.

7. Among the most helpful sources for this section were Benedict Alper, *Prisons Inside-Out* (Cambridge, Mass.: Ballinger, 1974); Gustave de Beaumont and Alexis de Tocqueville, *On the Penitentiary System in the United States and Its Applications in France* (Carbondale: Southern Illinois University Press, 1964); Orlando Lewis, *The Development of American Prisons and Prison Customs, 1776–1845* (Montclair, N.J.: Patterson-Smith, 1967); Leonard Orland, ed., *Justice, Punishment, and Treatment* (New York: Free Press, 1973); J. Goebel, *Felony and Misdemeanor* (Philadelphia: University of Pennsylvania Press, 1976); George Rusche and Otto Kircheimer, *Punishment and Social Structure* (New York: Russell & Russell, 1939); Samuel Walker, *Popular Justice* (New York: Oxford University Press, 1980); Newman, *The Punishment Response*; David Rothman, *Conscience and Convenience* (Boston: Little, Brown, 1980); George Ives, *A History of Penal Methods* (Montclair, N.J.: Patterson-Smith, 1970); Robert Hughes, *The Fatal Shore* (New York: Knopf, 1986); Leon Radzinowicz, *A History of English Criminal Law,* vol. 1 (London: Stevens, 1943), 5.

8. *Crime and Punishment in America, 1999,* Report 229 (Washington, D.C.: National Center for Policy Analysis, 1999).

9. Ibid.

10. Robert Davis, Barbara Smith, and Laura Nickles, "The Deterrent Effect of Prosecuting Domestic Violence Misdemeanors," *Crime and Delinquency* 44 (1998): 434–442.

11. Christopher D. Maxwell, Joel H. Garner, and Jeffrey A. Fagan, *The Effects of Arrest in Intimate Partner Violence: New Evidence from the Spouse Assault Replication Program* (Washington, D.C.: National Institute of Justice, 2001).

12. Patrick Langan and David Levin, *Recidivism of Prisoners Released in 1994* (Washington, D.C.: Bureau of Justice Statistics, 2002).

13. Charles Logan, *Criminal Justice Performance Measures for Prisons* (Washington, D.C.: Bureau of Justice Statistics, 1993), 3.

14. Alexis Durham, "The Justice Model in Historical Context: Early Law, the Emergence of Science, and the Rise of Incarceration," *Journal of Criminal Justice* 16 (1988): 331–346.

15. Andrew von Hirsh, *Doing Justice: The Choice of Punishments* (New York: Hill and Wang, 1976).

16. Shawn Bushway, "The Impact of an Arrest on the Job Stability of Young White American Men," *Journal of Research in Crime and Delinquency* 35 (1998): 454–479.

17. Lawrence W. Sherman, David P. Farrington, Doris Layton MacKenzie, Brandon Walsh, Denise Gottfredson, John Eck, Shawn Bushway, and Peter Reuter, *Evidence-Based Crime Prevention* (London: Routledge and Kegan Paul, 2002); see also Arnulf Kolstad, "Imprisonment as Rehabilitation: Offenders' Assessment of Why It Does Not Work," *Journal of Criminal Justice* 24 (1996): 323–335.

18. Charles Logan and Gerald Gaes, "Meta-Analysis and the Rehabilitation of Punishment," *Justice Quarterly* 10 (1993): 245–264.

19. Richard McCorkle, "Research Note: Punish and Rehabilitate? Public Attitudes Toward Six Common Crimes," *Crime and Delinquency* 39 (1993): 240–252; D. A. Andrews, Ivan Zinger, Robert Hoge, James Bonta, Paul Gendreau, and Francis Cullen, "Does Correctional Treatment Work? A Clinically Relevant and Psychologically Informed Meta-Analysis," *Criminology* 28 (1990): 369–404.

20. Francis Cullen, John Paul Wright, Shayna Brown, Melissa Moon, and Brandon Applegate, "Public Support for Early Intervention Programs: Implications for a Progressive Policy Agenda," *Crime and Delinquency* 44 (1998): 187–204.

21. Paula Ditton and Doris James Wilson, *Truth in Sentencing in State Prisons* (Washington, D.C.: Bureau of Justice Statistics, 1999).

22. Jo Dixon, "The Organizational Context of Criminal Sentencing," *American Journal of Sociology* 100 (1995): 1157–1198.

23. Michael Tonry, *Reconsidering Indeterminate and Structured Sentencing Series: Sentencing and Corrections: Issues for the 21st Century* (Washington, D.C.: National Institute of Justice, 1999).

24. Michael Tonry, *The Fragmentation of Sentencing and Corrections in America* (Washington, D.C.: National Institute of Justice, 1999).

25. Ibid., 11.

26. Robin Lubitz and Thomas Ross, *Sentencing Guidelines: Reflections on the Future* (Washington, D.C.: National Institute of Justice, June 2001).

27. Minnesota Sentencing Guidelines Commission, 2002; www.msgc.state.mn.us/msgcwork.htm.

28. Ibid.

29. Michael Tonry, "The Failure of the U.S. Sentencing Commission's Guidelines," *Crime and Delinquency* 39 (1993): 131–149.

30. Michael Tonry, "Racial Politics, Racial Disparities, and the War on Crime," *Crime and Delinquency* 40 (1994): 475–494.

31. Joan Petersilia and Susan Turner, *Guideline-Based Justice: The Implications for Racial Minorities* (Santa Monica, Calif.: Rand, 1985).

32. Elaine Wolf and Marsha Weissman, "Revising Federal Sentencing Policy: Some Consequences of Expanding Eligibility for Alternative Sanctions," *Crime and Delinquency* 42 (1996): 192–205.

33. Tonry, "The Failure of the U.S. Sentencing Commission's Guidelines," 131.

34. Michael Tonry, *Sentencing Matters* (New York: Oxford University Press, 1996), 5.

35. Henry Scott Wallace, "Mandatory Minimums and the Betrayal of Sentencing Reform: A Legislative Dr. Jekyll and Mr. Hyde," *Federal Probation* 57 (1993): 9–16.

36. Paula M. Ditton and Doris James Wilson, *Truth in Sentencing in State Prisons* (Washington, D.C.: Bureau of Justice Statistics, 1999).

37. Matthew Durose and Patrick A. Langan, *State Court Sentencing of Convicted Felons, 1998* (Washington, D.C.: Bureau of Justice Statistics, February 2001).

38. Brent Smith and Kelly Damphouse, "Terrorism, Politics, and Punishment: A Test of Structural-Contextual Theory and the Liberation Hypothesis," *Criminology* 36 (1998): 67–92.

39. For a general look at the factors that affect sentencing, see Susan Welch, Cassia Spohn, and John Gruhl, "Convicting and Sentencing Differences Among Black, Hispanic, and White Males in Six Localities," *Justice Quarterly* 2 (1985): 67–80.

40. Tracy Nobiling, Cassia Spohn, and Miriam DeLone, "A Tale of Two Counties: Unemployment and Sentence Severity," *Justice Quarterly* 15 (1998): 459–486.

41. Stewart D'Alessio and Lisa Stolzenberg, "Socioeconomic Status and the Sentencing of the Traditional Offender," *Journal of Criminal Justice* 21 (1993): 61–77.

42. Cecilia Saulters-Tubbs, "Prosecutorial and Judicial Treatment of Female Offenders," *Federal Probation* 57 (1993): 37–41.

43. See, generally, Janet Johnston, Thomas Kennedy, and I. Gayle Shuman, "Gender Differences in the Sentencing of Felony Offenders," *Federal Probation* 87 (1987): 49–56; Cassia Spohn and Susan Welch, "The Effect of Prior Record in Sentencing Research: An Examination of the Assumption That Any Measure Is Adequate," *Justice Quarterly* 4 (1987): 286–302; David Willison, "The Effects of Counsel on the Severity of Criminal Sentences: A Statistical Assessment," *Justice System Journal* 9 (1984): 87–101.

44. Cassia Spohn, Miriam DeLone, and Jeffrey Spears, "Race/Ethnicity, Gender, and Sentence Severity in Dade County, Florida: An Examination of the Decision to Withhold Adjudication," *Journal of Crime and Justice* 21 (1998): 111–132.

45. Ellen Hochstedler Steury and Nancy Frank, "Gender Bias and Pretrial Release: More Pieces of the Puzzle," *Journal of Criminal Justice* 18 (1990): 417–432.

46. Dean Champion, "Elderly Felons and Sentencing Severity: Interregional Variations in Leniency and Sentencing Trends," *Criminal Justice Review* 12 (1987): 7–15.

47. Darrell Steffensmeier, John Kramer, and Jeffery Ulmer, "Age Differences in Sentencing," *Justice Quarterly* 12 (1995): 583–601.

48. Darrell Steffensmeier, Jeffery Ulmer, and John Kramer, "The Interaction of Race, Gender, and Age in Criminal Sentencing: The Punishment Cost of Being Young, Black, and Male," *Criminology* 36 (1998): 763–798.

49. *Payne v. Tennessee*, 111 S.Ct. 2597, 115 L.Ed.2d 720 (1991).

50. Robert Davis and Barbara Smith, "The Effects of Victim Impact Statements on Sentencing Decisions: A Test in an Urban Setting," *Justice Quarterly* 11 (1994): 453–469; Edna Erez and Pamela Tontodonato, "The Effect of Victim Participation in Sentencing on Sentence Outcome," *Criminology* 28 (1990): 451–474.

51. Rodney Kingsworth, Randall MacIntosh, and Jennifer Wentworth, "Sexual Assault: The Role of Prior Relationship and Victim Characteristics in Case Processing," *Justice Quarterly* 16 (1999): 276–302.

52. Michael Tonry, *Malign Neglect: Race, Crime, and Punishment in America* (New York: Oxford University Press, 1995), 105–109.

53. *Coker v. Georgia*, 433 U.S. 584, 97 S.Ct. 2861, 53 L.Ed.2d 982 (1977).

54. "Many State Legislatures Focused on Crime in 1995, Study Finds," *Criminal Justice Newsletter*, 2 January 1996, 2.

55. The most recent data on capital punishment used here is from Tracy Snell, *Capital Punishment 2000* (Washington, D.C.: Bureau of Justice Statistics, 2001).

56. See, for example, *Lopez v. Singletary*, 719 So. 2d 287 (Fla. 1998).

57. Stephen Markman and Paul Cassell, "Protecting the Innocent: A Response to the Bedeau-Radelet Study," *Stanford Law Review* 41 (1988): 121–170.

58. Snell, *Capital Punishment*, 2.

59. Stephen Layson, "United States Time-Series Homicide Regressions with Adaptive Expectations," *Bulletin of the New York Academy of Medicine* 62 (1986): 589–619.

60. James Galliher and John Galliher, " A 'Commonsense' Theory of Deterrence and the 'Ideology' of Science: The New York State Death Penalty Debate," *Journal of Criminal Law & Criminology* 92 (2002): 307.

61. Steven Stack, "Publicized Executions and Homicide, 1950–1980," *American Sociological Review* 52 (1987): 532–540; for a study challenging Stack's methods, see William Bailey and Ruth Peterson, "Murder and Capital Punishment: A Monthly Time-Series Analysis of Execution Publicity," *American Sociological Review* 54 (1989): 722–743.

62. Steven Stack, "The Effect of Well-Publicized Executions on Homicide in California," *Journal of Crime and Justice* 21 (1998): 1–12.

63. David Friedrichs, "Comment—Humanism and the Death Penalty: An Alternative Perspective," *Justice Quarterly* 6 (1989): 197–209.

64. Kathleen Maguire and Ann L. Pastore, eds., *Sourcebook of Criminal Justice Statistics*, 2002; www.albany.edu/sourcebook/.

65. For an analysis of the formation of public opinion on the death penalty, see Kimberly Cook, "Public Support for the Death Penalty: A Cultural Analysis" (Paper presented at the annual meeting of the American Society of Criminology, San Francisco, November 1991).

66. Alexis Durham, H. Preston Elrod, and Patrick Kinkade, "Public Support to the Death Penalty: Beyond Gallup," *Justice Quarterly* 13 (1996): 705–736.

67. See, generally, Hugo Bedeau, *Death Is Different: Studies in the Morality, Law, and Politics of Capital Punishment* (Boston: Northeastern University Press, 1987); Keith Otterbein, *The Ultimate Coercive Sanction* (New Haven, Conn.: HRAF Press, 1986).

68. "Illinois Ex-Prosecutors Charged with Framing Murder Defendants," *Criminal Justice Newsletter* 28 (1997): 3.

69. Jim Yardley, "Convicted in Murder Case, Man Cleared Seven Years Later," *New York Times*, 29 October 1998, A3.

70. House Subcommittee on Civil and Constitutional Rights, *Innocence and the Death Penalty: Assessing the Danger of Mistaken Executions* (Washington, D.C.: Government Printing Office, 1993).

71. David Stewart, "Dealing with Death," *American Bar Association Journal* 80 (1994): 53.

72. "The Innocence Protection Act," editorial, *America* 187 (23 September 2002): 2–3.

73. Michael Radelet and Hugo Bedeau, "Miscarriages of Justice in Potentially Capital Cases," *Stanford Law Review* 40 (1987): 121–181.

74. Stewart, "Dealing with Death."

75. "A Victim's Progress," *Newsweek*, 12 June 1989, 5.

76. William Doerner, "The Impact of Medical Resources on Criminally Induced Lethality: A Further Examination," *Criminology* 26 (1988): 171–77.

77. Elizabeth Purdom and J. Anthony Paredes, "Capital Punishment and Human Sacrifice," in *Facing the Death Penalty: Essays on Cruel and Unusual Punishment*, ed. Michael Radelet (Philadelphia: Temple University Press, 1989), 152–153.

78. Kimberly Cook, "A Passion to Punish: Abortion Opponents Who Favor the Death Penalty," *Justice Quarterly* 15 (1998): 329–346.

79. Steven Barkan and Steven Cohn, "Racial Prejudice and Support for the Death Penalty by Whites," *Journal of Research in Crime and Delinquency* 31 (1994): 202–209; Robert Bohm and Ronald Vogel, "A Comparison of Factors Associated with Uninformed and Informed Death Penalty Opinions," *Journal of Criminal Justice* 22 (1994): 125–143.

80. Kathleen Maguire and Ann Pastore, *Sourcebook of Criminal Justice Statistics, 1995* (Washington, D.C.: Government Printing Office, 1996), 183.

81. Gennaro Vito and Thomas Keil, "Elements of Support for Capital Punishment: An Examination of Changing Attitudes," *Journal of Crime and Justice* 21 (1998): 17–25.

82. John Whitehead, Michael Blankenship, and John Paul Wright, "Elite Versus Citizen Attitudes on Capital Punishment: Incongruity Between the Public and Policy Makers," *Journal of Criminal Justice* 27 (1999): 249–258.

83. William Bowers and Glenn Pierce, "Deterrence or Brutalization: What Is the Effect of Executions?" *Crime and Delinquency* 26 (1980): 453–484.

84. Keith Harries and Derral Cheatwood, *The Geography of Executions: The Capital Punishment Quagmire in America* (Lanham, Md.: Rowman and Littlefield, 1997).

85. Jonathan R. Sorensen and Rocky L. Pilgrim, "An Actuarial Risk of Assessment of Violence Posed by Murder Defendants," *Journal of Criminal Law and Criminology* 90 (2000): 1251–1271.

86. Marian Williams and Jefferson Holcomb, "Racial Disparity and Death Sentences in Ohio," *Journal of Criminal Justice* 29 (2001): 207–218.

87. Jon Sorenson and Danold Wallace, "Prosecutorial Discretion in Seeking Death: An Analysis of Racial Disparity in the Pretrial Stages of Case Processing in a Midwestern County," *Justice Quarterly* 16 (1999): 559–578.

88. Lawrence Greenfield and David Hinners, *Capital Punishment, 1984* (Washington, D.C.: Bureau of Justice Statistics, 1985).

89. Gennaro Vito and Thomas Keil, "Capital Sentencing in Kentucky: An Analysis of the Factors Influencing Decision Making in the Post-Gregg Period," *Journal of Criminal Law and Criminology* 79 (1988): 493–503; David Baldus, C. Pulaski, and G. Woodworth, "Comparative Review of Death Sentences: An Empirical Study of the Georgia Experience," *Journal of Criminal Law and Criminology* 74 (1983): 661–685; Raymond Paternoster, "Race of the Victim and Location of Crime: The Decision to Seek the Death Penalty in South Carolina," *Journal of Criminal Law and Criminology* 74 (1983): 754–785.

90. Raymond Paternoster, "Prosecutorial Discretion and Capital Sentencing in North and South Carolina," in *The Death Penalty in America: Current Research,* ed. Robert Bohm (Cincinnati: Anderson, 1991), 39–52.

91. Vito and Keil, "Capital Sentencing in Kentucky," 502–503.

92. David Brown, "Man Is Executed in Carolina: Second of a White Who Killed a Black," *Boston Globe,* 25 January 1995, 3.

93. Geoffrey Rapp, "The Economics of Shootouts: Does the Passage of Capital Punishment Laws Protect or Endanger Police Officers?" *Albany Law Review* 65 (2002): 1051–1084.

94. Robert Johnson, *Death Work: A Study of the Modern Execution Process* (Pacific Grove, Calif.: Brooks/Cole, 1990).

95. William Bailey, "Disaggregation in Deterrence and Death Penalty Research: The Case of Murder in Chicago," *Journal of Criminal Law and Criminology* 74 (1986): 827–859.

96. Gennaro Vito, Pat Koester, and Deborah Wilson, "Return of the Dead: An Update on the Status of Furman-Commuted Death Row Inmates," in *The Death Penalty in America: Current Research,* ed. Robert Bohm (Cincinnati: Anderson, 1991), 89–100; Gennaro Vito, Deborah Wilson, and Edward Latessa, "Comparison of the Dead: Attributes and Outcomes of Furman-Commuted Death Row Inmates in Kentucky and Ohio," in *The Death Penalty in America: Current Research,* ed. Robert Bohm (Cincinnati: Anderson, 1991), 101–112.

97. John Cochran, Mitchell Chamlin, and Mark Seth, "Deterrence or Brutalization? An Impact Assessment of Oklahoma's Return to Capital Punishment," *Criminology* 32 (1994): 107–134.

98. William Bailey, "Deterrence, Brutalization, and the Death Penalty: Another Examination of Oklahoma's Return to Capital Punishment," *Justice Quarterly* 36 (1998): 711–734.

99. Joseph Schumacher, "An International Look at the Death Penalty," *International Journal of Comparative and Applied Criminal Justice* 14 (1990): 307–315.

100. David Stout, "Clemency Denied, Paraguayan Is Executed," *New York Times,* 15 April 1998.

101. Don Terry, "California Prepares for Faster Execution Pace," *New York Times,* 17 October 1998, A7.

102. *Furman v. Georgia,* 408 U.S. 238, 92 S.Ct. 2726, 33 L.Ed.2d 346 (1972).

103. *Gregg v. Georgia,* 428 U.S. 153, 96 S.Ct. 2909, 49 L.Ed.2d 859 (1976).

104. Ibid., at 205–207, 96 S.Ct. at 2940–2941.

105. *McLesky v. Kemp,* 428 U.S. 262, 96 S.Ct. 2950, 49 L.Ed.2d 929 (1976).

106. *Coker v. Georgia,* 430 U.S. 349, 97 S.Ct. 1197, 51 L.Ed.2d 393 (1977).

107. *Dawson v. Delaware,* 503 U.S. 159, 112 S.Ct. 1093, 117 L.Ed.2d 309 (1992).

108. *Wilkins v. Missouri* and *Stanford v. Kentucky,* 492 U.S. 361, 109 S.Ct. 2969, 106 L.Ed.2d 306 (1989).

109. *Atkins v. Virginia,* No. 00-8452, 2002.

110. *Witherspoon v. Illinois,* 391 U.S. 510, 88 S.Ct. 1770, 20 L.Ed.2d 776 (1968).

111. *Wainwright v. Witt,* 469 U.S. 412, 105 S.Ct. 844, 83 L.Ed.2d 841 (1985).

112. *Lockhart v. McCree,* 476 U.S. 162, 106 S.Ct. 1758, 90 L.Ed.2d 137 (1986).

113. *Ring vs. Arizona,* No. 01-488 (2002).

114. Walter C. Reckless, "Use of the Death Penalty," *Crime and Delinquency* 15 (1969): 43; Thorsten Sellin, "Effect of Repeal and Reintroduction of the Death Penalty on Homicide Rates," in *The Death Penalty,* ed. Thorsten Sellin (Philadelphia: American Law Institute, 1959); Robert H. Dann, "The Deterrent Effect of Capital Punishment," *Friends Social Service Series* 29 (1935): 1; William Bailey and Ruth Peterson, "Murder and Capital Punishment: A Monthly Time-Series Analysis of Execution Publicity," *American Sociological Review* 54 (1989): 722–743; David Phillips, "The Deterrent Effect of Capital Punishment," *American Journal of Sociology*

86 (1980): 139–148; Sam McFarland, "Is Capital Punishment a Short-Term Deterrent to Homicide? A Study of the Effects of Four Recent American Executions," *Journal of Criminal Law and Criminology* 74 (1984): 1014–1032; Richard Lempert, "The Effect of Executions on Homicides: A New Look in an Old Light," *Crime and Delinquency* 29 (1983): 88–115.

115. Jon Sorenson, Robert Wrinkle, Victoria Brewer, and James Marquart, "Capital Punishment and Deterrence: Examining the Effect of Executions on Murder in Texas," *Crime and Delinquency* 45 (1999): 481–493.

116. Isaac Ehrlich, "The Deterrent Effect of Capital Punishment: A Question of Life or Death," *American Economic Review* 65 (1975): 397.

117. For a review, see William Bailey, "The General Prevention Effect of Capital Punishment for Non-Capital Felonies," in *The Death Penalty in America: Current Research,* ed. Robert Bohm (Cincinnati: Anderson, 1991), 21–38.

Courts and Terrorism

Terrorist suspects have been tried in criminal courts under U.S. law for quite some time. The U.S. government has prosecuted the perpetrators of the 1993 World Trade Center bombing, the conspirators in a failed plot involving New York City tunnels, and those responsible for the 1998 bombings of two U.S. embassies in Africa. However, each new case provides a challenge to a legal system that is geared more for common law crimes such as murder and rape than international terrorist conspiracies. One of the most notorious cases under review at the time of this writing is that of Zacarias Moussaoui, a French-born Moroccan suspected of being the so-called twentieth hijacker in the September 11 attacks.

Moussaoui entered the United States in February 2001 and immediately enrolled in a flight school in Norman, Oklahoma, and then later at the Pan Am International Flying Academy in Eagan, Minnesota. His instructors became suspicious and called the FBI, which detained him on August 17, 2001, on immigration charges. After the World Trade Center attack, he was held as a material witness and then later charged with conspiracy. Moussaoui is currently charged with six criminal counts of conspiracy: to commit acts of terrorism across international boundaries, to destroy aircraft, to commit aircraft piracy, to use weapons of mass destruction, to murder U.S. employees, and to destroy U.S. property.

At the time of his arrest, FBI agents found flight manuals for the Boeing 747-400, a flight-simulator computer program, binoculars, two knives, fighting shields, and a laptop computer. They later learned that Moussaoui was suspected by the French government of involvement with Islamic extremists. The FBI team applied to Washington for a special warrant to go into Moussaoui's computer but were turned down: as it turned out, his disk contained information about spraying pesticide from a plane. Moussaoui was also carrying the phone number in Dusseldorf, Germany, of Ramzi bin al-Shibh, head of an al Qaeda cell that included Mohammed Atta, the leader of the September 11 attack. There is also evidence that al-Shibh sent Moussaoui money to pay for his flying lessons. (Al-Shibh is now in U.S. custody; he was captured during a shootout in Karachi, Pakistan, on September 13, 2002.)

Moussaoui denied any involvement in the crime. His lawyers contacted the French government and asked them to intervene in the case and to get him repatriated to France to stand trial there, arguing that he could not receive a fair trial in the United States but this was denied. The U.S. trial was slated to begin on October 14, 2002, but was postponed until June 2003 so that there would be more time to prepare a case.

The case against Moussaoui illustrates the difficulty prosecutors have in prosecuting suspected terrorists before they actually commit a violent act. Moussaoui's behavior followed patterns similar to that of the actual hijackers: attending flight-training school, inquiring into crop-dusting procedures, and receiving funding from suspected al Qaeda leaders. Yet many people attend flight school, studying crop dusting is not a crime, and his al Qaeda contacts are unlikely to be willing to testify against him in a court of law. There does not appear to be any physical evidence linking him to a conspiracy. On the other hand, it might not be difficult to sway a post–September 11 jury that Zacarias Moussaoui was part of a criminal conspiracy, even if the evidence is circumstantial. For example, reports have been circulated in highly regarded newspapers such as the *Washington Post,* that al Qaeda captives have told U.S. officials that Moussaoui met with Khalid Shaikh Mohammed, the suspected mastermind of the September 11 attacks, in late 2000 or early 2001 in Afghanistan. Even allegations of such a meeting may be enough to sway a jury.

Military Tribunals

Not all suspected terrorists will be tried in criminal courts if the government has its way. In November 2001 President Bush issued an executive order authorizing military tribunals rather than criminal courts to try foreigners accused of terrorism.

Military tribunals are typically convened during wartime to try extraordinary cases, usually involving foreigners, especially those accused of espionage. They are not bound by procedures followed in civilian courts. For example, they are closed to the public and allow a two-thirds majority of a jury that is made up of military officers to confer a sentence, even capital punishment. The Defense Department announced it was considering the following procedures when and if military tribunals are used:

- They will use juries of three to seven panelists, all of them military officers.
- They will require a two-thirds vote for conviction and sentencing, except where the death penalty is involved, in which case seven panelists must reach a unanimous decision.
- They will admit evidence including secondhand evidence and hearsay so long as it would have "probative value to a reasonable person."
- They will not require prosecutors to establish the "chain of custody" of evidence—that is, to account for how the evidence was transported from where it was found to the courtroom.
- They will provide defendants with military lawyers but allow them to hire civilian attorneys at their own expense.
- They will not allow defendants to appeal decisions in federal courts, but instead petition a panel of review, which may include civilians as well as military officers, to review decisions. The President, as commander-in-chief, will have final review.

The government contends that military tribunals would let the government try suspected terrorists quickly, efficiently, and without jeopardizing public safety, classified information, or intelligence-gathering methods and operations. The tribunals would protect American jurors, judges, and witnesses from the potential dangers of trying accused terrorists. Critics argue that military tribunals would deprive defendants of rights long held by American citizens. For example, Barbara Olshansky, of the Center for Constitutional Rights, has stated the following:

The military order gives the President the power to identify the particular persons who will be tried by military commission, to create the rules that the commission will operate under, to appoint those who will be the judges, prosecutors, and defense lawyers, to decide the sentence upon conviction, and to decide all appeals. The entire process can be held in secret, including execution; there is no mechanism to provide for any accountability to Congress, the courts, or the American public. In this way, the order provides the President, and in some instances the Secretary of Defense, with the greatest array of legal powers to be

exercised in the justice system that has ever been vested in a single person, office, or branch of government since the birth of this nation. In fact, the order is breathtaking in its abandonment of the doctrine of separation of powers and in its forsaking of cherished constitutional principles.

Although there may not be much public sympathy for former Taliban and al Qaeda fighters, it seems likely that the American people would not be pleased if one of our citizens were tried in a foreign court and deprived of the legal rights that other citizens of that nation enjoyed.

At the time of this writing, no military tribunal has been convened, and it remains to be seen whether this legal device will actually be employed. ■

Sources: Presidential Order, Detention, Treatment, and Trial of Certain Noncitizens in the War Against Terrorism, www.whitehouse.gov/news/releases/2001/11/20011113-27.html; Council on Foreign Relations, "What Is a Military Tribunal?" www.terrorismanswers.com/responses/tribunals.html; Barbara Olshansky, *American Justice on Trial: Who Loses in the Case of Military Tribunals?* (New York: Center for Constitutional Rights, 2002); "Moussaoui Trial Put Off Until June," *New York Times,* 1 October 2002, A1; Dahlia Lithwick, "What Was Moussaoui's Crime?" *New York Times,* 2 August 2002, A21; Raymond Bonner and Douglas Frantz, "French Suspect Moussaoui in Post-9/11 Plot," *New York Times,* 28 July 2002, A22; Katharine Q. Seelye, "War on Terror Makes for Odd Twists in Justice System," *New York Times,* 23 June 2002, A16; John Lumpkin, "Moussaoui Tied to September 11 Mastermind," *Washington Post,* 20 November 2002, 1.

To find out more about terrorism,
go to http://cj.wadsworth.com and click on "Terrorism Update."

Corrections and Alternative Sanctions

Kathy Boudin, onetime member of the radical Weather Underground, was convicted of murder and robbery in connection with a 1981 Brink's armored car heist in New York in which a security guard and two police officers were killed. When Boudin came up for parole in 2001, her request was denied by a New York State parole board. She was ordered held for at least another two years. Parole officials said that her release would "undermine respect for the law."

Boudin, fifty-eight, is serving a sentence of twenty years to life. She was part of the getaway team for six armed radicals who robbed the Brink's truck of $1.6 million. After the parole review, her lawyer said, "It's a sad day for Kathy. She was sentenced to twenty years by a judge who sat on her case for two and a half years and knew all the facts, and she did her twenty years with honor. For the system now not to keep its promise to someone who has been on exemplary behavior for two decades undermines respect for the law." Supporters of Boudin had argued that she had turned her life around while in prison, working to help inmates with AIDS and earning a master's degree in adult education while behind bars. A mother, Boudin also developed a program on parenting behind bars and helped write a handbook for inmates whose children are in foster care. During her more than seventeen years at the Bedford Hills facility in New York, Boudin had just three minor discipline infractions and none since 1989. Although the parole board noted her good behavior in prison, they said that "due to the violent nature and circumstances" of her crime, "your release at this time would be incompatible with the welfare of society and would serve to deprecate the seriousness of the criminal behavior."

Ironically, a year after Kathy Boudin was denied parole on December 7, 2002, her son Chesa Boudin, was given a prestigious Rhodes scholarship. He could not even share the good news. As a maximum-security inmate in the New York State prison system, Boudin is barred from receiving telephone calls or e-mail messages. She only learned about her son's triumph by reading a newspaper article days after the world learned of his appointment.

The Boudin case is notorious, but it is by no means unusual. The correctional system not only must house the nation's most dangerous people but also must decide when they are rehabilitated and ready to return to society. Do you believe it was correct to keep Kathy Boudin in prison longer or did her exemplary behavior warrant early release?

The following three chapters explore the correctional system and process. The first focuses on community corrections and the expanding field of restorative justice; the subsequent two focus on institutional corrections. ■

Criminal Justice Confronts Terrorism: Corrections and Terrorism

11 Community Sentences: Probation, Intermediate Sanctions, and Restorative Justice

Chapter Outline

Criminal Justice Links

Criminal Justice Viewpoints

Courtesy of CNN

ON DECEMBER 12, 2001, actress Winona Ryder was apprehended by Saks Fifth Avenue store detectives as she attempted to leave the premises with clothes, socks, hats, hair accessories, and handbags worth some $5,500. After she was taken into custody, store detectives found her in possession of designer tops and handbags, all bearing holes where security tags had been removed. Store detectives later found security tags in the pocket of a coat in a section of the store that Ryder had been seen to visit while in the store. Three of them contained materials that matched holes in two handbags and a hair bow that were allegedly stolen by Ryder. During her trial on shoplifting charges in October and November 2002, prosecutors alleged she went to the store equipped with scissors and tissue paper with intent to steal. Jury members were shown a store security tape that showed her being detained on a dark street after she left the store weighed down with bags. The store's security manager testified that after her arrest Ryder told him she was doing research for a role in an upcoming movie and that the director had told her to shoplift to prepare for the role. Her attorney told jurors that Saks had Ryder's credit card and that she had told them to keep her account open on that day. Movie stars routinely take stock and are billed later; perhaps she assumed that her account would be charged?

On November 6, 2002, Ryder was found guilty of grand theft and vandalism. After the trial was over, Ann Rundle, the prosecutor who tried the case, was quoted as saying, "We never thought about jail time....We won't be asking for it. We simply want Ms. Ryder to take responsibility for her conduct."[1] Since it was not a violent crime, Rundle said, a more likely and appropriate sentence would be some combination of probation, community service, and restitution. "And that's what we're going to ask for." ▪

 *To view the CNN video clip of this story, go to the book-specific Web site at* http://cj.wadsworth.com/siegel_essen4e.

The Winona Ryder case illustrates the difficulty of reaching appropriate sentences in the criminal justice system. Although some people may believe she was given special treatment because she is a celebrity, it is actually a rare occurrence for first-time offenders to be incarcerated for shoplifting. If they were, the correctional system would be even more crowded than it is today. Ryder's treatment reflects the evolution of punishment into more enlightened rulings that has continued for thousands of years.

The core value of the probation, alternative sanction, and restorative justice sentence is that many of those convicted in criminal courts are deserving of a second chance; most present little threat to society. If they can be reintegrated into the community and given the proper treatment they are unlikely to recidivate. Considering these circumstances, it seems foolish to incarcerate them in an overcrowded and dangerous prison system, which can damage younger inmates and lock them into a life of crime. It may be both more effective and less costly to have them remain in the community under the supervision of a trained court officer, where they can receive treatment that will help them turn around their lives. Rehabilitation would be aided immensely if those who commit crime could be made to understand the problems their actions cause their family, friends, and community.

Considering the potential benefits and cost-effectiveness of a community sentence, it is not surprising that the number of community sentences is at an all-time high. There are now a great variety of community sentences, including traditional probation sentences and probation plus sentences (also called *alternative* or *intermediate sanctions*), which typically involve probation plus a fine, forfeiture, restitution, so-called shock probation, split sentencing, intensive probation supervision, house arrest, electronic monitoring; or residential community corrections. These programs are designed to provide greater control over an offender and to increase the level of sanction without resorting to a prison sentence. In addition, restorative justice sentences are now being implemented that involve the offender in new forms of treatment designed to reintegrate them back into society.

Both traditional probation and the newer forms of community sentences have the potential to become reasonable alternatives to many of the economic and social problems faced by correctional administrators: they are less costly than jail or prison sentences; they help the offender maintain family and community ties; they can be structured to maximize security and maintain public safety; they can be scaled in severity to correspond to the seriousness of the crime; and they can feature restoration and reintegration rather than punishment and ostracism. No area of the criminal justice system is undergoing more change and greater expansion than community sentencing.

This chapter reviews these criminal sanctions. It begins with a brief history of probation and covers probation as an organization, sentence, and correctional practice. Then it focuses on such intermediate sanctions as intensive supervision, house arrest, and electronic monitoring. Finally, the chapter turns to a discussion of the concept of restorative justice and programs based on its principles.

Probation

probation A sentence entailing the conditional release of a convicted offender into the community under the supervision of the court (in the form of a probation officer), subject to certain conditions for a specified time. The conditions are usually similar to those of parole. (*Note:* Probation is a sentence, an alternative to incarceration; parole is administrative release from incarceration.) Violation of the conditions of probation may result in revocation of probation.

Probation is a criminal sentence mandating that a convicted offender be placed and maintained in the community under the supervision of a duly authorized agent of the court. Once on probation, the offender is subject to certain rules and conditions that must be followed to remain in the community. The probation sentence is managed by a probation department, which supervises offenders' behavior and treatment and carries out other tasks for the court.

The History of Probation

The roots of probation can be traced back to the traditions of the English common law. During the Middle Ages, judges wishing to spare deserving offenders from the pains of the then commonly used punishments of torture, mutilation, and death used their power to grant clemency and stays of execution. The common-law practice of **judicial reprieve** allowed judges to suspend punishment so that convicted offenders could seek a pardon, gather new evidence, or demonstrate that they had reformed their behavior. Similarly, the practice of **recognizance** enabled convicted offenders to remain free if they agreed to enter into a debt obligation with the state. The debt would have to be paid only if the offender was caught engaging in further criminal behavior. Sometimes **sureties** were required—these were people who made themselves responsible for the behavior of an offender after he was released.

Early U.S. courts continued the practice of indefinitely suspending sentences of criminals who seemed deserving of a second chance, but it was John Augustus of Boston who is usually credited with originating the modern probation concept.[2] As a private citizen, Augustus began in 1841 to supervise offenders released to his custody by a Boston judge. Over an eighteen-year period, Augustus supervised close to two thousand probationers and helped them get jobs and establish themselves in the community. Augustus had an amazingly high success rate, and few of his charges became involved in crime again.

In 1878 Augustus's work inspired the Massachusetts legislature to pass a law authorizing the appointment of a paid probation officer for the city of Boston. In 1880 probation was extended to other jurisdictions in Massachusetts, and by 1898 the probation movement had spread to the superior (felony) courts.[3] The Massachusetts experience was copied by Missouri (1887), by Vermont (1898), and soon after by most other states. In 1925 the federal government established a probation system for the U.S. district courts. The probation concept soon became the most widely used correctional mechanism in the United States.[4]

Why Probation?

Although the term today has many meanings, probation usually indicates a nonpunitive form of sentencing for convicted criminal offenders and delinquent youth, emphasizing maintenance in the community and treatment without institutionalization or other forms of punishment.[5]

The philosophy of probation is that the average offender is not actually a dangerous criminal or a menace to society. Advocates of probation suggest that when offenders are institutionalized instead of being granted community release, the prison community becomes their new reference point; they are forced to interact with hardened criminals and the "ex-con" label prohibits them from making successful adjustments to society. Probation provides offenders with the opportunity to prove themselves, gives them a second chance, and allows them to be closely supervised by trained personnel who can help them reestablish proper forms of behavior in the community. Probation is not limited to minor or petty criminals; a significant proportion of people convicted of felony offenses receive probation, including even some murderers and rapists.[6]

Probation usually involves suspension of the offender's sentence in return for the promise of good behavior in the community under the supervision of the probation department. As practiced in all fifty states and by the federal government, probation implies a contract between the court and the offender in which the former promises to hold a prison term in abeyance while the latter promises to obey a set of rules or conditions mandated by the court. If the rules are violated, and especially if the probationer commits another criminal offense, probation may be

judicial reprieve The common-law practice that allowed judges to suspend punishment so that convicted offenders could seek a pardon, gather new evidence, or demonstrate that they had reformed their behavior.

recognizance During the Middle Ages, the practice of letting convicted offenders remain free if they agreed to enter a debt relation with the state to pay for their crimes.

sureties During the Middle Ages, people who made themselves responsible for the behavior of offenders released in their care.

To learn more about the early history of probation and the movement toward professionalism, go to InfoTrac College Edition and read Anne Meis Knupfer, "Professionalizing Probation Work in Chicago, 1900–1935," *Social Service Review,* December 1999 v73 i4 p478.

Probation is not only used extensively in the United States but is quite popular abroad. Go to InfoTrac College Edition and read about probation in Holland: Donald G. Evans, "Spotlight on Probation in The Netherlands," *Corrections Today,* July 2002 v64 i4 p104(2).

Read about probation in England at
www.syps.org.uk/syindex.htm

revocation An administrative act performed by a parole authority that removes a person from parole, or a judicial order by a court removing a person from parole or probation, in response to a violation on the part of the parolee or probationer.

revoked; **revocation** means that the contract is terminated and the original sentence is enforced. If an offender on probation commits a second offense that is more serious than the first, he or she may also be indicted, tried, and sentenced on the second offense. However, probation may be revoked simply because the rules and conditions of probation have not been met; it is not necessary for an offender to commit another crime.

Each probationary sentence is for a fixed period of time, depending on the seriousness of the offense and the statutory law of the jurisdiction. Probation is considered served when offenders fulfill the conditions set by the court for that period of time; they can then live without state supervision.

Awarding Probation

Probationary sentences may be granted by state and federal district courts and state superior (felony) courts. In some states, juries may recommend probation if the case meets certain legally regulated criteria (for example, if it falls within a certain class of offenses as determined by statute). Even in those jurisdictions that allow juries to recommend probation, judges have the final say in the matter and may grant probation at their discretion. In nonjury trials, probation is granted solely by judicial mandate.

In most jurisdictions, all juvenile offenders are eligible for probation, as are most adults. Some state statutes prohibit probation for certain types of adult offenders, usually those who have engaged in repeated and serious violent crimes, such as murder or rape, or those who have committed crimes for which mandatory prison sentences have been legislated.

The most common manner in which a probationary sentence is imposed is a direct sentence to probation (about half). It is also common (about one-quarter of probationers) for the judge to formulate a prison sentence and then suspend it if the offender agrees to obey the rules of probation while living in the community (a **suspended sentence**).[7] The term of a probationary sentence may extend to the limit of the suspended prison term, or the court may set a time limit that reflects the sentencing period. For misdemeanors, probation usually extends for the entire period of the jail sentence, whereas felonies are more likely to warrant probationary periods that are actually shorter than the suspended prison sentences. Some offenders (about 10 percent) receive some form of split sentence in which they must first serve a jail term before being released on probation. In about 10 percent of all cases, the imposition of the sentence to probation is suspended.[8] This step is usually taken to encourage the defendant to pursue a specific rehabilitation program, such as treatment for alcohol abuse. If the program is successfully completed, then further legal action is not usually taken.

Probation provides an opportunity for nondangerous offenders to receive treatment in the community. A probation sentence is often combined with a variety of other sentencing alternatives. Here, former county clerk Juanita Wright is comforted by her daughter Paula Hughes prior to her sentencing on embezzlement charges, May 17, 2000, in Ashland County Common Pleas Court in Ashland, Ohio. The seventy-eight-year-old grandmother pleaded guilty to embezzling $178,000 in county funds over a ten-year period. She received thirty days in jail, eleven months house arrest, four hundred hours of community service, five years probation, and a $5,000 fine and repayment of the embezzled funds out of her retirement account. In addition, she would have to undergo treatment for a gambling addiction, take financial management classes, and get a job.

suspended sentence A prison term that is delayed while the defendant undergoes a period of community treatment. If the treatment is successful, the prison sentence is terminated.

The Extent of Probation

There are approximately two thousand adult probation agencies in the United States. Slightly more than half are associated with a state-level agency, while the remainder are organized at the county or municipal level of government. About thirty states combine probation and parole supervision into a single agency.

Today, more than 3.9 million adults are on federal, state, or local probation.[9] Among offenders on probation, slightly more than half had been convicted for committing a felony, 45 percent for a misdemeanor, and 1 percent for other infractions. In 1980, 1.1 million people were on probation, so the number of probationers has more than tripled in two decades. And although the growth rate has slowed down, the probation caseload increased about 3 percent between 2000 and 2001. Some states, such as Texas and California, are now maintaining hundreds of thousands of probationers in their caseloads. Without probation, the correctional system would rapidly become even more overcrowded, overly expensive, and unmanageable. Exhibit 11.1 provides a profile of the average probationer.

Eligibility for Probation

Several criteria are used in granting probation. On one level, the statutes of many states determine the factors that a judge should take into account when deciding whether to grant probation. Some states limit the use of probation in serious felony cases and for specific crimes whose penalties are controlled by mandatory sentencing laws. However, the granting of probation to serious felons is common; about half of all probationers were convicted on felony offenses.

Some states have attempted to control judicial discretion by creating guidelines for granting probation (see Chapter 10). Judges often follow these guidelines, but probation decision making is varied: an individual offender granted probation in one jurisdiction might not be if tried in another. Probation is most often granted by a discretionary decision based on the beliefs and attitudes of the presiding judge and the probation staff.

A significant issue involving eligibility for probation is community supervision of convicted felons. Many people believe that probation is given to minor or first offenders who are deserving of a break. This is not actually the case. Many serious criminal offenders are given probation sentences, including people convicted on homicide (about 5 percent), rape (about 20 percent), and robbery (12 percent) charges.[10]

Although originally conceived as a way to provide a second chance for young offenders, probation today is also a means of reducing the population pressures on an overcrowded and underfunded correctional system. So there are two distinct sides to probation, one involving the treatment and rehabilitation of nondangerous

The most recent data on the extent of probation is provided by the Bureau of Justice Statistics at www.ojp.usdoj.gov/bjs/pandp.htm

---

Exhibit 11.1 Profile of the probationer

- Women represented a slightly larger percentage of the probation population in 2001 than in 1990. Women were 22 percent of adults on probation in 2001 (870,000), up from 18 percent in 1990.
- At year-end 2001 about half of all probationers were white (2,175,600), a third were black (1,228,700), and an eighth were of Hispanic origin (469,800). Persons of other races made up about 2 percent of probationers (58,600).
- Half of all probationers were convicted of a felony; a quarter were convicted of a drug law violation.
- More than half of those on probation (54 percent) had a direct sentence to probation, 25 percent had received a sentence to incarceration that had been suspended, and 9 percent had received a split sentence that included incarceration followed by probation. An additional 10 percent had entered probation before completion of all court proceedings (including those who entered probation before final verdict).
- Approximately three of every four probationers were under active supervision and were required to report regularly to a probation authority in person, by mail, or by telephone. The percent of probationers required to report regularly has dropped steadily, from 83 percent in 1990 to 79 percent in 1995 and 74 percent in 2001.

Source: Lauren E. Glaze, *Probation and Parole in the United States, 2001* (Washington, D.C.: Bureau of Justice Statistics, 2002).

offenders deserving of a "second chance" and the other the supervision and control of criminals who might otherwise be incarcerated.

Conditions of Probation

When probation is fixed as a sentence, the court sets down certain conditions for qualifying for community treatment. Some conditions are standard and are applied in every probation case (that is, "Do not leave the jurisdiction"), but the sentencing judge usually has broad discretion to set specific conditions on a case-by-case basis. A presiding judge may not of course impose capricious or cruel conditions, such as requiring an offender to make restitution out of proportion to the seriousness of the criminal act.[11] For example, in one Illinois case, an appeals court ruled that requiring a probationer to make a public apology in the local newspaper for driving drunk was too punitive and a more drastic requirement than those authorized by the state's probation laws.[12]

Judges may, however, legally impose restrictions tailored to fit the probationer's individual needs and to protect society from additional harm. For example, a child molester can be forbidden to associate with minor children.[13] In one case, a probationer was actually banished from the county in which he lived on the grounds that he was a popular figure among drug-using adolescents to whom he sold cocaine; barring him from his residence also gave him an opportunity for a fresh start.[14] Probationers' community supervision may be revoked if they fail to comply with these conditions and to obey the reasonable requests of the probation staff to meet their treatment obligations.[15]

The most common of these special conditions include residential placement, alcohol- or drug-abuse treatment and testing, mental health counseling, house arrest, and community service (the last two conditions are discussed later in this

© 2002 AP/Wide World Photos

Conditions of probation may be tailored to the special circumstances of probationers. Here, Sangamon County Adult Probation Director Michael Torchia shows off Cyber Sentinel software, which could be added to the computers of sex offenders who are on probation and used to alert authorities to illicit activities, January 4, 2002, in Springfield, Illinois. Cyber Sentinel was developed to record chat room conversations, instant messages, e-mails, and images that are sexually explicit so that parents can see what their children are doing online.

Exhibit 11.2 Special probation rules suggested for convicted sex offenders

- Your employment must be approved by the probation agency.
- You shall participate in treatment with a therapist approved by the probation department.
- You shall participate in periodic polygraph examinations.
- You shall not have contact with children under age 18.
- You shall not frequent places where children congregate, such as schoolyards, parks, playgrounds, and arcades.
- You shall maintain a driving log (mileage; time of departure, arrival, return; routes traveled and with whom; etc.).
- You shall not drive a motor vehicle alone without prior permission of your supervising officer.

- You shall not possess any pornographic, sexually oriented, or sexually stimulating visual, auditory, telephonic, or electronic media and computer programs or services that are relevant to your deviant behavior pattern.
- You shall reside at a place approved by the supervising officer, including supervised living quarters.
- You shall abide by a curfew imposed by the supervising officer and comply with electronic monitoring, if so ordered.
- You shall not have contact, directly or through third parties, with your victims.
- You shall abstain from alcoholic beverages and participate in periodic drug testing.

Source: Adapted from Kim English, Suzanne Pullen, and Linda Jones, *Managing Adult Sex Offenders in the Community—A Containment Approach* (Washington, D.C.: National Institute of Justice, 1997), 5.

chapter); almost half of all probationers are given one or more special conditions. Exhibit 11.2 lists suggested rules for convicted sex offenders.

Administration of Probation Services

Probation services are organized in a variety of ways, depending on the state and the jurisdiction in which they are located. Some states have a statewide probation service, but each court jurisdiction actually controls its local department. Other states maintain a strong statewide authority with centralized control and administration. Thirty states combine probation and parole services in a single unit; some combine juvenile and adult probation departments, whereas others maintain these departments separately.

The typical probation department is situated in a single court district, such as juvenile, superior, district, or municipal court. The relationship between the department and court personnel (especially the judge) is extremely close.

In the typical department, the chief probation officer (CPO) sets policy, supervises hiring, determines training needs, and may personally discuss with or recommend sentencing to the judge. In state-controlled departments, some of the CPO's duties are mandated by the central office; training guidelines, for example, may be determined at the state level. If, on the other hand, the department is locally controlled, the CPO is invested with great discretion in the management of the department.

The line staff, or the probation officers (POs), may be in direct and personal contact with the entire supervisory staff, or they may be independent of the CPO and answer mainly to the assistant chiefs. Line staff perform the following major functions:

1. Supervise or monitor cases assigned to them to ensure that the rules of probation are followed.
2. Attempt to rehabilitate their cases through specialized treatment techniques.
3. Investigate the lives of convicted offenders to enable the court to make intelligent sentencing decisions.
4. Occasionally collect fines due the court or oversee the collection of delinquent payments, such as child support.
5. Interview complainants and defendants to determine whether criminal action should be taken, whether cases can be decided informally, whether diversion should be advocated, and so on. This last procedure, called *intake,* is common in juvenile probation.

Careers in Criminal Justice

Probation Officers

Probation officers—who in some states may be referred to as community supervision officers—monitor the behavior of offenders through personal contact with them and their families. Officers also may arrange for offenders to get substance abuse rehabilitation or job training. Probation officers usually work with either adults or juveniles exclusively. Only in small, usually rural, jurisdictions do probation officers counsel both adults and juveniles.

Another part of the probation officer's job involves working in the courts. Officers investigate the background of offenders brought before the court, write presentence reports, and make sentencing recommendations for each offender; review sentencing recommendations with offenders and their families before submitting the recommendations to the court; and testify in court regarding their findings and recommendations. Probation officers also attend hearings to update the court on an offender's probation compliance status and on the offender's efforts at rehabilitation. Occasionally, probation officers in the federal court system work as pretrial services officers, conducting pretrial investigations and making bond recommendations for defendants.

The number of cases a probation officer has depends on both the counseling needs of offenders and the risks they pose to society. Higher-risk offenders and those who need more counseling usually command more of an officer's time and resources. Those who work with these offenders handle fewer cases. Caseloads also vary by agency jurisdiction. Consequently, officers may handle twenty to more than three hundred active cases at a time.

Working Conditions

Probation officers usually work a standard forty-hour week, but they may be required to work longer or to be on call twenty-four hours a day to supervise and assist offenders at any time. In addition, meeting with offenders who are on probation or parole may require extensive travel or fieldwork. However, this burden may be eased somewhat for workers whose agencies allow them to telecommute from home via computers and other equipment and to make use of other technology, such as electronic monitoring devices worn by offenders, which allow officers to monitor their activities from a distance.

Probation officers may find their jobs stressful for a variety of reasons. They work with convicted criminals, some of whom may be dangerous. In the course of supervising offenders, officers usually interact with many other individuals, including family members and friends of their clients, who may be angry, upset, or uncooperative. Officers also may be required to collect and transport urine samples of offenders for drug testing.

Although stress makes the job difficult at times, the work also can be rewarding. Many probation officers gain personal satisfaction from counseling members of their community and helping them become productive citizens.

Employment and Earnings

Jobs for probation officers are more plentiful in urban areas. There are also more jobs in states that have numerous men and women on probation—such as California and Texas, which currently have the largest such populations. The median annual salary for probation officers today is about $36,000. Officers who work in urban areas usually have higher earnings than those working in rural areas.

Job Outlook

Employment of probation officers is projected to grow through 2008. Vigorous law enforcement is expected to result in a continuing increase in the prison population. Overcrowding in prisons also has swelled the probation population as judges and prosecutors search for alternative forms of punishment.

In addition to openings due to growth in the population, many other openings will result from the need to replace workers who leave the occupation permanently, including the large number expected to retire over the next several years.

Qualifications, Training, and Advancement

Prospective probation officers must be in good physical condition and be emotionally stable. Most agencies require applicants to be at least twenty-one years old, and for federal employment, not older than thirty-seven. Those convicted of felonies may not be eligible for employment.

Probation officers need strong writing skills because of the large number of reports they must prepare. Familiarity

To read about professional probation associations, go to InfoTrac College Edition and read Donald G. Evans, "Probation: Strength Through Association," *Corrections Today,* August 1995 v57 i5 p100(5).

Some POs view themselves as "social workers" and maintain a treatment orientation; their goal is to help offenders adjust in the community. Others are "law enforcers" who are more concerned with supervision, control, and public safety. An officer's style is influenced by both personal values and the department's general policies and orientation toward the goals of probation.[16]

Might you be interested in a career as a probation officer? Read the Careers in Criminal Justice feature above.

Probation officers may engage in a variety of activities, some of which may be very grisly. Here, a state probation officer and another worker unload tools from a truck at the site of the Tri-State Crematory in Noble, Georgia, February 21, 2002. State officials found numerous bodies on the grounds of the crematory and the home of Ray Brent Marsh. The bodies had been dumped there instead of being cremated.

with computers often is required. Job candidates also should be knowledgeable about laws and regulations pertaining to corrections.

Educational requirements for probation officers vary by state, but a bachelor's degree in social work or criminal

justice usually is required. In addition, some states require probation officers to have one year of work experience in a related field or one year of graduate study in criminal justice, social work, or psychology. Most probation officers must complete a training program sponsored by their state government or the federal government. Most work as trainees for about six months. Candidates who successfully complete the training period obtain a permanent position. Some states require applicants to take a certification test during or after training. Applicants usually must also pass written, oral, psychological, and physical examinations.

Agencies that employ probation officers have several levels of officers and correctional treatment specialists, as well as supervisors. A graduate degree—such as a master's degree in criminal justice, social work, or psychology—may be helpful for advancement.

Critical Thinking

1. Considering the fact that an important aspect of probation work is treatment, should probation officers be required to take courses in counseling, psychology, and so on? Or is it more important that they serve as monitors who enforce probation rules by, for example, ensuring that clients attend treatment programs at counseling centers or mental health clinics? Put another way, do you believe that probation officers should be hands-on treatment providers?
2. Should a probation officer be charged with arresting clients and taking them into custody if they violate a probation order? Would that make their role too similar to that of a police officer?

 InfoTrac College Edition Research
To learn more about the occupational duties of a probation officer, go to InfoTrac College Research Edition and read Andrew D. Alpert, "Probation Officers and Correctional Treatment Specialists," *Occupational Outlook Quarterly,* Fall 2001 v45 i3 p28.

 To find out more about careers in criminal justice, go to the book-specific Web site at http://cj.wadsworth.com/siegel_essen4e.

Duties of Probation Officers

Staff officers in probation departments are usually charged with four primary tasks: investigation, intake, diagnosis, and treatment supervision.

In the investigative stage, the PO conducts an inquiry within the community to discover the factors related to the criminality of the offender. The **presentence investigation** is conducted primarily to gain information for judicial sentences, but

Many states have their own probation professional organization. Here is the Web site for the one in New York: www.nyspoa.com/

presentence investigation An investigation performed by a probation officer attached to a trial court after the conviction of a defendant. The report contains information about the defendant's background, education, previous employment, and family; his or her own statement concerning the offense; prior criminal record; interviews with neighbors or acquaintances; and his or her mental and physical condition (that is, information that would not be made public record in the case of guilty plea or that would be inadmissible as evidence at a trial but could be influential and important at the sentencing stage).

intake The process in which a probation officer settles cases at the initial appearance before the onset of formal criminal proceedings; also, process in which a juvenile referral is received and a decision is made to file a petition in the juvenile court, release the juvenile, or refer the juvenile elsewhere.

Use "probation treatment supervision" as a subject guide on InfoTrac College Edition.

in the event that the offender is placed on probation, the investigation becomes a useful testimony on which to base treatment and supervision.

Intake is a process by which POs interview cases that have been summoned to the court for initial appearances. Intake is most commonly used with juvenile offenders but may also be used with adult misdemeanant cases. During juvenile court intake, the petitioner (the juvenile) and the complainant (the private citizen or the police officer) may work with the PO to determine an equitable resolution of the case. The PO may settle the case without further court action, recommend restitution or other compensation, initiate actions that result in a court hearing, or recommend unofficial or informal probation.

Diagnosis is the analysis of the probationer's personality and the subsequent development of a personality profile that may be helpful in treating the offender. Diagnosis involves evaluating the probationer, based on information from an initial interview (intake) or the presentence investigation for the purpose of planning a proper treatment program. The diagnosis should not merely reflect the desire or purpose of labeling the offender neurotic or psychopathic, for example, but should "codify all that has been learned about the individual, organized in such a way as to provide a means for the establishment of future treatment goals."[17]

Treatment Supervision Based on a knowledge of psychology, social work, or counseling, and the diagnosis of the offender, the PO plans a treatment program that will, it is hoped, allow the probationer to fulfill the probation contract and make a reasonable adjustment to the community.

In years past, the probation staff had primary responsibility for supervision and treatment. Probation officers today rarely have hands-on treatment responsibility and instead employ the resources of the community to carry out this function.

The treatment function is a product of both the investigative and diagnostic aspects of probation. It is based on the PO's perceptions of the probationer, including family problems, peer relationships, and employment background. Treatment may also involve the use of community resources. For example, a PO who discovers that a client has a drinking problem may find a detoxification center willing to accept the client. A chronically underemployed offender may be given job counseling or training, and a person undergoing severe psychological stress may be placed in a therapeutic treatment program. In the case of juvenile delinquency, a PO may work with teachers and other school officials to help a young offender stay in school. The need for treatment is critical and the vast size of probation caseloads, especially the large numbers of narcotics abusers, often overwhelms the availability of community-based substance abuse programs.[18]

Failure to supervise probationers adequately and determine whether they are obeying the rules of probation can result in the officer and the department being held legally liable for civil damages. For example, if a probationer with a history of child molestation attacks a child while working as a school custodian, the probationer's case supervisor could be held legally responsible for failing to check on the probationer's employment activities.[19]

Presentence Investigations An important task of POs is the investigation and evaluation of defendants coming before the court for sentencing. The court uses presentence investigation reports in deciding whether to grant probation, incarcerate, or use other forms of treatment.

The style and content of presentence investigations may vary among jurisdictions and also among individual POs within the same jurisdiction. Some departments require voluminous reports covering every aspect of the defendant's life; other departments, which may be rule oriented, require that officers stick to the basic facts, such as the defendant's age, race, sex, and previous offense record. Each department also has its own standards for presentence investigations.

At the conclusion of most presentence investigations, a recommendation is made to the presiding judge that reflects the department's sentencing posture on the case at hand. This is a crucial aspect of the report, because the probation department's recommendation is followed in many but not all cases.

Risk Classification   **Risk classification** involves classifying and assigning cases to a level and type of supervision on the basis of the clients' particular needs and the risks they present to the community. For example, some clients may receive frequent (intensive) supervision, whereas others are assigned to minimum monitoring by a PO.

A number of risk assessment approaches are used, but most employ such objective measures as the offender's age, employment status, drug abuse history, prior felony convictions, and number of address changes in the year prior to sentencing. Efforts are under way to create more effective instruments using subjective information obtained through face-to-face interviews and encounters.[20]

Does classification make a dramatic difference in the success of probation? Though there is little clear-cut evidence that classification has a substantial impact on reducing recidivism, its use has become commonplace and administrators believe that it may be a useful tool in case management and treatment delivery. The scales may validate the PO's self-perception of being a rational and scientific decision maker.[21] The classification of offenders aids the most important goal of supervision: reducing the risk the probationer presents to the community. In addition, classification schemes are in sync with desert-based sentencing models: the most serious cases get the most intensive supervision.[22]

risk classification   Classifying probationers so that they may receive an appropriate level of treatment and control.

How Successful Is Probation?

Probation is the most commonly used alternative sentence for a number of reasons: it is humane, it helps offenders maintain community and family ties, and it is cost-effective. Incarcerating an inmate costs over $20,000 per year, whereas probation costs about $2,000 per year.[23]

Although unquestionably inexpensive, is probation successful? If most probation orders fail, the costs of repeated criminality would certainly outweigh the cost savings of a probation sentence. Overall, most probation orders do seem successful. National data indicate that about 60 percent of probationers successfully complete their probationary sentence while about 40 percent percent either are rearrested, violate probation rules, or abscond.[24] Most revocations occur for technical violations that occur during the first three months of the probation sentence.[25] Although a 40 percent failure rate seems high, even the most serious criminals who receive probation are less likely to recidivate than those who are sent to prison for committing similar crimes.[26]

Felony Probation   Though probationers are less likely to recidivate than former prison inmates, the fact that many felons who commit violent offenses are granted probation is an issue of some concern. Tracking the outcome of felony probation was the goal of Joan Petersilia and her colleagues at the RAND Corporation, a private think tank, when they traced 1,672 men convicted of felonies who had been granted probation in Los Angeles and Alameda counties in California.[27] In this now-classic study, Petersilia found that 1,087 (65 percent) were rearrested; of those rearrested, 853 (51 percent) were convicted; and of those convicted, 568 (34 percent) were sentenced to jail or prison. Of the probationers who had new charges filed against them, 75 percent were charged with burglary, theft, robbery, and other predatory crimes; 18 percent were convicted of serious, violent crimes.

© 2002 AP/Wide World Photos

Former skating star Tonya Harding is shown here at a probation revocation hearing. She denied drinking alcohol, which would be a violation of the conditions of her probation following an assault conviction. Overall, about 60 percent of probationers successfully complete their probationary sentence whereas about 40 percent either are rearrested, violate probation rules, or abscond.

To read more about the RAND Corporation, go to www.rand.org/

The RAND researchers found that probation is by far the most common sentencing alternative to prison, used in about 60 to 80 percent of all criminal convictions. However, the crimes and criminal records of about 25 percent of all probationers are indistinguishable from those of offenders who go to prison. These data indicate that many people given prison sentences could have been granted community sentences, and vice versa. This is a disturbing example of the role discretion plays in sentencing decisions.

Who is most likely to fail on probation? Young males who are unemployed or who have a very low income, a prior criminal record, and a history of instability are most likely to be rearrested. In contrast, probationers who are married with children, have lived in the area for two or more years, and are adequately employed are the most likely to be successful on probation.[28] Among female probationers, those who have stable marriages, are better educated, and are employed full- or part-time are more likely to complete probation orders successfully than male probationers or women who are single, less educated, and unemployed. Prior record is also related to probation success: clients who have a history of criminal behavior, prior probation, and previous incarceration are the most likely to fail.[29]

Why Do People Fail on Probation? Probationers bring with them a lot of emotional baggage that may reduce their chances of successful rehabilitation. Many are felons who have long histories of offending; more than 75 percent of all probationers have had prior convictions. Others suffer from a variety of social and psychological disabilities. Surveys indicate that a significant number (16 percent) suffer from mental illness.[30] Whether mentally ill or mentally sound, probationers are likely to have grown up in households in which family members were incarcerated, and so have lived part of their lives in foster homes or state institutions. Many had parents or guardians who abused drugs; they also suffered high rates of physical and sexual abuse. They are now unemployed or underemployed, and almost half are substance abusers. Considering their harsh and abusive backgrounds and their current economic distress and mental illness, it comes as no surprise that many find it difficult to comply with the rules of probation and forgo criminal activity.

As mentioned earlier, although the recidivism rate of probationers seems high, it is still lower than the recidivism rate of prison inmates.[31] To improve probation effectiveness, it could be supplemented with more stringent rules, such as curfews, and closer supervision. Even though such measures can dramatically increase the cost of probation, they would still be far less expensive than the cost of incarceration.

Legal Rights of Probationers

A number of important legal issues surround probation, one set involving the civil rights of probationers and another involving the rights of probationers during the revocation process.

Civil Rights   The U.S. Supreme Court has ruled that probationers have a unique status and therefore are entitled to fewer constitutional protections than other citizens. One area of law involves the Fifth Amendment right of freedom from self-incrimination. The Supreme Court dealt with this issue in the case of *Minnesota v. Murphy* (1984).[32] In *Murphy,* the Supreme Court ruled that the probation officer–client relationship is not confidential, as physician-patient or attorney-client relationships are. If a probationer admits to committing a crime to his or her probation supervisor, the information can be passed on to the police or district attorney. Furthermore, the *Murphy* decision held that a probation officer could even use trickery or psychological pressure to get information and turn it over to the police.

A second area of law involving probationers is search and seizure. In *Griffin v. Wisconsin* (1987), the Supreme Court held that a probationer's home may be searched without a warrant on the grounds that probation departments "have in mind the welfare of the probationer" and must "respond quickly to evidence of misconduct."[33] But what if a probationer is believed to have committed another crime and the search is for evidence and not to protect his or her "welfare?" In *United States v. Knights* (2001), the Supreme Court upheld the legality of a warrantless search of a probationer's home for the purposes of gathering criminal evidence. In *Knights,* the Court ruled that the home of a probationer who is suspected of a crime can be searched without a warrant if the search was based on (a) reasonable suspicion that he had committed another crime while on probation and (b) that a condition of his previous probation was that he would submit to searches. The Court reasoned that the government's interest in preventing crime, combined with Knights's diminished expectation of privacy, required only a *reasonable suspicion* to make the search fit within the protections of the Fourth Amendment. Although the Court recognized that society has a legitimate interest in the rehabilitation of probationers, it embraced the state's argument that a probationer is more likely to commit a crime than a nonprobationer.[34]

To find out more about the *Knights* case, go to InfoTrac College Edition and read Jonathan T. Skrmetti, "The Keys to the Castle: A New Standard for Warrantless Home Searches in *United States v. Knights,*" *Harvard Journal of Law & Public Policy,* Summer 2002 v25 i3 p1201(13).

Revocation Rights   During the course of a probationary term, a violation of the rules or terms of probation or the commitment of a new crime can result in probation being revoked, at which time the offender may be placed in an institution. Revocation is not often an easy decision, since it conflicts with the treatment philosophy of many probation departments.

When revocation is chosen, the offender is notified, and a formal hearing is scheduled. If the charges against the probationer are upheld, the offender can then be placed in an institution to serve the remainder of the sentence. Most departments will not revoke probation unless the offender commits another crime or seriously violates the rules of probation.

Because placing a person on probation implies that probation will continue unless the probationer commits some major violation, the defendant has been given certain procedural due process rights at this stage of the criminal process. In three significant decisions, the U.S. Supreme Court provided procedural safeguards to apply at proceedings to revoke probation (and parole). In *Mempa v. Rhay* (1967), the Court unanimously held that a probationer was constitutionally entitled to counsel in a revocation-of-probation proceeding where the imposition of sentence had been suspended.[35] Then, in 1972, the Supreme Court in the case of *Morrissey v. Brewer* handed down an important decision detailing the procedures required for parole revocation.[36] Because the revocations of probation and parole are similar, the standards in the *Morrissey* case affected the probation process as well. In *Morrissey* the Court required an informal inquiry to determine whether there was probable cause to believe the arrested parolee had violated the conditions of parole, as well as a formal revocation hearing with minimum due process requirements. However, in *Morrissey* the Court did not deal with the issue of right to counsel. Chief Justice Warren Burger stated, "We do not reach or decide the question whether the parolee is entitled to the assistance of retained counsel or to appointed counsel if he is indigent."

The question of the right to counsel in revocation proceedings came up again in the 1973 case of *Gagnon v. Scarpelli*.[37] In that decision, which involved a probationer, the Supreme Court held that both probationers and parolees have a constitutionally limited right to counsel in revocation proceedings. The *Gagnon* case can be viewed as a step forward in the application of constitutional safeguards to the correctional process. The provision of counsel helped give control over the unlimited discretion exercised in the past by probation and parole personnel in revocation proceedings.

With the development of innovative probation programs, courts have had to review the legality of changing probation rules and their effect on revocation. For example, courts have in general upheld the demand that restitution be made to the victim of crime.[38] Because restitution is designed to punish and reform the offender, rather than simply repay the victim, the probationer can be made legally responsible for paying restitution.

In *United States v. Granderson* (1994), the Supreme Court helped clarify what can happen to a probationer whose community sentence is revoked. Granderson was eligible for a six-month prison sentence but instead was given sixty months of probation. When he tested positively for drugs, his probation was revoked. The statute he was sentenced under required that he serve one-third his original sentence in prison. When the trial court sentenced him to twenty months, he appealed. Was his original sentence six months or sixty months? The Supreme Court found that it would be unfair to force a probationer to serve more time in prison than he would have if originally incarcerated and ruled that the proper term should have been one-third of the six months, or two months.[39]

The Future of Probation

Probation remains the sentence of choice for about one-half of all felony cases.[40] Because it costs far less to maintain an offender in the community than in prison, and because prison overcrowding continues, there is constant economic pressure to grant probation to serious felony offenders. Even if probation is no more successful than prison, it costs less and is therefore extremely attractive to policymakers. However, some believe that the risk of probation failure is too high and that judges should think carefully before sentencing felons to probation.

Probation will continue to be a sentence of choice in both felony and misdemeanor cases because of its great cost savings in a time when many state budgets are being reduced. In fact, defraying the cost of probation may be possible by asking clients to pay fees for probation services, a concept that would be impossible with prison inmates. At least twenty-five states now impose some form of fee on probationers to defray the cost of community corrections. Massachusetts initiated **day fees,** which are based on the probationer's wages (the usual fee is between one and three days' wages each month).[41] Texas requires judges to impose supervision fees unless the offender is truly unable to pay; fees make up more than half the probation department's annual budget.[42]

Probation is unquestionably undergoing dramatic changes. During the past decade, it has been supplemented and used as a restrictive correctional alternative. Expanding the scope of probation has created a new term, **intermediate sanctions,**

day fees A program requiring probationers to pay in part for the costs of their treatment.

intermediate sanctions The group of punishments falling between probation and prison; "probation plus." Community-based sanctions, including house arrest and intensive supervision, serve as alternatives to incarceration.

to signify penalties that fall between traditional community supervision and confinement in jail or prison. These new correctional services are discussed in the following section.

Intermediate Sanctions

Community corrections has traditionally emphasized offender rehabilitation. The probation officer has been viewed as a caseworker or counselor whose primary job is to help the offender adjust to society. Offender surveillance and control has seemed more appropriate for law enforcement, jails, and prisons than for community corrections.[43]

But since 1980 a more conservative justice system has reoriented toward social control. Although the rehabilitative ideals of probation have not been abandoned, new programs have been developed that add a control dimension to community corrections. These programs can be viewed as "probation plus," since they add restrictive penalties and conditions to community service orders. Being more punitive than probation, intermediate sanctions can be sold to conservatives, while they remain attractive to liberals as alternatives to incarceration.[44]

Intermediate sanctions include programs that are usually administered by probation departments: intensive probation supervision, house arrest, electronic monitoring, restitution orders, shock probation or split sentences, and residential community corrections.[45] Some experts also include high-impact shock incarceration, or boot camp experiences, within the definition of intermediate sanctions, but since these programs are usually operated by correctional departments they are discussed separately in Chapter 12. Intermediate sanctions also involve sentences administered independently of probation staffs: fines and forfeiture, pretrial programs, and pretrial and posttrial residential programs. Intermediate sanctions therefore range from the barely intrusive, such as restitution orders, to the highly restrictive, such as house arrest accompanied by electronic monitoring and a stay in a community correctional center.

What are the advantages of creating a system of intermediate sanctions? Primary is the need to develop alternatives to prisons and jails, which have proved to be costly, ineffective, and injurious. Little evidence exists that incapacitation is either a general deterrent to crime or a specific deterrent against future criminality. Some correctional systems have become inundated with new inmates. Even states that have extensively used alternative sanctions have experienced rapid increases in their prison population; the pressure on the correctional system if alternative sanctions had not been an option is almost inconceivable. Other nations have embraced alternative sanctions, and despite rising crime rates they have not experienced the explosion in the prison population that has occurred in the United States. This issue is explored further in the Race, Gender, and Culture feature.

Advantages of Intermediate Sanctions

Intermediate sanctions also have the potential to save money. Although they are more expensive than traditional probation, they are far less costly than incarceration. If those offenders given alternative sanctions would have otherwise been incarcerated, the extra cost would be significant. In addition, offenders given intermediate sanctions generate income, pay taxes, reimburse victims, perform community service, and provide other cost savings that would be nonexistent had they been incarcerated. Intermediate sanctions are not likely to pay an immediate "corrections dividend" because many correctional costs are fixed, but they may reduce the need for future prison and jail construction.

Intermediate sanctions also help meet the need for developing community sentences that are fair, equitable, and proportional.[46] It seems unfair to treat both a

Race, Culture, and Gender in Criminal Justice

Alternatives to Incarceration Abroad

While the crime rate has been declining in the United States for nearly a decade, get-tough measures such as "three strikes, you're out" have resulted in a steadily increasing prison population. Western European countries have crime rates similar to the United States, but their incarceration rates are much lower; criminal penalties there are not nearly as harsh as in the United States. This disparity in punishment has not been lost on researchers such as legal scholar Michael Tonry, who has explored the differences between the United States and other Western democracies.

Tonry points out that crime trends seem to have an important impact on U.S. incarceration policies. As the crime rate goes up, so too does the media coverage of crime stories. Political figures, especially those running for office, feed off the media coverage and make crime an election focus. Because these events fuel public anxiety, there is an outcry for punitive measures to be taken against criminals. Politicians are happy to oblige their constituents and pass tough sanctions against criminals to show their sensitivity to the voters.

Tonry finds that crime has taken on increasing political importance since the 1964 presidential election. In the 1990s the overused phrase "get tough on crime" crossed party lines as lawmakers promised to implement harsh measures against criminals, regardless of whether the measures would actually reduce crime or were really needed. As crime rates fall, both the politicians and the public credit the get-tough stance for success, though little evidence shows that draconian measures actually reduce crime. For example, crime rates were already trending downward before harsh reform laws such as mandatory minimum sentencing and truth-in-sentencing laws were created; yet conservatives believe that these get-tough measures helped reduce crime rates.

Western European nations have taken a different approach to crime control. When rates of crime rose in European democracies, lawmakers focused on making punishment fair rather than harsh. Rather than mandatory sentencing, individual circumstances and the reasons for committing a crime are considered. Western European lawmakers also focus on punishments that are utilitarian and effective in reducing crime, rather than punitive and retributive. They often rely on community sentences such as day fines, which are based on the offender's earnings and economic circumstances. The money collected from day fines not only punishes the offender but also serves to benefit society. Western European judges have also been more likely to sentence offenders to community service. Community service, which was created in the United States, has quickly become the sentence of choice for minor crimes in European nations. Where community service hours can number in the thousands for an American criminal, European sentences often limit the number of hours to 240.

Critical Thinking

Incarceration sentences in Europe are substantially shorter than in the United States. No European country has implemented mandatory sentences or truth in sentencing. Almost all efforts to control or reduce judicial discretion have met with disapproval. Tonry points out this may be due to Western European judges and prosecutors being career civil servants, free from political concerns. Not having to worry about an upcoming election allows them to focus on what they believe is just, rather than what is politically expedient. Would you encourage such practices in the United States? Why or why not?

 ### InfoTrac College Edition Research

To learn more about community sentences abroad, read Donald G. Evans, "Ontario's New Probation Supervision Model," *Corrections Today 60* (1998): 126, and Donald G. Evans, "'What Works' in the United Kingdom," *Corrections Today 60* (1998): 124.

Sources: Michael Tonry, "Why Are U.S. Incarceration Rates So High?" *Crime and Delinquency 45* (1999): 419–438; Michael Tonry, "Parochialism in U.S. Sentencing Policy," *Crime and Delinquency 45* (1999): 48–66.

rapist and a shoplifter with the same type of probationary sentence, considering the differences in their crimes. As Figure 11.1 illustrates, intermediate sanctions can form the successive steps of a meaningful "ladder" of scaled punishments outside of prison, thereby restoring fairness and equity to nonincarceration sentences.[47] For example, forgers may be ordered to make restitution to their victims, and rapists can be placed in a community correctional facility while they receive counseling at a local psychiatric center. This feature of intermediate sanctions allows judges to fit the punishment to the crime without resorting to a prison sentence. Intermediate sentences can be designed to increase punishment for people whose serious or repeat crimes make a straight probation sentence inappropriate, yet for whom a prison sentence would be unduly harsh and counterproductive.[48]

In the broadest sense, intermediate sanctions can serve the needs of a number of offender groups. The most likely candidates are convicted criminals who would normally be sent to prison but who pose either a low risk of recidivism or who are of little threat to society (such as nonviolent property offenders). Used in this sense, intermediate sanctions are a viable solution to the critical problem of prison overcrowding.

Intermediate sanctions can also reduce overcrowding in jails by providing alternatives to incarceration for misdemeanants and cut the number of pretrial detainees who currently make up about half the inmate population.[49] Some forms of bail already require conditions, such as supervision by court officers and periods of home confinement (conditional bail), that are a form of intermediate sanctions.

Intermediate sanctions can also potentially be used as halfway-back strategies for probation and parole violators. Probationers who violate the conditions of their community release could be placed under increasingly more intensive supervision before actual incarceration is required. Parolees who pose the greatest risk of recidivism might receive conditions that require close monitoring, or home confinement. Parole violators could be returned to a community correctional center rather than a walled institution.

In the following sections, the forms of intermediate sanctions currently in use are more thoroughly discussed.

Fines

Fines are monetary payments imposed on offenders as an intermediate punishment for their criminal acts. They are a direct offshoot of the early common-law practice of requiring that compensation be paid to the victim and the state (wergild) for criminal acts. Fines are still commonly used in Europe, where they are often the sole penalty, even in cases involving chronic offenders who commit fairly serious crimes.[50]

In the United States, fines are most commonly used in cases involving misdemeanors and lesser offenses. Fines are also frequently used in felony cases where the offender benefited financially.

Fines may be used as a sole sanction or combined with other punishments, such as probation or confinement. Judges commonly levy other monetary sanctions along with fines, such as court costs, public defender fees, probation and treatment fees, and victim restitution, to increase the force of the financial punishment. However, there is evidence that many offenders fail to pay fines and that courts are negligent in their efforts to collect unpaid fees; it has been estimated that defendants fail to pay upward of $2 billion in fines each year.[51]

In most jurisdictions, little guidance is given to the sentencing judge directing the imposition of the fine. Judges often have inadequate information on the offender's ability to pay, resulting in defaults and contempt charges. Because the standard sanction for nonpayment is incarceration, many offenders held in local jails are confined for nonpayment of criminal fines. Although the U.S. Supreme Court in *Tate v. Short* (1971) recognized that incarcerating a person who is financially unable to pay a fine discriminates against the poor, many judges continue to incarcerate offenders for noncompliance with financial orders.[52]

Research indicates that, given the facts of a case, judges do seem to use fines in a rational manner: low-risk offenders are the ones most likely to receive fines instead of a jail sentence; the more serious the crime, the higher the amount of the

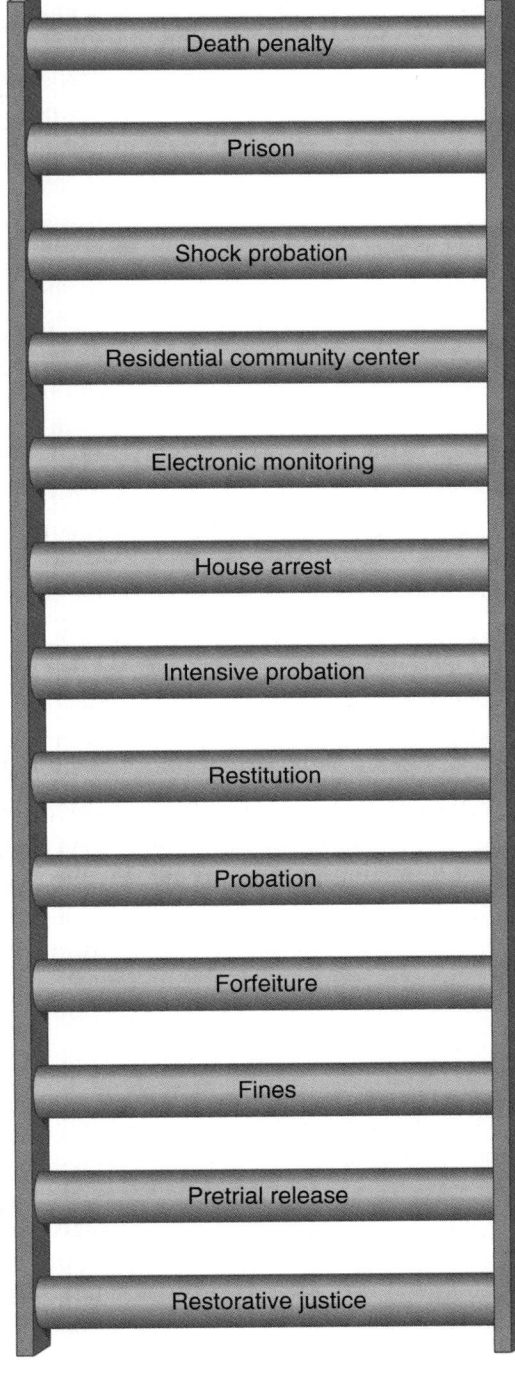

Figure 11.1
The punishment ladder

fine Levying a money payment on offenders to compensate society for their misdeeds.

The use of fines as a criminal penalty has escalated in an era of corporate misconduct. Federal prosecutor Andrew Weissman, left, talks outside the federal courthouse in Houston, October 16, 2002. Joining Weissman are prosecutor Sam Buell, center, and Leslie Caldwell, head of the Enron task force. Arthur Andersen LLP was sentenced to five years' probation and fined $500,000—both maximum penalties—for obstruction of justice in its handling of Enron Corp.–related documents, which prosecutors said were doctored or destroyed to thwart a federal probe of the energy company's finances.

fine. Offenders who are fined seem less likely to commit new crimes than those who receive a jail sentence.[53]

Day Fines   Because judges rely so heavily on offense seriousness to fix the level of fines, financial penalties may have a negative impact on success rates. The more serious the offense and the higher the fine, the greater the chances that the offender will fail to pay the fine and risk probation revocation. To overcome this sort of problem, some jurisdictions, such as New York City, began experimenting with **day fines.**[54]

> **day fine**   A fine geared to the average daily income of the convicted offender in an effort to bring equity to the sentencing process.

A concept that originated in Europe, day fines are geared to an offender's net daily income. In an effort to make them equitable and fairly distributed, fines are based on the severity of the crime, weighted by a daily-income value taken from a chart similar to an income tax table; the number of the offender's dependents is also taken into account. The day fine concept means that the severity of punishment is geared to the offender's ability to pay.

Day fines hold the promise of becoming an equitable solution to the problem of setting the amount of a fine according to the offender's ability to pay. However, there is little conclusive evidence whether the day fine program actually works as intended.[55]

Forfeiture

> **forfeiture**   The seizure of personal property by the state as a civil or criminal penalty.

Another intermediate sanction with a financial basis is criminal (in personam) and civil (in rem) **forfeiture.** Both involve the seizure of goods and instrumentalities related to the commission or outcome of a criminal act. The difference is that criminal forfeiture proceedings target criminal defendants and can only follow a criminal conviction. In contrast, civil forfeiture proceedings target property used in a crime and do not require that formal criminal proceedings be initiated against a person or that the person be proven guilty of a crime.[56] For example, federal law provides that after arresting drug traffickers, the government may seize the boats they used to import the narcotics, the cars they used to carry the drugs overland, the warehouses in which the drugs were stored, and the homes paid for with the drug profits; on conviction, the drug dealers lose permanent ownership of these "instrumentalities" of crime.

Forfeiture is not a new sanction. During the Middle Ages, "forfeiture of estate" was a mandatory result of most felony convictions. The Crown could seize all of a felon's real and personal property. Forfeiture derived from the common-law concept of "corruption of blood" or "attaint," which prohibited a felon's family from inheriting or receiving his property or estate. The common law mandated that descendants could not inherit property from a relative who may have attained the property illegally: "[T]he Corruption of Blood stops the Course of Regular Descent, as to Estates, over which the Criminal could have no Power, because he never enjoyed them."[57]

Forfeiture was reintroduced to U.S. law with the passage of the Racketeer Influenced and Corrupt Organization (RICO) and the Continuing Criminal Enterprises Acts, both of which allow the seizure of any property derived from illegal enterprises or conspiracies. Although these acts were designed to apply to ongoing criminal conspiracies, such as drug or pornography rings, they are now being applied to a far-ranging series of criminal acts, including white-collar crimes. More than one hundred federal statutes use forfeiture of property as a punishment.

Although law enforcement officials at first applauded the use of forfeiture as a hard-hitting way of seizing the illegal profits of drug law violators, the practice has been criticized because the government has often been overzealous in its application. For example, million-dollar yachts have been seized because someone aboard possessed a small amount of marijuana; this confiscatory practice is referred to as **zero tolerance**. This strict interpretation of the forfeiture statutes has come under fire because it is often used capriciously, the penalty is sometimes disproportionate to the crime involved, and it makes the government a "partner in crime."[58] It is also alleged that forfeiture unfairly targets a narrow range of offenders. For example, it is common for government employees involved in corruption to forfeit their pensions; employees of public companies are exempt from such punishment.[59] There is also the issue of conflict of interest: because law enforcement agencies can use forfeited assets to supplement their budgets they may direct their efforts to cases that promise the greatest "payoff" rather than ones that have the highest law enforcement priority.[60]

Restitution

Another popular intermediate sanction is **restitution,** which can take the form of requiring offenders either to pay back the victims of crime (**monetary restitution**) or serve the community to compensate for their criminal acts (**community service restitution**).[61] Restitution programs offer offenders a chance to avoid a jail or prison sentence or a lengthier probation period. It may help them develop a sense of allegiance to society, better work habits, and some degree of gratitude for being given a second chance. Restitution serves many other purposes, including giving the community something of value without asking it to foot the bill for an incarceration stay and helping victims regain lost property and income.

If monetary restitution is called for, the probation department usually makes a determination of victim loss and develops a plan for paying fair compensation. To avoid the situation in which a wealthy offender can fill a restitution order by merely writing a check, judges will sometimes order that compensation be paid out of income derived from a low-paid social service or public works job.

Community service orders usually require duty in a public nursing home, shelter, hospital, drug treatment unit, or works program; some young vandals may find

To read more about the conflict of interest inherent in a forfeiture policy, go to InfoTrac College Edition and read R. T. Naylor, "License to Loot? A Critique of Follow-the-Money Methods in Crime Control Policy," *Social Justice,* Fall 2001 v28 i3 p121(32).

zero tolerance   The practice of seizing all instrumentalities of a crime, including homes, boats, and cars. It is an extreme example of the law of forfeiture.

restitution   A condition of probation in which the offender repays society or the victim of crime for the trouble the offender caused.

monetary restitution   A sanction that requires that convicted offenders compensate crime victims by reimbursing them for out-of-pocket losses caused by the crime. Losses can include property damage, lost wages, and medical costs.

community service restitution   An alternative sanction that requires an offender to work in the community at such tasks as cleaning public parks or working with disabled children in lieu of an incarceration sentence.

that they must clean up the damage they caused to the school or the park. Judges sometimes have difficulty gauging the length of community service orders. One suggestion is that the maximum order should be no more than 240 hours and that this should be considered the equivalent of a six- to twelve-month jail term.[62] Whether these terms are truly equivalent remains a matter of personal opinion.

Judges and probation officers have embraced the concept of restitution because it appears to benefit the victim, the offender, the criminal justice system, and society.[63] Financial restitution is inexpensive to administer, helps avoid stigma, and provides compensation for victims of crime. Offenders ordered to do community service work have been placed in schools, hospitals, and nursing homes. Helping them avoid a jail sentence can mean saving the public thousands of dollars that would have gone to maintaining them in a secure institution, frees up needed resources, and gives the community the feeling that equity has been returned to the justice system.

Does restitution work? Most reviews rate it as a qualified success. It is estimated that most of the clients successfully complete their restitution orders and that most have no subsequent contact with the justice system.[64]

© 2002 AP/Wide World Photos

Restitution may be ordered in addition to other criminal penalties. Clinton Haskins is led by the Albany County sheriff's deputy, May 23, 2002, in Laramie, Wyoming, after being sentenced to fourteen to twenty years in prison for killing eight college students in a drunken-driving collision. Haskins, twenty-two, was also ordered to pay $80,000 in restitution to the families of the victims and fined $8,008.

shock probation A sentence in which offenders serve a short prison term before they begin probation, to impress them with the pains of imprisonment.

split sentence A practice that requires convicted criminals to spend a portion of their sentence behind bars and the remainder in the community.

Shock Probation and Split Sentencing

Shock probation and **split sentences** are alternative sanctions designed to allow judges to grant offenders community release only after they have sampled prison life. These sanctions are based on the premise that if offenders are given a taste of incarceration sufficient to shock them into law-abiding behavior, they will be reluctant to violate the rules of probation or commit another crime.

In a number of states and in the Federal Criminal Code, a jail term can actually be a condition of probation, known as split sentencing. About 10 percent of probationers are now given split sentences. The shock probation approach involves resentencing an offender to probation after a short prison stay. The shock comes because the offender originally received a long maximum sentence but is then eligible for release to community supervision at the discretion of the judge (usually within ninety days of incarceration).

Some states have linked the short prison stay with a boot camp experience, referred to as *shock incarceration,* in which young inmates undergo a brief but intense period of military-like training and hard labor designed to impress them with the rigors of prison life.[65] (Boot camp programs are discussed in greater detail in Chapter 12.) Shock probation and split sentencing have been praised as ways to limit prison time, reintegrate the client quickly into the community, maintain family ties, and reduce prison populations and the costs of corrections.[66] An initial jail sentence probably makes offenders more receptive to the conditions of probation, because it amply illustrates the problems they will face if probation is violated.

But split sentences and shock probation programs have been criticized by those who believe that even a brief period of incarceration can interfere with the purpose of probation, which is to provide the offender with nonstigmatizing, community-based treatment. Even a short-term commitment subjects probationers to the destructive effects of institutionalization, disrupts their life in the community, and stigmatizes them for having been in jail.

Intensive Probation Supervision

Intensive probation supervision (IPS) programs are another important form of intermediate sanctions. These programs are also referred to as *intensive supervision programs.*) IPS programs, which have been implemented in some form in about forty states and today include about one hundred thousand clients, involve small caseloads of fifteen to forty clients who are kept under close watch by probation officers.[67]

The primary goal of IPS is *decarceration:* without intensive supervision, clients would normally be sent to already overcrowded prisons or jails. The second goal is *control:* high-risk offenders can be maintained in the community under much closer security than traditional probation efforts can provide. A third goal is *reintegration:* offenders can maintain community ties and be reoriented toward a more productive life while avoiding the pains of imprisonment.

In general, IPS programs rely on a great degree of client contact to achieve the goals of decarceration, control, and reintegration. Most programs have admissions criteria based on the nature of the offense and the offender's criminal background. Some programs exclude violent offenders; others will not take substance abusers. In contrast, some jurisdictions do not exclude offenders based on their prior criminal history.

IPS programs are used in several ways. In some states, IPS is a direct sentence imposed by a judge; in others, it is a postsentencing alternative used to divert offenders from the correctional system. A third practice is to use IPS as a case management tool to give the local probation staff flexibility in dealing with clients. Other jurisdictions use IPS in all three ways, in addition to applying it to probation violators to bring them halfway back into the community without resorting to a prison term.

The Effectiveness of IPS   Evaluations indicate that IPS programs are generally successful, deliver more services than would normally be received by probationers, are cost-effective, and produce recidivism rates equal to or better than those of offenders who have been confined. However, evaluations have so far not been definitive, often ignoring such issues as whether the program met its stated goals, whether IPS is more attractive than other alternative sanctions, and which types of offenders are particularly suited for IPS. For example, IPS seems to work better for offenders with good employment records than it does for the underemployed or unemployed.[68] Younger offenders who commit petty crimes are the most likely to fail on IPS; ironically, people with these characteristics are the ones most likely to be included in IPS programs.[69]

Indications also exist that the failure rate in IPS caseloads is high, in some cases approaching 50 percent; IPS clients may even have a higher rearrest rate than other probationers.[70] It should come as no surprise that IPS clients fail more often because, after all, they are more serious criminals who might otherwise have been incarcerated and are now being watched and supervised more closely than probationers. Probation officers may also be more willing to revoke the probation of IPS clients because they believe the clients are a risk to the community and, under normal circumstances, would have been incarcerated. Why risk the program to save a few "bad apples?"

Although evidence that it can significantly reduce offending rates is still insufficient, IPS might be an attractive alternative to traditional correctional methods if it can be restricted to offenders who would most likely have been incarcerated without the availability of the IPS program. IPS may also be more effective if it is

intensive probation supervision (IPS) A type of intermediate sanction involving small probation caseloads and strict monitoring on a daily or weekly basis.

combined with particular treatment modalities such as cognitive-behavioral treatment, which stresses such life skills as problem solving, social skills, negotiation skills, management of emotion, and values enhancement.[71]

After thoroughly reviewing the impact of IPS, Betsy Fulton and her associates concluded that IPS programs are among the most popular alternatives to imprisonment in the United States and that, although IPS has not provided a solution to prison crowding, it is useful for those not meriting imprisonment but at high risk for probation.[72]

House Arrest

house arrest A form of intermediate sanction that requires that the convicted offender spend a designated amount of time per week in his or her own home—for example, from 5 P.M. Friday until 8 A.M. Monday.

The **house arrest** concept requires convicted offenders to spend extended periods of time in their own home as an alternative to an incarceration sentence. For example, persons convicted on a drunk-driving charge might be sentenced to spend between 6 P.M. Friday and 8 A.M. Monday and every weekday after 5:30 P.M. in their home for six months. According to current estimates, more than ten thousand people are under house arrest.

As with IPS programs, there is a great deal of variation in house arrest initiatives: some are administered by probation departments, while others are simply judicial sentences monitored by surveillance officers. Some check clients twenty or more times a month (such as the Florida Community Control Program), while others do only a few curfew checks. Some use twenty-four-hour confinement, while others allow offenders to attend work or school.

No definitive data exist indicating that house arrest is an effective crime deterrent, nor is there sufficient evidence to conclude that it has utility as a device to lower the recidivism rate. One evaluation of the Florida program found that nearly 10 percent of the house arrest sample had their probation revoked for technical violations within eighteen months of their sentencing.[73] Another evaluation of the same program found that recidivism rates were almost identical to a

© 2002 AP/Wide World Photos

The house arrest concept requires convicted offenders to spend extended periods of time in their own homes as an alternative to an incarceration sentence. Dontee Stokes, center, leaves jail May 17, 2002, with family members after being released on $150,000 bail in Baltimore. Stokes, twenty-six, accused of shooting a priest he had accused of molesting him, was released after a psychiatrist testified that he posed no danger to himself or others. Stokes was to remain under house arrest and fitted with an electronic monitoring device.

matched sample of inmates released from secure correctional facilities; four out of five offenders in both forms of correction recidivated within five years.[74] Although these findings are troublesome, the advantages of house arrest in reducing costs and overcrowding in the correctional system probably make further experimentation inevitable.

Electronic Monitoring

For house arrest to work, sentencing authorities must be assured that arrestees are actually at home during their assigned times. Random calls and visits are one way to check on compliance with house arrest orders. However, one of the more interesting developments in the criminal justice system has been the introduction of **electronic monitoring (EM)** devices to manage offender obedience to home confinement orders.[75]

Electronically monitored offenders wear devices that send signals to a control office; the devices are worn around their ankles, wrists, or necks. Two basic types of systems are used: active and passive. *Active systems* constantly monitor offenders by continuously sending a signal to the central office. If offenders leave their home at an unauthorized time, the signal is broken, and the "failure" is recorded. In some cases, the control officer is automatically notified electronically through a beeper. In contrast, *passive systems* usually involve random phone calls generated by computers to which the offenders have to respond within a particular time (such as thirty seconds). In addition to probationers, EM can be used at the front end of the system with bailees and at the back end with parolees.

The various kinds of EM devices are described in Exhibit 11.3.

electronic monitoring (EM) Requiring a convicted offender to wear a monitoring device as part of his or her community sentence. Electronic monitoring is typically part of a house arrest order and enables the probation department to ensure that the offender is complying with court-ordered limitations on his or her freedom.

Exhibit 11.3 Available electronic monitoring systems

- *Identity verification devices* range from personal identification numbers to biometric verification that recognizes different parts of the human body to ensure the reporting person is the intended offender.
- *Remote alcohol detection devices* require users to blow into the device, which is usually in the offender's home, to measure blood alcohol content. The results are recorded by a computer to determine compliance with conditions of alcohol consumption.
- *Ignition interlock devices* are linked to the electrical systems of automobiles. The driver must expel deep lung air into the device to operate the vehicle. If the driver's blood alcohol content registers above a predetermined level deemed unsafe to drive, the vehicle will not start.
- *Programmed contact systems* are used to contact and verify the location of offenders in their homes or elsewhere. They utilize a central computer that either receives telephone calls from or makes calls to offenders in one or more locations.
- *Continuous signaling devices* are battery-powered and transmit a radio signal two or more times per minute. These are placed on the offender's wrist or ankle with a tamper-resistant strap, and must be worn at all times. A receiver detects the transmitter's signals and conveys a message via telephone report to a central computer when it either stops receiving the radio frequency or the signal resumes. Receivers can detect transmitter signals from a range of up to,

and in some cases, exceeding, 150 feet when installed in a typical home environment.
- *Victim notification systems* alert the victim when the offender is approaching that person's residence. A transmitter is worn by both the offender and the victim, and a receiver is placed at both residences.
- *Field monitoring devices,* or "drive-by" units, are another type of continuous signaling technology. Probation or parole officers or other authorities use a portable device that can be hand-held or used in a vehicle with a roof-mounted antenna. When within two hundred to eight hundred feet of an offender's ankle or wrist transmitter, the portable device can detect the radio signals of the offender's transmitter.
- *Group monitoring units* allow supervisors to monitor several offenders in the same location, such as for verifying attendance of multiple offenders in a day-reporting program or monitoring offenders confined in a residential group setting.
- *Location tracking systems,* also known as global positioning systems, offer yet another way to monitor offenders. Receivers detect satellite signals that include the exact time the signal is sent and the identity of the satellite sending the signal. This information is processed to determine the person's location. This more expensive technology usually is used for high-risk offenders. It can determine when an offender leaves an area where he or she is supposed to be (inclusion zone) or enters an area where he or she is not allowed to be (exclusion zone)

Source: Ann Crowe, "Electronic Supervision: From Decision Making to Implementation," *Corrections Today* 64 (2002): 131–132.

Electronic monitoring supporters claim the EM has the benefits of relatively low cost and high security, while helping offenders avoid the pains of imprisonment in overcrowded, dangerous state facilities. Electronic monitoring is capital-intensive rather than labor-intensive. Since offenders are monitored by computers, an initial investment in hardware rules out the need for hiring many more supervisory officers to handle large numbers of clients. It is not surprising, then, that the public supports EM as a cost-effective alternative to prison sentences that have proven ineffective.[76]

There are some indications that EM can be an effective addition to the galaxy of intermediate sanctions, providing the judiciary with an enhanced supervision tool.[77] For example, when Kevin Courtright and his associates examined the cost-saving potential of using house arrest with EM as an alternative to incarceration for a drunk-driving population in a Pennsylvania county, they found that the program saved money and avoided new construction costs without widening the net of social control.[78] However, not all evaluations have been successful, and some find that offenders monitored on EM are no less likely to recidivate than those released without such supervision.[79]

Some civil libertarians are troubled by the fact that EM can erode privacy and liberty. Do we really want U.S. citizens watched over by a computer? What are the limits of EM? Can it be used with mental patients? HIV carriers? Suicidal teenagers? Those considered high-risk future offenders?

Although promising to reduce the correctional population, EM actually has the potential to substantially increase it by turning homes into prisons. Furthermore, neither its effectiveness nor its acceptance by state agencies has been fully determined. For example, one survey of supervision agencies in Texas found that about two-thirds still did not use EM, primarily because of its presumed cost and perceptions that it is ineffective.[80] Consequently, the future of EM is still uncertain.

Residential Community Corrections

residential community corrections (RCC) A nonsecure facility, located in the community, that houses probationers who need a more secure environment. Typically, residents are free during the day to go to work, school, or treatment, and return in the evening for counseling sessions and meals.

The most secure intermediate sanction is a sentence to a **residential community corrections (RCC)** facility. Such a facility has been defined as "a freestanding nonsecure building that is not part of a prison or jail and houses pretrial and adjudicated adults. The residents regularly depart to work, to attend school, and/or participate in treatment activities and programs."[81]

Traditionally, the role of community corrections was supplied by the nonsecure halfway house, which was designed to reintegrate soon-to-be-paroled prison inmates back into the community. Inmates spend the last few months in the halfway house, acquiring suitable employment, building up cash reserves, obtaining an apartment, and developing a job-related wardrobe.

The traditional concept of community corrections has expanded. Today, the community correctional facility is a vehicle to provide intermediate sanctions as well as a prerelease center for those about to be paroled from the prison system. For example, RCC has been used as a direct sentencing option for judges who believe particular offenders need a correctional alternative halfway between traditional probation and a stay in prison. Placement in an RCC center can be used as a condition of probation for offenders who need a nonsecure community facility that provides a more structured treatment environment than traditional probation. It is commonly used in the juvenile justice system for youths who need a more secure environment than can be provided by traditional probation yet who are not deemed a threat to the community and do not require a secure placement.

Probation departments and other correctional authorities have been charged with running RCC centers that serve as a pre-prison sentencing alternative. In addition, some RCC centers are operated by private, nonprofit groups that receive referrals from the county or district courts and from probation or parole departments. For example, Portland House, a private residential center in Minneapolis, operates as an alternative to incarceration for young adult offenders. The twenty-five residents regularly receive group therapy and financial, vocational, educational, family, and personal counseling. Residents may work to earn a high school equivalency degree. With funds withheld from their earnings at work-release employment, residents pay room and board, family and self-support, and income taxes. Portland House appears to be successful. It is significantly cheaper to run than a state institution, and the recidivism rate of clients is much lower than that of those who have gone through traditional correctional programs.[82]

Besides acting as sole sentences and halfway house, RCC facilities have also been residential pretrial release centers for offenders who are in immediate need of social services before their trial and as halfway-back alternatives for both parole and probation violators who might otherwise have to be imprisoned. In this capacity, RCC programs serve as a base from which offenders can be placed in outpatient psychiatric facilities, drug and alcohol treatment programs, job training, and so on. Some programs make use of both inpatient and outpatient programs to provide clients with specialized treatment, such as substance abuse management.[83]

One recent development has been the use of RCC facilities as **day reporting centers (DRCs)**.[84] Day reporting centers provide a single location to which a variety of clients can report for supervision and treatment. Used in Georgia, Delaware, Utah, and other jurisdictions, DRCs utilize existing RCC facilities to service nonresidential clients. They can be used as a step up for probationers who have failed in the community and a step down in security for jail or prison inmates.[85] For example, the Atlanta Day Reporting Center, opened in June 2001, was developed as a joint project by the Georgia Parole Board and the Department of Corrections. It provides 125 probationers and parolees with structured daily programs in GED preparation, substance abuse recovery, and cognitive skills training. Although offenders return to their homes at night, the center intensifies training and support and therefore affords many of the well-documented benefits of traditional halfway houses.[86]

More than two thousand state-run community-based facilities are in use today. In addition, up to twenty-five hundred private, nonprofit RCC programs operate in the United States. About half also house inmates who have been released from prison (halfway houses) and use the RCC placement as a method to ease back into society. The remainder are true intermediate sanctions, including about four hundred federally sponsored programs.

Despite the thousands of traditional and innovative RCC programs in operation around the United States, relatively few efforts have been made to evaluate their effectiveness. Those evaluations that do exist suggest that many residents do not complete their treatment regimen in RCC facilities, violating the rules or committing new offenses. Those that do complete the program have lower recidivism rates than the unsuccessful discharges.[87]

One reason why it is so difficult to assess RCC facilities is that programs differ considerably with respect to target population, treatment alternatives, and goals. Although some are rehabilitation-oriented and operate under loose security, others are control-oriented and use such security measures as random drug and alcohol testing. Although critics question their overall effectiveness, RCC facilities appear to work for some types of offenders, and some treatment orientations seem to work better than others. It is possible that rather than being used as a "last resort" community alternative before sentence to a jail or prison, RCC placement might actually work better with first-time offenders who have relatively little experience with the criminal or juvenile justice systems.[88]

day reporting center (DRC) A nonresidential community-based treatment program.

Can Intermediate Sanctions Work?

Intermediate community-based sanctions hold the promise of providing cost-effective crime control strategies without widening the net of the criminal justice system. They reduce overreliance on incarceration and exploding correctional construction costs.[89] Nonetheless, there are indications that, as currently situated, intermediate sanctions are no more effective in reducing recidivism than traditional forms of probation; because of the more intense monitoring involved, intermediate sanctions may result in more offenders being discovered to have committed technical violations.[90] Revocation for technical reasons helps increase rather than decrease the correctional population, an outcome in opposition to the stated goals of alternative sentencing.[91]

Some criminal justice professionals welcome the use of intermediate sanctions as a practical alternative to prison, whereas others are skeptical about the ability of community sentences to reduce the correctional population significantly. Skeptics John DiIulio and Charles Logan argue that it is a myth that prison crowding can be reduced, that new construction can be avoided, and that annual operating costs can be cut if greater advantage is taken of intermediate sanctions. The great majority of those under correctional supervision, they assert, have already been on probation and will eventually be supervised in the community. In other words, most convicted criminals are already experiencing an "intermediate sanction" for at least some part of their sentence. Of inmates currently in state prisons, 67 percent were given probation as an intermediate sanction one or more times on prior convictions, and over 80 percent have had prior convictions resulting in either probation or incarceration. On any day of the week, argue DiIulio and Logan, you will find three times as many convicts under alternative supervision as you will under the watchful eye of a warden. And most of those in the warden's custody are probably there at least partly because they did not do well under some prior alternative.[92]

In contrast to this view, Michael Tonry and Mary Lynch suggest that intermediate sanctions can be a useful correctional tool. Not everyone who commits a crime is the same, and they should not receive identical punishments. Clients for intermediate sanction programs might be chosen from those already incarcerated, eliminating the threat of net widening. It might be possible, they suggest, to create "exchange rates" that create equivalent sentences for prison and community alternatives, such as three days in home confinement instead of one day in jail. Although intermediate sanctions are not a panacea for all offenders (as Tonry and Lynch put it, "There is no free lunch"), they conclude that for offenders who do not present unacceptable risks of violence, well-managed intermediate sanctions offer a cost-effective way to keep them in the community.[93]

Restorative Justice

Some crime experts believe that, ironically, rather than reducing crime and recidivism, policies based on getting "tough on crime" can cause crime rates to fluctuate higher and offenders to commit more crime. Punishment does not work because it destroys the offender's dignity and piece of mind. Traditional community-based correctional models such as probation have proven ineffective. And when they are supplemented by the new alternative/intermediate sanctions the effect is to add a punitive aspect that can further hinder rehabilitation efforts. Instead, restorative justice advocates suggest a policy based on (1) restoring the damage caused by crime and (2) creating a system of justice that includes all the parties harmed by the criminal act: the victim, the offender, the community, and society.[94]

Although the restoration movement has many sources, one of the key pillars is the influential book by Australian criminologist John Braithwaite: *Crime, Shame, and Reintegration.*[95] Braithwaite's ideas are discussed in the Policy, Programs, and Issues in Criminal Justice feature that follows.

The Concept of Restoration

According to the restorative view, crimes can seem quite different, ranging from a violent assault to a white-collar fraud scheme. Nonetheless, they all share one common trait: they bring harm to the community in which they occur. The tradi-

Policy, Programs, and Issues in Criminal Justice

Reintegrative Shaming

John Braithwaite, a prominent Australian criminologist, notes that shame is a powerful tool of informal social control. Countries such as Japan, in which conviction for crimes brings an inordinate amount of personal shame, have extremely low crime rates. In contrast, citizens in cultures in which crime is not shameful, such as the United States, cast themselves as victims of the justice system. Because their punishment comes at the hands of strangers, like police and judges, who are being paid to act, they fail to understand the harm their actions caused. The adversary system turns their case over to lawyers and prosecutors who argue legal rules while ignoring the plight of the victim and the community. In nations that rely on shame and personal responsibility, such as Japan, criminal prosecution proceeds only when the normal process of public apology, compensation, and the victim's forgiveness breaks down.

Braithwaite divides the concept of shame into two distinct types. The most common form of shaming typically involves stigmatization that occurs during a process of degradation in which the offender is branded as an evil person and cast out of society. Shaming can occur at a school disciplinary hearing or a criminal court trial. Bestowing stigma and degradation is doomed to failure: people who suffer humiliation at the hands of the justice system are turned into outcasts with little choice but to reject society. They may join with fellow rejects and collectively resist social control. For example, the student boy who is expelled from high school joins a teenage gang. Despite these dangers, there has been an ongoing effort to brand offenders and make their "shame" both public and permanent; most states have passed sex offender registry and notification laws, which make public the names of those convicted of sex offenses and warn neighbors of their presence in the community. Such efforts leave little hope of successful reintegration into conventional society.

Braithwaite argues that crime control can be better achieved through a policy of *reintegrative shaming*. Here disapproval is limited to the offender's evil deeds, and not to the offender himself. Law violators must be made to realize that while their actions have caused harm they are still valuable people—people who can be reaccepted by society. A critical element of reintegrative shaming occurs when the offenders begin to understand and recognize their wrongdoing and shame themselves. To be reintegrative, shaming must be brief and controlled and then followed by ceremonies of forgiveness, apology, and repentance.

To prevent crime, society must encourage reintegrative shaming and eschew vengeance, stigma, and labeling. For example, the incidence of domestic violence might be reduced by mounting a crusade to shame spouse abusers and help them understand the harm they have caused. Similarly, parents who use reintegrative shaming techniques in their child-rearing practices may improve parent-child relationships and ultimately reduce the delinquent involvement of their children. Efforts like these can humanize a system of justice that today relies on repression rather than forgiveness.

Critical Thinking

Considering the reasons why people commit crime in the first place, is it reasonable to believe that a reintegrative shaming policy can restore them to conventional society? Can there be a simple solution to the crime problem such as reintegrative shaming if offenders actually suffer from multiple social and personal problems, including impulsivity, long-term substance abuse, and economic deprivation?

InfoTrac College Edition Research

Read an article by John Braithwaite on InfoTrac College Edition: "Shame and Criminal Justice," *Canadian Journal of Criminology*, July 2000 v42 i3 p281.

Sources: John Braithwaite, *Crime, Shame, and Reintegration* (Melbourne, Australia: Cambridge University Press, 1989); Anthony Petrosino and Carolyn Petrosino, "The Public Safety Potential of Megan's Law in Massachusetts: An Assessment from a Sample of Criminal Sexual Psychopaths," *Crime and Delinquency* 45 (1999): 140–158; Carter Hay, "An Exploratory Test of Braithwaite's Reintegrative Shaming Theory," *Journal of Research in Crime and Delinquency* 38 (2001): 132–153.

tional justice system has done little to involve the community in the justice process. What has developed is a system of coercive punishments administered by bureaucrats that is inherently harmful to offenders and reduces the likelihood they will ever again become productive members of society. This system relies on punishment, stigma, and disgrace. What is needed instead is a justice policy that repairs the harm caused by crime and includes all parties which have suffered from that harm, including the victim, the community, and the offender. Exhibit 11.4 sets out the principles of the restorative justice approach.

An important aspect of achieving these goals is that offenders accept accountability for their actions and responsibility for the harm their actions caused.

Exhibit 11.4	The basic principles of restorative justice

- Crime is an offense against human relationships.
- Victims and the community are central to justice processes.
- The first priority of justice processes is to assist victims.
- The second priority is to restore the community, to the degree possible.
- The offender has a personal responsibility to victims and to the community for crimes committed.
- The offender will develop improved competency and understanding as a result of the restorative justice experience.
- Stakeholders share responsibilities for restorative justice through partnerships for action.

Source: Anne Seymour, "Restorative Justice/Community Justice," in the National Victim Assistance Academy textbook (Washington, D.C.: National Victim Assistance Academy, 2001); updated July 2002.

Only then can they be restored as productive members of their community. Restoration involves turning the justice system into a "healing" process rather than a distributor of retribution and revenge.

Most people involved in offender-victim relationships actually know one another or were related in some way before the criminal incident took place. Instead of treating one of the involved parties as a victim deserving sympathy and the other as a criminal deserving punishment, it is more productive to address the issues that produced the conflict between these people. Rather than take sides and choose whom to isolate and punish, society should try to reconcile the parties involved in conflict.[96] The effectiveness of justice ultimately depends on the stake a person has in the community (or a particular social group). If a person does not value her membership in the group, she will be unlikely to accept responsibility, show remorse, or repair the injuries caused by her actions.

The Process of Restoration

The restoration process begins by redefining crime in terms of a conflict among the offender, the victim, and affected constituencies (families, schools, workplaces, and so on). Therefore, it is vitally important that the resolution take place in the context in which the conflict originally occurred rather than be transferred to a specialized institution that has no social connection to the particular community or group. In other words, most conflicts are better settled in the community than in a court.

By maintaining "ownership" or jurisdiction over the conflict, the community is able to express its shared outrage about the offense. Shared community outrage is directly communicated to the offender. The victim is also given a chance to voice his or her story, and the offender can directly communicate his or her need for social reintegration and treatment. In a sense, then, many different parties have a stake in the justice process; these are the primary and secondary "stakeholders" in crime and justice.

Restoration Programs

All restoration programs involve all the parties involved in a criminal act: the victim, the offender, and the community. Although processes differ in structure and style, they generally include the following:

1. Recognition by offenders that they have caused injury to personal and social relations, and a determination and acceptance of responsibility (ideally accompanied by a statement of remorse).

The Center for Restorative Justice & Peacemaking provides links and information on the ideals of restoration and programs based on its principles: http://ssw.che.umn.edu/rjp/default.html

2. A commitment to both material (for example, monetary restitution) and symbolic reparation (for example, an apology),
3. A determination of community support and assistance for both victim and offender.

The intended result of the process is to repair injuries suffered by the victim and the community while assuring reintegration of the offender.

Negotiation, mediation, consensus-building, and peacemaking have been part of the dispute resolution process in European and Asian communities for centuries.[97] Native American and Native Canadian people have long used the type of community participation in the adjudication process (for example, sentencing circles, sentencing panels, elders panels) that restorative justice advocates are now embracing.[98]

In some Native American communities, people accused of breaking the law meet with community members, victims if any, village elders, and agents of the justice system in a **sentencing circle**. All members of the circle express their feelings about the act that was committed and raise questions or concerns. The accused can express regret about his or her actions and a desire to change the harmful behavior. People may suggest ways the offender can make things up to the community and those who were harmed. A treatment program, such as Alcoholics Anonymous, may be suggested, if appropriate.

Restorative justice is now being embraced on many levels in the justice system.

Schools Some schools have employed restorative justice practices in order to deal with students who are involved in drug and alcohol abuse without having to resort to more punitive measures such as expulsion. School in Minnesota, Colorado, and elsewhere are now trying to involve students in "relational rehabilitation" programs, which strive to improve offenders' relationships with key figures in the community who may have been harmed by their actions.[99]

Police Restorative justice has also been implemented when crime is first encountered by police. The new community policing models discussed in Chapters 4 and 5 are an attempt to bring restorative concepts into law enforcement. Restorative justice relies on criminal justice policymakers listening to and responding to the needs of those who will be affected by their actions, and community policing relies on policies established with input and exchanges between officers and citizens.[100]

Courts In the court system, restorative programs usually involve diverting the formal court process. Instead, these programs encourage meeting and reconciling the conflicts between offenders and victims via victim advocacy, mediation programs, and sentencing circles, in which crime victims and their families are brought together with offenders and their families in an effort to formulate a sanction that addresses the needs of each party. Victims are given a chance to voice their stories and offenders can help compensate them financially or provide some service (for example, fix damaged

To read more about sentencing circles, go to

www.ojp.usdoj.gov/nij/restjust/CH5/3_sntcir.htm

sentencing circles A type of sentencing in which victims, family members, community members, and the offender participate in an effort to devise fair and reasonable sanctions that are ultimately aimed at reintegrating the offender back into the community.

© 2001 AP/Wide World Photos

Restorative justice advocate Gary Geiger speaks to students about mediation at Guilderland High School in New York. Restorative justice advocates believe that rather than punish criminals, a policy based on (a) restoring the damage caused by crime and (b) creating a system of justice that includes all the parties harmed by the criminal act—the victim, offender, community, and society—may help reintegrate the offender back into society.

Exhibit 11.5 Victim concerns about restorative justice

- Restorative justice processes can cast victims as little more than props in a psychodrama focused on the offender, to restore him and thereby render him less likely to offend again.
- A victim, supported by family and intimates while engaged in restorative conferencing, and feeling genuinely free to speak directly to the offender, may press a blaming rather than restorative shaming agenda.
- The victims' movement has focused for years on a perceived imbalance of "rights." Criminal defendants enjoy the presumption of innocence, the right to proof beyond a reasonable doubt, the right not to have to testify, and lenient treatment when found guilty of crime. Victims were extended no rights at all in the legal process. Is restorative justice another legal giveaway to criminals?
- Victims' rights are threatened by some features of the restorative justice process, such as respectful listening to the offender's story and consensual dispositions. These features

seem affronts to a victim's claim of the right to be seen as a victim, to insist on the offender being branded a criminal, to blame the offender, and not to be "victimized all over again by the process."
- Many victims do want apology, if it is heartfelt and easy to get, but some want, even more, to put the traumatic incident behind them; to retrieve stolen property being held for use at trial; to be assured that the offender will receive treatment he is thought to need if he is not to victimize someone else. For victims such as these, restorative justice processes can seem unnecessary at best.
- Restorative processes depend, case by case, on victims' active participation, in a role more emotionally demanding than that of complaining witness in a conventional criminal prosecution; this is itself a role avoided by many, and perhaps most, victims.

Source: Michael E. Smith, *What Future for "Public Safety" and "Restorative Justice" in Community Corrections?* (Washington, D.C.: National Institute of Justice, 2001).

property).[101] Again, the goal is to enable offenders to appreciate the damage they have caused, to make amends, and to be reintegrated back into society. The Policy, Programs, and Issues feature that follows discusses restorative justice in different states.

The Challenge of Restorative Justice

Although restorative justice holds great promise, there are also some concerns.[102] Restorative justice programs must be wary of the cultural and social differences that can be found throughout our heterogeneous society. What may be considered "restorative" in one subculture may be considered insulting and damaging in another.[103] Similarly, so many diverse programs call themselves "restorative" that it is difficult to evaluate them, because each one may be pursuing a unique objective. In other words, there is still no single definition of what restorative justice is.[104]

Possibly the greatest challenge in carrying out the goals of restorative justice is the difficult task of balancing the needs of offenders with those of their victims. If programs focus solely on the victim's needs they may risk ignoring the offender's needs and increasing the likelihood of re-offending. Sharon Levrant and her colleagues suggest that restorative justice programs that feature short-term interactions with victims fail to help offenders learn prosocial ways of behaving. Restorative justice advocates may falsely assume that relatively brief interludes of public shaming will change deeply rooted criminal predispositions.[105]

In contrast, programs that focus on the offender may turn off victims and their advocates. Some victim advocacy groups have voiced concerns about the focus of restorative justice programs. (See Exhibit 11.5.)

These are a few of the obstacles that restorative justice programs must overcome in order to be successful and productive. Yet, because the method holds so much promise, criminologists are now conducting numerous demonstration projects to find the most effective means of returning the ownership of justice to the people and the community. ■

Policy, Programs, and Issues in Criminal Justice

Restorative Justice in the Community

A number of new and innovative community programs based on restorative justice principles, three of which are discussed here, are being tested around the nation.

Minnesota

Minnesota has been a groundbreaker in restorative justice. Its department of corrections created the Restorative Justice Initiative in 1992, hiring Kay Pranis as a full-time restorative justice planner in 1994—the first such position in the country. The initiative offers training in restorative justice principles and practices, provides technical assistance to communities in designing and implementing practices, and creates networks of professionals and activists to share knowledge and provide support.

Besides promoting victim-offender mediation, family group conferencing, and neighborhood conferencing, the department has introduced sentencing circles. Citizen volunteers and criminal justice officials from Minnesota have participated in training in the Yukon Territory, Canada, where peacemaking circles have been held since the late 1980s. In Minnesota the circle process is used by the Mille Lacs Indian Reservation and in other communities in several counties. The circle process usually has several phases. First, the community justice committee conducts an intake interview with offenders who want to participate. Then, separate healing circles are held for the victim (and others who feel harmed) and the offender. The committee tries to cultivate a close personal relationship with victims and offenders and to create support networks for them. In the end, a sentencing circle, open to the community, meets to work out a sentencing plan.

Vermont

A pilot reparative probation program began in Vermont in 1994, and the first cases were heard by a reparative citizen board the following year. Three features distinguish this restorative justice initiative from most others in the United States: the department of corrections designed the program, it is implemented statewide, and it involves a sizable number of volunteer citizens. The process is straightforward. Following an adjudication of guilt, the judge sentences the offender to probation, with the sentence suspended and only two conditions imposed: the offender will commit no more crimes and will complete the reparative program. The volunteer board members meet with the offender and the victim and together discuss the offense, its effects on victim and community, and the life situations of victim and offender. All participants must agree on a contract, to be fulfilled by the offender. It is based on five goals: the victim is restored and healed, the community is restored, the offender understands the effects of the crime, the offender learns ways to avoid reoffending, and the community offers reintegration to the offender. Since reparative pro-

bation targets minor crimes, it is not meant as a prison diversion program. In a single year, forty-four reparative citizen boards handle about twelve hundred cases, accounting for more than one-third of the probation caseload. More than three hundred trained volunteers serve as board members. Ten coordinators handle case management and organization for the boards. The goal is to have the boards handle about 70 percent of the targeted probation cases. That only about 17 percent of offenders fail to complete their agreements or attend follow-up board meetings is a measure of the program's success. These offenders are referred back to the courts.

Travis County, Texas

Texas law now authorizes that each county develop a community justice council and community justice task force. The task force includes representatives of criminal justice agencies, social and health services, and community organizations. With task force assistance, the council, consisting of elected officials, handles planning and policymaking and prepares a community justice plan.

Many efforts are directed at juvenile offenses. In Austin, the juvenile probation office offers victim-offender mediation for young people in trouble. For misdemeanors, juveniles may be diverted from court to neighborhood conference committees. These consist of panels of trained adult citizens who meet with juvenile offenders and their parents and together develop contracts tailored to the case.

Critical Thinking

Restorative justice may be the model that best serves alternative sanctions. How can this essentially humanistic approach be sold to a general public that now supports more punitive sanctions? For example, is it feasible that using restorative justice with nonviolent offenders would free up resources for the relatively few dangerous people in the criminal population? Explain.

InfoTrac College Edition Research

To learn more about the restorative justice approach, go to InfoTrac College Edition and read Gordon Bazemore, "Restorative Justice and Earned Redemption: Communities, Victims, and Offender Reintegration," *American Behavioral Scientist* 41 (1998): 768; Tag Evers, "A Healing Approach to Crime," *The Progressive* 62 (1998): 30; Carol La Prairie, "The Impact of Aboriginal Justice Research on Policy: A Marginal Past and an Even More Uncertain Future," *Canadian Journal of Criminology* 41 (1999): 249.

Source: Leena Kurki, *Incorporating Restorative and Community Justice into American Sentencing and Corrections* (Washington, D.C.: National Institute of Justice, 1999).

SUMMARY

Probation can be traced to the common-law practice of granting clemency to deserving offenders. The modern probation concept was developed by John Augustus of Boston, who personally sponsored two thousand convicted inmates over an eighteen-year period. Today, probation is the community supervision of convicted offenders by order of the court. It is a sentence reserved for defendants whom the magistrate views as having potential for rehabilitation without needing to serve prison or jail terms. Probation is practiced in every state and by the federal government and includes both adult and juvenile offenders.

In the decision to grant probation, most judges are influenced by their personal views and the presentence reports of the probation staff. Once on probation, the offender must follow a set of rules or conditions, the violation of which may lead to revocation of probation and reinstatement of a prison sentence. These rules vary from state to state but usually involve such demands as refraining from using alcohol or drugs, obeying curfews, and terminating past criminal associations.

Probation officers are usually organized into countywide departments, although some agencies are statewide and others are combined parole-probation departments. Probation departments have instituted a number of innovative programs designed to bring better services to their clients. These include restitution and diversionary programs, intensive probation, and residential probation.

In recent years, the U.S. Supreme Court has granted probationers greater due process rights; today, when the state wishes to revoke probation, it must conduct a full hearing on the matter and provide the probationer with an attorney when that assistance is warranted.

To supplement probation, a whole new family of intermediate sanctions has been developed. These range from pretrial diversion to residential community corrections. Other widely used intermediate sanctions include fines and forfeiture, house arrest, and intensive probation supervision. Electronic monitoring (EM) involves the offender wearing a device under home confinement. Although some critics complain that EM smacks of a Big-Brother-is-watching-you mentality, it would seem an attractive alternative to a stay in a dangerous, deteriorating, secure correctional facility. A stay in a community correctional center is one of the most intrusive alternative sentencing options. Residents may be eligible for work and educational release during the day while attending group sessions in the evening. Residential community correction is less costly than more secure institutions, but there is little conclusive evidence that it is effective in reducing recidivism.

Although it is too soon to determine whether all these programs are successful, they provide a hope of being low-cost, high-security alternatives to traditional corrections. Alternatives to incarceration can help reduce overcrowding in the prison system and spare nonviolent offenders the pains of a prison experience. Even if alternatives are not much more effective than a prison sentence in reducing recidivism rates, they are far less costly and can free up needed space for more serious offenders.

A promising approach to community sentencing is restorative justice. These programs stress healing and redemption rather than punishment and deterrence. Restoration means that the offender accepts accountability for her actions and the responsibility for the harm her actions caused. Restoration involves turning the justice system into a "healing" process rather than a distributor of retribution and revenge. Restoration programs are now being used around the nation and involve mediation, sentencing circles, and other methods.

For an up-to-date list of Web links, go to
http://cj.wadsworth.com/siegel_essen4e.

KEY TERMS

probation 350	intake 358	restitution 367	house arrest 370
judicial reprieve 351	risk classification 359	monetary restitution 367	electronic monitoring (EM) 371
recognizance 351	day fees 362	community service restitution 367	
sureties 351	intermediate sanctions 362		residential community corrections (RCC) 372
revocation 352	fine 365	shock probation 368	
suspended sentence 352	day fine 366	split sentence 368	day reporting center (DRC) 373
presentence investigation 358	forfeiture 366	intensive probation supervision (IPS) 369	sentencing circles 377
	zero tolerance 367		

INFOTRAC COLLEGE EDITION EXERCISES

SOME PEOPLE BELIEVE that offenders have taken from society and should be forced to give back. Is this part of restorative justice? To find out the answer, read Gregg W. Etter and Judy Hammond, "Community: Service Work as Part of Offender Rehabilitation," *Corrections Today,* December 2001 v63 i7 p114(3).

CAN RESTORATIVE JUSTICE WORK? Does it affect men and women equally? Read Stephanie Coward-Yaskiw, "Restorative Justice: What Is It? Can It Work? What Do Women Think?" *Horizons,* Spring 2002 v15 i4 p22(4).

QUESTIONS

1. What is the purpose of probation? Identify some conditions of probation and discuss the responsibilities of the probation officer.

2. Discuss the procedures involved in probation revocation. What are the rights of the probationer? Is probation a privilege or a right? Explain.

3. Should a convicted criminal make restitution to the victim? Why or why not? When is restitution inappropriate?

4. Should offenders be fined based on the severity of what they did or according to their ability to pay? Is it fair to base day fines on wages? Why or why not? Should offenders be punished more severely because they are financially successful? Explain.

5. Does house arrest involve a violation of personal freedom? Does wearing an ankle bracelet smack of "Big Brother?" Would you want the government monitoring your daily activities? Could this be expanded, for example, to monitor the whereabouts of AIDS patients? Explain.

6. Do you agree that criminals can be restored through community interaction? Considering the fact that recidivism rates are so high, are traditional sanctions a waste of time and restorative ones the wave of the future?

NOTES

1. Rick Lyman, "Winona Ryder Found Guilty of Two Counts in Shoplifting Case," *New York Times,* 6 November 2002, A1.

2. For a history of probation, see Edward Sieh, "From Augustus to the Progressives: A Study of Probation's Formative Years," *Federal Probation* 57 (1993): 67–72.

3. Ibid.

4. David Rothman, *Conscience and Convenience* (Boston: Little, Brown, 1980), 82–117.

5. See, generally, Todd Clear and Vincent O'Leary, *Controlling the Offender in the Community* (Lexington, Mass.: Lexington Books, 1983).

6. Matthew Durose and Patrick A. Langan, *State Court Sentencing of Convicted Felons, 1998* (Washington, D.C.: Bureau of Justice Statistics, February 2001).

7. Lawrence Bonczar and Lauren Glaze, *Probation and Parole, 1998* (Washington, D.C.: Bureau of Justice Statistics, 1999).

8. Ibid.

9. Data in this section come from Lauren E. Glaze, *Probation and Parole in the United States, 2001* (Washington, D.C.: Bureau of Justice Statistics, 2002).

10. Jodi Brown and Patrick Langan, *Felony Sentences in the United States, 1996* (Washington, D.C.: Bureau of Justice Statistics, 1999).

11. *Higdon v. United States,* 627 F.2d 893 (9th Cir., 1980).

12. *People v. Johnson,* 175 Ill.App.3d 908, 125 Ill. Dec. 469, 530 N.E.2d 627 (1988).

13. *Ramaker v. State,* 73 Wis.2d 563, 243 N.W.2d 534 (1976).

14. *United States v. Cothran,* 855 F.2d 749 (11th Cir., 1988).

15. *United States v. Gallo,* 20 F.3d 7 (1st Cir., 1994).

16. Todd Clear and Edward Latessa, "Probation Officers' Roles in Intensive Supervision: Surveillance Versus Treatment," *Justice Quarterly* 10 (1993): 441–462.

17. Ibid.

18. David Duffee and Bonnie Carlson, "Competing Value Premises for the Provision of Drug Treatment to Probationers," *Crime and Delinquency* 42 (1996): 574–592.

19. Richard Sluder and Rolando Del Carmen, "Are Probation and Parole Officers Liable for Injuries Caused by Probationers and Parolees?" *Federal Probation* 54 (1990): 3–12.

20. Patricia Harris, "Client Management Classification and Prediction of Probation Outcome," *Crime and Delinquency* 40 (1994): 154–174.

21. Anne Schneider, Laurie Ervin, and Zoann Snyder-Joy, "Further Exploration of the Flight from Discretion: The Role of Risk/Need Instruments in Probation Supervision Decisions," *Journal of Criminal Justice* 24 (1996): 109–121.

22. Clear and O'Leary, *Controlling the Offender in the Community,* 11–29, 77–100.

23. Joan Petersilia, "An Evaluation of Intensive Probation in California," *Journal of Criminal Law and Criminology* 82 (1992): 610–658.

24. Glaze, *Probation and Parole in the United States, 2001.*

25. M. Kevin Gray, Monique Fields, and Sheila Royo Maxwell, "Examining Probation Violations: Who, What, and When," *Crime and Delinquency* 47 (2001): 537–557.

26. Cassia Spohn and David Holleran, "The Effect of Imprisonment on Recidivism Rates of Felony Offenders: A Focus on Drug Offenders," *Criminology 40* (2002): 329–359.

27. Joan Petersilia, Susan Turner, James Kahan, and Joyce Peterson, *Granting Felons Probation: Public Risks and Alternatives* (Santa Monica, Calif.: Rand, 1985).

28. Kathryn Morgan, "Factors Influencing Probation Outcome: A Review of the Literature," *Federal Probation 57* (1993): 23–29.

29. Kathryn Morgan, "Factors Associated with Probation Outcome," *Journal of Criminal Justice 22* (1994): 341–353.

30. Paula M. Ditton, *Mental Health and Treatment of Inmates and Probationers* (Washington, D.C.: Bureau of Justice Statistics, 1999).

31. Spohn and Holleran, "The Effect of Imprisonment on Recidivism Rates of Felony Offenders: A Focus on Drug Offenders."

32. *Minnesota v. Murphy,* 465 U.S. 420, 104 S.Ct. 1136, 79 L.Ed.2d 409 (1984).

33. *Griffin v. Wisconsin,* 483 U.S. 868, 107 S.Ct. 3164, 97 L.Ed.2d 709 (1987).

34. *United States v. Knights,* 122 S.Ct. 587 (2001).

35. *Mempa v. Rhay,* 389 U.S. 128, 88 S.Ct. 254, 19 L.Ed.2d 336 (1967).

36. *Morrissey v. Brewer,* 408 U.S. 471, 92 S.Ct. 2593, 33 L.Ed.2d 484 (1972).

37. *Gagnon v. Scarpelli,* 411 U.S. 778, 93 S.Ct. 1756, 36 L.Ed.2d 656 (1973).

38. *United States v. Carson,* 669 F.2d 216 (5th Cir., 1982).

39. *United States v. Granderson,* 114 Ct. 1259, 127 L.Ed.2d 611 (1994).

40. Matthew Durose and Patrick A. Langan, *State Court Sentencing of Convicted Felons, 1998* (Washington, D.C.: Bureau of Justice Statistics, February 2001).

41. "Law in Massachusetts Requires Probationers to Pay 'Day Fees,'" *Criminal Justice Newsletter,* 15 September 1988, 1.

42. Peter Finn and Dale Parent, *Making the Offender Foot the Bill: A Texas Program* (Washington, D.C.: National Institute of Justice, 1992).

43. Richard Lawrence, "Reexamining Community Corrections Models," *Crime and Delinquency 37* (1991): 449–464.

44. Todd Clear and Patricia Hardyman, "The New Intensive Supervision Movement," *Crime and Delinquency 36* (1990): 42–60.

45. For a thorough review of these programs, see James Byrne, Arthur Lurigio, and Joan Petersilia, eds., *Smart Sentencing: The Emergence of Intermediate Sanctions* (Newbury Park, Calif.: Sage, 1993). Hereinafter cited as *Smart Sentencing.*

46. Norval Morris and Michael Tonry, *Between Prison and Probation: Intermediate Punishments in a Rational Sentencing System* (New York: Oxford University Press, 1990).

47. Michael Tonry and Richard Will, *Intermediate Sanctions* (Washington, D.C.: National Institute of Justice, 1990).

48. Ibid., 8.

49. Michael Maxfield and Terry Baumer, "Home Detention with Electronic Monitoring: Comparing Pretrial and Postconviction Programs," *Crime and Delinquency 36* (1990): 521–556.

50. Sally Hillsman and Judith Greene, "Tailoring Fines to the Financial Means of Offenders," *Judicature 72* (1988): 38–45.

51. George Cole, "Monetary Sanctions: The Problem of Compliance," in *Smart Sentencing,* 51–64.

52. *Tate v. Short,* 401 U.S. 395, 91 S.Ct. 668, 28 L.Ed.2d 130 (1971).

53. Margaret Gordon and Daniel Glaser, "The Use and Effects of Financial Penalties in Municipal Courts," *Criminology 29* (1991): 651–676.

54. "'Day Fines' Being Tested in New York City Court," *Criminal Justice Newsletter,* 1 September 1988, 4–5.

55. Doris Layton MacKenzie, "Evidence-Based Corrections: Identifying What Works," *Crime and Delinquency 46* (2000): 457–472.

56. John L. Worrall, "Addicted to the Drug War: The Role of Civil Asset Forfeiture as a Budgetary Necessity in Contemporary Law Enforcement," *Journal of Criminal Justice 29* (2001): 171–187.

57. C. Yorke, *Some Consideration on the Law of Forfeiture for High Treason,* 2d ed. (1746), 26; cited in David Fried, "Rationalizing Criminal Forfeiture," *Journal of Criminal Law and Criminology 79* (1988): 328–436.

58. Fried, "Rationalizing Criminal Forfeiture," 436.

59. James B. Jacobs, Coleen Friel, and Edward O'Callaghan, "Pension Forfeiture: A Problematic Sanction for Public Corruption," *American Criminal Law Review 35* (1997): 57–92.

60. Worrall, "Addicted to the Drug War."

61. For a general review, see Burt Galaway and Joe Hudson, *Criminal Justice, Restitution, and Reconciliation* (New York: Criminal Justice Press, 1990); Robert Carter, Jay Cocks, and Daniel Glazer, "Community Service: A Review of the Basic Issues," *Federal Probation 51* (1987): 4–11.

62. Morris and Tonry, *Between Prison and Probation,* 171–175.

63. Frederick Allen and Harvey Treger, "Community Service Orders in Federal Probation: Perceptions of Probationers and Host Agencies," *Federal Probation 54* (1990): 8–14.

64. Sudipto Roy, "Two Types of Juvenile Restitution Programs in Two Midwestern Counties: A Comparative Study," *Federal Probation 57* (1993): 48–53.

65. Joan Petersilia, *The Influence of Criminal Justice Research* (Santa Monica, Calif.: Rand, 1987).

66. Ibid.

67. Jodi Brown, *Correctional Populations in the United States, 1996* (Washington, D.C.: Bureau of Justice Statistics, 1999), 39.

68. James Byrne and Linda Kelly, "Restructuring Probation as an Intermediate Sanction: An Evaluation of the Massachusetts Intensive Probation Supervision Program" (Final report to the National Institute of Justice, Research Program on the Punishment and Control of Offenders, Washington, D.C., 1989).

69. James Ryan, "Who Gets Revoked? A Comparison of Intensive Supervision Successes and Failures in Vermont," *Crime and Delinquency 43* (1997): 104–118.

70. Peter Jones, "Expanding the Use of Noncustodial Sentencing Options: An Evaluation of the Kansas Community Corrections Act," *Howard Journal 29* (1990): 114–129; Michael Agopian, "The Impact of Intensive Supervision Probation on Gang-Drug Offenders," *Criminal Justice Policy Review 4* (1990): 214–222.

71. Angela Robertson, Paul Grimes, and Kevin Rogers, "A Short-Run Cost-Benefit Analysis of Community-Based Interventions for Juvenile Offenders," *Crime and Delinquency* 47 (2001): 265–284.

72. Betsy Fulton, Edward Latessa, Amy Stichman, and Lawrence Travis, "The State of ISP: Research and Policy Implications," *Federal Probation* 61 (1997): 65–75.

73. S. Christopher Baird and Dennis Wagner, "Measuring Diversion: The Florida Community Control Program," *Crime and Delinquency* 36 (1990): 112–125.

74. Linda Smith and Ronald Akers, "A Comparison of Recidivism of Florida's Community Control and Prison: A Five-Year Survival Analysis," *Journal of Research in Crime and Delinquency* 30 (1993): 267–292.

75. Robert N. Altman, Robert E. Murray, and Evey B. Wooten, "Home Confinement: A '90s Approach to Community Supervision," *Federal Probation* 61 (1997): 30–32.

76. Preston Elrod and Michael Brown, "Predicting Public Support for Electronic House Arrest: Results from a New York County Survey," *American Behavioral Scientist* 39 (1996): 461–474.

77. Joseph Papy and Richard Nimer, "Electronic Monitoring in Florida," *Federal Probation* 55 (1991): 31–33.

78. Kevin E. Courtright, Bruce L. Berg, and Robert J. Mutchnick, "The Cost-Effectiveness of Using House Arrest with Electronic Monitoring for Drunk Drivers," *Federal Probation* 61 (1997): 19–22.

79. Mary Finn and Suzanne Muirhead-Steves, "The Effectiveness of Electronic Monitoring with Male Parolees," *Justice Quarterly* 19 (2002): 293–313.

80. Brian McKay, "The State of Sex Offender Probation Supervision in Texas," *Federal Probation* 66 (2002): 16–21.

81. See, generally, Edward Latessa and Lawrence Travis III, "Residential Community Correctional Programs," in *Smart Sentencing*, 65–79.

82. Updated with personal correspondence, Portland House personnel, September 22, 2002.

83. Harvey Siegal, James Fisher, Richard Rapp, Casey Kelliher, Joseph Wagner, William O'Brien, and Phyllis Cole, "Enhancing Substance Abuse Treatment with Case Management," *Journal of Substance Abuse Treatment* 13 (1996): 93–98.

84. Dale Parent, *Day Reporting Centers for Criminal Offenders: A Descriptive Analysis of Existing Programs* (Washington, D.C.: National Institute of Justice, 1990); Jack McDevitt and Robyn Miliano, "Day Reporting Centers: An Innovative Concept in Intermediate Sanctions," in *Smart Sentencing*, 80–105.

85. David Diggs and Stephen Pieper, "Using Day Reporting Centers as an Alternative to Jail," *Federal Probation* 58 (1994): 9–12.

86. For information on the Atlanta program, see www.pap.state.ga.us/2001%20Annual%20Report%20Web/day_reporting_centers.htm.

87. David Hartmann, Paul Friday, and Kevin Minor, "Residential Probation: A Seven-Year Follow-Up of Halfway House Discharges," *Journal of Criminal Justice* 22 (1994): 503–515.

88. Banhram Haghighi and Alma Lopez, "Success/Failure of Group Home Treatment Programs for Juveniles," *Federal Probation* 57 (1993): 53–57.

89. Richard Rosenfeld and Kimberly Kempf, "The Scope and Purposes of Corrections: Exploring Alternative Responses to Crowding," *Crime and Delinquency* 37 (1991): 481–505.

90. For a thorough review, see Michael Tonry and Mary Lynch, "Intermediate Sanctions," in *Crime and Justice: A Review of Research*, vol. 20, ed. Michael Tonry (Chicago: University of Chicago Press, 1996), 99–144.

91. Francis Cullen, "Control in the Community: The Limits of Reform?" (Paper presented at the International Association of Residential and Community Alternatives, Philadelphia, November 1993).

92. John DiIulio and Charles Logan, "The Ten Deadly Myths About Crime and Punishment in the U.S.," *Wisconsin Interest* 1 (1992): 21–35.

93. Tonry and Lynch, "Intermediate Sanctions."

94. Kathleen Daly and Russ Immarigeon, "The Past, Present, and Future of Restorative Justice: Some Critical Reflections," *Contemporary Justice Review* 1 (1998): 21–45.

95. John Braithwaite, *Crime, Shame, and Reintegration* (Melbourne, Australia: Cambridge University Press, 1989).

96. Gene Stephens, "The Future of Policing: From a War Model to a Peace Model," in *The Past, Present and Future of American Criminal Justice*, eds. Brendan Maguire and Polly Radosh (Dix Hills, N.Y.: General Hall, 1996), 77–93.

97. Kay Pranis, "Peacemaking Circles: Restorative Justice in Practice Allows Victims and Offenders to Begin Repairing the Harm," *Corrections Today* 59 (1997), 74.

98. Carol LaPrairie, "The 'New' Justice: Some Implications for Aboriginal Communities," *Canadian Journal of Criminology* 40 (1998): 61–79.

99. David R. Karp and Beau Breslin, "Restorative Justice in School Communities," *Youth & Society* 33 (2001): 249–272.

100. Paul Jesilow and Deborah Parsons, "Community Policing as Peacemaking," *Policing & Society* 10 (2000): 163–183.

101. Gordon Bazemore and Curt Taylor Griffiths, "Conferences, Circles, Boards, and Mediations: The 'New Wave' of Community Justice Decision Making," *Federal Probation* 61 (1997): 25–37.

102. John Braithwaite, "Setting Standards for Restorative Justice," *British Journal of Criminology* 42 (2002): 563–577.

103. David Altschuler, "Community Justice Initiatives: Issues and Challenges in the U.S. Context," *Federal Probation* 65 (2001): 28–33.

104. Lois Presser and Patricia Van Voorhis, "Values and Evaluation: Assessing Processes and Outcomes of Restorative Justice Programs," *Crime and Delinquency* 48 (2002): 162–189.

105. Sharon Levrant, Francis Cullen, Betsy Fulton, and John Wozniak, "Reconsidering Restorative Justice: The Corruption of Benevolence Revisited?" *Crime and Delinquency* 45 (1999): 3–28.

12 Corrections: History, Institutions, and Populations

Chapter Outline

Criminal Justice Links

Criminal Justice Viewpoints

IN THE PAST FEW YEARS, the American Civil Liberties Union has reported on numerous problems in county jails around the United States. Consider the following examples:

- Hundreds of inmates sleep shoulder-to-shoulder on bedrolls crammed into every open space on the concrete floors in Atlanta's Fulton County Jail. The strains of its huge population are aging the facility prematurely, worsening the conditions that could lead to expensive litigation. The walls leak when it rains. Toilets don't work. Medical care is wanting. Daily jail costs exceed $126,000 for the more than four thousand inmates. Their numbers are expected only to increase—especially because of changes in state mandatory sentencing laws such as the two-strikes law, which requires a life sentence for a second violent felony conviction. Those laws are expected to reduce defendants' willingness to admit guilt in plea deals, forcing more trials.

- Issuing a strong rebuke to a local sheriff's department, a federal jury awarded $5,000 in damages to a woman who was strapped naked, spread-eagle fashion, on a wooden board while in custody at an Iowa county jail. The woman, identified in legal papers as "Jane Doe" to protect her privacy, was represented by the Iowa Civil Liberties Union.

- Asserting that the El Paso County Jail in Colorado Springs has failed to protect and provide adequate resources for prisoners with mental health problems, the American Civil Liberties Union of Colorado filed a federal class-action lawsuit against prison officials. Representatives charged that the jail has been unable to fulfill its constitutional duty to protect prisoners from the risk of self-harm or suicide and to provide for their serious mental health needs. Inmates endure unconscionable neglect. At worst, they endure conditions that are inhumane, degrading, humiliating, dangerous, and sometimes fatal. The jail has faced scrutiny from the ACLU since May 1998, when pretrial detainee Michael Lewis died while strapped face-down on a restraint board. For days prior to his death, he had been hallucinating and suffering from psychosis, probably caused by a change in his usual medications. He had been on a waiting list to see the facility's psychiatrist, who visited only every other week. Eight additional prisoners have died in the jail since then; in almost every case the deceased prisoner was suicidal, seriously mentally ill, or displaying symptoms of psychosis from overdose or withdrawal. ■

To view the CNN video clip of this story, go to the book-specific Web site at http://cj.wadsworth.com/siegel_essen4e.

The social and institutional problems listed here are not unique to the nation's jails but can occur in almost any correctional facility in the United States. Many are underfunded, understaffed, and lacking in the programs needed to provide true offender rehabilitation.

Today, the correctional system has branches in the federal, state, and county levels of government. Felons may be placed in state or federal penitentiaries (prisons), which are usually isolated, high-security structures. Misdemeanants are housed in county jails, sometimes called reformatories or houses of correction. Juvenile offenders have their own institutions, sometimes euphemistically called schools, camps, ranches, or homes. Usually, the latter are nonsecure facilities, often located in rural areas, and provide both confinement and rehabilitative services for young offenders.

Other types of correctional institutions include ranches and farms for adult offenders and community correctional settings, such as halfway houses, for inmates who are about to return to society. Today's correctional facilities encompass a wide range, from super-maximum-security institutions, such as the federal prison in Florence, Colorado, where the nation's most dangerous felons are confined, to low-security camps that house white-collar criminals convicted of such crimes as insider trading and mail fraud.

One of the great tragedies of our time is that correctional institutions—whatever form they may take—do not seem to correct. They are, in most instances, overcrowded, understaffed, outdated warehouses for social outcasts. Overcrowding is the most significant crisis faced by the prisons today: they now contain more than 1.3 million inmates. Prisons and jails are more suited to control, punishment, and security than to rehabilitation and treatment. It is a sad but unfortunately accurate observation that today's correctional institution has become a revolving door, and all too many of its residents return time and again. Although no completely accurate statement of the recidivism rate is available, it is estimated that more than half of all inmates will be back in prison within six years of their release.

Even though the penal institutions seem unsuccessful, great debate continues over the direction of their future operations. Some penal experts maintain that **prisons** and **jails** are not really places for rehabilitation and treatment, but should be used to keep dangerous offenders apart from society and give them the "just deserts" for their crimes.[1] In this sense, prison success would be measured by such factors as physical security, length of incapacitation, relationship between the crime rate and the number of incarcerated felons, and inmates' perceptions that their treatment is fair and proportionate. The dominance of this correctional philosophy is illustrated by the facts that (1) presumptive and mandatory sentencing structures are now used in such traditionally progressive states as California, Massachusetts, and Illinois; (2) the number of people under lock and key has risen during the past decade even though the crime rate has declined; and (3) political candidates who are portrayed by their opponents as advocates of inmate rehabilitation soon find themselves on the defensive among voters.

Although the conservative tide in corrections is self-evident, many penal experts still maintain that prisons can be useful places for offender rehabilitation.[2] Many examples of the treatment philosophy still flourish in prisons: educational programs allow inmates to get college credits; vocational training has become more sophisticated; counseling and substance abuse programs are almost universal; and every state maintains some type of early-release and community correctional programs.

In this chapter we explore the correctional system, beginning with the history and nature of correctional institutions. Then, in Chapter 13 we examine institutional life in some detail.

Despite its spotty track record, the cost of the corrections system keeps escalating. To find out more about this issue, go to InfoTrac College Edition and read Elizabeth B. Guerard, "Analysis: Prison Spending Outpaces Higher Education," *Education Daily,* August 30, 2002 v35 i165 p3(2).

prison A state or federal correctional institution for incarceration of felony offenders for terms of one year or more.

jail A place to detain people awaiting trial, to serve as a lockup for drunks and disorderly individuals, and to confine convicted misdemeanants serving sentences of less than one year.

The American Correctional Association is a multidisciplinary organization of professionals representing all facets of corrections and criminal justice, including federal, state, and military correctional facilities and prisons, county jails and detention centers, probation/parole agencies, and community corrections/halfway houses. It has more than than twenty thousand members. To learn about what the group does, go to www.corrections.com/aca/

The History of Correctional Institutions

Use "correctional history" as a subject guide on InfoTrac College Edition.

As you may recall, the original legal punishments were typically banishment or slavery, restitution (wergild), corporal punishment, and execution. The concept of incarcerating convicted offenders for long periods of time as a punishment for their misdeeds did not become the norm of corrections until the nineteenth century.[3]

Although the use of incarceration as a routine punishment began much later, some early European institutions were created specifically to detain and punish criminal offenders. Penal institutions were constructed in England during the tenth century to hold pretrial detainees and those waiting for their sentence to be carried out.[4] During the twelfth century, King Henry II of England constructed a series of county jails to hold thieves and vagrants prior to the disposition of their sentence. In 1557 the workhouse in Brideswell, England, was built to hold people convicted of relatively minor offenses who would work to pay off their debt to society; those committing more serious offenses were held there prior to their execution.

Le Stinche, a prison in Florence, Italy, was used to punish offenders as early as 1301.[5] Prisoners were enclosed in separate cells, classified on the basis of gender, age, mental state, and crime seriousness. Furloughs and conditional release

van Gogh, Vincent: *Prisoner's Round* (detail), 1890, Pushkin Museum of Fine Arts, Moscow. Scala/Art Resource, New York.

"Prisoners Exercising," by Vincent van Gogh. Painted in 1890, this work captures the despair of the nineteenth-century penal institution. The face of the prisoner near the center of the picture looking at the viewer is van Gogh's.

were permitted, and perhaps for the first time, a period of incarceration replaced corporal punishment for some offenses. Although Le Stinche existed for five hundred years, relatively little is known about its administration or whether this early example of incarceration was unique to Florence.

The first penal institutions were foul places devoid of proper care, food, or medical treatment. The jailer, usually a shire reeve (sheriff), an official appointed by king or noble landholder as chief law enforcement official of a county, ran the jail under the "fee system." This required inmates to pay for their own food and services. Those who could not pay were fed scraps until they literally starved to death:

> In 1748 the admission to Southwark Prison was eleven shillings and fourpence. Having got in, the prisoner had to pay for having himself put in irons, for his bed, of whatever sort, for his room if he was able to afford a separate room. He had to pay for his food, and when he had paid his debts and was ready to go out, he had to pay for having his irons struck off, and a discharge fee.... The gaolers [jailers] were usually "low bred, mercenary and oppressive, barbarous fellows, who [thought] of nothing but enriching themselves by the most cruel extortion, and [had] less regard for the life of a poor prisoner than for the life of a brute."[6]

Jail conditions were deplorable because jailers ran them for personal gain; the fewer the services they provided, the greater their profit. Early jails were catchall institutions that held not only criminal offenders awaiting trial but also vagabonds, debtors, the mentally ill, and assorted others.

From 1776 to 1785 a growing inmate population that could no longer be transported to North America forced the English to house prisoners on **hulks,** abandoned ships anchored in harbors. The hulks became infamous for their degrading conditions and brutal punishments, but were not totally abandoned until 1858. The writings of John Howard, the reform-oriented sheriff of Bedfordshire, drew attention to the squalid conditions in British penal institutions. His famous book, *The State of the Prisons in England and Wales* (1777), condemned the lack of basic care given English inmates awaiting trial or serving sentences.[7] Howard's efforts to create humane standards in the British penal system resulted in the Penitentiary Act, by which Parliament established a more orderly penal system, with periodic inspections, elimination of the fee system, and greater consideration for inmates.

hulk A mothballed ship that was used to house prisoners in eighteenth-century England.

American Developments

Although Europe had jails and a variety of other penal facilities, it was in the United States that correctional reform was instituted. The first American jail was built in James City in the Virginia colonies in the early seventeenth century. However, the "modern" American correctional system had its origins in Pennsylvania under the leadership of William Penn.

At the end of the seventeenth century, Penn revised Pennsylvania's criminal code to forbid torture and the capricious use of mutilation and physical punishment. These penalties were replaced with imprisonment at hard labor, moderate flogging, fines, and forfeiture of property. All lands and goods belonging to felons were to be used to make restitution to the victims of crimes, with restitution being limited to twice the value of the damages. Felons who owned no property were required by law to work in the prison workhouse until the victim was compensated.

Penn ordered that a new type of institution be built to replace the then widely used public forms of punishment: stocks, pillories, gallows, and branding irons. Each county was instructed to build a house of corrections similar to today's jails. County trustees or commissioners were responsible for raising money to build the jails and providing for their maintenance, although they were operated by the local sheriff. Penn's reforms remained in effect until his death in 1718, when the criminal penal code was changed back to open public punishment and brutality.

It is difficult to identify the first American prison. Alexis Durham has described the opening of Connecticut's Newgate Prison in 1773 on the site of an abandoned copper mine. Newgate, which closed in the 1820s, is often ignored by correctional historians.[8] In 1785, Castle Island Prison was opened in Massachusetts and operated for about fifteen years.

The Quaker Influence   The origin of the modern correctional system, however, is usually traced to eighteenth-century developments in Pennsylvania. In 1776, postrevolutionary Pennsylvania again adopted William Penn's code and in 1787 a group of Quakers led by Benjamin Rush formed the Philadelphia Society for Alleviating the Miseries of Public Prisons. The aim of the society was to bring some degree of humane and orderly treatment to the growing penal system. The Quakers' influence on the legislature resulted in limiting the use of the death penalty to cases involving treason, murder, rape, and arson. Their next step was to reform the institutional system so that the prison could serve as a suitable alternative to physical punishment.

The only models of custodial institutions at that time were the local county jails that Penn had established. These facilities were designed to detain offenders, to securely incarcerate convicts awaiting other punishment, or to hold offenders who were working off their crimes. The Pennsylvania jails placed men, women, and children of all ages indiscriminately in one room. Liquor was often freely sold.

Under pressure from the Quakers to improve these conditions, the Pennsylvania state legislature in 1790 called for the renovation of the prison system. The ultimate result was the creation of a separate wing of Philadelphia's **Walnut Street Jail,** which had been in operation since 1776 as a local facility, to house convicted felons, except those sentenced to death. The legislation creating a state **"penitentiary house"** ushered in ten years of reform and attracted worldwide notice. Some prisoners were placed in solitary cells, where they remained in isolation and did not have the right to work; the majority of the several hundred inmates lived together in large common rooms.[9] The new system is credited with producing a rapid decrease in the crime rate—from 131 convictions in 1789 to 45 in 1793.[10] The prison became known as a school for reform and a place for public labor. The Walnut Street Jail's equitable conditions were credited with reducing escapes to none in the first four years of its existence (except for fourteen on opening day).

The Walnut Street Jail was not a total success. Overcrowding undermined the goal of solitary confinement of serious offenders, and soon more than one inmate was placed in each cell. The isolation had a terrible psychological effect on inmates, and eventually inmates were given in-cell piecework on which they worked up to eight hours a day. Despite these difficulties, similar institutions were constructed in New York (Newgate in 1791) and New Jersey (Trenton in 1798).

The Auburn System   As the nineteenth century got under way, both the Pennsylvania and the New York prison systems were experiencing difficulties maintaining the ever-increasing numbers of convicted criminals. Initially, administrators dealt with the problem by increasing the use of pardons, relaxing prison discipline, and limiting supervision.

In 1816 New York built a new prison at Auburn, hoping to alleviate some of the overcrowding at Newgate. The Auburn Prison design became known as the **tier system** because cells were built vertically on five floors of the structure. It was also referred to as the **congregate system** since most prisoners ate and worked in groups. Later, in 1819, construction was started on a wing of solitary cells to house unruly prisoners. Three classes of prisoners were then created: one group remained continually in solitary confinement as a result of breaches of prison discipline; the second group was allowed labor as an occasional form of recreation;

Walnut Street Jail   In 1790 a separate wing of Philadelphia's Walnut Street Jail was built to house convicted felons. This was the forerunner of the secure correctional system in the United States.

penitentiary house   A secure correctional facility, based on the Quaker concept that incarcerated criminals should do "penitence."

Eastern State Penitentiary became the most expensive and most copied building of its time. It is estimated that more than three hundred prisons worldwide are based on the penitentiary's wagon-wheel, or "radial" floor plan. Some of America's most notorious criminals were held in its vaulted, sky-lit cells, including Al Capone. After 142 years of consecutive use, Eastern State Penitentiary was abandoned in 1971.
www.EasternState.com/

tier system   The structure of early prisons having numerous floors or wings that stacked cells one over another.

congregate system   The Auburn Prison, one of the nation's first correctional facilities, was a congregate system, since most prisoners ate and worked in groups.

Auburn system The prison system developed in New York during the nineteenth century that stressed congregate working conditions.

The penitentiary movement spread around the world. In Australia, Fremantle Prison was built by convicts between 1850 and 1860. Convicts were brought to western Australia to help in the building of roads, bridges, port facilities, and public buildings. To read about the history of the institution and to get a virtual tour, go to www.fremantleprison.com.au

and the third and largest class worked and ate together during the day and were separated only at night.

The philosophy of the **Auburn system** was crime prevention through fear of punishment and silent confinement. The worst felons were to be cut off from all contact with other prisoners, and although they were treated and fed relatively well, they had no hope of pardon to relieve their solitude or isolation. For a time, some of the worst convicts were forced to remain totally alone and silent during the entire day; this practice caused many prisoners to have mental breakdowns, resulting in many suicides and self-mutilations. This practice was abolished in 1823.

The combination of silence and solitude as a method of punishment was not abandoned easily. Prison officials sought to overcome the side effects of total isolation while maintaining the penitentiary system. The solution adopted at Auburn was to keep convicts in separate cells at night but allow them to work together during the day under enforced silence. Hard work and silence became the foundation of the Auburn system wherever it was adopted. Silence was the key to prison discipline; it prohibited the formulation of escape plans, it prevented plots and riots, and it allowed prisoners to contemplate their infractions.

The Pennsylvania System Pennsylvania took the radical step of establishing a prison that placed each inmate in a single cell for the duration of his sentence. Classifications were abolished because each cell was intended as a miniature prison that would prevent the inmates from contaminating one another.

The new Pennsylvania state prison opened in 1826. Called the Western Penitentiary, it had an unusual architectural design. It was built in a circle, with the cells positioned along its circumference. Built back to back, some cells faced the boundary wall while others faced the internal area of the circle. Its inmates were kept in solitary confinement almost constantly, being allowed out for about an hour a day for exercise. In 1821 construction began on a second, similar penitentiary using the isolate system in Philadelphia: this was the Eastern State Penitentiary, which opened in 1829.

Inmates in a nineteenth-century prison return from a work detail in lockstep.

Supporters of the **Pennsylvania system** believed that the *penitentiary* was truly a place to *do penance*. By advocating totally removing the sinner from society and allowing the prisoner a period of isolation during which to reflect alone on the evils of crime, the supporters of the Pennsylvania system reflected the influence of religion and religious philosophy on corrections. Solitary confinement (with in-cell labor) was believed to make work so attractive that upon release the inmate would be well-suited to resume a productive existence in society.

Pennsylvania system The prison system developed during the nineteenth century that stressed total isolation and individual penitence as a means of reform.

Incarceration Philosophies

Why did prisons develop at this time? One reason was that during this period of "enlightenment," a concerted effort was made to alleviate the harsh punishments and torture that had been the norm. The interest of religious groups, such as the Quakers, in prison reform was prompted in part by humanitarian ideals. Another factor was the economic potential of prison industry, which was viewed as a valuable economic asset in times of a short labor supply.[11]

The concept of using harsh discipline and control to "retrain" the heart and soul of offenders is the subject of an important book on penal philosophy: *Discipline and Punish,* by French sociologist Michel Foucault.[12] Foucault's thesis is that as societies evolve and become more complex, they create increasingly more elaborate mechanisms to discipline their recalcitrant members and make them docile enough to obey social rules. In the seventeenth and eighteenth centuries, discipline was directed toward the human body itself, through torture. However, physical punishment and torture turned some condemned men into heroes and martyrs. Prisons presented the opportunity to rearrange, not diminish, punishment—to make it more effective and regulated. In the development of the nineteenth-century prison, the object was to discipline the offender psychologically; "the expiation that once rained down on the body must be replaced by a punishment that acts in the depths of the heart."[13]

Regimentation became the standard mode of prison life. Convicts did not simply walk from place to place; rather, they went in close order and single file, each looking over the shoulder of the preceding person, faces inclined to the right, feet moving in unison.[14]

When discipline was breached in the Auburn system, punishment was applied in the form of a rawhide whip on the inmate's back. Immediate and effective, Auburn discipline was so successful that when one hundred inmates were used to build the famous Sing Sing Prison in 1825, not one dared try to escape, although they were housed in an open field with only minimal supervision.[15]

Many fiery debates occurred between advocates of the Pennsylvania system and adherents of the Auburn system. Those supporting the latter boasted of its supposed advantages; it was the cheapest and most productive way to reform prisoners. They criticized the Pennsylvania system as cruel and inhumane, suggesting that solitary confinement was both physically and mentally damaging. The Pennsylvania system's devotees, on the other hand, argued that their system was quiet, efficient, humane, and well-ordered and provided the ultimate correctional facility.[16] They chided the Auburn system for tempting inmates to talk by putting them together for meals and work and then punishing them when they did talk. Finally, the Auburn system was accused of becoming a breeding place for criminal associations by allowing inmates to get to know one another.

The Auburn system eventually prevailed and spread throughout the United States; many of its features are still used today. Its innovations included congregate working conditions, the use of solitary confinement to punish unruly inmates, military regimentation, and discipline. In Auburn-style institutions, prisoners were marched from place to place; their time was regulated by bells telling them to wake up, sleep, and work. The system was so like the military that many of its early administrators were recruited from the armed services.

Although the prison was viewed as an improvement over capital and corporal punishment, it quickly became the scene of depressed conditions; inmates were treated harshly and were routinely whipped and tortured. Prison brutality flourished in these institutions, which had originally been devised as a more humane correctional alternative. In these early penal institutions, brutal corporal punishment took place indoors, where, hidden from public view, it could become even more savage.[17]

Prisons at the Turn of the Twentieth Century

The prison of the late nineteenth century was remarkably similar to that of today. The congregate system was adopted in all states except Pennsylvania. Prisons were overcrowded, and the single-cell principle was often ignored. The prison, like the police department, became the scene of political intrigue and efforts by political administrators to control the hiring of personnel and dispensing of patronage.

Prison industry developed and became the predominant theme around which institutions were organized. Some prisons used the **contract system,** in which officials sold the labor of inmates to private businesses, which then set up shops and supervised the inmates inside the prison itself. Under the **convict-lease system,** the state leased its prisoners to a business outside the prison walls for a fixed annual fee and gave up supervision and control. Finally, some institutions had prisoners produce goods for the prison's own use.[18]

The development of prison industry quickly led to the abuse of inmates, who were forced to work for almost no wages, and to profiteering by dishonest administrators and businessmen. During the Civil War era, prisons were major manufacturers of clothes, shoes, boots, furniture, and the like. Beginning in the 1870s, opposition by trade unions sparked restrictions on interstate commerce in prison goods.

Reform Movements Prison operations were also reformed. The National Congress of Penitentiary and Reformatory Discipline, held in Cincinnati in 1870, heralded a new era of prison reform. Organized by penologists Enoch Wines and Theodore Dwight, the congress provided a forum for corrections experts from around the nation to call for the treatment, education, and training of inmates.

One of the most famous people to attend the congress, Zebulon R. Brockway, warden at the Elmira Reformatory in New York, advocated individualized treatment, the indeterminate sentence, and parole. The reformatory program initiated by Brockway included elementary education for illiterates, designated library hours, lectures by faculty members of the local Elmira College, and a group of vocational training shops. From 1888 to 1920, Elmira administrators used military-like training to discipline the inmates and organize the institution. The military organization could be seen in every aspect of the institution: schooling, manual training, sports, supervision of inmates, and even parole decisions.[19] The cost to the state of the institution's operations was to be held to a minimum.

Although Brockway proclaimed Elmira to be an ideal reformatory, his actual achievements were limited. The greatest significance of his contribution was the injection of a degree of humanitarianism into the industrial prisons of that day (although there were accusations that excessive corporal punishment was used and that Brockway personally administered whippings).[20] Although many institutions were constructed across the nation and labeled reformatories based on the Elmira model, most of them continued to be industrially oriented.[21]

Advent of Community Corrections As the nineteenth century drew to a close some states began experimenting with community-based corrections to ease the transition back into society. The forerunner of this development began in Ireland in the 1850s, when Sir Walter Crofton, Ireland's prison director, set up a system

contract system (convict) The system used early in the twentieth century by which private industry contracted with prison officials for convict labor and set up shops on prison grounds for them to work.

convict-lease system The system whereby the state leased its prisoners to a business for a fixed annual fee and gave up supervision and control.

The Oregon State Penitentiary is the oldest prison and the only maximum security institution currently operated by the state of Oregon. To read about its history, go to www.doc.state.or.us/institutions/osp/histidx.htm

whereby penitentiary inmates spent the last portion of their sentences living in an intermediate institution and working in the outside community. Crofton's methods proved so popular that under Quaker influence, New York City opened the Isaac T. Hopper Home in 1845 as a shelter for released inmates. The Hopper home was followed by a shelter for women released from the Detroit House of Correction, opened by Zebulon Brockway in 1868; the Philadelphia House of Industry, opened in 1889; and Hope Hall, a refuge for ex-inmates in New York, opened by Maud Ballington Booth in the 1890s.[22]

Prisons in the Twentieth Century   The early twentieth century was a time of contrasts in the prison system of the United States.[23] At one extreme were those who advocated reform, such as the Mutual Welfare League led by Thomas Mott Osborne. Prison reform groups proposed better treatment for inmates, an end to harsh corporal punishment, the creation of meaningful prison industries, and educational programs. Reformers argued that prisoners should not be isolated from society and that the best elements of society—education, religion, meaningful work, self-governance—should be brought to the prison. Osborne went so far as to spend one week in New York's notorious Sing Sing Prison to learn firsthand about its conditions.

Opposed to the reformers were conservative prison administrators and state officials who believed that stern disciplinary measures were needed to control dangerous prison inmates. They continued the time-honored system of regimentation and discipline. Although the whip and the lash were eventually abolished, solitary confinement in dark, bare cells became a common penal practice.

In time, some of the more rigid prison rules gave way to liberal reform. By the mid-1930s, few prisons required inmates to wear the red-and-white-striped convict suit and substituted nondescript gray uniforms. The code of silence ended, as did the lockstep shuffle. Prisoners were allowed "the freedom of the yard" to mingle and exercise an hour or two each day.[24] Movies and radio appeared in the 1930s. Visiting policies and mail privileges were liberalized.

Prison Industry   A more important trend was the development of specialized prisons designed to treat particular types of offenders. For example, in New York the prisons at Clinton and Auburn were viewed as industrial facilities for hardcore inmates; Great Meadow was an agricultural center to house nondangerous offenders; and Dannemora was a facility for the criminally insane. In California, San Quentin housed inmates considered salvageable by correctional authorities, whereas Folsom was reserved for hard-core offenders.[25]

Prison industry also evolved. Opposition by organized labor helped put an end to the convict-lease system and forced inmate labor. By 1900 a number of states had restricted the sale of prisoner-made goods on the open market. The worldwide Great Depression that began in 1929 prompted industry and union leaders to pressure state legislators further to reduce competition from prison industries. A series of ever-more restrictive federal legislative initiatives led to the Sumners-Ashurst Act (1940), which made it a federal offense to transport out of state goods made in prison for private use, regardless of the laws of the state receiving the goods.[26] The restrictions imposed by the federal government helped to curtail prison industry severely for forty years. Private entrepreneurs shunned prison invest-

American Correctional Association

Elmira Reformatory, training course in drafting, 1909. Inmates stand at drafting tables as guards watch and a supervisor sits at a fenced-off desk at the front of the hall. Elmira was one of the first institutions to employ education and training programs.

ments because they were no longer profitable; the result was inmate idleness and make-work jobs.[27]

Despite some changes and reforms, the prison in the mid-twentieth century remained a destructive penal institution. Although some aspects of inmate life improved, severe discipline, harsh rules, and solitary confinement were the way of life.

The Modern Era   The modern era has been a period of change and turmoil in the nation's correctional system. Three trends stand out. First, between 1960 and 1980, what is referred to as the *prisoners' rights movement* occurred. After many years of indifference (a policy referred to as the *hands-off doctrine*), state and federal courts ruled in case after case that institutionalized inmates had rights to freedom of religion and speech, medical care, procedural due process, and proper living conditions. Inmates won rights unheard of in nineteenth- and early twentieth-century prisons. Since 1980, however, an increasingly conservative judiciary has curtailed the expansion of inmate rights.

Second, violence within the correctional system became a national concern. Well-publicized riots at New York's Attica Prison and the New Mexico State Penitentiary drew attention to the potential for death and destruction that lurks in every prison. Prison rapes and killings have become commonplace. The locus of control in many prisons shifted from the correctional staff to violent inmate gangs. In reaction, some administrators have tried to improve conditions and provide innovative programs that give inmates a voice in running the institution. Another reaction has been to tighten discipline and build new super-maximum-security prisons to control the most dangerous offenders. The problem of prison overcrowding has made attempts to improve conditions extremely difficult.

Third, the view that traditional correctional rehabilitation efforts have failed has prompted many penologists to reconsider the purpose of incapacitating criminals. Between 1960 and 1980, it was common for correctional administrators to cling to the **medical model**, which viewed inmates as "sick people" who were suffering from some social malady that prevented them from adjusting to society. Correctional treatment could help "cure" them and enable them to live productive lives once they returned to the community. In the 1970s, efforts were also made to help offenders become reintegrated into society by providing them with new career opportunities that relied on work-release programs. Inmates were allowed to work outside the institution during the day and return in the evening; some were given extended furloughs in the community. Work release became a political issue when Willie Horton, a furloughed inmate in Massachusetts, raped a young woman. Criticism of its "liberal" furlough program helped George Bush defeat Governor Michael Dukakis of Massachusetts for the U.S. presidency in 1988; in the aftermath of the Horton case, a number of states, including Massachusetts, restricted their furlough policies.

Prisons have come to be viewed as places for control, incapacitation, and punishment, rather than as sites for rehabilitation and reform. Advocates of the no-frills, or penal harm, movement believe that if prison is a punishing experience, would-be criminals will be deterred from crime and current inmates will be encouraged to go straight. Nonetheless, efforts to use correctional institutions as treatment facilities have not ended, and such innovations as the development of private industries on prison grounds have kept the rehabilitative ideal alive.

The alleged failure of correctional treatment, coupled with constantly increasing correctional costs, has prompted the development of alternatives to incarceration, such as intensive probation supervision, house arrest, and electronic monitoring (see Chapter 11). What has developed is a bifurcated correctional policy: keep as many nonviolent offenders out of the correctional system as possible by means of community-based programs; incarcerate dangerous, violent offenders for long periods of time.[28] These efforts have been compromised by a growing get-

medical model   A view of corrections holding that convicted offenders are victims of their environment who need care and treatment to transform them into valuable members of society.

tough stance in judicial and legislative sentencing policy, accented by mandatory minimum sentences for gun crimes and drug trafficking. Despite the development of alternatives to incarceration, the number of people under lock and key has skyrocketed.

In the following sections, we review the most prominent types of correctional facilities in operation today.

Jails

The nation's jails are institutional facilities with five primary purposes: (1) they detain accused offenders who cannot make or are not eligible for bail prior to trial; (2) they hold convicted offenders awaiting sentence; (3) they serve as the principal institution of secure confinement for offenders convicted of misdemeanors; (4) they hold probationers and parolees picked up for violations and waiting for a hearing; (5) they house felons when state prisons are overcrowded.

A number of formats are used to jail offenders. About fifteen thousand local jurisdictions maintain short-term police or municipal lockups that house offenders for no more than forty-eight hours before a bail hearing can be held; thereafter, detainees are kept in the county jail. In some jurisdictions, such as New Hampshire and Massachusetts, a house of corrections holds convicted misdemeanants, and a county jail holds pretrial detainees. Today, the jail is a multipurpose correctional institution whose other main functions are set out in Exhibit 12.1.

According to the most recent statistics, about 700,000 offenders are being supervised by jail facilities.[29] Of these, about 10 percent, or 70,000, are in alternative programs outside the jail facilities, while another 630,000 persons are actually housed in local jails. About half of the jailed inmates are unconvicted, awaiting formal charges (arraignment), bail, or trial. The remaining half are convicted offenders who are serving time, awaiting parole or probation revocation hearings, or were transferred from a state prison because of overcrowding.

Jails are usually a low-priority item in the criminal justice system. Because they are often administered on a county level, jail services have not been sufficiently regulated, nor has a unified national policy been developed to mandate what constitutes adequate jail conditions. Consequently, many jails have developed into squalid, crumbling holding pens.

The mission of the Corrections Connection is to provide a comprehensive and unbiased online community for professionals and businesses working in the corrections industry and to "inform, educate, and assist" corrections practitioners by providing best practices, resources, weekly news, products and services, career opportunities, the ability to post and review bids, partnership opportunities, innovative technologies, and educational tools. Contact the group at
www.corrections.com

Exhibit 12.1 Jail functions and services

- Receive individuals pending arraignment and hold them awaiting trial, conviction, or sentencing
- Readmit probation, parole, and jail-bond violators and absconders
- Temporarily detain juveniles pending transfer to juvenile authorities
- Hold mentally ill persons pending their movement to appropriate health facilities
- Hold individuals for the military, for protective custody, for contempt, and for the courts as witnesses
- Release convicted inmates to the community on completion of sentence
- Transfer inmates to federal, state, or other authorities
- House inmates for federal, state, or other authorities because of crowding of their facilities
- Relinquish custody of temporary detainees to juvenile and medical authorities
- Sometimes operate community-based programs as alternatives to incarceration
- Hold inmates sentenced to short terms (generally under one year)

Source: Darrell K. Gilliard and Allen J. Beck, *Prison and Jail Inmates at Midyear 1996* (Washington, D.C.: Bureau of Justice Statistics, 1997).

Jails are considered to be holding facilities for the county's undesirables rather than correctional institutions that provide meaningful treatment. They may house indigents who, looking for a respite from the winter's cold, commit a minor offense; the mentally ill who will eventually be hospitalized after a civil commitment hearing; and substance abusers who are suffering the first shocks of confinement. The jail rarely holds "professional" criminals, most of whom are able to make bail.[30] Instead, the jail holds the people considered detached from and disreputable in local society, who are frequently arrested because they are considered "offensive" by the local police. A recent survey in New York City found that on any given day more than twenty-eight hundred people with serious mental illness are being confined in jail, about 20 percent of the total inmate population.[31] The purpose of the jail is to "manage" these persons and keep them separate from the rest of society. By intruding in their lives, jailing them actually increases their involvement with the law.

Jail Populations

A national effort has been made to remove as many people from local jails as possible through the adoption of both bail reform measures and pretrial diversion. Nonetheless, jail populations have been steadily increasing, due in part to the increased use of mandatory jail sentences for such common crimes as drunk driving. Jail populations also respond to prison overcrowding; correctional departments sometimes use local jails to house inmates for whom there is no room in state prisons.

Since 1990 the nation's jail population on a per capita basis has increased by over a third. During this period the number of jail inmates per one hundred thousand residents rose from 163 to 222; if those under community supervision are included, the rate was 247 offenders per one hundred thousand U.S. residents in 2001. However, the most recent data indicate that jail populations are finally stabilizing. It is possible that the effects of a declining crime rate are finally being felt by the jail population.[32]

Who Are Jail Inmates?

Although removing juveniles from adult jails has long been a national priority, it is likely that over fifty thousand youths are admitted to adult jails each year. As of 2002, about eight thousand persons under age eighteen were housed in adult jails on a given day. Almost 90 percent of these young inmates have been convicted or are being held for trial as adults in criminal court.

Males still predominate, making up about 90 percent of the jail population. However, the female jail population is growing at a much faster rate. On average, the adult female jail population has grown 6.3 percent annually since 1990, whereas the adult male inmate population has grown 3.8 percent. The female/male jail inmate ratio reflects developments in the crime rate: as you may recall from Chapter 2, female crime rates are increasing at a faster pace than male crime rates.

As of 2001, a majority of local jail inmates were either black or Hispanic. White non-Hispanics made up 42 percent of the jail population; black non-Hispanics, 41 percent; Hispanics, 15 percent; and members of other races only about 1.6 percent of the jail population. In 2001, relative to their number in the U.S. population, black non-Hispanics were over five and a half times more likely than white non-Hispanics, over two and a half times more likely than all Hispanics, and over nine times more likely than persons of other races to have been held in a local jail.

There is also a strong association between prior physical and sexual abuse and jail inmate status: about 13 percent of males and 47 percent of female inmates report having experienced either physical or sexual abuse.[33] It is not surprising then that about 16 percent of those in local jails report either having a mental condition or an overnight stay in a mental hospital at least once in their lives.[34]

Jail Conditions

Jails are the oldest and most deteriorated institutions in the criminal justice system. Because they are usually run by the county government (and controlled by a sheriff), it is difficult to encourage taxpayers to appropriate money for improved facilities. In fact, jails are usually administered under the concept of "custodial convenience," which involves giving inmates minimum standards of treatment and benefits while controlling the cost of operations. Jail employees are often underpaid, ill-trained, and lacking in professional experience.

A number of factors lead to overcrowded and ineffective jails. One is the concerted effort being made to reduce or control particular crime problems, including substance abuse, spousal abuse, and driving while intoxicated (DWI). For example, some jurisdictions have passed legislation requiring that people arrested on suspicion of domestic violence be held in confinement for a number of hours to "cool off" before becoming eligible for bail. Other jurisdictions have attempted to deter drunk driving by passing mandatory jail sentences for people convicted of DWI; such legislation can quickly result in overcrowded jails.[35]

New-Generation Jails

To relieve overcrowding and improve effectiveness, a jail-building boom has been under way. Many of the new jails are using modern designs to improve effectiveness; these are referred to as *new-generation jails*.[36] Traditional jails are constructed and use what is referred to as the *linear/intermittent surveillance model*. Jails using this design are rectangular, with corridors leading to either single- or multiple-occupancy cells arranged at right angles to the corridor. Correctional of-

© 2002 AP/Wide World Photos

Because of a lack of resources and budget cuts, some jails have developed into squalid, crumbling holding pens and others are extremely overcrowded. Here, an inmate in the Garfield County Jail fills out paperwork needed to get a lawyer for an upcoming court date in Enid, Oklahoma, May 7, 2002. Many Oklahoma jails, including Garfield County's, must balance shrinking jail space with an increase in inmate population.

ficers must patrol to see into cells or housing areas, and when they are in a position to observe one cell they cannot observe others; unobserved inmates are essentially unsupervised.

In contrast, new-generation jails allow for continuous observation of residents. There are two types: direct and indirect supervision jails. *Direct supervision jails* contain a cluster of cells surrounding a living area or "pod," which contains tables, chairs, televisions, and other material. A correctional officer is stationed within the pod. The officer has visual observation of inmates and maintains the ability to relate to them on a personal level. By placing the officer in the pod, there is an increased awareness of the behaviors and needs of the inmates. This results in a safer environment for both staff and inmates. Since interaction between inmates is constantly and closely monitored, dissension can be quickly detected before it escalates. During the day, inmates stay in the open area (dayroom) and typically are not permitted to go into their rooms except with permission of the officer in charge. The officer controls door locks to cells from the control panel. In case of trouble or if the officer leaves the station for an extended period of time, command of this panel can be switched to a panel at a remote location, known as *central control*. The officer usually wears a device that permits immediate communication with central control in case of trouble, and the area is also covered by a video camera monitored by an officer in the central control room. *Indirect supervision jails* use similar construction; however, the correctional officer's station is located inside a secure room. Microphones and speakers inside the living unit permit the officer to hear and communicate with inmates. Although these institutions have not yet undergone extensive evaluation, research shows that they may help reduce postrelease offending in some situations.[37]

Prisons

The federal Bureau of Prisons and every state government maintain closed correctional facilities, also called prisons, penitentiaries, or reformatories.[38] It is a vast and costly system. According to the Bureau of Justice Statistics, the local, state, and federal governments between them spend about $49 billion per year on corrections, an amount that has risen a whopping 946 percent since 1977![39]

The prison is the final repository for the most troubled criminal offenders. Many come from distressed backgrounds and have little hope or opportunity; all too many have emotional problems and grew up in abusive households. A majority are alcohol- and drug-dependent at the time of their arrest. Those considered both dangerous and incorrigible may find themselves in super-maximum-security prisons, where they spend most of their days confined to their cells.

Types of Prisons

As of 2002, there were more than fifteen hundred public and private adult correctional facilities housing state prisoners. In addition, there were eighty-four federal facilities and twenty-six private facilities that housed federal inmates. Usually, prisons are organized or classified on three levels—maximum, medium, and minimum security—and each has distinct characteristics.

Maximum-Security Prisons
Housing the most notorious criminals and the subject of films and stories, **maximum-security prisons** are probably the institutions most familiar to the public. Famous "max prisons" have included Sing Sing, Joliet, Attica, Walpole, and the most fearsome prison of all, the now-closed federal facility on Alcatraz Island known as The Rock.

A typical maximum-security facility is fortress-like, surrounded by stone walls with guard towers at strategic places. These walls may be twenty-five feet high,

maximum-security prison A correctional institution that houses dangerous felons and maintains strict security measures, high walls, and limited contact with the outside world.

In maximum-security prisons correctional staff are made aware that each inmate may be a dangerous violent criminal, and that as a result, the utmost in security must be maintained. In keeping with this philosophy, prisons are designed to eliminate hidden corners where people can congregate, and passages are constructed so they can be easily blocked off to quell disturbances.

and sometimes inner and outer walls divide the prison into courtyards. Barbed wire or electrified fences are used to discourage escapes. High security, armed guards, and stone walls give the inmate the sense that the facility is impregnable and reassure the citizens outside that convicts will be completely incapacitated.

Inmates live in interior, metal-barred cells that contain their own plumbing and sanitary facilities and are locked securely either by key or electronic device. Cells are organized in sections called *blocks,* and in large prisons, a number of cell blocks make up a wing. During the evening, each cell block is sealed off from the others, as is each wing. Thus, an inmate may be officially located, for example, in Block 3 of E Wing.

Every inmate is assigned a number and a uniform on entering the prison system. Unlike the striped, easily identifiable uniforms of old, the maximum-security inmate today wears khaki attire not unlike military fatigues. Dress codes may be strictly enforced in some institutions, but closely cropped hair and other strict features are vestiges of the past.

During the day, the inmates engage in closely controlled activities: meals, workshops, education, and so on. Rule violators may be confined to their cells, and working and other shared recreational activities are viewed as privileges.

The byword of the maximum-security prison is *security*. Guards and other correctional workers are made aware that each inmate may be a dangerous criminal or violent, and that as a result, the utmost security must be maintained. In keeping with this philosophy, prisons are designed to eliminate hidden corners where people can congregate, and passages are constructed so that they can be easily blocked off to quell disturbances. Some states have constructed **super-maximum-security prisons** (supermax prisons) to house the most predatory criminals. These high-security institutions can be independent correctional centers or locked wings of existing prisons.[40] Some supermax prisons lock inmates in their cells twenty-two to twenty-four hours a day, never allowing them out unless they are shackled.[41] The Criminal Justice and Technology feature discusses these supermax prisons.

super-maximum-security prison The newest form of a maximum-security prison that uses high-level security measures to incapacitate the nation's most dangerous criminals. Most inmates are in twenty-three hours per day lockdown.

Ultra-Maximum-Security Prisons

At least thirty-four American states now operate super-maximum or ultra-maximum security prisons or units, also known as supermax prisons, providing nearly twenty-thousand beds and accounting for 1.8 percent of the states' prison population. These high-security institutions can be independent correctional centers or locked wings of existing prisons operating under such names as the "secure housing unit" or "maximum control unit."

The first federal supermax prison was located in Marion, Illinois; it was infamous for its tight security and isolate conditions. Marion has been supplanted by a new 484-bed facility in Florence, Colorado. This new prison has the most sophisticated security measures in the United States, including 168 video cameras and 1,400 electronically controlled gates. Inside the cells all furniture is unmovable: the desk, bed, and TV stand are made of cement. All potential weapons, including soap dishes, toilet seats, and toilet handles, have been removed. The cement walls are five-thousand-pound quality, and steel bars are placed so they crisscross every eight inches inside the walls. Cells are angled so that inmates can see neither each other nor the outside scenery (see Figure A). This cuts down on communications and denies inmates a sense of location, in order to prevent escapes.

Getting out of the prison seems impossible. There are six guard towers at different heights to prevent air attacks. To get out, the inmates would have to pass through seven three-inch-thick steel doors, each of which can be opened only after the previous one has closed. If a guard tower is ever seized, all controls are switched to the next station. If the whole prison is seized, it can be controlled from the outside. It appears that the only way out is through good works and good behavior, based on which an inmate can earn transfer to another prison within three years.

A national survey of supermax prisons conducted by the American Correctional Association found that although the cost of running these institutions is generally higher than in less secure facilities they tend to be popular with correctional administrators, who believe that isolating troublemakers helps them maintain order. The survey's major findings include these:

- Thirty-four prison systems are now either operating or will soon open new supermax facilities. Four others are considering the need for supermax facilities or are actively pursuing construction funds.
- Thirty-six prison systems cited the need to better manage violent and seriously disruptive inmates as a primary factor in their jurisdictions' development of supermax housing; seventeen of these systems include gang members as appropriate candidates for supermax housing.
- Jurisdictions vary greatly in the length of time inmates are confined in supermax facilities and the criteria for admission and release. Approval authority for admission and release of inmates varies from the warden or superintendent to the director/commissioner of the prison system.
- There are only minimal correctional programs, limited to television and video programming and other relatively limited methods. Transitional programming is available only in some jurisdictions.
- Jurisdictions differ in whether mentally ill and developmentally disabled inmates are placed in supermax housing.

Critiquing the Supermax Prison

Threat of transfer to a supermax institution is used to deter inmate misbehavior in less restrictive institutions. Civil rights watchdog groups charge that these prisons violate United Nations standards for the treatment of inmates. They are usually located in rural areas, which makes staffing difficult in the professional areas of dentistry, medicine, and counseling. Senior officers would rather not work in these institutions, leaving the most difficult inmates in the hands of the most inexperienced correctional officers.

A recent survey by Leena Kurki and Norval Morris found that although conditions vary from state to state, many supermaxes subject inmates to nearly complete isolation and deprivation of sensory stimuli. Although the long-term effects of such conditions are still uncertain, Kurki and Morris believe that they are likely to be extremely harmful, especially for those who suffer from preexisting mental illness or those with subnormal intelligence.

The development of the ultra-max prison represents a shift from previous correctional policy, which favored dispersing the most troublesome inmates to different prisons in order to prevent them from joining forces or planning escapes. The supermax model finds that housing the most dangerous inmates in an ultra-secure facility eases their control while reducing violence levels in the general prison population. Kurki and Morris, however, argue that while the supermax prison is considered the ultimate control mechanism for disruptive inmates, individuals are actually less to blame for prison violence and disruption than are dysfunctional prison regimes and misguided prison administrators, which make prisons the violent institutions they are.

Critical Thinking

1. Ultra-max prisons are reminiscent of the old Pennsylvania system, which made use of solitary confinement and high security. Is this inhumane in our more enlightened age? Why or why not?
2. Should all convicted terrorists be kept in supermax prisons, or should these facilities be reserved only for those proven to be violent and dangerous to other inmates?

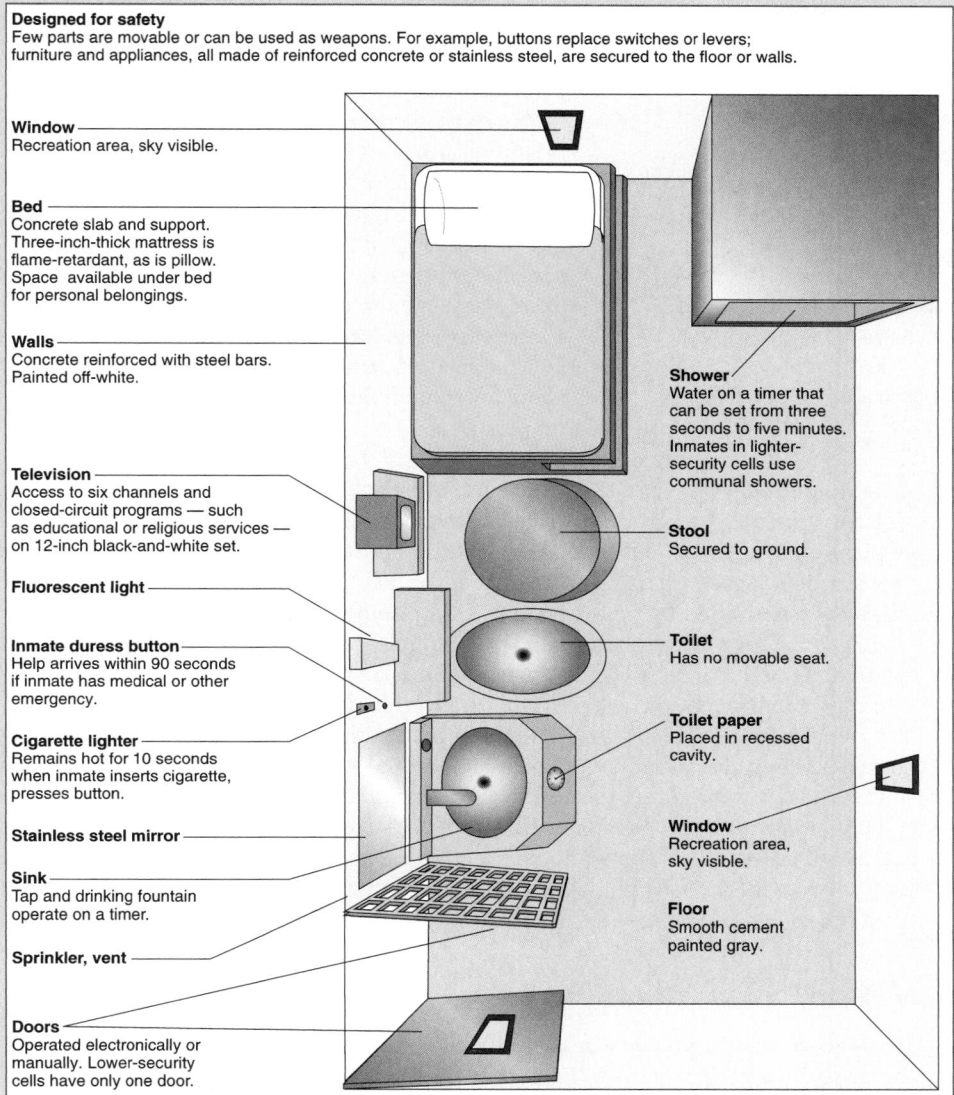

Designed for safety
Few parts are movable or can be used as weapons. For example, buttons replace switches or levers; furniture and appliances, all made of reinforced concrete or stainless steel, are secured to the floor or walls.

Window
Recreation area, sky visible.

Bed
Concrete slab and support. Three-inch-thick mattress is flame-retardant, as is pillow. Space available under bed for personal belongings.

Walls
Concrete reinforced with steel bars. Painted off-white.

Television
Access to six channels and closed-circuit programs — such as educational or religious services — on 12-inch black-and-white set.

Fluorescent light

Inmate duress button
Help arrives within 90 seconds if inmate has medical or other emergency.

Cigarette lighter
Remains hot for 10 seconds when inmate inserts cigarette, presses button.

Stainless steel mirror

Sink
Tap and drinking fountain operate on a timer.

Sprinkler, vent

Doors
Operated electronically or manually. Lower-security cells have only one door.

Shower
Water on a timer that can be set from three seconds to five minutes. Inmates in lighter-security cells use communal showers.

Stool
Secured to ground.

Toilet
Has no movable seat.

Toilet paper
Placed in recessed cavity.

Window
Recreation area, sky visible.

Floor
Smooth cement painted gray.

Figure A
Typical cell in a super-maximum-security prison
Some of the toughest felons in the federal prison system are held in a new penitentiary in Florence, Colorado. It is designed to be the most secure ever built by the government. Many inmates live in isolation, except for an hour a day of recreation. A high-security cell in the 575-bed facility has these features.

Source: Louis Winn, United States Penitentiary, Administrative Maximum, Florence, Colorado.

InfoTrac College Edition Research
To read about the conditions in the new super-maximum-security prisons, go to InfoTrac College Edition and read "Cruel and Unusual Punishment," *Harper's Magazine,* July 2001 v303 i1814 p92.

Sources: Leena Kurki and Norval Morris, "The Purpose, Practices, and Problems of Supermax Prisons," in Michael Tonry, ed., *Crime and Justice: An Annual Edition* (Chicago: University of Chicago Press, 2001), 385–422; Richard H. Franklin, "Assessing Supermax Operations," *Corrections Today* 60 (1998): 126–128; Chase Riveland, *Supermax Prison: Overview and General Considerations* (Longmont, Colo.: National Institute of Corrections, 1998); Federal Bureau of Prisons, *State of the Bureau, 1995* (Washington, D.C.: U.S. Government Printing Office, 1996); Dennis Cauchon, "The Alcatraz of the Rockies," *USA Today,* 16 November 1994, 6a.

© 2002 AP/Wide World Photos

Though often similar in appearance to maximum-security prisons, medium-security prisons have security measures that are neither so tense nor so vigilant. Medium-security prisons are also surrounded by walls, but there may be fewer guard towers or other precautions.

medium-security prison A less secure institution that houses nonviolent offenders and provides more opportunities for contact with the outside world.

minimum-security prison The least secure institution that houses white-collar and nonviolent offenders, maintains few security measures, and has liberal furlough and visitation policies.

Medium-Security Prisons Similar in appearance to maximum-security prisons, in **medium-security prisons** the security and atmosphere are neither so tense nor so vigilant. Medium-security prisons are also surrounded by walls, but there may be fewer guard towers or other security precautions. For example, visitor privileges may be more extensive, and personal contact may be allowed, whereas in a maximum-security prison visitors may be separated from inmates by acrylic plastic sheets or other barriers (to prohibit the passing of contraband). Although most prisoners are housed in cells, individual honor rooms in medium-security prisons are used to reward those who make exemplary rehabilitation efforts. Finally, medium-security prisons promote greater treatment efforts, and the relaxed atmosphere allows freedom of movement for rehabilitation workers and other therapeutic personnel.

Minimum-Security Prisons Operating without armed guards or walls, **minimum-security prisons** usually house the most trustworthy and least violent offenders; white-collar criminals may be their most common occupants. Inmates are allowed a great deal of personal freedom. Instead of being marched to activities by guards, they are summoned by bells or loudspeaker announcements and they assemble on their own. Work furloughs and educational releases are encouraged, and vocational training is of the highest level. Dress codes are lax, and inmates are allowed to grow beards or mustaches or demonstrate other individual characteristics.

Minimum-security facilities may have dormitories or small private rooms for inmates. Prisoners are allowed to own personal possessions that might be deemed dangerous in a maximum-security prison, such as radios.

Minimum-security prisons have been criticized for being like "country clubs"; some federal facilities for white-collar criminals even have tennis courts and pools (they are called derisively "Club Fed"). Yet they remain prisons, and the isolation and loneliness of prison life deeply affect the inmates.

Prison Inmate Characteristics

Surveys of prison inmates indicate that, as might be expected, the personal characteristics of prison inmates reflect common traits of arrestees: inmates tend to be young (about half are under age thirty), single, poorly educated, disproportionately male, and minority group members.[42] Many were either underemployed or unemployed prior to their arrest; many had incomes of less than $10,000 and suffer drug abuse and other personal problems.

Gender Gender differences in the prison population are considerable. Women are underrepresented in prison, and not solely because they commit less serious crimes. The Uniform Crime Reports arrest statistics indicate that the overall male-to-female arrest ratio is today about 3.5 male offenders to 1 female offender; for violent crimes, the ratio is closer to 6 males to 1 female. Yet female inmates account for only about 10 percent of the prison population. Whereas the typical male inmate is a violent offender, most female inmates have committed property offenses.

Race and Ethnicity At year-end 2001 there were 3,535 sentenced black male prisoners per 100,000 black males in the United States, compared to 1,177 sentenced Hispanic male inmates per 100,000 Hispanic males and 462 white male

inmates per 100,000 white males. Thus, the prison system is populated disproportionately by minorities; black males in the United States are now incarcerated
at a higher rate than in South Africa before the election of Nelson Mandela. An
estimated 10 percent of black males ages twenty-five to twenty-nine were in
prison in 2001. This condition severely decreases the life chances of African-
American men, has a devastating effect on the black community, and is an ongoing national concern.[43]

Type of Offense   What did the inmates do to earn their sentences? About half
of all inmates are serving time for violent crimes. Overall, the largest growth in
state inmates between 1990 and 2000 was among violent offenders, whose
numbers grew by more than 273,000; the number of drug offenders grew by
101,400. As a percentage of the total growth in the inmate population between
1990 and 2000, violent offenders accounted for 53 percent of the growth, drug
offenders 20 percent, property offenders 12 percent, and public-order offenders
15 percent.

Substance Abuse   A strong association exists between substance abuse and inmate status. For example, one study of four hundred Texas inmates found that almost 75 percent suffered from lifetime substance abuse or dependence disorder,
which is characterized by psychologists as (1) abuse of drugs for at least one continuous month (or repeated symptoms to occur over a longer period), (2) "failure
to fulfill major role obligations," and (3) "substance-related legal problems."[44]
About 80 percent of inmates report using drugs at some time during their lives,
and more than 60 percent are regular users. About half of the inmates report being
either drunk, high, or both when they committed the crime that landed them in
prison. Considering this background, it should come as no surprise that more inmates die from HIV-related disease than from prison violence.[45]

Physical Abuse/Mental Illness   Like jail inmates, prison inmates also report a
long history of physical abuse and mental health problems: about 19 percent report some form of physical abuse, including 57 percent of female offenders.[46] In
addition, about 16 percent of state prison inmates report having some form of
mental problems.[47] Mentally ill inmates are more likely to be arrested for violent
offenses and to have suffered a variety of personal and emotional problems than
the general inmate population. The picture that emerges is that prisons hold those
people who face the toughest social obstacles in society. Only a few members of
the educated middle class wind up behind bars, and these people are usually held
in low-security prisons, the "country club" institutions.

Alternative Correctional Institutions

In addition to prisons and jails, a number of other correctional institutions are
operating around the United States. Some have been in use for quite some time,
whereas others have been developed as part of innovative or experimental
programs.

Prison Farms and Camps

Prison farms and camps are used to detain offenders. These types of facilities are
found primarily in the South and the West and have been in operation since the
nineteenth century. Today, about forty farms, forty forest camps, eighty road
camps, and more than sixty similar facilities (vocational training centers, ranches,

and so on) exist in the nation. Prisoners on farms produce dairy products, grain, and vegetable crops that are used in the state correctional system and other governmental facilities, such as hospitals and schools. Forestry camp inmates maintain state parks, fight forest fires, and do reforestation work. Ranches, primarily a western phenomenon, employ inmates in cattle raising and horse breeding, among other activities. Road gangs repair roads and state highways.

Shock Incarceration in Boot Camps

shock incarceration A short prison sentence served in boot camp–type facilities.

boot camp A short-term militaristic correctional facility in which inmates undergo intensive physical conditioning and discipline.

A recent approach to correctional care that is gaining popularity around the United States is **shock incarceration** in **boot camps.** Such programs usually include youthful, first-time offenders and feature military discipline and physical training (Figure 12.1). The concept is that short periods (90 to 180 days) of high-intensity exercise and work will "shock" the inmate into going straight. Tough physical training is designed to promote responsibility and improve decision-making skills, build self-confidence, and teach socialization skills. Inmates are treated with rough intensity by drillmasters who may call them names and punish the entire group for the failure of one member. Discipline is so severe that some critics warn that it can amount to "cruel and unusual punishment" and generate costly inmate lawsuits.[48]

There is wide variation in the more than seventy-five programs now operating around the United States.[49] Some programs also include educational and training components, counseling sessions, and treatment for special-needs populations, whereas others devote little or no time to therapeutic activities. Some receive program participants directly from court sentencing, whereas others choose potential candidates from the general inmate population. Some allow voluntary participation and others voluntary termination.[50]

Shock incarceration programs can provide some important correctional benefits. New York houses inmates in these programs in separate institutions and provides most (but not all) "graduates" with extensive follow-up supervision. Although recidivism rates for these programs in New York are similar to those of traditional prisons, there are indications that both inmates and staff view shock incarceration as a positive experience.[51] It is estimated that the New York program has saved taxpayers hundreds of millions of dollars because boot camps are cheaper to build and maintain than traditional prisons. Other evaluations have found that a boot camp experience can improve inmates' attitudes and have the potential for enhancing their postcorrection lifestyle.[52]

Shock incarceration has the advantage of being a lower-cost alternative to overcrowded prisons because inmates are held in nonsecure facilities and sentences are short. Both staff and inmates seem excited by the programs, and even those who fail on parole report that they felt the shock incarceration was a valuable experience.[53] Of course, if shock incarceration is viewed as an exciting or helpful experience by its "graduates," they could be encouraged to recidivate, since the threat of the prison experience has been weakened.

Boot camps use strict discipline regimes, which some critics find demeaning to inmates. Here, at the Prison Boot Camp in Illinois, one correctional officer bangs the metal wastebasket against the cement floor. Two officers yell at the new inmate, demanding that he hurry and gather his newly cut hair into the basket. They hurl a barrage of nonprofane insults at him. Profanity by correctional officers as well as inmates is forbidden at the boot camp.

Evaluating Shock Incarceration Is shock incarceration a correctional panacea or another fad doomed to failure? The results so far are mixed. The costs of boot camps are no lower than those of traditional prisons on a daily basis, but because sentences are shorter they provide long-term savings. Some programs suffer high failure-to-complete rates, which

Rita finishes 50 sit-ups and springs to her feet. At 6:30 A.M. her platoon begins a 5-mile run, the last portion of this morning's physical training. After 5 months in New York's Lakeview Shock Incarceration Correctional Facility, the morning workout is easy. Rita even enjoys it, taking pride in her physical conditioning.

When Rita graduates and returns to New York City, she will face 6 months of intensive supervision before moving to regular parole. More than two-fifths of Rita's platoon did not make it this far; some withdrew voluntarily, and the rest were removed for misconduct or failure to participate satisfactorily. By completing shock incarceration, she will enter parole 11 months before her minimum release date.

The requirements for completing shock incarceration are the same for male and female inmates. The women live in a separate housing area of Lakeview. Otherwise, men and women participate in the same education, physical training, drill and ceremony, drug education, and counseling programs. Men and women are assigned to separate work details and attend network group meetings held in inmates' living units.

Daily Schedule

A.M.

5:30	Wake up and standing count
5:45–6:30	Calisthenics and drill
6:30–7:00	Run
7:00–8:00	Mandatory breakfast/cleanup
8:15	Standing count and company formation
8:30–11:55	Work/school schedules

P.M.

12:00–12:30	Mandatory lunch and standing count
12:30–3:30	Afternoon work/school schedule
3:30–4:00	Shower
4:00–4:45	Network community meeting
4:45–5:45	Mandatory dinner, prepare for evening
6:00–9:00	School, group counseling, drug counseling, prerelease counseling, decision-making classes
9:00	Count while in programs
9:15–9:30	Squad bay, prepare for bed
9:30	Standing count, lights out

Figure 12.1
Shock incarceration
Typical daily routines and schedule in a boot camp program.

Source: Cherie Clark, David Aziz, and Doris Mackenzie, *Shock Incarceration in New York: Focus on Treatment* (Washington, D.C.: National Institute of Justice, 1994), 5.

makes program evaluations difficult (even if graduates are successful, it is possible that success is achieved because troublesome cases drop out and are placed back in the general inmate population). What evaluations exist indicate that the recidivism rates of inmates who attend shock programs are in some cases no lower than for those released from traditional prisons.[54]

Many of these evaluations have been conducted by Doris Layton Mackenzie and her associates. One study with James Shaw found that, although boot camp inmates may have lower recidivism rates than probationers and parolees, they have higher rates of technical violations and revocations.[55] Even though these results are disappointing, Mackenzie reports, as already noted, that staff and inmates alike find boot camp to be a valuable experience.[56] With Alex Piquero she also found that carefully managed boot camp programs can make a big dent in prison overcrowding.[57] Nonetheless, Mackenzie's extensive evaluations of the boot camp experience generate little evidence that they can significantly lower recidivism rates. Programs that seem to work best, such as those in New York, stress treatment and therapeutic activities, are voluntary, and are longer in duration.[58]

Community Correctional Facilities

community treatment The attempt by correctional agencies to maintain convicted offenders in the community instead of a secure facility; it includes probation, parole, and residential programs.

halfway house A community-based correctional facility that houses inmates before their outright release so that they can become gradually acclimated to conventional society.

One of the goals of correctional treatment is to help reintegrate the offender back into society. Placing offenders in a prison makes them more likely to adapt an inmate lifestyle than to reassimilate conventional social norms. As a result, the **community treatment** concept began to take off in the 1960s. State and federal correctional systems created community-based correctional models as an alternative to closed institutions. Many are **halfway houses** to which inmates are transferred just before their release into the community. These facilities are designed to bridge the gap between institutional living and the community. Specialized treatment may be offered, and the residents use the experience to cushion the shock of reentering society.

As you may recall, commitment to a community correctional center may also be used as an intermediate sanction and sole mode of treatment. An offender may be assigned to a community treatment center operated by the state department of corrections or to probation. Or the corrections department can contract with a private community center. This practice is common in the treatment of drug addicts and other nonviolent offenders whose special needs can be met in a self-contained community setting that specializes in specific types of treatment.

Halfway houses and community correctional centers can look like residential homes and in many instances were originally residences; in urban centers, older apartment buildings can be adapted for the purpose. Usually, these facilities have a central treatment theme—such as group therapy or reality therapy—that is used to rehabilitate and reintegrate clients.

Another popular approach in community-based corrections is the use of ex-offenders as staff members. These individuals have made the transition between the closed institution and society and can be invaluable in helping residents overcome the many hurdles they face in proper readjustment.

Despite the encouraging philosophical concept presented by the halfway house, evaluation of specific programs has not led to a definite endorsement of this type of treatment.[59] One significant problem has been a lack of support from community residents, who fear the establishment of an institution housing "dangerous offenders" in their neighborhood. Court actions and zoning restrictions have been brought in some areas to foil efforts to create halfway houses.[60] As a result, many halfway houses are located in decrepit neighborhoods in the worst areas of town—certainly a condition that must influence the attitudes and behavior of the inmates. Furthermore, the climate of control exercised in most halfway houses, where rule violation can be met with a quick return to the institution, may not be one that the average inmate can distinguish from his former high-security penal institution.

Despite these problems, the promise held by community correctional centers, coupled with their low cost of operations, has led to their continued use into the new millennium.

Private Prisons

Correctional facilities are now being run by private firms as business enterprises. In some instances, a private corporation will finance and build an institution and then contract with correctional authorities to provide services for convicted criminals. Sometimes the private concern will finance and build the institution and then lease it outright to the government. This model has the advantage of allowing the government to circumvent the usually difficult process of getting voters to approve a bond issue and raising funds for prison construction. Another common method of private involvement is with specific service contracts; for example, a private concern might be hired to manage the prison health-care system, food services, or staff training.

On January 6, 1986, the U.S. Corrections Corporation opened the first private state prison in Marion, Kentucky—a three-hundred-bed minimum-security facility for inmates who are within three years of parole. Today, more than twenty companies are trying to enter the private prison market, five states are contracting with private companies to operate facilities, and more than ten others—including Oregon, New Mexico, and Florida—have recently passed laws authorizing or expanding the use of private prison contractors.[61]

A recent review of private prisons by Richard Harding finds that they now play an important correctional role in United States, Australia, and the United Kingdom. Harding finds clear evidence that the development of private prisons has stimulated improvement in the correctional system, but also that private prisons can experience the same failures and problems as public institutions.[62]

Private prisons are in operation abroad. To read about a private women's prison in Australia, see Amanda George, "Tales of a Private Women's Prison: Writ in Women's Lives," *Hecate*, May 2002 v28 i1 p145(9), on InfoTrac College Edition.

Can Private Prisons Work?   Some evaluations of recidivism among inmates released from private and public facilities find that recidivism rates are actually lower among the private prison group than the state prison inmates.[63] Inmates released from private prisons who reoffend commit less serious offenses than those released from public institutions. These findings help support the concept of the private correctional institution. Nonetheless, some experts question reliance on private prisons, believing that their use raises a number of vexing problems. For example, will private providers be able to evaluate programs effectively knowing that a negative evaluation might cause them to lose their contract? Will they skimp on services and programs in order to reduce costs? Might they not skim off the "easy" cases and leave the hard-core inmate to the state's care? And will the need to keep business booming require widening the net to fill empty cells? Must they maintain state-mandated liability insurance to cover inmate claims?[64] So far, private and state institutions cost about the same to operate.[65]

Private corrections firms also run into opposition from existing state correctional staff and management, who fear the loss of jobs and autonomy. Moreover, the public may be skeptical about an untested private concern's ability to provide security and protection. Private corrections also face administrative problems. How will program quality be controlled? To compete on price, a private facility may have to cut corners to beat the competition. Determining accountability for problems and mishaps will be difficult when dealing with a corporation that is a legal fiction and protects its officers from personal responsibility for their actions.

Legal Issues   There are also unresolved legal problems: Can privately employed guards patrol the perimeter and use deadly force to stop escape attempts? Do private correctional officers have less immunity from lawsuits than state employees? The case of *Correctional Services Corp. v. Malesko*, 534 U.S. 61, 122 S.Ct. 515 (2001), helps define the rights and protections of inmates in private correctional facilities. Malesko had a heart condition but was forced to walk stairs rather than take an elevator. When he suffered a heart attack he sued the Correctional Services Corp. (CSC), which was operating the prison, under the federal civil rights act, alleging that the denial of proper medical care violated his civil rights. Citizens are generally allowed to seek damages against federal agents who violate their civil rights. However, the U.S. Supreme Court ruled that although Malesko could sue an individual employee of the private correctional corporation for allegedly violating his constitutional rights, he could not sue the correctional corporation itself. This decision shields the private prison corporation from suits brought under the federal civil rights statute. The *Malesko* decision upholds the concerns of some critics, who view the private prison as an insidious expansion of state control over citizens: a state-supported entity that actually has more freedom to exert control than the state itself.[66]

In the abstract, a private correctional enterprise may be an attractive alternative to a costly correctional system, but these legal, administrative, and cost issues

Use "prison management companies" as a subject guide on InfoTrac College Edition.

need to be resolved before private prisons can become widespread.[67] A balance must be reached between the need for a private business to make a profit and the integrity of a prison administration that must be concerned with such complex issues as security, rehabilitation, and dealing with highly dangerous people in a closed environment.[68]

Correctional Populations

The nation's vast system of penal institutions now holds about 2 million people (counting jail and community corrections populations) and employs more than 250,000 to care for and guard them (see Table 12.1).

The nation's prison population has had a number of cycles of growth and decline.[69] Between 1925 and 1939, it increased at about 5 percent a year, reflecting the nation's concern for the lawlessness of that time. The incarceration rate reached a high of 137 per 100,000 U.S. population in 1939. Then, during World War II, the prison population declined by 50,000 as potential offenders were drafted into the armed services. By 1956 the incarceration rate had dropped to 99 per 100,000 U.S. population.

The postwar era saw a steady increase in the prison population until 1961, when 220,000 people were in custody, a rate of 119 per 100,000. During the Vietnam era (1961 to 1968), the prison population actually declined by 30,000. The incarceration rate remained rather stable until 1974, when the current dramatic rise began. Between 1995 and 2002, the number of male state and federal prisoners grew 24 percent, reaching 1,313,000 in 2001, whereas the number of female prisoners increased 36 percent, reaching 93,031, or 6.6 percent of all state and federal prisoners. The number of prisoners who were convicted for committing violent crimes increased at a particularly high level compared with recent trends for drug and property crimes (Figure 12.2).

Table 12.1  Correctional population, 2002

As of January 1, 2002 there were more than 2,100,000 United States residents incarcerated in the following facilities:

State and federal prisons	1,324,465
Local jails	631,240
Juvenile detention facilities	108,965
U.S. territorial prisons	15,852
U.S. Immigration and Naturalization facilities	8,761
Armed services (military) prisons	2,436
Indian Country jails	1,912

Source: Paige Harrison and Allen Beck, *Prisoners in 2001* (Washington, D.C.: Bureau of Justice Statistics, 2002).

Figure 12.2
State prison populations by offense type, 1980–2000
Over half of the increase in state prison populations since 1990 is due to an increase in the prisoners convicted of violent offenses.

Sources: Correctional Populations in the United States, Annual (Washington, D.C.: Bureau of Justice Statistics, 2002); Paige Harrison and Allen Beck, *Prisoners in 2001* (Washington, D.C.: Bureau of Justice Statistics, 2002).

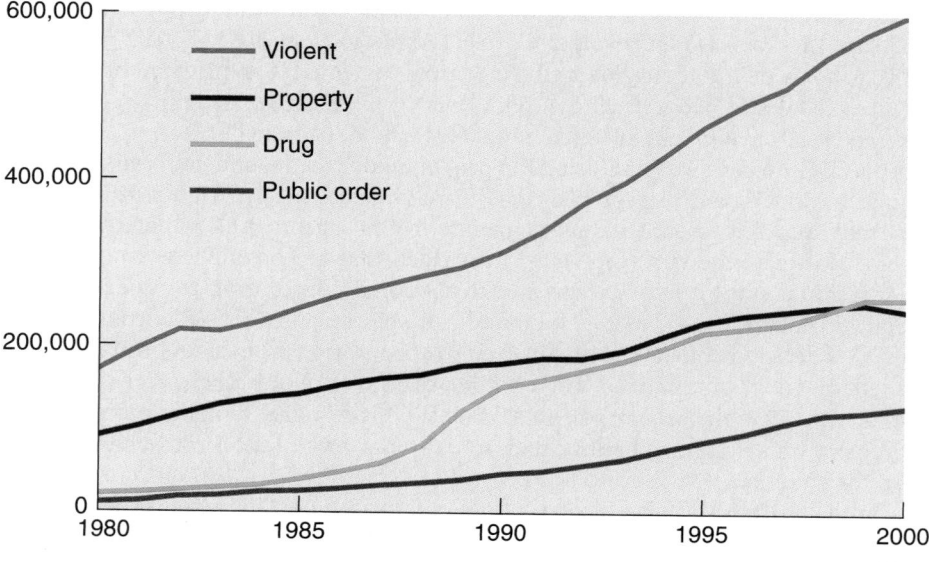

State prison population, 1980–2000

In 2002, the prison population finally began to stabilize and actually began to decline in the latter half of the year. Whether this is a short-term correction or long-term trend remains to be seen.[70]

Prison populations are also rising overseas. Go to InfoTrac College Edition and read about recent developments in Holland: Kees Boeij, "Developments in The Netherlands Penitentiary System," *Corrections Today*, February 2002 v64 i1 p50(4).

Explaining Prison Population Trends

Why did the prison population grow so rapidly over the past decade even though the crime rate fell? One reason may be politicians responding to the general public's more punitive response to criminal offenders. Public concern about drugs and violent crime has not been lost on state lawmakers. Mandatory sentencing laws, which have been implemented by a majority of states and the federal government, increase eligibility for incarceration and limit the availability for early release via parole. Although probation and community sentences still predominate, structural changes in criminal codes and crime rates helped produce an expanding correctional population. The amount of time served in prison has increased because of such development as truth-in-sentencing laws that require inmates to serve at least 85 percent of their sentence behind bars.[71]

As you may recall from Chapter 10, the conviction rate is increasing for crimes that are traditionally punished with a prison sentence, such as robbery and burglary. In addition, get-tough policies have helped curtail the use of parole and have reduced judicial discretion to impose nonincarceration sentences.[72] Some states have implemented laws mandating that violent juveniles be waived, or transferred, to the adult court for treatment.[73] Thousands of juveniles are being tried as adults each year and may end up in adult prisons.

Prison Overcrowding

Inmates are routinely housed two and three to a cell or in large dormitory-like rooms that hold more than fifty people. Military bases and even tents have been used to house overflow inmates. In addition to detainees and misdemeanants, thousands of people convicted of felonies are being held in local jails because of prison crowding, as we have already seen. State correctional authorities have attempted to deal with the overcrowding problem by building new facilities, using construction techniques that limit expenditures, such as modular and preassembled units. Precast concrete cells are fabricated as fully finished units and can be installed quickly. There is also an increasing need to maintain security in overcrowded facilities, and as the earlier Criminal Justice and Technology feature shows, correctional administrators may rely on high-tech advances to maintain order.

Cost of Incarceration   So many people are now going to prison that the federal government estimates that a significant portion of the nation's population will at one time or another be behind prison gates. About 5 percent of the population, or more than thirteen million people, will serve a prison sentence some time during their lives. Men are over eight times more likely than women to be incarcerated in prison at least once during their lives. Among men, African Americans (28.5 percent) are about twice as likely as Hispanics (16.0 percent) and six times more likely than whites (4.4 percent) to be admitted to prison during their lives. Among women, 3.6 percent of African Americans, 1.5 percent of Hispanics, and 0.5 percent of whites will enter prison at least once.[74] The extreme racial differences in the imprisonment rate are a key concern of the justice system. Do these differences reflect racial discrimination in the sentencing process? What might be done to reduce or eliminate this significant social problem?

Despite such ominous signs, the nation's prison population may be "maxing out." Budget cutbacks and belt tightening may halt the expansion of prison construction and the housing of ever-more prisoners in already crowded prison facilities.[75] Although new modular construction techniques and double- and triple-bunking of inmates make existing prisons expandable, the secure population

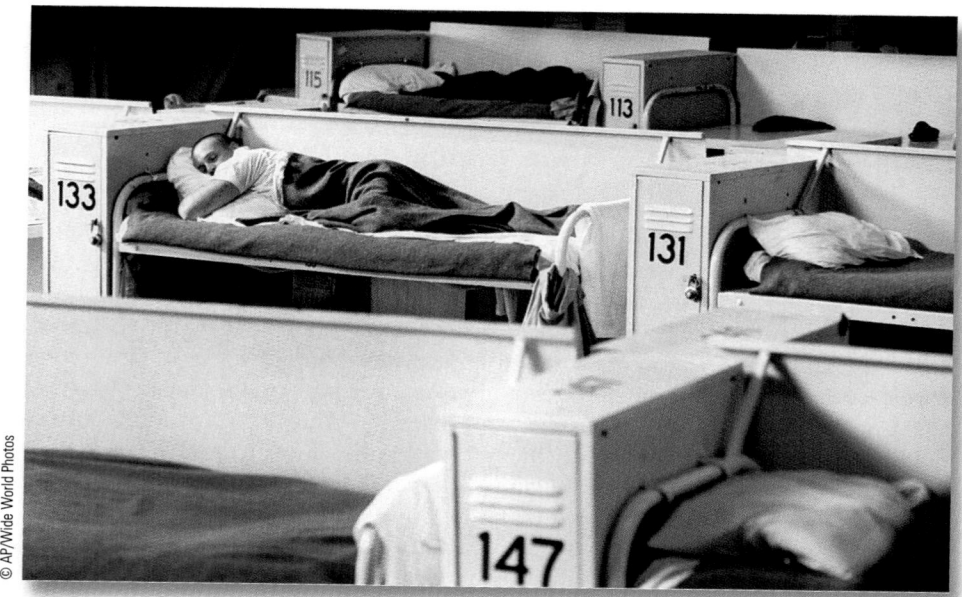

There is an ongoing correctional crowding crisis. Here, an inmate naps on a bunk bed in a gym that has been converted to house prisoners at Deuel Vocational Institute near Tracy, California. More than six hundred inmates are crammed into the half-century-old structure, one measure for coping with prison system overcrowding.

probably cannot expand endlessly. As costs skyrocket, some states are now spending more on prisons than on higher education. The public may begin to question the wisdom of a strict incarceration policy. There may also be fewer criminals to incarcerate. The waning of the crack cocaine epidemic in large cities may hasten this decline, because street crimes will decline and fewer offenders will be eligible for the long penalties associated with the possession of crack.[76] As noted earlier, fewer people are now receiving a prison sentence than five years ago, and if this trend holds the prison population will eventually decline.

In the final analysis, change in the correctional population may depend on the faith judges and legislators place in incarceration as a crime control policy. As long as policymakers believe that incarcerating predatory criminals can bring down crime rates, then the likelihood of a significant decrease in the institutional population seems remote. If there is little evidence that this costly system does lower crime rates, then less costly and equally effective alternatives may be sought. ■

SUMMARY

Today's correctional institutions can trace their development from European origins. Punishment methods developed in Europe were modified and improved on by American colonists, most notably William Penn. He replaced the whip and other methods of physical punishment with confinement in county institutions or penitentiaries.

Later, as needs grew, the newly formed states created their own large facilities. Discipline was harsh within them, and most enforced a code of total and absolute silence. The Auburn system of congregate working conditions during the day and isolation at night has been adopted in our present penal system.

The correctional population has grown dramatically in the past few years. Although the number of inmates diminished in the late 1960s and early 1970s, it has since hit an all-time high. This development may reflect a toughening of sentencing procedures nationwide.

A number of institutions currently house convicted offenders. Jails are used for misdemeanants and minor felons. Because conditions are so poor in jails, they have become a major trouble spot for the criminal justice system.

Federal and state prisons—classified as minimum, medium, and maximum security—house most of the nation's incarcerated felons. However, their poor track record has spurred the development of new correctional models, specifically the boot camp, the halfway house, and the community correctional center. Nonetheless, the success of these institutions has been challenged by research efforts indicating that their recidivism rates are equal to those of state prisons. One newer development has been the privately run correctional institution. These are jails and prisons operated by private companies, which receive a fee for their services. Used in a limited number of jurisdictions, they have been the center of some controversy. Can a private company provide better management of what has traditionally been a public problem?

The greatest problem facing the correctional system today is overcrowding, which has reached a crisis level. To help deal with the problems of overcrowding, corrections departments have begun to experiment with modular prison construction and the use of intermediate sanctions.

For an up-to-date list of Web links, go to http://cj.wadsworth.com/siegel_essen4e.

KEY TERMS

prison 386	congregate system 389	medical model 394	minimum-security prison 402
jail 386	Auburn system 390	maximum-security prison 398	shock incarceration 404
hulk 388	Pennsylvania system 391	super-maximum-security prison 399	boot camp 404
Walnut Street Jail 389	contract system (convict) 392	medium-security prison 402	community treatment 406
penitentiary house 389	convict-lease system 392		halfway house 406
tier system 389			

INFOTRAC COLLEGE EDITION EXERCISES

PRISON ADMINISTRATORS are beginning to pay more attention to the communications and other technologies that have been developed for correctional facilities. Technology has been used in some cases for security purposes and in others to keep down costs. To find out more about the emerging technologies, read the following articles on InfoTrac College Edition: Ann H. Crowe, "Electronic Supervision: From Decision Making to Implementation," *Corrections Today,* August 2002 v64 i5 p130(3); Steve Morrison, "Best Practices: Technology in Corrections," *Corrections Today,* July 1999 v61 i4 p84(8).

INFOTRAC COLLEGE EDITION has many interesting articles on the history of prisons and penal institutions. Read the following piece and then do a search on "prison history" to find other informative material: John W. Roberts, "A Century's Legacy: Five Critical Developments in the Evolution of American Prisons, 1900–2000," *Corrections Today,* August 2000 v62 i5 p102.

QUESTIONS

1. Would you allow a community correctional center to be built in your neighborhood? Why or why not?

2. Should pretrial detainees and convicted offenders be kept in the same institution? Explain.

3. What can be done to reduce correctional overcrowding?

4. Should private companies be allowed to run correctional institutions? Why or why not?

5. What are the drawbacks to shock incarceration?

NOTES

1. See David Fogel, *We Are the Living Proof,* 2d ed. (Cincinnati: Anderson, 1978); Andrew von Hirsch, *Doing Justice: The Choice of Punishments* (New York: Hill and Wang, 1976); R. G. Singer, *Just Deserts—Sentencing Based on* *Equality and Desert* (Cambridge, Mass.: Ballinger, 1979). The most widely cited source on the failure of rehabilitation is Robert Martinson; see Douglas Lipton, Robert Martinson, and Judith Wilks, *The Effectiveness of Correctional*

Treatment: A Survey of Treatment Evaluation Studies (New York: Praeger, 1975).

2. Ted Palmer, *Correctional Intervention and Research* (Lexington, Mass.: Lexington Books, 1978); Michael Gottfredson, "The Social Scientist and Rehabilitative Crime Policy," *Criminology* 20 (1982): 29–42.

3. Among the most helpful sources in developing this section were David Duffee, *Corrections: Practice and Policy* (New York: Random House, 1989); Harry Allen and Clifford Simonsen, *Correction in America*, 5th ed. (New York: Macmillan, 1989); Benedict Alper, *Prisons Inside-Out* (Cambridge, Mass.: Ballinger, 1974); Harry Elmer Barnes, *The Story of Punishment*, 2d ed. (Montclair, N.J.: Patterson-Smith, 1972); Gustave de Beaumont and Alexis de Tocqueville, *On the Penitentiary System in the United States and Its Applications in France* (Carbondale: Southern Illinois University Press, 1964); Orlando Lewis, *The Development of American Prisons and Prison Customs, 1776–1845* (Montclair, N.J.: Patterson-Smith, 1967); Leonard Orland, ed., *Justice, Punishment, and Treatment* (New York: Free Press, 1973); J. Goebel, *Felony and Misdemeanor* (Philadelphia: University of Pennsylvania Press, 1976); Georg Rusche and Otto Kircheimer, *Punishment and Social Structure* (New York: Russell & Russell, 1939); Samuel Walker, *Popular Justice* (New York: Oxford University Press, 1980); Graeme Newman, *The Punishment Response* (Philadelphia: Lippincott, 1978); David Rothman, *Conscience and Convenience* (Boston: Little, Brown, 1980).

4. Frederick Pollock and Frederic Maitland, *History of English Law* (London: Cambridge University Press, 1952).

5. Marvin Wolfgang, "Crime and Punishment in Renaissance Florence," *Journal of Criminal Law and Criminology* 81 (1990): 567–584.

6. Margaret Wilson, *The Crime of Punishment*, Life and Letters Series, no. 64 (London: Jonathan Cape, 1934), 186.

7. John Howard, *The State of the Prisons in England and Wales*, 4th ed. (1792; reprint ed., Montclair, N.J.: Patterson-Smith, 1973).

8. Alexis Durham III, "Newgate of Connecticut: Origins and Early Days of an Early American Prison," *Justice Quarterly* 6 (1989): 89–116.

9. Personal communication, Professor Norman Johnston, February 19, 2002. See his book *Forms of Constraint: A History of Prison Architecture* (Champagne: University of Illinois Press, 2000).

10. Johnston, *Forms of Constraint*, 29.

11. Dario Melossi and Massimo Pavarini, *The Prison and the Factory: Origins of the Penitentiary System* (Totowa, N.J.: Barnes & Noble, 1981).

12. Michel Foucault, *Discipline and Punish* (New York: Vintage Books, 1978).

13. Ibid., 16.

14. David Rothman, *The Discovery of the Asylum* (Boston: Little, Brown, 1970).

15. Orland, *Justice, Punishment, and Treatment*, 143.

16. Ibid., 144.

17. Walker, *Popular Justice*, 70.

18. Ibid., 71.

19. Beverly Smith, "Military Training at New York's Elmira Reformatory, 1880–1920," *Federal Probation* 52 (1988): 33–41.

20. Ibid.

21. See Z. R. Brockway, "The Ideal of a True Prison System for a State," in *Transactions of the National Congress on Penitentiary and Reformatory Discipline*, reprint ed. (Washington, D.C.: American Correctional Association, 1970), 38–65.

22. John Roberts, "A Century's Legacy: Five Critical Developments in the Evolution of American Prisons, 1900–2000," *Corrections Today* 62 (2000): 102–112.

23. This section leans heavily on Rothman, *Conscience and Convenience*.

24. Ibid., 23.

25. Ibid., 133.

26. 18 U.S.C., sec. 1761.

27. Barbara Auerbach, George Sexton, Franlin Farrow, and Robert Lawson, *Work in American Prisons: The Private Sector Gets Involved* (Washington, D.C.: National Institute of Justice, 1988), 72.

28. See, generally, Jameson Doig, *Criminal Corrections: Ideals and Realities* (Lexington, Mass.: Lexington Books, 1983).

29. Allen J. Beck, Jennifer Karberg, and Paige M. Harrison, *Prison and Jail Inmates at Midyear 2001* (Washington, D.C.: Bureau of Justice Statistics, 2002).

30. John Irwin, *The Jail: Managing the Underclass in American Society* (Berkeley: University of California Press, 1985).

31. Correctional Association of New York, *Prison and Jails: Hospitals of Last Resort* (New York: Correctional Association of New York, 1998).

32. Data in this and the following sections come from Beck, Karberg, and Harrison, *Prison and Jail Inmates at Midyear 2001*.

33. Caroline Wolf Harlow, *Prior Abuse Reported by Inmates and Probationers* (Washington, D.C.: Bureau of Justice Statistics, 1999).

34. Paula M. Ditton, *Mental Health and Treatment of Inmates and Probationers* (Washington, D.C.: Bureau of Justice Statistics, 1999).

35. Fred Heinzlemann, W. Robert Burkhart, Bernard Gropper, Cheryl Martorana, Lois Felson Mock, Maureen O'Connor, and Walter Philip Travers, *Jailing Drunk Drivers: Impact on the Criminal Justice System* (Washington, D.C.: National Institute of Justice, 1984).

36. Brandon Applegate, Ray Surette, and Bernard McCarthy, "Detention and Desistance from Crime: Evaluating the Influence of a New Generation of Jail on Recidivism," *Journal of Criminal Justice* 27 (1999): 539–548.

37. Ibid.

38. Data in this section come from Allen J. Beck and Paige M. Harrison, *Prisoners in 2000* (Washington, D.C.: Bureau of Justice Statistics, 2001).

39. Sidra Lea Gifford, *Justice Expenditure and Employment in the United States, 1999* (Washington, D.C.: Bureau of Justice Statistics, 2002).

40. Human Rights Watch, *Prison Conditions in the United States*; www.hrw.org/wr2k2/prisons.html.

41. "Suit Alleges Violations in California's 'Super-Max' Prison," *Criminal Justice Newsletter*, 1 September 1993, 2.

42. Allen J. Beck, Darrell Gilliard, Lawrence Greenfeld, Caroline Harlow, Thomas Hester, Louis Jankowski, Tracy Snell, James Stephan, and Danielle Morton, *Survey of Prison Inmates, 1991* (Washington, D.C.: Bureau of Justice Statistics, 1993).

43. Marc Mauer, "Men in American Prisons: Trends, Causes, and Issues," *Men's Studies Review* 9 (1992): 10–12.

44. Roger Peters, Paul Greenbaum, John Edens, Chris Carter, and Madeline Ortiz, "Prevalence of DSM-IV Substance Abuse and Dependence Disorders Among Prison Inmates," *American Journal of Drug and Alcohol Abuse* 24 (1998): 573–580.

45. Craig Hemmens and James Marquart, "Fear and Loathing in the Joint: The Impact of Race and Age on Inmate Support for Prison AIDS Policies," *Prison Journal* 78 (1998): 133–152.

46. Harlow, *Prior Abuse Reported by Inmates and Probationers,* 1.

47. Ditton, *Mental Health and Treatment of Inmates and Probationers,* 1.

48. James Anderson, Laronistine Dyson, and Jerald Burns, *Boot Camps: An Intermediate Sanction* (Lanham, Md.: University Press of America, 1999), 1–17.

49. Doris Layton Mackenzie, Robert Brame, David McDowall, and Claire Souryal, "Boot Camp Prison and Recidivism in Eight States," *Criminology* 33 (1995): 327–357.

50. Ibid., 328–329.

51. "New York Correctional Groups Praise Boot Camp Programs," *Criminal Justice Newsletter,* 1 April 1991, 4–5.

52. Velmer Burton, James Marquart, Steven Cuvelier, Leanne Fiftal Alarid, and Robert Hunter, "A Study of Attitudinal Change Among Boot Camp Participants," *Federal Probation* 57 (1993): 46–52.

53. Doris Layton Mackenzie, "Book Camp Prisons: Components, Evaluations, and Empirical Issues," *Federal Probation* 54 (1990): 44–52; see also "Boot Camp Programs Grow in Number and Scope," *NIJ Reports* (November/December 1990): 6–8.

54. See, for example, Dale Sechrest, "Prison 'Boot Camps' Do Not Measure Up," *Federal Probation* 53 (1989): 15–20.

55. Doris Layton Mackenzie and James Shaw, "The Impact of Shock Incarceration on Technical Violations and New Criminal Activities," *Justice Quarterly* 10 (1993): 463–487.

56. Mackenzie, "Boot Camp Prisons."

57. Doris Layton Mackenzie and Alex Piquero, "The Impact of Shock Incarceration Programs on Prison Crowding," *Crime and Delinquency* 40 (1994): 222–249.

58. Mackenzie, Brame, McDowall, and Souryal, "Boot Camp Prisons and Recidivism in Eight States," 352–353.

59. Correctional Research Associates, *Treating Youthful Offenders in the Community: An Evaluation Conducted by A. J. Reiss* (Washington, D.C.: Correctional Research Associates, 1966).

60. Kevin Krajick, "Not on My Block: Local Opposition Impedes the Search for Alternatives," *Corrections Magazine* 6 (1980): 15–27.

61. "Many State Legislatures Focused on Crime in 1995, Study Finds," *Criminal Justice Newsletter,* 2 January 1996, 2.

62. Richard Harding, "Private Prisons," in Michael Tonry, ed., *Crime and Justice: An Annual Edition* (Chicago: University of Chicago Press, 2001), 265–347.

63. Lonn Lanza-Kaduce, Karen Parker, and Charles Thomas, "A Comparative Recidivism Analysis of Releases from Private and Public Prisons," *Crime and Delinquency* 45 (1999): 28–47.

64. Ira Robbins, *The Legal Dimensions of Private Incarceration* (Chicago: American Bar Association, 1988).

65. Travis Pratt and Jeff Maahs, "Are Private Prisons More Cost-Effective Than Public Prisons? A Meta-Analysis of Evaluation Research Studies," *Crime and Delinquency* 45 (1999): 358–371.

66. Ahmed A. White, "Rule of Law and the Limits of Sovereignty: The Private Prison in Jurisprudential Perspective," *American Criminal Law Review* 38 (2001): 111–147.

67. Lawrence Travis, Edward Latessa, and Gennaro Vito, "Private Enterprise and Institutional Corrections: A Call for Caution," *Federal Probation* 49 (1985): 11–17.

68. Patrick Anderson, Charles Davoli, and Laura Moriarty, "Private Corrections: Feast or Fiasco," *Prison Journal* 65 (1985): 32–41.

69. Data in this section come from Bureau of Justice Statistics, *Prisoners, 1925–1981* (Washington, D.C.: Government Printing Office, 1982).

70. Paige Harrison and Allen Beck, *Prisoners in 2001* (Washington, D.C.: Bureau of Justice Statistics, 2002).

71. Todd Clear, *Harm in American Penology: Offenders, Victims, and Their Communities* (Albany: State University of New York Press, 1994).

72. Daniel Nagin, "Criminal Deterrence Research: A Review of the Evidence and a Research Agenda for the Outset of the 21st Century," in *Crime and Justice: An Annual Review,* ed. Michael Tonry (Chicago: University of Chicago Press, 1997).

73. For more on this issue, see Marcy Rasmussen Podkopacz and Barry Feld, "The End of the Line: An Empirical Study of Judicial Waiver," *Journal of Criminal Law and Criminology* 86 (1996): 449–492.

74. Thomas P. Bonczar and Allen J. Beck, *Lifetime Likelihood of Going to State or Federal Prison* (Washington, D.C.: Bureau of Justice Statistics, 1997).

75. Timothy Noah, "Prison Population Boom Sputters to Halt as States Lack Funds to House Criminals," *Wall Street Journal,* 3 February 1992, A7.

76. Andrew Lang Golub, Farrukh Hakeem, and Bruce Johnson, *Monitoring the Decline in the Crack Epidemic with Data from the Drug Use Forecasting Program, Final Report* (Washington, D.C.: National Institute of Justice, 1996).

13 Prison Life

Criminal Justice Links

Criminal Justice Viewpoints

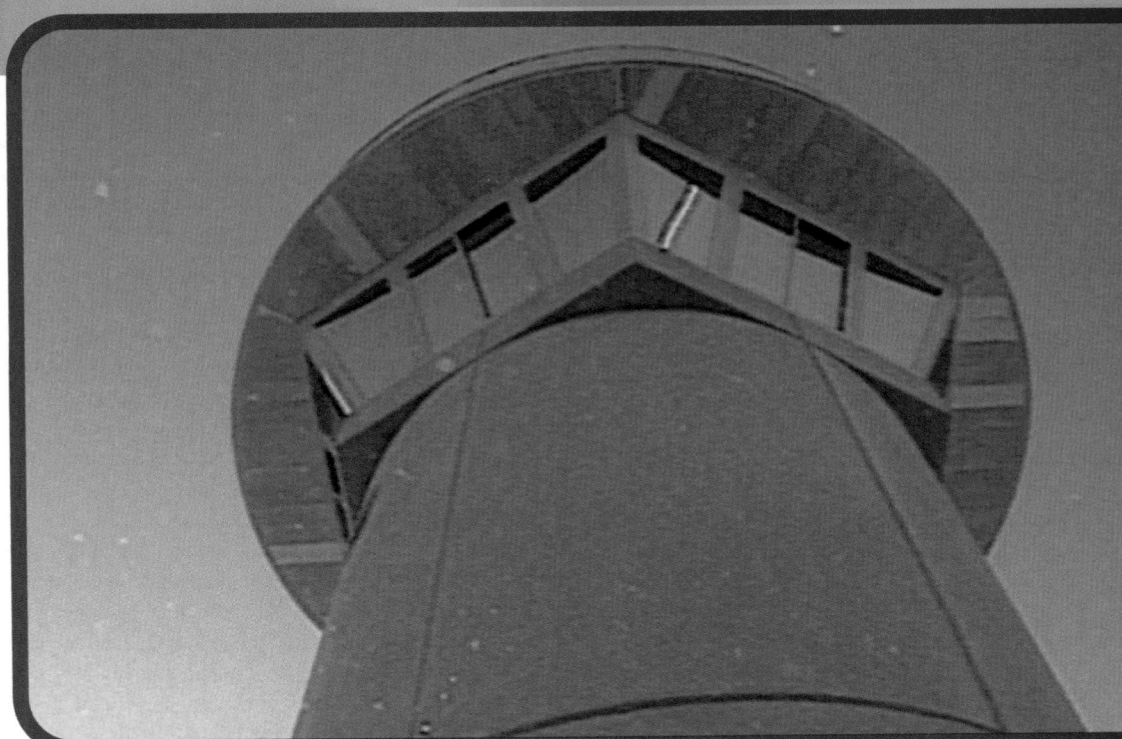

OVER THE CENTURIES, there has been significant debate over why people should be punished and what type of punishment is most appropriate to correct, treat, or deter criminal offenders. The style and purpose of criminal corrections have gone through many stages and have featured a variety of penal sanctions. Today, the most fearsome house of corrections is the notorious super-maximum-security prison.

Life is tough in the nation's fifty super-maximum-security prisons. Inmates are left alone in their cells for up to twenty-two to twenty-four hours a day. They have few visitors, they exercise alone, and they are kept under very high levels of surveillance and control. There is no hope of treatment or education; there are no jobs or vocational training. In other institutions, such harsh conditions are reserved for the most disruptive inmates, to be endured for a few days or even a week or two, but they are the daily condition of the typical prisoner in a "supermax" prison. Inmates must endure them for their entire sentences. According to watchdog group Amnesty International, many aspects of these living conditions violate international standards and some amount to cruel, inhuman, or degrading treatment. Prolonged isolation in conditions of reduced sensory stimulation can cause severe physical and psychological damage. Health experts who have examined prisoners in isolation have documented symptoms including acute anxiety and panic attacks, hallucinations, sudden violent outbursts, self-mutilation, difficulty with concentration and memory, deteriorating vision, and weight loss.

How can such inmates develop the ability to live with other human beings when they are eventually released and returned to society? And what effect does living under such harsh conditions have on their psyche? It is not surprising, considering these circumstances, that most inmates in all types of prisons are not rehabilitated, and a majority return to prison soon after their release. ■

 *To view the CNN video clip of this story, go to the book-specific Web site at* http://cj.wadsworth.com/siegel_essen4e.

"no-frills" policy   A correctional policy that stipulates that prisons are aimed at punishing and not coddling inmates. A "no-frills" orientation usually means a strict regimen of work and discipline, and reduced opportunities for recreation and education.

The spotty record of correctional rehabilitation is not surprising considering the overcrowded correctional system. A significant number of facilities are old, decrepit, archaic structures: of the prisons in this country, 25 were built before 1875, 79 between 1875 and 1924, and 141 between 1925 and 1949. In fact, some of the first prisons ever constructed, such as the Concord Reformatory in Massachusetts, are still in operation.

Although most prisons are classified as medium security, more than half of all inmates are held in large, maximum-security institutions. Despite the continuous outcry by penologists against the use of fortresslike prisons, institutions holding a thousand or more inmates still predominate. Prison overcrowding is a significant problem. As noted in Chapter 12, the prison system now holds over 1.3 million people. Many institutions are operating above stated capacity. Recreation and workshop space has been turned into dormitories housing thirty or more inmates in a single room. Most prison experts agree that a minimum of sixty square feet is needed for each inmate, but many prisons fail to reach this standard.

This giant system, designed to reform and rehabilitate offenders, is instead undergoing a crisis of massive proportions. Institutions are so overcrowded that meaningful treatment efforts are often a matter of wishful thinking; recidivism rates are shockingly high. Inmates are resentful of the deteriorated conditions, and correctional officers fear that the institution is ready to explode. In addition, some correctional administrators have begun to adopt a **"no-frills" policy** in prison, removing privileges and making prisons truly places of punishment. The no-frills movement is a response to lawmakers' claims that crime rates are high because inmates no longer fear imprisonment. This chapter presents a brief review of some of the most important issues confronting the nation's troubled correctional system.

Men Imprisoned

According to prevailing wisdom, prisons in the United States are **total institutions.** This means that inmates locked within their walls are segregated from the outside world, kept under constant scrutiny and surveillance, and forced to obey strict official rules to avoid facing formal sanctions. Their personal possessions are taken from them, and they must conform to institutional dress and personal appearance norms. Many human functions are strictly curtailed—heterosexual sex, friendships, family relationships, education, and participation in groups become privileges of the past.

total institution   A regimented, dehumanizing institution such as a prison in which like-situated people are kept in social isolation, cut off from the world at large.

Living in Prison

Inmates quickly learn what the term *total institution* really means. When they arrive at prison, they are stripped, searched, shorn, and assigned living quarters. Before they get there, though, their first experience occurs in a classification or reception center, where they are given a series of psychological and other tests and evaluated on the basis of their personality, background, offense history, and treatment needs. Based on the classification they are given, they will be assigned to a permanent facility. Hard-core, repeat, and violent offenders will go to the maximum-security unit; offenders with learning disabilities may be assigned to an institution that specializes in educational services; mentally disordered offenders will be held in a facility that can provide psychiatric care; and so on.

Once they arrive at the long-term facility, inmates may be granted a short orientation period and then given a permanent cell assignment in the general population. Due to overcrowding, they may be sharing a cell designed for a single inmate with one or more others. All previous concepts of personal privacy and dignity are soon forgotten. Personal losses include the deprivation of liberty, goods and services, heterosexual relationships, autonomy, and security.[1] Inmates may be subject to verbal and physical attack and threats, with little chance of legal redress. Although the criminal law applies to inmates as to any other citizen, it is rarely enforced within prison walls.[2] Therefore, part of living in prison involves learning to protect yourself and developing survival instincts.

Inmates in large, inaccessible prisons may find themselves physically cut off from families, friends, and associates. Visitors may find it difficult to travel great distances to see them; mail is censored and sometimes destroyed.

Adjusting to Prison Inmates go through a variety of attitude and behavior changes, or cycles, as their sentence unfolds. During the early part of their prison stay, inmates may become easily depressed while considering the long duration of the sentence and the loneliness and dangers of prison life. They must learn the ins and outs of survival in the institution: Which persons can be befriended, and which are best avoided? Who will grant favors and for what repayment? Some inmates will request that regular payments be made to them in exchange for protection from homosexual rape and beatings. To avoid victimization, inmates must learn to adopt a lifestyle that shields them from victimization.[3] They must discover areas of safety and danger. Some learn how to fight back to prove they are not people who can be taken advantage of. While some kill their attackers and get even longer sentences, others join cliques that provide protection and the ability to acquire power within the institution.

Inmates may find that some prisoners have formed cliques, or groups, based on ethnic backgrounds or personal interests; they are also likely to encounter Mafia-like or racial terror groups that must be dealt with. Inmates may find that power in the prison is shared by correctional officers and inmate gangs; the only way to avoid being beaten and raped may be to learn how to beat and rape.[4] If they are weak and unable to defend themselves, new inmates may find that they are considered "punks"; if they ask a guard for help, they are labeled a "snitch." After that, they may spend the rest of their sentence in protective custody, sacrificing the "freedom of the yard" and rehabilitation services for personal protection.[5]

Despite all these hardships, many inmates learn to adapt to the prison routine. Each prisoner has his own method of coping, he may stay alone, become friends with another inmate, join a group, or seek the advice of treatment personnel. Inmates may soon learn that their lifestyle and activities can contribute to their being victimized by more aggressive inmates: the more time they spend in closely guarded activities, the less likely they are to become the victims of violence; the more they isolate themselves from others who might protect them, the greater their vulnerability to attack; the more visitors they receive, the more likely they are to be attacked by fellow inmates jealous of their relationships with the outside world.[6]

New inmates must learn to deal with the guards and other correctional personnel; these relationships will determine whether the inmates do "hard time" or "easy time." For example, when inmates housed in open institutions are sent out to work on roads or to do farm work, they may be forced to wear stun belts for security while they do their outdoor activities. Once confined in a stun belt, the inmate can receive a shock of fifty thousand volts and three to four milliamps for a period of eight seconds. Although not fatal, the shock is very painful, and victims are immediately incapacitated. Burns, which may take months to heal, may develop where the electrodes touch the skin above the left kidney. Critics charge that stun guns are brutal and can be used by correctional workers to terrorize or torture inmates whom they dislike or find offensive.[7]

Regardless of adaptation style, the first stage of the inmate's prison cycle is marked by a growing awareness that he can no longer depend on his traditional associates for help and support and that, for better or worse, the institution is a new home to which he must adjust. Unfortunately for the goal of rehabilitation, the predominant emotion that inmates must confront is boredom. The absence of

Sexual abuse is a constant danger in prison. Read about the threat at Christopher Man and John Cronan, "Forecasting Sexual Abuse in Prison: The Prison Subculture of Masculinity as a Backdrop for 'Deliberate Indifference,'" *Journal of Criminal Law and Criminology,* Fall 2001 p127(59), on InfoTrac College Edition.

Erik Freeland/*U.S. News & World Report*

Counselor Charlie Doty talks to an inmate in a Kentucky prison. Counseling and treatment are standard fare in most prisons. Whether prison-based rehabilitation can succeed in reducing recidivism rates is the subject of constant debate. The so-called failure of rehabilitation has encouraged harsh penal measures such as mandatory life sentences for "three-time losers."

anything constructive to do, the forced idleness, is what is often so frustrating and so damaging.[8]

Conflict and Hustling Early adjustment to prison life involves becoming familiar with and perhaps participating in the black market, the hidden economy of the prison—the *hustle*. Hustling provides inmates with a source of steady income and the satisfaction that they are beating the system.[9] Hustling involves sales of such illegal commodities as drugs (uppers, downers, pot), alcohol, weapons, or illegally obtained food and supplies. When prison officials crack down on hustled goods, it merely serves to drive up the price—giving hustlers greater incentive to promote their activities. Drugs and other contraband are smuggled into prison by visitors, carried in by inmates who are out on furlough or work-release programs, or bought from corrupt prison officials. Control of the prison drug trade is often the spark that creates violence and conflict.

Inmates must also learn to deal with the racial conflict that is a daily fact of life. Prisoners tend to segregate themselves, and if peace is to reign in the institution, they learn to stay out of each other's way. Often, racial groupings are quite exact; for example, Hispanics will separate themselves according to their national origin (Mexican, Puerto Rican, Colombian, and so on). Because racial disparity in sentencing is common in many U.S. courts, prisons are one place where minorities often hold power.

Inmates may find that the social support of inmate peers can make incarceration somewhat less painful. They may begin to take stock of their situation and enter into educational or vocational training programs if they are available. Many turn to religion. They heed the inmate grapevine to determine what the parole board considers important when deciding to grant community release. They may become more politically aware in response to the influence of other inmates, and the personal guilt they may have felt may be shifted to society at large. Why should they be in prison when those who are equally guilty go free? They learn the importance of money and politics. Eventually, they may be called on by new arrivals to aid them in adapting to the system.

Even in the harsh prison environment, inmates may learn to find a niche for themselves. They may be able to find a place, activity, or group in which they can feel comfortable and secure.[10] An inmate's niche is a kind of insulation from the pains of imprisonment, enabling him to cope and providing him with a sense of autonomy and freedom. Finding a niche may insulate inmates from attack, and research in fact indicates that prison victimization may be less prevalent than commonly believed. Not surprisingly, the victims of prison violence seem less psychologically healthy, more fearful than nonvictims, and less able to avoid the pains of imprisonment.[11]

Of course, not all inmates learn to cope. Some inmates repeatedly violate institutional rules. One reason is that many inmates both in the United States and abroad suffer from serious psychological and emotional problems. A recent review of inmate mental health in twelve countries including the United States found that almost 4 percent of the male inmates suffered from psychotic illnesses, 10 percent were diagnosed with major depression, and 65 percent had a personality disorder, including 47 percent with antisocial personality disorder. Prisoners were several times more likely to have psychosis and major depression, and about ten times more likely to have antisocial personality disorder, than the general population.[12] The prevalence of psychological problems in the inmate population makes coping problematic.

Predicting who will become an institutional troublemaker is difficult, but rule-breaking behavior has been associated with being a younger inmate with a low IQ, possessing numerous juvenile convictions, being a repeat offender, and having victimized a stranger. Inmates who have limited intelligence and little self-control may not be able to form adaptive coping mechanisms and manage the stress of being in prison.[13]

The Inmate Social Code

For many years, criminal justice experts maintained that inmates formed their own world with a unique set of norms and rules, known as the **inmate subculture**.[14] A significant aspect of the inmate subculture was a unique **inmate social code**, unwritten guidelines that expressed the values, attitudes, and type of behavior that older inmates demanded of young ones. Passed on from one generation of inmates to another, the inmate social code represented the values of interpersonal relations in the prison.

National attention was first drawn to the inmate social code and subculture by Donald Clemmer's classic book *The Prison Community*, in which he presented a detailed sociological study of life in a maximum-security prison.[15] Referring to thousands of conversations and interviews, as well as to inmate essays and biographies, Clemmer was able to identify a unique language, or *argot*, that prisoners use. In addition, Clemmer found that prisoners tend to group themselves into cliques on the basis of such personal criteria as sexual preference, political beliefs, and offense history. He found complex sexual relationships in prison and concluded that many heterosexual men will turn to homosexual relationships when faced with long sentences and the loneliness of prison life.

Clemmer's most important contribution may have been his identification of the **prisonization** process. This he defined as the inmate's assimilation into the existing prison culture through acceptance of its language, sexual code, and norms

inmate subculture The loosely defined culture that pervades prisons and has its own norms, rules, and language.

inmate social code Unwritten guidelines that express the values, attitudes, and types of behavior that older inmates demand of young ones. Passed on from one generation of inmates to another, the inmate social code represents the values of interpersonal relations within the prison.

prisonization Assimilation into the separate culture in the prison that has its own set of rewards and behaviors. This loosely defined culture that pervades prisons has its own norms, rules, and language. The traditional culture is now being replaced by a violent gang culture.

Exhibit 13.1 Elements of the inmate social code

1. *Don't interfere with inmates' interests.* Within this area of the code are maxims concerning serving the least amount of time in the greatest possible comfort. For example, inmates are warned never to betray another inmate to authorities; in other words, grievances must be handled personally. Other aspects of the noninterference doctrine include "Don't be nosy," "Don't have a loose lip," "Keep off the other inmates' backs," and "Don't put another inmate on the spot."

2. *Don't lose your head.* Inmates are also cautioned to refrain from arguing, quarreling, or engaging in other emotional displays with fellow inmates. The novice may hear such warnings as "Play it cool," and "Do your own time."

3. *Don't exploit inmates.* Prisoners are warned not to take advantage of one another—"Don't steal from cons," "Don't welsh on a debt," and "Be right."

4. *Be tough and don't lose your dignity.* Although Rule 2 forbids conflict, once it starts an inmate must be prepared to deal with it effectively and thoroughly. Maxims include, "Don't cop out," "Don't weaken," and "Be tough; be a man."

5. *Don't be a sucker.* Inmates are cautioned not to make fools of themselves and support the guards or prison administration over the interest of the inmates—"Be sharp."

Source: Gresham Sykes, *The Society of Captives* (Princeton, N.J.: Princeton University Press, 1958).

of behavior. Those who become the most "prisonized" will be the least likely to reform on the outside.

Using Clemmer's work as a jumping-off point, a number of prominent sociologists have set out to explore more fully the various roles in the prison community. The most important principles of the dominant inmate culture are listed in Exhibit 13.1.

Although some inmates violate the code and exploit their peers, the "right guy" is someone who uses the inmate social code as his personal behavior guide. He is always loyal to his fellow prisoners, keeps his promises, is dependable and trustworthy, and never interferes with inmates who are conniving against the officials.[16] The right guy does not go around looking for a fight, but he never runs away from one; he acts like a man.

Some prison experts believe that the prison experience transforms people and forces them to accept the inmate culture, but others argue that the culture is actually imported from the outside world.[17] In other words, inmate culture is affected as much by the values of newcomers and events on the outside as it is by traditional inmate values. Both socialization and importation may also possibly help define the way inmates adapt to the prison culture. For example, inmates who view violence as an acceptable alternative before entering prison are the ones most likely to adopt the inmate social code.[18]

The effects of prisonization may be long-term and destructive. Many inmates become hostile to the legal system, learning to use violence as a means of solving problems and to value criminal peers.[19] For some this change may be permanent; for others it is temporary, and they may revert to their "normal" life after release.

The New Inmate Culture

The importation of outside values into the inmate culture has had a dramatic effect on prison life. Although the "old" inmate subculture may have been harmful because its norms and values insulated the inmate from change efforts, it also helped create order in the institution and prevented violence among the inmates. People who violated the code and victimized others were sanctioned by their peers. An understanding developed between guards and inmate leaders: the guards would let the inmates have things their own way; the inmates would not let things get out of hand and draw the attention of the administration.

© Nina Berman/Aurora

Even in the harsh prison environment, inmates may learn to find a niche for themselves. They may be able to find a place, activity, or group in which they can feel comfortable and secure. An inmate's niche is a kind of insulation from the pains of imprisonment, enabling him to cope and providing him with a sense of autonomy and freedom.

The old system may be dying or already dead in most institutions. The change seems to have been precipitated by the black power movement in the 1960s and 1970s. Black inmates were no longer content to play a subservient role and challenged the power of established white inmates. As the black power movement gained prominence, racial tension in prisons created divisions that severely altered the inmate subculture. Older, respected inmates could no longer cross racial lines to mediate disputes. Predatory inmates could victimize others without fear of retaliation. Consequently, more inmates than ever are now assigned to protective custody for their own safety.

In the new culture, African-American and Latino inmates are much more cohesively organized than whites.[20] Their groups sometimes form out of religious or political affiliations, such as the Black Muslims; out of efforts to combat discrimination in prison, such as the Latino group La Familia; or from street gangs, such as the Vice Lords or Gangster Disciples in the Illinois prison system and the Crips in California. Where white inmates have successfully organized, it is in the form of a neo-Nazi group called the Aryan Brotherhood. Racially homogeneous gangs are so cohesive and powerful that they are able to supplant the original inmate code with one of their own.

To read about the California prison system, go to
www.cdc.state.ca.us/index.htm

Women Imprisoned

Before 1960 few women were in prison. Women's prisons were relatively rare and were usually an outgrowth of male institutions. Only four institutions for women were built between 1930 and 1950; in comparison, thirty-four women's prisons were constructed during the 1980s as crime rates soared.

At the turn of the twentieth century, female inmates were viewed as morally depraved people who flouted conventional rules of female behavior. The treatment of white and African-American women differed significantly. In some states, white women were placed in female-only reformatories designed to improve their deportment; black women were placed in male prisons, where they were put on chain gangs and subject to beatings.[21]

As 2002 began, 93,031 women were in state or federal prisons—6.6 percent of all prison inmates. Since 1995 the number of male prisoners has grown

24 percent (reaching 1,313,000 in 2001), while the number of female prisoners has increased 36 percent.[22]

The female offender population has increased so rapidly for a number of reasons. Women have accelerated their crime rate at a faster pace than men. The get-tough policies that produced mandatory and determinate sentencing statutes also helped reduce the judicial discretion that has traditionally benefited women. As Meda Chesney-Lind points out, women are swept up in the get-tough movement and no longer receive the benefits of male chivalry. The use of sentencing guidelines means that such factors as family ties and employment record, two elements that usually benefitted women during sentencing, can no longer be considered by judges.[23] Chesney-Lind notes that judges seem willing once again to view female offenders as "depraved" and outside the ranks of "true womanhood."[24]

Female Institutions

State jurisdictions have been responding to the influx of female offenders into the correctional system by expanding the facilities for housing and treating them.[25] Women's prisons tend to be smaller than those housing male inmates.[26] Although some female institutions are strictly penal, with steel bars, concrete floors, and other security measures, the majority are nonsecure institutions similar to college dormitories and group homes in the community. Women's facilities, especially those in the community, commonly offer a great deal of autonomy to inmates and allow them to make decisions affecting their daily lives.

However, like men's prisons, women's prisons suffer from a lack of adequate training, health, treatment, and educational facilities. Psychological counseling often takes the form of group sessions conducted by laypeople, such as correctional officers. Most trained psychologists and psychiatrists restrict themselves to such activities as conducting intake classifications and court-ordered examinations and prescribing mood-controlling medication. Although many female inmates are parents and had custody of their children before incarceration, little effort is made to help them develop better parenting skills. And as Table 13.1 shows, while most female (and male) inmates have at least one child, less than a quarter actually get an annual visit. Who takes care of these children while their mothers are incarcerated? Most children of incarcerated women are placed with their fa-

Table 13.1   Incarcerated parents and their children

In 1999, an estimated 721,500 state and federal prisoners were parents to 1,498,800 children under age 18.
- About 40 percent of fathers and 60 percent of mothers in state prison reported weekly contact with their children.
- A majority of both fathers (57%) and mothers (54%) in state prison reported never having a personal visit with their children since admission.
- More than 60 percent of parents in state prison reported being held more than 100 miles from their last place of residence.

Minor Children	Percent of Prisoners, 1999	
	State	Federal
Any	55.4%	63.0%
1	23.8	24.0
2	15.8	18.5
3 or more	15.8	20.5
None	44.6%	37.0%
Estimated number of minor children, 1999	1,324,900	173,900

Type of Contact	Percent of State Inmate Parents Reporting Monthly Contact with Their Children, 1999	
	Male	Female
Any	62.4%	78.4%
Phone	42.0%	53.6%
Mail	49.9	65.8
Visits	21.0	23.8

Source: Christopher Mumola, *Incarcerated Parents and Their Children* (Washington, D.C.: Bureau of Justice Statistics, 2000).

ther, grandparent, other relative, or a family friend. About 10 percent wind up in foster homes or state facilities.

Job-training opportunities are also a problem. Where vocational training exists, it is in areas with limited financial reward, hindering adjustment on release. Female inmates, many of whom were on the economic margin before their incarceration began, find little room for improvement during their prison experience.[27] Surveys also indicate that the prison experience does little to prepare women to reenter the workforce after their sentence has been completed. Gender stereotypes still shape vocational opportunities.[28] Female inmates are still being trained for "women's roles," such as child rearing, and not given the programming to make successful adjustments in the community.[29]

Female Inmates

Like their male counterparts, female inmates are young (most are under age thirty), minority group members, unmarried, undereducated (more than half are high school dropouts), and either unemployed or underemployed.

Incarcerated women also have had a troubled family life. Significant numbers were at-risk children, products of broken homes and the welfare system; over half have received welfare at some time during their adult lives. Many claim to have been physically or sexually abused at some point in their lives. This pattern continued in adult life: many female inmates were victims of domestic violence. It is not surprising that many display psychological problems. One recent survey found that 4 percent of incarcerated women in twelve nations including the United States had psychotic illnesses, 12 percent suffered from depression, and 42 percent had a personality disorder, including 21 percent with antisocial personality disorder.[30]

A significant number of female inmates report having substance abuse problems. About three-fourths have used drugs at some time in their lives, and almost half were involved with addictive drugs, such as cocaine, heroin, or PCP. There is actually little difference in major drug use between male and female offenders when measured over their life span or at the time of their current arrest. The incarceration of so many women who are low criminal risks yet face a high risk of exposure to HIV (human immunodeficiency virus, which causes AIDS) and other health issues because of their prior history of drug abuse presents a significant problem. For example, one recent study of incarcerated women found that one-third of the sample reported that before their arrest they had traded sex for money or drugs; 24 percent of the women reported trading sex for money or drugs "weekly or more often."[31] Such risky behavior significantly increases the likelihood of their carrying the AIDS virus or other sexually transmitted diseases.

The picture that emerges of the female inmate is troubling. After a lifetime of emotional turmoil, physical and sexual abuse, and drug use, it seems improbable that overcrowded, underfunded correctional institutions can forge a dramatic turnaround in the behavior of at-risk female inmates.

To learn more about the problems faced by women in prison, go to InfoTrac College Edition and read Susie Day, "Cruel But Not Unusual: The Punishment of Women in U.S. Prisons," *Monthly Review*, July 2001 v53 i3 p42.

Sexual Exploitation   There are numerous reports of female prisoners being sexually abused and exploited by male correctional workers who either use brute force or psychological coercion to gain sexual control over inmates.[32] Staff-on-inmate sexual misconduct covers a wide range of behaviors, from lewd remarks to voyeurism to assault and rape. A recent survey by the federal government's General Accounting Office (GAO) found that the federal government, forty-one states, and the District of Columbia have been forced to pass laws criminalizing some types of staff sexual misconduct in prisons. The GAO's in-depth analysis of the three correctional systems with the largest number of female inmates—the federal Bureau of Prisons, the California Department of Corrections, and the Texas Department of Criminal Justice—found that sexual misconduct persists despite efforts to correct problems and train staff.[33]

Cynthia Hardin in the prison yard at Gatesville, Texas. Although there are far fewer women in prison than men, the rate of female incarceration is accelerating faster.

Criminologist Meda Chesney-Lind finds that the movement to eliminate gender inequality has triggered an increase in sexual abuse in male-dominated institutions. She cites the example of New York State, which created a policy of videotaping male inmates while they were being strip-searched; for the sake of gender equality, the state instituted a policy of also taping women's strip searches. The videotaping was done while male officers were in the vicinity, and the female inmates sued and won damages when they suspected that the videos were being watched by prison officials. Such sexually charged situations are particularly damaging to women who have a history of sexual and physical abuse. Because male correctional officers now are commonly assigned to women's prisons, there have also been major scandals involving the sexual exploitation and rape of female inmates. Few if any of these incidents are reported, and perpetrators rarely go to trial. Institutional workers cover for each other, and women who file complaints are offered little protection from vengeful guards.[34]

Adapting to the Female Institution

Daily life in women's prisons differs somewhat from that in male institutions. For one thing, unlike male inmates, women usually do not present an immediate physical danger to staff and fellow inmates. Relatively few engage in violent behavior, and incidents of inmate-initiated sexual aggression, so common in male institutions, are rare in women's prisons.[35] Recent research conducted in the California prison system finds that few female inmates either experience the violent atmosphere common in male institutions or suffer the racial and ethnic conflict and divisiveness.[36] Although female inmates may experience less discomfort than males, that does not mean their experience is a bed of roses. When Mark Pogrebin and Mary Dodge interviewed former female inmates who had done time in a western state they discovered that an important element of prison life for many women was dealing with fear and violence. Some reported that violence in women's prisons is common and that many female inmates undergo a process of socialization fraught with danger and volatile situations.[37]

The rigid, anti-authority inmate social code found in many male institutions does not exist in female institutions.[38] Confinement for women, however, may produce severe anxiety and anger because of separation from families and loved ones and the inability to function in normal female roles. Unlike men, who direct their anger outward, female prisoners may turn to more self-destructive acts to cope with their problems. Female inmates are more likely than males to mutilate their own bodies and attempt suicide. For example, one common practice among female inmates is self-mutilation, or "carving." This ranges from simple scratches to carving the name of their boyfriend on their body or even complex statements or sentences ("To mother, with hate").[39]

Another form of adaptation to prison used by women is the make-believe family. This group contains masculine and feminine figures acting as fathers and mothers; some even act as children and take on the role of brother or sister. Formalized marriages and divorces may be conducted. Sometimes one inmate holds multiple roles, so that a "sister" in one family may "marry" and become the "wife" of another inmate. It is estimated that about half of all female inmates are members of make-believe families.[40]

Why do make-believe families exist? Experts suggest that they provide the warm, stable relationships otherwise unobtainable in the prison environment. People both in and out of prison have needs for security, companionship, affection, attention, status, prestige, and acceptance that can be filled only by having primary group relationships. Friends fill many of these needs, but the family better represents the ideal or desire for these things in a stable relationship.

Correctional Treatment Methods

Almost every prison facility uses some mode of treatment for inmates. This may come in the form of individual or group therapy programs or educational or vocational training.

Despite good intentions, rehabilitative treatment inside prison walls is extremely difficult to achieve. Trained professional personnel usually command high salaries, and most institutions do not have sufficient budgets to staff therapeutic programs adequately. Usually, a large facility may have a single staff psychiatrist or a few social workers. A second problem revolves around the philosophy of *less eligibility,* which has been interpreted to mean that prisoners should always be treated less well than the most underprivileged law-abiding citizen. Translated into today's terms, less eligibility usually involves the question "Why should inmates be treated to expensive programs denied to the average honest citizen?" Enterprising state legislators use this argument to block expenditures for prison budgets, and some prison administrators may actually agree with them.

Finally, correctional treatment is hampered by the ignorance surrounding the practical effectiveness of one type of treatment program over another. What constitutes proper treatment has not yet been determined, and studies evaluating treatment effectiveness have suggested that few, if any, of the programs currently used in prisons actually produce significant numbers of rehabilitated offenders.

This section presents a selected number of therapeutic methods that have been used nationally in correctional settings and identifies some of their more salient features.

Individual and Group Counseling

Prison inmates typically suffer from a variety of cognitive and psychosocial deficits, such as poor emotional control, social skills, and interpersonal problem solving; these deficits are often linked to long-term substance abuse. Modern counseling programs help them to control emotions (for example, understanding why they feel the way they do; how not to get too nervous or anxious; solving their problems creatively), to communicate with others (for example, understanding what people tell them; communicating clearly when they write), to deal with legal concerns (keeping out of legal trouble; avoiding breaking laws), to manage general life issues (finding a job; dealing with difficult co-workers; being a good parent), and to develop and maintain social relationships (having good relations with others; making others happy; making others proud).[41] To achieve these goals, correctional systems use a variety of intensive individual and group techniques, including behavior modification, aversive therapy, milieu therapy, reality therapy, transactional analysis, and responsibility therapy.

Treating the Special-Needs Inmate

special-needs inmate Those correctional clients who require special care and treatment, such as the elderly, mentally ill, drug-addicted, or AIDS-infected.

One of the challenges of correctional treatment is to care for **special-needs inmates.** These individuals have a variety of social problems. Some are mentally ill but have been assigned to prison because the state has toughened its insanity laws. Others suffer mental problems developed during their imprisonment. An additional 1 to 6 percent of the inmate population is mentally retarded. Treating the mentally ill inmate has required the development and use of new therapies in the prison environment. Although some critics warn of the overuse of "chemical straitjackets"—psychotropic medications—to keep disturbed inmates docile, prison administrators have been found to have a genuine concern for these special-needs inmates.[42]

Restrictive crime control policies have also produced another special-needs group: elderly inmates who require health care, diets, and work and recreational opportunities that are different from those of the general population. Some correctional systems have responded to the growing number of elderly inmates by creating facilities tailored to their needs.[43] It is now estimated that more than twenty-two thousand inmates are over age fifty-five, an increase of more than 40 percent since 1990.[44]

To read how corrections departments are trying to treat drug-dependent inmates, go to
www.ojp.usdoj.gov/docs/psrsa.txt

The Drug-Dependent Inmate Another special-needs group in prison includes drug-dependent inmates. Although most institutions attempt to provide drug and alcohol treatment, these efforts are often inadequate.

Although the ideal drug treatment has yet to be identified, experimental efforts around the country include counseling sessions, instruction in coping strategies, employment counseling, and strict security measures featuring random urinalysis.

The AIDS-Infected Inmate The AIDS-infected prisoner is another acute special-needs inmate. Two groups of people at high risk of contracting HIV are intravenous drug users who share needles and males who engage in homosexual sex, two lifestyles common in prison. Although the numbers are constantly changing, the rate of HIV infection among state and federal prisoners has stabilized at around 2 percent and there are about twenty-five thousand HIV-infected inmates.

Correctional administrators have found it difficult to arrive at effective policies to confront AIDS. Although all state and federal jurisdictions do some AIDS testing, only eighteen states and the federal Bureau of Prisons conduct mass screenings of all inmates. Most states test inmates only if there are significant indications that they are HIV-positive. About 40 percent of all state prison inmates have never been tested for AIDS.

Most correctional systems are now training staff about AIDS. Educational programs for inmates are often inadequate because administrators are reluctant to give them information on the proper cleaning of drug paraphernalia and safe sex (since both drug use and homosexual sex are forbidden in prison).

Educational and Vocational Programs

Besides treatment programs stressing personal growth through individual analysis or group process, inmate rehabilitation is also pursued through vocational and educational training. Although these two kinds of training sometimes differ in style and content, they can also overlap when, for example, education involves practical, job-related study.

The first prison treatment programs were in fact educational. A prison school was opened at the Walnut Street Jail in 1784. Elementary courses were offered in New York's prison system in 1801 and in Pennsylvania's in 1844. An actual school system was established in Detroit's House of Corrections in 1870, and the Elmira Reformatory opened a vocational trade school in 1876. Today, most institutions provide some type of educational program. At some prisons, inmates can obtain a high school diploma or a general educational development (GED) certificate through equivalency exams. Other institutions provide an actual classroom education, usually staffed by certified teachers employed full-time at the prison or by part-time teachers who also teach full-time at nearby public schools.

Folsom Prison inmate Mathew Briggs looks over a computer tech manual at the prison's computer repair workshop in Folsom, California. Briggs is one of the dozens of prison inmates throughout the state who spend forty hours a week taking classes, studying to get their standardized computer certification, and refurbishing computers that will be sent to schools statewide.

The number of hours devoted to educational programs and the quality and intensity of these efforts vary greatly. Some are full-time programs employing highly qualified and concerned educators, whereas others are part-time programs without any real goals or objectives. Although worthwhile attempts are being made, prison educational programs often suffer from inadequate funding and administration. The picture is not totally bleak, however. In some institutions, programs have been designed to circumvent the difficulties inherent in the prison structure. They encourage volunteers from the community and local schools to tutor willing and motivated inmates. Some prison administrators have arranged flexible schedules for inmate students and actively encourage their participation in these programs. In several states, statewide school districts serving prisons have been created. Forming such districts can make better-qualified staff available and provide the materials and resources necessary for meaningful educational programs.

Every state correctional system also has some job-related services for inmates. Some have elaborate training programs inside the institution, whereas others have instituted prerelease and postrelease employment services. Inmates who hope to obtain parole need to participate in prison industry. Documenting a history of stable employment in prison is essential if parole agents are to convince prospective employers that the ex-offender is a good risk, and postrelease employment is usually required for parole eligibility.[45]

A few of the more important work-related services are discussed in the following sections.

Basic Prison Industries Prisoners are normally expected to work within the institution as part of their treatment program. Aside from saving money for the institution, prison work programs are supposed to help inmates develop good habits and skills. Most prominent among traditional prison industries are those designed to help maintain and run the institution and provide services for other public or state facilities, such as mental hospitals. These include the following:

- *Food services.* Inmates are expected to prepare and supply food for prisoners and staff. These duties include baking bread, preparing meat and vegetables, and cleaning and maintaining kitchen facilities.
- *Maintenance.* The buildings and grounds of most prisons are cared for by inmates. Electrical work, masonry, plumbing, and painting are all inmate activities. Of a less skilled nature are such duties as garbage collection, gardening, and cleaning.
- *Laundry.* Most prisons have their own inmate-run laundries. Quite often, prison laundries also furnish services to other state institutions.
- *Agriculture.* In western and southern states, many prisons farm their own land. Dairy herds, crops, and poultry are all managed by inmates. The products are used in the prison and in other state institutions.

Vocational Training Most institutions also provide vocational training programs. In New York, for example, more than forty-two trade and technical courses are provided in organized training shops under qualified civilian instructors. Some of these courses not only benefit the inmate but also provide services for the institution. New York has trained inmates to become dental laboratory technicians; this program provides dentures for inmates and saves the state money. Another New York program trains inmates to become optical technicians and has the added benefit of providing eyeglasses for inmates. Other New York correctional training programs include barber training, computer programming, auto mechanics, auto body work, and radio and television repair. The products of most of these programs save the taxpayers money, and the programs provide the inmates with practical experience. Many other states offer this type of vocational programming.

Prison education is important in Europe. Read about some efforts there at
http://users.tibus.com/epea/

Despite the promising aspects of such programs, they have also been seriously criticized: inmates often have trouble finding skill-related, high-paying jobs on their release; equipment in prisons is often secondhand, obsolete, and hard to come by; some programs are thinly disguised excuses for prison upkeep and maintenance; and unions and other groups resent the intrusion of prison labor into their markets.

Work Release   To supplement programs stressing rehabilitation via in-house job training or education, more than forty-four states have attempted to implement **work release** or **furlough** programs. These allow deserving inmates to leave the institution and hold regular jobs in the community.

Inmates enrolled in work release may live at the institutions at night while working in the community during the day. However, security problems (for example, contraband may be brought in) and the usual remoteness of prisons often make this arrangement difficult. More typical is the extended work release, where prisoners are allowed to remain in the community for significant periods of time. To help inmates adjust, some states operate community-based prerelease centers where inmates live while working. Some inmates may work at their previous jobs, while others seek new employment.

Like other programs, work release has its good and bad points. Inmates are sometimes reluctantly received in the community and find that certain areas of employment are closed to them. Citizens are often concerned about prisoners "stealing" jobs or working for lower than normal wages; consequently, such practices are prohibited by federal Public Law 89-176, which controls the federal work release program.

On the other hand, inmates gain many benefits from work release, including the ability to maintain work skills, to maintain community ties, and to make an easier transition from prison to the outside world. For those who have learned a skill in the institution, work release offers an excellent opportunity to test out a new occupation. For others, the job may be a training situation in which new skills are acquired. A number of states have reported that few work release inmates abscond while in the community.

Helping Female Offenders   Critics have charged that educational and vocational programs are especially deficient in female institutions, which typically have offered only remedial-level education or occasional junior college classes. Female inmates were not provided with the tools needed to succeed on the outside because the limited vocational training stressed what was considered traditional "women's work": cosmetology, secretarial work, and food services.

Today, forty-seven states have instituted some sort of vocational training programs for women; the other three states provide supplemental services for their few female inmates. Although the traditional vocation of sewing is the most common industrial program, correctional authorities are beginning to teach data processing, and female inmates are involved in such other industries as farming, printing, telemarketing, and furniture repair. Clearly, greater efforts are needed to improve the quality of work experiences for female inmates.

Private Prison Enterprise   Opposition from organized labor ended the profitability of commercial prison industries, but a number of interesting efforts have been made to vary the type and productivity of prison labor.[46] The federal government helped put private industry into prisons when it approved the Free Venture Program in 1976. Seven states, including Connecticut, South Carolina, and Minnesota, were given grants to implement private industries inside prison walls. This successful program led to the Percy Amendment (1979), federal legislation that allowed prison-made goods to be sold across state lines if the projects complied with

work release   A prison treatment program that allows inmates to be released during the day to work in the community and returned to prison at night.

furlough   A correctional policy that allows inmates to leave the institution for vocational or educational training, for employment, or to maintain family ties.

Although some critics want to end work release, the program is supported by the ACLU:
www.aclu.org/news/2002/
n042402b.html

Some employers have created programs for ex-offenders. Ronald Cook works at the Bellagio Hotel in Las Vegas. A former inmate of a Nevada boot camp, he took a job as a cook's assistant and has worked his way up the ladder. The opportunity has helped him turn his life around.

To learn more about prison industry, use the phrase as a key term on InfoTrac College Edition.

strict rules, such as making sure unions were consulted and preventing manufacturers from undercutting the existing wage structure.[47] The new law authorized a number of prison industry enhancement pilot projects. These were certified as meeting the Percy Amendment operating rules and were therefore free to ship goods out of state; by 1987, fifteen projects had been certified.

Today, private prison industries have used a number of models. One approach, the *state-use model,* makes the correctional system a supplier of goods and services that serves state-run institutions. For example, the California Prison Industry Authority (PIA) is an inmate work program that provides work assignments for approximately seven thousand inmates and operates seventy service, manufacturing, and agricultural industries in twenty-three prisons. These industries produce a variety of goods and services, including flags, printing services, signs, binders, eyewear, gloves, office furniture, clothing, and cell equipment. PIA products and services are available to government entities, including federal, state, and local government agencies. Court-ordered restitutions or fines are deducted from the wages earned by PIA inmates and are transferred to the Crime Victims' Restitution Fund. PIA inmates receive wages between 30 cents and 95 cents per hour, before deductions.[48] In another approach, the free-enterprise model, private companies set up manufacturing units on prison grounds or purchase goods made by inmates in shops owned and operated by the corrections department. In the corporate model, a semi-independent business is created on prison grounds whose profits go to the state government and inmate laborers.[49] Despite widespread publicity, the partnership between private enterprise and the prison community has been limited to a few experimental programs. However, it is likely to grow in the future.

Postrelease Programs   A final element of job-related programming involves helping inmates obtain jobs before they are released and keep them once they are on the outside. A number of correctional departments have set up employment services designed to ease the transition between institution and community. Employment program staff assess inmates' backgrounds to determine their abilities, interests, goals, and capabilities. They also help them create job plans essential to receiving early release (parole) and successfully reintegrating into the community. Some programs maintain community correctional placements in sheltered environments that help inmates bridge the gap between institutions and the outside world. Services include job placement, skill development, family counseling, and legal and medical assistance.

Inmate Self-Help

Recognizing that the probability of failure on the outside is acute, inmates have attempted to organize self-help groups to provide the psychological tools needed to prevent recidivism.[50] Membership in these programs is designed to improve inmates' self-esteem and help them cope with common problems, such as alcoholism, narcotics abuse, or depression.

Some groups are chapters of common national organizations, such as Alcoholics Anonymous. Other groups are organized along racial and ethnic lines. For example, there are chapters of the Chicanos Organizados Pintos Aztlan, the Afro-American Coalition, and the Native American Brotherhood in prisons stretching from California to Massachusetts. These groups try to establish a sense of brotherhood so that members will work together for individual betterment. They hold literacy, language, and religion classes and offer counseling, legal advice, and pre-release support. Ethnic groups seek ties with outside minority organizations, such as the National Association for the Advancement of Colored People (NAACP), the Black Muslims, the Urban League, La Raza, and the American Indian Movement, as well as the religious and university communities.

A third type of self-help group helps inmates find the strength to make it on the outside. The best known is the Fortune Society, which claims more than seven thousand members. Staffed by ex-offenders, the Fortune Society provides counseling, education, and vocational training to parolees. It even helps supervise offenders in the community in alternative-to-incarceration programs. They run a substance-abuse treatment unit that provides individual and group counseling to clients sent by the New York City Department of Probation, provide HIV-prevention information, and work as an advocate group to improve prison conditions.[51]

Can Rehabilitation Work?

Despite the variety and number of treatment programs in operation, questions remain about their effectiveness. In their oft-cited research, Robert Martinson and his associates (1975) found that a majority of treatment programs were failures.[52] Martinson found in a national study that, with few exceptions, rehabilitative efforts seemed to have no appreciable effect on recidivism; his research produced a "nothing works" view of correctional treatment.

Martinson's work was followed by efforts showing that some high-risk offenders were more likely to commit crimes after they had been placed in treatment programs than before the onset of rehabilitation efforts.[53] A slew of reviews have claimed that correctional treatment efforts aimed at youthful offenders provide little evidence that rehabilitation can occur within correctional settings. Evidence is scant that treatment efforts—even those that include vocational, educational, and mental health services—can consistently lower recidivism rates.[54]

The so-called failure of correctional treatment has helped promote a conservative view of corrections in which prisons are considered places of incapacitation and punishment, not treatment centers. Current policies stress eliminating the nonserious offender from the correctional system while increasing the probability that serious, violent offenders will be incarcerated and serve longer sentences. This view supports the utility of mandatory and determinate sentences for serious offenders and the simultaneous use of intermediate sanctions, such as house arrest, restitution, and diversion, to limit the nonserious offender's involvement in the system.

Although the concept of correctional rehabilitation is facing serious challenges, many experts still believe strongly in the rehabilitative ideal.[55] Recent analysis of education, vocation, and work programs indicate that they may be able to lower recidivism rates and increase postrelease employment.[56] Inmates who have completed higher levels of education find it easier to gain employment upon release and consequently are less likely to recidivate over long periods.[57] Programs that teach interpersonal skills, provide individual counseling, and make use of behavioral modification techniques have produced positive results both in the community and inside correctional institutions.[58] Other researchers have shown through careful analysis that, although not all programs are successful for all inmates, many treatment programs are effective and that participants, especially younger clients, have a better chance of success on the outside than those who forgo treatment. If administered properly, correctional treatment programs have success rates in the magnitude of 20 to 35 percent.[59] Exhibit 13.2 describes the characteristics associated with the most successful programs.

Exhibit 13.2 **What works in correctional rehabilitation?**

Rehabilitation is effective in reducing the criminal behavior of at least some offenders. The evidence suggests that correctional treatment programs follow some basic principles in order to reduce recidivism:

- They must be carefully designed to target the specific characteristics and problems of offenders that can be changed in treatment (dynamic characteristics) and those that are predictive of the individual's future criminal activities (criminogenic), such as antisocial attitudes and behavior, drug use, and anger responses.
- They must be implemented in a way that is appropriate for the participating offenders and must employ therapeutic techniques that are known to work (that is, they are designed by knowledgeable individuals, programming is provided by appropriately educated and experienced staff, adequately evaluated programs are used) and require offenders to spend a reasonable length of time in the program considering the changes desired (they deliver sufficient dosage).
- Offenders who are at the highest risk of recidivism must be placed in the most intensive programs.
- Programs must use treatment methods based on theoretical models such as behaviorism, social learning, or cognitive-behavioral theories of change that emphasize positive reinforcement for prosocial behavior. They must also be individualized as much as possible.

Rehabilitation programs that are successful tend to have the following characteristics:

- They are structured and focused.
- They use multiple treatment components, focus on developing skills, and employ behavioral (including cognitive-behavioral) methods, with reinforcements for clearly identified, overt behaviors, as opposed to nondirective counseling focusing on insight, self-esteem, or disclosure.
- They provide substantial, meaningful contact between the treatment personnel and the participant.
- They are of sufficient integrity to ensure that what is delivered is consistent with the planned design.

Among the programs that work best are the following:

- Intensive, behavior-based programs that target drug use, a behavior that is clearly associated with criminal activities
- Programs that combine in-prison therapeutic communities with follow-up community treatment
- Cognitive-behavioral therapy
- Programs that focus on changing participants' thoughts and attitudes, either through moral development (moral reconation) or problem solving (reasoning and rehabilitation)
- Non-prison-based sex-offender treatment programs, which offer treatment in a local hospital or other residential setting
- Vocational education programs provided in prison or residential settings

Research on vocational education programs demonstrates that these programs are effective in reducing the recidivism of offenders:

- Multicomponent correctional industry programs
- Community employment programs

Sources: Lawrence W. Sherman, Denise Gottfredson, Doris MacKenzie, John Eck, Peter Reuter, and Shawn Bushway, *Preventing Crime: What Works, What Doesn't, What's Promising: A Report to the United States Congress* (Washington, D.C. National Institute of Justice); Doris Layton MacKenzie, "Evidence-Based Corrections: Identifying What Works," *Crime and Delinquency* 46 (2000): 457–471.

Treatment Problems   While the research is promising, correctional treatment is too often hampered by a lack of funds and facilities. Even where programs exist, there has been low participation of inmates (both men and women) in work, vocational, mental health, substance abuse, and parent counseling programs.[60] For example, one federal survey found that although more than 80 percent of inmates report using drugs and almost 60 percent reported using drugs in the month before their arrest, only one-third of state inmates and one-quarter of federal prisoners said they had participated in drug or alcohol treatment or other substance abuse programs since admission. Reported levels of drug treatment since admission were lower for both state (10 percent) and federal (9 percent) prisoners than those reported in 1991 (25 percent and 16 percent, respectively).[61] Similarly, as Table 13.2 shows, about 40 percent of inmates diagnosed as being mentally ill receive no treatment in state prison; 60 percent of mentally ill jail inmates receive no treatment.

Table 13.2	Treatment of mentally ill inmates	
	Mentally Ill Inmates Receiving Mental Health Treatment	
	State Prison	**Jail**
Any treatment	60.5%	40.9%
Medication	50.1	34.1
Counseling	44.1	16.2

Source: Paula M. Ditton, *Mental Health and Treatment of Inmates and Probationers* (Washington, D.C.: Bureau of Justice Statistics, 1999).

Guarding the Institution

Control of a prison is a complex task. On the one hand, a tough, high-security environment may meet the goals of punishment and control but fail to reinforce positive behavior changes. On the other hand, too liberal an administrative stance can lower staff morale and place inmates in charge of the institution.

For many years, prison guards were viewed as ruthless people who enjoyed their positions of power over inmates, fought rehabilitation efforts, were racist, and had a "lock psychosis" developed from years of counting, numbering, and checking on inmates. This view has changed in recent years. Correctional officers are now viewed as public servants who are seeking the security and financial rewards of a civil service position.[62] Most are in favor of rehabilitation efforts and do not hold any particular animosity toward the inmates. The correctional officer has been characterized as a "people worker" who must be prepared to deal with the problems of inmates on a personal level and also as a member of a complex bureaucracy who must be able to cope with its demands.

Corrections officers play a number of roles in the institution. They supervise cell houses, dining areas, shops, and other facilities as well as perch up on the walls, armed with rifles, to oversee the yard and prevent escapes. Corrections officers also sit on disciplinary boards and escort inmates to hospitals and court appearances.

The greatest problem faced by correctional officers is the duality of their role: maintainers of order and security and advocates of treatment and rehabilitation. Added to this basic dilemma is the changing inmate role. In earlier times, corrections officers could count on inmate leaders to help them maintain order, but now they are faced with a racially charged atmosphere in which violence is a way of life. Today, correctional work is filled with danger, tension, boredom, and little evidence that efforts to help inmates lead to success. Research indicates that next to police officers, the correctional worker is the most high-risk job in the United States and abroad.[63] And unlike police officers, correctional officers apparently do not form a close-knit subculture with unique values and a sense of intergroup loyalty. Correctional officers experience alienation and isolation from inmates, the administration, and each other. Interestingly, this sense of alienation seems greatest in younger officers; evidence exists that later in their careers officers enjoy a revival of interest in their work and take great pride in providing human services to inmates.[64] It is not surprising that correctional officers perceive significant levels of stress related to such job factors as lack of safety, inadequate career opportunities, and work overload.[65]

Many state prison authorities have developed training programs to prepare guards for the difficulties of prison work. Guard unions have also commonly been formed to negotiate wages and working conditions with corrections departments.

Female Correctional Officers

The issue of female correctional officers in male institutions comes up repeatedly. Today, an estimated five thousand women are assigned to all-male institutions.[66] The employment of women as guards in close contact with male inmates has spurred many questions of privacy and safety and a number of legal cases. In one important case, *Dothard v. Rawlinson* (1977), the U.S. Supreme Court upheld Alabama's refusal to hire female correctional officers on the grounds that it would put them in significant danger from the male inmates.[67] Despite such setbacks, women now work side by side with male guards in almost every state, performing the same duties. Research indicates that discipline has not suffered because of the inclusion of women in the guard force. Sexual assaults have been rare, and more negative attitudes have been expressed by the female guards' male peers than by inmates. Most commentators believe that the presence of female guards can have an important beneficial effect on the self-image of inmates and improve the guard-inmate working relationship.

Interestingly, little research has been conducted on male correctional officers in female prisons, although almost every institution housing female offenders employs male officers. What research there is indicates that male officers are generally well received, and although there is evidence of sexual exploitation and pri-

© 2002 AP/Wide World Photos

Tatum Lodish, a prison guard, opens a gate in the Berks County Prison near Reading, Pennsylvania. Lodish graduated in 1997 with a bachelor's degree in criminal justice and the intention of working with troubled teenagers. But for the past eight months, the twenty-three-year-old has been a correctional officer at the prison.

vacy violations, female inmates generally believe that the presence of male correctional officers helps create a more natural environment and reduce tension. Both male and female inmates are concerned about opposite-sex correctional workers intruding on their privacy, such as being given assignments in which they may observe inmates dressing or bathing or in which they may come into physical contact, such as during searches or pat-downs.

The difficulties faced by correctional officers, both male and female, has been captured in a new book called *Newjack* (slang for a rookie officer), which is the subject of the following Criminal Justice and the Media feature.

Prison Violence

On August 9, 1973, Stephen Donaldson, a Quaker peace activist, was arrested for trespassing after participating in a pray-in at the White House. Sent to a Washington, D.C., jail for two nights, Donaldson was gang-raped approximately sixty times by numerous inmates. Donaldson later became president of Stop Prisoner Rape, a nonprofit organization that advocates for the protection of inmates from sexual assault and offers support to victims. On July 18, 1996, at the age of forty-nine, Stephen Donaldson died from infections complicated by AIDS, after he contracted HIV through prisoner rapes.[68]

Conflict, violence, and brutality are sad but ever-present facts of institutional life. Violence can involve individual conflict: inmate versus inmate, inmate versus staff, staff versus inmate. As this chapter has already indicated, one common threat is sexual assault. Research has shown that prison rapes usually involve a victim who is viewed as weak and submissive and a group of aggressive rapists who can dominate the victim through their collective strength. Sexual harassment leads to fights, social isolation, fear, anxiety, and crisis. Nonsexual assaults may stem from an aggressor's desire to shake down the victim for money and personal favors, may be motivated by racial conflict, or may simply be used to establish power within the institution.

Violence can also involve large groups of inmates, such as the famous Attica riot in 1971, which claimed thirty-nine lives, or the New Mexico State Penitentiary riot of February 1980, in which the death toll was thirty-three. More than three hundred prison riots have occurred since the first one in 1774, 90 percent of them since 1952.[69]

A number of factors can spark such damaging incidents. They include poor staff-inmate communications, destructive environmental conditions, faulty classification, and promised but undelivered reforms. The 1980 New Mexico State Penitentiary riot drew national attention to the problem of prison riots. The prison was designed for 800 but actually held 1,135 prisoners; conditions of overcrowding, squalor, poor food, and lack of medical treatment abounded. The state government had been called on to improve guard training, physical plant quality, and relief from overcrowding but was reluctant to spend the necessary money.

Although revulsion over the violent riots in New Mexico and the earlier riot in New York's Attica prison led to calls for prison reform, prison violence has continued unabated. About seventy-five to one hundred inmates are killed by their peers each year in U.S. prisons, six or seven staff members are murdered, and some 120 suicides are recorded.

Individual Violence

What are the causes of prison violence? There is no single explanation for either collective or individual violence, but theories abound.[70] One position holds that inmates are often violence-prone individuals who always used force to get their

To read about the history of correctional violence, go to InfoTrac College Edition and access Curtis R. Blakely, "A History of Correctional Violence: An Examination of Reported Causes of Riots and Disturbances," *Corrections Today*, February 1999 v61 i1 p80(1).

Criminal Justice and the Media

Newjack

The daily operations of criminal justice are not only portrayed on TV and in the movies but are also the focus of the print media. Although the number of novels focusing on police work are too numerous to count, there is also an extensive "true crime" literature. One unique addition to this literature was recently produced by Ted Conover, a well-known author (*Whiteout, Coyotes*), who wanted to write about what it meant to be a correctional officer in a maximum-security prison.

Conover soon found out that there is no way a civilian (and especially a writer) would be allowed to enter a prison and be given the needed access to inmates and correctional personnel. So, to get the data he needed, he applied to become a correctional officer, was given a position, and underwent seven weeks of training at the Correctional Officer Training Academy in Albany, New York. After graduation he was ready, so he thought, to become a *newjack*—a rookie correctional officer. He was assigned as a gallery officer, one who oversees a prison pod in Sing Sing Prison. This infamous 170-year-old institution, one of the first built in the United States, is the kind of maximum-security institution where men instantly size each other up to see who can be dominated and who will dominate.

On his first day on the job, Conover was asked to stand before a camera, holding up a piece of paper showing his name and Social Security number. When he asked why, he was told that these pictures were "hostage shots," kept on file in case a correctional officer was injured or taken

hostage, at which time the photographs would be released to the press. At first he laughed, but then realized that "hostage shots" aren't all that funny and that correctional officers may be injured or killed at any moment. It came as no surprise that while some of his colleagues were hard-working and sincere, others were brutal and vicious.

Conover soon learned that correctional officers can't show a trace of fear, because it attracts abuse from inmates and a loss of respect among fellow officers. Inmates will grant their respect if the correctional officer is firm but willing to make an exception to the rules once in a while. If there are too many exceptions, however, the respect vanishes as the residents start taking advantage. He found that inmates are described as the "lowest of the low," while officers describe themselves as "warehousers" and "babysitters." Some recollected what they called the "good old days," when they could beat up inmates at will; some suggested that there are still isolated institutions where a correctional officer can beat up an inmate with immunity.

Conover could feel the aggression, frustration at the procedures, and perpetually tense interaction between inmates and correctional personnel that permeated the institution. Officers bragged how at some institutions unruly inmates are savagely beaten and that they wouldn't mind doing the same at Sing Sing. Horrified at first, he soon realized that he himself had a violent side that he never knew existed and learned the tricks that could be used to protect himself when his aggression emerged. He learned to yell "stop resisting" as he roughed up an inmate in order to

own way; in addition, many of them suffer from personality disorders. Recent research shows that among institutionalized offenders, psychopathy is the strongest predictor of violent recidivism and indifferent response to treatment.[71] In the crowded, dehumanizing world of the prison, it is not surprising that people with extreme psychological distress may resort to violence to dominate others.[72]

A second view is that prisons convert people to violence by their inhuman conditions, including overcrowding, depersonalization, and the threat of sexual assault. Even in the most humane prisons, life is a constant put-down, and prison conditions are a threat to the inmates' sense of self-worth; violence is an expected consequence of these conditions.

Violence may also result because prisons lack effective mechanisms to enable inmate grievances against either prison officials or other inmates to be handled fairly and equitably. Prisoners who complain about other inmates are viewed as "rats" or "snitches" and are marked for death by their enemies. Similarly, complaints or lawsuits filed against the prison administration may result in the inmate being placed in solitary confinement—"the hole." The frustration caused by living in a prison in a climate that promotes violence—that is, one that lacks physical security and adequate mechanisms for resolving complaints and where the code of silence protects violators—is believed to promote individual violence by inmates who might otherwise be controlled.

avoid brutality charges; he was shown how logbooks could be fudged in order to conceal undeserved discipline. He considered some of his duties demeaning and ugly, especially body cavity searches; he was attacked and punched in the head by an inmate and forced to wrestle with powerful muscle-bound men. All for about $23,000 per year.

Conover experienced what he considered to be the essence of correctional life: unending tedium interrupted by a sudden adrenaline rush when an "incident" occurs. He began to understand why correctional officers develop a feeling that they are in confinement themselves. It is a consequence of dealing day and night with men who can do almost nothing for themselves on their own and who depend on their gallery officer to take care of their most personal needs. Instead of feeling tough and in control, at the end of the day the correctional officer feels like a waiter who has served a hundred tables or a mother with too many dependent children. Because of their dependence, the inmates are often made to feel like infants, and those who do not take to it well may revert to violence to ease their frustration. The potential for violence in the prison setting is so great that it makes even routine assignments seem dangerous. Yet Conover was astonished that there were not even more violent incidents considering that eighteen hundred rapists, murderers, and assaulters were trapped together in this hellish environment.

Conover found that some inmates are intelligent and sensitive. One, named Lawson, pointed out that the United States is now planning prisons that will be built in twelve years. By planning that far into the future, he told Conover, the government is planning on imprisoning people who are now children; instead of spending millions on future prisons, he asked, why not spend thousands on education and social services to ensure that these children will not be just another statistic? Conover could not think of an adequate answer.

Probably most disturbing to Conover was the effect the institution had on his personal life. Though he got to go home to his wife and children, he could not leave his prison experiences at the "gate"; prison gets into your skin, he says. If you stayed long enough, "some of it seeped into your soul." His wife was troubled by the changes she saw in him and begged him to quit; he in turn had to beg her to let him finish out the year. If a man like Conover could experience such personal stress, knowing that he was a writer incognito on temporary assignment, what must the stress be like for professional officers who do not have the luxury of another career waiting over the horizon?

Critical Thinking

Can a writer truly experience what it is like to be a prison guard when he is only playing a role, one that he can step out of any time he chooses? If a writer wanted to experience college life and enrolled at your school, would he or she truly begin to understand what it means to be a student?

● InfoTrac College Edition Research

 To learn more about the life of a correctional worker use the term as a subject guide on Infotrac College Edition.

Source: Ted Conover, *Newjack: Guarding Sing Sing* (New York: Random House, 2000).

Collective Violence

There are two distinct theories of the cause of collective violence. The first, called the *inmate-balance theory,* suggests that riots and other forms of collective action occur when prison officials make an abrupt effort to take control of the prison and limit freedoms. Crackdowns occur when officials perceive that inmate leaders have too much power and take measures to control their illicit privileges, such as gambling or stealing food.[73]

According to the *administrative-control theory,* collective violence may also be caused by prison mismanagement, lack of strong security, and inadequate control by prison officials. Poor management may inhibit conflict management and set the stage for violence. Repressive administrations give inmates the feeling that nothing will ever change, that they have nothing to lose, and that violence is the only means for change.

Overcrowding caused by the rapid increases in the prison population has also been linked to prison violence. As the prison population continues to climb, unmatched by expanded capacity, prison violence may increase.

It is possible that in the future prison officials may lean on technology to control the prison environment. This issue is discussed in the following Criminal Justice and Technology box.

Criminal Justice and Technology

Technocorrections: Contemporary Correctional Technology

Contemporary technological forces are converging with the forces of law and order to create *technocorrections*. The correctional establishment—the managers of the jail, prison, probation, and parole systems—and their sponsors in elected office are seeking more cost-effective ways to increase public safety as the number of people under correctional supervision continues to grow. A correctional establishment that takes advantage of all the potential offered by the new technologies to reduce the costs of supervising criminal offenders and minimize the risk they pose to society will define the field of technocorrections. The following paragraphs describe some recent advances in detail.

Ground-Penetrating Radar

Special Technologies Laboratories (STL) of Santa Barbara, California, has developed a new technology called ground-penetrating radar (GPR), which is able to locate tunnels inmates use to escape. GPR works almost like an old-fashioned Geiger counter, held in the hand and swept across the ground by an operator. Instead of detecting metal, however, the GPR system detects changes in ground composition, including voids such as those created by a tunnel.

Heartbeat Monitoring

The weakest security link in any prison has always been the *sally port,* where trucks unload their supplies and where trash and laundry are taken out of the facility. Over the years, inmates have hidden in loads of trash, old produce, laundry—any possible container that might be exiting the facility. Now it is possible to prevent escapes by monitoring inmates' heartbeats! The Advanced Vehicle Interrogation and Notification System (AVIAN)—being marketed by Geo Vox Security of Houston, Texas—works by identifying the shock wave generated by the beating heart, which couples to any surface the body touches. The system takes in all the frequencies of movement, such as the expansion and contraction of the engine or rain hitting the roof, and determines if there is a pattern similar to a human heartbeat.

Satellite Monitoring

Pro Tech Monitoring Inc. of Palm Harbor, Florida, has developed a system to monitor offenders by satellite using cellular technology combined with the federal government's global positioning system of satellites. While in the community, each offender wears an ankle bracelet and carries a three-pound portable tracking device (a so-called smart box), programmed with information on his or her geographical restrictions. For instance, a sex offender may be forbidden to come within five miles of his victim's home or workplace, or a pedophile may be barred from getting close to a school. A satellite monitors the geographic movements of the offender, either in real time or by transmitting the information to the smart box for later retrieval. The smart box and the ankle bracelet sound an alarm when boundaries are breached, alerting potential victims.

Sticky Shocker

This is a less-than-lethal projectile that uses stun gun technology to temporarily incapacitate a person at stand-off range. The Sticky Shocker is a low-impact, wireless projectile fired from compressed gas or powder launchers and is accurate to within ten meters.

Backscatter Imaging System for Concealed Weapons

This system utilizes a backscatter imager to detect weapons and contraband. The primary advantage of this device over current walk-through portals is that it can detect nonmetallic as well as metallic weapons. It uses low-power X rays equal to about five minutes of exposure to the sun at sea level. Although these X rays penetrate clothing, they do not penetrate the body.

Body-Scanning Screening System

This is a stationary screening system to detect nonmetallic weapons and contraband in the lower body cavities. It uses simplified magnetic resonance imaging (MRI) as a noninvasive alternative to X-ray and physical body cavity searches. The stationary screening system makes use of first-generation medical MRI.

Transmitter Wristbands

Developed by Technology Systems International, these wristbands broadcast a unique serial number via radio frequency every two seconds so that antennas throughout the prison can pick up the signals and pass the data via a local area network to a central monitoring station PC. The wristbands can sound an alert when a prisoner gets close to the perimeter fence or when an inmate doesn't return from a furlough on time; they can even tag gang members and notify guards when rivals get into contact with each another.

Personal Health Status Monitor

It may be getting easier to monitor inmates who are at risk of committing suicide. Correctional authorities are now developing a personal health status monitor that, in its initial form, will use acoustics to track the heartbeat and respiration of a person in a cell. The monitor does not actually need to be located on the person; because it is the size of two packs of cigarettes, it can be placed on the ceiling or just outside a cell. The device is similar to ones that are installed inside infant cribs in hospitals.

More advanced health status monitors are now being developed that can monitor five or more vital signs at once, and based on the combination of findings, can produce an assessment of an inmate's state of health. This more advanced version of the personal health status monitor may take another decade to develop, but the current version may already help save lives that would otherwise be lost to suicide.

All-in-One Drug Detection Spray

For the past several years Mistral Security of Bethesda, Maryland, has marketed drug detection sprays for marijuana, methamphetamines, heroin, and cocaine. A specially made piece of paper is wiped on a surface; when sprayed with one of the aerosol sprays, it changes color within fifteen seconds if as little as four to twenty micrograms of the drugs are present. A new detection device is now being developed that uses a single spray that will test for all drugs at once. The test paper will turn different colors depending on which drugs the spray contacts, and several positive results will be possible with a single use of the spray.

Radar Vital Signs Monitor/Radar Flashlight

Researchers at Georgia Tech have developed a handheld radar flashlight that can detect the respiration of a human in a cell from behind a twenty-centimeter hollow-core concrete wall or an eight-inch cinder block wall. It instantly gives the user a bar-graph readout that is viewed on the apparatus itself. Other miniature radar detectors give users heartbeat and respiration readings. The equipment is expected to be a useful tool in searches for people who are hiding, because the only thing that successfully blocks its functioning is a wall made of metal or conductive material. The radar detectors can also be used in telemedicine

and for individuals on whom electrodes would be difficult to apply. Future applications for this technology include advanced lie detectors and using the human heartbeat as a biometric for personnel identification.

Personal Alarm Location System

It is now possible for prison employees to carry a tiny transmitter linking them with a computer in a central control room. In an emergency, they can hit an alarm button and transmit to a computer that automatically records whose distress button has been pushed. An architectural map of the facility instantly appears on-screen, showing the exact location of the unfortunate staff member. Although sensors are only placed inside the prison, the Personal Alarm Location System (PALS) works up to three hundred feet outside prison walls. It locates within a range of four meters inside the room where the duress button is pushed, and also locates signals in between floors. The PALS system also has an option that tracks the movement of employees who have pressed their duress buttons. If an officer moves after hitting the duress button, the red dot that represents him or her on the computer screen will move as well. The PALS system, now being used in six correctional institutions in the United States and Canada, is scheduled to be adopted in others.

Future Technology

Not yet employed but in the planning stage are the following technological breakthroughs:

- *The angel chip.* This microchip would be implanted underneath the skin of the user and would contain vital and identifying information. To avoid future legal entanglements, it is being developed by Sun Microsystems with the assistance of the American Civil Liberties Union.
- *Noninvasive drug detection.* A swab or patch being developed; when placed on the skin, it absorbs perspiration and detects the presence of illegal drugs.

Sources: Mark Robert, "Big Brother Goes Behind Bars," *Fortune,* 146 (September 30, 2002): 44; Tony Fabelo, *Technocorrections: The Promises, the Uncertain Threats,* Sentencing & Corrections: Issues for the 21st Century Series (Washington, D.C.: National Institute of Justice, 2000); Irwin Soonachan, "The Future of Corrections: Technological Developments Are Turning Science Fiction into Science Fact," *Corrections Today* 62 (2000): 64–66; Steve Morrison, "How Technology Can Make Your Job Safer," *Corrections Today* 62 (2000): 58–60; Gabrielle deGroot, "Hot New Technologies," *Corrections Today* 59 (1997): 60–63.

Prisoners' Rights

Before the early 1960s it was accepted that on conviction an individual forfeited all rights not expressly granted by statutory law or correctional policy; inmates were civilly dead. The U.S. Supreme Court held that convicted offenders should expect to be penalized for their misdeeds and that part of their punishment was the loss of freedoms ordinary citizens take for granted.

One reason why inmates lacked rights was that state and federal courts were reluctant to intervene in the administration of prisons unless the circumstances of a case clearly indicated a serious breach of the Eighth Amendment protection against cruel and unusual punishment. This judicial policy is referred to as the **hands-off doctrine.** The courts used three basic justifications for their neglect of prison conditions:

1. Correctional administration was a technical matter best left to experts rather than to courts ill-equipped to make appropriate evaluations.
2. Society as a whole was apathetic to what went on in prisons, and most individuals preferred not to associate with or know about the offenders.
3. Prisoners' complaints involved privileges rather than rights. Prisoners were considered to have fewer constitutional rights than other members of society.[74]

hands-off doctrine The legal practice of allowing prison administrators a free hand to run the institution even if correctional practices violate inmates' constitutional rights; ended with the onset of the prisoners' rights movement in the 1960s.

As the 1960s drew to a close, the hands-off doctrine was eroded. Federal district courts began seriously considering prisoners' claims concerning conditions in the various state and federal institutions and used their power to intervene on behalf of the inmates. In some ways, this concern reflected the spirit of the times, which saw the onset of the civil rights movement, and subsequently was paralleled in such areas as student rights, public welfare, mental institutions, juvenile court systems, and military justice.

Beginning in the late 1960s, such activist groups as the NAACP Legal Defense Fund and the American Civil Liberties Union's National Prison Project began to search for appropriate legal vehicles to bring prisoners' complaints before state and federal courts. The most widely used device was the federal Civil Rights Act, 42 U.S.C. 1983:

> *Every person who, under color of any statute, ordinance, regulation, custom, or usage of any State or Territory subjects, or causes to be subjected, any citizen of the United States or other person within the jurisdiction thereof to the deprivation of any rights, privileges, or immunities secured by the Constitution and laws shall be liable to the party injured in an action at law, suit in equity, or other proper proceeding for redress.*

The legal argument went that, as U.S. citizens, prison inmates could sue state officials if their civil rights were violated—for example, if they were the victims of racial or religious discrimination.

The U.S. Supreme Court first recognized the right of prisoners to sue for civil rights violations in cases involving religious freedom brought by the Black Muslims. This well-organized group had been frustrated by prison administrators who feared its growing power and desired to put limits on its recruitment activities. In the 1964 case of *Cooper v. Pate,* however, the Supreme Court ruled that inmates who were being denied the right to practice their religion were entitled to legal redress under 42 U.S.C. 1983.[75] Although *Cooper* applied to the narrow issue of religious freedom, it opened the door to providing other rights for inmates.

The subsequent prisoners' rights crusade, stretching from 1960 to 1980, paralleled the civil rights and women's movements. Battle lines were drawn between prison officials hoping to maintain their power and resenting interference by the courts and inmate groups and their sympathizers, who used state and federal courts as a forum for demanding better living conditions and personal rights.

Each decision handed down by the courts was viewed as a victory for one side or the other; this battle continues today.

Substantive Rights

Through a slow process of legal review, the courts have granted inmates a number of **substantive rights** that have significantly influenced the entire correctional system. The most important of these rights are discussed in the following sections.

Access to Courts, Legal Services, and Materials Without the ability to seek judicial review of conditions causing discomfort or violating constitutional rights, the inmate must depend solely on the slow and often insensitive administrative mechanism of relief within the prison system. Therefore, the right of easy access to the courts gives inmates hope that their rights will be protected during incarceration. Courts have held that inmates are entitled to have legal materials available and be provided with assistance in drawing up and filing complaints. Inmates who help others, so-called **jailhouse lawyers,** cannot be interfered with or harassed by prison administrators.

Freedom of the Press and of Expression Correctional administrators traditionally placed severe limitations on prisoners' speech and expression. For example, they read and censored inmate mail and restricted their reading material. With the lifting of the hands-off doctrine, courts have consistently ruled that only when a compelling state interest exists can prisoners' First Amendment rights be modified; correctional authorities must justify the limiting of free speech by showing that granting it would threaten institutional security. In a 2001 case, *Shaw v. Murphy*, the Supreme Court ruled that inmates do not have a right to correspond with other inmates even if it concerns legal advice. If prison administrators believe such correspondence undermines prison security, the First Amendment rights of inmates can be curtailed.[76]

Freedom of Religion Freedom of religion is a fundamental right guaranteed by the First Amendment. In general, the courts have ruled that inmates have the right to assemble and pray in the religion of their choice, but that religious symbols and practices that interfere with institutional security can be restricted. Administrators can draw the line if religious needs become cumbersome or impossible to carry out for reason of cost or security. Granting special privileges can also be denied on the grounds that they will cause other groups to make similar demands.

Medical Rights In early prisons, inmates' right to medical treatment was restricted through the "exceptional circumstances doctrine." Using this policy, the courts would hear only those cases in which the circumstances totally disregarded human dignity, while denying hearings to less serious cases. The cases that were allowed access to the courts usually represented a situation of total denial of medical care.

To gain their medical rights, prisoners have resorted to class action suits (suits brought on behalf of all individuals affected by similar circumstances, in this case, poor medical attention). In the most significant case, *Newman v. Alabama* (1972), the entire Alabama prison system's medical facilities were declared inadequate.[77] The Supreme Court cited the following factors as contributing to inadequate care: insufficient physician and nurse resources, reliance on untrained inmates for paramedical work, intentional failure in treating the sick and injured, and failure to conform to proper medical standards. The *Newman* case forced corrections departments to upgrade prison medical facilities.

It was not until 1976, in *Estelle v. Gamble*, that the Supreme Court clearly mandated an inmate's right to have medical care.[78] Gamble had hurt his back in a

substantive rights Through a slow process of legal review, the courts have granted inmates a number of civil rights, including the rights to receive mail and medical benefits and to practice their religion.

jailhouse lawyer An inmate trained in law or otherwise educated who helps other inmates prepare legal briefs and appeals.

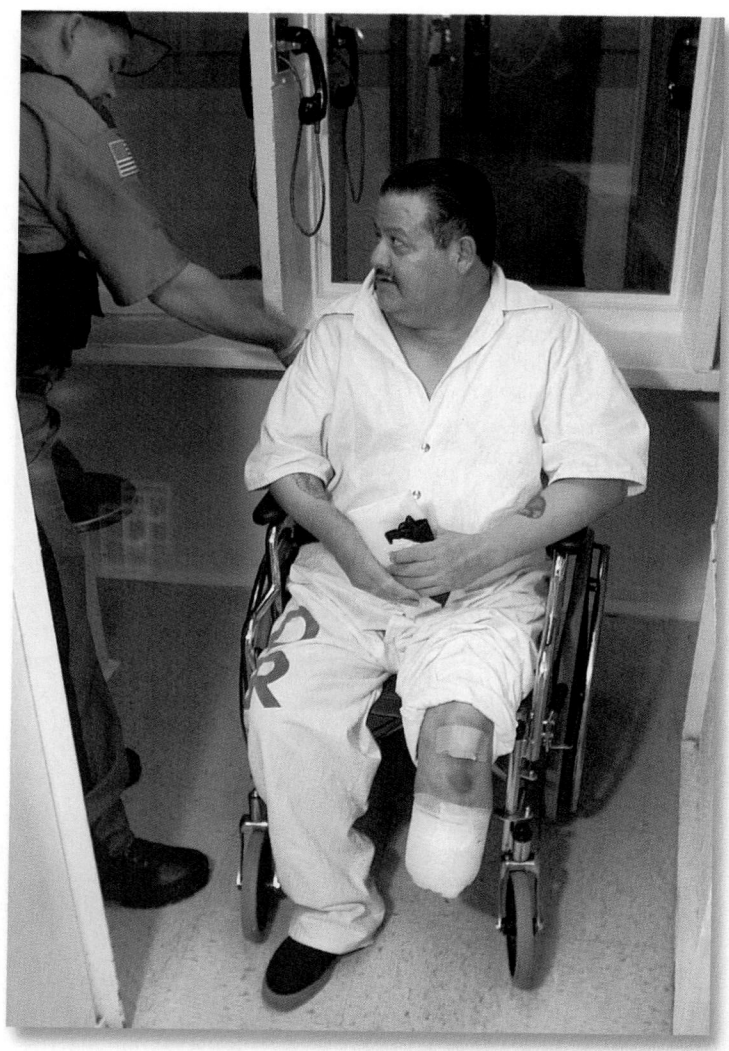

What are the medical rights of inmates? Should they be given the same level of care as any American citizen? Death row inmate Rodolfo Hernandez was denied an artificial limb by Texas authorities even though his leg was amputated due to complications arising from diabetes.

cruel and unusual punishment Physical punishment or punishment that is far in excess of that given to people under similar circumstances and is therefore banned by the Eighth Amendment. The death penalty has so far not been considered cruel and unusual if it is administered in a fair and nondiscriminatory fashion.

Texas prison and filed suit because he contested the type of treatment he had received and questioned the lack of interest that prison guards had shown in his case. The Supreme Court said, "Deliberate indifference to serious medical needs of prisoners constitutes the 'unnecessary and wanton infliction of pain,' proscribed by the Eighth Amendment."[79] Gamble was allowed to collect monetary damages for his injuries. The *Gamble* decision means that lower courts can decide, on a case-by-case basis, whether "deliberate indifference" to an inmate's medical needs has occurred and what damages the inmate is entitled to.

Cruel and Unusual Punishment The concept of **cruel and unusual punishment** is founded in the Eighth Amendment of the U.S. Constitution. The term itself has not been specifically defined by the Supreme Court, but the Court has held that treatment constitutes cruel and unusual punishment when it does the following:

- Degrades the dignity of human beings.[80]
- Is more severe (disproportional) than the offense for which it has been given.[81]
- Shocks the general conscience and is fundamentally unfair.[82]
- Is deliberately indifferent to a person's safety and well-being.[83]
- Punishes people because of their status, such as race, religion, and mental state.[84]
- Is in flagrant disregard of due process of law, such as punishment that is capriciously applied.[85]

State and federal courts have placed strict limits on disciplinary methods that may be considered inhumane. Corporal punishment all but ended after the practice was condemned in *Jackson v. Bishop* (1968).[86] Although the solitary confinement of disruptive inmates continues, its prolonged use under barbaric conditions has been held to be in violation of the Eighth Amendment. Courts have found that inmates placed in solitary have the right to adequate personal hygiene, exercise, mattresses, ventilation, and rules specifying how they can earn their release.

In a recent case, *Hope v. Pelzer,* the Supreme Court ruled that correctional officials who knowingly violate the Eighth Amendment rights of inmates can be held liable for damages.[87] The *Hope* case is set out in the following Law in Review feature.

Overall Prison Conditions Prisoners have long had the right to the minimal conditions necessary for human survival, such as the necessary food, clothing, shelter, and medical care to sustain human life. A number of attempts have been made to articulate reasonable standards of prison care and to make sure they are carried out. Courts have held that, although people are sent to prison for punishment, it does not mean that prison should be a punishing experience.[88] In the 1994 case of *Farmer v. Brennan,* the court ruled that prison officials are legally liable if, knowing that an inmate faces a serious risk of harm, they disregard that risk by failing

Hope v. Pelzer

Facts

Larry Hope, an Alabama prison inmate, was twice handcuffed to a hitching post for disruptive conduct. During a two-hour period one May, he was offered drinking water and a bathroom break every fifteen minutes, and his responses were recorded on an activity log. He was handcuffed above shoulder height, and when he tried moving his arms to improve circulation, the handcuffs cut into his wrists, causing pain and discomfort. After an altercation with a guard at his chain gang's worksite that June, Hope was subdued, handcuffed, placed in leg irons, and transported back to the prison, where he was ordered to take off his shirt, thus exposing himself to the sun, and spent seven hours on the hitching post. While there, he was given one or two water breaks but no bathroom breaks, and a guard taunted him about his thirst. Hope filed a suit against three guards charging them with violating his civil rights. Without deciding whether placing Hope on the hitching post as punishment violated the Eighth Amendment, the lower courts found that the guards were entitled to qualified immunity from lawsuits on the grounds that Hope could not show that their behavior violated "clearly established statutory or constitutional rights of which a reasonable person would have known."

Decision

On appeal, the Supreme Court ruled that Hope's allegations established an Eighth Amendment violation. It ruled that among the "unnecessary and wanton" inflictions of pain (constituting cruel and unusual punishment, forbidden by the amendment) are those that are "totally without penological justification." This determination is made in the context of prison conditions by ascertaining whether an official acted with "deliberate indifference" to the inmate's health or safety, a state of mind that can be inferred from the fact that the risk of harm is obvious. The Court reasoned that any safety concerns had long since ended by the time Hope was handcuffed to the hitching post, because he had already been subdued, handcuffed, placed in leg irons, and transported back to prison. He was separated from his work squad and not given the opportunity to return. Despite the clear lack of emergency, the guards knowingly subjected him to a substantial risk of physical harm, unnecessary pain, unnecessary exposure to the sun, prolonged thirst and taunting, and a deprivation of bathroom breaks that created a risk of particular discomfort and humiliation.

Qualified immunity ensures that before they are subjected to a lawsuit, officers are on notice that their conduct is unlawful. A reasonable officer would have known that using a hitching post as Hope alleged was unlawful. The obvious cruelty inherent in the practice should have provided respondents with some notice that their conduct was unconstitutional. In addition, binding legal precedent from earlier cases should have given them notice that several forms of corporal punishment are impermissible, including handcuffing inmates to fences or cells for long periods, and that "physical abuse directed at [a] prisoner after he terminate[s] his resistance to authority would constitute an actionable Eighth Amendment violation."

Significance of the Case

The *Hope* case shows that correctional officers can be sued if their behavior violates an inmate's constitutional rights and that they or any reasonable person should have surmised that the behavior was in violation of accepted practices. Courts have recognized the need to protect government employees from meritless litigation that may interfere with the exercise of lawful job-related discretion—that is, they have been given qualified immunity. But government officials are not immune from damages if their behavior violates basic human rights. If it does, then the courts must determine whether a reasonable officer would have thought that the alleged act was lawful in light of clearly established law and the factual information they possessed at the time. If the courts find their behavior was unreasonable, they are liable for damages. The fact that officers can be sued is critical because most state and local governments indemnify their employees against such judgments, and also assume the costs of their defense. Judgments such as this can cost states millions of dollars.

Critical Thinking

In order to prove cruel and unusual treatment in prison, the courts have ruled that there must be a showing of "unnecessary and wanton" inflictions of pain, especially those that are "totally without penological justification." In the context of prison conditions, it must be determined whether a prison official acted with "deliberate indifference" to the inmate's health or safety. Do you believe the facts of *Hope* met this condition?

InfoTrac College Edition Research

Use "cruel and unusual punishment" as a subject guide on InfoTrac College Edition to learn more about this topic.

Source: Hope v. Pelzer et al., Docket 01-301, decided June 27, 2002.

to take measures to avoid or reduce it. Furthermore, prison officials should be able to infer the risk from the evidence at hand; they need not be warned or told.[89]

Although inmates retain the right to reasonable care, if there is a legitimate purpose for the use of governmental restrictions, they may be considered constitutional. For example, it might be possible to restrict reading material, allow strip searches, and prohibit inmates from receiving packages from the outside if the restrictions are legitimate security measures. If overcrowded conditions require it, inmates may be double-bunked in cells designed for a single inmate.[90]

Leaving Prison

At the expiration of their prison term, most inmates return to society and try to resume their lives there. For some inmates, their reintegration into society comes by way of parole—the planned community release and supervision of incarcerated offenders before the expiration of their full prison sentences. In states where determinate sentencing statutes have eliminated discretionary parole, offenders are released after having served their determinate sentence, less time off for good behavior and other credits designed to reduce the term of incarceration. Their release may involve supervision in the community, and rule violations can result in return to prison for the balance of their unexpired sentence.

In a few instances, inmates are released after their sentence has been commuted by a board of pardons or directly by a governor or even the president of the United States. About 15 percent of prison inmates are released after serving their entire maximum sentence without any time excused or forgiven. And despite the efforts of correctional authorities, about seven thousand inmates escape every year from state and federal prisons (the number of escapes is actually declining, due in part to better officer training and more sophisticated security measures).[91]

Regardless of the method of their release, former inmates face the formidable task of having to readjust to society. This means regaining legal rights they may have lost on their conviction, reestablishing community and family ties, and finding employment. After being in prison, these goals are often difficult to achieve.

To learn more about today's prison release methods, use the term "parole" as a subject guide on InfoTrac College Edition.

parole The early release of a prisoner from imprisonment subject to conditions set by a parole board. Depending on the jurisdiction, inmates must serve a certain portion of their sentences before becoming eligible for parole. The conditions of parole may require the individual to report regularly to a parole officer, to refrain from criminal conduct, to maintain and support his or her family, to avoid contact with other convicted criminals, to abstain from using alcohol and drugs, to remain within the jurisdiction, and so on. Violations of the conditions of parole may result in revocation of parole, in which case the individual will be returned to prison. The concept behind parole is to allow the release of the offender to community supervision, where rehabilitation and readjustment will be facilitated.

Parole

The decision to **parole** is determined by statutory requirement. In some states parole is granted by a parole board, a duly constituted body of men and women who review inmate cases and determine whether offenders have reached a rehabilitative level sufficient to deal with the outside world. The board also dictates what specific parole rules parolees must obey. In other jurisdictions, the amount of time a person must remain in prison is a predetermined percentage of the inmate's sentence, assuming there are no infractions or escape attempts. Referred to as *mandatory parole release,* the inmate is released when the unserved portion of the maximum prison term equals his or her earned good time (less time served in jail awaiting trial). In some states, sentences can be reduced by more than half with a combination of statutory and earned good time. If the conditions of their release are violated, mandatory releasees can have their good time revoked and be returned to the institution to serve the remainder of their unexpired term. The remaining inmates are released for a variety of reasons, including expiration of their term, commutation of their sentence, and court orders to relieve overcrowded prisons.

People on Parole In 2001, there were more than 650,000 people on parole, up 30 percent since 1990. About 312 adults per 100,000 adult U.S. residents were on state-supervised parole in 2000, compared to 271 in 1990.[92] The popularity of determinate sentencing has radically changed the way people are being released from prison. The number of state inmates released from prison as a result of parole

If you were on the parole board would you free one of the women who helped Charles Manson in his murderous spree? Sheron Lawin, member of the Board of Prison Terms, left, listens to Leslie Van Houten, right, after her parole was denied at the California Institution for Women in Corona, California. Van Houten, fifty-three, has served over thirty years in prison for her involvement in the Tate-LaBianca killings.

board decision making has dropped from 39 percent of all releases in 1990 to about 24 percent today; during the same period, mandatory releases increased from 29 percent to 41 percent of all parole releases.[93]

The U.S. Parole Commission maintains a Web site at
www.usdoj.gov/uspc/

The Parole Board

In those states that have maintained discretionary parole, the authority to release inmates is usually vested in the parole board. State parole boards have four primary functions:

1. To select and place prisoners on parole
2. To aid, supervise, and provide continuing control of parolees in the community
3. To determine when the parole function is completed and to discharge from parole
4. To determine whether parole should be revoked, if violations of conditions occur

Most parole authorities are independent agencies with their own staff and administration, and a few parole boards are part of the state department of corrections. Arguments for keeping the board within a corrections department usually include improved communication and more intimate knowledge about offenders.

Most boards are relatively small, usually numbering fewer than ten members. Their size, coupled with their large caseloads and the varied activities they are expected to perform, can prevent board members from becoming as well acquainted with the individual inmates as might be desired.

Parole Hearings

The actual (discretionary) parole decision is made at a parole-granting hearing. At this hearing the full board or a selected subcommittee reviews information, may meet with the offender, and then decides whether the parole applicant has a reasonable probability of succeeding outside of prison. Each parole board has its own way of reviewing cases. In some, the full board meets with the applicant; in others, only a few members do that. In a number of jurisdictions, a single board member can conduct a personal investigation and submit the findings to the full board for a decision.

At the hearing, parole board members consider such information as police reports of the crime, the presentence investigation, psychological testing and scores developed by prison mental health professionals, and institutional reports of disciplinary actions, treatment, and adjustment.[94] Letters may be solicited from the inmate's friends and family members. In some jurisdictions, victims may appear and make statements of the losses they suffered.

By speaking directly to the applicant, the board can also promote and emphasize the specific types of behavior and behavior changes it expects to see if the inmate is to eventually qualify for or effectively serve parole.

The inmate's specific rights at a parole-granting hearing also vary from jurisdiction to jurisdiction. In about half of the parole-granting jurisdictions, inmates are permitted counsel or are allowed to present witnesses on their behalf; other jurisdictions do not permit these privileges. Because the federal courts have declared that the parole applicant is not entitled to any form of legal representation, the inmate may have to pay for legal services where this privilege is allowed. In almost all discretionary parole-granting jurisdictions, the reasons for the parole decision must be given in writing, and in about half of the jurisdictions, a verbatim record of the hearing is made.

In the case of *Pennsylvania Board of Probation and Parole v. Scott*, the U.S. Supreme Court held that the exclusionary rule for illegally obtained evidence did not apply to parole revocation proceedings. The Court reasoned that the social costs of excluding incriminating evidence outweigh any benefits of protecting parolees from invasion of their privacy. *Scott* then allows evidence to be used in a parole revocation hearing that would be excluded from a criminal prosecution.[95]

The Parolee in the Community

Once released into the community, a parolee is given a standard set of rules and conditions that must be obeyed. As with probation, the offender who violates these rules may have parole revoked and be sent back to the institution to serve the remainder of the sentence. Once in the community, the parolee is supervised by a trained staff of parole officers who help him or her search for employment and monitor the parolee's behavior and activities to ensure that the conditions of parole are met.

Parole is generally viewed as a privilege granted to deserving inmates on the basis of their good behavior while in prison. Parole has two conflicting sides, however. On the one hand, the paroled offender is allowed to serve part of the sentence in the community, an obvious benefit for the deserving offender. On the other hand, since parole is a "privilege and not a right," the parolee is viewed as a dangerous criminal who must be carefully watched and supervised. The conflict between the treatment and enforcement aspects of parole has not been reconciled by the criminal justice system, and the parole process still contains elements of both.

To overcome these roadblocks to success, the parole officer may have to play a much greater role in directing and supervising clients' lives than the probation officer. In some instances, parole programs have become active in creating new postrelease treatment-oriented programs designed to increase the chances of parole success. For example, the Kansas parole department has adopted a restorative justice approach and is now having parolees work in community service settings upon their release. Jobs may include work at soup kitchens, homeless shelters, and halfway houses; reports indicate the program is quite successful.[96] In other instances, parole agencies have implemented law enforcement–oriented services that work with local police agencies to identify and apprehend parolees who may have been involved in criminal activity. The California Department of Corrections (CDC) established the Special Service Unit, which among its others tasks acts as a liaison with local police agencies in helping them solve major crimes when inmates or state parolees are the known or suspected offenders.[97]

Intensive Supervision Parole   To aid supervision, some jurisdictions are implementing systems that classify offenders on the basis of their supervision needs. Typically, a point or guideline system (sometimes called a *salient factor score*) based on prior record and prison adjustment divides parolees into three groups: (1) those who require intensive surveillance, (2) those who require social service rather than surveillance, and (3) those who require limited supervision.

In some jurisdictions, parolees in need of closer surveillance are placed on **intensive supervision parole (ISP)**. These programs use limited caseload sizes, treatment facilities, the matching of parolee and supervisor by personality, and shock parole (which involves immediate short-term incarceration for parole violators to impress them with the seriousness of a violation). ISP clients are required to attend more office and home visits than routine parolees. ISP may also require frequent drug testing, a term in a community correctional center, and electronic monitoring in the home. More than seventeen thousand parolees are under intensive supervision, fourteen hundred of these are monitored electronically by computer.

Although ISP seems like an ideal way of limiting already overcrowded prison populations, there is little evidence that ISP programs are effective; in fact, they may produce a higher violation rate than traditional parole supervision. Limiting caseload size allows parole officers to supervise their clients more closely and spot infractions more easily.[98]

intensive supervision parole (ISP)
A limited-caseload program for those parolees who need intensive surveillance. Parolees are required to meet more often with parole officers than routine parolees and may also have frequent drug testing, serve a term in a community correctional system, and be electronically monitored.

The Effectiveness of Parole

Persons released from prison face a multitude of difficulties. They remain largely uneducated, unskilled, and usually without solid family support systems—and to this the burdens of a prison record are added. Not surprisingly, most parolees fail, and rather quickly—rearrests are most common in the first six months after release.

Despite all efforts to treat, correct, and rehabilitate incarcerated offenders, the fact remains that a majority return to prison shortly after their release. A recent (2002) federal study of nearly three hundred thousand prisoners released in fifteen states in 1994 provides data that underscore the problem. Of the total number of releasees, 67.5 percent were rearrested within three years of leaving prison for a felony or serious misdemeanor.[99] About 47 percent were reconvicted for a new crime and 25 percent were resentenced to prison for a new crime. Within three years, about 52 percent were back in prison, serving time for a new prison sentence or for a technical violation of their release, such as failing a drug test, missing an appointment with their parole officer, or being arrested for a new crime.

Who was most likely to fail on parole or other release mechanisms? Released prisoners with the highest rearrest rates were robbers (70.2 percent), burglars (74.0 percent), larcenists (74.6 percent), motor vehicle thieves (78.8 percent), those in prison for possessing or selling stolen property (77.4 percent), and those in prison for possessing, using, or selling illegal weapons (70.2 percent). Ironically, those committing murder, sexual assault, or rape had the lowest recidivism rates.

The cost of recidivism is acute. The 272,111 offenders discharged in 1994 had accumulated 744,000 charges within three years of release; put another way, about a quarter of a million U.S. citizens are victimized each year by people released on parole in just fifteen states! Another federal survey of 156,000 parole violators serving time in the nation's prison system estimated that these offenders committed at least 6,800 murders, 5,500 rapes, 8,800 assaults, and 22,500 robberies while under supervision in the community for an average of thirteen months.[100]

Why Do People Fail on Parole?

Parole failure is still a significant problem and a growing portion of the correctional population consists of parolees who failed on the outside. Why has the phenomenon of parole failure remained so stubborn and hard to control? One reason may be the very nature of the prison experience itself. The psychological and economic problems that lead offenders to recidivism are rarely addressed by a stay in prison. Despite rehabilitation efforts, the typical ex-convict is still the same undereducated, unemployed, substance-abusing lower-class male he was when arrested. Being separated from friends and family, not sharing in conventional society, associating with dangerous people, and adapting to a volatile lifestyle probably have done little to improve the offender's personality or behavior. And when he returns to society, it may be to the same destructive neighborhood and social groups that prompted his original law-violating behavior. It seems naïve to think that incarceration alone can help someone overcome these lifelong disabilities. As correctional expert Stephen Duguid maintains, by their very nature prisons seek to impose and maintain order and conformity rather than help inmates develop skills such as independence and critical thinking, factors that may be essential once the inmate is forced to cope outside the prison's walls.[101]

It is also possible that parole failure is tied to the releasee's own lifelong personal deficits. Most research efforts indicate that a long history of criminal behavior, an antisocial personality, and childhood experiences with family dysfunction are all correlated with postrelease recidivism.[102] Many releasees have suffered from a lifetime of substance abuse or dependence disorder.[103] A history of physical and sexual abuse has also been linked to recidivism.[104] One study of youthful ex-offenders trying to make it on the outside found that many experience delayed emotional and cognitive development due to early drug use; most have never learned to use problem-solving or coping skills outside of the correctional setting, and most remain drug-dependent.[105]

Once on the outside, these problems do not easily subside. Some ex-inmates may have to prove that the prison experience has not changed them: taking drugs or being sexually aggressive may show friends that they have not lost their "heart."[106] In contrast, parolees who have had a good employment record in the past and who maintain jobs after their release are the most likely to avoid recidivating.[107]

Ex-inmates may find their home life torn and disrupted when they are finally released. Wives of inmates report that they had to face the shame and stigmatization of having an incarcerated spouse while withstanding a barrage of calls from jealous husbands on the "inside" who tried to monitor their behavior and control their lives. Family visits to the inmate became traumatic and strained relationships because they often involved strip searches and other invasions of privacy.[108] Sensitive to these problems, some states have instituted support groups designed to help inmates' families adjust to their loneliness and despair.[109]

The specter of recidivism is especially frustrating to the American public: it is so difficult to apprehend and successfully prosecute criminal offenders that it seems foolish to grant them early release so they can prey on more victims. This problem is exacerbated when the parolee is a chronic, frequent offender. Research indicates that many of these returning prisoners are less prepared for reintegration and less connected to community-based social structures than in the past.[110] There seems to be a strong association between prior and future offending: the parolees most likely to fail on release are the ones who have failed in the past; chronic offenders are the ones most likely to re-offend. This issue takes on even greater importance when the community-level problems created by returning inmates are considered. This subject is discussed in the following Policy, Programs, and Issues feature.

The Problems of Reentry

Because of America's two-decade-long imprisonment boom, more than five hundred thousand inmates are now being released back into the community each year. As criminologist Joan Petersilia warns, there are a number of unfortunate consequences to this release back into the community because many of those being released have not received adequate treatment and are unprepared for life in conventional society. The risks they present to the community include increases in child abuse, family violence, the spread of infectious diseases, homelessness, and community disorganization.

The increased reentry risks can be tied to legal changes in how people are released from prison. In the past, offenders were granted early release only if a parole board believed they were rehabilitated and had ties to the community—such as a family or a job. Inmates were encouraged to enter treatment programs to earn parole. Changes in sentencing law have resulted in the growth of mandatory release and limits on discretionary parole. People now serve a fixed sentence and the discretion of parole boards has been blunted. Inmates may be discouraged from seeking involvement in rehabilitation programs (they do not influence the chance of parole), and the lack of incentive means that fewer inmates leaving prison have participated in programs to address work, education, and substance use deficiencies. For example, only 13 percent of inmates who suffer addiction receive any kind of drug abuse treatment in prison. Nor does the situation improve upon release. Many inmates are not assigned to supervision caseloads once back in the community; about one hundred thousand released inmates go unsupervised each year.

Petersilia argues that back in the community, offenders may increase their criminal activity because they want to "make up for lost time" and resume their criminal careers. Most leave prison with no savings, no immediate entitlement to unemployment benefits, and few employment prospects. One year after release, as many as 60 percent of former inmates are not employed in the regular labor market, and there is increasing reluctance among employers to hire ex-offenders. Unemployment is closely related to drug and alcohol abuse. Losing a job can lead to substance abuse, which in turn is related to child and family violence. Mothers released from prison have difficulty finding services such as housing, employment, and child care, and this causes stress for them and their children. Children of incarcerated and released parents may suffer confusion, sadness, and social stigma, and these feelings often result in difficulties in school, low self-esteem, aggressive behavior, and general emotional dysfunction. If the parents are negative role models, children fail to develop positive attitudes about work and responsibility. Children of incarcerated parents are five times more likely to serve time in prison than are children whose parents are not incarcerated.

Prisoners have significantly more physical and mental health problems than the general population because of lifestyles that often include crowded or itinerant living conditions, intravenous drug use, poverty, and high rates of substance abuse. Inmates with mental illness (about 16 percent of all inmates) also are increasingly being imprisoned—and then released. Even when public mental health services are available, many mentally ill individuals fail to use them because they fear institutionalization, deny they are mentally ill, or distrust the mental health system. The situation will become more serious as more and more parolees are released back into the disorganized communities whose deteriorated conditions may have motivated their original crimes.

Fear of a prison stay has less of an impact on behavior than ever before. As the prison population grows, the negative impact of incarceration may be lessening. In neighborhoods where "doing time" is more a rule than the exception, it becomes less of a stigma and more of a badge of acceptance. It also becomes a way of life from which some ex-convicts do rebound. Teens may encounter older men who have gone to prison and have returned to begin their lives again. With the proper skills and survival techniques, prison is considered "manageable." Although a prison stay is still unpleasant, it has lost its aura of shame and fear. By becoming commonplace and mundane, the "myth" of the prison experience has been exposed and its deterrent power reduced.

Critical Thinking

1. All too often, government leaders jump on the incarceration bandwagon as a panacea for the nation's crime problem. Is it a "quick fix" whose long-term consequences may be devastating for the nation's cities, or are these problems counterbalanced by the crime-reducing effect of putting large numbers of high-rate offenders behind bars?

2. If you agree that incarceration undermines neighborhoods, can you think of some other, indirect ways that high incarceration rates help increase crime rates?

InfoTrac College Edition Research

Alternatives to prison are now being sought because high incarceration may undermine a community's viability. What do you think? For some interesting developments, check out these articles on InfoTrac College Edition: Joe Loconte, "Making Criminals Pay: A New York County's Bold Experiment in Biblical Justice," *Policy Review*, January-February 1998 v87 p26, and Katarina Ivanko, "Shifting Gears to Rehabilitation," *Corrections Today*, April 1997 v59 i2 p20.

Source: Joan Petersilia, "When Prisoners Return to Communities: Political, Economic, and Social Consequences," *Federal Probation* 65 (2001): 3–9.

Exhibit 13.3 **Rights lost upon release from prison**

- Fourteen states permanently deny felons the right to vote; eighteen states suspend the right until after the correctional sentence has been completed.
- Nineteen states terminate parental rights.
- Twenty-nine states consider a felony conviction to be legal grounds for a divorce.
- Six states deny felons the opportunity for public employment.
- Thirty-one states disallow convicted felons the right to serve on juries.
- Twenty-five states prevent convicted felons from holding public office.
- Federal law prevents ex-convicts from owning guns. In addition, all states except Vermont employ additional legal measures to prevent felons from possessing firearms.
- Forty-six states require that felons register with law enforcement agencies. This requirement is up sharply in recent years; in 1986 only eight states required felons to register.
- Civil death, or the denial of all civil rights, is still practiced in four states.

Source: Kathleen Olivares, Velmer Burton, and Francis Cullen, "The Collateral Consequences of a Felony Conviction: A National Study of State Legal Codes Ten Years Later," *Federal Probation 60* (1996): 10–17.

Losing Rights   Ex-inmates may also find that going straight is an economic impossibility. Many employers are reluctant to hire people who have served time. Even if a criminal record does not automatically prohibit all chance of employment, why would an employer hire an "ex-con" when other applicants are available? If they lie about their prison experience and are later found out, ex-offenders will be dismissed for misrepresentation. Research shows that former inmates who gain and keep meaningful employment are more likely to succeed on parole than those who are unemployed or underemployed.[111] One reason that ex-inmates find it so difficult to make it on the outside is the legal restrictions they are forced to endure. These may include bars on certain kinds of employment, limits on obtaining licenses, and restrictions on their freedom of movement. One survey found that a significant number of states still restrict the activities of former felons.[112] Some of the more important findings are listed in Exhibit 13.3.

In general, states have placed greater restrictions on former felons as part of the get-tough movement. However, courts have considered individual requests by convicted felons to have their rights restored. It is common for courts to look at such issues as how recently the criminal offense took place and its relationship to the particular right before deciding whether to restore it.

A number of experts and national commissions have condemned the loss of rights of convicted offenders as a significant cause of recidivism. Consequently, courts have generally moved to eliminate the most restrictive elements of postconviction restrictions.[113] ■

SUMMARY

On entering a prison, offenders must make tremendous adjustments to survive. Usual behavior patterns or lifestyles are radically changed. Opportunities for personal satisfaction are reduced. Passing through a number of adjustment stages or cycles, inmates learn to cope with the new environment.

Inmates also learn to obey the inmate social code, which dictates certain behavior and attitudes. If inmates break the code, they may be unfavorably labeled.

Inmates are eligible for a large number of treatment devices designed to help them readjust to the community once they are released. These include educational programs on the basic, high school, and even college levels, as well as vocational training programs. In addition, a number of treatment programs have offered inmates individualized and group psychological counseling.

Despite such measures, prisons remain forbidding structures that house desperate men and women. Violence is common in prisons. Women often turn their hatred inward and hurt themselves, and male inmates engage in collective and individual violence against others. The Attica and New Mexico State Penitentiary riots are examples of the most serious collective prison violence.

In years past, society paid little attention to the incarcerated offender. Most inmates confined in jails and prisons were basically deprived of the rights guaranteed them under the Constitution. Today, however, the judicial system is actively involved in the administration of correctional institutions. Inmates can take their grievances to courts and seek due process and equal protection under the law. The courts have recognized that persons confined in correctional institutions have rights—which include access to the courts and legal counsel, the exercise of religion, the rights to correspondence and visitation, and the right to adequate medical treatment.

Most inmates return to society before the completion of their prison sentence. The majority earn early release through time off for good behavior or other sentence-reducing mechanisms. In addition, about 40 percent of all inmates are paroled before the completion of their maximum term. Most state jurisdictions maintain an independent parole board whose members decide whether to grant parole. Their decision making is discretionary and is based on many factors, such as the perception of the needs of society, the correctional system, and the client. Once paroled, the client is subject to control by parole officers, who ensure that the conditions set by the board (the parole rules) are maintained. Parole can be revoked if the offender violates the rules of parole or commits a new crime.

Ex-inmates have a tough time adjusting on the outside, and the recidivism rate is disturbingly high. One reason is that many states restrict their rights and take away privileges granted to other citizens.

For an up-to-date list of Web links, go to http://cj.wadsworth.com/siegel_essen4e.

KEY TERMS

"no-frills" policy 416	prisonization 419	hands-off doctrine 440	cruel and unusual punishment 442
total institution 416	special-needs inmate 426	substantive rights 441	parole 444
inmate subculture 419	work release 429	jailhouse lawyer 441	intensive supervision parole (ISP) 447
inmate social code 419	furlough 429		

INFOTRAC COLLEGE EDITION EXERCISES

IS IT POSSIBLE for prison authorities to introduce policies that really have an impact on crime rates? Although some experts may remain skeptical, authorities in Oklahoma believe they have found the answer. Read the following article on InfoTrac College Edition to discover their blueprint for success: Frank Keating, "The Oklahoma Turnaround: How One State Rethought Prison Policies—and Reduced Crime," *Corrections Today*, August 2002 v64 i5 p96(3).

HOW HAS PAROLE CHANGED in the era of "three strikes" and determinate sentencing? Read the following article to find the answer: George M. Anderson, "Parole Revisited," *America*, March 4, 2002 v186 i7 p10.

QUESTIONS

1. Considering the dangers that males face during their prison stay, should nonviolent inmates be placed in separate institutions to protect them from harm?

2. Should women be allowed to work as guards in male prisons? What about male guards in female prisons? Why or why not?

3. Should prison inmates be allowed a free college education while noncriminals are forced to pay tuition? Why or why not? Do you believe in less eligibility for prisoners? Explain.

4. Define parole, including its purposes and objectives. How does it differ from probation?

5. What is the role of the parole board?

6. Should a former prisoner have all the civil rights afforded the average citizen? Explain.

7. Should people be further penalized after they have paid their debt to society? Why or why not?

NOTES

1. Gresham Sykes, *The Society of Captives* (Princeton, N.J.: Princeton University Press, 1958).

2. David Eichenthal and James Jacobs, "Enforcing the Criminal Law in State Prisons," *Justice Quarterly* 8 (1991): 283–303.

3. John Wooldredge, "Inmate Lifestyles and Opportunities for Victimization," *Journal of Research in Crime and Delinquency* 35 (1998): 480–502.

4. David Anderson, *Crimes of Justice: Improving the Police, Courts, and Prison* (New York: Times Books, 1988).

5. Robert Johnson, *Hard Time: Understanding and Reforming the Prison* (Monterey, Calif.: Brooks/Cole, 1987), 115.

6. Wooldredge, "Inmate Lifestyles and Opportunities for Victimization."

7. Lawrence Hinman, "Stunning Morality: The Moral Dimensions of Stun Belts," *Criminal Justice Ethics* 17 (1998): 3–6.

8. Kevin Wright, *The Great American Crime Myth* (Westport, Conn.: Greenwood Press, 1985), 167.

9. Sandra Gleason, "Hustling: The Inside Economy of a Prison," *Federal Probation* 42 (1978): 32–39.

10. Hans Toch, *Living in Prison* (New York: Free Press, 1977), 179–205.

11. Angela Maitland and Richard Sluder, "Victimization and Youthful Prison Inmates: An Empirical Analysis," *Prison Journal* 77 (1998): 55–74.

12. Seena Fazel and John Danesh, "Serious Mental Disorder in 23,000 Prisoners: A Systematic Review of Sixty-Two Surveys," *Lancet* 359 (2002): 545–561.

13. Leonore Simon, "Prison Behavior and Victim-Offender Relationships Among Violent Offenders" (Paper presented at the annual meeting of the American Society of Criminology, San Francisco, November 1991).

14. John Irwin, "Adaptation to Being Corrected: Corrections from the Convict's Perspective," in *Handbook of Criminology*, ed. Daniel Glazer (Chicago: Rand McNally, 1974), 971–93.

15. Donald Clemmer, *The Prison Community* (New York: Holt, Rinehart & Winston, 1958).

16. Gresham Sykes and Sheldon Messinger, "The Inmate Social Code," in *The Sociology of Punishment and Corrections,* eds. Norman Johnston, Leonard Savitz, and Marvin Wolfgang (New York: Wiley, 1970), 401–408.

17. John Irwin and Donald Cressey, "Thieves, Convicts, and the Inmate Culture," *Social Problems* 10 (1962): 142–155.

18. Brent Paterline and David Petersen, "Structural and Social Psychological Determinants of Prisonization," *Journal of Criminal Justice* 27 (1999): 427–441.

19. Ibid., 439.

20. James B. Jacobs, ed., *New Perspectives on Prisons and Imprisonment* (Ithaca, N.Y.: Cornell University Press, 1983); idem, "Street Gangs Behind Bars," *Social Problems* 21 (1974): 395–409; idem, "Race Relations and the Prison Subculture," in *Crime and Justice,* vol. 1, eds. Norval Morris and Michael Tonry (Chicago: University of Chicago Press, 1979), 1–28.

21. Nicole Hahn Rafter, *Partial Justice* (New Brunswick, N.J.: Transaction Books, 1990), 181–182.

22. Paige Harrison and Allen Beck, *Prisoners in 2001* (Washington, D.C.: Bureau of Justice Statistics, 2002).

23. Meda Chesney-Lind, "Patriarchy, Prisons, and Jails: A Critical Look at Trends in Women's Incarceration" (Paper presented at the International Feminist Conference on Women, Law and Social Control, Mont Gabriel, Québec, July 1991).

24. Meda Chesney-Lind, "Vengeful Equity: Sentencing Women to Prison," in *The Female Offender: Girls, Women and Crime* (Thousand Oaks, Calif.: Sage, 1997).

25. Elaine DeCostanzo and Helen Scholes, "Women Behind Bars: Their Numbers Increase," *Corrections Today* 50 (1988): 104–106.

26. This section synthesizes the findings of a number of surveys of female inmates, including DeCostanzo and Scholes, "Women Behind Bars"; Ruth Glick and Virginia Neto, *National Study of Women's Correctional Programs* (Washington, D.C.: Government Printing Office, 1977); Ann Goetting and Roy Michael Howsen, "Women in Prison: A Profile," *Prison Journal* 63 (1983): 27–46; Meda Chesney-Lind and Noelie Rodrigues, "Women Under Lock and Key: A View from Inside," *Prison Journal* 63 (1983): 47–65; Contact, Inc., "Women Offenders," *Corrections Compendium* 7 (1982): 6–11.

27. Merry Morash, Robin Harr, and Lila Rucker, "A Comparison of Programming for Women and Men in U.S. Prisons in the 1980s," *Crime and Delinquency* 40 (1994): 197–221.

28. Pamela Schram, "Stereotypes About Vocational Programming for Female Inmates," *Prison Journal* 78 (1998): 244–271.

29. Morash, Harr, and Rucker, "A Comparison of Programming for Women and Men in U.S. Prisons in the 1980s."

30. Seena Fazel and John Danesh, "Serious Mental Disorder in 23,000 Prisoners: A Systematic Review of 62 Surveys," *Lancet* 359 (2002): 545–561.

31. Gary Michael McClelland, Linda Teplin, Karen Abram, and Naomi Jacobs, "HIV and AIDS Risk Behaviors Among Female Jail Detainees: Implications for Public Health Policy," *American Journal of Public Health* 92 (2002): 818–826.

32. "Sex Abuse of Female Inmates Is Common, Rights Group Says," *Criminal Justice Newsletter,* 16 December 1996, 2.

33. General Accounting Office, *Women in Prison: Sexual Misconduct by Correctional Staff* (Washington, D.C.: Government Printing Office, 1999).

34. Meda Chesney-Lind, "Vengeful Equity: Sentencing Women to Prison," in *The Female Offender: Girls, Women, and Crime* (Thousand Oaks, Calif.: Sage, 1997).

35. Candace Kruttschnitt and Sharon Krmpotich, "Aggressive Behavior Among Female Inmates: An Exploratory Study," *Justice Quarterly* 7 (1990): 370–389.

36. Candace Kruttschnitt, Rosemary Gartner, and Amy Miller, "Doing Her Own Time? Women's Responses to Prison in the Context of the Old and New Penology," *Criminology* 38 (2000): 681–718.

37. Mark Pogrebin and Mary Dodge, "Women's Accounts of Their Prison Experiences: A Retrospective View of Their Subjective Realities," *Journal of Criminal Justice* 29 (2001): 531–541.

38. Edna Erez, "The Myth of the New Female Offender: Some Evidence from Attitudes Toward Law and Justice," *Journal of Criminal Justice* 16 (1988): 499–509.

39. Robert Ross and Hugh McKay, *Self-Mutilation* (Lexington, Mass.: Lexington Books, 1979).

40. Alice Propper, *Prison Homosexuality* (Lexington, Mass.: Lexington Books, 1981).

41. Dianna Newbern, Donald Dansereau, and Urvashi Pitre, "Positive Effects on Life Skills Motivation and Self-Efficacy: Node-Link Maps in a Modified Therapeutic Community," *American Journal of Drug and Alcohol Abuse* 25 (1999): 407–410.

42. Ira Sommers and Deborah Baskin, "The Prescription of Psychiatric Medication in Prison: Psychiatric Versus Labeling Perspectives," *Justice Quarterly* 7 (1990): 739–755.

43. Judy Anderson and R. Daniel McGehee, "South Carolina Strives to Treat Elderly and Disabled Offenders," *Corrections Today* 53 (1991): 124–127.

44. American Bar Association, *The State of Criminal Justice* (Washington, D.C.: ABA, 1996).

45. Howard Skolnik and John Slansky, "A First Step in Helping Inmates Get Good Jobs After Release," *Corrections Today* 53 (1991): 92.

46. This section leans heavily on Barbara Auerbach, George Sexton, Franklin Farrow, and Robert Lawson, *Work in American Prisons: The Private Sector Gets Involved* (Washington, D.C.: National Institute of Justice, 1988).

47. Public Law 96-157, sec. 827, codified as 18 U.S.C., sec. 1761(c).

48. Courtesy of the Prison Industry Authority, 560 East Natoma Street, Folsom, Calif. 95630-2200.

49. Diane Dwyer and Roger McNally, "Public Policy, Prison Industries, and Business: An Equitable Balance for the 1990s," *Federal Probation* 57 (1993): 30–35.

50. This section leans heavily on Mark Hamm, "Current Perspectives on the Prisoner Self-Help Movement," *Federal Probation* 52 (1988): 49–56.

51. For more information, contact the Fortune Society, 39 West 19 Street, New York, N.Y. 10011; (212) 206-7070. The e-mail address is info@fortunesociety.org.

52. Douglas Lipton, Robert Martinson, and Judith Wilks, *The Effectiveness of Correctional Treatment: A Survey of Treatment Evaluation Studies* (New York: Praeger, 1975).

53. Charles Murray and Louis Cox, *Beyond Probation: Juvenile Corrections and the Chronic Delinquent* (Beverly Hills, Calif.: Sage, 1979).

54. Steven Lab and John Whitehead, "An Analysis of Juvenile Correctional Treatment," *Crime and Delinquency* 34 (1988): 60–83.

55. Francis Cullen and Karen Gilbert, *Reaffirming Rehabilitation* (Cincinnati: Anderson Publications, 1982).

56. David Wilson, Catherine Gallagher, and Doris MacKenzie, "A Meta-Analysis of Corrections-Based Education, Vocation, and Work Programs for Adult Offenders," *Journal of Research in Crime and Delinquency* 37 (2000): 347–368.

57. Mary Ellen Batiuk, Paul Moke, and Pamela Wilcox Roundtree, "Crime and Rehabilitation: Correctional Education as an Agent of Change—A Research Note," *Justice Quarterly* 14 (1997): 167–180.

58. Mark Lipsey and David Wilson, "Effective Intervention for Serious Juvenile Offenders: A Synthesis of Research," in *Serious and Violent Juvenile Offenders: Risk Factors and Successful Interventions,* eds. Rolf Loeber and David Farrington (Thousand Oaks, Calif.: Sage, 1998).

59. Paul Gendreau and Claire Goffin, "Principles of Effective Correctional Programming," *Forum on Correctional Research* 2 (1996): 38–41.

60. Morash, Harr, and Rucker, "A Comparison of Programming for Women and Men in U.S. Prisons in the 1980s."

61. Christopher J. Mumola, *Substance Abuse and Treatment, State and Federal Prisoners,* 1997 (Washington, D.C.: Bureau of Justice Statistics, 1999).

62. Lucien X. Lombardo, *Guards Imprisoned* (New York: Elsevier, 1981); James Jacobs and Norma Crotty, "The Guard's World," in *New Perspectives on Prisons and Imprisonment,* ed. James Jacobs (Ithaca, N.Y.: Cornell University Press, 1983), 133–141.

63. Claire Mayhew and Duncan Chappell, "An Overview of Occupational Violence," *Australian Nursing Journal* 9 (2002): 34–35.

64. John Klofas and Hans Toch, "The Guard Subculture Myth," *Journal of Research in Crime and Delinquency* 19 (1982): 238–254.

65. Ruth Triplett and Janet Mullings, "Work-Related Stress and Coping Among Correctional Officers: Implications from the Organizational Literature," *Journal of Criminal Justice* 24 (1996): 291–308.

66. Peter Horne, "Female Corrections Officers," *Federal Probation* 49 (1985): 46–55.

67. *Dothard v. Rawlinson,* 433 U.S. 321 (1977).

68. Christopher D. Man and John P. Cronan, "Forecasting Sexual Abuse in Prison: The Prison Subculture of Masculinity as a Backdrop for 'Deliberate Indifference,'" *Journal of Criminal Law and Criminology* (2001): 127–166.

69. David Duffee, *Corrections, Practice and Policy* (New York: Random House, 1989), 305.

70. Randy Martin and Sherwood Zimmerman, "A Typology of the Causes of Prison Riots and an Analytical Extension to the 1986 West Virginia Riot," *Justice Quarterly* 7 (1990): 711–737.

71. Grant Harris, Tracey Skilling, and Marnie Rice, "The Construct of Psychopathy," in Michael Tonry, ed., *Crime and Justice: An Annual Edition* (Chicago: University of Chicago Press, 2001), 197–265.

72. For a series of papers on the position, see A. Cohen, G. Cole, and R. Baily, eds., *Prison Violence* (Lexington, Mass.: Lexington Books, 1976).

73. Bert Useem and Michael Resig, "Collective Action in Prisons: Protests, Disturbances, and Riots," *Criminology* 37 (1999): 735–760.

74. National Advisory Commission on Criminal Justice Standards and Goals, *Corrections* (Washington, D.C.: Government Printing Office, 1973), 18.

75. *Cooper v. Pate,* 378 U.S. 546 (1964).

76. *Shaw v. Murphy* (99-1613), 2001.

77. *Newman v. Alabama,* 92 S.Ct. 1079, 405 U.S. 319 (1972).

78. *Estelle v. Gamble,* 429 U.S. 97 (1976).

79. Ibid.

80. *Trop v. Dulles,* 356 U.S. 86, 78 S.Ct. 590 (1958); see also *Furman v. Georgia,* 408 U.S. 238, 92 S.Ct. 2726, 33 L.Ed.2d 346 (1972).

81. *Weems v. United States,* 217 U.S. 349, 30 S.Ct. 544, 54 L.Ed. 793 (1910).

82. *Lee v. Tahash,* 352 F.2d 970 (8th Cir., 1965).

83. *Estelle v. Gamble,* 429 U.S. 97 (1976).

84. *Robinson v. California,* 370 U.S. 660 (1962).

85. *Gregg v. Georgia,* 428 U.S. 153 (1976).

86. *Jackson v. Bishop,* 404 F.2d 571 (8th Cir. 1968).

87. *Hope v. Pelzer,* et al., No. 01—309. June 27, 2002.

88. *Bell v. Wolfish,* 99 S.Ct. 1873–1974 (1979); see "*Bell v. Wolfish:* The Rights of Pretrial Detainees," *New England Journal of Prison Law* 6 (1979): 134.

89. *Farmer v. Brennan,* 144 S.Ct. 1970 (1994).

90. *Rhodes v. Chapman,* 452 U.S. 337 (1981); for further analysis of *Rhodes,* see Randall Pooler, "Prison Overcrowding and the Eighth Amendment: The Rhodes Not Taken," *New England Journal on Criminal and Civil Confinement* 8 (1983): 1–28.

91. *Prison Escape Survey* (Lincoln, Neb.: Corrections Compendium, 1991).

92. Bureau of Justice Statistics, "Forty-Two Percent of State Parole Discharges Were Successful," news release, 3 October 2001.

93. Timothy A. Hughes, Doris James Wilson, and Allen J. Beck, *Trends in State Parole, 1990–2000* (Washington, D.C.: Bureau of Justice Statistics, 2001).

94. Ronald Burns, Patrick Kinkade, Matthew Leone, and Scott Phillips, "Perspectives on Parole: The Board Members' Viewpoint," *Federal Probation* 63 (1999): 16–22.

95. Duncan N. Stevens, "Off the Mapp: Parole Revocation Hearings and the Fourth Amendment," *Journal of Criminal Law and Criminology* 89 (1999): 1047–1060.

96. Gregg Etter and Judy Hammond, "Community Service Work as Part of Offender Rehabilitation," *Corrections Today* 63 (2001): 114–117.

97. Brian Parry, "Special Service Unit: Dedicated to Investigating and Apprehending Violent Offenders," *Corrections Today* 63 (2001): 120.

98. Thomas Hanlon, David N. Nurco, Richard W. Bateman, and Kevin E. O'Grady, "The Response of Drug Abuser Parolees to a Combination of Treatment and Intensive Supervision," *Prison Journal* 78 (1998): 31–44; Susan Turner and Joan Petersilia, "Focusing on High-Risk Parolees: An Experiment to Reduce Commitments to the Texas Department of Corrections," *Journal of Research in Crime and Delinquency* 29 (1992): 34–61.

99. Patrick A. Langan and David J. Levin, *Recidivism of Prisoners Released in 1994* (Washington, D.C.: Bureau of Justice Statistics, 2002).

100. Robyn L. Cohen, *Probation and Parole Violators in State Prison, 1991: Survey of State Prison Inmates, 1991* (Washington, D.C.: Bureau of Justice Statistics, 1995).

101. Stephen Duguid, *Can Prisons Work? The Prisoner as Object and Subject in Modern Corrections* (Toronto: University of Toronto Press, 2000).

102. James Bonta, Moira Law, and Karl Hanson, "The Prediction of Criminal and Violent Recidivism Among Mentally Disordered Offenders: A Meta-Analysis," *Psychological Bulletin* 123 (1998): 123–142.

103. Roger Peters, Paul Greenbaum, John Edens, Chris Carter, and Madeline Ortiz, "Prevalence of DSM-IV Substance Abuse and Dependence Disorders Among Prison Inmates," *American Journal of Drug and Alcohol Abuse* 24 (1998): 573–580.

104. Catherine Hamilton, Louise Falshaw, and Kevin D. Browne, "The Link Between Recurrent Maltreatment and Offending Behavior," *International Journal of Offender Therapy & Comparative Criminology* 46 (2002): 75–95.

105. Bonnie Todis, Michael Bullis, Miriam Waintrup, Robert Schultz, and Ryan D'Ambrosio, "Overcoming the Odds: Qualitative Examination of Resilience Among Formerly Incarcerated Adolescents," *Exceptional Children* 68 (2001): 119–140.

106. J. E. Ryan, "Who Gets Revoked? A Comparison of Intensive Supervision Successes and Failures in Vermont," *Crime and Delinquency* 43 (1997): 104–118.

107. Hanlon, Nurco, Bateman, and O'Grady, "The Response of Drug Abuser Parolees to a Combination of Treatment and Intensive Supervision."

108. Laura Fishman, *Women at the Wall: A Study of Prisoners' Wives Doing Time on the Outside* (New York: State University of New York Press, 1990).

109. Leslee Goodman Hornick, "Volunteer Program Helps Make Inmates' Families Feel Welcome," *Corrections Today* 53 (1991): 184–86.

110. Jeremy Travis and Joan Petersilia, "Reentry Reconsidered: A New Look at an Old Question," *Crime and Delinquency* 47 (2001): 291–313.

111. Hanlon, Nurco, Bateman, and O'Grady, "The Response of Drug Abuser Parolees to a Combination of Treatment and Intensive Supervision."

112. Kathleen Olivares, Velmer Burton, and Francis Cullen, "The Collateral Consequences of a Felony Conviction: A National Study of State Legal Codes Ten Years Later," *Federal Probation* 60 (1996): 10–17.

113. See, for example, *Bush v. Reid,* 516 P.2d 1215 (Alaska, 1973); *Thompson v. Bond,* 421 F.Supp. 878 (W.D. Mo., 1976); *Delorne v. Pierce Freightlines Co.,* 353 F.Supp. 258 (D. Or., 1973); *Beyer v. Werner,* 299 F.Supp. 967 (E.D. N.Y., 1969).

Corrections and Terrorism

What should be done with captured Taliban, al Qaeda, and other terrorist fighters? There is not only a question about how they should be treated by the court system but also some question about how they should be dealt with by the corrections system.

The fighters captured in Afghanistan were first held at Camp X Ray, located at the American military base in Guantánamo, Cuba. The first detainees arrived at Camp X Ray on January 11, 2002.

Their legal status was uncertain. Although they were not, strictly speaking, criminal offenders, the U.S. government also refused to grant them prisoner-of-war status, which would entitle them to treatment governed by the Geneva Convention, including legal representation. The United States instead referred to these suspected terrorists by the vague term of "illegal combatants," entitled neither to attorneys, hearings, or other rights freely given to criminal defendants. This decision brought about protests from Germany, the Netherlands, the European Union, and human rights groups.

X Ray was run by the U.S. military command, and every effort was made to humanize the suspected terrorists' ordeal. When they arrived they were subject to a routine not unlike that for people entering a high-security prison. They were given a chemical washdown and a physical. The detainees also were fingerprinted and photographed. Meals were served three times a day in the cells; a typical breakfast included milk, a bagel with cream cheese and butter, a boiled egg, fruit, and water. The detainees received warm showers, toiletries, water, clean clothes, blankets, regular, culturally appropriate meals; they were given prayer mats and the right to practice their religion. Detainees were issued a bar of soap, a bottle of shampoo, a toothbrush and toothpaste, and flip-flop sandals. To address religious concerns, an Islamic call to prayer was broadcast over the camp's public address system, and U.S. troops placed signs near the cells pointing East so Muslim prisoners could pray in the direction of Mecca.

Despite these efforts, civil rights advocates became incensed when photographs emerged showing arriving detainees kneeling on the ground with earmuffs blocking their hearing, surgical masks covering their noses, and blackout goggles. Amnesty International likened the eight-foot-by-eight-foot chain-link cells at Camp X Ray to cages.

As the inmates continued to be detained at X Ray, it became apparent that the U.S. government was in no hurry to charge them with specific crimes or set up military tribunals to try their cases. The Pentagon reported that they were working to develop rules for these tribunals, because such a process has not been used since World War II.

As of March 27, 2002, there were three hundred detainees in the camp, representing at least thirty-three different countries. When on August 1, 2002, federal district judge Colleen Kollar-Kotelly dismissed a lawsuit brought by two groups of terrorist detainees, ruling that U.S. courts have no jurisdiction over prisoners in Cuba, it became obvious that the detention would be long term. She held that the detainees had no constitutional protections since Guantánamo is not formally part of the United States.

Camp Delta

As the number of detainees grew and it became apparent that their stay would be prolonged, the military began to build a larger and more complex prison compound, referred to as Camp Delta. With the opening of Camp Delta, Camp X Ray was closed on April 29, 2002. Three hundred detainees previously held there were transferred to the new camp on April 28, 2002. The rest were transferred on April 29, 2002.

Camp Delta was constructed as a 612-unit detention facility built on the site of a former facility made up of cinder-block buildings used years earlier during a Haitian refugee operation. Each unit measures eight feet by six feet eight inches. The facility has indoor plumbing with each unit having its own flush toilet, metal bedframe, and sink with running water. Areas at Camp Delta are also better controlled than Camp X Ray, and detainees are out of the sun more.

As of June 26, 2002, there were 536 detainees at Camp Delta. With military officials running out of detention space, construction work began on August 8, 2002, on a new wing for the Camp Delta prison camp.

C. Sherburne/PhotoLink/Getty Images

An additional 204 cells were added, thus bringing the number of cells in the compound to a total of 816. Some reports indicate that the camp will eventually have more than 2,000 cells.

At the time of this writing it seems unlikely that the terrorist suspects will be transferred to a stateside prison. Camp Delta will be the home of those captured in Afghanistan for far into the future.

Sources: Katharine Q. Seelye, "Threats and Responses: The Detainees; Guantánamo Bay Faces Sentence of Life as Permanent U.S. Prison," *New York Times,* 16 September 2002, A1; "Guantánamo Camp Grows," *New York Times,* 9 August 2002, A4; Neil A. Lewis, "Traces of Terror: The Prisoners; Judge Rebuffs Detainees at Guantánamo," *New York Times,* 1 August 2002, A20; "Detainees Treated Humanely, Officials Say," http://europe.cnn.com/2002/US/01/21/xray.conditions/, 23 January 2002; Frank Davies, "White House Considers Detaining Suspected Terrorists Indefinitely," *Knight Ridder/Tribune News Service,* 24 January 2002, K5608. Description of Camp Delta provided by Global Security, Inc., www.globalsecurity.org/military/facility/guantanamo-bay_x-ray.htm

To find out more about terrorism, go to http://cj.wadsworth.com and click on "Terrorism Update."

Juvenile Justice

In 2001, fourteen-year-old Nathaniel Brazill was convicted of second-degree murder for shooting his favorite teacher between the eyes after the teacher, Barry Grunow, age thirty-five, refused to let him into his classroom on the last day of school to say goodbye to two girls. By rejecting a verdict of first-degree murder, the jurors spared the boy from a sentence of life in prison without parole.

At his sentencing hearing, Nathaniel, facing twenty-five years to life, told the judge and the victim's family that he had never intended to shoot his favorite teacher and was sorry for the killing. "Words cannot really express how sorry I am, but they're all I have," the boy said. He called his victim a great man and teacher. "As I look back on that day I wish it had not happened and that I could bring Mr. Grunow back," said Nathaniel. "Regardless of what anyone thinks, I never intended to harm Mr. Grunow."

Typically, youngsters such as Nathaniel are tried in the juvenile justice system, an independent process that is designed to provide care and treatment to underage youth who are in trouble with the law. Yet, because of the seriousness of his crime, Nathaniel's case was transferred to the adult system, where he was tried and punished in the same manner as an adult. Should a boy as young as he be sent to an adult prison, where the emphasis is on punishment, not rehabilitation? Teenagers in adult prisons are the target of sexual exploitation and physical assault from older inmates; furthermore, being around older inmates can turn youthful offenders into hardened criminals. Yet Nathaniel was convicted of murder; does he deserve special treatment with an emphasis on rehabilitation?

Agencies of the juvenile justice system are continually faced with such dilemmas. Because of the importance of their work and the unique contribution they make, the topic of Part Five is the process of juvenile justice and its agencies. ■

14 The Juvenile Justice System

14 The Juvenile Justice System

Chapter Outline

Criminal Justice Links

Criminal Justice Viewpoints

IN 2002 THE NATION was shocked when taped confessions of two young boys were played in a Pensacola, Florida, courtroom during their murder trial. In calm, matter-of-fact tones, angelic-looking Derek King, fourteen, and his younger brother Alex, thirteen, were seen in a police video describing how on November 26, 2001, they planned an attack on their father and then beat him to death with a baseball bat. Terry King, a forty-year-old printer, was bludgeoned as he slept, legs crossed, in a recliner; afterwards, his house was burned down to destroy evidence. On the tape Derek says, "I made sure he was asleep. I got the bat and I hit him over the head. . . . I hit him once and I heard him moan. I was afraid he might wake up and see us, so I kept hitting him. I hit around ten times."

Derek was concerned that his father, who was a strict disciplinarian, was "staring" them down and planning on beating them for some misdeed. Derek said he was concerned that Alex, who could have passed for an eight-year-old, could not defend himself.

"I told Alex if it gets real serious that I would get physical with Dad," Derek said. "Alex told me that he was weak and he didn't have strength to fight my father off."

During the bizarre trial, the boys claimed that the statements they made were false. They had made up the tale to protect forty-year-old Ricky Marvin Chavis who, they claimed, was having a sexual relationship with Alex. Defense lawyers claimed that Chavis, a family friend, was the real killer, motivated by the fear that the boy's father was learning about his sexual relationship with Alex. The jury, however, did not believe the boys and they were convicted of murder. Chavis, tried separately, was found not guilty.

In another strange twist to the case, on October 17, 2002, the judge who tried the King brothers set aside their conviction, saying that the prosecutor's tactic of trying Chavis separately violated their rights to due process because the prosecution presented two theories about the crime, with no clear indication of who it believed committed the killing. Rather than overturn the conviction out of hand, the judge ordered the prosecution and defense to try to resolve the case in mediation, saying he would order a new trial only if they could not do so and prosecutors did not win an appeal. After some negotiation, the boys pled guilty to third-degree murder—a killing that occurs unintentionally during a crime, in this case an assault and battery. Derek King received an eight-year sentence; Alex received seven years. ■

To view the CNN video clip of this story, go to the book-specific Web site at http://cj.wadsworth.com/siegel_essen4e.

juvenile justice system The system of agencies and organizations that deal with youths who commit acts of juvenile delinquency (crimes under a given age) and acts of noncriminal behavior (truancy and incorrigibility).

The King case received significant media attention in 2002 because of its sensational and twisted facts and circumstances. Though highly unusual, it does illustrate the fact that many youths engage in serious criminal acts, even murder. And although most juvenile offenders are tried in a separate and independent **juvenile justice system**, those who commit the most serious crimes can be transferred to the adult system and face adult penalties. The King case is representative of the very difficult choices that agents of the juvenile justice system are continually asked to make: How should troubled children be treated? What can be done to save dangerous young offenders? Should youthful law violators be given unique treatment because of their age, or should they be treated in a similar fashion to an adult committing the same crime?

Independent of, yet interrelated with the adult criminal justice system, the juvenile justice system is primarily responsible for dealing with juvenile and youth crime, as well as with incorrigible and truant children and runaways. First conceived at the turn of the twentieth century, the juvenile justice system was viewed as a quasi-social welfare agency that was to act as a surrogate parent in the interests of the child; this is referred to as the **parens patriae** philosophy. Today, some authorities still hold to the original social welfare principles of the juvenile justice system and argue that it is primarily a treatment agency that acts as a wise parent, dispensing personalized, individual justice to needy children who seek guidance and understanding. They recognize that many children who are arrested and processed to court come from the lowest economic classes. These at-risk children have grown up in troubled families, attend inadequate schools, and live in deteriorated neighborhoods. They are deserving of care and concern, not punishment and control.

parens patriae Power of the state to act on behalf of the child and provide care and protection equivalent to that of a parent.

In contrast to this view, those with a crime control orientation suggest that the juvenile justice system's parens patriae philosophy is outdated. They point to nationally publicized incidents of juvenile violence, such as the shootings at Columbine High School in Colorado, as indicators that serious juvenile offenders should be punished and disciplined rather than treated and rehabilitated. They note that juveniles seventeen years and under commit about 17 percent of all murders in the United States.[1] It is not surprising then that they applaud when court rulings enhance the state's ability to identify and apprehend youthful law violators. For example, in 1995 the U.S. Supreme Court held in *Vernonia School District v. Acton* that public school athletes in middle and high schools can be required to submit to random drug testing even though the student did not engage in suspicious behavior.[2] Then on June 27, 2002, the Court ruled in the case of *Pottawatomie County v. Earls* that it is permissible to allow a school drug-testing policy that establishes random, suspicionless urinalysis testing of any students participating in extracurricular activities.[3] These and similar rulings encourage those who want the state to be given a free hand to deal with juveniles who are disruptive at school and in the community.

It remains to be seen whether the juvenile justice system will continue on its path toward identification and control or return to its former role as a treatment-dispensing agency. There are also those who call for a totally new approach to the juvenile justice system, using the **balanced and restorative justice model**, which calls for offender-victim reconciliation, personal accountability, and community-based program development.[4]

balanced and restorative justice model A new model of juvenile justice focusing on victim restoration, improving offender abilities, and protecting the public. Offenders, victims, and the community are all active participants.

This chapter reviews the history of juvenile justice and discusses the justice system's processing of youthful offenders.

The History of Juvenile Justice

The modern practice of legally separating adult and juvenile offenders can be traced back to two developments in English custom and law: the development of poor laws and the chancery court. Both were designed to allow the state to take control of the lives of needy but not necessarily criminal children.[5] They set the precedent for later American developments.

As early as 1535 the English passed statutes known as **poor laws,** which in part mandated the appointment of overseers who placed destitute or neglected children with families who then trained them in agricultural, trade, or domestic services; this practice was referred to as *indenture*. The Elizabethan poor laws of 1601 created a system of church wardens and overseers who, with the consent of the justices of the peace, identified vagrant, delinquent, and neglected children and took measures to put them to work. Often this meant placing them in poorhouses or workhouses or, more commonly, apprenticing them until their adulthood. The indenture, or involuntary apprentice, system set the precedent, which continues today, of allowing the government to take control of youths who have committed no illegal acts but who are deemed unable to care for themselves.

In contrast, chancery courts were concerned primarily with protecting property rights and welfare of more affluent minor children who could not care for themselves—children whose position and property were of direct concern to the monarch. They dealt with issues of guardianship and the use and control of property. Chancery courts operated under the parens patriae philosophy, which held that children were under the protective control of the state and that its rulers were justified in intervening in their lives.[6] In the famous English case *Wellesley v. Wellesley,* a duke's children were taken from him in the name of parens patriae because of his scandalous behavior.[7]

The concept of parens patriae came to represent the primacy of the state and its power to act in "the best interests of the child." The idea that the state was legally obligated to protect the immature, the incompetent, the neglected, and the delinquent subsequently became an important influence on the development of the U.S. juvenile justice system in the twentieth century.

Care of Children in Early America

The forced apprenticeship system and the poor laws were brought from England to colonial America. Poor laws were passed in Virginia in 1646 and in Connecticut and Massachusetts in 1678 and continued in force until the early nineteenth century. They mandated care for wayward and destitute children. However, those youths who committed serious criminal offenses continued to be tried in the same courts as adults.

To accommodate dependent youths, local jurisdictions developed almshouses, poorhouses, and workhouses. Crowded and unhealthy, these accepted the poor, the insane, the diseased, and vagrant and destitute children. Middle-class civic leaders, who referred to themselves as **child savers,** began to develop organizations and groups to help alleviate the burdens of the poor and immigrants by sponsoring shelter care for youths, educational and social activities, and the development of settlement houses. In retrospect, their main focus seems to have been on extending governmental control over a whole range of youthful activities that previously had been left to private or family control, including idleness, drinking, vagrancy, and delinquency.[8]

The Child-Saving Movement

The child savers were responsible for creating a number of programs for indigent youths, including the New York House of Refuge, which began operations in 1825.[9] Its creation was effected by prominent Quakers and influential political leaders, such as Cadwallader Colden and Stephen Allen. In 1816 they formed the Society for the Prevention of Pauperism, which was devoted to the concept of protecting indigent youths who were at risk to crime by taking them off the streets and reforming them in a family-like environment.[10]

poor laws   Seventeenth-century laws in England that bound out vagrants and abandoned children as indentured servants to masters.

child savers   Late nineteenth-century reformers in America who developed programs for troubled youths and influenced legislation creating the juvenile justice system.

Boys on the steps of an abandoned tenement building in New York City, about 1889. The child savers were concerned that, if left alone, children such as these would enter a life of crime. Critics accused them of class and race discrimination and thought they sought to maintain control over the political system.

Though privately managed, the New York State legislature began providing funds to the New York House of Refuge partly through a head tax on arriving transatlantic passengers and seamen, plus the proceeds from license fees for New York City's taverns, theatres, and circuses. These revenue sources were deemed appropriate, since supporters blamed immigration, intemperance, and commercial entertainment for juvenile crime.

The New York House of Refuge, actually a reformatory, opened January 1, 1825, with only six boys and three girls, but within the first decade of its operation 1,678 inmates were admitted. Most kids were sent because of vagrancy and petty crimes and were sentenced or committed indefinitely, and some remained until they reached adulthood. At first, the institution accepted inmates from across the state of New York, but when the Western House of Refuge was opened in Rochester, New York, in 1849, residents were selected by domicile: those residing in the eastern part of the state were sent to New York City, those in the western part to Rochester.

Once a resident, a large part of an adolescent's daily schedule was devoted to supervised labor, which was regarded as beneficial to education and discipline. Inmate labor also supported operating expenses for the reformatory. Male inmates worked in shops that produced brushes, cane chairs, brass nails, and shoes. The female inmates sewed uniforms, did laundry, and carried out other domestic work. A badge system was used to segregate inmates according to their behavior. Although students received rudimentary educational skills, greater emphasis was placed on evangelical religious instruction; non-Protestant clergy were excluded. The reformatory had the authority to bind out inmates through indenture agreements to private employers; most males were farmworkers and most females were domestic laborers.

The Refuge Movement Spreads

When the House of Refuge opened, the majority of children admitted were status offenders placed there because of vagrancy or neglect. Children were placed in the institution by court order, sometimes over parents' objections. Their length of stay depended on need, age, and skill. Critics complained that the institution was run like a prison, with strict discipline and absolute separation of the sexes. Such a harsh program drove many children to run away, and the House of Refuge was forced to take a more lenient approach. Despite criticism, the concept enjoyed expanding popularity. In 1826, the Boston City Council founded the House of Reformation for juvenile offenders.[11] The courts committed children found guilty of criminal violations, or found to be beyond the control of their parents, to these schools. Because the child savers considered parents of delinquent children to be as guilty as convicted offenders, they sought to have the reform schools establish control over the children. Refuge managers believed they were preventing poverty and crime by separating destitute and delinquent children from their parents and placing them in an institution.[12]

The child savers also influenced state and local governments to create independent correctional institutions to house minors. The first of these reform schools opened in Westboro, Massachusetts, in 1848 and in Rochester, New York, in 1849. Other states soon followed suit—Ohio in 1850 and Maine, Rhode Island,

and Michigan in 1860. Children lived in congregate conditions and spent their days working at institutional jobs, learning a trade where possible, and receiving some basic education. They were racially and sexually segregated, discipline was harsh and often involved whipping and isolation, and the physical care was of poor quality.

In 1853 New York philanthropist Charles Loring Brace helped develop the **Children's Aid Society** as an alternative for dealing with neglected and delinquent youths. Brace proposed rescuing wayward youths from the harsh environment of the city and providing them with temporary shelter and care. He then sought to place them in private homes in rural communities where they could engage in farming and agricultural work outside the influence of the city. Although some placements proved successful, others resulted in the exploitation of children in a strange environment with few avenues of escape.

Children's Aid Society A child-saving organization began by Charles Loring Brace; it took children from the streets in large cities and placed them with farm families on the prairie.

Establishment of the Juvenile Court As the nation expanded, it became evident that private charities and public organizations were not caring adequately for the growing number of troubled youths. The child savers lobbied for an independent, state-supported **juvenile court,** and their efforts prompted the development of the first comprehensive juvenile court in Illinois in 1899. The Illinois Juvenile Court Act set up an independent court to handle criminal law violations by children under sixteen years of age, as well as to care for neglected, dependent, and wayward youths. The act also created a probation department to monitor youths in the community and to direct juvenile court judges to place serious offenders in secure schools for boys and industrial schools for girls. The ostensible purpose of the act was to separate juveniles from adult offenders and provide a legal framework in which juveniles could get adequate care and custody. By 1925 most states had developed juvenile courts. The enactment of the Illinois Juvenile Court Act of 1899 was a major event in the history of the juvenile justice movement in the United States.

juvenile court A court that has original jurisdiction over persons defined by statute as juveniles and alleged to be delinquents or status offenders.

Although the efforts of the child savers to set up independent juvenile courts were originally seen as liberal reforms, modern scholars commonly view them as attempts to control and punish. Justice historians have suggested that the reform movement actually expressed the vested interests of the "ruling class."[13] Thus, according to this revisionist approach, the reformers applied the concept of parens patriae for their own purposes, including the continuance of middle- and upper-class values, the control of the political system, and the furtherance of a child labor system consisting of lower-class workers with marginal skills.

The Development of Juvenile Justice

The juvenile court movement quickly spread across the United States. In its early form it provided youths with quasi-legal, quasi-therapeutic, personalized justice. The main concern was the "best interests of the child," not strict adherence to legal doctrine, constitutional rights, or due process of law. The court was paternalistic, rather than adversarial. For example, attorneys were not required. Hearsay evidence, inadmissible in criminal trials, was commonly employed in the adjudication of juvenile offenders. Children were encouraged to admit their "guilt" in open court in violation of their Fifth Amendment rights. Verdicts were based on a "preponderance of the evidence," instead of being "beyond a reasonable doubt." Juvenile courts then functioned as quasi-social service agencies.

Reform Schools Youngsters found delinquent in juvenile court could spend years in a state training school. Though priding themselves as nonpunitive, these early reform schools were generally punitive and based on the concept of reform through hard work and discipline. In the second half of the nineteenth century, the emphasis shifted from massive industrial schools to the cottage system. Juvenile offenders were housed in a series of small cabins, each one holding twenty to forty children, run by "cottage parents," who attempted to create a homelike atmosphere. The first cottage system was established in Massachusetts, the second in Ohio. The system was generally applauded for being a great improvement over the industrial training schools. The general movement was away from punishment and toward rehabilitation through attending to the needs of the individual and by implementing complex programs of diagnosis and treatment.[14] By the 1950s the influence of such therapists as Karen Horney and Carl Rogers promoted the introduction of psychological treatment in juvenile corrections. Group counseling techniques became standard procedure in most juvenile institutions.

To read about decision making in the early juvenile justice system, go to David Wolcott, "'The Cop Will Get You': The Police and Discretionary Juvenile Justice, 1890–1940," *Journal of Social History,* Winter 2001 v35 i2 p349(24), on Info-Trac College Edition.

Legal Change   In the 1960s and 1970s the U.S. Supreme Court radically altered the juvenile justice system when it issued a series of decisions that established the right of juveniles to receive due process of law: the Court established that juveniles had the same rights as adults in important areas of trial process, including the right to confront witnesses, notice of charges, and the right to counsel.[15] Exhibit 14.1 illustrates some of the most important legal cases bringing procedural due process to the juvenile justice process.

Exhibit 14.1   Leading constitutional cases in juvenile justice

Kent v. United States (1966) determined that a child has due process rights, such as having an attorney present at waiver hearings.

In re Gault (1967) ruled that a minor has basic due process rights, including: (1) notice of the charges with respect to their timeliness and specificity, (2) right to counsel, (3) right to confrontation and cross-examination, (4) privilege against self-incrimination, (5) right to a transcript of the trial record, and (6) right to appellate review.

In re Winship (1970) determined that the level of evidence for a finding of "juvenile delinquency" is proof beyond a reasonable doubt.

McKeiver v. Pennsylvania (1971) held that trial by jury in a juvenile court's adjudicative stage is not a constitutional requirement.

Breed v. Jones (1975) rules that a child has the protection of the double-jeopardy clause of the Fifth Amendment and cannot be tried twice for the same crime.

Fare v. Michael C. (1979) held that a child's request to see his probation officer at the time of interrogation did not operate to invoke his Fifth Amendment right to remain silent. According to the Court, the probation officer cannot be expected to offer the type of advice that an accused would expect from an attorney. The landmark *Miranda v. Arizona* case ruled that a request for a lawyer is an immediate invocation of a person's right to silence, but this rule is not applicable for a request to see the probation officer.

Eddings v. Oklahoma (1982) ruled that a defendant's age should be a mitigating factor in deciding whether to apply the death penalty.

Schall v. Martin (1984) upheld a statute allowing for the placement of children in preventive detention before their adjudication. The Court concluded that it was not unreasonable to detain juveniles for their own protection.

New Jersey v. T.L.O. (1985) determined that the Fourth Amendment applies to school searches. The Court adopted a "reasonable suspicion" standard, as opposed to the stricter standard of "probable cause," to evaluate the legality of searches and seizures in a school setting.

Thompson v. Oklahoma (1988) ruled that imposing capital punishment on a juvenile murderer who was fifteen years old at the time of the offense violated the Eighth Amendment's constitutional prohibition against cruel and unusual punishment.

Stanford v. Kentucky and *Wilkins v. Missouri* (1989) concluded that the imposition of the death penalty on a juvenile who committed a crime between the ages of sixteen and eighteen was not unconstitutional and that the Eighth Amendment's cruel and unusual punishment clause did not prohibit capital punishment.

Vernonia School District v. Acton (1995) held that the Fourth Amendment's guarantee against unreasonable searches is not violated by the suspicionless drug testing of all students choosing to participate in interscholastic athletics. The Supreme Court expanded the power of public educators to ensure safe learning environments in schools.

United States v. Lopez (1995) ruled that Congress exceeded its authority under the Commerce Clause when it passed the Gun-Free School Zone Act, which made it a federal crime to possess a firearm within one thousand feet of a school.

Sources: *Kent. v. United States,* 383 U.S. 541, 86 S.Ct. 1045, 16 L.Ed.2d 84 (1966); *In re Gault,* 387 U.S. 1, 87 S.Ct. 1248 (1967); *McKeiver v. Pennsylvania,* 403 U.S. 528, 91 S.Ct. 1776 (1971); *Breed v. Jones,* 421 U.S. 519, 95 S.Ct. 1779 (1975); *Fare v. Michael C.,* 442 U.S. 707, 99 S.Ct. 2560 (1979); *Eddings v. Oklahoma,* 455 U.S. 104, 102 S.Ct. 869, 71 L.Ed. 2d 1 (1982); *Schall v. Martin,* 467 U.S. 253, 104 S.Ct. 2403 (1984); *New Jersey v. T.L.O.,* 469 U.S. 325, 105 S.Ct. 733 (1985); *Thompson v. Oklahoma,* 487 U.S. 815, 108 S.Ct. 2687, 101 L.Ed. 2d 702 (1988); *Stanford v. Kentucky,* 492 U.S., 109 S.Ct. 2969 (1989); *Vernonia School District v. Acton,* 515 U.S. 646 115 S.Ct. 2386, 132 L.Ed. 2d 564 (1995); *Wilkins v. Missouri,* 492 U.S. 361, 109 S.Ct. 2969 (1989); *United States v. Lopez,* 115 S.Ct. 1624 (1995).

Besides the legal revolution brought about by the Supreme Court, Congress passed the Juvenile Justice and Delinquency Prevention Act of 1974 (JJDP act) and established the federal Office of Juvenile Justice and Delinquency Prevention (OJJDP).[16] This legislation was enacted to identify the needs of youths and to fund programs in the juvenile justice system. Its main goal was to separate wayward, nondangerous youths from institutions housing delinquents and to remove adolescents from institutions housing adult offenders. In 1996, in a move reflecting the growing national frustration with serious delinquent offenders, the act was amended to make it easier to hold delinquents in adult penal institutions.

Juvenile Justice Today

Today, the juvenile justice system has jurisdiction over two distinct categories of offenders: delinquents and status offenders.[17] **Juvenile delinquency** refers to children who fall under a jurisdictional age limit, which varies from state to state, and who commit an act in violation of the penal code. **Status offenders** include truants and habitually disobedient and ungovernable children (see Figure 14.1). They are commonly characterized in state statutes as persons or children in need of supervision (PINS or CHINS). Most states distinguish such behavior from delinquent conduct to lessen the effect of any stigma on children as a result of their involvement with the juvenile court. In addition, juvenile courts generally have jurisdiction over situations involving conduct directed at (rather than committed by) juveniles, such as parental neglect, deprivation, abandonment, and abuse.

The states have also set different maximum ages below which children fall under the jurisdiction of the juvenile court. Many states include all children under eighteen years of age, others set the limit at seventeen, and still others at sixteen.

juvenile delinquency Participation in illegal behavior by a minor who falls under a statutory age limit.

status offender A juvenile who has been adjudicated by a judge of a juvenile court as having committed a status offense (running away, truancy, or incorrigibility).

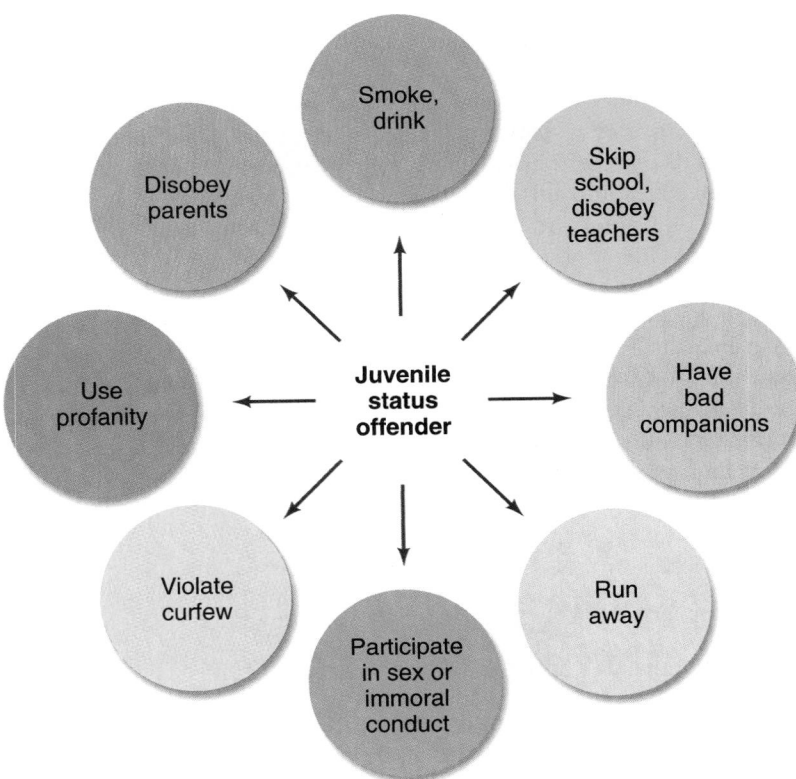

Figure 14.1
Status offenses

Does scaring youth help keep them out of trouble? Shape-Up participants tour cell house 5, dubbed "The Zoo," at the Colorado Territorial Prison. The two-day program is designed to show delinquent teens what life is like inside prison and how to avoid it. Reviews of such programs have been mixed, and there is some evidence that participants actually commit more crime than nonparticipants!

The Office of Juvenile Justice and Delinquency Prevention is an excellent resource for information on the juvenile justice system: http://ojjdp.ncjrs.org/

Some states exclude certain classes of offenders or offenses from the juvenile justice system. For example, youths who commit serious violent offenses such as rape or murder may be automatically excluded from the juvenile justice system and treated as adults on the premise that they stand little chance of rehabilitation within the confines of the juvenile system. Juvenile court judges may also transfer, or waive, repeat offenders whom they deem untreatable by the juvenile authorities.

The juvenile justice system has evolved into a parallel yet independent system of justice with its own terminology and rules of procedure. Exhibit 14.2 describes the basic similarities and differences between the juvenile and adult justice systems. Exhibit 14.3 points out how the language used in the juvenile court differs from that used in the adult system.

Today, the juvenile justice system is responsible for processing and treating almost two million cases of youthful misbehavior annually. Each state's system is unique, so it is difficult to give a precise accounting of the justice process. Moreover, depending on local practice and tradition, case processing often varies from community to community within a single state. Keeping this in mind, the following sections provide a general description of some of the key processes and decision points in juvenile justice. Figure 14.2 illustrates a model of the juvenile justice process.

Police Processing of the Juvenile Offender

According to the Uniform Crime Reports, police officers arrest more than 1.5 million juveniles under age eighteen each year, including almost 500,000 under age fifteen.[18] Most larger police departments have separate, juvenile detectives who handle delinquency cases and focus their attention on the problems of youth. In

Exhibit 14.2 Similarities and differences between juvenile and adult justice systems

Similarities

- Discretion used by police officers, judges, and correctional personnel
- Right to receive Miranda warning
- Protection from prejudicial lineups or other identification procedures
- Procedural safeguards when making an admission of guilt
- Advocacy roles of prosecutors and defense attorneys
- Right to counsel at most key stages of the court process
- Availability of pretrial motions
- Plea negotiation/plea bargaining
- Right to a hearing and an appeal
- Standard of proof beyond a reasonable doubt
- Pretrial detention possible
- Detention without bail if considered dangerous
- Probation as a sentencing option
- Community treatment as a sentencing option

Differences

- The primary purpose of juvenile procedures is protection and treatment; with adults, the aim is to punish the guilty.
- Jurisdiction is determined by age in the juvenile system, by the nature of the offense in the adult system.
- Juveniles can be apprehended for acts that would not be criminal if committed by an adult (status offenses).
- Juvenile proceedings are not considered criminal; adult proceedings are.
- Juvenile court proceedings are generally informal and private; adult court proceedings are more formal and are open to the public.
- Courts cannot release to the press identifying information about a juvenile, but must release information about an adult.
- Parents are highly involved in the juvenile process but not in the adult process.
- The standard of arrest is more stringent for adults than for juveniles.
- Juveniles are released into parental custody; adults are generally given bail.
- Juveniles have no constitutional right to a jury trial; adults do. Some states extend this right to juveniles by statute.
- Juveniles can be searched in school without probable cause or a warrant.
- A juvenile's record is generally sealed when the age of majority is reached; an adult's record is permanent.
- A juvenile court cannot sentence juveniles to county jails or state prisons, which are reserved for adults.
- The U.S. Supreme Court has declared that the Eighth Amendment prohibits the death penalty for juveniles ages 15 and under, but not for juveniles ages 16 and 17.

Exhibit 14.3 Comparison of terms used in adult and juvenile justice systems

	Juvenile Terms	Adult Terms
The person and the act	Delinquent child	Criminal
	Delinquent act	Crime
Preadjudicatory stage	Take into custody	Arrest
	Petition	Indictment
	Agree to a finding	Plead guilty
	Deny the petition	Plead not guilty
	Adjustment	Plea bargain
	Detention facility; child-care shelter	Jail
Adjudicatory stage	Substitution	Reduction of charges
	Adjudicatory or fact-finding hearing	Trial
	Adjudication	
Postadjudicatory stage	Dispositional hearing	Sentencing hearing
	Disposition	Sentence
	Commitment	Incarceration
	Youth development center; treatment center; training school	Prison
	Residential child-care facility	Halfway house
	Aftercare	Parole

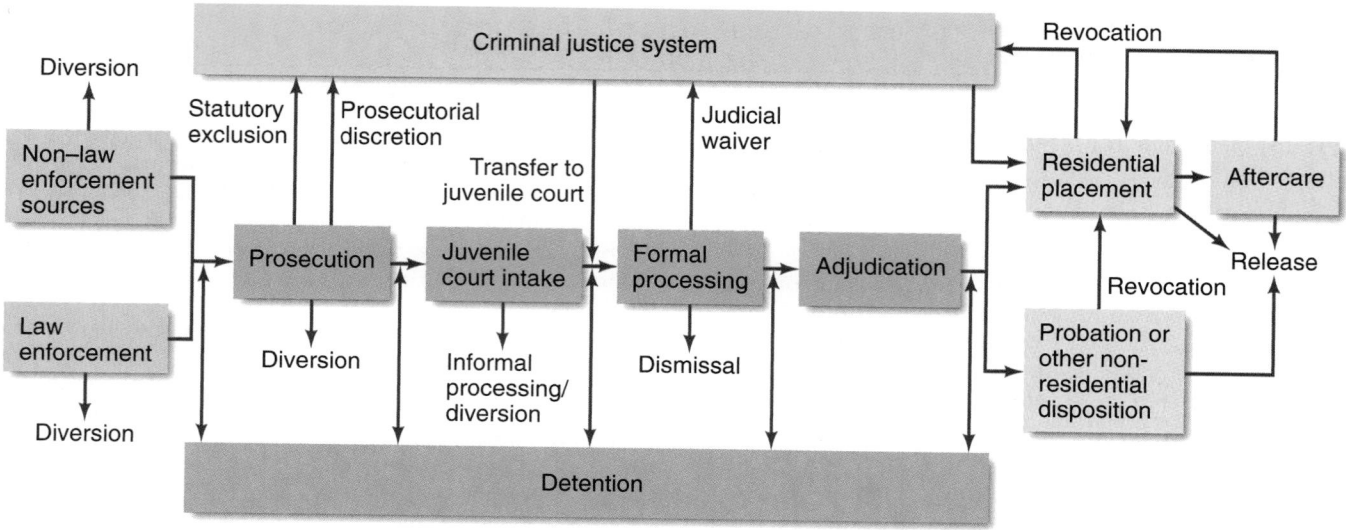

Figure 14.2
Case flow through the juvenile justice process

Source: This figure can be accessed online through the Office of Juvenile Justice and Delinquency Prevention: www.ojjdp.ncjrs.org/facts/casejpg.html.

addition to conducting their own investigations, they typically take control of cases after an arrest is made by a uniformed officer.

Most states do not have specific statutory provisions distinguishing the arrest process for children from that for adults. Some jurisdictions, however, give broad arrest powers to the police in juvenile cases by authorizing the officer to make an arrest whenever it is believed that the child's behavior falls within the jurisdiction of the juvenile court. Consequently, police may arrest youths for behavior considered legal for adults, including running away, curfew violations, and being in possession of alcohol.

Use of Discretion

When a juvenile is found to have engaged in delinquent or incorrigible behavior, police agencies are charged with the decision to release or to detain the child and refer her to juvenile court. Because of the state's interest in the child, the police generally have more discretion in the investigatory and arrest stages of the juvenile process than they do when dealing with adult offenders.

This discretionary decision—to release or to detain—is based not only on the nature of the offense but also on police attitudes and the child's social and personal conditions at the time of the arrest. The following is a partial list of factors believed to be significant in police decision making regarding juvenile offenders:

- The type and seriousness of the child's offense
- The ability of the parents to be of assistance in disciplining the child
- The child's past contacts with police
- The degree of cooperation obtained from the child and parents and their demeanor, attitude, and personal characteristics
- Whether the child denies the allegations in the petition and insists on a court hearing

Research indicates that most police decisions involve discretion.[19] The most recent of these studies, which analyzed juvenile data collected as part of the Project on

Policing Neighborhoods—a comprehensive study of police patrols in Indianapolis, Indiana, and St. Petersburg, Florida—found that only 13 percent of police encounters with juveniles resulted in arrest.[20] As shown in Table 14.1, the most likely disposition of police encounters with juveniles is a command or threat to arrest (38 percent), followed by searching or interrogating the suspects (24 percent). Furthermore, these studies show that many juvenile offenders are never referred to the juvenile court.

Table 14.1	Disposition of police encounters with juveniles

Disposition	Juveniles (%)
Release	14
Advise	11
Search/interrogate	24
Command/threaten	38
Arrest	13

Source: Robert E. Worden and Stephanie M. Myers, *Police Encounters with Juvenile Suspects* (Albany: Hindelang Criminal Justice Research Center and School of Criminal Justice, State University of New York, 2001), Table 3.

Legal Rights

Once a juvenile has been taken into custody, the child has the same Fourth Amendment right to be free from unreasonable searches and seizures as an adult does. Children in police custody can be detained prior to trial, interrogated, and placed in lineups. However, because of their youth and inexperience, children are generally afforded more protections than adults. Police must be careful that the juvenile suspect understands his constitutional rights, and if there is some question, must provide access to a parent or guardian to protect the child's legal interests. For example, police often questioned juveniles in the absence of their parents or an attorney. Any incriminatory statements or confessions made by juveniles could be placed in evidence at their trials. That is no longer permissible, and children have the same (or more) Miranda rights as adults, as was confirmed in the case of *Fare v. Michael C.* (1979).[21] Today, police will interrogate a juvenile without an adult present only if they believe that the youth is unquestionably mature and experienced enough to understand her legal rights.

To read more about a police juvenile division, go to the Web page of the Pasadena, California, Police Department:

www.ci.pasadena.tx.us/police/investigations/juveniles/juveniles.htm

The Juvenile Justice Process

After the police have determined that a case warrants further attention, they will bind it over to the prosecutor's office, which then has the responsibility for channeling the case through the juvenile court. The juvenile court plays a major role in controlling juvenile behavior and delivering social services to children in need.

The most recent data available indicate that U.S. juvenile courts process an estimated 1.8 million delinquency cases (cases involving juveniles charged with criminal law violations) each year. The number of delinquency cases handled by juvenile courts increased 44 percent during the ten-year period between 1989 and 1998. During this time, cases involving crimes against people (such as assaults and robberies) increased 88 percent; public order offenses (prostitution, traffic offenses) increased 73 percent, and property offense cases increased 11 percent.[22] There has also been a rapid increase in drug offenses, which more than doubled between 1993 and 1998; drug offense cases accounted for 11 percent of all delinquency cases in 1998, compared with 8 percent in 1994; the number of drug offense cases processed during 1998 was 108 percent greater than in 1993 and 148 percent greater than 1989.[23] Like the crime rate, the number of youths processed to juvenile court has stabilized during the past few years; the most recent data available indicate a decline of about 3 percent between 1997 and 1998.[24] There were distinct gender- and race-based differences in the juvenile court population. About three-quarters of all juvenile cases in 1998 involved a male. However, the percentage of females processed by juvenile courts has increased about 25 percent during the past decade. Similarly, about 30 percent of the juvenile court population was made up of African-American youth, although they make up only about 15 percent of the general population.

To read about the prosecution of juvenile gun offenders, go to

www.ncjrs.org/html/ojjdp/jjbul2000_03_5/pag4.html

The Intake Process

After police processing, the juvenile offender is usually remanded to the local juvenile court's intake division. At this juncture, court intake officers or probation personnel review and initially screen the child and the family to determine if the child needs to be handled formally or whether the case can be settled without the necessity of costly and intrusive official intervention. Their report helps the prosecutor decide whether to handle the case informally or bind it over for trial. The intake stage represents an opportunity to place a child in informal programs both within the court and in the community. The intake process also is critically important because more than half of the referrals to the juvenile courts never go beyond this stage.

The Detention Process

After a juvenile is formally taken into custody, either as a delinquent or as a status offender, the prosecutor usually makes a decision to release the child to the parent or guardian or to detain the child in a secure shelter pending trial.

detention The temporary care of a child alleged to be a delinquent or status offender who requires secure custody, pending court disposition.

Detention has always been a controversial area of juvenile justice. Far too many children have been routinely placed in detention while awaiting court appearances. Status offenders and delinquents have been held in the same facility, and in many parts of the country, adult county jails were used to detain juvenile offenders. The Juvenile Justice Act of 1974 placed emphasis on reducing the num-

Most children taken into custody by the police are released to their parents or guardians. Some are held overnight until their parents can be notified of the arrest. Police officers normally take a child to a place of detention only after other alternatives have been exhausted. Many juvenile courts in urban areas have staff members, such as intake probation officers, who are on duty twenty-four hours a day to screen detention admissions.

ber of children placed in inappropriate detention facilities, and although successful, the practice continues.

Despite efforts to reduce detention, caseloads increased 25 percent between 1989 and 1998, reflecting the increase in juvenile court cases from 1.2 million in 1989 to 1.8 million in 1998. Another reason was the surge in the detention of female offenders, whose numbers increased 56 percent compared with 20 percent for males. The large increase was tied to the growth in the number of delinquency cases involving females charged with violent offenses (15 percent).[25]

Detention caseloads increased more for white juveniles than black juveniles. Between 1989 and 1998, the number of cases involving detention increased more for white juveniles (33 percent, from 149,000 to 198,000) than for black juveniles (15 percent, from 100,900 to 115,800), most likely because the use of detention in cases involving violence and drug offenses increased more for whites than blacks. The increase in detention for juveniles charged with violent person offenses was three times greater for whites than blacks (95 percent versus 30 percent), and the increase for drug offenses was twelve times greater.

Legal Issues   Most state statutes ordinarily require a hearing on the appropriateness of detention if the initial decision is to keep the child in custody. At this hearing, the child has a right to counsel and may be given other procedural due process safeguards, notably the privilege against self-incrimination and the right to confront and cross-examine witnesses. Most state juvenile court acts provide criteria to support a decision to detain the child. These include (1) the need to protect the child, (2) whether the child presents a serious danger to the public, and (3) the likelihood that the juvenile will return to court for adjudication. Whereas in adult cases the sole criterion for pretrial release may be the offender's availability for trial, juveniles may be detained for other reasons, including their own protection. Normally, the finding of the judge that the child should be detained must be supported by factual evidence. In the 1984 case of *Schall v. Martin,* the U.S. Supreme Court upheld the right of the states to detain a child before trial to protect his welfare and the public safety.[26]

Reforming Detention   There has been an ongoing effort to reform detention. The most important reform has been the successful effort to remove status offenders from lockups containing delinquents. After decades of effort, almost all states have passed laws requiring that status offenders be placed in nonsecure shelters, rather than secure detention facilities, thereby reducing their contact with more dangerous delinquent youth.

Another serious problem is the detention of youths in adult jails. The practice is common in rural areas where there are relatively few separate facilities for young offenders.[27] The OJJDP has given millions of dollars in aid to encourage the removal of juveniles from adult lockups. These grants have helped jurisdictions develop intake screening procedures, specific release or detention criteria, and alternative residential and nonresidential programs for juveniles awaiting trial. By 1980 amendments to the act mandating the absolute removal of juveniles from jails had been adopted. Despite such efforts, many states are not complying with the removal provisions, and thousands of youths are annually detained in adult jails. Whatever the actual number jailed today, placing young offenders in adult jails continues to be a significant problem in the juvenile justice system. Juveniles detained in adult jails often live in squalid conditions and are subject to physical and sexual abuse. The practice is widely condemned, but eliminating the confinement of juveniles in adult institutions remains a difficult task.[28] Many youths who commit nonserious acts are still being held in adult jails—for example, runaways who are apprehended in rural areas; and minority juveniles may be spending greater amounts of time in jail than white offenders for the same offense.[29]

With offices based at Eastern Kentucky University and at Michigan State University, the National Juvenile Detention Association (NJDA) exists exclusively to advance the science, processes, and art of juvenile detention services through the overall improvement of the juvenile justice profession. Go to the Web site at
www.njda.com/default.html

To read about the bail process in Canada, go to InfoTrac College Edition and read Kimberly N. Varma, "Exploring 'Youth' in Court: An Analysis of Decision Making in Youth Court Bail Hearings," *Canadian Journal of Criminology*, April 2002 v44 i2 p143(22).

Bail

If a child is not detained, the question of bail arises. Federal courts have not found it necessary to rule on the issue of a juvenile's constitutional right to bail because liberal statutory release provisions act as appropriate alternatives. Although only a few state statutes allow release on money bail, many others have juvenile code provisions that emphasize the release of the child to the parents as an acceptable substitute. A constitutional right to bail that on its face seems to benefit a child may have unforeseen results. For example, money bail might impose a serious economic strain on the child's family while conflicting with the protective and social concerns of the juvenile court. Considerations of economic liabilities and other procedural inequities have influenced the majority of courts confronting this question to hold that juveniles do not have a right to bail.

Plea Bargaining

Before trial, juvenile prosecutors may attempt to negotiate a settlement to the case. For example, if the offender admits to the facts of the petition, she may be offered a placement in a special community-based treatment program in lieu of a term in a secure state facility. Or a status offense petition may be substituted for one of delinquency so that the adolescent can avoid being housed in a state training school and instead be placed in a more treatment-oriented facility.

If a bargain can be reached, the child will be asked to admit in open court that he did in fact commit the act of which he stands accused. State juvenile courts tend to minimize the stigma associated with the use of adult criminal standards by using other terminology, such as "agree to a finding" or "accept the petition" rather than "admit guilt." When the child makes an admission, juvenile courts require the following procedural safeguards: (1) the child knows of the right to a trial, (2) the plea or admission is made voluntarily, and (3) the child understands the charges and consequences of the plea.

Waiver of Jurisdiction

Prior to the development of the first modern juvenile court in Illinois in 1899, juveniles were tried for violations of the law in adult criminal courts. The consequences were devastating; many children were treated as criminal offenders and often sentenced to adult prisons. Although the subsequent passage of state legislation creating juvenile courts eliminated this problem, the juvenile justice system did recognize that certain forms of conduct require that children be tried as adults. Today, most jurisdictions provide by statute for **waiver**, or transfer, of juvenile offenders to the criminal courts. The decision of whether to waive a juvenile to the adult, or criminal, court is made in a **transfer hearing.**

The transfer of a juvenile to the criminal court is often based on statutory criteria established by the state's juvenile court act, so waiver provisions vary considerably among jurisdictions. Most commonly considered are the child's age and the nature of the offense alleged in the petition. For example, some jurisdictions require that children be over a certain age (typically, fourteen) before they can be waived. Some mandate that the youth be charged with a felony before being tried as an adult, whereas others permit waiver of jurisdiction to the criminal court regardless of the seriousness of the offense (for example, when a child is a petty albeit chronic offender).

Legal Controls Because of the nature of the waiver decision and its effect on the child in terms of status and disposition, the U.S. Supreme Court has imposed procedural protections for juveniles in the waiver process. In *Kent v. United States* (1966), the Supreme Court held that the waiver proceeding is a critically impor-

waiver (juvenile) A practice in which the juvenile court waives its jurisdiction over a juvenile and transfers the case to adult criminal court for trial. In some states a waiver hearing is held to determine jurisdiction, while in others juveniles may be automatically waived if they are accused of committing a serious crime such as murder.

transfer hearing A preadjudication hearing in a juvenile court to determine whether a juvenile offender should be detained in juvenile court or transferred to criminal court for prosecution as an adult.

tant stage in the juvenile justice process and that juveniles must be afforded minimum requirements of due process of law at such proceedings, including the right to legal counsel.[30] Then in *Breed v. Jones* (1975), the Court held that the prosecution of juveniles as adults in the California Superior Court violated the double jeopardy clause of the Fifth Amendment if they previously had been tried on the same charge in juvenile court.[31] The Court concluded that jeopardy attaches when the juvenile court begins to hear evidence at the adjudicatory hearing; this requires that the waiver hearing take place prior to any adjudication.

Youths in Adult Courts   Today, all states allow juveniles to be tried as adults in criminal courts in one of four ways:

1. *Concurrent jurisdiction.* The prosecutor has the discretion of filing charges for certain offenses in either juvenile or criminal court.
2. *Excluded offenses.* State laws exclude from juvenile court jurisdiction certain offenses that are either very minor, such as traffic or fishing violations, or very serious, such as murder or rape.
3. *Judicial waiver.* After a formal hearing at which both prosecutor and defense attorney present evidence, a juvenile court judge may decide to waive jurisdiction and transfer the case to criminal court. This procedure is also known as *binding over* or *certifying* juvenile cases to criminal court.
4. *Reverse waiver.* State laws mandate that certain offenses be tried in adult court; however, judges may decide that the case be tried in juvenile court.

© 2002 AP/Wide World Photos

Nathaniel Abraham, shown here talking to his attorney, was eleven years old when he committed murder. Should kids as young as Abraham be tried as adults? At what age should they be sent to an adult prison? Abraham was the youngest American child ever to be tried and convicted as an adult for murder, but instead of being sent to an adult institution he was sentenced to seven years in a maximum-security juvenile center. Prosecutors unsuccessfully requested that he face additional time in an adult prison.

Nearly every state has provisions for handling juveniles in adult criminal courts, and the trend is to make the waiver broader.[32] In thirty-one states, once a juvenile is tried in adult court, she is no longer eligible for juvenile justice on any subsequent offense. In order to get tough on juvenile crime, these efforts have limited the judge's ability to consider the individual circumstances that apply in each case.

The Extent of Waiver   The number of delinquency cases judicially waived to criminal court peaked in 1994 with 12,100 cases an increase of more than 50 percent over the number of cases waived in 1989 (8,000). Since 1994, however, the number of cases waived to criminal court has actually declined 33 percent to 8,100 cases, representing less than 1 percent of the formally processed delinquency caseload. One reason may be that the number of youth waived for drug cases is in decline, falling from 4.1 percent (1,800 cases) in 1991 to 1.1 percent (1,300 cases) in 1998.[33] The proportion of youths waived for personal offenses involving violence is now equal to the waived cases involving property crimes.

The Effect of Waiver   The problem of youths processed in adult courts is a serious one. About eight thousand juvenile delinquency cases are now being transferred to the adult courts each year. What is accomplished by treating juveniles like adults? Studies of the impact of the recent waiver statutes have yielded inconclusive results. Some juveniles whose cases are waived to criminal court are actually sentenced more leniently than they would have been in juvenile court. In many states, even when juveniles are tried in criminal court and convicted on the charges, they may still be sentenced to a juvenile or youthful offender institution, rather than to an adult prison. Some studies show that only a small percentage of juveniles tried as adults are incarcerated for periods longer than the terms served by offenders convicted on the same crime in the juvenile court; others have found that waived juveniles actually serve more time behind bars.[34] For example, they spend more time in juvenile detention awaiting trial. In the end, what began as a get-tough measure has had the opposite effect while costing taxpayers more money.[35]

Transfer decisions are not always carried out fairly or equitably and there is evidence that minorities are waived at a rate that is greater than their representation in the population.[36] About 40 percent of all waived youth are African Americans, even though they represent less than a third (31 percent) of the juvenile court population.[37]

Critics view these new methods of dealing with juvenile offenders as inefficient, ineffective, and philosophically out of step with the original concept of the juvenile court. Supporters view the waiver process as a sound method of getting the most serious juvenile offenders off the streets while ensuring that rehabilitation plays a less critical role in the juvenile justice system. Kids are most likely to be transferred to criminal court if they have injured someone with a weapon or if they have a long juvenile court record.[38] No area of juvenile justice has received more attention recently than efforts to redefine the jurisdiction of the juvenile court.[39]

The Trial

There are usually two judicial hearings in the juvenile court process. The first, typically called an **initial appearance**, is similar to the arraignment in the adult system. The child is informed of the charges against him, attorneys are appointed, bail is reviewed, and in many instances cases are settled with an admission of the facts, followed by a community sentence. If the case cannot be settled at this initial stage, it is bound over for trial.

During the adjudicatory or trial process, often called the *fact-finding hearing* in juvenile proceedings, the court hears evidence on the allegations stated in the delinquency petition. In its early development, the juvenile court did not emphasize judicial rule making similar to that of the criminal trial process. Absent were such basic requirements as the standard of proof, rules of evidence, and similar adjudicatory formalities. Proceedings were to be nonadversarial, informal, and noncriminal. Gradually, however, the juvenile trial process was the target of criticism because judges were handing out punishments to children without affording them legal rights. This changed in 1967 when the U.S. Supreme Court's landmark *In re Gault* decision radically altered the juvenile justice system.[40] In *Gault*, the Court ruled that the concept of fundamental fairness is applicable to juvenile delinquency proceedings. The Court granted critical rights to juvenile defendants, most importantly, (1) the notice of the charges, (2) the right to counsel, (3) the right to confront and cross-examine witnesses, (4) the privilege against self-incrimination, and (5) the right to a transcript of the trial record.

The *Gault* decision completely altered the juvenile trial process. Instead of dealing with children in a benign and paternalistic fashion, the courts were forced to process juvenile offenders within the framework of appropriate constitutional procedures. And though *Gault* was technically limited to the adjudicatory stage, it has spurred further legal reform throughout the juvenile system. Today, the right to counsel, the privilege against self-incrimination, the right to treatment in detention and correctional facilities, and other constitutional protections are applied at all stages of the juvenile process, from investigation through adjudication to parole. *Gault* ushered in an era of legal rights for juveniles; see again Exhibit 14.1, which summarizes some of the most important cases.

After *Gault* the Supreme Court continued its trend toward legalizing and formalizing the juvenile trial process with the decision in *In re Winship* (1970), which held that a finding of delinquency in a juvenile case must be made with the same level of evidence used in an adult case: beyond a reasonable doubt.[41]

Although the informality of the traditional juvenile trial court was severely altered by *Gault* and *Winship*, the trend of increased rights for juveniles was some-

For another take on the waiver decision go to Patricia Smith, "Juvenile Justice? In the 1990s, Many States Passed Laws That Made It Easier to Try Teens as Adults. Does Youth Crime Deserve 'Adult Time?'" *Junior Scholastic*, February 25, 2002 v104 i13 p10(3), on InfoTrac College Edition.

initial appearance A juvenile's first appearance before the juvenile court judge in which the charges are reviewed and an effort is made to settle the case without a trial. If the child does not have legal counsel an attorney will be appointed.

To read about the *Gault* case, go to http://caselaw.lp.findlaw.com/scripts/getcase.pl?court=us&vol=387&invol=1

what curtailed when the Supreme Court held in *McKeiver v. Pennsylvania* (1971), that children do not have the same right to a jury trial as an adult.[42] The Court reasoned that juries were not an essential element of justice and if used in juvenile cases would end confidentiality.

Once an adjudicatory hearing has been completed, the court is normally required to enter a judgment against the child. This may take the form of declaring the child delinquent or a ward of the court or possibly even suspending judgment to avoid the stigma of a juvenile record. Following the entering of a judgment, the court can begin its determination of possible **dispositions** for the child.

Alternatives to the Juvenile Trial

There has also been a movement to create alternatives to the traditional juvenile court adjudication process. One interesting approach has been the development of teen courts to supplement the traditional juvenile court process. Teen courts are the subject of the following Policy, Practices, and Issues in Criminal Justice feature.

Disposition and Treatment

At the dispositional hearing, the juvenile court judge imposes a sentence on the juvenile offender based on her offense, prior record, and family background. Normally, the judge has broad discretionary power to issue a range of dispositions from dismissal to institutional **commitment**. In theory, the dispositional decision is an effort by the court to serve the best interests of the child, the family, and the community. In many respects, this postadjudicative process is the most important stage in the juvenile court system because it represents the last opportunity for the court to influence the child and control his behavior.

To ensure that only relevant and appropriate evidence is considered by the court during trial, most jurisdictions require a separate hearing to consider an appropriate disposition. The bifurcated hearing process ensures that the adjudicatory hearing is used solely to determine the merits of the allegations, whereas the dispositional hearing determines whether the child is in need of rehabilitation.

To read about *McKeiver,* go to
http://caselaw.lp.findlaw.com/scripts/getcase.pl?navby=search&court=US&case=/us/403/528.html

disposition For juvenile offenders, the equivalent of sentencing for adult offenders. The theory is that disposition is more rehabilitative than retributive. Possible dispositions may be to dismiss the case; release the youth to the custody of his or her parents; place the offender on probation; or send him or her to an institution or state correctional institution.

commitment Decision of judge ordering an adjudicated and sentenced juvenile offender to be placed in a correctional facility.

Peer courts are becoming a popular alternative to traditional juvenile courts. Here, youth peer court prosecutor Dante Ballensky, a freshman at Mazama High School, confers with David Schutt, the court's judge, and a Klamath County deputy district attorney, during a session of court in Klamath Falls, Oregon, on June 26, 2000.

Policy, Programs, and Issues in Criminal Justice

Teen Courts

To relieve overcrowding and provide an alternative to traditional forms of juvenile courts, more than three hundred jurisdictions are now experimenting with teen courts. These differ from other juvenile justice programs because young people rather than adults determine the disposition in a case. Cases handled in these courts usually involve young juveniles (ages ten to fifteen) with no prior arrest records who are being charged with minor law violations (shoplifting, vandalism, and disorderly conduct). Typically, young offenders are asked to volunteer to have their case heard in a teen court rather than the more formal court of the traditional juvenile justice system.

As in a regular juvenile court, teen court defendants may go through an intake process, a preliminary review of charges, a court hearing, and sentencing. In a teen court, however, other young people are responsible for much of the process. Charges may be presented to the court by a fifteen-year-old "prosecutor." Defendants may be represented by a sixteen-year-old "defense attorney." Other youth may serve as jurors, court clerks, and bailiffs. In some teen courts, a youth "judge" (or panel of youth judges) may choose the best disposition or sanction for each case. In a few teen courts, youths even determine whether the facts in a case have been proven by the prosecutor (similar to a finding of guilt). Offenders are often ordered to pay restitution or perform community service. Some teen courts require offenders to write formal apologies to their victims; others require offenders to serve on a subsequent teen court jury. Many

courts use other innovative dispositions, such as requiring offenders to attend classes designed to improve their decision-making skills, enhance their awareness of victims, and deter them from future theft.

Though decisions are made by juveniles, adults are also involved in teen courts. They often administer the programs, and they are usually responsible for essential functions such as budgeting, planning, and personnel. In many programs, adults supervise the courtroom activities, and they often coordinate the community service placements, where youth work to fulfill the terms of their dispositions. In some programs, adults act as the judges while teens serve as attorneys and jurors.

Proponents of teen court argue that the process takes advantage of one of the most powerful forces in the life of an adolescent: the desire for peer approval and the reaction to peer pressure. According to this argument, youth respond better to prosocial peers than to adult authority figures. Thus, teen courts are seen as a potentially effective alternative to traditional juvenile courts that are staffed with paid professionals such as lawyers, judges, and probation officers. Teen court advocates also point out that the benefits extend beyond defendants. Teen courts may benefit the volunteer youth attorneys and judges, who probably learn more about the legal system than they ever could in a classroom. The presence of a teen court may also encourage the entire community to take a more active role in responding to juvenile crime. In sum, teen courts offer at least four potential benefits:

---

treatment The rehabilitative method used to effect a change of behavior in the juvenile offender, in the form of therapy, or educational or vocational programs.

In theory, the juvenile court seeks to provide a disposition that represents an individualized **treatment** plan for the child. This decision is normally based on the presentence investigation of the probation department, reports from social agencies, and possibly a psychiatric evaluation. The judge generally has broad discretion in dispositional matters but is limited by the provisions of the state's juvenile court act. The following are typical juvenile court dispositions:

1. Suspended judgment
2. Probation
3. Placement in a community treatment program
4. Commitment to the state agency responsible for juvenile institutional care

In addition, the court may place the child with parents or relatives, make dispositional arrangements with private youth-serving agencies, or order the child committed to a mental institution.

Disposition Outcomes   In 1998 (the most recent data available) juveniles were adjudicated delinquent in 63 percent of the 1,000,300 cases brought before a judge. Once adjudicated, juveniles in 58 percent (365,100) of the cases were placed on formal probation; in 26 percent (163,800) of the cases, they were placed in a residential facility.[43] Eleven percent of adjudicated cases resulted in other dispositions, such

1. *Accountability.* Teen courts may help to ensure that young offenders are held accountable for their illegal behavior, even when their offenses are relatively minor and would not likely result in sanctions from the traditional juvenile justice system.
2. *Timeliness.* An effective teen court can move young offenders from arrest to sanctions within a matter of days rather than the months that may pass with traditional juvenile courts. This rapid response may increase the positive impact of court sanctions, regardless of their severity.
3. *Cost savings.* Teen courts usually depend heavily on youth and adult volunteers. If managed properly, they may handle a substantial number of offenders at relatively little cost to the community.
4. *Community cohesion.* A well-structured and expansive teen court program may affect the entire community by increasing public appreciation of the legal system, enhancing community–court relationships, encouraging greater respect for the law among youth, and promoting volunteerism among both adults and youth.

The teen court movement is just beginning and its effectiveness is still a matter of debate. Recent evaluations of teen courts have found that they did not "widen the net" of justice by handling cases that in the absence of the peer court would have been subject to a lesser level of processing. However, research by Kevin Minor and his associates on teen courts in Kentucky, and by Paige Harrison and her colleagues in New Mexico, indicate that recidivism levels range from 25 to 30 percent. Considering that these cases usually involve offenses of only moderate seriousness, the findings do not suggest that the program can play a significant role in reducing teenage crime rates.

Critical Thinking

1. Could teen courts be used to try serious criminal acts such as burglary and robbery?
2. Is a conflict of interest created when teens judge the behavior of other teens? Does the fact that they themselves may one day become defendants in a teen court influence decision making?

InfoTrac College Edition Research

To read more about teen courts, go to InfoTrac College Edition and read Kathiann M. Kowalski, "Courtroom Justice for Teens—by Teens," *Current Health 2: A Weekly Reader Publication,* April 1999 v25 i8 p29(1).

Sources: Jeffrey A. Butts and Janeen Buck, "Teen Courts: A Focus on Research," *Juvenile Justice Bulletin October 2000* (Washington, D.C.: Office of Juvenile Justice and Delinquency Prevention, 2000); Kevin Minor, James Wells, Irinia Soderstrom, Rachel Bingham, and Deborah Williamson, "Sentence Completion and Recidivism Among Juveniles Referred to Teen Courts," *Crime and Delinquency 45* (1999): 467–480; Paige Harrison, James Maupin, and G. Larry Mays, "Are Teen Courts an Answer to Our Delinquency Problems?" *Juvenile and Family Court Journal 51* (2000): 27–33; Paige Harrison, James R. Maupin, and G. Larry Mays, "Teen Court: An Examination of Processes and Outcomes, *Crime and Delinquency 47* (2001): 243–264.

as referral to an outside agency, community service, or restitution. Between 1989 and 1998, the number of cases in which the court ordered an adjudicated delinquent to be placed in a residential facility increased 37 percent, while the number of formal probation cases increased 73 percent.[44] Although the juvenile court has been under pressure to get tough on youth crime, probation is still the disposition of choice in even the most serious cases. Fewer youths are being waived to the adult court today than a decade ago; conversely, more on being placed on probation.[45]

There were racial differences in out-of-home placements. About 24 percent of adjudicated cases involving white youth resulted in out-of-home placement, compared with 30 percent of cases involving black youth and 25 percent involving other minority youth.[46]

Juvenile Sentencing Reform

Over the past decade, juvenile justice experts and the general public have become aroused about the serious juvenile crime rate in general and about violent acts committed by children in particular. As a result, some law enforcement officials and conservative legislators have demanded that the juvenile justice system take a more serious stand with dangerous juvenile offenders. In the past two decades, many state legislatures have responded by toughening their juvenile codes. Some

Percent of cases detained

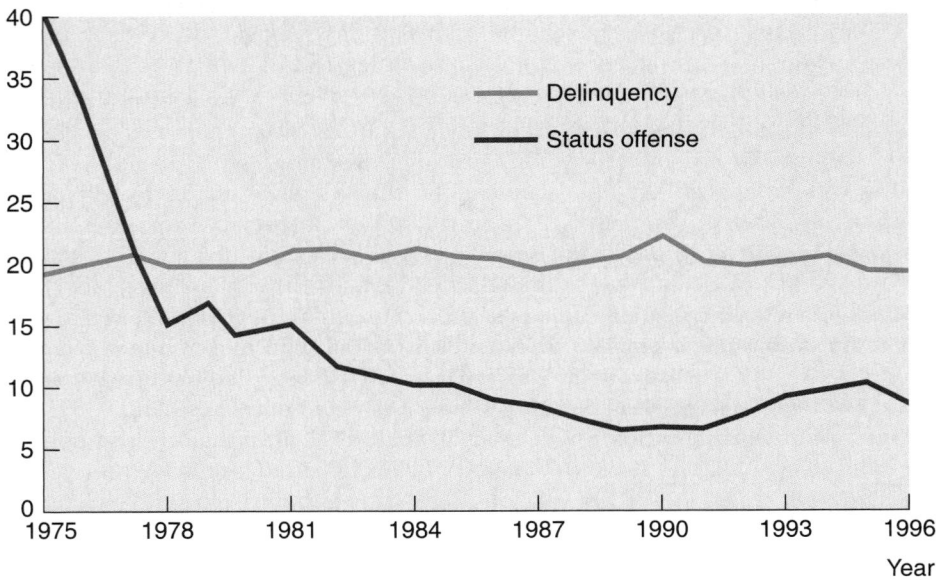

- In 1975 status offense cases were twice as likely as delinquency cases to involve secure detention between the time of referral to court and case disposition.

- By 1992 the likelihood that a status offense case would involve detention was less than half that for delinquency cases.

- In 1975 an estimated 143,000 status offense cases involved detention—in 1996, the figure was 39,100.

Figure 14.3
Court data show a substantial decline in the use of detention in status offense cases.

Source: Howard Snyder and Melissa Sickmund, *Juvenile Offenders and Victims: 1999 National Report* (Washington, D.C.: Office of Juvenile Justice and Delinquency Prevention, 1999), 207.

jurisdictions have passed mandatory or determinate incarceration sentences for juveniles convicted of serious felonies. The get-tough approach even allows the use of the death penalty for minors transferred to the adult system.[47] Many jurisdictions, however, have not abandoned rehabilitation as a primary dispositional goal and still hold to the philosophy that placements should be based on the least detrimental alternative. This view requires that judges employ the least intrusive measures possible to safeguard a child's growth and development.[48]

A second reform has been the concerted effort to remove status offenders from the juvenile justice system and restrict their entry into institutional programs. Because of the development of numerous diversion programs, many children who are involved in truancy and incorrigible behavior who ordinarily would have been sent to a closed institution are now being placed in community programs. There are far fewer status offenders in detention or institutions than ever before (see Figure 14.3).

A third reform effort has been to standardize dispositions in juvenile court. As early as 1977, Washington passed one of the first determinate sentencing laws for juvenile offenders, resulting in other states adopting similar statutes.[49] All children found to be delinquent are evaluated on a point system based on their age, prior juvenile record, and type of crime committed. Minor offenders are handled in the community. Those committing more serious offenses are placed on probation. Children who commit the most serious offenses are subject to standardized institutional penalties. As a result, juvenile offenders who commit such crimes as rape or armed robbery are being sentenced to institutionalization for two, three, and four years. This approach is different from the indeterminate sentencing under which children who have committed a serious crime might be released from institutions in less than a year if correctional authorities believe that they have been rehabilitated.

The Juvenile Correctional Process

After disposition in juvenile court, delinquent offenders may be placed in some form of correctional treatment. Although many are placed in the community, more than one hundred thousand are now in secure facilities.

Probation

Probation is the most commonly used formal sentence for juvenile offenders, and many states require that a youth fail on probation before being sent to an institution (unless the criminal act is quite serious). Probation involves placing the child under the supervision of the juvenile probation department for the purpose of community treatment. Conditions of probation are normally imposed on the child by either statute or court order. There are general conditions, such as those that require the child to stay away from other delinquents or to obey the law. More spe-

© A. Ramey/Photo Edit

Juvenile probation officers provide supervision and treatment in the community. The treatment plan is a product of the intake, diagnostic, and investigative aspects of probation. Treatment plans vary in approach and structure. Some juveniles simply report to the probation officer and follow the conditions of probation. In other cases, juvenile probation officers supervise young people more intensely, monitor their daily activities, and work with them in directed treatment programs. Here, a juvenile probation officer and police officer talk with Crips gang members in California.

cific conditions of probation include requiring the child to participate in a vocational training program, to attend school regularly, to obtain treatment at a child guidance clinic, or to make restitution. Restitution can be in the form of community service—for example, a youth found in possession of marijuana might be required to work fifty hours in a home for the elderly. Monetary restitution requires delinquents to pay back the victims of their crimes. Restitution programs have proven successful and have been adopted around the country.[50]

Juvenile probation is an important component of the juvenile justice system. Juvenile courts place more than 80 percent of adjudicated delinquents on some form of probation. It is the most widely used method of community treatment. The cost savings of community treatment, coupled with its nonpunitive intentions, are likely to keep probation programs growing.

Institutionalization

The most severe of the statutory dispositions available to the juvenile court involves commitment of the child to an institution. The committed child may be sent to a state training school or private residential treatment facility. These are usually minimum-security facilities with small populations and an emphasis on treatment and education. Some states, however, maintain facilities with populations over one thousand.

Most state statutes vary when determining the length of the child's commitment. Traditionally, many jurisdictions committed the child up to majority, which usually meant twenty-one years of age. This normally deprived the child of freedom for an extensive period of time—sometimes longer than an adult sentenced for the same offense would be confined. As a result, some states have passed legislation under which children are committed for periods ranging from one to three years.

To better handle violent juvenile offenders, some states have created separate or intermediate juvenile systems. Under such statutes, fourteen- to seventeen-year-olds charged with certain violent felonies are treated as adults, and if convicted, sentenced to new intermediate prisons, separated from both adult and regular juvenile offenders, for terms of two to five years.[51]

Ninety-five percent of incarcerated juveniles are held for delinquent offenses—offenses that would be crimes if committed by adults. Thirty-five percent are held for person-oriented offenses; about 20 percent for alcohol, drug, and public order offenses; and more than 40 percent for property crimes.[52] Just over 5 percent are confined for a juvenile status offense, such as truancy, running away, or incorrigibility. The efforts made in recent years to keep status offenders out of institutions seem to have paid off.

Population Trends   At last count, there were almost 110,000 juveniles being held in public (70 percent) and private (30 percent) facilities in the United States.[53] The juvenile custody rate varies widely among states: the District of Columbia makes the greatest use of custodial treatment, incarcerating just over 700 delinquents in public and private facilities per 100,000 juveniles in the general population. In contrast, about half of the states had rates of about 300 juveniles per 100,000. Some states rely heavily on privately run facilities, while others place many youths in out-of-state facilities. Whereas most delinquents are held in public facilities, most status offenders are held in private facilities.

The typical resident of a juvenile facility is a fifteen- to sixteen-year-old white male incarcerated for an average stay of five months in a public facility or six months in a private facility. Private facilities tend to house younger youths, whereas public institutions provide custodial care for older youths, including a small percentage of youths between eighteen and twenty-one years of age. As already noted, most incarcerated youths are person, property, or drug offenders.

The Council of Juvenile Correctional Administrators (CJCA) is dedicated to the improvement of juvenile correctional services and practices. Its Web site is at www.corrections.com/cjca/

Many incarcerated youth have serious social and psychological problems. To learn more, read Deborah Shelton, "Failure of Mental Health Policy—Incarcerated Children and Adolescents," *Pediatric Nursing,* May-June 2002 v28 i3 p278(4), on InfoTrac College Edition.

Minorities in Juvenile Institutions   Minority youths are incarcerated at a rate two to five times that of white youths. The difference is greatest for black youths, with a custody rate of 1,004 per 100,000 juveniles; for white youths the rate is 212.[54] Research has found that this overrepresentation is not a result of differentials in arrest rates, but often stems from disparity at early stages of case processing.[55] Of equal importance, minorities are more likely to be confined in secure public facilities rather than in open private facilities that might provide more costly and effective treatment.[56]

Minority youths accused of delinquent acts are less likely than white youths to be diverted from the court system into informal sanctions and are more likely to receive sentences involving incarceration.

Deinstitutionalization

Some experts in delinquency and juvenile law question the policy of institutionalizing juvenile offenders. Many believe that large institutions are too costly to operate and only produce more sophisticated criminals. This dilemma has produced a number of efforts to remove youths from juvenile facilities and replace large institutions with smaller community-based facilities. For example, Massachusetts closed all its state training schools more than twenty years ago (subsequently, however, public pressure caused a few secure facilities to be reopened). Many other states have established small residential facilities operated by juvenile-care agencies to replace larger units.

Despite the daily rhetoric on crime control, public support for community-based programs for juveniles still exists. Although such programs are not panaceas, many experts still recommend more treatment and less incarceration for juvenile offenders. Utah, Maryland, Vermont, and Pennsylvania, for example, have dramatically reduced their reform school populations while setting up a wide range of intensive treatment programs for juveniles. Many large, impersonal, and expensive state institutions with unqualified staff and ineffective treatment programs have been eliminated.

Status Offenders   There has been an ongoing effort for almost thirty years to deinstitutionalize status offenders (DSO).[57] This means removing noncriminal youths from institutions housing delinquents in order to prevent them from interacting with violent or chronic offenders.

Since its inception, the DSO approach has been hotly debated. Some have argued that early intervention is society's best hope of forestalling future delinquent behavior and reducing victimization. Other experts maintain that legal control over status offenders is a violation of youths' rights. Still others have viewed status-offending behavior as a symptom of some larger trauma or problem that requires attention. These diverse opinions still exist today.

Since Congress passed the JJDP act in 1974, all fifty states have complied with some aspect of the deinstitutionalization mandate. Millions of federal, state, and local dollars have been spent on the DSO movement. Vast numbers of programs have been created around the country to reduce the number of juveniles in secure confinement. What remains to be done, however, is to study the effect DSO has had on juveniles and the justice system.

Aftercare

Aftercare marks the final stage of the formal juvenile justice process. Its purpose is to help youths make the transition from residential or institutional settings back into the community. Effective aftercare programs provide adequate supervision and support services to help juvenile offenders avoid criminal activity. Examples of programs include electronic monitoring, counseling, treatment and community service referrals, education, work training, and intensive parole supervision.

Most juvenile aftercare involves parole. A juvenile parole officer provides the child with counseling, school referral, vocational training, and other services. Children who violate the conditions of parole may have their parole revoked and be returned to the institution. Unlike the adult postconviction process, where the U.S. Supreme Court has imposed procedural protections in probation and parole revocations, juveniles do not have such due process rights. State courts have also been reluctant to grant juveniles rights in this area and those that have, generally refuse to require that the whole array of rights be made available as they are to adult offenders. Since the *Gault* decision, however, many states have adopted administrative regulations requiring juvenile agencies to incorporate due process, such as proper notice of the hearing and the right to counsel in postconviction proceedings.

Former Attorney General Janet Reno is a firm advocate of prevention in the juvenile justice system. Read what she has to say at Janet Reno, "Prevention as Public Policy," *Reclaiming Children and Youth,* Winter 2002 v10 i4 p207(2), on InfoTrac College Edition.

Preventing Delinquency

Although the juvenile justice system has been concerned with controlling delinquent behavior, there are now important efforts being made to prevent delinquency before it occurs. *Delinquency prevention* refers to intervening in a young people's lives prior to their engaging in delinquency in the first place; that is, preventing involvement in delinquency at all. In the past, delinquency prevention was the responsibility of treatment-oriented agencies such as the day care providers, YMCA and YWCA, Boys and Girls Clubs of America, and other private and public agencies. Today, there are many community-based treatment programs involving a combination of juvenile justice and treatment agencies. A few prominent examples of these are discussed in some detail in the following paragraphs.

Community Strategies

Today, comprehensive community-based delinquency prevention programs are taking a systematic approach or using a comprehensive planning model to develop preventive interventions. This includes an analysis of the delinquency problem, an identification of available resources in the community, development of priority delinquency problems, and the identification of successful programs in other communities and tailoring them to local conditions and needs.[58] Not all comprehensive community-based prevention programs follow this model, but there is evidence to suggest that this approach will produce the greatest reductions in juvenile delinquency.[59]

Many jurisdictions are developing new intervention programs for at-risk teenage youths. Some are treatment-oriented programs that rely on rehabilitation ideals. For example, the Children At Risk (CAR) program was set up to help improve the lives of young people at high risk for delinquency, gang involvement, substance abuse, and other problem behaviors. It was delivered to a large number of young people in poor and high-crime neighborhoods in five cities across the country. It involved a wide range of preventive measures, including case management and family counseling, family skills training, tutoring, men-

Wilderness programs give young people a sense of confidence and purpose by involving them in outdoor expeditions. They provide an opportunity for juveniles to confront the difficulties in their lives while achieving positive personal satisfaction. Here, a group of young people at the Piedmont Wilderness Institute in Clinton, South Carolina, learn team building as they work together to accomplish the task of getting eight of them onto the platform without spilling the water in the can.

toring, after-school activities, and community policing. The program was different in each neighborhood. A study of all five cities showed that one year after the program ended, the young people who underwent it, compared with a control group, were less likely to have committed violent delinquent acts and used or sold drugs. Some of the other beneficial results for those in the program included less association with delinquent peers, less peer pressure to engage in delinquency, and more positive peer support.[60]

Communities That Care Other large-scale comprehensive community-based delinquency prevention programs include Communities That Care (CTC)[61] and the SafeFutures Initiative.[62] Both programs are funded by OJJDP. The CTC strategy emphasizes the reduction of risk factors for delinquency and the enhancement of protective factors against delinquency for different developmental stages from birth through adolescence.[63] CTC follows a rigorous, multilevel planning process that includes drawing upon interventions that have previously demonstrated success and tailoring them to the needs of the community.[64]

SafeFutures Initiative The SafeFutures Initiative operates much like CTC—for example, emphasizing the reduction of risk factors for delinquency and protective factors against delinquency, using what works, and following a rigorous planning model to implement different interventions. It also works to build or strengthen existing collaborations among the many community groups and government departments working to prevent delinquency. The SafeFutures Initiative is targeted both at youths who are at high risk for delinquency and those who are already adjudicated offenders (see Exhibit 14.4).

Enforcement Strategies

While these programs are primarily treatment-oriented, many new programs combine treatment with enforcement. Some important ones are now targeting teen gun use. Easy availability of guns is a significant contributor to teen violence. Research indicates a close tie between gun use, control of drug markets, and teen violence. Gang-related homicides almost always involve firearms. Unless significant efforts are made to control the spread of handguns, teenage murder rates are likely to continue to rise.

Parenting Resources for the 21st Century links parents and other adults responsible for the care of a child with information on issues covering the full spectrum of parenting. It provides information on delinquency prevention in the community:
www.parentingresources.ncjrs.org/

Exhibit 14.4 SafeFutures program to reduce juvenile delinquency and youth violence

Nine program areas constitute SafeFutures:
1. After-school programs
2. Juvenile mentoring programs (JUMP)
3. Family strengthening and support services
4. Mental health services for at-risk and adjudicated youth
5. Delinquency prevention programs in general
6. Comprehensive community-wide approaches to gang-free schools and communities
7. Community-based day treatment programs
8. Continuum-of-care services for at-risk and delinquent girls
9. Serious, violent, and chronic juvenile offender programs (with an emphasis on enhancing graduated sanctions)

Source: Elaine Morley, Shelli B. Rossman, Mary Kopczynski, Janeen Buck, and Caterina Gouvis, *Comprehensive Responses to Youth at Risk: Interim Findings from the SafeFutures Initiative* (Washington, D.C.: Office of Juvenile Justice and Delinquency Prevention, 2000), x.

At least thirty-five states have adopted legislation dealing with guns and children. In 1995 alone, nineteen states passed laws requiring schools to expel or suspend students for possessing weapons on school grounds.[65] At the federal level, laws have also been passed to restrict the possession, sale, and transfer of guns to juveniles. The Gun-Free Schools Act of 1994 requires local educational agencies receiving financial assistance to expel for one year any student who brings a firearm to school. The Youth Handgun Safety Act (part of the Omnibus Violent Crime Control and Law Enforcement Act of 1994) prohibits the possession or private transfer of a handgun to a juvenile. Although this legislation was enacted by the federal government, it is the state and local officials who can deal most effectively with juvenile gun violations.

The following Policy, Practices, and Issues feature describes one of the most successful of the local efforts.

Keep the Juvenile Court?

Over the past century, the juvenile court has struggled to provide treatment for juvenile offenders while guaranteeing them constitutional due process. Over the last century, the juvenile court system has been transformed from a rehabilitative to a quasi-criminal court. Many states are toughening juvenile codes. With limited resources and procedural deficiencies, there is little likelihood of much change in the near future.

The system has been so overwhelmed by violent juvenile crime and family breakdown that some judges and politicians have suggested abolishing the juvenile system. Even those experts who want to retain an independent juvenile court have called for its restructuring. Crime control advocates want to reduce the court's jurisdiction over juveniles charged with serious crimes and liberalize the prosecutor's ability to try them in adult courts. In contrast, child advocates suggest that the court scale back its judicial role and transfer its functions to community groups and social service agencies.[66] Despite these differing opinions, the juvenile court will likely remain a critical societal institution; there are few viable alternatives. This issue is addressed in the following Policy, Practices, and Issues in Criminal Justice feature. ■

Operation Ceasefire

One of the most successful police-inspired delinquency prevention programs is Operation Ceasefire. Implemented in Boston, Massachusetts, this program aims to reduce youth homicide victimization and youth gun violence. Despite being a police-led program, Operation Ceasefire involves many other juvenile and criminal justice and social agencies, including probation and parole; Bureau of Alcohol, Tobacco and Firearms (ATF); gang outreach and prevention street workers; and the Drug Enforcement Administration (DEA). This group of agencies became known as the Ceasefire Working Group.

The program has two main elements:

1. A direct law-enforcement focus on illicit gun traffickers who supply youth with guns
2. An attempt to generate a strong deterrent to gang violence

A wide range of measures was used to reduce the flow of guns to youth, including pooling the resources of local, state, and federal justice authorities to track and seize illegal guns and targeting traffickers of the guns most used by gang members. The response to gang violence was pulling every deterrence "lever" available, including shutting down drug markets, serving warrants, enforcing probation restrictions, and making disorder arrests. The Ceasefire Working Group delivered its message clearly to gang members: "We're ready, we're watching, we're waiting: Who wants to be next?"

An evaluation of the program from before it started to the time it ended showed a substantial reduction in youth homicide victims, youth gun assaults, and overall gang violence across the city. Compared to other large U.S. and New England cities, the majority of which also experienced a reduction in youth homicides over the same time period, it was found that the significant reduction in youth homicides in Boston was due to Operation Ceasefire.

Following the success of the Boston program, the Office of Juvenile Justice and Delinquency Prevention (OJJDP) launched a comprehensive initiative to reduce juvenile gun violence in four cities (Baton Rouge and Shreveport, Louisiana; Oakland, California; and Syracuse, New York). Called the Partnerships to Reduce Juvenile Gun Violence Program, problem-oriented policing strategies are at the center of the program, but other intervention strategies are also important, such as delinquency prevention (job training and mentoring), juvenile justice sanctions, and a public information campaign that is designed to communicate the dangers and consequences of gun violence to juveniles, families, and community residents. An evaluation of the implementation of the program found that three of the four cities were successful in developing comprehensive strategies. An evaluation of the effectiveness of the program in reducing juvenile gun violence is under way. With a successful implementation and inclusion of many of the components of the Boston program, this program offers promise in reducing juvenile violence.

Critical Thinking

1. What other areas of juvenile delinquency prevention might benefit from the policies and procedures used by Operation Ceasefire? Could it be used, for example, to reduce teenage substance abuse?
2. Do you believe that get-tough policies will work better with teenagers than treatment-oriented programs, which provide alternatives to crime?

InfoTrac College Edition Research

To read about Operation Ceasefire, go to Gordon Witkin, "Swift and Certain Punishment: How to Keep Young Toughs from Committing Violent Acts," *U.S. News & World Report,* December 29, 1997 v123 n25 p67(2) on InfoTrac College Edition. To research the topic further, use "delinquency prevention" as a subject guide.

Sources: Anthony A. Braga, David M. Kennedy, Elin J. Waring, and Anne Morrison Piehl, "Problem-Oriented Policing Deterrence, and Youth Violence: An Evaluation of Boston's Operation Ceasefire," *Journal of Research in Crime and Delinquency* 38 (2001): 195–225; David M. Kennedy, Anthony A. Braga, and Anne Morrison Piehl, "Developing and Implementing Operation Ceasefire," in *Reducing Gun Violence: The Boston Gun Project's Operation Ceasefire* (Washington, D.C.: NIJ Research Report, 2001); David M. Kennedy, "Pulling Levers: Chronic Offenders, High-Crime Settings, and a Theory of Prevention," *Valparaiso University Law Review* 31 (1997): 449–84; David M. Kennedy, "Pulling Levers: Getting Deterrence Right," *National Institute of Justice Journal* (July): 2–8 (1998); David Sheppard, Heath Grant, Wendy Rowe, and Nancy Jacobs, *Fighting Juvenile Gun Violence* (Washington, D.C.: OJJDP Juvenile Justice Bulletin, 2000); Alan Lizotte and David Sheppard, *Gun Use by Male Juveniles: Research and Prevention* (Washington, D.C.: OJJDP Juvenile Justice Bulletin, 2001), 7.

Should We Abolish the Juvenile Court?

In an important work, *Bad Kids: Race and the Transformation of the Juvenile Court,* legal expert Barry Feld makes the rather controversial suggestion that the juvenile court system should be discontinued and replaced by an alternative method of justice. He suggests that the current structure of the juvenile court almost makes it impossible for it to fulfill or achieve the purpose for which it was originally intended.

Feld maintains that the juvenile court system was created in an effort to foster an atmosphere and process that was more lenient than that used against adult criminals. Although this was a worthwhile goal, the court system was doomed to fail even from the beginning, because it was thrown into the role of providing child welfare while at the same time being an instrument of law enforcement, two missions that are often at cross-purposes. During its history, various legal developments have further undermined its purpose—most notably the *In re Gault* ruling, which ultimately led to juveniles receiving similar legal protections as adults and to children being treated like adults in all respects. The juvenile court vision of leniency was further undermined by the fear and consequent racism created by post–World War II migration and economic trends, which led to the development of large enclaves of poor and underemployed African Americans living in northern cities. Then, in the 1980s, the sudden rise in gang membership, gun violence, and homicide committed by juveniles further undermined the juvenile court mission and resulted in legislation creating mandatory sentences for juvenile offenders and mandatory waiver to the adult court. As a result, the focus of the court has been on dealing with the offense rather than treating the offender. In Feld's words, the juvenile court has become a "deficient second-rate criminal court." The welfare and rehabilitative purposes of the juvenile court have been subordinated to its role as law enforcement agent.

Can juvenile courts be reformed? Feld maintains that it is impossible because of their conflicting purposes and shifting priorities. The money spent on serving the court and its large staff would be better spend on child welfare, which would target a larger audience and prevent antisocial acts before they occur. In lieu of juvenile court, youths who violate the law should receive full procedural protections in the criminal court system. The special protections given youth in the juvenile court could be provided by altering the criminal law and recognizing age as a factor in the creation of criminal liability. Because youths have had a limited opportunity to develop self-control, their criminal liability should also be curtailed or restricted.

Is Feld's rather dour assessment of the juvenile court valid and should it in fact be abolished? No, according to John Johnson Kerbs, who suggests that Feld makes assumption that may not fit the reality of the American legal system. First, Kerbs finds that it is naïve to assume the criminal courts can provide the same or greater substantive and procedural protections as the juvenile court. Many juvenile court defendants are indigent, especially those coming from the minority community, and it may be impossible for them to obtain adequate legal defense in the adult system. Second, Feld's assumption that criminal courts will take a defendant's age into close consideration may be illusory. In this "get tough" era, it is likely that criminal courts will provide harsher sentences, and the brunt of these draconian sentences will fall squarely on the shoulders of minority youth. Research efforts routinely show that African-American adults are unduly punished in adult courts. Sending juvenile offenders to these venues will most likely further enmesh them in an already unfair system. Finally, Kerbs finds that the treatment benefits of the juvenile courts should not be overlooked or abandoned. There is ample research, he maintains, that shows that juvenile courts can create lower recidivism rates than criminal courts. Though the juvenile court is far from perfect and should be improved, it would be foolish to abandon a system that is aimed at helping kids find alternatives to crime rather than one that produces higher recidivism rates, lowers their future prospects, and has a less than stellar record of providing due process and equal protection for the nation's most needy citizens.

Critical Thinking

What's your take on this issue? Should the juvenile court be abolished? Since the trend has been to transfer the most serious criminal cases to the adult court, is there still a purpose for an independent juvenile court? Should the juvenile court be reserved for nonserious first offenders?

● InfoTrac College Edition Research

Before you make up your mind about the future of juvenile courts, read Joseph V. Penn, "Justice for Youth? A History of the Juvenile and Family Court," *Brown University Child and Adolescent Behavior Letter,* September 2001 v17 i9 p1.

Sources: Barry C. Feld, *Bad Kids: Race and the Transformation of the Juvenile Court* (New York: Oxford University Press, 1999); John Johnson Kerbs, "(Un)equal Justice: Juvenile Court Abolition and African Americans," *Annals, AAPSS,* 564 (1999): 109–125.

SUMMARY

The juvenile justice system is concerned with delinquent children, as well as with those who are beyond the care and protection of their parents. Juveniles involved in antisocial behavior come under the jurisdiction of juvenile or family court systems. These courts belong to a system of juvenile justice agencies, including law enforcement, child care, and institutional services.

When a child is brought to the juvenile court, the proceedings are generally nonadversarial and informal. Representatives from different disciplines, such as lawyers, social workers, and psychiatrists, all play major roles in the judicial process.

In recent years the juvenile court system has become more legalistic by virtue of U.S. Supreme Court decisions that have granted children procedural safeguards. However, neither rehabilitation programs nor the application of due process rights has stemmed the growing tide of juvenile antisocial behavior. Perhaps the answer lies outside the courthouse in the form of job opportunities for juveniles, improved family relationships, and more effective school systems. How to cope with the needs of children in trouble remains one of the most controversial and frustrating issues in the justice system.

In the immediate future, the goals of the juvenile justice system are likely to be (1) reorganization of the juvenile system, (2) increased use of the juvenile waiver, (3) development of intermediate juvenile systems to handle violent offenders, and (4) tougher sentences.

For an up-to-date list of Web links, go to
http://cj.wadsworth.com/siegel_essen4e.

KEY TERMS

juvenile justice system 460	child savers 461	status offender 465	initial appearance 474
parens patriae 460	Children's Aid Society 463	detention 470	disposition 475
balanced and restorative justice model 460	juvenile court 463	waiver (juvenile) 472	commitment 475
poor laws 461	juvenile delinquency 465	transfer hearing 472	treatment 476

INFOTRAC COLLEGE EDITION EXERCISES

INFOTRAC COLLEGE EDITION provides numerous articles on juvenile justice. You can use it to review many of the topics discussed in this chapter. For example, if you want to research the issues related to the abolition of the juvenile court, read Barry C. Feld, "Abolish the Juvenile Court: Youthfulness, Criminal Responsibility, and Sentencing Policy," *Journal of Criminal Law and Criminology* 88 (1997): 68–136, or Stephen J. Morse, "Immaturity and Irresponsibility," *Journal of Criminal Law and Criminology* 88 (1997): 15–67. For information on detention and incarceration issues, check out Steven H. Rosenbaum, "Civil Rights Issues in Juvenile Detention and Correctional Systems," *Corrections Today* 61 (1999): 148.

QUESTIONS

1. Should status offenders be treated by the juvenile court? Explain. Should they be placed in confinement for running away or cutting school? Why or why not?

2. Should a juvenile ever be waived to adult court at the risk that the child will be incarcerated with adult felons? Why or why not?

3. Do you support the death penalty for children? Explain.

4. Should juveniles be given mandatory incarceration sentences for serious crimes, as adults are? Explain.

5. Is it fair to deny juveniles a jury trial? Why or why not?

6. Do you think the trend toward treating juveniles like adult offenders is desirable? Explain.

NOTES

1. Federal Bureau of Investigation, *Crime in the United States, 2000* (Washington, D.C.: U.S. Government Printing Office, 2001); Howard Snyder and Melissa Sickmund, *Juvenile Offenders and Victims: 1999 National Report* (Washington, D.C.: Department of Justice, Office of Juvenile Justice and Delinquency Prevention, 1999). Hereinafter cited as *Juvenile Offenders and Victims.*

2. *Vernonia School District v. Acton,* 515 U.S. 646, 115 S.Ct. 2386, 132 L.Ed.2d (1995).

3. *Board of Education of Independent School District No. 92 of Pottawatomie County v. Earls* (No. 01-332) 2002.

4. Gordon Bazemore, "What's 'New' About the Balanced Approach," *Juvenile and Family Court Journal* 48 (1997): 1–21; see also Office of Justice Programs, "Balanced and Restorative Justice for Juveniles: A Framework for Juvenile Justice in the 21st Century" (Washington, D.C.: Department of Justice, Office of Juvenile Justice and Delinquency Prevention, 1997).

5. Material in this section depends heavily on Sanford J. Fox, "Juvenile Justice Reform: A Historical Perspective," *Stanford Law Review* 22 (1970): 1187–1205; Lawrence Stone, *The Family, Sex, and Marriage in England: 1500–1800* (New York: Harper & Row, 1977); Philippe Aries, *Century of Childhood: A Social History of Family Life* (New York: Vintage Press, 1962); Douglas R. Rendleman, "Parens Patriae: From Chancery to the Juvenile Court," *South Carolina Law Review* 23 (1971): 205–229; Wiley B. Sanders, "Some Early Beginnings of the Children's Court Movement in England," in *National Probation Association Yearbook* (New York: National Council on Crime and Delinquency, 1945); Anthony M. Platt, "The Rise of the Child-Saving Movement: A Study in Social Policy and Correctional Reform," *Annals of the American Academy of Political and Social Science* 381 (1979): 21–38; idem, *The Child Savers: The Intervention of Delinquency* (Chicago: University of Chicago Press, 1969); Robert S. Pickett, *House of Refuge: Origins of Juvenile Reform in New York State, 1815–1857* (Syracuse, N.Y.: Syracuse University Press, 1969).

6. Douglas Besharov, *Juvenile Justice Advocacy: Practice in a Unique Court* (New York: Practicing Law Institute, 1974), 2; see also Jay Albanese, *Dealing with Delinquency: The Future of Juvenile Justice* (Chicago: Nelson-Hall, 1993).

7. 4 Eng.Rep. 1078 (1827).

8. Platt, *The Child Savers,* 11–38.

9. See generally, Anne Meis Knupfer, *Reform and Resistance: Gender, Delinquency, and America's First Juvenile Court* (London: Routledge, 2001).

10. This section is based on material from the New York State Archives, *The Greatest Reform School in the World: A Guide to the Records of the New York House of Refuge: A Brief History 1824–1857* (Albany: New York State Archives, 2001); Sanford J. Fox, "Juvenile Justice Reform: A Historical Perspective," *Stanford Law Review* 22 (1970): 1187.

11. Robert S. Pickett, *House of Refuge: Origins of Juvenile Reform in New York State, 1815–1857* (Syracuse, N.Y.: Syracuse University Press, 1969).

12. Robert Mennel, "Origins of the Juvenile Court: Changing Perspectives on the Legal Risks of Juvenile Delinquents," *Crime and Delinquency* 18 (1972): 68–78.

13. Platt, *The Child Savers,* 116.

14. LaMar T. Empey, *American Delinquency: Its Meaning and Construction* (Homewood, Ill.: Dorsey Press, 1978), 515.

15. *Kent v. United States,* 383 U.S. 541, 86 S.Ct. 1045, 16 L.Ed.2d 84 (1966); *In re Gault,* 387 U.S. 1, 87 S.Ct. 1428, 18 L.Ed.2d 527 (1967): juveniles have the right to notice, counsel, confrontation, and cross-examination and to the privileges against self-incrimination in juvenile court proceedings. *In re Winship,* 397 U.S. 358, 90 S.Ct. 1068, 25 L.Ed.2d 368 (1970): proof beyond a reasonable doubt is necessary for conviction in juvenile proceedings. *Breed v. Jones,* 421 U.S. 519, 95 S.Ct. 1779, 44 L.Ed.2d 346 (1975): jeopardy attaches in a juvenile court adjudicatory hearing, thus barring subsequent prosecution for the same offense as an adult.

16. Public Law 93-415 (1974).

17. For a comprehensive view of juvenile law, see, generally, Joseph J. Senna and Larry J. Siegel, *Juvenile Law: Cases and Comments,* 2d ed. (St. Paul: West, 1992).

18. Federal Bureau of Investigation, *Crime in the United States, 2001* (Washington, D.C.: Government Printing Office, 2002), 220.

19. Richard J. Lundman, "Routine Police Arrest Practices," *Social Problems* 22 (1974): 127–141; Robert E. Worden and Stephanie M. Myers, *Police Encounters with Juvenile Suspects* (Albany: Hindelang Criminal Justice Research Center and School of Criminal Justice, State University of New York, 2001).

20. Worden and Myers, *Police Encounters with Juvenile Suspects;* Joan McCord, Cathy Spatz-Widom, and Nancy A. Crowell, eds., *Juvenile Crime, Juvenile Justice.* Panel on Juvenile Crime: Prevention, Treatment, and Control (Washington, D.C.: National Academy Press, 2001), 163.

21. *Fare v. Michael C.,* 442 U.S. 707 (1979).

22. Anne L. Stahl, *Delinquency Cases in Juvenile Courts, 1998* (Washington, D.C.: Office of Juvenile Justice and Delinquency Prevention, 2001).

23. Anne L. Stahl, *Drug Offense Cases in Juvenile Courts, 1989–1998* (Washington, D.C.: Office of Juvenile Justice and Delinquency Prevention, 2001).

24. Anne L. Stahl, *Delinquency Cases Juvenile Courts, 1998* (Washington, D.C.: Office of Juvenile Justice and Delinquency Prevention, 2001).

25. Paul Harms, *Detention in Delinquency Cases, 1989–1998* (Washington, D.C.: Officer of Juvenile Justice and Delinquency Prevention, 2002).

26. *Schall v. Martin,* 467 U.S. 253, 104 S.Ct. 2403, 81 L.Ed.2d 207 (1984).

27. See Juvenile Justice and Delinquency Prevention Act of 1974, 42 U.S.C., sec. 5633.

28. Ira Schwartz, Linda Harris, and Laurie Levi, "The Jailing of Juveniles in Minnesota," *Crime and Delinquency* 34 (1988): 131; also Barry Krisberg and Robert DeComo, *Juveniles Taken into Custody—1991* (San Francisco: National Council on Crime and Delinquency, 1993), 25.

29. Schwartz, Harris, Levi., "The Jailing of Juveniles in Minnesota," 134.

30. 383 U.S. 541, 86 S.Ct. 1045, 16 L.Ed.2d 84 (1966).

31. 421 U.S. 519, 528, 95 S.Ct. 1779, 1785, 44 L.Ed.2d 346 (1975).

32. Alan Karpelowitz, *State Legislative Priorities—1995* (Denver: National Conference of State Legislatures, 1995), 10.

33. Charles M. Puzzanchera, *Delinquency Cases Waived to Criminal Court, 1989–1998* (Washington, D.C.: Office of Juvenile Justice and Delinquency Prevention, 2001).

34. Dale Parent, *Key Issues in Criminal Justice: Transferring Serious Juvenile Offenders to Adult Courts* (Washington, D.C.: National Institute of Justice, 1997).

35. Barry Feld, "The Juvenile Court Meets the Principle of the Offense: Legislative Changes in Juvenile Waiver Statutes," *Journal of Criminal Law and Criminology 78* (1987): 471–533; see also John Kramer, Henry Sontheimer, and John Lemmon, "Pennsylvania Waiver to Adult Court" (Paper presented at the annual meeting of the American Society of Criminology, San Francisco, November 1991); authors confirm that juveniles tried in adult courts are generally male, age seventeen or older, and disproportionately minorities.

36. Puzzanchera, *Delinquency Cases Waived to Criminal Court, 1988–1998*; Jeffrey Fagan, Martin Forst, and T. Scott Vivona, "Racial Determinants of the Judicial Transfer Decision: Prosecuting Violent Youth in Criminal Court," *Crime and Delinquency 33* (1987): 359–386; J. Fagan, E. Slaughter, and E. Hartstone, "Blind Justice: The Impact of Race on the Juvenile Justice Process," *Crime and Delinquency 53* (1987): 224–258; J. Fagan and E. P. Deschenes, "Determinants of Judicial Waiver Decisions for Violent Juvenile Offenders," *Journal of Criminal Law and Criminology 81* (1990): 314–347; see also James Howell, "Juvenile Transfers to Criminal Court," *Juvenile and Family Justice Journal 6* (1997): 12–14.

37. Anne L. Stahl, *Delinquency Cases in Juvenile Courts, 1997* (Washington, D.C.: Office of Juvenile Justice and Delinquency Prevention, 2000); Puzzanchera, *Delinquency Cases Waived to Criminal Court, 1988–1998*.

38. Howard N. Snyder, Melissa Sickmund, and Eileen Poe-Yamagata, *Juvenile Transfers to Criminal Court in the 1990s: Lessons Learned from Four Studies* (Washington, D.C.: Office of Juvenile Justice and Delinquency Prevention, 2000).

39. Parent, *Key Issues in Criminal Justice*.

40. 387 U.S. 1, 87 S.Ct. 1428, 18 L.Ed.2d 527 (1967).

41. 397 U.S. 358, 90 S.Ct. 1068, 25 L.Ed.2d 368 (1970).

42. 403 U.S. 528, 91 S.Ct. 1976, 29 L.Ed.2d 647 (1971).

43. Paul Harms, *Robbery Cases in Juvenile Court, 1989–1998* (Washington, D.C.: Office of Juvenile Justice and Delinquency Prevention, 2002).

44. Stahl, *Delinquency Cases in Juvenile Courts, 1998*.

45. Harms, *Robbery Cases in Juvenile Court, 1989–1998*.

46. Charles Puzzanchera, *Juvenile Court Placement of Adjudicated Youth, 1989–1998* (Washington, D.C.: Office of Juvenile Justice and Delinquency Prevention, 2002).

47. Victor Streib, *Death Penalty for Juveniles* (Bloomington: Indiana University Press, 1987); also Paul Reidinger, "The Death Row Kids," *American Bar Association Journal 70* (1989): 78; also, "Note: The Death Penalty and the Eighth Amendment: An Analysis of *Stanford v. Kentucky*," *Yale Law Review 35* (1990): 641.

48. See Joseph Goldstein, Anna Freud, and Albert Solnit, *Beyond the Best Interest of the Child* (New York: Free Press, 1973).

49. See Michael Serrill, "Police Write a New Law on Juvenile Crime," *Police Magazine* (September 1979): 47; see also A. Schneider and D. Schram, *Assessment of Juvenile Justice Reform in Washington State*, vols. 1–4 (Washington, D.C.: Department of Justice, Institute of Policy Analysis, 1983); T. Castellano, "Justice Model in the Juvenile Justice System—Washington State's Experience," *Law and Policy 8* (1986): 479.

50. Anne Schneider, *Guide to Juvenile Restitution* (Washington, D.C.: Department of Justice, 1985).

51. "Colorado OKs New Way to Handle Violent Juvenile Offenders," *Criminal Justice Newsletter 9* (1993): 4.

52. Melissa Sickmund, Howard N. Snyder, and Eileen Poe-Yamagata, *Juvenile Offenders and Victims: 1997 Update on Violence* (Washington, D.C.: Department of Justice, Office of Juvenile Justice and Delinquency Prevention, 1997), 18.

53. Melissa Sickmund and Yi-chun Wan, "Census of Juveniles in Residential Placement Databook," 2001; www.ojjdp.ncjrs.org/ojstatbb/cjrp.

54. Ibid.

55. Howard N. Snyder and Melissa Sickmund, *Juvenile Offenders and Victims: 1999 National Report* (Pittsburgh, Penn.: National Center for Juvenile Justice, 1999), 192.

56. Ibid., 195.

57. National Conference of State Legislatures, *A Legislator's Guide to Comprehensive Juvenile Justice, Juvenile Detention, and Corrections* (Denver: National Conference of State Legislators, 1996).

58. J. David Hawkins, Richard F. Catalano, and Associates, *Communities That Care: Action for Drug Abuse Prevention* (San Francisco: Jossey-Bass, 1992).

59. Richard F. Catalano, Michael W. Arthur, J. David Hawkins, Lisa Berglund, and Jeffrey J. Olson, "Comprehensive Community- and School-Based Interventions to Prevent Antisocial Behavior," in *Serious and Violent Juvenile Offenders: Risk Factors and Successful Interventions*, eds. Rolf Loeber and David P. Farrington (Thousand Oaks, Calif.: Sage, 1998).

60. Adele V. Harrell, Shannon E. Cavanagh, and Sanjeev Sridharan, *Evaluation of the Children At Risk Program: Results One Year After the End of the Program* (Washington, D.C.: NIJ Research in Brief, 1999).

61. Hawkins, Catalano, and Associates, *Communities That Care*.

62. Elaine Morley, Shelli B. Rossman, Mary Kopczynski, Janeen Buck, and Caterina Gouvis, *Comprehensive Responses to Youth At Risk: Interim Findings from the SafeFutures Initiative* (Washington, D.C.: Office of Juvenile Justice and Delinquency Prevention, 2000).

63. Catalano, Arthur, Hawkins, Berglund, and Olson, "Comprehensive Community- and School-Based Interventions to Prevent Antisocial Behavior," 281.

64. James C. Howell and J. David Hawkins, "Prevention of Youth Violence," in *Youth Violence: Crime and Justice: A Review of Research*, vol. 24, eds. Michael Tonry and Mark H. Moore (Chicago: University of Chicago Press, 1998), 303–304.

65. Office of Justice Programs, *Reducing Youth Gun Violence* (Washington, D.C.: Department of Justice, Office of Juvenile Justice and Delinquency Prevention, 1996).

66. Fox Butterfield, "Justice Besieged," *New York Times*, 21 July 1997, A16.

Glossary

actus reus An illegal act. The actus reus can be an active act, such as taking money or shooting someone, or a failure to act, such as failing to take proper precautions while driving a car.

adjudication The determination of guilt or innocence; a judgment concerning criminal charges. The majority of offenders charged plead guilty; of the remainder, some cases are adjudicated by a judge and a jury, some are adjudicated by a judge without a jury, and others are dismissed.

adversarial procedure The procedure used to determine truth in the adjudication of guilt or innocence in which the defense (advocate for the accused) is pitted against the prosecution (advocate for the state), with the judge acting as arbiter of the legal rules. Under the adversary system, the burden is on the state to prove the charges beyond a reasonable doubt. This system of having the two parties publicly debate has proved to be the most effective method of achieving the truth regarding a set of circumstances. (Under the accusatory, or inquisitorial, system, which is used in continental Europe, the charge is evidence of guilt that the accused must disprove; the judge takes an active part in the proceedings.)

appellate court A court that reconsiders a case that has already been tried in order to determine whether the measures used complied with accepted rules of criminal procedure and were in line with constitutional doctrines.

arraignment The step at which accused offenders are read the charges against them and are asked how they plead. In addition, the accused are advised of their rights. Possible pleas are guilty, not guilty, nolo contendere, and not guilty by reason of insanity.

assigned counsel A lawyer appointed by the court to represent a defendant in a criminal case because the person is too poor to hire counsel.

Auburn system The prison system developed in New York during the nineteenth century that stressed congregate working conditions.

Bail Reform Act of 1984 Federal legislation that provides for both greater emphasis on release on recognizance for nondangerous offenders and preventive detention for those who present a menace to the community.

bail The monetary amount for or condition of pretrial release, normally set by a judge at the initial appearance. The purpose of bail is to ensure the return of the accused at subsequent proceedings.

balanced and restorative justice model A new model of juvenile justice focusing on victim restoration, improving offender abilities, and protecting the public. Offenders, victims, and the community are all active participants.

beat A defined patrol area.

bench trial The trial of a criminal matter by a judge only. The accused waives any constitutional right to trial by jury.

Bill of Rights The first ten amendments to the U.S. Constitution.

biosocial theory The school of thought holding that human behavior is a function of the interaction of biochemical, neurological, and genetic factors with environmental stimulus.

blameworthy The culpability or guilt a person maintains for participating in a particular criminal offense.

blue curtain The secretive, insulated police culture that isolates officers from the rest of society.

booking process The administrative record of an arrest, listing the offender's name, address, physical description, date of birth, and employer; the time of arrest; the offense; and the name of the arresting officer.

Photographing and fingerprinting of the offender are also part of the booking process.

boot camp A short-term militaristic correctional facility in which inmates undergo intensive physical conditioning and discipline.

broken windows model The term used to describe the role of the police as maintainers of community order and safety.

brutalization effect The belief that capital punishment creates an atmosphere of brutality that enhances, rather than deters, the level of violence in society. The death penalty reinforces the view that violence is an appropriate response to provocation.

Burger v. Kemp The 1987 U.S. Supreme Court decision upholding that no conflict of interest results when a defense attorney represents two defendants charged with the same crime as long as counsel acts competently and effectively.

Carriers case A fifteenth-century case that defined the law of theft and reformulated the concept of taking the possession of another.

challenge for cause Removing a juror because he or she is biased or has prior knowledge about a case, or for other reasons that demonstrate the individual's inability to render a fair and impartial judgment in a case.

charge In a criminal case, the judge's instruction to the jurors before deliberation.

child savers Late nineteenth-century reformers in America who developed programs for troubled youths and influenced legislation creating the juvenile justice system.

Children's Aid Society A child-saving organization began by Charles Loring Brace; it took children from the streets in large cities and placed them with farm families on the prairie.

chivalry hypothesis The view that the low female crime and delinquency rates are a reflection of the leniency with which police treat female offenders.

choice theory The school of thought holding that people will engage in delinquent and criminal behavior after weighing the consequences and benefits of their actions. Delinquent behavior is a rational choice made by a motivated offender who perceives the chances of gain outweigh any perceived punishment or loss.

chronic offender A delinquent offender who is arrested five or more times before he or she is eighteen and who stands a good chance of becoming an adult criminal; these offenders are responsible for more than half of all serious crimes.

circumstantial (indirect) evidence Evidence not bearing on the fact in dispute but on various indirect circumstances from which the judge or jury might infer the existence of the fact (for example, if the defendant was seen in the house with wet clothing, that is circumstantial evidence that the person had walked in the rain).

civil law All law that is not criminal, including torts (personal wrongs), contract, property, maritime, and commercial law.

commitment Decision of judge ordering an adjudicated and sentenced juvenile offender to be placed in a correctional facility.

common law Early English law, developed by judges, that incorporated Anglo-Saxon tribal custom, feudal rules and practices, and the everyday rules of behavior of local villages. Common law became the standardized law of the land in England and eventually formed the basis of the criminal law in the United States.

community service restitution An alternative sanction that requires an offender to work in the community at such tasks as cleaning public parks or working with disabled children in lieu of an incarceration sentence.

community treatment The attempt by correctional agencies to maintain convicted offenders in the community instead of a secure facility; it includes probation, parole, and residential programs.

complaint A sworn allegation made in writing to a court or judge that an individual is guilty of some designated (complained of) offense. This is often the first legal document filed regarding a criminal offense. The complaint may be "taken out" by the victim, the police officer, the district attorney, or another interested party. Al-though the complaint charges an offense, an indictment or information may be the formal charging document.

concurrent sentence A prison sentence for two or more criminal acts that are served simultaneously, and run together.

conflict theory The view that human behavior is shaped by interpersonal conflict and that those who maintain social power will use it to further their own needs.

conflict view of crime (or *critical view of crime*) The belief that the law is controlled by the rich and powerful who shape its content to ensure their continued economic domination of society. The criminal justice system is an instrument of social and economic repression.

confrontation clause The constitutional right of a criminal defendant to see and cross-examine all the witnesses against him or her.

congregate system The Auburn Prison, one of the nation's first correctional facilities, was a congregate system, since most prisoners ate and worked in groups.

consecutive sentence A prison sentence for two or more criminal acts that are served one after the other, or that follow one another.

consensus view of crime The belief that the majority of citizens in a society share common ideals and work toward a common good and that crimes are acts that are outlawed because they conflict with the rules of the majority and are harmful to society.

constable In medieval England, an appointed official who administered and supervised the legal affairs of a small community.

contingent exclusionary rule A plan that would allow evidence seized in violation of the Fourth Amendment to be used in a court of law. It would apply when a judge finds police testimony questionable, but also concludes that the release of the guilty would be unpleasant and unwarranted. Rather than simply excluding the evidence, the judge could request that the prosecution or police pay a fee, similar to a fine, in order to use the evidence in court. Exclusion of the evidence would be contingent on the failure to pay the damages set by the court.

contract system (attorney) Providing counsel to indigent offenders by having attorneys under contract to the county handle all (or some) such cases.

contract system (convict) The system used early in the twentieth century by which private industry contracted with prison officials for convict labor and set up shops on prison grounds for them to work.

convict-lease system The system whereby the state leased its prisoners to a business for a fixed annual fee and gave up supervision and control.

court of last resort A court that handles the final appeal on a matter. The U.S. Supreme Court is the official court of last resort for criminal matters.

courtroom work group The phrase used to denote that all parties in the adversary process work together in a cooperative effort to settle cases with the least amount of effort and conflict.

crime A violation of societal rules of behavior as interpreted and expressed by a criminal legal code created by people holding social and political power. Individuals who violate these rules are subject to sanctions by state authority, social stigma, and loss of status.

crime control perspective A model of criminal justice that emphasizes the control of dangerous offenders and the protection of society. Its advocates call for harsh punishments as a deterrent to crime, such as the death penalty.

criminal justice The decision-making points from the initial investigation or arrest by police to the eventual release of the offender and his or her reentry into society; the various sequential criminal justice stages through which the offender passes.

criminal law The body of rules that define crimes, set their punishments out, and mandate the procedures in carrying out the criminal justice process.

criminal procedure The rules and laws that define the operation of the criminal proceedings. Procedural law describes the methods that must be followed in obtaining warrants, investigating offenses, effecting lawful arrests, conducting trials, introducing evidence, sentencing convicted offenders, and reviewing cases by appellate courts.

cross-examination The process in which the defense and the prosecution interrogate witnesses during a trial.

cruel and unusual punishment Physical punishment or punishment that is far in excess of that given to people under similar circumstances and is therefore banned by the Eighth Amendment. The death penalty has so far not been considered cruel and unusual if it is administered in a fair and nondiscriminatory fashion.

culture of poverty   The crushing lifestyle of slum areas produces a culture of poverty, passed from one generation to the next, marked by apathy, cynicism, feelings of helplessness, and mistrust of social institutions, such as schools, government agencies, and the police.

cynicism   The belief that most people's actions are motivated solely by personal needs and selfishness.

day fees   A program requiring probationers to pay in part for the costs of their treatment.

day fine   A fine geared to the average daily income of the convicted offender in an effort to bring equity to the sentencing process.

day reporting center (DRC)   A nonresidential community-based treatment program.

deadly force   The ability of the police to kill suspects if they resist arrest or present a danger to the officer or the community. The police cannot use deadly force against an unarmed fleeing felon.

death-qualified jury   The process during jury selection of removing any juror in a capital case who acknowledges that he or she will not convict knowing that there is a potential for the death penalty being applied. The U.S. Supreme Court has ruled that prosecutors have the right to discharge those jurors who would not consider the death penalty under any circumstances.

decriminalization   Reducing the penalty for a criminal act but not actually legalizing it.

deinstitutionalization   The movement to remove as many offenders as possible from secure confinement and treat them in the community.

demeanor   The way in which a person outwardly manifests his or her personality.

deposit bail   The monetary amount set by a judge at a hearing as a condition of pretrial release, ordering a percentage of the total bond required to be paid by the defendant.

detention   The temporary care of a child alleged to be a delinquent or status offender who requires secure custody, pending court disposition.

determinate sentence   A fixed term of incarceration, such as three years' imprisonment. Determinate sentences are felt by many to be too restrictive for rehabilitative purposes; the advantage is that offenders

know how much time they have to serve—that is, when they will be released.

deterrent effect   Stopping or reducing crime by convincing would-be criminals that they stand a significant risk of being apprehended and punished for their crimes.

developmental theory   The view that social interactions developed over the life course shape behavior. Some interactions, such as involvement with deviant peers, encourage law violations, whereas others, such as marriage and military service, may help people desist from crime.

direct examination   The questioning of one's own (prosecution or defense) witness during a trial.

directed verdict   The right of a judge to direct a jury to acquit a defendant because the state has not proven the elements of the crime or otherwise has not established guilt according to law.

discretion   The use of personal decision making and choice in carrying out operations in the criminal justice system. For example, police discretion can involve the decision to make an arrest; prosecutorial discretion can involve the decision to accept a plea bargain.

displacement   The process by which the presence of police officers in one area causes criminals to move to another, less well-guarded neighborhood.

disposition   For juvenile offenders, the equivalent of sentencing for adult offenders. The theory is that disposition is more rehabilitative than retributive. Possible dispositions may be to dismiss the case; release the youth to the custody of his or her parents; place the offender on probation; or send him or her to an institution or state correctional institution.

diversion   A noncriminal alternative to trial, usually featuring counseling, job training, and educational opportunities.

DNA profiling   The identification of criminal suspects by matching DNA samples taken from their person with specimens found at the crime scene.

double marginality   The social burden African-American police officers carry by being both minority group members and law enforcement officers (see Nicholas Alex, *African American in Blue,* 1969).

Drug Abuse Resistance Education (DARE)   A school-based antidrug program initiated by the Los Angeles Police Department and now adopted around the United States.

Drug Enforcement Administration (DEA)   The federal agency that enforces federal drug control laws.

due process perspective   Due process is the basic constitutional principle based on the concept of the privacy of the individual and the complementary concept of limitation on governmental power; a safeguard against arbitrary and unfair state procedures in judicial or administrative proceedings. Embodied in the due process concept are the basic rights of a defendant in criminal proceedings and the requisites for a fair trial. These rights and requirements have been expanded by appellate court decisions and include (1) timely notice of a hearing or trial that informs the accused of the charges against him or her; (2) the opportunity to confront accusers and to present evidence on one's own behalf before an impartial jury or judge; (3) the presumption of innocence under which guilt must be proven by legally obtained evidence and the verdict must be supported by the evidence presented; (4) the right of an accused to be warned of constitutional rights at the earliest stage of the criminal process; (5) protection against self-incrimination; (6) assistance of counsel at every critical stage of the criminal process; and (7) the guarantee that an individual will not be tried more than once for the same offense (double jeopardy).

electronic monitoring (EM)   Requiring a convicted offender to wear a monitoring device as part of his or her community sentence. Electronic monitoring is typically part of a house arrest order and enables the probation department to ensure that the offender is complying with court-ordered limitations on his or her freedom.

entrapment   A criminal defense that maintains the police originated the criminal idea or initiated the criminal action.

equity   The action or practice of awarding each person his or her just due; sanctions based on equity seek to compensate individual victims and the general society for their losses due to crime.

exclusionary rule   The principle that prohibits using evidence illegally obtained in a trial. Based on the Fourth Amendment "right of the people to be secure in their persons, houses, papers, and effects, against unreasonable searches and seizures," the rule is not a bar to prosecution because legally obtained evidence may be available that may be used in a trial.

Federal Bureau of Investigation (FBI)   The arm of the U.S. Justice Department that investigates violations of federal law, gathers crime statistics, runs a comprehensive crime laboratory, and helps train local law enforcement officers.

felony A more serious offense that carries a penalty of incarceration in a state prison, usually for one year or more. Persons convicted of felony offenses lose such rights as the rights to vote, hold elective office, or maintain certain licenses.

felony court A state or federal court that has jurisdiction over felony offenses—serious crimes that carry a penalty of incarceration in a state or federal prison for one year or more.

fine Levying a money payment on offenders to compensate society for their misdeeds.

First Amendment The U.S. constitutional amendment that guarantees freedom of speech, religion, press, and assembly and the right of the people to petition the government for a redress of grievances.

foot patrol Police patrols that take officers out of cars and put them on a walking beat in order to strengthen ties with the community.

forfeiture The seizure of personal property by the state as a civil or criminal penalty.

furlough A correctional policy that allows inmates to leave the institution for vocational or educational training, for employment, or to maintain family ties.

general deterrence A crime control policy that depends on the fear of criminal penalties. General deterrence measures, such as long prison sentences for violent crimes, are aimed at convincing the potential law violator that the pains associated with the crime outweigh the benefits.

Gideon v. Wainwright The 1963 U.S. Supreme Court case that granted counsel to indigent defendants in felony prosecutions.

good faith exception The principle of law holding that evidence may be used in a criminal trial, even though the search warrant used to obtain it is technically faulty, if the police acted in good faith and to the best of their ability when they sought to obtain it from a judge.

grand jury A group (usually consisting of twenty-three citizens) chosen to hear testimony in secret and to issue formal criminal accusations (indictments). It also serves an investigatory function.

grass eaters A term to describe police officers who accept payoffs when everyday du-

ties place them in a position to be solicited by the public.

halfway house A community-based correctional facility that houses inmates before their outright release so that they can become gradually acclimated to conventional society.

hands-off doctrine The legal practice of allowing prison administrators a free hand to run the institution even if correctional practices violate inmates' constitutional rights; ended with the onset of the prisoners' rights movement in the 1960s.

hearsay evidence Testimony that is not firsthand but related information told by a second party.

hot spots of crime Places from which a significant portion of all police calls originate. These hot spots include taverns and housing projects.

house arrest A form of intermediate sanction that requires that the convicted offender spend a designated amount of time per week in his or her own home—for example, from 5 P.M. Friday until 8 A.M. Monday.

hue and cry A call for assistance in medieval England. The policy of self-help used in villages demanded that everyone respond if a citizen raised a hue and cry to get their aid.

hulk A mothballed ship that was used to house prisoners in eighteenth-century England.

hundred In medieval England, a group of one hundred families that had the responsibility to maintain the order and try minor offenses.

in forma pauperis "In the manner of a pauper." A criminal defendant granted permission to proceed in forma pauperis is entitled to assistance of counsel at state expense.

incapacitation The policy of keeping dangerous criminals in confinement to eliminate the risk of their repeating their offense in society.

indeterminate sentence A term of incarceration with a stated minimum and maximum length, such as a sentence to prison for a period of from three to ten years. The prisoner would be eligible for parole after the minimum sentence has been served. Based on the belief that sentences should fit the criminal, indeterminate sentences allow individualized sentences and provide for sentencing flexibility. Judges can set a high

minimum to override the purpose of the indeterminate sentence.

index (Part I) crimes The eight crimes that, because of their seriousness and frequency, the FBI reports the incidence of in the annual Uniform Crime Reports. Index crimes include murder, rape, assault, robbery, burglary, arson, larceny, and motor vehicle theft.

indictment A written accusation returned by a grand jury charging an individual with a specified crime after determination of probable cause; the prosecutor presents enough evidence (a prima facie case) to establish probable cause.

indigent Person who is needy and poor or who lacks the means to hire an attorney.

inevitable discovery rule Evidence seized in violation of the Fifth Amendment's self-incrimination clause may be used in a court of law if a judge rules that it would have been found or discovered even if the incriminating statements had never been made.

information Like the indictment, a formal charging document. The prosecuting attorney makes out the information and files it in court. Probable cause is determined at the preliminary hearing, which, unlike grand jury proceedings, is public and attended by the accused and his or her attorney.

initial appearance A juvenile's first appearance before the juvenile court judge in which the charges are reviewed and an effort is made to settle the case without a trial. If the child does not have legal counsel an attorney will be appointed.

initial hearing The stage in the justice process during which the suspect is brought before a magistrate for consideration of bail. The suspect must be taken for an initial hearing within a "reasonable time" after arrest. For petty offenses, this step often serves as the final criminal proceedings, either by adjudication by a judge or the offering of a guilty plea.

inmate social code Unwritten guidelines that express the values, attitudes, and types of behavior that older inmates demand of young ones. Passed on from one generation of inmates to another, the inmate social code represents the values of interpersonal relations within the prison.

inmate subculture The loosely defined culture that pervades prisons and has its own norms, rules, and language.

insanity A legal defense that maintains a defendant was incapable of forming criminal intent because he or she suffers from a defect of reason or mental illness.

intake The process in which a probation officer settles cases at the initial appearance before the onset of formal criminal proceedings; also, process in which a juvenile referral is received and a decision is made to file a petition in the juvenile court, release the juvenile, or refer the juvenile elsewhere.

intensive probation supervision (IPS) A type of intermediate sanction involving small probation caseloads and strict monitoring on a daily or weekly basis.

intensive supervision parole (ISP) A limited-caseload program for those parolees who need intensive surveillance. Parolees are required to meet more often with parole officers than routine parolees and may also have frequent drug testing, serve a term in a community correctional system, and be electronically monitored.

intent An action that on its face indicates a criminal purpose—for example, breaking into a locked building or trespassing on someone's property; a guilty mind.

intermediate sanctions The group of punishments falling between probation and prison; "probation plus." Community-based sanctions, including house arrest and intensive supervision, serve as alternatives to incarceration.

internal affairs The branch of the police department that investigates charges of corruption or misconduct made against police officers.

jail A place to detain people awaiting trial, to serve as a lockup for drunks and disorderly individuals, and to confine convicted misdemeanants serving sentences of less than one year.

jailhouse lawyer An inmate trained in law or otherwise educated who helps other inmates prepare legal briefs and appeals.

judicial reprieve The common-law practice that allowed judges to suspend punishment so that convicted offenders could seek a pardon, gather new evidence, or demonstrate that they had reformed their behavior.

jury trial The process of deciding a case by a group of persons selected and sworn in to serve as jurors at a criminal trial, often as a six- or twelve-person jury.

just desert The philosophy of justice asserting that those who violate the rights of others deserve to be punished. The severity

of punishment should be commensurate with the seriousness of the crime.

justice of the peace Established in 1326 England, the office was created to help the shire reeve in controlling the county and later took on judicial functions.

juvenile court A court that has original jurisdiction over persons defined by statute as juveniles and alleged to be delinquents or status offenders.

juvenile delinquency Participation in illegal behavior by a minor who falls under a statutory age limit.

juvenile justice system The system of agencies and organizations that deal with youths who commit acts of juvenile delinquency (crimes under a given age) and acts of noncriminal behavior (truancy and incorrigibility).

Knapp Commission A public body that led an investigation into police corruption in New York and uncovered a widespread network of payoffs and bribes.

landmark decision A decision handed down by the U.S. Supreme Court that becomes the law of the land and serves as a precedent for similar legal issues.

Law Enforcement Assistance Administration (LEAA) Funded by the federal government's Safe Streets Act, this agency provided technical assistance and hundreds of millions of dollars in aid to local and state justice agencies between 1969 and 1982.

legalization The removal of all criminal penalties from a previously outlawed act.

life history A research method that uses the experiences of an individual as the unit of analysis, such as using the life experience of an individual gang member to understand the natural history of gang membership.

lower court A generic term referring to a court that has jurisdiction over misdemeanors and conducts preliminary investigations of felony charges.

mala in se A term that refers to acts that society considers inherently evil, such as murder or rape, and that violate the basic principles of Judeo-Christian morality.

mandatory sentence A statutory requirement that a certain penalty shall be set and carried out in all cases on conviction for a specified offense or series of offenses.

Manhattan Bail Project The innovative experiment in bail reform that introduced and successfully tested the concept of release on recognizance.

maximum-security prison A correctional institution that houses dangerous felons and maintains strict security measures, high walls, and limited contact with the outside world.

meat eaters A term used to describe police officers who actively solicit bribes and vigorously engage in corrupt practices.

medical model A view of corrections holding that convicted offenders are victims of their environment who need care and treatment to transform them into valuable members of society.

medium-security prison A less secure institution that houses nonviolent offenders and provides more opportunities for contact with the outside world.

mens rea Guilty mind. The mental element of a crime or the intent to commit a criminal act.

methadone A synthetic narcotic used as a substitute for heroin in drug-control efforts.

minimum-security prison The least secure institution that houses white-collar and nonviolent offenders, maintains few security measures, and has liberal furlough and visitation policies.

Miranda warning The result of two U.S. Supreme Court decisions (*Escobedo v. Illinois* and *Miranda v. Arizona*) that require police officers to inform individuals under arrest that they have a constitutional right to remain silent, that their statements can later be used against them in court, that they can have an attorney present to help them, and that the state will pay for an attorney if they cannot afford to hire one. Although aimed at protecting an individual during in-custody interrogation, the warning must also be given when the investigation shifts from the investigatory to the accusatory stage—that is, when suspicion begins to focus on an individual.

misdemeanor A minor crime usually punished by less than one year's imprisonment in a local institution, such as a county jail.

Missouri Plan A way of picking judges through nonpartisan elections as a means of ensuring judicial performance standards.

Mollen Commission An investigatory body formed in New York City in 1993 to scrutinize police misconduct.

monetary restitution A sanction that requires that convicted offenders compensate crime victims by reimbursing them for out-of-pocket losses caused by the crime. Losses can include property damage, lost wages, and medical costs.

National Crime Victimization Survey (NCVS) The ongoing victimization study conducted jointly by the Justice Department and the U.S. Census Bureau that surveys victims about their experiences with law violation.

neighborhood-oriented policing (NOP) Community policing efforts aimed at individual neighborhoods.

no bill The action by a grand jury when it votes not to indict an accused suspect.

"no-frills" policy A correctional policy that stipulates that prisons are aimed at punishing and not coddling inmates. A "no-frills" orientation usually means a strict regimen of work and discipline, and reduced opportunities for recreation and education.

nolle prosequi The term used when a prosecutor decides to drop a case after a complaint has been formally made. Reasons for a nolle prosequi include evidence insufficiency, reluctance of witnesses to testify, police error, and office policy.

nolo contendere A plea of "no contest"; the defendant submits to sentencing without any formal admission of guilt that could be used against him or her in a subsequent civil suit.

nonindex (Part II) crimes All other crimes except the eight index crimes recorded by the FBI. The FBI records all arrests made by police of Part II crimes.

nonintervention perspective A justice philosophy that emphasizes the least intrusive treatment possible. Among its central policies are decarceration, diversion, and decriminalization. In other words, less is better.

official crime statistics Compiled by the FBI in its Uniform Crime Reports, these are a tally of serious crimes reported to police agencies each year.

order maintenance (peacekeeping) The order-maintenance aspect of the police role involves peacekeeping, maintaining order and authority without the need for formal arrest, "handling the situation," and keeping things under control by using threats, persuasion, and understanding.

parens patriae Power of the state to act on behalf of the child and provide care and protection equivalent to that of a parent.

parole The early release of a prisoner from imprisonment subject to conditions set by a parole board. Depending on the jurisdiction, inmates must serve a certain portion of their sentences before becoming eligible for parole. The conditions of parole may require the individual to report regularly to a parole officer, to refrain from criminal conduct, to maintain and support his or her family, to avoid contact with other convicted criminals, to abstain from using alcohol and drugs, to remain within the jurisdiction, and so on. Violations of the conditions of parole may result in revocation of parole, in which case the individual will be returned to prison. The concept behind parole is to allow the release of the offender to community supervision, where rehabilitation and readjustment will be facilitated.

penitentiary A state or federal correctional institution for incarceration of felony offenders for terms of one year or more.

penitentiary house A secure correctional facility, based on the Quaker concept that incarcerated criminals should do "penitence."

Pennsylvania system The prison system developed during the nineteenth century that stressed total isolation and individual penitence as a means of reform.

peremptory challenge The dismissal of a potential juror by either the prosecution or the defense for unexplained, discretionary reasons.

plea bargaining The discussion between the defense counsel and the prosecution by which the accused agrees to plead guilty for certain considerations. The advantage to the defendant may be a reduction of the charges, a lenient sentence, or (in the case of multiple charges) dropped charges. The advantage to the prosecution is that a conviction is obtained without the time and expense of lengthy trial proceedings.

police brutality Usually involves such actions as the use of abusive language, unnecessary use of force or coercion, threats, prodding with nightsticks, stopping and searching people to harass them, and so on.

police chief The top administrator of the police department, who sets policy and has general control over all operating branches.

police officer style The belief that the bulk of police officers can be classified into ideal personality types. Popular types include crime fighters, who desire to enforce only serious crimes, such as robbery and rape; law enforcers, who use a broad definition of police work; social agents, who see their job as a helping profession; and watchmen, who do as little as possible. The actual ex-

istence of ideal police officer types has been much debated.

police-community relations Programs developed by police departments to improve relations with the community and develop cooperation with citizens. The forerunner of the community policing model.

poor laws Seventeenth-century laws in England that bound out vagrants and abandoned children as indentured servants to masters.

preliminary hearing (probable cause hearing) The step at which criminal charges initiated by an information are tested for probable cause; the prosecution presents enough evidence to establish probable cause—that is, a prima facie case. The hearing is public and may be attended by the accused and his or her attorney.

preponderance of the evidence The level of proof in civil cases; more than half the evidence supports the allegations of one side.

presentence investigation An investigation performed by a probation officer attached to a trial court after the conviction of a defendant. The report contains information about the defendant's background, education, previous employment, and family; his or her own statement concerning the offense; prior criminal record; interviews with neighbors or acquaintances; and his or her mental and physical condition (that is, information that would not be made public record in the case of guilty plea or that would be inadmissible as evidence at a trial but could be influential and important at the sentencing stage).

presentment The report of a grand jury investigation, which usually includes a recommendation of indictment.

pretrial detention Holding an offender in secure confinement before trial.

pretrial diversion A program that provides nonpunitive community-based alternatives to more intrusive forms of punishment such as jail or prison.

pretrial procedure A proceeding held before an official trial, such as a pretrial hearing, bail review, and pretrial diversion to a noncriminal program.

preventive detention The practice of holding dangerous suspects before trial without bail.

prison A state or federal correctional institution for incarceration of felony offenders for terms of one year or more.

prisonization Assimilation into the separate culture in the prison that has its own set of rewards and behaviors. This loosely defined culture that pervades prisons has its own norms, rules, and language. The traditional culture is now being replaced by a violent gang culture.

pro se The defense of self-representation.

proactive policing A police department policy emphasizing stopping crimes before they occur rather than reacting to crimes that have already occurred.

probable cause The evidentiary criterion necessary to sustain an arrest or the issuance of an arrest or search warrant; less than absolute certainty or "beyond a reasonable doubt" but greater than mere suspicion or "hunch." Probable cause consists of a set of facts, information, circumstances, or conditions that would lead a reasonable person to believe that an offense was committed and that the accused committed that offense. An arrest made without probable cause may be susceptible to prosecution as an illegal arrest under "false imprisonment" statutes.

probation A sentence entailing the conditional release of a convicted offender into the community under the supervision of the court (in the form of a probation officer), subject to certain conditions for a specified time. The conditions are usually similar to those of parole. (*Note:* Probation is a sentence, an alternative to incarceration; parole is administrative release from incarceration.) Violation of the conditions of probation may result in revocation of probation.

problem-oriented policing A style of police operations that stresses proactive problem solving, rather than reactive crime fighting.

proof beyond a reasonable doubt The standard of proof needed to convict in a criminal case. The evidence offered in court does not have to amount to absolute certainty, but it should leave no reasonable doubt that the defendant committed the alleged crime.

prosecutor Representative of the state (executive branch) in criminal proceedings; advocate for the state's case—the charge—in the adversary trial, for example, the attorney general of the United States, U.S. attorneys, attorneys general of the states, district attorneys, and police prosecutors. The prosecutor participates in investigations both before and after arrest, prepares legal documents, participates in obtaining arrest or search warrants, decides whether to charge a suspect and, if so, with which of-fense. The prosecutor argues the state's case at trial, advises the police, participates in plea negotiations, and makes sentencing recommendations.

psychoanalytic view This position holds that criminals are driven by unconscious thought patterns, developed in early childhood, that control behaviors over the life course.

psychopathic (antisocial, sociopathic) personality Psychopaths are chronically antisocial individuals who are always in trouble, and who do not learn from either experience or punishment. They are loners who engage in frequent callous and hedonistic behaviors, are emotionally immature, and lack responsibility, judgment, and empathy.

public defender An attorney generally employed by the government to represent poor persons accused of a crime at no cost to the accused.

public safety doctrine Statements elicited by police violation of the Fifth Amendment's self-incrimination clause may be used in a court of law if a judge rules that the questioning was justified in order to maintain public safety. So, for example, it would be permissible for police to ask a suspected terrorist where he planted a bomb and then use his statement in a criminal trial even though he had never been apprised of his Fifth Amendment (Miranda) rights.

real evidence Any object produced for inspection at the trial (weapon, photograph).

recidivism Repetition of criminal behavior; habitual criminality. Recidivism is measured by (1) criminal acts that resulted in conviction by a court when committed by individuals who are under correctional supervision or who had been released from correctional supervision within the previous three years and (2) technical violations of probation or parole in which a sentencing or paroling authority took action that resulted in an adverse change in the offender's legal status.

recognizance During the Middle Ages, the practice of letting convicted offenders remain free if they agreed to enter a debt relation with the state to pay for their crimes.

rehabilitation perspective A model of criminal justice that views its primary purpose as helping to care for people who cannot manage themselves. Crime is an expression of frustration and anger created by social inequality that can be controlled by giving people the means to improve their lifestyle through conventional endeavors.

release on recognizance (ROR) A non-monetary condition for the pretrial release of an accused individual; an alternative to monetary bail that is granted after the court determines that the accused has ties in the community, has no prior record of default, and is likely to appear at subsequent proceedings.

residential community corrections (RCC) A nonsecure facility, located in the community, that houses probationers who need a more secure environment. Typically, residents are free during the day to go to work, school, or treatment, and return in the evening for counseling sessions and meals.

restitution A condition of probation in which the offender repays society or the victim of crime for the trouble the offender caused.

restorative justice perspective A view of criminal justice that advocates peaceful solutions and mediation rather than coercive punishments.

revocation An administrative act performed by a parole authority that removes a person from parole, or a judicial order by a court removing a person from parole or probation, in response to a violation on the part of the parolee or probationer.

risk classification Classifying probationers so that they may receive an appropriate level of treatment and control.

search warrant An order issued by a judge, directing officers to conduct a search of specified premises for specified objects or persons and bring them before the court.

self-defense A legal defense in which defendants claim that their behavior was legally justified by the necessity to protect their own life and property or that of another victim from potential harm.

self-incrimination Personal utterances or statements that can be used as evidence in a criminal matter. The Fifth Amendment prohibits law enforcement officials from using force or coercion to obtain incriminating statements from suspects in criminal cases.

self-report survey A research approach that requires subjects to reveal their own participation in delinquent or criminal acts.

sentencing circles A type of sentencing in which victims, family members, community members, and the offender participate in an effort to devise fair and reasonable sanctions that are ultimately aimed at reintegrating the offender back into the community.

sheriff The chief law enforcement officer in a county.

shire reeve In medieval England, the senior law enforcement figure in a county; the forerunner of today's sheriff.

shock incarceration A short prison sentence served in boot camp–type facilities.

shock probation A sentence in which offenders serve a short prison term before they begin probation, to impress them with the pains of imprisonment.

six-person jury The criminal trial of a defendant before a jury of six persons as opposed to a traditional jury of twelve persons.

Sixth Amendment The U.S. constitutional amendment containing various criminal trial rights, such as the right to public trial, right to trial by jury, and the right to confrontation of witnesses.

social control The ability of society and its institutions to control, manage, restrain, or direct human behavior.

social learning The view that behavior patterns are modeled and learned in interactions with others.

social process theory The view that an individual's interactions with key social institutions—family, school, peer group—shapes behavior.

social structure theory The view that a person's position in the social structure controls behavior. Those in the lowest socioeconomic tier are more likely to succumb to crime-promoting elements in their environment society, whereas those in the highest tier enjoy social and economic advantages that insulate them from crime-producing forces.

socialization The process in which a person learns to adapt to the cultural and social institutions in society.

source control Eradicating the drug problem through a policy of destroying crops and manufacturing plants located in source countries before they can be shipped to the United States.

special-needs inmate Those correctional clients who require special care and treatment, such as the elderly, mentally ill, drug-addicted, or AIDS-infected.

specific deterrence A crime control policy suggesting that punishment should be severe enough to convince convicted offenders never to repeat their criminal activity.

split sentence A practice that requires convicted criminals to spend a portion of their sentence behind bars and the remainder in the community.

stare decisis To stand by decided cases. The legal principle by which the decision or holding in an earlier case becomes the standard by which subsequent similar cases are judged.

status offender A juvenile who has been adjudicated by a judge of a juvenile court as having committed a status offense (running away, truancy, or incorrigibility).

sting operation An undercover police operation in which police pose as criminals to trap law violators.

stop and frisk The situation when police officers who are suspicious of an individual run their hands lightly over the suspect's outer garments, to determine whether the person is carrying a concealed weapon. Also called a patdown or threshold inquiry, a stop and frisk is intended to stop short of any activity that could be considered a violation of Fourth Amendment rights.

Strickland v. Washington The 1984 U.S. Supreme Court decision upholding that defendants have the right to reasonably effective assistance of counsel (that is, competent representation).

strict liability crime Illegal act whose elements do not contain the need for intent or mens rea; usually, acts that endanger the public welfare, such as illegal dumping of toxic wastes.

substantive criminal law A body of specific rules that declare what conduct is criminal and prescribe the punishment to be imposed for such conduct.

substantive rights Through a slow process of legal review, the courts have granted inmates a number of civil rights, including the rights to receive mail and medical benefits and to practice their religion.

super-maximum-security prison The newest form of a maximum-security prison that uses high-level security measures to incapacitate the nation's most dangerous criminals. Most inmates are in twenty-three hours per day lockdown.

sureties During the Middle Ages, people who made themselves responsible for the behavior of offenders released in their care.

suspended sentence A prison term that is delayed while the defendant undergoes a period of community treatment. If the treatment is successful, the prison sentence is terminated.

teleconferencing Using audio and video linkups to allow people to communicate from distant locations.

tier system The structure of early prisons having numerous floors or wings that stacked cells one over another.

time-in-rank system For police officers to advance in rank they must spend an appropriate amount of time, usually years, in the preceding rank; that is, to become a captain an officer must first spend time as a lieutenant.

tithing In medieval England, a group of ten families who collectively dealt with minor disturbances and breaches of the peace.

tort The law of personal wrongs and damage. Tort-type actions include negligence, libel, slander, assault, and trespass.

total institution A regimented, dehumanizing institution such as a prison in which like-situated people are kept in social isolation, cut off from the world at large.

transfer hearing A preadjudication hearing in a juvenile court to determine whether a juvenile offender should be detained in juvenile court or transferred to criminal court for prosecution as an adult.

treatment The rehabilitative method used to effect a change of behavior in the juvenile offender, in the form of therapy, or educational or vocational programs.

true bill The action by a grand jury when it votes to indict an accused suspect.

truth in sentencing A new sentencing scheme which requires that offenders serve at least 85 percent of their original sentence before being eligible for parole or other forms of early release.

Uniform Crime Report (UCR) The FBI's yearly publication of where, when, and how much serious crime occurred in the prior year.

venire The group called for jury duty from which jury panels are selected.

verdict A finding of a jury or a judge on questions of fact at a trial.

vice squad Police officers assigned to enforce morality-based laws, such as those on prostitution, gambling, and pornography.

victim impact statement A postconviction statement by the victim of crime that may be used to guide sentencing decisions.

victimless crime An act that is in violation of society's moral code and therefore has been outlawed—for example, drug abuse, gambling, and prostitution. These acts are linked together because, although they have no external victim, they are considered harmful to the social fabric.

vigilantes A citizen group who tracked down wanted criminals in the Old West.

voir dire The process in which a potential jury panel is questioned by the prosecution and the defense in order to select jurors who are unbiased and objective.

waiver (juvenile) A practice in which the juvenile court waives its jurisdiction over a juvenile and transfers the case to adult criminal court for trial. In some states a waiver hearing is held to determine jurisdiction, while in others juveniles may be automatically waived if they are accused of committing a serious crime such as murder.

Walnut Street Jail In 1790 a separate wing of Philadelphia's Walnut Street Jail was built to house convicted felons. This was the forerunner of the secure correctional system in the United States.

watch system During the Middle Ages in England, men were organized in church parishes to guard at night against disturbances and breaches of the peace under the direction of the local constable.

wergild Under medieval law, the money paid by the offender to compensate the victim and the state for a criminal offense.

widening the net of justice The charge that programs designed to divert offenders from the justice system actually enmesh them further in the process by substituting more intrusive treatment programs for less intrusive punishment-oriented outcomes.

work release A prison treatment program that allows inmates to be released during the day to work in the community and returned to prison at night.

writ of certiorari An order of superior court requesting that the record of an inferior court (or administrative body) be brought forward for review or inspection.

writ of habeas corpus A judicial order requesting that a person detaining another produce the body of the prisoner and give reasons for his or her capture and detention. Habeas corpus is a legal device used to request that a judicial body review the reasons for a person's confinement and the conditions of confinement. Habeas corpus is known as "the great writ."

zero tolerance The practice of seizing all instrumentalities of a crime, including homes, boats, and cars. It is an extreme example of the law of forfeiture.

Table of Cases

Name Index

Subject Index